THE

Donald Sassoon is Emeritus Professor of Comparative European History at Queen Mary, University of London. His previous books include *One Hundred Years of Socialism* (1996), *Mona Lisa* (2001) and *The Culture of the Europeans* (2006), all widely translated. He gives lectures at universities and conferences all over the world.

DONALD SASSOON

The Anxious Triumph

A Global History of Capitalism, 1860–1914

PENGUIN BOOKS

PENGUIN BOOKS

UK | USA | Canada | Ireland | Australia
India | New Zealand | South Africa

Penguin Books is part of the Penguin Random House group of companies whose addresses can be found at global.penguinrandomhouse.com

First published by Allen Lane 2019
Published in Penguin Books 2020

002

Printed in Great Britain by Clays Ltd, Elcograf S.p.A.

A CIP catalogue record for this book is available from the British Library

ISBN: 978-0-141-98655-5

www.greenpenguin.co.uk

Penguin Random House is committed to a sustainable future for our business, our readers and our planet. This book is made from Forest Stewardship Council® certified paper.

For Marina.
All successful social systems appear to be alike;
each unsuccessful social system appears to be
unsuccessful in its own way (with thanks to Tolstoy)

Contents

PART FOUR
Facing the World

Acknowledgements

My thanks go to Marina Lewycka for reading the manuscript carefully, advising, editing, encouraging, disagreeing and agreeing, and everything else; Lauro Martines, a wise man, for reading the manuscript and offering wise advice; Paul Auerbach for doing the same; Candida McDonogh for her brilliant editing; Richard Mason for his brilliant copyediting; Toby Mundy, of course, as well as Stuart Proffitt; the Maison des Sciences de l'Homme for having me in Paris almost every year; the Leverhulme Trust for a grant enabling me to take a year's leave of absence; the University of Padua for a visiting professorship in 2017; the British Library and the Bibliothèque Nationale de France.

List of Tables

List of Tables

Introduction

Globalization is the name we currently give to the progressive integration of the world, a process that started centuries go. It denotes not only a massive expansion of trade and production but also a remarkable and unprecedented growth and convergence in consumption. Increasingly, we buy similar products, eat similar food (hamburgers, pizzas, sushi, pasta, fries, 'Chinese' food, curries, tacos, couscous), drink the same beverages (cola, coffee, tea, beer), wear the same clothes (jeans, T-shirts, sneakers) with the same brands (Levis, Quicksilver, Nike, etc.), read the same best-sellers (J. K. Rowling, Dan Brown, Ken Follett), listen to similar music, and watch the same kind of television programmes.

Underpinning this worldwide system is an equally global ideology, market capitalism, which no longer needs defending, though it is constantly attacked. In its western heartland, no significant countervailing force opposes capitalism. In the rest of the world, opposition is muted. In the emerging economies of China, Brazil, and India there is little opposition to capitalism per se; public debate centres on the variety of capitalism that should prevail. Islamic fundamentalism, seen by some as the remaining challenger of the so-called 'new world order', has little to say about the economy.

The aim of this book is not to revisit the initial stages of capitalism, but to investigate the period between the second half of the nineteenth century and the Great War, when capitalism triumphed and became universally accepted, when most of its opponents acknowledged that it was inevitable, perhaps even desirable. It will examine how the elites responded to the challenge of industrial capitalism and how industrial progress could be achieved while keeping dissent to a minimum by creating a sense of national community, or a patriotic spirit, or using the state to regulate capitalism, or by conquering new territories.

In the eyes of many liberal ideologues the profit-maximizing entrepreneur was and is the real hero of capitalist development. He battles against politicians, bureaucrats, petty legislation, uppity workers and voracious trade unions. He identifies a sought-after demand; he works out how to satisfy it; he develops new production methods, thus increasing productivity; he bullies or begs banks into lending him money for investment; or he risks his own family fortune or his own hard-earned savings. Finally, having created jobs for a usually ungrateful workforce and having satisfied customers who did not know they needed something, he finds he has to protect his rightfully earned gains from the rapacious hands of the tax collector. Thanks to this entrepreneur and him alone, society and civilization have moved one small step forward towards happiness and prosperity. He is, above all others, the real creator of real wealth.

This is, of course, a free-enterprise fantasy, almost on a par with that held by anti-capitalists of yore, for whom capitalists were sleazy, heartless, cigar-chomping, arrogant, callous, money-obsessed rich thugs, devoid of human decency and delighted to grind the faces of the poor (to use a biblical expression, see Isaiah 3:15).

In reality entrepreneurs, like workers, come in all shapes and sizes. They do not have a single aim, do not speak with a single voice, have no unified political strategy. Some try to obtain as much as possible from the state; others are not interested; most hate politicians and politics but need them; and most assume that their interests are the same as those of the wider collective. Politicians agree, for it does not require great perception and intuition to see that prosperous capitalism is better than failed capitalism: more jobs, more money, more taxes, more consensus.

Capitalism is a process difficult to define since the presence of a few capitalists and of a few capitalist enterprises does not make a society 'capitalist'. That what we call 'the Industrial Revolution' started in the United Kingdom is uncontroversial. What is controversial is when capitalism started. Processes, unlike wars and regimes, do not start on a precise date. There were people one might call 'capitalists' well before one could speak of an industrial revolution. Imagine, for instance, a weaver in ancient Mesopotamia, who hires workers, provides them with the tools and the raw materials, and pays them a salary. This entrepreneur would be recognized by Karl Marx himself as a 'capitalist' since he owns the means of production (the capital), pays wages to his workers, and derives what Marx would have called 'surplus value' from selling the cloth, yet no one would say that ancient Mesopotamia was a capitalist economy, even though there were 13,200 weavers in its main city, Ur, in c. 2000 BC at the time of the third Sumerian dynasty; the basis of the economy was in agriculture, and trade and production were mainly in luxury goods such as terracotta plaques.[1] In ancient Rome, slaves often worked in mines and in the fields and as servants in the homes of patrician families. There were also entrepreneurs such as Quintus Remmius Palaemon, a former slave (mentioned, disparagingly, by Suetonius in his *De illustribus grammaticis*, as being arrogant and 'especially notorious for acts of licentiousness with women').[2] Palaemon, who lived at the time of emperors Tiberius and Claudius, made considerable money not only from his teaching and his vineyard but also from his clothes-making workshop. He thus had a presence in all the main economic sectors: agriculture, manufacturing, and the service sector.[3]

One should not underestimate the technological sophistication of the economy of Ancient Rome: there was considerable use of money; trade was thriving; and production and productivity levels were probably as high as in medieval Europe, a thousand years later.[4] But, again, no one would suggest that Imperial Rome was a capitalist society. Artisans and entrepreneurs were regarded as second-class citizens, which is why we know so little about them. The blown glass, metal weapons, and ceramic pots produced by these early 'capitalists' were closely regulated by the authorities. Here too agriculture remained the fundamental economic activity, and artisans and manufacturers were a small minority.[5]

In Carolingian Europe (ninth century AD) there was considerable trade, not only in the Mediterranean but also in northern Europe (the North Sea, the Baltic Sea, and the Rhineland). This tended to focus on luxury goods manufactured by craftsmen, but it was remarkably global, stretching from old Viking trading outposts in present-day Denmark to Baghdad, centre of a trading network that stretched all the way to India and China.[6] In those days the Muslim and the Byzantine worlds were far more 'advanced' than northern Europe, while the British Isles certainly lagged behind the continental countries.

In Bologna, in 1294, there were 1,700 *cordovaneri* (leather workers) organized in corporations whose main aim was to block competition. Inside each corporation, though there were inequalities, there was a desire to maintain a reasonable equilibrium between the various masters to ensure stability and contain competition, which is why it was forbidden to poach workers from other producers or to store excessive quantities of raw material.[7]

In Florence, between c. 1340 and c. 1530, the wool industry had capitalist characteristics – labourers constituted between one-third and one-half of the workforce of the city.[8] These workers, part of the labouring classes or *popolo minuto* (some of whom were immigrant workers from as far as Ragusa – present-day Dubrovnik – Flanders, Naples and Cologne), were excluded from the management of the city, paid high taxes, received low wages, and were deprived of rights. The most important proletarian revolt of the Middle Ages occurred in Florence between 1378 and 1382: the *tumulto dei Ciompi*, the revolt of the

Ciompi (wage workers employed mainly in the wool industry). This revolt led to the formation, in the summer of 1378, of a short-lived 'workers' government'. There were precedents, of course: in 1252 textiles workers in Ghent, in eastern Flanders, went on strike and were brutally repressed, but the Ciompi rebellion was far more significant.[9]

This 'early' form of capitalism was largely self-regulated. Even in Venice, where state control was strict, the corporations kept some autonomy.[10] Centuries later, when Napoleon conquered the city and handed it over to Austria in exchange for a peace treaty in 1797, there were still 114 corporations in Venice with a total membership of 31,664.[11] But the total population had long been in decline and so had exports (as had happened in other once rich Italian cities from Milan to Genoa and Florence). As the Venetian state became weaker so did local enterprises and commerce, and by 1808 the corporations no longer existed.

Yet neither the Industrial Revolution nor capitalism started in Bologna during the thirteenth century or Florence in the fourteenth century. The typical unit of production remained the small workshop run by a single artisan employing some apprentices, using simple tools. The merchants could also use the 'putting out' system, which consisted in providing workers, in their own homes, with raw materials, tools, even partially woven cloth, and then selling their products. This avoided what would have been the expensive and risky creation of larger units of production, such as factories.[12] There were 'big' entrepreneurs, real tycoons, even in medieval Europe, people such as Francesco di Marco Datini in Tuscany, Jacques Coeur from Bourges in France, and Benedetto Cotrugli in Ragusa, then under Venice, one of the pioneers of double-entry bookkeeping, but they were exceptions.[13]

Totally unregulated 'capitalism', even at the origins of industry, could not exist. In ancient Babylon, the Hammurabi Code (c. 1750 BC) determined the level of wages a hired craftsman should be paid: 'If any one hire a skilled artizan, he shall pay as wages of the . . . five gerahs, as wages of the potter five gerahs, of a tailor five gerahs . . . per day.'[14] Regulation could, of course, go the other way and penalize labourers who chose to seek a better job, as in fifteenth-century England when labour mobility was controlled under the guise of combating 'vagrancy'. Such legislation endured well into the eighteenth century not only in England but also in most of western Europe.[15]

The state mattered. And some states mattered to other states as well, for commercial or financial hegemonic powers were able to impose, consciously or not, international rules for global commerce. If you wanted to trade, you had to accept externally imposed criteria. Thus Venice,

Bruges, and then Antwerp in the fifteenth century, Amsterdam in the seventeenth century, London in the nineteenth and the United States in the second half of the twentieth century were 'hegemonic' precisely because traders involved in foreign trade had to follow their rules.[16]

Medieval Italian cities possessed particular advantages: in the fourteenth century, northern Europe was still underdeveloped and Islam was declining, thus enabling Italian merchants to monopolize the trade of luxury items made in the east and export them to northern Europe.[17] In a continent that was overwhelmingly rural, this trade was concentrated in cities, the heart of politics and culture; and since trade and commerce are even more unstable than agriculture, there was considerable anxiety.[18]

Flanders was not far behind Italy. The Dutch Republic, born in 1581, became a remarkable commercial and financial power, particularly in the course of the seventeenth century when it acquired some of the features of a capitalist economy, producing and exporting luxury cloth and beer and soon becoming also Europe's main supplier of credit and finance.[19] In the period 1676–1700 over half of Amsterdam's bridegrooms 'declared an occupation with an industrial or artisanal character'. Fourteen per cent of married men in Amsterdam were involved in textile production.[20] Here too the state played an important role. In the seventeenth century Dutch cities (where effective political power resided) had an industrial policy: to attract industries by offering advantages to entrepreneurs and protecting established industries by prohibiting the removal of important raw material such as wool.[21] Half of the population resided in the towns and were employed in manufacturing, and the Netherlands were 'the most highly urbanized, most highly industrialized regions in Europe'.[22] Then, in the course of the eighteenth century, during wars with England, the Dutch Republic declined.[23]

This coincided with the rise of industrial England. England had industries from before the period conventionally taken as the beginning of the Industrial Revolution (1760). There were small cloth manufacturers producing in workshops attached to their houses, employing apprentices and craftsmen. In Yorkshire and elsewhere in England, there was the beginning of a metal 'industry'. Travelling in the mid-1720s, Daniel Defoe noted that in 'populous' Sheffield the houses were 'dark and black, by the continued Smoke of the Forges, which are always at work', and that there were plenty of cutlers.[24] The urban population of England grew exponentially in the decades preceding the Industrial Revolution. By 1800, England was more urbanized than any other European country apart from the Dutch Republic.[25] By 1850, in this respect it dwarfed them all.[26]

What contributed to the torch of 'progress', particularly technological advance, passing to the West and to Britain in particular? Why this 'great divergence', as Kenneth Pomeranz called it, between the West and the East?[27] Coal production has been described as one of the main causes behind British success.[28] The evidence is compelling: British coal production was 2,950 thousand tons in 1700 and 15,045 thousand tons in 1800, way ahead of all other countries.[29] But there were plenty of other factors. Was it culture, laws, and religion; well-established property rights; technology; high wage levels in Europe, forcing entrepreneurs to innovate; maritime exploration and conquests; banks, double-entry bookkeeping, letters of credit? Or just the remarkable set of technological innovations that characterized the eighteenth century in Britain: the steam engine (Thomas Newcomen, 1712, and James Watt, 1781), the spinning jenny (James Hargreaves, 1764), which enabled the industrialization of weaving, the water frame (Richard Arkwright, 1769), and coke smelting which enabled the conversion of coal into coke and the production of cast iron (Abraham Darby, 1709–10, and later John Wilkinson)? It was not just the innovations, often seen as near-miraculous moments of genius or of luck, the work of talented amateurs, but the hard work of testing them, applying them, making them work, refining them and so on, which made the difference.[30] Was British society particularly open to such entrepreneurship and innovation, encouraged by the British state, or perhaps by high wages, which led to labour-saving innovations?[31] Was it the slave trade, which Marx credited in *Das Kapital* with providing such enormous profit? 'Liverpool waxed fat on the slave trade.'[32] This was a common view at the time.[33] Or was it that, while the rest of the world and certainly the rest of Europe was in turmoil in the final decades of the eighteenth century and the beginning of the nineteenth, Britain was stable and solid, rewarded enterprise, favoured innovation, was freer, and could rely on skilled workers and technicians (including many who came from abroad)? All such factors mattered, though their relative importance is a constant matter of controversy. Above all, the British, or some of them, believed in progress. They were, not necessarily consciously, children of the Enlightenment and the pioneers of an Industrial Enlightenment, even though many of the famous inventors had little knowledge of what we now call the Enlightenment.[34]

In the period 1800 to 1830 when the Industrial Revolution was in full swing and the country had virtually no competitors, the United Kingdom grew by an average of 1.4 per cent a year. France did a little better (but starting from a lower level) with an average of 1.8 per cent after 1840. In fact growth in the nineteenth century in Europe was low – around 1 per cent.[35] Even the United States averaged only a little more than 1 per cent between 1860 and 1910, and this was not evenly spread throughout the country, given its size, but it was enough to overtake Britain, as early as the 1850s, in industrial production.[36] By 1890 the USA had become the leading manufacturing power in the world. As in Britain, coal extraction was a key factor, in the area from Pennsylvania to Kentucky. Iron-ore mines were discovered in the northern Midwest. Pittsburgh became the steel town par excellence while the post-bellum South and the American West remained undeveloped.

Britain has now long lost her position of pre-eminence and we do not know how long the present Western 'lead' will last, or indeed precisely what we mean by 'lead'. Is it just military supremacy? The rate of technological breakthrough? Cultural power? A greater concern for human rights? Or is it simply a matter of wealth? Western modernity was imposed on much of the rest of the world after 1800, and sometimes it was eagerly welcomed. And today the objective of many (though not all) outside the West is neither the now extinct *Homo sovieticus* nor *Homo islamicus* but *Homo occidentalis*.[37]

The state and its institutions are not automatic champions of economic development: the state must be a willing and purposeful actor. In some circumstances it can be an obstacle to productivity growth and innovation, even an instrument for maintaining a particular anti-industrial class in power or entrenching bureaucratic interests.[38] But institutions matter. Capitalism needs a strong state, and it must be a state that is willing and able to promote capitalism. This had been the case in Europe: in the nineteenth century in Belgium and in Russia and elsewhere the state developed the railways; in France and in Italy it mobilized loans and offered guarantees;[39] in Britain, it regulated the raising of capital by introducing the Limited Liability Act of 1855, a formal system of company registration, auditing, and a process of bankruptcy.[40] The post office was in state hands virtually everywhere. In England it had been a monopoly since the seventeenth century, a monopoly considerably strengthened in the nineteenth century when mail delivery expanded considerably. A uniform penny postage was introduced in 1840 ensuring delivery anywhere within the country irrespective of distance – the first country to do this.[41] By the mid-1850s mail delivery in Britain had been brought completely under state control, thus establishing, in effect, a nationalized industry. The telegraph system followed in 1870.

With the purchase of a 40 per cent holding of Suez Canal shares in 1875 'the British government became the largest single shareholder in the greatest international public utility in the world'.[42] Finally, on the eve of the First World War, the government (technically the Admiralty, whose First Lord was then Winston Churchill) bought the majority shareholding of Anglo-Persian Oil Company (which became BP in 1954), saving it from bankruptcy.[43]

So states and capitalism grew increasingly intermeshed, but it is not clear when a society can be called 'capitalist'. Presumably manufacturing should have acquired a substantial weight. But what is substantial? How can one calculate the level of industrialization? If we use pig-iron production (gross figures and not per capita) we find that, in 1800, the United Kingdom with 190,000 tons was the leader, but it was followed by 'backward' Russia with 160,000 tons, then France (120,000 tons), then Sweden and Germany with 50,000 tons each, and, not far behind, the United States (40,000 tons) and Belgium and Austria with 30,000 tons each.[44] Yet it would be difficult to argue that Russia, in 1800, was the second industrial country in the world or that in 1850 it was more capitalist than Belgium. A league table on a per capita basis would obviously not see Russia near the top.

It was understood that civilization was connected with industry and industry with power, yet no single power dominated Europe. Britain was the leading industrial power and her navy ruled the waves, but her army was of no great importance in continental Europe. The major industrial continental state in the late nineteenth century, Germany, was never in a position to establish political supremacy, not even after defeating France in 1870. Belgium was an industrial state, but too small to matter in wider European affairs. Portugal, Holland and Sweden had lost the power and the wealth they once possessed, as had Spain, which, by the end of the century, had also lost her empire. In 1880, Latin America, Africa and Asia – taken together – accounted for only 20 per cent of world trade.[45] How different from the situation in 2010, when Europe's share of world exports was 17 per cent and that of the United States only 12 per cent![46]

In the nineteenth century, Europe was divided, then as now, into a multiplicity of states (see Chapter 1), but it would be wrong to treat it simply as an uncoordinated bickering Tower of Babel, fatally divided by protectionism and national identities.[47] Besides, industrial development does not coincide precisely with state boundaries: advanced sectors often coexist with backward ones. If we ignore national borders, and hence politics, mid-nineteenth-century European industrial society would include areas in Lancashire, Yorkshire, the Midlands, and parts of southern Scotland (the Glasgow area), parts of German-speaking Switzerland, francophone Belgium, Alsace and Lyon in France, the Ruhr in Germany, Piedmont and parts of Lombardy in Italy. There were regions in the 'periphery' of Europe which, had they been states, would have been in the top league of industrializing countries. Thus in what had just become the Austro-Hungarian Empire (1867), there was a significant industrial sector but largely confined to Bohemia and Moravia (now the Czech Republic).[48] France may have been backward compared to Britain and Germany, but Alsace, at least in the decades following the Napoleonic Wars, outperformed Britain.[49]

The British lead was evident in 1850 when the United Kingdom produced a staggering 2,390,000 tons of pig iron, but the United States was second, at some distance, with 670,000 tons, followed by France with 450,000 tons. Russia (with 220,000 tons) still managed to outdistance Germany (210,000), the Austrian Empire, Belgium, and Sweden.[50] Pig-iron production gives an indication of the huge take-off into industrialization: in fifty years the UK increased production by 12.5 times, Germany quadrupled it and France doubled it. By 1900 the UK had lost its European lead in steel production to Germany, and the USA was already producing as much steel as the UK and Germany combined.[51] If one chooses cotton spindle production, then the British lead over all other countries put together lasted until circa 1890; then the 'rest of the world' overtook Great Britain.[52]

What if one chooses numbers of those employed in industry? Here too we encounter problems: countries today still generally regarded as 'capitalist' have a relatively low level of people employed in industry (and that includes white-collar workers in industry). World Bank figures for 2010–14 suggest the USA has circa 17 per cent employed in industry, the UK does a little better with 19.2 per cent, Portugal, Italy and Germany are around 28 per cent, which happens to be the world average, Poland has 30 per cent, less than Iran (32–34 per cent), while China is by far the most 'industrial' country in the world with 44 per cent of its people employed in manufacturing.[53] Today, being 'industrial' is no longer the hallmark of an advanced economy. In fact, as the UN acknowledges, the boundaries between manufacturing and other sectors 'can be somewhat blurry'.[54]

At the end of the nineteenth century, the nine large conurbations with more than 500,000 consumers (Amsterdam, Paris, the Ruhr,

Birmingham, Glasgow, Lancashire, Yorkshire, Hamburg, and London) formed an area of greater industrial concentration than the corresponding one in the United States (New York, Boston, Philadelphia, Pittsburgh, St Louis, and Chicago).[55] There was some specialization: cotton in Lancashire, in Scotland, and later in Lille and Rouen; wool in Scotland, Yorkshire, Catalonia, and parts of northern France; steel in Yorkshire, Wales, and the Midlands, but also in parts of France and Germany. Before 1880 large factories were rare. There were some giants, such as the Schneider steel works at Le Creusot in France, employing 9,950 workers in 1867, and the Krupp works in Essen (8,500 workers in 1865), but most enterprises were relatively small – employing on average fewer than ten workers.[56] The financing of these enterprises was largely done by the entrepreneurs themselves. Banks played a role only for major projects, often with a state guarantee. And there was a constant flow of people and capital across barely controlled state borders.

By the 1880s the 'modern' encompassed virtually the entire world, not, of course, in the sense that the whole world had become 'modern' – far from it – but in the sense that modernity had become a near-universal goal. The modern is, of course, largely an ideological construct. Westerners took some of the political, cultural, and economic features of their most industrial regions and countries and defined them as modern. As they became modern a cult of tradition developed. This cult was 'modern' too since in traditional societies no one *chooses* to venerate traditions; they are just part of the cultural environment. Glancing back towards the past is a deliberate choice. As Théophile Gautier noted in 1867 in a review of a book on the Danish sculptor Bertel Thorvaldsen: 'On the one hand the most extreme modernity, on the other an austere love for the antique.'[57] But modernity has many meanings. For John Stuart Mill it was linked to commerce and international trade, which put people in contact 'with persons dissimilar to themselves, and with modes of thought and action unlike those with which they are familiar'.[58]

When modern capitalism started, there was little resistance to it. In Britain, during the Napoleonic Wars, there were the luddites, workers resisting their harsh conditions and the increase in food prices more than (as is commonly believed) the imposition of new technology, but they were quickly repressed. The Chartists, whose struggle was virtually over by 1857, wanted more democracy. The unions wanted higher wages. The socialist movement wanted social reforms and the regulation of the labour market. Yet the new economic system was seen as the inevitable future for the whole of humanity, a future full of hope but also of anxieties. Capitalism was seen as the natural consequence of everything that had gone before, even though it was 'a startling departure from the norms that had prevailed for four thousand years'.[59]

There was nothing inexorable or predestined about the rise of capital. And this may account for the anxieties that have troubled and are still troubling those who live within its compass. Anxiety is an enduring trait of capitalist societies, but it is part of the system, not external to it. In the past, the vagaries of the weather and the ever-present threat of famine, war, and pestilence were the main sources of anxiety for the majority of the population who lived on the land. For most people, unacquainted with the notion of progress, anything new, anything unexpected was a cause for alarm. Then one could blame God, the sinners among us, or just bad luck. Not so with modern capitalism; since it is so obviously a human system that rests, apparently, on the accumulation of a mass of individual decisions, it creates losers and winners by constantly innovating. This chronic instability is the foundation of its advance, not a fault in the system or an incidental by-product.

The period surveyed here was one of capitalist triumph. It was a global triumph. By 1900 Great Britain was no longer almost alone as an industrial power, as had been the case earlier in the nineteenth century. Germany was catching up and the United States had done so. In the decades before 1914 no single capitalist state was 'hegemonic' either militarily or economically. But the end of the First World War saw the extraordinary rise of the only true superpower of the modern era: the United States. Its pre-eminence was due not only to its outstanding growth in the decades preceding the war, but also to its continuous rise between the wars. In 1928 a British Foreign Office memorandum noted with a mixture of alarm and admiration that the USA was 'a phenomenon for which there is no parallel in our modern history . . . almost invulnerable, and at least our equal in prosperity, vital energy, technical equipment and industrial science'.[60] The phrase 'at least our equal' was self-delusion: the USA was, by then, clearly superior in wealth, science, energy, etc. The British Empire was on the way out, though many pretended otherwise at the time, blinded by wishful thinking.

Japan had initiated its peculiar process of industrialization from above in 1868. France was worrying it was not catching up fast enough. In the Tsarist Empire the main debate was how to industrialize without endangering the autocratic regime. New states were being created. Territories were being colonized by industrial powers. Industrialize or perish seemed to be the prevailing slogan. Many perished, but many prospered.

Today we in the West are richer than we have ever been, but more unequal. In some places – the USA and the UK – inequalities are particularly pronounced. The old social democratic dream of narrowing inequalities has been almost abandoned along with social democracy. Is this a problem? To have to walk while others ride in carriages – as in the mid-nineteenth century – is certainly a greater inequality than to drive a small car while being overtaken by others in their Maserati. Owners of small cars may envy (or despise) the owners of fast cars, but the power of mobility of the two groups, controlled by speed limits and traffic rules, is substantially similar (during rush hour a cyclist may be faster than either). The gap between the few who toured Europe in the nineteenth century and those who never had a day of rest is certainly greater than the present one between those who go on a cheap package holiday and those who can afford a luxury cruise. Visible monetary inequalities may increase while – at least in the wealthier parts of the world – the inequality of effective capabilities may decrease.

Most people seem to accept that the present economic arrangements of society are the only ones available. Capitalism works. Yet there appears to be a pervasive disaffection. Politicians are despised. They know it (and some despise the electorate in turn) and seek to regain consensus by emulating popular celebrities, emphasizing their personalities and cultivating their use of the media – the triumph of form over content. Fewer people vote and an increasing percentage of those who do so vote for parties that blame immigrants for whatever ills the people might be suffering.

While there are problems, these look to many as temporary glitches, not the death-knell of the system – an unlikely prospect since not even the outlines of its successor are discernible. Since there is no visible alternative, the system looks everlasting. True, there are still many who live in squalor and destitution. But – in the West – they constitute a minority, albeit a privileged one in comparison to those in large parts of the Third World who have barely enough to eat. The poor in late capitalist societies are no threat to the system. The occasional riot, the explosion of popular rage, the violence that surfaces irregularly is almost a recognition that no serious political challenge can be levelled against the market economy. Once, it was believed that the 'wretched of the earth' would revolt against the system. Now we know better. When they do revolt it is because they are frustrated at being left out of the system, not because they want to subvert it. Those who are not part of the enchanted world of consumer capitalism – still the majority of the world's population – knock at its door in an unprecedented wave of migration.

Today the great wealth accumulated by business elites causes envy and scandal, but the remedies proposed (tax them, control them, shame them) do not question the validity of capitalism, only one of its unpalatable outcomes. Indeed, depriving 'fat cats' of their greedily acquired fortune presupposes that this would not endanger the system. If it did, would such dispossession really be advocated?

Besides, the seriously rich of today do not visibly grind the faces of the poor into the dust. Unlike some Victorian entrepreneurs or nineteenth-century American robber barons, most capitalists in the West rarely employ oppressed and underpaid workers directly. Those who work for the new plutocrats in finance and the new 'clean' dot-com industries are usually fairly comfortable themselves. The oppressed and underpaid are far away, in distant countries, or working for subcontractors of the likes of Apple, one of the most profitable companies in the world. The software ideas and packages that power the smart phones, the iPads, the iPhones, the Kindles and the iPods, as well as the numerous play stations, are conceived in the West. The actual computers, phones, and tablets – the hardware – are made by firms such as Foxconn, the main affiliate of Hon Hai and one of the largest, possibly *the* largest electronics manufacturer in the world. Foxconn is headquartered in Taiwan but has factories in India, Brazil, Mexico, and other countries, and above all in Shenzhen, near Hong Kong, a centrepiece of 'socialism with Chinese characteristics' – the official name for the new market economy. It employs, in China, one million workers and is the largest private employer in China with young migrant workers between the ages of 16 and 29 constituting over 85 per cent of its workforce, and often working over the legal minimum of sixty hours a week.[61] The gap in conditions between workers in emerging economies and those in 'the West' remains remarkable. There is a chain that joins together those who work for miserable wages in what was called the Third World and those in the West whose incomes are wildly high; but the chain is so long as to be almost invisible.

This was not the case in Victorian Britain. In a striking chapter in *Capital*, Karl Marx, dripping with outrage and indignation, reports the death from overwork of Mary Anne Walkley, a 20-year-old milliner.[62] Mary Anne worked, on average, sixteen hours a day without a break, but during the 'season' (March to July) the workshop had to produce elegant dresses for noble ladies in time for a ball in honour of the Princess of Wales. At one point Mary Anne had to work continuously for over twenty-six hours, with thirty other girls in one small room. Her death was reported in all the main newspapers. *Punch*,

THE HAUNTED LADY, OR "THE GHOST" IN THE LOOKING-GLASS.

MADAME LA MODISTE.—"*We would not have disappointed your Ladyship, at any sacrifice, and the robe is finished* À MERVEILLE."

whose ethos was mildly Tory, was just as indignant as Marx. Its famous cartoon by John Tenniel, published in the magazine on 4 July 1863 and entitled *The Haunted Lady, or 'The Ghost' in the Looking-Glass*, depicting Mary Anne's death, thunders against the rich as loudly as any radical pamphlet. The noble lady, wearing, presumably, the dress that caused Mary's death, looks at herself in the mirror only to see, to her consternation, the moribund body of the exhausted seamstress. The woman behind the lady is reassuring: 'We would not have disappointed your Ladyship, at any sacrifice, and the robe is finished *à merveille*.'

This was in 1863 – more or less when this book starts – at a time when Mary Anne and her fellow sufferers worked less than a mile away from the consumers of the produce of their labours – the distance from Soho to Mayfair. Over one hundred and fifty years later the Mary Annes of this world still exist, but far from the putative cause of their misery, though the distance is somewhat tempered by the power of the modern media. In the contemporary 'advanced' world, Mary Anne's descendants – the Western workers of today – are relatively prosperous; they live a long life; they work shorter hours; they have holidays; they have education; expenditure on food is a relatively small proportion of their income; they have culture on tap (television, music, internet); they have pensions; they have healthcare. Far from threatening the foundations of society, as many *bien pensants* feared, they have become its archetypal supporters. And who can blame them? The process of democratization turned them into citizens with equal rights. Economic growth has granted them access to the consumer society, which many value more than the suffrage.

Today there are still many poor people in the West, but few regard them as victims of an exploitative system. Being a minority marks them out as losers – the 'left behind' – in a world where the winners seem to be the majority. They can blame themselves and their fecklessness or they can blame their bad luck or they can blame foreign immigrants – but not capitalism, since capitalism, visibly, has provided well for the majority. And there is enough wealth around so that those the Victorians called the 'undeserving poor' can be kept alive on state benefits, albeit increasingly grudgingly; hence the ever-increasing number of mendicants and homeless and the widespread use of 'food banks' even in rich countries such as the United States (where they started), Germany, France and the United Kingdom.

The victory of market capitalism was sealed by the democratization of consumption. Some communist economies, the Soviet Union and Czechoslovakia for instance, had been successful in laying the foundation of an industrial society, but none matched the achievements of modern consumer capitalism. When the Berlin Wall fell in November 1989, some of the media reported ironically that those who were among the first to jump across the breach between East and West went shopping, as if some dramatic pilgrimage of thanksgiving would have been more appropriate for such a history-making event: 'Clamor in the East: Jubilation in Berlin; A Day for Celebration and a Bit of Shopping' intoned *The New York Times* on 11 November 1989. In more hallowed times, prayers in a cathedral to celebrate freedom regained would have been an almost universal choice.

Ten years before the fall of the Wall, in December 1978, at the plenary session of the Central Committee of the Communist Party of China, Deng Xiaoping, the new 'paramount leader', had launched the 'Reform and Opening Up' policies that would put the country on a path towards a market economy, albeit one with 'Chinese characteristics'. That was a clear and clear-headed move towards a consumer society. Symbolically, at the same session of the Central Committee, the opening in Shanghai of the first Coca-Cola plant was also announced.[63] Mao Zedong had been dead for just over two years.

In the final decades of the nineteenth century, such a clear triumph for capitalism was not generally anticipated. By the 1880s, throughout the world of independent states – including most of Europe, almost all of North, Central, and South America, Japan, China, and some countries in Asia and Africa (such as Ethiopia) – there was a common recognition that it was necessary to 'modernize', that is to say, to embrace industrial capitalism. But its advance caused considerable anxiety, even in prosperous England; and not only, as one might expect, among suffering workers and threatened peasants, but also among the middle classes themselves, who were afraid of potentially seditious workers, of economic uncertainty, of rapidly changing status, of Jews and Irish, of cholera and smallpox, and, above all, of the poor.

They were right to be scared. The Industrial Revolution that had begun in England and was sweeping throughout the West, and the concomitant move of workers from the countryside into the cities, was bringing about an unparalleled upheaval in social structure. This was not simply a change of jobs. It involved abandoning a life of tranquil poverty in a settled community for the unstable conditions of urban life, at times in another country. Usually, though not always, this meant better housing and better food, but it also meant anxiety about the future.

Optimism and anxiety go together since it is not unreasonable to assume that the years of abundance will be followed by years of scarcity. It is, after all, an ancient view, narrated in the Old Testament. As Joseph explained to Pharaoh, the seven years of abundance will be followed by seven years of famine: 'and all the plenty shall be forgotten in the land of Egypt; and the famine shall consume the land' (Genesis 41:25–31) – a kind of pre-capitalist 'boom and bust'. Such anxiety had been even more marked in the early part of the nineteenth century when England was like a huge ship sailing into uncharted waters. What would industrialization produce? How severe would the business cycles be (identified by the French economist Clément Juglar in his *Des Crises commerciales et leur retour périodique en France, en Angleterre et aux États-Unis* in 1862). Pessimism was rife among the intellectual classes. Malthus, in his *Essay on the Principle of Population* (1798), thought that population growth, unless held back by war or disease, would outstrip growth of production, particularly of food, causing widespread famine. Since he was writing before the first population census (1801), he could not be certain of his figures, but we are pretty sure that the population *did* increase: in 1721 the population of England (not Scotland, Wales and Ireland) was over 5 million; by 1761 it was 6 million and by the census of 1801 it was 8.6 million.[64]

Some, such as Thomas Carlyle, lamented the horrors of modernity, explaining in his essay 'Signs of the Times' (1829) that 'It is the Age of Machinery . . . Our old modes of exertion are all discredited, and thrown aside.'[65] And after ten pages of whining he added:

> The truth is men have lost their belief in the Invisible, and believe, and hope, and work only in the Visible; . . . This is not a Religious age. Only the material, the immediately practical, not the divine and spiritual, is important to us. The infinite, absolute character of Virtue has passed into a finite, conditional one; it is no longer a worship of the Beautiful and Good; but a calculation of the Profitable . . . Our true Deity is Mechanism. It has subdued external Nature for us, and we think it will do all other things.[66]

Two decades earlier, in 1802, William Wordsworth had composed a famous sonnet ('The World Is Too Much with Us') which begins thus:

> The world is too much with us; late and soon,
> Getting and spending, we lay waste our powers;
> Little we see in Nature that is ours;
> We have given our hearts away, a sordid boon!

Those who lamented the dawn of capitalism, the empire of money, the dangers of modernity continued to complain throughout the nineteenth century, usually, but not always, from a religious angle. Juan Donoso Cortés, who inspired Pope Pius IX's anti-liberal 1864 document *Syllabus Errorum*, discussing liberalism and socialism in the context of the revolutions of 1848, lamented in one of his last essays, published in 1851, that:

> The revolutions of modern times have . . . an unconquerable and destructive force which the revolutions of ancient times did not possess; and this destructive force is necessarily satanic, since it cannot be divine.

Corruption, he continued, is the god of Liberalism: 'All combine to bribe the people with their promises, and the people, in turn, intimidate every one by their clamors and threats.'[67] Such invectives marked much of the nineteenth century, particularly in France: from Joseph de Maistre's tirades against science and the Enlightenment (*Examen de la philosophie de Bacon*, 1836) to Louis de Bonald (1754–1840) and Louis Veuillot (1813–1883) – all traditional Catholics who supported the principle of Papal supremacy. For them, the 'new', the 'modern' were harbingers of disaster.

By the middle of the century the doom-mongers were beginning to give way to the optimists. The ship of British industry had found its course towards the seductive pleasures of modernity. With varying degrees of reluctance and enthusiasm other countries, France, later Germany and Japan, had to follow, fearing to be left behind, but anxieties plagued them too.

By the 1860s, at least in Europe, the debate among political elites developed within a specific framework: the recognition that industrialization was an unavoidable imperative, and the fear (for the socialists, the hope) that this would destabilize the political system. These elites divided themselves into various broad political tribes: liberals (then by far the most important group), enlightened conservatives, reactionaries, and socialists. Each had its own narrative about capitalism, and, of course, each narrative overlapped with the others.

The liberal tribe embraced capitalism enthusiastically, as an end in itself. Capitalist industrialization would wipe away feudal residues such as aristocratic and clerical privileges; liberate entrepreneurship; enable economic growth and prosperity; and strengthen the nation (often the new nation) militarily and politically. It would enable progress and promote science. These liberals were the true heirs to the Enlightenment. They celebrated the individual as the maker of his own destiny, breaking away from the limits imposed by birth and caste.

By the 1880s, however, most liberals even in Britain had abandoned their previous commitment to the untrammelled development of market forces. Such notions were no longer held dogmatically, as a matter of faith, but only pragmatically when it suited the development of one's own national capitalism. Most liberals and intelligent conservatives recognized that capitalism could also be a devastating force, and sought to temper its disruptive effects with policies of social and political reforms. Liberalism itself promoted reforms in fin-de-siècle Europe, starting at the centre of liberalism itself: Great Britain.

Here, by the end of the century, individualistic liberalism was giving way to a new 'collectivist' liberalism. This envisaged a positive role for the state in the solution of social problems and the establishment of a just society. The road was open for the great reforming Liberal administrations of the years 1906–14 that laid the foundation of the British welfare state. The proponents of untrammelled capitalism were on the defensive even in Great Britain.

While Britain was moving towards the new 'caring and softer' liberalism, on the continent the older, 'authentic' liberal position was still regarded as the last word in political ideology by much of the intelligentsia. It is often the case that laggard countries, countries worried that they are failing to keep up with others, seek to modernize themselves on the basis of ideas that have become obsolete in the advanced ones. Thus, in France, by the 1890s, liberals dominated the universities and the political and economic establishment. While their British counterparts were having second thoughts about the joys of free-market forces, French liberals still assumed that state intervention would cause more harm than good. The state, they believed, should never have been entrusted with the railways and the post office where it would face pressure for higher wages from its own employees, and for lower prices from consumers. And, to cap it all, politicians, keen to ingratiate themselves with their supporters, would spend tax revenues without inhibition.

These liberals were not wrong. French politicians, like their counterparts in Germany and Italy and elsewhere, paid lip service to the principles of economic liberalism, while exchanging public funds for votes. It became a well-established practice. Democratization empowered groups, such as artisans, small farmers, and shopkeepers, who feared the advance of capitalism. Democracy enabled them to lobby politicians and extract from them promises of tax concessions or restriction of competition.[68] Local politicians spent their days beseeching the government to spend money on behalf of their electorate before offering a few hurried prayers to market forces in their after-dinner speeches. Governments responded by introducing some taxes, reducing others, initiating public works programmes, and subsidizing this or that enterprise.

The economists who argued that there should be no political interference with capitalism did not understand a simple truth: capitalism was not simply an economic system, but a way of organizing social relations. In order to thrive, capitalism required the existence of a supportive infrastructure and a wide consensus around itself that the capitalists themselves, often forced to think for the short term, could not possibly achieve on their own.

The state and its institutions were needed, above all, by the new social class, the bourgeoisie, in the sense that the emerging capitalist system needed a centralized state with a civil service and a standing army and a legal system that regulated commerce, enforced contracts, kept workers at bay, and developed communication infrastructures.[69] The old aristocracy (and the peasantry) of the eighteenth century were not so dependent on state structures.

Such consensus could only be built by political power. How could this be achieved – in democracies – without vote-seeking policies? And if this required higher public expenditure and some degree of interference in the market mechanism, that was a price well worth paying for capitalist progress. This, of course, could not be calculated with any exactitude. The door was opened for endless arguments over whether or not the state had over-reached itself. Even old-fashioned liberals were not sure where the boundaries of state interference should be erected. All agreed that the state should have – as Max Weber put it later – a monopoly of the means of force. Most also agreed that some basic infrastructures could only be built and maintained by the state, such as roads and bridges. Education generated more debate. In principle, liberals were happy for those who could afford it to have most of it, but they also feared that if the state refrained from running schools, the priests would do so – hence the rapid development of compulsory and free state education in most European countries.

What was happening outside Europe?

In Latin American countries, between 1870 and 1930, the so-called 'Liberal' era was one where natural resources were exported while opening the economy to European capital and labour. Since these countries were export-oriented they were vulnerable to external shocks, but there was an overwhelming consensus on the economy until the First World War. The ruling classes were divided politically: liberals versus conservatives, centralists versus federalists, and Catholics versus the anticlerical. But they were all in agreement about free trade, accepted some protection for domestic activity, and encouraged foreign investment and immigration.

Enlightened conservatism rather than liberalism prevailed in Russia in the second half of the nineteenth century, with a succession of finance ministers (Mikhail Reutern, Nikolai Bunge, Ivan Vyshnegradsky, and Sergei Witte) who realized only too well that in order to defend the autocracy it was necessary to modernize the country. That spirit of intelligent and enlightened conservatism was epitomized at the time by diverse European leaders and politicians – conservatives such as Bismarck in Germany and Disraeli in Britain but also liberals such as Giolitti in Italy and Gladstone in Britain. In Japan, Ōkubo Toshimichi, one of the champions of the Meiji Restoration, and Ōkuma Shigenobu, the great modernizing Prime Minister, embraced change to preserve what they regarded as essential. All of these and more radical politicians (such as Theodore Roosevelt in the United States) understood something that few conservatives today appreciate: that for the old order to survive it is necessary to perceive early on which reforms are inevitable and implement them on one's own terms and under one's own direction, before they become irresistible, unavoidable, and ungovernable. One must not leave reforms to the last moment, when revolution threatens, and it is too late. Alexis de Tocqueville explained this so well:

> It is not always going from bad to worse that leads to revolution. What happens most often is that a people that put up with the most oppressive laws without complaint, as if they did not feel them, rejects those laws violently when the burden is alleviated. The regime that a revolution destroys is almost always better than the one that immediately preceded it, and experience teaches that the most dangerous time for a bad government is usually when it begins to reform . . . The evil that one endures patiently because it seems inevitable becomes unbearable the moment its elimination becomes conceivable.[70]

If necessary, conservative reformers must co-opt the opposition, embrace their cause to make sure that nothing essential changes. In Giuseppe Tomasi di Lampedusa's great novel *Il gattopardo* the young Tancredi reassured his uncle, the novel's protagonist Prince Fabrizio di Salina, that he had joined Garibaldi's revolutionary expedition to Sicily in 1860 to contain its radicalism: '*Se non ci siamo anche noi, quelli ti combinano la repubblica. Se vogliamo che tutto rimanga com'è, bisogna che tutto cambi. Mi sono spiegato?*' ('If we are not there as well, they will set up a republic. If we want everything to remain the same, everything must change. Do you understand?')[71]

Aligned against liberals and conservatives we find 'the reactionaries' – I use the term descriptively, not pejoratively. Originally the reactionaries, including those mentioned above such as Thomas Carlyle, as well as a galaxy of French and Italian Catholics, wished to return to a pre-industrial age. The old days were always better and change is always a change for the worse. As the historian Michael Bentley wrote about diehard British Tories in the nineteenth century:

> Conservatism has a close and necessary relationship with the end of the world. That everything slides from a better condition to a worse is not merely the Tory's allegation, after all; it is an important reason for his existence.[72]

The 'reactionaries' longed for an idealized past in which everyone knew their place. They saw every novelty as undesirable (they were not always wrong). They disapproved of the new power of markets because it privileged the power of money instead of aristocratic values. Markets enabled anyone with money to obtain status, enhancing individualism. Although the reactionaries were beating the retreat in the last decades of the nineteenth century, their views influenced all politics, and still do. By decrying change they slowed it down. Lord Salisbury, the great anti-democratic Prime Minister of late Victorian Britain, explained the position admirably:

> The perils of change are so great, the promise of the most hopeful theories is so often deceptive, that it is frequently the wiser part to uphold the existing state of things, if it can be done, even though, in point of argument, it should be utterly indefensible.[73]

Of course, the reactionaries could never hope to win – they lost all the battles they fought – but they had considerable support among the members of the lower orders who felt threatened by the new capitalist social order. Unable to gather sufficient strength to put the clock back, they tried to stop it from ticking on. They made reforms difficult. They put obstacles in the way of democracy, civil rights, female emancipation. They defended traditions as a matter of conviction, thus often ensuring that reforms would be promulgated only when they were seen as absolutely necessary. Their views, however ahistorical, were widely shared and still survive. And while change is one of the few constant elements in the history of the world, a sceptical attitude towards it is not unhealthy since every modification, whether gradual or speedy, is seldom to the advantage of all.

Religion underpinned the beliefs of many reactionaries, who, at least in Europe, included many Roman Catholics. They too were dismayed by modernity. They assumed that religion required the survival of the old rural order, where everyone accepted with grace what fate had ordained. But, as the century progressed, many Christians, popes as well as Protestant bishops, realized that a return to the old status quo was utopian and that the world could not stand still. They moved away from the reactionaries and adopted some of the views of enlightened conservatives. These Christians believed that religion should have social goals and that the everyday life of ordinary mortals should be made more endurable even in this vale of tears. While remaining committed to a religious view of human society, to hallowed traditions, and social deference, they also knew that such attitudes were no longer sufficient in the face of advancing capitalist modernity – a threat they could no longer dispel by ignoring it.

The socialists, above all in Germany, where they were strongest, wanted everything to change and nothing to stay the same, but, like the liberals, they accepted the inevitability of capitalism, which they regarded as a temporarily progressive force. They shared with liberals a commitment to capitalist modernity and industrialization. They praised capitalism's systematic destruction of tradition. They celebrated the disruption of rural life, with its absurd superstitions and arcane religious beliefs. Following Marx and Werner Sombart, they were convinced that destruction, in this case the destruction of the traditional world, would generate a new spirit of creativity – what Sombart referred to as *schöpferische Zerstörung* (creative destruction) – a concept later theorized by Joseph Schumpeter, for whom the process of creative destruction was 'the essential fact about capitalism'.[74]

Socialists did not celebrate capitalism as an end in itself but as the anticipation of the society of the future, a society without classes and privileges. The capitalist social order, they believed – following Marx – was the necessary antechamber to a socialist society. Some were confident that capitalism would eventually enter into a terminal crisis and collapse under the burden of its own contradictions, enabling humanity to reconstruct society anew. Others believed that only a revolutionary uprising, a final onslaught on the citadel of capitalism, could give birth to the new society. In practice such doctrinal disputes did not matter as much as the participants believed. Revolutionaries and reformists alike were convinced that their chances were intimately connected to the physical expansion in the numbers of the working class and hence dependent on the expansion of capitalism. Most socialist parties were formed in the last decades of the nineteenth century, but almost exclusively in western and central Europe and where Europeans had settled (as in the United States, Australia, and New Zealand). They were weak or non-existent elsewhere.

In the minds of many socialists the model for a socialist party was the German *Sozialdemokratische Partei Deutschlands*. Created in 1863 it soon became the most successful socialist party in the world in terms of organization, doctrine, and electoral strength.

In France the fragmented socialist movement took some time in separating itself from the radical republican tradition. By the 1880s the Third Republic, born in 1870, had defeated those who wished to re-establish a monarchical regime. Only then did France develop a socialist party, but one that remained deeply divided between various factions, at least until its formal unification in 1905.

In Britain the powerful trade union movement, throughout the nineteenth century, refrained from forming a socialist party, in the belief that the Liberal Party would be able to deliver substantial gains for the labour movement: the British unions had no objections to capitalism per se, only to some of its manifestations (exploitation, unfairness, inequalities). What was required was a political system in which the economic struggle between labour and capital could be carried out within a framework of rules more favourable to the workers. In this sense continental parties were not so different. Although their programmes wanted the abolition of private ownership of the means of production, their immediate aims were the expansion of democracy, the development of a regulatory framework for capitalism, and social reforms. Socialist politics was always paradoxical. The socialists wanted the abolition of capitalism, but the reforms they advocated tended to strengthen it. The more successful they were in their reformist aims the more the final aim of abolishing capitalism receded.

Thus a powerful though disparate range of forces was formed at the end of the nineteenth century, united by a common desire to ameliorate the fate of those affected by capitalism, and by a recognition of the inevitability of capitalist modernity, divided only by a different attitude on its desirability. These various political 'families' (liberal, reactionary, socialist), of course, never existed in a pristine state, each patrolling its boundaries with zeal and fervour. In the murky and ever-changing world of politics one often fights with borrowed concepts and with ideas developed on the hoof, making friends with former enemies, revising positions hitherto staunchly defended, and justifying what was, only yesterday, apparently unjustifiable. Thus in Britain, once they realized that the extension of the suffrage was inevitable, the Conservatives under Disraeli introduced the Reform Bill in 1867 enfranchising almost the whole of the male working class. In Austria-Hungary, pro-capitalist cosmopolitan liberals, faced with reactionary aristocrats, anti-capitalist Social Democrats, anti-Semitic lower middle-class Social Christians and the nationalism of the Slavic minorities, sought (and obtained) the support of the imperial house of Habsburg to protect their positions and modernize the empire.[75]

What of religion? Social Christianity was a significant force but mainly in (western) Europe. It acquired weight and renown in Latin America only in the last decades of the twentieth century. The Roman Catholic Church remained a bastion of reaction until the last decade of the nineteenth century – a role it continued to play in some countries well into the twentieth. The Russian Orthodox Church was equally a support system for Tsarism, though, here as elsewhere, there were always dissident voices, such as those of Georgy Gapon, an Orthodox priest who was a working-class leader in St Petersburg in 1905.

Protestantism, in its various forms, had always been more socially aware. In its Methodist and Quaker manifestations it inspired many trade unionist and labour activists in late nineteenth-century Britain, while the Anglican Church remained solidly Tory. In the United States, Evangelical and Baptist churches played a leading role among abolitionists. Christianity was also a source of strength and resistance among the slaves themselves and an important component of the American populist movement against the big corporations. (American fundamentalists turned pro-capitalist only in the last few decades of the twentieth century.) Considering the relatively recent alliance between neo-liberal thought and creationism – the rejection of Darwin's theory of evolution in favour of the biblical account – it is ironic that, in the nineteenth century, much pro-capitalist thought in the United States was influenced by a derivative of Darwinism – social Darwinism – as epitomized by William Graham Sumner's *What Social Classes Owe to Each Other* (1883), which extolled capitalism precisely because it was *not* based on traditional ties but on rational contract.[76] Conversely, some strands of progressive thought were implacably opposed to Darwinism, such as that represented by William Jennings Bryan, the leading populist politician, enemy of banks and trusts, a devout Presbyterian, and liberals such as Samuel Wilberforce, son of William Wilberforce, the leader of the anti-slave-trade movement in Great Britain.

*

My narrative opens around 1860, when Europe still regarded itself as the centre of the world and had not yet begun its long voyage towards the periphery. But since capitalist modernization involved most of the planet, this book will avoid, I hope, excessive Eurocentrism. The main focus will be on the decades leading up to the First World War, those halcyon days before the era of murderous wars and massacres of civilians, the decades that the French and others called *la Belle Époque*, the Americans the 'Gilded Age', and the British the 'Great Victorian Boom'.[77] That was the period where global capitalism truly emerged, the period of the first great modern economic globalization. After the 1914–18 war globalization subsided and even went into reverse, capitalism retreating 'into the igloos of its nation-state economies and their associated empires'.[78] Globalization re-emerged after 1945, reaching new heights in the decades following 1980.[79] Similarly, capital mobility was very high in the period between 1870 and 1914, dropped during the 1930s, and then expanded gently from 1945 until 1971, before taking off rapidly in the subsequent decades.[80]

In the decades to 1900, countries that regarded themselves as laggards, determined to catch up with the lead country (Great Britain), had no choice but to strengthen their national state. The idea that capitalist development should be left to entrepreneurs was seldom taken seriously. Capitalists themselves asked to be protected by their state. In any case, in most countries, there were not many capitalists and few willing or able to take risks without state protection. Capitalists had to be nurtured and protected. By the end of the twentieth century, capitalism had grown and matured. Where it was strong and sturdy, the capitalists and their apologists sought, Oedipally, to free themselves from the embrace of the state, demanding a 'return' to the minimal state they imagined existed 'in the good old days'. The fantasy of better days – 'Before the Fall' – is a recurring myth in world history, as Walt Whitman wrote in *Leaves of Grass* (1888):

> Then for the teeming quietest, happiest days of all!
> The brooding and blissful halcyon days!

In the 1880s the prevailing view among the politically conscious was that for liberal capitalism to thrive, it was necessary to strengthen the state. And since the disruption accompanying industrialization would be considerable, the mobilization of people required unprecedented resources, and the benefits were not immediate, it was necessary to involve an important section of the population, perhaps the majority, in economic development. For this to occur, capitalism had to become a collective project. It had to mobilize the people, the whole nation.

Capitalism, as we have seen, is never a matter of mere economics. Its expansion generates social and political problems; its failure to expand creates even more problems, albeit of a different nature. The ruling elites must find ways of ensuring that capitalism develops without excessive political and social disruption and confound those who seek to dethrone them. What is required is the formation of a *national community*, one in which all groups, regardless of their differences, have a stake in capitalist development. This requires a steady and continuous improvement in the conditions of life of the many, so that individuals regard their own problems as temporary, and can hope that, however bad the present, the future will be better, thus partaking of the optimistic ideology of progress – the ideological foundation of capitalism.

But material improvements for the majority take time and are often not sufficiently well distributed. In any case, the formation of a national community cannot proceed simply by increasing prosperity. A feeling of national togetherness, of social solidarity, requires more than simply the hope of greater wealth in the future. At the end of the nineteenth century, various strategies were deployed, not always consciously, to construct a national community: nationalist state-building, democratization, colonialism and foreign expansion, and social reforms.

These themes provide the backbone of the book.

Part One ('The Condition of the World') consists of two chapters. The first surveys the proliferation of states in the nineteenth century, new states such as Germany, Romania, and Italy (Belgium and Greece had been created a few decades earlier); states restructured on a new basis such as the Austrian Empire, which became the 'dual monarchy' of Austria-Hungary in 1867, following its defeat by Prussia; and enlarged states such as the USA. These joined older states such as Britain, France, Spain, and Japan. The second chapter examines social conditions, contrasts the situation in the countryside and in cities, and how the rich and the poor lived and what they ate: in other words the kind of society capitalism had to work with.

Part Two ('Becoming Modern', Chapters 3–9) provides a comparative analysis of the involvement of the state in the economy throughout the world in the decades preceding the First World War. It examines the novel allure of industry, the new role of the state in managing the economy, the question of taxation, and, above all, the anxieties caused by the perception that some countries were more advanced than others, anxieties focused on the modern image of America and exemplified by the great debates on modernization that marked the Tsarist Empire.

Part Three ('Involving the Demos', Chapters 10–16) deals with various strategies devised to cope with the disruptions and anxieties of capitalist industrialization: nation-building and its limits (who is part of the 'nation' and who is not); democratization, that is, the extension of the suffrage and the development of political, social, and economic rights, including welfare rights that gradually transformed people into citizens, and the role of religion in this process.

Democratization enhanced the appeal of nationalism, essentially a nineteenth-century construct. The precise make-up of nationalism would differ from country to country, but the early exponents of European and Latin American nationalism assumed that it would be democratic (in the nineteenth-century sense of the word, that is, with numerous exclusions). Nationalism could become the ideological glue that held the people together regardless of other differences, by excluding 'the others' not on religious or class grounds, as was traditional in pre-modern societies, but on a more or less invented ethnic basis. Not for nothing had Marx and Engels concluded their famous 1848 *Manifesto* with their rallying cry to the *Proletarier aller Länder* ('proletarians of all countries') to unite, an internationalist appeal that went quite unheeded – not surprisingly since, in the same text, they called upon the proletariat, if it wanted to 'acquire political supremacy', to become 'the leading class of the nation' and 'constitute itself the nation'.

Nation-building could also involve projecting the nation's power overseas by acquiring colonies (principally by Great Britain, France, Belgium, and, much later, Germany, Japan, and Italy), or internally by extending its territories contiguously, for instance the Tsarist Empire to the east and the United States to the west, or by protecting national capitalism with tariffs in the hope that it would benefit some strata of the population. Such themes are dealt with in Part Four ('Facing the World', Chapters 17–20). Colonialism, of course, existed in various forms independently of industrial capitalism. The Dutch, Spanish, and Portuguese empires were in reality remnants of an earlier era when these countries had considerable power. During the nineteenth century, Spain lost most of its empire, while Portugal and the Netherlands managed to keep some of their colonies, at great expense. They contributed little to national pride or to industrialization.

Colonialism contributed to nation-building in a number of ways: by providing an outlet for colonial administrators and emigrants; by promoting trade; by developing the military; and by building up pride in one's country as truly superior (*la mission civilisatrice*, the white man's burden, and other such fantasies). Along with democratization, taxation, and the welfare state, it contributed to the extraordinary development of the state under capitalism and of capitalism under the state, since colonialism is a form of extension of the state into overseas territories.

Yet between the state and capitalism there can be no harmonious relation but only constant conflict. The state, even when it is federal, devolved, and even when there is a division of power, is necessarily a monolith. There can be only one command centre with rules decided by the state itself. Capitalism, on the other hand, is anarchic, has no centre, no single will. The state is anchored within a territory. Capitalism has global tendencies both in its production and its consumption. It runs where it can, where there are profits, opportunities, openings. Every failure of one capitalist is another capitalist's success. Every crisis has winners. Every triumph is temporary. As Schumpeter wrote, capitalism is like a hotel where the clients 'are forever changing'.[81]

And while the form of organization of capital is ever more global, the regulatory agency, the state, is constrained by other states. Of course, states get together, make agreements, sign treaties, establish rules, but there is no super-state able to impose its control, whereas capitalism can reach out all over the planet precisely because it is not a monolith, because it has no centre, because it engenders rivalries and thrives on competition.

PART ONE

The Condition of the World

I
New States, Old States

Has there ever been a time when the world was made up of small communities living in isolation, under the illusion that they were unique? If there ever was, such beliefs, bred by poverty, ignorance, and almost non-existent technology, were regularly shattered by enterprising men and women who travelled outside their villages, discovered new worlds, exchanged goods and ideas, and subjugated other men and women.

The 'shrinking' of our planet began some 70,000 years ago, perhaps more, when, after several unsuccessful attempts, a technologically aware *Homo sapiens* began to spread from Africa to the Eurasian landmass, and reached Australia and the Americas, colonizing virtually the entire surface of the earth, except for some permanently frozen spaces and a few small islands. The key to this was the technological advance of travelling by boat and ship, though of course it is possible to cover great distances just by walking. If one walked just 20 kilometres every day, one would be able to cover the distance from Cape Town to Helsinki, Vladivostok, and then to Singapore in just over four years.

These highly mobile human beings, whose most significant difference with other mammals was their ability to use language, eventually discovered how to grow food and how to cook flesh. They built empires, spread religions and belief systems, and traded with each other.[1]

Much later, travellers and invaders from Asia, Europe, and the Arab world systematically explored other lands, in which they occasionally settled. Thus, beginning in the eighth century, the Vikings colonized vast swathes of Europe; in the thirteenth century, the Mongols arrived in what is today Hungary and Poland; at the same time the Maoris settled in New Zealand from eastern Polynesia. The great Chinese explorer Zheng He (1371–1434) travelled on his enormous 'treasury ships' (at the time the largest in the world) and traded perhaps as far as the east coast of Africa and north into Kamchatka. Such sea explorations, which could have created a Chinese empire overseas, were stopped in 1433 by the

Ming emperors, who regarded such expenditure as wasteful at a time when China was under renewed threat from the Mongols and needed resources for domestic production, internal stability, and colonization.[2] The powerful Chinese state could put a stop to exploration, as no European state was able to: though it traded extensively and had settlers elsewhere, it never developed an overseas empire. Over the last five hundred years or so, Europeans have settled in vast numbers in Africa, the Americas, and Australasia. Even in pre-Colombian America, indigenous peoples, such as the Aztec, though cut off from Africa, Asia, and Europe, traded extensively.[3] The Silk Road, the ancient trade route that connected China to the Mediterranean, was a major example of trade, as was the slave trade of the eighteenth century.

Globalization is thus an ancient process and not something that sprang up upon an unsuspecting world in the last few decades. In the 'olden days', however, only a few were involved in global processes. A traveller such as Marco Polo, the fabled merchant who went, or so he claimed, all the way to China and came all the way back to Venice in the thirteenth century, was part of a tiny minority. Until the sixteenth–seventeenth century what peasants consumed was largely produced within a few miles of their home, and most marriages were equally local. The vast majority of markets were places that could be reached in twenty-four hours. The wider circle for most people was a region, not a state. The globalized economy then involved only the one per cent of total production that was transported by ship.[4]

The globalization that occurred in the last decades of the nineteenth century was, however, quite different. While people have long traded from distant places, buying goods in one place and selling them in another at a higher price, the late nineteenth century saw the start of a global market for capital and the globalization of manufacturing, in other words the modern internationalization of capitalism.[5] So though globalization was a process with a long history, the intensity with which it developed from the 1860s onwards, helped by conquest, economic development, and the revolution in communication, was new. The most important difference between the First Great Globalization (1860–1910) and the Second (1980–) is the acceleration of time.[6]

A new word was invented during the Second Great Globalization to highlight what is new in what is old. Until the late 1980s, the term 'globalization' was hardly ever used. Sporadic sightings of this now-so-popular concept occurred before 1990, usually in connection with 'global firms' and global marketing. In 1983, Theodore Levitt, in a famous if somewhat over-hyped article in the *Harvard Business*

Review, wrote of 'The globalization of markets'.[7] Before 1990, the catalogue of the Library of Congress listed only a dozen or so books in English with the word 'globalization' in the title, none published before 1987. But since then what used to be called international or transnational was suddenly called 'global'.

After 1990 the term 'globalization' was deployed with a crescendo of enthusiasm. Twenty-four titles containing the word appeared between 1990 and 1995, a further 86 by 2000, another 913 between 2001 and 2005, and a further 1,330 in the years between 2006 and 2010. In 1964, *Le Monde* used the word *mondialisation* in only one article. By 1992 the paper had published almost 200 articles containing the term, and in 2000 there were over 800.[8]

'Globalization' sells. In 1996, Susan Strange was already complaining, with some justification, that this was yet another of those 'vague and woolly' words freely bandied about, whose precise meaning is seldom clearly defined, and that 'all too often, it is a polite euphemism for the continuing Americanization of consumer tastes and cultural practices'.[9] Globalization became an ill-defined state of affairs loathed and feared by some, celebrated by others as a new stage in the evolution of humanity from a primitive world of separate communities to a single 'global village' (the expression was used by Marshall McLuhan in *The Gutenberg Galaxy*, published in 1962 – well before the age of the internet).

Globalization, of course, has been going on for many centuries through the channels of trade, religion, crime, food, even disease. Ancient trade routes covered much of the globe. Religions travelled widely, often on the back of conquest and colonialism: Christianity from the Mediterranean to Asia, Africa, and the Americas; Islam from the Arabian Peninsula as far as Spain in the west and Indonesia in the east; Buddhism from India to China and Japan. Crime too travelled as criminals (pirates) became increasingly mobile, keeping up with technology, as do modern mafia organizations. After 1500, food became global as the New World alerted everyone to the existence of potatoes, tomatoes, cocoa, peppers (including chilli), peanuts, and maize. It is rather remarkable that only four years after Peru was conquered by Francisco Pizarro's armed men (1532) the first potato (the tuber is indigenous to the Andes) was eaten in Spain. By 1597 it was cultivated in London, and soon became popular in Ireland. Rice cultivation in the United States was introduced by the slaves who planted rice when and where they could, as they had done in west Africa for generations.[10] Along with food and people, diseases travelled too, causing more deaths in the New World than the atrocities directly perpetrated by European colonists. But the globalization of diseases was hardly new. Bacteria on fleas, fleas on rats, rats in ships travelled along trading routes, arriving in Europe from Asia and causing, in the fourteenth century, the traumatic death of perhaps one-third of the population.

The globalization of food is a topic of study in itself since it includes products that became part of the staple diet across the world, food such as potatoes, maize, rice, and cassava. Coffee made its way in the fifteenth century from the port of Mocha in Yemen, via Turkey, towards the Mediterranean, the Middle East, India, and Java. It was eventually drunk at the court of Louis XIV, served on Chinese porcelain, sweetened with sugar grown on slave plantations in São Tomé and Brazil.[11] Luxury food was soon 'global'. At dinner parties at the house of Thomas Cromwell, chief minister to Henry VIII in the 1530s, the cook would use such exotic delicacies as ginger, nutmeg, figs, oranges, and marzipan.[12] Then it was the turn of the bourgeoisie to eat 'international' food. In 1833 the celebrated Paris restaurant Aux Frères Provençaux offered a menu that today we would call 'world cuisine': oysters from Ostend (Belgium), ducks 'farcis à l'anglaise', prawns in 'soya de Chine', and various meals from different parts of France, from Dieppe in the north (mussels) to Provence, where the owners came from.[13] Fruit salad was already called a 'Macédoine' – an allusion to the multi-ethnic nature of Alexander's Macedonian Empire. At the restaurant Lapérouse, established in 1766 (and still on the Quai des Grands Augustins), one could eat, in 1891, *Barbue sauce hollandaise* (a fish called brill in English and *rombo liscio* in Italian) and *Puddings d'abricots à la Vénitienne* (bread pudding with apricots).[14] The bourgeois classes of the nineteenth century could drink coffee from the Americas or Africa, fill their pipe with tobacco from Virginia or Kentucky, wear shirts made from Egyptian or American cotton, and eat chocolate made with cocoa imported from Africa or the Americas.[15] Upper-class ladies were wearing hats made of beaver and vicuña, or of raw materials from Canada, Peru, west Africa, the Sudan, and the Levant, made fashionable in the eighteenth century by French hat-makers.[16]

In 1876 the first refrigerated ship sailed from Argentina to France with frozen beef. The further drop in transport costs between 1870 and 1914 led to a remarkable convergence in prices – Liverpool wheat prices still exceeded those in Chicago by 58 per cent in 1870, but by only 18 per cent in 1895.[17] Advances in transport made the world smaller: the fastest liner in 1842 had a speed of 10 nautical miles per hour; by 1912 it could do 18 nautical miles per hour. The opening of the Suez Canal

(1869) almost halved the distance between London and Bombay: in the 1840s it took between five and eight months to get to India, but in 1912 the trip could be done in two weeks.[18]

Ideas too travelled. Contemporary cosmopolitans can look back to ancient celebrations of international interconnectedness, from John Donne's famous line from his *Meditation* XVII (1623), 'No man is an island, entire of itself; every man is a piece of the continent, a part of the main'; to Jeremy Bentham's first use of the word 'international' (1780) to denote 'the branch of law which goes commonly under the name of the law of nations'; to Immanuel Kant's *Project for a Perpetual Peace* (1795), which envisaged a world of sovereign states (*ius gentium*), at peace with each other but also one in which men would be regarded as citizens of a universal state (*ius cosmopoliticum*); to the Marquis de Condorcet's *Esquisse* (1795), which looked forward to a time when the 'sun will shine only on free peoples who will know no master but reason and when tyrants, slaves and priests will exist only in history'.[19]

These dreams are still to be fulfilled, but in 1864 the first international agreement was signed that limited the absolute sovereignty of the state; that was the Geneva Convention, which allowed for the protection of soldiers wounded in battle. It had been immediately preceded by the first supra-national humanitarian organization, the Red Cross (1863). Since then there has been a proliferation of trans-national organizations and agreements, such as the International Telegraph Union (1865), the Universal Postal Union (1874), and an international agreement adopting the metric system signed by seventeen states in 1875 (the *Convention du Mètre*) and now adopted by all countries in the world except Burma, Liberia, and the United States.[20] By 1914 there were 112 international organizations.[21] The number has steadily increased ever since.

Time-keeping also has become global in the sense that a single clock is used to measure time in different parts of the world. Dates are the same everywhere, even though the date universally adopted is that of the Christian calendar, which non-Christian cultures also use, often alongside their own.

In the twentieth century, international organizations such as the United Nations, the OECD, the World Trade Organization, the World Bank, the International Monetary Fund, and the International War Crimes Tribunal arose out of increasing cooperation among almost all countries in the world. There are also regional associations – prevalently dealing with trade – such as the European Union, SAFTA (South Asian Free Trade Area), MERCOSUR (Common Market of South America),

NAFTA (North American Free Trade Agreement), ASEAN (Association of Southeast Asian Nations), and the African Union. But such organizations do not substitute themselves for states. On the contrary they are agreements between sovereign states and they come in two forms: economic alliances, in which case almost always about free trade within the regions (as the *Zollverein*, the German customs union, in the nineteenth century from 1833); or military alliances such as NATO, dominated by the United States. In fact, while the equality of states, just like the equality of people, was often declared, the reality is that power in the international arena has remained in the hands of a few states: whether the Great Powers of the so-called Concert of Nations in the nineteenth century or what today we call the 'international community', meaning, most of the time, a US-led West.

Market capitalism and representative democracy are regarded by their supporters as suitable for all people, without exceptions (the parallel with religious belief is striking). But capitalism is wider than liberal democracy. Although almost all the hardware and software associated with the computer and internet revolutions – IBM, Hewlett Packard, IBM, Dell, Intel, Cisco, Microsoft, Apple, Google, e-Bay, Twitter, Facebook, YouTube, Amazon, and Wikipedia – originated in America, an increasing proportion of the physical goods (such as computers and electronic tablets) are manufactured outside 'the West', above all in China, which exports half the computers of the world.[22] The ever-increasing speed of travel, the waves of migration, and, above all, the formidable speed of cultural exchange and communication (radio, television, and the internet), have been among the more salient aspects of the shrinking of our planet. The international division of labour studied and theorized by the eighteenth- and nineteenth-century economists Adam Smith and David Ricardo has developed to levels then unimaginable.

The general acceptance, at least formally, of the concept of universal human rights, an aspiration seldom mentioned a few decades ago, suggests the establishment of common moral standards. This is a recent achievement. When, in 1853, the Comte de Gobineau published his racist *Essai sur l'inégalité des races humaines*, his views were not regarded as particularly provocative. Global warming and the perils associated with a significant increase in the world's temperature have strengthened the view that we are all in the same boat, burning slowly and surely, but together.

Today internationalism and cosmopolitanism are seen by many as worthy of praise. Yet this was not so in the first half of the twentieth century, when internationalists and cosmopolitans were often denounced – and, in some places, shot. Indeed, in the nineteenth century even progressive literary critics such as Vissarion Belinsky, a Russian Westernizer, attacked some writers for their 'rootless cosmopolitanism' – an early, perhaps the first, use of this expression.[23] And he did not mean Jews. The term 'cosmopolitan', however, is ancient. Diogenes, asked where he came from, is reported to have said (by a Greek biographer writing in the first half of the third century AD): 'I am a citizen of the world' (*kosmopolitês*).[24] Less grandly, the term was adopted as the title of an international magazine first published in 1886 in the United States: *The Cosmopolitan*, originally a 'family' magazine, but aimed mainly at women with articles on fashions, cooking, and household management – sex advice came later. Fashion, one of the regular features of the magazine, already straddled countries and continents.

Today the forces of nationalism are stronger than those of cosmopolitanism. Politics is still overwhelmingly national politics. Citizens may not trust politicians but they trust their own more than those of other countries. They expect their governments to protect their own interests above those of foreigners. In the era of globalization it is felt that to belong to a strong state is an advantage – which may not always be true, since strong states also give rise to strong feelings of antagonism: it is probably safer to be an Austrian anywhere in the Middle East than an American.

The nineteenth century may have been the age of nationalism but the twentieth was the age of nation states, and the era of nationalism is very far from coming to an end. In 1900 there were just over fifty formally sovereign states (without counting various sultanates such as the Upper Aulaqi Sheikhdom, now part of the Republic of Yemen, and statelets such as Andorra, still extant), including the United States, Canada, and Haiti, plus nineteen states in Europe, seventeen in Latin America, and only six in Africa and seven in Asia (see Table 1).

By 1960 there were over one hundred sovereign states, and today there are more than two hundred. Yet despite its successes, nationalism has nowadays lost the unquestioned positive connotations it possessed in the nineteenth century. Although today's schoolchildren may be taught about their glorious past, they are also often taught to be tolerant of and to value other cultures. This narrative usually comes from intellectual elites, the most cosmopolitan section of the population, who speak more than one language, travel easily, and are curious about other people's mores. Nationalists are perceived by them to be provincial, narrow-minded, and obsessed with defending their own culture, while

Table 1 Sovereign States in the World, 1900

Argentina	Luxembourg
Austria-Hungary	Mexico
Belgium	Montenegro
Bhutan	Morocco
Bolivia	Nepal
Brazil	Netherlands
Canada	Nicaragua
Chile	Norway
China	Orange Free State
Colombia	Ottoman Empire
Costa Rica	Paraguay
Denmark	Persia
Dominican Republic	Peru
Ecuador	Portugal
El Salvador	Romania
Ethiopia	Russia
France	Serbia
Germany	Siam
Greece	South African Republic
Guatemala	Spain
Haiti	Swaziland
Honduras	Sweden
Italy	Switzerland
Japan	United Kingdom
Korea	United States
Liberia	Uruguay
	Venezuela

cosmopolitans glory in their ability to transcend borders and frontiers, in being 'citizens of the world'. Yet, when it comes to culture and politics, the majority of the inhabitants of each nation state tend to be unaware of those of even neighbouring countries (unless it is American politics, which is constantly discussed by the international media, while American cultural products, particularly music, films, and television fiction are widely exported). Such abject ignorance about neighbouring nations is true even in highly advanced countries with fine schools and ancient universities. Thus Jean Racine, the seventeenth-century dramatist, who is studied in all French schools, is virtually unheard of in neighbouring Germany and Italy. Similarly, a majority of Germans and French have never heard of Dante.[25] People still live in their nation as if they were in a village.

Some theorists, such as the Japanese management expert Kenichi Ohmae, go so far as to say that we live in a 'borderless world' and that since the great problems of our age are global, they can only be solved by a global or trans-national approach. They say that nation states are empty vessels, mere illusions belonging to the past, and 'unnatural business units' in a global economy: what matters now are 'region states', geographical units such as northern Italy, Wales, San Diego, Hong Kong, and Silicon Valley.[26] Yet, at one time, Ohmae thought that Japan, far from being borderless, could unilaterally extend its borders and its sovereignty over coastal areas to 200 nautical miles – an 'act of state' that made Japan less dependent on 'foreign' fish.[27] We are still far, after all, from the borderless state. The idea that nation states are doomed by ever-growing internationalization is barely new. In 1910, Gustave Hervé, then an international socialist and not yet a rabid nationalist and admirer of Mussolini, stated it forcefully in his pamphlet *L'internationalisme*: 'Modern motherlands have just been created and already they are threatened by internationalism.' He confidently predicted that if the nineteenth century was the century of nationalism, in the twentieth century internationalism would prevail.[28]

So how important are nation states in the era of globalization? It could be argued that if states did not count, their decisions would not be so important for the world economy. But would anyone make such a strange claim for the American decision in 1971 to devalue the dollar, or for the member states of the European Union to establish a single market under the Maastricht Treaty in 1992, or the decision in 1978 by the Chinese Communist Party to reform the economy, or, in 2016, that of Britain to leave the European Union?

The debate over whether the state is growing or shrinking rages on, fuelled by the difficulty in defining the state. Some point out that after years of almost unimpeded growth, the advent of neo-liberalism has led states to retrench themselves, cutting down on public spending on welfare, health, and education, and abandoning their control over the commanding heights of the economy they had developed in the thirty years of post-1945 growth. Here the statistics are not univocal. State spending remains surprisingly stable. General statements about 'the state' and its future often show a lack of understanding of the variety of states and their ever-changing relationship to each other. The Franco-Spanish border, now just a line on a map, was only too tangible to someone trying to flee from the Nazis. On the night of 25 September 1940 the great social theorist Walter Benjamin killed himself because he was told that he would not be able to cross the border and reach safety. Today, anyone can just walk across it.

How and why have states proliferated over the last 150 years? The new states were formed either by secession – breaking away violently or peacefully from a wider unit (e.g. former British colonies, Norway from Denmark, Slovenia from Yugoslavia) – or by unification imposed from above, as was the case with Italy and Germany in the second half of the nineteenth century. Secession is by far the norm, absorption is rare.

Each new state, however small, maintains all the paraphernalia of sovereignty largely established in the nineteenth century: passports, borders, armies, uniformed police, currencies, national anthems, national days, and central banks – later even airlines, national football teams, and entrants in the Eurovision Song Contest or the Miss World competition.

There is one conspicuous exception to all this. A number of European states have adopted a single currency (beginning with eleven members in 1999 and reaching nineteen in 2015) and abolished border controls among each other with the Schengen Agreement of 1985. Yet all sovereign states, including those in the European Union, celebrate a 'national' culture, have at least one or more national television channels that give priority to national news, and impart their national history in schools where children are taught to be proud of their country, even though most would agree that there is no personal merit in being born in any one particular place. They are given a somewhat embellished account of the birth and development of their nation.

The litany is fairly similar – a literary genre – poised between lachrymose self-pitying victimhood and vainglorious accounts of heroic deeds. 'We', it says, have been around for centuries, or even more (1066 in Britain; 966 in Poland; since Romulus and Remus in Italy; since Plato and Aristotle in Greece; since the days of Abraham in Israel). We have written glorious pages of history and they would have been even more glorious had it not been for the dastardly acts of our oppressors. Eventually we achieved our freedom, our independence, our happiness, and we, who are unlike everyone else (for we are Croats and not Slovenians, Italians and not Austrians, French and not Germans, Ukrainians and not Russians, etc.), can finally be like everyone else: members and possessors of a country, a nation, defenders of a remarkable literature, a major culture, a beautiful language, and a unique landscape.

We tend to think that a state is defined by its borders, but the borders and boundaries of most of today's sovereign states are a relatively recent creation. This is as true in European states as across the globe. An Italian state has existed, in any shape or form, only since 1861, but even this is too distant a date since Venice and its region were incorporated into Italy only in 1866 and its capital, Rome, only in 1870; the current borders with Austria have been extant only since 1919. Although an island, the present boundaries of Great Britain are even more recent. They are certainly not as old as 1066, as children used to be taught in British schools. Great Britain has been in existence only since 1707 with the Act of Union between Scotland and England. The UK's borders changed again in 1801 when Ireland became part of the United Kingdom, and again in 1922 when the southern part of the island of Ireland became the Irish Free State. England, on the other hand, when it existed as a state, was relatively ancient, at least by European standards: by the end of the Middle Ages it had a shared language and strong state structures covering a clearly defined territory under clearly defined laws. But for a period, before 1066, under King Canute (Knut the Great), England was part of a northern Scandinavian kingdom with Denmark and Norway. After 1066 and the Norman Conquest, England was part of a polity that included a part of France at least until the late Middle Ages; after 1707 there was no longer a state called 'England'.

History has dealt with borders and population in a cavalier way and determined that a place could be part of a state for reasons that had nothing at all to do with national feelings – a relatively simple task since in most cases such feelings did not exist. Had Immanuel Kant been born in 1946 in Kaliningrad rather than in 1724 in Königsberg (as it then was), he might have been a Russian philosopher rather than a German one. Had Arthur Schopenhauer been born in Polish Gdansk in 1946 rather than in German Danzig – as it was when he was born in 1788 – he would have been Polish. The inhabitants of Corsica are now French, whether they like it or not (and some don't), only because France acquired it in 1770 – previously it was an independent republic that had freed itself from the 'yoke' of the Republic of Genoa. Had this not happened, Napoleon (born in 1769) might have been little more than a local strongman, since it is unlikely that Corsica could have conquered anything at all, let alone most of Europe. The people of Nice are French today because the city and its surrounding territory (plus what is now called French Savoy) were handed over by the Kingdom of Piedmont to the French in 1860 – had that not happened the Italian Riviera would have been much more extensive, tourists in Marseille might be regaling themselves with *zuppa di pesce* instead of *bouillabaisse*, and its inhabitants would have supported Italy's national football team and not that of France. The city of St Louis in Senegal is an older French city than Lille since St Louis became French in 1659, whereas Lille was acquired by the French Crown nine years later, in 1668, by the Treaty of Aix-la-Chapelle. France's boundaries have continued to change even after the Second World War when overseas territories such as Guadeloupe and Martinique have been incorporated as part of France. The country's borders have been unstable throughout the centuries. Alsace, minus Strasbourg, was attached to France only at the end of the Thirty Years War (1648), as was (in 1659) the county of Artois. Lorraine became French only because Louis XV married Maria Leszczyńska, the daughter of the Duke of Lorraine (who had himself obtained Lorraine only in 1738 in compensation for renouncing the Polish throne). Yet for much of the twentieth century the children of Lorraine (who, until recently, spoke various German patois at home) were taught in French schools not only that they were French but that, as such, they were descendants of *nos ancêtres les Gaulois* ('our ancestors the Gauls'). Even this belief that the Gauls were the ancestors of the modern French is recent. Gaul was unmentioned throughout the Middle Ages.[29] The choice of the Gauls as the ancestors of the French nation was made during the nineteenth century.[30] Current scholarship seriously doubts that there was ever even a single Gaulish nation. Indeed, the Gauls have not left any written texts whatsoever and all we know about the great 'national' hero Vercingetorix comes from his conquerors, the Romans.[31] The amazing sales of the comic strip *Astérix* since 1959 have surely reinforced the belief in *nos ancêtres les Gaulois.*

French boundaries may have been unstable but they look as solid as rock when compared to those of Poland. This is not surprising since Poland is in the middle of the northern European plain, a near-flat landscape with few natural geographic limits. What is more surprising (unless one is familiar with the fervid imagination of nationalists) is that the Polish state celebrated 'its thousand-year history' in 1966 – 'history' having begun with the Christianization of the country and the baptism of King Mieszko I (the leader of the powerful Polanie tribe, one of many). In 1966 the country was still under communism, but the idea of the millennium rallied all and sundry, communists and patriots, Catholics and agnostics.[32] Yet, the borders of the country celebrating its longevity had expanded and shrunk constantly. In 1634 'Poland' was very large, including what is now Lithuania (another independent sovereign state with extravagant claims of longevity, in this case since 1253), as well as bits of Moldavia and Prussia. The Polish-Lithuanian Commonwealth, as it was known, stretched from the Baltic to the Black Sea. Then Poland began to shrink, partitioned over several decades between Russia, Austria, and Prussia. After the Napoleonic Wars much of what is Poland today came to be incorporated into the Tsarist Empire, and only regained its independence after the Russian Revolution, with boundaries quite different from those of the old Polish-Lithuanian Commonwealth. After the Second World War, Poland shifted to the West as it acquired former 'German' territory and lost some to the Soviet Union (now in independent Ukraine, whose boundaries have been and continue to be equally elastic and hotly contested). As Norman Davies remarks: 'Despite the Poles' own fervent belief in the *macierz* or "motherland", it is impossible to identify any fixed territorial base which has been permanently, exclusively, and inalienably, Polish.'[33]

Some states appear to have a truly long history, as is the case with Japan, with more or less the same boundaries for centuries, an easier feat if you are an island or, in this case, four large islands and a few thousand smaller ones. Nevertheless the idea of Japan as a nation state (*kokka*) lay dormant, in spite of the unification of the country in 1590 under the regency of Toyotomi Hideyoshi, and primary loyalties belonged with local clans (*han*), who continued to fight it out for centuries. The few thousand islands also made a difference, acting as 'zones of continuous economic and cultural exchange' and delaying the drawing of proper 'modern' borders until the middle of the nineteenth century. So even the state of Japan is a modern artefact.[34]

The United States declared its sovereignty first and embarked on expansion later. The boundaries of the USA in 1776 have little in common with those of 2019. One could almost say that British settlers, having declared their independence from the mother country, and become Americans, continued the westward conquest the British had started.

Thus each nation state builds its own special 'national' history, however chequered. For instance, Montenegro (or, in Slavonic, Crna Gora, 'Black Mountain'; Montenegro is the Venetian name) is one of the 'newest' European states, but it had been sovereign before the First World War (though its tiny borders changed over time), having successfully resisted complete subordination to Ottoman rule. It was amalgamated into Yugoslavia in 1919, and regained its independence in 2006 when it seceded from what was left of Yugoslavia (i.e. from Serbia). It acquired its own constitution, but not its own currency, having decided to use the euro even though it was not actually in the European Union. It had a diplomatic corps and its own armed forces but not its own language since everyone speaks Serbo-Croat. Local nationalists nevertheless insisted that their version of Serbian should be called Montenegrin, an assertion of identity that older states such as Belgium, Switzerland, and the USA have refrained from since they seem happy to use other names for the languages their citizens speak. No one speaks Belgian, Swiss or American but Montenegrins, apparently, speak Montenegrin. The country also has a new national anthem, *Oj, svijetla majska zoro* ('Oh, Bright Dawn of May'), based on a nineteenth-century folk tune with words that have been changed to fit the prevailing politics. Montenegro has fewer than 700,000 inhabitants – fewer than Birmingham in England or Tucson in Arizona but more than at least twenty other sovereign states (including EU members such as Malta and Luxembourg). Formally speaking, Montenegro is as 'sovereign' as the United States, but in practice sovereignty is limited by the power of other countries. Its inhabitants can affirm their pride in their country, but this is not much different from the inhabitants of Cornwall or Lombardy being proud to be Cornish or Lombard, even though neither has ever been a sovereign state.

Our new brave globalized world is thus also a world of 'them and us', of states, large and small (mainly small), trying to make their presence manifest, taking offence, being proud, and defending, sometimes hypocritically, the sanctity of their borders against secessionist claims by even smaller 'nations' simmering within and aspiring to get out. This is the situation Georgia faces with the recalcitrant inhabitants of South Ossetia and Abkhazia who do not feel they share the same ancestry as those Georgian nationalists who, in a remarkable flight of imagination, trace theirs to the Hittites in 1600 BC, or to the more recent kingdom of Egrisi (sixth–seventh century BC) – which was itself the outcome of local chieftains fighting it out for their own power and aggrandizement. Thus Kalistrat Salia's *Histoire de la nation géorgienne* (1980), based on the works of nationalist ideologues such as Ivane Javakhishvili masquerading as historians, celebrates Georgians as an ancient people ('one of the most beautiful races in the world') who, in spite of external threats and invaders, managed to preserve their national personality, their language, and their culture.[35] Ukrainian nationalism stands on similarly shaky foundations, which is one reason why so little was done by Ukrainians to achieve independence from Russia until the Soviet Union collapsed (on Russia's initiative). Some Ukrainian nationalist historians, such as the popular Yurii Kanyhin, strongly endorsed by the first president of Ukraine (and former communist), Leonid Kravchuk (1991–4), even claimed that Ukrainians are mentioned in the Bible and are descended from Noah.[36] In fact, there never has been an exclusively Ukrainian nation.

With the collapse of the Soviet Union, engineered by the Russians themselves under Boris Yeltsin, it became routine to rediscover one's nation even if, when the collapse occurred, some, such as Uzbekistan, were reluctant to become independent. Once independence was obtained, history books were rewritten reversing the previous 'consensus', tracing Uzbek origins to prehistoric times and making Timur (Tamerlane in the West), once a cruel tyrant and responsible for the death of millions, the founding hero of the country. His equestrian statue now graces the spot where Karl Marx's statue once stood. It is quite common for nationalist feelings to increase *after* independence is obtained. Nationalism is usually a minority affair until there is a state that continues the nationalists' work, which is why one can speak of, say, Iraqi or Nigerian nationalism in the late twentieth century. It would be absurd to do so in the nineteenth century since neither existed.

*

There are far more states today than in 1860 or even 1880, but before 1800 there were more states than in 1880. There is an ebb and flow in the coming into being and the disappearing of states, which suggests that it is better to avoid any deterministic view as to their future. There may be more. There may be fewer. Catalonia and perhaps Scotland might be sovereign states one day.

Sovereignty of states is another disputed term, one whose meaning has changed in the course of the centuries to such an extent that there can be no all-embracing definition. A state must be sufficiently centralized to ensure that all its constituent parts are 'united under the same law and the same name', as Livy put it in *Ab urbe condita*. This is what most people understand as a sovereign state.[37] In more modern times a functioning state should be able to impose its will sufficiently to be able to collect taxes. If it cannot force or persuade its citizens that they should pay up so that their state can function, it is a 'failed' state.

Some argue that sovereignty needs to be recognized by others, and this is largely true, but we know that any state able to defend itself is, in fact, a sovereign state whether or not it is recognized by anyone. China, when not recognized by the United States, and Israel, not recognized by most Arab states, are certainly sovereign states.

Sovereignty is something you acquire when you are strong enough and eager for it, or others are weak and unable to stop you. You may lose or fail to acquire sovereignty when you are feeble and vacillating, or others are stronger. This is, more or less, how states have developed since the last decades of the nineteenth century when the number of sovereign states was at its lowest.

The great empires of the nineteenth century, such as the colonial empires of the French, the British, and the Dutch, and the newly formed Belgian Empire, the short-lived Napoleonic Empire, and the pre-existing Russian and Ottoman Empires, left as their fundamental legacy the elimination of thousands of self-governing units, tribal areas, principalities, duchies, bishoprics, and city states (sometimes loosely connected by the decentralized Holy Roman Empire) – an operation we could regard as a gigantic geopolitical tidying-up but that some might see as an unfair removal of self-government. Borders that would become sacrosanct were often defined from a great distance by more powerful countries. Thus, in 1862, the Tsarist regime imposed on the Chinese a border according to topography, rather than ethnicity, thereby dividing peoples such as the Kirghiz and leaving a problem that festered well into the twentieth century.[38]

Even more momentous was the establishment of the so-called Durand Line in 1893 between the British (Sir Mortimer Durand was a British diplomat) and Abdur Rahman Khan, the ruler of Afghanistan. This effectively cut through the Pashtun tribal areas (as well as those of other tribes), resulting in the Pashtun people being divided between Afghanistan and present-day Pakistan (then part of British India). The Pashtun had lived in the area for centuries, perhaps more. Tribal division was only one of the many problems facing the country, problems that made it almost impossible for Afghanistan to emerge as a modern state: it was not colonized (so no national liberation movement emerged), it was landlocked, isolated, economically backward, and though united by religion it was divided by language.[39]

Elsewhere state construction was dominated by the interests of the Great Powers. Thus the secret Anglo-French agreement of 1916, known as the Sykes-Picot Agreement, defined future spheres of influence in the Ottoman Empire, while the Treaties of Sèvres (1920) and Lausanne (1923) resulted in the present, highly contested borders of three states that had never existed before then: Iraq, Lebanon, and Syria. Parts of what is today Israel were designated as a 'national home' for the Jews by the British foreign secretary. A part of the area known as Palestine was subsequently carved up as 'Israel' in 1948 by the United Nations and soon enlarged through military activity and the ethnic cleansing of part of the Palestinian population.

In sub-Saharan Africa too, state-building was externally determined. Before the advent of colonialism, there were some 10,000 polities exhibiting as diverse a range of organization as their equivalent in pre-modern Europe: kingdoms, city states, small isolated communities, trading towns, empires. Under colonialism, thousands of self-governing units were wiped away and boundaries drawn across well-established lines of communications. As a result the Maasai were cut in half by the Kenya-Tanzania border; the Bakingo (or Kongo people) found themselves in states called Gabon, Congo, and Angola; the Yoruba (who number over 30 million people, more than most European nations) could be found in Nigeria, Benin, and Togo.[40] Nigeria itself, the most populous state in Africa, was the result of the amalgamation of two British protectorates by their governor, Sir Frederick Lugard, into one colony (1912–14). The name had been suggested by the renowned journalist and colonial editor of *The Times*, Flora Shaw (who married Lugard in 1902), in an article in *The Times* in which she suggested that 'the name "Nigeria" . . . may, without offense to any neighbours, be accepted as co-extensive with the territories over which the Royal Niger Company has extended British influence'.[41] Nigeria became independent in 1960 and kept the name invented by Flora Shaw in 1897. Its first national anthem, 'Nigeria, We Hail Thee', adopted in 1960, was written by two British women (it was replaced in 1978 by the present anthem, 'Arise, O Compatriots').

The forty-nine states formed in the decades after the colonialists vacated sub-Saharan Africa (see Table 2) and whose boundaries were drawn – with some exceptions – by white occupiers became sovereign states with their own flags, national anthems, and football teams. And they have survived, some better than others, into the twenty-first century.

The multiplicity of ethnic groups across borders may not explain the enormity of civil conflicts in Africa after decolonization, since wars *between* African states (as distinct to civil wars) have not been as pronounced or intense as the intra-European wars of the first half of the twentieth century. One can blame African rulers for all sorts of sins, but it was a wise move when they decided not to revise the borders fixed by the colonialists and thus accept them de jure as well as de facto by signing the Charter of the Organization of African Unity (now the African Union).

The decision to accept the colonial borders has been, on the whole, respected with a precision few other international agreements can

Table 2 States in Sub-Saharan Africa, 2019*

Angola	Ethiopia	Niger
Benin	Gabon	Nigeria
Botswana	Gambia	Rwanda
Burkina Faso	Ghana	Sao Tome and Principe
Burundi	Guinea	Senegal
Cameroon	Guinea-Bissau	Seychelles
Cape Verde	Kenya	Sierra Leone
Central African Republic	Lesotho	Somalia
Chad	Liberia	South Africa
Comoros	Madagascar	South Sudan
Congo (Democratic Republic of)	Malawi	Sudan
Congo (Republic of)	Mali	Swaziland
Côte d'Ivoire	Mauritania	Tanzania
Djibouti	Mauritius	Togo
Equatorial Guinea	Mozambique	Uganda
Eritrea	Namibia	Zambia
		Zimbabwe

*African countries not part of sub-Saharan Africa: Morocco, Algeria, Tunisia, Libya, Egypt, as well as Western Sahara – claimed by Morocco. The UN definition of sub-Saharan is used here.

claim – though there were important exceptions: the Ethiopia-Somalia war over Ogaden (1977–8), the Tanzania-Uganda war (1978–9), and the civil wars in Sierra Leone (1991–2002) and Congo (1998–2003) where other African states (notably Liberia in the case of Sierra Leone) have intervened to help this or that side in the conflict. The acceptance of colonial boundaries, however, has led to the worst conflicts in Africa, but in the form of civil wars rather than interstate wars. This was partly a consequence of the difficulty of creating 'nations' out of heterogeneous cultural materials in a relatively short period of time. But this is also true for the world as a whole: in 2001 most conflicts in the world were civil wars.[42] Internal conflicts in African countries have included the former Belgian Congo (now the Democratic Republic of Congo), the former French Congo (today the Republic of Congo), Angola, Rwanda, Sierra Leone, Sudan, Ethiopia/Eritrea, Algeria, Libya, and Mali, and they took an enormous toll in human lives. Most but not all of these conflicts have taken the form of secessionist struggles, such as the Polisario movement in the western Sahara, the Ogaden liberation movement in Ethiopia, and many others. The most serious attempt at secessions were those of Biafra from Nigeria (1967–70) and Katanga (with direct military help from Belgium) from the Democratic Republic of the Congo (1960–63). They were both defeated, at huge human cost. Unlike Europe or Asia, Africa has produced only two new countries since decolonization. The first was Eritrea, independent in 1993, but a country whose independence had been originally curtailed by Ethiopia in 1952 and not by a European power. The second was South Sudan, which achieved statehood in 2011 after a referendum. Both Eritrea and South Sudan are currently in disastrous conditions.

Although not as pulverized as pre-colonial Africa, pre-Napoleonic Europe too was a remarkably fragmented entity consisting of dozens of statelets under the domination, protection or toleration of larger states – some of these tiny entities still survive either as gambling preserves (Monte Carlo), or tax-dodging havens (Monte Carlo again or Lichtenstein), or a dispensary for cheap alcohol (Andorra) or the producer of pretty stamps (San Marino).

*

The idea of a nation is constructed out of a mish-mash of myth, legend, history, and wishful thinking. The inhabitants of those self-governing units that prevailed before 1800 were seldom self-conscious members of a nation, but were held together by a sovereign, or a religion or a language or by force of arms or the self-interest of the local elites, or because it was in the interest of foreign powers to let them survive. Central Europe, in particular, was a complex conglomeration of such states and statelets.

Within the boundaries of what today we call Italy, there were at the time of the French Revolution almost twenty such self-governing units. By 1870 all these states and statelets had been amalgamated into a single state: Italy, a state with a history it claimed to be ancient and a language, Italian, only a minority of its inhabitants could speak or spoke habitually. This state joined a system of European states that turned out to be generally stable on its western flank but unstable on the eastern one (the main exceptions to the rule of western stability after 1880 were the birth of the Republic of Ireland in 1922 and the formalization of Norwegian and Icelandic independence – see below). The following tables and maps show how European sovereign states multiplied between 1901 and 2010.

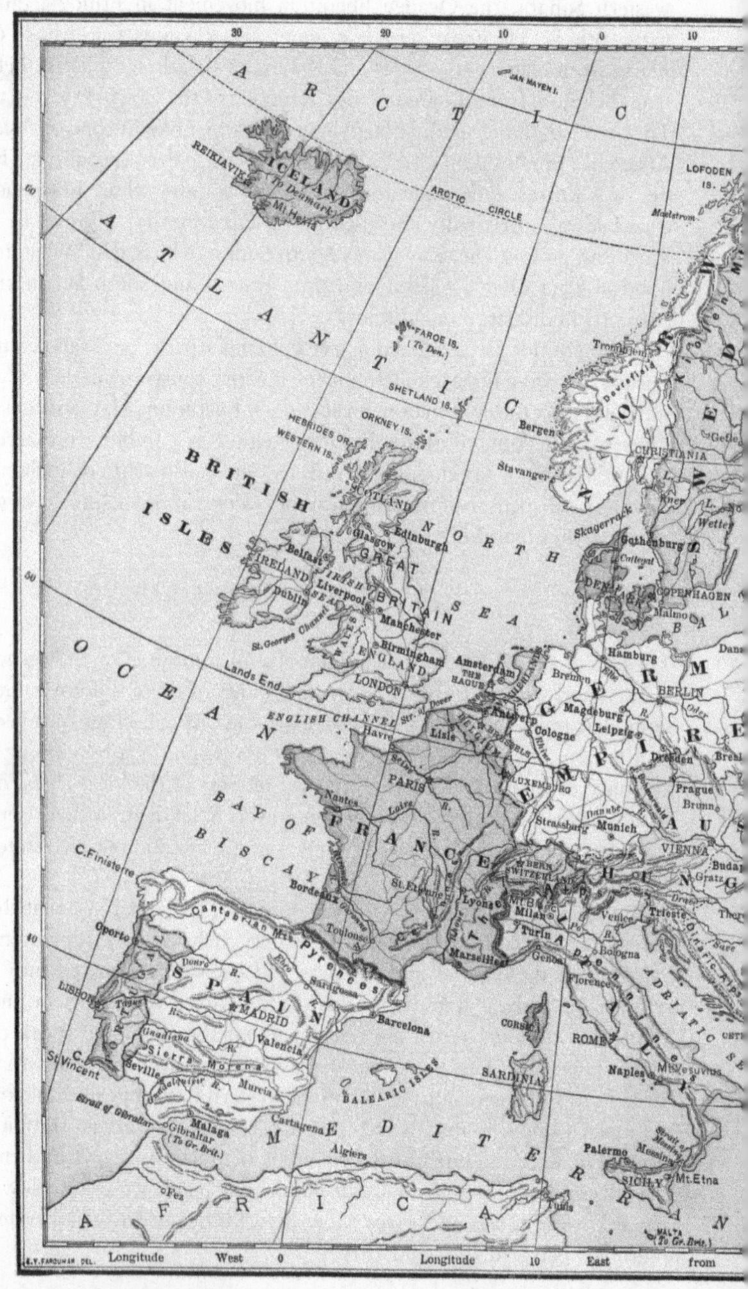
ARCTIC
JAN MAYEN I.
ICELAND
(To Denmark)
REIKIAVIK
Mt. Hekla
ARCTIC CIRCLE
LOFODEN IS.
Maelstrom
ATLANTIC
FAROE IS.
(To Den.)
SHETLAND IS.
ORKNEY IS.
HEBRIDES OR WESTERN IS.
BRITISH ISLES
SCOTLAND
Edinburgh
Glasgow
Belfast
IRELAND
Dublin
IRISH SEA
St. Georges Channel
GREAT BRITAIN
Liverpool
Manchester
WALES
Birmingham
ENGLAND
LONDON
Lands End
NORTH SEA
Trondhjem
Dovrefjeld
Bergen
Stavanger
CHRISTIANIA
Skagerrack
Cattegat
Gothenburg
DENMARK
COPENHAGEN
Malmo
Wetter
Gefle
OCEAN
ENGLISH CHANNEL
Str. of Dover
Amsterdam
THE HAGUE
NETHERLANDS
Antwerp
BELGIUM
BRUSSELS
Lille
Havre
Bremen
Hamburg
BERLIN
Magdeburg
Cologne
Leipzig
Dresden
GERMAN EMPIRE
LUXEMBURG
Prague
Brunn
Strassburg
Munich
Danube
VIENNA
PARIS
Seine
Loire
Nantes
FRANCE
BAY OF BISCAY
C. Finisterre
Bordeaux
St. Etienne
Lyons
Toulouse
Marseilles
BERN
SWITZERLAND
Mt. Blanc
Milan
Turin
Venice
Trieste
Genoa
Bologna
Florence
ROME
Naples
Mt. Vesuvius
ADRIATIC SEA
Dinaric Alps
Cantabrian Mts.
Pyrenees
Oporto
Douro
Ebro
Saragossa
LISBON
Tagus
SPAIN
MADRID
PORTUGAL
Barcelona
Guadiana
Valencia
Sierra Morena
C. St Vincent
Seville
Guadalquivir R.
Murcia
Strait of Gibraltar
Gibraltar
(To Gr. Brit.)
Malaga
Cartagena
BALEARIC ISLES
CORSICA
SARDINIA
MEDITERRANEAN
Algiers
Fez
AFRICA
Tunis
Palermo
Messina
Strait of Messina
SICILY
Mt. Etna
MALTA
(To Gr. Brit.)
E. V. FARQUHAR DEL.
Longitude West 0 Longitude 10 East from
30
20
10
0
10
60
50
40

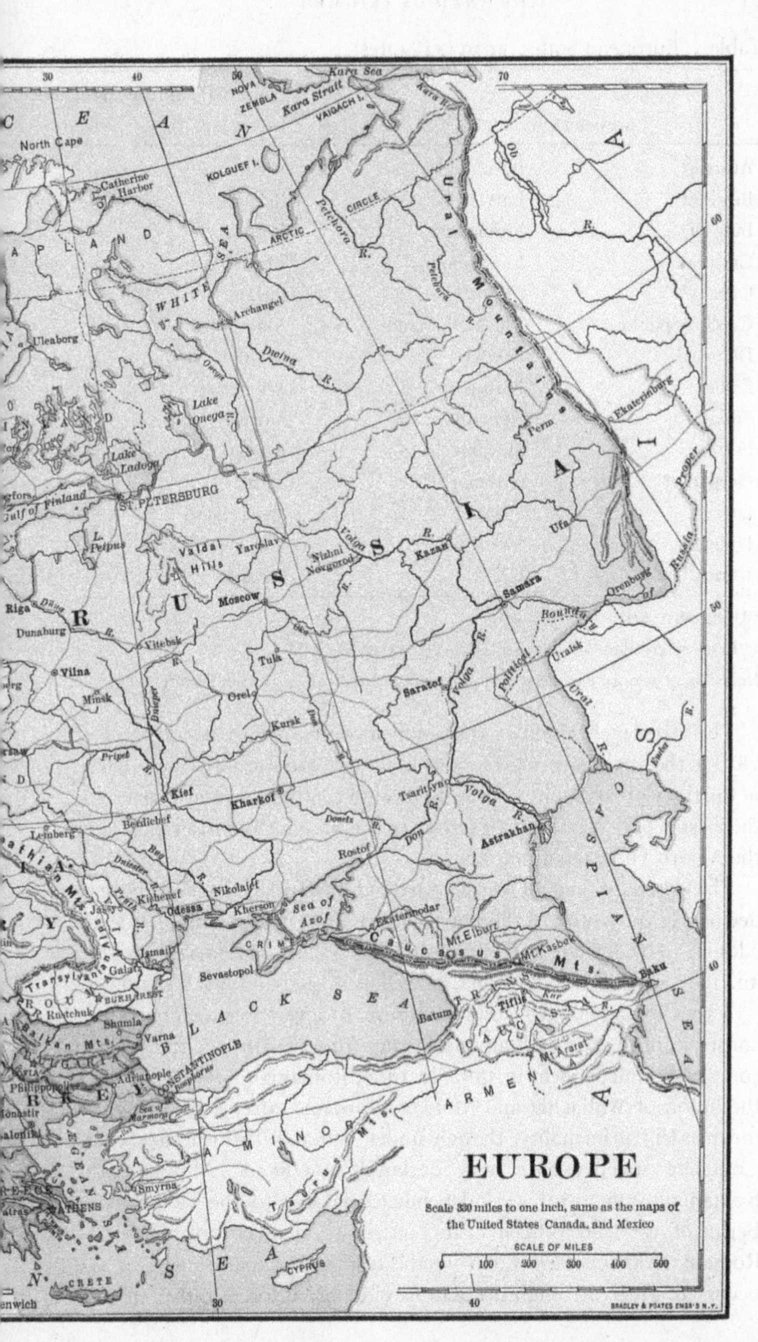
EUROPE
Scale 330 miles to one inch, same as the maps of the United States Canada, and Mexico
SCALE OF MILES
BRADLEY & POATES ENGR'S N.Y.

Table 3 European States, 2019 (42 States)

European Union (28)		Outside the European Union (14)
Austria*	Italy*	Albania
Belgium*	Latvia*	Belarus
Bulgaria	Lithuania*	Bosnia
Croatia	Luxembourg*	*Kosovo
Cyprus*	Malta*	Iceland
Czech Republic	The Netherlands*	Macedonia
Denmark	Poland	Moldova
Estonia*	Portugal*	*Montenegro
Finland*	Romania	Norway
France*	Slovakia*	Russia
Germany*	Slovenia*	Serbia
Greece*	Spain*	Switzerland
Hungary	Sweden	Turkey
Ireland*	UK**	Ukraine

* Using euro currency

** In the referendum of 2016, the UK voted to leave the EU

Note: There were 19 European states in 1900, including the Ottoman Empire

The awesomely complex transition from the twenty or so states of 1880 to the forty-two or so of today is almost entirely due to the collapse of the three great empires of the nineteenth century as a consequence of the First World War: the vast Ottoman Empire, the Tsarist Empire, and the Austro-Hungarian Empire.

The Ottoman Empire, whose heartland was Turkey, had long been in decline: in the course of the nineteenth century it 'lost' Albania, Macedonia, Greece, Crete and Cyprus, Wallachia and Moldavia, Bulgaria, and most of present-day Serbia, as well as Bosnia and Herzegovina.

Serbia, already largely autonomous in 1830, was able to adopt a new constitution in 1869 without interference from the Turks,[43] and became completely independent in 1882. In 1866, Romania (itself the result of the union of Wallachia and Moldavia) became, after a plebiscite, an independent principality, though under nominal Turkish suzerainty. Complete independence was declared in 1881.[44] Although the Romanian state owes its independence largely to the Congress of Berlin of 1878, its official history attributes a much greater role to Romanians themselves. Likewise the territorial expansion of Greece occurred largely through the actions of external forces rather than of the Greeks themselves. The Aeolian Islands were given to them by Great Britain in 1864, Thessaly was obtained by the Treaty of Berlin in 1878, and parts of Macedonia, Crete, and Epirus during the Balkan wars of 1912–13.[45]

At the Congress of Berlin of 1878 the Great Powers (Great Britain, France, Germany, Russia, Austria-Hungary, and Italy) convened to stabilize Europe after the Ottoman collapse. None of the Balkan countries participated: delegates from Greece, Serbia, Montenegro, and Romania were only allowed to attend in silence the session in which their fate was decided.[46]

The Treaty of Berlin recognized the independence of Serbia and Montenegro. Bulgaria became an autonomous principality and a fully independent kingdom in 1908. Albania achieved independence from the Ottomans after the Balkan War of 1912. Thus, the so-called 'Balkanization' of the Balkans pre-1914 was largely due to the disintegration of the Ottoman Empire, and further Balkanization occurred after 1918 with the fall of the Austro-Hungarian Empire, but was limited by the creation of Yugoslavia in 1945. Finally, the disintegration of Yugoslavia in the 1990s led to further multiplication of states.

In north Africa, the Ottoman Maghrebi provinces were lost to the French in the course of the nineteenth century and Libya (then known as Tripolitania and Cyrenaica) to the Italians in 1911. Egypt, the jewel in the Ottoman's crown, had become virtually independent when Ismail Pasha came to power as hereditary ruler of Egypt (1863) with the title of Khedive, a title not granted to other provincial governors, and obtained the right to conclude treaties and raise loans.[47] Thus Turkey, whose presence in Europe had extended under Suleiman the Magnificent to the gates of Vienna (1529), and whose expansion had been definitively stopped in 1683, again just outside Vienna, was reduced to a rump state across the Bosphorus straits with a population that was almost completely Muslim.[48]

While the Ottoman Empire continued to shrink, the Tsarist Empire, whose formal birth had occurred in 1721 when Muscovite Russia became the Russian Empire under Peter the Great, continued the consolidation of its rule in Asia. By the end of the nineteenth century it included Russia, much of what had been Poland, Ukraine, Moldova, Belarus, the Baltic States and Finland, and also Armenia, Georgia, and Azerbaijan, as well as what are today known as Kazakhstan, Kyrgyzstan, Tajikistan, Turkmenistan, and Uzbekistan. It probably contained more Muslims than the Ottoman Empire.

The immediate successor of the Tsarist Empire, the Soviet Union, did not modify the borders of its predecessors significantly. It lost Poland and Finland (Finland became an autonomous Grand Duchy in the Russian Empire from 1809 until the end of 1917) as well as the Baltic states (Lithuania, Estonia, and Latvia, which they reoccupied after the Second World War). The fall of communism, however, brought about an entirely new situation. Countries whose claims to nationhood had been more linguistic and cultural than political (Ukraine and Belarus, for instance, but also Armenia, Georgia, and Azerbaijan, as well as the Asian Republics) had to rapidly develop a brand of nationalism relevant to their newly acquired statehood, won without a significant struggle of national liberation. Russia, much reduced in size for the first time, appeared to belong exclusively to Russians. Yet, far from being mono-ethnic, the new Russian Federation is home to a considerable variety of ethnic groups, and, as in the Tsarist Empire, numerous languages (twenty-four officially recognized), and nationalisms. These are either strongly secessionist (such as that of Chechnya) or demand protection from Russia against new threatening nationalisms (such as South Ossetia and Abkhazia) – just as Georgia under King Giorgi XII demanded to be incorporated into the Tsarist Empire in 1801 when it feared neighbouring Muslim nations more than it feared Russian hegemony.[49]

The Austro-Hungarian Empire, which included Austria, Hungary, Bohemia, Slovenia, and Croatia, continued to expand right up to 1914, notably at the expense of Turkey with the annexation of Bosnia and Herzegovina. By contrast with the Ottoman and Tsarist Empires, it was itself a somewhat recent creation, formed out of the old Austrian Empire created in 1804 when Francis II, the last Holy Roman Emperor, became the Emperor of Austria with the name Francis I. After its defeat by Germany in 1866 (when it lost Venetia to Italy and hegemony in Germany), the Austrian Empire reconstituted itself by sharing the task of governing what was an increasingly complex multinational state with Hungary. This was the so-called Compromise, or Ausgleich, of 1867.

The 1867 Compromise entrenched the Hungarian nation, now in charge of all its internal affairs with its own parliament. However, this parliament, by giving virtual control to the ethnic Hungarians, discriminated against the Croats and Slovakian minority. Thus within every majority there is always a minority that, once its minority status is enshrined formally, will struggle to get out.

Of the twenty states that existed in Europe in 1880 only nine (Switzerland, the United Kingdom, France, Portugal, Spain, Sweden, Denmark, and the Tsarist and Ottoman Empires) had existed in the eighteenth century and only seven of these survived into the twenty-first century. But continuity had hardly been the norm even in apparently long-lasting states.

Between the Congress of Vienna of 1815 and 1870 the boundaries of France remained stable. Then, in 1870, having lost the war with Prussia, France was forced to cede Alsace and Lorraine to the newly born German Empire. But ceaseless and traumatic political changes made France the least stable country in nineteenth-century western Europe. In the hundred years prior to 1870, it had gone through an astonishing range of permutations: an absolute monarchy up to 1789; an interregnum between the fall of the *Ancien Régime* and the proclamation of a Constitutional Monarchy in 1791; a radical (Jacobin) republic between 1792 and 1794; a moderate republic between 1794 and 1799; a military dictatorship from 1799 to 1804 under Napoleon; and then the Napoleonic Empire between 1804 and 1815. This was followed by a constitutional monarchy under two successive dynasties, the Bourbon (1814–30) and then the Orléans (1830–48). Then there was the Second Republic (1848–52); the Second Empire of Napoleon III (1852–70); a period of civil upheaval (the Paris Commune of 1870–71); and then, finally, the Third Republic (1870), which was consolidated only in 1880.

Spain more than matched France in political strife. Ruled directly or indirectly by Napoleonic France between 1808 and 1814, the country was plagued by a succession of civil wars leading to the Vicálvaro Revolution of 1854 and the 'Glorious' Revolution of 1868 (*La Gloriosa*), the moderate monarchy of King Amadeo (1870–73), the brief First Republic of 1873–4, and the restoration of the monarchy in 1874.

Nothing as dramatic as this occurred elsewhere. Portugal remained stable, but lost Brazil in 1822 and declined inexorably though holding on to its African empire until the 1970s – after most British, French, Belgian, and Dutch colonies became independent. Switzerland acquired the Valais, Neuchâtel, and Geneva in 1815 thanks to the Congress of Vienna and became a stable country only in 1848 when it settled its internal conflicts by adopting a federal system.

In northern Europe the situation was less complex but also far from static. Denmark lost Norway in 1814 (to the Swedish Crown) and the provinces of Schleswig and Holstein to Prussia in 1864. Iceland obtained autonomy from Denmark in 1874 but became independent only in 1944. Two new major states were created in the course of the nineteenth century: Italy in 1861 and Germany in 1871. Belgium and Greece had been created in 1830, though Greece in the 1830s was far smaller than it is now and much of its present-day territory still lay in the Ottoman Empire.

There were, of course, plenty of 'nations' in nineteenth-century Europe without a sovereign state, and many, such as the Welsh, the Flemish, the Catalonian, the Breton, the Corsican, and the Basque, still exist. And, in the late nineteenth century, though there was an abundance of racialist theories pertaining to ethnicity, many had serious doubts that there was such a thing as an ethnic definition of nation.[50]

So Great Britain was the European success story of the nineteenth century. It did not lose territory, it gained an empire, it continued to industrialize and to stave off social unrest by extending the franchise significantly, first in 1832 and then in 1867, the mid-point between these two dates being punctuated by the defeat of the Chartist movement, the most serious political unrest in the history of modern Britain. Thus, contrary to the terminology that contrasts the Old World (Europe) to the New (the Americas), many of the states that existed in Europe in 1880 were no older than those of North or Latin America. The paradox is that the regional association we call today the European Union, which has few of the attributes of a state, is the strongest and closest inter-state association in the world, but it is located in the continent with the greatest degree of political fragmentation. This fragmentation is not new. Since time immemorial, no single state or conqueror has been able to unify Europe or even to build a large and stable empire such as China, which survived for at least two thousand years, or the Mughal in India for at least two hundred years.

European fragmentation, already pronounced in the nineteenth century, reached new heights in early twenty-first century Europe. By 2015 (as can seen in Table 3 above) there were, in Europe, forty-two states including Turkey but excluding statelets and all former Russian republics east of Turkey (excluding, for instance, Armenia, Georgia, and Azerbaijan, which are members of the Council of Europe – adding them would simply strengthen the point about fragmentation). Of these sovereign states twenty-eight were in the European Union. The increase in European states since 1980 – when there were 'only' thirty – was entirely due to the end of communism, as the Soviet Union and Yugoslavia broke up and the Czech Republic and Slovakia separated. There was only one merger: the DDR was (re-) united with the Federal Republic of Germany. No one expects any new mergers while further secessions or separation (Belgium, Scotland, Catalonia) are possible.

Beyond Europe the formation of states proceeded in a different way, though often brought about by European settlers. In complete contrast to the constant redrawing of states and nations in Europe, the United States exhibited a formidable degree of continuity. Independent since

1776, it adopted in 1787 a Constitution, the oldest in the world, that is still substantially the same today. Its main formal political arrangements (President, Senate, House of Representatives, federal system, relatively autonomous judiciary) have remained unchanged. Yet, throughout the nineteenth century everything else changed including key aspects of what makes a nation: territory and population. Few countries of a respectable size have undergone the extraordinary demographic transformations that have characterized the USA. What was, in 1800, substantially a former colony peopled mainly by settlers from the British Isles (circa 4.3 million), their slaves (893,000 and 108,000 former slaves), and a constantly decimated population of indigenous inhabitants (for which we do not have reliable figures) became, on the eve of the Civil War (1861) a country many times more populous: 27 million whites, 3.9 million slaves, and 488,000 freed slaves.[51] It was more multi-ethnic than any European country (except, perhaps, the Austro-Hungarian Empire where ethnicity and territory often coincided), with more than 13 per cent of the population born abroad.

Furthermore, the United States was virtually refounded by the bloodiest war it ever fought, the Civil War of 1861–5, with twice the American casualties suffered in the Second World War (circa 620,000 deaths in both South and North during the Civil War and just over 400,000 in WWII) – proportionately, of course, the difference was even more serious since the US population in 1940 was much greater than in 1860 (132 million in 1940 against 31.4 million in 1860, including almost 4 million slaves).[52]

The Civil War not only put an end to the plantation system but also to any further secessionist tendencies. Since then there has been not the slightest threat of secession (hardly anyone takes seriously the Alaskan Independence Party or the Texas Nationalist Movement). In any case the American Constitution does not allow for secession.

A further dramatic change was the completion of internal colonization. Strictly speaking, the creation of the United States, even if we stick to the formal recognition of territories as being part of the Union, was an extended process. The formation of the USA was completed between 1850 when California became a state (thus bringing westward expansion to an end) and 1912 when Arizona became the 48th state and the last contiguous territory to be annexed. Wars with Mexico settled the southern border. Alaska and Hawaii joined the Union in 1959 but this entailed minor demographic change (though, in the case of Alaska, considerable territorial expansion, most of it of frozen lands).

The conquest of the west was described by the historian Frederick Jackson Turner in a famous paper he delivered at the American Historical Association in Chicago in 1893 as the event that led to the formation of a unique 'American' character, for, as the settlers advanced, killed Indians and buffaloes, built homesteads and railways, they shed, Turner claimed, the germs of Europeanness they carried and emerged, finally, as true Americans:

> Little by little [the colonist] transforms the wilderness, but the outcome is not the old Europe, not simply the development of Germanic germs . . . here is a new product that is American . . . Moving westward the frontier became more and more American . . . Thus the advance of the frontier has meant a steady movement away from the influence of Europe, a steady growth of independence on American lines.[53]

The creation of Canada was almost as complex, though it became a de facto state in the 1860s, earlier than the majority of present-day European states. In 1841 the British government joined together two separate colonies: English-speaking Upper Canada (present-day Ontario) and French-speaking Lower Canada (present-day Quebec). British Colombia was added in 1873. Newfoundland was preserved as a colony until 1907 when it acquired dominion status. It joined Canada only in 1949 after a referendum won by pro-Canadians by a relatively small margin (52 per cent to 48 per cent).

Latin America is a continent with exceptionally stable state boundaries (compared to Europe or Africa) but with often exceptionally unstable internal regimes. The direct impetus for independence was the Napoleonic invasion of Spain and Portugal in 1807 and the Peninsular War that followed. This undermined Spanish authority and enabled the Spanish settlers (and, in Brazil, the Portuguese) to declare independence in the subsequent decade. The power of the settlers (like those in North America) was due to the near-impossibility for Spain to control her possessions.[54] Eventually the settlers took over and declared independence. The dissolution of the Spanish Empire in Latin America thus brought about the existence of over twenty states.

Dissolutions of empires (Ottoman, Austro-Hungarian, Tsarist/Soviet, British, French, and Spanish) are the fundamental causes behind the existence of the majority of today's states, but the Latin American case, like the earlier case of the United States, and later of Canada, Australia, and New Zealand, offers a variant: states that came into being because settlers (almost always European settlers) obtained independence from the mother country, quite unlike the African and Asian instances where, by and large, it was the indigenous population that wrested independence from the colonial power.

After losing much territory to the USA in the 1830s and 1840s, including Texas, Arizona, New Mexico, and parts of California, Mexican boundaries remained relatively stable but, between 1822 and 1872, the country had fifty-two different governments and thirty-six heads of state. Most Latin American countries had at least twenty governments in their first fifty years. The Dominican Republic, independent from 1844, had twenty-five governments, seventeen heads of state, and six constitutions in its first fifty years.[55]

Even an enormous increase in population did not lead to territorial instability. In 1900, compared to Europe or North America the total population of Latin America was small: 61 million (not much more than the population of Germany at the time, 56 million).[56] Today the population of Latin America is greater than that of the European Union.

Although territorially fragmented, Latin America exhibited a remarkable linguistic and religious unity: there were only two dominant languages (Portuguese in Brazil and Castilian everywhere else) and one dominant religion, Catholicism. The exceptions to this are minor and confined to territories that, strictly speaking, cannot be classified as part of 'Latin' America: English is the main language in most of the Caribbean islands as well as in Guyana, French prevails in Haiti and in French Guyana, Dutch in Surinam. There are, of course, a large number of subsumed native languages, some endangered or spoken by few people, others, such as Quechua, the main Native American language family, which is spoken by some 10 million people and whose multiplicity of dialects are spread across the Andes.

The borders of Latin American states, like those of Africa, were drawn without any consideration for the indigenous people, decimated by disease and oppression, and who never constituted a serious countervailing force or threat to the settlers (here the situation approximates that of the United States and Australia). Popular insurrections and military coups had as their main objective the governance of each country, not the domination of others, and they did not destabilize Latin American states. Simón Bolívar's efforts in 1819–31 to create larger states such as Gran Colombia (which would have included Colombia, Ecuador, Venezuela, and Panama) were unsuccessful. As he exclaimed:

> In America there is no good faith, not even between nations. Our treaties are scraps of paper, our constitutions empty texts; our elections pitched battles; our freedom, mere anarchy; and life pure torture.[57]

However, by and large Spanish-imposed borders proved long-lasting. The advantage with borders created mainly for administrative reasons, as was the case with Latin America, is that they occasionally reflected geographical constraints (mountains, deserts, forests). Without indigenous native revolts, these turned out to be more stable than those created by a succession of treaties among Great Powers, or by ethnic, religious conflicts, or by ancient wars of conquest and annexation – as in much of Europe. This may explain the relatively low level of external conflicts once independence had been gained. There were, of course, inter-state disputes in nineteenth-century Latin America.[58] The most important of these was the Paraguayan war of 1865–70 fought between the Triple Alliance (Brazil, Argentina, and Uruguay) and Paraguay, resulting in extremely high casualties on the Paraguayan side. But this aside, other wars, including the War of the Pacific (1879–83) that pitted Chile against a Peruvian-Bolivian coalition, were relatively small compared to the European carnages of the twentieth century, the Chinese wars of the nineteenth century, or the American Civil War. The Battle of Arica, fought between Chile and Peru (1880) and regarded as the most important battle of the War of the Pacific, resulted in 'only' 1,500 casualties.

As in Africa, borders were relatively stable, but, inside them, political instability was virulent and, at times, violent, though the commitment to the republican form of government was never seriously questioned, with some minor exceptions. In Mexico, General Agustín de Iturbide had himself designated as Emperor Agustín I in 1822, and though his 'empire' was extensive (it included not just Mexico but the whole of Central America as well as what are today California, Texas, Arizona, New Mexico, Nevada, Colorado, and Utah), he lasted only a few months. Brazil had a king (King João I of Portugal, who fled the Napoleonic armies in 1808) who left the Brazilian throne to his son Pedro I. Pedro was in turn succeeded by the long-lasting and 'enlightened' Pedro II (1825–89), who abdicated when a relatively peaceful military coup brought about the republic.[59]

The domestic instability of Latin America states bore little relation to the class struggle as conceived in Europe: there was no sturdy industrial system, and the proletariat was supine or non-existent and concentrated prevalently in the mining or food industries. The most important cleavage was between urban and agrarian interests and this often took the form of a struggle between Church and State or between centralizers and devolutionists. The contrast between liberals and conservatives owed little to ideology, though liberals tended to be anti-clerical Westernizers who favoured free trade.

The dualism of Latin America has been much remarked upon: a society of agricultural workers and peasants with little connection to wider political realities and an elite of landlords and mining barons who fought it out, often peacefully, for political control. Such dualism, of course, also prevailed in much of Europe. The main difference, however, is that in Europe no country, not even those regarded as 'backward' such as Tsarist Russia, remained unaffected by industrialization. Latin America did not need to industrialize (though Argentina's important food industry is an exception), since by exporting its primary products (such as guano from Peru, sugar from Brazil, coffee from Brazil, Colombia, El Salvador, and Costa Rica, wheat from Chile) its elites could obtain a lifestyle similar to that of their counterparts in Europe and in North America. There had been frequent attempts to industrialize but to little effect. Thus, in 1823–5, in Peru, shortly after Simón Bolívar had declared independence from Spain, there were timid attempts to purchase British machinery to equip local enterprises, but soon this flow of imports was reduced to the usual luxuries and semi-luxuries such as French and English textiles, books, and assorted Parisian goods.[60]

In parallel with what occurred later in post-colonial Africa, the military struggle required to break the links with Spain in the nineteenth century brought to the fore a class of military strongmen, or *caudillos*, who dominated much of the politics of Latin America until the 1870s and beyond. Since industrialization was not a policy any of the elites pursued with any vigour, political conflicts were essentially conflicts within the leading groups in society.

The common traits we noted among Latin American countries (languages, religion, Iberian origins, etc.) do not seem to have produced a political integration of the region comparable to that of the European Union, even though linguistic, religious, and political divisions in Europe have been and still are considerable. This gives some substance to Benedict Anderson's claim that modern nationalism (in the sense of resistance to any pooling of sovereignty) was born in Latin America. It shows that, however artificial the borders and minor the differences, bureaucratic construction and propaganda do marvels for the establishment of patriotic fervour.[61]

*

State formation in North and South America as well as Australia and New Zealand (in the last quarter of the nineteenth century still part of the British Empire but, like Canada, virtually autonomous) largely reflected the activities of European settlers who subjugated or wiped out the original inhabitants and formed their own states. State formation in sub-Saharan Africa was completely different. It was the result of a two-stage process: colonization, mainly in the second half of the nineteenth century, and decolonization in the second half of the twentieth. In Africa all attempts to establish settlers' states, as in South Africa and Rhodesia (Zimbabwe), eventually failed.

Asia and the Middle East offered yet another pattern. With the exception of Israel, no Asian or Middle Eastern state was the result of settlers establishing their own state. Some states were the direct result of colonialism, but the colonial powers had to work through existing elites and reach some kind of negotiated settlement. Others were states which pre-dated colonialism and maintained a strong element of continuity with the ancient world, such as China, Japan, Vietnam, Cambodia, Iran, Madagascar, and Tunisia. In many cases modern boundaries have no direct correspondence with older ones; thus India and Pakistan, as presently constituted, have never previously existed. In Iraq, Syria, Jordan, and Lebanon state boundaries were decided by European powers.

China is one of the oldest states in the world with 2,000 years of continuous history, though for most of its history it could not be called a 'nation state' in the modern nineteenth- and twentieth-century sense.[62] The first emperor (*huangdi*) of a unified China was Qin Shi Huang, founder of the short-lived Qin Dynasty in 221 BC, but the China he ruled did not have the same borders as the China of today. The 2,000 years of Chinese history saw many dynasties including foreign ones. A Mongol, Kublai Khan, founded the Yuan Dynasty (1271–1368) and, in 1662, the Manchus founded the last dynasty, that of the Qing, which ruled until 1911 when the Chinese Republic was born. Not only the borders of the state altered frequently in the course of the centuries, but there were wars, rebellions, unrest, turmoil; nevertheless the continuity of the bureaucracy was remarkable as were the set of rules, based on Confucius's teaching after the initial period of so-called 'legalism' under Qin Shi Huang.

Although never a colony, China was hardly a sovereign state between the 1840s and the establishment of the People's Republic of China in 1949, the period the Chinese call, fairly justifiably, the 'century of humiliation'.[63] It was more than humiliation; it was a century of disasters: the Opium Wars, the cession of the so-called 'treaty' ports, the loss of Hong Kong to the British. This was followed by the Taiping Rebellion, a bloody and brutal civil war (1850–64) and the Second Opium War (1856–60), the forcible opening of the whole country to trade including opium, then the Japanese invasion of 1895 and the loss of Taiwan, then the Boxer Rebellion, an anti-foreign uprising (1899–1901) that led to further foreign intervention.

The end of the empire in 1911 led to further chaos: a failed attempt to reinstate a monarchy (1915–16); a protracted period of internecine warfare in the 1920s among regional warlords; the establishment of a nationalist government in 1928 under Chiang Kai-shek in partial control of the country; conflicts with the communists in the 1930s; Japan's invasion of China in 1937; further conflict between nationalists and communists after the Second World War, leading to the communist victory and the establishment of the People's Republic of China in 1949, while Chiang Kai-shek's armies retreated to Taiwan.

This makes the continuity of China's history all the more remarkable. As early as the Qin Dynasty (that of the First Emperor) there was a quasi-unified legal code (though not yet Confucian), a unified measurement system, and the standardization of Chinese characters. The Chinese state changed very little compared to most of the European states, let alone those of Africa and the Americas. Modern states tend to be recent inventions, often the product of European colonialism. Some new states, such as Israel, claim to be old when they are in fact a variant of settlers' states (like Australia or the USA), one without a 'mother-country'. The movement for the 'return' of the Jews to 'Israel' advocated a return to a territory that for the 2,000 years before 1947 had contained very few Jews, and that does not correspond to either of the two ancient Jewish kingdoms of Judea and Israel. A United Kingdom of Israel – that of Saul, David, and Solomon – existed, if at all (there is only questionable biblical evidence for it), for only 120 years. Zionism was substantially a European nationalist movement led by Jews who adopted a religious language since very little else, except persecution and religion, united them. The term 'Zionism' was coined by Nathan Birnbaum (who eventually became an orthodox Jew and turned against Zionism). The modern movement was initiated by rabbis: two Sephardic, Yehuda Bibas and Judah Alkalai, and one Ashkenazi, Hirsch Kalischer. The best-known spokesman for the movement, widely but wrongly regarded as its founder, was Theodor Herzl (1860–1904), who was perhaps an atheist and certainly a secular, non-religious Jew.[64] In his 1896 pamphlet *The Jewish State* (*Der Judenstaat*), Herzl raised the possibility that the Jewish state could be constituted in Argentina, should the authorities agree. Or even in Palestine, should 'His Majesty the Sultan' agree. 'To give us Palestine', then, Herzl wrote, '. . . we should there form a portion of a rampart of

Europe against Asia, an outpost of civilization as opposed to barbarism. We should as a neutral State remain in contact with all Europe, which would have to guarantee our existence.'[65]

The 'Jews' State' was clearly viewed by Herzl as a European settlers' state peopled by unskilled labourers, organized under some kind of military discipline, and imported from the Jewish communities of Russia and Romania, with funds raised from rich Jewish bankers.[66] There was not, in Herzl's pamphlet, any understanding that the settled land might already contain an existing population, and he wrote, mindlessly, '... the Jews, once settled in their own state, would probably not have any more enemies'.[67]

Some African states avoided, at least for a while, the fate of colonization. Ethiopia succeeded in remaining independent after the Battle of Adua of 1896 when it defeated the Italians, but was eventually occupied by them in 1936. The occupation did not last long since the country was liberated in 1941 by the British. Escaping from Western colonialism, however, does not seem to have benefited Ethiopia particularly: famine, civil war, and despotic governments have plagued the country as much as some of its neighbours. But even Ethiopia was not an ancient country. At the beginning of the nineteenth century the Ethiopian monarchy existed only in name. The real rulers of the country were provincial chieftains, or *ras*. Only in 1855 was the country effectively ruled by an emperor ('King of Kings'), Tewodros II (1855–68); later one of his successors, Menelik II (1889–1913), further enlarged it.[68] So Ethiopia too, like Germany and Italy, had recently established borders. Today's states are mostly recent; old nations are hard to come by.

At the beginning of the twentieth century there were only two sovereign countries in sub-Saharan Africa, Liberia and South Africa, and neither were ruled by indigenous people. Liberia had in fact been colonized in 1847. The settlers were black Americans (mainly freed slaves), who were backed by a group of wealthy white Americans under the aegis of the aptly named American Colonization Society, formed in 1816. The black colonialists behaved liked their white counterparts. They defrauded the indigenous people, whose hostility they encountered. They 'built stockades in the North American frontier tradition, with cannon mounted'.[69] They imposed a regime of servitude on the local inhabitants, forcing them to work in appalling circumstances in rubber plantations. The descendants of these black settlers (only 3 per cent of the population in 1980) monopolized the government and the domestic market economy until a military coup in 1980. The ensuing civil war (1989–2003) caused 200,000 deaths out of a population of 3 million.

In 1909 an Act of the British Parliament created the Union of South Africa, a Dominion with at least nominal independence and that included the former territories of the Cape and Natal colonies, as well as the republics of Orange Free State and the Transvaal. It became fully sovereign only in 1931. Until 1994, South Africa was in fact ruled by white settlers, who increasingly strengthened racial segregation after independence, culminating in the formal adoption of the apartheid system in 1948.

*

Thus most of the two hundred or so states that are members of the United Nations today have a recent history. State formation coincides with the recent history of globalized capitalism. The economic imperative of the state managing the economy was the key mechanism that favoured the growth of states. Capitalism is often seen as trying to straddle the world, but this is an abstract notion. In reality each variety of capitalism must be nurtured by a state and shaped according to local conditions. There is no single path. Strong states have helped the development of capitalism. Weak states have faced problems industrializing. States that are not effective states, states that became states recently, or that have been subjected by other states, fare worst of all.

But what were the conditions of life of the population of states before capitalism developed? What was it like to be an ordinary inhabitant of those states that were invented or reinvented in the course of the nineteenth century? To this we now must turn.

2
The Lives of the People

INTRODUCTION

In the last decades of the nineteenth century, at the heart of western Europe, in France, then as now one of the richest countries in the world, many rural families lived in a single room in appalling hygienic conditions. These citizens of the Third Republic slept in their daily clothes, which they changed perhaps only once a month. Most only washed their hands and face. Drinking water was scarce. The daily diet of many French peasants consisted of soup, some lard, and bread. Peasant cuisine, unlike the romantic image that some urbanites have of it today (simple and healthy unadulterated food, close to the earth, a world we have lost, etc.) was poor, devoid of nutritional value, lacking in vitamins, and unhygienic.[1]

In the north of the country, the more prosperous farmers, part of the 3.5 million who owned their land, were eating meat regularly, but the rest lived in misery, not so distant from the present-day living conditions of people in the Third World.[2] In fact peasants in the Third World, even in the 1930s, were probably better off than some of their French counterparts in the 1870s – as we can see from Pierre Gouron's account of the living conditions of poor peasants in the Tonkin Delta in 1936.[3]

This rural world coexisted with a developing capitalism. Was that, as the optimists believed, the age of progress? The case is strong. It was the age of cotton spinning, of the steam engine, and of railroads; textiles became cheaper, communication easier, and the world smaller. Later in the century a further spate of innovations made life more bearable and the economy far more productive: the application of electricity, the internal combustion engine, running water with indoor plumbing, a chemical revolution, a revolution in information (the telephone, the phonograph, the cinema). This formidable technological evolution laid the path for successive decades of increases in productivity and led to a hitherto unequalled period of economic growth.[4]

The nineteenth century was also the age of the abolition of the slave trade; the introduction of (some) democracy; the age of science and social science (Darwin and Marx); of opera (Verdi and Wagner); of the great novels (Tolstoy, Dostoyevsky, Flaubert, and Dickens); the age of national liberation (Giuseppe Garibaldi, Simón Bolívar, but also Abraham Lincoln). It was, of course, the age of industrialization; the age of the birth of global capitalism and hence also the age of the 'new' imperialism, of colonialism, of the Opium Wars. Many of these developments were of benefit only to a minority. The conditions of the rest would improve, if at all, only in the twentieth century. It is certain, however, that in the nineteenth century more people than ever survived in spite of wars, famines, and diseases. It took 250 years, from 1500 to 1750, for the world's population to increase by just over 300 million, that is from 460 million in 1500 to 770 million in 1750. By 1900 it had reached 1,630 million. In 1950 there were 2,500 million people on the planet. By 1987 the population had doubled again. By 2018 there were 7,600 million people in the world.[5]

In 1900 'capitalist' Europe was still overwhelmingly rural; by 2000, peasants had almost disappeared. The workers of the world, who were supposed to follow Marx's call to arms, losing little but their chains, were very few when the *Communist Manifesto* was written (1848), almost all of them in western Europe and North America. By the end of the twentieth century, the majority of industrial workers were not in the 'West' but in the 'Rest' – what was once known as the Third World.

THE RURAL WORLD

In Europe, even in 1900, the rural world still dominated everywhere, except in Great Britain and, to a lesser extent, Holland, Germany, and Belgium. France, not far behind them in industrial capacity, was still a largely agrarian society. Nearly 70 per cent of its inhabitants lived in the countryside. Small businessmen accounted for 11 per cent of the population, but the majority of these were shopkeepers and peddlers, hardly better off than many small farmers.[6]

In 1910 only 10 per cent of the inhabitants of the Russian Empire lived in cities and only in 1961, in what was by then the Soviet Union, would the country become mainly urban. In Sweden, in 1870, only 13 per cent of the population lived in urban areas. By 2015, 86 per cent did so.[7]

In Britain, between 1790 and 1840, the conditions of agricultural labourers hardly improved. In the course of the subsequent decades there was some amelioration, but it was interrupted by the fall of prices during the so-called long depression of 1873–96.[8]

In the early nineteenth century, in villages near Zurich, soon to become one of the wealthiest regions in the world, the peasant's main meal consisted of a kind of porridge to which some milk had been added.[9] A country with the characteristics of Switzerland in 1800 would today be classified by the United Nations as qualifying for international aid.[10]

In the 1870s, in the countryside of what is now the Emilia-Romagna region, where much of what is now most famous in Italian cuisine originates (Parma ham, parmesan cheese, tortellini, ravioli, etc.), and home to luxury cars such as Ferrari, Maserati, and Lamborghini, people in the countryside hardly ever drank wine, ate little bread, and had to be content with a kind of polenta, a few vegetables and, occasionally, a little meat. This is what was reported in the famous *Inchiesta agraria e sulle condizioni della classe agricola* ('Inquiry into Agriculture and the Conditions of the Agrarian Class') conducted by Count Stefano Jacini, an enlightened conservative politician, and published in 1884.[11] Similar observations can be found in the travel journal of the British diplomat William N. Beauclerk, who sojourned in Italy in the 1880s: 'Meat and wine seldom form a part of the food of the peasants', who were reduced to a diet of coarse bread, chestnuts, and herbs.[12]

Housing was dismal and, for casual labourers, terrible. Near Rome, according to the Jacini Inquiry, casual labourers lived 'like cattle':

> Occasionally they find an old house, or an ancient inn or some edifice in ruins, and they crowd in there, one on top of the other without distinction of sex or age, defenceless against the weather and with none of the comforts which are indispensable to human existence.

These were the lucky ones; others simply slept in caves and in holes dug in the hills:

> Inside these caves, for months at a time, these families live without privacy, with no beds, no latrines, just like animals. It is a sorry spectacle which faces the traveller who passes by these primitive dwellings. Women who barely look human, masses of half-naked children surround the visitor begging.[13]

They lived on a miserable diet: polenta with no salt, bread made with maize flour shaped as a pizza, occasionally with some lard or ricotta or stale olive oil. The food, such as it was, was often rotten. Further south, conditions were worse. Bread made with wheat flour was rare, in fact wheat consumption was fairly limited then, even in wheat-growing areas such as the northern Mediterranean.[14] Most peasants ate bread made with maize or chestnuts. Pasta was then eaten only by the more prosperous.[15] In 1891 the health officer of Capracotta, a small town (5,000 inhabitants) in the Molise region of south-central Italy, reported that the people lived in tiny hovels, huddled together with their domestic animals: pigs, horses, sheep, and cows.[16] Twenty years later, in Sicily, the situation had barely improved. The Faini Parliamentary Commission (1907–10) noted that in a typical peasant home animals and humans slept together: the grandparents, the children, the grandchildren, the mule, the donkey, the chickens, and sometime the pig.[17] Even as recently as the mid-1930s, Carlo Levi, a doctor and painter exiled in the Italian rural south for anti-Fascist activities, noted in his famous account – *Christ Stopped at Eboli* – that the local inhabitants appeared quite alien to him (as he appeared to them):

> as I talked with the peasants, I observed their faces and their build: short, dark, with round faces, large eyes and thin lips, their archaic aspects did not resemble that of the Romans, or of the Greeks, or of the Etruscans, or of the Normans, or of any of the other conquerors who had passed through their lands. They reminded me of some very ancient Italic figures. I reflected that their lives had not changed since the oldest of times. History has swept over them without touching them . . .[18]

The south may have been in 'western Europe' but its peasants were barely aware of being Italians. The literacy gap in Italy was particularly pronounced. While in Piedmont, in 1911, only 11 per cent were illiterate, the percentage in Sardinia was 58 per cent and in the deep south, in Calabria, the worst-performing region, it was 69 per cent. Yet, before the unification of the country in 1861, the north–south gap was less pronounced.[19]

On the southernmost tip of the Italian peninsula, in Calabria, even after Italian unification, most sharecroppers were serfs in all but name since they were kept in a state of subjugation by the enormous supply of labour that gave the landlords the upper hand whenever the contracts for the renting of land were up for renewal. Many peasants emigrated to Belgium, France, Argentina, and the United States. Some became bandits. The rest lived in perpetual fear – fear of the weather, fear of the landlord, fear of each other, fear of everything.[20] In the countryside the weight of tradition and anxiety about change dominated life.

This should cause no surprise. Where so much was beyond the control of human beings, it was reasonable to trust in God, to be afraid of novelty, and to pray regularly. And not to trust anyone, hence the proliferation of sayings in local dialect such as *Non diri all'amico toi quantu sai cà 'ncunu jornu tu nimico l'ài* ('Do not tell your friend what you know, one day he may be your enemy').[21]

Throughout much of mid-nineteenth-century Europe the standard fare of poor peasants was a porridge made with some stomach-filling starch such as maize to which an occasional 'treat' of vegetables or meat would be added. This they ate in the morning, in the middle of the day, and in the evening – day after day, year after year.[22] The nutritional value of a maize-based diet was far inferior even to that of wheat. Not surprisingly it was one of the main causes of pellagra – a vitamin-deficiency disease prevalent across southern and eastern Europe.[23] In 1891 it killed 4,303 people in Italy, though far more were killed by tuberculosis, typhus, and malaria.[24] We don't in fact know how many died of tuberculosis in the nineteenth century. In France, there were no reliable statistics before 1886 and only for towns of over 5,000 inhabitants. Rural deaths were calculated only in 1906.[25] But it is likely that by then, in France alone, some 90,000 died every year of TB.[26]

The belief that rural communities were kept together by shared values and a kind of ancient cohesion is a romantic myth that contrasts the individualism of the city to the collectivism of the village. Georg Simmel did have a point when he wrote in 1903 that it was in the city that individuals sought liberation and distinguished themselves from one another, that it was the city which enabled individuals to be individuals and free themselves from historical ties.[27] A dark view of the towns prevailed well before industrialization. In his treatise on education, *Émile* (1762), Jean-Jacques Rousseau lamented that 'young women from the provinces are soon taught to despise the happy simplicity of their lives, and rush to Paris to share in our corruption. Vice . . . is the sole object of their journey; ashamed to find they are so much behind the noble licentious behaviour of Parisian ladies, they crave to be worthy of being part of the city.'[28] In his poem 'The Deserted Village' (1770), Oliver Goldsmith describes the consequence of the forcible enclosure of common land (one of the preconditions of the Industrial Revolution) with the image of a young woman forced to abandon her village to migrate to the town, where she is now poor and 'houseless' and 'shivering':

She once, perhaps, in village plenty blessed,
Has wept at tales of innocence distressed;
Her modest looks the cottage might adorn,

Sweet as the primrose peeps beneath the thorn:
Now lost to all; her friends, her virtue fled,
Near her betrayer's door she lays her head . . .

In the 1850s a Bavarian journalist and university professor, Wilhelm Heinrich Riehl, depicted cities both as symbols and as sources of the worst aspects of the modern world when he wrote: 'Europe is becoming sick as a result of the monstrosity of its big cities.' Riehl regarded cities as the home of a rootless proletariat devoid of traditions and familial ties, living in solitude and alienation (a refrain that still endures).[29]

A few decades later, as Germany, and most of Europe, was rapidly urbanizing, cities continued to be regarded by many as socially destructive. The German clergyman Christian Rogge expressed widely held anti-urban concerns when he wrote that if the big city 'becomes a dwelling place for masses of criminals', mass degeneration will occur and 'an army of prostitutes and pimps will eat away at its foundations'. Others warned that socialist agitation in the big city would spread to the countryside.[30]

Similar complaints were manifested by the urban intelligentsia throughout Europe. The world seemed to be full of innocent girls from the countryside who, the minute they stepped into the city, turned into wanton harlots. As a French saying goes: *Toute bretonne perd la foi au moment où elle met le pied sur le quai de la gare de Montparnasse* ('Breton girls lose their faith the moment they arrive at the railway station of Montparnasse'). Migrant workers became criminals, thieves, beggars, and prostitutes. They were the dangerous class. Most, of course, became honest urban dwellers rightly attracted by the better life that even the dismal cities of the nineteenth century offered. This was particularly important to young women for whom life in the countryside consisted in overwork, insecurity, fear of not finding the 'right man', namely, someone who might work hard and not beat them up too often. In France, women had a crucial role in persuading men to abandon the land and village life, and if the young men could not be persuaded, the girls left alone: in some parts of France, among agricultural workers, three times more men than women stayed behind.[31]

As the rural world disappeared, a rose-tinted view of it surfaced, abundantly described in literature. Thus Count Leinsdorf in Robert Musil's *The Man Without Qualities* contrasted the unwelcoming world of cities, the threats of progress, to the happy tranquillity of the countryside:

His Grace was decidedly averse to what he called mere literature. It stood for something he associated with Jews, newspapers, sensation-hungry

> booksellers, and the liberal, hopelessly garrulous paid hirelings of the bourgeoisie . . . What he was thinking of . . . was fields, the men who worked them, little country churches, and that great order of things which God had bound as firmly together as the sheaves on a mown field, an order at once comely, sound, and rewarding . . .[32]

Cursing cities is an ancient custom. The prophet Zephaniah thundered against Jerusalem:

> Ah, soiled, defiled, oppressing city!
> It has listened to no voice;
> it has accepted no correction.
> It has not trusted in the LORD;
> it has not drawn near to its God.
> (Zephaniah 3:1–2)

Yet, great civilizations were all based on cities – Babylon, Memphis, Athens, Rome, Venice, Timbuktu, Kyoto, Beijing, Samarkand – while the countryside was a Hobbesian jungle where life was brutish and short. Centuries ago as today, cities were, almost always, the centre of modernity, however one defined modernity at a particular time. Yet the city depends on the countryside whether near, as was normally the case, or far away, as is often the case now. The city obtains from the countryside food and workers, hence it needs trade and migration. A city, Fernand Braudel explained in lyrical tones, would cease to exist unless people were attracted by its lights, its freedoms (real or only apparent), better wages, and also because life in the countryside has become difficult, even intolerable.[33] Cities are dependent on the rural world but this dependency coexists with a dramatic cultural separation: urban dwellers look down on those who live in the country. To be an urban dweller is to be a *citizen*, a *civis*, a civilized human, a member of the city, of the *polis* (and hence polite in English, *polie* in French, and also *urbane*); to be in the country is to be a 'villain', a *villano* (Italian), *villain* (French), *villanus* (Latin), in other words a rural worker, bound to the soil of a villa, i.e. a farm – someone dictionaries define as an 'ignorant, rude, or unsophisticated person'.

In the eighteenth century and earlier, per capita income differentials among European countries, and between Europe and the rest of the world, were relatively minimal. A huge gap between the richest and poorest countries begins to appear only in the nineteenth century, in other words, with industrial capitalism.[34] It is thus not surprising that in the 'periphery' of Europe, outside the hallowed boundaries of 'the

West', the situation for those who lived on the land was even worse. The population of the Russian Empire grew rapidly from 74 million in 1860 to 161 million in 1910 (some of this increase was due to annexations), and between 1885 and 1897 the population actually dropped due to crop failures and the subsequent famine.[35] Death rates per 1,000 inhabitants were 36.5 when the serfs were emancipated in 1861; by 1913 they had improved a little to 27.1 per 1,000.[36]

In 1897 (the date of the first Russian census) the majority of the Cossack population of Ukraine was illiterate, and largely rural. These provinces had no distinct national institutions, though they produced a considerable proportion of the country's coal, steel, and cereals. Most Ukrainians were poor peasants using simple wooden tools and living under straw roofs. The incidence of typhus, dysentery, and diphtheria among them was the same as that of central Russia. Rich Ukrainian families intermarried with wealthy noble Russian families and were assimilated into an imperial elite, but few of these Russified nobles maintained a practical interest in their native land.[37]

In Moldavia and Wallachia (present-day Romania) the situation was no better. A French diplomat travelling in the area in 1848 manifested his dismay that 'at the doors of Bucharest . . . entire families . . . live huddled together, far from daylight, in underground cabins. Then, near such misery, as a natural counterpoint, cheerful villas, splendid and opulent monasteries, built on the wooded hillside, present themselves to my sight.'[38] In Romania, wooden ploughs were still employed at the end of the nineteenth century, fertilizers and even beasts of burden were barely used, and there was no systematic crop rotation – just as in Flanders in the twelfth century.[39] Decades later, conditions in the countryside were still dismal. In 1879, 10 per cent of conscripts were found by the medical authorities to be infirm. Charles Arion, who reported these data in 1895, added: 'The condition of the peasants between 1864 and 1879 can be summed up in two words: crushed by taxation and submission to the tyranny of the first newcomer, a Jew or a Greek, agent of the landlord.'[40]

DISMAL CITIES

Industrialization and migration from the land accelerated the historic decline of the peasantry. Urbanization was rapid, though it was not as closely correlated with industrialization as one might think. Cities have existed for thousands of years. They are not a modern invention, and are not the harbingers of capitalism. Ur in Mesopotamia, it is estimated, had a population of 65,000 in 2000 BC, Babylon had 200,000 people in 430 BC, and Rome reached 450,000 in 100 BC. At the height of its power, in the second century AD, Rome may have had one million inhabitants, the largest European city before London in 1800.[41] Around AD 800 there were seven cities in the world with over 200,000 inhabitants: Chang'an (now Xi'an), Luoyang (one million each), and Hangzhou in China; Kyoto in Japan; then, further to the west, Baghdad (with probably 700,000 inhabitants), Constantinople (the only European example), and Alexandria.[42] Pre-Columbian America was more urbanized than Europe around 1500: Tenochtitlán (now Mexico City), a clean, elegant city, had perhaps 250,000 inhabitants, whereas Paris, then the largest city in Europe, only 225,000.[43]

By 1700 the city in the world with the largest population was probably Constantinople, followed by Beijing and Isfahan; London, then as now western Europe's largest city, was the fourth largest, Paris fifth. By 1800, London had almost caught up with Beijing and was followed by Canton, Constantinople, and Paris; Naples was eighth – all other cities in the league of largest cities were in Asia.[44] Rapid urbanization, however, is a modern phenomenon. Between 1850 and 1910 the level of urbanization in Europe (towns being defined as agglomerations of at least 5,000 inhabitants) rose from less than 15 per cent to 32 per cent (see Table 4).[45]

Table 4 Urban Population as a Percentage of Total Population*

	1870	1890	1913
United Kingdom	53.3	64.0	69.7
Belgium	38.8	48.0	58.0
Holland	38.5	46.3	51.3
Germany	24.5	34.5	51.0
Italy	25.0	31.0	41.5
France	24.3	30.7	39.5
Switzerland	17.5	24.5	39.3
Spain	22.5	30.5	39.3
Balkans**	11.8	12.5	22.6
Russia	9.2	11.6	14.6

* Urban region: at least 5,000 inhabitants

** Bulgaria, Greece, Romania, and Serbia

Source: Paul Bairoch, 'Une nouvelle distribution des populations: villes et campagne', p. 221.

Urbanization led to the partial demise of rural industry.[46] In pre-industrial times, the rural village used to be flexibly structured: the movement to towns used to have a largely seasonal character, with rural workers working in towns during the winter when they were not busy in the fields. The factory system, however, requires a continuous and fairly standardized work practice and precise skills. Migration from the countryside soon acquired an increasingly permanent character.[47]

With the growth of towns and industry a new cleavage developed. Many peasants became workers (or domestic servants, a major occupation in the nineteenth century), but those who remained in the countryside were less cut off from the rest of the world than before. The globalization of the world made itself felt even there.

In fact peasants had been in movement for much of the nineteenth century. Some went to 'their' cities, but many migrated to 'foreign' cities, a global urbanization movement that shows no sign of abating. The favoured destination was the Americas. As a result the white population of the United States grew rapidly, partly due to a high fertility rate, partly to declining mortality rates, but above all due to the massive levels of immigration that accounted for between 25 per cent and 33 per cent of total population growth in the last quarter of the nineteenth century, including 28 million of the 40 million Europeans who migrated to the Americas.[48] Most immigrants were employed in the rapidly expanding industrial sector. Even in 1810, American industrial development was on a level with that of France, Switzerland, and Belgium.[49] If, before the Civil War, the USA was a largely agrarian economy (44 per cent of free males were classified as farmers in 1850), by 1900 it had become an industrial country, in which one third of the population lived in cities of 100,000, where farmers accounted for less than 20 per cent of the total population, and blue-collar workers 35.8 per cent.[50] Despite this demographic shift, the USA was still the world's main agricultural producer.

Until the 1870s the European migration to the United States came mainly from Britain, Germany, and Scandinavia – all groups that (except for the Irish Catholics) assimilated fairly easily with the existing, overwhelmingly Protestant white population. Those who arrived later, after 1880, came mainly from eastern and southern Europe. They were Jews, Catholics, and Orthodox Christians. By the early 1900s these new immigrants constituted two-thirds of all arrivals.[51] They did not assimilate so easily – hence the enduring existence of 'hyphenated Americans' (Polish-Americans, Jewish-Americans, Italian-Americans, etc.) even in the closing decades of the twentieth century. Many migrants did not settle but returned to their country of origin, some because they had 'succeeded' and returned to buy a business or land or retire, others because they had failed or were homesick or because new opportunities had arisen back home. Half the Italian emigrants who left Italy between 1880 and 1950 returned home.[52] What attracted European migrants to the USA was not its democracy or its modernity, but, quite simply, the prospect of improving their standard of living: 'America meant more than anything else abundant and better food, superior houses, clothing, medical care, and education.'[53] Nevertheless those who went to the USA were a minority of those who emigrated: during the nineteenth century, for every European who left Europe, nine moved *within* Europe: Irish to England, Italians to France and Belgium, Jews from the Tsarist Empire to Germany and France.[54]

Immigrants left the parlous conditions of the countryside, but what they found in cities was seldom better. An investigation published by two radical French journalists, the brothers Léon and Maurice Bonneff, tells of their visit to a working-class home in Lille in 1908. The home is in a narrow and muddy street; the staircase has no ramp; inside lies an emaciated woman. She is twenty-six years old but looks fifty. The room where she lives with her husband and their five children is four metres by two. She is illiterate. Her husband leaves for work at five in the morning and returns at seven in the evening. She coughs uninterruptedly, has tuberculosis, and will not live long.[55] In 1902 the local hospital estimated that malnutrition was the direct cause of TB in 68 per cent of the 519 workers affected. The situation barely improved in the succeeding six years.[56] In Houplines, near the Belgian border, the Bonneff brothers visited the home of a textile worker where meat was eaten only twice a year, namely on 1 May, the international day of the working class, and on 14 July, the anniversary of the Revolution – but only because the municipality distributed it to the needy.[57]

In his 1819 poem 'Peter Bell the Third' (a satire on Wordsworth), Shelley had decreed that 'Hell is a city much like London'. Decades later, for many people it was still hellish. In 1873, not far from Kensington Palace, the birthplace of Queen Victoria, stood Jennings' Buildings, a slum consisting of eighty-one two-storey wooden tenements, with over 1,500 people in accommodation meant for 200. They shared forty-nine toilets. There was no drainage, and, until 1866, no drinking water. As a result, the mortality rate was over twice that of their wealthier neighbours in Kensington.[58]

Maud Pember Reeves, a member of the Fabian Society, in her famous report *Round About a Pound a Week* (1913) on the conditions of working-class households in Lambeth, offered a detailed account of the problems facing a young working-class mother. Life was a constant struggle to care for her family: 'That the diet of the poorer London children is insufficient, unscientific, and utterly unsatisfactory is horribly true. But that the real cause of this state of things is the ignorance and indifference of their mothers is untrue.'[59] Yet, while the housing conditions were terrible (vermin infestation, overcrowding, rudimentary cooking, and sanitary facilities), families seemed to be eating meat fairly regularly (with the husband, the main – often the sole – breadwinner, taking the lion's share of the meat and fish).[60]

Such reports may overstate the state of deprivation of the working class. According to two economists, by the 1880s consumption of meat, at least in the big cities (Paris, Lyon, and Grenoble), was not uncommon even among the lower income groups.[61] Still, in spite of the economic progress of the next fifty years, even in the mid-1950s many working-class French households had no water, no gas, no inside toilets even on the outskirts of Paris.[62]

In pre-industrial Britain wages and living standards among workers were among the highest in the world, and, by the mid-nineteenth century, the situation was significantly better than on the continent.[63] Friedrich Engels, writing in the 1840s in what was far from being an uncritical account of the benefits of British capitalism, explained: 'The better paid workers, especially those in whose families every member is able to earn something, have good food as long as this state of things lasts: meat daily and bacon and cheese for supper.'[64] This was probably better than the diet of most French or German workers, though a French report published in 1840 suggests that among workers in Normandy, Lyon, and Reims it was not uncommon to eat meat along with *la soupe grasse* and white bread.[65]

Nutrition might have been better among English workers than elsewhere, but Engels had no doubt that, from the perspective of both health and ecology, cities – London in particular – were a disaster:

> the atmosphere of London can never be so pure, so rich in oxygen, as the air of the country; two and a half million pairs of lungs, two hundred and fifty thousand fires, crowded upon an area three to four miles square, consume an enormous amount of oxygen, which is replaced with difficulty, because the method of building cities in itself impedes ventilation . . . The lungs of the inhabitants fail to receive the due supply of oxygen, and the consequence is mental and physical lassitude and low vitality.

He added:

> The filth and stagnant pools of the working-people's quarters in the great cities have, therefore, the worst effect upon the public health, because they produce precisely those gases which engender disease; so, too, the exhalations from contaminated streams. But this is by no means all. The manner in which the great multitude of the poor is treated by society today is revolting.[66]

Other foreign visitors were equally alarmed by the conditions of British workers. In *De la misère des classes laborieuses en Angleterre et en France* (1840), Eugène Buret, while extolling the wealth of Britain ('One cannot fail to be impressed by the opulence of this nation; wealth is unveiled in thousands of ways before the astonished traveller . . . material life has reached the pinnacle of refinement'), noted that such extreme wealth coexisted with the 'most terrible misery . . . Not far from the monuments to British opulence are the sad monuments to its poverty.'[67] Visiting Shoreditch and Bethnal Green in East London, he noted the horrible shacks where people live amid dirt, stink, and 'moral turpitude' (*infamie*). There is no sewage, no rubbish disposal, no lighting: 'it is the most absolute laissez-faire one can imagine'.[68] And, Buret added, all the English can say is 'That's the Irish for you', since a significant proportion of the slum dwellers were Irish immigrants. French cities may not be as elegant and clean as English ones, he continued consolingly, but at least we are spared the horrors of English poverty, since the poor, he added, are not as miserable in France as they are in England.[69] Such poverty was not caused by the employers, Buret concluded, but by the system, by the *puissance des choses*, the power of things – an idea approvingly cited by Marx in one of his early writings.[70] Buret himself was not above some racist blame-mongering since he believed that most 'mobile' wealth was in the hands of the Jews, 'these clever usurpers of the wealth of nations! One sign from them, a furrowed brow, is sufficient to cause turmoil in all the markets of the world.'[71] Such remarks were not unusual even a few decades later. In 1885, T. H. S. Escott, editor of the *Fortnightly Review*, noted that 'English society, once ruled by an aristocracy, is now dominated by a plutocracy. And this plutocracy is to a large extent Hebraic in composition.'[72] Yet the conditions of the Jewish immigrants in London's East End were dire. One in three, according to the *Spectator* (23 April 1887), was on poor relief and their mortality rate was higher than that of the long-standing resident.[73]

Hippolyte Taine, who had written a five-volume history of English literature, was shocked by how boring London was. In one of the opening pages of his *Notes sur l'Angleterre* (1872) he wrote:

> A rainy Sunday in London: shops closed, streets almost empty; it looks like a huge and clean cemetery. The few passers-by, beneath their umbrellas, in this desert of squares and streets, are like returning anxious ghosts; it's horrible.[74]

Later on, encountering young prostitutes near Haymarket and the Strand, he wrote:

> Every hundred steps one encounters some twenty girls; some ask for a glass of gin; others say, 'Sir, it's for paying the rent.' It's not an exhibition of debauchery but misery, and what misery! . . . it breaks the heart; it was like observing a procession of the dead. This is a plague, the true plague of English society.[75]

A Belgian journalist and social reformer, Édouard Ducpétiaux, writing five years after Buret, in 1845, noted how miserable were the working classes in prosperous Belgium and how their children were as cruelly exploited as in Great Britain, punished for the smallest fault and deprived of the most elementary education. The miners did not save any of their earnings, because 'most of them fear to die without having spent all they had earned'.[76]

Writing about the conditions of the urban poor was then an even more popular genre than it is now. In the 1830s the French Académie des Sciences Morales et Politiques asked Dr Louis René Villermé and his colleague Benoiston de Chateauneuf to examine the conditions of workers in French factories. Villermé concentrated on textile works in the north and east of the country, textile manufacturers being then by far the largest employers in the country. He was particularly alarmed by the conditions of children and their high mortality rate. Half of them die, he wrote, before reaching the age of two.[77] Villermé's investigations, which took four years to complete, took him to factories where he noted down everything he saw, enabling him to establish, for the first time, that the working classes endured very long working days and lived in extreme poverty.[78]

Villermé was probably influenced by the report of Dr James Phillips Kay, *The Moral and Physical Condition of the Working Classes*, on the conditions in cotton manufacturing in Manchester (1832), which Engels quotes approvingly. Kay confirmed that Manchester workers ate meat three times a week, though 'the quantity consumed . . . is not great'.[79] But the situation was grim anyway. 'The population,' Kay explained, 'is crowded into one dense mass, in cottages separated by narrow, unpaved, and almost pestilential streets; in an atmosphere loaded with the smoke and exhalations of a large manufacturing city.' None of this, he added, could possibly be the result of the 'commercial system', as capitalism was often then called. The strife between capital and labour is 'unnatural' since 'capital is but accumulated labour'. These evils result not from the 'commercial system', which 'promotes the advance of civilization', but from 'foreign and accidental causes', from alcoholism, from the 'absence of religious feeling', and, above all, from the Irish, who brought with them 'the contagious example of ignorance', and whose 'barbarous habits and savage want of economy, united with the necessarily debasing consequences of uninterrupted toil, have demoralized the people'.[80] He seemed to ignore the fact that children employed in Lancashire textile mills were regularly beaten.[81] In 1849, James Kay was made a baronet.

Of course, worse than being employed, even in these conditions, was being unemployed. In that case, in Britain as elsewhere, the situation was dreadful. On 5 April 1867 the London *Standard*, a conservative London newspaper, in an article approvingly quoted by Karl Marx in *Capital*, reported:

> A frightful spectacle was to be seen yesterday in one part of the metropolis. Although the unemployed thousands of the East-end did not parade with their black flags en masse, the human torrent was imposing enough. Let us remember what these people suffer. They are dying of hunger. That is the simple and terrible fact. There are 40,000 of them . . . In our presence, in one quarter of this wonderful metropolis, are packed – next door to the most enormous accumulation of wealth the world ever saw cheek by jowl with this are 40,000 helpless, starving people. These thousands are now breaking in upon the other quarters; always half-starving, they cry their misery in our ears, they cry to Heaven, they tell us from their miserable dwellings, that it is impossible for them to find work, and useless for them to beg.[82]

And, as Gladstone himself had admitted as a young MP twenty-four years earlier in the House of Commons (13 February 1843), even those in employment consumed less while the rich got richer:

> It is one of the most melancholy features in the social state of this country, that we see, beyond the possibility of denial, that while there is at this moment a decrease in the consuming powers of the people, an increase of the pressure of privations and distress – there is at the same time a constant accumulation of wealth in the upper classes, an increase of the

> luxuriousness of their habits, and of their means of enjoyment, which, however satisfactory it may be as affording evidence of the existence and abundance of one among the elements of national prosperity, yet adds bitterness to the reflections which are forced upon us by the distresses of the rest of our fellow countrymen . . .[83]

The urban workers in Britain were doing poorly, but that was still better than others elsewhere in Europe. In the 1870s, Pasquale Villari, an Italian historian and politician who knew England well, and whose wife, Linda White, was English, wrote that however immense the misery in London, 'anyone who claims that the London poor are worse off than those of Naples, either does not know the former or does not know the latter'.[84]

Some compared the conditions of the English poor not to Naples but to darkest Africa. With, perhaps, some excessive emphasis, the founder of the Salvation Army, William Booth (not to be confused with the sociologist of poverty, Charles Booth) – having read Henry Morton Stanley's *Through the Dark Continent* (1878) – wrote in *In Darkest England and the Way Out* (1890):

> But while brooding over the awful presentation of life as it exists in the vast African forest, it seemed to me only too vivid a picture of many parts of our own land. As there is a darkest Africa is there not also a darkest England? . . . May we not find a parallel at our own doors, and discover within a stone's throw of our cathedrals and palaces similar horrors to those which Stanley has found existing in the great Equatorial forest?[85]

Drawing a parallel between England and 'darkest Africa' was a common trope. The socialist and feminist novelist Margaret Harkness had done the same in her novel *In Darkest London* (1889).[86]

In his path-breaking survey of 1889 on the London poor, *Life and Labour of the People of London*, Charles Booth divided the population into eight classes. The bottom four, the poor, including 'the lowest' class, 'the occasional labourers, loafers, and semi-criminals' (class A), the casual earners ('the very poor' – class B), and the 'poor', who either had 'intermittent earnings' (class C) or 'small regular earnings' (class D). He estimated that in East London 35 per cent of the population could be described as poor or very poor.[87] The life of class A was:

> the life of savages, with vicissitudes of extreme hardship and occasional excess. Their food is of the coarsest description, and their only luxury is drink . . . They render no useful service, they create no wealth . . . They degrade whatever they touch.[88]

In the Whitechapel district of East London, almost 2,500 people belonged to this class, out of a total of just over 73,500.[89] The four categories of the poor were, between them, almost 40 per cent of the total – yards away from the City of London, then, as now, the financial centre of the world.

The East End was poor but even poorer, according to Charles Booth's classification, was Holborn, where almost 50 per cent lived in poverty. Holborn was followed by various East End districts, but even Westminster had a 35 per cent level of poverty, while Islington was at 31 per cent. Chelsea, with 24 per cent, was in those days on a level with Hackney and Stoke Newington (23 per cent). Best of all was Hampstead with a poverty level of only 13.5 per cent.[90] The 'poor' Booth was describing were the 'working poor' or the 'respectable poor', not his 'class A' feckless poor. Nor were they the small underclass of the extremely poor of the 1840s described by Henry Mayhew in his *London Labour and the London Poor* (1851), the bottom fortieth of society. Booth's 'working' and 'respectable' poor were the true victims of the Industrial Revolution, yet they were also poised to derive increasing benefits from it in the course of the successive century, inhabiting Birmingham, Manchester, Sheffield, and industrial Scotland.[91] This dismal view of London was enhanced by Jack London's popular *The People of the Abyss* (1903), based on several months' stay in the East End, where he contrasted 'hordes of beastly wretchedness and inarticulate misery' to the life of 'a millionaire brewer who lives in a West End palace, sates himself with the sensuous delights of London's golden theatres, hobnobs with lordlings and princelings, and is knighted by the king'.[92]

Everywhere distinctions were made between respectable workers and casual labourers. In 1901, in Italy, there were, according to the census, one million casual labourers in the north alone. They were regarded as a dangerous class and described in police reports as if they were aliens: one is described as having thick eyelashes, the face of a 'cretin', and the women are described as promiscuous.[93]

Most British people were not poor, but a minority were. Thus under the headline 'The Unemployed', the *Hampshire Chronicle* of 16 January 1904 intoned:

> Never a winter passes without this melancholy title for a record of want and suffering appearing daily in our journals. It is a pitiable thing, an evil that the wisest statesmen and the richest and most generous philanthropists at their best seem only able to alleviate.[94]

Much of the scandal about living conditions of the poor was because the poor were a minority. Consumption of food increased regularly in the United Kingdom in the years 1860 to 1913 (see Table 5).

Table 5 Weekly Per Capita Consumption, 1860–1913

	1860	1909–13
Meat and bacon (lb)	1.8	2.5
Fresh milk (pint)	1.75	3.2
Sugar (lb)	0.7	1.4
Tea (oz)	0.8	2.1
Butter (oz)	2.7	4.8

Source: Mary Mackinnon, 'Living Standards, 1870–1914', in Roderick Floud and Donald McCloskey (eds), *The Economic History of Britain since 1700*, vol. 2: *1860–1939*, 2nd edn, Cambridge University Press 1994, p. 279.

By the beginning of the century, however, in Britain, very nearly all households had a diet that provided sufficient energy for sustained work, though perhaps not much more than that.[95] London was a paupers' paradise compared to St Petersburg, according to the statistically based study by Dr G. I. Arkhangel'skii, editor of *Archiv sudebnoi meditsiny i obshchestvennoi gigieny* (Archive of Forensic Medicine and Social Hygiene), a medical journal founded in 1865 that discussed regularly and consistently the health problems of the lower classes of St Petersburg.[96] It was, wrote Arkhangel'skii, 'the most deadly of all major European cities'. The causes were the usual ones: overcrowding and poor hygienic conditions to which was added an unusually high level of alcoholism.[97]

Americans were probably already better off, on average, even than those in the more prosperous European countries. They were eating meat regularly even at the height of the Civil War, and the European immigrants who arrived in the 1880s found that they could afford to buy food that, in Europe, was available only to the more prosperous.[98] Peter Maretich, a Croatian immigrant to the United States, explained that, back in the old country, at the end of the nineteenth century, they were lucky to eat meat once a week; their breakfast consisted of corn meal with milk, and their dinner of potatoes or noodles, with a little bread but no butter, 'But when we get to this country we had meat every day if we want to.' When asked why they had left Croatia, Maretich replied that hunger had forced them out.[99]

In 1875 in Massachusetts, a family of seven (parents plus five children ranging from one to twelve years of age) would have had a varied diet that included the occasional fish and meat, as well as butter, gingerbread, molasses, and tea. The father, an unskilled labourer of French-Canadian extraction, would earn $385 a year supplemented by the $145 earned by the oldest son (a 12-year-old) and $120 by the second son (10 years old). The mother stayed at home to care for the children. Although far better fed than their European counterparts, the family did not live well; they spent well over half their income on food; they dressed poorly; and the children were pale.[100]

The Jews who crowded 'Jewtown' in the Lower East Side in New York were certainly better off than they had been in the Tsarist Empire – and there were no pogroms. But they were far from thriving. As the journalist and photographer Jacob A. Riis reported in *How the Other Half Lives* (1890):

> Penury and poverty are wedded everywhere to dirt and disease, and Jewtown is no exception. It could not well be otherwise in such crowds, considering especially their low intellectual status. The managers of the Eastern Dispensary, which is in the very heart of their district, told the whole story when they said: 'The diseases these people suffer from are not due to intemperance or immorality, but to ignorance, want of suitable food, and the foul air in which they live and work.'[101]

Perhaps Riis saw only the poverty, or matters had improved remarkably in the following twenty years, because there were, by 1913, in the 57 blocks that made up the Jewish Lower East Side, 112 candy and ice-cream stores, 78 barbers, 93 butchers' shops, and 43 bakeries.[102]

An important move towards the consumer society occurs when a significant part of one's disposable income is left after paying for the obvious necessities of life: food, housing, and clothing. In 1901 the *average* American family would earn $769 a year. A worker would earn $0.23 per hour, which meant that working fifty hours a week every week of the year would enable him to bring home $600. Of this, 42.5 per cent was spent on food, 14 per cent on clothing, and 23.3 per cent on housing (rent, heating); in other words 79.8 per cent of the household's income would go on necessities. In the larger French cities such as Lyon and Grenoble, 26 per cent of the working-class budget was spent on food (1913 figures).[103] Of course even this was a remarkable improvement over the eighteenth-century French labourer, who spent half of his income on bread and 16 per cent on vegetables, fats, and wine.[104]

Between 1876 and 1885, in Germany, the proportion of working-class income spent on food remained more or less the same (about 47 per cent, the same as in the USA), the percentage spent on housing dropped a little (20.4 to 18.2 per cent), and that on clothing rose from 9.8 to 13 per cent. This means that these three items represented 77.9 of total expenditure in 1876 and 78.2 per cent in 1885 – almost unchanged.[105]

By the year 2000, the proportion of average income spent on food in the United States was down to 13.1 per cent (and 40 per cent of this 13 per cent was consumed on food prepared outside the home, i.e. restaurants and take-aways); 4.2 per cent was spent on clothing and 32.8 per cent on housing (more than in 1901). This left a full 50 per cent of household income available for holidays, entertainment, a car, television, radios, computer games, and other items that had become necessities of life for almost all Americans.[106]

In 1905, Simon Patten, an American economist, was already welcoming the first 'ready to eat' foods. 'These,' he wrote, 'were less monotonous, more palatable, and very easily prepared' and 'perhaps the cheapest, in proportion to nutrition and to labor-power saved, that have yet to be found'.[107] He equally welcomed 'The "specials" offered by cash groceries at seven, six, and five cents', for these extended 'the circle of purchasers and the poor man's wife finds their ragged contents very satisfactory when served with her dull meat stew'. Now, he enthused, the working men could have cereal for breakfast, with milk, and sugar; and they could eat tomatoes and preserved food.[108]

The United States was well ahead of Europe in the development of branded products one could eat (though the idea of putting food such as fish in tins had been pioneered by French and British inventors at the beginning of the nineteenth century). In the 1870s the Heinz brothers started producing a sauce called ketchup, whose origins are Chinese.[109] In the 1880s, Singer sold sewing machines, Underberg sold a herb liqueur in a special, recognizable bottle. On 8 May 1886 in Atlanta, Georgia, John Styth Pemberton started selling a drink based on extracts of kola nuts which, allegedly, could cure hangovers and headaches. He called it Coca-Cola. In 1894, John Harvey Kellogg invented the cornflakes that still bear his name. In January 1912, Procter and Gamble introduced a vegetable shortening called Crisco which, according to the advertisement placed in the *Ladies' Home Journal*, was a 'scientific discovery which would affect every kitchen in America'.[110] Developments such as these and the greater abundance of food in the West would mean that the three-course meal became common in Europe and North America. Later in the twentieth century a multiplication of snacks led to all-day eating sprees, the primary cause of an illness almost unheard of in the nineteenth century (except among the rich): obesity.

Overeating was not a problem for workers even in prosperous Milan, where, in 1879, they lived on what was a not necessarily unhealthy diet of rice, beans, onions, and fried cabbage.[111] But there were problems. Their wages were low and the municipal authorities did little for housing. The immigrants who poured into Milan throughout the 1870s and 1880s unsurprisingly met with hostility from the resident working class, since their arrival increased the competition for housing and other resources.[112] The influx of workers into cities caused massive housing crises almost everywhere, while the unhygienic conditions of such dwellings were regularly denounced in various surveys.[113]

To be a wage worker at the end of the nineteenth century was a situation of course envied by the 'really poor', but it could be a calamity. Wage workers found themselves in a situation of extreme dependency and uncertainty, a predicament they did not choose but into which they were forced by poverty. They were often artisans ruined by machinery, farmers whose land could no longer support them or who could no longer compete against the more technologically aware. As wage workers they could lose their jobs at a stroke, because of illness or disability, including disability contracted during work, or because of the vicissitudes of the business cycle, or because of the inefficiency of their employer.[114]

In the poor countries of eastern Europe, factory workers and miners lived in conditions far worse than the rural workers in the West. At the turn of the century in the Donbass, in eastern Ukraine, in factory districts, there were virtually no sanitary facilities such as running water and sewerage. The residents used water from wells, rivers, and reservoirs that was usually contaminated by industrial waste. Many drank water from the river, as they had done in pre-industrial days. Excrement commonly littered the ground.[115] As a result typhus and cholera repeatedly swept through the Donbass working population.

Worst of all were the living conditions of those who worked in the mines, and not just those digging coal. In the salt mines of Lungro in Calabria the conditions were particularly appalling. The mines reached a depth of 220 metres but the mechanical means of bringing the salt to the surface only extended to 118 metres; the remaining distance had to be covered by miners carrying the salt on their backs. Women and children were used in this work as late as 1888.[116]

In large firms, even one run along paternalistic lines by 'caring' entrepreneurs such as the Schneiders, owners of the steel works of Le Creusot in Burgundy, France, workers still toiled under inhuman conditions. In 1897, Jules Huret, a socialist journalist working for the conservative daily *Le Figaro*, described the Creusot foundry as if it were a vision of hell: chimneys spitting smoke and flames and the air polluted by the smell of sulphur. The faces of the workers looked thin and grey, eyes were red, their eyelashes burnt. They ate a bread 'blackened by their hands' (*le pain que leurs mains noircissent*), and they got up every day at six, and worked every day for twelve hours, from dawn to dusk with no rest, and why? – *parce qu'un jour sans travail est pour eux un jour sans pain* ('because one day without work is one day without bread').[117] This was true in Paris too, where a regime of overwork followed by unemployment was the pattern.[118]

On the other side of the globe, in Japan, matters were no better. A rotting smell pervaded the slums. In Tokyo, in the 1890s, at a time of great economic development, Matsubara Iwagoro, a young journalist, inspired by Charles Booth's investigation into the London poor and by Victor Hugo's *Les Misérables*, had decided to live in what he called 'Poverty Street'. He wrote that 'there are narrow lanes and alleys that have no outlet, and by the wayside stand closets, which have to serve several families, and vitiate the air. Why is this permitted? Because the landlord wants to build as many houses as he can on the ground he owns.'[119] Matsubara spent the night in a hostel for the poor where 'the sultry air was filled with nauseous odours from the bodies of the coolies, so that one could scarcely breathe. The fleas came charging in legions, the mosquitoes got through the rents of the net, and there was fear of worse vermin.'[120] Another journalist, Yokoyama Gennosuke, claimed that the smell in the Asakusa district of Tokyo was 'indescribable', that it caused migraines, and that it made it impossible to linger in the area for more than half an hour.[121]

Paris did not smell any better than Tokyo or New York before Napoleon III's prefect, Baron Haussmann, improved the sewage system remarkably. Writing in 1848, Henri Lecouturier, author of the radical *Paris incompatible avec la République. Plan d'un nouveau Paris où les révolutions seront impossibles*, wrote that 'Most of the streets of this marvellous Paris are just like dirty bowels full of infected water . . . A crowd, pale and ill, crosses them constantly.'[122]

It was not just the smell, it was the people. A sense of disgust towards the workers overcame the socialist and feminist writer and activist Flora Tristan (Paul Gauguin's grandmother) when visiting a working-class home in Paris: 'I have learned so much in a fortnight living with these workers – they are horrible when seen from up close.'[123] A few weeks later she was even more disgusted:

> Who can serve the poor people so gross, so ignorant, so vain, so unpleasant to mix with, so disgusting when up close! Many compare the people to animals, but animals, even wild ones, would be a thousand times less unpleasant . . . And those stupid rich live calmly in the midst of a people in this state of degradation. This is madness.[124]

The rich may have lived in tranquillity, but the authorities were anxious. The police prefect, in a letter to the French Ministry of the Interior (11 September 1831), signalled that the misery was so great that its victims were likely to turn to violence.[125]

One way to resolve the overcrowding was simple: encourage people to leave the cities. In 1851 the City of London (as distinct from the wider conurbation) had 132,354 inhabitants, all crowding into the fabled square mile; sixty years later there were only 27,402.[126] In 2015 the numbers were down to 8,072 and poverty was not their problem.[127] Greater London, meanwhile, grew from one million in 1801 (already the largest city in Europe) to 2.2 million in 1851, to 6.2 million in 1901, peaking at 8.1 million in 1951.[128] Then the population dropped slightly due to suburbanization before returning to vigorous growth thanks to immigration. By 2014 it had reached 8.6 million.[129] Nowadays most of the top urban agglomerations are in Asia. They include Guangzhou (Canton), Tokyo, and Shanghai.

The romantic view that people moved from an allegedly salubrious countryside to the rotten life of the cities is, however, as simplistic as the starry-eyed celebration of towns against the idiocy of rural life. A study based on autobiographies of English industrial workers in the 1820s and 1830s points out that many of those who left the countryside never cast a nostalgic backward glance, never lamented the simplicity or health of rural life, and never returned.[130]

But even those who were enthusiastic about the long-term benefits of industrialization could not avoid allowing their pride in the achievements of technology to be tempered by a foreboding of the losses inflicted on the environment. Thus the radical journalist and free-trade supporter William Cobbett, writing in the 1820s in his *Rural Rides* (published in 1830):

> All the way along, from Leeds to Sheffield, it is coal and iron, and iron and coal. It was dark before we reached Sheffield; so that we saw the iron furnaces in all the horrible splendour of their everlasting blaze . . . It is a surprising thing to behold . . . whatever other nations may do with cotton and with wool, they will never equal England with regard to things made of iron and steel. This Sheffield, and the land all about it, is one bed of

> iron and coal. They call it black Sheffield, and black enough it is; but from this one town and its environs go nine-tenths of the knives that are used in the whole world . . .[131]

This 'wondrous works of their hands' came at a terrible cost: it was estimated by J. C. Hall in the *British Medical Journal* (March 1857) that Sheffield metal grinders rarely lived beyond the age of 35.[132]

Cities were not centres of modern rationality. Many urban dwellers, particularly in southern Europe, were hardly more enlightened than their rural counterparts. Axel Munthe, a Swedish doctor who worked in cholera-stricken Naples in 1884, lamented the battles he had to fight against the 'primitive superstitions' of many of its inhabitants who distrusted doctors and medicines.[133] In Caltanissetta, in Sicily, in 1886, only a few homes had toilets, and these discharged the waste into the sewers; otherwise excrement was usually thrown into the street.[134] The writer and traveller Maxime Du Camp, who followed Giuseppe Garibaldi's 1860 expedition to southern Italy, described the Sicilian town of Messina as a den of superstitions, run by priests who scared their congregation with stories of devils attracted by the local sulphur. He described Maida, a town near Catanzaro in Calabria, as inhabited by semi-savages. Du Camp found the place reminiscent of oriental towns he had visited (with Gustave Flaubert), with dogs running wild, naked children caked in dirt, pigs in the middle of the street, and women singing melancholic songs while their friends combed their hair looking for lice.[135]

In France, in the middle of the nineteenth century, the population that could be classified as destitute, kept alive only by private philanthropy and public assistance, was just under 10 per cent.[136] The link between pauperism and industrialization was by then well established. In 1835, Alexis de Tocqueville, in his *Mémoire sur le paupérisme*, asserted that industrial society increased the numbers of those who had to rely on private or public benefaction. Rich countries, such as England (which Tocqueville had visited in 1833), contained the greatest number of people in a state of destitution: 'If you go through the English countryside, you feel you are in the Eden of modern civilization.' Roads were well-kept, the houses solid and clean, the cattle well fed. But once inside towns, 'you will discover that one-sixth of the population live on public charity'.[137]

Some forty years later a not dissimilar verdict was recorded by a different traveller. Kume Kunitake, chronicler of the Iwakura embassy sent round the globe by the Japanese government in 1871, noted that 'Britain had been able to become the wealthiest country in the world . . .

because its people's industriousness exceeds that of other nations.' But, he added, 'the numbers of the poor are probably greater than in almost any other country'.[138]

There had been laws in England to deal with the destitute for a long time, but the old form of charity, the Poor Laws (1601), were an impediment to the development of industry, not because they made the poor lazy but because, to obtain public assistance, people had to be registered in the parish in which they resided and this was an obstacle to the mobility of labour. The Poor Law Amendment Act of 1834 forced the poor to accept work in workhouses whose conditions were such as to make even work in factories acceptable.[139] Causing the poor to be even more miserable if they did not accept any work was seen, then as now, as a way of reducing poverty. The advantage, from the point of view of capitalism, is that it accelerated the process of urbanization, since the workhouses were in urban centres, and, of course, they kept wages down. The drawback was that urban taxpayers had to pay more to maintain them. By the middle of the century, according to travellers' reports, a similar repressive attitude towards the poor existed even in prosperous Geneva, where 5 per cent of the inhabitants were on public assistance.[140]

Matters did not seem to have improved significantly by the end of the nineteenth century, at least not for the very poor – though precision is impossible in a field where statistics are unreliable and the definition of poverty uncertain. In 1899 in York, northern England, according to the famous survey conducted by Seebohm Rowntree, almost 10 per cent of the population of the city were below what Rowntree defined as 'the primary poverty line' (the 'really really poor'), a further 13 per cent were below the secondary poverty line (the poor), and a further 21.5 per cent were not far from the first two groups.[141] After further calculation, Rowntree concluded that 'nearly 30 per cent of the population are found to be living in poverty'.[142]

Why were they poor? Although Rowntree suggested that gambling and drinking were a main cause of secondary poverty, people found themselves in real poverty when the main breadwinner had died, or was incapacitated, or unemployed, or because the families were too large, or the wages too low.[143] These causes might be seen as unexceptional now, but it was believed then (as many still believe now) that people were poor because they did not want to work. The belief that poverty might be caused by circumstances outside the control of the poor clashed with the apparent evidence that society was not at fault. If it were, why were some people poor and others, born in similar circumstances, not?

Charles Booth in his 1891 investigation had no doubt: the main causes of destitution, he wrote, were 'drink, immorality, laziness and pauper associations or heredity'.[144] But, like Rowntree, he tried not to be judgemental: 'It may be their own fault that this is so; that is another question,' he wrote, adding, with the balanced tone of the impartial sociologist (one of the first), 'my first business is simply with the numbers who, from whatever cause, do live under conditions of poverty or destitution.'[145]

THE PROSPEROUS

In practice, between the truly rich (the landowners, major bankers, and industrialists) and the really poor (those with no jobs, the so-called dangerous classes) there was a variety of social groups, each separated from the next by minor differences in income and status (semi-skilled workers, skilled workers, shopkeepers, clerks, etc.).

The nobility enjoyed an entirely different lifestyle from the rest. This was true not only of the aristocracy in London, Paris, Naples, Berlin, and other major cities, but also of petty aristocrats in peripheral areas. The French geologist Barthélemy Faujas-Saint-Fond, who travelled to Scotland in 1784, a century before the period I am describing, gives us a fascinating account of the breakfast table of his host 'Monsieur Mac-Liane', the son of the Laird (Lord) of Torloisk, in the Isle of Mull. 'Mac-Liane' was, in all likelihood, General Allan MacLean, who had taken part in the Jacobite rebellion and the defence of Quebec from the American revolutionary armies. He was far from rich (Faujas-Saint-Fond writes that the house was simple), but the food he offered his French guest was quite remarkable in both quantity and range. Perhaps he was trying to impress; he certainly did so. Breakfast was at 10 a.m. and consisted of smoked beef, salted herrings, butter, milk, and cream, what is evidently porridge (boiled *farine d'avoine*), milk mixed with egg yolk, sugar, and rum (some kind of eggnog), gooseberry jam, blueberries, local fruits, tea, coffee, various kinds of bread, and Jamaica rum. At 4 p.m. they had dinner: a great bowl of soup of beef, mutton and fowl with oats, onions, parsley, and peas, followed by black pudding with lots of pepper and ginger, 'excellent' grilled beef slices, 'high quality' roasted mutton, potatoes cooked in meat juices, chickens, cucumbers, and ginger chutney, milk, Madeira, 'poudingue' of barley flour, cream, and Greek raisins. All this was laid on the table at the same time along with beer and wine. When dinner was over, they were served port, sherry, Madeira, and punch; two cheeses, a Cheshire and a local; and finally tea, bread, and butter.[146] Faujas-Saint-Fond then tells us that the ordinary inhabitants of Mull (7,000 people) were mainly shepherds and fishermen who went around without shoes or hat (in the north of Scotland!) and just ate oats and potatoes, though those who fished also smoked the salmon they caught; that the women were ugly (unlike MacLean's daughter, whom he describes several times as *jolie, d'une taille élégante, de la plus charmante figure*), which he attributes to the climate, the food, and the lack of proper clothes and shelter.[147]

The life of the rich, especially the nouveau riche in the middle of the nineteenth century, impressed the middle classes. In 1867 the Polish-born Danish painter Elisabeth Jerichau-Baumann wrote to her husband, the sculptor Jens Adolf Jerichau, of the dinner she had while a guest at the country house of Baron Carl Joachim Hambro (Milton Abbey in Dorset, purchased by Hambro in 1852). Amazed at the 'unnatural life of the rich' (Hambro, who was Danish too, was the founder of Hambros Bank), she marvelled at the landscape designed by Capability Brown in the eighteenth century, and then described the dinner table:

> Everything imaginable ad nauseam in the way of delicacies offered: melons, strawberries, grapes, figs, etc., and then the inevitable champagne. And against this a background of thousands of poor starving children lacking the barest necessities.[148]

In 1900 the prosperity that would be characteristic of the West in the second half of the twentieth century had only begun to reach the lower middle classes. Much of their expenditure was spent not on consumer goods but on food and rent: 80 per cent in the case of Parisian skilled workers (1907 survey), 65 per cent in the case of artisans.[149] And, of course, there was progress. By 1910, on average a Frenchman consumed four times more wine than his counterpart in 1831, three times more beer, seven times more sugar, eleven times more tea, and thirty times more chocolate.[150]

The middle classes, particularly the urban middle classes, were the main beneficiaries of the growth of industry and thus, not surprisingly, they were the backbone of modernity, and sometimes even of democracy. They were the true heirs to the Enlightenment, not necessarily because they were enlightened, though some were, but because the middle class was the only class truly at home in the new world of progress. Inequalities were still very high, though perhaps only as high as now. At the beginning of the twentieth century the 90,000 households that made up the British middle classes had a yearly income oscillating between £300 and £1,000, while an unskilled worker, working a six-day week, would earn £56 a year.[151] By 1908, those earning above £700 a year (3.1 per cent of the population) could be deemed rich, while those earning between £160 and £700 were merely 'comfortable'.[152] In Chicago, in the late nineteenth century, the earnings of a white-collar worker were twice those of a skilled labourer (the gap since then has all but disappeared).[153] Yet such was the degree of uncertainty about the future that the middle class saved obsessively, and expenditure for pleasure was restricted to the minimum. Pleasure, after all, was for the really prosperous.

It must be remembered that everyday items of consumption taken for granted even by the very poor at the end of the twentieth century were still semi-luxuries at the end of the nineteenth. Take tea. The yearly consumption of tea in western and central Europe in 1840 was about four ounces per year per person (today in Turkey, the world leader, it is three kilos; in the UK and in Ireland around two kilos). At that time the Chinese drank two and a half times as much, hardly surprising since tea was, after all, 'their' drink.[154] In 1800 the British annual consumption of sugar, then a luxury, was just over eight kilos per capita (21.9 grams a day), the average continental European only one kilo per capita (2.7 grams a day).[155] By 2015, to the chagrin (or perhaps joy) of dentists, the average American per capita consumption of sugar per day was 126.4 grams, out-sugaring Germany (102.9 grams) and the Netherlands (102.5 grams). The British were seventh in the world, consuming 93.2 grams per capita a day, while Indians were at the bottom of the countries surveyed at only 5.1 grams a day (still nearly twice continental European consumption in 1800). The World Health Organization recommendation is 50 grams a day.[156]

Around 1900 the lower middle classes could consume some such 'luxuries', but they lived in small dwellings, deprived of comforts. Shopkeepers lived at the back of the shop with the kitchen used as a dining room and sometimes as a bedroom.[157] They eventually became more prosperous, narrowing the gap within the middle classes. Although numbers are difficult to estimate, it is likely that by the end of the nineteenth century what was once a plentiful supply of domestic servants began to decrease. Middle-class ladies, once the managers of the household, turned into housewives as it became more difficult to recruit maids and cleaners. The phrase, 'you can't find servants nowadays', was already a cliché at the end of the nineteenth century. In Paris many ladies of the solid bourgeoisie had only one maid and had to do the shopping themselves, occasionally, it seemed, helped by their husbands. The fate of servants was dismal, though arguably an improvement over the homes they were born into.

Eliza Lynn Linton provided us with a description of the bleak fate that awaited the typical maid in the London of the 1870s, all the more interesting since the author was a ferocious anti-feminist who raised 'moral objections against the active political woman', declaring it was 'an absolute truth' that the 'raison d'être of a woman is maternity'.[158] In a letter (26 January 1898) to William Woodall, a Liberal politician and supporter of women's suffrage, she wrote that the advent of female suffrage together with full manhood suffrage would bring about 'mob rule heightened by the hysteria of the feminine element'.[159] Be that as it may, Eliza Linton was unenthusiastically married for less than ten years, had no children of her own, and was a well-paid and remarkably successful writer and journalist. *But* she had feelings for servants. In an article in *The Cornhill Magazine* in 1874 she wrote:

> the kindest-hearted mistress treats it as an impertinence when her maids stipulate for rights, say in the matter of a fixed holiday . . . She [the maid] is liable to be rung up at all hours; her very meals are not secure from interruption; she has no time that is absolutely her own; and even her sleep is not sacred. In the dead of night something may be wanted, and she must get up to bring or to do it . . . She lives under ground or just below the roof. Damp, drains, want of efficient ventilation, with the constant presence of draughts, surround her in winter . . . Her food is of poorer quality and less appetizing than the family's . . . She comes up from the country and is plunged at once from the fresh air and free expanse of her old surroundings into the dismal darkness of a London kitchen . . . No followers, no friends in the kitchen, no laughing to be heard above stairs . . . this is English domestic service.[160]

The large number of servants among the nobility was not (only) a matter of being ostentatious: it was imposed by the low level of household technology. Since there was no running water, it had to be pumped up by servants. Everything needed to be washed by hand. Hot water had to be carried to the masters' bathrooms after heating it on the stove. Chamber pots had to be emptied regularly. In the evening ladies really needed someone to help them remove their boots, as well as their corsets tied by a complex system of laces. In the morning a similar ritual took place for dressing. Socks were expensive, so there was constant darning. There was no central heating, so fires had to be lit at various times according to a pattern set by the masters. Knives were not of stainless steel, so they had to be cleaned and dried with great care. When cars became available, they needed to be dried by the chauffeur after every rainfall to avoid rust. Since there were no well-stocked local shops, the rural nobility had to consume vegetables and fruits grown on their estate; this required a small army of gardeners. Before the First World War at the Château de Cheverny by the Loire, each male member of the family had a valet, each lady a chambermaid; in the kitchen the cook had a 'saucier' to make the sauces as well as various scullery maids and sous-chefs.[161] All these servants had to be fed and clothed. This was so expensive that in 1914 the owners opened the château to a paying public. Today Cheverny employs even more people than at the beginning of the twentieth century, but that is because it is now a business, a place visited by tourists (an added bonus is that Cheverny was the inspiration for the Château de Moulinsart in the popular Tintin comic books). Such tourism would not have been possible had not the 'masses' become more prosperous and had there not been 'socialist' reforms such as paid holidays, one of the few achievements of the Popular Front government in 1936.

Of course, lesser aristocrats and most bourgeois employed a fraction of those employed at Cheverny, but even in 1914 there were in Paris some 200,000 domestic servants: 11 per cent of the population.[162] In Britain domestic service was the largest employer of female labour not just until the eve of the First World War but even in 1945.[163] In 1881 one Londoner in fifteen was a servant (one in twenty-two for the whole of England). There were over 750,000 servants in Britain in 1851 and the numbers grew to a peak of almost 1.4 million in 1891 (though some historians set the peak in 1871).[164]

What also changed over the course of the nineteenth century was the relationship between masters (or, rather, mistresses) and servants. Protective paternalism gradually faded away. The maid's relationship with the 'masters' became mainly economic.[165] One must, of course, beware of a mental image of 'domestic servants' derived from films, novels, and television serials. Domestic service is a generic term that covers (in census reports) 'general servant', 'housekeeper', 'nurse', 'cook', etc.[166] Besides, many employers were not middle class and did not have live-in servants but recruited young women from the workhouse and obtained their labour in exchange for a meal and a few coins.[167]

In Britain the typical middle-class family at the turn of the century employed two or three servants, one of whom would be a maid (answering the door, helping the lady of the house to dress, serving dinner). The others cooked and cleaned. By having two or three deferential servants, the growing ranks of the middle classes could bask in the illusion that they were approaching the lifestyle of the aristocracy.[168]

Small entrepreneurs, though better off than the majority of the population, were, then as now, in a constant state of anxiety, partly because they were worried by the competition from larger firms, but also because they were envious of the salaried bourgeoisie, especially those in public employment. The latter spent more on rent, on the education of their children, on books and newspapers, than most traders and merchants.[169] And they also had a more secure future. Not for nothing their allegiance to the existing political order was almost unassailable.

What of those, the overwhelming majority, who had no servants? Take just a single and simple task indispensable before the introduction of indoor plumbing. Before, water required for washing, cleaning, and cooking had to be brought into the house several times a day. The water, once boiled, would be used to wash heavy articles such as sheets and tablecloths, using detergent that might be harmful to the skin. They needed to be rubbed, wrung, then dried on a line, and, finally, ironed.[170] A North Carolina Farmer's Alliance organizer calculated, in 1886, that a woman might walk 150 miles a year carrying water – water-carrying in North Carolina as in India was regarded as a woman's task.[171] Then there was the cooking, which took far longer than today, since chickens had to be plucked, bread needed to be baked – and finally there was looking after the children. A woman's work was really never done.

DEATH AND DISEASE

Urbanization was a great killer.[172] Towns, already unhealthy in preindustrial times, became even unhealthier with industrialization and urbanization. Urban infant mortality rates were higher than in rural parts at least until the beginnings of the twentieth century.[173] Cities, after all, are places easily devastated by disease since people are far more concentrated than in rural areas. This higher mortality rate would have caused the urban population to decrease if deaths exceeded births, but there was a constant stream of people to the cities to find work, thus replenishing the spaces left empty by the dead. This was the case, for instance, in Sweden, where most towns had a birth deficit as late as the first half of the nineteenth century.[174]

Migrating from the rural to the urban world increased one's chances of dying for much of the nineteenth century. In Italy, France, and elsewhere infant mortality was higher in cities than in the countryside.[175]

In 1811 life expectancy at birth in London was only 30 years. In the countryside one could expect to live, on average, until 41. Then things improved, albeit slowly. By 1911 life expectancy at birth in London was 52; in the countryside it was 55: the gap had narrowed considerably but had not been eliminated.[176] Cities were murderous in the United States too. In his State of the Union address of 6 December 1904, Theodore Roosevelt lamented: 'The slum exacts a heavy total of death from those who dwell therein; and this is the case not merely in the great crowded slums of high buildings in New York and Chicago, but in the alley slums of Washington.'[177]

Towns were described as 'graveyards'.[178] In Berlin in 1880 more than 100,000 people lived in cellar flats (*Kellerwohnungen*), usually dark and humid and where the death rate was highest.[179] In both Germany and England the urban mortality figures were above the national average until the tide turned in the 1870s.[180] Average life expectancy at birth in the Prussian countryside in 1877 was around 38 (for males, females did a little better), but in towns less than 33. Only by 1905 did it become a little healthier to live in Prussian towns than outside them.[181] Yet urbanization was unstoppable. In 1871, 36 per cent of the German population lived in towns; by 1914 it was 60 per cent.[182]

In the urban streets of the 1870s and 1880s the dirt was not just caused by human excrement and the lack of sewers, but by what was then the prevalent mode of transportation: horses. While many today complain (rightly) about the pollution caused by the internal combustion engine, in pre-car days, in New York, horses daily excreted a considerable amount of manure and urine, and when they died their carcasses were often left in the streets for days.[183] Pigs were allowed to roam in towns because they ate garbage. It was more dangerous to drink water or milk than to drink beer. Lactose intolerance, common in Japan and China, ensured that their populations were spared the disastrous effects of drinking milk in the pre-pasteurization era.[184] Drinking tea was also safer than plain water, not for any particular property of tea leaves but simply because of the requirement of boiling the water first.[185]

In 1882, New York was one of the richest cities in the world, yet only 2 per cent of its houses had running water (in France, as late as 1946, 31 per cent of homes in urban centres had no water or electricity).[186] In its slums as many as eight persons shared a single small room. Workers in American coal mines and in the steel industry worked 60-hour weeks in dirty and dangerous conditions, exposed to lethal gas and smoke.

Food was dangerous, far more so than today when people are worried about GM foods and pesticides. Since regulations were few, meat often came from diseased animals, lard contained carbonate of soda, and chocolate was often coloured. After the Public Health Act of 1848 (in response to Edwin Chadwick's struggle against insanitary conditions in many cities), there were further initiatives, particularly in the 1850s and 1860s, when Dr Arthur Hill Hassall, a physician, brought to public attention food adulteration later listed in his *Food: Its Adulterations, and the Methods for their Detection* (1876). Hassall had found *Cocculus indicus* (the source of a poisonous substance) in beer, sulphate of copper in pickles and preserves, lead and mercury in confectionery, blancmange coloured by copper arsenite. No wonder chronic gastritis was a common disease in the nineteenth century.[187] This led to the 1860 Food and Drink Adulteration Act, which made the adulteration of food and drink a criminal offence; the first of many public health measures. Then there were a series of Vaccination Acts establishing free vaccination for all children (1840, 1853, 1867, 1871, 1873, 1898, and 1907); the 1866 Sanitary Act and the 1875 Public Health Act, which compelled local authorities to ensure that there was an adequate water supply, drainage, and sewage disposal; and a string of regulations aimed at controlling 'offensive trades', reporting infectious diseases, and improving the quality of food (ten years later typhoid rates in England had fallen by 50 per cent).[188]

In the United States the unhealthy and dangerous conditions of the Chicago meat-packing industry denounced in Upton Sinclair's best-selling novel *The Jungle* (1906) helped the passage of the Pure Food and Drug Act (1906), a historic piece of federal legislation initiated by President Theodore Roosevelt, which led to the establishment of the Food and Drug Administration.[189] Thus in 'liberal' America public intervention in public health was considerable. By 1900 the overwhelming majority of the fifty largest cities in the America had public waterworks and by 1910, '70 per cent of cities with populations of more than 30,000 had shifted from private to municipal water services'.[190] As a comparison, in 2016, in India, 75.8 million people (5 per cent of the population) had no access to clean water, causing the death from diarrhoea of over 140,000 children.[191] Furthermore, according to UNICEF, there were, in 2014, one billion people in the world defecating in the open, 597 million of whom were in India.

It paid to be rich. Mortality in London's poor Whitechapel in the nineteenth century was much higher than in the prosperous West End.[192] The gap still exists today, but it has considerably narrowed, though poverty (or more specifically, inequality) still shortens one's life considerably.[193] By the end of the century the chances of dying in cities were not much higher than in the countryside. It was no longer so certain, as much traditional historiography tells us, that Paris was the tomb of sturdy provincial migrants.[194]

The middle classes, of course, lived longer than the workers and the peasants and the poor, as they do now, but they did not live long by our standards and not as comfortably. They generally died rapidly of infection instead of being kept alive by the wonders of medicine to die slowly of degenerative diseases as we do.

Compared to today, even the rich and famous did not live long in the nineteenth century. In 1800 people aged over 65 were less than 5 per cent of the population.[195] A quick (anecdotal and unscientific) look at the longevity of some of Europe's and America's best-known writers suggests that life was short for them too. While Alessandro Manzoni and Thomas Hardy lived until the age of 88, and Victor Hugo, Giovanni Verga, Leo Tolstoy, and Wordsworth made it past 80, many others were not so lucky: Byron died at 36 (of a fever contracted at war the previous year); Shelley at 30 (drowning); Keats at 26 (tuberculosis and/or mercury poisoning); Pushkin at 37 (in a duel); Balzac at 51 (ill-health); Baudelaire at 46 (opium? alcoholism?); Edgar Allan Poe at 40 (opium and alcoholism); Emily Dickinson at 56 (kidney disease); Jane Austen at 42 (typhus? TB?); George Eliot at 61 (kidney disease); Dostoyevsky at 60 (pulmonary emphysema); Heinrich Heine at 63 (lead poisoning); Charlotte Brontë at 39 (dehydration and malnourishment while pregnant); Flaubert and Stendhal at 59 (the first of a cerebral haemorrhage, the second of medication used to treat his syphilis); Vissarion Belinsky at 37 (TB); and Anton Chekhov at 44 (TB). The idea that people were unlikely to live beyond their sixties lasted into the twentieth century: Adolf Hausrath, in his essay on the historian Heinrich von Treitschke, written in 1914, says: 'Treitschke died at the age of sixty-two, older or nearly of the same age as his teachers – Häusser, Mathy, and Gervinus, all of whom we invariably regard as venerable old men.'[196] The Bible was more optimistic about the length of our lives, promising seventy years. As Psalm 90:10 says: 'The days of our lives *are* seventy years.' Seventy years seemed reasonable: Dante's *Divina Commedia* begins with the words *Nel mezzo del cammin di nostra vita* ('Midway upon the journey of our life'), meaning he was thirty-five.

Given the conditions of life even in rich European countries, it was not surprising that mortality rates were still very high in the 1880s. There was, however, a dramatic improvement, at least in Europe, in longevity (see Table 6).

Table 6 Life Expectancy at Birth in Selected European Countries

	1880		1910	
	Men	Women	Men	Women
England and Wales	44.3	47.1	51.1	55.4
France	41.0	47.1	48.5	52.2
Germany	36.3	39.2	47.4	50.7
Italy	33.3	34.0	44.3	45.7
European Russia (includes Dnieper, Ukraine, and Belarus)	26.3	29.1	34.7	37.8
Switzerland	40.6	43.2	50.6	54.0
Sweden	48.7	50.0	55.2	57.6

Source: Alfred Perrenoud and Patrice Bourdelais, 'Le recul de la mortalité', p. 77.

There was a parallel, though not consistent, decline in infant mortality (see Table 7).

Table 7 Infant Mortality Rate in Selected Countries, 1881–1911

	Prussia	England and Wales	France	Belgium	Netherlands	Sweden	Italy
1881	199	130	165	155	182	113	n/a
1891	201	149	161	162	169	108	188
1901	200	151	142	142	149	103	165
1911	188	130	117	167*	137	72	153

Source: R. I. Woods, P. A. Watterson, and J. H. Woodward, 'The Causes of Rapid Infant Mortality Decline in England and Wales, 1861–1921, Part I', pp. 343–66.

*The figure for Belgium in 1911 is far higher due to an exceptional outbreak of dysentery among the young.[197]

So over thirty years things were looking up, particularly if one survived the first five years of life (where mortality was extremely high, especially in cities). Then, after 1875, matters deteriorated for adults, at least for the 'respectable', employed working classes, perhaps because of the lower nutritional value of cheaper food from abroad (white flour from the USA, tinned meat from Argentina, sugar from the West Indies).[198] In Norway and Sweden around 1875 the mortality rate *before* the fifth birthday was about 20 per cent against 25 per cent in England and 30 per cent in France, but in Italy, just after unification (1861), it was as much as 47 per cent.[199]

The longer life achieved today is due to a remarkable and costly improvement in nutrition, education, the environment, and public health, though the relative importance of these factors is debated.[200] To put it plainly, for countries as for individuals, it is better to be rich than to be poor, since prosperity enables one to have a better diet, a more hygienic home, and a cleaner environment, thus increasing one's resistance to or reducing encounters with diseases.

Progress of this kind often requires public intervention. In the nineteenth century, improvements in health were not only the result of economic growth (the beneficial workings of 'the market') but of the conscious and direct intervention of public bodies.[201] In 1875 the British government passed the Public Health Act to reduce unhygienic living conditions so as to combat the spread of diseases such as cholera and typhus, and began improving its public health system. Ten years later typhoid rates in England had fallen by half. Between 1880 and 1920 hundreds of American cities municipalized their water systems (293 in 1880 to nearly 8,000 in 1932). The death rate from typhoid plummeted, in some instances by 70 per cent.[202] Improvements in public health, sewers, sterilization, pasteurization, purification of water were a major factor in improving life expectations. By 1900 public water supplies were available to over 40 per cent of Americans and sewers to almost 30 per cent. Filtered water, available to only 30,000 people in the USA in 1880, became available to 10 million by 1910, bringing about a drastic reduction of typhoid mortality.[203]

In some cases richer did not mean healthier. Scotland, considerably poorer than England, had a lower infant mortality rate throughout the nineteenth century. And, as we can see from the table above, Italy did better than Prussia. Today Kerala does better than wealthier regions in India.[204] In 2010 life expectancy at birth in Costa Rica was better than in the much richer United States.[205] Sweden led the world in life expectancy from the eighteenth century (when it was not rich) until about 1978, when it was one of the richest. Then Japan, which in the 1920s had health standards similar to those of Egypt, took the lead.[206] Nor is democracy necessarily better for one's health. In 2014 fifteen Baltimore neighbourhoods (mainly black) had a life expectancy worse than that of North Korea (70.6 in 2015). A baby born in the wealthy suburb of

Roland Park, in the north of the city, was likely to live to the age of 84 (the US average is 79). One born three miles away, in downtown Seton Hill, was expected to die at the age of 65, nineteen years earlier.[207] Other studies have confirmed the huge disparity in life expectancy in the USA.[208] In 1979 (before economic reform had even started) life expectancy at birth in communist China was 64, better than democratic India (52), better than the average for low-income countries (50), and even better than the then average of middle-income countries (61).[209] In 2015 communist China (and communist Vietnam) was still ahead of democratic India (76 and 68.3), and communist Cuba, with 79.1 years, was only marginally below the USA with 79.3 years.[210]

Around 1860 the eight great killer diseases (whooping cough, measles, scarlet fever, diphtheria, smallpox, typhoid, typhus, and tuberculosis) were responsible for 30 per cent of the total annual deaths in England and Wales. By the beginning of the twentieth century their share had dropped to under 20 per cent thanks to a combination of factors, including public health acts and preventive medicine.[211]

The importance of state action was not underestimated by most contemporaries. Edmund A. Parkes, an English military physician and hygienist and veteran of the Crimean War, had no doubts over 'the necessity of state interference', adding that 'In all civilized countries' there are laws 'removing conditions which injure the health of the people', and suggesting that England should have stronger laws of that kind.[212]

Those who still believe in progress can take comfort: today's poor, on the whole, live longer than yesterday's rich. In 2004 life expectancy in sub-Saharan Africa was 46.1 – the lowest in the world, but still higher than that in almost all European countries in 1880.[213] Progress, then as today, was very uneven. In spite of fairly strong growth rates in 1880–1900, life expectancy in Russia and Italy remained well behind Germany, France, the United States, and Great Britain. Of course, in Latin America it was even worse: between 1865 and 1895 in Brazil, Chile, Colombia, Costa Rica, and Panama the life expectancy of a child at birth was a dismal 26.9.[214] We do not have reliable data on mortality rates in late nineteenth-century Asia but they were probably worse than Europe's and certainly far worse than now. What we do know is that, with the exception of the Irish Famine of 1845–51, in western Europe in the nineteenth and twentieth centuries there were no serious peacetime famines, unlike European Russia, where famine devastated whole areas in 1891–2, 1921–2, and 1932–3. The typical diet in France at the start of the eighteenth century was as poor as that of

Rwanda in 1965 (then the most malnourished country in the world, according to the World Bank).[215] Even in what are now regarded as the more prosperous areas of western Europe there were serious differences: the average Belgian in the early nineteenth century consumed 2,500 calories per day while the average Norwegian consumed only 1,800, a figure that persisted in nearly all of Asia, Africa, and most of Latin America until the 1950s.[216] Today the World Health Organization recommends a daily intake of 2,000 calories for the average person.

Killer diseases, such as smallpox, typhus, malaria, and tuberculosis, spread far better in towns than in the countryside, though in the course of the nineteenth century the spread of smallpox was increasingly controlled by vaccine. A relatively new disease, cholera, devastated cities throughout the world in the nineteenth century. It began on the Ganges Delta and continued its deadly journey, reaching Russia in the early 1820s and then western Europe.[217] Expanding trade enabled it to reach China and then the Americas; devoted pilgrims took it to Mecca, where it killed 15,000 people in 1846.[218] Those who survived took the disease back home. In Egypt it killed 30,000 in 1848 and twice that many in 1865.[219] Cholera continued its murderous march, killing 24,000 in Paris before it went on to Brussels. Between 1847 and 1851 it had killed a million people in Russia.[220] In the period 1865–8 it killed 160,000 in Italy.[221] In Naples alone 42,000 people died of it in the second half of the nineteenth century (10 per cent of its population). The virulence of the epidemic was not due to the cholera germ by itself but to the debilitated state of much of the population and the dismal hygienic conditions caused by bad housing, poor sanitation, and a rudimentary or non-existent sewage system.[222] In Hungary the cholera epidemic of the 1870s noticeably slowed down population growth.[223]

In 1854 in London's Soho, 616 were killed by the contaminated water pumped in what is today Broadwick Street, the source later being famously identified by Dr John Snow. In 1866 almost 4,000 Londoners died of cholera, mainly in the East End of London, including 916 just in the one week ending 4 August.[224] In 1892 the killer disease hit Hamburg, a rich city, leaving 9,000 dead.[225] The problem in Hamburg was that the local elite was committed to a policy of laissez-faire and neglected public health; the dead were victims of what today we would call 'neo-liberal' economics. When Robert Koch visited the city during the epidemic he contrasted unfavourably the conditions of the workers of Hamburg with those of Alexandria and Calcutta: 'I forget that I am in Europe,' he said.[226] Eighty years later, when the same bacteria (associated with infected shellfish) struck again Naples and Bari (1973) and

Portugal (1974), it killed very few people, mainly because social conditions had improved remarkably.[227]

Outside Europe epidemics were worse. In 1855 there was an outbreak of bubonic plague in Yunnan. It advanced along the tin and opium routes, reaching the Gulf of Tonkin. Chinese junks and, later, faster ships carried the disease, reaching Guangzhou (Canton) and Hong Kong in 1894. Two years later it surfaced in India, hitting port cities from Calcutta to Mumbai and Karachi. Thousands died. In 1899 the plague hit Alexandria, then Buenos Aires in 1900 and other Latin American cities. South Africa and Australia were not spared.[228] It reached San Francisco in 1900. Since most of the city's victims were in Chinatown, Chinese immigrants, depicted as filthy and diseased, were blamed.[229] In fact almost everywhere the poor were blamed for the plague – their poverty, squalor, poor hygienic conditions and the overcrowding of their dwellings providing the necessary evidence. In some instances, such as in Sydney, in addition to the Chinese, the causes of the disease were attributed to the wrath of God or paper currency.[230] Some, quite rightly, blamed the rats (though it was actually their fleas that carried the disease). Some advocated public health measures. Public health scientists such as the justly celebrated Louis Pasteur and Robert Koch, pioneers of 'germ' theory, received the backing of their respective countries (France and Germany). This may be hardly surprising in our age, when the state intervenes compelling us to wear seatbelts when we drive cars, but in the nineteenth century making laws compelling people to be vaccinated or securing the purity of water and food was controversial.[231]

So accustomed were the inhabitants of even the wealthiest nations of the world to the catastrophic effects of pandemics in the decades preceding the Second World War that they paid relatively little attention to them.[232] The great influenza of 1918–19, which killed far more people in Europe and the Americas than the preceding 'Great War', has hardly been commemorated in novels and films; it is not remembered in monuments and songs, nor is it remembered in rituals anywhere – unlike the victims of the First World War. Mexico may have been then still in the midst of years of revolutionary upheavals, but many more died of the flu pandemic of 1918 that wiped out hundreds of thousands of people, 'the most devastating blow to human life in Mexico in 350 years'.[233]

Things did get better, at least in Europe, but slowly. In 1806 a newly born boy in France could expect to die before the age of 33, a girl would last a few more years. By 1850 the situation had already improved: longevity was lengthened by ten years for men, by five for women. Progress in the next fifty years, however, was minimal: just over one extra year for men and less than four for women.[234]

In the United States mortality rates had started to decline in 1870.[235] In part this was due to the somewhat improved circumstances of the now liberated slaves, since slaves worked from childhood until death, often in field gangs and in appalling conditions.[236] Nevertheless, even after abolition their conditions remained far below that of Europe's poor. Those who stayed in the South worked as sharecroppers on the same fields still owned by their former masters.[237] They had few skills, no economic resources, and faced a dour and obtuse racism that no equivalent ethnic group had to face in Europe during the nineteenth century.

Only the Native Americans, pitilessly decimated (such massacres later celebrated in numberless films), fared worse. The population of Native Americans collapsed between 1500 and 1800 while that of Europe continued to increase, particularly that of Great Britain, which trebled during these three centuries in spite of the constant emigration to North America.[238] The natives were killed not only by the colonists themselves but, and in greater numbers, by the new diseases. In what Alfred Crosby has called 'the Columbian Exchange', the colonizers, from Spain and Portugal as well as France and England, exported to Europe these new foods, such as maize, potatoes, various kinds of beans, peanuts, tomatoes, etc.. They imported into the Americas diseases such as smallpox, measles, whooping cough, typhus, and chicken pox, which vastly increased the mortality of the native population of the New World. Indigenous Americans were the chief victims of this new globalization, since 'The most spectacular period of mortality among the American Indians occurred during the first hundred years of contact with the Europeans and Africans.'[239] The main reason was that the Indians had 'little or no resistance to many diseases brought from the Old World'.[240] Encountering the Europeans was the equivalent of being invaded by contaminated monsters from outer space as in a sci-fi horror film.

In pre-Columbian America, north of Mexico, there might have been between 5 and 18 million Native Americans, and about 75 million in the entire New World.[241] By the time the conquest of the 'West' had been accomplished by settlers there were very few natives left in the USA. In California alone, the indigenous population plunged from 85,000 to 35,000 between 1852 and 1860. By 1890 fewer than 18,000 Californian Native Americans were still alive.[242] In Brazil, at the beginning of European colonization there were probably 5 million people divided into self-governing units. Diseases and massacres then took their toll and those who remained in 2010 were 896,917 individuals, or 0.47 per cent of the population.[243]

INDUSTRY

By the beginning of the nineteenth century, agricultural productivity had barely increased since the Middle Ages. This was not necessarily a problem. All it meant was that several members of a farming household had to produce not only what was necessary to feed themselves but also enough to feed other members unable to work because they were too young or too old.[244] Those too old or feeble were kept alive out of intergenerational solidarity (sooner or later, those who worked, if they did not die young, would become old in turn). In the absence of a welfare state, to have many children was a rational choice: it was one's pension, one's insurance against old age. And since so many died at birth or soon after birth, it was necessary to have as many children as possible. The sooner they could work the better.

France was an exception to this pattern. In the nineteenth century its population, compared to other, similar countries, was stagnant because of an exceptionally low birth rate. This made for a tight labour market, which legal restrictions on child labour made tighter still.[245]

Why did the French breed so little? The usual explanation is that, quite deliberately, many French farmers opted for a small family to preserve the size of their land, which otherwise would be divided, according to legislation, among too many heirs. This was particularly marked in the first half of the nineteenth century, when French peasants seemed particularly prone to the use of contraceptives, unlike peasants elsewhere.[246] This remains the most likely explanation, since there was no significant difference in the percentage of women of childbearing age in France as compared to Germany, England, and Italy in 1870, nor in the age of marriage.[247] In the years before the outbreak of the First World War, a new cause of low birth rates was identified: the excessive length of military service delayed the beginning of the reproductive cycle by keeping young men away from young women (and husbands from their wives).[248] One of the effects of the slow rise of the population in France was that few of them emigrated.[249] Germans and Poles, Italians and Jews, Irish and Chinese, English and Scots left their homes and went to the United States, to Latin America, to the colonies. The French, by and large, stayed in France.

In fact France, in the nineteenth century, was an importer of labour, receiving more immigrants than any other European country. By 1886 there were over one million foreign workers in France – 7 per cent of those employed in industry. By 1891 12 per cent of wage workers were foreigners.[250] The immigrants came mainly from Belgium, then one of the most industrialized countries in western Europe, and from Italy (one of the least). In 1872, and still in 1911, Belgians and Italians constituted 61 per cent of the immigrant working population. There were more Belgians than Italians, but the former were skilled miners while the Italians were a kind of sub-proletariat who, as is often the case with such groups, were the target of local racism. Other immigrants came from Spain, Portugal, and from central and eastern Europe, including many Jews from the Tsarist Empire.[251] During the recovery from the crisis of the 1870s, there was also a considerable increase in the number of internal migrants. This was a largely unskilled labour force, feeling uprooted and disoriented in big cities, and many suffering from tuberculosis.[252] Female employment increased too: women were 30 per cent of the workforce in 1866 and 37.7 per cent in 1906.[253] Most of the industrial employment was concentrated in small firms.[254]

Industrialized Europe, at the end of the nineteenth century, consisted of a relatively few islands of manufacturing in an ocean of agriculture. These outposts were the United Kingdom, Belgium, the Netherlands, parts of Germany, parts of Scandinavia, and parts of France. Then there were the latecomers: the rest of Scandinavia, the rest of Germany, parts of Italy. Elsewhere industrialization was just in its infancy. For instance in the middle of the nineteenth century only 8 per cent of the population of Wallachia and Moldavia (the main components of modern Romania) was employed in manufacturing.[255] Even in 1900 there was no proper capitalism in what had by then had become Romania: the capital stock of industrial enterprises with more than twenty-five workers represented only 1.5 per cent of the total for the country.[256]

But the latecomers, since they started from a lower base, were growing rapidly – or at least some of them. In 1870 the share of total European GDP (Gross Domestic Product) in north-western Europe was 26.3 per cent (with a population just under 16 per cent of the total). By 1913 it had gone down slightly to 24.4 per cent while central and eastern Europe was surging ahead (from 46 per cent to 53.2 per cent). Russia, Romania, and Bulgaria were growing more rapidly than the Mediterranean countries.[257]

In 1850, in terms of income per capita, Spain was still richer than Germany and Portugal richer than Sweden. By 1870, Germany was well ahead of Spain and one of the richest countries in Europe, while Portugal was one of the poorest.[258]

Table 8 Per Capita GDP in Some European Countries and the USA, 1870–1913*

	1870	1913
United Kingdom	3,328	5,030
Belgium	2,722	4,263
USA	2,454	5,301
Netherlands	2,417	3,539
Switzerland	2,098	4,270
Germany	2,006	4,181
Denmark	1,929	3,768
Italy	1,838	2,721
France	1,746	3,245
Austria-Hungary	1,584	2,576

*$ in 1990 international prices

Source: Stephen Broadberry and Alexander Klein, 'Aggregate and Per Capita GDP in Europe, 1870–2000'.

The richest countries in Europe in 1870 were still rich on the eve of the First World War (see Table 8).

The figures should not be taken too literally since the methodology used relies on uncertain figures (Italy could not have been richer than France in 1870) and GDP is a relatively recent statistical figure developed by Simon Kuznets in 1934. What matters is the relative gap between the top ten countries. Whereas today they are all fairly close, the gap was then very wide: in 1913 the income of the average French person was still only 60 per cent of that of the average British; that of the average American twice that of the average Italian or Norwegian. The clearest sign of things to come, however, was the remarkable performance of the United States, whose per capita GDP had become the highest in the world in 1913. By 1950 the USA had outdistanced even the richest European states, except for Switzerland. Only in the 1970s and 1980s would the Europeans catch up once again (see Table 9).

In the period 1870–1913 annual growth rates in the industrial West were 2.5 per cent, just a little better than in the period 1820–70 (2.4) or 1913–50 (2.0), but much less than in 1950–73 (4.9).[259] If we take Europe as a whole, growth rates between 1830 and 1910 were 1.7 per cent per annum, the kind of growth rates that until recently we would regard as

Table 9 Per Capita GDP in Some European Countries and the USA, 1950*

USA	9.561
Switzerland	9.071
UK	6.879
Sweden	6.539
Denmark	6.404
Belgium	5.472
Norway	5.376
Netherlands	5.285
France	4.943
Finland	4.362
Germany	4.075

*$ in 1990 international prices

Source: Stephen Broadberry and Alexander Klein, 'Aggregate and Per Capita GDP in Europe, 1870–2000'.

stagnation. Yet there is no question that income growth in the period of industrialization, even in a bad period, was considerably higher than the growth of per capita income in previous centuries: between 1500 and 1800 per capita income increased by less than 0.3 per cent.[260]

In late nineteenth-century Europe the fastest growing countries were concentrated in the north (Scandinavia). The so-called 'laggards' were all in eastern Europe and the Mediterranean.[261]

By the eve of the First World War, the countries that exceeded the European GNP average were the Scandinavian countries, Finland, Germany, Switzerland, France, Belgium, the United Kingdom, Austria-Hungary, Russia, the Netherlands, and probably Romania. Of course, volume of GNP per se is not necessarily of great significance, since a country with a large population should have a larger GNP than one with a small population. Thus China in 1880 had probably the highest GNP in the world and in 1913 Russian GNP, with 20.4 per cent of total European GNP, was higher than that of Britain with 17.2 per cent, as was Germany's at 19.4 per cent, while France and Austria-Hungary followed at some distance with 10.7 and 10.1 per cent respectively.[262] Some of the rich counties, such as the UK and the Netherlands (including Belgium), France, and Switzerland were already rich in 1800, but Portugal, one of the richest in 1800 (thanks to its colonies), was by 1913 among the poorest in Europe, exporting mainly wine, cork, and sardines.[263] Some countries went from poor to rich.

Thus Finland, part of the Tsarist Empire, at the beginning of the 1860s had a per capita GDP 25 per cent lower than the average for the rest of Europe. The famine of 1866–8, the last great European famine of the nineteenth century, aggravated the situation. Yet, by 1914, Finland had caught up with the average.[264] The UK, on its own, accounted for 20 per cent of Europe's GNP in 1890, up from 'only' 9 per cent in 1800.[265] To have colonies was a bonus but not a determining factor. By 1913 other countries were catching up.

In terms of the international economic situation, the most significant development in the nineteenth century was the rise of Europe. In 1800, Europe's GNP per capita was 20 per cent higher than that of what was later called the Third World. By 1860 it was twice that of the Third World and by 1900 more than three times as much.[266]

Had capitalist growth been equally distributed among the inhabitants of each industrial country, there would have been fewer reasons for the anxiety of being 'left out'. There would have been a massive disruption of traditional lifestyles, and there would have been, as there always are, winners and losers; but the widespread improvement in living standards, if distributed evenly, would have considerably assuaged the population in industrial countries. However, there was no such equanimity. Capitalism cannot generate, spontaneously, anything resembling an equality of outcomes. A reasonable distribution of income is far from incompatible with capitalism, but since individual capitalists pursue private and not social benefits, unless there is a systematic political intervention in favour of redistribution, the pursuit of private interests leads towards greater inequality. Yet political intervention can only be limited, since one of the motivations behind the private accumulation of wealth is that of being better off than others. Massive redistribution is unlikely to favour capital accumulation – which is not to say that some levelling policies would necessarily be dysfunctional. On the other hand massive inequalities are also dysfunctional, and not just for obvious political reasons but also for the economic one that if much of the growth accrues only to the very top, overall demand decreases. The rich save more than the poor, and saving is bad for growth, as Keynes often pointed out. 'The fundamental psychological law . . . is that men are disposed . . . to increase their consumption as their income increases, but not by as much as the increase in their income.'[267]

Inequalities did increase with industrialization. The common measure used to compute inequality is the Gini coefficient, a formula devised in 1912 by the Italian mathematician Corrado Gini. The nearer the coefficient is to zero the more equality there is, and the nearer to 100 the less equal the country is. Current studies show that many advanced capitalist countries have a more equal distribution of income than less developed ones. Thus, in 2010–13 Scandinavian countries exhibited a greater degree of equality than others: Denmark, Sweden, and Norway hover around the 25 mark while the European Union average is 30.9 (2014 figures).[268] However, matters are not that simple. In 2013, Ukraine was much poorer than Britain, France, and Italy, but more equal than any of them, at 24.6, against 30.1 for France, 31.9 for Italy, and 32.4 for the United Kingdom. 'Inequality', as Angus Deaton writes, 'is often a *consequence* of progress.'[269] Income distribution in Slovakia (Gini coefficient: 26) was on a level with that of Norway. The United States was more unequal than any European country (Gini: 45), and only a little more unequal than Malawi, one of the poorest countries in the world (Gini: 39). Communist China, with 46.9, was more unequal than capitalist America, and Nigeria (43.7) was almost as unequal. Obviously there can be equality in prosperity (e.g. Japan and Sweden) as well as in misery (Ukraine and Malawi). On average the international Gini coefficient rose by one point every decade from 1820 to 1950, then decreased between 1950 and 1992.[270] After 1990, according to Thomas Piketty, income inequalities increased again and, in Anglo-Saxon countries (the UK, USA, Australia, and Canada) they increased sharply after 1980.[271] But income inequality was already high in the early nineteenth century, when the Industrial Revolution started. The Gini coefficient rose with industrialization until the First World War, when it reached 61 (worst than almost all African countries and all Latin American countries). Inequalities slowed between the wars but in 1950 the world Gini coefficient was still very high: 64. This was higher than all countries in the world in the late 1990s except for Namibia (74.3).[272] Now (2017) no country is as unequal as the world average for 1950, but most of today's heavily unequal countries are in Latin America and in Africa.

Health *disparities* are roughly the same today as they were in the early nineteenth century.[273] Of course, the peoples of the world are healthier now and live longer, nor are the poor of today as poor in absolute terms as they were in the nineteenth century. The number of those in extreme poverty, 84 per cent in 1820, dropped to 24 per cent in 1992.[274] Today we often speak of relative poverty. To use this concept, rather than that of absolute poverty, is a sign of an affluent age: by definition, relative poverty, in unequal societies, can never be eradicated. In many advanced capitalist societies, what the poor receive today in social assistance is better – in terms of purchasing power – than what many workers obtained in wages in 1880, for it enables them to own goods that in the 1950s were regarded as the prerogative of the rich, goods such as refrigerators, telephones, and television sets.

Discussing inequalities, it should be noted, is hardly a novel issue. In 1880 a champion of economic liberalism in France, Paul Leroy-Beaulieu, not only believed that the concentration of wealth was a matter of the recent past and was unlikely to last but that the real danger for the future would be that there will not be enough inequality and that life will become boring if everyone is the same.[275]

If we talk about the absolute poor, the really, really poor, the destitute, then their number in the world increased with industrialization at least until the end of the twentieth century, when Chinese economic growth led to the removal from the poverty line of some 400 million people. Had the growth rate of income been the same across and within countries since 1820, the number of 'extremely' poor people ($1 a day expressed in 1985 purchasing power parity) in 1992 would have been only 150 million instead of 1.3 billion, or 3.6 per cent instead of 24 per cent.[276] What we do not know is the extent to which inequalities favoured growth. Much of the ideological divide at the end of the twentieth century, and since, centres around this question: is there a trade-off between equality and economic development?

Capitalism requires two contradictory elements: the first is a thriving market of increasingly prosperous workers whose demand for commodities becomes a formidable incentive for investment; the second is workers prepared to work a lot for little. Capitalism sells to the prosperous workers what has been produced with the labour of the miserable ones. This works particularly well in international trade and is what occurred when some countries industrialized before others, thus widening the gap. The industrial and technological gap between the United Kingdom and China in 1820 was serious, yet in 1800 Chinese standards of living were comparable to those of the rest of western Europe, particularly in the richer areas such as the Lower Yangtze Delta, which comprises Shanghai, Nanjing, and Zhejiang province.[277] Indeed, the Lower Yangtze Delta was, between 1350 and 1750, one of 'the most consistently dynamic economies' in the world.[278] Robert Fortune, a Scottish botanist who travelled extensively in China during the middle of the nineteenth century, was struck by the abundance of food at the disposal of ordinary Chinese. He opined that:

> in no country in the world is there less real misery and want than in China . . . In Scotland, in former days – and I suppose it is much the same now – the harvest labourer's breakfast consisted of porridge and milk, his dinner of bread and beer, and porridge and milk again for supper. A Chinaman would starve upon such food.[279]

Adam Smith had no doubt that China was rich, as he repeatedly emphasized in *The Wealth of Nations*: 'China has been long one of the richest, that is, one of the most fertile, best cultivated, most industrious, and most populous, countries in the world'; 'China is a much richer country than any part of Europe'; 'In China, a country much richer than any part of Europe'.[280]

But China's lead shrank continuously after 1750, partly because its agricultural productivity had not increased, partly because it had not developed its industry. By 1910 the United Kingdom was six times richer than China and, in 1950, ten times richer. In fact, throughout most of the nineteenth century, the UK became increasingly more prosperous than its European rivals.[281] This was one of the key factors that sealed the victory of the pro-industrialization elites at the beginning of our story. Industry equalled prosperity, power, and political stability. By 1913 workers in industry earned more in Great Britain than anywhere else in Europe, though less than in the United States.[282] Almost everywhere in the capitalist world, long working hours in sweatshops still prevailed, but, in most of the advanced countries, the wages of unskilled workers increased steadily, if slowly, between 1880 and 1914, while the cost of their main staple, bread, declined.[283]

Amid the dismal conditions, the lack of hygiene, the spread of diseases, life was, by our standards, brutish and short, but longer and less brutish than before. So there was the possibility that the emerging industrial capitalist society was benefiting not only the owners of capital but also those who had to sell their labour. Few knew or even guessed that in the subsequent decades after 1914 much of the world would be plagued by wars of unparalleled cruelty and devastation. Even fewer would have anticipated that such wars would pave the way for the most rapid growth in the history of capitalism during the decades after 1945. Much foretelling simply assumes that what happened before will happen in the future. Because matters had improved since 1800 it was reasonable to assume that they would go on improving at roughly the same pace. There is a difference, however, between the fate of humanity as a whole and the fate of each and every human. Progress is never progress for all. It is this awareness which meant that life under capitalism was a constant source of anxiety, anxiety for the poor and unemployed – never sure whether they would get a job; anxiety for the employed – never sure whether they would keep it; anxiety for the rich – unsure whether they would remain rich; anxiety for the capitalists – uncertain whether they would be winners or losers in the ever more dynamic turmoil of competitive capitalism.

PART TWO

Becoming Modern

3
Westernizing the East

In the last decades of the nineteenth century, the concept of the 'West' was identified with western Europe, the beacon of the world, the template of modernity. And modernity then meant industrial capitalism. On a number of indices, the United States was already an industrial powerhouse and hence part of 'the West', even though, in 1880, it was not yet so widely evident that the next century would become the American Century. Geography notwithstanding, large parts of Italy, all of Portugal, all of Greece, all of Ireland, and much of Spain were not part of this world. Japan had just begun its march towards industrial capitalism: an 'eastern' nation reaching out to become western.

The opposition between an abstract East and West has been 'as old as written history' or, at least as Ancient Greece and Rome.[1] It was further strengthened by the division between the Roman Catholic West and the Eastern Orthodox Church. The identification of 'Europe' with western Europe and the concomitant negative view of the East (but not of the Far East) had been a common trope since the days of the Enlightenment, though occasionally Islam was viewed positively by eighteenth-century secular philosophers, as a purer revealed religion, devoid of the imperfections of Judaism and Christianity.[2]

Voltaire, in his *Histoire de Charles XII* – an eighteenth-century literary success – published in 1731 and translated almost immediately into English – assumed, not wrongly, that his readers would be those who lived in 'civilized' western Europe and not in the cold areas of the North, let alone the distant and remote areas of eastern Europe.[3] Muscovites, he explained, were less civilized than the Mexicans before the arrival of Hernán Cortés, ignorant of all arts and commerce, innumerate, and their Christianity contaminated by all sorts of superstitions.[4] In his *Histoire de l'Empire de Russie sous Pierre le Grand*, published thirty years later, Voltaire pointed out that reformers such as Tsar Peter the Great did not try to emulate Persia or Turkey but looked for a model in 'our part of Europe', 'where all kind of talents are celebrated for eternity'.[5]

The West meant enlightenment, progress, secularism, and human rights, and even the rights of women. Montesquieu in his *De l'esprit des lois* (1748) asserted that customs such as polygamy (which he regarded as primitive) indicated that it was in Asia that 'despotism feels, so to speak, so natural', so at home.[6] The way women were treated in non-European countries was seen as an index of backwardness. Towards the end of the nineteenth century Yan Fu, a westernizing Chinese scholar, wrote that of all the 'noxious practices' that plagued China, two stood out, one the addiction to opium, the other the practice of binding the feet of women.[7] A few decades earlier, Karl Marx, in a letter to Ludwig Kugelmann (12 December 1868), declared that 'Anybody who knows anything of history knows that great social changes are impossible without the feminine ferment. Social progress can be measured exactly by the social position of the fair sex . . .'[8]

Such views were often put forward by western men unaware of the double standards they were deploying. Thus Lord Cromer, British consul general in Egypt from 1883 to 1907, convinced of the inferiority of Islamic religion and society, held the view that the Muslim segregation of women (keeping them veiled and in ignorance) was the 'fatal obstacle' to the development of civilization in Egypt, the main cause of its 'complete failure' as a social system.[9] But once back in Britain, far from championing women, Cromer became President of the Men's League for Opposing Women's Suffrage. In this as in so much else, he was not on the side of history well before women achieved the suffrage. The Married Women's Property Act 1882 finally allowed women to own property in their own right, while the Guardianship of Infants Act 1886 increased women's chances of receiving custody of their children after a divorce.[10]

It was not the case that 'the feminine ferment' (to use Marx's words) was a western prerogative. In the late nineteenth and early twentieth centuries, female poets such as Qiu Jin (1875–1907), in her manifesto *A Respectful Proclamation to China's 200 Million Women Comrades*, raged against footbinding and the denial of education to girls. In one of her poems she wrote:

> Unbinding my feet I clean out a thousand years of poison,
> With heated heart arouse all women's spirits.[11]

She was executed in 1907 for conspiring against the Qing Dynasty. The anarchist and feminist He Zhen tackled labour and sexuality in the years leading up to the Chinese revolution of 1911, stressing the centrality of the liberation of women, and the crucial role they would play in any revolution.[12] Women were on the march even in some Islamic countries. In Iran they were actively involved in the defence of the achievements of the modernizing constitutional revolution of 1906. Morgan Shuster, writing in 1912, witnessed the demonstrations of Iranian women in favour of the Constitutional Reform and against Russian and British interference:[13]

> having themselves suffered from a double form of opposition, political and social, they were the more eager to foment the great nationalist movement for the adoption of constitutional forms of government and the inculcation of Western political, social, commercial, and ethical codes.[14]

The 'Europe' that was seen as emblematic of civilization was a social space defined by the lifestyles and attitudes of a privileged minority of urban dwellers, not that of the brutish, stunted, ill, and barely literate mass of its inhabitants. Some members of the elites of the Ottoman Empire and Japan wanted modernity, but they also wanted to preserve their 'soul', their culture, their tradition, and thought that the fabled Western package could be dismantled into its various components and that one could pick and choose.

The success of the West, its primacy, had been relatively recent and not earlier than the closing decades of the eighteenth century, when areas such as East Asia were not much behind Europe in being able to develop an industrial system.[15] The technological advantages that some parts of Europe possessed around 1850 were not as obvious in 1750 as they would be later; in fact, manufacturing in some parts of India or China were more advanced than in some parts of western Europe.[16] Nor was there a particularly significant gap between north-western Europe and the more advanced regions of China in terms of consumption levels or life expectancy. The work of Joseph Needham (the multi-volume *Science and Civilisation in China*) shows that China was well ahead of Europe in most branches of science until the eighteenth century. Printing had been introduced centuries before Gutenberg. In 200 BC the Chinese were casting iron, a technology that reached Europe only around 1400. Chinese paper technology took one thousand years to reach the West.[17] Under the golden age of the Song Dynasty (960–1279) the compass was introduced (a century before it surfaced in the West); the navy was the largest in the world; paper money was issued before anywhere else; rice cultivation, thanks to new irrigation systems, increased exponentially; the population reached 100 million in 1100 (more than in the whole of Europe); textile production improved, particularly of cotton and silk; gunpowder was perfected; there was expansion of shipbuilding, of ceramic production, and of iron and steel; finally a remarkably meritocratic examination method to select state functionaries was established and a system of indirect taxes collection was set up.[18] Much of this golden age was due to state intervention and much of this intervention was due to threats from external forces, above all the Mongols, who, led by Kublai Khan, took over China and established the Yuan Dynasty in 1271.[19] Under the following dynasty, that of the Ming emperors (1368–1644), China became a proto-industrial society producing cotton, silk, ceramics, and paper on an industrial scale, creating a thriving market economy.[20]

Around 1800, China was still more prosperous than most of Europe.[21] Already in the eighteenth century the agriculture of Jiangnan (the area south of the Yangtze River including Shanghai) was one of the 'most commercial and externally oriented agricultures in the pre-modern world'. It was a major producer and exporter of silk and cotton, producing more cotton cloth than Britain.[22] By the mid-nineteenth-century one in five of Jiangnan's inhabitants lived in towns (out of a population of 436 million).[23] This put Jiangnan ahead of European countries in terms of urbanization, except for the United Kingdom, Belgium, and the Netherlands; and its population at that time was greater than any country in Europe except for Tsarist Russia.[24] Guangdong (Canton) was not far behind Jiangnan. By the 1860s there were 30,000–40,000 weavers belonging to the silk guild in Nanhai County (Guangdong) alone.[25] It is thus not surprising that Jiangnan was the site of the main effort of the Chinese Empire to industrialize in the second half of the nineteenth century and is now China's major industrial and commercial region.[26]

As late as the 1750s, the Chinese were just as well educated as average Europeans: in the eighteenth century the Chinese lower classes had greater access to education than their equivalents in the West.[27] Even in the nineteenth century, literacy rates were relatively high in Qing China: between 30 and 45 per cent of men and between 2 and 10 per cent of women.[28]

In the nineteenth century it was commonplace in intellectual quarters to assume that China was relatively prosperous even while disparaging her artistic achievements. Thus Ernest Renan, in the 1850s, wrote that China at the end of the eighteenth century was more advanced than all others, yet, when it came to art 'China has nothing which warrants the name of art' ('*la Chine n'a rien qui puisse mériter le nom d'art*').[29]

There might have been something true in Hegel's remark (one of the many unverifiable remarks so frequent in his writings) that 'The History of the World travels from East to West', though the second part of the sentence, '. . . for Europe is absolutely the end of History, Asia the beginning', is questionable.[30]

Traditional China consisted of an enormous territory ruled by a central authority, deeply introspective, not needing anything at all from the outside world, and discouraging rationalist inquiries and innovations.[31] There had been exceptions: both the Kangxi emperor (1654–1722) and the Qianlong emperor (1711–99) were open to western influences, especially in the arts, but on the whole China tended to absorb rather than import. Foreign invasions such as that from Mongolia, which established the Yuan Dynasty (13th–14th century), and from Manchuria, which established the Qing Dynasty (1644–1911), did not lead to foreign rule but rather to the absorption of foreign rulers into the Chinese political framework.[32] In fact from the thirteenth century to the end of the Chinese Empire (1911) the only period in which China was ruled by native Han emperors was from 1368 to 1644 (the Ming Dynasty) – 276 years. In a sense the ethnic origin of Chinese emperors mattered little: it was assumed that they were not just rulers of China but emperors of the world, lords of humanity, sons of heaven.[33]

In 1793, George III sent a diplomat, George Macartney, bearing many gifts, to seek to convince the Chinese to relax barriers to trade. The letter sent by the Qianlong emperor to the king has remained famous:

> our Celestial Empire possesses all things in prolific abundance and lacks no product within its own borders. There was therefore no need to import the manufactures of outside barbarians in exchange for our own produce. But as the tea, silk and porcelain which the Celestial Empire produces, are absolute necessities to European nations and to yourselves, we have permitted, as a signal mark of favour, that foreign hongs [merchants] should be established at Canton, so that your wants might be supplied and your country thus participate in our beneficence.

He then asked not to be importuned again, adding: 'I do not forget the lonely remoteness of your island, cut off from the world by intervening wastes of sea, nor do I overlook your excusable ignorance of the usages of our Celestial Empire.'[34]

This was widely interpreted as a sign of Chinese arrogance and refusal to modernize, though it is possible that the Qianlong emperor was simply seeking to buy time and prepare a more sturdy defensive system.[35] Indeed, as Macartney departed, the emperor made sure the military might of China was on display at all times.[36]

The belief that China did not need anything endured for decades. Robert Hart, the British Inspector General of the Chinese Imperial Maritime Customs Service, a true expert on China and resident there for almost fifty years, wrote in 1901 that:

> Trade, it is true, has grown, and the revenue derived from it has multiplied; but as yet it is far, far from what our predecessors looked for; and the reason is not that the Chinese Government actively opposed foreign commerce, but that the Chinese people did not require it. Chinese have the best food in the world, rice; the best drink, tea; and the best clothing, cotton, silk and fur. Possessing these staples and their innumerable native adjuncts, they do not need to buy a penny's worth elsewhere; while their Empire is in itself so great, and they themselves so numerous, that sales to each other make up an enormous and sufficient trade, and export to foreign countries is unnecessary.[37]

The Chinese Empire, once 'the centre of the universe', received its *coup de grâce* from the West when the British and the French, followed by Russia and the United States, forced the Chinese authorities to allow the traffic of opium into their country by waging the so-called Opium Wars (1839–42 and 1856–60). The spread of opium, which had already established itself in the Chinese army in 1832, climbed steadily among the people throughout the nineteenth century and, massively, among the peasantry in the 1870s.[38] By 1900 a high government official, Zhang Zhidong, wrote that 'Opium has spread with frightful rapidity and heart-rending results throughout the provinces. Millions upon millions have been struck down by the plague . . . wrecking the minds and eating away the strength and wealth of its victims.'[39]

Not realizing their weakness, the Chinese had at first tried to resist foreign arrogance with words that could not be backed by deeds. In 1839, alarmed by the penetration of opium into China, under the protection of British military force, the imperial commissioner, Lin Zexu (Lin Tse-hsü), was sent to Guangzhou (Canton) to stamp out the opium trade. Opium dealers were arrested, their cargo was confiscated and destroyed, culminating in over one million kilos being thrown into the sea in a lengthy operation that was concluded on 26 June (now UN International Day against Drug Abuse). Then Lin Zexu, realizing that the problem had to be tackled at source, wrote a famous letter to Queen Victoria:

among the crowd of barbarians . . . there are those who smuggle opium to seduce the Chinese people and so cause the spread of the poison to all provinces. Such persons who only care to profit themselves, and disregard the harm to others, are not tolerated by the laws of heaven and are unanimously hated by human beings. His Majesty the Emperor, upon hearing of this, is in a towering rage . . . Yet [these] barbarian ships . . . come here for trade for the purpose of making a great profit . . . By what right do they then in return use the poisonous drug to injure the Chinese people? Even though the barbarians may not necessarily intend to do us harm, yet in coveting profit to an extreme, they have no regard for injuring others. Let us ask, where is your conscience? . . . Of all that China exports to foreign countries, there is not a single thing which is not beneficial to people . . . Is there a single article from China which has done any harm to foreign countries? Take tea and rhubarb, for example; the foreign countries cannot get along for a single day without them . . . If China, again, cuts off this beneficial export, what profit can the barbarians expect to make? . . . How can you bear to go on selling products injurious to others in order to fulfil your insatiable desire?[40]

There was no reply. But the British retaliated forcefully in favour of their freedom to trade throughout China, including in drugs (at the time opium was legal in most countries, including Great Britain, something of which commissioner Lin Zexu was not aware, as he probably did not realize that most Westerners could get by for far longer than 'a single day' without rhubarb). It was the beginning of the Opium War.

There were, of course, dissident voices in Britain, notably that of the young William Gladstone, who, on 8 April 1840, attacked the government, pointing out that the Chinese 'gave you notice to abandon your contraband trade. When they found that you would not, they had a right to drive you from their coasts on account of your obstinacy in persisting in this infamous and atrocious traffic.' Adding that he could not think of 'a war more unjust in its origins, a war more calculated in its progress to cover this country in permanent disgrace . . .'[41] A civil servant, Robert Montgomery Martin, member of the legislative council in Hong Kong, fulminated in 1846:

Have we simply remained passive, and allowed the crimes and the murders caused by the opium trade to go on silently, unnoticed and unapproved by Her Majesty's government? . . . Better – far better – infinitely better – abjure the name of Christianity; call ourselves heathens – idolaters of the '*golden calf*' – worshippers of the 'evil one' . . . Why the 'slave trade' was merciful compared to the 'opium trade'. We did not destroy the bodies

> of the Africans . . . But the opium seller slays the body after he has corrupted, degraded, and annihilated the moral being of unhappy sinners . . . No blessing can be vouchsafed to England while this national crime is daily calling to Heaven for vengeance . . . We stand convicted before the nations of the world . . .[42]

Karl Marx, quoting this passage in 1858, pointed out the irony that:

> the representative of the antiquated world appears prompted by ethical motives, while the representative of overwhelming modern society fights for the privilege of buying in the cheapest and selling in the dearest markets . . .[43]

During the final phase of the Second Opium War, in 1860, British and French troops under the orders of Lord Elgin (the worthy son of the Lord Elgin who had removed the marbles from the Parthenon some decades earlier) destroyed Beijing's summer palace, or *Yuanming yuan* (the Gardens of Perfect Brightness). The Treaties of Nanking (1842) and Tientsin (1858) and the Conventions of Peking (1860) imposed free trade on China; coerced it to open a number of ports to Western trade; required it to cede Hong Kong to Britain; abolished all internal taxes, thus ensuring that Western goods could transit freely inside China; allowed missionaries and Western merchants unimpeded access to the country, the former to proselytize, the latter to make money. To cap these indignities China had to pay indemnities to Britain and France out of Chinese customs revenues.[44] After 1895 the Chinese government was forced to grant railway and mining concessions to various Western nations and to Japan. By 1911, 41 per cent of the railway mileage in China was owned by foreigners. Numerous mining concessions were granted between 1896 and 1913 to the British, Germans, Russians, Americans, Belgians, etc.[45] Just before the First World War there were no fewer than forty-eight treaty ports where foreigners had the absolute right to settle, trade, and enjoy immunity from local prosecution for any crime they might commit. Some of these treaty ports had no reason to exist except for furthering the national pride of certain European states who wished to show that they were part of the European power system, as was the case with the Italian concession of Tianjin (Tientsin), in which Italy had no real interest.[46]

Zhōngguó – the Middle Kingdom – the 'land within the four seas' (i.e. the 'world'), whose history stretched back two thousand years, had become a quasi-colony of the West. Weak against external enemies, China was equally weak at home. The absence of a strong central government meant that no single authority could prevent provincial and military officials and corrupt landlords from appropriating an increasing share of public wealth. As the old Chinese proverb says: 'The mountains are high and the emperor is far away.' Peasant discontent was common. This turned into a major revolution, the Taiping Rebellion (1850–64), arguably the world's most destructive and 'bloodiest civil war'.[47] It resulted in the death of at least 20 million people, perhaps more, mainly due to war-induced starvation and diseases. The ideology of the Taiping was a curious mix of Christianity and older Chinese radical thought. Its programme was a harbinger of twentieth-century peasant communism – the end of landlordism, the distribution of land, equality between the sexes, and a ban on opium and gambling. The rebellion was crushed not so much by the central government but by the provincial administrations whose power was threatened.[48] The repression was harsh and led to the growth of provincial power at the expense of the centre.[49]

China further lost control over its own destiny as it endured the emigration of a significant proportion of its population (35 million in the nineteenth century), the famine of 1876–9, the Sino-Japanese War of 1894–5, which resulted in the loss of Korea and Taiwan, and the Boxer Rebellion of 1899–1901. There were also natural catastrophes unparalleled in Europe: in 1855, during the Taiping Rebellion, the Yellow River changed its course, causing catastrophic floods. Although the great river had flooded many times, it was the first time it had taken a different path since 1194. It continued to be unstable, freely wandering from its usual trajectory during the rainy seasons; there followed another disastrous flood in 1889.[50] Peasant unrest continued, concurrent with the progressive breakdown of the Qing imperial state. In Hunan many followed the Taiping rebels, but probably more in the hope of doing away with landlord exploitation than for ideological reasons. Banditry and tax resistance became widespread.[51] In north China heavy rains destroyed crops in 1872, followed by the great north China famine of 1876–9, and more floods in 1890–95.[52] In the course of the nineteenth century millions of Chinese died of famine and millions more were displaced.[53]

By the end of the century China had been forced to sign further 'unequal treaties' not only with the United Kingdom, but also with the United States, Russia, France, Germany, Japan, and other countries. To all intents and purposes, the country had lost sovereignty. The failure to modernize was the major reason. In the first half of the nineteenth century the Qing emperors had done all they could to prevent the modernization of the country. By 1860 reforms, after the ravages brought about by the Opium Wars and the Taiping Rebellion, seemed inevitable. In 1861 the advent of Tongzhi, the new emperor, then a mere child, was acclaimed as the beginning of a new era in Chinese history. But while in Japan reforms (under the reassuring name of the Meiji *Restoration* of 1868) changed the country for ever, the Tongzhi Restoration was a half-hearted affair of the upper classes rallying round the tottering throne of their ruler (who was five when he acceded to the throne; effective power at court was in the hands of his mother the Empress Dowager Cixi).[54] The 'restoration' did not sap the traditional Confucian basis of Chinese society, but neither was Confucianism used as a basis for reforms.[55] The Tongzhi's economic goal was to restore the traditional agrarian economy because the vast majority of the population lived on the land and the government derived most of its income from a land tax. The principles of 'exalt agriculture' (*chung nung*) and 'disparage commerce' (*ping shang*) continued to be regarded as the only desirable basis for the Chinese economy. The goal was an austere and stable agrarian society, not a modern industrial society (the goal of the Japanese after 1868).[56] The de facto leader of the restoration, Zeng Guofan, who as a general had fought against the Taiping, wrote a letter of instruction to local officials:

> If the farmers suffer too long the field will be barren and uncultivated. If the army has no food, it will certainly give trouble to the people. If the people have no food they will certainly follow the bandits. If the bandits have no food, they will become roving bandits and create disorder on a large scale, and there will be no end to it. Therefore the first duty of magistrates today is to 'exalt agriculture'.[57]

Stability remained a forlorn hope. China continued, for one hundred years and beyond, to be constantly disrupted by civil wars, foreign intervention, and social unrest. There were some changes: after 1860 there was a movement in favour of adopting Western methods of education, and a new line of thinking emerged in 1875, when the authorities stressed the importance of enriching the people.[58] There was some industrialization: shipbuilding, textiles, armaments; students were sent abroad, railways were built, and steelworks started production. Although less vigorously than in Meiji Japan, the Chinese government did take on modern tasks such as reforming the banking system and currency, standardizing weights and measure, raising taxes, creating a proper police force, and building modern infrastructure such as telegraphs.[59] But it was all rather unsystematic. The central government remained in the hands of those, like Empress Dowager Cixi, who were hostile to modernization.[60]

China could not industrialize 'spontaneously', as the British are alleged to have done. Small enterprises remained small. Industrialization was conducted by the state or by foreigners. The strength of the West led to a growing feeling in China that the 'West wind is blowing East', that change was being forced upon the Chinese by the impact of the West. After the burning of the Summer Palace by British troops in 1860, the Chinese authorities finally set up a Foreign Office, the *Zongli Yamen*, accepted foreign diplomats, and (in 1873) no longer required them to kowtow to the emperor. Pressures to modernize came from friendly Westerners such as Robert Hart.[61] In a memorandum to the *Zongli Yamen*, entitled 'Observation by an outsider', he stressed the importance of railways, steamships, and the telegraph, explaining that this would make China strong and better able to resist international servitude.[62] Although the Customs Service had been imposed by the Western powers on China, and buttressed foreign privileges and extraterritorial rights, Robert Hart was technically an employee of the Chinese government, with a profound sense of loyalty and obligation to the Chinese. When he took over the post of Inspector General, he wrote to his staff: 'The first thing to be remembered by each is that he is the paid agent of the Chinese Government for the performance of specified work, and to do that well should be his chief care.'[63]

Painfully slowly, China modernized like a wounded giant, kicked and tormented, and deeply divided. By 1911 the country had been able to build only 8,900 kilometres of railway lines.[64] By comparison Russia had 66,000 kilometres and Italy, so much smaller, 16,400 kilometres. Even the construction of such a puny railway network had been difficult and had been opposed by reactionaries. The modernizing *North China Herald* of 22 April 1867 summed up the conflict thus: 'To us, railways mean free intercourse, enlightenment, commerce and wealth; to the mandarins, they suggest rowdyism, the overthrow of time-honoured customs and tradition, disturbance and pain.'[65]

Why was modernization in China such a painful process? In *The Religion of China: Confucianism and Taoism* (1915), Max Weber explained that Confucianism and Taoism had been obstacles to capitalist development in China, and though he was careful to add that 'It is obviously not a question of deeming the Chinese "naturally ungifted" for the demands of capitalism', he thought that 'a rational economy and technology of a modern occidental character was simply out of the question'.[66]

Well before Weber, some members of the Chinese intelligentsia recognized that China could no longer pretend to be the representation of Celestial Perfection. The scholar Feng Guifen, in an essay included in his collection *Chiao-pin-lu k'ang-i* (*Personal Protests from the Study of Chiao-pin*, 1861), wrote that though China is larger than Russia (or so he thought), the United States, France, and Great Britain:

> we are shamefully humiliated by those four nations in the recent treaties – not because our climate, soil or resources are inferior to theirs, but because our people are really inferior . . . Why are they small and yet strong? Why are we large and yet weak? We must try to discover some means to become their equal.[67]

He pointed to four areas of inferiority: use of manpower, agriculture, the art of 'maintaining a close relationship between the ruler and the people', and the ability of linking theory and practice. 'The way to correct these four points lies with ourselves, for they can be changed at once if only our Emperor would set the general policy right. There is no need for outside help in these matters.'

The road to reform was exceedingly difficult. Inspired by Feng Guifen, the scholar (and general – see above) Zeng Guofan, one of the great conservative modernizers of the nineteenth century, launched a series of initiatives aimed at importing Western know-how.[68] This was all the more important since Zeng was completely committed to the preservation of traditional Confucian hierarchies, to order and tranquillity in a world that had been repeatedly plunged into turmoil by wars, chaos, and natural catastrophes. Yet to achieve such essential goals he believed modernization was necessary.[69]

But there was no period of relative calm during which China could adapt to the necessary reforms. The calamities continued: further humiliation by Japan in the Sino-Japanese War of 1894–5, leading to the loss of Taiwan and the end of Chinese control over Korea. Japan, with the Meiji Restoration, had successfully reformed, and it had now joined the Western club by defeating China. The shock to China's self-esteem was considerable. What had once been 'an inaccessible and insignificant island kingdom at the eastern edge of Chinese Civilization' (and which had been heavily culturally indebted to China) had now become like a 'Western Power'.[70] Japan too modified its image of China. The latter was no longer the revered land of sages and learning imagined by intellectuals, but a country peopled by an undisciplined rabble led by untrustworthy leaders.[71]

In China, Zhang Zhidong, a leading reformer and government official, warned that 'the country is now in extreme danger' and lamented that 'Chinese officials and people elect to remain blind, stubborn, and proud as of old . . . If we do not change soon what will become of us? European knowledge will increase more and more and Chinese stupidity will become more dense . . . The foreigners will suck our blood . . . will swallow us down body and soul.'[72] Frightened at the possibility of the country being dismembered, a reform movement – the so-called Hundred Days Reform Movement of June to September 1898 – emerged. It was ostensibly led by the young Guangxu emperor (who had succeeded Tongzhi in 1875 and was Empress Dowager Cixi's nephew) but was inspired by Kang Youwei, then China's leading reformer. It advocated a revolution from above, as Japan and even Prussia had achieved, with the state taking charge of promoting the economy.[73] It was stopped in its tracks by conservative opponents backed by Empress Dowager Cixi. The defeat by Japan had made reforms imperative, as a growing section of public opinion realized. China, after all, had lost yet again, yet again had to pay indemnities, yet again had to give up sovereignty, and had been humiliated, yet again.[74] The reformers' plans were adopted in principle by the emperor, but not the recommendation that there should be a constitution, a national assembly, and that the emperor and the people should rule 'jointly'.[75] Emperor Guangxu was placed under house arrest and his closest advisers were executed.[76] What had particularly alarmed the empress were proposals to modernize the state bureaucracy.[77]

Eventually, the Imperial Court was compelled to accept change. The Boxer Rebellion (the appellation 'Boxer' is Western) was an anti-foreign, nationalist movement led by the Righteous Harmony Militia, purporting to support the Qing rulers and brandishing the slogan: 'Protect our country, drive out foreigners, and kill Christians.'[78] In 1899 the rebels began to attack Western legations and missions, virtually forcing the Qing to authorize war against the foreign presence in China. Stories of Chinese cruelty and savagery made their way into the Western press. In London the *Daily Mail* reported on 7 July 1900 that the entire diplomatic community in Beijing had been put to the sword.[79] This false story reinforced support for an eight-nation expeditionary force – Britain, the United States, France, Germany, Italy, Japan, Russia, and Austria-Hungary – to intervene for 'humanitarian' reasons. On 14 August 1900 they seized Beijing, forcing the Empress Dowager Cixi and the Guangxu emperor to flee to Xi'an. They were allowed to return only after signing an agreement to pay 450 million ounces of silver over thirty-nine years.[80] In January 1901, utterly defeated and humiliated, the emperor, directed by a reluctant Empress Dowager Cixi, issued an edict which declared that:

> The weakness of China is caused by the strength of convention and the rigid network of regulations. We have many mediocre officials but few men of talent and courage . . . The appointment of men of talent is restricted by regulations which are so rigid that even men of extraordinary talent are missed. What misleads the country can be expressed in one word, selfishness (*ssu*), and what suffocates all under heaven is precedent (*li*).[81]

By now it had become obvious to all, even to the most pig-headed of reactionaries, that stagnation was not an option, and the Imperial Court, long divided between conservatives led by the Empress Dowager Cixi and reformers such as Prince Gong, reluctantly decided to embrace modernity and launch a new set of reforms inspired by Feng's self-strengthening movement. In any case, the Qing court had long stopped being in charge of events, limiting itself to reacting to them.[82] In 1901 a letter was circulated among the provincial officials of the vast empire eliciting proposals for reforms. The response of two important provincial governors (and leading reformers), Zhang Zhidong (Chang Chih-tung) and Liu Kunyi (Liu K'un-i), turned out to be particularly influential:

> In general there are three important factors in building a nation: good administration, wealth and strength . . . The reorganization of the Chinese political system is to serve as an instrument for bringing about better administration. The adoption of Western methods is for the purpose of attaining wealth and strength.[83]

So China attempted to follow in the footsteps of Japan, swallowing its pride and learning from the West, from Western universities, Western schools, and Western military academies.[84]

The pressures for reform accelerated further after Japan's victory against Russia in 1905.[85] That a European country should be defeated by Japan was a sign that modernization 'worked' and that modernization included some forms of popular involvement, however limited. Reformers such as Liang Qichao, active during the Hundred Days Reform Movement of 1898, returned from their Japanese exile to advocate a constitutional monarchy.[86]

In December 1905 the Qing government sent a high-level mission to Japan, England, the United States, Germany, and France to study political reforms. The East was learning from the West, while Europeans (and Americans) did not take the slightest interest in Japanese or Chinese culture, displaying once more the provincialism of the hegemon. China's reform movement was still conservative. The slogan of the reformers was 'import from the West its practice not its ideas', as in the formula (*tĭ-yòng*) popularized by Zhang Zhidong in his *Exhortation to Learning* (1898), 'the old learning is the fundamental thing; the new learning is for practical use.' The old learning was China's. It was fundamental (*tĭ*). The practical (*yòng*) knowledge was Western.[87] Zhang Zhidong was no wild progressive. As Viceroy of Huguang he had ordered, in 1900, the execution of Tang Caichang, who had advocated a constitutional monarchy.[88] Zhang Zhidong had ruled out democracy (which leads to disorder and will bring 'not a single benefit but a hundred evils') and personal liberty ('that is even more absurd'). But he urged his countrymen to learn from the barbarians in order to control the barbarians: 'if we wish to make China strong . . . we must study Western knowledge'.[89]

Qing officials thought that the development of industry could not be left to the initiative of private entrepreneurs. But in the second half of the nineteenth century new kinds of merchants emerged known as compradors, dependent on foreign firms and foreign trade, who also brought new ideas into the Chinese merchant class.[90]

One of the leading reformers was in fact a 'comprador' merchant called Cheng Kuan-ying (usually reformers were senior civil servants and intellectuals).[91] Cheng Kuan-ying advocated *shang-chan*, which means economic warfare (as opposed to *ping-chan*, military confrontation) but is usually translated as economic competition. He was among those who believed that reforming China meant reforming the institutions which held back its economic development rather than developing its military power to withstand Westerners and the Japanese.[92] So it was necessary to elevate the social status of the merchant, reform the tax system, change the examination system, modernize agriculture, promote commerce and industry, and establish technological schools.[93] In other words, provide some of the conditions for capitalist development.

In 1902, Adam Smith's *The Wealth of Nations* was first translated into Chinese. The primary concern of Yan Fu, the translator (who also translated John Stuart Mill's *On Liberty*, Montesquieu's *De l'esprit des lois*, and was inspired by social Darwinism), was the wealth and power of China, which, he felt, had been damaged not only by foreign imperialism but by the attitude of Chinese intellectuals who despised commerce and trade.[94] Merchants were ranked lowest in the social order by classical Confucianism, which scorned businessmen even though commerce had played such an important role in Chinese history.[95] On their own, however, these despised businessmen could not industrialize the country. Yan Fu was convinced that since 'the wealth and power of modern Europe are attributed by experts to the science of economics' and that 'Economics began with Adam Smith, who developed the great principle . . . that in serving the greater interest, the interest of both sides must be served', then China had to learn from Adam Smith.[96] The West, explained Yan Fu, exalted dynamism, and assertiveness; its commitment to liberty released the potential of individuals. That's why the West was rich and powerful. China should turn her back on 'the way of the Sages' and the traditionalism that kept her people weak and ignorant.[97] The Chinese could not simply borrow technology from the West but had to transform their entire society and government. Westerners were a new kind of 'barbarians' (*yi*), with their own culture. They were different from the old barbarians who had invaded China in ancient times and who had only physical strength and so could be civilized by the superior culture of the Chinese.[98] These sentiments became part of the so-called 'New Culture Movement', an anti-traditional intellectual school whose foremost representative was Lu Xun. His *A Madman's Diary* (1918), inspired by Gogol's short story, was influential for its satirical attack on Confucian culture.

By 1918, Yan Fu, disillusioned with the West, had turned conservative and went back to Confucius and Mencius:

> I have been the witness of seven years of Republic in China and four years of a terrible war in Europe . . . I have come to realise that all the progress of the West in the last three centuries has led its peoples to become inhuman, to kill each other, to lose integrity and a sense of honour. I think now of the teachings of Confucius and Mencius; they seem to me the embodiment of universal wisdom and the bringers of much benefit to our country.[99]

Despite this Yan Fu was praised by Mao Zedong, on the morrow of the communist victory in 1949, as one of the four national figures who, before the birth of the Communist Party, had turned to the West to find 'the truth', the others being Hong Xiuquan, the leader of the Taiping Rebellion, Kang Youwei, the architect of the so-called Hundred Days Reform Movement of 1898, and Sun Yat-sen, the leader of the Chinese revolution of 1911.[100]

The so-called *Xinzheng* (New Policy) between 1906 and 1911 manifested itself when leading officials were dispatched, once again, to Europe and the United States to find out what was best about those cultures, as Japan had done decades before.[101] But what successful Western states and Japan possessed, and China did not, was the institutional capacity to project their power throughout society.[102] Not only was the state not strong enough but the country never had the kind of institutions – banks, joint-stock companies – or legislative framework that might have helped entrepreneurs to develop capitalism.[103] Furthermore the enormous outflow of funds to pay the indemnities arising from the Boxer wars and the war against Japan resulted in increased taxation and weakened considerably the possibility of reforms (even though by then there was a much greater consensus behind them).[104]

Not surprisingly the reform movement in China faltered yet again. The problems were too immense for a small ruling class that had long ruled over a very large population (400 million by 1900). It was necessary, it was felt, to devolve further power to local government and create 'new' citizens.[105] The Empress Dowager Cixi issued an edict in November 1906 promising a constitution, a national assembly, and to curb the powers of the central state.[106] But reforms arrived too late to save the imperial system. In 1908, Emperor Guangxu died in mysterious circumstances, still in palace detention under orders from his aunt the empress, who may have had him poisoned with arsenic, while she herself was on her deathbed, just to make sure he would never rule.[107] She died the following day, having appointed as her successor the two-year-old Puyi, who became the last emperor of China. Reforms continued anyway, the throne having become almost an irrelevancy. A new constitution was promulgated in 1908.[108]

A nationalist movement, led by Sun Yat-sen (the 'father' of modern China), continued to gather ground, leading to the collapse of the Qing state in 1911. The Qing Dynasty had ruled since 1644, longer than any European royal house, and had been the last rulers of an empire that had unified China in 221 BC. The last days of the last emperor, after well over two thousand years, had finally arrived. The new Chinese republic was led by Sun Yat-sen. The republic continued the tasks set by previous reformers. Thus, the New Policy of 1906 to 1911 was not the last gasp of a dying system but the foundation of a new state.[109] Building it, however, took far longer than anyone expected. The country remained in a constant state of turmoil throughout the twentieth century: first a civil war, as regional landlords fought each other; then, just as China was about to be united under the Kuomintang, the Japanese invasion of Manchuria (1931), the war of resistance against Japan (1937–45); then, after yet another bloody civil war, the communists took over and re-established sovereignty in 1949. Not that calm prevailed in the 'Middle Kingdom': the Great Leap Forward (the 'Three Bitter Years', 1958–61) resulted in a massive famine; and then the Great Cultural Revolution disrupted the economy for almost another decade.[110] Finally, after 1978, there was a turn to a market economy denoted, somewhat defensively, as 'socialism with Chinese characteristics'.

Before the nineteenth century, the East had looked down on the West or, rather, had not bothered to look at all, since there was little to learn from it. China had been the technological world leader until about 1400.[111] Then Europeans, having long felt inferior, at last turned the tables and European admiration turned to disdain. China, they discovered, was an empire in decay, stagnant and backward, able to offer the surging West only some trade and some souls to be saved.[112] Yet the West feared China even when China was down: one of the most distinguished nineteenth-century sinologists, the diplomat Sir Thomas Wade, contributor to the romanization of mandarin (the famous Wade-Giles transliteration system), insisted that China must never be allowed to have a fleet or a strong army.[113] And in 1850, Lord Palmerston as Foreign Minister noted, in a similar vein, that China was one of 'These half-civilized governments' which 'require a dressing every eight to ten years to keep them in order'.[114]

Previously, however, in the seventeenth and eighteenth centuries, the West had been transfixed by Qing China: oriental gardens and pagodas decorated Kew and Tivoli; porcelain and lacquered cabinets were imported or imitated; rooms were decorated in the 'Chinese' style in palaces and castles throughout Europe from the Winter Palace in St Petersburg to Kilkenny Castle in Ireland; rococo artists, such as Antoine Watteau, were inspired by Chinese motifs; Chinese 'wisdom' (there is always a good deal of fantasy in all worship) was admired by great thinkers of the age, notably Voltaire and Leibniz, both also admirers of Confucius.[115] Voltaire's chapter on China in his *Essai sur les moeurs* is full of praise for the distant country.[116] Hegel declared that China 'is this wondrously unique empire that astonished Europeans, and has continued to do so . . .'[117] Later in the nineteenth century, not just China worship but also general admiration for non-Western societies and for the 'Orient' (usually but not always the Middle East) became a reaction against the vulgarity of Western culture, against the ugliness of its coal-based industrialization. In France there was a proliferation of societies aimed at cultivating the knowledge of the 'Orient', such as the Société des peintres orientalistes français, founded in Paris in 1893.

Of course what writers and artists of the Orient such as Flaubert, Pushkin, David Roberts (a Scottish painter famous for his sketches of the Middle East), and Delacroix hoped to discover was a Western invention, their invention. There was often a feeling of condescending superiority in this admiration, as Edward Said explained in his famous *Orientalism* (1978); nevertheless there was much to admire. The Chinese had refined the division of labour without it becoming a question of factory production. Silks, stone carvings, and metalwork were produced in large workshops by a minute specialization where each aspect of the production process was in the hands of an individual workman. By the beginning of the Han Dynasty (206 BC–AD 220) the Chinese were able to weave complex patterns in silk that remained the envy of the West for centuries.

In 1697 Gottfried Leibniz, in his Preface to *Novissima Sinica*, comparing China and Europe, lamented that the European did not try to learn from the Chinese who '. . . vies with us in many other ways in almost equal combat . . . they surpass us (though it is almost shameful to confess this) in practical philosophy'.[118] From the seventeenth century, reports written by Jesuits who had gone out to convert 'heathens' extolled their wealth and taste, their sophisticated culture and art, their astonishing bureaucracy, and their apparently benevolent and tolerant rulers (more tolerant than Christian rulers – admittedly not a difficult feat). Matteo Ricci (known by the Chinese as Li Madou), one of the first Jesuits to reside in China, from 1582 until his death in Beijing in 1610, admired many aspects of Chinese culture, though he was perplexed at its apparent 'immorality'. While distancing himself from Buddhism and neo-Confucianism, he held the view that traditional Confucianism and Christian beliefs were not incompatible.[119] David Hume, writing in 1752, thought that China was 'one of the most flourishing empires in the world, though it had very little commerce beyond its own territories'.[120] The Chinese state, before it was fatally damaged by nineteenth-century wars and foreign interventions, was quite sturdy: it promoted new crops; it dealt with flood control; it manipulated currencies; it developed a banking system, and attempted to cope (less and less successfully) with what, traditionally, Chinese governments were supposed to do above all else: preventing or dealing with 'natural' disasters and famines.[121] Natural disasters were regarded as signs that the Mandate of Heaven, the right to rule, could be in jeopardy.

The relatively high level of economic development reached by China in the eighteenth century did not endure in the nineteenth. Much of its industry, except for ceramics, was still at the handicraft stage at a time when it had to face the damaging competition of Western industries.[122] While Western states were favouring capitalist development, the imperial state was erecting obstacles to it. Thus, when in 1801, some merchants in Pingquan (Zhili) applied for permission to open copper mines (mining was forbidden or restricted), the imperial response was negative. The authorities were worried about what would happen once the mines were depleted and the workforce dispersed: 'Can there be no risk that they will stir up trouble?' So mining in that region was banned 'in perpetuity'.[123] Such anxieties about development were deeply engrained. Scholars such as Yü Yueh (1821–1905) thought technology would be harmful in the long run because it quickly consumed natural resources that were limited in supply (and how right he was, though such views were, until recently, regarded as eccentric). In the 1870s, Liu Ping-chang, governor of Kiangsi, cited this (apparently ecological) reason for continuing to oppose modern mining. Others such as Wang Ping-hsieh (an intellectual who opposed foreign influence) claimed that the introduction of Western technology would exacerbate social injustice.[124]

Why China failed to produce an industrial revolution to match that of Great Britain has long been a matter of controversy among economic historians, who have only recently begun to observe their distance from the previous excessively Eurocentric perspective.[125] China's GNP in 1820 was estimated to have been one-third that of the rest of the world. By 1949 it had collapsed to 1 per cent, though by 2013 it had climbed back to 12.3 per cent.[126]

In Japan things developed differently. The country, earlier than China, had been swept by a wave of enthusiasm for Western progress, though its adoption of Western mores proceeded quite differently. There was a 'revolution' in favour of modernity and industrialization but it looked more like a palace coup rather than a rebellion led by several of the *tozama han* (*han* are domains ruled by quasi-independent lords) to 'return' the emperor to power. This was the Meiji Restoration (*Taisei Hōkan*) of 1868.[127] Considering the importance of this event, it was, by all standards, a remarkably non-violent affair. The Meiji 'revolutionaries', unlike their counterparts in the United States or France, or, fifty years later, the Russian communists, did not have a global ideology or universalist slogans and had no wish or ambition to inspire people in the rest of the world. They did very little to benefit their own class; quite the contrary, they removed its privileges. They were nationalists who aspired to protect Japan and secure its place in the world. It was, of course, the nationalism of the elite, not one born of a popular sense of political solidarity. This nationalism, which had arisen largely as a response to external threats, had been compelled to confront its main obstacle: the Tokugawa feudal system. Under this system, the common people, the peasantry, were outside the state and expected to do little else other than to pay taxes; merchants were expected to worry only about enriching themselves; and the sole political class was that of the samurai, who were expected to mind the affairs of the state.[128] The Meiji Restoration blew all this apart and created the basis for the modern Japanese nation and hence for modern Japanese nationalism. In 1860, Yokoi Shōnan, a reformer and a scholar (assassinated in 1869 by a conservative samurai), offered his verdict on the previous 260 years of Tokugawa rule when he exclaimed that Commodore Matthew Perry (whose fleet had compelled Japan to open its ports to Western trade in 1852–4) had indeed been 'correct in regarding this country as a country without any government'.[129]

Although the new Meiji government included some advocates of the anti-Western 'expel the barbarians' policy, even they soon realized that the only true defensive policy was the modernization of Japan. The Meiji Restoration was thus a 'bourgeois revolution' but one carried out by the lower ranks of the samurai class and members of the intelligentsia. Capitalists and merchants played no role at all, nor did 'the people' since there was very little popular social unrest.[130]

The rule of the emperor (*tenno*, or Heavenly Sovereign) had traditionally been purely formal, with even fewer powers than a constitutional monarch in the West. The real power was in the hands of the Tokugawa *Bakufu* (the feudal quasi-military ruler called by Westerners the Shogun). This had been made possible by the establishment of a new state structure. Power could no longer be shared between the Imperial Court and the *Bakufu*. As Iwakura Tomomi (later a leading member of one of Japan's exploratory missions to the West) said: 'You can't have two suns in one heaven . . . Hence it is my desire that we should act vigorously to abolish the *Bakufu*.'[131] After January 1868 the administration was formally handed over to the young *tenno* Meiji (the 122nd Emperor of Japan), who was only sixteen.[132] A new central authority emerged under the patriotic slogan of *fukoku kyōhei* ('enrich the nation; strengthen the army').[133] The modernization of the country in the Western sense was a consequence. Members of the old ruling class were enticed into the construction of capitalism – a kind of unconscious co-optation similar to what Antonio Gramsci would have called a 'passive revolution'. The Kōbushō (the Ministry of Industry), at breakneck speed, and with no grand preordained plan, imported and applied Western technology, constructed the first railways, created, against fierce opposition, a nationwide telegraph network, employed hundreds of foreign engineers and experts, and used many of them to train Japanese counterparts.[134]

The Meiji leaders resembled contemporary elites in the Third World, torn between admiration for the West and a hatred of it. They represented a major rupture with the past, undoing over two centuries of self-imposed isolation since the days, in the seventeenth century, when Tokugawa Iemitsu, the third Shogun, expelled all Westerners, except for the Dutch, and imposed a regime of strict state control over Japan's trade and communication with the outside world. The objective behind the self-imposed isolation was the same as that behind its eventual termination: the desire to preserve Japan from foreign conquest. Thus Aizawa Seishisai, the historian and thinker, wrote in his *New Theses* (*Shinron*, 1825): 'When those barbarians plan to subdue a country not their own, they start by opening commerce and watch for a sign of weakness. If an opportunity is presented, they will preach their alien religion to captivate the people's hearts.'[135] He was right: it was the deployment of force by Commodore Matthew Perry and his US fleet that had shattered Japan's isolation and provided the impetus for reform. At first, in the 1850s and 1860s, the impact with the West sparked off a xenophobic movement under the slogan *Sonnō jōi* ('Revere the Emperor, Expel the Barbarians'). The government did not try to restrain the activities of militant nationalists, since they shared the same pro-emperor ideology, and the government feared Western-oriented radicals more than these romantic traditionalists.[136] Even Kōno Hironaka, the Liberal leader, had been, at first, attracted by the 'Expel the Barbarians' movement. He then read John Stuart Mill's *On Liberty* (he said while he was on horseback) and then, as he wrote, 'in a flash' his entire way of thinking was 'revolutionized': 'Now all these earlier thoughts of mine, excepting those concerned with loyalty and filial piety, were smashed to smithereens.'[137]

This attitude gave way to a general pro-Western enthusiasm in a period known as *bunmei kaika* ('civilization and enlightenment'), which manifested itself in the building of Western-style homes, the wearing of Western clothes (compulsory for government officials, but seldom adopted by ordinary Japanese), and the import of beef. The ban on Christianity was lifted in 1873.[138]

The delegation led by Iwakura Tomomi (1871–3), the first of many, visited the West to deal not only with diplomatic matters but also to study aspects of Western government and cultures. It found sources of inspiration in many countries. Japan imported from France fashion items, the school district system, the criminal code (the Napoleonic Code), and even the French jurist Gustave Boissonade, soon dubbed 'the father of Japanese Law', even though he could barely speak Japanese after twenty years in Japan. From Germany they took the civil code and the organization of the army; from Britain, the Navy, the telegraph and the railways; and from the United States, the universities.[139] A Western-style peerage system was created with titles such as prince, marquis, count, viscount, and baron. Even the emperor started wearing Western-style military uniform like European monarchs.[140]

Modernization proceeded apace because all factions in the ruling groups agreed that the state needed to be strengthened.[141] The impulse was political: the regime opted for industrial development to protect the independence of the country as a military necessity vital to avoid Japan being turned into a colony.[142] Until recently Japan had been militarily weak. Without allies, without a fleet, without a modern army, and without industry it faced powerful Western nations.[143] In Japan the dominant class was not a bureaucracy committed to Confucian values (as in China) but a warrior class, impressed by the superiority of Western military might.[144] The process of industrialization became largely determined by military requirements and the military themselves, generals or admirals, headed governments for twenty-one of the thirty-six years between 1901 and 1937.[145]

The era when Japan regarded itself as singular among nations was over. Imitation became frenetic, but not for the first time in the country's history. In the fifth century, religion (Confucianism, Buddhism), architecture, administrative practices, and writing had been imported from China, often via Korea.[146] 'One of the great traits of the Japanese character,' wrote Manjirō Inagaki, a diplomat and scholar who had studied at Cambridge in 1888 to 1890 under John Seeley, the historian of the British Empire, 'is that they never hesitate to adopt new systems and laws if they consider them beneficial for their country.'[147] Some were less starry-eyed. The novelist Natsume Sōseki (who had lived for a couple of years in London and hated it), in his 1911 lecture 'The Civilization of Modern-Day Japan', pointed out that Japan's modernization had to compress one hundred years into ten, and that as a result the Japanese, in a kind of self-colonization, felt as if they were 'dressing up in borrowed clothing, putting up a false front'.[148]

The period of extreme pro-Western sentiments gave way to a more sober assessment of foreign successes, but there was never a significant reversal of policies.[149] It meant combining – as the expression *Wakon yōsai* implies – the Japanese spirit with Western technology. Yukichi Fukuzawa, a leading pro-business liberal intellectual of the Meiji period and founder of Keio University as a school for Western studies in 1858, stressed in his influential pamphlets (*An Encouragement of Learning*, 1872–6, and *An Outline of Theories of Civilization*, 1875) that while national sovereignty was the main goal of Japan, ultimately national power depended on the level of acceptance of modern civilization and rejection of the xenophobia of the *Sonnō jōi* movement. 'The more this movement of expel-the-foreigners increased,' he wrote in his autobiography, 'the more we would lose our national power, to say nothing of prestige.'[150] The Japanese had to learn to become civilized to avoid succumbing to 'aggressive foreigners'. That meant adopting modernity, industrialization, and independent thought.[151] He exhorted the Japanese to abandon their old customs and transform Japan into 'a new Western nation'.[152]

Not that Fukuzawa was uncritical of the West. A participant in Japan's first mission to the United States in 1859, his reaction was characteristic of a Japanese first impact with a modern, wasteful consumer society that cared little for tradition and had little respect for relatives; he was surprised that no one seemed to know or care about what happened to the family of George Washington. He was shocked that no one seemed to practise traditional values such as thrift: 'everywhere I found lying old tins, empty cans, and broken tools. This was remarkable for us, for in Yedo, after a fire, there would appear a swarm of people looking for nails in the ashes.'[153]

There were divisions within the reform movement. Some, such as Fukuzawa and Hironaka, were inspired by English liberalism; others, such as Katō Hiroyuki, were admirers of the Prussian autocratic model.[154] All wings of the movement, however, were united in their desire to adopt Western methods to save Japan from the spectre of China's fate. The Japanese were alarmed by the Chinese experience (Opium Wars, Taiping Rebellion) and were determined not to replicate it. Takasugi Shinsaku, a Chōshū samurai leader who sojourned in Shanghai for two months in 1862, was appalled by Chinese subservience to foreigners: 'When British and French walk along the street, Chinese move aside and get out of their way. Shanghai is Chinese territory, but it really belongs to the British and the French . . . This is bound to happen to us too.'[155] The inescapable conclusion was that the old policy of seclusion from the West would provide no protection.[156] One could almost say that Japan was scared into capitalism by the spectacle of what had occurred to China. What was remarkable about the opening up of Japan was that it took place with relatively little civil strife.

By the end of the century Japan possessed technicians, professors, doctors, managers, army officers. It had succeeded in forming an indigenous elite capable of leading the country towards industrialization, at a time when Turks and Chinese, Argentinians and Brazilians had not. What was particular about the Japanese elites was that they were strongly united, with few marked divisions between landed and urban interests (and Japan was ethnically far more homogeneous than its European counterparts). Theirs was a real technocracy committed to modernity. Their counterparts elsewhere often encountered opposition from important segments of the establishment: bishops and landlords in Latin America, nawabs in India, Confucian scholars in China, and mullahs in Turkey and Egypt. Japan did not have the great coal deposits that fuelled British, German, and American expansion. She did not have a particularly fertile soil. Nor did she rely on foreign loans (as did Russia and, indeed, many other European countries).[157] In fact, at first the government tried to ward off foreign investors, aware that foreign loans could be the first steps to being taken over[158] (as Egypt had been by the British after its debt default in 1879–81).

Japan could not afford to wait for capitalism to develop spontaneously. Japanese merchants were averse to risk taking and reluctant to invest in anything new, preferring making silk to making steel, so the Meiji government stepped in, actively constructing the Japanese bourgeois class, investing in industry by establishing and funding pilot plants to produce steam engines and machinery for mines, subsidizing industries such as cotton spinning, and encouraging the formation of banks.[159]

More public money was available for investment from the indemnities forced upon China after the 1895 war. Western capital flooded in only subsequently.[160] Yet Japanese firms remained Japanese, under Japanese control. This was partly because the state's share of total investment was much higher than in Europe and, like continental Europe, it devoted considerable resources to education. Once Japan was on the path to industrialization, the most valuable resource was her abundant supply of cheap, educated, hard-working labour.[161] Thus 'early Japanese capitalism may be described as of the hothouse variety, growing under the shelter of state protection and subsidy'.[162]

From 1896 to 1899 the government initiated heavy subsidies aimed at transforming Japanese shipbuilding into one of the most important industries in the world.[163] Throughout the Meiji era (1868–1912) there was more employment in government-owned heavy industries than in private ones, even though the government began to sell major enterprises to the private sector as early as the mid-1880s.[164] Almost all railway construction was undertaken by the government with very little foreign borrowing; national and municipal governments undertook

85 per cent of the borrowing, foreign direct investment was a paltry 5.5 per cent.[165] Only towards the 1880s, when private capital was reassured, did capitalists, foreign as well as Japanese, join in.[166] Soon, the state-run conglomerates were handed out at rock-bottom prices (an early example of privatization) to a new industrial capitalist class.

The level of concentration in Japanese business was particularly high: Sumitomo, Mitsui, Mitsubishi and Yasuda, the big four *zaibatsu* (rather appropriately the term means 'moneyed clique'), were all the product of the Meiji period (though some had earlier roots).[167] Japanese capitalists, created by the state, remained grateful, obedient, and loyal to it. Competition played a secondary role in Japanese economic growth. In his autobiography the liberal intellectual Yukichi Fukuzawa tells us that when he was asked to translate an economics textbook from English into Japanese he could not find the equivalent for 'competition', so he invented the term *kyōsō* (literally 'race-fight' or contest), and he had to explain to a bemused official that such a bellicose word better represented the Western concept.[168]

Contrary to the mythology of free-enterprise ideologues, state intervention worked. By the 1880s and 1890s the economy had taken off and, by the beginning of the twentieth century, Japan was one of the fastest-growing economies in the world.[169] The results were startling: in the years after 1886, the years of the Japanese take-off (1868–86 had been a preparatory stage), Japanese GNP doubled. In Italy, for example, in a comparable period, GNP increased by 'only' 30 per cent.[170]

The state had played a strong role under the Tokugawa, before the Meiji restoration.[171] As the historian Hattori Shiso pointed out in the 1930s, there was an embryonic capitalism as early as 1830. Two of the three largest shipyards owned and operated by the Meiji regime had been built before the Restoration.[172] The isolationism of the Tokugawa, the policy of 'national seclusion', was actually a form of economic protectionism that facilitated the process of development.[173] When events required state intervention, the pre-Meiji regime did not hesitate to intervene: during the inflation of the 1860s the shogunate issued a spate of decrees to control the price of rice, oil, timber, copper, manure, and commodity prices in general.[174]

There was, inevitably, a conservative backlash. Reactionaries argued, with some justification, that one could not rebuild a society as if nothing had happened before, as if customs and traditions did not matter, as if the past had all been a tragic mistake, or as if one should simply develop, *ab initio*, a foreign model.[175] But this movement was ephemeral, and, paradoxically, Japan established a model of economic development which, in the nineteenth century, remained unequalled. Since industrialization appeared to be state-directed, it may seem that the state became stronger and more interventionist. In reality what changed was the kind of intervention. Some of the Meiji reforms of the period 1868–72 lessened controls: abolition of guilds, freedom to engage in any occupation, permission for farmers to sell crops and land without restriction.[176] In other words old feudal and corporatist restrictions were lifted and pro-industrialization measures introduced.

The peasantry was taken by surprise by the speed of change – a change that did not benefit them.[177] There was some peasant unrest, especially in the first years after the Restoration, and some was even violent, but the speed of the transition, the autocratic manner in which it was accomplished, the fact that it did not begin as a response to popular demands, the high degree of unity within the ruling class, the fact that the army (the samurai class) thought they would benefit (in contrast to China where the bureaucracy knew they would lose from any change), meant that Japan moved from something one could call feudalism to something one could call capitalism in a relatively peaceful and smooth way.[178] The military-caste samurai, though soon deprived of their right to be the only armed force, began to do business, or at least some of them did.[179] The entrepreneurs of the first half of the Meiji period included adventurers who had made some money when the ports were opened up as well as *seishō* (merchants by the grace of political connections) who benefited from the privatization of government enterprises after 1881.[180]

The old merchant classes, however, proved to be a disappointment; they were unwilling to take chances, to trade abroad, or to risk capital in untried projects. So the government had to do it for them. This is why the Ministry of Industry, set up in 1870, created the pilot enterprises that became a model for the private sector, absorbing unavoidable start-up costs and attracting foreign technicians. The old money changers of the feudal times, like the merchants, proved to be unsuitable for the new order. The creation of a modern banking system was an urgent necessity. That too was constructed by the Meiji state with the Banking Act of 1872 (modelled on the American Banking Act of 1863).[181]

Japan had been an 'urban' society for a long time. As early as 1700 it was one of the most urbanized societies in the world (though a considerable proportion of the urban lower classes were, in fact, servants).[182] In 1731, Edo (Tokyo) was one of the largest cities in the world. Human capital formation and educational resources were already advanced in the first half of the nineteenth century.[183] There was a high rate of literacy.[184]

The West too seemed aware of Japanese potential even before the Meiji 'Restoration'. In August 1860, *Harper's Monthly* declared that the Japanese 'seemed to have an aptitude for acquiring the civilization of the West to which no other Oriental race can lay claim'. China, on the other hand, was regarded as 'so corrupt, so wretchedly degraded, and so enfeebled by misgovernment, as to be already more than half sunk in decay'.[185]

The Japanese state funded the industrial economy largely out of the proceedings of a land tax. At the turn of the century other sources of tax revenue materialized but they were mainly agriculturally based (taxes on sugar, alcoholic drinks, textiles, soya, and tobacco). And the countryside suffered in other ways, as young women from the rural sector were drafted into the rapidly developing light industry, particularly in textiles.[186] In fact, quite unlike the West, 80 per cent of the industrial workforce, heavily concentrated in textiles, consisted of female labour. In 1901 in the Nagano region 91 per cent of the workers in the top 205 textile factories were women, usually the daughters of impoverished peasants, recruited from the countryside to work in the spinning mills.[187]

Even so, by 1914, the Japanese economy was still overwhelmingly agrarian and its main exports largely primary products such as tea, cotton yarn, and raw silk.[188] Raw silk indeed dominated Japan's exports, though, as the country developed, its share declined from 60 per cent in 1868 to 46 per cent in the early 1920s. Lacking the natural energy resources for an industry-based economic growth, the Japanese state helped the national economy by establishing (by 1910) formal control over Taiwan, Korea, southern Sakhalin, and other islands, thus obtaining raw materials that were in scarce supply in Japan.[189]

Although there was no outright protectionism, the government deliberately favoured national products, and laws and regulations encouraged Japanese citizens to purchase the products and services of native industries, while discouraging Westerners from setting up factories in Japan. In Japan, more than anywhere else in the nineteenth century, without the state there would have been no capitalism. Of the many causes for the diverging paths of Japan and China, the most important one was the difference in the strength, organization, and direction of the state.

The Chinese reform movement of the 1890s had not been able to transform the state into an effective machine to mobilize resources for industrialization.[190] In fact, before the Sino-Japanese War of 1894–5, the little industrial investment there was in China had to come from the Qing administration.[191] Japan succeeded where China failed because it had been able to construct a strong central authority that could impress its will on the periphery. China, behind the pomp of the Imperial Court, was fragmented into semi-autonomous provincial authorities whose power had grown at the expense of the centre.

In Europe, private initiative was essential but on its own would have led, at best, to the industrialization of very few countries: probably Britain, perhaps Belgium and Switzerland. In Asia, to be like the West it was necessary to have a strong state building capitalism from above. In Japan this was understood as early as 1868. It took over a century for China to master this lesson. Once she had done so, she appeared unstoppable, poised to overtake the West in a global race for economic dominance. The outcome, as is always the case in history, is uncertain since all things are impermanent. In the words of the Ming Dynasty poet Yang Shen (1488–1559) in 'The Immortals by the River': 'The gushing waters of the Yangzi River pour and disappear into the East, washing away past heroes: their triumphs and failures, all vanish into nothingness in an instant.'

4
The Allure of Industry

Industrialization progressed around the globe with varying degrees of success, in ways that were patchy, unpredictable, and not predetermined. While Japan and China were in ferment, the Ottoman Empire was too. In 1839 the proponents of 'reorganization' (Tanzimat), led by Sultan Mahmud II (1785–1839), decided that modernization from above was necessary in order to halt the constant decline of the empire. Resistance within the elites, however, was greater here than in Japan and the reforms were essentially concerned with the social and legal aspects of Westernization, rather than the economy. In fact, the Ottoman Empire had no real economic policies and, until the 1860s, little conception that one of the hallmarks of modernity was government responsibility for the economy.[1]

There were symbolic gestures, however, and these had significance. Mahmud II ordered his portrait to be hung in public places (like a Western monarch), though it was not an Islamic custom.[2] He adopted Western forms of dress, even though as recently as 1823 an order had been issued to Grigore Ghica, the Voivode (Lord) of Wallachia, to refrain from wearing 'French' (i.e. Western) clothes.[3] The Western image of the Turks as 'unspeakable' (Gladstone's term), and the empire as a degenerate nest of bloodthirsty tyrants or lustful 'Orientals', was challenged.[4] Roads and bridges were built, public health and education promoted, but such initiatives were limited. The amount spent on public works, education, health, and so on was a small percentage of state spending.[5] For the majority of the population, the state manifested itself through conscription and taxation.[6]

The huge debts incurred to pay for the Crimean War (1853–6) had gravely damaged the imperial finances. Sultan Abdülhamid II, one of Mahmud II's successors, who reigned from 1876 until his deposition in 1909 (the last effective Ottoman ruler), knew that a strong economy was essential and that he had to modernize infrastructures and communications. But military and administrative expenditures during his reign averaged about 60 per cent of government spending, 30 per cent of which went towards servicing the enormous public debt.[7] The depression in world agricultural prices in the 1870s further strained Ottoman finances. In the face of a dearth of funds, the government was forced to grant monopolies to European concerns in many important mining and other projects. To a certain extent, the Ottoman government was able to use European vested interests to perpetuate its own policies, but the capitulatory commercial and legal privileges enjoyed by European powers, backed by threats of force, left the Ottoman government with little room to manoeuvre. The Sultan chose to continue the free-trade policy embodied in the 1838 Anglo-Turkish commercial Convention, though there was little in it for the Ottoman Empire – its aim was to secure for Britain an increased share of the Middle Eastern market: the Ottoman Empire thought it could not afford to clash with the British Empire. The phrase 'the sick man of Europe', attributed to Tsar Nicholas I, was not an inaccurate depiction of the Ottoman Empire.

Later in the century, problems multiplied. In 1873–4 a massive famine ravaged central Anatolia. This was followed by the war with Russia (1877–8), which ended in defeat and population and territorial losses. The so-called 'Great Depression of 1873–96' led to a loan default and a weakening of Ottoman trade with the rest of the world, which by then had become very important to the economy of the empire.[8] Between 1881 and 1903 it was involved in constant debt renegotiations with European powers and bankers, occasionally being able to play off creditors against creditors but never establishing a longer-term plan for its financial affairs.[9] The consequence was ever-increasing control by European powers over Ottoman finance, leading in 1881 to the establishment of the Ottoman Public Debt Administration.[10]

The time was ripe for change. In 1908 a group of officers, intellectuals, and exiles known as the Young Turks staged what amounted to a coup, forcing Sultan Abdülhamid II to restore the constitution of 1876 that he had suspended in 1878 and introduce a relatively democratic system. Inspired by the West, they were a typical 'Third World' elite group who wanted to modernize the Ottoman Empire to protect it from the West. Originally they regarded religion as an obstacle to progress, though they later used Islam to unite the country, aspiring to make Turkey the 'Japan of the Middle East'.[11]

Political reforms, which is what the Young Turks achieved, are seldom sufficient to stop decline. In fact, they often accelerate it, unsurprisingly since they themselves are often a symptom of decline. By 1914, having lost nearly all of its European territories in the Balkan Wars, the empire depended almost exclusively on exporting agricultural produce.[12] Such decadence contributed to ever-growing resistance to the rule of the sovereign.[13]

The impetus for reforming the empire was not so much the fear of backwardness per se but, as with Japan, the fear of being taken over by Western powers, including Russia. Unlike Japan, however, the Ottoman Empire was a multinational imperium subject to centrifugal pressures from its provinces, above all from the Balkans and from Egypt. Like the Russian and Chinese empires, the Ottoman Empire knew little peace in the nineteenth century and collapsed after the First World War (the Russian Empire had already collapsed in 1917, the Chinese Empire in 1911).

It was not just modernizing Turks, Iranians, and Egyptians who looked to Europe along with the Japanese and the Chinese. The European 'periphery' (i.e. eastern Europe) also looked towards the 'centre' – England, France, and Germany – and so did the South (Italy, Greece, Spain, and Portugal). In the twentieth century all would look to the United States, and always with the same questions: how can we be like them without being like them? What to take and what to keep? Ideological imports from the West, namely from western Europe and the United States, have been a constant element of the global political struggle in the twentieth century, including, most obviously, the idea of communism. Even the West's most vociferous opponents in the contemporary era, such as the ideologue of the Islamic Revolution in Iran, the Ayatollah Ruhollah Khomeini, imported the idea of a national state and, indeed, of a republic, from the West, as well as the concept of the political party.[14] And Khomeini himself was following in the footsteps of the Constitutional Revolution of 1906, which used Western values (popular representation and constitutionalism) to challenge Western hegemony.

Ideas are the easiest items to import and the second half of the nineteenth century saw a flourishing global trade in this adaptable commodity. The importers of ideas are often intellectuals from 'backward' regions, aware and embarrassed by their backwardness, who cling to the Romantic belief that ideas can change things.

Paradoxically, even the idea of nationalism could be imported. Russian intellectuals, for instance, read Fichte's *Speeches to the German People* (1808) and Hegel's *Philosophy of History* (1837) in which a particular place was assigned to every 'historical' nation (with the *Urvolk*, the original people, being, obviously, the Germans), and 'applied' these ideas to Russia, with Russia, of course, at the heart of things. As Pavel Milyukov (Paul Milyoukov), a liberal Westernizer, wrote in 1905:

> Thus, by a curious irony of history, the first and only nationalistic theory ever developed in Russia lay on the foundations of western European philosophic thought; and we must add that this theory was very old in western Europe when it was first heralded by Russian nationalists.[15]

The Russian intelligentsia was united in the need to go forward in opposition to the autocracy, but was divided on what could and should be done. As we will discuss in greater depth later, the division was between the Slavophiles, who thought Russia could evolve in its own, non-Western way, and the Westernizers, who believed that there was one path to follow and that the laggards had to go where the pathbreakers had gone before. This great debate was replicated elsewhere, especially in eastern European countries. Let us examine the Romanian case.

In Romania, in the early twentieth century, literary critics such as Eugen Lovinescu and economists such as Ştefan Zeletin argued that their country had no choice but to replicate the Western road, 'the road to civilization', while the traditionalists insisted on the allegedly unique agrarian character of Romania.[16] But the idea of importing industrialization was already current, unsurprisingly, since, even on the eve of the First World War, four-fifths of the population still lived off agriculture and only 3 per cent worked in industry.[17]

In 1881 the nationalist liberal historian Alexandru Dimitrie Xenopol (and later theoretician of the far-right anti-Semitic Iron Guards) wrote that precisely because Romania was a 'laggard' state, industrialization had to be imposed from above, directed by the state on a large scale, rather than relying on craft and artisan entrepreneurship.[18] In fact, in countries like Romania, most major changes, such as the abolition of feudalism, were a direct result of Western influence.[19]

The country did not have a class of merchants eager to emancipate themselves from the shackles of semi-feudal relations. Romanian elites were largely preoccupied with national unity and, later, its preservation. Nationalism preceded economic modernity.[20] The members of the petty nobility ('the lesser boyars') preferred the secure employment of state service to the risks associated with entrepreneurship. The educated offspring of traders and artisans soon followed their examples.[21] The nineteenth-century Romanian economy was characterized by a decline of artisanal industry and its replacement by manufactured imports. Much of the commerce was controlled by foreigners.[22] The country's middle class was a small proportion of the population. In addition the proportion of pupils in Romanian schools in the early 1870s was dismal: there were only 82,145 pupils, whereas advanced Belgium (with a similar population) had 545,000.[23] Eventually, however, the cultural policies of the state were successful and more and more people were educated.[24]

Romanian liberals, who might have been in favour of capitalist modernity, lamented the rise of a 'foreign' entrepreneurial class (mainly Germans and Jews), though, of course, economic rationality required their presence. To cement the unity of the nation, Romania did what many new nations do (and go on doing): she expanded the public sector, thus creating jobs for the scions of the 'native' middle classes and of the lower nobility. The result was an elephantine bureaucracy, open to corruption and bribery, paying salaries which, though low, made up one-third of the national budget.[25] So the Romanian state grew by borrowing heavily.[26]

There was no real urban labour market; most rural labourers were sharecroppers, and only one in seven agrarian producers sold the crop regularly for cash. All this added to the complaints of the liberals regarding the lack of 'maturity' of the peasantry (i.e. their lack of entrepreneurial spirit).[27] Liberals thought that it was possible to modernize agriculture, improve the peasants' standard of living, diversify the economy, and become a 'civilized' state. The conservatives were convinced that Romania was destined to remain an agrarian country for the foreseeable future.[28]

This was also their wish. Their ideal was a situation in which Romania would export wheat, thus providing enough wealth for its upper class to live it up in Western style; the peasantry could be kept docile by being fed with *mămăligă* – a porridge of maize – while the more precious wheat could be exported. This powerful and large landowning class (reminiscent of its equivalent in Latin America) preferred to live in Bucharest or spend their time abroad. They were an example of one of the most important obstacles to industrialization throughout the world: a self-satisfied aristocratic class which, thanks to their hold on land and primary products, had no reason to invest in industry, but were content to use their wealth to buy luxuries made elsewhere, so that even their consumption did not benefit the local economy. They often had no incentive to use their capital even for the modernization of their own estates, let alone the modernization of the state.

Their wealth had enabled them to 'catch up' with the West, or at least with France, while the country remained backward. Even as early as 1848, according to Hippolyte Desprez (a French diplomat who had travelled extensively in Romania), the Romanian upper classes felt at home in Paris, Vienna, and in Italy, and lived in Bucharest as their counterparts lived in the great capitals of Europe: 'the salons of Bucharest are the same of ours'.[29] They took little interest in technological development or in how to improve agriculture. They leased their estates for fixed sums and spent the revenue on themselves. By 1900 these leaseholders, or *arendaşi*, many of whom were Jews from the Habsburg Empire, controlled a considerable part of the landowners' estates.[30] Needless to say this only contributed to increasing the anti-Semitism of the peasants. The continuing peasant misery, barely improved by the great agrarian reform of 1864, and the succession of smaller reforms that followed, maintained the rural sector in a state of constant seething discontent.[31] The reform had introduced capitalist agriculture to the countryside, eliminated the communal village, and given the best land to the landlords. By 1905, 0.6 per cent of all landowners owned almost half the land. The actual cultivation was done by the *arendaşi*, who paid a rent on the property and then tried to recover it by squeezing the maximum out of the peasants. By 1900 the *arendaşi* controlled more than half the land over 500 hectares.

The basis of this transformation was the amazing growth of wheat production and export: annual export increased more than five times between 1880 and 1906, when it formed 82.5 per cent of the value of Romania's total exports.[32] But there were problems ahead and not only for Romania. Technology was transforming agriculture, so that, by the end of the nineteenth century, the agriculture–industry distinction was becoming less relevant, especially in America, where farming was being rapidly industrialized. John Deere had pioneered the use of the smooth-sided steel plough in the United States as early as 1837. By 1892, John Froelich had developed the first petrol-powered tractor. After clearing much of American land of its original inhabitants, technological breakthroughs and innovations in marketing meant the birth of agribusiness. Wheat, for instance, was now shipped, mixed with that of other growers, as part of a homogeneous commodity to be traded by merchants and bought by anonymous and distant consumers.[33] This was an aspect of modernity highlighted by social theorists such as Georg Simmel: 'The modern metropolis . . . is supplied almost entirely by production for . . . entirely unknown purchasers who never personally enter the producer's actual field of vision.'[34]

The United States, Hungary, and Romania were all major exporters of wheat, but American wheat was produced with what was then sophisticated technology that permitted ever-increasing productivity. This severely damaged Romanian exports. Hungary fared better than Romania because it had the technology to transform wheat into flour and export it.[35]

In Romania, as elsewhere, the main political division was between Liberals and Conservatives. Roughly speaking, the former were stronger in cities, the latter in the countryside, but it was more complex than that. The Liberals were in favour of autarkic protectionist development (since they wanted to promote Romanian industrialists); the Conservatives were open to foreign investment that would not damage their agrarian interests. So the Liberals were statist and protectionists whereas the Conservatives feared a strong state and were in favour of free trade. The Conservatives were pro-Jews and pro-foreign influence. The Liberals were anti-Semitic and nationalist.

In 1900, faced with a considerable deficit, the Conservatives, led by Petre Carp, one of Romania's leading politicians, granted foreign companies concessions to extract the country's recently discovered oil, the importance of which was becoming obvious. The Liberals reacted with nationalist slogans: 'America to the Americans, Europe to the Europeans and Romania to the Romanians'. But when the Liberals, led by Dimitrie Sturdza, formed a government in 1901, they changed track and opened negotiations with foreign interests.[36] By 1914 the Romanian economy was dominated by foreign capital – German, Dutch, Austrian, American, and French.[37]

The backward nature of Romanian development suited the Conservatives. The free-trade policies they favoured would help perpetuate the agrarian character of the Romanian economy since they would facilitate access to foreign markets for the grain and cattle they produced. The Liberals wanted protectionism in the hope that Romanian industry would grow behind a tariff wall. Their hopes were dashed: there was hardly any industrialization (unlike in Russia). Romanian peasants were not threatened by industrialization, because there was too little of it, rather they were threatened because they had too little land and the market for their produce had been shrinking ever since 1875 when the international price for wheat collapsed. Eventually, in 1907, a peasant tax revolt took place, but it was brutally repressed (see Chapter 12).

The kind of economic progress that eventually occurred in Romania relied substantially on the state. Rural inhabitants did not benefit from it. Poverty persisted and Romania remained, by European standards, an underdeveloped country with 82 per cent of the population still living in the countryside in 1912.[38] There was of course considerable urbanization, particularly in Wallachia. The population of Bucharest more than doubled between 1860 and the end of the century, but this was due largely to administrative and commercial developments rather than industrial growth. There was also some modest mechanization of agriculture, partly spurred by American competition.[39]

Nationalists, in Romania as elsewhere, were plagued by contradictory ideas. On the one hand they wanted their country to be a strong nation, with its own culture, language, and traditions. They constantly constructed a national culture of rural values and peasant memory, resistant to the anonymity of urban life. At the same time they wanted to be a modern nation, like all the others, but modernity entailed industry, progress, urbanization, openness to the rest of the world. They looked both ways, towards a mythical past and towards a future full of hope. They were like the *Angelus Novus*, Paul Klee's painting (see over), so famously celebrated by Walter Benjamin:

> His eyes are opened wide, his mouth stands open and his wings are outstretched. The Angel of History must look just so. His face is turned towards the past . . . But a storm is blowing from Paradise, it has caught itself up in his wings and is so strong that the Angel can no longer close them. The storm drives him irresistibly into the future, to which his back is turned, while the rubble-heap before him grows sky-high. That which we call progress is *this* storm.[40]

One of the leading Romanian nationalists and briefly prime minister in 1931, Nicolae Iorga, in the journal *Sămănătorul* protested in 1906 that a large number of the plays performed at the National Theatre of Bucharest were in French: this foreign language crushes us, he wrote, it subjugates us, it humiliates us, it divides our people between those who speak our despised language and the others, the good and the great and the rich who speak another language, those who live, love and die in this other language.[41] As if Romania, like all other nations, was not in any case divided between the rich and the poor, between those who went to the theatre and the vast majority who did not.

Hard economic facts were also at work. The decline in world wheat prices forced the Romanian Liberals, the main force behind modernization, to push for an acceleration of industrialization – hence the expansion of rural education under the education minister Spiru Haret (in the hope of turning the peasant into an 'educated producer'), the Popular Banks laws of 1903, and the establishment of village cooperatives (*obştii săteşti*) in 1904.[42]

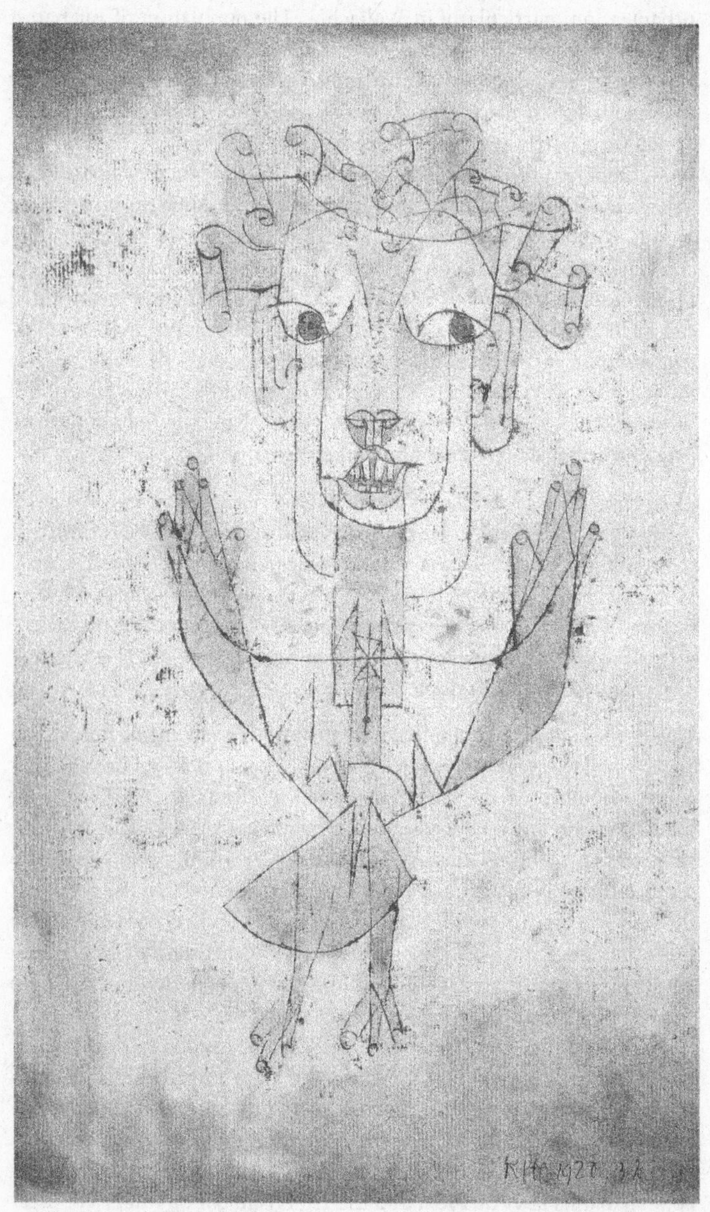

Romanian Liberals, like Liberals in other east European countries, wanted a strong state with a strong constitution and a proper bureaucracy, the establishment of property rights in land, and labour replacing the corvée and servile obligations with wage labour.[43] The problem was that there was no proper banking system and local landlords were not investing. So they borrowed, as did the state. By the beginning of the twentieth century, Romania was one of the leading debtor nations in Europe, with a public debt standing at 116 per cent of national product (1870–1880s), though Serbia's debt was even worse at 120 per cent.[44]

The role of the state in developing capitalism was crucial, it was agreed, and not just in Romania. Scientific knowledge was vital for modern economic growth, but had capitalism been just a question of technology, it could have been imported from the West in a less traumatic way. However it was also, and mainly, a question of politics. And this was the real problem facing China and Russia, Romania and the Ottoman Empire, as they faced the West: too little state.

To be prosperous it is not necessary to be a manufacturing industrial nation. White European settlers' colonies – with the United States as the significant exception – never became major manufacturing countries. In Canada, New Zealand, and Australia, primary products (farming, fishing, and mining) dominated the economic landscape, while their populations remained prosperous by any standards.

The same cannot be said for Latin America, however, which, like Australia and New Zealand, exported primary products mainly to Great Britain, France, Germany and the United States while importing manufactured goods.[45] Even in Argentina, the wealthiest country in Latin America, private wealth was not used to develop industry. Although richer, at the end of the nineteenth century, than Sweden or Norway and with a much larger population (which would have provided a home market), Argentina had a lower level of manufacturing than either of them.[46] Its significant exports, frozen meat, wheat, and maize, provided Argentina with a higher standard of living than anywhere else in Latin America.[47] Indeed, on the eve of the First World War, in 1912, Argentina, in GDP per capita, was on a par with the main western European countries, and higher than France and Germany, below only Belgium, the Netherlands, Switzerland, and Great Britain – hence the high level of immigration, particularly from Italy.[48] Uruguay was not far behind Argentina. Here the contrast with Japan is telling. Japan too, like many Latin American countries, was an exporter of primary products (raw silk and tea). But in Chile the export of nitrates enriched those who controlled it; in Brazil the export of coffee enriched the growers. In Japan the revenue from raw silk and tea was used to buy foreign machinery.[49]

Latin America, or, rather, its elites, became integrated into the world system while remaining peripheral to it, and dependant on the fortunes of industry in the 'West', while local production consisted almost entirely of handicrafts.[50] Of course there was some industrialization before the First World War, but it was limited to products such as cotton textiles in Mexico, Brazil, and Peru.[51] In some countries, such as Chile, there was a transition from the traditional rural estates (the hacienda system) to some kind of agrarian capitalism and the formation of a rural proletariat.[52] Nevertheless most Latin American countries, though backward compared with the West in terms of industrialization, did better than colonies such as India.

There were major differences between the success of former non-settler colonies such as India in launching their products into the world market, and countries that were not colonies. For example, Indian products (mainly textiles) were in practice excluded from world trade by the British. India was unable to withstand British competition even in its own market: while it produced almost all its textiles in 1833, by 1877 it was producing only 35–42 per cent of what it consumed. Mexico, not a colony, and which produced 60 per cent of the textiles it consumed in 1879, saw this share reach 78 per cent in the period 1906–8.[53]

In non-industrialized countries, exports remained firmly confined to primary products. Mexico had a variety of exports (and the luck to be near a market the size of the USA). In 1913 coffee accounted for 50 per cent of Brazilian and Venezuelan exports. In Chile the main export was nitrates; in Honduras bananas; in Peru guano and nitrates (and later sugar and copper); in Argentina it was maize (22 per cent of exports), and meat (20 per cent). Cuba produced 25 per cent of the world's sugar cane.[54] In Ecuador it was cacao but also straw hats (known as panama hats), quinquina (a popular aromatic herb used, among others, by the French in making the popular aperitif Dubonnet), and tobacco. These four products made up 90 per cent of Ecuador's exports in the middle of the nineteenth century.[55]

As José Luis González, one of the leading Puerto Rican writers of the twentieth century, exclaimed: 'Industry! . . . What interest could have awakened the group of old factories that produced poorly or expensively if consumption could be satisfied by importing from Europe [mainly Britain] or the United States?'[56]

The more a country exported, the more its cosmopolitan and highly urbanized landowning elite enjoyed a higher standard of living and could bask in the benefits of modernization.[57] They imitated their counterparts in the United States and Europe in their lifestyles and consumption patterns, down to the spread of country clubs such as the Hurlingham in Buenos Aires (developed by the British in 1908 and named after a London sports club) and the Chimont in Montevideo (developed by Americans in 1910). At the same time, unsurprisingly, there was a rejection of *nordomanía*, as the uncritical attitude towards the USA was called. José Enrique Rodó's essay *Ariel*, published in 1900, had an immense influence in Latin America. It called for a revival of an idealized Latin American spirit, while indicting American utilitarianism and democratic mediocrity.[58] Like many thinkers in the periphery, Rodó (a major Uruguayan modernist writer) exhibited an elitist distaste for the multitude, which can be an instrument of barbarism or civilization, and the spirit of vulgarity (*el espíritu de vulgaridad*) of American democracy.[59]

After 1870 this dependency on foreign manufactures decreased, but it took the crisis of 1929 to lead to the establishment of state-led import-substituting policies in a somewhat unsuccessful attempt to lessen imports.[60] Until then, during what came to be known as the 'Liberal' era, Latin America, unlike the United States, remained vulnerable to external shocks.[61] Throughout the nineteenth century, economic issues were seldom central to Latin American debates. What moved the elites was the struggle between centralism and federalism and between Church and State. A pragmatic form of free trade had been widely accepted, tempered by some protection for domestic activity, while both foreign investment and immigration were encouraged.[62]

Latin American governments were weak, even though authoritarian forms of rule prevailed. While territorial stability was remarkable, political instability was uncommonly pronounced. Change occurred through military coups or fraudulent elections. But this did not perturb big business, which had become more or less independent from the political level (thanks, no doubt, to the weakness of the latter).[63] What really impinged on enterprises was not the state within which it was operating but what happened in the wider global economy. This confirmed the peripheral status of Latin America, which largely managed to be modern, though with little or no industry.

Modernity was mixed with backwardness in most European countries, too. For instance, in fin-de-siècle Italy, though most of the country was still relatively 'backward', what would become known as the 'industrial triangle' (Milan-Turin-Genoa) already possessed many of the preconditions for industrial development, including reasonably high literacy rates.[64] The economy was becoming more diversified, taking in not just textiles and steel (the latter in Terni, Umbria – a project initiated by the state), but also rubber (Pirelli 1872), chemicals (Montecatini 1888), cars (FIAT began production in 1899), electricity (Edison 1884), and engineering (Cantoni Krumm & Co. in 1874, then Franco Tosi in 1894). The working class was still small: 15 per cent of the labour force, according to the 1901 census, and even this was an overestimate since this figure included artisans and owners of workshops, so that in reality industrial workers were probably some 10 per cent of the working population.[65] Elsewhere in Italy modernity took the form of rapid urbanization without a corresponding industrial growth, usually due to the growth of commerce and public-sector jobs.[66] During industrialization the gap between north and south increased, partly because the south was incapable of setting up its own enterprises, partly because northern and foreign capital did not invest in the south.[67] Public utilities, in a metropolis such as Naples with over 500,000 inhabitants in 1900, were in the hands of foreigners: the French controlled the gas supply; the Swiss electricity; the main water supply was in the hands of a British company; the tram system was Belgian.[68]

Some countries were relatively high on the industrial league table, while still being socially backward. Thus Russia combined considerable industrial development with an extremely backward agriculture. Serfdom itself had been abolished only in 1861, while in much of Europe it had been done away with long before: 1788 in Denmark, 1771 in Savoy, 1789 in France (where, at the time, there was very little actual serfdom left), 1798 in Switzerland. In Britain the abolition of serfdom had taken place in the fourteenth century. (There were some countries in which serfdom was abolished even later than in Russia; Romania, for example, where it was abolished formally in 1864, and Tibet, where it was abolished only in 1959.)[69] In Prussia most feudal rights were abolished late, by 1850, but there was already a powerful class of landlord farmers.[70]

Industry was advancing, slowly and tentatively, in Russia but not (yet) in Greece or Spain or in the Ottoman Empire. Agriculture was central to the Greek economy: before 1914 agricultural products constituted the main export of Greece (75 per cent in 1887 and 78 per cent in 1912, and they are still a major component of Greek exports one hundred years later). These were mainly wine, raisins, olives, olive oil, and tobacco – none of which required much industrial technology. All you needed to do was to dry the grapes for raisins, ferment them for wine, roll the tobacco leaves, and press the olives for the oil. As late as 1874, even road construction remained rudimentary and investments were mainly involved in distribution and finance.[71] Taxes were collected on behalf of the Ottoman Empire by local notables (*proestoi*), the basis of a later clientele system. In the 1880s some of the preconditions for industrialization came into being (a transport system, a unified internal market, and a strengthening of the mechanism for state intervention), but the Greek working class remained tiny, and peasants remained on the land or emigrated to the United States (the number who left every year was greater than the total number of workers employed in the Greek industry).[72] Under Charilaos Trikoupis, several times Prime Minister in the 1880s and 1890s, there was considerable modernization of the military, judiciary, and civil service, but the most significant industrial development was in shipping. By 1920 the Greek fleet was one of the largest in the world.[73] In 2015 it still was the largest in deadweight tonnage (a measure of how much vessels can transport), though many are registered in other countries such as Panama for tax reasons.[74] Greece did have a remarkable entrepreneurial class, but it was scattered in various parts of the Ottoman Empire, just like the Lebanese and the Armenians, leaving the country with little industry.[75]

Like Greece, Spain had very little to export to advanced countries such as France, Great Britain, and Belgium, except for its agricultural products like wine (between 1880 and 1914 Spain was the leading wine-exporting country in Europe).[76] The control of Spanish mines (as well as the rail infrastructure) was in the hands of foreigners, mainly British, French, and German, with the complicity of corrupt local elites.[77] This was no minor affair since, in the last quarter of the nineteenth century, Spain produced more than 23 per cent of the world lead, 16 per cent of its copper, and large quantities of iron ore and sulphur. Then, at the beginning of the twentieth century, decline set in and other competitors emerged.[78] These vast resources might have been used to help bridge the gap between backward Spain and the rest of the West. But they weren't. The state was too bureaucratic to be of much use and the banking system was primitive – two reasons why Spain failed to have an industrial revolution in the nineteenth century.[79] As early as 1891 an engineer, Pablo de Alzola, lamented that the mineral industries had failed to promote economic growth.[80] The limited industrialization that existed was confined to Catalonia and the Basque country.[81] Elsewhere industrial development proceeded at a very slow pace and remained so weak that it could not provide sufficient stimulus to increase production in agriculture. Labour remained, unproductively, in the countryside, acting as a restraint on the Spanish economy, as it also did in the case of Portugal.[82]

The growth of industry in Europe in the decades leading up to the First World War was concentrated in a few regions of the West. Outside the West (and Japan) there was hardly any modern manufacturing. Industrialization remained firmly in the hands of western Europeans and Americans. Only Japan just about challenged this hegemony as the table below makes clear (see Table 10).[83]

The circumstances surrounding each industrial country were varied. This is hardly surprising. Within the world of advancing capitalism there was remarkable diversity: new countries (Germany and Italy) and old ones (Britain and Sweden), landlocked countries (Switzerland) and islands (Japan and Britain), large countries (the USA and Russia) and small ones (Belgium and Switzerland), multinational (Russia) and fairly ethnically homogeneous states (Sweden and Japan). Some small countries could follow bigger ones by producing manufactured exports for their markets, as was the case for Belgium and Switzerland, whose exports per capita were far higher than any other country, including Britain, throughout the period 1880 to 1914.[84] In the same period Sweden achieved the highest rate of growth per capita GNP in Europe.[85] Other small peripheral countries did not do well. Most of the Balkan nations that became independent only in the second half of the nineteenth century faced problems of nation-building while being constrained by unfavourable economic circumstances. Their subsequent history turned out to be most unfavourable to economic prosperity and, as a result, even today they suffer from relative economic backwardness. They lagged behind western Europe before the First World War, between the wars, during communism and after communism.

On the eve of the First World War what we came to call the 'Third World' accounted for less than 2–3 per cent of the world's industrial output.[86] Western growth was remarkable only in comparison with that of the periphery, and not in comparison with the growth it would experience in the decades after the Second World War, the real Golden Age of Capitalism, when the advanced economies of Europe and North America grew by leaps and bounds.

Table 10 League Table of Industrial Development, 1810–1910

	1810	1840	1860	1880	1900	1910
1	UK	UK	UK	UK	USA	USA
2	Belgium	Belgium	Belgium	Belgium	UK	UK
3	USA	USA	USA	USA	Belgium	Belgium
4	France	Switzerland	Switzerland	Switzerland	Switzerland	Germany
5	Switzerland	France	France	Germany	Germany	Switzerland
6	Germany	Germany	Germany	France	France	France
7	Sweden	Sweden	Sweden	Sweden	Sweden	Sweden
8	Spain	Spain	Spain	Spain	Spain	Spain
9	Italy	Italy	Italy	Italy	Italy	Italy
10	Russia	Russia	Russia	Russia	Russia	Russia
11	Japan	Japan	Japan	Japan	Japan	Japan

Source: Paul Bairoch, 'Niveaux de développement économique de 1810 à 1910'.

5
The State

The idea that minimal state intervention was best was seldom seriously propounded by the political elites in the second half of the nineteenth century (or indeed until sometime around 1980), though it was by many intellectuals. It was generally agreed that the state should play an active role in removing obstacles to growth and at the same time try to alleviate some of the social problems growth created. As globalization proceeds states find it increasingly difficult to control all aspects of a nation's affairs, particularly international financial transactions. But states matter and will go on mattering for the foreseeable future, which is why not even their opponents would be so bold as to say that state treaties like NAFTA (the North American Free Trade Agreement) and the European Union Treaty of 1992 (the Maastricht Treaty) are irrelevant, or that the decision by Richard Nixon to unpeg the dollar from gold in 1971 (effectively abolishing the Bretton Woods agreement) had little impact.

The state was crucial in creating the preconditions of economic transformation, including a set of legislative institutions regulating competition, because capitalism, unlike other economic systems, has strong anarchic tendencies. Taming the beast to save the beast was essential. Capitalists do not control capitalism. They are themselves prisoners of a set of social and economic relations within which they try to improve their position against their competitors. The distribution of winners and losers owes something to the relative distribution of entrepreneurial skills, but it is also due to exogenous elements, even to luck (such as the availability of raw materials), and past decisions taken by others. To some extent success in capitalism as in politics depends on the circumstances facing individuals and their capacity to exploit them to their advantage, or as Machiavelli explains in Chapter 6 of *The Prince*, on the combination of *fortuna* (circumstances) and *virtù* (one's own capacity and skill). This is where politics comes in. The stability of the state and its own success in expanding its power or protecting itself from enemies came increasingly to depend on the economic performance of its own home-grown entrepreneurial class. At the same time it was essential for entrepreneurs to be protected by a strong state. The two worked in symbiosis.

What if there were no entrepreneurs? 'Enlightened' sovereigns like the German-born Catherine of Russia (r. 1762–96) thought that one should create them, producing a 'middling class' like Britain's. That was the way of strengthening the state, she wrote: 'The object of commerce is to export and import goods for the benefit of the State.'[1] Her Manifesto of 22 July 1763, distributed throughout Europe, encouraged, over the following six years, the immigration of thousands of entrepreneurs and craftsmen attracted by loans and concessions.[2] A lack of an entrepreneurial middle class was a standard explanation, at least in the nineteenth century, for the lack of industry. It was believed that the problem with the Ottoman Empire, for example, was that it had too many aristocrats and not enough merchants, which is why it imported or developed a middle class from the Greek, Armenian, and Jewish communities.[3]

In Japan too, as we have seen, the protagonists of modernization believed that since native industrialists were weak the government had to assume their role. The Chinese authorities too tried to modernize in the early 1870s, setting up enterprises called *kuan-tu shang-pan* (literally, firms under government-supervised management). The reformer Cheng Kuan-ying (see Chapter 3) advocated some form of protectionism or *shang-chan*, explaining that, given the strength of the West, it was better to compete using *shang-chan* than *ping-chan* (military confrontation).[4] However, such attempts failed, hampered by Western encroachments, military intervention, and the exaction of indemnities.[5]

Japan, but also Russia and Prussia, and even Britain, could not possibly have developed as they did without the vigorous leadership of the state. A truly modern country requires a properly functioning state, an efficient bureaucracy, a set of institutions, preferably some elements of popular control, clearly defined property rights (public or private), an industrial economy, and an educated population. A truly modern country needs to be able to raise its own funds for infrastructural investment or attract them from investors and lenders. Infrastructural projects have had to be further buttressed by an adequate health system as well as a proper educational system and mechanisms to maintain and enforce law and order. A weak state will not be able to raise funds, attract investment, or prevent public spending from ending up in the hands of corrupt politicians. In other words, a strong state is an economic resource. One could almost view the state as an economic enterprise that produces protection and security for its citizens, a kind of legitimate racketeer.[6]

At the close of the nineteenth century those unable to adapt, such as the Ottoman Empire, suffered a lengthy decay before their inevitable collapse. Others, such as the Chinese Empire, were repeatedly humiliated by arrogant foreigners before collapsing as well. Those who adapted, such as Japan, became major powers.

Traditions might be defended or invented to justify the new – a pretence at which the British and the Japanese excelled. The purpose was not to slow down or impede the march of progress but to reassure all and sundry that change would not be traumatic. And progress could be measured in one way only: the extent to which one had moved away from pre-industrialism into the exciting new world of capitalism; for of all the desirable and defining traits associated with modernity, an industrialized capitalist economy was the most obvious.

Other traits, such as a corresponding legal system and an efficient state, what Marx called the *Überbau*, 'the superstructure' – a term he only used in the few pages of his 1859 Preface to *Zur Kritik der Politischen Ökonomie* – were key factors that made industrialization possible. It is difficult to imagine sustained industrialization and economic growth without a properly functioning state. Even the neo-liberal programme known as the Washington Consensus, which became so famous in the 1980s, included major political factors such as fiscal discipline, strong property rights, privatization, and competitive exchange rates.[7] Neo-liberals too require an efficient state. However, as Adam Przeworski put it, it is naive to assume that once the central elements of the neo-liberal programme are in place, 'manna will fall from heaven'.[8] And, in any case, one kick-starts industrialization, historically speaking, with little democracy and few civil rights. Stalin's Soviet Union achieved a remarkable degree of industrialization without the whiff of an independent judiciary, or clear property rights, or an independent central bank – let alone democracy – though the eventual outcome was not a success. South Korea and Taiwan grew rapidly in the 1960s, 1970s, and 1980s under the aegis of dictatorships. Chinese economic growth since 1980 owes absolutely nothing to the prescriptions of the International Monetary Fund, the US Treasury, the World Bank (which eventually abandoned its attachment to the 'consensus'), *The Wall Street Journal*, *The Economist*, or any form of 'shock therapy' (sudden liberalization) à la Russia.[9] In fact, any attraction the so-called Western model may have had has no hold on the Chinese elites.[10] The same can be said about the economic success of Japan, or the Four Asian Tigers (Hong Kong, Singapore, Taiwan, and South Korea) in the 1960s and 1970s, which was kick-started by state protectionism. Even the axiom that clearly defined property rights are essential to development does not seem to apply to China, where the successful TVEs (Township and Village Enterprises) in the 1970s and 1980s were a kind of hybrid of municipal enterprises and cooperatives with an unfocused structure and without clear property rights.[11] Control here, unlike in the former communist economies of the USSR and eastern Europe, was in the hands of the regional governments. The more the process involved the regions, the more successful was the development process.[12] The countries that industrialized in the nineteenth century, and Britain that industrialized in the late eighteenth and early nineteenth centuries, would have failed the Washington Consensus test.[13] More recently, countries that followed the Washington Consensus, such as many Latin American ones, did not grow as fast as those that did not, such as China.[14]

Yet many social scientists cannot resist proposing a universally applicable model. Distinguished economists such as William J. Baumol and his colleagues, for instance, writing in 2007, explained that the main elements required for 'a well-oiled entrepreneurial economy' were a well-functioning financial system, flexible labour markets, property rights, and incentives for entrepreneurs – elements that seldom co-existed in the most rapidly developing economies at the time of writing.[15] Nor was it clear how to define a 'well-functioning financial system', since what seemed to be functioning in 2007, for example, did not look so good on 15 September 2008, when Lehman Brothers collapsed (the largest financial bankruptcy in American history).

In reality, the application of particular formulae depends not only on the will of decision-makers but, far more importantly, on the way a particular country is inserted into the global economy. Thus small countries are more likely to reform their labour markets if they are exposed to international competition, which explains why such labour-market reforms were promulgated far more energetically in smaller countries such as Finland, Denmark, Sweden, New Zealand, and Ireland than in larger economies such as France or Germany.[16] In the United Kingdom labour-market rigidities had been far more determined by trade unions than by the legislation, which is why as trade union power decreased, labour markets became more flexible.

The first road to capitalism had been the British one, and this might explain why, at the end of the nineteenth century, most liberals wanted to follow the United Kingdom. This was all the more alluring since Britain was rich and powerful and freer than other countries – the delicious combination of civil rights (for many) and wealth (for some) seemed proof that there are times when one can have one's cake and eat it. However, on the continent and in the United States, most liberals were vigorous proponents of the strong state. Liberals such as the influential German economist Friedrich List (*The National System of Political Economy*, 1841) promoted national progress and the advance of capitalism – but not laissez-faire or the 'free' markets of the British. What mattered above all was industry. He wrote:

> A purely agricultural nation cannot develop to a high degree its home and foreign trade, its communications, its shipping; it cannot increase its prosperity as its population increases; it cannot make sensible progress in its moral intellectual, social and political culture; it cannot acquire great political power; it cannot exercise any important influence over the civilization and progress of less advanced nations; nor can it found colonies . . .[17]

And to develop industry, it was necessary, at least initially, to protect one's economy by stopping foreign competition. The key was the state and not just any state but a strong state:

> the activity of individuals is powerless to preserve the commerce, industry, and wealth of a State, if the general conditions of society are not favourable; and if individuals do not owe the greatest part of their productive power to the political organization, and to the power of the country in which they reside.[18]

List lambasted what he called 'the cosmopolitan school' (i.e. Adam Smith, David Ricardo, Jean-Baptiste Say, and their followers) for three essential errors: firstly, 'a chimerical cosmopolitanism which does not comprehend nationality and which has no regard for national interests'; secondly, 'a dead materialism which regards everywhere the exchangeable value of things'; and, thirdly, a 'disorganizing' individualism which, 'disregarding the nature of social labour . . . depicts individual industry as it would develop itself if unrestrained in society, that is with the whole human family, were it not separated into different nations'.[19] Between the individual and mankind, he explained, there is the nation with its particular language and history and origins. It is through the nation that the individual acquires civility. Some nations were barely civilized; the task of political economists was to help them out of their predicament. Adam Smith's 'school', Friedrich List went on:

> has admitted as realized a state of things to come. It presupposes the existence of universal association and perpetual peace, and from it infers the great benefits of free trade . . . History proves that political union always precedes commercial union . . . In the actual state of the world, free trade would bring forth, instead of a community of nations, the universal subjection of nations to the supremacy of the greater powers in manufactures, commerce, and navigation.[20]

List overestimated the extent to which the doctrine of laissez-faire was held by the classical economists of the British school. This is not surprising, since Adam Smith, David Ricardo, and others are generally credited with the theoretical ancestry of today's neo-liberals, even though considerable scholarship has been expended in trying to rescue Adam Smith from their over-enthusiastic embraces. The concept of 'an invisible hand' – for which Smith became famous and infamous – is mentioned only three times in his entire oeuvre.[21] In *The Wealth of Nations*, the concept is mentioned once; the context is the unflattering description of the entrepreneur as a self-absorbed and largely unconscious operator able to see only his own narrow interest:

> He generally . . . neither intends to promote the public interest, nor knows how much he is promoting it . . . and he is in this, as in many other cases, led by an invisible hand to promote an end which was no part of his intention . . . By pursuing his own interest, he frequently promotes that of the society more effectually than when he really intends to promote it. I have never known much good done by those who affected to trade for the public good.[22]

As Donald Winch explained, this contrast between 'the private intentions or the professed aims of individuals' and 'the unintended social or public consequences' of their actions (and not an alleged celebration of individualism, as present-day neo-liberals claim) enabled Smith and his successors (including Karl Marx) to analyse a commercial world, that of capitalism, 'characterized by impersonal and anonymous relationships'.[23] Smith was far from being an unwavering supporter of 'capitalists'. Nor did he think that individualism was the basis of capitalism. In fact, he regarded capitalism as a cooperative system. This was the main point of his examination of the division of labour in *The Wealth of Nations*.

Adam Smith, as a good liberal, was particularly alarmed by the possibility of industrialists banding together to fix prices and advocated some form of state regulation. 'People of the same trade,' he wrote, 'seldom meet together, even for merriment and diversion, but the conversation ends in a conspiracy against the public, or in some contrivance to raise prices.' Regulation (what today we would call anti-trust legislation), he admitted, might be difficult but nothing should be done to encourage such practices.[24]

Smith was unaware that an industrial society was about to erupt and drive the whole of the country. Nor did he think that societies could grow for ever. In fact, he thought China had already reached the end goal: 'China seems to have been long stationary, and had, probably, long ago acquired that full complement of riches which is consistent with the nature of its laws and institutions.'[25] This is not such a surprising view if we consider that China, in 1820, had the highest share of world GDP: 32.9 per cent.[26]

Adam Smith, however, was a staunch opponent of 'mercantilism' or protectionism, a state policy aimed at promoting (and protecting) one's own state economy at the expense of that of other states – the very same policy Friedrich List would later propound, though for List protectionism was a step to allow one's economy to grow, not a permanent policy. And List was right to highlight Smith's 'cosmopolitanism', since Smith himself was aware of the potentially cosmopolitan nature of capitalists. The fundamental difference between the owner of land and the owner of stock, in his view, was that the former is a citizen of the country, whereas 'the proprietor of stock is properly a citizen of the world and is not necessarily attached to any particular country'.[27] We can easily recognize today's financial operators in this characterization of a new cosmopolitan class of rich *déracinés* who, as the novelist Marina Lewycka put it in her *Various Pets Alive and Dead*, are a 'young high-flying free-floating no-baggage global elite, whose title is wealth, whose passport is brains, whose only nation is money'.[28]

Adam Smith, like many university professors, did not like or admire capitalists – whom he called dealers or manufacturers or merchants. He never used the word 'capitalist' (though the term was in use, notably in the works of Jean-Baptiste Say) and preferred the term 'commercial society' to 'capitalism', just as Marx never used the term *kapitalismus* in *Das Kapital* (though he used the term 'capitalist mode of production').[29] Smith was critical of a state that cravenly complied with the wishes of manufacturers. In Book I of *The Nature and Causes of the Wealth of Nations* (1776), he wrote that the interests of merchants 'is always in some respects different from, and even opposite to, that of the public. To widen the market, and narrow the competition, is always in the interest of the dealers.'[30] In fact, markets, far from adjusting to change automatically, if unchecked, would lead to monopolies:

> The constant view of such companies is always to raise the rate of their own profit as high as they can; to keep the market, both for the goods which they export, and for those which they import, as much understocked as they can; which can be done only by restraining the competition, or by discouraging new adventurers from entering into the trade.[31]

The point of the economy was not profit. Consumption, the goal of the consumer, is the sole end and purpose of all production. As he wrote in *The Wealth of Nations*:

> The maxim is so perfectly self-evident, that it would be absurd to attempt to prove it. But in the mercantile system, the interest of the consumer is almost constantly sacrificed to that of the producer; and it seems to consider production, and not consumption, as the ultimate end and object of all industry and commerce.[32]

This principle was echoed by John Maynard Keynes, 160 years later, in his *General Theory of Employment, Interest, and Money*, when, having asserted that 'All production is for the purpose of ultimately satisfying a consumer', he added that 'Consumption – to repeat the obvious – is the sole end and object of all economic activity.'[33]

The centrality of consumption in Adam Smith was well known even among non-economists. The poet Pushkin in the 1830s writes of his rather shallow anti-hero Yevgeny Onegin that 'he rated Adam Smith highly':

> Who knew it all: how states exist,
> How to transform them, make them wealthy,
> And why they have no need of gold
> If they have things that can be sold.[34]

Although an economic liberal, Smith was aware of the circumstances where only government policy could prevent or ameliorate human suffering and situations where government intervention was necessary to protect the most disadvantaged.[35] He allowed for numerous exceptions to the rule of non-interference by the state in the economy: public works, such as roads and bridges, were better performed by the state; new domestic industries could be protected from foreign competition, at least until they developed (the so-called infant industry argument, though the term was not used by Smith); states should also regulate the currency, and use taxes to modify behaviour, for example levying taxes on harmful alcoholic drinks, such as hard liquor, to encourage the consumption of less damaging ones, such as beer.[36] He certainly did not like capitalists, much preferring 'the small proprietor' who 'knows every part of his little territory, views it with all the affection which property, especially small property, naturally inspires, and who . . . is generally of all improvers the most industrious, the most intelligent, and the most successful'.[37]

In spite of such views and social concerns, for most of the nineteenth century (and even more now) Adam Smith was regarded as an intransigent supporter of laissez-faire and described by people like Friedrich List as the champion of absolute free markets. But he was not, and nor were other pillars of eighteenth- and nineteenth-century British liberalism, such as David Hume, Jeremy Bentham, David Ricardo, and John Stuart Mill, who today we would call 'neo-liberals'. Hume, in an essay written in 1752, departed somewhat from the principles of free trade:

> All taxes, however, upon foreign commodities, are not so regarded as prejudicial or useless, but those only which are founded on the jealousy above mentioned. A tax on German linen encourages home manufacturers, and thereby multiplies our people and industry. A tax on brandy increases the sale of rum, and supports our southern colonies.[38]

John Stuart Mill, in *Principles of Political Economy* (1848), thought that the 'necessary functions of government' were 'considerably more multifarious than most people are at first aware of'.[39] He listed as exceptions to the rule of laissez-faire: education, poor relief, hospitals, various public services, the limitation of the hours of work, and the regulations of the conditions of work.[40]

Edmund Burke had been more restrictive. In a memorandum for Prime Minister William Pitt in November 1795 (published posthumously in 1800) he wrote that one of the key problems of law-making was to determine 'What the State ought to take upon itself to direct by the public wisdom, and what it ought to leave, with as little interference as possible, to individual discretion.'[41] This is a famous passage, a little misquoted by John Maynard Keynes in 'The End of Laissez-Faire' (1926).[42] The fuller context of Edmund Burke's memorandum contains a rosier picture of Great Britain than others had sought to present, that of 'one nation' – to use an expression coined later – 'united in prosperity':

> The consideration of this ought to bind us all, rich and poor together, against those wicked writers of the newspapers who would inflame the poor against their friends, guardians, patrons, and protectors. Not only very few . . . have actually died of want, but we have seen no traces of those dreadful exterminating epidemics which, in consequence of scanty

> and unwholesome food, in former times not infrequently wasted whole nations. Let us be saved from too much wisdom of our own, and we shall do tolerably well.

Having set the context Burke sought to establish the limits of state interference:

> the state ought to confine itself to what regards the state or the creatures of the state: namely, the exterior establishment of its religion; its magistracy; its revenue; its military force by sea and land; the corporations that owe their existence to its fiat; in a word, to everything that is *truly and properly* public, to the public peace, to the public safety, to the public order, to the public prosperity . . . Statesmen who know themselves will . . . proceed only in this the superior orb and first mover of their duty, steadily, vigilantly, severely, courageously . . . They ought to know the different departments of things – what belongs to laws, and what manners alone can regulate.[43]

But that was in 1795 and the words were those of a leading member of the conservative wing of the Whigs. When the state is in the hands of one's opponent, when it is an oppressive force, when one is a revolutionary, then the idea of an end to the state is somewhat appealing. Thus Tom Paine, towards the beginning of his *Common Sense* (1776), declared 'Society in every state is a blessing, but Government, even in its best state, is but a necessary evil; in its worst state an intolerable one.'[44] Friedrich Engels looked forward to the withering away of the state under communism: 'the government of persons is replaced by the administration of things . . . The state is not "abolished", it withers away.'[45] Lenin reiterated this semi-utopian concept in *State and Revolution* in August 1917, before the actual Bolshevik seizure of power in October. But when one is in power or close to power the priority for government becomes, as Keynes, pragmatically and perhaps wisely, declared, 'not to do things which individuals are doing already . . . but to do things which at present are not done at all'.[46]

To find in Britain a true advocate of the minimalist state after 1860 one has to go to the tough-talking libertarian 'philosopher' Herbert Spencer. It was he who coined the expression 'the survival of the fittest' (often wrongly attributed to Darwin): 'This survival of the fittest, which I have here sought to express in mechanical terms, is that which Mr. Darwin has called "natural selection or the preservation of favoured races in the struggle for life".'[47] Spencer's anti-statism would sound today somewhat eccentric, loved only by dogmatic ultra-libertarians.

So extreme was Spencer that he held the view that the state should not step in to help prevent epidemics. One should not take it for granted, he explained in *The Man versus the State* (originally published in *Contemporary Review* in 1884), 'that all suffering ought to be prevented, which is not true: much suffering is curative, and prevention of it is prevention of a remedy'.[48] In his days he was regarded as one of the great social thinkers of his age. In 1891 the Scottish philosopher David George Ritchie, in the midst of a tirade against Spencer, felt obliged to admit that 'Mr. Spencer is perhaps the most formidable intellectual foe with whom the New Radicalism has to reckon.'[49]

Ritchie thought, like many modern liberals as well as sensible people, that one should defend good government against bad government and not be against government in principle.[50] Spencer did not have such problems: helping the poor is bad, always. His thought, such as it was, was admirably suited to the American scene in the late nineteenth century, since it sounded scientific and comprehensive. In the America of the 1880s it was impossible to be active in the social sciences and political philosophy without mastering Spencer.[51] In France between 1871 and 1881 he was the most popular author in the *Revue scientifique* and more than twenty articles of his were published in the *Revue philosophique*.[52] In Italy the new positivist thinkers read him avidly, particularly those such as Cesare Lombroso, Achille Loria, and Enrico Ferri, associated with the *Sinistra storica* (the Historic Left), politically in the ascendant.[53] In China, Westernizers like Yan Fu (who translated Spencer) were full of admiration.[54] In Japan, most of the builders of the new Meiji state were dazzled by his system-building prowess.[55] Between 1877 and 1900 more than thirty of his works were translated into Japanese; Japanese readers were particularly interested in his views on progress and individual rights.[56] In 1885 the Arabic science journal *Al-Muqtataf* called Spencer 'one of the greatest philosophers of the age'.[57] In Mexico he was more influential than Auguste Comte.[58] In Australia the politician Bruce Smith, in his appropriately named *Liberty and Liberalism: A protest against the growing tendency towards undue interference by the state, with individual liberty, private enterprise and the rights of property* (1887), included many respectful references to Spencer's works.

But the positive judgement of his contemporaries did not outlast Spencer. The peak of his fame was reached in the 1870s and 1880s.[59] During his lifetime he and his supporters in the Liberty and Property League were regarded as a little extreme, while his *The Man versus the State* (1884) was an embarrassment to moderate individualists.[60] Today

Spencer's expression, 'the survival of the fittest', is commonly attributed to Darwin while Spencer himself is virtually forgotten and mostly unread. His views apparently were not fit enough to survive in the marketplace of ideas.

The authentic laissez-faire liberals had fought their battle somewhat earlier, in the 1840s and 1850s. They had started from the simple assumption that the freedom of the individual was the foundation of the 'good' social order. Their most exemplary champions were reformers of the so-called Manchester School, whose main proponents were Richard Cobden and John Bright (for whom, in any case, free trade mattered far more than laissez-faire). They and their counterparts elsewhere favoured a minimalist state that would limit itself to law and order and the enforcement of contracts, though even they accepted the case for some regulation of the labour market, especially in matters of child labour and public goods, such as road maintenance and the preservation of forests.

While strict liberal economics was widely acclaimed, it was never put into effect. Politics, even in England, compelled pragmatic liberals to acknowledge that such ideas could not be defended with excessive vigour. The most august political representative of laissez-faire liberalism, William Gladstone, became, when Prime Minister, an advocate of limited state interventionism and social reformism.

Thus by the second half of the nineteenth century, non-interventionist liberalism was being questioned even in Britain. Liberals such as John Stuart Mill claimed that there were circumstances in which human improvement (progress) and protection of individual rights required interference with private property. Mill's posthumously published *Chapters on Socialism* contained a passionate attack on the iniquities of the capitalist system, the idleness of the rich, and the miserable conditions of the working classes. Although he accepted the idea of profit and competition, he claimed that the aim of production should be the common good, and the means of production be held in common. From the 1880s onwards a new breed of liberalism was stalking Britain: the 'New Liberalism'. By the 1880s laissez-faire 'had been definitively abandoned by the liberal mainstream and socialism in its general ethical sense had become part of the liberal terminology'.[61] Henry Sidgwick in his *Elements of Politics* (1891) tried to put forward a moderate individualism by listing the things that should be done by the state: protection of children, enforcement of professional standards, disease control, making certain types of information available.[62] And in 1883 the *Pall Mall Gazette* lamented that 'even the liberals speak of laissez-faire with scorn'.[63]

Sidney Webb, in an article in 1892, pointed out that adhesion to laissez-faire had become the prerogative of only one faction of the Liberal Party grouped around Gladstone, whose idea of social reforms was that they should enable some members of the lower classes to become small capitalists and not, as the trade unions wanted, to 'raise the social condition of the class itself'.[64] Within the party, however, continued Webb, there was emerging a radical 'collectivist' faction whose new principle was that 'the best Government is that which can safely and advantageously administer most'.[65] The struggle between the old fashioned laissez-faire Manchester Liberals and the new radicals, Webb pointed out, was at the heart of the difficulties of modern liberalism: 'the citadel of individualist Liberalism is being besieged on all sides by the Labour forces'.[66]

Economic liberalism in mid-nineteenth-century Britain had meant, in practical terms, the abolition of the Corn Laws (thereby lowering the price of imported foodstuffs and containing labour costs). This was achieved in 1846. It was British liberalism's greatest victory.

The liberal state was soon also expected to safeguard savings (and hence financial institutions) and the stability of the currency (to protect savers), to refrain from interfering in disputes between wage workers and capitalists (though in practice it often did and often on the side of the capitalists), and to uphold some welfare principles, such as social insurance, particularly if the costs were to be borne by the employers. Many liberals were prepared to countenance some protectionism. Most businessmen are not, contrary to popular belief, 'natural' liberals. Their inclination is towards order and peace. They tend to be anxious and feel vulnerable, understandably so since they seldom know what is going to happen next. When they wave the banner of liberalism, they do so not out of ideology but in defence of their interests. As for state intervention, there never was a united opposition to it by the business community, for it is in the nature of such a 'community' to have relatively few common interests except the enforcement (by the state) of the political framework that makes their existence possible. It is pretty obvious that even the most ideological of neo-liberal capitalists expect the state in which they live to safeguard credit, not to use inflation to decrease public debt, and not to default on debt, though states, of course, have occasionally been forced into such policies.

Politicians understood this well. In a speech on 28 April 1885, Joseph Chamberlain, then still a Liberal and still a minister in Gladstone's government, enumerated the main social evils of the time whose solution, he thought, could only come from government:

> Children are stunted in their growth and dulled in their intellects for want of proper nourishment . . . The ordinary conditions of life among a large proportion of the population are such that common decency is absolutely impossible; and all this goes on in sight of the mansions of the rich . . . in presence of wasteful extravagance.
>
> Government is only the organisation of the whole people for the benefits of all its members, and that the community may – ay, and ought to – provide for all its members benefits which it is impossible for individuals to provide by their solidarity and separate efforts . . . It is only the community acting as a whole that can possibly deal with evils so deep-seated as those to which I have referred.[67]

Far from favouring 'small government', the Victorians systematically intervened in all areas of public and private life, and not just in those such as morality that the term 'Victorian values' suggests. The extent of Victorian social legislation was impressive (see Chapters 14 and 15).

Interventionism was even more popular in Germany where prominent intellectuals had taken on board Friedrich List's prescriptions and, by the beginning of the 1870s, when Germany was being consolidated as a unitary state, became concerned with social reforms in favour of the working classes. Labelled ironically *Kathedersozialisten* (socialists in academic chairs) by their opponents, members of the so-called German Historical School of Economics and the *Verein für Socialpolitik* (Social Policy Association), founded in 1872, led by Gustav von Schmoller, Adolph Wagner, and Étienne Laspeyres, were almost unanimously critical of the so-called British school (Adam Smith, David Ricardo, etc.), whom they regarded as unreconstructed laissez-faire liberals. Schmoller regularly attacked the perceived inadequacies of the school's contemporary followers because they could not explain the social problems of the 1890s, the new forms of business enterprises, or the unintended consequences of competition.[68] Lujo Brentano, another leading German *Kathedersozialisten*, founded in 1900 the International Association for Labour Legislation, a precursor of the International Labour Organization, and advocated a high-wage and short-hours economy, though he was unenthusiastic about an eight-hour day throughout the country.[69]

Capitalism had been developing in Germany before unification, due in part to the pro-business legislation promulgated by some of the German states in the 1850s and 1860s. This had enhanced the confidence of industrialists and created the climate for industrial development after unification: state-sponsored railways, chemical, electrical, and optic industries. Many landlords had started running their estates along capitalist lines.[70]

'Bourgeois' radicals, à la *Kathedersozialisten*, and assorted intellectual groups who regarded robust interventionism as the only road towards industrialization and who defined themselves as 'modern', emerged throughout Europe: in Britain the Fabian Society; in Spain those known as the *generación del 98*, who lamented the loss of Spain's colonies while urging their countrymen to move forward (see Chapter 11); in Austria the fearless public intellectual Karl Kraus, who used his journal *Fackel* to attack German nationalism (as he had attacked and mocked Theodor Herzl's Zionism), liberal economics, and almost everything he regarded as hypocritical (which was almost everything); in Bohemia 'the Realists' led by Tomáš Masaryk, soon to join the Young Czech Party (1891); in Romania the socialist group around Constantin Dobrogeanu-Gherea (originally Solomon Katz), who realized the limited hopes of a socialist movement in an agrarian country; and in Hungary the Society for the Social Sciences around the journal *Huszadik Század*, which sought to introduce its readers to emergent 'modern' ideas such as positivism and Marxism.[71]

The Italian counterpart of these movements consisted mostly of members of the southern liberal positivist intelligentsia, the so-called *meridionalisti*. They denounced socialism ('the main enemy'), but realized that pure laissez-faire would not resolve the miserable conditions of existence of the southern peasantry. Alongside southern intellectuals such as Pasquale Villari, Giustino Fortunato, and Francesco Saverio Nitti, there were also those such as Luigi Luzzatti (briefly Prime Minister, 1910–11), grouped around the Padua-based *Il giornale degli economisti* (also followers of the German *Kathedersozialisten*).[72] The rhetorical commitment to liberalism (and positivism) of the Italian press, the urban bourgeoisie, and the intelligentsia gives a distorted image of the real ideology of the *meridionalisti* and their northern allies. The liberating energies of free capitalism were never seen as the remedy to prevailing social problems. Consequently, the Italian state resorted, alternatively, to two distinct strategies: the stick of repression and centralization, wielded chiefly by Francesco Crispi (Prime Minister, 1887–91, 1893–6), and the carrot of consensus and mediation, embraced above all by Giovanni Giolitti, Prime Minister for most of the period 1903 to 1914.

The Italian elites were correspondingly divided. The northern military elites as well as the southern landowning gentry were indifferent to or afraid of industrialization, negative towards the rise of a large proletariat, and frightened by the idea of modernity. But there was also a less blinkered elite of professionals, intellectuals, and entrepreneurs who wanted Italy to be more like the 'advanced' countries of Europe – Britain, France, or Germany. After the so-called liberal *Sinistra storica* (historic left) won the election in 1876, the suffrage, until then uncommonly narrow, was expanded. In the event, the *Sinistra storica* was not enormously different from the preceding conservative *Destra storica* (historic right).[73] As Antonio Gramsci wrote in his *Prison Notebooks*, 'The left succeeded in being only a safety valve. It largely continued the policies of the right with the personnel and the words of the left.'[74] The 'left', though, was a little more progressive and anticlerical than the 'right'. While the left defended the interests of the commercial and industrial bourgeoisie, it also recognized that the poor could present a threat unless the state did something for them, wanted to work for greater harmony between the classes, and believed that class conflict belonged to the proto-industrial past or, at least, to backward or early capitalism.[75]

The *Sinistra storica* was unlucky: its advent to power coincided with the initial phase of the so-called Long Depression of 1873 to 1896. This is probably why it abandoned gradually any attachment to liberal economics it might have had. The incompetence of the Italian bourgeoisie forced the state to take the initiative in promoting growth, helped by the military elites (including the monarchy), who had finally understood that international prestige required economic growth. This, in addition to the costs of national unification and the debts inherited from pre-unification states, meant that the country had a significant public debt, so much so that a French journalist called his account of contemporary Italy, *Voyage au pays du déficit*: 'Bankruptcies are followed by bankruptcies; catastrophe leads to a further ten catastrophes; from every side all one can hear is wailing and gnashing of teeth.'[76] Inevitably, there were also a considerable number of financial scandals involving public funds.[77]

The negative view of the Italian bourgeoisie, unable and unwilling to perform what was supposed to be its historic task – the task of modernization and industrialization – ran like a leitmotif in Italian political thought, from Gramsci and Giolitti to Fascist thinkers such as Nello Quilici, who wrote in 1930 that, unlike in France and Great Britain, in Italy the bourgeoisie lives in fear of change and modernity, which is why it surrendered without resistance to Fascism: 'it thought only of its wallet'.[78]

There were, of course, genuine obstacles to industrialization: Italy was long and thin, mountainous, with limited natural resources and a restricted home market. It was only around 1890, when the international economic situation began to improve and a new style of economic management emerged under the influence of Giovanni Giolitti, the dominant political personality of the pre-war years, that a period of innovation and industrialization ensued, thanks to state intervention. The state regulated the railways, guaranteeing their profitability, and entrusted the management to private groups for a period of twenty years. Soon even the iron and steel industries, regarded by entrepreneurs as a highly speculative and risky venture, came to be guaranteed by the state.[79]

The state busied itself with the most varied tasks throughout Europe. A pre-existing centralist tradition had enabled Napoleon III and his prefect, Baron Haussmann, to increase the sewage system fivefold in Paris, resulting in virtually every street in Paris being connected to it while, above ground, there was a regular system of street cleaning and refuse collection: 'Paris soon became the envy of the civilized world' with more street cleaners than those of London and Berlin.[80]

French liberals were occasionally pragmatic. Even Paul Leroy-Beaulieu, the ultra-liberal French economist (albeit pro-colonialist), faced with the chronically low rate of birth of the French, suggested, in his pro-natalist *La question de la population* (1913), that those with larger families (i.e. those with three or four children) should be given priority when applying for public-sector jobs.[81]

Nevertheless, the real advocates of laissez-faire in the nineteenth century were French rather than British, people like Jean-Baptiste Say, one of the few economists who was also an entrepreneur, Frédéric Bastiat, and Léon Walras, who elaborated a general equilibrium theory (the doctrine that markets collectively will tend to equilibrium). The tone of these French intellectuals (unlike that of French politicians) was far more ideological than that of British economists. The British were writing in a society that was breaking all previous economic boundaries and pragmatism tempered their liberalism. The French, on the other hand, regarded themselves as economic laggards burdened by the weight of over two centuries of centralism – a red line of continuity that linked Jean-Baptiste Colbert, Louis XIV's Finance Minister, to the Jacobin revolution and beyond.

Frédéric Bastiat was later referred to by Karl Marx, writing in his incandescent mode, as 'the most superficial . . . representative of the apologetic of vulgar economy', a 'modern bagman of free trade', and 'a dwarf economist . . . truly comical'.[82] Keynes called him 'the most extravagant and rhapsodical expression of the political economist's religion'.[83] Around 1848, Bastiat founded an association modelled on the Anti-Corn Law League of Richard Cobden and John Bright, but he far surpassed them in his distaste for the state. In his *Harmonies économiques*, published in 1850 (the year of his death), he complained that private services were being converted into public ones, that the government was 'confiscating' (i.e. taxing) over one-third of the income of its citizens, making the law an instrument of spoliation. He observed, with dismay, that the government had proclaimed itself to be a universal force – today we would say totalitarian. It is surprising, he added, that revolutions were not more frequent.[84] What should governments do? For Bastiat, not much: defence, public security ('defending our freedom'), and administering common property (such as forests and roads). Beyond this every government intervention was an injustice.[85] Nor, he added, could one ever say that the state provides a 'free' service, such as education (neither free nor compulsory in mid-nineteenth-century France). Someone, somewhere pays, he explained, pre-empting contemporary ultra-libertarians by more than 150 years, many of whom, such as the 'anarcho-capitalist' Murray Rothbard, worshipped him. In bypassing the market, Bastiat wrote, the state gives everyone the same product whether they want it or not, regardless of individual preferences.[86] He defended himself against critics who, he wrote, accused him of being heartless, since he praised the market while 'before our eyes there is suffering, misery, the proletariat, pauperism, children being abandoned, malnutrition, crime, inequalities', only stating when faced with a sick society, '*Laissez-faire, laissez-passer; tout est pour le mieux dans le meilleur des mondes possibles.*' His defensive riposte (invoking Leibniz and Voltaire) was 'We see evil just as our opponents do but have a different solution.'[87] The solution was the minimalist state.

In Belgium, liberals of the same ilk, huddling together around journals such as *L'Économiste belge* and its editor Gustave de Molinari, also claimed that it was not the business of the state to ensure that virtue should reign on earth, that social inequalities were indispensable. For such inequalities enabled the accumulation of wealth whereas social equality would generate social misery.[88] De Molinari even went as far as suggesting that law and order could be privatized and subject to the laws of the market.[89] By 1880, fifty years after the creation of the Belgian state, its self-satisfied bourgeoisie was completely in charge.[90] Led by Walthère Frère-Orban, the Belgian liberals were distinguished by an unremitting economic liberalism, a strong anticlericalism, a reluctance to aid the colonial policies of the king, and a profound distaste for the expansion of the suffrage. It was, however, the beginning of the end for Belgian Liberals. In 1884 the surprising victory of the Catholic Party, coupled with the advance of the socialists, put paid to their hegemony. The expansion of the suffrage further strengthened the Catholics (as well as the socialists). All the while, Belgium continued its industrial economic growth, prosperity reaching wider groups in the population and the ultra-liberalism of its first decades giving way to social legislation, while capitalism became more and more concentrated. In other words, the country became both more capitalist and more 'collectivist'.[91]

The other great national bastion of economic liberalism was in a country even more laggard than France: Austria. The so-called 'Austrian School' (a term then used pejoratively by German academics) was led by Carl Menger, whose *Principles of Economics* (1871) inspired some of the most important free-market champions of the twentieth century: Eugene von Böhm-Baker, Ludwig von Mises and, above all, Friedrich Hayek. But even Carl Menger was not quite as much against state interference as some of his followers made him out to be.

As is often the case, the more intransigent advocates of ultra-liberalism were not cautious academics but popular writers and journalists, people such as James Wilson (the first editor of *The Economist*, 1843–59) and Harriet Martineau (who, however, accepted numerous exceptions to laissez-faire).[92] They preached a simplistic version of economic liberalism – one that John Stuart Mill, writing on Martineau, thought was a little over the top, though it 'possesses considerable merit'.[93]

Unlike journalists, academic economists knew that life was complicated and were keeping their distance from authentic laissez-faire. As John Maynard Keynes explained later, revisiting these debates in his essay 'The End of Laissez-Faire', most leading economists, far from upholding the doctrine of laissez-faire, directed their attention 'to the elucidation of the leading cases in which private interest and social interest were not harmonious', while still retaining the traditional assumption that:

> the ideal distribution of productive resources can be brought about through individuals acting independently by the method of trial and error in such a way that those individuals who move in the right direction will destroy by competition those who move in the wrong direction.[94]

As for politicians and state functionaries, even the liberals tended to be interventionists, for it was (and is) difficult for them to declare that 'nothing can be done' without talking themselves out of a job. Pro-interventionism was especially prominent in France where the liberal Republicans who controlled the National Assembly after 1880 systematically strengthened the economic powers of the state. State interventionism had already began in earnest earlier, with the launch in 1878 of the Freycinet Plan (Charles de Freycinet was then Minister for Public Works; later he became Prime Minister) to ensure the development of the railways either by directly subsidizing private enterprise or by the state investing directly in railroad construction.[95]

In the United States too the federal government was a key factor in the original impetus for railways, providing capital as well as a protective legal environment that shielded the companies from the consequences of poor judgement and corruption. As William G. Roy explained: 'It is difficult to imagine that the railroad companies could have been built as extensively or as quickly without vast government support.'[96]

This was also the case in Russia. The key role in Russian economic growth was played by the state with the significant help of foreign banks.[97] In the 1860s and 1870s private rail companies had been state subsidized with negative consequences: rampant speculation and abuse by private companies increased debt and general incompetence. This led even those deeply committed to private initiative, like Nikolai Bunge, later Minister of Finance and then Prime Minister under Alexander III, to advocate nationalization and state management of the railways.[98]

French state functionaries (and politicians) had studied their economics at the feet of liberal academics but, once in charge of the state machine, they used it – sometimes energetically, sometimes reluctantly. Convinced that, theoretically, state intervention was wrong, even when the result seemed advantageous to all – as with the railways – they resolved the conundrum by granting the monopoly to a private company.[99] Of course, when the economy was in trouble, as it was during the Long Depression, liberal principles were further downplayed and French public subsidies to the private sector were, in the period 1873 to 1895, four times greater than in the years 1850 to 1873.[100]

Capitalism had become *the* economic form of organization of the nation state, regardless of what theorists claimed. Any improvement in consumption, in France as elsewhere, was attributed to the economic policies of the state, even when the state was only indirectly responsible. When things did not go well, it was the state and politicians who were blamed, even if they had little to do with it (for instance if international prices changed). The destinies of politics (the state) and capitalism were (and continue to be) irrevocably bound up together.

The interconnectedness between state and economy – between 'our' state and 'our' economy – had by then become quite evident. Even today when the word 'globalization' is on every opinion-maker's lips, there is not a single government in the world that does not regard one of its main duties – probably its *main* duty – to be that of managing 'its' economy. No international organization, not even the European Union, has come near to establishing the kind of control and rules that the nation state still deploys. Our world is one of nation states, advancing not towards a global state but towards a global system of states.

Strengthening the state inevitably involved expanding the bureaucracy and hence the number of state functionaries whose commitment towards the state was due not only to loyalty but also to personal self-interest in the security of their jobs. Of course state-dependent personnel have existed for a long time: soldiers, officers, tax collectors, scribes, monks, and priests are ancient figures, but they were never either so numerous or so closely dependent. China, at the beginning of the Christian era, already had over 130,000 bureaucrats (in a population of roughly 60 million), most of whom had been selected by competitive examination.[101] But this was only 0.21 per cent of the population; the OECD average is today 15 per cent. In the West, bureaucracy was highly undeveloped at least until the nineteenth century. The growth of bureaucracies is a twentieth-century phenomenon that originated in the nineteenth century. Large states for obvious reasons require bureaucracies, particularly when their diversity involves a policy of cooptation of groups (a form of glorified bribery). Thus when the *Ausgleich* or Compromise of 1867 established Hungary as a nation within the Austrian Empire (which changed its name to the Austro-Hungarian Empire), and Francis Joseph became King of Hungary, as well as Emperor of Austria, and when Hungary became virtually self-administered, a bureaucratic class of significant proportion arose, doubling in size between 1890 and 1910. By 1914 the Hungarian public sector employed 3.5 per cent of the labour force, three times the number of Britain's civil servants and more than twice the number in Germany. The economy remained backward, and the more backward it was the more public-sector jobs were created to appease the job-seeking sons of the middle and lower middle classes.[102] Of course, these figures pale into insignificance when compared with those of today's advanced states. In the years 2000 to 2008 the public sector (government plus public corporations) employed almost 30 per cent of the labour force in Norway and Denmark, over 20 per cent in Sweden, Finland, France, and most of the other main OECD countries, around

15 per cent in the UK and the USA, while Greece, Japan, and Korea had less than 10 per cent.[103]

The wider problem with terms such as 'state' and 'nation state' (the latter being a state pretending to enclose within its boundaries all the members of a nation) is that they subsume entities exhibiting vast differences in size, in population, and in organizational efficiency. Luxembourg, Japan, the United States, and Thailand are all, technically, 'sovereign' states, though the way in which they are 'sovereign' is very different.

Yet each state is modern in at least one sense: it has 'the people' at its heart. Its purpose or 'project', at least formally, even in a dictatorship, is to ensure an improvement in the conditions of life of 'its' people. Its rulers may think mainly about their own power, their own wealth, and their own families, but the ideological rhetoric of the modern state is essentially 'democratic'; its rulers must claim to act on behalf of the 'people'. This is not to say that the rhetoric had not been deployed in earlier times, but only with the modern state did it become universalized. The 'people' came to exist as a political force, real or potential, mainly at the end of the nineteenth century, along with industrial capitalism. This is when the people needed to be placated, cajoled, or coerced. They could not be ignored. Improving their conditions became an imperative alongside the older imperative of defending the country. Here too economic considerations prevailed, for rich countries could defend themselves better than poor ones. Thus capitalism became a matter of state policy – far too important to be left to the whims of entrepreneurs or the vagaries of the market. Capitalism was never a purely private process.

Some social theorists saw this clearly, particularly in Germany – obsessed with catching up with Britain – and where a solid body of academic opinion urged the state to encourage the development of a dynamic capitalism.[104] The rejection of capitalism, once de rigueur in many intellectual and conservative circles, became less and less common after 1900.[105] Max Weber in his inaugural lecture at Freiburg University in May 1895, a lecture imbued with what one might call 'national capitalist' ideology, declared that the goal of the economic policies of the state should be to defend the German people as a whole and not as individuals because 'our state is a *nation state* [*Nationalstaat*]'. And he added that the 'economic policy of a German state, and, equally, the criterion of value used by a German economic theorist, can therefore only be a German policy or criterion'.[106] In other words, capitalism was a collective enterprise aimed at improving the conditions of the members of the *national* community, not a social system that would enable individuals to get richer.[107] Production for production's sake was not all-important. What really mattered was the production of German values.[108] In Weber's later writings, including *The Protestant Ethic and the Spirit of Capitalism* (1904–5), while perturbed by the growing bureaucracy, the stifling of the individual, and the replacement of the personal relationships of traditional society with impersonal class conflict, he recognized that politics was necessarily becoming increasingly dominated by economic and materialist concerns.[109]

The British had known this for a while, and without any help from Weber. Since the end of the eighteenth century it was commonly accepted in British government circles that policy, including foreign policy, would have to take into account economic requirements. Its trade expanded into 'an international vacuum . . . cleared by the activities of the British navy'.[110] In July 1757, Lord Holderness, a government minister, explained that:

> we must be Merchants while we are Soldiers, that our Trade depends upon a proper exertion of our Maritime Strength; that Trade and Maritime force depend upon each other, and that the Riches which are true Resources of this Country depends upon its Commerce.[111]

The country might appear as if its policy was always in the hands of haughty aristocrats inexperienced in the vulgar business of commerce, but no British Prime Minister ever ignored the fact that the country was dependent on overseas trade. William Pitt the Younger, the youngest ever Prime Minister and one of the best (becoming PM for the first time at the age of twenty-four in 1783), remarked that 'British policy is British trade'. Lord Palmerston, Foreign Secretary in the 1840s and Prime Minister in the 1850s, told the House of Commons that to be accused of being indifferent to commercial interests was like being accused of lacking common sense. Finally Lord Clarendon, who came from an old aristocratic family of courtiers, diplomats, and politicians, and who never dealt in anything as sordid as trade and commerce, once he became Foreign Secretary in 1853 explained that he regarded commerce as one of his leading priorities, adding that 'the magnitude of our commercial relations has created an interest that did not exist before'.[112] It was not aristocrats who were running the country, but, overwhelmingly, businessmen who had gone into politics either as Liberals or as Conservatives.[113]

Everyone knew that the key to British success was trade. Between 1700 and 1780 English foreign trade nearly doubled. Between 1780 and 1800 it trebled.[114] The key variables behind Britain's rise to global pre-eminence as an industrial power were a strong navy, economic protectionism (or mercantilism as it was called), and a proper tax system. All of these required an uncommonly strong state. Once these were achieved, economic liberalism, of a pragmatic kind, became associated with Britain. Elsewhere, liberal thought in the course of the nineteenth century had undergone a major transformation, becoming far more *étatique* (statist), recognizing, for better or for worse, the intimate connection between politics and capitalist social relations. The first who attempted to theorize this nexus had been Karl Marx, but he was far from being a lone eccentric battling in a sea of philistinism, as some of his followers (and perhaps Marx himself) thought. Marx was a man of his era, grappling with a conception of the state that was not entirely dissimilar from that of many of his liberal contemporaries. And even those liberals who advocated a strongly non-interventionist state did so on the grounds that a free market would promote industrialization better, and would improve the conditions of the life of the majority.

Such improvements were no longer attributed to fate or God's will but to politics. By the early 1900s most of the press, including most conservative newspapers, agreed that only an industrial society could support a large population and secure national defence. Once the newspapers began to equate industry with national prestige they became pro-industrial. An industrial policy had become a central part of national identity. And the main way to fund it was taxation.

6
Taxation

Taxation is no novelty. Taxes or duties were collected in Ancient Egypt, Greece, and Rome. According to the legend, Lady Godiva (who did really live in the eleventh century) rode naked into Coventry to convince her husband to abandon the excessively high taxes he levied (thus combining some form of early feminism with tax protest). Clause 12, the key section of Magna Carta (1215), required the king to levy taxation only with the 'general consent', meaning that of the nobility and the clergy. In other words taxation was about political power.

As Edmund Burke lucidly explained in his *Reflections on the Revolution in France* (1790): 'the revenue of the state is the state. In effect, all depends upon it, whether for support or for reformation . . . the revenue, which is the spring of all power, becomes in its administration the sphere of every active virtue.'[1] This statement needs to be qualified for the twentieth century, since a state massively involved in production, as was the Soviet Union, made tax-raising of lesser importance (the main mechanism there was a turnover tax, similar to VAT). In Europe in feudal times, in the absence of a centralized state, lords confirmed their membership of the dominant class by claiming exemption from taxation (the 'privilege'). Peasants paid taxes to landlords in exchange for 'protection' while the connection between landlords and the sovereign was, in the final analysis, a matter of military strength and political alliances.[2] The obligations (rent) due by peasants to landlords were far more burdensome than the taxes workers pay now. Those who today complain of the high rate of taxation might consider that in 1755 French peasants had to provide the value of 33 per cent of their product to their lords. François Quesnay in his *Tableau économique* (1766) set the figure at 40 per cent. In the Middle Ages in Austria, Russia, and Prussia, peasants spent two-thirds of their working time meeting their feudal obligations.[3] In the 1780s, in villages in Galicia (Austrian Empire) peasants could pay up to 85.9 per cent of their gross product to their landlords.[4] Other studies suggest that, towards the end of the nineteenth century, the Christian peasants in Macedonia kept only 37 per cent of their product and paid the rest to their Muslim landlords and to the Ottoman government.[5]

Needless to say, peasants did not like paying taxes, and at times their anger erupted in violent protest. Thus the 1381 poll tax in England was widely evaded and led to revolt.[6] But peasant turmoil rarely, if ever, turned into serious revolutionary uprisings. The great revolutions of the past – the French, the American, and even the English Civil War – were sparked by the anti-tax resentment of the *middle classes* – not of the peasantry. Although no one is overjoyed at the prospect of paying taxes, taxes cannot really be levied in any significant amount without the consent, however grudging, of those who are taxed. One might almost say that democracy and taxation go together. The modern state, even when run by aristocrats, in order to be able to raise revenue, had to pander to the bourgeoisie. To obtain bourgeois consent the governing class had to allow some form of representation or consultation.[7]

That taxes were a delicate matter and that they could antagonize people was abundantly clear to Machiavelli, who advised the Prince (see Chapter 16 of *The Prince*, 'De liberalitate et parsimonia') to avoid being too spendthrift, because this would require taxing the people, and to 'do everything he can to get money' (*fare tutte quelle cose che si possono fare per avere danari*), thus soon making himself 'odious to his subjects . . . and he will be little valued by any one' (*odioso con sudditi, e poco stimare da nessuno*). The point is to be careful with funds at first, make sure that there is plenty of money in the state's coffers, and then have enough resources to defend the state against aggression or pay for projects without having to tax the people unduly. In other words: have a large budget surplus.

In his *Second Treatise of Government* (1690) John Locke wrote that 'they must not raise taxes on the property of the people, without the consent of the people, given by themselves, or their deputies'.[8] Jean-Jacques Rousseau in the *Discours sur l'économie politique* (his entry in volume 5 of the *Encyclopédie* of 1755) held a similar view, noting that 'taxes can only be legitimately levied with the consent of the people or of its representatives'.[9] The French *Déclaration des droits de l'homme et du citoyen* (1789) devoted two out of its seventeen articles to taxation (Articles 13 and 14). It should be said that the principle of equity (taxes should be proportionate to the ability to pay) existed already under the *Ancien Régime*.[10] In the modern era, taxation became central to government policies and to the relation between the individual and the state, since it transformed private earnings or wealth into a public or state resource. Without taxation there can be no economic policy. There can be no defence. There can be no state education or pensions or welfare or public-health measures or road-building or major infrastructure.

In 1919, Max Weber, discussing the modern state in his much-discussed lecture 'Politics as a Vocation', famously defined it, echoing Hobbes's *Leviathan* (without mentioning him), as 'a human community that (successfully) claims the monopoly of the legitimate use of physical force within a given territory'.[11] But to use force it is necessary to be able to pay for this: no funds, no monopoly of force. The two are intrinsically linked. To privilege the 'legitimate use of violence' as the central concept defining the modern state is to downplay the fact that the fundamental economic instrument at the disposal of the state – a 'proper' state, that is, one with an efficient bureaucratic machinery and a reasonably high degree of legitimacy – is taxation. Taxation is a procedure whereby the state takes money from citizens in exchange for services deemed to be in the collective interest. As Oliver Wendell Holmes Jr (of the US Supreme Court) is supposed to have said, 'Taxes are the price we pay for civilized society' (1927). Even genuine free-market liberals who have a jaundiced view of taxation regard it, at best, as a necessary evil. Jean-Baptiste Say, a classical liberal with a pronounced anti-tax bias, did not deny the necessity of taxes: the best taxes, he wrote, were the lowest, the most equitable, the most useful or moral, and those that were the least unfavourable to production.[12]

So people pay taxes. Why? Compulsion and fear of penalties, of course, play a significant role. Many taxes are unavoidable since they are embedded in the price one pays for goods (duties tax, excise tax, value-added tax) or deducted from one's pay. The history of taxation is full of examples of attempts to introduce taxes on all kind of items: in 1535, Henry VIII introduced a 'beard tax', as did Peter the Great of Russia in 1698 (in order to modernize the country). England, France, and Scotland, at different times between the eighteenth and twentieth centuries had 'window taxes' (a tax on the number of windows in one's home, leading to some windows being bricked up to avoid paying it). In 1784 a 'brick tax' was introduced in Great Britain to help pay for the American wars (leading to an increase in the size of bricks).

The principle that taxes are necessary in order to obtain public goods is not seriously challenged. Those who evade taxes are freeriders who would admit that if many others behaved the same way, all would suffer. It follows that tax compliance is not only due to coercion but also to some degree of trust in the state.[13] I pay because the state is, in a way, 'my' state and I trust it will deliver the services I require: borders will be protected, criminals will be pursued, order will be maintained, rules will be enforced, rubbish will be collected, schools will be funded and, more recently, pensions, welfare, and healthcare will be provided. Thus tax collecting is a good index of the success achieved in the development of a national community; a 'failed' state is a state unable to collect taxes, a state where tax collectors are open to bribery, where ordinary people conspire with others to avoid paying taxes, and where tax evasion is seen as acceptable and legitimate.[14] The breakdown of law and order leading to civil disorder is only the final manifestation of the fiscally failed state. As Joseph Schumpeter wrote in a famous essay ('The Crisis of the Tax State', 1918): 'If the tax state [*Steuerstaat*] were to fail . . . the modern state would itself change its nature; the economy would have to be driven by new motors along new paths; the social structure could not remain what it is . . . everything would have to change.'[15]

Some taxes are easier to levy than others. Successful states are those able to raise a wide range of taxes, not only taxes on property, goods, and commodities, but also taxes on income. Taxation depends on a widely diversified system of collection that will not hurt people unduly. As Jean-Baptiste Colbert, Louis XIV's great Finance Minister (1665–83), is supposed to have said, *L'art de l'imposition consiste à plumer l'oie pour obtenir le plus possible de plumes avec le moins possible de cris* ('The art of taxation consists in plucking the goose so as to obtain the maximum number of feathers with the minimum amount of screams').[16]

The British state was able to extract taxation thanks to an extremely centralized system that encountered very little opposition at home.[17] In the eighteenth century the country moved from the inefficient tax system of the Restoration to a system marked 'by the orderly collection of public moneys by a predominantly professional body of state officials'.[18] By then the British fiscal system had become more efficient than any of its counterparts on the continent.[19] Britain was, by that time, the most successful tax state in Europe. English superiority in this matter was due to the relatively weaker position of the English monarchs (as compared to monarchs elsewhere) vis-à-vis their subjects. This forced them to make concessions towards enhancing the fiscal powers of Parliament. In France this happened only in 1789. By then it was too late.[20] The Netherlands, richer than Britain in the eighteenth century, had a fragmented political structure and thus no national taxing authority.

None of this means, of course, that the British were enthusiastic taxpayers. Thomas Mortimer in *The Elements of Commerce, Politics and*

Finances (1772) – subtitled 'designed as a supplement to the education of British youth' – while defending the necessity of taxation ('It is the duty of good subjects to pay all taxes legally imposed, and never to defraud the public revenue'), added 'I am sorry to say that British subjects too generally make light of this obligation', and added later that 'all taxes, of what nature soever, are paid, in every kingdom, with bad grace'.[21] British taxation met far greater resistance from those who had settled in the American colonies, who no longer trusted remote London to use public revenues to their advantage and who were themselves distant enough to resist compliance. It was the beginning of the American Revolution.

Britain became engaged in important aspects of state-building following the Act of Union with Scotland (1707) and with Ireland (1801). Having been, in Elizabeth I's days, a second-rate state, militarily speaking, it became a major naval power in the course of the eighteenth century. An important component of British success was the soundness of its finances. It could tax more and better, and because it could do so, it could also borrow cheaply, since a state's best collateral lies in its ability to levy taxes. Contemporaries were aware of this. Immanuel Kant pointed out that the credit system made wars possible because it enabled countries to borrow. This 'ingenious system,' he added, 'invented by a *commercial people* in the present century, provides a military fund which may exceed the resources of all other states put together'.[22] This 'commercial people' were, of course, the British.

Taxation enabled the British state to make its weight felt in the conduct of international trade by subsidizing exports. Taxes on expenditure, such as levies on salt or beer or certain other items of consumption, had been around since the time of the Roman occupation. But Britain introduced direct income tax only in 1799, during the Napoleonic Wars, the first Western country to do so (the absolute first, almost 1,800 years previously, was China when the emperor Wang Mang, founder of the Xin Dynasty, introduced a 10 per cent tax in AD 10).[23] By 1815, taxation in Great Britain was higher than anywhere in the world, largely because of the costs associated with the Napoleonic Wars – wars that were regarded as inevitable and necessary by British taxpayers (i.e. by the middle and upper classes). British taxes on revenue remained relatively high even afterwards, though they declined gently (as a percentage of GNP) until around 1880, thus making them more acceptable. Then they started to rise again. This suggests that the British government achieved a reasonably high level of trustworthiness among taxpayers throughout the nineteenth century. Income tax, after all, is very expensive to extract unless the vast majority of taxpayers comply voluntarily; and they are likely to do so if they regard the tax as 'fair' and the money well spent.[24]

A further reason for the acceptability of taxes in Britain, however, was that those who were subject to direct income tax (reintroduced in 1842) had been able to vote in parliamentary elections since the Reform Act of 1832. Taxpayers had been enfranchised and could have voted (and did vote) for a tax-cutting government keen to dismantle the fiscal-military state that had arisen during the Napoleonic Wars.[25] In other words, one was all the more willing to pay taxes if one could vote for lower taxes. Indeed, radicals who wanted to extend the suffrage assumed that the newly enfranchised electorate would vote for lower taxes. Those who feared democracy warned that the poor would use their newly acquired political power to 'rob the rich' and redistribute wealth radically. There was also the issue of privacy: one had to declare one's income, let the state pry into one's financial affairs. The liberal feminist Harriet Martineau was horrified:

> for, while every tax is disagreeable . . . there is something transcendently disgusting in an income tax which not only takes a substantial sum immediately out of a man's pocket, but compels him to expose his affairs to a party that he would by no means choose for a confidant.[26]

In fact, income tax was regularly renewed not because it was popular, quite the contrary, but because the alternative (indirect taxes) would have had even fewer supporters. Once again war intervened to help the state to raise money: the Crimean War (1853–6) saved the income tax. The war was won, the expenses incurred did not cause great hardship, and the economy did well. This entrenched income tax once and for all. Lord Palmerston, when out of office, had opposed income tax; once he became Prime Minister he became its champion. If the people wanted Britain to win wars, he explained with a candour few contemporary politicians exhibit, they must be prepared to pay for them.[27] In 1913 the United Kingdom spent (per capita) on the navy almost three times more than Germany and France, though France spent more than anyone else on the army (and three times more than Russia).[28] The result was that on the eve of the First World War, Britain had the mightiest navy in the world.

It was not all a matter of consensus – coercion was applied too. The British state was stronger than its counterparts on the continent and hence better able to inquire into people's incomes and force them to pay. Other states, such as the French, had to rely more, for tax-gathering purposes, on the formal display of wealth.[29] Nevertheless, even in the

United Kingdom the prevailing form of taxation was the unfair but more easily obtainable tax on consumption rather than tax on income (unfair because those on low income spend a greater proportion of their earnings on consumption). In 1900, 68 per cent of the revenue of the British state came from taxes on expenditure against only 10.3 per cent on income, a third of what it would be in 1979.[30]

Those on the continent who looked up to Britain as a haven for freedoms and liberties did not always realize that such liberties came, literally, at a price. Tax-raising was a fiendishly complicated business then as now. Among philosophical liberals, there was no doubt that the rich should pay more tax than the poor. Adam Smith thought so. In fact, he thought that it was not 'very unreasonable that the rich should contribute to the public expense, not only in proportion to their revenue, but something more than in that proportion'.[31] Jeremy Bentham and John Stuart Mill both thought so too.[32] But, contrary to the present situation, many on what was then 'the left' were less favourable to taxation than 'the right'. The radical Thomas Paine in *The Rights of Man* (1792) denounced taxation:

> If, from the more wretched parts of the old world, we look at those which are in an advanced stage of improvement we still find the greedy hand of government thrusting itself into every corner and crevice of industry, and grasping the spoil of the multitude. Invention is continually exercised to furnish new pretences for revenue and taxation. It watches prosperity as its prey, and permits none to escape without a tribute.[33]

The moderate Burke, on the other hand, in his *Reflections on the Revolution in France* (1790), declared that prosperous states were those who succeeded in keeping a proper balance between revenue and taxation, but he was far from being against taxation.[34] Montesquieu in *De l'esprit des lois* (1748) wrote that taxes are what citizens pay to protect the money they keep.[35] Intelligent politicians, such as Sergei Witte, Russian Minister of Finance (1892–1903) and long-time reformer, knew perfectly well that a sound fiscal policy required, in a country such as Russia, a prosperous and healthy peasantry – though tireless attempts to improve the conditions of rural life were unsuccessful, to the detriment of fiscal policy.[36]

France found it difficult to levy a tax on income. A debate on direct income tax started in 1870, but most French politicians were bitterly opposed to it (out of fear of being voted out) and preferred to tax things rather than income. Adolphe Thiers, President of the nascent Third Republic (1870), regarded an income tax as a socialist measure, a tax on the rich, a piece of demagogy.[37] French taxation remained antiquated and unfair, because it was based overwhelmingly on indirect taxes (including a tax on windows, established at the time of the Revolution, abolished in Britain in 1851, but in France only in 1926). These failings were often remarked on by the German press, which railed that the Third Republic was manifestly unable to come to grips with modern taxation.[38]

The French government led by Léon Bourgeois from 1895 to 1896 tried to introduce a progressive income tax under the notion of *solidarisme* along with social reforms but the opposition in parliament was too great. Compared to Imperial Germany and Imperial Britain, republican France remained a low-tax country until the First World War. As a percentage of GDP, French taxation declined between 1880 and 1913 from 11.2 per cent to 8.9 per cent whereas, in the same period, German taxes went up from 10 to 17.7 per cent, Japanese from 9 to 14.2 per cent, and British taxes from 9.9 to 13.3 per cent.[39] Matters changed only in 1914 when Joseph Caillaux, the Finance Minister, after years of fighting for a general income tax finally succeeded in obtaining it in July 1914 with war looming.

The question had been debated for over forty years.[40] The Caillaux proposal had been approved by the Chamber in 1909, but it was turned down by the Senate.[41] What had perturbed the French senators and the people they represented (the richer members of society) was the prospect of a strong state snooping on one's private affairs. Much of the struggle faced by Caillaux was about this anxiety, harbinger of things to come, since the actual size of the tax proposed was relatively small and the exceptions numerous – thus many farmers had been exempted because the majority of deputies hailed from rural constituencies; and professionals had been exempted because many deputies were professional themselves.[42]

Before the Second World War taxation was still low in developed countries: around 10 per cent of GDP.[43] By 2007 it averaged 35 per cent, ranging from 28.3 per cent in the United States to 48.7 per cent in Denmark.[44] High-tax countries (where taxes constitute between 25 and 50 per cent of GDP) are usually democratic countries with extensive individual freedoms.

Where industrial development was state funded, as in Meiji Japan, farmers and landlords bore the brunt of taxation and agriculture was made to pay the cost of industrialization. The peasants were the chief victims of the Meiji changes. The abrupt transition from what was regarded as the feudal period consisted of exposing agriculture to the forces of the money economy by permitting the sale of land. No real land reform took place, but the new land tax (implemented in 1879) fell on the owner of land and not on the cultivator and had to be paid to the central government. The land tax was an unusually high proportion of government revenue (69.4 per cent in the period 1885–9), thus contributing in no small measure to social strife in the countryside.[45] By 1900 the land tax had dropped to 25 per cent of state revenue; even the tax on alcohol produced more.[46]

At the end of the nineteenth century most states were not strong enough to be able to expand the range of taxes collected; they were weak or under the tutelage of foreign powers, or forced into unequal terms of trade, or had to pay high interest rates for foreign loans, or had poor internal markets.[47] Britain, Japan, and France were exceptions. Romania was closer to the norm. Politically speaking, this was a relatively modern country: it possessed a parliament, held elections, had a constitution, and had a relatively free press, but its economy could not provide an adequate fiscal basis for its development. In other independent eastern European countries before the First World War (such as Bulgaria, Montenegro, and Serbia), since parliament was reluctant to increase taxes, the state used force to obtain the money it needed. Parliamentary power was debased as deputies sought favours from the bureaucracy on behalf of their electorate.[48] So weak was the Romanian state that the hundreds of laws passed in the last two decades of the nineteenth century to encourage economic development failed to improve the unimpressive performance of the economy.[49]

The problem with weak states is that they do not dare to tax their citizens or to enforce taxation. They fear no one will support new taxes in the hope of greater benefits in the future. Before unification, for example, the southern Italian states, previously under the Bourbon kings, had a very low level of taxation. Unification meant that southerners were going to be taxed more. The consequent rapid growth of banditry in the south at the end of the nineteenth century was partly due to high taxation.[50] In the Ottoman Empire, in the second half of the nineteenth century, political weakness manifested itself in the empire's inability to raise taxes. It tried to meet its ever increasing financial obligation by printing money and selling bonds in London, Paris, and Vienna and was forced to borrow more at ever increasing interest rates. By 1875–6 the empire had, to all intents and purposes, defaulted. In 1881 the European creditor countries seized effective control of the Ottoman finances by establishing the Ottoman Public Debt Administration. This was quite effective, but the substantial problem remained: the Ottoman was a failed state, unable to establish a proper taxation system, and by the time the First World War broke out it was once again on the verge of bankruptcy.[51] It did not survive the war.

Weak states, unable to raise sufficient revenues from taxes, resorted to their own commercial monopolies. Thus in Tsarist Russia, in the decades leading to the First World War, only a fraction of total state revenues were collected from direct taxes, much lower than in Britain, Germany, Austria-Hungary, and even France, then still without an income tax. Much of the rest came from indirect taxes on various products, or from the state monopoly on the sale of spirits.[52] This monopoly was created after agonizing discussions. As Sergei Witte explained in his memoirs, Tsar Alexander III had been concerned about alcoholism in Russia (vodka production was virtually uncontrolled) and resolved to 'effect a measure, absolutely unprecedented and vast in scope', namely the establishment of a state monopoly on vodka.[53] Nikolai Bunge (Finance Minister, 1881–6) thought this was unpractical. His successor, Ivan Vyshnegradsky (Finance Minister, 1887–92), was equally unenthusiastic. But the next Finance Minister, Sergei Witte, managed to tax vodka. As he reputedly wrote: 'I transferred the entire vodka traffic into the hands of the government.'[54] The connection between alcoholism and mortality is seen starkly in the death rate in Russia: in 1861 it was higher than in western Europe one hundred years earlier, and it was still double that of western Europe on the eve of the First World War.[55] And, one should add, the situation is still dire today.[56] Vladimir Kokovtsov, Finance Minister under Witte and Pyotr Stolypin (and later Prime Minister himself), introduced an income tax and abolished the redemption payments still extant from the days of the Emancipation Decree (November 1905). The main opposition to income tax came from landowners, who wanted taxes to be under the tutelage of the *zemstva* (the forms of local self-government they dominated). Taxation had become a major factor in Russia's political battle.[57]

China had taxed its people for two thousand years. The Imperial State was seen as a gigantic bureaucratic machine run by unenlightened despots. Tax resistance was rife.[58] The central government's main tax revenue was from custom duties, which was almost entirely dependent on China's commerce with the rest of the world.[59] In the nineteenth century the collection of taxes was still farmed out, and the supervision of tax collectors was so unsystematic that it was impossible to know how much was collected since some of it never reached the central government but was shared with 'officials, bandits, provincial politicians, secret societies, warlords, and others . . .'[60] The weakening of central authority during the Taiping Rebellion (1850–64) made matters even worse.[61] As Jonathan Spence explained, the Imperial Court, the bureaucracy, the provincial officials, and the merchants each had their own interests to safeguard, making it difficult to develop the kind of coordinated policies that had been so successful in Japan during the Meiji Restoration.[62]

As states expanded their functions, they also expanded their fiscal systems. The development of the welfare state inevitably contributed to an increase in taxation. As Richard Musgrave, author of *The Theory of Public Finance* (1959), for long the standard textbook on fiscal matters, explained in 1997, as if to warn an increasingly vociferous anti-tax lobby: 'like it or not, government and its public finances are here to stay'. Taxes are needed to repair market failures, to address issues of distribution, to help in the conduct of economic policy. Taxes may not be popular, he added, but they are indispensable 'partners to the market system'.[63]

The systematic increase in taxes has continued throughout the modern period, reaching heights that would have horrified the Victorians. Not even the neo-liberal counter-revolution associated with Reaganism and Thatcherism reversed the trend: the OECD average of tax revenue as a percentage of GDP, which was 25.4 per cent in 1965, went up to 34.1 per cent in 2011. Even in the United States, home of a strong anti-tax movement, the percentage barely changed in that period.[64] Capitalism, especially effective capitalism, needs the oxygen of taxation.

7
Laggards and Pathbreakers

The path to industrialization was undertaken at different speeds in different countries and, in some countries, even the preconditions for industrialization were difficult to establish. In 1500 the leading region had been central and northern Italy. Then economic leadership passed on to the Dutch Republic. By 1700, Dutch per capita income was twice that of Great Britain. Then, by 1820, the country (by then no longer the Dutch Republic but the United Kingdom of the Netherlands) was overtaken by Britain. As Eric Hobsbawm put it:

> There was a moment in the world's history when Britain can be described, if we are not too pedantic, as its only workshop, its only massive importer and exporter, its only carrier, its only imperialist, almost its only foreign investor, and for this reason its only naval power and the only one which had a genuine world policy.[1]

By 1900, the United States had become the world economic leader.[2] In 1870, however, the United Kingdom was still well ahead of everyone else.[3] It manufactured half the world's pig iron, 3.5 times more than the USA, four times as much as Germany, and five times more than France.[4] And it was, of course, way ahead of countries in the 'periphery'. Such wealth caused envy. Charles Masterman in *The Condition of England* (1909) was splenetic against the English rich and their arrogance:

> When the Englishman goes abroad, the customs of the country, the opinion of the people amongst whom he lives, count for nothing. He comes to Biarritz to live his life, the traditional English life, made up of bounteous feeding, of violent physical exercise, of clubs, and of bridge . . . all just blandly tolerant of the occasional presence of the native inhabitant in this frontier post of Empire.[5]

Self-satisfaction had preceded actual industrial development. Already in 1740 the Scottish poet James Thomson penned the lyrics of what would virtually become the anthem of the Royal Navy in which freedom from tyranny appeared to be Britain's particular advantage over all others nations:

> The nations, not so blest as thee,
> Must, in their turns, to tyrants fall;
> While thou shalt flourish great and free,
> The dread and envy of them all.
> Rule, Britannia! rule the waves:
> Britons never will be slaves.

At that time Britain did not yet rule the waves, but it did soon after and not just the waves but world commerce and industry. Such supremacy had not been inevitable. Matters could have gone differently. At the end of the seventeenth century the economies of the Dutch Republic, England, and France were at a similar level of development. Even in the eighteenth century the British were not as rich as the Dutch; the country was not as large in size or population as France; and it did not have an empire the size of Spain's. Yet, already in 1750 less than half the population of England was employed in agriculture. To reach that stage, western and northern Europe had to wait until the second half of the nineteenth century, and southern Europe (Italy, Spain, and Portugal) had to wait until the twentieth century.[6] Britain became a pathbreaker because it innovated technologically and because it was able and willing to borrow innovations made elsewhere and exploit them commercially far more than other countries.[7] Obstacles to industrialization (political, religious, geographical, etc.) were few and the country had luck too: huge known coal resources.

Unlike many of the continental states Britain possessed a large homogeneous market with no internal barriers to trade (unlike the still-to-be unified Italy, though the German states benefited from a customs union, the *Zollverein*). British urbanization was rapid: in 1831 less than one-tenth of the population lived in sizeable urban centres; by 1901 it was one-quarter.[8] Yet the country was not in constant turmoil even demographically. Between 1851 and 1911 the proportion of those employed in manufacturing and domestic work in Victorian Britain was fairly stable but it doubled in absolute numbers, and employment in agriculture dropped drastically, while the numbers of those employed in public service and the professions increased.[9] The remarkable stability in the proportion of the working class disguises major internal shifts such as those from textiles to other sectors of manufacturing such as steel.[10] The sector that was really growing was that of the public sector and white-collar workers in general.

Abroad, British economic growth was widely seen as a direct result of what came to be called 'Manchester' liberalism, the main force lobbying for the repeal of the Corn Laws and the transformation of Britain into a Free Trading Nation – even though, as we have seen, Britain was truly liberal in foreign trade only in the second half of the nineteenth century. Richard Cobden, the main spokesman of the Anti-Corn Law League (founded in Manchester in 1838), became known throughout Europe and was much admired by Frédéric Bastiat, who translated many of Cobden's speeches (see Chapter 5).

But it was not just free trade that excited Europeans. Britain seemed to win on many fronts. Since the Reform Act of 1832 it had become the most democratic and freest country in Europe. Thanks to its industries and its exports, it offered the prospect of increasing wealth for all its inhabitants. Compared to other countries (France, prone to regime change, the United States and its civil war, China and the Taiping Rebellion, and the not yet united Italy and Germany) it was internally secure and politically stable. Its main internal threat, the Chartists, had been quelled, with relatively little violence, by 1850.

And, last but not least, the British state, after the Glorious Revolution of 1688 and the consolidation of true parliamentary rule, was not in conflict with the requirement of capitalist accumulation. England was an authentic modern capitalist country, one where the role of the state consisted not in defending the interests of a particular dynasty (as was the case, say, in pre-revolutionary France) in alliance (or in conflict) with a landowning class, but in enhancing the country's economic performance.

Britain was admired for its alleged economic liberalism, but this did not lead other countries to adopt the doctrine in practice. In the nineteenth century the continental theorists of the minimalist state – the progenitors of today's 'neo-liberals' – were regarded, by most politicians, as eccentrics. Throughout most of Europe, in Hungary as in Poland, in France as in Germany, in Italy as in Russia, the consensus among the elites was that industrialization required the strengthening of the nation state; liberal political institutions (fair trial, secure rights, some form of democratic representation) were part of the deal, the economically minimalist state was not. The objective of reformers was to weaken, even eliminate, the restrictions of traditional society and on these ruins build a strong state. Everyone seemed to understand that in order to 'import' the British Industrial Revolution one should not 'adopt the official policy – or, rather, the lack of policy – which was associated with the pioneer episode in industrialisation'.[11] The historical task of the modern state, of the state that wished to become 'modern', was to promote capitalist growth: the British policy of laissez-faire was a luxury they could not afford.

British entrepreneurship (as opposed to the policies of the British state), however, was a major example for French steel magnates such as François de Wendel, Eugène Schneider, and Georges Dufaud, who regularly visited Great Britain.[12] And so did Germany's Alfred Krupp, who went to Sheffield in 1839 in order to 'learn the secrets of England's supremacy in the manufacture of steel'.[13] In the middle of the nineteenth century the world produced only 70,000 annual tons of steel; 40,000 tons in the United Kingdom alone. To put this in perspective: in 2013, Greece, which ranked fiftieth in the world league of steel producers, produced 1.2 million tons, that is, thirty times more than Britain in 1850. Then, after 1856, a number of technological advances such as Henry Bessemer's converter enabled a massive expansion of the industry.[14] It also meant that, since these innovations could be quickly used by everyone, the days of British supremacy were numbered.

Britain continued to do well even when other countries were catching up: in the 1870s productivity growth in critical industries such as iron and steel was still higher in Britain, though the United States had surpassed it by the 1890s.[15] Even industrially important regions such as Bohemia and Moravia in the Austro-Hungarian Empire were well behind the United Kingdom in 1910, since their per capita industrial production was 66 per cent of Britain's, though far better than Poland, which was still 22 per cent.[16]

At the beginning of the nineteenth century, productivity in France was a little better than in Britain, but by the last quarter of the century Britain was clearly in the lead.[17] French agriculture, until the end of the nineteenth century, was barely active in international markets, except for a few well-known luxury products, such as champagne and fine wines.[18] France was industrializing faster than most countries, though not as fast as her nearest rivals. Between 1882 and 1907 the number of German workers increased from 10 million to 16 million; but in France there were only 3,385,000 wage earners employed by 778,000 small entrepreneurs (4.4 workers per employer). Had French agriculture been less protected by tariffs, there would have been a far greater rural exodus.

Nevertheless by 1879 French industry, in terms of its contribution to the national economy, had almost caught up with agriculture. In 1890 the share of industry was still 29 per cent (almost the same as in 1820), while agriculture was 35.1 per cent. By 1913 industry's share had overtaken that of agriculture (38.6 per cent and 35.3 per cent respectively).[19] Services and transport recruited another 23 per cent of the workforce, with 3.2 per cent in the public sector.[20]

France, as a manufacturing country, was overtaken first by Germany in 1880, then by the United States in 1914 and, by 1930, by Japan.[21] Of course, by 2011 every country, except the USA, was overtaken by China in world manufacturing output. And it is estimated that China will eventually overtake the USA in terms of its share of the world economy – not surprisingly given its massive population.[22] In 2011 the old pathbreaker, the United Kingdom, once the leading economic power in the world, was ninth after the USA, China, India, Japan, Germany, Russia, Brazil, and France.[23] The richest countries in the world, in terms of GDP per capita, are now small countries, almost special cases, countries such as Luxembourg, Qatar, and Singapore, whether one goes by IMF or World Bank data.[24]

But what about the so-called laggards? The 'advanced' countries do not wait passively to be overtaken; they do everything they can to keep on top. The others, those that lag behind, lag differently. Countries that have little in common are lumped together because the one characteristic they share is that they are not in the top group. Italy, in 1870, was certainly a laggard country, but so was Paraguay, and far more so. As countries 'caught up', new and more complex differentiations emerged.

One of the key differentiators was the emergence of bourgeois democratic states. In 1880 most European countries still lagged behind the early starters (England and Belgium). Those who were close behind were Germany, France, Denmark, Sweden, and parts of the Austro-Hungarian Empire. In some countries belonging to this group, such as Denmark and Sweden, the establishment of bourgeois democracy occurred without revolution or violence, or internal or external strife. No revolution was required to unhinge the shackles of the old order; no struggle for national independence, as in Germany or Italy, had been necessary since these countries were already nation states; no external enemy threatened their sovereignty (though Denmark lost Schleswig-Holstein to Prussia in 1864). Modernizing reforms had been promulgated granting freedom of religion, greater equality for women, local self-government, a new criminal code, and constitutional reform.[25]

Scandinavian economies were also on the move. Until the middle of the nineteenth century, Swedish exports consisted largely of primary products, wood in particular.[26] This export, led by the constantly increasing demand from the United Kingdom, turned out to be the engine for Swedish economic growth.[27] Norway exported fish as well as timber and Denmark specialized in food exports. Then the three Scandinavian countries developed industries directly or indirectly connected to their exports: iron and steel in Sweden, wood processing in Norway and Sweden, and food processing in Demark. All, and Sweden more than the others, achieved extremely high growth rates, catching up, in terms of per capita income, with the leading western European countries.[28] Because of Sweden's use of primary products, a capitalist economic development less dependent on the state was possible there and state intervention could be limited to infrastructure projects.[29] But the state, or in this case the State Church (*Svenska kyrkan* – established by King Gustav I in 1526), played a key role in promoting one of the central conditions for economic growth: the development of a highly literate and educated population. The Church Law of 1686 had in fact decreed that everyone should be able to read the Bible. This made Sweden, by the mid-nineteenth century, one of the most literate countries in Europe. The real benefit of a population of competent Bible-readers was a skilled working class that contributed to the wood industry first and later to other, more sophisticated industries, and eventually to an advanced banking and financial sector.[30] Swedish agriculture too underwent significant changes in the course of the nineteenth century with the development of large capitalist farms, particularly in Skåne County at the southern tip of Sweden where a new class of landless agricultural workers emerged.[31]

Whereas the Scandinavian economies were too small to perturb Great Britain, Germany, by the end of the nineteenth century, emerged as a new and fearsome competitor. Had the country remained a conglomeration of statelets dominated by Prussia in the east and by Bavaria and Austria in the south, Britain would not have had much to fear, just as it never had to fear Switzerland or Sweden. But, after 1871, Germany had become the strongest state in continental Europe, and the customs union of German states, which had existed in Germany previously under the banner of the *Zollverein*, now had a powerful political entity as a protector, a new unified Reich.

The Germans rejoiced. Werner Sombart, writing in 1913, announced, with a note of pride, that Germany was almost on a par with the United States as the land where the new spirit of capitalism had reached its utmost development (thanks to the organizational abilities of the Germans and their attitude towards science).[32] And, with some satisfaction, he explained that the old pathbreaker, England, was on the decline. There, he claimed:

> Clear thinking has ceased to be an active and compelling influence in economic activities . . . The spirit of enterprise, interest in business, and love of industry are all declining . . . The Englishman finds pleasure in luxury, in an aristocratic manner of living, and above all in sport.[33]

For a long time the British had tried to come to terms with the 'puzzling signs' that their own economic fate was without historical precedent and possibly fraught with danger.[34] Now its undisputed lead was being disputed. The British intelligentsia was still complacent, but alarmist voices were raised, even though British decline was then more imagined than real and the country was as prosperous as ever.

In 1907, Austin Harrison, a journalist who was briefly editor of the *Observer* and later of *The English Review* (1909–23), wrote, somewhat torn between alarm and admiration, that since his last visit to Berlin he had noticed that German living standards had improved remarkably, leading to a development of 'a truly prodigious kind: in shipping, national wealth, industry, commerce, population, production, consumption, prosperity'.[35] Women were well dressed; one rarely saw real poverty, or drunken women; and 'the children of the poor are much better dressed than our own'.[36] While 'a few decades ago' Germany was divided into 'petty principalities, petty Courts, petty policies, petty Philistinism', now Germany was one country.[37]

Ernest E. Williams was equally alarmist about Britain's predicament. His '*Made in Germany*' (1896) was an influential and popular contribution to the literature on British decline, a literature that has been developing ever since, repeating the same clichés, unaware that it had all been said before. Williams balanced the laziness of the British workers with the incompetence of the British entrepreneur and contrasted both, unfavourably, with German workers and entrepreneurs:

> Ask your tailor whether he would rather employ an Englishman or a German? and why? His answer will be conclusive . . . the cost of running a factory is less when the men are regular . . . the great cause of German success is an alert progressiveness, contrasting brilliantly with the conservative stupor of ourselves.[38]

Arthur Shadwell's *Industrial Efficiency* (1906) continued in the same vein, lamenting that 'the once enterprising manufacturer has grown slack, he has let the business take care of itself, while he is shooting grouse or yachting in the Mediterranean'. The British worker is almost as bad since, Shadwell continued in what would become a familiar whinging mode, his motto is 'Get as much and do as little as possible', his main business being 'football or betting'. Among the culprits, then as now, were seen to be excessive and obsolete regulations that handicapped the manufacturer. Government departments were 'too indolent to . . . adapt regulations to changing conditions' while 'everybody is bent on pleasure and amusement . . . We are a nation at play. Work is a nuisance, an evil necessity to be shirked and hurried over as quickly as possible . . .'[39] To strengthen his argument Shadwell quoted the occasionally bizarre views of foreigners writing letters to the British press. Here is 'A German Resident' writing in *The National Review* (June 1905):

> the majority of your workers read little but the sporting press, and care for little but betting and sport . . . You are even getting ready, I see, to feed the children of the poor, and next I suppose you will clothe them as well, winding up by maintaining their parents . . . you seem bent upon producing a nation of degenerate paupers, not of sturdy men . . . Your politicians appear ready to promise anything to the working-man, provided it is at somebody else's expense . . . You call this democratic government; I call it the rule of the nursery. The children are to govern the wise and far-seeing men – to ruin your State in gratifying their own selfish caprices.[40]

Then there is a Mr Taylor from New York, who explained in the *Daily Telegraph* the real reason behind English decline:

> The plain truth is the English are suffering the physical diseases which arise from excess and immorality. Your females show their physical degeneration by their excessive increase in stature, which has always been a characteristic of those ancient races which have been killed off the face of the earth by their luxuries and vices; for as human females increase in size so also they decrease in vigour, endurance and fruitfulness.[41]

And a Russian in the *Pall Mall Gazette*:

> it is too late for you to take any action that will save your race from speedy extinction, because during the last thirty years the English people have become mentally, morally, and physically rotten to the core. If your male population only were defective there might be some chance of your regeneration; but your women have decayed also, as is clearly proved by the miserably feeble, imbecile, crippled and neurotic children which they bring into the world to be future English citizens.[42]

Of course, the British elites still believed they were top of the world, while elites in other countries tended to be envious Anglophiles. But the

Germans felt that they were really catching up. By 1900, Germany had a larger share of trade with other industrial countries than Britain.[43] The great Anglo-German rivalry that preceded the Great War had an economic underpinning. And this was the novelty. Until then Britain's great rival had been France. Now industrial competition had become more important than the political one or, to put it differently, economics had become the main determinant of politics. If you were on top, economically speaking, you tried to remain on top. If you were near the top, you tried to make it to the top. If you were outside the magic circle of 'top countries', you tried to enter it. In the world of capitalism standing still is an unaffordable luxury, hence the British anxiety about decline and decadence. The use of the word 'decadence', whether in *The Times* or in books, accelerates constantly from 1800 to 1900, before calming down. The use of the word 'decline' gently decreased between 1810 and 1920, then increased (with a pause during the Second World War) before decreasing again in the 1980s, paradoxically, just as capitalist growth declined.[44]

There were laggards with a long way to go. Italy, for instance, though far from the bottom of the league in terms of European development (she did better than most), had a textile industry that was almost entirely pre-capitalist in terms of organization and was dominated by small entrepreneurs of rural origin craving the support of the state.[45] Alessandro Rossi, one of the country's few large-scale textile industrialists (founder of Lanerossi in 1873), though convinced of the benefits of large-scale industry, particularly his own, was equally convinced that the state should protect industry (particularly his). When it came to the so-called 'social question', the euphemism for helping the poor, he was an economic liberal. The state should keep out of welfare. This should be left in the hands of philanthropic entrepreneurs like himself. The way to inspire workers was through a policy of paternalism (prizes, pensions, homes, schools). Yet Rossi was a modern entrepreneur able to combine tradition and innovation and able to link up with the most advanced European business centres.[46] The commitment to what we would call today 'compassionate capitalism' was aimed at keeping the state out of the way, unless capitalism and capitalists were in trouble, in which case the state had to intervene and save them both.

Which foreign model to choose became a permanent preoccupation of Italian elites, though, in general, the idea was to pick and choose whatever was convenient. Odd explanations for backwardness were provided by people regarded as economic luminaries. Thus Luigi Einaudi, later President of the Italian Republic (1948–55), wrote in

1899 that the reason why the standard of living in Italy was lower than elsewhere in Europe was because of the high population density (a way of saying that there were too many people). Actually, density was higher in far more prosperous Belgium and Great Britain.[47] And Einaudi added that if Italy wanted to avoid the fate of Iberian or Balkan people, it should imitate England and Germany rather than France by adopting more liberal economic policies.[48] Obviously he had failed to realize that both England and Germany had turned towards liberal interventionism.

In fact, the Italian state was far from inactive, whether run by conservatives (the so-called *Destra Storica*, the 'historic right') or the liberals. Public expenditure in the years leading up to the First World War was a considerable 16–18 per cent of GNP.[49] The money was spent on traditional law-and-order duties and education, but also on public works (the railways above all, as well as the telegraph and the postal services) and on some of the infrastructure necessary for capitalist development. Private enterprise was often subsidized by the state in the form of loans and guarantees. In the Italian South there was further intervention in agriculture in the hope of alleviating poverty and keeping the landlords on the side of the new Italian state.[50]

Everyone agreed on the link between industry and modernity, and on the necessity to bridge the gap with the wealthier European countries, but also with the idea that the road to prosperity, if it were to involve a wider group of people than the elites, would go a long way towards ensuring a greater degree of legitimacy for the recently united Italy. This project, or hope, of democratization via industrial production and industrial consumption was made clear, as Ilaria Barzaghi shows with a wealth of illustrations, at the 1881 Esposizione Industriale Nazionale held in Milan in 1881, only twenty years after national unification.[51]

In other Mediterranean countries, deprived of even the backward capitalism that existed in Italy, the prospects were negative. That was the case with Spain and Greece, but Portugal too stagnated in the decades leading up to the First World War, partly because of bad harvests (Portugal was highly dependent on its agriculture), partly because of the drop of remittances from Brazil.[52] Its internal market was small, but it could have used the revenue of some of its exports (cork, tinned fish, wine) to fund manufacturing, yet its chances to excel in this were poor, given the competition from the more advanced European countries. Little was spent on education in spite of the country having one of the lowest literacy rates in Europe.[53] Humiliated by Britain in Africa, debilitated by a chronic governmental instability (fifty-four cabinets between 1834 and 1905 and ten between 1905 and 1910), plagued by corruption at the highest levels, and further weakened by social unrest, the Portuguese monarchy collapsed shortly after the assassination of King Carlos I in 1908. A republic was proclaimed in 1910.[54] The decisive force in the Portuguese 'revolution' had been the middle classes and an intelligentsia ideologically committed, as was that of Spain and much of Latin America, to anticlerical liberal republicanism, which made them even more distant from the traditional peasantry.

Yet some 'laggard' countries caught up in what might seem to be unpropitious circumstances. Finland, for instance, had been part of the Tsarist Empire as a Grand Duchy since 1809. The country was poor. In 1860, Finland's per capita GDP was 25 per cent lower than the European average. Only 4 per cent of the population was engaged in manufacture. Then industrial output grew by more than 5 per cent every year.[55] By 1914 it had caught up with the average European GDP per capita, thanks to the growth of agriculture and, above all, forestry.[56]

In Russia a different pattern emerged. Russian and Ukrainian peasants, more mobile than it is usually thought, migrated towards the Asian parts of the expanding Russian Empire, east of the Urals (particularly Siberia and Kazakhstan). These colonists did not, on the whole, destroy the local populations (these, unlike indigenous Americans, were not prone to the diseases the settlers brought with them). By gradually colonizing large areas of Asian Russia, the migrants could sustain an increase in population without having to make major changes to their way of life. They did not need to try to limit the size of their families; they did not need to migrate overseas; they did not need to innovate; they could remain backward. The persistence of Russian peasant society, 'that was still very much evident in 1897 was, to a large degree, a consequence of peasant migration and the settlement of Russia's frontiers between the mid-sixteenth and late-nineteenth centuries'.[57] There were, of course, major areas of the Tsarist Empire that were taking off into industrial growth and they coexisted with the backward zones, as in other parts of Europe.

The fate of 'laggards' in history is somewhat curious. They are impinged upon far more by the external world than the so-called pioneers. They are supposed to catch up yet they cannot replicate exactly the action of the pathbreakers, for the latter operate in an environment in which, by definition, they have few or no competitors. If you are on top and no one challenges you, there is no need to try to change anything (though perhaps you should). There is a reason why old elites are conservative. It is one thing to initiate change, as Britain did; it is another to have change thrust upon you. One needs to react. Laggards cannot wait for entrepreneurs to materialize out of nothing. The state must take the lead. In eastern Europe, the socio-economic pull of the West was such that it was the old elites which, however half-heartedly, tried to lead the industrial and political revolutions.[58]

The language used to describe the process of 'catching up' (just like the expression 'laggard') assumes a vision of stages: from under-developed to developed, from inferior to superior, from backward to advanced. Inevitably, this 'stagist' and determinist view tends to simplify a complex process. After all, British industrial growth followed a fairly lengthy period of agricultural progress and an equally remarkable period of commercial expansion. 'Stagist' views have been common throughout history. Ideas of progress based on the replication of past successes were held by Marx and many of his followers: 'The country that is more developed industrially,' asserted Marx in the Preface to *Capital*, 'only shows, to the less developed, the image of its own future.'[59] A similar position has also been held subsequently by anti-Marxists such as Walt Rostow in *The Stages of Economic Growth: A Non-Communist Manifesto* (1960), or by pre-Marxists such as Friedrich List (who envisaged a progression from pastoral life to agriculture to manufactures, etc., as set out in *The National System of Political Economy*). Adam Smith in the first of his *Lectures on Jurisprudence* (December 1762) suggested 'four distinct states which mankind pass thro: – 1st, the Age of Hunters; 2dly, the Age of Shepherds; 3dly, the Age of Agriculture; and 4^{thly}, the Age of Commerce'.[60] By the time of *The Wealth of Nations* (1776) he was down to three stages of 'natural' development. During the first, 'the greater part of capital of every growing society is, first, directed to Agriculture', then to manufactures, 'and, last of all, to foreign commerce'. However, he then added, 'this natural order of things' has, in all the modern states of Europe, been 'entirely inverted'.[61] Distinguished economic historians, such as Karl Polanyi, Alexander Gerschenkron, and Barrington Moore, were committed to a developmental conception, even though they all agreed that the ways out of under-development could be varied.[62] Policy differences so dependent on different conjunctures might explain why the search for a 'bourgeois' revolutionary model has proved so controversial and so fruitless. Barrington Moore's famous *Social Origins of Dictatorship and Democracy* (1966) was groundbreaking because it tried to construct a typology of evolution into industrialization and democracy by distinguishing three cases:[63]

1. Capitalist democracy (USA, UK, and France) resulting from the conflict between the industrial bourgeoisie and landed interests.
2. Authoritarian regimes (Germany and Japan) where the landed elites remain dominant and conduct a 'revolution from above'.
3. Communist regimes (Russia and China) resulting from a peasant revolution for land.

There is something rather Western and rather modern (i.e. post-Enlightenment) in such a developmental conception. As Patrick O'Brien pointed out, historians of economic development, traditionally, have found it difficult not to use the category of stages.[64] To demarcate the precise moment when one leaves a stage and enters a new one is far from simple, yet in the popular literature, the press, and in everyday political discourse the idea of stages (pre-this and post-that) is as strong as ever.

And there is a further problem: the vision of a First/Second/Third World was always one closely connected to the Cold War. The First World was the West, the second was the Communist world, and then there was the Rest. In reality the term Third World quickly came to assume the same meaning as under-developed, so that in fact there were two worlds: the developed and the under-developed or, to put it bluntly, the West and the Rest. But the 'Rest' was always far too wide-ranging a concept. As Colin Leys pointed out, one ends up putting very different countries in the under-developed basket: Haiti, Thailand, Rwanda, and China – all in this all-encompassing 'Third World' category.[65] The United Nations General Assembly has attempted to be less blunt, and in 1971 it listed the world's 'least developed countries' or LDCs. It was envisaged that this would work like some kind of football league table, with countries graduating from the status of 'least developed' to the less dismal 'developing'. Very few graduated and, at the bottom of the pile, according to almost any listing (see the IMF World Economic Outlook Database), virtually all the bottom countries are African. But the central assumption of development theory was still the ruling one: eventually, in the fullness of time, if they worked hard, developed a strong bourgeoisie, got rid of backward landlords, eliminated corruption, etc., they would be able to join the happy world of the better off.

Counterpoised to the idea of stages is that of cycles. The former asserts a vision of progress; the latter asserts that who is up must come down, that empires come and go, the United States declines and China returns. It is almost as if the idea of cycles reinforces our idea of natural justice, with the underdog rising while the top dog bites the dust. The idea of progress may be antithetical to the idea of cycles in history but they both share a deterministic element: the first believes that one can only go up, the second that what goes up must come down. Chinese historical culture was deeply committed to the idea that there was a natural cycle of flourishing and decay: the first chapter of the most widely read of Chinese classics, the fourteenth-century *The Romance of the Three Kingdoms*, opens with the announcement that 'The Empire, long divided, must unite; long united, must divide. Thus it has ever been.'[66] The prophecy, of course, may turn out to be true. The beauty with cyclical views is that they cannot be falsified. If one waits long enough the downside may well appear. If it doesn't, it simply means we have not waited long enough. Cyclical views, however, cannot really explain novelties such as industrialization. Nor can they explain what one must do to move away from pre-capitalism. One thing is certain: no country has done so entirely through the spontaneous workings of the markets – not even England.

The idea of a more or less fixed path to development, where each laggard catches up by replicating what the pioneers have done before, may seem commonsensical. It is, after all, the basis of what came to be known as the Washington Consensus (see Chapter 5). Such views, because of their seductive simplicity, have been adopted by many commentators who thought that a country could escape poverty if it followed the formula: privatization, small government, deregulation, free trade, etc.

Historians have been scathing about this for a long time. The simplistic reduction of developmental differences to a mathematical formula was criticized in 1952 by Charles Kindleberger, the economic historian, commenting on World Bank missions and their 'country reports'. Decades before the formulation of the Washington Consensus, he wrote, somewhat sarcastically, that these were 'essays in comparative statics. The missions bring to the underdeveloped world a notion of what a developed country looks like. They observe the underdeveloped country. They subtract the former from the latter. The difference is a program.'[67] His conclusion was that though the authors of these reports may have learned much from the countries they have visited, 'they do not yet know much about the process of economic development. I hasten to add that neither does anyone else.'

Not much new here. In the nineteenth century it was common practice for laggard countries to compare their economic structures with those of more successful models (usually an idealized version of Great

Britain). The stages of English economic development seemed 'so inescapable that whenever a developing country in the West happened to dispense with some of the prerequisites or to bypass some of its stages, its performance was usually presented as an exception proving the rule'.[68] Britain remained a model for a long time, even though there is little reason to suppose that the British road could be replicated or even that it was the 'best'.[69]

The problems of 'laggard' countries were seen to be for them to resolve. Thus in France it was common to blame the excessively individualistic mentality of local entrepreneurs, their dour rurality, their obsessive concern with family, their inability to 'think big', their narrowness of mind derived from their peasant roots, etc.[70] French banking, in comparison to the British, was said to be primitive and unable to provide industry with the necessary capital.[71] Also blamed was the scarcity of labour due to the low birth rate, the attraction of public employment, which, allegedly, starved the private sector of labour, and the multiplicity of small firms.[72] This was all the more surprising since France was regarded throughout Europe as politically advanced thanks to its revolution. Besides, the French Second Empire (1852–70) had laid the foundations for the regular and rapid development of industry in the decades following its demise. French industrialization followed a model suited to France, adapted to a large peasant population without a great surplus for consumer expenditure, a wealthy urban market, and export markets that absorbed the high quality goods for which France was long renowned.[73]

Between 1865 and 1895 French growth rates were low (an average of 0.6 per cent against 1.5 per cent in the preceding twenty years and 1.6 per cent in the next thirty years, and 1.9 per cent in the period 1929–63). There might not have been as sudden a sustained take-off, but at least development was more harmonious than elsewhere.[74] The low birth rate and consequent scarcity of labour, inevitably, caused wages to remain higher than in other countries.[75] Although consistently behind Great Britain and Germany, France was ahead of almost everyone else in the development of railways, telegraphs, and shipping – the pillars of industrialization (not that this calmed down French uneasiness at not being first). Besides, the low level of population increase meant that growth was largely due to an increase in productivity.[76] The Germans, just as prone as the French to exhibiting angst for not doing as well as others, regarded France as the main modern state on the continent, as their natural rival, and admired the speed at which France had recovered, economically and politically, from the defeat of 1870.[77] The country seemed richer than Germany.[78] Their banks, such as Crédit Lyonnais, the Société Générale (run by an English banker, Edward Charles Blount, from 1886 to 1901), the Banque de Paris et des Pays-Bas, were more powerful than the German ones. The Paris Bourse rivalled the London Stock Exchange. French capitalism was the capitalism of small firms only when compared to the United States and the United Kingdom. By defining 'giant' firms as those employing more than one thousand workers (of which there were some 3,000 in the world at the beginning of the twentieth century) and calculating the proportion of employees in manufacturing in the 'giant' firms, France ranked just below Germany and Sweden.[79]

Yet even in France the liberals looked up to Britain as the model to follow. French liberals not only admired the Manchester School but also political liberalism and its leading representative, William Gladstone. Gladstone has pride of place in the coverage of the *Revue des deux mondes* throughout the 1870s. Paul-Armand Challemel-Lacour, a leading French liberal, and a supporter of leading politicians Léon Gambetta and Jules Ferry, celebrated Gladstone as one of the few politicians able to see further than the short term and as a statesman who endeavoured to eliminate class differences 'due to the selfishness of the ones and the ignorance of the others', ready to use 'the public purse to help the working classes and to pacify them with equitable laws and plenty of employment'.[80] Another leading liberal, Léon Say, held the British parliamentary system to be the model France should follow if one wanted to create a great French Liberal Party.[81] There was little competition on the monarchist right, which produced no serious economic thought, at least until the end of the century.[82]

That Britain should have been a model is not surprising. The British themselves were quite conscious of this. It was not just a matter of greater wealth but also of a more *modern* way of life. In *The Progress of the World in Arts, Agriculture, Commerce, Manufactures, Instruction, Railways, and Public Wealth* (1880), the Irish author Michael Mulhall, in a work dedicated, without irony, 'to the press of Great Britain, which so zealously promotes the moral and material progress of the age', noted that the country was not just more prosperous ('our people are better fed, can do more work, and possess a greater amount of national wealth, than any other nation') but more civilized, less 'barbaric'. Mulhall celebrated the growth of schools and libraries, the expansion of institutions, the drop in crime rates (64 per cent between 1840 and 1877), the fact that 3 million women 'now earn their living' instead of 'depending on the men for support', and the increasing prosperity of the working classes.[83] Mulhall's comparative statistical work, one of the first of its kind, provided empirical substance to what everyone knew: though not as wealthy as the United States, Britain was, in 1894, the richest country in Europe and, by far, the foremost trading nation in the world.[84] It is no wonder that Anglophilia was strong on the continent, particularly among elites who were using the British model of liberalism to advance a specific programme of economic development.

Montesquieu had been an early Anglophile (he thought the British monarchy was the nearest to a real republic). Germaine de Staël, in her posthumous *Considérations sur les principaux événements de la Révolution française* (1818), compared England favourably to France. Thanks to its freedom and its stability England was spared the terrible experiences suffered by France in the preceding decades. England produced real heroes such as William Wilberforce, the champion of the abolition of the slave trade. England was far superior to France in the extent of press freedom, the respect for religion, the openness and depth of its culture, and the solidity of its political institutions. England was a country where merit prevailed over birth.[85] François Guizot, statesman, Protestant, historian, and admirer of England, in a letter written in 1857, piled on the praise, declaring that 'England is the avenue of dignity and human freedom. No nation, since the beginning of time, has become so great and wealthy without anger and bribery. She owes it to her Protestant Christianity and her parliamentary regime.'[86]

Learning lessons from 'abroad', namely from Britain, became the watchword. In Germany the most influential commentators on the British political scene – such as the economists and social reformers Lujo Brentano and Gerhart von Schulze-Gaevernitz – admired everything British, including the trade unions, because, unlike the German ones, they were non-political, busied themselves with improving wages and conditions, and had no intention of subverting capitalism.[87] Friedrich List, conscious of Germany's laggard status, writing in 1841, was effusive in his admiration for Great Britain:

> In all ages there have been cities or countries surpassing others in manufactures, trade and navigation; but the world has never witnessed a supremacy to be compared with that existing in our time . . . Far from having been stopped in its progress by England, the world has received from her its strongest impulse. She has served as a model to all nations in her internal and external policy; in her great inventions and grand enterprises of every kind; in the advancement of the useful arts; in the construction of roads, railways and canals; in the discovery and cultivation of lands in

> a state of nature, particularly in displaying and developing the natural wealth of tropical countries; and in the civilization of tribes, savage or subsiding into barbarism. Who can tell how far the world would have been behind if there had been no England? And if England even now should cease to exist, who can say how far mankind would retrograde?[88]

List was not a narrow nationalist. On the contrary, he wanted all nations to reach a similar level of prosperity and of common peaceful coexistence. Britain's early success had enabled its manufactured goods to invade much of Europe, eliciting the kind of envious and worried comments that later would be made of German, American, or Chinese products.

Admiration for Britain was not new. At the close of the eighteenth century a traveller, the geologist Barthélemy Faujas-Saint-Fond, marvelled at the excellence of British products, such as leather, beer, and, above all, Wedgwood earthenware (known in France as *fayance anglaise*), which, deservedly in his view, had become universally available from Paris to St Petersburg, in Holland, Sweden, Spain, and Italy.[89] He even mentioned the excellent dinner he had enjoyed at the Royal Society, though he was puzzled and a little upset by the lack of napkins, amazed by the terrible coffee, and alarmed by the huge consumption of port.[90]

Admiration for England, as virtually all continentals called the United Kingdom, was as strong as ever fifty years later. In 1845, as Britain was poised to repeal the Corn Laws, Camillo Benso, Count of Cavour, future Prime Minister of a united Italy, but then a simple deputy in the parliament of the Kingdom of Sardinia, wrote:

> The commercial revolution which is now taking place in England . . . will have a mighty impact on the Continent. By opening up the richest market in the world to foodstuffs, it will encourage their production . . . The need to provide for regular foreign demand will arouse the energy of these agricultural industries . . . Trade will then become an essential element in the prosperity of the agrarian classes, who will then naturally tend to join the supporters of the liberal system.[91]

Fifteen years earlier, the liberal economist Giuseppe Pecchio, in exile in England (he died in Brighton in 1835), wrote in his *Osservazioni semiserie di un esule sull'Inghilterra* (*Semi-serious Observations of an Exile in England*, translated into English in 1833) that 'There is scarcely a single nation in Europe which is not in her debt for the protection afforded', and that everything in England was better, including the roads and the canals, for there were more of them than in the rest of

Europe put together' and 'more civilization'. Even the lunatic asylums were better, including Bedlam, which was 'vast and sumptuous'.[92]

In the Italian intelligentsia, Anglophilia was the default position even after the unification of the country and particularly among the more conservative elements. After all, Britain had managed to be both rich and free and had changed gradually, unlike the French, who were in regular upheaval. The jurist Domenico Zanichelli constantly compared Britain favourably to France and Italy. In an 1883 lecture he celebrated the 'great spectacle' offered by Britain, 'the only European state where revolutionary doctrines did not succeed in establishing themselves, the only one which Napoleon could not defeat; all of this contributed to push the people towards orderly freedom'.[93] In another lecture, in 1886, in the presence of the King and Queen of Italy, he declared that 'Constitutional development in England is quite different from that of France, and history shows us that the English system is by far better than that of France'.[94]

The more developed countries offered the 'backward' countries of Europe, those on the 'periphery', an economic challenge and an opportunity: rapidly industrializing countries became importers of raw material and agricultural produce, and 'backward' countries could become exporters of raw materials, thus joining in world trade.[95] However, the countries of eastern Europe were not equipped to take up such a challenge; precisely because they were backward, they had no adequate institutional and economic frameworks, suffered from the persistence of feudal customs, lacked a sound financial system, had poor education, and no unified national market. Their elites were split between modernizers and traditionalists.[96] Eastern European countries remained behind western Europe before the First World War, between the wars, under communism, and after the fall of communism.[97]

The problem is not just one of industrial development. Not all the more advanced countries were industrialized. The United States, for example, was a major exporter of food, and Australia, not usually classified as a laggard, was and has remained largely an exporter of primary products. The problem is that the 'laggard' countries of eastern Europe were backward as agricultural producers too. And if they managed to export agricultural produce (as Romania and Hungary did with their grain), they only strengthened a backward agricultural sector ready eventually to be eclipsed by the higher agricultural productivity of advanced countries.

The case of Hungary was emblematic. The country (part of the Austro-Hungarian Empire) saw a great spurt towards industrialization only in the late 1880s with annual growth rates of 6–7 per cent.[98] Leading sectors were all in heavy industry, usually connected to the railways, public works, armaments, and therefore connected to the state-induced demand.[99] The main export, however, was wheat and, indeed, the years before 1875 were years of relative prosperity for wheat growers (who were seldom the small farmers). In the 1880s and 1890s Budapest was, next to Minneapolis, the second-largest flour-milling centre in the world.[100] Since there was money in wheat, other crops and sheep farming were abandoned whenever possible in favour of wheat. Then disaster struck: improvements in transportation and cultivation (such as railroad building in North America and commercial steam shipping) made American wheat far cheaper than that of Hungary. By the 1890s the cost of producing wheat in Hungary was 30 per cent above that of the United States. When international prices dropped by almost 50 per cent, poorer Hungarian farmers were hit badly. There followed the gradual abandonment of the land by the better-educated sons of the better off. It was the same story in Romania (see Chapter 4). And since the best jobs available were in the public sector and above all in the state bureaucracy, this is where they went. The larger and better-organized landlords formed pressure groups lobbying the state for tariffs to protect them against foreign wheat.[101] Once again ideology was trumped by sheer necessity. Sándor Wekerle (Finance Minister from 1887 to 1892 and then thrice Prime Minister of Hungary) was a liberal and committed to laissez-faire, but when he faced the beginnings of the agrarian crisis, admitted that 'Agriculture is unable to intensify production. The population is increasing and the excess can be absorbed only if the state is ready to intervene.'[102]

By 1914, Hungarian agriculture in output per capita was roughly the same as the rest of western Europe, albeit with lower productivity, and per capita industrial production was roughly the same as Italy.[103] Unlike Italy, however, Hungary was not a sovereign state but part of an empire, though integrated in a market of 40 to 50 million people.[104] The advantages of being part of a wider market (such as the European Union) at the expense of some loss in sovereignty would be constantly debated.

Each country entered modernity in its own way, though not always at a time of its own choosing; at times internal forces were dominant, at others external pressures were decisive.

So, if there were no well-trodden paths to follow, no recipe for success, no models to imitate, how was one to drag one's country into the era of so-called modernity, however and whoever defines modernity? Until it is well entrenched, modernity has few friends, but these are often powerful enough to be able to use force to drag the recalcitrant majority onto the path of the new. The operation is made easier by the relative lack of democracy that generally precedes the establishment of capitalism. It is, after all, rare that industrialization can advance without some human suffering. Or, as Marx put it, rather melodramatically: capital comes 'dripping from head to foot, from every pore, with blood and dirt'.[105] In eighteenth-century Britain, common land was forcibly enclosed by landlords. Money was made by transporting slaves to the Americas to pick the cotton that made Lancashire manufacturers rich (including Friedrich Engels's family firm, Baumwollspinnerei Ermen & Engels, which had cotton mills in Manchester and Oldham as well as in North Rhine-Westphalia). Much of this cotton cloth was then sold to India, which before the Industrial Revolution had been the main exporter of cotton. Landless peasants made their way to insalubrious cities where work could be found in the new factories. Others went across oceans to settle in what were colonies or former colonies – like the United States. More violence ensued as the native population in the Americas, Australia, and parts of Africa was exterminated or marginalized. The process of industrial growth was not accompanied by anything resembling full democracy – not in Britain in the 1830s, not in Russia in the 1930s, not in China in the 1980s and 1990s, not in Japan before 1945, not in Taiwan before 1996, not in South Korea before 1987, or in South Africa until 1994, and not in Spain until the end of the Franco dictatorship in the 1970s.

In all instances industrialization was guided from above by elites, sometimes enlightened and sometimes not, but often acting, in the words of Anatole Leroy-Beaulieu, a French specialist on Russia writing in 1881, with the vanguard spirit of members of the Russian nobility:

> The Russian nobility behaved like a General Staff who, impatient to rush ahead, launches into a gallop without looking back. Meanwhile its army, carrying its baggage and pulling its carriages is left behind, stuck in muddy marches, or tangled in the underbrush, deaf to the calls of the trumpet or clarion . . . So the elites of Russian society hurled themselves forward. Attracted by the fascinating lights of civilization, they rushed towards Europe, leaving the stragglers behind without a thought for those unable to follow, as if the whole country had been conscripted in its armed ranks, as if the whole of Russia shared the same goal as the world of St Petersburg.[106]

The Russian reformers were too precipitate, going much faster than the country was ready for. Yet they were not entirely wrong. Industrialization was more a matter of politics than economics. And examples mattered. When Britain began on the road to industrialization, it may have been the most democratic country in Europe, but this 'democracy' involved just, at best, the middle classes. The common people, as they were called, were not involved, even tangentially, in the business of political decision-making. It was only in the last decades of the nineteenth century that it would become difficult, though not impossible, for any European country to industrialize without seeking some kind of popular support (not necessarily through the electoral process). The people would have to be involved not just in the construction of an industrial society but of a national community.

How such a national community could be formed became a major political issue in the decades preceding the First World War. Various strategies were pursued. The most obvious was available only to the wealthiest countries: distributing rapidly the gains of industrialization by a rapid improvement in consumption. The conditions of existence in even the most prosperous European countries were low for the majority of the population, though in countries such as Britain, Germany, Belgium, and France the skilled working class was well on the way to becoming part of the system. On the whole, however, people would have to be harnessed to the capitalist project by ideological means as well as by material prosperity, by making the people feel they were part of a common project and also by establishing or reinforcing the limits to capitalist exploitation, such as the length of the working day, promoting public health, welfare, and free education – what we now call the welfare state. This, as we shall see in greater detail in Part Three, developed with greater intensity in the last decades of the nineteenth century.

Other ways of constructing a national community were deployed: nationalism, which sought to embrace every citizen; the acquisition of colonies, which provided not only national pride but also markets, a focus for emigration, and state-subsidized jobs; and, finally, the development of democratic structures subject to some form of popular control. Democracy, welfarism, nationalism, and imperialism thus became part of the capitalist project. The consumer society was yet to come. Even in Britain it took a long time for the benefits of industrial growth to trickle down to the wider population.

Eventually, capitalism extended its dominion over the globe. The cosmopolitan tendencies of capitalism had been noted by Marx and Engels as early as 1848 in the *Communist Manifesto*, when they declared:

> In place of the old local and national seclusion and self-sufficiency, we have intercourse in every direction, universal inter-dependence of

nations . . . National one-sidedness and narrow-mindedness become more and more impossible . . .[107]

But laggards also have advantages. In a relatively brief period of time they can use what others have invented or perfected over many decades. Thus Japan and Germany eventually caught up with the leading countries, the United Kingdom and the United States, partly thanks to borrowed technologies. Great Britain was no longer the pioneer in agricultural technology. Land productivity increased rapidly in Denmark and the Netherlands (dairy farming), in Germany (potatoes and sugar beet), and in the USA, thanks to the mechanization of agriculture. All these were economies where peasant owners – the champions of the principle of property rights – dominated.[108] Between 1840 and 1910 productivity in American agriculture had doubled, as did that of Sweden and Switzerland. Germany, an agricultural laggard in 1840 (in European terms), had surpassed Britain by 1910, but Russian agricultural productivity had barely improved.[109]

The truth of the matter is that the economic development of a country does not depend just on the country itself but on the entire world economy, including those countries that remain under-developed. How good you are depends also on how bad the others are. Moreover, the pioneers, by the mere fact of being first, alter the environment of others and often, at least in the short term, for the worse. As Marx and Engels explained in their early work, *The German Ideology* (1846):

the more the original isolation of the separate nationalities is destroyed . . . the more history becomes world-history . . . Thus, for instance, if in England a machine is invented which in India or China deprives countless workers of bread, and overturns the whole form of existence of these empires, this invention becomes a world-historical fact.[110]

Such a view of global interconnectedness had already been noted by Immanuel Kant: 'The peoples of the earth have thus entered in varying degrees into a universal community, and it has developed to the point where a violation of rights in one part of the world is felt everywhere.'[111] Fifty years later this had become a familiar theme, at least among specialists. The Austrian statistician Franz Xaver von Neumann-Spallart, writing in 1887, explained:

It is becoming ever more apparent that the economic condition of individual nations is determined by their dependence on all other nations, to which they are connected by countless ties . . . Today the course of trade in general is being decided outside the continental boundaries of Europe;

> it is being decided on one side of the far west, beyond the Atlantic Ocean, and on the other side in the far east . . .[112]

In 1891 the Reverend William Cunningham, President of the Economic Science and Statistics Section of the British Association, in his address entitled 'Nationalism and Cosmopolitanism in Economics' pointed out that at least in England:

> We no longer contemplate isolation from the rest of the globe; we only grumble because other people interpose barriers which check free commercial intercourse between all parts of the known world . . . We have given up all idea that the nation should be self-sufficing . . . we regard England as part of a greater whole . . . as one portion of a cosmopolitan economic organism . . .[113]

This unambiguously extolled celebration of interdependence in a globalized world, one century before the term globalization would become commonplace, entailed a vision of a future nation-less capitalism: 'patriotism is left out of sight, and capital is invested wherever there is an apparent promise of profits'. 'Capital tends to minimize the differences between nations . . .' noted Cunningham, and he added (almost echoing the famous concluding words of the *Communist Manifesto*): 'There thus comes to be a class sympathy between wage-earners in many lands, such as has never existed before in the history of the world.'[114]

Equally optimistic was Gustave Hervé, then a French socialist politician, who in 1910 pointed out that the development of science and communication (railways, steamships, and telegraph) in the second half of the nineteenth century had created a situation in which goods, capital, and people could circulate freely, cheaply, and securely, as if with a touch of a magic wand, and borders just seemed like a grotesque anachronism.[115]

Jean Jaurès, the French socialist leader, was equally aware that capital was becoming a free-floating system, able to transcend national boundaries. In a speech in December 1911 he explained that capital has 'the speed of movement, the freedom of flight of large migratory birds', adding '. . . over the frontiers of races and customs barriers industrial and financial capitalism cooperate in unison'.[116]

But what neither Cunningham, Marx, Jaurès, nor Hervé said was that potential class sympathy and internationalism were constantly undermined by the reality of international competition. (Two years later Hervé jettisoned socialism, turned into a rabid nationalist and, after the war, into a fascist.) Lower wages in one part of the world, though sometimes leading to an improvement in the conditions of life of local workers, might cause unemployment or force down wages elsewhere. This was perfectly clear to contemporaries. Thus Giovanni Dalla Vecchia, an Italian commentator writing in the liberal periodical *The Contemporary Review* about the bread riots in April 1898 in southern Italy, attributed their cause not just to taxation, political corruption, or even the failure to colonize Ethiopia, but also to the rise in the price of bread, itself a consequence of a distant event: 'the Hispano-American war'.[117]

Writing in the 1880s, Charles Booth noted the changes that had come over the population of Clerkenwell in central London. 'Half a century or so ago,' he wrote in his *Life and Labour of the People in London*, the local industries '. . . – watch and clock-making, gold-beating, diamond-cutting, and the manufacture of jewellery – were in a flourishing condition, and throughout this district masters and journeymen worked and lived in prosperity'. The trade was almost all carried out in private houses with the manufacturers living on the premises and having a workshop in the rear or in the basement. 'Now this is much changed. Under the stress of cheap foreign production the Clerkenwell trade has steadily declined.' The masters and their artisans had left, their place taken by 'a lower class': 'policemen, postmen and warehousemen at the top, casual labourers at the bottom'.[118]

Globalization had significant consequences even then. Urban centres, scattered throughout the world, from Shanghai to Buenos Aires, from Alexandria to Naples, were increasingly part of this newly emergent global economy.[119]

The gap between the pathbreaker and some of the laggards narrowed. By the end of the Victorian era English industry was faltering. In the years before the First World War, British growth was averaging less than that of the United States, Germany, and Sweden, and productivity was even lower than that of France.

The surge of the United States was particularly significant. Already in the 1860s the USA had caught up technologically with Britain. By 1870 primacy in technological innovation in Europe had shifted to Germany, which was also on the verge of becoming post-industrial: between 1883 and 1925 the number of white-collar workers increased five times whereas that of industrial workers 'only' doubled.[120]

Britain retained its lead in shipping, insurance, brokerage, banking, and was still the world's largest trading power.[121] In 1900 it still had the highest GDP per head in the world, but by 1914 it had been overtaken by the United States, Australia, and New Zealand.[122]

Why was Britain the pathbreaker? Modern capitalism, it is true, originated in Britain and the Low Countries, but it did so because of exceptional social and economic reasons. It did not have to happen. Had landlords in Britain been unable (for cultural or political reasons) to enclose, with parliamentary support, land hitherto held in common, they might not have been able to increase agricultural yield and promote innovation. Expelled labourers would not have become an industrial workforce and consumers of agrarian surplus.[123] Had there not been relatively high wages in Europe entrepreneurs would not have been forced to experiment with technological innovations.

Coal was widely perceived to have contributed massively to British industrial success, accompanied with an anxiety about the depletion of natural resources. The economist William Stanley Jevons in *The Coal Question* (1865) did not think that Britain's lead could possibly last because:

> to disperse so lavishly the cream of our mineral wealth is to be spendthrifts of our capital – to part with that which will never come back. And after all commerce is but a means to an end, the diffusion of civilization and wealth. To allow commerce to proceed until the source of civilization is weakened and overturned is like killing the goose to get the golden egg.[124]

These were not solely the preoccupations of a mere economist. On 3 May 1863, William Gladstone, then Chancellor of the Exchequer, in his Financial Statement to the House of Commons, explained the reasons behind British successes. What is remarkable about this speech is that success is not attributed, as it would be today by any of today's ministers with a rudimentary knowledge of public relations, to the hard work of the people or the prescience and intelligence of the government, but to the luck of having mineral resources. The chief cause of British success, he explained:

> is the possession of our mineral treasures. The fact, not merely of the possession of coal, but of the possession of vast stores of coal under such circumstances that we can raise it to the surface at a lower price than any other country in the world . . . It is, then, our possession of coal . . . that has given us this extraordinary pre-eminence in commercial and industrial pursuits.[125]

And such circumstances, Gladstone did not need to add, could come to an end. Of course, mineral resources were, at most, a major contributing factor to British success, but the insistence of contemporaries on the importance of coal shows that, while the Victorians may have given the appearance of being a self-satisfied lot, they were, in reality, anxious and perturbed. As Stefan Collini has written: 'Victorian intellectuals were self-consciously members of a society in the van of progress: the first arrivals in the future cannot be sure what to expect . . .'[126]

Today we think that capitalism is the norm because it is the norm in our era; because it is a state of affairs almost everyone seeks (dissidents are regarded as misfits); because the only recent alternative, communism, failed; because a return to a pre-capitalist era could only occur after a major ecological catastrophe. Yet, it is useful to remind ourselves that, 'historically speaking, non-development is the rule rather than the exception . . .'[127]

One could easily imagine an economy in which the producers are mainly peasants, who sell part of their product on the market so they can buy some of the goods they cannot produce themselves (for example, salt, the kind of commodity that can be obtained only if one is near a mine or near the sea). Most peasant production, however, is for consumption. Luxury products made by artisans are mainly purchased by the well-off. The income of the upper classes is the chief determinant of the size of this market. This income in turn is determined by the rent they can obtain from the peasants. The level of this rent is determined largely by non-economic variables such as the weather, as well as by cultural and political factors.[128] In theory, things could go on like this for ever. Things certainly went on like this for a very long time. Nothing would necessarily propel this economy into a capitalist one.

But something did. A number of factors converged, and once industrial growth in one area was underway, it transformed at once all other areas and countries into 'laggards', while Britain, a small country with a large navy, became 'advanced'. The world had become global not only in the sense that there was global trade (an ancient phenomenon) but also in the sense that a particular set of economic arrangements came to be seen as the key to success in all other spheres.

Which other European country could have done the same? The Netherlands, a major commercial power in the eighteenth century? France? Or a small country like Belgium? With its excellent mining resources and abundant labour force Belgium was the second most industrialized country in the world when it was created in 1830. It was ahead of France and not far behind Britain. Like Britain it was committed, by the middle of the nineteenth century, to the kind of economic liberalism which, at the time, meant essentially the elimination of tariffs on agricultural produce.[129]

But size matters. Eventually even pathbreaking Britain was not a big enough country. The new leader was America, whose growing power impressed industrialists everywhere. The supremacy of other countries enables domestic producers to scare their own government into doing something about protecting industry, subsidizing it, and making all sorts of concessions. Adversaries, real or imaginary, are often more useful than friends.

8
Russia: The Reluctant Laggard

Napoleon's wars provided a major impetus towards modernization, as is often the case with wars. Prussia, Spain, and the Italian states, unable to withstand the emperor, were propelled towards reform. Russia, which *did* withstand the French armies, remained an absolutist state for decades, until it lost a war, the Crimean (1853–6), and tentative reforms were promulgated to make the state a little less absolute. The complex relationship between political absolutism and economic backwardness has dominated Russia's hesitant and problematic modernization from the second half of the nineteenth century to the present day.

Intellectuals dreamt of the awakening of Russia. The country's greatest poet, Alexander Pushkin, in a poem written in 1818 (he was only nineteen) dedicated to Pyotr Chaadayev (author of the *Philosophical Letters*, which denounced Russia's laggard status) wrote:

My friends, let's trust! It will rise up,
This star of charming lucky fortune
And on the fragments of despotism
They'll write all our simple names.[1]

More pessimistic was another major Russian poet, Mikhail Lermontov, a contemporary of Pushkin's. In 'A Prophecy', written in 1830 (Lermontov was only 16) and published in 1862, he foretells the terrible fate awaiting Russia:

A year will come – of Russia's blackest dread;
Then will the crown fall from the royal head,
The throne of tsars will perish in the mud,
The food of many will be death and blood . . .[2]

In 1860, Russia was the least developed of the so-called Great Powers with only 860,000 people in industry, out of an adult population of 74 million.[3] Russia's defeat in the Crimean War revealed her backwardness even to those who sought to deny it: Russian battleships were inferior to those of the British and the French; Russian rifles were primitive, the Russian transportation system rudimentary. In 1855, Leo Tolstoy, in his *Sevastopol Sketches*, celebrated the courage and resilience of the Russian people in defending not the Tsar but Mother Russia.[4] Something had to be done, and the state had to do it. State-led growth remained largely determined by military considerations. 'The state,' wrote the economic historian Alexander Gerschenkron, 'moved by its military interest, assumed the role of the primary agent propelling the economic progress in the country.'[5] Boris Chicherin, a remarkable liberal conservative, spoke for many when he wrote in 1857: 'What good is the great valour of the Russian people when their energies are sapped by the general corruption of the state apparatus, by the virtually universal corruption they see on all sides?' The people should no longer be treated as a child, he continued, but 'as an adult who thinks and acts independently'. Not that he was suggesting a limitation of tsarist authority ('about which no one in Russia even thinks', he added), but a mechanism for the Tsar to find out what it was that 'his' people were thinking.[6]

The problem, from the point of view of progress, was that in Russia the entrepreneurial bourgeoisie were weak and saw no problem with autocracy, from which all they wanted was a little protection. Liberal ideas were advanced not by the entrepreneurs themselves but by dissident elements of the aristocracy and by the intelligentsia. The ever percipient Paul Milyoukov, writing in 1905, noted, with only a slight exaggeration, that whereas in Europe liberalism originated in the bourgeoisie:

> in Russia though it was directed against the landlord class, as elsewhere, it was started by the members of the same class of agrarian gentry and nobility, and the promoters of the movement, far from supporting the class interests, undermined the social position of the nobility and destroyed the very source of their political power.[7]

They were guided by philanthropic considerations and advanced political theories rather than class interest. 'Russian liberalism was not bourgeois, but intellectual . . .'[8]

The connection between reforms and economic development was obvious to all, but for a long time even the liberal Russian intelligentsia was ambivalent about industrialization, preferring to emphasize the social, cultural, and political problems of backwardness rather than the economic ones. As early as 1842 the radical Russian thinker Alexander Herzen accused Romantic intellectuals of behaving like Don

Quixote in their scorn for labour and machines and for the 'material tendency of the age'. '[E]nsconced upon their high belfries,' he lamented, they 'failed to observe the romance of industrialization which was unfolding on so grand a scale in North America.'[9] Yet even Herzen, anxious about the consequences of industrial growth, thought that it might be possible to skip the dreaded 'stage' of private capitalist accumulation and project the country directly into a kind of ill-defined socialistic economy based on the village commune, the *obshchina*. It was on this basis that, much later, the Socialist Revolutionary Party, the heir to the Narodniks (the Populists), came closest to the aspiration of the peasantry and their apparent desire to hold land in common.[10]

Like many intellectuals, Herzen wanted everything: to liberate the individual and to preserve the commune; to have a special Russia, proud of its traditions and yet imbued with English liberalism; to have development without any of its drawbacks.[11] He wanted both Western modernity and Slavic tradition:

> Only the mighty thought of the West . . . is able to fertilize the seeds slumbering in the patriarchal mode of the life of the Slavs . . . The workmen's guild and the village commune, the sharing of profits and the partition of fields, the meeting of the *mir* and the union of villages into self-governing *volost*, are all the corner-stones on which the mansion of our future, freely communal existence will be built. But these corner-stones are only stones . . . and without the thought of the West our future cathedral would not rise above its foundations.[12]

The great debate between the Slavophiles and the Westernizers dominated Russian thought throughout the nineteenth century. At the heart of the Slavophile outlook was an almost mystical belief in the Russian peasant, the muzhik, and the communal ownership of land through the village commune, the *mir* or *obshchina*, which was one of the central institutions of rural Russia. Slavophiles believed in 'the people' from a position of reaction to modernity, they believed in the idyllic village, the *obshchina*, where decisions were taken by the local *sobornost* or spiritual community, and where individualism had no role. They decried the Westernizing sentiments of Tsar Peter the Great (r. 1682–1725) and Catherine the Great (r. 1762–96). The Westernizers had cut the connection between the aristocracy and the people, the *narod*. They claimed the aristocracy had turned their back on the Russian people. They had turned to the West. They imitated the Europeans. They were in awe of the French, the Germans, and the English. They were ashamed of being Russian, of being Slavic. In the 1830s religious writers such as Konstantin Aksakov and the poet Aleksey Khomyakov glorified the distinctiveness of the Slavic East, in its pure and uncontaminated Christianity, in the absence of all traces of Roman law or of what they regarded as 'pagan' irrationalism.[13] One can, at once, recognize a form of resistance to modernity that is not peculiar to Russia. In Russia, however, it was articulated with particular intensity. There was a strong belief among Slavophiles that it was among the simple people, among the peasantry, not among the ruling classes, that the idea of Russia and of the Orthodox Church was preserved.[14]

The Slavophiles moved with the times. As true reactionaries they devised new ways to stop the new. They wanted to preserve the *obshchina* but they wanted it precisely because it was a traditional non-capitalist, non-individualistic way of organizing and maintaining the rural economy. This debate on the development of capitalism between Slavophiles and Westernizers was almost a dress rehearsal for the grand issues of the following century on whether the road to capitalism (or socialism) would be more or less the same for all.[15]

Like so many other concepts embraced by the Russian intelligentsia, the idea that the *obshchina* might be of great significance for Russian development had to be legitimized from abroad, by foreign visitors such as August von Haxthausen. His *Studien über die innern Zustände, das Volksleben und insbesondere die ländlichen Einrichtungen Russlands* (*Studies on the Internal Conditions, the People and especially the Rural Institutions of Russia*, 1847–52), translated into French and English shortly after publication, was widely read among the educated classes, even though he was far from being the first to extol the commune.[16] Von Haxthausen had an idyllic view of peasant life derived from proto-Romantics such as Jean-Jacques Rousseau and Johann Gottfried Herder. He believed that the muzhik, the peasant, was morally superior, the quintessential Russian. Von Haxthausen enthused particularly about the patriarchal nature of the *obshchina* in the belief that the principles of this communal institution might ease the shock of industrial development. He was reassured in this by his perception of the non-revolutionary nature of the muzhik, whom, he thought, condescendingly, had:

> a childlike fear and veneration for the Czar; he loves him with devoted tenderness . . . The celebrated expression 'Prikazeno' (It is ordered), has a magical power over him. Whatever the Emperor commands must be done . . . The profound veneration felt for the Czar is also shown in the care of everything belonging to him . . .[17]

Such views were eagerly embraced by those who either did not want Russia to undergo any form of capitalist development at all, or hoped that the promised land of industrialization would be reached in a novel and original way, less individualistic, less destructive of the past, less harsh, avoiding the horrors described by Karl Marx:

> the highest development of productive power together with the greatest expansion of existing wealth will coincide with depreciation of capital, degradation of the labourer, and a most straitened exhaustion of his vital powers. These contradictions lead to explosions, cataclysms, crises, in which . . . capital . . . is violently reduced to the point where it can go on.[18]

The fear of such upheaval may explain why so many, in Russia, put their hopes in the people, the *narod*, the repository of wisdom, the embodiment of the Great Russian Soul. As Nikolai Berdyaev wrote in *The Russian Idea* (written during the Second World War), 'There are in the Russian people germs . . . of common life, of a possible brotherhood of man, things which are not yet to be found among peoples in the West.'[19]

In Ivan Turgenev's 1867 novel *Smoke* (*Dym*) the Westernizer Sozont Potugin points out that, while a group of Englishmen would discuss technological innovations, the Germans the unification of their country, and the French their amorous adventures, the Russians would discuss:

> the significance and the future of Russia . . . then, of course the rotten West comes in for its share. It's a curious thing, it beats us at every point, this West – but yet we declare that it's rotten! And if only we had a genuine contempt for it . . . but . . . the opinion of the West is the only thing we value, the opinion, that's to say, of the Parisian loafers . . . but the habits of slavery are too deeply ingrained in us; . . . And our pride is slavish, and slavish, too, is our humility.

And the rant continued:

> and Russia for ten whole centuries has created nothing of its own, either in government, in law, in science, in art, or even in handicraft . . . But wait a little, have patience; it is all coming. And, why is it coming . . .? Why, because we . . . the cultured classes are all worthless; but the people . . . Oh, the great people! You see that peasant's smock? That is the source that everything is to come from. All the other idols have broken down; let us have faith in the smock-frock. Well, but suppose the smock-frock fails us? No, it will not fail.[20]

Fyodor Dostoyevsky has one of his characters, Stepan Trofimovich Verkhovensky in *The Devils* (1871), express an equally sarcastic view of the potentialities of the peasantry:

> Like all people in a hurry, we've been too hasty with our peasants . . . We've made them the rage; for several years a whole branch of our literature has fussed over them as if they were some newly discovered treasure. We've crowned their lice-ridden heads with laurel wreaths. During the last thousand years the Russian village has given us nothing more than the Komarinsky dance.[21]

Others, such as Nikolai Chernyshevski, a writer much admired by Marx and Lenin, while distancing himself from those 'exclusive worshippers of the Russian national character' who regarded the *obshchina* as 'an object of mystical pride', thought that the *obshchina* could enable Russian peasants to avoid the dismal fate of the Western proletariat, through a direct transition from the primitive Russian village to some kind of socialistic cooperative of workers.[22] History, Chernyshevski wrote, adapting a Latin proverb, is like a grandmother fond of her younger grandchildren, the *tarde venientibus*, the latecomers; she gives them not the *ossa*, the bones, but the *medullam ossium*, the marrow of the bones.[23] In his *What Is To Be Done?* (a didactic novel written in prison in 1862; the title was later adopted by Lenin for his famous pamphlet of 1901), the heroine, the emancipated Vera Pavlovna, dreams of a future ideal society, and opens a cooperative of dressmakers. Chernyshevski's tone, however, hints that she might be deceiving herself:

> she tried to convince herself of what she wanted to believe, that the shop could get along without her, so that, in time, other shops might be established of the same kind, entirely spontaneously; and why not? Wouldn't it be a good thing? It would be better than anything else; even without any leadership, outside of the rank of seamstresses, but by the thought and planning of the seamstresses themselves.[24]

Others thought the idea that Russia could skip the Western stage of industrialization was Romantic and utopian nonsense. The literary critic Vissarion Belinsky, towards the end of his life (he died in 1848, he was only thirty-seven), recognized, unlike Herzen, the progressive and inescapable nature of capitalism and mocked those who dreamed of skipping stages:

> To bypass the period of reform, to leap over it, as it were, and to return to the preceding stage – is that what they call distinctive development? A truly

ridiculous idea, if only because it cannot be done, just as one cannot change the order of the seasons or force winter to come after spring . . .[25]

Skipping stages, however, was a concept that even Karl Marx had entertained. In 1881 the Russian revolutionary Vera Zasulich, then in exile in Geneva, wrote to Marx asking him 'a life or death question . . . for our socialist party': would the *obshchina* be able to develop in a socialist direction (and in this case the socialist movement would have to pour their energies into it) or, 'after decades', would farming become capitalist and only after further 'centuries of development' would Russian capitalism catch up with the West?[26] The question was obviously framed to obtain the desired, affirmative, answer, namely, one in favour of skipping capitalism altogether. Marx took the request seriously. He had been pondering the problem of stages for a while. Four years earlier, in late 1877, he had written to the editor of *Otyecestvenniye Zapiski* (*Notes on the Fatherland*), a liberal literary magazine, complaining that Nikolay Mikhaylovsky, a leading Narodnik:

> feels obliged to metamorphose my historical sketch of the genesis of capitalism in Western Europe into a historic-philosophic theory of the *marche générale* imposed by fate upon every people, whatever the historic circumstances in which it finds itself . . . But I beg his pardon. (He is both honouring and shaming me too much.)[27]

When he replied to Vera Zasulich, Marx wrote at first four drafts of varying length (one of which was almost 4,000 words) before finally sending a brief response declaring that the development of capitalism via the expropriation of the agricultural producer is likely to be a purely western European phenomenon, that the analysis in *Das Kapital* provides no reasons either for or against the vitality of the Russian commune, and finally that the 'special study' he had made of it had convinced him that the 'commune is the fulcrum for social regeneration in Russia'.[28] The question may have been of burning interest in 1881, but Zasulich did not publish Marx's reply, and within a few years (Marx died in 1883) it had become clear to her (and to most Marxists) that the disintegration of the *obshchina* was unstoppable.[29]

Liberals, such as Paul Milyoukov, the leader and founder of the Constitutional Democratic Party (the Kadets), had other criticisms of the *obshchina* (or *mir*), which, he wrote, was:

> ruled by its elders; following customs . . . The *mir* even had the right to meddle in family affairs and to chastise its members by the whip or by exile. In reality the *mir* was an instrument for tax collecting by the central

> government. Abuses of power were rife within the village, the will of the strongest prevailed. The village representative to the *zemstvo* [rural council] was in practice a little dictator who had all the powers.[30]

The beginning of the end for the more utopian visions of the Slavophiles (one in which the *obshchina* would prevent capitalism and preserve the sanctity of Russia from Westernization) had already occurred much earlier, in 1855, with the death of Tsar Nicholas I.[31] The abolition of serfdom finally seemed within reach: the new Tsar, Alexander II, was a progressive aware that ending serfdom had become the goal of the entire intelligentsia, both Slavophile and Westernizing. Its enduring existence in the second half of the nineteenth century was widely regarded as the main cause of the abysmal economic backwardness of Russia. It had been condemned in widely influential novels such as *Anton-Goremyka* (1847; *Luckless Anton*) by the twenty-five-year-old Dmitry Grigorovich, but progress was by no means straightforward.

Well before the October Revolution the image of the bourgeoisie evoked powerful negative images in Russia, and not just among socialist radicals.[32] This coexisted with a longing to 'do as they do in the West', which had been expressed since the days of Peter the Great.

To do 'as they do in the West', however, it was necessary to liberate the peasantry from the shackles of feudalism. Or so it was thought. The emancipation of the serfs was thus advocated for a mixture of reasons: humanitarian reasons, Westernization, but perhaps the main one was that it would enable industrialization. As Alexander Gerschenkron explained, it was only with the emancipation of the serfs that the main (but not the only) condition for the abysmal economic backwardness of Russia was removed.[33] Since fewer people on the land had to produce food not just for themselves but also for a growing proletariat, capitalism required a rise in agricultural productivity. Here the real model was the American one, but this was a model few could follow. Yet there were similarities between backward Russia and advanced America: the emancipation of the serfs, decreed by the Tsar in 1861, almost coincided with the abolition of slavery in the United States (1865).

The emancipation of the serfs delivered 20 million people from bondage and from the arbitrary power of the landlord. Many peasants felt themselves cheated. The burden of debts was heavier than ever, since now they owed the redemption payments, and the so-called cut-off land (*otrezki*) kept by the former masters was roughly one-sixth of the area involved.[34]

The Emancipation Decree was followed by reforms. It seemed as if a new era was dawning for Russia. In the course of the following decades, universities became more autonomous; the judiciary more independent; education and the army were reformed; censorship was alleviated; jury trials were instituted for all (except the peasants – 80 per cent of the population!). Locally elected rural assemblies, known as *zemstva*, were instituted in 1864.[35]

In January 1881, Alexander II instructed Count Mikhail Loris-Melikov, the Minister of the Interior, to draw up plans for a limited constitution. Two months later the Tsar himself was assassinated by terrorists from the organization *Narodnaya Volya* (People's Will). The reform process faltered and never recovered its impetus. Alexander II's successors (the obtuse Alexander III, who ruled until 1894, and the even less enlightened Nicholas II) aspired to industrialization without reforms. These they accepted only when pushed, and remained one step or two behind the society they thought they dominated. Their closest advisers were deeply conservative: the Minister of the Interior, Count Dmitry Tolstoy (related to the writer), the *ober-prokuror* (Chief Procurator) of the Holy Synod, Konstantin Pobedonostsev, and Mikhail Katkov, editor of the influential *Moskovskie vedomosti* (*Moscow News*). These, and people like them, were so ferocious in their criticism of Western individualism and capitalist development, and so powerful, that they often succeeded in delaying what the liberals regarded as essential reforms. The climate of thought among conservatives was epitomized by the philosopher and literary critic Konstantin Leontiev, author of *The East, Russia, and Slavdom* (1885–6), who believed that despotism was necessary for a 'flowering life', regarded egalitarianism as one of the greatest modern evils, and opposed universal education.[36]

The Russian reactionaries were too reactionary even for a reactionary Tsar like Alexander III, who realized he had to accept some of the liberals' views. He appointed as his Finance Minister Nikolai Bunge, a supporter of free enterprise and of the West and a protégé of Loris-Melikov, the enlightened former Minister of the Interior.

In tsarist Russia, finance ministers were usually more powerful than prime ministers. They were Mikhail von Reutern (Finance Minister, 1862–78, under Alexander II); Nikolai Bunge (1881–6, under Alexander III, and then Prime Minister); Ivan Vyshnegradsky (1887–92, also under Alexander III); and the remarkable Count Sergei Witte (1892–1903, and later Prime Minister).[37] They somehow did not 'fit' within the normal circles of tsarist government. Reutern and Bunge were of

German origin; Witte was of Dutch descent, his wife was both a converted Jewess and a divorcee; and Vyshnegradsky came from a humble family of priests (though he eventually became very rich). They, and Bunge above all, were the true architects of Russia's painful and flawed industrialization, not an easy task since they were supposed to create a modern industrial society within the framework of an absolutist, backward political system. The Ministry of Finance, unlike the rest of the state machine, was a powerhouse.[38] These outstanding ministers, from Reutern onwards, carved a path radically different from that of their predecessor, Georg Kankrin, Nicholas I's perennial Finance Minister (1823–44), who thought that the railways were 'the malady of our age' and feared they might cause excessive mobility among the populace and favour the spread of egalitarianism.[39] Reutern broke with the past with his criticisms of the old order, and paved the way for a justification of liberal reforms in terms of realpolitik, national regeneration, and continuation of the autocracy.[40]

The problem these clever ministers faced was the indolence of the nobility, the lack of capital, the burden of debt that weighed on the emancipated peasantry, and the sheer incompetence of native capitalists. These had always been regarded as particularly obtuse – a view that led both Peter the Great and Catherine the Great to favour Jewish, Armenian, German, Tatar and Polish merchants rather than the native breed. In 1847 foreign merchants controlled over 90 per cent of foreign trade.[41] Perhaps this made it even more difficult for an indigenous capitalism to flourish.[42] Everything was done to attract foreign investment. The industrialization of eastern Ukraine (especially the Donbass region) would not have occurred without government intervention, but it would not have been so pronounced without foreign investment. By the beginning of the twentieth century, foreign steel mills produced 90 per cent of the iron and steel in the Donbass.[43]

In an ideal world a virtuous process should have taken place: some of the more intelligent peasants, liberated by the Emancipation Decree, more efficient and more 'modern', would get rich and buy up the land and the farms of poor and inefficient peasants; they would generate a surplus to sell to the nascent industrial proletariat, whose numbers would be increased by the exodus of former peasants (those who were poor, inefficient, etc.). But this process was slower than the optimists had hoped.

Almost as a counterpoint to the legendary optimism of Americans, Russian intellectuals wallowed in miserabilism. The ending of Modest

Mussorgsky's opera *Boris Godunov* (1868–73) – the composer wrote the libretto himself – is sung by 'the simpleton':

> Flow, flow bitter tears!
> Weep, weep, Orthodox soul!
> Soon the enemy will come and darkness will descend.
> Dark and impenetrable darkness.
> Woe, woe to Russia!
> Weep, weep, Russian people,
> Starving people![44]

And the lamentations went on: Nikolai Berdyaev, the Russian philosopher who, having been a Marxist in his youth, turned to Christianity, lamented in the 1930s that 'The fate of the Russian people in history has been an unhappy one and full of suffering.'[45]

The collectivist *obshchina*, which protected the poor peasants (the muzhiks), also made it difficult for them to sell their share of the land distributed by the Emancipation Decree of 1861. Even the champions of the Decree had insisted that the *obshchina* was essential for the proper functioning of post-emancipation agriculture, fearing the massive flight from the land that would have resulted from competitive capitalist agriculture.[46] Besides, much land (22 per cent in 1905) was still owned by the nobility.[47] Peasants, driven by hunger, rented some of it and so ended up working, once again, for landlords. For many muzhiks the emancipation brought little change.

Understanding their dismal condition Nikolay Nekrasov, in his famous poem *Who Can Be Happy and Free in Russia*? (published posthumously in 1879), tells the story of seven peasants trying to find a happy person in the Russian countryside. They fail miserably.[48] As Anatole Leroy-Beaulieu wrote, the modern world has been characterized by a struggle between the principle of individualism and that of collectivism or community. In Russia the second principle has traditionally been the dominant one, particularly in the countryside. Since no one can tell which of the two principles will prevail one must understand the hesitation of the Russian legislator before destroying an institution, that of collective property embodied in the *obshchina*, which realizes at least partially what in other countries seems to be a utopia.[49]

Soon agrarian violence erupted. Peasants moved away from their villages looking for temporary jobs.[50] The depression of the 1890s, the increase in the price of wheat, and the subsequent famine, added to the hardship and multiplied the economic difficulties faced by those who worked on the land, including some members of the nobility. The landowners demanded and obtained compensation, more privileges, more local government jobs and sinecures. They had to be placated. They were, after all, the autocracy's main allies.

The bourgeoisie, and not just in Russia, was criticized for lacking the proper capitalist spirit and not doing 'its duty', when it was not sufficiently entrepreneurial, progressive, forward-looking. When the bourgeoisie aped the aristocracy it was mocked (as it had been as early as 1670 by Molière in *Le Bourgeois gentilhomme*). The social pretensions of the bourgeoisie were mercilessly criticized and satirized throughout the nineteenth century (and still are), but a shift began to appear at the turn of the century. The bourgeoisie was no longer funny. It was dangerous.

Charles Normand, writing in 1908 about the *haute bourgeoisie* ('*cette aristocratie bâtarde*') of the seventeenth century, lambasted it for being even worse than the aristocracy:

> more improvident, more selfish, more set in its ways and more culpable than the nobility, it is . . . a mean-spirited class, greedy for profit, avid for posts and honours, entrenched in its privileges, and as forgetful of its origin and as envious of those whom birth had given a higher place.[51]

The pro-capitalist elites, especially those in a position of power, like Count Witte when Finance Minister, offered a formidable resistance to the pretensions of the nobility. Why shift precious resources away from railway construction and industrial development to help a largely useless and unproductive class? he mused.[52] At a special conference on the 'Needs of the Nobility' (1895–7), Witte predicted that within fifty years Russia would be dominated by bankers and industrialists, just like western Europe. If the nobility wanted to survive, he warned, they should pay less attention to shoring up their position as landowners and more to getting into proper business. The mining engineer Aleksandr Fenin, vice-president of the Association of Southern Coal and Steel Producers, wrote in his memoirs that 'the class of noble landowners', who might have turned to business, were highly prejudiced against industry. He complained of the 'malevolence' with which 'we "industrialists"' were viewed in Russia, and tells an anecdote about being visited by Tolstoy's wife, Sofia Andreevna. Upon learning that Fenin managed a coal mine, Sofia Andreevna 'dropped her eyes and uttered the following, straight from the heart: "You manage a coal mine! Well, everyone has to earn a living."'[53]

In his unusually frank memoirs Count Witte was even more severe. While acknowledging the existence of 'many truly noble and unselfish men and women' among the landed aristocracy, he declared that the majority was:

> a mass of degenerate humanity, which recognizes nothing but the gratification of its selfish interests and lusts, and which seeks to obtain all manner of privileges and gratuities at the expense of the taxpayers generally, that is, chiefly the peasantry.[54]

He complained that, when he was in charge of the Ministry of Finance and hence the funding of the railways, 'a great many members of our highest aristocracy' were constantly 'flocking to my reception room' seeking railway concessions:

> It was then that I found out of what inferior stuff all these people with ancient names were made. Unlimited greed seemed to be their chief characteristic. These men who at Court functions wore princely airs were ready to crawl on all fours in my office, provided they could obtain some financial advantage. For many years some of these scoundrels and hypocrites have been holding the highest Court positions . . .[55]

Witte, a technocrat who had worked for years in the administration of the railways (and was then Minister of Transport and, as Finance Minister, one of the champions of the great Trans-Siberian Railway), seemed to think – as Ricardo, Saint-Simon, Marx, and, later, Keynes did – that an intelligent bourgeois should not let upper-class scroungers stand in the way of capitalist development. Above all, it was necessary to use the state. Witte explained that:

> It was imperative to develop our industries not only in the interest of the people, but also of the State. A modern body politic cannot be great without a well-developed national industry. As Minister of Finances, I was also in charge of our commerce and industry. As such, I increased our industry threefold. This again is held against me. Fools! It is said that I took artificial measures to develop our industry. What a silly phrase! How else can one develop an industry?[56]

Yet the 'silly phrase' embodied the key classical liberal assumption: industry develops spontaneously with no 'artificial' political interference. Witte – unlike some of his predecessors – realized that a policy of industrial development required a reform of state institutions. The main principle of autocracy, he believed, should be the development of private initiative. Becoming rich was in itself an emancipatory process.[57]

Witte was far from isolated. Admiration for the West and despair at the Russian state was growing among the elites. This longing to be truly 'civilized', namely, truly 'European', could be discerned even in the lamentations of the most embittered of Slavophiles such as Dostoyevsky. Celebrating the Siege of Geók Tepé (1881) in central Asia, where Russian troops defeated Turkmen troops and massacred thousands of civilians, Dostoyevsky described Russia's role in Asia thus:

> Asia, perhaps, holds out greater promises to us than Europe. In our future destinies Asia is, perhaps, our main outlet! . . . We must banish the slavish fear that Europe will call us Asiatic barbarians . . . In Europe we were hangers-on and slaves, whereas we shall go to Asia as masters. In Europe we were Asiatic, whereas in Asia we, too, are Europeans.[58]

To be masters in Asia might have been some consolation but it was not a solution to Russia's woes. Even so, some thirty years earlier the Russian commander-in-chief in the Caucasus, Baron G. V. Rosen, thought that Transcaucasia could become a source of raw cotton for the domestic industry, and that the inhabitants could 'be our Negroes'.[59] But if you cannot join an exclusive club you can try to create your own. This was the position of Slavophiles such as Nikolay Danilevsky, a philosopher and naturalist (of the anti-Darwin kind). The sickness of Russia, he wrote in 1871, consisted in trying to be European. What it should do, instead, was to construct a younger civilization around a Greater Slav Nation with the Poles, the Czechs, the Slovenians, Croats, Bulgarians, etc.[60]

The solution to Russia's problem lay not in some kind of pan-Slavic mirage (Slavic nations such as Poland were unremittingly hostile towards Russia) but, as almost everyone knew, in the land question. If laggard Russia aspired to catch up with the 'West' something had to be done about the peasants. It took the 1905 Revolution to scare Tsar Nicholas II, who was even less intelligent and reform-minded than his father, into appointing Pyotr Stolypin Prime Minister in 1906 to carry out further land reforms. Yet, on the eve of the First World War, backward Russian agriculture still accounted for 50 per cent of national income.[61] Observers noted, undoubtedly with some exaggeration, that Russia's rural economy was cultivated by 'medieval methods' and was five hundred years behind the West.[62]

The backwardness of Russia's rural economy acted as a brake on industrialization. In the years 1861 to 1883 industrial output doubled but output per worker increased very slowly, if at all. Then, in the years leading up to the First World War, output grew more rapidly.[63] By the eve of the war Russia was fifth in the league table of industrial states (after the United States, Germany, Great Britain, and France), though in per capita output it was way down the table.[64]

The impact of the government on industry was massive: state enterprises, state railways, large government orders, government credit, tariffs, industrial and taxation policy – all combined to promote industrial capitalism. By the 1890s, as the Soviet economic historian Peter Lyashchenko wrote in 1939, the national economy of Russia had been brought into the 'world system' (his words) of capitalism, and it had become 'apparent even to the most convinced champions of pre-capitalist Russia that a retreat from capitalism with all its historically positive and negative elements was impossible'.[65]

This had been clear to Nikolai Bunge (Finance Minister, 1881–6, and Prime Minister from 1887 to 1895). In a 'Memorandum to the Tsar' he had submitted towards the end of his life (probably in 1894, he died in 1895) to Alexander III, he delineated what amounted to a nationalist reformist programme. In order to emancipate itself from the tutelage of other nations, he explained, Russia should strengthen its own national state structures, streamline the state machine, extend state institutions to all parts of the empire, improve the conditions of the peasants, centralize the state, and integrate minorities, such as the Jews. He advocated a broadening of the activity of local government bodies (the *zemstva*): rationalizing them, making them more responsive, more 'democratic' (though, of course, he does not use the word).[66] He had been appointed Finance Minister by Alexander III in 1881, the only reformist minister in the new government. Yet Bunge was able to achieve much: the regulation of working time for women and children, the strengthening of the *zemstvo* and factory inspectorate, and the creation, in 1883, of a Peasant Land Bank, which enabled some peasants to purchase their own farms. He overhauled the inefficient and largely private railway system by having the state acquire some private companies and establish control over the growing network. He also abolished the iniquitous poll (or 'soul') tax as well as the equally unpopular salt tax, making the tax system somewhat less inequitable (shifting the tax burden away from the rural population) – no mean feat in the reactionary atmosphere of the 1880s.[67] Some peasants did get rich, but not on the scale required for industrialization. And since it was obvious that the state had to step in to finance industrial development, the key question was the extent to which taxes could be levied on the peasantry. In the end, contrary to what economic historians such as Alexander Gerschenkron have suggested, agriculture was not unduly taxed or, at least, was taxed proportionately less than the urban sector:

'the urban-industrial sector furnished almost 70 per cent of the entire tax receipts'.[68] The workers paid for industrialization more than the peasants, but, of course, many of the workers had been, until recently, poor peasants.

Nikolai Bunge encountered the wrath of the reactionaries, particularly because of his labour legislation. Mikhail Katkov, in an editorial in his *Moskovskie vedomosti*, accused him of ignoring Russian realities and compounding the sin of 'following the West'. Eventually Bunge had to resign as Finance Minister, and was 'kicked upstairs' to be Prime Minister. He was followed as Finance Minister by Ivan Vyshnegradsky in 1887, the candidate of the reactionaries.[69] They were disappointed in him. Vyshnegradsky had come up from a humble, clerical background, had made a fortune administering joint-stock companies, and was a tooth-and-claw pro-capitalist. However, he was no one's pawn, and he continued the modernizing policies of Bunge, and even attempted to develop factory and labour legislation to protect the workers and to reduce child labour. A follower of Friedrich List's idea of 'national capitalism', Vyshnegradsky erected a formidable tariff barrier to nurture Russia's infant industries. He was forced to resign after his poor handling of the famine of 1891. The problems were huge. After all, this was a largely peasant agriculture lacking markets, capital, and the technology to raise productivity, and the economy did not produce enough savings to enable the state to invest in industrialization.[70]

Vyshnegradsky's successor was Count Witte, after Bunge the greatest architect of Russia's industrializing process, and, like Vyshnegradsky, an admirer of Friedrich List and author of a pamphlet about him published in 1889.[71] Since the key question remained the peasant question, Witte asked Alexander Rittikh (his special assistant for agriculture and later in charge of implementing land reforms) to investigate the conditions of the peasantry. The resulting *Memorandum on the Peasant Question* appeared in 1903 under Witte's name. It concluded that the *obshchina* had prevented the formation of a rural proletariat, and that, far from being the collectivist dreamland of the populists, it was in reality dominated by a rich minority of kulaks (who were already hated well before 1918, when Lenin demanded their suppression as 'bloodsuckers' and 'vampires', calling for 'Ruthless war on the kulaks! Death to them!'[72]).

The gap between Count Sergei Witte and Lenin was thus not quite as great as either imagined. In a way the Bolsheviks were both Slavophiles and Westernizers, since they condemned pitilessly the rural remnants of

Old Russia, including the *obshchina*, while assuming that they could skip the stage of Western capitalism on the road to communism.

Witte, as a minister of Imperial Russia, was just as scathing as Lenin in his disdain for the romanticism of those who wanted to preserve the *obshchina*. For him the *obshchina* was a relic of the primitive past that had survived because of the way in which the emancipation of the serfs had been fashioned. And while populists of various ilk proclaimed the muzhik, the poor peasant, to be a kind of latent communist, Witte, who had once been inclined to share the Slavophiles' positive view of the *obshchina*, wrote that Bunge had convinced him:

> that the medieval *obshchina* was a serious hindrance to the economic development of the country. In order to raise the productivity of peasant labour it was necessary, I found, besides removing the legal disabilities of the peasant class, to make the product of labour the full and assured property of the toiler and his heirs.[73]

In other words, development on the basis of small rural property ownership was the way forward. It would create, so it was thought, a class of conservative small landowners (as in the West) who would be grateful to the system and become its bulwark – all the more necessary after the destabilizing effects of the Revolution of 1905.

What almost all the elites wanted, however, was a modern industrial society, regardless of whether it was capitalist or socialist or some kind of peculiarly Russian one. Part of the success of Marxism in late nineteenth-century Russia (and in the Third World for much of the twentieth century) was that it was regarded as an unashamedly pro-industrial ideology that viewed the coming industrial modernity as an iron law of history, against which nothing could or should be done, and yet it promised industry without the painful necessity of capitalism. In the end Russia was industrialized mainly by the state with foreign money, or by foreigners with state money. Even attracting foreign capital for investment in Russia on the scale required was not easy. Some entrepreneurs blamed the government, others blamed the bureaucracy; all blamed the backwardness of the country, the lack of paved roads, sewers, and lighting even in the largest cities, and all because, as the journal *Industry and Trade* declared in 1909, of the 'primordial and universal hostility towards capital'.[74]

No foreigner would want to invest without strong guarantees from the Russian state, so the state borrowed to build infrastructures. From 1880 onward, it invested in the railways, took over private lines, and imposed a uniform tariff policy to encourage the movement of goods over long distances.[75] By 1903 Russian railways exceeded the size of the French and German networks (the territory was, of course, much larger).[76] Their development constituted the most important structural change in the Russian economy before the First World War.[77]

The reforms of the rural sector, initiated by Witte and developed by Stolypin after 1906, when the revolution of 1905 frightened even the obdurate Tsar into action, were all aimed at cutting, as Alexander Gerschenkron wrote, 'the umbilical cord that tied the individual peasant to the village community', by creating a mechanism to transfer land into private ownership. 'From the point of view of Russia's industrialization,' he continued, the 'potential positive effects were undeniable', since the reforms created an economically strong peasantry, a heightened demand for industrial capital goods, and an increase in the number of industrial workers through accelerated flight from the land.[78]

The reforms aimed to destabilize the *obshchina* and accelerate the shift towards capitalist agriculture, thus transforming a tradition-bound peasantry into modern farmers.[79] The peasantry might have to suffer for a while, 'stew in the factory boiler' was how Nikolai Ziber, a contemporary economist, put it, adding that this was inevitable if Russia was to become capitalist.[80] Needless to say, peasants were less relaxed about the abolition of the *obshchina*.[81] Stolypin's reforms did not really take into account what the peasants thought. His aim was to eliminate communal land, which, with the law of 1908, could be re-partitioned among the members of the commune if only one member demanded it because he wanted to leave. The idea was that the strong and enterprising would want their cash, move to the city, become workers or entrepreneurs (or drunkard do-nothings), leaving behind sturdy capitalist farmers.[82]

Were these reforms really so decisive for industrialization? This is almost impossible to establish because the First World War interrupted the process. However, between 1906 and 1915 one-fifth of all households left the *obshchina*, thus allowing the transformation of an area the size of England into small peasant holdings.[83] Were the very high growth rates achieved in the years preceding the war due to the Stolypin reforms of 1906 and to the growth of civilian domestic demand brought about by these reforms? This was the classic view held by Alexander Gerschenkron.[84] But not all agree. Advancing solid evidence, Peter Gatrell has argued that 'Contrary to the view of Gerschenkron, the Russian government continued to exercise a crucial influence on industrial activity, particularly in 1910–14.' Gatrell argues that the main cause behind the growth in those years was defence spending, not land reforms.[85] It is certainly the case that in the years leading up to the First World War, agriculture remained the most important sector of the Russian economy, both as a source of employment and as a contributor to national income, while even in 1913 industry employed only 5 per cent or so of the entire labour force, and that the rate of growth of real income per head in Russia between 1860 and 1913 was close to the European average (one per cent per year) and well below that of the United States, Germany, and Japan. Thus, in that period, Russia failed to catch up economically with the West. It was still an undeveloped country.[86]

State direction was the reason why Russian industrial capitalism was lopsided. Large factories were more significant in Russia than almost anywhere else in the world: in 1895 plants with more than 1,000 workers accounted for 31 per cent of those employed in industry (as compared with 13 per cent in Germany).[87] In 1902 it was even higher: those employing more than 1,000 workers employed 38 per cent of the workforce.[88] Cities did not play a prominent role in industrialization.[89] In fact, apart from Moscow and St Petersburg, industrialization took place mainly outside Russia proper; its centre was in eastern Ukraine, in the Donbass area, followed by Poland (near Warsaw, Białystok, and Łódź), Belarus (near Minsk), Latvia (near Riga), and Azerbaijan (Baku).[90]

Some of the credit for industrialization should be given to Sergei Witte's government but also to previous policies that developed the railways and stabilized the currency, enabling the government to borrow abroad, which in turn brought the country into the global economy. Of course only a much more radical transformation of agriculture and a decrease in the burden of taxation required to support the autocracy would have led to a more vigorous industrial development of Russia.[91] By the end of the century Russia was the world's largest debtor country, but it was also the fifth largest industrial power in the world, with a share of world output (8 per cent in 1900) ahead of that of France. In the years between 1885 and 1914 the annual increase in industrial production averaged 5.72 per cent, exceeding that of the United States (5.26 per cent), Germany (4.49 per cent), and Britain (2.11 per cent).[92] The high growth rates were not based on an increase in productivity, but were the consequence of massive investment in industry and a considerable increase in population, in so far as one can be certain, given the paucity of reliable statistics. The slow growth rate of agricultural productivity was the main force holding down the overall growth rate of productivity.[93]

Both Witte and Stolypin intended to create a class of small private landowners (as in France or the United States), which would entrench a healthy spirit of entrepreneurial conservatism and stabilize the countryside. Similar views about the benefits of a prosperous farming community circulated widely even in countries as different from Russia as Ireland, where the Land Acts of 1881 (introduced by Gladstone's Liberals) and 1885 (introduced by Lord Salisbury's Conservatives) were designed to enable tenants to purchase their farms from landlords, thus creating an economy of small peasant proprietors – 'in effect an agrarian revolution'.[94] But Stolypin, at least according to Witte in his self-serving memoirs, wanted to do so by forcefully disrupting the *obshchina* without granting the peasants full political rights.[95]

This was the paradox faced by Russian modernizers. Reform, both economic and political, was necessary for industrialization; yet the purpose of industrialization, at least in the mind of the tsarist reformers, was to strengthen the autocracy, with as little political reform as possible. No one seriously thought that Russian development could possibly take place 'spontaneously'. Russia, with its mixture of high and low development, became a great laboratory in which an 'industrial experiment' was constantly refined and modified, almost a template for the debates pursued throughout the world in the course of the twentieth century: how much state? How much individual entrepreneurship? How much democracy, if any? Under which conditions should one prevail over the other? What was the role of the state?

That the debate, in its most pristine form, should have originated in Russia is not entirely surprising. The country, like the United States, was really a continent. It contained both 'Western' and 'Eastern' elements. It had a highly educated intellectual class, aware of the deficiencies of their country and of its possibilities. It had had a statist and bureaucratic direction since the days of Peter the Great. It had a highly diversified economy: in 1877, according to a land census 24 per cent of rural property was in private hands, 33.5 per cent in communal hands, and 42.5 per cent in state, crown, and clergy hands.[96] Russia had great ambitions, but these seemed to be constantly thwarted by fate or by its rulers, its people, or by foreigners.

Be that as it may, the fact remained that, by 1907, the growth of prosperous independent farmers, with their own livestock, some machinery, and some savings, made discussions on a future role for the *obshchina* increasingly unreal and out of step with the real developments in Russia.[97] The *obshchina* was in its death throes. On this point Marxists such as Georgi Plekhanov in *Our Differences* (1885), and the early Lenin, who wrote *The Development of Capitalism in Russia* (1896–9), were right. Russia, like it or not, was on the road towards capitalism, a weak capitalism, to be sure, one perhaps devoid of thrusting native entrepreneurial spirit, one far too dependent on foreign investment, but capitalism nevertheless.

The Russian intelligentsia, like some of their counterparts in the West, believed capitalism had to be tamed before it could be unleashed. Fear of an uncontrolled social process was deeply embedded in Russian political culture. Eventually the intelligentsia accepted the inevitability of capitalism while criticizing the capitalists for their lack of social conscience.[98]

The people were less sure. Most, of course, were peasants who just wanted their own land, unencumbered by debts. Like many peasants, they hated the landlords more than they hated the state, which might explain the paradox that perturbed the Christian thinker Nikolai Berdyaev when he wrote in 1935 (by which time he was in exile in France, and no longer a Marxist) that the Russian people are 'State-minded, . . . submissively giving themselves to be material for founding a great empire, and yet at the same time inclined to revolt, to turbulence, to anarchy'.[99]

The problem that faced Russian modernizers was the same facing modernizers everywhere. As the Narodnik writer Vasilii Vorontsov explained in *The Fate of Capitalism in Russia* (1882), following the West entailed opening up one's economy, but in so doing there was a risk that the more efficient Western industries would choke Russia's new capitalism.[100] Was it better to rely on the peasant economy or import Western models? And how should the peasant economy evolve? Peter Struve, a so-called 'legal' Marxist (i.e. one sufficiently moderate to be able to publish their works openly), writing in 1894 and having declared the *obshchina* moribund and capitalism inevitable, asserted that Russian capitalism could only be developed on the basis of German-style Junker farms, namely, large landlords turning into capitalist farmers. Of course this would be a harsh transition since 'capitalism . . . is evil from the point of view of our ideals.'[101] Lenin too, writing in 1907, thought that capitalism was both inevitable and desirable and indeed already taking over the Russian economy. Partly following Struve, he contrasted the so-called German Junker path based on large landholding with the American model based on capitalist farmers. Unlike Struve, however, he disparaged the German way, believing that it would condemn 'the peasants to decades of most harrowing expropriation and bondage, while at the same time a small minority of *Grossbauern* ("big peasants") arises'. The American path, which Lenin regarded as far preferable, was one on which the small peasant evolves into a capitalist farmer.[102]

Nowhere else in Europe and nowhere in the United States was the intelligentsia so obsessed with discovering what might be the right path towards industrialization.

9
The American Challenge and the Love of Capital

For much of the nineteenth century Britain was the ideal of modernity, but this was increasingly challenged. The United States and France thought they were at least as modern as Britain, which was after all a monarchy, while a truly modern country, they thought, should be a republic. Besides, Britain did very little to project an image of modernity. On the contrary it sought to combine its undoubted scientific and industrial progress with an unremitting respect for traditions, many of which it invented with surprising zeal. But by the beginning of the twentieth century, neither Britain nor France was regarded as the epitome of modernity – the torch had passed to America, where so many Europeans had gone to improve their living conditions and make their fortune. The USA, the country with no past, had become the country of the future.

The thirty years or so that followed the American Civil War had changed the shape of the country dramatically. The United States became the leading manufacturing country in the world, overtaking Great Britain. The population had nearly doubled, thanks to massive immigration. Urbanization added a further fifty cities with over 50,000 inhabitants. Railway lines more than trebled, wheat production more than doubled, while steel production increased from 77,000 tons in 1870 to a staggering 11.2 million tons in 1900.[1] The American South, however, remained overwhelmingly rural: 88 per cent in 1880 and still 72 per cent in 1920, with cotton accounting for almost half of the region's total production.[2]

The myth of America was particularly strong in laggard countries such as Russia. As was to be expected, reformers were the most pro-American. The economist Ivan K. Ozerov, in two influential articles written in 1903, pointedly entitled 'Why Does America Advance So Quickly?' and 'What Does America Teach Us?', contrasted Russian sloth, bureaucratic arrogance, the absence of civil rights and legal security, and risk-averse entrepreneurs, as well as Russian workers accused of being drunk, illiterate, and lacking in discipline and work ethics, with American initiative, energy, sobriety, education, and the protection given to every individual:

> How can we awaken our energies, develop our slumbering strength; what magic slogan will summon forth the riches of our soil? Why, with our vast territories do we lack land; why, with a relatively sparse population do so many of our people have no opportunity to apply their labor?[3]

And the poet Alexander Blok, in a poem of 1913 entitled 'New America' ('Novaia Amerika'), imagined a Russia in the image of the new great model shining across the ocean:

> I see black factory chimneys towering
> And everywhere the hooters scream.
> . . . I see huge factories with many stories,
> And workers' cities clustering round.
> . . .
> Now crackles the coal, now the salt whitens,
> I hear molten iron hiss from afar,
> Now over thy empty steppes there brightens,
> My America, my new-risen star![4]

This was a laggard's conception of America – America as the future, quite different from the older usage of America as a mysterious continent to be explored, when John Donne called his mistress 'Oh my America! my new-found-land'.[5] Or a primitive continent that ignored the existence of money and hence of real labour, as John Locke declared in the *Second Treatise*: 'Thus in the beginning all the world was America, and more so than that is now; for no such thing as money was any where known.'[6]

By the end of the nineteenth century America had indeed become the future. The percipient W. T. Stead (an influential crusading British journalist who died aboard the *Titanic*) declared, in his *The Americanization of the World, or The Trend of the Twentieth Century* (1902), that the United States of America had now reached 'such a pitch of power and prosperity as to have a right to claim the leading place among the English-speaking nations', adding that there were now more 'white-skinned' people in the United States than in the whole of the British Empire. Towards the end of the book he showed qualms about the frenetic modernity of America and suggested that perhaps the obsession with rapid change and constant work might 'easily be carried to such a point as to make existence itself hardly worth having'.[7]

Each country had its own way of becoming like America, its own way of catching up, of becoming like the others, while remaining different, knowing that no two roads can be alike, hence the proliferation of claims to distinctiveness: *l'exception française*, American exceptionalism, *l'anomalia italiana*, the German *Sonderweg*, and the distinct road to a market economy announced in 1978 by Deng Xiaoping under the terms of 'socialism with Chinese characteristics' (*zhongguo you teside shehui zhuyi*).

As with most things in history, America's own path was unique and unrepeatable. It had its own sense of possessing an extraordinary destiny, something not all countries can have. Tocqueville noted that the 'position of the Americans is . . . quite exceptional, and it may be believed that no democratic people will ever be placed in a similar one'.[8] Walt Whitman was quite certain about this. In his 1867 poem 'As I Sat Alone by Blue Ontario's Shores', he wrote:

> Any period, one nation must lead,
> One land must be the promise and reliance of the future.[9]

The country's outstanding economic performance in both the nineteenth and the twentieth centuries was due to a multiplicity of factors, but the central one was the vast 'open' lands and territories, drawing forth Europe's pullulating rural 'swarms', which led to a formidable increase of its population. This constantly expanded the number of producers and consumers while containing wages. In 1790, shortly after the declaration of independence, there were fewer than 4 million inhabitants. By 1900 there were 76 million. In May 2017 there were over 325 million.[10] In the same time span Britain's population increased much more slowly: from fewer than 10 million in 1800 to 38 million in 1900, to 65 million in 2015. The growth in the population of France was even slower: 29 million in 1801, 40.7 million in 1901, and 66 million today.

The American Civil War of 1861 to 1865 has been seen as an epic conflict between slave-owners and the liberators of the slaves. Karl Marx saw it as 'the first grand war of contemporaneous history'.[11] It appeared to many as a conflict between an old, traditional society in the South and the new world of capitalism in the North. The political economy of the slave South clashed with that of the North based on free labour.[12] The southern plantation owners were either indifferent to capitalism or hostile towards it, even though they were connected to world capitalism. The profits made sustained a southern lifestyle to the detriment of slaves and poor whites (who derived some psychological benefit from being above the slaves). Southerners emphasized their largely invented aristocratic traits, the mission of the southern gentleman against the money-grubbing soulless mentality of northerners. Some denounced capitalism as a 'brutal, immoral, irresponsible wage slavery in which the masters of capital exploited and impoverished their workers without assuming personal responsibility for them'.[13] Northerners retorted by emphasizing the horrors of slavery, of life on the plantations, the nastiness of auctioning slaves and the brutal treatments inflicted.

As far as the industrial North was concerned, the southern slave economy could not have provided a large consumer market for northern products (since slaves did not earn wages), so there were sound economic reasons to be against it. There could, of course, have been a compromise between northern industrial interests and southern agricultural ones: tolerance for slavery in the South, and economic growth in the North. The North could have manufactured cotton cloth just like Britain, following the pattern already established before the Civil War. There was an intrinsic economic reason why the Civil War occurred, though wars seldom occur for purely economic reasons.[14]

Moreover, slaveholding plantations sometimes took a more scientific and modern approach to management than the factories of the North. Plantations 'became laboratories for agricultural experiment, and planters and overseers measured and monitored human capital with great precision'.[15] That slavery could be economically successful (and not as damaging to the slaves as it had been thought) had already been mooted by Robert Fogel and Stanley Engerman in their classic *Time on the Cross: The Economics of American Negro Slavery* (1974).[16] A plantation system operating by slavery was 'no anachronistic excrescence on industrial capitalism'.[17]

Slavery was profitable, but slave-owners wanted some ethical principles to defend slavery on moral grounds, arguing that it was better than wage labour and benefited both slaves and masters.[18] Economic rationality needed to be bolstered by ideology, vision, beliefs. The idea that God had created masters and slaves was fine for the masters, but the entire ideological basis of the American Revolution was that all men were created equal.[19] Indeed the entire basis of bourgeois capitalist society required some kind of affirmation of the importance of individual human effort against the idea of heredity.

Southern political economists were committed to laissez-faire policies as well as slavery, which they defended as being more humane towards the slaves than capitalism was towards its 'wage-slaves'.[20] Even after the end of the war many southerners, including many clergymen, insisted that slavery protected workers against the ravages of capitalism (just as the Russian Slavophiles believed that serfs were better protected by the *obshchina*, the village commune).[21] And yet the North won. And it won not because it was on the side of justice against nefarious slavery (though it was), but because it was technologically, financially and industrially superior to the South, had more people and better transport.[22] The victory of the North seemed a victory for Alexander Hamilton's late eighteenth-century vision of the American future (at a time when there was no industry to speak of) against Thomas Jefferson's and Andrew Jackson's reactionary populist approach. While Hamilton conjured up a grand vision of a commercial America, others, such as Benjamin Franklin, were sceptical.[23] Jefferson and his followers assumed an international division of labour where the Europeans, and Great Britain above all, would be the manufacturing powers, while the United States would be the great exporter of agricultural products. As Michael Lind put it: 'The United States, in effect, was to have been the world's largest banana republic, with cotton and tobacco in place of bananas.'[24]

The fear of urbanization, of what cities might do to the pioneering spirit, has pervaded American conservatism in its various aspects ever since, even though such anti-urban ideology clashes with the cult of modernity. Modernity on its own is too frightening a thing – even for Americans. Many of the Founding Fathers had a pronounced conservative bias against big cities, a bias that small-town America, 'so calmly philistine and so very, very solid in its certainties', as Irving Kristol put it in 1970, has maintained to this day and in its own inimitable way.[25]

The victory of the North over the South was a victory for abolitionism, though the war was fought originally with the more modest aim of preventing slavery expanding into the western territories. It was also a victory for democracy, since the freed slaves enjoyed the same political rights as whites, though not for long. Finally, it was also a victory for the ideal of small farms – of the nation's 10.5 million workers, 6.2 million worked on farms.[26] Hence the sentimental celebration by politicians, artists, and writers of 'thrifty villages', 'honest labor' – in other words, what was then (and for some still is) the American Dream.[27] As is often the case, reality shatters the dream, but there is seldom a return to the previous state of affairs. After the political conflicts in the period of immediate post-war Reconstruction when something approaching interracial democracy seemed to emerge, the post-emancipation South turned out to be still largely controlled by its previous masters and, long after the end of slavery, the 3 million former slaves and their descendants remained trapped in a system of segregation, disenfranchisement, and misery.[28] As Eric Foner wrote, 'the legacy of decades of plantation dominance' could not be erased in the two years of radical Reconstruction, for the planter class 'had no intention of presiding over its own dissolution'.[29]

Once, the slave-owning plantation owners had been the most powerful political class in the whole of America. After the Civil War they could lord it only in the South.[30] As for the black man who had been a slave, now he was a disenfranchised labourer. W. E. B. Du Bois, scholar, pan-Africanist, and civil rights activist, lamented that, following the Civil War, 'The slave went free; stood a brief moment in the sun; then moved back again toward slavery.'[31]

Slave plantations, both in the American South and in the West Indies, as Sven Beckert has shown, were an integral part of the world capitalist economy (more than the protected American North); but, in themselves, they were not capitalist and not particularly integrated into the developing American capitalism.[32] Two economies lived side by side: a strong plantation economy in the South and a developing industrial one in the North. They might have coexisted. But it was not to be. The Civil War turned out to be the first great international military victory of capitalism. It was, as William Roy put it, 'the precipitating event for the creation of the corporate infrastructure as we know it'. Barrington Moore called it 'the Last Capitalist Revolution'.[33] It paved the way for large-scale industrial corporations, the creation of a national currency and a national banking system, and the establishment of Wall Street as the centre of finance.[34] A flood of immigrants from the rural South (mainly former slaves) as well as from Europe ensured a steady supply of cheap labour to the burgeoning North. Few European immigrants settled in the South. Everyone went north, east, and west. The construction of the railways led to a boom in coal and steel and the expansion of the frontier brought farmers within the orbit of capitalist expansion.[35] Before 1850 those who settled in America came from Britain and northern Europe (Germany, Sweden, and Holland). Then between 1850 and 1880 some 300,000 European settlers arrived each year on America's shores. Between 1880 and 1900 the numbers shot up to 600,000 a year and in the early years of the twentieth century about one million a year arrived in America, mainly from Italy, the Russian Empire, including Poland, and parts of the Austro-Hungarian Empire.[36]

The idea that the transformation of America into the world's most formidable industrial power was due to 'small' government, to letting everyone's private individual initiative blossom and flourish, is an endearing and naive myth. The federal government always had a major role in American development. It was the largest landowner and aggressively subsidized the railways.[37] Between the Civil War and the First World War the government both at federal and state levels expanded its regulatory power. The Civil War drove up government spending from 2 per cent of GNP to 15 per cent (by 2015 it was almost 40 per cent).[38] The war also led to the creation of the first federal income tax, set at 3 per cent at the beginning of the war. By the end of the war it had risen to 5 per cent (10 per cent for incomes over $5,000).[39]

After the Civil War the American army was used increasingly for 'internal' colonization in a massive ethnic cleansing (the term was invented much later), in the continuing wars against the Indians, such as the Great Sioux War of 1876, now remembered principally for the Battle of the Little Bighorn, the site of Custer's famous last stand. The country became home to the purest form of 'naked' capitalist ideology. Between the Civil War and the First World War, American industrialization proceeded with a greater dose of brutality than in most European countries, probably because of the peculiarly violent nature of frontier culture, a civil war of unparalleled ferocity, and slavery. There were thousands of industrial disputes, strikes, lockouts, often repressed by force.[40] As the loyalty of the army could not be guaranteed against white workers on strike, so repression of such unrest was 'privatized'. The Pinkerton National Detective Agency, founded in 1850 by Allan Pinkerton, constituted a de facto private army to be deployed by capital against labour. By the 1880s and 1890s the Pinkerton Agency outnumbered the US army.[41] One should add that even in May 2016 American private security guards outnumbered the police by 1.1 million to 650,000 and that such disparity existed also in China, Russia, India, and the United Kingdom (the only Western European country today where police are outnumbered by private security guards).[42]

The economic organization of society in America became the envy of the world well before its consumer society. Its market was bigger than any in Europe; its productivity was higher; its marketing techniques were unequalled.[43] By the end of the nineteenth century, the United States was already the capitalist country par excellence while England remained full of aristocrats pretending to despise capitalism. American capitalism had taken its own particular path, which historians such as Louis Hartz (*The Liberal Tradition in America*) and Richard Hofstadter (*The American Political Tradition*) argued might be explained by the absence of a pre-capitalist past. The importance of *not* having an aristocracy and being freed from the burden of the past had been recognized much earlier by aristocrats of the intellect such as Goethe, representative of the enlightened cosmopolitanism of the early nineteenth century, who wrote in 'To the United States' (*Den Vereinigten Staaten*, 1827):

America, yours is a better fate
Than that of our old continent.
You have no decaying castles
And no basalts.
You are not troubled
By useless memories
And futile strife.[44]

Hegel wrote along similar lines: 'Emigrants to America have on the one hand an advantage in that they bring with them the whole treasure of European culture . . . without the burdens that the European states impose on individuals, without re-encountering the hardships they have left behind . . .'[45]

To pursue capitalism meant to pursue wealth and money. The idea that Americans were particularly in love with money (as if Europeans despised it) was already a cliché in the early nineteenth century: the Duchess Sanseverina, in Stendhal's *La Chartreuse de Parme* (1839), alerts the oh-so-innocent Fabrice to the peculiarities of American capitalist democracy, explaining to him the cult of the God Dollar and the respect one must have for street artisans who, with their votes, decide everything.[46] And Tocqueville noted later in his *Democracy in America*, 'I do not know another country where the love of money has such a large place in the hearts of men . . .'[47] What became a famous adage, 'Remember that time is money', was first coined by Benjamin Franklin at the beginning of his 'Advice to a Young Tradesman, Written by an Old One' (1748).[48] Charles Péguy, writing just before the First World War, but already a conservative Catholic, having been anticlerical, denounced the power of money in bitter tones: 'Never until today has money been so much the sole master and God. Never until today have the rich been so protected against the poor and the poor so unprotected against the rich.'[49]

Financiers were more despised than industrialists. Decent people made money out of making things. Bankers made money out of money – they grew nothing, made nothing, sold nothing. They were the objects of contempt well before the global downturn of 2007–8, when the large bonuses bankers subtracted from their shareholders caused such scandal. European literature in the nineteenth century and beyond is replete with negative images of those involved in finance, from the Baron Nucingen (an obvious allusion to Rothschild) in Balzac's *La Maison Nucingen* (1838), to Ebenezer Scrooge in Dickens's *A Christmas Carol* (1843), Augustus Melmotte in Trollope's *The Way We Live Now* (1875), Aristide Saccard in Zola's *L'Argent* (1890), and John Gabriel Borkman in Ibsen's eponymous play (1896). In his *Cantos* (Canto XLV) Ezra Pound intones a litany against 'usura', which, he claimed, made no contribution to the crafts or arts (listing Duccio, Botticelli's *La Calunnia*, Piero della Francesca, Giovanni Bellini, and Hans Memling, and totally ignoring the contribution to the arts made, for instance, by the bank Monte dei Paschi di Siena):

> Usura is a murrain, usura
> blunteth the needle in the maid's hand
> and stoppeth the spinner's cunning. Pietro Lombardo
> came not by usura
> Duccio came not by usura
> nor Pier della Francesca; Zuan Bellin' not by usura
> nor was 'La Calunnia' painted.
> Came not by usura Angelico . . .

Thomas Jefferson, as early as 1816, was denouncing bankers in no uncertain terms: 'I believe that banking institutions are more dangerous to our liberties than standing armies.'[50] Without banks, of course, as Jefferson knew well, there would be no capitalism. Without hands-on 'universal' banks (where the investment function is not separate from the commercial one, as in Britain), Germany, Switzerland, France, and Italy would not have industrialized as they did.[51]

As Noel Annan noted, 'one common assumption' held by many men of letters is that 'the career of moneymaking . . . is a despicable life in which no sane and enlightened person should be engaged; and that indeed such people are unworthy of a novelist's attention'.[52] In 'Economic Possibilities for our Grandchildren' (1930), John Maynard Keynes wrote:

> The love of money as a possession – as distinguished from the love of money as a means to the enjoyments and realities of life – will be recognised for what it is, a somewhat disgusting morbidity, one of those semi-criminal, semi-pathological propensities which one hands over with a shudder to the specialists in mental disease.[53]

Albert Hirschman opens his clever *The Passions and the Interests: Political Arguments for Capitalism before its Triumph* (1977) with the query (inspired by Max Weber): 'How did commercial, banking, and similar money-making pursuits become honorable at some point in the modern age after having stood condemned or despised as greed, love of lucre, and avarice for centuries past?'[54]

Industry too was often despised. The Swiss economist Jean-Charles de Sismondi declared in his *Études sur l'économie politique* (1837): 'I will always oppose the industrial system which ranks low human life.'[55] In America as well as everywhere else, modern capitalism was both a desirable goal and an object of loathing. However, hostility towards capitalism was more widespread in the Old World than in the New, where it had a home among old reactionaries as well as new radicals.

The French liberal social scientist Émile Boutmy was quoted, not altogether approvingly, by the historian Frederick Jackson Turner, as saying of the United States:

> The striking and peculiar characteristic of American society is that it is not so much a democracy as a huge commercial company for the discovery, cultivation, and capitalization of its enormous territory. The United States are primarily a commercial society, and only secondarily a nation.[56]

Tocqueville had noted the alienation and fragmentation so characteristic of American society:

> I see a multitude of men all equal and alike, turned on themselves to obtain the petty and vulgar pleasures with which they fill their souls. Each of them, living apart, is a stranger to the fate of all the others: his children and his own friends are for him the whole of humanity; as for his other fellow citizens, he is near them, but does not see them; he touches them, but does not feel them; he exists for himself and for himself alone, and if he still has a family, we could say he no longer has a country.[57]

But what also impressed Tocqueville during his visit from 1831 to 1833 was the industriousness of Americans as well as the small scale of their enterprises. Starry-eyed as he often was, he declared that 'what is most striking in the United States is not the extraordinary size of a few industrial enterprises; it's the innumerable multitudes of small firms.'[58]

In the first half of the nineteenth century the United States was probably as close to being a country of independent small producers and property owners as it ever has been.[59] Few wanted to become wage-earners: they wanted to be independent craftsmen, artisans, small entrepreneurs, not 'wage slaves'.[60] To be a wage labourer signified humiliation, lack of autonomy, degradation. Many Americans believed that independence could exist only in a society of small producers.[61] Yet, industrial slavery was a fate open to most Americans after the Civil War. As Henry George, radical journalist and scourge of landed and corporate interests, declared: 'We have not abolished slavery; we have only abolished one rude form of it, chattel slavery. There is a deeper and a more insidious form, a more cursed form yet before us to abolish, in this industrial slavery that makes a man a virtual slave.'[62] And in his famous tract *Progress and Poverty* (1879), he wrote: 'Labour has become a commodity, and the labourer a machine. There are no masters and slaves, no owners and owned, but only buyers and sellers. The higgling [haggling] of the market takes the place of every other sentiment.'[63]

The Civil War, terrible though it was, with tremendous human losses on both sides of about 620,000 individuals, had its compensations. The economy of the South was devastated, but in the North industry boomed, the stock market prospered, speculators speculated and became richer, agriculture flourished.[64] And cotton production, which had virtually stopped during the war, recovered so rapidly that the United States exported more cotton in 1880 than it had in 1860.[65]

Some reformers hoped that the South would follow the North on the road to industry, but this did not happen, at least not then: the transformation of a planter society into an industrial one is exceedingly difficult. The reformers lacked a vision of what was required while the planter class, though willing to adopt new technologies and new methods of production, were quite unwilling to let their land fall into black hands. Agrarian reform was unthinkable, though Radical republicans had a plan to seize millions of acres from the wealthiest planters and redistribute or sell them to freed slaves.[66] This was part of the political ferment of the Reconstruction period when not just white reformers but also many former slaves challenged the old planter class's attempts to maintain or retake power. But the reformers failed. True, things had changed and considerably so: the slaves were freed and became sharecroppers or emigrated to the North. The former slave-owners kept their local power, and lands confiscated from the planters during the war were returned to their original owners, but the planters now mattered less in the national economy. Before the Civil War they had mattered greatly: until 1850 southerners had held the presidency for all but thirteen years, occupied half the seats in the Senate and more than half the seats in the Supreme Court. They had been the nearest America had achieved to an aristocracy, an elite that might have competed with the northern capitalists for political favours and for access to political resources. After the Civil War, there was a dramatic decline in southern power: 'the political bloc coming to dominate the new nation state scarcely included the Southern landed elite'.[67] They remained rich but, at the federal level, powerless.[68] Hence their deep odium for 'Washington' and Big Government.

Before 1840, American society was predominantly pre-industrial; by the end of the century it had become a mature industrial society; and by 1914 it had become the world's industrial colossus.[69] American capitalism became large-scale, as the plantations had once been. In 1870, Standard Oil at Cleveland employed 2,500 people; Singer (sewing machines) employed almost as many in New York; the Cambria Iron Works near Pittsburgh, Pennsylvania, employed 6,000 people.[70] Everything was increasingly linked by railways. Change was, of course, uneven: almost all of the industry was concentrated in the Northeast and the Mideastern states of Ohio, Indiana, Illinois, Wisconsin, and Michigan.[71]

Such advances inspired Walt Whitman, who linked the opening up to the west achieved by the railroad to the opening of the Suez Canal in 1869:

> Singing my days,
> Singing the great achievements of the present,
> Singing the strong, light works of engineers,
> Our modern wonders, (the antique ponderous Seven outvied,)
> In the Old World, the east, the Suez canal,
> The New by its mighty railroad spann'd,
> The seas inlaid with eloquent, gentle wires,
> I sound, to commence, the cry, with thee, O soul,
> The Past! the Past! the Past!
> . . .
> I see over my own continent the Pacific Railroad, surmounting every
>   barrier;
> I see continual trains of cars winding along the Platte, carrying freight
>   and passengers;
> I hear the locomotives rushing and roaring, and the shrill steam-whistle,
> I hear the echoes reverberate through the grandest scenery in the world . . .[72]

But even Whitman was perturbed. He hailed, in 1871, 'with pride and joy', America's 'unprecedented materialistic advancement' at the end of the Civil War. Later he lamented the 'hollowness at heart' of his countrymen:

> Genuine belief seems to have left us . . . We live in an atmosphere of hypocrisy throughout . . . A lot of churches, sects, etc., the most dismal

> phantasms I know, usurp the name of religion . . . The depravity of the business classes of our country is not less than has been supposed, but infinitely greater. The official services of America, national, state, and municipal, in all their branches and departments, except the judiciary, are saturated in corruption, bribery, falsehood, maladministration . . . In business . . . the one sole object is, by any means, pecuniary gain . . . The best class we show, is but a mob of fashionably dressed speculators and vulgarians . . .

He celebrated the material achievements of the New World democracy but bemoaned its 'deceptive superficial popular intellectuality . . . everywhere, in shop, street, church, theatre, bar room, official chair, are pervading flippancy and vulgarity . . .'[73]

American anxieties about capitalism echoed those made by European intellectuals. The literary critic Charles-Augustin Sainte-Beuve, writing in 1839, complained about the development of an 'industrial' culture, one in which authors wanted to be paid, thought in purely commercial terms, and were overcome by the 'demon of literary property'.[74] In the 1860s Alexander Herzen, now disillusioned with France and the West, wrote in his memoirs:

> the theatre, holiday-making, inns, books, pictures, clothes: everything has gone down in quality and gone up fearfully in numbers. The crowd of which I was speaking is the best proof of success, of strength, of growth; it is bursting through all the dams, flooding and overflowing everything; it is content with anything and can never have enough.[75]

The anthropologist Charles Letourneau (general secretary of the Société d'anthropologie), writing in 1897, while accepting the need for manufacturing and commerce, pointed out that commerce could be a major cause of wars and, regretfully, announced that if it invaded the whole world there would be no time left for poetry.[76] Order, discipline, and precision, not poetry, were the hallmark of the new money-dominated world, along with uniformity and punctuality. As Georg Simmel wrote: 'If all clocks and watches in Berlin would suddenly go wrong in different ways, even if only by one hour, all economic life and communication of the city would be disrupted for a long time.'[77]

Previously, wrote Werner Sombart, production was meant to satisfy wants and bring about happiness, but with the dawn of the new century all this changed. The lone entrepreneur has given way to collectively run corporations, capitalists have become slaves to the need to expand: 'Speed and yet more speed . . . is the cry of the age. It rushes onward in one mad race.'[78] This was part of the complaint by intellectuals of both left and right that the formation of a 'mass' society was inevitably bringing about a collapse in standards, standards that they themselves defined.

The lamentation of the intelligentsia for the bad taste of the people continues to this day. Yet even those critics who approached capitalism with disdain were unwilling to do away with the industrial system. Important trends within the American public felt vulnerable, uneasy, and angry in the face of the considerable changes that economic growth brought about.[79] Such sentiments were common at the time of the so-called 'Gilded Age'. This appellation, derived from a satirical novel by Mark Twain and Charles Dudley Warner (*The Gilded Age: A Tale of Today*, 1873), suggested an era of superficial 'gilded' splendour to be contrasted with what might have been a real Golden Age. This negative image, not undeserved, was based, above all, on the behaviour of politicians, generally described as cynical and venal opportunists, seeking office in order to get rich. Such views, of course, are far from uncommon today, nor are they confined to the United States. In fact one would be hard put to find a country in which the prevailing view is to hold politicians in high esteem for their spirited defence of the public good and the denial of self-interest. The Gilded Age was probably no worse than any other in terms of the standing or quality of politicians.

Capitalist development in the United States went hand in hand with corruption, particularly as this was linked to the state and the development of the railways. The post-bellum South was as corrupt as the North, perhaps more so because its economy needed reconstructing and this could not happen without government money. But corruption, bribery, and the private use of public money were pervasive everywhere.[80] Legislatures throughout the North awarded special charters to railroad, mining, and manufacturing companies. Although American capitalists were in principle against state regulation, they welcomed state regulation of the railways – a fairly common contradiction, as self-interest regularly triumphs over principles. J. Pierpont Morgan and other magnates explained that, because of the great importance of railways, 'we cannot uphold a system of operating public highways . . . which is controlled absolutely by a few individuals who tax production and commerce at will, and who practically dictate what rewards the producer, manufacturer and merchant shall receive for his labour.'[81] Between 1862 and 1872 the federal government awarded large tracts of territory and millions of dollars in direct subsidies to railway companies.[82] By 1896 the amount of money received and spent by the railway system amounted to 15 per cent of GNP and exceeded public expenditure. Some 800,000 men, 3 per cent of the nation's entire workforce, were employed by the railways.[83] No wonder the railway barons were so powerful and no wonder many politicians were in their pockets. When greed is all-pervasive, it does not pay to be honest. By 1913, observers such as Werner Sombart could write: 'Whatever the results of the capitalist spirit may be, you will find them developed to their utmost in the United States today. There the strength of that spirit is as yet unbroken; there the whirlwind still rages.'[84] Yet, the data suggest that middle-class Americans had an increasingly unfavourable view of big business in the years 1880 to 1910, peaking in the mid-1890s.[85] Farmers were even more anti-business and were particularly against the railways, largely because of the exorbitant rates they charged.[86]

One of the ideas sustaining the new capitalist spirit was a cool-headed adaptation of social Darwinism and positive science. William Graham Sumner, an Episcopalian minister with a chair in political economy at Yale, and who believed that democracy was 'the pet superstition of the age', was the leading American follower of Herbert Spencer, who brought together economics and natural selection.[87] In his 1902 essay 'The Concentration of Wealth: Its Economic Justification', Sumner explained that millionaires were 'a product of natural selection'.[88] He was also one of the first to put forward a justification for the concentration of wealth, revived in more recent times under the quaint expression 'trickle-down economics' (or, in its educated form, supply-side economics), when he wrote that 'no man can acquire a million without helping a million men to increase their little fortunes all the way down through the social grades . . . it is an error that we fix our attention so much upon the very rich and overlook the prosperous mass . . .'[89] Sumner felt that government should deal only with 'the property of men and the honour of women'.[90] As usual, the intellectuals – both those in favour of capitalism and those against it – acted as provocateurs, testing 'advanced' ideas that practical politicians could not possibly implement in their pure form. Considering the relatively recent rise in the United States of a form of fundamental Christianity that espouses both neo-liberal principles and creationism – the rejection of Darwin's theory of evolution in favour of the biblical account – it is ironic that, traditionally, much pro-capitalist thought in America was influenced by social Darwinism (i.e. Herbert Spencer's Darwinism, not Darwin's), while some strands of fin-de-siècle American progressive thought, such as that represented by the populist leader William Jennings Bryan, were opposed to the theory of evolution.

America had not invented capitalism but it invented the capitalists. Not that Europe was deprived of capitalists, but these were seldom glamourized and were usually overshadowed by aristocrats, people for whom being rich was natural and effortless. In 1870 among the richest in Europe were the Rothschild banking family (of Jewish-German origins) and the steel magnate Eugène Schneider, who had become rich in one generation (his father, Antoine, had been a bankrupt notary).[91] These 'new' capitalists and others like them (pejoratively referred to as *nouveaux riches*) who dominated finance and industry did not really alter significantly the hierarchy in French society.[92] They simply bought their place in the world of the old elites. The new American elites were quite different. The great entrepreneurs were Jay Gould, Cornelius Vanderbilt, and E. H. Harriman (railways), John D. Rockefeller (railways, gas, Standard Oil, and National City Bank), J. P. Morgan (First National Bank, Chase Manhattan Bank, United Steel, and General Electric), James Buchanan Duke (American Tobacco Company), Henry O. Havemeyer (sugar), George Eastman (founder of Eastman Kodak), and Andrew Carnegie (US Steel).[93] These were the celebrated and despised 'robber barons', a term used pejoratively to denote capitalists in the nineteenth century and popularized in 1934 by Matthew Josephson in his classic *The Robber Barons: The Great American Capitalists, 1861–1901*, and then in endless Hollywood films.[94]

The 'robber barons' were increasingly reviled in the years following the Civil War, when a particular kind of anti-big-business populism haunted the United States – as if to occupy the space which, in Europe, was that of socialism. There was, in America as elsewhere, a strand of society that hated the rich. Edwin L. Godkin, founder of the radical weekly *The Nation* (1865), wrote in 1866 that America was 'a gaudy stream of bespangled, belaced, and beruffled barbarians . . .' and berated the rich for lacking both culture and imagination.[95] In 1876 a radical paper, the weekly *National Labor Tribune* (Pittsburgh), asked: 'Shall we let the gold barons of the nineteenth century put iron collars of ownership around our necks as did the feudal barons with their serfs in the fourteenth century?'[96] On the Christian side of the spectrum Washington Gladen, minister of the First Congregational Church in Columbus, Ohio, the outspoken leader of social Christianity, argued that unbridled competition was the antithesis of Christian love.[97]

Between the end of the Civil War and the mid-1890s two movements of agrarian protest emerged: the Granger movement, particularly active in the older wheat areas: Illinois, Wisconsin, Iowa, and Minnesota; and the Populists in newer ones such as Dakota, Nebraska, and Kansas.

The odium of the farmers was directed at bankers and speculators. 'The capitalist produced no wealth, the farmer argued, but merely manipulated it to the disadvantage of those engaged in physical work.'[98]

Meanwhile, the large corporations, through mergers, trusts, and cartels, tried to eliminate competition.[99] They organized cartels, entered into agreements, and, far from trying to compete, sought monopolistic positions. This, they thought, was part of the march of civilization. They believed that monopolies (theirs, in particular) would provide better goods at lower cost. They regarded unrestricted competition as an evil, 'a deceptive mirage' (the view of an American Tobacco Company executive), while Charles Francis Adams, Jr, president of the Union Pacific Railroad, announced that the principle of consolidation was a 'natural law of growth'.[100]

The workers, too, organized. Two national trade union organizations emerged in the 1870s and 1880s – the National Labor Union and the Knights of Labor. The unions, however, were weak, inevitably so, since their birth, not accidentally, coincided with a massive wave of immigration. The main political battle was between the representatives of the new urban corporate industrial elite (the Republican Party) and those of the agricultural frontier (the Democrats). The latter, as well as the short-lived People's Party (the Populists), represented the cotton and wheat farmers of the Plains hurt by falling prices in the 1880s. These wanted government assistance against the corporations and they wanted the government to regulate the economy in order to restore competition. They were defeated by the Republicans. But even the champions of large-scale 'corporate' capitalism rejected competitive markets and price competition. Pierpont Morgan, the world's most powerful banker at the end of the nineteenth century, wanted to bring the market's 'destructive' forces (destructive of his banking empire, that is) under control.[101]

John D. Rockefeller, the oil tycoon, had looked forward to an economy dominated by a few giant corporations (especially his own) cooperating to avoid 'wasteful' competition:

> Probably the greatest single obstacle to the progress and happiness of the American people lies in the willingness of so many men to invest their time and money in multiplying competitive industries instead of opening up new fields, and putting their money into lines of industry and development that are needed.[102]

And, with candour difficult to imagine today, he praised the state for helping his company, Standard Oil: 'One of our greatest helpers has been the State Department in Washington. Our ambassadors and ministers and consuls have aided to push our way into new markets to the utmost corners of the world.'[103]

'Real' capitalists were often ambivalent about laissez-faire. They somewhat understood that the free market, like socialism, was very nice in theory but seldom worked in practice. They wanted a state that protected them from competition, that is, from market forces. In the real world of capitalist enterprises, the protectionists prevailed. In the more rarefied sphere of ideas, the true liberals held sway. Capitalists needed a state to lord it above them, discipline them, nurture them, and to kill a few to save the rest: a real Hobbesian state overseeing the war of all against all. Stateless capitalism never had a chance.

The chief myth of Americanism was embodied in the popular 'dime' novels of Horatio Alger with their heart-warming stories of young orphans coming to the city from the country, who, with some hard work and plenty of amazing luck, became successful. These rags-to-riches stories (almost one hundred novels all telling more or less the same story) became The American Story. Some of the time, as was the case with Andrew Carnegie, the son of a Scottish weaver who lost his job to mechanization, it was even true. While such possibilities remained open to the blessed few, the more usual path to great wealth and power was to join a large corporation and make it to the top (the simplest and less laborious route being, of course, to inherit wealth from one's parents). Big companies continued to dominate American society, in spite of repeated attempts to curb their power by politicians like Theodore Roosevelt, who denounced their social irresponsibility and arrogance, and urged that Rockefeller's Standard Oil Company be dismembered because it accounted for 80 per cent of US oil production.

The federal government was in the business of helping business, especially big business, throughout the nineteenth century. Only towards the end of the century, when it was too late, did regulation kick in with the passage, in 1890, of the Sherman Antitrust Act. However, it did little to contain the Great Merger Wave of 1898 to 1902, when perhaps as much as one-half of American manufacturing capacity merged – probably because the Act, which was largely against cartels and price-fixing, actually encouraged mergers.[104]

That anti-competition practices should have started in the railways is not surprising: they were a very small number of large enterprises, with high initial costs, competing for the same business. Once the volume of traffic began to fall off (because the networks had been established) they tried to agree not to compete.[105] For obvious reasons it was almost impossible for the individual states to regulate the railways since they operated interstate.[106] This is the kind of combination the Sherman Antitrust Act was designed to prevent. Its language reflected the outlook of the small producers. It was not anti-capitalist, only against large-scale capitalism. Senator John Sherman, who introduced the bill that bears his name, declared that unless one heeded the appeal of the people who were feeling the impact of the giant corporations, the people would follow 'the socialist, the communist, and the nihilist'.[107]

However, as the political climate changed, the Sherman Act became a major weapon in the hands of President Theodore Roosevelt, who in 1904 won an antitrust suit against Northern Securities, a huge railways conglomerate that ranked second only to US Steel.[108] Elected triumphantly in 1904 for a full term with 56.4 per cent of the vote, Roosevelt continued to pursue progressive policies, including a wealth tax, and filing more than thirty-five antitrust actions in the oil, meat packing, and tobacco industries against escalating opposition in Congress.[109]

In 1909, Standard Oil was broken up and forced to sell all its thirty-three subsidiaries, a verdict confirmed by the Supreme Court in 1911. The company did not suffer unduly and had anyway been facing international competition from Royal Dutch Shell (which had amalgamated in 1907) and the Anglo-Persian Oil Company (which became BP in 1954). Rockefeller, by far the largest shareholder of Standard Oil, became even richer after being granted his share in all the new companies. Once the lengthy litigation was over, the shares escalated, increasing five times in the ten years after 1911.[110]

In the 1890s the main target of the anti-monopoly campaigners had been the railway industry, the linchpin of American capitalism. The railway owners argued that the problems of the industry could be mitigated if competition was contained. The Interstate Commerce Act of 1887, however, specifically outlawed pooling, in deference to anti-monopolistic feelings. The great railway strike of 1894 (the Pullman strike, named after the company making train carriages), opposed by the official unions, the American Federation of Labor (AFL), engendered considerable violence and anti-trade union repression. Troops were called in; thirty-four strikers were killed. George Pullman stood firm and the strike failed.[111] Nevertheless there were also positive results for the workers. A commission appointed by President Grover Cleveland (a pro-business Democrat) offered a compromise. It met the anti-competition requests of the railway barons but, by pointing out that the railways affected every American citizen – at a time when judges regarded virtually all strikes as illegal – established the principle of compulsory arbitration in labour disputes.[112]

That period was characterized by 'the bloodiest and most violent labor history of any industrial nation in the world'.[113] That American workers were not happy could be measured not only by recording the number of strikes, but also by the – economically more costly – evidence of rapid job turnover, absenteeism, and alcoholism.[114] Between 1880 and 1900 there were nearly 23,000 strikes in 117,000 firms in the United States. The violence and frequency of labour conflict had no effect in the highly competitive party-political arena. Politicians seldom did more than just express sympathy with the workers.[115]

Anxieties increased with the Depression of the 1890s. Some 'progressives' also asked for alcohol prohibition, immigration restrictions, and racial proscription. Yet most of these reformers accepted the basic premises of capitalism, and the changes proposed did not involve significant ideological realignment.[116]

For a while William Jennings Bryan, the Democratic candidate in the presidential election of 1896, came to represent political hostility towards American capitalism, though this did not stop William Randolph Hearst, the newspaper magnate (and the main inspiration for Orson Welles's film *Citizen Kane*), from backing him in 1900.[117] Bryan spoke of the need to stand 'against the encroachment of organized wealth', and in his acceptance speech for the Democratic nomination he declared that government agencies 'have been so often prostituted to purposes of private gain'.[118]

Supported by the Populists, Bryan came close to obtaining a majority in the presidential elections of 1896 (and again in 1900). Yet he was an unusual anti-capitalist and sworn enemy of big business, for he was also a devout Presbyterian, a prohibitionist, and a creationist (he had a major role in the famous Scopes 'Monkey' trial in 1925 when he stood against the teaching of evolution in Tennessee schools), and he was deeply suspicious of industrialization and nostalgic for disappearing rural values, believing that virtue resided in those who stayed close to the land. He was a pacifist, yet, when he was Woodrow Wilson's ineffectual Secretary of State (1913–15), he approved US military intervention in Mexico. Bryan obviously failed to impress the British ambassador in Mexico, who thought him 'like a horrid mass of jellified sentimentality from which a sharp beak occasionally pokes out and snaps'.[119]

In their struggle for the regulation of capitalism, Bryan and his Populist followers were supporting a growing trend. Interference in the market during the American Progressive Era (c. 1890–1920) was far greater at state level than at federal level, with the result that industrial states such as Wisconsin and New York were progressive, whereas others, such as Alabama, resisted protective labour legislation and crushed unionization to keep wages down.[120] Alabama did not have much industry and unions were not important. They mattered much more where industry was more advanced. Enlightened elites were quite aware of that. In 1904, Theodore Roosevelt used the language of conciliation with the trade unions:

> I believe that under modern industrial conditions . . . there should be organization of labor in order better to secure the rights of the individual wage-worker. All encouragement should be given to any such organization . . . Wage-workers have an entire right to organize and by all peaceful and honorable means to endeavor to persuade their fellows to join with them in organizations. They have a legal right . . . to refuse to work in company with men who decline to join their organizations.[121]

Large corporations and trusts remained unpopular in the United States, though some had some influential defenders, such as George Gunton. Once close to Theodore Roosevelt, Gunton regarded himself as a friend of the labour movement but thought that the real enemy of the workers were small firms. In his article 'The Economic and Social Aspect of Trusts' (1888) he tried to defend even a universally hated corporation such as Standard Oil on the grounds that its superior efficiency would lead to lower prices.[122]

The large manufacturing corporations, a rarity before 1890 and mainly associated with the railways, had become, by 1910, the dominant form of business, accounting for over half of the value of all manufacturing capital.[123] The high wages these firms were able to pay brought about the first large mass consumer market. And they paid high wages because the demand for labour grew at a faster rate than the flow of immigrants. The combination of a large domestic market, constant innovation, and rising productivity was unbeatable.

It may well be to the advantage of a single capitalist to exploit his workers, pay them absurdly low wages, make them redundant at the slightest whim of the business cycle, but, collectively, capitalists need prosperous workers able and willing to buy the goods produced; they need satisfied workers able and willing to turn up to the factory gates with, if not quite a smile on their faces, at least able and willing to work another day with some prospects that their conditions of existence will not deteriorate and will perhaps improve.

Henry Ford understood this perfectly well. Although an uncomplicated union-basher, an anti-Semite, and an admirer of Adolf Hitler (who decorated him in 1938), he was not a reactionary (there were few true reactionaries in North America). He was an authentic pioneer of twentieth-century capitalism. High wages were a way of bribing workers away from militancy. In January 1914, Ford announced he would pay his workers five dollars a day (far more than what similar firms paid) – the equivalent, adjusted for inflation, of $109.09 a day in 2010. (In 2010 an automotive worker earned on average $28.57 per hour or $228.56 for an eight-hour day – just over twice as much as in 1914.)[124] Ford's decision deeply perturbed financial circles and puzzled trade unionists, but it signalled that modernity could and would benefit the industrial working class. The five-dollar day, however, included a bonus (half of the daily wage) to be paid to workers who were disciplined, who performed well, and who abandoned their old 'values' carried over from Europe (whatever these might have been) in favour of 'Americanism'.[125] Henry Ford, who blended modernity with a paternalistic attitude towards his workers, explained that 'These men of many nations must be taught American ways, the English language, and the right way to live.' Married men should not take on lodgers. Workers should live in clean 'well-conducted homes, in rooms that are well lighted and ventilated' and not in slums. A Ford pamphlet intoned: 'Employees should use plenty of soap and water in the home, and upon their children, bathing frequently. Nothing makes for right living and health as much as cleanliness. Notice that the most advanced people are the cleanest.'[126] Religiosity was encouraged but not when it interfered with profits; thus, almost 900 Greek and Russian workers (6 per cent of the workforce) were dismissed because they celebrated 'their' Christmas, following the Julian calendar, thirteen days later than other Christians: 'If these men are to make their home in America they should observe American holidays,' declared Ford (though even he would have agreed that Jesus was not American).[127] As wages crept up in other companies and wartime inflation took its toll, the size of the bonus decreased as a proportion of the total pay and there was less of an inducement for workers to follow Ford's precepts.[128] American wages remained higher than European ones, though welfare was much lower in the United States than in advanced European countries.

As mentioned above, American capitalism, like British capitalism (and unlike Japanese and Russian), did not start big but small: a myriad of small enterprises dominated every sector of human activity.[129] This was not the result of market forces or native Yankee ingenuity, but rather of the management by the state of the way the land was settled. The federal government contributed decisively to the creation of a class of small landholders through the Homestead Act of 1862, when Abraham Lincoln's administration granted land hitherto uncultivated to those who wished to cultivate it (provided they had not fought with the South). Between 1880 and 1910 the farm population grew from 22 million to over 32 million.[130] At the same time the number of people living in cities increased. Normally, urbanization and depopulation of the countryside is the trend within each economy, but the United States attracted immigrants who settled both in the countryside and in the cities. This was the basis for a considerable industrial expansion. American farmers too were now involved in worldwide economic networks. They had to learn to behave like businessmen, or else sink. American farmers (including some of the more prosperous among the small ones) demanded and were eager to adopt new mechanized equipment such as the McCormick reaper, the McCormick harvester, and the steam tractor.[131] In 1883 alone McCormick sold 48,000 machines.[132] By using such industrial goods, American farmers raised their productivity dramatically, increasing the production of wheat between 1870 and 1900 four times, lowering export prices and destroying the livelihood of increasingly uncompetitive farmers in the USA, but causing even more destruction in Europe, particularly in eastern Europe. The main beneficiaries were, of course, the larger farms.

The myth of the frontier, celebrated by historians such as Frederick Jackson Turner in his famous 1893 Chicago lecture 'The Significance of the Frontier in American History', and glorified in endless books and films, depicted brave settlers going west to build a new Jerusalem against the odds (the drought, the cold, the outlaws, the Indians). This myth is contradicted by modern historians, who point out that homesteaders got the poorer land while the better land had already been acquired by speculators in order to resell it to others, or by richer farmers who could afford the new implements and machines. In 1886 a congressional committee discovered that twenty-nine companies, all foreign owned, controlled more than 20 million acres of farmland and one English company held 3 million acres in Texas alone.[133]

Unlike the rest of rural North America, California was not a place of small farms but of plantations and large estates. The workers were not individualist small farmers but exploited indentured Chinese and migrant Mexicans.[134] In industry, transport, and mining a similar process of concentration was underway. By 1918 the United States had 318,000 corporations. The largest 5 per cent earned almost 80 per cent of the total net income.[135] Hence the enduring appeal of an American form of right-wing populism (especially among disgruntled small farmers) angry at large corporations, cities, modernity, immigrants, and, above all, the federal government.

Capitalism may be constantly renewing itself but many of the companies that still dominated the corporate landscape at the end of the twentieth century had been founded in the nineteenth century – companies such as Eastman Kodak, Boston Food, which became, eventually, United Fruit (famous for Chiquita bananas), Johnson and Johnson (pharmaceutical and baby products), Coca-Cola, Westinghouse Electric, Sears Roebuck (department store chain), Avon (beauty products), and Hershey Food (the famous chocolate bars started to be sold in 1900). Then in the years preceding the First World War, car manufacturers appeared (Ford and General Motors), publishing (McGraw-Hill), Gillette (the first razor went on sale in 1903), Black and Decker (1910, in 1917 they invented the portable power drill), and the supermarket chain Safeway (the original store was founded in 1915 in Idaho). Of the largest 500 American firms at the end of the twentieth century, 144 originated in the period 1880 to 1910 (fifty-three in the 1880s, thirty-nine in the 1890s, and fifty-two in 1900s).[136]

American big business inspired fear in Europe, and rightly so. After all, the more mechanized, innovative, and efficient American agriculture was, the more European agriculture was in danger (as noted when discussing Hungary and Romania, see Chapter 4). Manufacturing countries too began to be afraid of the Americans. America gloried in its unlimited possibilities. American businesses advanced on the international scene steadily, even before the middle of the nineteenth century. In 1836 nine out of the fifty-five foreign firms operating in Guangzhou (Canton) were American. By 1851, at the Crystal Palace World Fair, American firms exhibited chemicals, reapers (McCormick), firearms (Samuel Colt), and starch (Colgate). The first great US international firm was Singer (sewing machines) followed by Standard Oil, General Electric, National Cash Register, and International Harvester. To save transport costs Singer in 1867 built a factory in Glasgow, where by 1881 it had three.[137]

Germans were afraid of an invasion of American-made goods and all the more so since the United States itself protected its manufactures behind a wall of tariffs.[138] The French too were scared. In 1898 the liberal economist Paul Leroy-Beaulieu argued that the entry of the USA into the global system was irrevocably changing the political framework within which the European powers operated. The population of America increased constantly, he noted, estimating that by 1950 there would be 120 to 130 million people – a slight underestimate since the figure for 1950 was 151,325,000. And if you added Great Britain and her colonies, he continued, there would be in the world some 200 to 220 million 'Anglo-Saxons'. Faced with this danger the continental European powers should end the arms race and proceed towards the constitution of a European Federation, one of whose objectives would be to ensure that only European powers continued to colonize Africa; another would be inter-European cooperation in Asia and the Pacific. And, in what appears to be a precursor of the European Economic Community, the main purpose of the federation would be to proceed towards a western European customs union that excluded the United States and the United Kingdom.[139] The idea of a united Europe had not been uncommon among European intellectuals in the nineteenth century (such as Giuseppe Mazzini, Victor Hugo, and Julius Fröbel), but it was usually linked with the idea of peace and not so obviously tied to a vision of a continent battling against American and British economic supremacy.

Americans too were anxious: would they really be able to sustain their growth and defeat European competition – the competition of a Europe that was edging towards protectionism, even including that great bastion of free trade, Great Britain? After all, they indicated, the Europeans, and the British in particular, still had some significant advantages: greater international experience in trade matters in markets they had themselves established and control of international banking and shipping.[140] Anxiety overcomes both laggards and pathbreakers.

liquid [illegible] would [illegible] Americans. And if he added Great Britain and her dominions, he continued, then would [illegible] of the world [illegible] so-called 'Anglo-Saxon' [illegible] with the [illegible] the continental European powers should end the [illegible] and [illegible] the convergence of [illegible] Federation, [illegible] those [illegible] and be to go [illegible] European powers, continued to [illegible] another [illegible] cooperation in Asia and the Pacific. And [illegible] what appears [illegible] of the European Economic Community, the main purpose of the Federation would be [illegible] towards a [illegible] Europe [illegible] that excluded the United States and the United Kingdom? The idea of a united Europe had not [illegible] among [illegible] the [illegible] Curzon, Mazzini, [illegible] and [illegible] it was still linked with [illegible] and [illegible] of a [illegible] against American and British economic [illegible].

Americans [illegible] would they really be able to [illegible] their growth [illegible] European [illegible] of a European [illegible] towards [illegible] including the [illegible] of [illegible] Europe? [illegible] the [illegible] and the [illegible] in particular still had some [illegible] of [illegible] they had themselves established and control of [illegible] banking [illegible] both [illegible] and [illegible].

PART THREE

Involving the Demos

10
Building the Nation

The great revolutions of the eighteenth century, the French and the American, and the British Industrial Revolution, were not driven by a desire to catch up with more advanced countries: France, the United States, and Great Britain *were* the more advanced countries. They thought they were the centre of the world. They were inventing a new modern politics. They had no lessons to learn and plenty to teach: the universality of the rights of men and citizens (France), the right of settlers to organize themselves and their taxes independently of a distant 'mother country' (USA), the establishment of an industrial society semi-autonomous from the state (Great Britain).

It seemed, then and now, that there was a kind of symmetry between democratization and capitalist growth. In Britain, the model for so many, citizenship was being developed throughout the nineteenth century, expanding gradually to include a greater proportion of the (male) working class, and women too acquired rights they had not possessed before.

In France the process of democratization was more erratic, but went deeper than Britain, particularly after the foundation and the stabilization of the Third Republic in the decade after 1870 and the introduction of universal male suffrage (as happened in Germany when the country was unified). In America the conception of a state of the whole people had been a founding principle of the United States themselves, albeit only in theory, since women were excluded from voting (like almost everywhere else), as were slaves and, after the Civil War, former slaves.

The revolutions that ensued elsewhere in the nineteenth century borrowed heavily from these pathbreakers. The settlers in Latin America followed in the footsteps of their counterparts in North America and broke with Spain and Portugal; nationalists in Germany and Italy constructed new states, hoping to emulate France and Great Britain; reformers in Japan reorganized an existing state to resist the West.

The idea of democracy, of having to achieve some form of popular consent, of having to carry the masses along, was never far from these developments. The liberal grandiloquence of the West (the French *Liberté, égalité, fraternité*, the American 'We hold these truths to be self-evident, that all men are created equal', the English 'rule of law' and 'parliamentary representation') resonated for the rest of the world not least because this wonderful rhetoric could be redeployed against actual and potential Western oppressors. Subsequently, throughout the twentieth century, whatever was done politically, whether by democracies or dictatorships, was done 'in the name of the people'. The initial shot may have been that of the newly formed United States of America – the preamble to its constitution started with the proud words: 'We the People' – but the sentiment was also to be found in an older nation, about to be dismembered, namely Poland, where Stanisław Poniatowski was proclaimed king in 1791 by the 'grace of God and *the will of the nation*'.[1] And earlier, in June 1789, Count Mirabeau, representative of the Third Estate (the first two Estates being the nobility and the clergy), warned (as legend has it) Louis XVI with the proud words: *Nous sommes ici par la volonté du peuple et nous n'en sortirons que par la force des baïonnettes* ('We are here by the will of the people and we will leave only if forced by bayonets'). Jean-Sylvain Bailly, astronomer and future mayor of Paris, joined in declaring proudly that *la nation assemblée ne peut recevoir d'ordre* ('the nation, assembled, cannot receive commands').

History, language, and religion all have an important role to play in building the nation. The new emerging nations usually pretended to be old since it was thought that the people could be held together more firmly if they possessed the memory of a shared past. Often such a past was invented. Some thinkers understood this perfectly well. Ernest Renan, in his famous 1882 lecture at the Sorbonne ('Qu'est-ce qu'une nation?'), explained that a nation was a 'great solidarity constituted by the common understanding of the sacrifices made in the past and those to be made in the future'. But this past, he added ominously, was often a constructed past, for it assumed 'oblivion' (*l'oubli*): '*historical error* [my emphasis] is a crucial factor in the creation of a nation, which is why progress in historical studies often constitutes a threat to the nation'.[2]

Renan added that 'the existence of a nation is like a daily plebiscite', meaning that national unity must be constantly constructed and reconstructed. As Anne-Marie Thiesse explains, 'the real birth of a nation occurs when a few individuals declare that the nation exists and decide to prove it.'[3] It is the work of an elite. Of course, nationalists did not just want to celebrate a nation, a community that holds itself to be a nation, but the transformation of the nation into a sovereign state, the idea being that the state embodied the people, something quite different from the states of old, embodied in a sovereign. Friedrich Nietzsche saw this clearly in 1881 when in *Thus Spoke Zarathustra* he exclaimed:

> The state? What is that? Well then! Now open your ears, for now I shall speak to you of the death of peoples. The state is the coldest of all cold monsters. Coldly it lies, too; and this lie creeps from its mouth: 'I, the state, am the people.'[4]

When the Italian nationalist republican activist and historian Carlo Cattaneo, writing in the 1840s (before Italy was a state), appealed to the Italians, he really meant the Italy of cultural elites, not the 'multitude divided in manifold warring nations, divided by casts, dialects, and greedy and bloodthirsty factions, who thrive in superstition, in selfishness, and in ignorance . . .'[5]

Massimo D'Azeglio, a Piedmontese politician and supporter of Italian unification, is supposed to have coined the famous aphorism, on the morrow of national unity: 'We have made Italy, now we have to make the Italians' – a recognition that, somehow, the people are constructed by politics rather than the other way round. D'Azeglio's actual words, however, were a little different: 'Italy's first objective,' he wrote, 'is the formation of Italians endowed with a strong and noble character. Unfortunately every day we move to the opposite pole; unfortunately we have made Italy, but not the Italians.'[6] What had gone wrong? Italy, he explained, had (re)-acquired its territory, but had not achieved real national unity: 'Italy's most dangerous enemies are not the Germans [i.e. the Austrians] but the Italians.' A new Italy was born, but the Italians were not yet really Italians or, at least, not the 'right' kind of Italian. The Italians needed to be taught how to acquire a sense of citizenship.[7]

In 1866 Pasquale Villari, historian and politician, in an article entitled 'Di chi è la colpa?' ('Who is to Blame?'), contrasted the remarkable performance of Bismarck's new Germany to that of Italy, whose real enemy was:

> colossal ignorance, the illiterate masses, bureaucrats who behave like machines, ignorant professors, childish politicians, intolerable diplomats, incompetent generals, workers without skills, patriarchal farmers, and a rhetoric which gnaws on our bones.[8]

Almost ten years later, in 1875, still lamenting the waste and the corruption, Villari complained: 'Even if we were united, free, independent and with our finances in order, we would still be a nation without meaning in the world. What we need is to acquire a new spirit and to have a new ideal manifesting itself before us . . .'[9] And in 1894 the social theorist Vilfredo Pareto echoed such negative views of Italians and their leaders (views that are just as prevalent now). He lambasted the state for being the servant of narrow interests, since 'the best' (*i migliori*), so far, look after only their own interests: 'Freedom has been extinguished except the freedom of politicians to steal; everything is done to destroy any feeling of rectitude and honesty existing in popular conscience.'[10]

A similar need for the 'right' people to construct the nation surfaced in an older country, China. Sun Yat-sen, 'father of modern China', leader of the 1911 revolution, revered by communists as well as their nationalist antagonists, was aware that a modern industrial country had to be democratic (*Mínquán*), but also that it must have national unity (*Mínzú*), and prosperity (*Mínshēng*). These three features (democracy, unity, and prosperity) constituted Sun's famed Three Principles of the People (*San-min chu-i*). The problem with China, according to Sun, was that its people had lost their sense of a nation and were like scattered sand. They needed to reconstruct themselves on the basis of their own past, their own ancient morality, and not on the basis of 'cosmopolitan' (i.e. foreign) ideologies (as if the idea of a republic had not come from the West).[11]

Sun Yat-sen thought that China needed unity and discipline more than individual freedom, which was secondary to national emancipation.[12] In 1924–5, shortly before his death, in his lectures 'The Three Principles of the People', he explained that there are three classes of men. Firstly, there are the innovators and discoverers, 'those who know and perceive beforehand'; then the promoters, 'those who know and perceive afterwards'; and, finally, those who neither know nor perceive, who cannot see anything and can only do as they are told.[13] The task of the enlightened minority is to guide these masses towards democracy. Their duty is to serve the less able and make them happy. This is what is meant, added Sun Yat-sen, sounding like the Plato of the myth of the cave in the *Republic*, by the saying that the clever must be 'slaves' to the imbeciles. This, he thought, was the problem of democracy; and since this is not a problem the West has resolved, there is little to imitate and China must find its own route: 'After the Revolution of 1911, the whole country went mad and insisted on applying in China the political democracy which westerners talked about, without any study of its real meaning.'[14] Once he had attributed the origin of his country's backwardness to the stagnation caused by an unreformed and unreformable imperial court. By 1920 he had concluded that the real enemy was Western imperialism. The nationalist revolution he had led to oust the Qing Dynasty could not move forward without challenging the West.[15]

Far more difficult was constructing a nation in which there was no common language, no common territory, and no common culture. This was the dilemma facing Jewish nationalism. As the Zionist leader Nahum Sokolov disarmingly observed in 1903: 'We don't even have a people yet.'[16] The task of the Zionists was to create a people out of a deeply divided community held together by persecution, but with no common ideology, culture, or religious practices (since fewer and fewer Jews observed traditional rituals). In the creation of a Jewish people the Zionists were helped, if that is the word, by anti-Semites. Theodor Herzl, whose pessimistic views as to the fate of liberalism in Europe led him to proclaim the need for a Jewish national home, wrote: 'anti-Semitism . . . will do the Jews no harm. I hold it to be a movement useful for the development of the Jewish character.'[17] The requisite impetus for Jewish migration to Palestine would be voluntary but, he added in his famous pamphlet, *The Jewish State*, help would come from the anti-Semites: 'They need only do what they did before, and they will create a desire to emigrate where it did not previously exist, and strengthen it where it existed before.'[18]

As often happens, nationalists, but not only nationalists, have a certain aversion to the people they seek to lead, blaming them for not being sufficiently willing to be led. Zionists needed to 'make the Jews' the way D'Azeglio wanted to 'make the Italians'. The closeness between Zionists and anti-Semites led Carl Schorske to point out Herzl's ideological kinship with the leading Viennese anti-Semites, such as Georg Schönerer and Karl Lueger.[19] An anti-Semitic discourse was quite common, at the time, even among the intellectual elites. Theodore Herzl himself, when describing an elegant soirée at the Berlin home of a wealthy businessman in 1885, lamented the presence of 'Some thirty or forty ugly little Jews and Jewesses. No consoling sight.' And, writing to his parents from Ostend, 'although there are many Viennese and Budapest Jews here, the rest of the vacationing population is very pleasant . . .'[20]

Constructing a nation remained a difficult yet essential task for the development of an industrial capitalist society. The multiplication of identities (national, religious, gender, regional, class, ethnic, professional, ideological, sporting affiliation, age, etc.) is not a recent phenomenon, but it is exacerbated by the greater dynamism of capitalist societies compared to those of the past. National identities, being relatively new, needed to be connected to older ones, such as linguistic or religious identities.

Language could be a complicating factor in nation-building. Within Italy there were major cultural differences and an enormous linguistic diversity (those who habitually spoke Italian were a small minority). In 1910 in the Austro-Hungarian Empire the various Slavs (Serbs, Czechs, Slovaks, Poles, Slovenes, and Ruthenians/Ukrainians) made up almost half of the population (46 per cent) whereas the German speakers made up only 23.9 per cent, the Hungarians (Magyar) 20.2 per cent, the Romanians 6.4 per cent, the Italians 2 per cent, and the Bosnian Muslims 1.2 per cent.[21] Belgium and Switzerland were and have remained linguistically divided. And, throughout Europe there are still plenty of minority languages within nation states, some regarded as 'proper' languages, others regarded as dialects (there is no way of distinguishing between the two), such as Welsh in the United Kingdom, German in the Italian South Tyrol (or Alto Adige as the Italians call it), Catalan and Basque in Spain, Swedish in Finland, etc.

In Germany, *Hochdeutsch* (High German) in 1800 was spoken by only one-third of the population. By 1900 it was understood by virtually everyone, though dialects continued to prevail, especially in the countryside. Polish was the most significant minority language in Germany, spoken by 3.4 million people.[22] Poles were an obvious target of cultural contempt and prejudice: they were Catholics in a largely Protestant region (what was then Prussia); they were mostly peasants or workers; and they felt Polish.[23] Other linguistic minorities in Germany were of less importance, though Germany's national minorities accounted for almost 8 per cent of the entire population.[24] There were other divisions: a widespread distrust of Prussia, the largest state, among the other German states; a growing class antagonism; and a strong urban–rural cleavage.[25] In France, as in most other countries, many did not habitually speak the national language, but rather a host of other languages relegated to the rank of 'primitive' dialects (however ancient they might be and, in some cases, such as Provençal and Breton, as solidly implanted as French).

Religion too could bring numerous problems to the task of nation-building. Of the independent states that existed in 1900, those where the elites and the overwhelming majority of the population shared the same religion were relatively few. They included Japan, Sweden, Norway, Denmark, Greece, Romania, Italy, Spain, and Portugal. They did not include the United Kingdom since there were plenty of Catholics (including the majority of the Irish) and Nonconformists in a formally Anglican country. The Tsarist Empire had numerous religious and ethnic minorities. The Austro-Hungarian Empire was three-quarters Catholic but no single 'nation' dominated demographically. Switzerland was divided by both language and religion.

In Germany religion was potentially a destabilizing factor. From a Prussian Protestant point of view the most important potential antagonism was that between the two-thirds of the inhabitants who were Protestant and the rest, who were mainly Catholic. However, this division never erupted into a serious violent conflict (as it did, on and off, in Ireland). Although Catholics were persecuted by Bismarck during the so-called *Kulturkampf*, Protestants did not storm Catholic holy sites; Catholics did not desecrate Protestant churches.[26] Catholics and Protestant conservatives did not like each other but they shared a mutual antipathy towards liberals and socialists. Pro-capitalist anti-clerical liberals and Marxist socialists were in antagonism on most issues except on the need to keep religion at bay. Socialist and socially aware Christians had not dissimilar views on social welfare. National unity seldom means conformity and total integration.

In France, where the majority of the population espoused a conventional form of Catholicism, the religious issue was resolved by creating a secular French nationality. The so-called *laïcité*, enshrined in French law only in 1905 after lengthy disputes akin to a non-violent civil war, became part of a national narrative that endures in France to this day. Of course, *laïcité* is constantly reinterpreted and means different things to different people. The way to examine it is not to decide how near or far from the idealized French model other countries are (the French version of a myth of exceptionalism that is common to other nationalisms), but to compare it to how the question of the relation between Church and State was resolved elsewhere.

Well before the French espousal of *laïcité*, the United States had disentangled 'the American nation' from any specific religion and, for obvious reasons, unlike most European countries, no single Church dominated. It was thus in the interest of the numerous Christian Churches and sects (non-Christian religions were of little importance in nineteenth-century America) to have a state that did not intervene in religious matters. God was not mentioned. It is said that when Alexander Hamilton was asked why the Constitution did not mention God, he answered 'We forgot.' More likely it was quite deliberate since religion and the divinity are never invoked in the *Federalist Papers*, of which Hamilton wrote fifty-one out of eighty-five, whereas in the previous century no political argument could be conducted without some reference to the Bible.

The original oath of allegiance to the American flag (1892), 'I pledge allegiance to the Flag . . . one Nation, indivisible, with liberty and justice for all', was formally adopted by Congress only in 1942, to be read in all schools. The words 'under God' inserted after 'one Nation' were added only in 1954. And only in 1956 a new national motto, 'In God We Trust', was deployed on all dollar banknotes, adding weight to the feeling that God had blessed American capitalism. By and large it was still a Protestant God. Even though the country became less and less Protestant as emigration from Catholic Europe (Ireland, Poland, and Italy) accelerated in the last decades of the nineteenth century and from Catholic Latin America over the past fifty years, political control has remained in the hands of Protestants. Only in 1960 was a non-Protestant, the Catholic John F. Kennedy, elected President. Religion remains very important to a majority of Americans. According to a Gallup poll the percentage of Americans who said that religion was important to them oscillated between 58 and 53 per cent between 1982 and 2016, with a peak of 61 per cent in 2003, though secularization may be on the increase.[27] Other countries had resolved the Church–State problem as early as the sixteenth century by 'nationalizing' the Church, that is to say, by establishing a Church under state control. In England the sovereign became the head of the Church of England. Sweden, Denmark, Norway, Iceland, and Finland followed with an established national state religion. Nations could be built 'against' religion (the French case) or by having a national religion. Mexico and Turkey established a secularism similar to the French *laïcité*, enforced by law in, respectively, 1917 and 1924.

The key instrument of French nation-building turned out to be the establishment of a state educational system that sought to 'make' the French by forcing the adoption of a common language and even inventing a common ancestry to be traced back to a mythical Gaul. The legislators and the architects of the French educational system restructured the identity of the nation in terms of an antagonism towards Germany and the Germans, being against monarchists and for *la République*, and against Catholics and for *laïcité*. This led to a constant rise in spending on education throughout the nineteenth century not just in France but in many other countries, though there were significant differences in the numbers of children enrolled in primary school in 1900: the United States had the highest number (939 per

1,000 children), followed by France (820), the United Kingdom (720), Japan (507), Italy (362), and Russia (149).[28]

Ernest Lavisse's *Histoire de France depuis les origines jusqu'à la Révolution* (1901) became a mandatory history textbook in French schools, instructing generations of children that the great duty of their lives would be to avenge the defeat of Sedan in 1870 by Prussia and defend the values of the French Revolution against all those who sought a return to the *Ancien Régime*.[29] The motherland, patriotism, and the honour of France were in evidence everywhere, from books aimed at a young readership to the newly inaugurated 14th of July, the day which since then has been taken as the day the Revolution started (there were other possible contenders). By contrast, a pacifist textbook written by Gustave Hervé, when he was a socialist (later he became a supporter of Mussolini), *Histoire de France pour les grands* (1910), was banned in all the schools of the Republic.

Italy could have been united by religion, but national unity had been achieved against the will of the Pope. Secular nationalism was politically dominant, though the majority of the population remained loyal to the Church. As in France, unity was constructed through education, propaganda, and centralization. In much of Latin America, overwhelmingly Catholic, anticlericalism was also a major force in building the nation, particularly in Mexico, Argentina, Brazil, and Chile.

In the United Kingdom there were four 'nationalities', but, in the nineteenth century, only one, the Irish, resisted inclusion into the (British) national family, and were themselves divided between Catholics and Protestants. The Welsh and the Scots appeared content with their subordinate status. The English did not seem to require nation-building myths and national heroes on a par with Vercingetorix, though in the nineteenth century an attempt was made to establish Boudicca (who led an uprising against the Romans just like Vercingetorix and Arminius) as a somewhat idealized ancestor of Queen Victoria. It never caught on. The problem was that, in traditional 'school' history, the Anglo-Saxons had been subjugated by the Normans and that, as a result, to be 'English' meant to be descended from both conquered and conquerors. The claim that all English were descended from a single ethnic group was never seriously peddled in the way French schoolchildren for generations recited together the unlikely claim *nos ancêtres les Gaulois* – a claim that originated only in 1875.[30] In Germany the idea of a common ancestry was also muted, though Romantic myth-making produced a national hero, Arminius (or Hermann), who fought against the Romans just like the 'French' Vercingetorix, but who was more successful since he defeated them in the Battle of the Teutoburg Forest.

In Poland nation-building was rendered unusually complicated by the fact that it was not clear who the Poles were and where the boundaries of Poland lay. As everywhere else, political activists were deeply divided. The socialists thought that the national question was divisive because it set workers in one nation against those belonging to another nation, thus uniting the 'wrong' people and putting in the same camp Polish workers and Polish aristocrats. The conservatives meanwhile tried to carve out for the more privileged classes (i.e. themselves) a space within the three empires (Tsarist, German, and Austro-Hungarian) then occupying putative Polish territory. The strongest political force, however, were the nationalists of the Polish National Democratic Party, which dominated the Polish parliament and whose leader, Roman Dmowski, argued that 'we are a nation, a unified indivisible nation, because we possess a common, collective consciousness, a shared national spirit'.[31] In Polish nation-building, as in most nationalist ideologies, historical truth counted for little. History was mined for events that could form a national narrative. Dmowski's nationalism, however, was of a new type, less connected to a Romantic myth of an ancient Polish nation, and more imbued with the modern idea of creating 'new Poles'.[32] Not every country could aspire to become a nation. Some nations were 'real', others were not. For Dmowski, Ukrainians, Belorussians, and Lithuanians were incapable of statehood and, consequently, should be subjected to Polish rule, while Poland's eastern borders should extend from the Baltic to the Black Sea.[33] Polish nationalism could be built around Catholic identity and stand against Orthodox Russia and Protestant Prussia.

The French 'solution' was to regard all identities (religious, regional, linguistic) as a private matter. This could be achieved, if at all, after a protracted struggle between the Catholic monarchist 'Right' and the Republican 'Left'. The Dreyfus Affair of 1894, in which a Jewish army captain was falsely accused of treason, was the terrain where this battle was fought. It saw the victory of the pro-Dreyfus camp, an uneasy coalition between modernist pro-capitalists and socialists of various hues. The losers had to abandon the old dream of turning the clock back to a monarchic Catholic nation and reconstitute itself as a new nationalist force of the right, virulently anti-German, despising parliament (since it divides the nation) and the Jews (guilty of not being sufficiently French). The ultra-nationalist Maurice Barrès even deployed a class rhetoric in an effort to appeal to French workers. In articles such as 'La lutte entre capitalistes et travailleurs' (*Le Courrier de l'Est*,

28 September 1890) he addressed the workers thus: 'You are isolated workers . . . hold hands with all other workers, your brothers.'[34] When the Dreyfus Affair erupted Barrès and his supporters branded Dreyfus a traitor because he was a Jew and because he was not really French, pointing out that even his great defender, the writer Émile Zola, was not quite French either, since his father was Italian. This new modern battleground was defined by questions of ethnicity and citizenship. The idea of 'race' acquired a new dimension. Barrès's journal, *L'Action Française*, redefined 'Frenchness' to exclude Protestants, Jews, and Freemasons.[35] Two-thirds of the articles it published between 1908 and 1914 attacked the Jews.[36] If the Jews tried to assimilate, in the words of Henri Vaugeois, one of the initiators of the movement, it was even worse since 'the Jew is all the more dangerous when he is cleaned up, adapted, civilized'.[37] This process of redefining French nationhood in racial terms enabled those hostile to the Republic to shed their monarchism, and become patriotic supporters of the (bourgeois) Republic.

In multinational empires building the nation was an obviously difficult task. One 'nation' could dominate the others, as Turks did in the Ottoman Empire and Russia in the Tsarist Empire. In the Habsburg Empire the unquestioned domination of Austria had come to an end with its defeat by Germany in 1866. The 'solution' to Austrian weakness was the so-called compromise of 1867 that gave birth to the Austro-Hungarian Empire, upgrading, so to speak, Hungary to equal status with Austria, but this left the question of nation-building unresolved and unresolvable.

The Tsarist Empire faced similar problems. According to the only census ever held under the Tsars (it excluded Finland, technically an autonomous Grand Duchy), in 1897, 146 languages and dialects were spoken in the empire; two-thirds of the inhabitants were 'Russians' – adding together 'great' Russians (55.6 million), 'little' Russians (Ukrainians, 22.4 million), and 'white' Russians (Belorussians, 5.8 million).[38] These spoke varieties of Slavonic, regarded themselves as Slavs, and were Orthodox (at the time Ukrainian Catholics were largely in the Austro-Hungarian Empire). Nationalist stirrings in Ukraine were confined to minority sections of the intelligentsia, as was the case in most countries. A great many landlords were of Polish descent, and many of the peasants had also once been petty nobles of Polish origin. They were deprived of their privileges by the Tsar after the failed uprising of 1830 and became assimilated, adopting the Ukrainian language and Russian Orthodoxy. Jews represented some 10 per cent of the population of Ukraine.[39]

Even counting all Ukrainians, Belorussians, and Russians as Russians, almost one-third of the population of the empire remained outside the 'Russian nation' and most of them were not Orthodox: Poland and Lithuania were Catholic; Latvia and Estonia (and Finland) were Protestant; in the Caucasus and central Asia there were probably more Muslims than in the Ottoman Empire. Even the Muslims were not a single group: there were the Azerbaijanis (mainly Shia), then there were the Volga and Crimean Tatars, the Kazakhs, the Uzbeks, the Kyrgyzs, etc.; there were Buddhists in Mongolia, Christians in the Caucasus (Georgians, Ossetians, and Armenians) as well as in Bessarabia (now mainly in Moldova).[40]

Meanwhile, the internationalist socialist movement was busily building the idea of an identity based on class rather than on nation. Did the class antagonism between capitalists and workers stand in the way of nation-building? The workers, like the putative citizens of the nations, needed convincing, inciting, organizing. After all, no one, not even a true proletarian, was a spontaneous socialist. The famous 1871 socialist hymn, the 'Internationale', written by Eugène Pottier, urges the *damnés de la terre* (the wretched of the earth) to stand up (*debout, debout*), not to accept their fate as an enslaved crowd (*foule esclave*), not to follow supreme saviours (*Ni Dieu, ni César*). But by 1914, nation-building had reached a stage such that socialists felt comfortable in the bourgeois capitalist nation that had given them the suffrage and (some) political power and (some) social reforms. So, when war broke out, the socialists, almost everywhere, and above all in well-established nations such as Germany and France, stood alongside the *patrie* of the so-hated capitalists. The great gap between capital and labour had narrowed in the face of a common external enemy, and an enemy of 'the nation'.

Nation-building is a cumulative process that depends on a series of relatively minor events: the creation of pan-national institutions, a central bank, a unified system of weights and measures, a single currency, and a new generation educated in the national stories and myths. There was plenty to be proud of in being French in 1900: the ancient history, the Revolution, popular mobilization, a culture that appeared then to dominate the continent, and the feeling of superiority that accompanies all of this. There was also plenty to be proud of in being German: the most powerful country in continental Europe, a world leader in scientific achievements, more universities than Great Britain. It made many think that, after all, it was better to be a German than to be a Bavarian or a Prussian. Besides, with the exception of being Prussian and perhaps Bavarian, other local identities in Germany (being from the Rhineland,

Hamburg, or Saxony) had virtually no national connotation, whereas Prussia was so dominant that Prussians accepted becoming Germans the way the English became British.

In nation-building the class division between bourgeois and aristocrats was even easier to bridge than that between workers and capitalists or between ethnic groups and religions. The nobility, as Arno Mayer has pointed out, were more cohesive and self-confident than the bourgeoisie, which 'never coalesced sufficiently seriously to contest the social, cultural and ideological pre-eminence of the old ruling class'.[41]

In most European countries there was a conflict between agrarian and industrial elites, but such elites were never monolithic. There never was a landed bloc facing, as in trench warfare, an industrial bloc. Besides, in the nineteenth century, if one had money and power one could join the aristocracy the way one joined a club. Once one was rich one could obtain a title, hence the tremendous expansion of the aristocracy throughout Europe in the 'bourgeois' nineteenth century, with bankers in the lead. The aristocracy, over the centuries, had diversified their interests. They had a disproportionate presence in the military, the bureaucracy, the Church, and in parliament. They could not behave as a monolithic class. Those in the bureaucracy often had a bias in favour of strong states. Those in the Church defended clerical privileges. Those in the military were often in favour of industrial growth. And, of course, the landowners upheld the interests of landowners, including those of non-aristocratic landowners. This old landed aristocracy was still around and included the richest people in nineteenth-century Europe, who had not yet been displaced by industrialists and bankers. They were perturbed by the rising tide of capitalist modernity and suspected that they were now on the wrong side of history. But wealth buys time, and though their status was constantly being challenged by the nouveau riche, the positions of power they had accumulated in previous centuries saw them in good stead for a further century.[42] The more intelligent among the aristocrats realized that future primacy would reside in economic power rather than social privilege (it is easier at the top to discern the future than when one is labouring down below).

In Prussia, from the second half of the eighteenth century, well before the industrialization process had started, a modern entrepreneurial and speculative spirit manifested itself among large landholders. The urban markets of western Europe increased the demand for grain and this was reflected in rising prices and land values. The possibility of rapid profits led many aristocrats to speculate on land. The agricultural crisis that followed the Napoleonic Wars led some of the more forward-looking aristocrats to adopt scientific methods of agriculture. By 1835 many Prussian landowners had been converted to modern agriculture. Soon advanced systems of drainage were developed, machinery was introduced and, after 1850, chemical fertilizers. These changes in agricultural production had profound consequences for the Prussian aristocracy. They led to a division between those who still viewed landed estates mainly as the source of aristocratic status and those who viewed them as an investment that had to be protected. And as capitalistic agriculture grew the gap separating the aristocracy from the middle classes narrowed.[43]

Those who owned much land were still rich.[44] They might have had less ready cash (their wealth being tied to the land), but they still wielded some power, and still commanded some respect. They too, however, had to adjust to the developing capitalist world. In Britain many members of the landowning classes, then the richest in Europe, retained their prosperity thanks to the financial sector.[45] The City of London thus always straddled two worlds, the pre-capitalist world of commerce and banking and the post-industrial world of the future. The City offered a way of getting rich, or remaining rich, while also remaining a gentleman, since one could remain distant from the sordid world of trade and the dirty world of manufacture. Not that there was a serious (i.e. political as opposed to cultural) conflict between industrial capital and 'gentlemanly' capital.[46] Elsewhere, the political problem within the establishment was in trying to reconcile urban and landed interests. This was true even where there was no authentic aristocracy (as in the United States and Latin America), or where it had been formally destroyed (republican France), or where commerce and/or the professions were in the hands of foreigners and 'alien' groups (such as the Jews) – as in parts of Austria-Hungary and Romania.

While the aristocracy increasingly adopted bourgeois lifestyles, the capitalists acquired titles and became noble. Impoverished nobles married the rich and became rich. In Belgium, for instance, the nobility remained politically influential but by the end of the nineteenth century the country was governed by an elite of businessmen.[47] Money mattered more than ever before, and so did bourgeois values. What these values might be was not clear then (and is still not clear now). Was it the assumption that the virtuous (bourgeois) man worked whereas, in traditional society, gentlemanly virtues consisted in not having to work?[48] Was thrift and prudence a bourgeois virtue, as was so often said? Yet successful capitalists were often those who had the courage to borrow and take a gamble. Some capitalists were virtuous, philanthropic, and ethical; others were power-hungry, avaricious, and greedy. There is no general rule.[49] Goethe's flawed hero, Faust, is at peace with himself not after accumulating vast wealth but when he finally perceives the possible fulfilment of his project for economic and human progress. Some capitalists, like some workers, may be ethical, but capitalism as a system has no necessary ethics, and only one aim, growth (like cancer cells).

Did the vast material inequality that accompanied the growth of capitalism interfere with the building of the nation? Bourgeois society implied two contradictory aspects: that we are all equal with the same chances of being unequal, and, as it inevitably followed, inequality was 'fair'. The modern bourgeois state was supposed to treat everyone equally without raising the question of real material inequalities; it was supposed to look after the 'general interest' as if society was a happy homogeneous whole; it was supposed to dispense justice while letting happiness remain a matter for the individual. We were all equal, all 'in it together', all part of the same commonwealth, of the same community, of the same society, of the same nation – all of us, rich and poor, educated and uneducated, the clever and the stupid, the talented and the inept, those raised in squalor and those born in prosperity. All could rally around the idea of nationhood.

While the ideology surrounding the development of capitalism was 'democratic', capitalism also increased income inequalities, though France and Britain were more unequal (in terms of income) than the more capitalist United States in the years 1900–1910.[50] Do inequalities make nation-building more complex? That is difficult to say, particularly since nation-building is a vague concept and almost impossible to measure. The proposition that inequalities weakened nations had been cogently expressed as early as 1752 by one of the sharpest minds of the Enlightenment, David Hume:

> A too great disproportion among the citizens weakens any state. Every person, if possible, ought to enjoy the fruits of his labour, in a full possession of all the necessaries, and many of the conveniences of life. No one can doubt but such an equality is most suitable to human nature, and diminishes much less from the *happiness* of the rich, than it adds to that of the poor.[51]

Benjamin Disraeli's famous novel *Sybil, or The Two Nations* (1845) highlighted the problem in a dramatic (and didactic) form. Charles Egremont, a young aristocrat, dons a disguise to investigate the conditions of the working classes. He is dismayed by the factory system.

In an encounter with a working-class radical (the father of the lovely Sybil) he is told that England is divided into two nations:

> between whom there is no intercourse and no sympathy; who are as ignorant of each other's habits, thoughts, and feelings, as if they were dwellers in different zones, or inhabitants of different planets; who are formed by a different breeding, are fed by a different food, are ordered by different manners, and are not governed by the same laws . . . THE RICH AND THE POOR.[52]

This was a common theme in the social novels of the time. Six decades after *Sybil*, in 1909, the Liberal MP Charles Masterman lamented the coexistence of 'public penury' with 'private ostentation' – a characterization similar to John Kenneth Galbraith's 'private opulence and public squalor' in *The Affluent Society* (1958). Masterman noted that the 'multitude', the 'masses', the 'crowd', the '80 per cent' of the population, live in complete separation from the elites (the 'conquerors') and the middle classes (the 'suburbans'):

> . . . it is a people . . . who never express their own grievances, who rarely become articulate . . . It is a people which, all unnoticed and without clamour or protest, has passed through the largest secular change of a thousand years: from the life of the fields to the life of the city.[53]

For Disraeli and his followers the creation of 'one nation' did not mean bridging the gap between rich and poor. It meant integrating the poor into the nation so that they would be content and made to feel they had a stake in it. In his celebrated Crystal Palace speech of 24 June 1872, Disraeli explained that 'the Tory party, unless it is a national party, is nothing'. Its goals were not only the preservation of the institutions of the country (law and order, religion, the monarchy, the Empire, etc.) but also 'the elevation of the condition of the people'. Disraeli gloried in the fact that the Conservatives had been able to reduce working hours 'without injuring the wealth of the nation'. The Liberals had opposed these reforms, arguing that they would lead to unemployment and impoverishment.[54] Social, 'compassionate' conservatism was then strong and probably contributed to the phenomenon of the working-class Tory. Some Tories understood this perfectly: Lord John Manners, a supporter of Disraeli, in a letter to him (24 October 1866) about the extension of the Factory Acts, wrote of the need to cultivate 'the Working Classes'.[55]

How effective was this 'compassionate conservatism' – as we would call it today? Was it anything more than a desire to use working-class discontent against the Liberals? Was it propelled by a vague fear of revolution?[56] The subsequent history of the Conservative Party is the history of its transformation into a pro-capitalist party, rendered easier by the fact that, though its parliamentary representation, even in the 1860s, was based mainly on rural constituencies, its basic economic ideas, as with those of the Liberal Party, were embedded in an orthodox political economy built on the principles of individualism and predisposed against government intervention.[57]

Being worried about the gap between the 'two nations' was not just a Tory peculiarity. Gladstone, when Chancellor of the Exchequer, in his Financial Statement to the House on 16 April 1863, noted that the country had experienced a 'vast increase in wealth', indeed an '*extraordinary and almost intoxicating growth*' due, he surmised, to technological improvements and legislation. But he then added, ominously, 'The augmentation I have described . . . is an augmentation entirely confined to the classes possessed of property', something he disapproved of, though he added, consolingly, that perhaps this may be of 'indirect benefit to the labourer' (later referred to as the 'trickle-down effect'). Yet he was confident that the *average* condition of the British labourer had improved remarkably in the last two decades.[58] Karl Marx could not fail to mention this speech in *Das Kapital* while ungraciously calling Gladstone 'this unctuous minister'.[59]

Alessandro Garelli, an Italian academic, who remarked on the 'strange scene' of wealth and misery constantly growing side by side in the United Kingdom, worried about inequalities in post-unification Italy too, lamenting that the wealth accumulated by the wealthy has produced a terrible new misery among the poor.[60] He warned that 'our workers' are still full of good intentions, all they want is to improve their conditions of existence; they do not want to abolish wages, they want higher wages.[61] In other words they were not socialists – not yet.

Inequalities also perturbed liberals such as J. A. Hobson, who pointed out that the majority of the working class did not have sufficient resources for a 'decent human life', adding that greater equality as a result of stimulating home consumption might 'make our industries largely independent of the need of finding new markets in parts of the world where we stir national animosities involving incalculable risks . . .'[62]

And in 1909, Winston Churchill, then a cabinet minister in a Liberal government, in a speech supporting David Lloyd George's so-called People's Budget (5 September 1909), asserted that the 'unnatural gap between rich and poor' was 'the greatest danger to the British Empire'. Such a danger, he explained:

> is not to be found among the enormous fleets and armies of the European Continent, nor in the solemn problems of Hindustan; it is not the Yellow peril nor the Black peril nor any danger in the wide circuit of colonial and foreign affairs. No, it is here in our midst, close at home . . . It is there you will find the seeds of Imperial ruin and national decay – the unnatural gap between rich and poor . . . the constant insecurity in the means of subsistence and employment which breaks the heart of many a sober, hard-working man, the absence of any established minimum standard of life and comfort among the workers, and, at the other end, the swift increase of vulgar, joyless luxury – here are the enemies of Britain. Beware lest they shatter the foundations of her power.[63]

The rhetoric, in this case, should not disguise the solidity of the evidence. Social reformers and investigators such as Charles Booth and Seebohm Rowntree had based their disquiet about social problems and poverty upon detailed surveys on, respectively, the poor of London (*Life and Labour of the People of London*, 1889–91) and of York (*Poverty: A Study of Town Life*, 1901).

William Booth (founder of the Salvation Army and no relation to Charles Booth), in his *Darkest England and the Way Out* (1890), appealed to the propertied classes to help lift the English poor out of poverty, out of their 'darkest Africa', by following the example set by Bismarck's social reforms, warning them not to 'simply shrug our shoulders, and pass on . . . leaving these wretched multitudes in the gutters where they have lain so long. No, no, no; time is short.'[64]

The Bitter Cry of Outcast London (1883), a particularly influential pamphlet by the reverend Andrew Mearns, advocated that 'the State must . . . secure for the poorest the rights of citizenship and the right to live in something better than fever dens – the right to live as something better than the uncleanest of brute beasts'.[65]

The idea that there was some kind of savagery in capitalism (hence the frequent allusions to darkest Africa and to wild beasts) was becoming commonplace. It was not surprising that Upton Sinclair called his best-selling novel on the conditions in the meat-packing industry in Chicago *The Jungle* (1906). What was shocking for many was the fact that misery could be so extensive in countries such as England and the United States, which were the richest in the world.

Of course, such sentiments were more likely to be expressed in a prosperous country than in a poor one where inequalities of wealth could be attributed to natural and ancient causes. The conditions of the workers were worse in barely industrialized countries such as Romania, where, in 1914, the working class numbered only 10 per cent of the population, and where working conditions were abominable, where workers had no protection, and no laws regulated the hours of labour.[66]

A key motivation for reform was to regard the poor and the unfortunate not as 'strangers in our midst' but as fellow citizens. Social reform and the creation of a national community went together. This was the case not just in Europe but also in distant Japan, where radicals and social investigators expressed feelings similar to those of British social reformers. The discovery that the poor even existed required public intervention. Socialist intellectuals such as Kotoku Shusui appealed to 'Scholars, entrepreneurs, ministers, police chiefs', pointing out that 'many of . . . our fellow nationals are leading monstrous lives almost like animals'.[67] The literary critic Taoka Reiun, whose interest in social inequality was enhanced by reading Victor Hugo, also urged the integration of the poor into the nation, warning that 'The so-called civilization and enlightenment of the nineteenth century entailed much civilization for the rich', but it made the gap between rich and poor greater.[68]

Few defended inequalities but, among those who did, exponents of economic liberalism were more pre-eminent than outspoken reactionaries. Thus, in 1880, Paul Leroy-Beaulieu explained that the excessive concentration of wealth was a thing of the recent past. The free market, he declared confidently, will smooth away inequalities, adding, almost but not quite in jest, that the real danger for the future was that there would not be enough inequality and that life would become boring with everyone being the same.[69] Leroy-Beaulieu, in this as in much else, was wrong in upholding the political myth (admittedly widely held) that the Third Republic was an egalitarian republic of small owners.[70] In fact, inequalities increased in France throughout the nineteenth century and up to the First World War, much of this increase in inequality occurring during the period 1860 to 1913, mostly because of the growth of large industrial and financial estates.[71] Inequality in Paris increased substantially after 1867: the top 1 per cent climbed from owning 52 per cent of the wealth in 1867 to a staggering 72 per cent in 1913.[72] There was not much *égalité* or *fraternité* in the Third Republic, but plenty of *liberté* to get rich.

That was the modernity that dazzled much of the world, as many years later American modernity would inspire so many in spite of its urban ghettoes and rural poverty. The new, recently arrived Americans, like those who had settled earlier, wanted to become their own boss. Abraham Lincoln, in his speech to the Wisconsin Agricultural

Society (30 September 1859), thought that in America, for the new immigrant, wage labour was just a stepping stone to becoming their own master: 'The prudent, penniless beginner in the world, labors for wages awhile, then saves enough to buy some land for himself.'[73] But, Lincoln's wishes notwithstanding, most immigrants remained wage-workers, at the bottom of the pile, just above those with no work.

Inequality was a constant element in the development of American capitalism. Andrew Carnegie, the American steel magnate and philanthropist, did note the 'contrast between the palace of the millionaire and the cottage of the laborer', but he added consolingly that this was a 'product of civilization', 'not to be deplored, but welcomed as highly beneficial . . . Much better this great irregularity than universal squalor. Without wealth there can be no Maecenas . . . A relapse to old conditions would be disastrous – not the least so to him who serves – and would sweep away civilization with it.'[74] This inequality, he claimed with the self-confidence of the rich, is 'temporary'. The vast wealth will trickle down 'by degrees' largely through private benefaction, the way Carnegie did it.[75] And, eventually, the nation will be united in prosperity.

11

A Yearning for Democracy Sweeps the World

A wave of reformist unrest erupted in 'laggard' countries as diverse as China (the Xinhai Revolution, 1911), Turkey (the Young Turks Revolution, 1908), Mexico (the 1910 revolution against Porfirio Díaz's dictatorship), Iran (the Constitutional Revolution of 1905–7), the Portuguese republican revolution of October 1910, the modernization of Thailand (then called Siam, the name Thailand was adopted in 1939) at the turn of the century by the 'Great Beloved King' Chulalongkorn the Great, which led to the abolition of slavery and serfdom. In Russia, after the failed revolution of 1905, there was a wave of reforms leading to the legalization of political parties, elected bodies in local government, and a major agrarian reform. An important factor in this turmoil was the impact of the industrialization of Europe and its quest for raw materials and foodstuffs, notably in the Ottoman Empire.[1]

National elites tried to force through political and economic reforms under the banner of modernity. Sometimes these reforms resulted in increased inequality, since these pre-capitalist societies had never idealized *égalité*. Fear of conquest or domination by foreign powers was often an incentive for reform. Thailand, one of the few uncolonized countries in Asia, was afraid of French imperialism. In Portugal, still an imperial though powerless country, British colonial claims in Africa prompted the republican coup against the dithering monarchy. Japan, Iran, and China feared Western colonialism in general; Latin Americans feared the United States, hence the famous lament, often attributed to Porfirio Díaz: *¡Pobre México! ¡Tan lejos de Dios y tan cerca de los Estados Unidos!* ('Poor Mexico! So far from God and so close to the United States!'); Russia and the Ottoman Empire feared western European powers. Fear was one of the main constituent factors behind the movement of reforms from above.

In many instances the process of change was initiated by the military, the army often being a prefiguration of the modern political party:

centralized, disciplined, and able to recruit among diverse social classes. The pre-eminence of the military was particularly important in two distinct if different areas, the Middle East (in Egypt and the Ottoman Empire) and Latin America.

The Ottoman Empire was in gradual decline. The authorities in Constantinople, like those in China, were constantly urged to reform, but were unable to move fast enough. Some timid steps were taken. With the Ottoman Reform Edict of 1856, the Ottomans, realizing their debt towards the European powers during the Crimean War, accepted the principle of civic equality.[2] Twenty years later, in 1876, Sultan Abdülhamid II, who had just acceded to the throne, promised to introduce constitutional reforms, but the constitution that was drafted, based on that of Belgium (1831), allowed for no constraint on the Sultan's powers, thus undermining the powers of the elected assembly. What was new was the declaration that all would really be equal before the law regardless of religion.[3]

The external threat that had helped accelerate the pace of reforms also impeded them: the Russian military intervention of 1877–8 put paid to Ottoman constitutionalism.[4] So in effect the constitution lasted for only a couple of years. Besides, the elected chamber had shown itself to be too independent, thus confirming the fears of traditionalists who thought that reforms, once started, would inevitably lead to the collapse of the entire imperial system. An era of repression followed as Abdülhamid purged, exiled, and assassinated his opponents while developing an expensive and complex system of patronage and clienteles.[5] Osman's empire (Ottoman being the Europeanized form for the House of Osman) had, in fact, become a kind of police state that used not just networks of informers and strict censorship but also the postal and telegraph services to monitor the activities and daily life of its citizens – as democratic states, such as the USA and the UK, continue to do to this day.

The Ottoman regime's mistake was to try to break the link between democratic reforms and economic development, hoping to obtain prosperity without democracy, with the result that neither was achieved. The administrators of the empire (like those of the Chinese Empire) feared that the penetration of capitalist relations would increase the power of the merchant classes and decrease theirs, but knew that economic stagnation would also affect them adversely. Ottoman handicrafts had continued to suffer, since the 1830s, from the massive imports of cheaper, machine-made European goods. To such longer-term failures of the Ottoman regime were added more contingent factors such as the harsh winter of 1907 and the consequent spiralling cost of food. Such tension led to the Young Turks Revolution of 1908.[6]

This would not have been possible had not the Young Turks been able to unite various oppositional factions under the name of the Committee of Union and Progress (CUP, *İttihad ve Terakki Cemiyeti*), founded in Paris in 1889. Their 'modernity' was heralded in the opening paragraph of their manifesto that appealed to *both* women and men and denounced the government for violating human rights 'such as justice, equality and liberty'. The condition of women came to the fore, as it always does when modernizing movements emerge, and a variety of feminist organizations sprang up, to the amazement of foreign visitors.[7] The Young Turks also attempted the seemingly impossible task of uniting the various minorities under the umbrella of the 'fatherland'. They were successful since, by 1908, they had forced Abdülhamid II to reinstate the suspended constitution and concede elections. This was the so-called Young Turks Revolution. The constitution was amended (1909), reducing considerably the prerogatives of the Sultan.[8] Abdülhamid was finally deposed and the Ottoman Empire became, belatedly, a constitutional monarchy, but its days were numbered. Nation-building in the Ottoman multinational empire was impossible. It was only after the First World War that a Turkish nation arose out of the dismantling of the empire.

The Young Turks, themselves members of the intellectual and political elite, had taken power ostensibly to re-establish parliamentary government and the constitution of 1876, but democratization was soon halted. The Young Turks, like their counterparts in China, Mexico, Egypt, and elsewhere, were authoritarian modernizers who distrusted the masses, as most revolutionaries do without discarding the *idea* of appealing to the people. They were secularists, prefiguring the Kemalist revolution of 1923. They advocated the separation of state and religion and hoped that Islamic education could be modernized, a hope that Mustafa Kemal, the future Atatürk, 'Father of the Turks', thought was utopian, preferring to close the religious schools altogether.[9]

The consequences of the Balkan Wars of 1912 to 1913, during which the Ottomans lost Macedonia and Thessaloniki (the birthplace of Atatürk), showed how precarious the empire had become – though it had been declining for over a century. Already in 1877, Lord Salisbury, then Secretary of State for India, had looked forward to the dismemberment of the Ottoman Empire, saying that it was absurd to go on 'treating and respecting the Turkish Empire as a living organism, when everybody else was treating it as a carcass'.[10] In the years preceding the First World War, the European powers, like vultures, picked at the bones of the Ottoman Empire: Austria-Hungary annexed Bosnia and Herzegovina, Greece captured Crete and Thessaloniki, and Italy occupied Libya and the Dodecanese Islands, including Rhodes. Only the military coup of 23 January 1913 led by the Young Turks prevented the loss of the last European remnant of the empire, Eastern Thrace, to Bulgaria.[11] The military continued to dominate Turkish politics throughout most of the twentieth century and were instrumental in building the Turkish nation. Most nations have been constructed as a result of wars, or the threat of war: Napoleonic France, the Third French Republic, Bismarck's Germany, the Soviet Union, China, the United States after the Civil War, Austria, Italy, most postcolonial states, Yugoslavia, and Israel.

Iran, however (Persia was the name more commonly used by foreigners), was far more dominated by Western powers than the Ottomans were. Under the Anglo-Russian Agreement of 1907, the country had been carved up into spheres of influence: the Russian in the north, including Tehran, and the British in the south-east ('protecting' Afghanistan and Baluchistan).The merchant community, dismayed at the taxes it had to pay, wanted tariffs against foreign imports, especially textiles. But the Shah (King Mozaffar ad-Din), whose extravagant lifestyle had contributed to overburdening the country with debt, was in hock to foreigners and could rule only by constantly negotiating with various notables and local leaders. Protectionism never stood a chance.[12]

Once again the push for change in Iran came from abroad: the victory of Japan over Russia in 1905 had proved the strength of constitutional and reformed states, while the subsequent abortive Russian Revolution of 1905 'expanded the realm of possibilities . . . a constitutional revolution in Iran became imaginable'.[13] In the summer of 1906 a series of demonstrations in Tehran led by an alliance of clerics and merchants convinced Mozaffar ad-Din to convene a National Consultative Assembly.[14] The 1906 revolution left important legacies in Iran: there was some modernization in financial practices, in the judiciary, in public education, in elections to parliament or Majlis (Arabic for 'a place of sitting'), in the development of political organizations; some women were able to take part in politics and founded the first women's newspaper.[15]

However, the powerful clerics wanted a constitution quite different from that desired by the modernizing secular forces.[16] They wanted to limit the powers of the state – just like their Christian counterparts in

Italy, Austria, and Germany – whereas the secular forces wanted to create a strong state capable of overcoming Iran's backwardness and leading the way towards an industrial society.[17] In the ensuing turmoil an Iranian constitution was established – as in Turkey – on the basis of the Belgian constitution of 1831.[18]

As we saw in Chapter 10, nation-building is easier when there is some kind of linguistic or religious unity. Iran was far less ethnically diverse than the Ottoman Empire, while Islam, being correspondingly stronger, was useful to reformers in their struggle against foreign domination.[19]

It became evident to the new ruler, Mohammad Ali Shah Qajar, who had succeeded his father in 1907, that the new constitutionalism could not be fought by appealing to loyalty to the monarch, but only by reviving and mobilizing popular support around Islam. Abroad, the Shah's image was dismal. He was, in the words of W. Morgan Shuster, 'perhaps the most perverted, cowardly, and vice-sodden monster that had disgraced the throne of Iran in many generations'. The front page of the *Illustrated London News* of January 1909 carried a picture of the Shah seated on the Peacock Throne with the caption 'the "Kings of Kings" has declared that his country is unripe for either a Constitution or a National Council'.[20]

Forced into exile in Odessa, Mohammad Ali staged a comeback with Russian help.[21] He dispersed the elected Majlis, but, without them, could not raise the tax revenues to pay off his debts to the British and the Russians, so he had to reconvene the Majlis while facing unrest in a number of provinces.[22] He was ousted again in July 1909 by the constitutionalist forces and was succeeded by his son, Ahmad Shah, who was eleven at the time. It looked as if the modernizers had won, though the country had been weakened by constant upheavals, as the exiled Shah tried to stage one final comeback in 1910 and failed again. The British, once supporters of the constitutionalist and nationalist forces, changed tack on the grounds that it was not worth, as the (Liberal) Foreign Secretary, Sir Edward Grey, said, '[keeping] up a quarrel with Russia in order to curry favour with the Persians', since they (the British) had signed an agreement with the Russians (1907) on their respective spheres of influence in the region.[23] In fact, Great Britain had never really cared that much about Iran. Lord Salisbury himself had observed twenty years earlier that 'Were it not for our possession of India, we should trouble ourselves but little over Persia.'[24] The main 'specialist' on Iran in the British establishment was Lord Curzon, author of *Persia and the Persian Question*, written in 1892, who was deeply prejudiced against the Iranians, whom he regarded as inherently duplicitous and perfidious.[25] Few listened to the leading British academic specialist on Iranian culture, Edward G. Browne, who, in his pro-Iranian book *The Persian Revolution of 1905–1909* (1910), explained that the nationalist-constitutionalist forces were 'essentially the patriotic party, which stands for progress, freedom, tolerance, and above all for national independence and "Persia for the Persians"'.[26]

The Majlis had attempted to reform the country's finances by collecting taxes from wealthy grandees, and they stopped the Shah from borrowing from Russia and Great Britain; they hired a financial expert, W. Morgan Shuster, an American, as Treasurer-General (Americans were seen in a favourable light, unlike the highly distrusted Europeans).[27] Shuster, who arrived in Iran in December 1911, had previously organized the customs of Cuba and the Philippines, de facto US colonies, which is why he was occasionally, if wrongly, regarded as an American stooge. Shuster took his job seriously, attempting to collect taxes and stamp out corruption, and operated as if Iran were a truly independent country. He acted as if he owed his loyalty exclusively to his employers, the Majlis, and managed to antagonize the Russians, the British, and even the French (whose priority was the development of an alliance against Germany).[28] But the Majlis had no support whatsoever from any European power. Eventually the Russians sent an ultimatum to the Majlis asking them to dismiss Shuster and not to hire foreign subjects without asking Russia and Great Britain.[29] At first the Majlis refused and were supported by a popular boycott of British and Russian goods.[30] Without a proper army the country was unable to resist and eventually the Majlis were forced to accept the Russian ultimatum. Shuster went back to the United States in January 1912, a bitter man. His mission had lasted only seven months. He wrote in his memoirs of the events, *The Strangling of Persia*, that the country 'was the helpless victim of the wretched game of cards which a few Europeans powers, with the skill of centuries of practice, still play with weaker nations'.[31]

In Egypt, too, democracy was stirring. Although technically part of the Ottoman Empire, the country was autonomous. Egypt had become, by 1848, among the top ten cotton producers in the world, with France and Britain as her main trading partners, thanks to the state-directed reforms of the great khedive Muhammad Ali ('founder of modern Egypt' – a soldier of Albanian birth who conducted his governmental affairs in Turkish). The wealth derived from cotton might have been used as the springboard for a state-directed industrialization – as in Japan.[32] Indeed, Muhammad Ali destroyed some of the privileges of the landlords and distributed cultivation rights to the *fellahin* (the peasants).[33] Soon he was the agricultural master of Egypt as well as its chief industrialist, employing in his factories some 40,000 workers.[34] But the British–Ottoman Treaty forced free trade on Egypt, destroying its mechanized industry (which, had Egypt been a stronger state, should have been protected). Egypt's cotton industry was devastated. The Egyptian state was strong at home but weak internationally and 'no match for British interests and designs'.[35] Muhammad Ali's grandson Ismail Pasha ('Ismail the Magnificent') continued the task of modernizing the country, becoming increasingly independent from the Ottoman Empire. He opened the Suez Canal in 1869, and introduced a modern co-educational school system, encouraging the emergence of a native elite and the involvement of Europeans in the economic and cultural life of the country.[36] By the 1860s, expressions such as *tamaddun* (civilization) and *taqaddum* (progress) had become common among Egyptian intellectuals, particularly with the minority that had a Christian background.[37] However, modernizing on the back of huge debts contracted with the British and the French proved too great an obstacle.

In the years before the First World War, during the heyday of British imperialism, the British consul was the de facto ruler of Egypt. Evelyn Baring (who became Lord Cromer in 1892), consul for twenty years from 1887, had two priorities: the first was to assert British control and the second to convince London politicians that the British (i.e. himself) would be better at ruling Egypt than the Egyptians.[38] In 1887 he wrote to Lord Salisbury, the Prime Minister, that he doubted that there could be:

> a sudden transfer of power in a quasi-civilized State to a class so ignorant and incapable as the pure Egyptians. These latter have for centuries past been a subject race . . . Neither for the present do they appear to possess any of the qualities which would render it desirable, either in their own interests or in those of the civilized world in general, to raise them to the category of autonomous rulers.[39]

Cromer wanted to vet all ministers in the Egyptian 'government'. Gladstone himself, then Prime Minister, was alarmed by Cromer's arrogance.[40] Soon the khedive gave up any pretence of being able to resist British demands. The old guard of Egyptian politicians was now completely demoralized.[41] Cromer did his best to prevent the development of an Egyptian middle class or a cotton industry in Egypt for fear of the 'serious consequences . . . [for the] . . . huge trade in cotton now carried on between England and this country'.[42] If asked to choose between the interests of Lancashire cotton and those of Egypt, Cromer, in spite of spending three decades in Egypt, would always choose Lancashire. However, without a strong enough state Egypt could never become the Japan of the Middle East. The major modernizing project it had undertaken in the nineteenth century, the Suez Canal, which halved the distance between England and India, turned out to be a blessing in disguise since it made Egypt of vital importance to Britain and its empire.[43]

Thus the Ottoman, Iranian, and Egyptian aspirations towards constitutional rule and democratic reform were part of a global movement which, paradoxically, was often thwarted by the so-called pioneers of democracy. Today we call this the 'international community', or the West.

A central aspect of this new 'democratic' era was that some sort of lip service had to be paid to 'the people'. Even a brutally frank authoritarian discourse would be phrased in populist and popular terms. Thus, in Latin America the oligarchies that had broken with Spain, often led by caudillos such as Juan Manuel de Rosas in Argentina or Antonio López de Santa Anna in Mexico, or authoritarian politicians such as Diego Portales in Chile, and, later, 'elected' dictators such as Porfirio Díaz in Mexico, claimed they had the interests of the people at heart. (Those who fought against these caudillos also used the language of democracy.) The caudillos themselves required an army of loyal followers to whom they would distribute state resources while themselves possessing an economic base in the form of landed estates they had obtained by force or inherited, as was the case with many of the caudillo of the Plata region such as Rosas.[44]

The Mexican Revolution of 1910 had goals that were unmistakably 'modern': 'representative democracy', the subservience of Church to State, the development of secular education, agrarian reform, regulation of employment and the extension of the public sector, especially over resources that might fall under the control of foreign companies.[45] The Mexican Revolution was a revolution of the New World, like the North American one. It was not aimed at eliminating an *ancien régime* as the Constitutional Revolution in Iran, the Young Turks in the Ottoman Empire, and the 1911 revolution in China had been. Its target was a modern dictatorship, that of Porfirio Díaz, a regime which had all the hallmarks of modern liberalism: a strong belief in national unity, secularism, republicanism, and individualism.[46] Democracy had been a formal element of this liberal Mexican state. Díaz was almost constantly re-elected between 1876 and 1910, albeit by means of a formidable array of methods, from threats and coercion to bribery and cooptation. Parliament was a rubber stamp. As Henry Lane Wilson, the American ambassador to Mexico, wrote in 1914: 'Díaz was not a tyrant, but a benevolent autocrat who understood the Mexican people and knew them to be unfitted for self-government.'[47]

The old Mexican Constitution of 1857, extant during the entire period of the Porfiriate (as Porfirio Díaz's rule came to be known), did not recognize the indigenous natives as true Mexican citizens; defended private ownership of land, much of which was communally held by the people of the villages; and was anticlerical in a deeply Catholic country.[48] Nevertheless, it was also the kind of constitution any European democrat would have recognized: it enshrined human rights, male suffrage, the separation of executive and judiciary powers, federalism, and the separation of Church and State. Of course, in practice, little of this was respected. Whereas in the Ottoman and Tsarist Empires reformers asked for a constitution, the revolutionaries in Mexico in 1910 demanded the implementation of the existing constitution in a political conflict between elites, where each used the people as a weapon in the struggle.[49]

Yet the people were not absent. The great land reforms that characterized the Mexican experience saw a popular involvement unequalled elsewhere. In Russia, for instance, the emancipation of the serfs had been fundamentally a revolution from above. In Mexico, on the eve of the 1910 revolution, villagers petitioning the authorities for land used all legal (and sometimes illegal) means, searched land titles, marked boundaries, and asked the authorities to mediate disputes over land ownership.[50]

Porfirio Díaz's dictatorship was not just an arbitrary one-man rule but was rather a modernizing 'liberal' quasi-dictatorship. (True, elections were usually rigged, but Díaz had genuine support.) Porfirian liberals strengthened the executive branch not only to promote economic development and growth, but also to uphold social policies that could protect the poor. Lands were often distributed to poor Indians in an effort to relieve them of their dismal conditions. The turmoil of 1910 to 1913 – the end of the Porfiriate, revolution, the election of Francisco Madero, his assassination in 1913, and the military *coup d'état* by Victoriano Huerta with the probable complicity of the American ambassador to Mexico, Henry Lane Wilson – resulted in the long-term rule of the aptly named *Partido Revolucionario Institucional* (Institutional Revolutionary Party), which ruled uninterruptedly for seventy-one years and was re-elected often with extravagantly large majorities.

By 1917, Mexico had promulgated social and political rights similar to those of the more progressive European states: land reform; male suffrage; some form of welfare; and rights for workers to organize themselves into unions and to go on strike; protection for women and children; the eight-hour day; and a minimum wage. The example was followed by many Latin American countries. Of course, the extent to which such rights were implemented remained an issue.

The Mexican Revolution was a harbinger of other twentieth-century secularist and nationalist revolutions. Until the advent of the Khomeini Revolution in Iran in 1979, such national revolutions were overwhelmingly secular and often anti-religious, propounding a language which, as in Mexico in 1910, constantly referred to the 'people', whom the revolution claimed to have liberated.[51] Of course, the people often remained dissatisfied. Revolutionary rhetoric inevitably exalted the possibility of impossible messianic changes.

The chronic instability of so many Latin American countries was often due to significant differences between rural conservative elites and urban-based liberal ones. The two sides at times entered into an *acuerdo entre caballeros* (a gentlemen's agreement) and monopolized power, but when the compromise was broken, instability ensued.[52] On both sides rhetoric invoked 'the people' but treated them like pawns in a complex political game. Harsh repression of the people was often deployed, as in Chile in 1907 when troops murdered over a thousand defenceless striking miners as well as their wives and children in Iquique (the Santa María School massacre). Yet neither liberals nor conservatives were unduly worried by militant workers. Neither the industrial proletariat nor socialism was a significant force in Latin America.[53]

Popular consensus for nation-building, real or presumed, was also invoked elsewhere: in recently unified states such as Germany and Italy; in recently consolidated ones, such as the United States after the Civil War; even in well-established states such as France and Britain; in 'nations' that wished to become nations while being part of other, larger states, such as Poland and Ireland; and in old countries in decline such as Portugal and Spain. Such a distinction between old dying nations and 'true' living nations had been evoked by Lord Salisbury, then Prime Minister, in a famous speech to the Primrose League (a Conservative organization committed to 'uphold and support God, Queen, and Country') on 4 May 1898. In it he divided the nations of the world into dying nations (such as Spain, Portugal, China, and Turkey) and living ones such as the United States and Germany and, of course, Great Britain (Salisbury was unsure about France and Italy).[54]

Spain was, it is true, compared to most western European countries, economically backward, politically unstable, and troubled by coups and counter-coups. The economic situation was dire. After years of civil strife state finances were in disarray.[55] After the republican interlude of 1873–4 the military-led restoration of the Bourbon dynasty turned out to be a conservative 'liberal' regime where the conservative Antonio Cánovas del Castillo (six times Prime Minister between 1874 and 1897, when he was murdered by an Italian anarchist) alternated in power with a liberal, Práxedes Mateo Sagasta (eight times Prime Minister between 1870 and 1902). This was the so-called *turno pacifico* (peaceful turn), a semi-formal arrangement aimed at keeping the army out of politics and sharing the spoils in what was a highly corrupt system with some of the trappings of democracy. Social conditions remained dire: there was chronic under-nourishment and many were plagued by cholera and flu epidemics (1885–90). Tuberculosis was the main cause of death in urban centres; 71 per cent of Spaniards were illiterate.[56] In 1898, Spain lost its remaining colonies – Cuba, Puerto Rico, and the Philippines – to the United States. Some Europeans, such as the French geographer Maurice Zimmermann, began to worry at the rise of the new American power.[57]

The demoralization that pervaded the country after the *desastre del '98* – as the losses of the colonies were called – gave way to a period of intense soul-searching, nationalism, and economic protectionism, even though the economic consequences of the *desastre* were relatively trivial.[58] There was little popular sorrow for these losses – something which puzzled the intelligentsia, particularly those who were so traumatized that they became known as the *generación del '98*, whose despair gave rise to a spate of books, from Damían Isern's *Del desastre nacional y sus causas* (1899) to Ricardo Macías Picavea's *El problema nacional. Hechos, causas y remedios* (1899).[59]

In Catalonia, Spain's most modern (culturally and industrially) region, the disaster of 1898 was regarded as a defeat for Spain not for Catalonia.[60] Nation-building in Spain was difficult because the separatist movements prevailed where industry was strong, namely in Catalonia and the Basque country. This was unusual at the time in western Europe since separatism of this kind tended to be in poorer areas, which blamed the richer ones for their plight. And even this poor man's separatism was a minor affair: in Sicily it did not amount to much; in Corsica nationalism was a spent force; in Scotland and Wales it was, at the time, a matter for eccentrics; Bavaria seemed content to be part of Germany at least until after the First World War. Ireland was quite a different matter and, indeed, Irish nationalism remained a key player in British politics even after the formation of the Irish Free State in southern Ireland in 1922.

The anti-democratic argument in Spain (but also elsewhere, as we shall see in Chapter 13) was that it would be folly to grant the suffrage to the entire people since they were an inchoate mass whose lack of education and base desires made them easy prey for unscrupulous rabble-rousers. The people had to be educated and then, in the fullness of time, and only gradually, could they be allowed to elect their representatives. They would learn their duties. They would behave responsibly. They would stop blaming their rulers for what happened to them. They would arbitrate between competing elites in a peaceful way. Nevertheless, in 1890 a new electoral law granted suffrage to all Spanish men over the age of twenty-five, regardless of income (and well ahead of Britain, where universal men's suffrage was granted only in 1918).

In Russia, too, there was an unmistakable whiff of democracy. By the 1860s even Russian conservatives recognized that some political reforms were due. Some attributed the catastrophic defeat in the Crimean War (1853–6) to the lack of patriotic spirit of conscripted soldiers (mainly peasants) and believed that this, in turn, was due to the lack of involvement of the people in political life. Yuri Samarin, an ardent Slavophile, wrote, 'We will regain our proper place in the comity of European powers not in Vienna, not in Paris, and not in London but only inside Russia' by ending 'the isolation of the government from the people'.[61] There were 300,000 landowners in Russia, he explained, who lived in fear of a terrible revolution (and 'with reason' he added) and millions of peasants united in the belief that their common enemy was the nobility (though they still worshipped the Tsar).[62]

Like many conservatives who wanted 'to turn to the people', whom they regarded as a source of wisdom, religion, and tradition, Slavophiles such as Samarin had advocated the abolition of serfdom not out of some commitment to liberalism but in order to ensure that the autocracy would rest on a solid foundation of popular deference, all the better to withstand revolutionary populism. Other Slavophiles had welcomed the emancipation of the serfs too because they thought it would eliminate the seemingly insurmountable barrier between the serfs and their masters.[63]

By the turn of the century most Russian newspapers, whether liberal or conservative, supported the idea of equal rights and criticized the excessive privileges of the nobility.[64] An important paper such as

Peterburgskaia gazeta in 1905 carried interviews with workers protesting against conditions in factories and even articles sympathetic to radical reformers.[65] Even more alienated than the peasants (whose thoughts can only be surmised) were members of the young radical *intelligentsia* – a word borrowed from the German *die Intelligentz*, but already widely circulating in Russia.[66] Their rejection of the existing order had no parallel in the rest of Europe. Many of these young intellectuals were 'nihilists' (a word popularized by Turgenev in his famous 1862 novel *Fathers and Sons*). Some became terrorists, forming groups such as *Narodnaya Volya* (People's Will), responsible for a spate of assassinations. Many of their victims were obvious targets of hatred, including the Education Minister Nikolai Bogolepov (1901), who had cracked down on students; the Interior Minister Dmitry Sipyagin (1902); his successor Vyacheslav von Plehve (1904), who had persecuted minorities – Armenians, Jews, and Finns – as well as militant workers and who had fervently supported the war against Japan (1904–5); Grand Duke Sergei Alexandrovich, Governor General of Moscow and brother of Tsar Alexander III (1905), who had been a repressive hardliner responsible for the expulsion of some 20,000 Jews from Moscow in 1891; and, finally, the Prime Minister Pyotr Stolypin (1911), who had closed down the First Duma (the legislative assembly), modified electoral rules in a conservative direction, executed terrorists under martial law, and operated in complete disregard of established legislation.

Their most illustrious victim, however, was the liberal and reforming Tsar Alexander II, who was killed in 1881. During his long, twenty-six-year rule Alexander had been responsible for the emancipation of the serfs, the promulgation of a new penal code (adapted from the French Code Napoléon), the reorganization of the judiciary, and the setting up of units of self-government in the countryside: the *zemstva*. True, he had suppressed Polish nationalism, but promoted that of Finland. Just before Alexander II's assassination, Count Mikhail Loris-Melikov, the new Minister of the Interior, had persuaded him to promote further liberalization.

It was too late. By assassinating Alexander II, the *Narodnaya Volya* set back the reform process by years, but then their goal was a revolution and the end of the autocracy, not its reform. One of their unwitting allies was Konstantin Pobedonostsev, the powerful Chief Procurator of the Holy Synod of the Russian Orthodox Church from 1880 to 1905. Pobedonostsev was a true reactionary and *éminence grise* at Court. When Alexander III ascended the throne, Pobedonostsev, who had been his tutor (he was later also tutor to Nicholas II, the last Tsar), wrote

Alexander a letter warning him to resist change and not to listen to 'the old siren songs':

> for God's sake, do not believe, Your Majesty, do not listen. This spells destruction, the destruction of both Russia and yourself . . . The mad villains who destroyed your father will not be satisfied with any concession . . . the evil seed can be extracted only in a struggle with them for life and death, with iron and blood.[67]

Not for Pobedonostsev the seduction of democracy: 'In a democracy,' he explained, 'the real rulers are the dexterous manipulators of votes, with their placemen, the mechanics who so skilfully operate the hidden springs which move the puppets in the arena of democratic elections. Men of this kind are ever ready with loud speeches lauding equality; in reality, they rule the people as any despot or military dictator might rule it.'[68]

Pobedonostsev was, in his peculiar way, a nihilist of the ultra-pessimistic kind. He believed that Man was hopelessly bad: his salvation could be achieved only by being ruled with an iron rod.[69] The Tsar ruled because he was appointed by God to rule. The divine right of kings did not require, by definition, any popular legitimacy, only God's. Parliaments, liberalism, democracy, separation of Church and State, social progress, and so on would all lead, irrevocably, to the dismemberment of the Tsarist Empire.

Pobedonostsev, an intelligent and deeply cultured conservative, was, of course, despised by the intelligentsia, though much admired by Dostoyevsky. He was neither easily forgotten nor forgiven: in 1910, three years after his death, the poet Alexander Blok included in his lengthy poem *Vozmezdie* ('Retribution'), his spiritual testament, a particularly poignant lament on the dispiriting effect the Chief Procurator of the Holy Synod had had on Russian society:

> In these mute and distant years
> A dull gloom filled all hearts.
> Pobedonostsev had unfurled
> His owlish wings over Russia.
> There was neither day nor night,
> Only the shadows of giant wings.[70]

Alexander III followed Pobedonostsev's advice. His reign (1881–94) saw few reforms. One was the decree of 1882 (extended in 1885) regulating the work of children and women in a number of unhealthy occupations (widely ignored).[71] This had been sparked by the strike of

1885 at the Morozov textile factory at Orekhovo-Zuyev, which had been crushed by the army. Afterwards, the description of the appalling exploitation of the workers (many former peasants) that surfaced in the courtroom led to the acquittal of the strikers.[72]

Such independence of the judiciary was not a novelty. Much of the credit for it must go to Alexander II. Thus when, in 1878, the revolutionary Vera Zasulich shot and seriously wounded Colonel Fyodor Trepov, the governor of St Petersburg and former police chief, the jury found her not guilty (though the evidence was unassailable). Even a convicted terrorist could become a popular liberal heroine. On 16 January 1906, Maria Spiridonova, a Social Revolutionary, then only twenty-one years old, killed Gavril Luzhenovsky, a provincial counsellor notorious for his brutal suppression of rural unrest. At the trial she claimed that she had been tortured and sexually abused by Luzhenovsky's bodyguards.[73] Described by the liberal press as a 'flower of spiritual beauty that only the highest culture of Russia could produce', she was condemned to only eleven years of exile in Siberia. Liberated in 1917 she continued being a revolutionary but was executed in 1941 on the orders of Stalin.[74]

Such was the cult of the people in Tsarist Russia that Alexander III's successor, Nicholas II, blamed the intellectuals and not the people for fostering dissent. Count Witte, in his memoirs, recounts that once, on hearing someone mentioning the 'intelligentsia', the Tsar exclaimed: 'How I detest that word! I wish I could order the Academy to strike it off the Russian dictionary.'[75]

Even the reactionaries worshipped an idealized version of the people. Dostoyevsky, in an entry in his diary on his celebrated oration on the unveiling of the monument to Alexander Pushkin (8 June 1880), declared that the greatness of Pushkin's poetry consisted in being born out of the Russian people, out of its *narodnyi* (native) spirit and:

> not in so-called 'European' education (which, it may be noted in passing, we never did possess); it was not in the deformities of the outwardly adopted European ideas and forms, that Pushkin found this beauty, but exclusively in the people's spirit and *in it alone*.[76]

Meanwhile the people, the real people, not the 'people' imagined by the intelligentsia, could no longer be kept at bay. When the autocratic Interior Minister Plehve was blown to pieces on 28 July 1904, there was such a distinct lack of regret even among conservatives that the Austro-Hungarian ambassador felt he had to report back to Vienna the fact that it had been such a non-event.[77] Count Witte was equally unregretful, perhaps even gleeful, at the assassination of Prime Minister

Stolypin: 'This statesman was the embodiment of political immorality and the members of his Cabinet were not far superior to him. He ruled Russia by violating every law and he disdained no means, however reprehensible, to keep himself in power',[78] adding later, 'No other statesman has ever succeeded in drawing upon himself the enmity of so many men and women.'[79]

Seriously worried, Nicholas II appointed Prince Sviatopolk-Mirsky as Interior Minister to succeed the murdered Plehve. Mirsky, who had a reputation for liberalism, had reluctantly accepted, hoping that the Tsar would finally see sense. To his dismay the Tsar, still trying to hold on to the past, declared that 'under no circumstances will I ever agree to a representative form of government, for I consider it harmful to the trust God gave me'.[80] The decree he subsequently signed (under pressure from Witte, then Prime Minister) promised greater autonomy to the judiciary, greater tolerance to religious dissenters, and greater powers to the *zemstva*, which, though under the control of the nobility, did some good. As Pavel Milyukov, the leader of the liberal Kadets (or Constitutional Democrats), said:

> [The *zemstva*] founded schools, built hospitals, helped the peasantry in every kind of agricultural improvement, and developed domestic industries . . . they were the first to come to the villages with messages of health, sanitation, enlightenment, and with sound reasons for private economy. Whatever has been done for culture in the Russian villages was done by the Zemstvos – and that in spite of every sort of obstruction . . . on the part of the central government.[81]

Tsar Nicholas II was somewhat less enthusiastic. Some ten years earlier, in January 1895, in a speech to *zemstvo* representatives, he declared, according to Milyukov, 'in a strong, clear voice, and with a remarkably resolute manner':

> I am aware that in certain meetings of the Zemstvos voices have lately been raised by persons carried away by absurd illusions as to the participation of the Zemstvo representatives in matters of internal government. Let all know that . . . I intend to protect the principle of autocracy as firmly and unswervingly as did my late and never-to-be-forgotten father.

The liberals replied with an open letter warning:

> Your speech has provoked a feeling of offense and depression; but the living social forces will soon recover from that feeling . . . You first began the struggle; and the struggle will come.[82]

Russia was on the move. In December 1904 workers had gone on strike at the armaments and shipbuilding Putilov plant in St Petersburg. These workers, who had been peasants until recently, still revered the Tsar, attributing the problems afflicting Russia to wicked advisers who kept him in the dark. It was a common way of being both loyal and subversive (if only the Tsar, may God bless his soul, knew our wretched conditions, etc.). They sent Nicholas II a 'humble and loyal address' explaining that 'we are enslaved, enslaved under the patronage and with the aid of your officials', and decrying the 'bureaucratic administration composed of embezzlers of public funds' who had involved the country 'in a humiliating war'.[83]

Their demands, however, were far from humble. They wanted elected workers' soviets (councils) in all factories to examine, along with management, workers' grievances. It was the birth of Soviet power. To back these demands, on 22 January 1905 (9 January according to the Julian calendar), a massive march took place led by Georgy Gapon, a charismatic priest. There were 50,000 participants, some say 100,000. Many of the workers took their families along as if to show that they did not intend any violence. The police fired on the demonstrators, leaving at least a hundred dead, perhaps more. It was Bloody Sunday. That was, to quote a Chinese proverb famously used by Mao in 1930, the single spark that started a prairie fire. The fire would engulf Russia for decades to come.

In September 1905 the military defeat by Japan jolted the autocracy into reforms (just as the Crimean War had done fifty years previously) and everything changed. To be defeated by what was (wrongly) regarded as a backward Asian state was unbearable. The domestic repercussions were enormous. The crew of the battleship *Potemkin* mutinied in Odessa. Social Democrats, including the Bolsheviks, a hitherto insignificant force, grew in strength and influence. Nationalist parties emerged or became stronger in Finland, Poland, the Baltic provinces, Georgia, and Ukraine (it was only in 1905 that the Russian Academy of Sciences decreed that Ukrainian was a real language and not a mere dialect of Russian).[84] Russia was in disarray as demonstrations, counter-demonstrations, and random pogroms multiplied. The autocracy was scared. Nothing like this had been seen at the time anywhere else in Europe. Concessions flowed accompanied by further turmoil and strikes.

Until 1905 there had been no significant working-class movement in the country, though there had been strikes and unrest.[85] This apparent docility may have contributed to preventing the kind of labour legislation that reformers demanded. If the workers did not complain, why change anything? Let the radical intelligentsia preach to the wind, amid the apathy of the muzhiks in the countryside or the *rabochikh* (workers) in the cities. Meanwhile, the industrialists continued to pursue their narrow material interests, exhibiting an obtuse absence of a social vision. They believed that it would be counter-productive to improve the conditions of the working class since they had been peasants until recently and therefore were immature and ignorant. Concessions could be made only when the working class had become more educated and capitalism more advanced.[86] No wonder no one listened to what the industrialists had to say. Their natural party, the Kadets (or KD, the Constitutional Democrats), the party of the liberal intelligentsia, led by Pavel Milyukov, were dismayed by the 'narrow' class interests of Russian landlords and industrialists.[87]

Russian liberalism was chronically weak. It was split into three tendencies, the Kadets, the Progressists, and the Octobrists, but even united it would not have amounted to much. The differences were minor and mainly to do with the question of agency, in other words who would lead the change. The Octobrists thought enlightened landlords and the urban upper middle classes would have the leading role. The Progressists rejected the possibility of an alliance between the bourgeoisie and the nobility; progress would only be achieved through the bourgeoisie. The Kadets were the most radical of the three and wanted a democratic system. What united all three of the groups was the idea that capitalism would be the inevitable outcome of Russian development (here even the Marxists, including Lenin and Plekhanov, agreed). Although they rejected the idea of a social revolution, the Kadets wanted a political revolution that would transform the Tsar into a constitutional ruler (as in Germany and Great Britain).[88]

Even Nicholas II realized that further concessions had to be made. Prompted, once again by Count Witte, he issued what came to be known as the 17 October 1905 Manifesto, written by Witte, pledging basic freedoms of speech, press, and religion, an elected Duma with considerable powers ('no law can become effective without approval of the State Duma') but a limited franchise.[89] 'In those days,' wrote Witte:

> even the conservatives advocated a constitution. In fact, there were no conservatives in Russia on the eve of October 17, 1905 . . . Many also suspected – and their suspicions proved eminently true – that the constitution had been granted by the Emperor in a fit of panic and that as soon as his

position improved he would so manipulate the constitution as to annul it and turn it into a ghastly farce.[90]

The period from mid-October to early December 1905 came to be known as the 'Days of Freedom'. But as the government relented, the prestige of the opposition grew, especially in the main cities. Workers' councils (soviets) were formed. In St Petersburg they elected Leon Trotsky as one of their leaders. In the countryside the Socialist Revolutionary Party (which had emerged from *Narodnaya Volya*) became a mass organization backed by rapidly developing peasant unions. The *zemstva* demanded an elected national assembly. Then, in December 1905, a particularly threatening uprising in Moscow, acting 'as a red rag to the bull of the counter-revolution', was crushed.[91] It was the end of the honeymoon. The regime clamped down everywhere: in southern Russia against the peasants, in Russian cities against the workers, in Poland against the nationalists.

Sergei Witte had urged the Tsar to accelerate constitutional reforms, but his influence was diminishing rapidly. Witte wanted to save the autocracy as much as the Tsar did but he thought that reforming it was the way forward, whereas the Tsar believed that the slightest change would bring the entire edifice down. Of Nicholas II, Witte wrote: 'A ruler who cannot be trusted, who approves to-day what he will reject to-morrow, is incapable of steering the Ship of State into a quiet harbour. His outstanding failing is his lamentable lack of will power.'[92] Witte was convinced that Russia could follow the West but only with a proper legal structure that would stop the peasants being in thrall to the arbitrariness of local powers.[93]

Terrorism escalated but, as is always the case, the terrorists were never in control of the consequences of their actions and never able to shape them. Like a sudden flood or a natural disaster, what the terrorists did was left to be exploited by others who were politically more astute, leaving the terrorists under the illusion that they 'had made a difference' without ever understanding what that the difference might have been.

Finally, a new Duma was elected (it took months) with a complicated franchise that depended not only on payment of taxes or property qualification but also on one's status. The outcome was that electoral power remained distributed unequally: workers were only 2.5 per cent of the electorate, the peasants 42 per cent, but the landowners 32 per cent.[94]

The Kadets became the largest party, gaining about one-third of the seats, while the Trudoviks (Labour Party) were second. Witte's supporters did not fare as well. The far left, namely the Socialist Revolutionaries as well as the much smaller Social Democrats (which then included both Menshevik and Bolsheviks factions), boycotted the election.

This Duma lasted two months. Contrary to what had been promised, its powers were largely advisory, as the Tsar reminded everyone in his address from the throne.[95] In 1907 a second Duma was elected, one far more representative than the first and not boycotted by Socialist Revolutionaries or Social Democrats.

This Duma too had very limited powers. Everything it did was subject to the approval of the State Council of Imperial Russia, half of whose members were appointed by the Tsar (who had a further right of veto).[96] The Tsar openly manifested his disdain of the Duma by telling the German ambassador that the deputies 'behave in a manner beneath all contempt, who think about nothing else except how to revile each other and fight against each other'.[97] He was not entirely wrong: the delegates were rowdy and disorderly.[98] As the Duma tried to assert its power, the suffrage was modified again to give more weight to the supporters of the Tsar – in effect a 'constitutional' *coup d'état*. The Third Duma, elected by a much smaller electorate, ran its full course (1907–12). The landowners (30,000 families) now held 40 per cent of the seats.[99]

Tsardom had failed to reform itself. Russia was more than ever in turmoil. There was an enormous increase in the publication of books, newspapers, and journals of varying political persuasions. New civic associations emerged. Capitalism, and with it the middle classes and 'bourgeois' society, was growing.[100] Yet the Tsar was out of touch with this new Russia. The regime's narrow basis of consensus would lead to its definitive downfall in 1917, changing the course of European and world history. The problem was that there was no political mechanism able to transform dissent into constructive opposition and the peoples of the Tsarist Empire into a nation. The people could be consulted, but could not rule.

Reforms proceeded at a snail's pace, particularly in the countryside, where the object was to develop agrarian capitalism. The Tsar, far from being the Tsar of all Russians (his official title was 'Emperor and Autocrat of All the Russias'), was now little more than the Tsar of the landowners.

Building democracy in these circumstances would have been difficult even if the regime had chosen, wholeheartedly, to trust the people, not a prevalent feeling, at the end of the nineteenth century, even in the rest of 'civilized' Europe. Building democracy would not have necessarily generated a stronger capitalist-industrial growth, but it would have involved the people in the construction of a more unified country. Democracy, however, would have revealed the deep splits in Russian society at a time when the throne of the Tsars was tottering. It is possible to build an industrial society in an authoritarian manner, as Stalin proved decades later, but to do so required a far stronger state than that run by the Tsars.

12
Keeping the 'Outsiders' Out

Capitalism does not need nations, though it needs states. It needs capital and workers and cares little for the 'national' origins of either. Milton Friedman, in one of his most libertarian moments, concluded his 1991 Wriston Lecture by declaring that:

> The great virtue of a free market system is that it does not care what color people are; it does not care what their religion is; it only cares whether they can produce something you want to buy. It is the most effective system we have discovered to enable people who hate one another to deal with one another and help one another.[1]

However, the survival of capitalism, as we have seen, requires political and social conditions, such as a functioning political system, namely a state or a legal framework, as well as social cohesion, optimism, the belief that things will get better, a certain degree of loyalty towards the state and a feeling that one will be protected by it. In a real world – capitalism or no capitalism – people are never simply buyers and sellers, indifferent to each other, to their identities, to their hopes, to their hatred, but require a feeling of national togetherness.

Nation-building sometimes, though not always, requires exclusions since it asks the question 'Who is in, who is out?' Assimilation may not always be available. When it is, it may not always work. Outsiders may resist modernity, defending their culture, their traditions, and their religion. Some, within such groups, can't wait to break out of 'their' culture and be like everyone else. The Jews, for instance, were and are deeply divided among themselves. In the past, when they were forced to live together enclosed or self-enclosed in their own community and ghettos, they had been united by religion, a wish to live apart, and the anti-Semitism of those around them, but with 'emancipation' and their acquisition of rights, matters became more complex. Some desperately wanted assimilation, others desperately wished to remain separate. Most opted for a halfway house and became 'secular Jews'.

Outsiders such as Jews often represented a problem for other submerged nationalisms. Thus in the Tsarist Empire there were those who advocated the unification of all Slavs (Russians, Ukrainians, Poles, Bulgarians, Serbs, etc.). But what to do with the Jews? Could they ever become Russians? Even a conservative ideologue like Mikhail Katkov (Pobedonostsev's predecessor) thought that the Russianization of the Jews was a possibility since in other countries, such as France and Britain, they seemed able to be patriotic.[2] Prime Minister Nikolai Bunge in his 'Memorandum to the Tsar' (1894) noted that there was no point blaming the Jews for not integrating, since they were so discriminated against.[3]

In the Russian Empire, Jews had been traditionally confined by law to the Pale of Settlement, a territory that roughly corresponded with the old Polish-Lithuanian Commonwealth. This included parts of western Russia, Poland, Lithuania, Belarus, Moldova, and Ukraine, and thus cities such as Odessa, Vilnius, Warsaw, Białystok with its two-thirds Jewish population, Lublin (half-Jewish), and Łódź (one-third Jewish).[4] In 1856, Tsar Alexander II, shortly after his accession, decided to review all decrees discriminating against Jews 'with the general goal of fusing this people with the indigenous population'.[5] Selected 'valuable' Jews were allowed to settle outside the Pale, in cities such as Moscow and St Petersburg, and discriminatory rules that drafted Jews into the armed forces at a higher rate and a younger age than non-Jews were abolished.[6] By 1897 there were over 5 million Jews in the Tsarist Empire – almost 4 per cent of the total population, probably half the Jewish population on the planet. Elsewhere in Europe there were 2 million Jews in Austria-Hungary, more than half a million in Germany, including those in recently conquered Alsace, 200,000 in the United Kingdom, and 115,000 in France.[7] In France, Germany, and Britain they were relatively assimilated and integrated. In the Austro-Hungarian Empire they were supporters of the empire, in the sense that they owed no allegiance to any of the nations of Austria-Hungary: not to Bohemia or Moldavia; not to Hungary or Austria; and they did not regard themselves as Czech or German. And they were, as Carl Schorske explained, 'the supra-national people of the multi-national state'.[8] They were perfectly at home in this liberal, cosmopolitan environment.

In Russia the situation was far more complex. Drafting Jews into the Russian nation proved near-impossible. Even some members of the intelligentsia – both liberal (such as the poet Nikolay Nekrasov) and reactionary (such as Dostoyevsky) – exhibited marked anti-Semitic sentiments, assuming that most Jews were merciless exploiters of the toiling masses. In his *Diary of a Writer*, Dostoyevsky, after pages and pages manifesting his scorn for the Jews, while denying he was a 'Jew-hater', complained about '*Judaism* and the *Jewish idea* which is clasping the whole world'.[9] Nekrasov in his 1866 poem 'Ballet' scorned 'commercial' minorities, the Jews, of course, but also the Germans and the Greeks, (he lamented there were no Russian merchants: 'Has the bitter cold frightened them away?'), and added contempt for mercenary Russian girls whose:

> ideal is the golden calf,
> Embodied in the gray-haired Jew,
> Whose filthy hand causes these bosoms
> To quiver with gold.[10]

Nekrasov was possibly thinking of the Jewish 'capitalists' operating successfully in Russia, for example Samuel Polyakov from Belarus, the banker Leopold Kronenberg from Poland, and members of the Ephrussi family from Berdychiv in Ukraine, all contractors who had built the Russian railways.

The early 1880s saw a wave of pogroms, the first widespread manifestation of popular violence against Jews in the Russian Empire.[11] Contrary to the widely held view that the Russian authorities inspired, or aided and abetted, anti-Jewish rioting, the government of Alexander III actually 'feared all popular violence, including pogroms'.[12] Even the arch-reactionary Konstantin Pobedonostsev sent a circular letter to the clergy in the Pale urging them to deter the population from attacking the Jews.[13] When a pogrom started in Lugansk (Ukraine) in 1905 the demonstrators, carrying both the red flag and portraits of the Tsar, were stopped by government troops.[14]

There had been 'pogroms' in Odessa previously (in 1821, 1859, 1871), initiated by the local Greek community,[15] but, otherwise, pogroms were rare in Russia before 1881 (when Alexander II was assassinated).[16] The new pogroms were mainly in urban centres where the Jews were often the largest group. In Kishinev (in what is now Moldova) in 1903, forty-seven Jews were murdered, houses burned, and shops looted.[17] Many of those responsible were workers, particularly miners.[18] Kishinev was followed by numerous pogroms in 1905 to 1906. One of the worst was in Odessa, where Jews constituted one-third of the population, in the wake of the Tsar's October Manifesto of 1905 that extended fundamental rights to Jews. Hundreds of Jews were killed, perhaps as many as eight hundred.[19]

These pogroms represented a novel type of anti-Semitism connected to the new governmental policy of absorbing the Jews.[20] One of the outcomes was a massive Jewish emigration: between 1881 and 1914 almost two million Jews emigrated from Russia, the vast majority to the United States, very few to Palestine. Zionism held virtually no appeal for the overwhelming majority of Jews. The Second 'Aliyah' (1904–14), as Zionists called the migration of Jews to what was then Palestine (Aliyah means 'ascent', namely ascent to Israel), was in fact a dismal failure in terms of numbers. In the decade preceding the First World War only 35,000 Jews went to Palestine.[21] Most left again as soon as they could and only 2,500 decided to remain.[22] These became the backbone of the Zionist movement in what would become Israel; they revived Hebrew as a spoken language, founded schools, and established the first kibbutz in 1909.

Jews had a particular advantage over other persecuted peoples: by 1917 a major power, Great Britain, looked favourably on their settlement in Palestine. The famous Balfour Declaration of 1917 (not an official document but a paragraph in a letter addressed by the Foreign Secretary, Arthur Balfour, to the Zionist Federation in Britain via Lord Rothschild) gave preferential treatment to Jewish immigration in Palestine over the wishes and interests of the local population. In the words of Arthur Koestler, 'it was one of the most improbable political documents of all time. In it one nation solemnly promised to a second nation the country of a third.'[23] After the war the Balfour Declaration was incorporated in the British Mandate over Palestine while declaring that Britain would safeguard the civil and religious rights of the non-Jewish inhabitants (i.e. 90 per cent of the resident population), but without mentioning their political rights or any organization that might represent them.[24]

The relatively small numbers of victims of Russian pogroms, a few thousand at the most, moreover, suggests that the pogroms themselves were not the major cause of the emigration of 2 million Jews, though certainly they were an added incentive. There were plenty of other good reasons for Jews to leave Russia: conscription by the Tsar, lack of opportunities, and above all poverty and the prospect of a good future – just like the other millions of Europeans who emigrated to the United States not out of fear for their lives but hoping for a better life. For the vast majority of Jews the new (American) capitalist paradise was far more appealing than the ancient land of Abraham of biblical and Zionist lore.

Many Jews in Russia joined revolutionary movements, some because they were part of a rebellious intelligentsia, some because they were proletarians, some because they felt alienated from the regime.[25] Count Witte, Finance Minister and later Prime Minister (whose second wife was Jewish), was in no doubt that it was the discrimination and abuses suffered by the Jews which caused their radicalization: 'From the pusillanimous people that the Jews were some thirty years ago there sprang men and women who threw bombs, committed political murders and sacrificed their lives for the revolution.' He recalled that he had warned the Jewish leaders that they should show some loyalty to the regime and that 'instead of dreaming of revolutionary freedom' they should demand the right not to be discriminated against.[26] The Ministry of Finance opposed anti-Jewish policy because of the important role Jews could play in industrialization; here it clashed with the Ministry of the Interior, for whom more Jews meant social unrest. The Russian authorities distributed circulars in Poland and Ukraine warning that pogroms might diminish production in factories.[27]

Since Russian industrialization proceeded more rapidly in the western territories of the empire, the Pale, Jews appeared to benefit directly, at least in terms of employment, from industrialization. In the Donbass region in Eastern Ukraine, in particular, industry was booming in the 1890s, attracting thousands of Jews. Soon they constituted between 20 and 35 per cent of the population.[28] This internal migration was partly due to the relative prosperity of the native peasantry (relative to central and northern Russia): why go down a mine or work in a factory when you have a good field to till?[29]

The Donbass became an area of exceptionally high working-class militancy. However, ethnic divisions (in addition to Jews, Russians, and Ukrainians there were also Greeks, Gypsies, Tatars, Turks, and Poles) made class solidarity very difficult, and the Great Russian and Ukrainian industrial workforce increasingly resented the Jewish presence.[30] If nation-building was not easy, building class consciousness was even more problematic.

A further element complicated the situation: educated Jews chose Russification over other national identities such as Ukrainization, thus increasing anti-Semitism among non-Russian nationalists. Jewish socialists in Vilna preferred to speak Russian rather than Polish, to the dismay of Polish nationalists.[31] Assimilation was one thing, but it was not clear which nation Jews should assimilate into: Russia, Poland, or Lithuania.

The Populist (Narodnik) revolutionary *Narodnaya Volya*, in a proclamation of 30 August 1881 'To the Ukrainian People', drafted by Gerasim Grigorevich Romanenko on behalf of its executive committee, intoned:

> The people in the Ukraine suffer worst of all from the Jews. Who takes the land, the woods, the taverns from out of your hands? The Jews. From whom does the muzhik, often with tears in his eyes, have to beg permission to get to his own field, his own plot of land? – the Jews . . . The Jew curses you, cheats you, drinks your blood . . . Soon the revolt will be taken up across all of Russia against the tsar, the *pany* [landlords], the Jews.[32]

These sentiments were quickly condemned by other leading Narodniks, who thought that any popular enmity towards Jews should be turned into a revolutionary hatred of the ruling classes, but there is little doubt that many Narodniks held anti-Semitic feelings.[33] Left-wing anti-Semitism was not unique to Russia. In Germany, for example, socialists often equated Jews with capitalism.[34]

The pogroms in Russia in the late nineteenth century seemed to confirm the widely held western European view that the empire was still stuck in the Middle Ages, but, in fact, the rest of Europe conformed to the Russian pattern. Anti-Jewish riots, when they took place, originated from the people while the main protectors of Jews were the central authorities (thus the centrally directed Nazi genocide of 1941–5 was a new phenomenon and not just in its sheer scale). In 1819 an anti-Jewish riot occurred in Würzburg (Bavaria) that lasted three days and caused many Jews to flee the town in spite of the intervention of police and army. The Würzburg events seemed to be a signal for further anti-Jewish riots in other German towns such as Frankfurt and Hamburg that spread as far as Copenhagen. They were known as the 'Hep Hep' riots from the student slogan *Hep! Hep! Jude verrecke!* ('Hep, Hep, die Jew!').[35] George Eliot called her philo-Semitic essay published in 1879, her last published work, 'The Modern Hep! Hep! Hep!'[36]

These riots, just as those in Russia in the 1880s, were not remnants of some ancient medieval antagonism: they were embedded in modernity, sparked by the fears and stress that a rapidly changing economic situation brings about. The possibility of an improvement in the legal conditions of Jews was sufficient to provoke the hostility of lower-class elements of society as well as that of journalists and professors.[37] Adolf Wagner, the socially inclined Christian economist (not the far more famous composer Richard Wagner), complained in 1884 that 'the new economic conditions have allowed a foreign race to exploit our economic relations; a race whose motto "Gain as much as possible" fits in well with the new economics.'[38]

In Poland the nationalist leader Roman Dmowski raised the call to boycott Jewish businesses. This did not endear him to Jewish voters and, in 1912, he lost his seat in the Duma to a Jewish socialist.[39] By 1914, however, Dmowski and his party were a major political force in Poland.[40] He advocated an alliance with Russia against the Germans designed to protect the Poles from 'Ukrainians, Lithuanians, Jews, *e tutti quanti*'.[41] Yet, he did not think Jews should be eliminated or expelled. In his *Germany, Russia and the Polish Question* (*Niemcy, Rosya i kwestya polska*, 1908) he described them as highly motivated and intelligent, among the most educated, the most economically entrepreneurial, and among the most revolutionary.[42] But in spite of such qualities they remained 'foreign elements' to be tolerated only as long as they did not plot the destruction of the Polish nation.[43] After the First World War, Dmowski became increasingly anti-Semitic, regarding Woodrow Wilson and David Lloyd George as puppets of 'the Jews' and the League of Nations as a Jewish plot.[44] Yet Dmowski remained such a significant figure that in 2006 a gigantic statue of him was erected in the centre of Warsaw, an icon of Polish ultra-nationalism.[45]

The age of mass politics, largely urban, gave rise not only to the politics of class, as socialists hoped and conservatives feared, but to the politics of identity. In a dynamic society where 'fate' or 'the gods' could no longer be blamed for failure, the search for scapegoats was as intense as ever and prone to manipulation by unscrupulous politicians. In previous centuries, pogroms against religious minorities and against the Jews in particular had often been connected to natural calamities, famines or pestilence. In the new age of democracy anxieties about one's station in life could give rise to similar discontent. In Poland, middle-class frustration with the socio-economic upheavals of capitalism had by the end of the century become intertwined with political anti-Semitism.[46] The urban lower-middle classes, who were mainly engaged in artisanal manufacture, were losing the economic battle with capitalists, few of whom were Polish. Industry was foreign-owned, with German, British, French, and Belgian capital playing an increasing role in the industrialization of Poland.[47] Given the very high presence of Jews in Poland (Warsaw by 1904 was one of the most Jewish cities in the world with over 300,000 Jewish inhabitants), it is not entirely surprising that any anti-foreign feelings eventually led to overt manifestations of anti-Semitism particularly in the most industrialized part of Poland.[48]

There were outbursts of anti-Semitism even in parts of Europe where there were hardly any Jews. In 1904 there were only thirty-five Jewish families in Limerick in the west of Ireland, an insignificant number in proportion to the population, but this did not stop the local priest, in his sermons, from accusing the Jews of having murdered both St Stephen and St James (which was probably true since they were both Jewish and both died in Jerusalem in the first century AD) and of trying to take over Ireland the way they had taken over France. This led to acts of aggression against Jews in the streets of Limerick and the boycott of their business.[49] A few years later, in 1911, in Tredegar, in South Wales, Jewish shops were attacked and looted against a background of industrial unrest.[50]

In London's East End, where 40,000 Jews huddled in the 1880s, there was obviously more concern and scope for racist sentiments. Thus, John Colomb, Conservative MP for Tower Hamlets, set the tone in a speech in the House of Commons (10 March 1887) where he complained that no other great states 'permit the immigration of destitute aliens without restriction' and called for it to be stopped. The *Pall Mall Gazette* (February 1886) warned that 'foreign Jews are becoming a pest and a menace to the poor native born East Ender'.[51] In 1903 a former president of the street sellers' association complained that the Jewish immigrants monopolized certain trades.[52] Arnold White, an English journalist with strong populist imperialist sentiments, noted in *The Modern Jew* (Heinemann, 1899) that Jewish immigration was threatening the British way of life. An agent of the German-Jewish philanthropist Maurice von Hirsch, he also supported Hirsch's efforts to create a Jewish colony in Argentina: Jews could have their own territory as long as it was far from England. There was, unquestionably, anti-Semitism in 'liberal' Britain, yet it was also the only country in the nineteenth century that elected a Prime Minister of Jewish birth, with an unmistakable Jewish name (Disraeli) and an appearance that conformed to the stereotype of the Jew.

In Hungary anti-Semitism was more ingrained. In 1848 when Budapest erupted in favour of 'Liberty, Equality, Fraternity' there was also anti-Semitic rioting in Pozsony (Pressburg in German), then regarded as part of Hungary (but now Bratislava, the capital of Slovakia). The riots were sparked by the granting of full civil rights to Jews in March of that year. This led Lajos Kossuth, the 'Father of Hungarian Democracy', to ask that the demand for full equality be postponed: 'let [the Jews] be patient a little longer in the interest of the homeland and the freedom of the people'.[53] They were patient for a further nineteen years and finally obtained their emancipation in 1867, but no thanks to Hungarian nationalists, for it was the Emperor Franz Joseph who sought

Jewish support by suppressing overt anti-Semitism and ennobling rich Jews.[54] Nevertheless, in the 1870s and 1880s there were sporadic anti-Semitic incidents, fuelled in part by the resentment of petty landowners whose land had been bought by Jews.[55] As for the newly ennobled capitalists (by the end of the century 346 Hungarian Jewish families had obtained noble titles), they provided the regime with much support.[56] 'Liberal' and philo-Semite came to be nearly synonymous in Hungarian common parlance.[57]

Hungarians were right to feel anxious. The compromise of 1867 with Austria had given Hungary real powers within the new Austro-Hungarian Empire, but 'true' Hungarians, who almost completely dominated their own parliament, were only just over half the population of Hungary. In 1906 the Germans consisted of 12.7 per cent, the Slovaks 11.4 per cent, with the rest being made up by Romanians, Ukrainians (Ruthenians), Jews, Croats, and Serbs.[58]

If local entrepreneurs cannot be found, one can always import them, hence the wave of Jewish immigrants from Russia and Poland (mostly in Moldavia) as well as Greeks. In the Old Kingdom (Romania or Vechiul Regat) made up of Wallachia and part of Moldavia, which had united in 1859 after the Treaty of Paris of 1856, the Jews were a major urban presence and a significant segment of the petty commercial and artisanal sector of the economy.[59]

By the beginning of the twentieth century Jews, though they were only 3.3 per cent of the Romanian population, accounted for 19 per cent of the urban population – 32 per cent in Moldavia (with Wallachia one of the main constituent parts of Romania) and half the population of Iaşi, Moldavia's capital. The Romanian press reported this as if it were a genuine invasion.[60] The Jews were resented by conservatives, who regarded them as agents of capitalism and responsible for the ills of modernity.[61] In 1867, just as Romania had come into being, the Minister of the Interior, Ion Brătianu, a liberal, took harsh measures against Jewish immigration, denying Jews the right to settle in the countryside, to own rural property or to practise certain professions. Foreigners may not have been able to kick-start Romania on the road to industrialization but they certainly dominated its commerce. Just to make sure that entrepreneurial spirits were kept out of politics the new Romanian constitution (formally modelled on that of Belgium, regarded as the most liberal in Europe) disenfranchised foreigners (unless they were Christians) from acquiring citizenship, effectively barring the Jews from political life. This overt discriminatory practice was eventually abolished in 1879 at the insistence of the Congress of Berlin (and

Bismarck in particular after some serious lobbying by the Paris-based Alliance Israélite Universelle). In practice very few Jews succeeded in obtaining Romanian citizenship or even desired it.[62] Brătianu had complained that Europe did not understand the situation in Romania, that it was not possible to resolve the 'Jewish Question' immediately, and that to allow Jews to become Romanian would mean the end of Romanian nationhood.[63]

In 1907, following the imposition of a new tax, a major peasant revolt took place that at first took a specifically anti-Semitic form since a large proportion (40 per cent) of estate farmers or *arendaşi* (originally money-lenders or small businessmen who had invested in the land), at least in northern Moldavia, where the revolt started before spreading into Wallachia, were Jewish. When asked what was his main grievance, an inhabitant of Botoşani replied that it was the lack of land and that this was the fault of foreigners, especially of Jews, 'who have seized absolutely all the estates and have made the price of arable land go up in the most horrible way'.[64] The revolt was put down brutally: 11,000 peasants were killed.[65] More than ever the peasantry felt themselves to be outside the Romanian nation. What they wanted was not a nation but land.

The anti-Semitism increasingly espoused in Europe was neither of the old Christian form nor of the new pseudo-scientific variety, though it used whatever argument was available. Its real strength was in its connection with nascent forms of demotic nationalism, what Carl Schorske called 'politics in a new key'.[66] Modern political anti-Semitism became one of the features of this new politics. Some of the Jews reacted by turning towards Zionist separatism.

Migrants are often disliked, and successful migrants are disliked even more. The Jews suffered as did other 'non-national' minorities, such as the Germans, the Greeks, and the Armenians in the Ottoman, Austro-Hungarian, and Tsarist Empires, and later the Chinese in much of South-East Asia, and the Gujarati Indians in east Africa.

Abuse came from all quarters. The august journal of the Jesuits, *Civiltà cattolica*, virtually the unofficial organ of the Pope, launched regular tirades against the Jews, such as this one in 1880:

> The Jews – eternal insolent children, obstinate, dirty, thieves, liars, ignoramuses, pests and the scourge of those near and far – . . . immediately abused [their newfound freedom] to interfere with that of others. They managed to lay their hands on . . . all public wealth . . . and virtually alone they took control not only of all the money . . . but of the law itself in those countries where they have been allowed to hold public offices.[67]

Leading intellectuals espoused similar views. Antoine Blanc de Saint-Bonnet, a reactionary philosopher, in *Restauration française* (1851) blamed the Jews for inventing commerce.[68] The more radical and certainly more liberal Werner Sombart (later he was ambivalent about Nazism) in *The Jews and Economic Life* (*Die Juden und das Wirtschaftsleben*, 1911) denounced Jewish money and (contra Max Weber) maintained that Judaism was even more suited to capitalism than Protestantism.[69] Édouard Drumont, founder of the Anti-Semitic League of France (1889) and author of the best-selling *La France juive* (1886), explained that the Jew, an 'instinctive' merchant, will not miss an opportunity to cheat his fellows. Fortunately, Drumont continued, one could always recognize 'the Jew' by the 'famous nose', the ears sticking out, one arm shorter than the other, the flat feet, 'the moist and soft hand of the hypocrite and the traitor' (*la main moelleuse et fondante de l'hypocrite et du traitre*); and, of course, they smell.[70] The success of *La France juive* was considerable, also because the kind of generic anti-Semitism it promoted was widely accepted. It did not even provoke the consternation of socialists, not even that of Jean Jaurès, who became the leader, in 1902, of the French Socialist Party.[71] The nationalist historian Heinrich von Treitschke declared that Jews 'bear a heavy responsibility for the vile materialism of our time'.[72] Just as alarmed was Theodor Fritsch, author of *Die Juden im Handel und das Geheimnis ihres Erfolges* (*The Jews in Commerce and the Secret of their Success*, 1913).[73] Paul de Lagarde, a German scholar of the Orient, who, it must be said, hated almost everyone – Catholics, liberals, moderate Protestants, Bismarck, and Imperial Germany – regarded the Jews as the agents of a 'gigantic conspiracy aimed at the heart of Germany'.[74] Some socialists too, for instance Pierre-Joseph Proudhon and Charles Fourier, manifested anti-Semitic sentiments.[75] The great social reformers Sidney and Beatrice Webb, writing in 1897, held the view (then almost banal, now somewhat eccentric) that the 'races' of wage earners could be divided into three groups: 'the Anglo-Saxon skilled artisan', who will 'not work below a customary minimum Standard of Life'; the Negro who will work for low wages, but who will not work at all 'once their primitive wants are satisfied'; and, finally, the Jew, who 'will accept the lowest terms rather than remain out of employment', but then, as he 'rises in the world' and acquires new wants, 'no amount of income causes him to slacken his indefatigable activity'. And this is why they explained that Jewish workers are 'the poorest in all Europe', while individual Jews are 'the wealthiest men of their respective countries'.[76] A race-based view of the world was exceedingly common.

In many quarters, the sinister power of the Jews was discerned behind that of the bankers in a common trope that united anti-Semites of all political stripes. Thus the Proudhonian and anticlerical socialist Auguste Chirac produced a diatribe against the Jews in his 1883 *Les rois de la république*, targeting, as usual, Rothschild, 'the man, the race, who today exercise . . . a kingly power . . . not in the general interest but in his own exclusive interest'.[77] The liberal anti-imperialist J. A. Hobson was similarly impressed by the alleged powers of the Rothschilds. In his *Imperialism* (1902) he wrote that European finance was controlled 'chiefly by men of a single and peculiar race, who have behind them many centuries of financial experience', that they were 'in a unique position to control the policy of nations', and that no 'great war could be undertaken by any European State, or a great State loan subscribed, if the house of Rothschild and its connections set their face against it'.[78] The obsession with the occult powers of Rothschild had, like many obsessions, only a relative connection with reality. Jews were certainly disproportionately represented in French banking and the more famous big bankers were Jews of German extraction who had acquired aristocratic titles: Baron Jacques de Reinach, Baron d'Erlanger, Baron Maximilien Königswarter, Count Cahen d'Anvers, Jacques de Günzburg (of Russian origin) and, of course, the Rothschilds.[79] However, the largest banks were truly 'old French', banks such as the Crédit Lyonnais, founded in 1863, which by 1900 had become the largest bank in the world.[80] Besides the Rothschilds (whose power had much diminished towards the end of the century) there were other important banking families, not all Jewish, for instance Hope & Co, a bank founded by Scots and based in Amsterdam, and the Anglo-German Baring Bank. Historically, Jews had very little to do with the invention of banking. Italians were the founders of arguably the world's oldest bank, Monte dei Paschi di Siena (1472), while Berenberg Bank was founded in Hamburg in 1590, by Protestants fleeing persecution in the Low Countries.

On the whole, Jews were safest under Islam. In medieval Islam there were no special laws for Jews as there were in Christendom and Jews under Islam were in a better economic position than in medieval Christendom.[81] In the nineteenth century, under the Ottoman Empire, there were numerous attacks on Jews accused of ritual murder but they 'almost invariably originated among the Christian population' and the Jews were usually protected by the authorities.[82]

Conversion was never forced upon them just as it was not on the other non-Muslim subjects of the Ottoman or the Mughal Empire.

However, Jews, like Christians, Zoroastrians, Yazidis, and other non-Muslims, had second-class status within the Ottoman Empire, the so-called 'dhimmi' status (the word means 'protected'). In practice that meant equality on matters of property and contract, though a special tax was levied. During the Balkan Wars (1912–13) the Jewish citizens of the Ottoman Empire remained loyal to the Ottomans, mistrusting, probably rightly, the Christian-based nationalism that dominated Balkan League states.[83]

The real victims of Turkish nationalism were the Armenians not the Jews. The massacre in 1915 of over one million Armenians became one of the first modern genocides and was preceded by numerous acts of violence against Armenians under the orders or the complicity of the Sultan, such as the massacre of some 200,000 Armenians between 1894 and 1896.[84] Ottoman Armenians, just like the Jews, were, on the whole, more prosperous than ordinary Ottoman subjects, being more urban and more involved in commercial and craft activities. The rising Turkish nationalism required a uniform nation.[85] As its historian Raymond Kévorkian has written: 'the murder of the Armenians was bound up with the construction of the Turkish nation'.[86]

One would have thought that prejudice and anti-immigrant feelings would be less pronounced where the majority of the inhabitants were immigrants. In South America, for instance, the white settlers were so dominant and the indigenous people so weak and impoverished that nation-building remained a matter for the whites. Those discriminated against were the indigenous population, Asian immigrants, and former slaves (in Brazil slavery was abolished only in 1888, having imported more Africans, in the course of the previous two centuries, than the United States).

In the United States nation-building was a task of a different magnitude. The biggest conflagration had been between northerners and southerners – a conflict that had nothing to do with ethnic divisions but with the economics and ethics of slavery and the powers of the federal government. The price paid by the North to the South for national reconciliation (and hence nation-building) was to allow the discrimination against blacks to continue, especially in the South. Ethnic rivalries (Irish, Italians, Poles, Jews, and others) continued to plague the United States, all to the advantage of the white Anglo-Saxon Protestant elite. The brunt of white violence, however, was borne by the blacks.

One example, among the hundreds available: against a background of economic and social tensions over jobs, sparked by the alleged rape of a white woman by a black, widespread riots against blacks took place in Atlanta in September 1906. Local newspapers had conducted a vigorous campaign encouraging violence against black people. The *Atlanta Evening News* declared in a headline that it stood 'forever on the rock of protection of our southern white women regardless of condemnation at home or abroad'.[87] Much of the northern press north condemned southern racism. The *Washington Star* called the Atlanta riots 'the Odessa of America'; the *Philadelphia Press* judged the riot 'a deplorable exhibition of race ferocity and savagery'.[88] The event received international coverage, including a front-page illustration in the mass-circulation French daily *Le Petit Journal* of 7 October 1906.[89]

Racial prejudice and racist language continued for decades. As recently as 1948 Strom Thurmond, running for president as the States Rights Democratic Party candidate declared:

> I want to tell you, ladies and gentlemen, that there's not enough troops in the army to force the Southern people to break down segregation and admit the Negro race into our theaters, into our swimming pools, into our homes, and into our churches.[90]

Thurmond obtained less than 3 per cent of the vote but was elected senator for South Carolina in 1954 and remained in the Senate for forty-eight years. He was still in office at the age of 100, by which time he had accepted desegregation and voting rights for blacks.

Non-white immigrants too felt the blows of American xenophobia. The Union Pacific railroad employed Chinese and white immigrants in their coal mines in Rock Springs, Wyoming. In a dispute between the white miners (members of the Knights of Labor, then the largest American trade union) and their Chinese counterparts, on 2 September 1885 some of the white miners rioted, burned down the Chinese quarter and killed twenty-eight of its inhabitants. This sparked a series of anti-Chinese riots the length and breadth of the Rocky Mountains.[91] Anti-Chinese legislation had been formidable even before the incident. In California and much of the Far West there were special taxes against the Chinese (even a laundry tax) and they were excluded from schools, from public-works programmes, denied the right to own land and even to testify in a court against whites.[92] In 1862 the governor of California, Leland Stanford, in his inaugural address to the legislature, declared:

> There can be no doubt but that the presence of numbers among us of a degraded and distinct people must exercise a deleterious influence upon the superior race, and, to a certain extent, repel desirable immigration. It will afford me great pleasure to concur with the Legislature in any

> constitutional action, having for its object the repression of the immigration of the Asiatic races.[93]

These views were quite commonplace at the time. Leland Stanford was also a hypocrite: his anti-immigration rants did not prevent him, as president of railroad companies such as the Central Pacific (he was a classic 'robber baron'), from employing thousands of Chinese workers. Stanford University is named after him, unsurprisingly, since he funded and founded it.

Discrimination against the Chinese, in a country that welcomed immigrants from everywhere in Europe, had already been established in law by the Chinese Exclusion Act of 1882, was extended in 1892, and made permanent in 1902 – the only US immigration law openly discriminating on grounds of race. It was repealed only in 1943, while the Californian state law prohibiting non-whites from marrying whites was upheld until 1948 when the California Supreme Court declared it unconstitutional. Elsewhere in America such legislation survived until 1967, when the United States Supreme Court ruled that all anti-miscegenation laws were unconstitutional.

The Chinese Exclusion Act was supported by the official labour movement, the American Federation of Labor (AFL). It demanded that Chinese and 'Orientals' be kept out of the country since they brought 'nothing but filth, vice, and disease'. The head of the AFL, Samuel Gompers (a Jew), told his members in 1901 that 'every incoming coolie . . . means so much more vice and immorality injected into our social life'.[94] In 1905 Gompers declared that 'the caucasians are not going to let their standard of living be destroyed by negroes, Chinamen, Japs, or any others'.[95] This union racism played a major role in the development of American organized labour.[96] The Chinese Exclusion Act was, however, opposed by the Industrial Workers of the World (the 'wobblies'), a radical union formed in 1905 which, unlike the AFL, recruited mainly unskilled immigrant labourers.

In 1902, Samuel Gompers and Herman Gutstadt published a racist pamphlet called *Meat vs. Rice. American Manhood Against Asiatic Coolieism. Which Shall Survive?* (reprinted in 1908 by the Asiatic Exclusion League), quoting with approval remarks made in 1879 by James G. Blaine (twice Secretary of State, abolitionist, presidential candidate, Speaker of the House): 'I am opposed to the Chinese coming here. I am opposed to making them citizens . . . You cannot work a man who must have beef and bread alongside a man who can live on rice.'[97]

Henry George, the radical reformer, author of the best-selling *Progress and Poverty: An Inquiry into the Cause of Industrial Depressions and of Increase of Want with Increase of Wealth: The Remedy* (1879), railed against the Chinese: 'their moral standard is as low as their standard of comfort', they were 'filthy in their habits' and 'incapable of understanding our religion' or 'our political institutions'.[98] The progressive journalist Jacob Riis in his famous social exposé *How the Other Half Lives* (1890) wrote that the Chinese in New York 'are in no sense a desirable element of the population' and 'serve no useful purpose here, whatever they may have done elsewhere', though, since they were here, we 'should make the best of it' and ensure that they can bring their families.[99]

Archibald Coolidge, professor of history at Harvard and editor-in-chief of the distinguished journal *Foreign Affairs*, in his influential text *The United States as a World Power* (1908), replete with vacuous bar-room generalizations about race, thought that the natives of Africa were mere savages and that those of the Middle East and India were better, but the more their living conditions improved the more they were likely to become impatient.[100] He was also worried about the mixing of races in the United States:

> Dogs, for instance, can often be profitably crossed . . . but if kinds that are too alien to one another are bred together, the product is a worthless mongrel. May not something of the same sort hold true of human beings?[101]

Much of the anti-Chinese prejudice was extended to the Japanese. In 1901, Henry Gage, Governor of California, warned that Japanese immigration was a menace to American workers just as much as the Chinese were. White workers formed the Asiatic Exclusion League 'to preserve the Caucasian race upon American soil'.[102] In 1888 the newly formed American Economic Association offered a prize of $150 for the best essay on 'The Evil Effects of Unrestricted Immigration'.[103] The winner was the Chicago professor Edward Webster Bemis, who argued in various lectures that immigrants were over-represented among criminals and the insane.[104]

American Indians, decimated by diseases imported from Europe and by settlers' violence, were kept in reservations, though various attempts were made to 'Americanize' them. Thomas Jefferson Morgan, commissioner of Indian Affairs (1889–93), aimed to build a one-nation identity among Native American children by means of compulsory education and placing them with white families during the holidays in order to turn them into good Christians and good Americans. By 1900, 10 per cent of Native American children had been placed in special schools where American history, seen as a history of progress, challenged Native American traditions regarded as backward.[105]

In the 1880s immigration from eastern and southern Europe increased sharply and so did anti-immigrant feeling among well-established American settlers. New immigrants were seen as an economic threat. Two groups were singled out: the Italians and the Jews. The Italians were regarded as bloodthirsty criminals, quick with the knife; besides they were Catholics and, if not Catholics, dangerous anarchists. A lynching of Italians occurred in New Orleans on 14 March 1891, the largest lynching in American history, when a group of vigilantes slaughtered eleven Italians who were being tried for the murder of David Hennessey, the chief of police. The *New York Times* of 15 March 1891 approved heartily: 'Chief Hennessy Avenged; Eleven of his Italian Assassins Lynched by a Mob'. Equally approving were the *Washington Post* and the *San Francisco Chronicle* as well as *The Times* of London. Later a grand jury condoned the lynching, as did the governor of Louisiana.[106]

As for the Jews, they were filthy peddlers whose God was money, out to take over native business.[107] American populists made the identification between Jews and the power of money only too readily.[108] They were certainly not the only ones. The distinguished historian Henry Adams, whose grandfather (John Quincy Adams) and great-grandfather had been President of the United States, wrote in 1895 that 'in ten years . . . Jews will completely control the finances and Government of this country . . .'[109] Views like these led to quotas being imposed against Jews in colleges and universities, hospitals and law firms. The appointment of the distinguished Jewish jurist Louis Brandeis to the Supreme Court was bitterly contested – ironically he was the author of *Other People's Money and How the Bankers Use It* (1914), which criticized investment bankers, especially J. P. Morgan.

Building the American nation on the basis of some kind of 'Anglo-Saxon' nativism, leaving out blacks, orientals, Latinos, Catholics, and Jews, ultimately proved futile, its absurdity heightened by the slow but unrelenting demographic change that would made the phrase 'White Anglo-Saxon Protestant' (WASP) more a term of mild abuse than one of proud self-satisfaction.

In Australia, too, white supremacist beliefs were regarded as normal among the political elites. In 1901 the White Australia Policy, limiting immigration to whites only via a dictation test in any European language (the Australian Labour Party had wanted to exclude explicitly Asians and Africans), was introduced by the country's first Prime Minister and leader of the Protectionist Party, Edmund ('Toby') Barton, who declared:

> I do not think that the doctrine of the equality of man was really intended to include racial equality. These races are, in comparison with white races . . . unequal and inferior. The doctrine of the equality of man was never intended to apply to the equality of the Englishman and the Chinaman.[110]

Barton's idea of the 'white races' did, at least, include women and, in 1902, his government extended female suffrage throughout all parts of the country.

The European labour movement was also not immune to racism. In France, for instance, at the Congrés Ouvrier of Lyon in 1878 a delegate referred to the Arabs as '*ce peuple ignorant et fanatique*', and in the socialist daily *L'Humanité* (7 August 1913) Maurice Allard, a socialist and anticlerical MP, referred to 'primitive and grotesque blacks' with whom he claimed to have far less in common than with the Germans.[111] Xenophobia in the trade unions was rife, reflecting the worries of many French workers about the influx of Belgian and Italian workers (in 1886 there were over one million foreign workers in France).[112] Between 1881 and 1893, some thirty Italians were killed in a series of anti-Italian pogroms, mainly in the south of France. Clashes between French and Italian workers in Aigues-Mortes, north-west of Marseille (the capital of xenophobia), in 1893 resulted in the deaths of ten Italians.[113]

The arch-liberal economist Paul Leroy-Beaulieu was even worried about the Chinese, of whom there were hardly any in France (only 283 recorded out of a population of nearly 40 million, according to the 1911 census). In his *Essai sur la repartition des richesses* he argued against shortening the working day, saying that the 'yellow men' were 'willing to sell their labour for less and work for longer hours'. He warned: 'Beware of the Orientals whose ideal of happiness is a bowl full of rice.'[114]

At least a bowl of rice meant cheap wages. With the end of slavery in America, the liberal weekly *The Economist* wondered how 'the dark races' could be 'induced to obey white men willingly'.[115] Of course, racism has long been part of the history of humanity, not least among so-called civilized peoples, including some remarkable minds, such as Hegel, who indulged, in his lectures on the 'philosophy of world history', in low-level stereotypes without even realizing it. In Africa, Hegel explained, 'human development is arrested'. Africans exhibit 'sensuous enjoyment, great muscular strength to sustain labour, child-like good nature, but also unreflective and unfeeling ferocity . . .'[116] And it gets worse: 'The Negro . . . exhibits the natural man in his completely wild and untamed state . . . there is nothing harmonious with humanity to be found in this type of character.'[117]

Immanuel Kant wrote of the American Indian who, being 'too weak for hard labor, too indifferent for industry and incapable of any culture . . . ranks still far below even the Negro, who stands on the lowest of all the other steps that we have named as differences of the races'.[118] Voltaire, the author of the famous *Treatise on Tolerance* (1763), wrote in the less well-known and much longer *Essai sur les moeurs et l'esprit des nations* (1756) about the 'Negroes': 'Their round eyes, their flat nose, their lips always large, their odd-looking ears, their woollen head, even the measure of their intelligence, makes them prodigiously different from other men.'[119]

A century later such stereotypes were still produced by distinguished intellectuals. Ernest Renan, in the first chapter of his *Histoire générale et système comparé des langues sémitiques* (1855) ranked the 'Semitic race' well below the 'Indo-European'.[120] The great liberal John Stuart Mill, in his *Considerations on Representative Government* (1861), noted, with little regard for logic or evidence, that 'The most envious of all mankind are the Orientals . . . Next to the Orientals in envy, as in inactivity, are some of the Southern Europeans . . .', while noting 'the striving, go-ahead character of England and the United States . . .'[121] The young Mahatma Gandhi, on 26 September 1896, speaking in Bombay in order to gather support for the Indian community in South Africa, where as a lawyer he defended Indians against laws that regarded them no better than blacks ('kaffirs' in the pejorative language of the time), declared:

> Ours is one continual struggle against a degradation sought to be inflicted upon us by the Europeans, who desire to degrade us to the level of the raw Kaffir whose occupation is hunting, and whose sole ambition is to collect a certain number of cattle to buy a wife with and, then, pass his life in indolence and nakedness.[122]

Ranking civilizations as well as 'races' was common at the time. Thus Churchill spoke of the 'gulf which separates the African negro from the immemorial civilizations of India and China'. Subjugation was one way of helping the 'negroes'. Another, explained Churchill, was to put them in 'Large reservations of good, well-watered land where the Africa aboriginal for whom civilization has no chance may dwell secluded and at peace.'[123]

Anti-immigration feelings were present even in countries with a relatively low level of immigration, such as England. Margaret Harkness's novel *Out of Work* (1888), published under the pseudonym of 'John Law', tells the story of a carpenter, Jos Corney, during the depression of the 1870s and 1880s, who tries to find some work in the docks only to be told all the jobs are going to 'them furriners [foreigners] . . . Why should they come here, I'd like to know? London ain't what it used to be; it's just like a foreign city. The food ain't English; the talk ain't English. Why should all them foreigners come here to take the food out of our mouths, and live on victuals we wouldn't give to pigs?'[124]

Immigration did not need to be massive to give rise to racist prejudice. Between 1908 and 1911, Joseph Havelock Wilson, the Liberal MP and leader of the National Sailors' and Firemen's Union (NSFU), waged a campaign against Chinese labour in British shipping, framing the issue in terms of a universal conflict between the white and yellow races.[125] Yet in 1911 there were only 300 Chinese in London and 403 in Liverpool, and there were fewer Chinese working on British ships (4,595) than Scandinavians (5,948).[126] The image of the Chinese in England was imbued with racial stereotypes (immoral, violent people whose values were incompatible with those of whites).[127] M. P. Shiel's best-selling novel *The Yellow Danger* (1898) played its part, as did the creation of Fu Manchu, the criminal genius and opium addict, in Sax Rohmer's popular novels, the first of which was serialized in 1912–13.[128]

Outsiders have always suffered. But industrialization increased migration and hence the number of outsiders. It was an inevitable result of 'progress': greater mobility, better transportation, new lands to settle, and the realization of personal ambition. It was less and less likely that someone would live his or her entire life where they were born. The signs of this new modernity had been detected decades earlier. John Stuart Mill, in his *Principles of Political Economy* (1848), noted:

> It is hardly possible to overrate the value . . . of placing human beings in contact with persons dissimilar to themselves, and with modes of thought and action unlike those with which they are familiar. Commerce is now, what war once was, the principal source of this contact . . .[129]

Much of this movement of people was involuntary in the sense that the migrants were pushed by the need to improve their circumstances, in some cases not having enough to eat (though migrants tended to be better off than those who remained, as one needed to be able to fund one's voyage), in other cases by persecution and war. In most cases it was a combination of poor prospects at home and better ones overseas. Thus in Germany, for example, in the early 1880s many of the annual 170,000 individuals who migrated to the United States were pushed by economic discontent at home and the prospect of land in America.[130]

Immigration controls are a modern invention, part of the history of modern capitalism. Throughout most of the nineteenth century emigration (much of which was from Europe) was not restricted. By the end of the nineteenth century there were restrictions in many countries as industrialized nation states had passed legislation that required immigrants to register, to have some skills and to pay a tax. Governments asserted their sovereign right to exclude people from crossing their borders or stop them registering – the Netherlands in 1887, Sweden in 1894, Argentina in 1902, Chile in 1918, France after 1893, the United States after 1891.[131] In Britain the Aliens Act of 1905, intended mainly against Jews from the Tsarist Empire, imposed border controls for the first time. In 1905 the eminent constitutional lawyer A. V. Dicey wrote that the aim of the legislation was 'to restrain any form of competition which may come into conflict with the immediate interest of . . . English wage-earners'.[132] Laws such as these concentrated power in the hands of the state. Previously, at least in Britain, immigration control took the form of expulsion in cases decided by local authorities or voluntary agencies. Thus two Jewish organizations repatriated some 31,000 Jews to eastern Europe between 1881 and 1906.[133]

Some ethnic groups were banned or had severe restrictions imposed on them. Venezuela banned non-Europeans; the United States banned orientals; Prussia deported some 40,000 Polish workers in 1885.[134] These bans were usually supported by trade unions, while employers, understandably enough, opposed them. Max Weber noted that the people who were replacing the Germans on the sugar-beet estates of East Prussia were able to submit to conditions that Germans would not accept. Recruited by agents, they 'cross the frontier in tens of thousands in spring and leave again in autumn'.[135] Weber, who was always more of a nationalist than a liberal, advocated closing the eastern frontier. 'From the standpoint of the nation,' he wrote, 'large-scale enterprises which can only be preserved at the expense of the German race deserve to go down to destruction.'[136]

This lament was all in vain. Between 1890 and 1914 some 2 million people had moved to the western provinces of the German Empire, in particular the Rhineland.[137] In the United Kingdom, Irish migration, which had increased sharply after the famine of 1846–50, continued steadily until, by 1911, there were more than 550,000 Irish in Great Britain.[138] They were regarded as a source of disease and a burden on the taxpayer, a 'collection of demoralised paupers and criminals threatening the well-being of the nation'.[139]

Between 1871 and 1914 a total of 34 million migrants left Europe for the Americas, 25 million of whom became permanent settlers.[140] Migrants to the Americas originated from various parts of Europe both industrialized and rural, their origins changing in the course of the years. In the 1870s the top labour-exporting European countries (relative to population) were the United Kingdom, Norway, and Portugal; by 1913 the top labour-exporters were Italy, Portugal, Spain (and the United Kingdom again).[141] The overall movement of people has continued to increase, with ups and down. By 1990 international migrants numbered 154 million. In 2013, according to the United Nations, this figure reached 232 million.[142] Middle Eastern wars further increased the flow of refugees.

As new nations appeared and were constructed, and older ones were redefined and reconstructed, the 'demos' itself changed ceaselessly, acquiring ever more rights, including the right to citizenship and, with it, the right to vote.

13
Suffrage

The discontent facing nascent capitalism took many forms. There was discontent from the industrial workers: wages were too low, working conditions too harsh. There was discontent from rural workers whose situation was often worse than those in industry, and much of it was suppressed or disguised because many migrated. There was discontent from the middle classes, always anxious about their chronically unstable position. Yet none of this really threatened the stability of advanced capitalist countries in the decades leading to the First World War. Only in unindustrialized countries such as the Tsarist Empire were there serious near-revolutionary threats, notably in 1905. There was indeed little trouble in Great Britain, France, Belgium, the Netherlands, Japan, and Germany, though at the time, as is often the case, an air of unexceptional hysteria prevailed among the established classes always fearful of any real or imagined challenge to their position.

On 13 November 1887 in Trafalgar Square in London a large demonstration took place against unemployment and British repression in Ireland. It was organized by the Social Democratic Federation and the Irish National League and joined by eminent personalities including George Bernard Shaw, the feminist Annie Besant, the anarchist Charlotte Wilson, and William Morris of the Social Democratic Federation. It was the first 'Bloody Sunday' in a long history of bloody Sundays in Europe and North America (Wikipedia lists twenty), although there were few injured and no dead. In North America, at the time, the most famous instance of repression was the Haymarket 'Massacre' on 4 May 1886 following a demonstration in favour of the eight-hour day. The violence never surged out of control but eleven people died, seven of whom were policemen.

Belgium was more rebellious and the casualties were greater: on 29 March 1886, in Roux, in French-speaking Belgium, the army was called in to quell a miners' strike that had turned into a riot, resulting in many dead.[1] On 1 May 1891 in Fourmies, an industrial town in the north of France, the army intervened to disband a demonstration in favour of the eight-hour, resulting in nine people killed, including a twelve-year-old, and thirty wounded.[2] The ruling elites, haunted by the fear of communism, socialism, and anarchism were, as is often the case, anxious and ready to use repression. The 'spectre haunting Europe' was not just a poetic image used by Karl Marx and Friedrich Engels to describe communism in the opening lines of their famous manifesto.

Matters were more serious in Italy. In 1894 a *stato d'assedio* (state of emergency) in Sicily was proclaimed by Francesco Crispi, then both Prime Minister and Interior Minister, against the so-called *Fasci siciliani*. This was a largely rural movement with no connections with what was later the Fascist movement. The name alluded to the strength gained from solidarity: *fasci* means bundle – a single stick can be broken but not a bundle of sticks. The *Fasci siciliani*, which grew significantly between 1891 and 1893, was made up of agricultural workers, tenant farmers, and sharecroppers, though there were some industrial workers, especially those in textiles, hurt by higher industrial productivity in the north of the country. Their conditions could be dire. An impoverished rural worker told the journalist Adolfo Rossi that he could find work for only half the year: 'So how do you cope, the rest of the time? We gather grass, we cook it and eat it without salt.'[3]

According to the southern historian and politician Pasquale Villari, writing at the time, by November 1893 the movement had a membership of more than 300,000.[4] The *fasci* wanted fair rents, higher wages, and lower local taxes. Many Sicilian workers and peasants had looked forward to a better life after Italian unification, but such hopes had been dashed. Of course, the landless wanted land. In the words of a Sicilian dialect saying, similar in sentiment to those of land workers everywhere: *La terra e' di cu' la zappa, no di cu' porta cappa* ('The land belongs to those who till the soil, not to those who wear a cape').[5]

The agrarian question and the enormous disparity in power and wealth between landlords and rural workers could not have been resolved, as Francesco Crispi's predecessor, the liberal Prime Minister Giovanni Giolitti, hoped, by the state refusing to take sides. By being neutral the state was, in effect, leaving untouched the power of landlords. Crispi eventually intervened, and brutally, against the *fasci*.

The Sicilian movement was largely non-violent (land occupation, demonstrations, etc.). One of its leaders, Rosario Garibaldi Bosco, always denied ever planning an insurrection, though probably because he thought the time was not ripe.[6] The subsequent repression was harsh. Between December 1893 (when Giolitti resigned) and January 1894, troops killed ninety-two activists during demonstrations. Only one soldier died.[7] In the two weeks following the start of the emergency (1 January 1894), about a thousand activists were sent to detention centres in various islands of the south without trial.[8] At the same time thousands of 'subversives', designated as such by local mayors, were removed from electoral registers, thus reducing the electorate from circa 250,000 to just under 125,000.[9] A new crime, incitement to class hatred, was introduced that was clearly aimed at anarchists and socialists. Class hatred, declared Prime Minister Crispi (a southerner himself), becomes dangerous when the lower orders (*la plebe*) take literally propositions such as 'property is theft'.[10] A public prosecutor blamed anarchists for inciting 'the ignorant plebs' to reject all laws, all authority, marriage, the family, private property, the state, and the motherland, and to embrace revolution, arson, murders, robberies, and massacres.[11] In reality concessions could have placated the *Fasci siciliani*: where local taxes were decreased there were fewer demonstrations.[12]

Unrest continued throughout southern Italy. Giuseppe Zanardelli, Prime Minister from 1901 to 1903, responding, in 1901, in the Chamber of Deputies to those who accused him of being soft on strikers, declared that labour conflicts did not seriously threaten people or property and that frequent strikes did not require repression.[13] Yet in the province of Foggia, strikes by railway workers resulted in the death of eight strikers in September 1902, three in May 1904, and four in March 1905, all killed by government troops.

There had also been unrest in 1898 against a steep increase in the price of grain, and hence of bread (partly due to the increase in international wheat prices after the Spanish-American wars). The protests were relatively peaceful but in May 1898, in Milan, Italy's second city after Naples, the army, under General Bava Beccaris, gunned down unarmed demonstrators causing perhaps as many as one hundred dead.[14] Socialist leaders, including Filippo Turati and Anna Kuliscioff, were jailed. Bava Beccaris was decorated by King Umberto I (who was, in turn, killed by an anarchist in 1900).

At the end of the century there was widespread anxiety about social unrest, and understandably so since it is almost impossible to foresee the long-term consequences of any event. Strikes may degenerate into a riot; a riot may degenerate into a revolution. Or repression may quell a protest once and for all, and matters may remain calm and without major consequences. With hindsight it is easy to be wise. At the time there was anxiety as well as hope. Proponents of universal suffrage argued that if everyone could vote there would be less popular discontent. The Belgian Socialist leader, César de Paepe, in his pamphlet on universal suffrage declared that 'If we want universal suffrage, it is in order to avoid a revolution.'[15]

Of course, the *bien pensants* were anxious not only about unrest but also about universal suffrage, since no one could tell what the masses would do with their votes. They were less anxious about extending the suffrage to the 'respectable workers' but terrified of extending it to the 'dangerous classes' (i.e. the poor). Yet by the First World War, even universal *manhood* suffrage had become the norm in the so-called 'civilized world', though there were numerous exceptions. The road had been long, even though the direction to take had been worked out centuries ago by some, such as the Levellers during the Putney Debates of 1647 who wanted the suffrage extended to most males. David Hume, in 1752, argued that some form of popular representation, albeit of 'tradesmen and merchants', that is 'the middling rank of men', is the 'firmest basis of liberty' and 'good for peace and prosperity'.[16]

Yan Fu, a leading Chinese intellectual (see Chapter 3), wrote in 1895 that the superiority of the West resided in the particular link between the people and their government and that this link depended on the fact that they elected representatives, and that these representatives were not 'imposed by superior authorities': 'When the English speak of England and the French of France . . . they speak as when we speak of our parents with a sincere ardour and attachment which appears to come from a deep love.'[17] And he added: 'In case of war between us and westerners, their people will fight for a public thing, a common good, while the Chinese people will fight like slaves for the benefit of their masters.'[18]

Maybe Yan Fu had read *Letters to a Chinese Official* by the American populist politician and scourge of large corporations, William Jennings Bryan, who, while admitting that wealth influenced the outcome of American elections, extolled the sense of unity and power that was acquired through the suffrage: 'The people choose their representatives, retain them in office as long as they like and depose them when they please.'[19]

Building the nation and building the citizenry were seen as part of the same process. But is there a direct connection between the expansion of the suffrage and the level of industrialization? The connection between modern industry and the suffrage is to be made, but it is not obvious. The common idea was that the suffrage was a European invention, born in old and stable countries of which Britain was the paragon. The evidence only partly confirms the assumption. In the race towards universal manhood suffrage, the pioneers were not the British, but European states such as Belgium, Switzerland and Germany or settlers in new states such as the USA, Australia and New Zealand (though in all these cases many were excluded on ground of race.) Almost all Latin American countries had universal manhood suffrage before 1914. Some had it in the mid-nineteenth century, though they reintroduced restrictions later, notably Colombia and Peru.[20] Others, such as Uruguay, Brazil, Peru, and Cuba, extended the suffrage to women before the Second World War (and hence before Italy, France, and Belgium); others, such as Argentina, Chile, and Venezuela, after 1945, Mexico in 1953, and Paraguay only in 1961.[21]

The table below (p. 316) gives an idea of the spread of the suffrage for national elections in selected countries before 1914. In some cases the suffrage had been expanded for local elections in advance of national ones. For instance, in the United Kingdom, under the Municipal Franchise Act 1869, unmarried women paying local taxes could vote in local elections; in the United States, women could vote in some territories (i.e. before statehood) such as Wyoming in 1869 and Utah in 1870; in Canada women in Manitoba could vote in 1916 ahead of federal enfranchisement (1918); after 1959, women could vote in some Swiss cantons but gained the vote for federal elections only in 1971.

There were often exclusion clauses other than that of gender: being too young, not being a citizen, belonging to the 'wrong' race or religion, being too poor or not rich enough, being a convicted criminal, being illiterate, etc. Exclusion by age has remained the most obvious and the least controversial since a minimum voting age is unavoidable. In the period we are examining the usual 'majority' age was twenty-one or higher. Only later in the twentieth century would this be lowered to eighteen. No one ever contemplated disenfranchising the very old; and lack of mental awareness (dementia, etc.) was seldom a criterion for disenfranchisement, though in the UK certified 'lunatics' are barred from voting along with convicted criminals and members of the House of Lords.

Literacy tests were often a way of disenfranchising the lower classes. Thus in Brazil the Saraiva Law of 1881 enfranchised all men, including blacks, as long as they could pass a literacy test. Since the overwhelming majority of Brazilians (and blacks in particular) were illiterate, they were effectively disenfranchised. In fact, Brazil was an interesting case study of having elections without democracy since elections were regularly held under the empire (1822–89), the First Republic (1889–1930), and subsequent dictatorships, but they were often fraudulent, voters were intimidated and outcomes predetermined, even though a higher proportion of the population could vote than in Great Britain.[22] Indeed, elections in Latin America 'were almost exclusively defined by fraud or violence', though it does not follow that they were useless, since their purpose was to find a modus vivendi between competing elites.[23]

Ecuador abolished the literacy test only in 1978 (by then there had been seventeen constitutions since 1830). Yet as early as 1861, Ecuador had abolished all property requirements for the suffrage. Women were enfranchised in 1929, the same year as in Great Britain and well before France.[24] In Argentina, as elsewhere, only citizens could vote, but the ratio of citizens to non-citizens was rather skewed since many of the inhabitants were newly arrived immigrants. Those qualified (i.e. adult males holding citizenship) represented only 20 per cent of the total population.[25]

Women were usually 'citizens' but of second rank. They were part of the nation, in the sense that they were French, English, German, Italian, and so on, but they could not vote and many of their other rights (such as the right to own property) were curtailed. In Britain it was only in 1882 with the Married Women's Property Act that women were allowed to own property individually after marriage.

Nowadays the limitation of the suffrage to the male population does not exist anywhere in the world: if there are elections at all, everyone can vote – even in Saudi Arabia (since 2015), where people can vote only in municipal elections. Before the First World War, however, women were allowed to vote in general elections only in New Zealand, Australia, Finland, and Norway. Some men, such as John Stuart Mill, advocated female suffrage (*The Subjection of Women*, 1869, written with his wife Harriet Taylor) on equal terms with men without abolishing property or financial qualifications – a position held by suffragettes such as Emmeline Pankhurst. The founding programme of the Second International (1889) was in favour of universal female suffrage, a position reaffirmed at its Seventh Congress held in Stuttgart in 1907 when the first International Conference of Socialist Women was launched.

In spite of the long struggle for the enfranchisement of women, female suffrage has not brought about a major change in party alignment. Although women originally perhaps tended to vote more conservatively than men, the difference was minor. Class, religious and regional issues have been of greater importance. Even today there is still no considerable women-based party, the way there are class or religion-based or ethnic or regionally based parties.

Here is a table depicting the spread of universal manhood suffrage and universal suffrage in some countries:

Table 11 The Spread of the Suffrage for General Elections before 1914: Selected Countries

Country	Universal Manhood Suffrage for Central/Federal Assemblies	Female Suffrage
Australia	The (self-governing) colony of South Australia (the only colony, out of six, without a 'convict past') introduced universal manhood suffrage in 1856. Other colonies followed. The Franchise Act of 1902 extended the franchise to all men and women for federal elections. Aborigines obtained the vote only in 1962.	1902
Austria-Hungary	1907 universal manhood suffrage in the Austrian part of the Austro-Hungarian Empire. Suffrage remained restricted in Hungary.	1918
Belgium	After the general strike of 1893 universal manhood suffrage was introduced (but some had more than one vote). Proportional representation introduced in 1899; universal manhood suffrage introduced in 1919 and war widows allowed to vote.	1948
Canada	Chinese, Japanese, and other 'Asiatic' people and aboriginal people excluded in decades leading to the First World War. Only in 1960 were all the descendants of the original inhabitants allowed to vote. Some provinces had female suffrage before 1918.	1918
Denmark	Universal manhood suffrage 1849 (suffrage in 1834 confined to male property owners).	1915
Finland	Until 1917, Finland was an autonomous principality within the Russian Empire. It adopted universal suffrage in 1906.	1906
France	The Convention nationale of 1792 was elected by all males. Then suffrage was restricted until the Constitution of the Third Republic in 1875, which established universal manhood suffrage. Universal suffrage established in 1944.	1944

Country	Universal Manhood Suffrage for Central/Federal Assemblies	Female Suffrage
Germany	Universal manhood suffrage: 1871.	1919
Iran	In 1962 the Shah introduced female suffrage as part of the reforms of his modernizing 'White Revolution'. The Revolution of 1979 (led by the Ayatollah Khomeini) maintained women's right to vote.	1963
Italy	Universal manhood suffrage: 1913.	1946
Japan	Universal manhood suffrage: 1925.	1946
Netherlands	Universal manhood suffrage: 1917.	1919
New Zealand	In 1867 Maori men had four reserved seats and acquired voting rights on equal terms only in 1948. Women were allowed to stand for parliament only after 1919.	1893
Norway	Universal manhood suffrage: 1898.	1913
Portugal	The 1822 Constitution granted universal manhood suffrage, excluding illiterates; there were some financial restrictions.	1931
Spain	Universal manhood suffrage: 1869, repealed in 1878, reinstated in 1890.	1931
Sweden	Universal manhood suffrage: 1909 with some restrictions; extended to all in 1919.	1919
Switzerland	Universal manhood suffrage: 1848. Women not enfranchised until 1959. Allowed gradually in various cantons. Universal suffrage only in 1971.	1971
United Kingdom	Universal manhood suffrage in 1918 for men over 21 and women over 30. Full equality in 1928.	1928
United States	1825: all but three states had universal manhood suffrage; in 1856 property qualifications were removed everywhere. Voting restricted to white males only in most states. 1917: first woman (Jeannette Rankin) to be elected in either House. 1920: Nineteenth Amendment enfranchising women. The Voting Rights Act 1965 makes illegal racial discrimination in voting.	1918

In reality the mere extension of the suffrage is not an adequate index of democratization, nor was the suffrage ever, as a sceptical Karl Marx put it, 'the miraculous magic wand for which the republican duffers had taken it . . .'.[26]

Other factors come into play:

1. *The Actual Power of the Elected Assembly.* What if the elected assembly has few powers? What if the executive (the government and the sovereign) can ignore it? Does an unelected chamber have powers of veto? Finland had universal suffrage before any country in Europe (1906) but it was a semi-autonomous Grand Duchy within the Russian Empire. The real ruler was the Tsar (with the title of Grand Duke), who could and did ignore the will of the electorate, turning down most of the legislative proposals in the years after 1906 (making a rare exception in the case of the regulation of working hours in bakeries).[27]

   In terms of the suffrage, Germany in 1871 was more democratic than Britain in 1914 since all males could vote, but the Reichstag had fewer powers than the House of Commons, partly because Germany was a federal state and partly because the Kaiser had greater powers than the British monarch. The British House of Commons was faced with a hereditary House of Lords that could veto all legislation until the Parliamentary Act of 1911 (after which the Lords could only delay non-financial bills). Today the House of Lords, though almost totally non-hereditary, is still the only unelected chamber in Europe, indeed one of the few in the world along with those of countries such as Belize, Lesotho, Canada, Oman, and Saudi Arabia.

2. *Electoral Mechanism.* The way seats are allocated is a major factor in deciding who wins and who loses an election. An absolutely proportional system leads to a parliament that is the 'mirror of the nation', to use a metaphor coined by the nineteenth-century Scottish jurist James Lorimer, but it is unlikely to produce a single-party majority, thus making compromises inevitable.[28] If rural areas are over-represented, as they often were and are, it is more difficult for urban-based parties (such as the Socialists) to win power. For instance, in 1907 in Germany the Social Democratic Party (SPD) lost twenty-six seats but gained hundreds of thousands of votes. In Germany

at the time it took only 18,000 votes to elect a Conservative but 70,000 to elect a Social Democrat.[29]

3. *Political Freedoms.* This is crucial. Can the electorate choose freely between genuinely independent political parties? Are there laws that stop or make it difficult to form a political party? Is there a free press? Do all the candidates have a similar access to the media, to newspapers, to places where they can speak? Is the ballot really secret? A 'father of liberalism' such as Montesquieu thought that open voting was essential to maintain the rule of the aristocracy over the unenlightened *petit peuple.*[30]

The ballot became secret in Australia in 1856 and in New Zealand in 1870. Great Britain introduced it only in 1872, Belgium in 1877, Germany in 1903, and France in 1913.[31] In Imperial Germany big employers such as Krupp could sack workers for voting the wrong way. When the ballot became secret in 1903, Krupp workers could finally vote for the Social Democrats – and one-quarter of them did so.[32] Personal expenditure limits for candidates were introduced in Imperial Germany, where they had been championed by the 'popular' parties, notably the SPD and the Catholic Zentrum.[33]

There may also be de facto impediments in elected deputies taking their seats. For instance, Catholics were prevented from sitting in the House of Commons until the passage of the Roman Catholic Relief Act of 1829. Jews had to wait a little longer. In 1847 an elected MP, Lionel Rothschild, was not allowed to sit in the House, because he refused to swear the oath of allegiance 'on the true faith of a Christian'. Several attempts were made to modify the practice but all were vetoed by the House of Lords. Only in 1858 could Lionel de Rothschild (who, meanwhile, had been re-elected several times) take his seat. Those elected as republicans (for instance members of Sinn Fein in Northern Ireland) are required to swear allegiance to the monarchy – an oath they have so far refused to swear and so they cannot take part in parliamentary proceedings.

Finally, there is also the issue of payment for members of parliament. In the nineteenth century it was usual for parliamentarians not to receive any salary or expenses. Consequently only people with an independent income could afford to be elected and to pay not just for their upkeep but also for the cost of elections, travelling, entertaining, networking etc.

4. *Political Power.* Some people and organizations are more powerful, have more money, can influence those who can influence others, have a disproportionate weight in the media, or belong (by birth, accident, or design) to influential networks. In 2015 the British government came under criticism for having an excessive representation of people who went to the same public school (Eton). So it should not be surprising that even after considerable electoral reform in the mid-1880s, 5 per cent of the Lower House in the Austro-Hungarian Parliament were aristocrats when aristocrats already occupied the whole of the Upper House.[34]

   Then there is the question of political corruption. Are voters bribed or threatened? Are elections rigged? How widespread is political corruption? In the late nineteenth century, between 1865 and 1884, even in the so-called 'mother of parliaments', the title the British invented for its parliament, there were cases of corruption at elections in at least sixty-four English boroughs.[35]

And there are more problems: what if only a few electors bother to vote? What if voting is made difficult by the sparse numbers of voting stations? What if one is forced to queue for a long time? What if the level of information available to the electorate is limited?

The difficulty in establishing a democracy index is apparent from contemporary attempts to do this. The 2012 Democracy Index established by the Economist Intelligence Unit listed twenty-five countries as being 'fully democratic', followed by a number of 'flawed democracies', 'hybrid regimes', and 'authoritarian regimes'.[36] France turns out to be a 'flawed democracy' like Portugal, Greece, and Italy, even though the turnout in the 2012 and 2017 presidential elections in France was around 80 per cent while the turnout for presidential elections in the United States (a 'full democracy') is usually around 60 per cent, in spite of the enormous sums of money spent by the leading candidates.[37] By 2014, France was promoted by the Economist Intelligence Unit to the lower echelons of 'full democracy' and one wonders which flaws were put right in two years, yet the fix must not have been very convincing because by 2016 France was flawed again, along with Belgium and Japan, and just below Cabo Verde, while even the USA was downgraded to 'flawed democracy'. The United Kingdom remains a 'full democracy' despite having a hereditary head of state and a non-elected upper house. Russia ranks as a fully fledged 'authoritarian regime', though it has elections, an (embattled) opposition, and at least some independent newspapers. Although no one would view Russia as a full democracy, it seems that ranking it 122nd in 2012 (squeezed between Jordan and Ethiopia – where the ruling party and its allies 'won' all parliamentary seats in the 2010 and 2015 elections) and 132rd in 2014 (well below Belarus and Cuba) may be unduly severe. It calls into question the simplistic and naive methodology of surveys such as these. Perhaps there should there be an index of such surveys: very flawed, deeply flawed, etc. These issues exemplify the difficulties facing the comparative analyst of democracy, one of the most used and misused concepts of modern times – perhaps because it is one of the most important. Above all the notion that there is a 'will of the electorate' must be a fiction since the whole point of elections is that the 'people' are divided and that they do not and cannot express a single will. Elections are an act whereby the 'people' reveal their differences and divisions. Ultimately, the value of the democratic mechanism is that it legitimizes the victorious candidates.

In France the road to democracy was particularly complex due to the significant changes of regimes in the period between the French Revolution and the final establishment of the Third Republic. For the first half of the nineteenth century the norm in France and in almost all 'democratic' countries was a restricted suffrage based on income and property, thus withholding power from the broad masses who might use it in the 'wrong' way.

The idea that owning property uniquely qualified one to vote has a long and distinguished pedigree. William Blackstone, the eighteenth-century jurist and a progressive Tory, wrote in his celebrated and massively influential *Commentaries on the Laws of England* that since those who are indigent cannot be expected to protect property, they should be excluded from voting.[38] Immanuel Kant, in 1793, also thought that only 'citizens' should be allowed to vote. Who were the citizens? Citizens were those who were their own masters, he explained, and the propertyless cannot be their own masters, because they serve others.[39] Although in favour (in principle) of equal rights of individuals, he was really defending inequality of outcomes: 'this thoroughgoing equality of individuals within a state . . . is quite consistent with the greatest inequality in terms of the quantity and degree of their possessions . . .'[40] He then added: 'The quality requisite to this, apart from the *natural* one (of not being a child or a woman), is only that of *being one's own master* (*sui iuris*), hence having some *property* . . . that supports him . . .'[41]

It was better to have a restricted suffrage, which is a real check on the executive, than give ineffectual votes to everyone, explained the liberal thinker Benjamin Constant in the *Mercure de France* on 18 January 1817.[42] In an earlier text ('Principes de politique', now part of the collection *Écrits politiques*), having praised the labouring classes ('*Je ne veux faire aucun tort à la classe laborieuse*') and declared them just as much part of the nation as all the others, Constant explained that in order to exercise the suffrage properly it was necessary to have the time to acquire wisdom and proper judgement ('*l'acquisition des lumières, la rectitude du jugement*'). Thus only the possession of property can make men capable of exercising their political rights ('*La propriété seule rend les hommes capables de l'exercice des droits politiques*').[43] And if one is going to have a hereditary monarchy then one must also have a chamber based on the principle of heredity alongside an elected assembly.[44] The best model, declared Constant, as did almost all French liberals of the time, was Great Britain.[45]

The fear of the mob, namely of unpredictable people, was commonplace among progressive opinion. Thus the Abbé (Emmanuel) Sieyès, one of the protagonists of the French Revolution, stated in no uncertain terms that 'the mob belongs to the aristocracy', meaning that the people would be under the hegemony of the nobility.[46] If we were dealing with a 'new people' ('*un peuple neuf*'), he explained, then one would unhesitatingly advocate equality of rights, but, since we are dealing with people who have had to endure centuries of oppression, one must take further precautions against the enemies of freedom.[47] There were major dissenting voices. Jean-Paul Marat, in particular, was alarmed. If the suffrage is restricted to such an extent that only the rich will be citizens, he argued in his newspaper *L'Ami du peuple* (30 June 1790), then the people will be at their mercy: 'What would we have gained if, having destroyed the aristocracy of the nobles, it is replaced by the aristocracy of the rich. And if we have to suffer under the yoke of these new parvenus, we might as well have maintained the privileges of the old order.'[48]

The first elections after the Revolution were based on property qualifications. There was no major drive for universal suffrage at least until 1830 when the Bourbon dynasty was overthrown and replaced with the Orléans dynasty, and even then universal suffrage was advocated only by minorities.[49] And the great liberal Alexis de Tocqueville, speaking in the Chamber of Deputies on 29 January 1848, worried that injustices would spark rebellion:

> Observe what is going on in the working classes . . . have you not noticed that their passions once political have become social? . . . that all those above them are incapable and unworthy of ruling them? that the present distribution of wealth is unjust? . . . and do you not think that when such opinions . . . penetrate deeply into the masses, that they will lead, I do not know when or how, to the most redoubtable of revolutions?[50]

When the French monarchy was finally overthrown the new provisional government of the Second Republic established by decree (March 1848) universal manhood suffrage. It was declared that 'The Republic excludes none of its sons, calls all to political life; it will be for you like a rebirth, a baptism, a regeneration.'[51]

The fear of the conservatives was not justified: the ballot was used to elect moderates and to defeat the more radical popular insurrection of July 1848. Then, later in December, the people elected Louis-Napoléon Bonaparte as the first French President of the Republic with almost 75 per cent of the vote. His subsequent *coup d'état* on 2 December 1851 (analysed famously by Karl Marx in his 1852 'instant book' *The Eighteenth Brumaire of Louis Napoleon*) was endorsed by a popular referendum or plebiscite with an unlikely 92 per cent of the vote, a further sign that even dictators had to pay some obeisance to the idea of democracy. A year later Louis-Napoléon became '*Napoléon III, Empereur des Français*', again with overwhelming popular backing.

Clearly there was little to fear from universal manhood suffrage. Democrats backed the extension of the suffrage out of principle, conservatives out of self-interest. The socialists were less sure. Some were optimistic. Egged on by Engels, the socialist Paul Lafargue (Karl Marx's son-in-law) wrote to the Socialist leader Jules Guesdes on 14 November 1892: 'Universal suffrage will become a formidable weapon now that the workers are beginning to learn how to exploit it.'[52] But not trusting the people was not just a prerogative of the aristocracy. A man of the left such as Eugène Sémérie, a supporter of the Paris Commune, wrote in *La République et le peuple souverain* (1871) of the 'absurd theory of popular sovereignty' whereby each vote is the same as any other. The real culprits were, of course, the peasants, the bastion of reaction. The peasant, he explained, is barely aware of the meaning of civic life ('*la vie civique*'): 'He understands nothing of the great human questions which inspire, perturb and arouse the cities.'[53] The historian

Hippolyte Taine wrote in *Du Suffrage universel et de la manière de voter* (1872) that 'the ignorance and credulity of the rural population are astonishing . . . The peasant spends the whole day in the fields and agricultural work stultifies human thought.'[54]

Gustave Flaubert, who held an aristocratic conception of politics ('the best should rule'), in letters to the eminent novelist George Sand, declared quite simply, '*Je hais la démocratie*', adding a few months later that he was 'tired of the ignoble worker, the inept bourgeois, the stupid peasant, and the hateful priest' ('*je suis las de l'ignoble ouvrier, de l'inepte bourgeois, du stupide paysant et de l'odieux ecclésiastique*').[55] He complained that free and compulsory education would only increase the number of '*imbéciles*',[56] and added that universal suffrage is 'more stupid than the divine right of kings . . . the masses, the greater number is *always* idiotic'.[57] Of course, Flaubert liked being *contre-courant*. Politically, he counted for very little and he knew it. By 1887 even Philippe d'Orléans, heir to the French Crown as the grandson of Louis Philippe I, the last King of France, formally embraced universal manhood suffrage, though few took him seriously.

Not surprisingly, reactionary nationalists such as the German historian Heinrich von Treitschke warned, in the 1890s, against the rule not just of the working classes but also of the middle classes, who 'will determine Europe's future' and who 'are not free from a certain preference for the mediocre'. He decried the 'yoke of public opinion', which 'presses heavier than elsewhere in the freest great States of modernity – in England and the United States'. The solution was to increase the role of the state 'that protected our forefathers with its justice'.[58] Every society is a natural aristocracy. 'Logic has decreed,' he explained, 'that millions of people work, forge and labour so that a few thousand can devote themselves to scholarship, the arts and poetry.'[59]

At least France, even in 1848, had universal manhood suffrage, which was not the case in the United Kingdom. Before the 1832 Reform Act, the UK, the world's 'oldest democracy', was remarkably undemocratic. The electorate was tiny and constituencies were unequal in size. Cities such as Sheffield, Leeds, and Manchester did not return any MPs while small towns in Cornwall returned two members. As Thomas Babington Macaulay famously said in the House of Commons on 5 July 1831 during the debate on parliamentary reform: 'For who can answer plain arithmetical demonstration? Under the present system, Manchester, with two hundred thousand inhabitants, has no members. Old Sarum, with no inhabitants, has two members.'[60]

The struggle for electoral reform had not been entirely peaceful. In

1816 a large gathering took place in Spa Field in Islington (London). It quickly turned into the so-called Spa Fields Riots. In 1819 a massive demonstration (60,000 people) gathered in St Peter's Field, Manchester, only to be attacked by the cavalry, leading to some ten to fifteen dead and hundreds injured (in an obvious reference to Waterloo, this became known as the Peterloo Massacre). The demonstration, which had been entirely peaceful, moved Shelley to celebrate it in his famous poem *The Mask of Anarchy* (1819):

Rise, like lions after slumber
In unvanquishable number!
Shake your chains to earth like dew
Which in sleep had fallen on you:
Ye are many – they are few!

Demands such as those that led to Peterloo were not always simply calls for electoral reform. Economic hardship usually figured, especially among the new industrial working classes whose strikes often turned into riots.[61] By the 1830s the situation had become incandescent as more riots followed the repeated vetoing of reforms by the House of Lords. In Bristol, in 1831, rioters demolished the Bishop's Palace (the bishops had long opposed any reforms), the Customs House and other important buildings. A dozen rioters died, a hundred were wounded: 'It was the last great urban riot in English history.'[62] Finally, the Prime Minister, the Whig Earl Grey, managed to get the 'Great Reform Act' through both houses. The Act increased the representation of those who lived in industrial areas and abolished the number of seats with small voting populations.

A further and far more significant step forward was taken with the Second Reform Act of 1867, which extended the suffrage to 30 per cent of adult males, in other words all 'householders', enfranchising most of the 'respectable' working class.

The Third Reform Act (the Representation of the People Act, 1884) further widened the franchise. This enlarged the electorate from 2.6 million to 5.6 million –about 60 per cent of the male population.[63]

Universal manhood suffrage was finally adopted in Britain only in 1918. Women over the age of thirty were enfranchised. Real equality between the sexes at elections came into force only in 1928. France, which had promulgated the *Declaration des droits de l'homme et du citoyen* in 1789, had real universal suffrage (i.e. women as well as men) only in 1944. In the United States, which had declared in 1776 that 'We hold these truths to be self-evident, that all men are created equal', women were enfranchised only in 1920 for federal elections (many states had introduced it earlier) with the passing of the Nineteenth Amendment to the Constitution – forty-one years after it had been introduced by Senator Aaron Sargent, whose wife, Ellen, was a prominent suffragette. The effective and practical enfranchisement of all blacks had to wait until the Voting Rights Act of 1965.

John Stuart Mill, who, unlike most of his peers, was in favour of allowing women to vote on the same terms as men, seemed to believe in some kind of inevitable class struggle between employers and employees. In *The Principles of Political Economy* (1848) he wrote that the working classes lacked the 'just pride which will choose to give good work for good wages'.[64] As he wrote in the preface to the third edition (1852), socialism was not practical, because of 'the extreme unfitness of the labouring classes . . . for any order of things which would make any considerable demand on either their intellect or their virtues'.

Other 'progressives' held similar doubts about the lower orders. Thus John Ruskin, after whom a college in Oxford intended for the education of the working classes was named, wrote in 1862 that the central policy of government is:

> *that the wise and kind, few or many, shall govern the unwise and unkind* . . . I once saw democracy finely illustrated by the beetles of North Switzerland, who by universal suffrage and elytric acclamation, one May twilight, carried it, that they would fly over the Lake of Zug; and flew *short*, to the great disfigurement of the Lake of Zug . . . over some leagues square, and to the close of the cockchafer democracy for that year.[65]

Ruskin's worry about the lack of education of the working classes increased during the debates on the Reform Bill of 1867 when he wrote on 17 February that workers should realize that they need ideas to bring about change: 'Your voices are not worth a rat's squeak, either in Parliament or out of it, till you have some ideas to utter with them.'[66] Almost as alarmed was Matthew Arnold, who, in *Culture and Anarchy* (1869), announced that the working class (which he called the Populace):

> which, raw and half-developed, has long-lain half hidden amidst its poverty and squalor . . . is now issuing from its hiding-place to assert an Englishman's heaven-born privilege of doing as he likes, and is beginning to perplex us by marching where it likes, meeting where it likes, bawling what it likes, breaking what it likes . . .[67]

Arnold, a true cultural elitist, was even more contemptuous of the aristocracy, whom he called 'the Barbarians', and the middle classes, whom he called 'Philistine'.

The anti-democratic position had been previously well established by Catholic writers and, in England, High Anglicans. William George Ward, a reactionary supporter of papal infallibility, with some sagacity, was casting aspersions on the double standard of the democrats (whom he called 'revolutionists'). He wrote in 1865:

> whenever the masses are on the whole orderly and devout, your true revolutionist despises them as ignorant, superstitious, and (if so be) priest-ridden . . . 'the people' means with him the aggregate of shallow public writers, and of restless busybodies, and of those generally who have received a certain smattering of what he absurdly calls education.[68]

The more mundane conservative position was uncomplicated: since people were unequal why should their vote count for the same? Thus, in 1851, the future Conservative Prime Minister Lord Salisbury (then Lord Cecil) declared that:

> Every community has natural leaders, to whom, if they are not misled by the insane passion for equality, they will instinctively defer. Always wealth, in some countries birth, in all intellectual power and culture, mark out the men to whom . . . a community looks to undertake its government.[69]

Later, in 1859, he still thought it was completely ridiculous that 'twenty struggling green-grocers' should carry more (voting) weight than 'a dozen of those colossal capitalists whose word is law to the bourse of Europe', adding, 'If you give the poor the power of taxing the rich at will, the rich will soon find the whole expenditure of the country saddled upon them.'[70]

A few years later, in 1864, and a few years before the Second Reform Act (enacted by his own party), Lord Salisbury was still fighting, along with many others, the good anti-democratic fight in the pages of the *Quarterly Review*. Of course, few, at the time, were outright supporters of 'democracy', but, as Paul Smith wrote, Salisbury was the 'cleverest and most virulent anti-democrat in the party'.[71] He was also a pragmatist who had said, in quite a different context (the Eastern Question), that 'the commonest error in politics is sticking to the carcasses of dead policies'.[72] Unsurprisingly, Salisbury eventually changed his mind on the suffrage and even had the audacity, some might call it chutzpah, to tell the House of Lords, in 1884, that he never had 'any adverse feeling to the extension of the suffrage on the ground of the presumed incapacity or unfitness of those to whom it has to be extended'. He even mused that eventually the suffrage might be extended to women and they could well inject stability, morality, and wisdom into British political life.[73]

Salisbury had assumed that, since legislation is mainly concerned with property, to give the suffrage to a poor man 'must infallibly give to that class a power *pro tanto* of using taxation as an instrument of plunder, and expenditure and legislation as a fountain of gain'.[74] Labour agitators in favour of extending the suffrage used the same logic linking the vote and property. James Bronterre O'Brien, the Irish Chartist leader, put it thus: 'Knaves will tell you that it is because you have no property, you are under-represented. I tell you on the contrary, it is because you are under-represented that you have no property . . .'[75]

The years of Chartist agitation (1838–48), partly caused by widespread disappointment at the limitations of the Reform Act of 1832, would be described by A. V. Dicey as a period when:

> The time was out of joint. The misery and discontent of city artisans and village labourers were past dispute . . . The horrors connected with factory life were patent. Widespread was the discontent of the whole body of wage-earners . . . there were acts of violence by trade unionists in the towns. The demand for the People's Charter was the sign of a social condition which portended revolution.[76]

The response was a set of gradual reforms, the work of both utilitarian liberals and Tory humanitarians. The threat from the working classes had occurred far earlier than in other countries, a reflection of the lead that Britain had in industrialization. The revolutions of 1848 on the continent were essentially middle-class revolutions led by liberals and nationalists whereas in Britain the Chartists, while demanding liberal reforms (universal manhood suffrage, a secret ballot, annual elections, etc.), were a national working-class movement. Robert Gammage, author of one of the first histories of Chartism, explained that 'the masses', contrasting the opulence of the 'enfranchised classes . . . with the misery of their own condition', arrived at the conclusion that 'their exclusion from political power is the cause of our social anomalies'.[77]

By 1864 liberals like Gladstone, then Chancellor of the Exchequer, once lukewarm about extending the suffrage, now accepted that 'there ought to be, not a wholesale, nor an excessive, but a sensible and considerable addition to that portion of the working classes – at present almost infinitesimal – which is in possession of the franchise'.[78] This was said in support of Edward Baines's private members' bill for the extension of the borough franchise. The bill was soundly defeated by 272 votes to 56, but Gladstone's speech was a turning point. Some pointed out that there was no need for further reforms. After all, working-class agitation for an extension of the franchise had quietened down; the old Chartist demand for universal suffrage was by then somehow muted. But the Reform League, which later led powerful demonstrations in 1866 and 1867 in Hyde Park, was ready to settle for an expansion of the suffrage falling short of universality. But Gladstone was far-sighted:

> but is it desirable that we should wait until they do agitate? In my opinion, agitation by the working classes, upon any political subject whatever, is a thing not to be waited for, not to be made a condition previous to any Parliamentary movement; but, on the contrary, it is a thing to be deprecated, and, if possible, anticipated and prevented by wise and provident measures.

A worried Queen Victoria wrote to Lord Palmerston expressing her fears that this 'imprudent declaration' may produce agitation in the country.[79] Gladstone, however, did not look back. On 27 April 1866 he fulminated against those who described working men 'as an invading army . . . as a band of enemies': 'these men whom you are denouncing . . . are your own flesh and blood'.[80] The British nation was becoming a community, at least in thought. The radical liberal MP John Bright in his Glasgow speech of 16 October 1866 called for manhood suffrage, declaring:

> The nation would be changed . . . The class which has hitherto ruled in this country has failed miserably. It revels in power and wealth, whilst at its feet, at terrible peril of its future, lies the multitude which it has neglected. If a class has failed, let us try the nation . . . I see . . . the glimmerings of a dawn of a better and nobler day for the country and for the people that I love so well.[81]

Although Queen Victoria did not understand that the times were changing, Disraeli, whom she much preferred to Gladstone for his wit and 'exotic' charm, did. By 1867 the Conservatives were back in power. The Prime Minister was Lord Derby but the pillar of the government was Disraeli, now Chancellor of the Exchequer. It was this administration that passed the 1867 Reform Act and it was this Act that changed British politics, trebling the number of voters.[82] Disraeli did not think the 1867 reform would introduce 'democracy': 'We do not . . . live – and I trust it will never be the fate of this country to live – under a democracy.'[83] And, still in 1867, he reassured a group of businessmen by declaring 'England is a country of classes, and the change that is impending in this country will only make those classes more united, more complete, and more cordial.'[84] Most Conservatives too needed reassuring. There were exceptions: H. A. M. Butler-Johnstone, a maverick Conservative saw the enfranchisement of workers as a necessary step for uniting the country. Speaking on the Reform debate in the House of Commons he declared that 'If this country was to be engaged in a life and death struggle with any of the nations of the world – if we had to defend our overland route to India – if we had to maintain our passage through Egypt – how should we fare if the whole country was not united?' Another Conservative, Viscount Sandon, declared that nothing was 'more dangerous' than depriving a 'great class' (the working classes) of their views in the House of Commons.[85]

The Conservatives' otherwise unenthusiastic support for the reform was due in part to the desire to maintain and expand their popular basis by pioneering a reform which, sooner or later, would have been passed anyway. In the short term this was a miscalculation. The Conservatives lost the 1868 election and Gladstone became Prime Minister. But Disraeli, like Gladstone, had an eye on the long term. As Dicey said in 1898: 'The lesson which Disraeli taught his party was the possibility, which he had long perceived, of an alliance between the Tories and English wage-earners; and the true basis of this alliance was their common dissent from individualistic liberalism.'[86] The Conservatives had little choice but to cultivate the urban middle classes, though they remained for decades overwhelmingly the party of rural Britain.[87] Eventually, in the course of the twentieth century, they became the party of capitalism, displacing the Liberals.

The liberal elites were by no means united behind the expansion of the suffrage. The liberal weekly *The Economist* continued to view any widening of the franchise with suspicion. What if the people's representatives adopted the views of the people and not the 'right' position (presumably that of *The Economist*).[88] In fact, conservative fears and radical hopes did not materialize. The radicals were dismayed at the lack of revolutionary (or even reformist) zeal shown by the newly enfranchised working-class electorate. Engels, writing to Marx, on the first elections held under the 1867 Reform Act, expressed his disappointment that in proletarian Manchester and Salford, three Tories were returned: 'The proletariat has once again made an awful fool of itself . . . Everywhere the proletariat is the rag, tag, and bobtail of the official parties, and if any party has gained strength from the new voters it is the Tories.'[89] Disraeli, who had said that he always regarded 'the labouring classes as essentially the most conservative interests in the country', would have had reasons to be smug.[90]

Conservatives continued to worry about the 'socialist threat' in the 1880s (even though there were hardly any socialists in the United Kingdom). By 1886 the scare seemed over. Socialists, social liberals, and 'collectivists', as socialists were often called at the time, continued to fight for the further democratization of the country but insisted that this should coincide with a constant improvement in the economic conditions of the lower classes. Thus Sidney Webb wrote in 1892 that 'The problem of our own time is to secure for the whole community not political but economic freedom. We must frankly recognise that our task is to convert, by the aid of the English genius for representative self-government, a political into a social democracy.'[91] Liberal imperialists (and anti-socialists) such as the Prime Minister Lord Rosebery lamented the fact that there were not many representatives of the working classes in Parliament.[92] Yet he did not suggest a remedy.

In the rest of the world issues around suffrage were moving too. During the 1880s, Belgian politics was dominated by two parties: the rural-based and conservative Confessional Catholic Party and the anticlerical Liberals. The dispute between them centred mainly on the question of secular education, the so-called School War (*la guerre scolaire*). The suffrage was still severely restricted. A socialist party emerged only in 1885/6, helped by the rise in unemployment and the hardship caused by an unduly severe winter.[93] Alfred Defuisseaux, one of the founders of the Belgian Socialist Party, produced a pamphlet, 'Le catéchisme du peuple' (1886), which sold some 300,000 copies, in the form of questions and answers (as in the Catholic catechism) such as these:

Q. Article 25 of the Constitution says: 'All powers come from the nation.' Is it true?

A. It is a lie.

Q. Why?

A. Because the nation is made up of 5,720,807 inhabitants. Let's say 6 million, and of these 6 million, only 117,000 are involved in making laws.

Q. How come 6 million are ruled by 117,000?

A. Because to vote you must pay 42.32 francs in taxes and in Belgium only 117,000 citizens pay this . . .[94]

The Socialists organized a demonstration (13 June 1886) in favour of universal manhood suffrage. This was followed in 1893 by a general strike (the first in Europe).[95] The result was a near-victory: all males could vote, though some had more than one vote depending on income and education. By 1906 the electorate had expanded from 136,000 to 850,000 and the Socialists obtained a quarter of the vote, though the Confessional Catholic Party further enshrined its hold on government.[96]

In Italy, too, what was a highly restricted suffrage (2.2 per cent of the adult population) was extended in 1882 to all adult males who were not illiterate *or* who paid a minimum tax. The result was that the suffrage was extended to almost 7 per cent of the population – still a very long way from the 'advanced' countries.[97] Giuseppe Zanardelli, the architect of the law (and also a champion of many social and civil reforms – he abolished capital punishment in 1889), thought that, in principle, all males should be allowed to vote as long as they possessed some '*cultura intellettuale*'. Hence the exclusion of the illiterates who did not pay taxes.[98]

Germany was, in terms of the extension of the suffrage, the most democratic country in Europe along with Greece and France. Elections were frequent (every three years) and virtually all seats were contested (unlike Britain where one-fourth were not).[99] But the Reichstag (the federal parliament) was not very powerful. It could not appoint the Chancellor or dismiss him, though it could make life difficult for him. And it did. Almost all significant pieces of legislation were modified by the Reichstag against the wishes of Bismarck and his government.[100] Foreign policy and overall taxation remained in the hands of the executive. Elections, however, contributed to the growing 'nationalization' of the German electorate in that there was increased popular participation in them. In 1871, when universal manhood suffrage was introduced, only 52 per cent cast their vote; by 1912 it was 85 per cent. The beneficiaries were the mainly rural Catholic Zentrum Party and the Socialists of the SPD.[101]

Democracy began a cautious advance even in deeply aristocratic Meiji Japan. At the purely formal level this was recognized when, on 6 April 1868, the young Meiji Emperor accepted a Charter Oath under which 'all classes, high and low' would be represented.[102] If taken seriously this would have meant the abolition of the entire caste establishment of the old Tokugawa system.[103] In reality the suffrage included all males but with such restrictive property qualifications that only one per cent of the population (half a million) could vote.[104] The new constitution, enacted in 1889, drafted by Itō Hirobumi, the first Prime Minister of Japan, ensured that, ultimately, power would remain concentrated in the hands of the Council of State (the *dajōkan*). It was necessary, Itō explained, to bolster the monarchy, otherwise 'politics will fall into the hands of the incontrollable masses; and then the government will become powerless, and the country will be ruined'.[105] The constitution contained 'Western' phrases, declaring that the government would govern 'with the consent of the National Assembly'. Some thought this was too daringly democratic but, given the highly restricted franchise, there was little to worry about.[106] The numbers of those enfranchised grew slowly over the years, though in 1914 the electorate was still below 10 per cent.[107] Real universal manhood suffrage was reached only in 1925.

Japan was irrevocably changing as a bourgeois ethos was beginning to descend on what Westerners (but not the Japanese) liked to call the 'land of the rising sun'. Members of the Japanese intelligentsia started questioning aristocratic values. While the government wanted the franchise to remain narrow, the opposition wanted it widened; but neither wanted genuine democracy. Those who called for a wider suffrage used the increasingly frequent argument that Western strength rested on greater democracy.[108] Yukichi Fukuzawa, the founder of Keio University and of the influential newspaper *Jiji-Shinpo* (see Chapter 3), opened his famous 1872 essay 'Encouragement of Learning' with a clear statement of equality: 'Heaven does not create persons above other persons, nor does it create persons below other persons.'[109]

In the United States the issue of who had the right to vote was particularly contested, thus underlining the importance of elections. The level of electoral participation in the first decades after independence was exceptionally high, especially by modern standards: there was an 80 per cent turnout in New Hampshire in 1814 and over 96 per cent in Alabama in 1819. By the middle of the nineteenth century, the USA and Canada had the highest turnout in the world.[110] Then turnout decreased, though with ups and downs. After the Civil War, it dropped severely in the defeated South from 50 per cent in 1872 to 30 per cent in 1908.[111] Turnout improved after that but remained low by Western standards: in the 2016 presidential election turnout was a paltry 60 per cent.

It was not clear who could decide the extension of the suffrage – the Federal Congress or the individual states. Since the Constitution was ambiguous, it was left to the US Congress to decide who was a citizen, while leaving each state the right to decide who could vote – hardly a recipe for clarity. For several decades after the adoption of the Constitution (1787) only white males with some property (5 per cent of the population) were enfranchised. In 1856 property restrictions for all white males were finally removed in the last state to preserve them: North Carolina. In 1857 the US Supreme Court ruled in *Dred Scott v. Sandford* that blacks, even if free, could not be American citizens. In 1866, after the Civil War and the abolition of slavery (enshrined in the first of the so-called Reconstruction Amendments, the Thirteenth), Congress passed the Civil Rights Act, extending citizenship and the right to vote to black men. President Andrew Johnson (who had succeeded Lincoln) twice attempted to block the measure. He was a man who believed that blacks should be kept 'in order' and be civilized by whites.[112] A two-thirds majority in Congress overruled him and, eventually, another Reconstruction Amendment, the Fifteenth (1870), enshrined in law the right of black men to be full citizens and hence to vote. Native Americans had to wait until the Indian Citizenship Act of 1924 before becoming fully fledged citizens with voting rights.

The Republicans, the leading force in the abolition of slavery, remained a minority force in the South for the rest of the nineteenth century (and most of the twentieth), though they dominated presidential politics. Between 1861 and 1933 all presidents but two (Grover Cleveland and Woodrow Wilson) were Republican.[113] In the decades following the Civil War the Republicans used their power to promote Northern business interests rather than civil rights in the South. In the South, the dominant Democrats restricted the suffrage to whites through measures such as poll taxes, voters' registration, and levels of education. When this failed they resorted to naked violence.[114] Literacy test were also instituted in Northern states in the years after 1889, mainly to keep immigrants off the electoral register. In the years following the First World War most of those born in the United States, including women and Native Americans, acquired the right to vote (in 1956, Utah was the last state to give Native Americans the vote).

However, the eventual enfranchisement of blacks and women did not bring about any significant change in the American political-party system. Throughout the nineteenth and twentieth centuries and into the twentieth-first, elections were fought almost exclusively between Republicans and Democrats. No serious third party emerged to challenge this duopoly. A contributing factor behind this apparent immobility was the instability of party ideologies. In the nineteenth century the Democratic Party was in favour of states' rights whereas Republicans were, in American political parlance, 'federalist'. In the course of the twentieth century the position reversed. Similarly, the Republicans who in the nineteenth century were the party of industrial progress had become by the late twentieth century the defenders of traditional values. Unfettered by anything resembling ideologies, embracing a somewhat à la carte belief system, the two parties, elected by a diminishing proportion of the electorate, seldom higher than 60 per cent since the beginning of the twentieth century, carved up the entire political system to an extent unparalleled in Europe.

In the United States class did not play a significant role. Voters cast their vote on the basis of geographical location, religious affiliation, ethnicity, or issues such as prohibition, and Sunday closing (and more recently abortion, gun control, and gay marriage).[115] In Europe the pattern was different. The enlargement of the franchise brought about a new party system, and, notably, the rise of two formidable forces: Social Democrats and 'social' Christians. The socialists were based on the working class and the trade unions but extended their influence well beyond these. Their ideology was somewhat schizophrenic. On the one hand they held a vision of a future post-capitalist society leading to a classless and stateless society; on the other they promulgated a series of reforms (welfare states, civil rights, control of markets) that strengthened the existing state of affairs and improved capitalism. On the one hand they denounced nationalism and appealed to the 'workers of the world'; on the other they were intransigent defenders of the nation state once it became the main instrument of reformist policies.

Only after the First World War did parties of the left become one of the two leading contenders for power in most of Europe's democratic countries. They were not insignificant before 1914: socialist parties obtained 47 per cent of the vote in Finland; over 30 per cent in Sweden, Norway, Belgium, and Germany; over 25 per cent in Austria and Denmark; and 16 per cent in France. In Great Britain, one of the most industrialized countries in Europe, the trade unions and the workers still favoured the Liberal Party over the recently formed Labour Party. Only after 1918 did they shift their position.

The second force that emerged in Europe after the enlargement of the franchise were the social Christian parties – parties such as the Anti-Revolutionary Party in the Netherlands, the Zentrum in Germany, and various agrarian or farmers' parties in the Scandinavian countries. In Belgium there was a powerful Catholic Party, which dominated politics during the decades prior to the First World War.

Social Christians were, in their own way, as ambivalent as the socialists. On the one hand they were committed to the defence of traditional values, especially those of the rural world, their electoral basis; on the other they had to engage with modernity, with capitalism, with consumerism and, in so doing, abandon their commitment to tradition.

Like the socialists, the social Christians despised the state as an alien force celebrating modernity and individualism, but, when in power, they used the state machinery uninhibitedly to favour the social groups who supported them, namely small farmers and artisans.

Suffrage had shifted with the rising prosperity brought by industrialization. Previously, voting restrictions were based on class, property, income – in other words fear of propertyless masses – whereas by the twentieth century, if they existed at all, they tended to be based on age, nationality, ethnicity, and gender. The suffrage exacerbated the contradictory nature of modern politics. Parties had to appeal to a fragmented electorate where each person had only one vote but different desires and different identities: class, region, religion, age, prejudices, etc. Parties had to be in favour of capitalism since that seemed to ensure a modicum of progress for the majority; but they were never sure what kind of capitalism would meet the aspirations of their electors. The world of electoral politics, born in the nineteenth century, reserved endless surprises for the politicians of the twentieth century. Neither the economy nor politics could stand still in the new modern era.

14
Private Affluence, Public Welfare

Voting is important in nation-building, but living standards are more important. It is difficult, though not impossible, to build a nation on empty stomachs. Nevertheless, throughout the decades leading up to 1914, the evolving consensus around capitalism was constructed largely on constantly growing prosperity. Of course, we were still far from the consumer society so often celebrated and occasionally criticized in the 1950s by social scientists such as David Riesman, Nathan Glazer, and Reuel Denney (*The Lonely Crowd: A Study of the Changing American Character*, 1950), and John K. Galbraith in *The Affluent Society* (1958), but the concept was in the air much earlier. The Christian socialist historian R. H. Tawney in *The Acquisitive Society* (1920) lambasted capitalism for producing so much 'waste' and so much stuff that 'should not have been produced at all', stuff 'which fill[ed] shop windows in Regent Street . . .'[1]

Keynes, writing in 1919, was more positive:

> perhaps a day might come when there would be enough to go round . . . In that day overwork, overcrowding, and underfeeding would come to an end, and men, secure of the comforts and necessities of the body, could proceed to the nobler exercise of their faculties.[2]

Even earlier, another economist, Simon Patten, in his 1905 Kennedy Lectures had noted the remarkable improvements in the condition and consumption of workers and assumed that it would be possible to eliminate poverty in a few decades.[3] He did not deny that 'the working people of industrial centres are ill paid, that employment is uncertain, housing is bad, sickness frequent, and that the abnormally short working life ends in an old age of poverty and fear', yet no one, he claimed, could deny the evidence of growing prosperity.[4]

Americans were already discussing the question of abundance and consumption at a time when few in Europe were doing so. Around

1900, as we have seen (Chapter 2), the average American family spent most of their income on food, fuel, and rent.[5] Yet, there were already signs of an emerging consumer society: a shorter working week, the display of goods in department stores, and the growth of popular entertainment.[6] Advertising began to be a real industry, even though, at the time, most traded goods were consumed predominantly by the top layers of society.[7] There was even the beginning of 'ethical' consumption, started by the National Consumers League, founded in 1891, which opposed child labour and poor working conditions, declaring that this stance should be reflected in the selections of goods one bought. This lead was followed in France by 'La ligue sociale d'acheteurs', started by Henriette Jean Brunhes, a socially inclined Catholic hostile to industrialism.[8] The League had a list of stores and suppliers that did not force their staff to work excessive hours or on Sunday.[9]

Americans could already detect the embryonic elements of a consumer society in which workers would be earning a 'living wage' and hence acquire dignity.[10] Conservatives were already moralizing about the profligacy of the poor, while social theorists such as Thorstein Veblen, in his celebrated *The Theory of the Leisure Class* (1899), castigated the consumption habits of the rich. Consumption, he claimed, was decreasingly aimed at satisfying genuine wants and increasingly directed at establishing status (though aristocrats had been at it for centuries). The consumption of the higher classes reinforced their domination: 'the consumption of luxuries, in the true sense, is a consumption directed to the comfort of the consumer himself, and is, therefore, the mark of the master'.[11]

David Hume was aware of this, but, less puritanically than Veblen, he thought the consumption of luxuries was a sign of civilization:

> The increase and consumption of all the commodities, which serve to the ornament and pleasure of life, are advantages to society . . . In a nation where there is no demand for such superfluities, men sink into indolence, lose all enjoyment of life, and are useless to the public . . .[12]

There is, as everyone knows, a cultural-class element in consumption: it is often the case that a worker who gets richer lives like a rich worker and not like a professional middle-class person.

Americans did not just produce more and better. They consumed. The department store was invented in Europe, but the Americans created a multiplicity of chain stores, large retailers that exploited their size by mass purchasing, sometimes using catalogues for mail orders – the precursor of online shopping – causing fierce resistance from shopkeepers, some of whom ceremoniously burned catalogues in public.[13] The key was in the marketing. Richard Sears created Sears, Roebuck & Co. in Chicago; F. W. Woolworth's small shop in 1879 became the largest retailer in the world; John Wanamaker, whose first store opened in Philadelphia in 1861, invented (it is said) the price tag, offered a money-back guarantee to his customers and allowed them to wander freely in the store examining the merchandise. In 1908, Henry Ford introduced the Model T Ford, having announced 'I will build a motor car for the great multitude . . . But it will be so low in price that no man making a good salary will be unable to own one – and enjoy with his family the blessing of hours of pleasure in God's great open spaces.'[14] Edward Filene, the department store magnate and philanthropist, had no doubts: consumption trumped democracy. 'The masses of Americans,' he declared in 1932, 'have elected Henry Ford. They have elected General Motors. They have elected the General Electric Company and Woolworth's and all the other great industrial and business leaders of the day.'[15]

In 1884 the National Cash Register Company was founded in Dayton, Ohio (the machine had been invented in 1879). It soon employed 1,000 people to produce 15,000 cash registers annually.[16] The supermarket trolley too was invented in America. It was devised in 1936 by Sylvan N. Goldman, who had noted that one of the obstacles to purchasing was not always financial or taste but simply a physical constraint: an individual could only carry a limited amount. One of his advertisements sang the praises of being able to 'wend your way through a spacious food market without having to carry a cumbersome shopping basket on your arm . . .'[17]

Much of what is still present on people's breakfast and dinner plates has its origin in pre-1914 America: Quaker Oats, Campbell soups, Heinz baked beans, Libby tinned and processed meat.[18] Shredded Wheat breakfast was already advertised in 1902, Whitman's Chocolate in 1902, and Wrigley's Spearmint Gum in 1913.[19] In 1906 the Battle Creek Toasted Corn Flake Company was created (it changed its name to Kellogg's in 1922) to develop the production of breakfast foods that would transform daily morning habits first in the United States and later in Europe.

Not all the innovations in everyday living started out in America: the first department store was Le Bon Marché, founded in Paris 1838 and completely redeveloped in 1852; the first automated vending machine selling food and drink opened in Berlin in 1895. Nevertheless it was in America that such innovations in the organization of consumption developed and expanded to unprecedented levels.

The true basis of the great consensus that legitimized American capitalism was the transformation of citizens into consumers. This developed in the decades after the Civil War. The system could work not just for the robber barons and the filthy rich but also for ordinary people. What was coming into being was not just an industrial society but a world of consumers united by their position in the marketplace and unconnected to religion and traditional values.[20]

Edward Bellamy's 1888 novel *Looking Backward: From 2000 to 1887* imagined a young American, Julian West, waking up in the year 2000 to discover that Boston had become a gigantic shopping centre where everyone had a home full of appliances such as telephones and machines producing recorded music.[21] They even had credit cards – a term used in the book, though the cards themselves were not introduced until the 1920s. In the novel, however, the cards were the mode of payment in what appeared to be a socialist society: 'A credit corresponding to his share of the annual product of the nation is given to every citizen . . . at the beginning of each year, and a credit card issued him with which he procures at the public storehouses . . . whatever he desires, whenever he desires it.'[22] Competition between firms had long been replaced by a single giant corporation, in effect the government. Bellamy had dreamt up a communist-capitalist utopia based on consumption in which the people shopped constantly, no one was poor, and everyone was happy.

Two opposing myths, one triumphant and optimistic, the other sombre and tragic, but both containing some truth, sought to explain the American miracle. The first narrative was essentially liberal: ordinary people free from the prejudices of the Old World and able to compete as individuals in the marketplace, repelled the growth of government and became prosperous, in fact, the most prosperous people in the world, while remaining free. By 1949 an average income in the United States was 1,453 dollars at a time when no other country exceeded 900 dollars; the runner-ups were Canada, New Zealand, and Switzerland (800–900 dollars), followed by Sweden and the United Kingdom (700–800 dollars).[23]

David M. Potter, a historian writing in 1954, waxed lyrical over the wonders of the American model: 'Everyone knows that we have, per capita, more automobiles, more telephones, more radios, more vacuum cleaners, more electric lights, more bathtubs, more supermarkets, more movie palaces and hospitals than any other nations.' Abundance was a conspicuous feature of American life, he continued. America had a greater measure of social equality and social mobility than any other society in human history. Business was conducted as if social barriers did not exist. But the citizen had to be 'educated to perform his role as a consumer, especially as a consumer of goods for which he feels no impulse of need'. The only institutions 'we have for instilling new needs, for training people to act as consumers, for altering men's values, and thus for hastening their adjustment to potential abundance is advertising. That is why it seems to me valid to regard advertising as distinctively the institution of abundance.' The perils of advertising, together with those of waste, were, in David Potter's somewhat starry-eyed narrative, the only cause for concern.[24]

The second narrative, favoured by left-wing and populist historians, described the United States as a country taken over by capitalists who were bent on destroying a developing democracy by naked force and bribery, who stamped upon the human spirit, and imposed a system based on greed and the accumulation of wealth in the hands of the few.[25] People were made to work hard in order to buy goods they do not need and which do not make them any happier. On the contrary, devoured by envy, they are unhappy when others have what they themselves do not have. Consumption sets individuals against individuals in a race no one can win since capitalism constantly creates new goods that make everything you had before quite obsolete. The only beneficiaries of this 'Joyless Economy' (the title of a book by the economist Tibor Scitovsky, published in 1976) are large corporations. The clash between these two narratives, writ large at the planetary level, still informs most politics.

A consumer society required a level of earnings greater than that needed to provide the 'basic' necessities such as food, clothing, heating, and lodging, though even these are culturally and financially determined (lobster or polenta?; any old jeans or Giorgio Armani's?; penthouse or trailer?). In France, as elsewhere, clothing was the first item that benefited from the reduction in the proportion of expenditure on food in the 1880s.[26]

In the United States in the 1880s, of the 12.5 million families recorded in the census, 12 per cent had an income greater than $1,200 a year (and 200,000 of these had an income higher than $5,000). One can thus surmise that most of non-food consumption was then directed towards the top 12 per cent, and most luxury consumption would be absorbed by the richest one per cent whose total income was larger than that of the poorest 50 per cent.[27] After 1910 the USA grew not only richer (as was the case with most European countries) but also increasingly unequal in terms of income until 1940. Income inequalities then dropped sharply only to start a new climb in the 1980s.[28]

The United States was well ahead of European countries in the construction of a consumer society. The wealthier European countries, as well as Canada, New Zealand, and Australia, followed, at some distance, catching up with the United States only in the decades after the Second World (along with various Asian enclaves of prosperity such as Singapore, Hong Kong, Qatar, South Korea, Japan, and Israel). Private consumption, on its own, does not provide a sufficient index of well-being because the real revenue of ordinary people is made up not only of their post-tax income but also of the benefits they get in kind or in cash. A worker with a take-home pay of, say, $300 a week, may appear to 'earn' more than one on $200. But if the latter is a citizen of a country with an advanced welfare state, free healthcare, free childcare, free education for the children, and a pension when she retires, all paid for from taxation, that is not so.

One can also look at this from the point of view of employers who, in the absence of any kind of state benefits, may have to pay their workers more than those living under a generous welfare system. In other words welfare can also be seen as a state subsidy for private sector wages. It became the role of democratic and socialist parties to promote welfare for those who had not risen far enough up the ladder of consumption.

Werner Sombart, in his 1906 classic *Why is there no Socialism in the United States?*, attributed the failure to develop a socialist party to the comfortable circumstances and high standard of living of the American worker (there was, as we shall see, a socialist party in the United States but presumably not big enough for Sombart). He wrote, 'All Socialist utopias came to nothing on roast beef and apple pie.'[29] Earlier than Sombart, on 24 October 1891, Friedrich Engels, in a letter to Friedrich Sorge (a socialist leader who had emigrated from Germany to the USA), discussing the apparent lack of radicalism of American workers, surmised that it was due to their higher standard of living (as compared to that of European workers).[30] And even earlier than Engels, the American journalist and founder of *The Nation*, Edwin L. Godkin, pointed out that the real issue lay in the attitude of the working man who, having realized that the capitalist he was confronting had once been a working man, could entertain the hope of becoming a capitalist.[31]

This explanation for the alleged lack of radicalism of American workers was based on the alleged social mobility of Americans in contrast to the rigid hierarchy of classes in Europe – the idea that only in America could a poor man, just landed on the East Coast, aspire to become a millionaire. Sombart's reasoning rests with the somewhat simplistic notion that poverty is a powerful force in the creation of a socialist party, a causal relationship for which there is little evidence. (European socialist parties tended to rely on the support of the best-paid, organized, and skilled workers, not the very poor.) Other plausible explanations for the lack of a strong socialist party in the United States (no feudalism, the two-party system, relative prosperity, the constantly moving frontier, massive immigration, and ethnic divisions, etc.) remain unsatisfactory.[32] Australia, which shared some similarities with the United States (ethnic problems, immigrant working class, lack of feudalism, similar electoral system, egalitarian ideals) did not follow the USA and developed a strong Labour Party, as did New Zealand.[33]

Socialist parties in the mould of the Second International were essentially a continental European phenomenon. They were almost non-existent in Latin America, Africa, or Asia. While there were parties everywhere espousing ideas of progress similar to those of traditional socialist parties, they did not attribute the key agency for advancing human progress to the working class, nor did they envisage a future classless society. Great Britain, though industrially more advanced than other European countries, had no strong socialist party until after 1918. So the United States, at least at the time, was not so 'exceptional' in not having a strong socialist party. In any case the Socialist Party of America (SPA) was, before the First World War, only a little weaker than the British Labour Party, founded in the same year (1901). By 1912 the SPA, with almost 120,000 members, had 1,200 elected local government officials and the mayors of important industrial cities such as Milwaukee (Wisconsin), home of the world's largest breweries, and Flint in Michigan, home before the First World War of Buick and General Motors.[34] The SPA boasted 323 papers and periodicals, including eight foreign-language dailies. The socialist paper *Appeal to Reason* (founded in 1895) had a weekly circulation of almost 400,000.[35] Eugene Debs, one of the founders of the Industrial Workers of the World, won over 900,000 votes (6 per cent of the total) as the candidate for the SPA in the 1912 presidential elections. His demands were quite uncompromising:

> We demand the abolition of capitalism and wage-slavery and the surrender of the capitalist class. We demand the complete enfranchisement of women and the equal rights of all the people regardless of race, color, creed or

> nationality. We demand that child labor shall cease once and forever and that all children born into the world shall have equal opportunity to grow up, to be educated, to have healthy bodies and trained minds, and to develop and freely express the best there is in them in mental, moral and physical achievement.[36]

American trade unions were then a powerful force, in spite of the constant stream of immigrants and the anti-union violence. They had the respect of their counterparts in Europe. Thus the first day of May, celebrated today as a workers' holiday throughout Europe and in many other parts of the world, but not, ironically, in the United States, was chosen to commemorate the demonstration in Haymarket Square in Chicago (1886) in favour of the eight-hour day. International Women's Day (now 8 March) was first decreed by the Socialist Party of America in solidarity with the strike of 1908 by the International Ladies' Garment Workers' Union, eventually one of the largest American unions. Social conflicts intensified. Workers organized unions, farmers established cooperatives. By the end of 1889 it might have been possible to imagine the unification of urban and rural protest groups into a kind of American populist-socialist party. Yet American unions chose not to follow the British example and form a labour party.[37]

Such efforts led instead to organizations such as the Farmers' Alliances and the People's Party (known as the 'Populists') founded in 1891 (though its founding convention was on 4 July 1892 when the Omaha Platform was adopted), whose aim was to challenge the economic and political power of the businesses and corporations that controlled the financing and distribution of agricultural produce.[38] In 1892 the Populists obtained 8.5 per cent of the vote in the presidential election. In 1896 they endorsed the Democratic presidential nominee, William Jennings Bryan, who obtained 46.7 per cent of the vote, though he lost the election (Bryan's main platform was a demand for the free and unlimited coinage of silver, an inflationary solution to the farmers' problem of low commodity prices). The Republicans (William McKinley) while endorsing the gold standard also pushed for protectionism. Bryan was openly critical of the Northeast and was reluctant to appeal to non-rural voters. During the subsequent four years of acute depression the People's Party rapidly declined.

The Progressive Party, created by Theodore Roosevelt, from the left of the Republicans, obtained 27.4 per cent in the 1912 presidential elections on a platform that included a national health service, social insurance, the eight-hour day, and a federal income tax. It was the highest percentage ever obtained by a third party in an American presidential election. Roosevelt's electoral campaign was unashamedly radical:

> There once was a time in history when the limitation of governmental power meant increasing liberty for the people. In the present day the limitation of governmental power, of governmental action, means the enslavement of the people by the great corporations, who can only be held in check through the extension of governmental power.[39]

The outgoing President William Howard Taft (who obtained 23 per cent) had also pursued left-of-centre policies (antitrust legislation, and the introduction of a corporate income tax). In fact, during his single term in office he launched twice as many antitrust suits as Roosevelt.[40] The new president, Woodrow Wilson, during his first term in office (1913–17) introduced the most progressive legislation in the United States before Franklin Roosevelt's New Deal. In 1900, Wilson had denounced trust busters as unrealistic reactionaries who want to return to a world that can no longer exist. By the time of his presidential campaign of 1912 he had come round to their views:

> we used to think in the old-fashioned days when life was very simple that all that government had to do was to put on a policeman's uniform and keep out of business. But now business is conducted by huge corporations and not individual entrepreneurs, it is a public affair in need of government regulation.[41]

In 1912, unlike in 2012, America was in tune with the kind of interventionist liberalism that prevailed in much of Europe. Here are the results for the four main candidates, none of whom was right-wing or conservative by today's standards:

Table 12 USA Presidential Election, 1912

Candidates	Party	Percentage
Woodrow Wilson	Democrat	41.8
Theodore Roosevelt	Progressive	27.4
William Howard Taft	Republican	23.2
Eugene Debs	Socialist	5.9

Much of the progressivism of early twentieth-century America may be regarded just as populist rhetoric, yet it was a sign that one had to be somewhat hostile to business to do well in elections.

Consistency did not always prevail. For instance, the same Theodore Roosevelt who was worried about large corporations in 1912 had been eulogizing about them in 1901 (when, at the age of forty-two, he became President after the assassination of William McKinley by an anarchist), just as Woodrow Wilson had done. In his first message to Congress in 1901, Roosevelt had declared that:

> The captains of industry who have driven the railway systems across this continent, who have built up our commerce, who have developed our manufactures, have on the whole done great good to our people. Without them the material development of which we are so justly proud could never have taken place . . . . The mechanism of modern business is so delicate that extreme care must be taken not to interfere with it in a spirit of rashness or ignorance. Many of those who have made it their vocation to denounce the great industrial combinations which are popularly, although with technical inaccuracy, known as 'trusts' appeal especially to hatred and fear.[42]

But he was soon attacking the 'trusts', declaring that the state had the duty to control the great corporations. It was the beginning of the so-called Progressive Era, full of promises about fairness, anti-monopoly legislation, regulating the railway industry, enacting laws against the adulteration of food (such as the Pure Food and Drug Act, 1906), mediating between coal miners and coal owners, and establishing national parks. Progressivism was not confined to the presidential office. One of the most remarkable exponents of the Progressive Era and of Midwestern reformism was Robert M. La Follette ('Fighting Bob'), a Republican (and later a Progressive) politician who was a congressman (1885–91), then Governor of Wisconsin (1901–6), finally Senator (1906–25) and who, as the presidential candidate for his Progressive Party in 1924, obtained 17 per cent of the vote. Following the depression of the 1890s, there were plenty of protests, particularly in cities such as Chicago and Milwaukee, against inadequate public services, unjust taxation, or corruption in local government.[43] What was missing in the various progressive platforms emerging in the United States was a conception of state welfare. Here the USA, then as now, was well behind the European countries.

Concern for the welfare of the poor is, per se, not new. In ancient Greece and Rome philanthropy was regarded as a duty of the nobility. Although encouraged in the Old Testament, giving to the poor is not one of the Ten Commandments. Islam is different: *Zakat*, one of the five pillars of Islam, is the compulsory and regular giving of 2.5 per cent of one's wealth to the poor. Competition between Protestants and Catholics in sixteenth-century Europe led to a spread of schemes for poor relief 'from Augsburg to Zurich by way of London, Paris, Nuremberg, Ypres, Madrid, Toledo, Venice and a great many places besides'.[44] In England, the Poor Laws, introduced in 1601 under Elizabeth I (though some poor relief already existed) and administered by parishes, continued in a constantly modified form down to the first half of the twentieth century. In the early nineteenth century almost 10 per cent of the population was covered by such poor relief.[45]

Poor relief was always a matter of controversy. At the end of the eighteenth century and at the beginning of the nineteenth, the intelligentsia, especially in Britain, turned vehemently against public charity. Thomas Malthus (a clergyman as well as an economist and demographer) thought that giving money to the poor would lead them to have more children and make them even poorer. The Poor Laws, he wrote in *An Essay on the Principle of Population* (1798), 'may have alleviated a little the intensity of individual misfortune' but 'they have spread the general evil over a much larger surface'.[46] It was not the business of the state, he explained, to use public revenue for the benefit of the unfortunate or undeserving few.[47] Two years later even Malthus was ready to admit that in some circumstances (e.g. famine) 'the system of poor laws' (which he still 'heartily' condemned) would be necessary.[48] Recent scholarship supports the view that, at least at times of bad harvest, and certainly from the mid-sixteenth to mid-seventeenth century, poor relief kept mortality down.[49] But at the time not just dreary pessimists like Malthus but even 'enlightened' liberal thinkers from Jeremy Bentham (*Observations on the Poor Bill*, 1797) to David Ricardo agreed that poor relief was counter-productive. Explicitly endorsing Malthus's views, Ricardo wrote that 'the poor laws' were not 'as the legislature benevolently intended . . . to amend the condition of the poor, but to deteriorate the condition of both poor and rich; instead of making the poor rich, they are calculated to make the rich poor.'[50] The campaign against the indolence of the poor, which is vigorously waged to this day, led to the great Poor Law Amendment Act 1834, perhaps the most important piece of social legislation of the nineteenth century, affecting almost every aspect of life and labour in Victorian Britain.[51]

Then as now the main preoccupation of the lawmakers was that any form of charity, state or otherwise, might be a disincentive to trying to find work. It was widely agreed that the so-called 'impotent' poor (i.e. the disabled or the elderly) should be provided for. The vagrant would be sent to a kind of prison. But what about the able-bodied poor? One must not protect the lazy. The solution was to make the conditions of recipients worse than those they would have encountered had they been working.[52]

In the course of the nineteenth century poor relief decreased rapidly everywhere in Europe.[53] While Britain had, at the end of the eighteenth century, the most wide-reaching poor laws, it was revolutionary France that first established the principle that society owes some form of subsistence to citizens in misfortune, either by providing work or the means of existence to those unable to work. The Convention nationale (i.e. the Constituent Assembly) had even tried in 1793 to abolish private philanthropy (in 1789 there were 27,000 charitable institutions; by 1848 the number was down to 1,800).[54] The reason given was that the relief of indigence should be the business of the state and not of private citizens: a citizen in a state of poverty should not be further humiliated by receiving charity from another citizen. To be helped was a *right*, explained Pierre-Roger Ducos, a member of the Convention nationale.[55] Article 21 of the Declaration of the Rights of Man and of the Citizen promulgated (but not adopted) in 1793 (not to be confused with the more important but less 'Jacobin' Declaration of August 1789) states that 'public relief is a sacred obligation. Society owes subsistence to citizens in misfortune, by providing work, or, for those unable to work, the means of existence.'

In 1791, Tom Paine in *The Rights of Man* had developed the idea of allocating public grants to families with children under the age of fourteen (a form of family allowance not introduced anywhere in the world before the twentieth century) and a pension to all those over fifty.[56] Two years later, the Marquis de Condorcet, Paine's fellow member of the Convention, devoted the last chapter of his *Esquisse d'un tableau historique des progrès de l'esprit humain* (published posthumously in 1795) to what a social insurance system might look like; how it could reduce inequality, insecurity, and poverty; and how it would be financed partly by 'people's own savings and partly by the saving of others'.[57]

This concern did not last. Already in Thermidor (July–August 1794), when reaction set in, another *conventionnel*, Jean-Baptiste-Joseph Delecroy, complained there were not enough public funds: 'It is time to get out of that rut where we have been confined by too generous a philanthropic attitude in the days of the Constituent Assembly.'[58] At the time liberals had a position on welfare that today would be associated with right-wing neo-conservatives. The great liberal economist Jean-Baptiste Say, in his *Cours complet d'économie politique practique* (1829), declared that society does not owe any help or subsistence to any of its members.[59] Alexis de Tocqueville in his *Mémoire sur le paupérisme* (1835) maintained that any regular system of help towards the poor will cause their number to grow, will increase misery, and bring about the deterioration of trade and industry. He contrasted public charity (of which he disapproved) to private philanthropy (of which he approved). Having examined England's poor laws, 'the only country in Europe which has systematized and massively applied the theories on public charity on a grand scale', the great liberal concluded that though rights are all very well, the right to public charity humiliated those who received it, unlike charity privately received.[60]

Forty years and four political regimes later (the Orléans monarchy, Second Republic, Second Empire, Third Republic), French liberals were still upset about public assistance. In 1872, Paul Leroy-Beaulieu, the editor of *L'Économiste français*, contrasted Britain unfavourably to France, arguing that in Britain public charity (unlike private charity) diminished human dignity, was costly and counter-productive, and that all leading British economists agreed with him – or so he said.[61] He accepted that the workhouse regime was very harsh.[62] Matters were far better in France where there is no public charity, where the poor are (rightly) left to look after themselves, and where, should a local authority want to help them, it would do so out of charity and not to repay a 'social debt', since the poor have no rights.[63] British workers, he explained (with little empirical evidence), just spend everything they earn knowing that they will be looked after when they are old.[64] British welfare legislation had gone too far. Working only ten hours a day and resting on Sundays and on holidays such as Christmas was not such a bad life, he opined; it left workers with plenty of leisure time, if only they knew what to do with it.[65]

As a consequence of this liberal anti-welfare attitude, France, though politically more radical than England or Germany, lagged behind in terms of social policies.[66] Even when the Republicans gained control of the Republic in 1879, no drastic move was made to increase poor relief.[67] Not until the late 1880s were some timid steps taken towards welfare.

The Third Republic was 'radical' only in intention or only in its anticlericalism. Not for nothing did Madeleine Rebérioux doubt its radicalism with a question mark in *La République radicale?*[68] The radicals had been mocked as radishes: 'rouges à l'extérieur, blancs à l'intérieur, et toujours près de l'assiette au beurre' ('red on the outside, white on the inside, and always near the butter dish').[69] Yet the radicals hardly ever had a majority and, in the years leading up to the First World War, depended on the *Alliance républicaine démocratique* (ARD), a party founded in 1901 by followers of Léon Gambetta, who was tied to the business world.[70] The ARD too, however, claimed to be 'radical' and 'democratic'.

The main radical-republican leaders of the Third Republic, Jules Ferry and Léon Gambetta, cared little for social reforms. Gambetta was a typical nineteenth-century traditional liberal who did not believe there was something called the social question and was wary of state intervention. Competition was the solution to everything. Gambetta's salient trait as a radical consisted in being anticlerical.[71] He, like Georges Clemenceau later, started his career on the 'far' left, scaring the establishment, and then, as happens only too often, was regarded as an opportunist, as indeed the *Républicains modérés* came to be known. Even under the Second Empire, in 1868, Gambetta had been convinced that the solution to the 'social question' could only be found in liberal capitalism; the problem with Louis-Napoléon's empire was that it was not sufficiently pro-capitalist.[72] In 1872 (the empire had collapsed in 1870) when he toured some of the cities in western France, such as Le Havre and Rouen, Gambetta hinted that there might be a 'social question' by saying 'there is no social solution because there is not a real social question: one must solve problems one at a time, with patience.'[73] And when he considered new social groups entering politics – what he called *les nouvelles couches sociales* – he meant, above all, shopkeepers, artisans, employees, teachers, and doctors, as distinct from the notables.[74] Gambetta was far more concerned with not losing the support of the rural world than in gaining that of the working class.

Jules Ferry, the other great protagonist of republican France, held a similar view in the 1860s when Louis-Napoléon was still on the throne. The prosperity of the masses depended on capitalism and not on state intervention. Free enterprise will lower the cost of foodstuffs and increase wages. The elimination of poverty is not the business of the state; the state should not bother with stuff like compulsory insurance but should encourage savings.[75]

This explains at least in part why France, having taken a somewhat timid step earlier than other countries, with a national pension fund in 1850 and an accident insurance fund in 1868, was overtaken by all comparable countries in welfare benefits and especially in pensions.[76] The opposition to state-funded poor relief united both French Catholics (i.e. the conservatives) and liberals – the former because state charity would undermine clerical charity, the latter because it would undermine individualism.[77] Even a relatively reformist Prime Minister such as Pierre Waldeck-Rousseau thought that pensions should be left to associations of workers who ought to join forces to pay a subscription for their old age.[78]

The French paradox is that everyone, or, at least, all socialists, radical-socialists, and socially minded Catholics claimed to be in favour of social policy, yet those in power remained firmly attached to generic liberal principles, though there were some telling exceptions: wine growers whose vines had been affected by phylloxera received public help.[79] The rural votes mattered too much to stand in the way of liberal principles. Deputies and ministers were particularly susceptible to lobbying and to pressures partly because, as in Italy, there was no strong party system (as there was in Great Britain), and partly because even though there was remarkable homogeneity among the members of the republican majority, governments were exceedingly unstable. The Third Republic may have lasted seventy years (1870–1940) but each government did not last long; there were around 120 of them and the record-holder, the 1899 Waldeck-Rousseau government 'de défense Républicaine', lasted only three years.

What moved many French republicans towards welfare was not so much the plight of the poor as the realization that if the state did not intervene it would leave 'charity' to the good works of the Roman Catholic Church, strengthening its prestige. Thus the social question became part of the anticlerical battle and France turned more decisively in favour of public welfare. In 1893 medical cover for the poorest was established by law.[80] In 1905, as the battle against clericalism had been won with the law separating Church and State, public assistance was introduced for the over-seventies and the disabled.[81]

The main opposition to public assistance was now confined to Catholics of various hues and the odd ultra-liberal. During the 1903 parliamentary debate on national insurance a leading monarchist, the Comte Paul-Henri Lanjuinais, declared that in a really free country the state should limit itself to maintaining law and order and national defence. Everything concerning public welfare should be left to private initiative and, failing this, to local authorities. Pro-republican Catholics around the newly formed party *Action libérale populaire* were just as opposed to public welfare. One of their deputies, Pierre-Marc Arnal, used the slippery-slope argument: if you grant 'them' the right to welfare, next they will ask for the right to work and before you know it the budget of the state will be spent on such 'adventures', to the delight of the socialists.[82] In fact the right to work, the *droit au travail*, had already been accepted in the Second Republic (1848) and would become an international right enshrined in the United Nations Universal Declaration of Human Rights.

Socialists, as was to be expected, were all in favour of state welfare. Léon Mirman, an independent, wanted welfare to be a right and not part of state philanthropy:

> It would be a new world. Imagine! An old man . . . will no longer feel humiliated, shameful as those who are today on public assistance, but will hold his head high, no longer a prayer on his lips, but the law in his hand; he will . . . be able to claim his rights . . . not requiring any recommendation, protection or patronage, neither from the clergy nor from a masonic lodge to obtain a pension . . .[83]

Thanks to Mirman the text of the law was systematically modified: expressions such as 'indigent' became *ayant-droit* (having the right) and *recevoir l'assistance* (to be in receipt of assistance) was turned into *droit à l'assistance* (right to assistance).[84]

When, towards the end of the century, the radical-republican government led by Léon Bourgeois tried to introduce a progressive income tax to pay for compensation for industrial accidents, medical cover, and pensions, many liberals denounced it as a frontal attack on private property.[85] Bourgeois had to explain that his proposal was aimed at defusing the socialist threat. The 'Red Peril', whether real or imaginary, is often a useful argument for reforms; after all, the point of reforms was to make revolutions impossible. In his book *Solidarité* (1896), Bourgeois explained that it was necessary to distance oneself from both economic liberalism and socialism in favour of a 'superior goal' – that of solidarity – and that this required state intervention. He was thus aligning himself with mainstream liberal interventionists in Germany, Italy, and Great Britain.[86] By 1912, however, the average amount received per assisted person in France was still only one-fifth of the British level and French housing conditions were among the worst in western Europe.[87]

Impenitent as ever, the ultra-liberal Leroy-Beaulieu remained firm in his denunciation of what later would be known in Britain and the United States as 'the nanny state' but was already known, according to him, as 'great motherly legislation' (in English in the text):

> Western civilization owes its growth to individual vigour, to individual initiative, courage, foresight . . . qualities which separate Europeans and Americans . . . from other races . . . the whole system of paternalistic legislation, as the English say, great motherly legislation, tends to suppress and eliminate such qualities . . . We think this to be a detestable system

> which transforms members of civilized nations into perpetual children, spineless and sleepy.[88]

The term 'grandmotherly legislation', and not 'great motherly legislation' as Leroy-Beaulieu would have it, had been used by liberals such as Jevons in his last work, *The State in Relation to Labour* (1882), but, by the time Leroy-Beaulieu was deriding it, it was no longer used even in Britain.[89] British liberals had moved decisively towards defending the principle of state welfare. Thus the utilitarian philosopher Henry Sidgwick, writing in 1891 in the footsteps of Jeremy Bentham and John Stuart Mill, used the term 'paternal', aware that it was 'used with more or less sarcasm', to describe the circumstances in which individuals were helped by the state.[90]

Although backward on many welfare issues, the French, however, were ahead of most other countries in assisting mothers and their children. They helped large families and funded maternity crèches. By 1904 even the organized working class, though still giving priority to improving wages and working conditions, established associations such as the *Alliance d'hygiène sociale* (1904–11), which encouraged physical education for workers and their children, provided hot lunches in schools for poor children, tried to enforce hygiene in working-class homes, instructed women on the benefits of breastfeeding, and looked after unwed mothers. It was one of the rare forays of the labour movement onto a terrain so far occupied by philanthropists, liberal activists, and intellectuals.[91]

Public assistance was doled out by local, not central government, and much of this went to hospitals for abandoned children. There was an anticlerical element behind this since local authorities were afraid that abandoned children would be rescued by parishes and fall prey to the ideological zeal of priests. No doubt such pro-natalist policies were also largely due to the rapid drop in French fertility rates. In 1800, France had been the most populous country in non-Russian Europe. By 1850 it had been overtaken by Germany (i.e. the territories that eventually formed the united Germany of 1870).[92] Immigration into France, largely from Belgium and Italy, as well as from eastern Europe, alleviated the situation only a little.[93] Encouraging large families was something that united republican nationalists as well as Catholics. After France's defeat in the Franco-Prussian War of 1870, anxieties about depopulation (*dénatalité*) grew. These increased pressure for the establishment of a less perfunctory welfare state. It became a 'family welfare state' or even a 'maternalist' welfare state, one in which the state's solicitude was directed not so much towards women per se but rather towards women as mothers and wives.[94] Prominent social theorists and politicians 'ceased to castigate the unwed mother for her immorality'.[95]

Around 1910 anxieties about a drop in the birth rate also plagued some northern European countries, leading to demands for maternity reforms. In Norway the feminist Katti Anker Møller proposed a state salary for mothers (she was also a leader in the campaign for the rights of children born out of wedlock and for the decriminalization of abortion).[96] Similar demands were put forward by Swedish social democrats in early 1900s.[97] Increasingly, women entered the official labour market. By 1891 the percentage of women in the economically active population was around 30 percent in France and Britain, and a little less in Germany.[98] This was the beginning of an unresolved controversy: would a state salary for mothers condemn women to domestic labour and discourage them from entering the labour market? Would the lack of support to mothers discourage them from having children?

Some Christian feminists defended private charity. Conceptión Arenal, the leading Spanish feminist of her time and the first woman to attend university in Spain, thought that social problems would be solved, she declared in 1875, only if the rich accepted their Christian obligation to provide charity and build an 'International of Love' (*Internacional del Amor*) against the 'International of Hate' (*Internacional del Odio*, i.e. Karl Marx's First International).[99]

In the years between 1880 and 1914, at least in Europe or in countries settled by Europeans, such as Australia and New Zealand (but not in the USA), modern welfare took off, along with the globalization of industrialization. In its initial stages, as we mentioned, such welfare developments owed little to social unrest. The growing power of socialism might have played an important role in welfare legislation but only after the establishment of universal male suffrage in 1909.

The state began to intervene where the private insurance system was the most absent: accidents, sickness, old age, and unemployment.[100] The 1904 programme of the Bulgarian Liberal Party called for free health care, a pharmacy in each community, free education.[101] It may have been just propaganda, but it was a sign that such measures might be electorally popular even in the 'periphery' of Europe.

Most capitalist countries had nation-wide insurance against industrial accidents before the First World War; the Americans and Canadians had to wait until the 1930s.[102] In vain had President Theodore Roosevelt demanded a law to force employers to pay for injuries suffered by their employees in the course of their work, declaring in a message to Congress (31 January 1908) that congressional reluctance to approve such legislation was an 'outrage' and 'humiliation' to the United States, that 'In no other prominent industrial country in the world could such gross injustice occur . . . Exactly as the working man is entitled to his wages, so he should be entitled to indemnity for the injuries sustained in the natural course of his labor.'[103]

National health insurance schemes of varying coverage were introduced before 1914 in European countries including Austria, Italy, France, Sweden, Belgium, Switzerland, Norway, and the United Kingdom. Between 1914 and 1945 such schemes were introduced in Australia, New Zealand, Spain, the Netherlands, and much later in Finland, Canada, and Portugal. The United States still lacks a universal health insurance scheme.

It is doubtful that public welfare, as is sometimes suggested, was introduced as a response to growing social unrest. It is equally possible that public assistance was, like the abolition of slavery in an earlier era, the result of the activities and pressures of enlightened reformers and activists. At the time the organized labour movement was not particularly interested in assistance for the poor, since its members were, prevalently, working men. Unions much preferred to fight for higher wages, the suffrage, and the eight-hour day, than the welfare demands contained in the 1889 programme of the Second International.

Nordic nations were no more troubled by radicalism than others, yet by the end of the nineteenth century they had established the foundation for the substantial Scandinavian welfare state of the twentieth century.[104] This early welfare legislation was the outcome of a political conflict between a rising agrarian bourgeoisie and, in Peter Baldwin's words, 'entrenched, but declining, bureaucratic and urban élites'.[105] In other words the early welfare legislation was a victory for the middle classes of the countryside. Danish farmers, who wished to avoid paying for the local poor, favoured a new pension system which, being non-contributory, was in fact a state subsidy for both workers and employers.[106] This is why Denmark produced, in 1891, an all-inclusive, non-contributory, tax-financed pension, the *Alderdomsunderstøttelsen* (Old Age Compensation Act). All Danish citizens over the age of sixty and in need of help would be entitled to a pension, though there were stringent conditions attached. New Zealand followed in 1898, Australia in 1901, and England in 1908. The first truly universal pension, involving all citizens, regardless of means, past contributions, and gender, and applicable to all those who were over sixty-seven or unable to work because of disability, became law in Sweden in 1913 after a long campaign initiated in 1884 by the liberal politician and newspaper publisher Adolf Hedin.[107]

In 1909 there was a political earthquake in Sweden. In previous Swedish elections the main division in politics had been between protectionists and free traders. Electoral turnout was usually very low, below 40 per cent: at most one-fifth of the all-male electorate voted. But in 1909, although the Liberal Party led by Karl Staaff, a progressive liberal, won with 40 per cent, the Social Democratic Party obtained 28.5 per cent and was for the first time represented in Parliament. The consensus was shifting to the left and it is this that led to the 1913 law. The principle of universalism embodied in this legislation became the cornerstone of the Scandinavian welfare model.

The best-remembered early welfare state, however, was not Sweden's but Germany's, probably because of the central importance of the Reich in European history. It elicited widespread admiration among social reformers. A book published in England in 1890, William Harbutt Dawson's *Bismarck and State Socialism*, was full of praise for Bismarck, regarded as the first European statesman who set out a grand strategy for resolving the 'social question'.[108] Bismarck, explained Dawson, 'has dispersed to the four winds of heaven the old doctrine that the State has nothing to do with economics'.[109] Bismarck was not quite as enthusiastic about social reform as Dawson makes out, but he certainly did not oppose it.

Without quite putting down his anti-socialist stick, Bismarck waved the carrot, promulgating strong social welfare policies, particularly in the sphere of pensions. From the point of view of the Reich these policies had the advantage of strengthening both financially and politically central government at the expense of the German states (since some of the funding for welfare would be through national federal, or Reich, taxes).[110] In June 1883 a means-tested health insurance scheme was introduced. It would pay medical expenses and replace the portion of income lost because of illness (two-thirds of the cost of the insurance paid by the workers and one-third by their employers). In July 1884 a law on industrial accidents was passed whereby employers would be obliged to pay the full contribution. Finally, in 1889, the Invalidity and Old-Age Insurance Law provided old age and disability pensions for all those over seventy. At the time very few people lived much longer than that, so it did not cost much and some workers were fired before they retired, thus losing their pensions.[111]

The three schemes were consolidated in 1911 in the so-called National Insurance Code. Paradoxically this welfare legislation, widely regarded as Bismarck's most significant achievement in domestic policy, does not receive a single mention in his memoirs.[112]

One of the main proponents of the principle of compulsory insurance was an industrialist, Carl Ferdinand Stumm, who was the main employer in the mining and the steel and iron industries in the Saarland. Mining already had compulsory insurance for invalidity and old age because mining had been a state monopoly. Stumm, a conservative deputy in the Reichstag, proposed that the principle should be extended to all industrial workers. Other reformers, such as Theodor Lohmann, the real protagonist in the construction of the German welfare system, thought that if the employers were forced to pay for the cost of accidents then they would make more efforts to ensure the safety of their workers.[113] Lohmann was a liberal who regarded workers as citizens to be reconciled through social reform, whereas Bismarck, a conservative, regarded them as subjects to be attached to the existing order. Bismarck eventually accepted a compromise in an empire-wide insurance scheme, realizing that it would strengthen the Reich.[114] Nation-building was never far from Bismarck's mind. Eventually his proposal was approved thanks to the support of the Catholic Zentrum, in spite of its hostility towards Bismarck for his anti-Catholic legislation.[115]

One effect of German welfare laws was to slow down the rate of emigration. Germans had emigrated in great numbers until the 1860s; after 1880 very few crossed the oceans.[116] By 1890, Germany was ahead of Britain in social legislation *and* had caught up in the industrial race. By some standards it was as democratic as (if not more democratic than) Britain. A virtuous circle – Capitalism plus Democracy plus Welfare – seemed now to be the perfect recipe for the new modern state.

Bismarck was a conservative forced to become revolutionary. He had started out with the intention of preserving Prussia; he ended up as the architect of German unity. He had started out to preserve the power of his class, the Junker or landed aristocracy, and ended up overseeing the triumph of German capitalism. He had started out trying to block the emergence of popular parties; he ended up witnessing the rise of the Catholic Zentrum and the socialist SPD. The unintended consequences of policies might not have surprised him. Deep down he was only too aware of the illusory nature of politics. As he wrote to his wife in 1859: 'it is all merely a matter of time; nations and individuals, folly and wisdom, war and peace, they come and go like waves, and the sea remains'.[117]

Bismarck's successor as Chancellor, Leo von Caprivi (1890–94), built on the social policy of his predecessor, calling it, as is often the case with politicians who claim to innovate (even when they don't), the *Neuer Kurs* (New Course). He banned the employment of children under thirteen, restricted the number of hours worked by thirteen- to eighteen-year-olds and by women, and established a minimum wage and arbitration in industrial disputes (with trade union representatives). Neither the Social Democrats nor the Catholics of the Zentrum were fobbed off with such mild reform.[118] But it went too far for the Conservatives. Everyone was dissatisfied, particularly the Kaiser, Wilhelm II. Caprivi further alienated farming interests by lowering duties on imported grain. All of this and particularly the hostility of the Junker contributed to Caprivi's fall. His successors were more hesitant in challenging the Junker, at least until the 1930s when Hitler crushed them definitively.

Reformers everywhere were particularly exercised by the housing question. The dismal housing conditions and the dangers this posed for the stability of society had been discussed throughout much of Europe for most of the nineteenth century, not only in highly urbanized and industrialized countries such as Britain and Germany, but also in the more industrial parts of Spain such as the Asturias. Fear of the workers was often a factor. For instance, the Asturian folklorist Aurelio de Llano in his 1906 pamphlet *Hogar y Patria. Estudio de casas para obreros* ('Home and Motherland. Study of Homes for Workers') thought that one should not isolate workers in working-class districts so that, by being near civilized people, they will be less likely to commit unjust acts against the ruling classes.[119] In Germany, Lujo Brentano, a left-liberal economist admirer of Britain (see Chapter 7), was strongly in favour of public housing to rectify the unsanitary conditions of the workers caused by rapid urbanization and pressed for legislation to help trade unions deal with such problems.[120] In France, according to a government survey of 1910 (*Statistique générale de France*), workers spent between one-tenth and one-fifth of their earnings in rent for dwellings deprived of simple hygiene.[121]

In Britain, Gladstone's radical 1881 Irish Land Acts protected tenants against unfair evictions and gave them rights on the land. Opponents saw this as the first step in a popular attack on property, an attack soon labelled 'collectivism' or 'state socialism'.[122] Yet it was a Conservative government (under Lord Salisbury) which, with the Purchase of Land (Ireland) Act (1885), set up a fund to lend money to tenants who wanted to buy their land – a real volte-face for the Conservatives.[123]

Lord Salisbury, though far from being a progressive conservative (we saw how opposed he was to the extension of the suffrage), was perturbed by the housing question. On 22 February 1883 (when leader of the opposition) he delivered one of the most important speeches on housing reform in the history of Victorian England.[124]

Later in November, shortly after the publication of the Reverend Andrew Mearns's pamphlet *The Bitter Cry of Outcast London*, in a lengthy and detailed article published in the new conservative journal the *National Review*, Salisbury denounced the overcrowding in working-class housing that caused 'grave injury, both to morality and health' for the thousands of families who 'have only a single room to dwell in, where they sleep and eat, multiply, and die'.[125] He advocated not only cheap government loans, but also the regulation of speculative builders whose houses:

> are built upon dust heaps; their drainage is not connected with the main sewer . . . they are unwholesome from damp; the bricks are put together with mortar which is little more than mud or sand . . . In short, they are the production of the jerry builder, the representative and the creature of fierce competition.[126]

The liberal *Manchester Guardian* denounced Salisbury's proposals as 'State Socialism pure and simple'. To combat his 'socialism', the *Manchester Guardian* was joined by the recently formed ultra-liberal Liberty and Property Defence League. Its 1884 pamphlet *The State and the Slums* (written by Edward Robertson) declared that overcrowding was much exaggerated, that better ventilation would not make much difference to the workers, it 'would only be a change in their discomfort. Foul air and evil smells they are used to.'[127] Salisbury was not deterred: sanitary legislation on its own, he declared, would not resolve the overcrowding. One needed more houses. But who should build them? The Liberty and Property Defence League and many liberals thought that housing should be left to the market. Salisbury, though not in favour of 'wild schemes of State interference', proposed a Royal Commission on the Housing of the Working Classes chaired by Sir Charles Dilke, a radical-liberal politician. The spirit of this report, in a somewhat watered-down version, led to the Housing of the Working Classes Act (1885), which was one of the first bills introduced by Salisbury as Prime Minister.

Salisbury's vital role in the housing reform movement of 1883 to 1885 has long been ignored by his biographers, though more recently Andrew Roberts devoted three pages to this in a 900-page-long biography.[128] Was Salisbury moved by fear of the masses or by moral outrage at the idea of people living in promiscuity or by Christian charity?[129] Probably all of these, especially the last (he affected a staunch Christianity) because in the 1880s he could not have been particularly worried about social unrest.[130] However, he was pressed from various sides (the recently formed Fabian Society, the Land Nationalization Society, and the English Land Restoration League) for greater government intervention.

Salisbury was building on a previous Conservative housing act, Disraeli's Artisans' and Labourers' Dwellings Improvement Act (1875), which allowed (but did not compel) local councils to clear slums and rebuild them. In reality few local authorities took advantage of the law and most were unable or unwilling to raise the finances (and taxes). The most famous exception was Birmingham under the leadership of Joseph Chamberlain, then a prominent Liberal.

These reforms were facilitated by the difficulties facing the British government in the Boer War (1899–1902) in southern Africa against the Dutch settlers who resisted British annexation of the Transvaal: it was felt that the British soldiers had been poor fighters because of the impoverished conditions in which they had been brought up. Rudyard Kipling, famously, in his poem 'The Islanders' (first published in *The London Weekly Times*, 3 January 1902) denounced the cricket-playing upper classes ('the flannelled fools at the wicket') who had sent unprepared and unfit volunteers to the war: 'Sons of the sheltered city – unmade, unhandled, unmeet – / Ye pushed them raw to the battle as ye picked them raw from the street.'

The Boer War and its outcome helped to stir the Conservatives towards an increase in state expenditure and a less antagonistic attitude towards trade unions. This led to the passing of the Conciliation Act (1896), the foundation stone of a voluntary arbitration service that would advise employers and unions on industrial relations. The Liberal Party, having been out of power for ten years following a spectacular defeat in 1895, returned to office in 1906, after campaigning on free trade rather than on welfare and trade union issues. They faced two threats to their position as one of the two main parties. The first was the election of twenty-nine Labour MPs. The second, a threat to the unity of the country, was the election of eighty-two MPs from the nationalist Irish Parliamentary Party, heir to the Home Rule League. Sometimes threats work and the new Liberal government turned out to be the most reforming British government of the period, perhaps of the century, the 1945–51 Labour government being a close rival. Taking a leaf from the German model, they introduced a non-contributory universal pension scheme (1908), unemployment insurance (1908–11), labour exchanges, holidays for some categories of workers, and minimum wages in mines (1912). In 1909 the Trade Board Act created Trade

Boards (which became Wages Council in 1945) in industries where low wages were concentrated. Much of this was to be paid for by raising taxes on the rich.

The debates about how to eliminate poverty in Britain perturbed the nation. Anxieties are never far from politics. The economic problems of the 1880s (itself part of the wider so-called 'Long Depression' of 1873–96) had increased the threat not from the organized working class but the 'disorganized' one: the poor, the lumpen proletariat, the outcast, the underclass, the 'residuum'. And what if, somehow, the 'dangerous' class coalesced with the 'respectable' working class?[131] After all, what happens in periods of economic crisis is precisely that many of the 'respectable' workers are forced into the underclass, but without losing the capacity to organize and protest that they possessed before. Such anxieties were boosted by the London 'riots' of 1886. These may not have been on the scale of continental riots, but in the United Kingdom private property had not been so disturbed since 1832.[132] The riots scared *The Times* (never a difficult enterprise), which was alarmed at the fact that 'the West End' of London 'was for a couple of hours in the hands of the mob'. The poor were a problem not just because they were poor but because they constituted a 'social plague'. The diseases attributed to poverty, it was said, weakened the population and imperilled national security. Reformers even exaggerated the figures of those affected by tuberculosis by reclassifying bronchitis as TB.[133]

Poverty, some reformers argued, could be alleviated by education. In the 1870s the education of the English poor had become the direct concern of the nation, and the state attempted to oblige parents to provide their children with elementary knowledge. The Elementary Education Act (1880) made school attendance compulsory. By 1891 primary education had become free.[134]

Other solutions were touted. Some social reformers suggested that the colonies could be used as a recipient for local undesirables. Charles Booth, the social investigator of the London poor, wrote that 'To the rich the very poor are a sentimental interest: to the poor they are a crushing load. The poverty of the poor is mainly the result of the competition of the very poor.' The solution was to send the very poor into labour colonies where they would work in a disciplined way, under some form of state slavery, in other words unpaid, in exchange for their sustenance.[135] Little came of such proposals, which were not the product of the imaginations of some ultra-reactionaries but of social reformers.

A new, wider electorate (see Chapter 13) could now scrutinize government policy. In Britain, in the years leading up to the 1906 elections, arguments in favour of free trade became increasingly constructed on the basis that it would improve the standards of the working class.[136]

The great Liberal welfare legislation of 1906–11 encountered only mild Conservative opposition. The Tories, smarting from the scale of their defeat in 1906, were still, at least technically, in alliance with the Liberal Unionist Party (founded by Liberals opposed to Irish Home Rule but in favour of social reform). When, in 1907, the Liberals introduced the Old Age Pensions Act, the Conservatives gave it a welcome and few campaigned against it in the election of 1910.[137]

The Conservatives did not even try to mutilate the Liberals' Trades Disputes Act (which established that trade unions could not be sued for damages arising out of a strike, thus reversing Conservative legislation); nor did they object strongly to the School Meals and School Health measures.[138] But they drew the line over the financing of this legislation by an increase in taxes.

The Liberal 1909–10 budget, which went down in history as 'the people's budget', pushed through the Commons by the Chancellor David Lloyd George and Winston Churchill, then a Liberal and President of the Board of Trade, was a brutally redistributive budget. It taxed both the incomes of the rich and their land. As Lloyd George declared on 29 April 1909 to the House of Commons:

> This is a war Budget. It is for raising money to wage implacable warfare against poverty and squalidness. I cannot help hoping and believing that before this generation has passed away, we shall have advanced a great step towards that good time, when poverty, and the wretchedness and human degradation which always follows in its camp, will be as remote to the people of this country as the wolves which once infested its forests.[139]

The Conservatives used their majority in the House of Lords to veto the budget. New elections were called (January 1910). The Liberals won again and passed the budget with the help of the Irish nationalists and the nascent Labour Party. A second election was called for December 1910 to push through a major piece of legislation: the Parliament Act (1911), which severely curtailed the powers of the House of Lords. The Liberals won again and, this time, the Lords were too scared to veto it. The construction of the British welfare state had begun in earnest. Its unlikely architects were what was once the main pro-capitalist force in Victorian Britain, the Liberal Party, in alliance with Irish nationalism.

Yet, even then, British welfarism should not be reduced to its 'state' element. The annual income and expenditure of registered and unregistered charities, friendly societies, benefit-paying trade unions, and other benevolent and self-help institutions, vastly exceeded the expenditure on social welfare of central government up until just before the First World War.[140]

It was realized that one could no longer just rely on private charity; even in poorer countries, such as Italy, the state had to intervene. Francesco Crispi, once a strong supporter of the 'revolutionary' Garibaldi, turned out as a Prime Minister (1887–91, 1893–6) to be authoritarian at home and colonialist abroad, which is why he is often regarded as a precursor of Mussolini. Nevertheless, unlike his more 'liberal' (in the economic sense) colleagues, he understood the need for social reforms. As Antonio Gramsci put it, 'he was the true man of the new bourgeoisie'.[141] Crispi himself would not have disagreed. He wrote to his fellow Sicilian politician Giuseppe Tasca-Lanza in August 1891 that the common people (he used the word *plebe*, then less insulting than it sounds now) should be reminded that it was the bourgeoisie who had united Italy, expelled foreign occupiers, and established basic freedoms. And while it was politically imperative that there should be no differences among the citizens, the *plebe* should be grateful and happy to be given a place at the 'banquet of life'.[142]

Crispi's visits to his remote southern constituency (Tricarico in Basilicata) had brought home to him, or so he wrote, the poverty of its inhabitants, the gap between the people and the institutions, the squalor, and the arrogance of local public officials: 'The organism of the state is corrupted. We must cure this body.'[143] When he became Prime Minister he promoted a major Public Health Act (1888), giving a central role to government-appointed prefects, thus bypassing locally elected officials. The law established for the first time in newly united Italy the principle that 'The health of both mind and body should be the responsibility of the government.' As Crispi declared to the Chamber of Deputies, 'On this depends . . . the greatness of nations.'[144] Two years later he proceeded to move against Church charities (12,000 of them!), claiming that much of their money was not spent on welfare and that most of them were totally unaccountable. From now on welfare would be secularized.[145]

Throughout Europe, more than in Japan or the United States, welfare reformism – what one might call the 'nationalization' of private charity – in the run-up to the First World War, united the majority of Liberal politicians, many Conservatives, the Roman Catholic Church, and the majority of Socialists. However, reformism could not be just about welfare, which, by and large, was something that involved the poor and the old. Of even greater importance was the 'social question' (then the accepted name for the labour question). Organized workers, after all, were a greater threat than those in need of welfare. Here, once again, the state had to take the commanding role and interfere in the relations between capitalists and workers. It is to this that we now turn.

15
Managing Capital and Labour

'The executive of the modern state is but a committee for managing the common affairs of the whole bourgeoisie,' declared Marx and Engels in *The Communist Manifesto*, unaware that this would later be taken as seriously as a biblical pronouncement. This has been interpreted by some of their followers, somewhat crudely, as suggesting that the 'bourgeois' state would always be on the side of the capitalists, that it could not be reformed and hence would have to be abolished. Yet Marx and Engels's blunt statement contains a grain of truth. The words 'the common affairs of the whole bourgeoisie' is a recognition that capitalism has a common interest, but that it would be safer if this was not left to the vagaries of the internecine competition that constantly pits capitalists against each other. A Leviathan is needed to regulate the competitive jungle, to enforce contracts, redress grievances, and, more generally, make sure that the conditions of existence of the system, and not just of this or that individual capitalist, endure. Relying on the occasional philanthropic capitalist is too risky for the long-term prospects of capitalism as a whole.

The 'state' that acts as a guarantor and that sets the rules does not have to be the state of the actual territory within which capitalists find themselves. An external and commercially powerful state could set the rules, often informally as was the case with the Dutch Republic in the seventeenth and eighteenth century, Great Britain in the eighteenth and nineteenth century, and the United States in the twentieth century. It could be an international organization such as the IMF or the World Bank, dominated by the most powerful hegemonic countries.

Modernity, 'progress', and capitalism, although they offered exciting prospects, were also frightening, with forebodings of unhappiness and suffering. These worries did not just exist in fully fledged capitalist countries, such as France or Britain, but also in others where the movement towards industrialization was seen as an unavoidable stage of progress. In nineteenth-century China liberals were dismayed by the social evils that capitalism seemed to bring about.[1] In Russia anti-capitalist attitudes developed early in the nineteenth century, even before industrialization had set in. They knew what was happening elsewhere and saw the consequences. Indeed, many Westernizers, such as the literary critic Vissarion Belinsky, held anti-capitalist ideas. Vasil Bervi-Flerovskiĭ, a populist writer, declared in *The Condition of the Working Class in Russia* (1869) that the conditions of factory workers were worse than those of the peasantry.[2] Populists, in Russia and even more so in America, approved of markets but not of capitalism. They approved of small firms and detested large ones. They wished capitalism had only produced the small entrepreneur, the smallholder, the small landowner, the small shopkeeper. They had looked forward to a capitalism of little guys not of big conglomerates. Small-time capitalists, merchants, and landowners hated the state when it interfered with them but wanted the state to protect them from the rapacious threats of large-scale manufacturing and finance. They hated finance (banks) even more than they hated big capitalists because they needed banks, borrowed money from them, and had to pay it back – with interest.

Global migration reproduced the essential condition for the reproduction of capitalism: the uprooting of workers from the land – any land – and the constant expansion of the market for commodities. No wonder that the enormous migration from countryside to cities of the period 1880 to 1910 coincided with the growing regulation of labour markets since workers too – increasingly organized – wanted some form of regulation of capitalism.

Of course, in liberal theory, the capitalist and the worker face each other in the labour market on a footing of equality. The former offers work at a given rate and with certain conditions. The latter can accept or reject it. If all workers reject the work, the capitalist will have to revise his offer, or cease being a capitalist. Eventually a bargain is struck. A wage is agreed, as is the length of the working day. Each side can quit at any time. Everyone is free. Any interference by the state into this bargain would be nonsensical, an encroachment on basic liberties.

Except that the parties are not equal.

The individual worker is powerless if there is always another worker ready to step in to take his place and work harder and for less. Matters change if workers bargain collectively and do not face the capitalist as individuals but as a united force – one of the many reasons why the language of solidarity and fraternity is favoured by the labour movement while that of individualism is extolled in pro-capitalist discourse.

This, of course, was rhetoric: capitalists, like socialists, required organization and cooperation, required people to work together, inside a firm, towards its expansion and ever greater profits. Capitalists were competing against other capitalists, but workers too were competing against other workers over jobs, over wages, and restricting employment to keep wages high. And though individual capitalists would always try to do with fewer workers, and, by introducing machines, to eliminate the need for some of them, capitalism as a system required an ever expanding market of consumers, of people working, earning money, and spending it on the products of capitalism. Nor was there much room for individualism in the traditional bourgeois family – a model of conformity, where the paterfamilias demanded the same kind of unquestioned obedience that a boss required in a factory.

Well before Karl Marx, Adam Smith was perfectly aware of the power differential between employers and trade unions and the inequalities in law between workers and capitalists:

> The masters, being fewer in number, can combine much more easily; and the law, besides, authorises, or at least does not prohibit their combinations, while it prohibits those of the workmen. We have no acts of parliament against combining to lower the price of work; but many against combining to raise it. In all such disputes the masters can hold out much longer . . . Many workmen could not subsist a week, few could subsist a month, and scarce any a year without employment. In the long run the workman may be as necessary to his master as his master is to him; but the necessity is not so immediate.[3]

A. V. Dicey concurred: 'an individual artisan or labourer does not bargain on fair terms . . . The sale of labour, in short, is felt to be unlike the sale of goods.'[4] In other words, labour is not a simple commodity. It needs to reproduce itself (himself, and herself, and the future labour force). Capitalist production is a social issue.

In the second half of the nineteenth century the state did not just intervene on welfare matters (as we saw in the previous chapter) but in labour disputes, on the length of the working day, in establishing who could work (children, women), in the quality of the commodity sold, and in the safety of workers. Regulation of production and commerce existed in the Middle Ages, but it was only in the nineteenth century that matters such as working hours and the establishment of a minimum age for workers became a major political matter. In some Swiss cantons, as early as 1848, laws were introduced that restricted men's work in factories to thirteen hours during the day and eleven hours at night. In 1877 the Swiss Federal Factory Act (*Eidgenössisches Fabrikgesetz*) established an eleven-hour day, restricted night work, made Sunday a day of rest, and banned children under fourteen from working in factories (they could work in the fields).[5]

In France social investigators such as Louis René Villermé (see Chapter 2 above) denounced the conditions of child labour in his *Tableau de l'état physique et moral des ouvriers employés dans les manufactures de coton, de laine et de soie* (1840). This was decisive for the law of 1841, which established that factories employing twenty or more workers should restrict child labour. At the time some 150,000 children, 12 per cent of the labour force, were working in French factories. Implementing the law was problematic since there was no factory inspectorate, and the law encountered opposition from both employers and working-class families.[6] Finally, in 1874 the regulation of child labour was applied to all factories and a salaried inspectorate was created. The implementation of the law, however, remained difficult.[7] The working day was still long and exhausting. According to a contemporary survey (*Salaire et durée du travail dans l'industrie française*), 90 per cent of those working in the Paris region and 60 per cent of those working elsewhere worked between nine and a half and eleven hours a day (hence the strength of the socialist struggle for the eight-hour day and the forty-hour week).[8] To some extent the relative lack of concern about the social question on the part of French politicians was due to the quietness of workers after the terrible repression that followed the Paris Commune of 1871.[9]

In Belgium, in 1886, shortly after the stunning electoral victory of the Catholic Party against the liberals, King Leopold II, in a speech from the throne, declared that one needed to regulate the work of women and children.[10] For the first three-quarters of the nineteenth century the average working day in that country was twelve hours, one of the longest in western Europe.[11] In 1889 new laws banned the employment of children under twelve and shortened the working week for women under the age of twenty-one and boys under sixteen (to seventy-two hours!).[12] In 1896, 50 per cent of the workforce worked more than ten hours a day and one-fifth worked eleven hours.[13] Trade unions had been legal in Belgium since 1830, but employers were allowed to sack union organizers. Only in the 1860s did unions start to gain strength, and a new electoral law (1894) enabled more socialists to be represented in Parliament. As a result, social legislation developed further while the stubborn liberalism of both Catholics and liberals began to give way to a more interventionist outlook.[14] Marx commented acidly, praising the struggle for a shorter working day in Great Britain: 'Belgium, the paradise of Continental Liberalism, shows no trace of this movement. Even in the coal and metal mines, labourers of both sexes, and all ages, are consumed, in perfect "freedom" at any period and through any length of time.'[15]

Marx was right: the pathbreaker in the reduction of the working day was Victorian Britain. In 1819 children in textile factories could not work more than twelve hours a day; this was reduced to nine hours in 1833; in 1847 working hours for women were restricted to ten. The French lagged behind: only in 1900 would the French achieve the British legal standard for women and children.[16]

Towards the final decades of the century Russia took some tentative steps towards regulation of the labour market (see Chapter 8). In 1882, Nikolai Bunge, then Finance Minister, introduced the first major laws limiting night work for children. In 1897 the maximum length of the working day was set at eleven and a half hours. Before that a fourteen-hour day had been normal and an eighteen-hour day was not uncommon; workers worked on Sundays in appalling conditions. The labour reforms had been, at least in part, a response to the labour unrest of 1884–5, itself a consequence of the repressive use of police by factory owners and the heavy fines imposed on workers for turning up late for work. In 1903 workers suffering injury at work were to be compensated, the first step towards accident insurance, and in 1912 a general law on accident and medical insurance finally emerged.[17] But the problem with laws regulating the labour market in many countries was their implementation. In Russia the state, though it appeared strong, was weak, like many authoritarian states.[18] Bunge, in his famous memorandum (1894), wrote that 'though desirable it is impossible to have in Russia the kind of factory legislation which is the norm in England'. He blamed it on the workers, a population in constant flux, consisting 'of all the rabble from the various ends of Russia . . .'.[19] Socialism, he explained, arises when social discipline is weak, when mankind ceases to be resigned, when the wealth of others is envied, and when men have doubts about justice and legality. To fight socialism it was necessary to establish not just justice for all but also to provide everyone with the chance of acquiring property and capital. And it was necessary to tie the interests of the workers to those of factory owners, 'who understand very little of the social question and the means for its solution'.[20] Industrialists viewed Bunge's factory laws as an unwarranted intrusion into their private affairs; they assumed that they should be able to do what they wanted with their workers and even regarded Bunge as a 'socialist' (already a generic term for anyone with mildly progressive views on labour issues).[21]

Bunge's successor, Ivan Vyshnegradsky, toned down many of Bunge's reforms. He then bequeathed his successor, Count Witte, a bill making factory owners responsible for the death or injury of an employee. When the matter came up for discussion in the Imperial Council, Konstantin Pobedonostsev (see Chapter 8) argued against it, saying the law was 'socialistic'. Witte explained in his memoirs that the Tsar 'as a rule . . . refused to support me in my effort to organize a system of factory inspection . . . all the efforts to improve the lot of factory workers in Russia by legislative means were strenuously opposed by the reactionaries'.[22]

The reduction in working time was opposed not only by capitalists unable to see beyond their immediate interest, but also by influential 'classical' economists such as Nassau W. Senior, who argued (*Letters on the Factory Act*, 1837) that the whole of an entrepreneur's profit was obtained in the last hour's work and so in any shortening of the working day would be 'destroyed'.[23] Some industrialists were less retrograde, notably the great social reformer and 'utopian' socialist Robert Owen, who, in 1817, had coined the famous slogan: 'Eight hours' labour, Eight hours' recreation, Eight hours' rest'. A few industrialists favoured a reduction of working time: some for philanthropic reasons; others because they were efficient and could compete better if a limit was imposed on their competitors' ability to extract the last drop of production from their exhausted workers; others, afraid of the power of the newly enfranchised electorate, wanted to appease their workers.

Thus in England, William Mather, a Liberal MP and an industrialist, had written in 1892 that 'Many of us who sat in the last parliament and did not support the Eight Hour Bill, had our majorities largely reduced solely in consequence of our opposition to it.'[24] A year later he introduced the eight-hour day at his ironworks in Salford. In spite of this he was defeated at the 1895 general election (though he was returned in February 1900). In Germany, at the turn of the century the optical scientist Ernst Abbe, co-owner of the famous Zeiss plants in Jena, introduced the eight-hour day in his factory as well as other measures aimed at improving the lives of his workers.

There were economically rational reasons as to why some capitalists might be in favour of greater state regulation. If, because of strong trade unions, or for other reasons, an employer found himself having to make concessions or pay higher wages, it might be quite desirable that all sections of industry should be subjected to the same regulations, all the more so if his firm was more efficient than the competition. In any case the shorter working day was and is essential to the overall growth of the capitalist system, since it enhances consumption.

The international labour movement wanted a far shorter working day than the ten to twelve hours that prevailed in the nineteenth century. The First International had demanded the eight-hour day as early as 1866. Karl Marx, in *Das Kapital*, scorning 'the pompous catalogue of the "inalienable rights of man"', demanded a 'modest Magna Carta of a legally limited working-day'.[25] The Second International, convened in Paris at its founding congress in 1889, made the eight-hour day a key element of its programme. American trade unions advanced such demands throughout the 1870s and 1880s (the eight-hour day had been introduced for federal employees as early as 1868). In Great Britain in 1890 and 1891 the Trade Union Congresses passed resolutions in favour of the eight-hour day. In 1890, in London's Hyde Park, a large demonstration (the organizers claimed 250,000 participants) marched in favour of it. One of the organizers was Will Thorne, the leader of the National Union of Gas Workers and General Labourers, which had won the eight-hour day the previous year. The more moderate trade unionists joined in out of fear of losing touch with their rank and file. As the Liberal MP George Howell put it, 'Goaded by the attacks of the Socialists and New Trade Unionists, the London Trades Council found itself obliged to participate in May Day celebrations in favour of . . . the Eight Hours and other idealist proposals.'[26]

The historian Gary Cross explained that the eight-hour day was a much more radical measure than the ten-hour limit advanced by earlier reformers. While ten hours was believed to be the norm, the eight-hour movement was more 'revolutionary' because it aimed to set a universal standard, regardless of productivity, age, and conditions.[27] Sidney Webb, in a Fabian pamphlet, declared that workers increasingly realised that:

> it is only by shortening their working day that they can share in the benefits of the civilization they have toiled to create. They have been educated; but their work leaves them no time to read. They have been given the vote; but they have no time to think.[28]

In Britain, Conservatives were just as likely as Liberals (sometimes more likely) to be in favour of legislation against sweated industries, low wages, and long hours, some even suggesting state interference in raising wages.[29] In fact, 'Between 1903 and 1910 the Conservative party became increasingly receptive to the idea of developing a distinctive policy on social reform.'[30] They were in favour of a vast increase in employment and promoted tariff reforms (i.e. protectionism) on the grounds that it would increase employment and protect jobs – with the slogan 'tariff reform means work for all'.[31]

The 'labour question' became increasingly central: novels proliferated denouncing the conditions of the working class. Here, for obvious reasons, British novelists had been first, with Charles Kingsley's *Alton Locke* (1850) about conditions in the textile industry; Elizabeth Gaskell's *Mary Barton* (1848) and *North and South* (1855); Charlotte Brontë's *Shirley* (1849); and Charles Dickens's *Oliver Twist* (1839) and *Hard Times* (1854). In France, Yves Guyot, radical journalist and politician, for twenty years editor-in-chief of the pro-laissez-faire *Journal des économistes*, ferociously anti-socialist, pro-Dreyfus, feminist, and anticlerical, wrote a novel in 1882, *La famille Pichot*, subtitled *Scènes de l'enfer social*, denouncing conditions in the mining industry and depicting the owners in lurid terms (wearing gold-rimmed monocles, cigar-smoking, only concerned about profits and not about the lives of 150 miners trapped down the pit, etc.).[32] None of this is surprising: Émile Zola would do the same in *Germinal* (1885) with far superior flair and talent but espousing a not dissimilar ideology. There were non-fiction books denouncing the conditions of workers, such as Georges Picot's *Les Moyens d'améliorer la condition de l'ouvrier* (1891) and Jules Huret's *Enquête sur la question sociale en Europe* (1892–7, see Chapter 2 above). In the United States the most celebrated and influential example of this genre of novels was Upton Sinclair's *The Jungle* (1906), first serialized in the socialist newspaper *Appeal to Reason*. In 1907, Jack London published a dystopian novel, *The Iron Heel*, in which America is ruled by large corporations run by an oligarchy (the 'Iron Heel'), which has destroyed all small businesses and set worker against worker. Well before Upton Sinclair and Jack London, there was a spate of books and pamphlets about the negative consequences of industrialization, such as Henry George's *Progress and Poverty* (1879), as well as novels about tramps (usually perceived as dangerous outcasts), such as Horatio Alger's *Tony the Tramp* (1876), George M. Baker's *A Tight Squeeze* (1879), and Lee Harris's *The Man Who Tramps* (1878).[33] In Germany, Wilhelm Raabe's ecologically anticapitalist novel, *Pfisters Mühle: Ein Sommerferienheft* (*Pfister's Mill: Notes from a Summer Vacation*, 1884), tells the story of how a new factory pollutes the stream on which the mill owned by the jovial and likeable Pfister stands, kills the flora and fauna, and makes the air unhealthy.[34]

There was plenty of evidence that extremely long hours were an important factor in accidents. In France in 1909, 2,395 individuals were killed at work and 434,000 were injured.[35] During an investigation in France in 1872 into a train accident caused by the driver falling asleep, it was discovered that the man had been working for thirty-eight consecutive hours.[36] The public was increasingly alarmed. Mutual societies, originally created to help unemployed railwaymen or their widows and orphans, soon turned into pressure groups lobbying for an improvement in the conditions of the railwaymen. One, created in 1883, even had as its honorary president a public intellectual of the stature of Victor Hugo.[37] In *Capital*, Karl Marx reported the frequency of newspaper reports about railway catastrophes with headlines such as 'Fearful and Fatal Accidents' and 'Appalling Tragedies'. *Reynolds' Newspaper* of 4 February 1866 reported 'as a very frequent occurrence' a driver who commenced work on the Monday morning at a very early hour, and, 'When he had finished what is called a day's work, he had been on duty 14 hours 50 minutes. Before he had time to get his tea, he was again called on for duty . . . The next time he finished he had been on duty 14 hours 25 minutes, making a total of 29 hours 15 minutes without intermission.'[38] There was considerable sympathy for railway workers, especially for the driver, who was regarded as a heroic figure (though not in Zola's *La bête humaine*, 1890), the first to die in the frequent accidents of the period, solitary – unlike other workers – and carrying some of the aura that airline pilots would later have.[39]

In Berlin the social Christian academic Adolf Wagner, shocked by the squalor of the working class (for which he blamed, among others, the Jews), declared in October 1871 that 'The system of free competition which permits work to be treated as a commodity and wages as the price for it, is not merely un-Christian, it is inhuman in the worst sense of the word.' He insisted on the need for ethical considerations in human affairs and state intervention in the economy.[40]

Eventually, throughout Europe, labour legislation was promulgated during a period of crisis (1873–96) that also coincided with the increased strength of trade unions and the growing enfranchisement of male workers. In Australia and New Zealand the eight-hour day had already been introduced in the late nineteenth century, but only in some trades. Australians had to wait until the 1920s; New Zealand never introduced a nation-wide law.

In most countries, across industries, there was little uniformity in working hours. For instance, in Italy and Canada people worked longer hours in textiles, mining, and services.[41] There was also a significant difference between countries. Thus, in 1913, Americans, Italians, and Dutch workers worked more hours a year (over 2,900 hours) than anywhere else. Australians worked the least (2,214 hours) and far less than the French.[42] This disproportion has endured today even in 'advanced' countries. In 2000, each American still worked longer than anyone elsewhere in the Western world (1,879 hours), while the Dutch, who worked so hard in 1890, could now relax with 'only' 1,347 hours a year. But there was also considerable convergence. In 1870, Britons worked less than other Europeans, the Belgians more, but by 1913 the Scandinavians and other Western countries had caught up.[43]

The eight-hour day is an achievement of the twentieth century. In most cases it was introduced immediately after the First World War: November 1917 in Russia, 1918 in Germany, Poland, Luxembourg, Czechoslovakia, and Austria; 1919 in Denmark, Hungary, Spain, France, Italy, Portugal, Bulgaria, Switzerland, Sweden, and Holland. The workers' unrest of the immediate post-war period and the success of the Bolsheviks in Russia were a crucial factor in the widespread adoption of this long-fought-for measure.

In Belgium, the United Kingdom, and the United States there was no country-wide legislation on the eight-hour day. In those countries, powerful trade unions achieved the eight-hour day in their own industry but did not put pressure on government for national legislation. The lack of state intervention in the social question, they felt, would be an added incentive for people to join unions and organize – which is why the eight-hour day was not made compulsory in the UK.

Class conciliation was advanced as a justification for labour reforms by British Conservatives such as Lord Shaftesbury, who, as Lord Ashley, introduced the Mines and Collieries Act of 1842, which banned the employment of women and young children in mines, and the Ten Hours Act (Factories Act, 1847), which restricted the hours of women and children. Karl Marx, in his inaugural address to the International Workingmen's Association in 1864, attributed this achievement to the 'admirable perseverance' of the English working classes, but forgot to mention Shaftesbury.

In 1874, after six years in opposition, Benjamin Disraeli and the Conservative Party introduced a new Factory Act (1874), which raised the minimum working age to nine and limited the working day for women and young people to ten hours in the textile industry, and the Conspiracy and Protection of Property Act (1875), which decriminalized picketing (thus strengthening the Molestation of Workmen Act, 1859) and the Employers and Workmen Act (1875), which enabled workers to sue employers in the civil courts if they broke legal contracts. In fact, the Conservative government elected in 1874 managed to pack eleven major pieces of social legislation into three years, more than any government until the Liberal government of 1906.[44] This legislation seemed to have granted the trade unions everything they had wanted and which Gladstone's ministry had refused them. In October 1875 the TUC even carried a motion of thanks to the (Tory) Home Secretary by a large majority. And the Conservatives, in turn, could tell industrialists that they had disposed of a major source of social conflict. On 29 June 1875, Disraeli wrote to Lady Bradford, 'We have settled the long and vexatious contest between capital and labour' and, on the same day, to Lady Chesterfield (Lady Bradford's sister), 'This . . . will gain and retain for the Tories the lasting affection of the working classes.'[45] (From 1873 until his death in 1881, Disraeli wrote some 1,600 letters to the two sisters.)

In fact, Victorian Britain, contrary to the stereotype of laissez-faire Britain so beloved by historically unaware modern neo-liberals, had the most interventionist government in the world. Its list of Acts of Parliament reforming labour relations included: the Railway Acts of 1842 and 1844, which set up a system of inquiries into accidents and which gave the government the right to fix fares and freight charges; the Mines Act of 1842, which restricted the employment of women and children underground; the Coal Mines Inspection Act of 1850, which established health and safety in the mines, against opposition from coal-mine owners, many of whom sat in the Lords. Then there were numerous Factory Acts (1833, 1844, 1847, 1850, 1856, 1870, 1871) regulating working hours for women and children, all consolidated with the Factory and Workshop Act (1878), described by A. V. Dicey as the 'most notable achievement of English socialism'.[46]

The 1876 Merchant Shipping Act prevented ship owners from sending unsafe ships to sea. The 1878 Factory and Workshop Act established that all workshops and factories employing more than fifty people should be inspected regularly by government inspectors rather than by local authorities (as previously). The 1897 Workmen's Compensation Act compelled an employer to compensate an employee injured at work, and his dependants if he was killed at work.[47] Finally, when it came to legislating between employers and workers, the turning points were the Trade Union Act of 1871 (when Gladstone was Prime Minister), which made trade unions legal, and that of 1875 (when Disraeli was Prime Minister), which made strikes legal.

All in all these measures were as significant a legislative revolution as the establishment and development of the welfare state between 1906 and 1910 and after 1945. As John Morley wrote in his famous *Life of Richard Cobden*, published in 1881, summarizing the voluminous social legislation of the previous decades: 'we find the rather amazing result that in the country where socialism has been less talked about than any other country in Europe, its principles have been most extensively applied'.[48] For liberals like Dicey the key factors in advancing such reforms were the moderation of the ruling classes and of trade union leaders. In his words the era of the 'despotic authority of individualism' had come to an end and Britain became increasingly 'socialist or collectivist'.[49]

Trade union strength was not directly related to that of socialist parties. Unions could be strong, as in Britain and, to a lesser extent, in the United States, where there was no strong socialist party. But unions, per se, do not challenge capitalism at all. Their task was (and is) to modify the distribution of the gains from capitalism. To the extent that they were successful in obtaining better conditions and higher wages for their members, they raised costs for firms. But raising costs is also a way of weeding out inefficient firms – part of the 'creative destruction' that drives capitalism. Increasing wages was also a way of expanding the size of the market. Poorly paid workers could not be good consumers. Producing with cheap workers and selling to well-paid ones is the ideal situation from the point of view of the entrepreneurs, but it is not something one can plan. The view that the pursuit of individual interests works in favour of the general welfare of capitalism is an act of faith and/or propaganda held by over-enthusiastic and naive supporters of free markets. Paying workers more than the going rate is an excellent business decision if one intends to steal workers from other employers because one's prospects are buoyant and to keep them loyal (it is, incidentally, the justification for paying footballers and bankers munificent sums, a justification far more valid for the former than for the latter).

Collective bargaining was established by the last decades of the nineteenth century at the local if not yet at the national level. It became the norm in the United Kingdom and Switzerland; it was occasionally used in Germany, Austria-Hungary, and Denmark, and, to a lesser extent, in the Netherlands, Catalonia, and Norway. Elsewhere it barely existed. In Japan, for instance, before 1895 there were hardly any unions. A socialist party was founded in 1906, well after most European socialist parties. It was banned the following year, after heavy repression and the accusation that it was seeking to murder the Emperor.[50] It was not until 1926 that collective bargaining was accepted.[51] Even in the decades after 1945 trade unions in Japan remained weak when compared to those in the West. Yet, everywhere unions grew in strength. As early as 1870, Britain had a higher trade union membership (in relative terms) than any other country.[52]

In France, home to economic liberalism, there were fewer reforms and less trade union recognition than in conservative Britain, though there was growing concern for the welfare of the working class. The dominant political factions, grouped under the banner of 'moderate' republicanism, initiated limited pro-labour legislation with the Waldeck-Rousseau law of 21 March 1884 (Waldeck-Rousseau was then the Minister of the Interior). This finally gave workers the right to join a trade union (the right to strike had already been established by Napoleon III in 1864), and was perhaps the only significant pro-labour law that Waldeck-Rousseau managed to get through.[53] Although Waldeck-Rousseau was a very moderate reformer, he was regarded by respectable liberal publications (*L'Économiste français*, the *Journal des économistes*, the *Revue des deux mondes*, the *Journal des débats*) as almost a socialist.[54] In reality, he was more afraid of social Catholicism than of socialism and fought for social reforms without ever having any real sympathy for those who would benefit from these.[55] By 1883 the bourgeois press (such as *L'Économiste français*) was almost resigned to trade unionism, particularly as Waldeck-Rousseau had obtained the support of the most important employers' organizations.[56]

During the 1890s there was a further slide to the left in France: at the municipal elections of 1892 the socialists won a majority in four towns, including cities as important as Marseille and Lille.[57] At the 1893 election the *Parti ouvrier français* and other socialists (French socialists, at the time, were deeply divided) increased their strength to forty-nine seats and a new radical government, supported by some socialists and led by Waldeck-Rousseau, reduced the length of the working day for children and women (though the measure was not properly enforced), and made employers responsible for labour accidents (1898).[58]

Even so the main trade union confederation, the CGT (*Confédération générale du travail*), created in 1895, still only had 700,000 members in 1914, fewer than the numbers in the United Kingdom in 1888.[59] This was partly in response to the first major wave of industrial conflict (1893) with some 170,000 strikers in that year compared to an average of 47,000 strikers in the period 1871–92.[60] Further waves of unrest occurred in 1905–6 and increased enormously in the years leading up to the First World War, of which just over half could be considered successful.[61] At that time only 10 per cent of the small factory proletariat in France was unionized, while in Great Britain the number was 26 per cent and in Germany a staggering 63 per cent.[62]

Nevertheless timid social legislation continued. Alexandre Millerand, Minister of Commerce in the Waldeck-Rousseau government of 1899 to 1902, was regarded as an opportunist by other socialists because he had agreed to enter a 'bourgeois' government.[63] His achievements were modest: an eleven-hour day leading to a ten-hour day, the enforcement of the law of working time for women and children, the establishment of consultative committees with workers, and a proposal for an old-age pension – all derisory advances compared to Germany or Britain, but not insignificant in the context of French social policy, and employers were alarmed.[64] In 1897, Émile Cheysson, a follower of the social Christian conservative thinker Frédéric Le Play, lamented the fact that being a boss (*un patron*) was an increasingly thankless task since all progress was forcing down prices and lowering profits; he added that 'Parliament is always on the side of the workers. Every law enacted or proposed adds a burden of inspections, fines, prison, compulsory taxes on industry . . .'[65]

Philanthropic paternalism was one classic response to working-class militancy – anything to avoid trade unions. Take Henri Schneider, owner of the Creusot steel works in Burgundy, and son of Eugène, the works' founder. Henri was interviewed by Jules Huret, author in 1897 of one of the main investigations on the social question in Europe (see Chapter 2), a socialist writing for the conservative *Le Figaro*. At Le Creusot, Huret explained, workers could obtain a mortgage (at high interest) from the Schneiders to build their homes; there were schools for the children of the workers; when they left school, they were trained in Schneider's training schools and then given employment at the steel works. If there was an accident there was free medical care; those who were injured were kept on with one-third pay; when they died the widow got a pension.[66]

It was a welfare state at company level. Le Creusot was a fully fledged company town employing some 16,000 workers. Henri Schneider himself was the mayor of Le Creusot for twelve years and then the local MP for another ten. A worker interviewed by Huret told him that Schneider was elected because the workers were afraid to vote for somebody else, and that workers who went to socialist meetings were dismissed one by one. Schneider's authoritarian paternalism, it turned out, was paralleled by his utter distaste for state interference, trade unions, and for any kind of labour legislation.[67] None of this stopped the strikes of 1899–1900, facilitated in part by an economic conjuncture favourable to the labour movement (the rise in demand for components for the railways and military rearmament) and to the growing power of the trade unions.[68] These were not strikes for increases in wages but for trade union rights and the end to the kind of paternalistic regime that had been the hallmark of the reign of the Schneider family.

Paternalistic capitalism developed rapidly in the United States (encountering problems): firms hoped to bribe their workers with company welfare and provided kindergartens, libraries, English lessons, company stores, housing – many businesses could not have attracted workers unless they could house them – and even bowling alleys.[69] At Pelzer, a small 'model' cotton factory town in South Carolina under the complete control of the Pelzer family, there was a school for the children of construction workers (almost all white and, until the turn of the century, not immigrants); a church shared by Baptists, Methodists, and Presbyterians; a town marshal employed by Pelzer to enforce paternalistic rules (no drunkenness, no dogs). The work contracts required attendance at school by all children until the age of twelve, and they were expected to take jobs in the mill once they had completed their education. At one point the US Steel Corporation owned 28,000 houses in which its employees lived.[70] In Pullman, a factory town near Chicago (founded by George Pullman) where the famous railway carriages were manufactured, the workers were provided with libraries, theatres, and churches. The owners controlled all local politics. Paternalistic policies were wound down after the 1894 strike and the subsequent violent repression.[71]

The richest man in Belgium, Raoul Warocqué, who had inherited the coalmines at Campine, was a philanthropist who distributed soup and bread to the poor, supported the Université Libre de Bruxelles, the *École des Mines*, an orphanage, a childcare facility, and a maternity hospital; and he was also the local mayor and deputy, a freemason, an anticlerical, an art collector, and a liberal supporting legislation favourable to workers, while opposing the right to strike.

Baron Alphonse de Rothschild, reputedly the richest man in France (banker, art collector, owner of railways, vineyards, racehorses), and who, according to the Jewish Encyclopaedia of 1906, gave large sums to charities committed to improving the conditions of the working class, was against any kind of protection for trade unions or strikers.[72] If the government were to protect trade unions and grant the right to strike, he told Jules Huret, 'in ten years' time there will be no commerce or industry left in France'. If workers worked only eight hours a day, they would drink or go to the cabaret the rest of the time. The workers who demanded the eight-hour day were the lazy and the incompetent ones.[73] Each has the capital he deserves due to his work, energy, and intelligence, declared the Baron, who had inherited all of his wealth.

In Germany, as elsewhere, the most important instances of paternalism were in the coal, iron, and steel industries, where disruption would be particularly costly. In the Saarland, Carl Ferdinand Stumm, a champion of the principle of compulsory insurance (see Chapter 14), ran his steel and mining works on military lines, requiring that workers obtain his permission before they marry, and he forbade the reading of certain newspapers and involvement with trade unions or social democratic politics. In exchange, so to speak, he paid better wages, provided interest-free mortgages as well as schools, nurseries, playgrounds, libraries, sports clubs, and needlework classes. Involvement in forbidden activities would be punished while punctuality and loyalty to the firm would be rewarded.[74]

Emil Kirdorf, the 'king of coal and steel', thought, in 1905, that it was 'regrettable that our workers are in a position to change their places at any time. I do not demand that legislation come to our assistance, but we must reserve the right to take measures in order to stop this frequent change of employment.'[75] In other words, workers should be like serfs, tied to their place of work, but at least serfs were not expected to move at the will of the company, as they often had if they worked for the railways.[76] Kirdorf, who lived a long life, was a Nazi supporter in the 1920s and was decorated by Hitler on his 90th birthday in 1937.

When workers went on strikes at Carnegie's Homestead Steel plant in Pennsylvania in 1892, asking that their union be recognized, Andrew Carnegie, the great philanthropist, along with his associate Henry Clay Frick, union-buster and art patron, broke the strike with the help of the private security firm Pinkerton. Carnegie is now better known for the thousands of public libraries he endowed as well as a whole range of educational institutions he funded. As for Henry Clay Frick, his remarkable, world-famous art collection is now housed in his former residence on New York's Fifth Avenue.

Paternalistic capitalism failed almost everywhere. The only possible exception was in Japan, where in the first decade of the twentieth century large companies, it was believed, should be loyal to loyal employees and guarantee them lifetime employment (*shūshin koyō*) and not get rid of them during an economic downturn. The paternalism of Japanese employers had traditional (feudal) roots, as explained in their daily paper, the *Economic Journal*, of 22 August 1891:

> In Japan relations between employer and employee are regulated by time-honored customs and moral principles. These are like relations between father and son, lord and vassal, or teacher and disciple. They should not be regarded in the same light as employment relations in the West.[77]

This system survived the interwar years and the Second World War. It developed substantially in the decades after 1945. As the long post-war Japanese boom subsided, the so-called lifetime employment began to break down. In the period we are examining there was no strong trade union movement and a Japanese socialist movement barely existed. Industrial conflicts were limited. Then, just as the Meiji elites sent missions to Europe and the United States to learn how to organize a modern society, so did those who sought to establish a modern labour movement. The *Shokko Giyukai* (Knights of Labor), a society aimed at promoting trade unions, sent representatives to the USA (the largest American trade union of the 1880s was called the Knights of Labor). On their return in 1896, they launched a 'Call to the Workers'. They warned that foreign capitalists, attracted by low Japanese wages, would come to exploit workers, and 'if you workers do not prepare to meet this challenge you will follow the same sad deplorable fate of European and American workers'.[78] In the same year the government established a commission to carry out an inquiry into the conditions of the working class.[79] What worried the Japanese authorities was that overworked workers might not be fit to be soldiers and meet the Meiji objective of *fukoku kyōhei* ('enrich the country; strengthen the army'). Although business leaders opposed intervention, the government was unusually firm. In 1911 it introduced norms for the protection of women and children and set up a factory inspectorate. Workers' welfare, however, was left to the discretion of employers.[80]

Even in Italy the state was abandoning its role as a minimalist *Nachtwächterstaat* ('Nightwatchman state', an expression coined by the socialist leader Ferdinand Lassalle in 1862) in favour of liberal interventionism.[81] The great liberal leader Giovanni Giolitti, in an attempt to push the country's economic elites into the twentieth century, accused the outgoing government of treating all workers' associations as dangerous, even though this was no longer how such things were viewed in 'civilized countries' – by which he meant Great Britain and France, liberal Italy's main models. Giolitti believed that socialism was best fought by improving the welfare of the poorer strata and encouraging small private property.[82] He wanted a capitalist society where the working classes would have a stake. Giolitti accepted the existence of trade unions, their value, and their right to be represented politically and exercise influence, as long as they did not exercise power. He hoped that the bourgeoisie would rule in perpetuity, but he knew it would be able to do so only if it became an 'enlightened' bourgeoisie.[83] The state should remain impartial in the conflict between capital and labour; each should have their own representation and be equal before the law. Trade unions reacted towards the government in a hostile way because of the hostility exhibited by successive governments. But, Giolitti went on to argue, unions were the legitimate representatives of the working classes. Political institutions should fear disorganized crowds, not organized workers. There was no reason why the state should object if workers were able to obtain higher pay thanks to their unions. It was not the business of the state to defend the entrepreneurial classes. After all, it would be wrong to depress salaries below their economically 'fair' level since countries where workers were well paid were in the vanguard of economic progress.[84] The formation of trade unions was part of the progress of civilizations, Giolitti explained in a famous speech on 4 February 1901.[85] Shown a cable in which a senator lamented that 'Today I, a senator of the Kingdom of Italy, had to use the plough myself because my workers, for centuries loyal to my family, are on strike with the assent of the government,' Giolitti replied: 'May I encourage you to continue to do so. You will thus be able to realize how fatiguing it must be and you will pay your workers better.'[86]

A renewed wave of labour unrest strong enough to worry the bourgeoisie had encouraged the development of Giolitti's policies. The unrest had been the result of laws restricting strikes and press freedoms promulgated in February 1899 and the subsequent decision of the Constitutional Court (*Corte di Cassazione*) to declare these laws unconstitutional. In 1900 a huge dock strike in Genoa led to the fall of the government and the beginning of a new phase in which the more moderate exponents of Italian liberalism, such as Giolitti, acquired influence and power.[87] The subsequent elections (June 1900) strengthened the Socialists, who obtained 13 per cent of the vote, 10 per cent more than previously. A month later, in July, King Umberto I was killed by an anarchist. A new reformist government led by Giuseppe Zanardelli was installed and Giolitti was appointed Interior Minister. He turned out to be the real architect of Italy's social policy.

He had explained his long-term vision to the electors of Caraglio, his Piedmontese constituency, in the following terms: at home, politics should maximize the welfare of the greatest number of citizens, encourage public education, industry, and agriculture, reduce public spending, help 'the toiling classes', and guarantee freedom. Abroad, Italy should pursue a policy of peace. Italy had no choice but to follow this 'democratic' course and reject what Giolitti called the 'imperial course'.[88]

Giolitti was five times Prime Minister in Italy's numerous pre-war coalition governments: 1892–3, 1903–5, 1906–9, 1911–14 (when universal manhood suffrage was introduced), and finally, after the war, in 1920–21. His most important parliamentary speech, however, was probably the one he gave when he became Minister of the Interior, in February 1901. In it he warned:

> We are at the beginning of a new historical period. One must be blind not to see it. New popular strata are entering our political life; every day there are new problems, and new forces arise with which any government must deal. The confusions in today's parliamentary groups show that what divides us now is no longer what used to divide us.[89]

A few months later he explained that the rapidly developing labour movement required the introduction of social legislation. The most 'serious error of the bourgeoisie', he told his parliamentary colleagues, would be to fail to understand that they must improve the conditions of the working classes, and show them that they have more to gain from the establishment than from 'those who want to use them for their own political ends'.[90]

Giolitti was a far-seeing and enlightened bourgeois (a rare case in Italy), who defended the state and the values of the Risorgimento, and who denounced – not for the first time – the numerous indirect taxes (on bread and salt, for instance) that hit the poor disproportionately. In the years leading up to the First World War, Italy began to develop the kind of social legislation that was already entrenched elsewhere: laws protecting working women and children (1902); compensation for workers' injuries (1904); public health legislation (1907); the establishment of *Cassa di maternità* (1910) for the protection of mothers; and the setting up of a Labour Inspectorate (1912) to ensure that labour legislation was enforced.[91] Social reforms, Giolitti claimed, with considerable sagacity, were perfectly compatible with capitalism. This is why, decades later, he received a positive encomium from an unusual source: Palmiro Togliatti, leader of the Italian Communist Party, who, in a speech in 1950, said that Giolitti was, of the men of his epoch, the one who had understood better which way Italian society should proceed.[92]

Giolitti was not alone in his battle to improve conditions. Francesco Saverio Nitti, a leading *meridionalista* (a loose group of Southern intellectuals), had already complained that Italian social legislation was the worst in Europe – an exaggeration, but then Nitti's models were Great Britain, France, and Germany, not Bulgaria and Spain.[93] His journal, *La Riforma sociale*, became the stronghold of liberal economists amenable to listening to the growing voice of the labour movement.[94] The Pope, with the encyclical *Rerum Novarum* of 1891, had also joined the reformist camp in competition with the Socialists. The defenders of the non-interventionist state were, increasingly, in a minority. These included people such as the liberal economist Luigi Einaudi (who became President of the Republic in 1948, though he had voted for the monarchy in the referendum of 1946); he dogmatically repeated the truisms of a previous era, attacking the corrupting aspects of state intervention and celebrating the hegemonic role of the entrepreneurial classes.[95] The Milan daily the *Corriere della Sera*, Italy's main newspaper and the de facto organ of the bourgeoisie, equally opposed Giolitti. The *Corriere* wanted a strong state hostile to the labour movement. As for the industrialists, they simply regarded Giolitti as a dupe or a servant of the Socialists.[96]

From 1900 to 1902 there was a clear improvement in the economic situation but, at the same time, an increase in labour conflicts, almost as if to prove Giolitti's idea that class conflict was part and parcel of capitalist modernization. If Giolitti, ultimately, failed in 'making the Italians', this was due to the weakness of the Italian state, not its excessive strength; to division among the ruling elites; the failure to bring down military spending; the obscurantism of the entrepreneurs; and to the provincialism of its intelligentsia. This, and much else, turned Giolitti's reformism into what some have called, with exaggerated severity, a 'reformism without reforms', *un riformismo senza riforme*.[97]

Legislation, trade unions, and paternalism were all ways to mitigate the 'red in tooth and claw' aspects of capitalism. The labour movement was usually regarded as the main opponent of capitalism. Yet it was a creature of capitalism: no capitalism, no workers. It was almost always a reformist movement against the harsher manifestations of capitalism, such as long hours and low wages, but not necessarily against the system per se. As wages increased and conditions improved, enmity against capitalism subsided, without ever disappearing. Trade unionists, wearing their trade union hats and not their revolutionary berets, were ready to accept capitalist relations and even profit-making as long as workers obtained their 'fair share'. What was 'fair' was a matter for negotiation, even involving bitter disputes with strikes and lock-outs, but it also meant that there could be such a thing as 'fair' capitalism. One just had to fight for it. And while capitalism needed workers, the *owners* of capital were unnecessary – the unanswerable argument of socialists. Of course, managers were needed, but one could always find them and pay them, and, if required, pay them well.

Eventually 'capitalists' became simply the owners of capital but, at the end of the nineteenth century, the separation of ownership and management was in its infancy, except in some enterprises, such as railways and oil, which required such large amounts of capital that no single person or even group of persons could finance them without the help of many investors; although, as Louis Brandeis pointed out before the First World War, a few men could control American corporations without owning them.[98] Even John Rockefeller, the richest man in the United States before the war, held only a fraction of Standard Oil shares.[99] In the twenty-first century, shareholders, whether the stereotypical old lady sitting on her shares in some far-flung part of the country or the impersonal investment funds (such as pension funds, mutual funds, hedge funds, etc.), have little effective control over the actual running of the company, nor do they wish to have any. All they want is for the shares to appreciate in value and for the dividends to be paid. Thus the actual owners of capital are, in fact, real business parasites.[100] As long as they are content, the managers, having, in effect, taken over from the owners of capital, can use their position of power to appropriate for themselves extravagant sums, in the guise of salaries and bonuses, which is the situation that faces us now. In the nineteenth century, savers would have put their money under the mattress in the knowledge that inflation barely existed, or in a bank to collect interest, or in property. They would have been called 'rentiers' and despised accordingly. Today they are ordinary citizens, even less knowledgeable than yesterday's rentiers, who entrust their savings and their pensions to financial advisers and fund managers.[101]

16
God and Capitalism

Religion had an important humanizing role to play because capitalism was becoming impersonal. The visible figure of the owner-entrepreneur who could behave in a tyrannical manner, but also with humanity (just like some slave-owners were 'good' and others 'wicked'), was becoming less central to the system. In capitalism both capitalists and workers were at the mercy of economic relations which they had not created, and which, though man-made, were as impersonal as the British court system denounced by Dickens in *Bleak House* when his character Mr Gridley exclaims in a rage: 'The system! I am told on all hands, it's the system. I mustn't look to individuals. It's the system.'[1]

If capitalism and the labour movement were relatively new, religious beliefs were as old as humanity. Religions, however, generally said little about the economic organization of society, though some economic activities were disliked or prohibited, for instance usury (in the sense of excessively high interest) by the Roman Catholic Church. Dante, in his *Divine Comedy*, had placed usurers in Hell to be burnt by a constant rain of fire. Yet the modern banking system was born in Catholic Italy, in the shadow of the throne of St Peter's. The Lutheran Reformation was more open-minded, though it objected to the sale of indulgences, to what today we might call the privatization of salvation: buy indulgences to get to heaven, or, as Martin Luther put it in one of his Ninety-Five Theses (no. 27), 'as soon as the money clinks into the money chest, the soul flies out of purgatory'.[2] But John Calvin discarded the prohibition of usury and might have been pleased, though not surprised, that his adopted city, Geneva, has become a major financial centre; since the sixteenth century it has been a thriving commercial hub. Islam (like Judaism) had no particular animosity towards commerce (the Prophet Muhammad was himself a merchant and so was his wife Khadija), but prohibited the taking of interest (yet through legal subterfuges and creative accounting some get round the prohibition). The Torah regarded usury as perfectly acceptable, as long as lending was done to non-Jews: 'Do not charge a fellow Israelite interest' (Deuteronomy 23:19–20).

Confucianism, with filial obedience as its cardinal principle, thought commerce was demeaning and vulgar but never suggested it should be banned. As the Master (Confucius) said: 'The superior man (the gentleman) seeks virtue, the inferior man (the small man) seeks material things' (*Analects* 4.11). During the latter part of the Zhou Dynasty (1046–256 BC) Confucius's followers divided the people into four groups. On top were the scholars (quite rightly), then the farmers, then the artisans, and, at the bottom, the merchants and traders (*shāng*). Even during the Ming and Qing Dynasties (1368–1644 and 1644–1911) commerce was seen as a vulgar occupation (as in some aristocratic Victorian circles), which is not to say that the Qing state was not extremely active in facilitating commercial growth.[3]

Hinduism too has four classes or *Varna* with the scholars (Brahmin) on top, followed by the Kshatriya (soldiers), the Vaishya (farmers and traders) and, at the bottom, the servants or *Shudra*, while the Untouchables, now called *Dalit*, were outside society. Buddhism has little to say about commerce, though it urged its followers to eliminate selfishness and an acquisitive mentality. Judaism, in spite of all the stereotypes about Jews and money, has no significant position on commerce, let alone capitalism.

The Russian Orthodox Church had been, in Richard Pipes's words, the 'servant of the state' since the days of Peter the Great: the Tsar appointed all the senior bishops and high-ranking lay personnel to the Holy Synod, which was a tool of the Tsar.[4] On industry and social questions the Russian Church produced little independent thinking. It was alienated from the intelligentsia and was not a popular institution; priests were held in low esteem even by the peasantry.[5] It completely failed to address itself to the problems of industrialization.[6] Liberalizing legislation in 1905 and 1906 established religious tolerance and granted other 'sects' – such as the Old Believers – certain rights, forcing churchmen to rethink their relationship with an increasingly fragmented society.[7] Of course, there were socially concerned clergy, such as Sergei Bulgakov, elected to the Duma in 1907 as a Christian socialist, and Father Georgy Gapon, who, in 1903, formed the Assembly of Russian Workers, and in 1905 led the demonstration of Bloody Sunday. But the Russian Church, on the whole, stamped down successfully on liberalizing tendencies.[8]

The obvious candidate for the most capitalist-friendly religion was Protestantism, especially Calvinism. This was theorized by Max Weber, in his celebrated *The Protestant Ethic and the Spirit of Capitalism*, a series of essays written in 1904–5. (Marx had somewhat preceded him by musing that Protestantism, 'by changing almost all the traditional holidays into workdays, plays an important part in the genesis of capital'.)[9] Weber was particularly interested in the doctrine of predestination, a core claim in Calvinism, since, with predestination, it was impossible to 'buy' one's way into the saved by good deeds or good works, or by repenting one's sins. Given the uncertainty of one's salvation, explained Weber, a Calvinist had to behave as if he was one of the elect: 'Restless work in a vocational calling was recommended as the best possible means to acquire the self-confidence that one belonged to the elect.'[10] Worldly success could be taken as a sign that one was going to be saved. Weber argued that since Calvinism was hostile to giving money to the poor (it encouraged indolence) and frowned on the idea of spending it on luxuries (sinful), and since one was supposed to work hard, the best thing one could do with one's money was to make more of it. This was the ethical basis of capitalism, explained Weber, which is why, or so he claimed, it was born in Protestant countries. The British historian and Christian socialist R. H. Tawney followed in Weber's footsteps with his *Religion and the Rise of Capitalism* (1926), where the true initiators of capitalism are the Puritans: Puritanism 'became a potent force in preparing the way for the commercial civilization which finally triumphed at the Revolution'.[11]

Such connections between religion and capitalism seem to be simplistic. If commerce and industry had never developed in Calvinist countries an explanation would immediately surface attributing such failures to the fatalistic and deterministic outlook of Calvinism, just as some have attributed the presumed lack of entrepreneurial spirit in India to Hinduism, karma, and mysticism. Yet there is no empirical evidence to show that Hindus who 'profess such beliefs have become fatalistic and other-worldly and as a result do not arrive on time for appointments, have a high frequency of absences from their jobs'.[12]

Weber never claimed that his argument was a total explanation for the rise of capitalism (as some of his followers maintained), but it rests anyway on dubious historical foundations. Capitalism, whether as merchant capitalism, finance capital or manufacturing capital, was thriving in much of Catholic Italy in the fourteenth and fifteenth centuries, particularly in Genoa, Venice, and Florence (see Introduction). In fourteenth-century Florence the wool guild alone accounted for some hundreds of firms, employing 10,000 workers. As the historian of Florence John Najemy writes: 'Measured by the number of entrepreneurs and labourers, the manufacture and sales of textiles constituted Florence's largest complex of economic activities.'[13] In eighteenth-century Ming China the region of Jiangnan (south of the Yangtze) was a major producer and exporter of silk and cotton. Catholic Belgium was the first industrial country in continental Europe, and Ghent, famous for its cotton mills, became known as the 'Manchester of Flanders'. Moreover, a careful comparison of economic growth in Protestant and Catholic cities and regions over the very long run (1300–1900) found that religion made no difference at all.[14] (The main difference was that the population in Protestant countries was more literate than that in Catholic countries.)[15]

In the later part of the twentieth century capitalism did well in Buddhist and Shinto Japan, as well as, even more recently, in Confucian-Communist China. Various communities throughout the world have excelled in commerce without any connection to Protestantism: the Lebanese in Latin America, the Chinese in South-East Asia, the Guajarati in east Africa, the Hausa merchants in west Africa and, of course, the Greeks in Alexandria as well as in the Tsarist Empire, the Armenians in the Ottoman Empire, and the Jews in much of Europe and the Middle East. The only thing such disparate groups have in common is that they were often a diaspora and a minority in their host population.

Admittedly, Weber's focus was on 'modern capitalism' and not the various manufacturing and commercial activities that had existed for centuries. This, for Weber, entailed a relatively free market and a certain degree of organization. In fact, organization seems to be the central aspect: the 'systematic utilization of skills or personal capacities on behalf of earnings in such manner that, at the close of business transactions, the company's money balances or "capital" exceeds the estimated value of all production costs':[16] a roundabout way of saying, 'maximizing profit'.

Religion did not like the pursuit of money for its own sake, and though not specifically anti-capitalist, it looked with some hostility at capitalism's manifestations and, above all, to its modernity. Religion, and Christianity in particular, for obvious historical reasons, was unavoidably linked to rural life. This is where most of the churches had been built, where the faithful could be found, where the priests lived, where one was at the mercy of the weather and the elements, and praying seemed a rational way of facing the unexpected. Capitalism was about cities, the class struggle, the cult of the individual, democracy, secularist values, and sinful entertainments. It was not conducive to family life. In a village families work in close proximity. In a city everyone works separately. Cities created circumstances where religiosity was more difficult and one lost one's faith only too easily. In 1869 rural churches in Germany were full. But in Berlin in the same year only one per cent of nominally Protestant workers went to church on Sundays; in Leipzig and Bremen it was much the same.[17]

Although the nineteenth century was and is seen as the century of secularism, secular advances were met by countervailing revivals of religiosity. In Weber's days, religion appeared to be on the wane, but it was on the wane, if at all, only among the elites and above all among the educated elites. America was more religious at the end of the nineteenth century than at the beginning. In Ireland there were twice as many priests in 1901, proportionately, than in 1800. There were far more nuns in Germany in 1908 than in 1866.[18] One in eight books published in Germany in the 1870s was a work of theology.[19]

As democracy expanded, religion too had to organize itself along the lines dictated by the evolution of the state. Once upon a time the Churches had to deal with absolute rulers, kings, princes, and emperors. Now they had to deal with parliaments, elections, voters, lobbies, and pressure groups. In some countries religion had to organize itself as a political party, begging for votes, just like liberals, socialists, and conservatives. This was not a universal position. In Britain, no confessional party ever emerged, even though the Conservative Party was regarded as the 'Anglican Party' and the Church of England as the 'Tory party at prayer'; and there was a close connection between the so-called Nonconformist Churches (which included Methodists, Presbyterians, Baptists, Quakers, and others) and the Liberal Party and, later, the Labour Party.

Hugh Price Hughes's *Methodist Times* and the Congregationalist William Robertson Nicoll's *British Weekly* (both founded in 1885–6) tried to persuade their readers to consider the social implications of their faith. The *Methodist Times* rejected the idea that poverty was the fruit of sin. In 1893 an assembly of the Congregational Union agreed that 'the rights of humanity must always take precedence over those of property' and that profits from coal mining 'made out of the labours of men receiving wages inadequate for the support of themselves and their families are obviously inconsistent with righteousness and fraternity . . .'.[20] Resistance was considerable, partly because members of the congregation tended to be middle class and hostile to anything that smacked of socialism, and partly because strict evangelicals maintained that the duty of a Christian was to reject the world not to reform it.[21] Compromise was often reached by reasserting the rights of property as well as the duty of Christians 'to diminish the inequalities which unjust laws and customs produce . . .'.[22] There was always much concern about the threat of socialism among the labouring classes.

Some members of these Nonconformist Churches, such as the Quakers, were extraordinarily active in business and founded the Lloyds banking group, Barclays Bank, the match-making concern Bryant and May, Clark rugs and later shoes, famous manufacturers of confectionery such as Cadbury and Rowntree and many others. Bethlehem Steel in the United States and, of course, Quaker Oats were also founded by Quakers.

The involvement of religion in politics was different from country to country. In Japan the official state religion in the years between the Meiji Restoration (1868) and 1945, Shinto, was used to celebrate nationalism and keep the country united, not unlike Anglicanism in England and Catholicism in Ireland and Poland, but there was no formal Shinto party. In fact, there never was in Japan an ecclesiastical force aspiring to match in any way the powers of the central government.[23]

In Italy, since national unification had taken place against his wishes, Pope Pius IX had forbidden Catholics from taking part in the politics of the new state. His letter *Non expedit* ('It is not convenient', 1874) prohibited the formation of a Catholic party. Good Catholics should not vote. If they did, they would be excommunicated and go to Hell. Gradually, the Church relented. Pius X, in his encyclical *Il Fermo Proposito* ('The Firm Purpose', 1905), encouraged Catholics to vote (he was worried about the advances of socialism). But it was only in 1919 that Benedict XV allowed the formation of a Catholic party, the *Partito Popolare Italiano*.

In Latin America the great divide was not socialism versus capitalism or liberalism, but secular liberalism versus the Church. There were no Catholic parties of note, though, obviously, Catholicism was (and is) a very strong force. In Ecuador, President García Moreno (1861–5, 1869–75) took a decisive stand against liberalism and attempted to set up a Christian state – in fact, under his authoritarian rule, remarkable social progress was made, particularly in education and road building (expropriating landlords where necessary).[24] In Brazil, Argentina, Chile and, above all, Mexico, anticlerical secularism emerged politically triumphant, while the masses remained deeply Catholic.[25]

While in Latin America both Catholics and liberals were in favour of the Republic, this was not so in France. Jules Ferry (who was both Education Minister and Prime Minister in the 1880s), in a letter in 1872, declared that the Republic has only one enemy: the clergy.[26] Léon Gambetta (also Prime Minister in the 1880s) agreed, declaring, in May

1876, that a patriotic Catholic was a 'rare thing'.[27] He had a point since, at the time, Catholics were staunchly monarchist and against the Third Republic. Church rhetoric was just as strident. The anticlerical paper *Le Républicain de la Loire et de la Haute Loire* in July 1876 reported that the curé of Estadens (Haute-Garonne) had declared from his pulpit: 'If the Republic triumphs churches will be destroyed, priests guillotined, a terrible civil war will break out.'[28]

There were in fact three ways of being on the right in late nineteenth-century France. The first consisted in being a true reactionary and longing for a return to the monarchy of pre-1789, the old-fashioned France of rural deference, family values, and Catholicism. This ideology (not always in conjunction with monarchism) was still held to decades later by writers such as Charles Maurras and Maurice Barrés, and had many supporters in Vichy France, above all its leader, Marshal Pétain.[29] The second way of being right-wing was to be a Bonapartist, which meant to be in favour of 'a strong man', if only they could find one. Their ideas survive to this day. The third way of being right-wing in late nineteenth-century France was to be a supporter of the Orléans Dynasty, that is, a liberal democratic monarchy tinted with Catholicism. Eventually, the commitment to the monarchy, even a democratic and constitutional one, was abandoned and the modern form of conservatism found a later incarnation in General de Gaulle.

Actual capitalists in France took very little interest in this controversy since it was not clear which side they should be on. Catholicism might have been the favoured choice, out of habit and a desire to keep everyone, especially the workers, in their place. But as the Republic was consolidated, capitalists switched to the republican side, partly because it was winning and partly because it had become abundantly clear that republicans were more interested in priest-bashing than in interfering with capitalism. Republican ideology, to the extent there was one, meant being generically in favour of reason, science, positivism, and progress, and that meant industry.[30] This was appealing to some industrialists, flattered to be told that their money-making activities were on the side of history, but others such as Schneider, the leading steel magnate (see Chapter 15), found solace in the doctrine of social Catholicism advocated by thinkers like Albert de Mun, the leading Catholic politician in France, for it confirmed the paternalistic model they had adopted in their own establishment.

Of course, Catholics were not a monolithic bloc. The more intransigent among them followed the commands of Pius IX's 1864 encyclical *Quanta Cura*, which condemned the idea of liberty of conscience.

Its annex, the *Syllabus Errorum*, castigated liberalism, modern civilization, and progress, and regarded socialism as a 'pest'.[31] This was not quite new. Pope Gregory XVI had already condemned liberalism with his *Mirari Vos* in 1832, as well as French Catholic 'liberals' such as Félicité Robert de Lamennais, one of the earliest champions of social Catholicism.

Theologians and Catholic intellectuals of the intransigent tendency (known in France, pejoratively, as *Ultramontanisme*) rejected individualism, rationalism, and the secular state, insisting on the absolute primacy of papal power. Catholic popularizers of this tendency, such as the journalist Eugène Veuillot, author of *Çà et là* (1860), rejoiced that France, lacking the mineral wealth of England, had been spared the abominations of industry. England, 'until it returns to Catholicism', will remain 'a depraved nation' with 'Men and women working naked on top of each other; children growing up in the depth of caves without ever hearing the word of God, surfacing occasionally only to get drunk with their parents.'[32] Equally reactionary was the now forgotten Antoine de Saint-Bonnet (1815–80), then an anti-Semite (see Chapter 12) and regarded highly as a thinker. Saint-Bonnet condemned capitalism because it was based on the exploitation of man by man, socialism because it was the heir to liberalism and Protestantism, and the Republic because it 'will be the ruin of the people and of the whole of humanity'. He condemned democracy and defended aristocratic rule (he was an aristocrat himself); the people, he complained, ruined by industry and banks, no longer dream of Heaven and seek instead earthly riches; they produce more just to consume more instead of loving each other.[33]

Intransigent Catholicism was not so distant from social Catholicism – its 'progressive' counterpart. Both shared an exaltation of tradition, a rejection of the present, a nostalgia for the rural world, a defence of the family, a hatred of the centralist state, a discontent with a society constantly on the move, a distaste for socialism and anarchism, and all the other 'ills' that followed the French Revolution. Albert de Mun, a traditional reactionary, opposed to universal suffrage, and an anti-Dreyfusard, was clearly on the 'left' on the 'social question', namely the question of the condition of the working class. In February 1885, in a speech at the Université Catholique de Louvain in Belgium, where he had considerable influence, he urged his followers:

> let us go to the workers, understand them, love them. Let us go to find out what causes their suffering and what they want . . . In their

isolation they are looking for friends who would help them rather than exploit them.[34]

The hardship caused by industrialization had been castigated by leading members of the Catholic clergy throughout the world, who often made common cause with the exploited workers: from Cardinal Bonald, the Archbishop of Lyon, to Wilhelm Emmanuel von Ketteler, the Bishop of Mainz, author of *Die Arbeiterfrage und das Christenthum* (*The Workers' Question and Christianity*, 1864), clearly influenced by the socialist leader Ferdinand Lassalle; Cardinal Henry Edward Manning, Archbishop of Westminster (whose funeral, in 1892, was followed by trade union banners); Gaspar Decurtins, a leader of the Swiss *Parti Catholique-Conservateur* (today's Christian Democratic Party), organizer of one of the first international congresses for the protection of workers in Zurich in 1897 (a precursor of the ILO); and Cardinal James Gibbons, Archbishop of Baltimore (1877–1921), who wrote that it was 'the right of the laboring classes to protect themselves' and it was everyone's duty to help them to find a 'remedy against avarice, oppression and corruption'.[35]

By the end of the 1880s, French social Catholicism began to diverge from the intransigents and to accept democracy and republicanism.[36] This *ralliement* to the Republic was promoted by Pope Leo XIII. The Pope started cautiously, with the encyclical *Libertas* (1888), where he declared that it was a calumny to say that the Church 'is the foe of individual and public liberty'.[37] It was followed by one of the most important encyclicals in the history of the papacy, *Rerum Novarum*, 'New Things' (15 May 1891). Leo XIII, unlike his obtuse predecessor, Pius IX, realized that industrialization and the concomitant massive exodus from the countryside was a historic revolution whereby hitherto docile peasants and rural workers would find in cities and factories, far from the watchful eye of the priest, a novel kind of class solidarity, and where they would be exposed to rival messianic creeds, such as anarchism and socialism, promising Heaven on Earth and not for the afterlife. Pope Leo XIII had embraced change. The Catholic Church, with 2,000 years of experience of survival, having sided with the reactionaries for most of the nineteenth century, was finally accepting modernity. The enemies had not changed. They were those the Pope had denounced in 1878 in his *Quod apostolici muneris* ('Of Our apostolic office'): 'men who, under various and almost barbarous names, are called socialists, communists, or nihilists, and who, spread over all the world, and bound together by the closest ties in a wicked confederacy' seek the overthrow of society.[38] What changed was the strategy.

In *Rerum Novarum*, significantly subtitled 'On the conditions of the workers' (*de conditione opificum*), Leo XIII advocated saving 'unfortunate working people from the cruelty of men of greed, who use human beings as mere instruments for money-making'. He insisted that wages and working conditions should not be left to the good intentions of the employers but should be negotiated, possibly with the mediation or intervention of the state. The aim was, of course, to maintain social peace, avoiding the 'mistaken notion' that 'class is naturally hostile to class', above all to make sure that the socialists do not exploit 'the poor man's envy of the rich'. And since a few rich men 'have been able to lay upon the teeming masses of the labouring poor a yoke little better than that of slavery itself', the authorities should intervene whenever working conditions are unjust, or 'repugnant' to the dignity of workers as 'human beings'. 'Wages', continued the Pope, should be high enough 'to support a frugal and well-behaved wage-earner'. And if 'through necessity or fear of a worse evil the workman accept harder conditions because an employer or contractor will afford him no better', then workers' unions are 'greatly to be desired'.[39]

This was the signal many Catholics had wanted: they could now compete with liberals and socialists in advocating social reforms, form new trade unions to wean workers away from those under socialist influence, and build organizations and civic associations dealing with urban problems. Intelligent conservatives realized the significance of this move at once. Ruggiero Bonghi, former Italian Minister of Education, in the journal *Nuova Antologia* immediately welcomed *Rerum Novarum*, remarking that 'Atheism has more and more influence among the working classes. The common people, those of the towns, but not yet those in the countryside, are the most reluctant to follow any kind of religious or spiritual authority.' They see God as the ally of capital and of the rich, he added, and, consequently, want to abolish God.[40]

French bishops welcomed the encyclical, aware of what Alphonse Martin Larue, Bishop of Langres, called 'the new conditions of industrial life'.[41] Finally, they could dispel what another French bishop, the Bishop of Bayonne, quaintly called in his pastoral letter announcing the encyclical, the *malentendu* (misunderstanding) between the 'peuple ouvrier', the working people, and the Church.[42] Socialists ignored the encyclical, especially in France, where labour activists were not very Catholic.[43] Leo XIII had thought principally of France when he wrote *Rerum Novarum*, and followed it with another encyclical specifically directed at the French, giving it a French title: *Au milieu des sollicitudes* (20 February 1892). In it he denounced even more forcefully the excesses of capitalism and the love of money.[44] But *Au milieu des sollicitudes* had also a specifically political objective: the Pope wanted to prevent the birth in France of the kind of monarchist Catholic party that Albert de Mun wanted to create, a party that would fight for social legislation 'in the name of Jesus Christ'.[45] The Pope, obviously a clever man, believed that this would unnecessarily inflame anticlerical republicans. Better to form a not overtly Catholic party that would espouse generic religious principles, attract Catholics, make its peace with the republic, and forget about the monarchy.

The advantage of being Pope is that, on the whole, good Catholics obey you, and Albert de Mun obeyed: there would be no specifically Catholic party in France. Leo XIII met him halfway. In the middle of the crisis caused by the Dreyfus Affair and the wave of anticlericalism that would lead to the separation of Church and State in France in 1905, he encouraged Albert de Mun to form a pro-Catholic party, as long as it was open to all 'honest people', as long as it was not formally Catholic, and as long as it was pro-Republic. It was the birth of *Action libérale populaire*, in 1901, soon to become the main opposition party. In 1903 de Mun explained to his followers that a Catholic party could only be the 'core' (*noyau*) of a wider party; it cannot be, on its own, a political party, it would not have sufficient electoral appeal and this is why, he added, the Pope was quite right to order him not to form one.[46]

One of the most important influences on French social Christians such as de Mun was Frédéric Le Play, a conservative thinker who belonged to the right-wing tradition of French authoritarianism. On social matters, however, Le Play was a reformist and even an early ecologist (as many conservatives were at the time) who denounced the destruction of forests for profit and gain.[47] He was an engineer turned sociologist and an admirer of the positivism of Auguste Comte. In his *La réforme sociale en France déduite de l'observation comparée des peuples européens* (1864), he denounced the dismal conditions of the working class and the rapid accumulation of wealth, which, he thought, made men lazy and prey to lust, selfishness, and so on. He held the view that work, after religion, property, and family, was what could best elevate humanity towards an *ordre moral*. For the aim of work was not wealth but virtue.[48] The virtues required by entrepreneurs were order and love of justice.[49] A religious sense of solicitude towards one's subordinates was one of the distinctive virtues of the truly superior classes. In other words those like Le Play who were often, and not wrongly, characterized as being nostalgic about the *Ancien Régime*, were in fact trying to achieve a new synthesis: no longer an uncritical admiration for the old order, but a desire to show the lower classes that their interests would best be served by those who espoused traditional religious values. This was all the more important given the remarkable degree of indifference towards their welfare exhibited by the liberal ideology of the politically dominant republican groups.

The disdain for liberalism by socially concerned Christians was almost universal. In Italy, Catholics followed the French pattern: both traditionalists and the socially concerned were united by a vague hostility towards the new industrial society. Carlo Maria Curci, one of the founders of the Jesuit journal *Civiltà cattolica*, found positive elements in socialism, declaring that it was not possible to find happiness just by accumulating goods.[50] Curci was astute enough to realize that there was no question of returning to a time before unification when the Pope ruled over central Italy. It was useless, Curci warned Catholics, to fight against the ideas of democracy and nationalism that had 'taken possession of the world'.[51] But in politics it does not always pay to be too prescient, and Curci was too left-wing too soon and was expelled from the Jesuits. Romolo Murri, a priest and an inspirer of Italian Christian Democracy, unsuccessfully urged the ecclesiastical authorities to create a Catholic party hostile to capitalism to block the further growth of socialism in Italy. 'The industrial proletariat,' wrote Murri, 'wanted to have a soul, a class consciousness. It remembered the miseries it suffered, the paltry wages it received . . .' Now, he went on, it is no longer on its knees, and appears '*terribile, feroce*'. 'This new class consciousness', continued Murri in the biblical style fashionable among Catholics at the time, though 'savage' and 'brutal', could be used by true Christians. The Church had waited too long and let the socialists have an early start in the struggle for the minds and hearts of the proletariat.[52] This was far too radical for the Church. Murri was suspended from the priesthood '*a divinis*' in 1907. Impenitent, he was elected to Parliament in 1909 for the *Lega Democratica Nazionale*, a (Catholic) organization not approved by the Pope. He was immediately excommunicated.

This itinerary was not unusual. In Poland, Izydor Kajetan Wysłouch (1869–1937) had started out as a socially concerned Catholic intellectual. As he became increasingly active, he became more radical, began to attack the Church for its immobility, and was eventually excommunicated.[53]

Christian hostility against economic liberalism was just as strong in non-Catholic countries, including Britain, where many religious people were more vociferous against the liberalism of the so-called Manchester School than against socialism (which, anyway, was not a force in

Victorian England). Charles Kingsley, chaplain to the Queen and celebrated novelist (*Westward Ho!*, 1855, and *The Water Babies*, 1863, about chimney sweeps), in a letter to his friend Thomas Hughes, a Christian socialist (author of the famous book *Tom Brown's School Days*, 1857), had urged the recognition of trade unions as early as 1852. Kingsley told Hughes that:

> the real battle of the time is – if England is to be saved from anarchy and unbelief, and utter exhaustion caused by the competitive enslavement of the masses – not Radical or Whig against Peelite or Tory . . . but the Church, the gentleman, and the workman, against the shopkeepers and the Manchester School.

He thought the task of 'true Conservatism' was 'to reconcile the workmen with the real aristocracy'.[54]

Kingsley was prejudiced against Jews, Catholics, Irish, blacks, and Americans, but he reserved his severest verdict for 'Manchester liberals':

> from whom Heaven defend us; for of all narrow, conceited, hypocritical, and anarchic and atheistic schemes of the universe, the Manchester one is exactly the worst. I have no language to express my contempt for it . . . To pretend to be the workers' friend by keeping down the price of bread, when all they want is to keep down wages, and increase profits, and in the meantime to widen the gulf between the working man and all that is time-honoured, refined, and chivalrous in English society . . . that is . . . the game of the Manchester School.[55]

Such denunciations, fairly typical at the time, did not bring about the formation of a religiously based anti-capitalist party in Britain: both the Conservatives and the Liberals offered a home, for most of the nineteenth century, to those who were hostile to unfettered capitalism, either from a pre-capitalist position (the Conservatives) or in favour of a reform of capitalism (the Liberals). Later in the twentieth century the Conservatives became the main pro-capitalist party, the Liberals dwindled, while the Labour Party absorbed and virtually monopolized anti-capitalist feelings. In reality quite a few socialist-inclined thinkers would probably have been equally at home in a social Christian party nostalgic for a pre-industrial age: John Ruskin (a troubled agnostic); Frederick Denison Maurice, a founder of British Christian Socialism and of the Working Men's College (1854); Keir Hardie (evangelical, founder of the Labour Party); Ramsay Macdonald (Church of Scotland and Labour's first Prime Minister in 1924); George Lansbury (a devoted

Anglican and leader of the Labour Party, 1932–5); as well as atheists such as Robert Blatchford, whose best-selling *Merrie England* (1893) identified socialism with rural life, and William Morris, described by Friedrich Engels as an 'emotional socialist', and whose *News from Nowhere* (1890), depicted an idyllic agrarian socialist England with no industry.[56] Much of what Morris wrote on politics could have been written by a Christian socialist, or indeed, by an anti-industrial Christian:

> I found that the causes of the vulgarities of civilization lay deeper than I had thought, and little by little I was driven to the conclusion that all these uglinesses are but the outward expression of the innate moral baseness into which we are forced by our present form of society.[57]

This ambivalence towards industry was also present in northern Europe, particularly where the Lutheran Church predominated, as in Finland, Iceland, Latvia, Estonia, and the Scandinavian countries, where those who were particularly concerned with the social question ended up in the ranks of social democracy, whose anticlericalism was fairly restrained. Those concerned with defending agrarian relations against industry ended up in specifically agrarian parties. Here religion was almost incidental. Thus Santeri Alkio, who founded the Agrarian League (*Maalaisliitto*) in Finland in 1906, was a strong Christian, though also an opponent of an established state Church. The Agrarian League had no confessional basis, its main ideology being a kind of linguistic nationalism (anti-Swedish and anti-Russian) and a populism tinged with liberalism.

Some of the agrarian parties that emerged in eastern Europe likewise had no overtly religious basis. In Bulgaria the Agrarian Union, which held its first congress in 1899, originally campaigned against a new land tax proposed by the ruling Liberal Party. By 1901 it had turned itself into a fully fledged party, the Bulgarian Agrarian Popular Union – the word 'popular' signalled its ambition to be a party of the whole people and not just of the peasantry.[58] By 1908 it was the largest opposition party in the country, albeit with only 11 per cent of the vote, since the opposition was unusually fragmented.[59] Its leader, Alexander Stamboliski, an anti-monarchist who became Prime Minister after the war, wrote at length on the importance of peasants and agriculture but kept Christianity in the background. He was a corporatist in the sense that he thought that the country should be run not by political parties (which he despised) but by representatives of economic interests, namely a group of people with the same occupation (artisans, wage workers, merchants, entrepreneurs, peasants, and so on, the sort of society some Italian Fascists tried to develop in the 1930s).[60]

The Czech Agrarian Party, formed in 1899 (it merged in 1905 with its Moravian and Silesian counterparts), sought to unite all country-dwellers against rising socialism. Thus alongside typical agrarian demands (tariffs policies that suited farmers' interests, removal of 'unfair' land taxes, and so on) the party took up traditional nationalist demands, such as equality of the Czech language with the German language and as much autonomy as possible within the Austro-Hungarian Empire, but religion played no formal part in its ideological make-up.[61] Its enemies were the 'bourgeois' parties such as the Czech National Party (*Národní strana*) or Old Czech Party, and the National Liberal Party (*Národní strana svobodomyslná*), also known as the Young Czech Party, which claimed to represent the nation as a whole.[62] There was also a Czech Catholic Party, led by the priest Jan Šrámek (later Prime Minister of the Czechoslovak government-in-exile during the Second World War). It emerged in the 1890s, far stronger in Moravia, where it obtained 36.6 per cent in the 1911 elections, than in Bohemia. Inspired by *Rerum Novarum*, it stood in antagonism to the marked anticlericalism of the Young Czech Party.[63] Its real growth, however, occurred when Czechoslovakia became an independent state after the First World War.

The rise of religious-based parties in eastern Europe was further encouraged by the agrarian crisis of the 1880s, which affected peasant smallholders and rural artisans. This enabled membership of some religious-based parties to grow, as was the case with the Catholic People's Party of Hungary (founded in 1894). This was 'anti-capitalist' in the sense that it wanted to restore 'the natural order' uprooted by liberalism and capitalism, which it decried as a form of gambling. But this party was never as strong as its Austrian counterpart, Karl Lueger's Christian Social movement, which we will discuss at greater length below.[64]

Organized political Christianity was stronger in Belgium than anywhere else, followed by German-speaking areas such as Germany, Austria, and Switzerland. In Switzerland a Catholic and rural party (rather than Protestant and urban) arose as early as 1848. It changed its name to *Katholische Volkspartei* in 1894 and to *Konservative Volkspartei* in 1912, and again in 1957 before in 1970 becoming the Swiss Christian Democratic Party, until recently one of the major Swiss parties.

Of greater significance was the emergence of a Catholic political party in Bismarck's new German Empire. This Germany was roughly two-thirds Protestant and one-third Catholic. Had Austria become part of Greater Germany (*Größdeutschland*) – as many German nationalists had hoped – Catholics and Protestants would have had more or less equal weight. As it turned out, 'smaller' Germany (*Kleindeutschland*) suited the Protestants better. Apart from the obvious religious differences, Catholics were far less 'bourgeois', in the sense of middle class or *Mittelschicht*, than the Protestants; Catholic workers were more religious than their Protestant counterparts; far better organized around a formidable network of associations, charities, music societies, clubs, and so on – a path the Social Democrats also took. Catholics were thus seen by Bismarck and his main political allies, the National Liberals, as potential threats to the authority and stability of the new empire, because, or so he claimed, they did not possess a national identity (Protestants, after all, were Lutheran and hence 'more German'). Catholics looked towards Rome and had accepted the new dogma of papal infallibility – decreed by the First Vatican Council (1869–70) – just as nineteenth-century nationalism recorded its clearest victories: the unification of Germany and the 'liberation' of Rome, the new capital of a new state, by Italian troops.

Faced with growing Protestant hostility, German Catholics, to protect their rights as a minority, formed their own party, the *Deutsche Zentrumspartei* or Zentrum. Bismarck interpreted all this as the continuation of an age-old conflict for power between 'kingship and the priestly caste'.[65] Anti-Catholicism became state policy. It became known as the *Kulturkampf* (struggle for culture in the sense of struggle for civilization). This 'struggle' was particularly intense in Prussia, where the majority of Catholics were Polish – the *Kulturkampf* had a decidedly anti-Polish subtext.[66] Laws against the Jesuits were enacted, enabling the authorities to deport them at will; priests not appointed by the state were arrested; Catholic schools were subjected to strict government supervision; and some church property was confiscated. Ultimately, the *Kulturkampf* proved a failure, since it politicized Catholics to an extent unimaginable before.[67] The Zentrum became the focus of Catholic loyalties at the expense of pastors and bishops.[68] Furthermore the Bismarckian state also lacked (and failed to develop) institutions for its anti-Catholic laws. German judges had a scrupulous regard for evidence, and their rigorous approach hindered the successful implementation of the *Kulturkampf*, which, anyway, encountered considerable public hostility.[69] In the Reichstag elections of 1874 the Zentrum doubled its vote. Bismarck's Germany was not as authoritarian as is commonly thought.[70]

Bismarck, ever the realist, dropped anti-Catholic repression and, in 1878, with the support of the once so reviled Zentrum Party, turned against the socialists of the Social Democratic Party, not by banning the party outright but by making life difficult for them (banning newspapers, strikes, meetings, etc.) with the so-called Anti-Socialist Laws. The Zentrum, once a subculture, was becoming part of the establishment. It was an 'identity' party with a clear overall aim: the defence of the religious interests of Catholics. Otherwise, as was the case with nationalist parties, it was far from clear what its politics should be. Its class basis was complex: there were few Catholic industrialists, but plenty of Catholic farmers, rural dwellers, shopkeepers, and even some workers (here the competition with the SPD was keen). Catholics, like Social Democrats, opposed high taxes and military expenditure and also wanted the eight-hour day. Catholics were 'anti-centralist' because they feared a centralizing state. In fact, Catholics everywhere were anti-statist because states everywhere were encroaching on education and family law (marriage, divorce), and after all the Roman Catholic Church was a transnational organization. The Zentrum, however, was far from being a tool of Rome, as its enemies insisted. In 1887, Leo XIII, as a gesture of conciliation towards Bismarck, put pressure on the Zentrum to support the government's military budget. The Zentrum refused. The Pope leaked his instructions and allowed Bismarck to publish them.[71] Most of the senior German clergy sided with the party. The Pope, they thought, was infallible only on theological rather than political matters.

Catholics and Social Democrats turned out to be the real victors of the 1890 Reichstag (federal parliament) election. The Social Democrats obtained 19.7 per cent of the vote, but only thirty-five seats. The Zentrum had 18.6 per cent but, thanks to a distribution that favoured rural areas, it obtained 106 of the 397 seats, making it the largest party in the Reichstag. So the least pro-capitalist parties had polled together almost 40 per cent of the vote. The National Liberal Party and the various conservative parties, Bismarck's staunchest allies in his 'wars' against Social Democrats and Catholics, lost heavily.[72] Bismarck wanted to renew the anti-socialist legislation but many, including many industrialists, were alarmed at the unending climate of confrontation with the unions and the Social Democrats. The bill to renew the legislation was thrown out by an unlikely and disparate coalition made up of Conservatives (who wanted a more anti-socialist law), Social Democrats, Catholics, and liberals.[73] Even the young Kaiser, Wilhelm II, preferred a more conciliatory approach towards the 'social question'. It was the end of the great Chancellor. He was sacked by Wilhelm in March 1890, having held office for twenty-seven years.

The Social Democrats (and the Zentrum) went from strength to strength. They obtained the most votes in every election leading up to the war and, in 1912, for the first time, also won the most seats (110 out of 397) with more than double the votes of the Zentrum Party. It was now, in every sense, the largest party in Germany. This was a pattern that would repeat itself throughout democratic Europe in the course of the twentieth century: pro-capitalism, pure and simple, was never a recipe for electoral success. To be a leading party one had to be a Christian Democratic Party, or a Social Democratic Party, or a nationalist 'one nation' party like the Gaullists and the Conservatives. Only after 1980, when neo-liberalism had become the hegemonic ideology, was it occasionally possible to win on the basis of being the 'best party' to manage the market economy.

In Catholic Austria there was a successful Christian Social Party (*Christlichsoziale Partei*), but it was strong only in the Austrian part of what was then the Austro-Hungarian Empire. Unlike the Zentrum it was strongly urban-based. Its birth was almost simultaneous with that of the other great mass party of fin-de-siècle Austria, the Social Democratic Workers' Party. Both were centred on Vienna, where Karl Lueger, a social Christian (and a ferocious anti-Semite), dominated local politics as mayor from 1897 until his death in 1910. Lueger's goal was the unification of the fragmented bourgeoisie, the *Bürgertum*, into an effective political party to meet the challenge of social democracy.[74] In 1907, thanks to universal manhood suffrage, the Christian Social Party became the largest parliamentary group in Austria's Lower House, though, at the subsequent election, that position was taken by the Social Democratic Workers' Party (*Sozialdemokratische Arbeiterpartei Österreichs*). So, in both Austria and Germany, no overtly pro-capitalist party succeeded in obtaining a majority in Parliament.

The Emperor Franz Joseph, as well as the central government, were alarmed at Lueger's extreme populism and anti-Semitism, and tried to block his rise by vetoing his election.[75] Lueger's party was the first anti-Semitic populist party of some importance. There were, of course, plenty of anti-Semites in Europe, but they were never organized in substantial political parties (Adolf Stoecker's *Christlichsoziale Partei* in Germany did not have a mass following). Lueger used anti-Semitism for political ends but the strength of the party rested on more complex foundations. Its main strength was among Catholic artisans in Austria who were hostile towards immigrants and Jews since these were, in the main, supporters of the Liberal Party and/or competing artisans. In the 1880s, before the party was formed, Lueger's populism was overtly hostile to big capital (originally he had been active in the left faction of the Progressive Party, a liberal party), and he demanded the regulation of private companies, protectionism to defend local industry, nationalization of insurance and credit systems, laws to protect the workers against big industry, and laws against political corruption.[76] By 1887 he had espoused political Christianity.[77]

In 1891 the newly launched Christian Social Party won major electoral successes in Vienna and, in 1897, when Lueger became mayor. In his inaugural address he outlined the kind of 'municipal socialism' he wanted for Vienna: municipalized utilities, including new gas and water works, improved care for the poor, and a greater share of tax revenues for the city.[78] By 1910, when Lueger died, a substantial share of the city budget depended on the profits from a vast network of municipal utilities and services. By 1913, Vienna had one of the best public transportation systems in the world.[79] Lueger was the kind of anti-capitalist who distinguished between good and bad capitalism. The party's appeal was a combination of Christianity, anti-Semitism, and elements of economic interventionism, including many from the Social Democratic programme.[80] It prefigured later fascist parties. Hitler wrote of Karl Lueger, 'my fair judgement turned to unconcealed admiration. Today, more than ever, I regard this man as the greatest German mayor of all times.'[81] Posterity has been kind to Karl Lueger. In 1926 his former opponent, the Social Democrat Karl Seitz, unveiled an imposing bronze statue of Lueger in Dr.-Karl-Lueger-Platz.[82] The square is still so named and the statue still stands.

The Christian Social Party was anti-liberal but so were the Social Democrats. The two parties detested each other, but they were both strong in Vienna, and Vienna was the bureaucratic centre of the empire.[83] The major banking centre was Budapest, once a provincial backwater but, in the decades leading to 1914, one of the most vibrant and fastest-growing cities of Europe (it was the eighth largest city on the continent).[84] The major industrial centres were in Bohemia and Moravia-Silesia, later part of Czechoslovakia and today's Czech Republic. After the dismemberment of the empire in 1918 and particularly after the Second World War, when Austria had become a small Alpine republic with a capital that had once been the capital of an empire, the two dominant parties continued to be the Christian Social Party and the Social Democrats (under various different names) for nearly a century.

Catholic parties were strong in Germany and Austria, but never supreme, at least not in the decades leading up to the First World War. They never formed a government. Elsewhere they barely existed, with the one major exception: Belgium. Faced with a strong anticlerical Liberal Party, dominant since the creation of the country in 1830, Catholics started to organize politically earlier than elsewhere, though it would take a long time for a proper Catholic party to emerge. What they objected to was not so much the iniquities of industrialization and capitalism as the determination of the Liberals to create a strongly secular state in control of education. There was substantial workers' unrest in 1885–6 led by the coalminers, and a constitutional crisis over the reform of the electoral system (1891–5).[85] The main political conflict, however, was over education and whether the Church or the State controlled schools. It was so acute that it came to be known as *La première guerre scolaire* (1879–84). The Liberal government had passed a law in 1879 establishing that there should be at least one secular school in each commune. The bishops reacted by announcing that the last rites would be withheld from teachers who taught in those schools and from parents who sent their children there – thus condemning them to burn in Hell for eternity. When the Catholics returned to power in 1884, they modified the law in their favour without, however, abolishing secular schools, as the more intransigent Catholics had hoped. The struggle over education continued throughout the twentieth century. There was a second *guerre scolaire* in the 1950s. Finally, in 1958, a compromise, still extant, was reached. Capitalism, industrialization, the economy, labour market regulation, and so on were never the central issues in this lengthy conflict.

In Belgium, the two-party system (Liberals versus Catholics) became, as the socialist movement developed in the last decades of the nineteenth century, a three-party fight. Liberals and Socialists cooperated on secularism, since both detested the Catholics ('popish gangs'), but disagreed on regulating markets. Liberals and Catholics hated each other but both feared the revolutionary appeal of the Socialists. Socialists and Catholics regarded the Liberals as their main enemy, though for quite different reasons. Since the Catholics were always in power after 1884, Liberals and Socialists ended up cooperating in trying to eliminate clerical control over education, with little success. To complicate things further, there was a regional dimension: the Catholics were stronger in Flanders (with the exception of industrial Ghent) whereas the Liberals and Socialists were stronger in French-speaking Wallonia.

Belgian Catholics, like Belgian Liberals, did little for the workers: the Child and Labour Act of 1889 on working hours, health, and safety, and limiting abuses at the workplace, was less significant than the legislation adopted in Britain by Liberals and Conservatives decades earlier. In 1903 there was the more significant Workplace Accident and Insurance Act. Until then courts and judges had been more active than politicians in promoting the welfare of workers.[86] The succession of Catholic-led governments in the period between 1884 and the First World War were generically pro-capitalist. The longest-serving Prime Minister in Belgium before 1914, Count Paul de Smet de Naeyer, in office 1896–1907, had no reason to be hostile to capitalism. He came from one of the wealthiest cotton manufacturing families of Ghent, and, before entering politics, had been the boss of the Société générale de Belgique, the largest enterprise in the country that dominated the railways, coal and steel, and played an active part in Belgian colonialism.

Socialists emerged in Belgium as a significant force only at the close of the century, as the suffrage expanded. The Socialist-led general strike of 1893 (the first general strike in Europe) in favour of universal manhood suffrage forced Catholics and Liberals to bow to the inevitable and concede the suffrage (though some people with more money and/or more education had more than one vote). Paradoxically, this helped the Catholics consolidate their power while dividing the non-Catholic vote almost equally between Socialists and Liberals.[87]

Some social legislation was promulgated by successive Catholic governments to maintain their not inconsiderable support among Catholic workers. Catholics themselves had organized trade unions well before the Pope's *Rerum Novarum*, in 1857 when the union of cotton weavers had been formed. As the Socialists became stronger, the Catholic faction within the union split and created in 1886 the aptly named Anti-Socialist Cotton Workers' Union (*Antisocialistische Katoenbewerkersbond*). Thus Catholic trade unionists were forced into politics by the Socialists. This led to the creation, in 1904, under the guiding spirit of Père Rutten, a Dominican friar, of the *Confédération des syndicats chrétiens*. To this day the Catholic trade union confederation remains stronger than that of the Socialists. The word 'socialist' frightened even the workers, which is why the Socialist Party called itself the *Parti ouvrier* or, in Flemish, *Belgische Werkliedenpartij* (Labour Party).

Catholics, *pace* Weber, turned out to be just as good at promoting capitalist ethics as the Protestants. They developed a consensual view of society as an organic whole modelled on the idea of the family. It allowed for differences in power and inequality to be justified in terms of the greater good. They thus shared some elements of socialism (the final goal of human brotherhood) and of liberalism (the justification of differences). In practice Christians were closest to the traditional populist view that defended small-scale private property (i.e. the farmers and shopkeepers) against 'soulless' large-scale capitalism and the Godless labour movement.

American populism also spoke out for the local against the central state, for the 'small' against the 'big' (corporations, trade unions, etc.). But one of the many differences between European countries and the United States is that, though religiosity was strongly present in American political discourse, the USA, in keeping with the doctrine of the separation of Church and State (the first state to adopt it), always lacked an explicitly religious party. Yet religion itself mattered a great deal more in America than in Europe. And it still matters: in their inaugural addresses American presidents routinely refer to God: John F. Kennedy (1961) affirmed that the rights of man come 'not from the generosity of the state but from the hand of God'; Jimmy Carter (1977) mentioned the Bible his mother had given him and 'a timeless admonition from the ancient prophet Micah'; Ronald Reagan (1981) expressed his wish that subsequent Inaugural Days should be declared a 'day of prayer'; Barack Obama (2009) explained that the proposition that all are equal, all are free, and all deserve a chance to 'pursue their full measure of happiness' was a 'God-given promise'. 'The Bible tells us,' Donald J. Trump (2017) declared, 'how good and pleasant it is when God's people live together in unity.'[88] It is difficult to find an inaugural address of an American President without a reference to God or the Bible. By contrast, God is hardly ever mentioned in official speeches by Charles de Gaulle (a fervent Catholic) or by the even more Catholic Konrad Adenauer (German Chancellor 1949–63) or by any of the main leaders of the Italian Christian Democratic Party that dominated Italian politics from 1945 to 1991 with the unswerving support of the Roman Catholic Church.

The American republic, though strictly secular, was never anticlerical. Religion was an important element uniting small farmers together but was never an autonomous political force. The separation of Church and State was designed not in order to keep the clergy out of politics (as in Europe) but so as not to take sides between the competing Churches and religions. And there were many of these. Note the constant development and multiplication of Churches throughout the nineteenth century: Mormons (1830), Seventh-Day Adventists (1863), Jehovah's Witnesses (1870s), Christian Scientists (1875), and many others, in addition to Churches and sects previously established or imported from Europe (mainly England), such as Evangelicalism, Quakers, Baptists, Plymouth Brethren (from Dublin in the 1820s), Episcopalian (the American adaptation of the Church of England), and, of course, Catholicism. This also meant the unusually high religious profile that political leaders, outside the two main parties, have had throughout the last two hundred years or so of American history, particularly in the fight against slavery and for civil rights. First, Nat Turner, who led a slave rebellion in 1831, and who, before his execution, explained that he was taking on the yoke of Christ and that he had been 'ordained for some great purpose in the hands of the Almighty'.[89] Then: Frederick Douglass (1818–95), former slave, great orator, abolitionist, and preacher for the African Methodist Episcopal Zion Church (mainstream Methodism was segregated); Harriet Tubman (1822–1913), abolitionist as well as active suffragette and also devout member of the African Methodist Episcopal Zion Church; the staunchly religious John Brown, who led the famous raid on the arsenal at Harpers Ferry in 1859 hoping to start an armed campaign against slavery (and whose body, according to the famous Civil War marching song, 'lies a-mouldering in the grave' while 'His soul's marching on!'); down to, a century later, the Reverend Martin Luther King, a Baptist preacher; and Malcolm X, who converted to Islam. On the 'other' side, on the side of slavery, was a now far less celebrated array of preachers and clergymen such as James Henley Thornwell (1812–62), who justified slavery on the basis of the Bible while being horrified at the condition of the English poor (he had been to England). He concluded that Europe was already facing, and the American North would soon face, all-out class war and revolutionary turmoil. Consequently, he regarded slavery as the Christian solution to the social question. In the bluntest possible language, he predicted that the capitalist countries would have to institute a wage-labour system so close to Southern slavery as to be indistinguishable from it.[90]

The Civil War was paved with good intentions or, at least, the pretence of good intentions. Both sides sought the moral high ground and, once they found it, killed each other until one side won. The Bible, being the archetypal 'open text', could be used by all sides, as Abraham Lincoln was only too aware. In his Second Inaugural Address (4 March 1865) he said of the contending parties that had just finished fighting each other in America's bloodiest war: 'Both read the same Bible and pray to the same God, and each invokes His aid against the other . . . The prayers of both could not be answered . . . The Almighty has His own purposes.' He then concluded with these much-cited conciliatory words: 'With malice toward none, with charity for all, with firmness in the right as God gives us to see the right, let us strive on to finish the work we are in . . .[91] Five weeks later he was assassinated.

Europe too had a tradition of using religion for political ends, but it was strongest before the Enlightenment. In the nineteenth century such use was rather limited. One can think of William Wilberforce, the evangelical Christian who led the campaign for the abolition of the slave trade, and some messianic preacher of only local relevance, such as Davide Lazzaretti (1834–78), one of Eric Hobsbawm's 'primitive rebels'.[92] Otherwise religion remained in the hands of institutions such as the Churches and political parties. Even Gladstone did not claim that God was a Liberal.

PART FOUR

Facing the World

17
Europe Conquers All

In 1847, after a campaign lasting more than fifteen years, the Emir (Prince) Abd el-Kader, leader of the resistance against the French occupation of Algeria, was finally vanquished and captured. This milestone in the colonization process was celebrated by Friedrich Engels, in the pages of the Chartist newspaper *The Northern Star*, as follows:

> it is . . . very fortunate that the Arabian chief has been taken. The struggle of the Bedouins was a hopeless one, and though the manner in which brutal soldiers, like Bugeaud, have carried on the war is highly blameable, the conquest of Algeria is an important and fortunate fact for the progress of civilisation . . . And if we may regret that the liberty of the Bedouins of the desert has been destroyed, we must not forget that these same Bedouins were a nation of robbers, whose principal means of living consisted of making excursions either upon each other, or upon the settled villagers, taking what they found, slaughtering all those who resisted, and selling the remaining prisoners as slaves. All these nations of free barbarians look very proud, noble and glorious at a distance, but only come near them and you will find that they, as well as the more civilised nations, are ruled by the lust of gain, and only employ ruder and more cruel means. And after all, the modern *bourgeois*, with civilisation, industry, order, and at least relative enlightenment following him, is preferable to the feudal lord or to the marauding robber, with the barbarian state of society to which they belong.[1]

Abd el-Kader, far from being a 'marauding robber', was a remarkable guerrilla fighter. He had admirers everywhere. William Thackeray, inspired by his plight, wrote a ballad in his honour ('The Caged Hawk', 1848):

> 'Twas not in fight they bore him down; he never cried *amàn*;
> He never sank his sword before the PRINCE OF FRANGHISTAN;

> But with traitors all around him, his star upon the wane,
> He heard the voice of ALLAH, and he would not strive in vain.[2]

Finally freed by the French in 1852, in exile in Damascus, Abd el-Kader dedicated himself to literature and theology. In 1860 he saved members of the local Christian community from a massacre by the Druzes, an achievement that earned him the respect of many in the West, including the Pope, Napoleon III, and Abraham Lincoln. The *New York Times* reported that 'It is no light thing for history to record, that the most uncompromising soldier of Mohammedan independence . . . became the most intrepid guardian of Christian lives and Christian honor in the days of his political downfall . . .'[3] And even before this achievement, even before his capture, a town in Iowa (Elkader) was named after him by its founders in 1846. It is still there, in Iowa, with its 1,273 inhabitants (2010 census).

The man who defeated Abd el-Kader, Maréchal Thomas Bugeaud, mentioned by Engels, was a pioneer of what is now known as a 'scorched earth' policy. He had warned the Algerians that if they did not submit:

> I will enter your mountains, I will burn your villages and your crops, I will cut down your fruit trees, then you will have only yourselves to blame; I will be, before God, completely innocent of such disasters; for I would have done much to spare you.[4]

Alexis de Tocqueville, the great liberal thinker, warmly approved:

> In France I have often heard people I respect, but with whom I disagree, deplore that we burn harvests, we empty granaries and even seize unarmed men, women and children. These, in my opinion, are unfortunate necessities that any people who wishes to wage war on the Arabs must accept.[5]

Tocqueville's commitment to the French occupation of Algeria was based on the idea of a *mission civilisatrice* (though the term had not yet been coined); but it was also based on the objective of preventing the formation of a modern Arab state close to France and led by a man he called, with admiration, the 'Muslim Cromwell'.

If the narrative espoused by *romantic colonialism* could be defined as the enterprise of far-sighted and enlightened settlers who, at great risk, bring the joys and benefits of civilization and modernity to miserable savages, *melancholic colonialism* is its more responsible development. As represented above by Engels and Tocqueville, it recognizes the cruelties and brutalities committed by settlers and colonialists, yet approves of the process, because, in the end, it is for the best in the best of all possible worlds.[6] Civilization, the Enlightenment's substitute for religion in whose name one can justify almost anything, was repeatedly invoked by imperialists (and not just by them). Such sentiments remained pervasive: 'You cannot have omelettes without breaking eggs,' explained Joseph Chamberlain, amid cheers, and deploying a not yet stale cliché at the Royal Colonial Institute half a century later, in 1897, 'you cannot destroy the practices of barbarism, of slavery, of superstition, which for centuries have desolated the interior of Africa, without the use of force . . .'[7] You did not need an empire to have a *mission civilisatrice*, as long as you had a 'manifest destiny', a term coined by the American journalist John O'Sullivan in 1845 when trying to justify the annexation of Texas: 'Texas is now ours . . .', and he added that no other nation (alluding to England and France) would 'in a spirit of hostile interference against us', try to thwart 'our policy', hamper 'our power', limit 'our greatness' and check 'the fulfillment of our manifest destiny. . .'.[8]

The possible future of Algeria, and the rest of the so-called Third World, had it not been 'civilized' by the West, has been debated ever since. Engels and Tocqueville, and those who followed them, liberals as well as Marxists, assumed that modernization was the way out of under-development. The methods might have been brutal, as both sides acknowledged, but the ultimate consequences would be beneficial, bringing modernity to the colonized, including, in the fullness of time, the highest fruits of civilization such as equality and human rights.

Against such views are ranked the cohorts of 'dependence theorists' who argue that poor states, once they are forcibly integrated into the world economy, make rich states richer while remaining poor.[9] While the optimist supporters of 'stages of development' theories claim that laggards must imitate pathbreakers, and thus overcome their traditional and backward structures, the pessimists of the dependency school argue that the real conflict is not internal to each country but between the core (the West) and the periphery (the Third World). Only by breaking the links of dependency can the laggards succeed in controlling their gradual insertion into the world economy. Otherwise they would be forcibly dragged into it under conditions they did not negotiate or create. There is plenty of evidence to argue either case – and both require some complex counter-factual calculations – which is why the controversy is unlikely to be resolved soon. Besides, dividing the world between advanced and backward areas is too crude. By the standards of Sweden, Brazil is 'under-developed', but to lump Brazil with Haiti does not seem useful.[10]

Dependency or no dependency, one thing is certain: the industrialization of the West in the nineteenth century brought about the de-industrialization of at least some of 'the Rest'. The reasons are connected to the process of industrialization that requires the constant expansion of markets. An increase in productivity due to improvement in technology will inevitably bring about a decisive competitive edge on the part of the 'advanced country'. The greater productivity of an English spinner in the period 1830–40 compared with that of an Indian textile craftsman, at a time when English wages were just a little higher than those of India, meant that England could flood India with its manufactured textiles and wipe out local markets.[11] Between 1780 and 1830 the production cost of a yard of cotton cloth in Britain fell by 83 per cent. British cotton production was extremely concentrated. It is estimated that, between 1800 and 1840, one-third of the population of Lancashire worked in the industry. Producers in Manchester, Oldham, Bury, Rochdale, and Whalley (each with over a hundred cotton factories) accounted for over half of British production. The cloth produced in this small area was then exported throughout the world.[12] This epitomized what globalization meant then: concentration of production in a few centres and consumption in a wider periphery. The consequence is that events in one part of the world, such as the American Civil War (1861–5), would provoke untold hardship in others such as cotton manufacturing in Lancashire where, by the end of 1863, half a million people were out of work.[13]

The influx of British goods into India led to the significant de-industrialization of India. Before the nineteenth century Indian textiles represented 60–70 per cent of India's total exports. As soon as the East India Company's monopoly was ended (1833), the influx of English textiles into India increased considerably and India became a significant market for Britain.[14] By 1857, as a result of what the British called the Indian Rebellion or Indian Mutiny and the Indians the First War of Independence, India became a colony and the British Raj ('rule' in Hindi) was born. By 1900, 78 per cent of British cotton was exported, much of it to India, which had been a leading producer of cotton for centuries.[15] The de-industrialization of India was celebrated by British cotton manufacturers. In 1860, Edmund Potter, an industrialist and MP (grandfather of Beatrix Potter), speaking at the Manchester Chamber of Commerce, announced to rapturous applause that Indian weavers were losing their jobs and were 'returning to the occupation we wish them to follow, namely, agricultural operations'.[16]

Rural cultivators perhaps realized that they were now at the mercy of the world market. This world market, however, was not the neoliberal fantasy of a market with no state interference. States, particularly imperial states, interfered ceaselessly. It is simply not the case, as neoliberals have claimed for so long, that government is the problem and markets are the solution.[17]

After taking over the province of Berar in India in 1853 (the main cotton-producing province, located in Hyderabad), the British developed it to meet the requirements of the home industry (i.e. Manchester) by introducing technology and building railroads to connect Berar to Bombay. Berar's natural landscape was turned upside down by a vast British effort 'to turn so-called "waste lands" into cotton farms'.[18] British economic interests prevailed to the extent that even the Cotton Commissioner for Berar appointed by the British, Harry Rivett-Carnac, was an agent of the Manchester Chamber of Commerce.[19] During the American Civil War, as the production of American cotton slumped, Indian cotton more than quadrupled in value.[20] Irrigation was cheap, since Berar's black soil was naturally rich for cotton. Britain only cared about Berar cotton, not Berar weavers.[21] Indian peasants were now at the mercy of the constant fluctuation of prices, whether of grain or cotton. If the international prices of grain increased, it made more sense for Indian growers to export their produce (via intermediaries) rather than to sell it to the home market. If the international price of cotton fell, cotton weavers could not afford food, particularly if this food could be exported. Indian wheat exports actually increased during the 1876–7 famine. This makes perfect economic sense: one sells to those who can afford to buy, not to those who are starving to death. In practice the people of the West were eating India's food.[22] The result of a combination of drought and world market dependency was a sequence of famines in the last decades of the nineteenth century with millions of deaths: 1866 in Orissa, 1869 in Rajputana, 1873–4 in Bihar, 1876–8 in southern India.[23]

William Digby, a champion of Indians under British rule and an advocate of racial equality, in his *'Prosperous' British India: A Revelation from Official Records*, published in 1901, used official statistics to demonstrate that the situation of the people of India deteriorated constantly under the British. In what amounts to a long and sustained denunciation of imperial rule, backed by an impressive array of figures and citations from official British documents, he estimated that there had been four times as many famines in the immediately preceding thirty years (under British rule) than in the previous century, and that the deaths in India caused by famines in the period 1891–1900 numbered 19 million.[24] Digby denounced the delusion of the British about their allegedly enlightened rule in India and the attempt to forget that originally 'we were in India to make money, and all shadow of pretence at even making money honestly was cast aside'.[25] Many of Digby's findings were used by Dadabhai Naoroji, the first Asian British MP (elected for the Liberal Party, 1892–5) and a founder of the Indian National Congress. Naoroji, a wealthy cotton merchant, claimed that the British had 'drained India of its wealth, impoverished its people, and subjected them to a series of devastating famines'.[26] He denounced the high salaries received by British colonial officials, the huge cost of an army whose task was that of maintaining British rule not just in India but also in neighbouring countries, and the tax burden inflicted on Indians without the benefit of direct representation.[27] The worst famine was yet to come: the Bengal famine of 1943–4, a man-made catastrophe that caused the deaths of perhaps 3 million people.[28] The new Viceroy, Archibald Wavell, pleaded in vain with the British cabinet and particularly with Churchill (in a letter, 24 October 1944), but with little success, writing that India's problems were being treated by the government 'with neglect, even sometimes with hostility and contempt'.[29] Churchill's racist contempt for the Indians was, of course, well known but does not seem to have tarnished his image as the saviour of Britain in the Second World War.[30]

The British did not just take over India gradually in the course of the nineteenth century because they thought it would lead to greater economic growth. They did so because the East India Company was no longer able to control India. Britain did not need a formal empire to penetrate Indian markets. After all they had traded successfully throughout the world without any need for direct administrative controls.[31] No one could seriously argue that the lengthy and haphazard British expansion in India, which had taken 250 years, was propelled by a single cause or a single will.[32] The same can be said for the French conquest of Algeria and Indochina.

Had India been a strong state, of course, it might have been able to protect its economy. But it wasn't and it didn't. India (and other similar colonies) suffered not because it was outside the world of Western empires. It suffered because it was part of it. It does not follow, however, that because what was later called the 'Third World' (the term was coined in 1952 as '*Tiers Monde*' by the French historian Alfred Sauvy) was impaired by the industrialization of the 'First', the 'First' benefited massively. The data seem to suggest that access to non-Western markets provided only an extra stimulus to the industrial growth of the developed world.[33] On the other hand, had there been no colonialism, some countries of the 'Third World' might well have become modern nations at an earlier stage, countries such as Egypt and Morocco as well as Mexico and Colombia.

Local entrepreneurial spirits were thwarted by imperialism. 'King' Jaja of Opobo in the eastern Niger delta (in today's Nigeria) became a wealthy trader in palm oil. In the 1880s he tried to ship it directly to Liverpool to avoid the cartel of British traders who regulated the price of palm oil to their advantage.[34] He was lured to a negotiation whereupon he was arrested and found guilty of blocking hinterland trade, an act that, according to Lord Salisbury, then Prime Minister but on holiday in France, amounted to kidnapping. Jaja was deported to St Vincent in the West Indies. Four years later he was permitted to go back home, but died on the return journey.[35] Jaja of Opobo had welcomed the presence of the British in west Africa and the trading opportunities this opened up. His mistake was to believe that one could deal with Europeans as equals.[36] Colonialism was a one-way street.

The situation was no better in Egypt, ruled by Ismail Pasha, grandson of the great modernizing khedive Muhammad Ali who had tried to establish a thriving domestic cotton industry.[37] The country was in dire straits because it owed vast sums to its formal suzerain, the Ottoman Empire, and because the price of its main export, cotton, had dropped significantly after the end of the American Civil War and the consequent American recovery. By 1875, Ismail Pasha's finances relied on the goodwill of the British and the French. Egypt's shares of the Suez Canal were sold to the British government, thus involving Britain even more in Egypt's internal affairs. The burden of debt on the *fellahin* (the Egyptian peasants) increased, sapping Ismail Pasha's remaining popularity. Europeans were appointed to the government to reassure creditors. Ismail Pasha accepted such imposition but he also encouraged agitation against the European powers, thus involving the army even more in Egyptian politics. To cap it all, Islamic reformers emerged, adding to the destabilizing forces surrounding Ismail's rule.[38] Ismail, now desperate, decided to throw in his lot with an elected assembly that had been hitherto divided and ineffectual. He declared, 'In my capacity as head of the government and an Egyptian, I consider it my duty to comply with the opinion of the nation . . .'[39] Neither Britain nor France (the main creditors) was impressed with this belated discovery of democracy. They put pressure on the ever weaker Ottoman Empire to depose Ismail Pasha (1879) and install his more pliable son Tewfiq.[40] Ismail, ousted, spent the rest of his life in exile in Naples. Anti-British feelings erupted into a revolt in 1881, largely conducted by nationalist officers (the 'Urabi revolt, so called after its leader, Colonel Ahmad 'Urabi). It was quickly crushed by the British and Egypt became a de facto British colony.[41]

Rallying the Egyptians was difficult since a wide variety of groups jockeyed for position: the old non-Egyptian elites, tied to the former khedives (Albanians, Ottomans, etc.); expatriate Europeans; Syrian Christians; junior officers; overtaxed *fellahin*; urbanized intellectuals; merchants; clerks; Jews, etc. Egyptian nationalism was of the modern variety: it wanted for itself what Europeans had and what they boasted about, namely, some form of democracy and an elected parliament. The assembly that came into being had little support among the traditional conservative masses. The modernizing elites could ignore the masses, as they often do, sometimes at their cost, but could not ignore Great Britain. The members of the elected assembly wanted to wrest some powers from the Ottomans and the British. They wanted to be a true parliament in control of the national budget or, at least, that half not already pledged to servicing its debts to Europeans.[42] This was more than the British and the French could bear. What if Egypt defaulted? This was the background to the British take-over of Egypt (nominally still part of the Ottoman Empire), which included the bombing of Alexandria in July 1882 by the British Mediterranean Fleet under Sir Beauchamp Seymour (as a recompense he was made Lord Alcester), the defeat of 'Urabi's troops, and the establishment of a British protectorate over Egypt, which lasted formally until 1922 and informally until the so-called Revolution of 23 July 1952, led by a group of army officers under the direction of Muhammad Naguib and Gamal Abdel Nasser.

Gladstone, who was Prime Minister in 1882, and whose government instructed Beauchamp Seymour 'to warn & then destroy' Egypt (in effect, bomb Alexandria), tried to invoke some kind of feeble ethical justification. In a letter to the Liberal MP John Bright on 14 July 1882, Gladstone wrote defensively that 'I have been a labourer in the cause of peace'. It was clear, however, and clear to John Bright, that the goal was to protect the interests of the British holders of Suez Canal bonds.[43] Gladstone was a reluctant imperialist, the reluctance more pronounced in opposition than in power. John Bright, the effective leader of the 'Peace Party', resigned from the cabinet in spite of entreaties from Gladstone: 'I object to the slaughter of some thousands of Egyptians on such grounds as have been offered in defence of our policy.'[44]

This was the beginning of a lengthy period of Egyptian subservience to the wider Western world. Its features were: a native elite (including the army) whose main model of modernity was Europe; a largely rural and traditionally minded population at odds with this elite; and subservience to foreign powers (Britain until 1950, then the USSR, and then the USA). A similar pattern would be replicated in many former colonies.

In Tunisia too (also nominally part of the Ottoman Empire), modernization attempts led to an ever increasing spiral of indebtedness towards France, Britain, and Italy. The European powers created an 'international' commission to oversee the repayment of the country's debt to themselves. Internal strife in Tunisia provided Jules Ferry, the French Prime Minister, with the excuse to send troops and seize power. He was backed by a near-unanimous vote in Parliament. To the dismay of Italy, which had hoped to gain a foothold in Tunisia, the French established a protectorate in 1881. At first Tunisia was not a formal colony. It was colonialism without responsibility: Tunisia kept its flag and its national anthem; Tunisians kept Tunisian nationality; and the coinage was in the name of the Bey (Sultan) who remained in office. Nevertheless all practical attributes of sovereignty, particularly foreign relations, were in the hands of the French.[45] The real ruler was the *French Résident général* appointed from Paris. The Bey's task was, in effect, to repay the debts contracted. The Treaty of Bardo signed with France in May 1881 stated plainly that the Bey's reforms would have to be approved by France and that no new loans could be contracted without the authorization of France.[46] In fact, the treaty was merely the terms of Tunisia's surrender and the Bey was given a few hours to accept it. Had he refused he would have been taken prisoner.[47] Two years later, in 1883, tribal unrest forced France to intervene again and with greater ferocity, ruling Tunisia, technically still a protectorate (though the word was not used in the Treaty of Bardo), almost like a colony until 1956.

Pro-colonialists argue that colonialism brought some advantages and not just to the colonial power. Niall Ferguson believes that 'without the spread of British rule' liberal capitalism and parliamentary democracy would not have been so successfully established throughout the world.[48] Some might wonder to what extent parliamentary democracy has really been established throughout the world, or why particular credit is due to the British, since very few parliamentary democracies seem to have copied the Westminster system. Nevertheless, it is true that not being colonized was not a recipe for economic or political success. Countries that were never colonies, such as Afghanistan, Nepal, Ethiopia (a colony for only a few years), and Liberia fared no better (and probably worse) than some of their colonized neighbours. But the forty-eight countries listed as the 'least developed countries' by the United Nations in 2012 have almost all been colonies: thirty-three in Africa, fourteen in Asia and Oceania, and one in the Caribbean (Haiti), though these countries were certainly not prosperous before colonialism.[49] One thing is certain: colonial countries would have had quite a different shape and history if they had not been colonized and no one can be sure what this would have been.

The gap between the two worlds was not purely one of wealth. It reflected an international division of labour: Europe and North America exported manufactured goods, agricultural produce such as wheat, and dominated finance and international trade, while the countries of the 'periphery' (i.e. not part of the West) were largely limited to the export of primary products: silk and tea from China, cotton from Egypt and India, sugar from Brazil, wool and beef from Argentina, nitrates and copper from Chile, and so on. None of the peripheral countries of the core itself (whether Russia, Spain, Italy or Romania or even Japan) felt they had a real option. They had to follow the pathbreakers – maybe in their own way, but they had to follow. Modern industrial capitalism belonged, then, to the West. Even Argentina, by far the most developed of Latin American countries, had, at the end of the nineteenth century, a relatively small manufacturing sector composed of small and medium-sized firms employing less than 20 per cent of the workforce.[50] Moreover, countries exporting primary products were at the mercy of changes in demand in the importing country. Thus once European beet sugar was produced in ever larger quantities (mainly in Germany and France), cane sugar became less important, to the detriment of Caribbean sugar cane and hence to planters and growers, many of whom had been forcibly transported from Africa as slaves. This was not before the production of sugar cane had destroyed many of the forests of those islands, never to be replaced.[51] Few of the one hundred or so countries subjected to colonial rule ever developed a proper manufacturing sector.[52]

There are significant differences between 'real' colonies, such as the Caribbean islands, and settlers' states, like the USA, Australia, and New Zealand, and originally the Latin American countries. The relationship between settlers and the 'mother-country' (Spain, England) was nothing like the relationship between conquered Africans or Indians and their European 'masters'. Settlers' states often had more in common with states that had escaped colonization, countries such as Japan, which caught up with the West in the 1960s, or Thailand. The Asian 'Tigers' that emerged after 1945 had never been classical colonies: not even Taiwan or South Korea (for decades under Japanese control), though when Korea was formally annexed by Japan in 1910 there were 170,000 Japanese settlers, almost all recent immigrants. By 1935 there were over almost 600,000, a number comparable to French settlers in Algeria.[53] One-quarter of the Japanese who settled in Korea worked in the colonial administration, so were not 'real' settlers, and other Japanese became small landlords employing Korean workers.[54] Japanese workers who wanted to go abroad went to California and Hawaii.[55] There was little cultural assimilation. The city-states of Singapore and Hong Kong were commercial and financial intermediaries and therefore more autonomous from China, or the British Crown, than if they had remained part of China or been part of Malaysia. China, the great success story in the race to industrialization since the 1980s, for all its woes, humiliations, and oppression, was never a colony.

Africans were not 'free' to follow their 'own' model of development, and never really had the option of delaying their integration in the world economy until their own economic structures were sturdy enough to resist subjugation. The only country in sub-Saharan Africa with an adequate infrastructure, state institutions, education system, financial network and so on (compared to its neighbours) was South Africa – a country that had freed itself from the clutches of the British Empire earlier than the rest of the continent, though one in which, until the final decade of the twentieth century, a minority of white settlers oppressed a black majority.

But was colonization itself the way forward for the pathbreakers? Although colonialism did not play a major role in the birth of the British Industrial Revolution it helped its development. Did Britain succeed in industrialization because it had inserted itself into the international system earlier than others? Karl Marx had no doubt about this being the case. Early colonialism, he thought, was a key variable to British development:

> The discovery of gold and silver in America, the extirpation, enslavement and entombment in mines of the aboriginal population, the beginning of the conquest and looting of the East Indies, the turning of Africa into a warren for the commercial hunting of black-skins, signalised the rosy dawn of the era of capitalist production. These idyllic proceedings are the chief moments of primitive accumulation. On their heels treads the commercial war of the European nations, with the globe for a theatre. It begins with the revolt of the Netherlands from Spain, assumes giant dimensions in England's Anti-Jacobin War, and is still going on in the opium wars against China, &c.[56]

It was, in fact, a commonplace view and certainly not just one held by Marxists, that industry and colonial expansion were somewhat connected. As Talleyrand put it in his memoirs: 'Agriculture does not conquer: it settles. Trade conquers: it needs to expand.'[57] Max Weber, in one of his last lectures, concurred that early colonization expanded markets and profits: 'the acquisition of colonies by the European states led to a gigantic acquisition of wealth in Europe for all of them . . . This accumulation was secured by force, without exception and by all countries.'[58] The standard Enlightenment view of international commerce was benign. So wrote Montesquieu in *De l'esprit des lois*: 'Commerce is a cure for the most destructive prejudices; for it is almost a general rule that wherever we find agreeable manners, there commerce flourishes; and that wherever there is commerce, there we meet with gentle manners.'[59]

The two Opium Wars, fought, ostensibly, to open up China to Western trade (1839–42 and 1856–60), were not gentle. Nevertheless there is little doubt that opium was a major source of revenue for British India. The profits were used to sustain the government of India, and to buy American cotton and Chinese tea and silk. All of this made China into one of Britain's main trading partners in the middle of the nineteenth century.[60] The duty levied on Chinese tea was almost alone sufficient to pay for the yearly expenditure of the British Navy.[61] The amazingly profitable commerce in opium played a central place in Britain's global trade 'from the purchase of US cotton for the Lancashire mills to the remittances of India to the United Kingdom'.[62] By the time of the Arrow War (the Second Opium War), opium earnings had grown to about 22 per cent of the gross revenue of the whole of British India. Before British rule, opium cultivation in India was negligible.[63] The Treaty of Nanjing reveals Victorian Britain's astonishing willingness to go to war and impose severe penalties on a foreign country in defence of what were British opium traders.[64]

Chinese anger, understandably, marked a whole generation of intellectuals and that anger is not forgotten to this day. The progressive scholar and journalist Liang Qichao, in his essay 'On the New Rules for Destroying Countries', written after the draconian Western sanctions that followed the Boxer Rebellion (1899–1901), listed sarcastically the 'rules' which could be deployed against China by the all-conquering West: sending the country into debt (Egypt), splitting it territorially (Poland), divide and rule (India), and using overwhelming force (Philippines and the Transvaal).[65] Late Qing China may not have been a colony but its economy was almost completely dominated by foreigners. Foreign banks, such as the Hong Kong Shanghai Banking Corporation (HSBC), founded in 1865, monopolized the banking sector and enjoyed extra-territoriality. Shipping was also controlled by foreigners (84 per cent in 1907), and again the largest firms were British. Four major foreign railway companies controlled 41 per cent of the entire railway track. Foreign interests also dominated mining and the postal service. Foreign control increased even after the nationalist revolution of 1911.[66] Korea, once a Chinese colony, was now a Japanese one. The Japanese had also conquered Taïwan and had extended their influence into Manchuria. Russia had a zone of influence in the north-east; Britain had one in Shanghai, Nanking, and in much of the Yangtze valley, as well as in Hong Kong and Kowloon in the south and in Tibet; Portugal still controlled Macao; and there was considerable French influence in Kunming and along the border with Indochina (a French colony).

Colonialism was a factor behind early industrialization and may have prevented others from joining the 'advanced' club, as dependency theorists claim. But was the significant expansion of overseas possession in the period we are discussing of such importance to economic development? Was the acquisition of colonies, in the 'Age of Empire', really functional to industrialization? Were the revenues from the new possessions significant, or was the expenditure excessive? Were post-1880 acquisitions as important as older, pre-industrial-age colonies? And were they acquired as part of a nation-building programme, to create social order and social peace at home?

This latter explanation particularly fits German and Italian colonialism. In 1882, the President of the German Colonial Association (*Deutscher Kolonialverein*), Prince Hohenlohe-Langenburg, declared that acquiring colonies would help in the struggle against social democracy.[67] But then, he would have said that, since lobbyists will use any argument available. Lothar Bucher, a close aide to Bismarck, argued that the real 'enemy' was not social democracy but Britain, and that the new German state should expand its economic activities overseas in competition with Great Britain to benefit German industry. Bismarck soon realized that this would add a significant burden to the national budget. He remained an unenthusiastic colonialist.[68]

There was no obvious pattern or connection between industrial capitalism and colonial acquisition, particularly after 1880. While trade and foreign investments were crucial for some countries, they did not require colonies. There was, after all, plenty of trade with Latin America and China as well as areas, such as Canada, Australia, and New Zealand, which, though not yet independent, were self-governing. Colonization seemed to be reaching a final stage.

The list of the main European acquisitions between 1880 and the First World War shows that Africa was the focus of late colonization (see Table 13). In 1879 some 90 per cent of Africa was still ruled by Africans. By 1912 very few Africans ruled themselves.[69] An anonymous writer for the *Fortnightly Review* could claim in 1890 that 'The partition of Europe, of Asia, and even of America, among the dominating races of the world has been the slow work of centuries; the serious scramble for Africa began only six years ago, and is now nearly complete.'[70] Where else but in Africa could colonies be established after 1880, since not much was left and the conquest of Africa was relatively cheap? As Joseph Chamberlain declared in 1893, smugly, 'It is a curious fact . . . that of all the nations in the world, we are the only one which has been able to carry out this work of civilisation without great cost to ourselves.'[71]

Colonization could not have taken place in Latin America. There white settlers had already freed themselves from Spain and Portugal – and European expansionism would have had to face the hostility of the United States following the Monroe Doctrine, which declared that any European attempt to colonize any part of South America would be viewed by the USA as an act of aggression (though one it could probably not have enforced). In any case, no European powers had either the intention or the strength to colonize any parts of Latin America. Great Britain, already dominant in some of those regions, especially Argentina, was satisfied with what came to be called 'an informal empire', far less costly then direct rule. Indeed, Britain had been an instigator of the Monroe Doctrine to keep other Europeans away.[72]

No new colonial expansion could have taken place in the Indian subcontinent (present-day India, Pakistan, Bangladesh, Sri Lanka, and Burma), since Great Britain was firmly in control. China, though not a colony, was open to Western trade and no single European power would have been able to take the country over without fierce resistance from China and opposition from other European powers. Most of the Middle East was part of the Ottoman Empire, whose dismemberment had started earlier in the century. Much of Asia, by 1900, had been taken over by the West. In 1898 the Philippines had been ceded by Spain to the United States for $20 million. Indonesia was a Dutch colony and Indochina (present-day Vietnam, Laos, and Cambodia) a French one. Thailand managed to play the French against the British and thus retain its independence. So, by 1880 there was not much left to colonize outside Africa.

Afghanistan, along with Persia, was being fought over by Russia and Great Britain (the famous 'Great Game' that endured for most of the nineteenth century) and, as the British discovered, was not worth the time or the expenditure. The Russians were extending their empire into central Asia, and the British assumed that their target was India. Several proxy wars were fought, mainly in Afghanistan. Britain, fearing Russian intentions, invaded Tibet (technically part of China's Qing Empire) in December 1903, egged on by Lord Curzon, India's Viceroy, who was now convinced that the Dalai Lama was about to enter an alliance with Russia, for a long time Curzon's great obsession. The British government itself had initially been reluctant to intervene, but Curzon exploited a bogus incident to sway the British Prime Minister, Arthur Balfour, the Secretary of State for India, and the entire British cabinet. British troops, or, rather, Indian Sikh sepoys and Nepalese Gurkhas, led by British officers under the overall command of Francis Younghusband, met fierce resistance from the Tibetans. Eventually, British military superiority triumphed: at the hot springs of Chumik Shenko, Tibetan forces, outgunned and outnumbered, suffered severe casualties (over 500 killed), compared to very few (twelve) on the British side. This episode became known as 'the massacre of Chumik Shenko'.[73]

The rise of German power finally led Russia and Britain to bury their differences and to forget about Tibet and Afghanistan. The Anglo-Russian Convention of 1907 recognized the two countries' respective spheres of influence, particularly over Iran, Afghanistan, and Tibet. The 'Great Game' was over at last, albeit temporarily, a monument to diplomatic incompetence and the obtuse frame of mind that characterized many of those, such as Lord Curzon, who ruled the empire.

There was, though, a newcomer in the colonial race: Japan. The only non-European industrial power apart from the United States, it had managed to put itself beyond the reach of Western greed thanks to its largely military-led process of industrialization. Previously, Japanese forays abroad were rare (the failed invasions of Korea between 1592 and 1598 by Toyotomi Hideyoshi and the informal annexation of the Ryukyu Islands in the seventeenth century being the most significant). But in the decades following the Meiji Restoration (1868) Japan entered the race in Asia, which it regarded as its 'natural' sphere of influence. Japan's 1895 war with China resulted in the capture of Port Arthur (Lüshunkou), where the Japanese army was responsible for the massacre of over a thousand civilians and the virtual annexation of Korea (formalized in

1910). The Treaty of Shimonoseki that ensued was extremely damaging for China: it had to cede Taiwan, pay a large indemnity, and open its borders to Japanese trade.[74] Ten years later, in 1905, Japan waged another war, this time against Russia. Its victory astounded the world, unused as it was to the spectacle of non-Europeans defeating a 'great' European power. Yukichi Fukuzawa, one of Japan's foremost writers, declared that this was 'the victory of a united government and people. There are no words that can express my pleasure . . .'[75]

In the 1870s the term 'Yellow Peril' had been used in the United States to denote the 'threat' represented by the immigration of Chinese workers (leading to the Chinese Exclusion Act of 1882). Now Japan, thanks to its newly acquired military might, had become, in the eyes of Westerners, a new colour-tinted race 'peril'. In retaliation, the poet Mori Ōgai coined the term *hakka* (white peril) in 1904:

> Yellow Peril in victory, barbarian in defeat;
> The White race makes a mockery of criticism.
> But who rejoices in the praise
> And who laments the slander?[76]

In Japan there was widespread optimism. The diplomat and scholar Manjirō Inagaki, writing in 1890, was looking forward to a world which, after the opening of the Panama Canal, would see Japan 'practically in the centre of the three large markets – Europe, Asia and America – and its commercial prosperity would be ensured'.[77] And he added, 'Japan has not only a splendid future before her with regard to commercial greatness, but has every chance of rising to the head of manufacturing nations.'[78] For many Japanese, acquiring an empire was part and parcel of being a modern power in the modern world.[79] The making of Japan as a nation state 'entailed the creation of new peripheries on the home islands as well as overseas'.[80] Inoue Kaoru, Japan's Foreign Minister, wrote in a memorandum (1887), 'what we must do is to transform our empire and our people, make the empire like the countries of Europe and our people like the peoples of Europe. To put it differently we have to establish a new European-style empire on the edge of Asia.'[81] Thus the occupation of Korea was part of the Japanese reframing of the European 'civilizing mission' in Japanese terms.[82]

Japanese imperialism, like other imperialisms, had been motivated by the desire to exclude other powers from Korea and to secure its trade. In Hirobumi Itō's narrative (Itō had several times been Prime Minister of Japan and then Governor of Korea), Japan occupied Korea to prevent Russia or China from conquering it – a kind of humanitarian intervention that did not convince most Koreans and obviously not An Jung-geun, a nationalist convert to Catholicism and now a Korean national hero, who assassinated Itō in 1909.[83] The justification by Japan for the take-over of Korea was similar in kind to that of Europeans: Koreans were barbarians who dealt with their criminals in an inhumane way by burying them up to their necks and letting them be devoured by insects.[84] Similarly, the inhabitants of Taiwan, ceded under duress by China to Japan in 1895, were routinely referred to as ferocious savages.[85] To colonize Taiwan, Japan had to fight a colonial war that lasted two decades, claimed more Japanese lives (not to mention Taiwanese lives) than the Sino-Japanese War, and consumed 7 per cent of Japanese national product. Eventually, after a lengthy campaign of terror and sheer brute force, superior Japanese technology prevailed.[86] Japan had joined the West in every sense.

Japan too had its anti-colonialists: Kōtoku Shūsui, a socialist, wrote *Imperialism, the Spectre of the Twentieth Century* (1901). However, far from being an economic analysis of imperialism (like J. A. Hobson's *Imperialism*, 1902, Rudolf Hilferding's *Finance Capital*, 1910, and Lenin's *Imperialism: The Highest Stage of Capitalism*, 1916), the text was imbued with a strong anti-militaristic and anti-nationalistic message: a people that allows itself to be manipulated by patriotism is narrow-minded and cannot claim to be civilized. Those who sacrifice education, the economy, and politics at the altar of patriotism should be regarded as criminals against humanity.[87] Kōtoku Shūsui contended that imperialism retarded economic progress and that Japan should renounce imperialism and, instead, expand trade and spread civilization.[88] Accused, almost certainly unjustly, of plotting to assassinate the Emperor (known in Japan as the 'High Treason Incident'), Kōtoku Shūsui was executed in 1911 along with many others, including his wife Kanno Sugako. A campaign of repression against left-wing organizations ensued, even though they did not pose any threat to the stability of the country since the influence of socialism in Japan was derisory: Japan's Interior Ministry estimated the total number of socialists in Japan to be 532.[89]

The Japanese 'empire' was tiny compared to the vast territories accumulated by Britain and France. Table 13 shows the remarkable list of acquisitions by Western countries between 1880 and 1914.

European imperialism was the business of a few nations and, among these, the lion's share, by far, was in the hands of the British. Taking size as a measure of empire (rather than population) it is evident

Table 13 Western Countries' Colonial Acquisitions, 1880–1914*

Acquired by Great Britain	
Middle East and North Africa	Bahrain; Kuwait; Egypt
Asia	Brunei; Hong Kong new territories
Sub-Saharan Africa	Botswana; Ghana; Kenya; Lesotho; Malawi; Uganda; British Somalia; Sudan; Swaziland; Zanzibar; Rhodesia (now Zambia and Zimbabwe)
Oceania	Papua New Guinea; Fiji (in 1874); New Hebrides (with France – now Vanuatu)
Acquired by France	
Middle East and North Africa	Tunisia; Morocco
Asia	Indochina
Sub-Saharan Africa	Mauritania; Mali; Ivory Coast; Niger; Haute-Volta (Burkina Faso); Dahomey (Benin); Madagascar; Tunisia; Senegal; French Congo (Congo-Brazzaville); Djibouti; French Guinea; Chad
Oceania	New Hebrides (with Great Britain – now Vanuatu); German New Guinea (acquired in 1914); Marshall Islands
Acquired by Germany (all lost after the First World War)	
Africa	Cameroon; Togoland; Ruanda-Burundi; Tanganyika (Tanzania); German South-West Africa (Namibia); German New Guinea (lost in 1914)
Acquired by other European countries	
Belgium	Congo Free State (private possession of King Leopold II until 1908 when it became a Belgian colony)
Italy	Eritrea; Somalia; Libya

*After the First World War the British and French Empires expanded further with the acquisition of territories such as Iraq, Palestine, Syria, Lebanon, Tanzania, and Cameroon, hitherto under the control of the defeated powers (Turkey and Germany). Australia acquired German New Guinea.

(see Table 14) that by 1913 European empires were in practice a British-French condominium in which the British were the dominant force:[90]

Table 14 Extra-European Territory Held by European Powers (in millions of sq. km)

	1878	1913
Great Britain	24.9	29.5
France	4.9	11.5
Portugal	2.2	2.2
Netherlands	2.1	2.1
Spain	1.0	0.8
Germany	0.5	3.5
Italy	0.0	2.5

Colonialism encountered some resistance: in southern India by Tipu Sultan at the close of the eighteenth century; in Haiti by Toussaint Louverture, who fought the French in 1801–2, believing in the values of the French Revolution only to be defeated by Napoleon and deported to France; in what is Ghana today by the Ashanti Empire against the British and their African allies in a succession of wars between 1824 and 1901; and by the Xhosa tribes in nine wars for most of the nineteenth century in the Dutch Cape Colony.[91] In 1879 the Zulu fought the British in South Africa at the Battle of Isandlwana, thoroughly defeating them before being subjugated. On 27 July 1880 the British were defeated at the Battle of Maiwand by the Afghan army led by Ayub Khan (now Afghanistan's national hero). In 1887 the Italians were defeated by the Ethiopians and then again in 1896 (see below). In 1906, in their colony in Natal, the British crushed a Zulu rebellion against taxation in which between 3,000 and 4,000 were killed.[92]

From 1905 to 1907 in German East Africa (Tanganyika, today's Tanzania), the Maji Maji fought against German colonial rule and attempts to compel the local population to grow cotton for export.[93] In 1898, Emilio Aguinaldo led Filipino forces against the Spaniards, defeating them. Originally he had been supported by the United States but was soon forced to fight the Americans themselves in a vain effort to obtain independence from what he had regarded as the 'land of liberty'.[94] American troops destroyed villages, tortured captives, and forced Filipinos into concentration camps.[95] Little of this colonial oppression and the resistance to it have found their way into American or European history school textbooks – even today, even when the facts are known and undisputable.[96] The same can be said of the extermination by conquest and disease of so many native Americans in both the northern and southern hemisphere; of the massacre of Tasmanians by British colonists from 1828 to 1832 (the so-called Black War); of the horrors of Belgian colonialism in the Congo; the punitive expedition of the British in Benin in 1897 that resulted in British troops killing thousands of people, setting the city of Benin on fire and stealing the famous Benin bronzes (many are now in the British Museum); and, last but not least, the German extermination of the Herero tribe in 1907 in South-West Africa (today's Namibia) – the first modern genocide.[97] The Herero were a semi-nomadic people who had resisted white settlers' attempts to fence off common land to raise cattle.[98] They were good fighters, so good that in 1904 a particularly determined military commander, Lothar von Trotha, a veteran of the suppression of the Boxer Rebellion in China, was chosen over the objections of the civilian authorities. Von Trotha decided that the whole of the Herero people should be annihilated. As he told a journalist, 'Against *Unmenschen* (non-human), one cannot conduct war humanely.'[99] Later that year he declared that the Herero people had to disappear from the German colony, either by fleeing to British territory or by being killed. The official goal was now genocide (though the term had not been coined), and genocide it was. Some 66–75 per cent of the 60,000 to 80,000 members of the tribe were killed.[100] The German government apologized in 2004, one hundred years after the event.[101]

Even more horrific than German colonization was that of Belgium in the Congo. King Leopold II had claimed that the conquest of the Congo and the creation of the *État Indépendant du Congo* (the Congo Free State, his private property, not Belgium's colony) was an improvement on what had happened under the rule of Muslim slave traders who controlled the territory. In fact, the system he presided over was the most monstrous example of modern colonization and 'more horrendous' than slave trading.[102] As a consequence of Leopold's paradigmatic 'predatory economy':

> the fields lay fallow. Agriculture dwindled . . . Native commerce came to a standstill. Crafts in the process of refinement for centuries, such as iron smithing or woodcarving, were lost. The native population became listless, enfeebled, and malnourished . . . It is impossible to say how many people died as a direct or indirect result of Leopold's rubber policies.[103]

Many died, were killed, raped, and tortured; villages were torched; and killing squads were sent out to force the natives to produce more rubber.

A Swedish missionary reported seeing dead bodies floating on the lake 'with the right hand cut off, and the officer told me . . . they had been killed . . . for the rubber'.[104] Thousands of people fled their villages out of fear of Leopold's soldiers. Their crops were burnt; their animals killed; starvation ensued.[105] The much-weakened population was thus far more susceptible to diseases such as smallpox and sleeping sickness. Men were sent into the forests in search of rubber for long periods of time while their wives and children were held hostages, half-starved. The outcry was such that, in 1908, the Belgian Parliament decided to terminate Leopold II's *mission civilisatrice*. During his twenty-three-year nefarious rule the king had become rich thanks to the rubber extracted and the ivory poached, but the Congo had lost half its inhabitants and 10 million people had died.[106]

The anti-colonialists shared common ground with the colonialists. They had imbibed the same culture, often the same language (French in Algeria and Vietnam; English in India), the same commitment to modernity, the same sense of class belonging. The Belgian socialist leader Émile Vandervelde wrote at length about the horrors of Belgian colonization in Congo, but he was an advocate of a 'rational' system of colonization that would allow the natives to own their own land and the Europeans to trade with them.[107] Similarly, Edmund D. Morel, an Anglo-French journalist who founded the Congo Reform Association (1904) and who denounced mercilessly the nefarious activities of the Belgians in the Congo, was not against colonization but against excessive exploitation.[108] The leading voice against colonialism in the Belgian Socialist Party (POB), that of Louis de Brouckère, editor of the party paper *Le Peuple* in 1907, amid his party's general indifference, veiled indignation with solid pragmatism: 'One must build railways, roads, a postal system, fortresses, guns, in a word the necessary tools to keep a country in a state of subjugation. But how much will all this cost? The Congo will not benefit us; it might benefit the bourgeoisie but not us.'[109]

Insofar as most ordinary 'native' people were concerned, colonialism often simply meant swapping one ruling class for another. Since they had always been ruled, they went on being ruled and being subservient to the new rulers as they had been to the old. There was no reason to rebel, plot, or conspire. Since there was no national consciousness, there was no wounded national pride. As long as the new rulers did not interfere with established norms, existing tradition, and local religions, or cause a deterioration in one's conditions of existence, there was no reason to object. The problem was not with the natives at the bottom but with those at the top. They faced a constant dilemma: should they cooperate with the colonialists, agreeing to share power albeit in a subordinate way; or should they resist in order to acquire power later?

As John Gallagher and Ronald Robinson explained in a now famous text, the extension of colonial empires could not have occurred in the way it did without some form of cooperation, collaboration, or instrumental engagement by local societies.[110] Europeans may have played the game of divide and rule, but indigenous forces also tried to exploit colonial rivalries to settle scores internally against rivals. The British, in particular, tailored imperial intervention to fit local divisions in order to confuse resistance and obtain compliance.[111] In India too, before the 1857 takeover, British rule consisted not in direct control but in having subordinate local allies and dependants and arbitrating between Indian states. In a sense the British inherited the system of controls of their predecessors, the Mughal rulers.[112]

On the eve of the First World War, in 1913, the British Empire took in a population of some 440 million, on a level with China, a number hugely boosted up by India, whose population was just over 300 million.[113] This amounted to a quarter of mankind, probably the largest empire ever. But Britain had had this empire for quite a while and its economy was the most globalized among the main industrial states. Why bother to take over more colonies whose value was far from obvious? One answer, the most traditional, was that it was not very costly to take them over and that in so doing one kept others out. The British dominated in three ways: one was by having more colonies than anybody else, then by trading with them more than anyone else, and finally by having, in addition to its formal empire, an informal one. Keeping the world open to British goods was central to British imperialism. As Joseph Chamberlain put it in his speech at the Birmingham Chamber of Commerce (1896): 'the greater part of Africa would have been occupied by our commercial rivals, who would have proceeded, as the first act of their policy, to close this great commercial market to the British Empire'.[114]

The reach of this empire was quite formidable. Of the 200-plus countries that exist today, sixty-three were once ruled by Britain, twenty more were occupied for shorter periods, and a further seven (such as Argentina and Chile) could be counted as part of its informal empire.[115] This 'empire', however, had no consistency and no unity: Canada was not ruled in the same way as India and India not in the same way as Egypt, which was not a real colony.[116]

Britain's colonial supremacy was partly due to the circumstances of potential rivals. Portugal and Spain, once possessors of great empires, were too poor to expand; and Spain did not even succeed in keeping what it had, losing Cuba, Puerto Rico, Guam, and the Philippines to the United States. Germany and Italy appeared too late on the scene to be major players in the colonial scramble. Some of their leading politicians, Bismarck in Germany and Giolitti in Italy, were reluctant to enter the colonial race.

Russia could expand eastwards, annexing Asian territories without transforming them into formal colonies. It established formal rule over Transcaucasia, thus completing its control over the vast Eurasian plain and moved into the Far East.[117] As for the United States, it expanded westward, fighting Indians and Mexicans. Russia and the USA were not 'classic' empires, though they could be said to constitute instances of 'internal' or 'contiguous' colonialism.

Other countries, such as Switzerland and Sweden, were industrializing in earnest without any need of an empire. Neither of the two states called empires, the Ottoman and the Austro-Hungarian, expanded in the slightest during the nineteenth century. They did not produce settlers. Few Turks settled in the European or Arabic parts of the Ottoman Empire. Few Austrians settled in Galicia or Hungary. In the years leading up to the First World War, the Ottoman Empire was losing territories and was well on the road to disintegration, while the Austro-Hungarian Empire was desperately trying to hold on to the recalcitrant nations within its borders. No one, whether in Vienna or in Constantinople, seriously advocated creating settlements in far-flung areas overseas.

So Britain's only possible rival was France. But while Britain had been remarkably stable throughout the nineteenth century, France had been astonishingly unstable since 1789, even losing a major war against Prussia in 1870.[118] All this contributed to Britain's success in the imperial stakes. In spite of such luck, towards the end of the nineteenth century, Britain's trading advantages were constantly decreasing as other countries were catching up.

Was any of this of material significance to the development of capitalism? Those who advocated colonies seemed certain of it. Jules Ferry, Prime Minister of France, stated it plainly in 1885 in a much-used quote: '*La politique coloniale est la fille de la politique industrielle.*'[119] Perhaps that was true of France, though many disagreed, but it was manifestly untrue of Germany, since German industrial success involved no colonies before 1884, and nothing of significance afterwards. Those Germans who were in favour of colonies argued that German industrial development required not just a united Germany but also a large empire. Leo von Caprivi, Bismarck's successor as

Chancellor, justified the aspiration to become a sea power and building the navy by stressing that commerce and industry were of great political and cultural importance.[120]

A popular argument, expressed by the nationalist historian Heinrich von Treitschke as well as by many others was that Germany, having 'lost' decades reconstructing her national identity, had now to enter a colonial race that others, above all the so detested 'arrogant' England, had started long ago.[121] There was also the hope that colonies would provide jobs and land for German settlers.[122] Treitschke too, who wanted a German empire for the greater glory of Germany, deployed practical arguments: 'For a nation that suffers from continued over-production, and sends nearly 200,000 of her children abroad, the question of colonisation is vital.'[123] Among the most vociferous colonialists were Admiral Alfred von Tirpitz, architect of German naval rearmament, and Carl Peters, Reichskommissar (Imperial High Commissioner) for East Africa (1891), responsible for atrocities (posthumously rehabilitated by Hitler, and celebrated in films and books during the Nazi period).[124] The central idea of German foreign policy in this post-Bismarck period was that of *Weltpolitik* ('global policy'), though, in reality, without much of a navy Germany could, at best, dream only of a *Europapolitik* and not a proper *Platz an der Sonne* (Place in the Sun).[125]

The pre-industrial Romantic idea of Germans returning to till the soil and finding their soul – this time in foreign lands – was absurd even in the nineteenth century, though not absurd enough not to be revived, far more disastrously, under Hitler's Third Reich. The Nazi *Hungerplan* for eastern Europe, however, was not aimed at anything outside Europe. It envisaged the starving to death or into submission of the Soviet Union and Poland, and the consequent implementation of the *Generalplan Ost*: the settling by pure-bred German farmers of the eastern territories thus freed.

However, leaving aside this grandiose scheme and its ideological justifications, the most immediate spur to German colonial acquisition in the 1880s was the so-called Long Depression of the 1870s. This crisis was generally seen as a crisis of overproduction, to overcome which a major export drive was proposed. Since Great Britain had a considerable advantage in overseas market, it was felt that colonial acquisitions would provide the desirable outlets, though this case for colonialism would hardly justify the German conquest of places of little trading value, such as Cameroon, Togoland, Ruanda-Burundi, and Tanganyika.

Politicians also argued that colonies would keep the state in the driving seat of economic policy; colonies might unite agrarian and industrial interests; might enable many to make money out of state procurement; might contain socialism; and might encourage a broad ideological consensus around the press, the Reichstag, and the civil service.[126] Public opinion, until whipped up by the press, cared little for colonies, but colonial enthusiasts and industrial interests, particularly shipbuilders, converged in pressure groups such as the *Deutscher Kolonialverein* (1882, German Colonial League) and later the *Deutsche Kolonialgesellschaft* (1887, German Colonial Society), the Naval League (*Deutscher Flottenverein*, 1898, with its 330,000 members), and the ultra-nationalist anti-Polish Pan-German League (*Alldeutscher Verband*, 1891), of which Max Weber was a member. Among the objectives of such pressure groups was that of turning workers into patriots, or, in the words of a supporter, of 'winning back the masses' by an extensive shipbuilding programme that would provide jobs as well as patriotic pride.[127] Friedrich Engels too, though from an entirely different political position, thought there was a connection between economic power and proletarian ardour. In a letter (30 August 1883) to the German socialist leader August Bebel, lamenting the lack of socialism among the English working class and their contentment at being just 'an appendage of the "Great Liberal Party"', Engels declared that 'participation in the world market was and is the economic basis of the English workers' political nullity'.[128]

All this may explain why Germany pursued colonial expansion, but it does not follow that such expansion was profitable. In fact, enthusiasm soon cooled down, for the new territories were a drain on government finances; industry did not benefit; and hardly any Germans wanted to become settlers.[129] The social composition of the organized colonial movement in Germany was largely made up of middle-class professionals, such as doctors, lawyers, and pharmacists, imbued with nationalism, who had no intention of becoming settlers but who thought that colonies were where dangerous proletarians and dispossessed peasants should go.[130] Although this was the age of mass migration, not many proletarians and peasants were willing to leave their homes to endure the heat, the insects, and the diseases of sub-Saharan Africa. They much preferred to go to the United States, to Latin America, to Australia and New Zealand, and to South Africa (which had good land, diamonds, and fewer mosquitoes). Some colonies would have been useful to send convicts to, as Napoleon III knew: in 1854 he closed expensive French prisons and sent the convicts to New Caledonia and French Guiana, thus shortening their lives and saving public funds. The Tsar sent his convicts to Siberia and the British sent theirs to Australia (where they thrived). But although colonialism provided an outlet for 'undesirables' by absorbing some of the unemployed from the upper and middle classes, a country does not conquer a vast empire just to solve its prison problems.

An empire did not profit the Netherlands either. The country was engaged in a long, bitter, unpopular, and totally useless war in the Sultanate of Aceh (1873–1903) in order to conquer Sumatra, part of Indonesia – a war that caused the deaths of 37,000 troops on the Dutch side (the majority Indonesian recruits) and over 60,000 natives.[131] There was no reason for this financially costly thirty-year war apart from prestige and pride as well as the fear that if the Dutch were to withdraw, the Americans, or the British, or the Germans, or the Japanese would intervene.[132] Control over the whole of Indonesia did nothing for the Dutch economy, which never regained the glorious days of the eighteenth century and lagged behind that of Belgium, whose empire was much smaller and whose industrialization had preceded the acquisition of Congo. The Netherlands did expand commercially throughout the nineteenth century, but its success was due more to the development of intra-European trade than to its colonies.[133]

Italy, like Germany, did not have an empire and could only hope to acquire what the British and French had left over – stuff of no great economic consequence. The Italians even failed to conquer Ethiopia, where they were defeated militarily by local armies, first at the Battle of Dogali in 1887 and then, even more decisively, by armies led by Menelik II at Adwa in 1896. Being defeated by 'natives' was a rare event in the history of modern European colonialism. (The British had been defeated too, as we have seen, but they eventually won the Afghan wars.) The Italians had chronically underestimated the Ethiopians, assuming that a 'primitive' kingdom could be no match for a modern European state.[134] Menelik was turned into a celebrity in the West with his own tableau in wax at the Musée Grévin in Paris and a colour lithograph in the magazine *Vanity Fair*.[135]

The motivations for Italian colonies were so weak that most of the country's establishment opposed their acquisition, calling their colonialism *un colonialismo da straccioni* (' a beggars' colonialism'). In any case Italy, without colonies, had almost levelled with Spain in terms of industrial development. In November 1886, Giovanni Giolitti, not yet in charge of the country's politics, explained patiently and wisely to his electors that an imperial policy was expensive; that it required armies and a navy; and it would confer more privileges to the aristocracy – not something he would recommend.[136] Other enlightened conservatives were equally scathing of Italy's attempts to build an empire, notably Count Stefano Jacini, author of the celebrated Agrarian Inquiry, who, in his *Pensieri sulla politica italiana* (1889), accused the government of 'megalomania' – the first modern use of the term – a disease he attributed to the *eccitabilità della nostra immaginazione meridionale* (the 'excitability of our southern imagination').[137]

Italy succeeded in acquiring Eritrea (1882), Somalia (1889), and Libya (1911–12). These, however, offered neither commercial advantages nor primary products worthy of note (oil was discovered in Libya only in the 1950s). Some politicians, in particular southerners such as Francesco Crispi (Prime Minister 1887–91, 1893–6), were strong supporters of colonial expansion.[138] The idea that colonial settlements would relieve overpopulation in Italy had become a prominent justification for acquiring an empire. Italians, it was mistakenly believed, would prefer to settle as conquerors in Eritrea and Somalia than to be received in the United States as 'huddled masses' and 'wretched refuse'.

Crispi's dream of colonial conquest as a means of resolving the inability of the growing Italian industry to absorb Italian labour turned out to be a chimera. Antonio Gramsci was scathing. In his *Prison Notebooks* he wrote that southern Italian peasants wanted land, and since Crispi could not give it to them, he hoped to give them colonial lands. Crispi's imperialism, he explained, had no economic basis in reality. Italy had no capital to export, like the advanced countries, so he hoped to export labour and calm down the land hunger of the southern peasantry.[139]

As in many other matters, the young Italian state turned out to be quite inadequate to the tasks it had set itself. Much of the (not large) budget devoted to colonization was earmarked for the armed forces and little was left for the necessary infrastructure that might have attracted private enterprise and personnel. The first 'model' settlers did not have the skills required, and the climate was quite different from that of southern Italy.[140] Italians continued to emigrate to the United States and Canada, to other European countries, and above all to Argentina, in ever larger numbers (an annual average of 679,000 in the years immediately preceding the First World War).[141] Few went to Africa. In the first decades after unification, Italy's main exports were to France and Germany and its imports came mainly from Austria, France, and the United Kingdom. By 1913 its extra-European trade had increased considerably, a further sign of the globalization of commerce even for countries not yet in the first ranks of the industrial race and without empires.[142] Opposition to Italy's forays in Africa had been manifest as early as 1888 when Andrea Costa, the first socialist member of parliament at a time when the Socialist Party had not yet been created, declared that the huge sums to be spent on African conquest could be better spent on the draining of swamps in Italy, thus encouraging 'our poor peasants' not to emigrate but to find work at home. When finally a socialist party emerged in 1892, such anti-colonialism encountered some internal dissent. In 1911 leading socialists, such as Leonida Bissolati and Ivanoe Bonomi, supported the Italian conquest of Libya precisely on the grounds that Libya would provide Italian peasants with land.[143] They were both expelled from the party in 1912.

Italy had begun to industrialize but Portugal failed even to start. It did have an old empire acquired well before the nineteenth century but it was the poorest country in western Europe. It exported primary products, such as cork and port wine – the latter trade dominated by the British, as the enduring names testify: Cockburn, Osborne, Sandeman, and Taylor. Portugal's population was tiny: 5 million in 1890, the same as London. Its bourgeoisie was involved in commerce rather than manufacturing. Its African possessions were tangential to its economy.[144]

Portugal's African empire looked big on paper, but, in the middle of the nineteenth century, it consisted of little more than the occupation of coastal areas and only a nominal control of the hinterland. The country's rulers dreamt of using their empire in a modern way. Plantations and mines would be developed and Portuguese emigration would be diverted from Brazil to Africa. The colonies would cease to be a financial burden. The whole grandiose project, the attempt to create a vast central African empire, foundered almost immediately.[145] In 1886, Portugal sought to claim the territory between Mozambique and Angola so as to have a stretch of African territory from ocean to ocean, suitably coloured in pink (*Mapa cor-de-rosa*). This clashed with the British project of an uninterrupted rose-tinted map (also the colour designating British possessions) stretching from Cairo to Cape Town. In January 1890, Lord Salisbury, then Prime Minister, sent Lisbon an ultimatum requesting unconditional Portuguese withdrawal from territories that are now Zimbabwe and Malawi, territories which had long been regarded as Portuguese. Lisbon, unable to face Britain militarily or diplomatically, gave way.[146] It had been an expensive disaster. Humiliated by its oldest and only ally, Britain, Portugal entered a period of national recrimination. Britain was depicted, not unreasonably, as Perfidious Albion. There was popular disenchantment with the Portuguese royal family, widely regarded as pusillanimous and corrupt.[147] Money lost value, some banks failed, public debt increased, investments declined.[148] In 1908, King Carlos I and his son and heir Luís Felipe were assassinated by a secret republican organization, the Carbonária, which claimed 40,000 members.[149] In 1910, Portugal became a republic.

Much of the land in the remaining Portuguese colonies – Guinea (now Guinea-Bissau), Mozambique, and Angola – was not settled by the Portuguese, few of whom wanted to become settlers and fight the Africans, who were better adapted to the climate and the insects.[150] Those few Portuguese who settled in the African colonies – 13,000 in Angola and 11,000 in Mozambique (1914) – lobbied Lisbon to extract concessions and subsidies.[151] They were detested everywhere, especially on plantations such as those of São Tomé and Principe, where they exploited an enslaved workforce (formal slavery having been officially abolished in 1876) in appalling conditions.

Spain fared even worse than Portugal, having 'lost' most of its empire to the United States in 1898. In reality these colonies were not very important and their loss was not detrimental to growth. The main consequence of such loss was political-cultural rather than economic. Spaniards could not use imperial grandeur to rebuild national identity. Instead, the country faced a lengthy period of autarchy under authoritarian regimes of various hues occasionally interrupted by brief periods of democracy.[152]

Ramiro de Maeztu, one of the most influential members of what came to be called the *generación del '98* that arose following the *desastre del '98* (see Chapter 11), declared that since 'the loss of our colonial markets makes clear how shallow and peripheral our economic evolution [was]', the only way Spanish manufacturing, for example, textiles, could prosper was to develop the internal market.[153] But, had Spain retained her empire or even been able to expand it she might, in any case, have been forced to adopt the same protectionist conclusions. The era of the first great modern globalization was dominated by such protectionist sentiments. Facing the world could be a terrifying prospect for countries whose greatness lay in the past.

For Americans, however, the future could only be glittering – in a sense, optimism was the real American ideology. Despite their anti-colonial rhetoric, they could not resist the temptation of establishing a protectorate over Cuba and the Philippines, which became de facto colonies. Americans too were becoming imperialists, as a French commentator pointed out in 1902.[154] The United States had already in 1875 established a treaty with the kingdom of Hawaii that made it a virtual colony, before annexing it formally in 1898. Hawaii acquired statehood only in 1959 (just two years before Barack Obama's birth). In 1899 the USA partitioned the Samoan islands by agreement with Germany. In 1900 it took part in the suppression of the Boxer Rebellion in China along with Britain, France, Japan, Russia, Germany, Italy, and Austria-Hungary.

The United States felt it had a 'duty' in places such as the Philippines or Hawaii on a par with the *mission civilisatrice* of European colonial states. In 1899, having just defeated Emilio Aguinaldo's Filipino liberation army, President McKinley declared 'The Philippines are ours not to exploit, but to civilize, to develop, to educate, to train in the science of self-government.'[155] In 1901, Woodrow Wilson, then still a professor at Princeton, echoed McKinley when he declared that since the USA had acquired the Philippines 'almost accidentally', it was 'our duty' to play a part in its future and that since:

> The East is to be opened and transformed, whether we will or no; the standards of the West are to be imposed upon it . . . It is our peculiar duty . . . to moderate the process in the interests of liberty: to impart to the peoples thus driven out upon the road of change . . . our own principles of self-help; teach them order and self-control . . . impart to them . . . the drill and habit of law and obedience which we long ago got out of the strenuous processes of English history . . .'[156]

McKinley's successor as President, Theodore Roosevelt, in his State of the Union address on 6 December 1904, noted that the Philippine people were at present 'utterly incapable of existing in independence at all or of building up a civilization of their own'. Eventually, with American help, they would 'rise higher and higher in the scale of civilization' and would be able to govern themselves. He then added candidly:

> There are points of resemblance in our work to the work which is being done by the British in India and Egypt, by the French in Algiers, by the Dutch in Java, by the Russians in Turkestan, by the Japanese in Formosa . . .[157]

The American takeover of the Philippines in 1898 was the inspiration for Kipling's famous 1899 poem 'The White Man's Burden' (subtitled 'The United States and the Philippine Islands'), which begins 'Take up the White Man's burden – / Send forth the best ye breed'.

Theodore Roosevelt, who has been described as 'the most impulsive, compulsive, dramatic, rambunctious . . . character ever to live in the White House', was, like many politicians at the time (in Europe and in the USA), a social reformist at home and an imperialist abroad. (He was also an undeserved winner of the Nobel Peace Prize in 1906 for his mediating efforts to end the Russo-Japanese War – hardly a momentous enterprise.)[158] In his four-volume work *The Winning of the West* (1889–96), he drew from the history of his country's struggle with the Indians the conclusion that a racial war to the finish was inevitable.[159] The triumph of the Anglo-Saxon race (a common trope at the time) was not inevitable. In a famous lecture he gave in 1899 ('The Strenuous Life') he declared that one must fight for greatness and not follow the bad example of:

> the timid man, the lazy man, the man who distrusts his country, the over-civilized man, who has lost the great fighting, masterful virtues, the ignorant man, and the man of dull mind, whose soul is incapable of feeling the mighty lift that thrills . . . shrink from seeing the nation undertake its new duties; shrink from seeing us build a navy and an army adequate to our needs; shrink from seeing us do our share of the world's work, by bringing order out of chaos . . . we cannot sit huddled within our own borders . . .[160]

Domestic reaction against the new American imperialism was muted and largely confined to those who, consistent with their libertarian and anti-statist attitude, regarded foreign adventure as a betrayal of what America 'stood for'. Thus, when the United States went to war with Spain over Cuba and the Philippines (1898), the arch-liberal William Graham Sumner warned that the USA risked following Spain and other European powers on the road of empire and eventual post-imperial ruin. Americans would become inflated with vanity and pride. They would assume, just like other colonialists, that the conquered inhabitants of the Philippines and Cuba would relish America's rule: 'this is grossly and obviously untrue. They hate our ways. They are hostile to our ideas. Our religion, our language, institutions and manners offend them.' And Sumner added: 'The most important thing which we shall inherit from the Spaniards will be the task of suppressing rebellions.'[161] The philosopher William James concurred. In a letter written in 1899 to his brother the novelist Henry James about the American acquisition of the Philippines, he declared that 'our national infamy is I fear undeniable . . .'[162] In 1899, William and Henry James and Sumner had joined the American Anti-Imperialism League in opposition to the occupation of Cuba, the Philippines, and Puerto Rico. The League was founded by George S. Boutwell, former Treasury Secretary, Senator and Governor of Massachusetts, and included among its supporters the satirical writer Ambrose Bierce, the steel magnate Andrew Carnegie, Samuel Clemens

(Mark Twain), the former President of the USA Grover Cleveland, the philosopher John Dewey, and the trade union leader Samuel Gompers.

Many European empires originated in a partnership between private companies and the state. The East India Company originated from the granting, in 1600, of a royal charter by Queen Elizabeth I, to a group of City merchants of the monopoly of trade with India and other parts of Asia. In 1602 the *Vereenigde Oost Indische Compagnie* was granted by the Dutch Parliament the monopoly of trade with Indonesia. In 1664 the *Compagnie française des Indes orientales* (a state company but with a private basis) was founded by Jean-Baptiste Colbert, Minister of Finance and architect of Louis XIV's centralized French state. These companies were not purely commercial; they also had political institutional functions since, in their territories, they could raise armies, establish an administration, exercise police powers, and collect taxes.

Throughout the seventeenth century other European states granted trade monopolies to private enterprises in the East Indies and elsewhere: Denmark in 1616, Portugal in 1628, and Sweden in 1731. By the end of the nineteenth century most of these private enterprises had been wound down and states became directly responsible for the colonies. However, Britain continued to use the private-company model when it deemed it suitable. The British South Africa Company, established in 1889 under Cecil Rhodes, had its own army, fought wars against local kingdoms, and occupied a territory corresponding to present-day Zimbabwe and Zambia. The *Manchester Guardian*, in its obituary in 1902, described him as being constantly implicated in unscrupulous pursuits and, as a consequence, became 'a wrecker instead of a constructor of South African development'.[163] Rhodes's statue still stands at Oriel College, Oxford – the beneficiary of huge sums from his will.

The historical verdict on the most famous of these imperial private enterprises, the East India Company, can only be negative, vindicating the judgement of contemporaries such as Adam Smith, Edmund Burke, and Jeremy Bentham that the Company was despotic and corrupt.[164] In 1789, Bentham, mischievously, even suggested that the East India Company erect a statue of Warren Hastings, de facto Governor of India from 1772 to 1785, who was accused of corruption and eventually acquitted:

> To this Governor a statue is erecting by a vote of East India Directors and Proprietors: on it should be inscribed – *Let it but put money into*

> *our pockets, no tyranny too flagitious to be worshipped by us.* To this statue of the Arch-malefactor should be added, for a companion, that of the long-robed accomplice: the one lodging the bribe in the hand of the other. The hundred millions of plundered and oppressed Hindoos and Mahometans pay for the one: a Westminster Hall subscription might pay for the other.[165]

'The British,' exclaimed Burke in 1783, had established 'an oppressive, irregular, capricious, unsteady, rapacious, and peculating despotism' that had no regard for the well-being of the Indians.[166] Adam Smith, in the *Wealth of Nations*, denounced the Company for having extended its 'dominion or their depredations' over some of 'the richest and most fertile countries in India', which were 'all . . . wasted and destroyed'. Consequently, it was now (1784) in 'greater distress than ever; and, in order to prevent immediate bankruptcy, it is once more reduced to supplicate the assistance of government', and all now agree to 'what was indeed always abundantly evident': that the East India Company was altogether 'unfit to govern its territorial possessions'.[167] The Company survived into the nineteenth century, facing increasing financial problems. By 1813 the British government, now hostile, stripped the Company of almost all its trading privileges and monopolies, leaving it with only the unglamorous function of providing personnel as agents of the Crown in India.[168] In 1833 the Charter Act (formally the Government of India Act, 1833) removed all remaining privileges, including the China monopoly, from the East India Company.[169] The Company's trading days were over. James Silk Buckingham, a former editor of the *Calcutta Journal*, who led the campaign to end the monopoly, declared in that year that the idea of giving a commercial undertaking 'the political administration of an empire peopled with a hundred million of souls was so preposterous' that if it were proposed now it would be regarded as absurd.[170] Yet the Company, even after it lost its commercial business, continued to exercise British rule over much of South Asia – a kind of privatized armed force working on behalf of the Crown. It did so rather badly and was widely held responsible for the Indian Rebellion of 1857. With the Government of India Act in 1858, the Company was dissolved and the administration of India became not just de facto but also de jure the business of the British state, in other words, a colony.[171]

After 1860, British exports to the empire increased at a faster rate than its trade with the rest of the world, cushioning the negative effects of the Long Depression of the 1870s and 1880s and the growing competition from continental Europe and the United States.[172] However, as early as the 1870s, the total value of British exports to Europe and the USA began to fall seriously. In the ten non-European countries in which 82 per cent of British capital was invested, exports fell by almost 50 per cent in the years 1870 to 1913.[173] Fortunately for Britain, there was an empire where it could dump its exports, though, of course, Britain's share of exports going to the empire was slowly decreasing between the 1860s and 1913.[174] Britain's best customers (in per capita terms) were the British themselves, suitably transplanted as settlers in Australia, New Zealand, and Canada. Unlike Americans (well on the way to industrialization), these 'British' settlers did not compete with British manufacturing but supplied the mother country with mineral and agricultural goods in exchange for British industrial products.

The closeness between these 'white' Dominions, as they were soon called, and Great Britain should not be underestimated. Americans really regarded themselves as a separate nation and all the more so as immigrants from other European countries changed the demographic balance. Australians, Canadians, and New Zealanders, however, continued to think of themselves as British and did not hesitate to send their men to fight for Britain in the great wars of 1914–18 and 1939–45, and kept the British monarch as their head of state well into the twenty-first century. Only by the 1970s did many Australians no longer think of themselves as 'basically British'.[175] By then, of course, a majority of Australians had non-British ancestors.

The pro-imperial economic argument became less plausible as economic growth accelerated in the thirty years after 1945 when both Great Britain and France lost their empires. The French financial daily *Les Échos* in a scaremongering article of 12 March 1956 entitled 'La France sans l'Algérie?' declared that the loss of Algeria would cause such a level of unemployment that 'the political balance of France would be rapidly destroyed'.[176] They were wrong. In October 1960 a group of conservative intellectuals produced a manifesto against other intellectuals who were against the war declaring that the French army in Algeria had been pursuing for years *une mission civilisatrice sociale et humaine*.[177] Six months later, on 11 April 1961, President Charles de Gaulle, with the war in Algeria in its seventh year, discovered that decolonization was in the national interest: 'In today's world . . . France has no interest in keeping under her law and rule an Algeria which has chosen another destiny.'[178]

Similarly, in the Netherlands it was feared that the loss of Indonesia would be a catastrophe. Yet, after the Netherlands 'lost' Indonesia in

Table 15 Independence from the United Kingdom of Colonies and Protectorates

1967	Aden
1968	Mauritius; Swaziland; Nauru
1970	Tonga; Fiji
1971	Bahrain; Qatar; United Arab Emirates
1973	Bahamas
1974	Grenada
1976	Seychelles; Gilbert and Ellice Islands
1978	Dominica; Solomon Islands
1979	St Vincent and the Grenadines; St Lucia
1980	New Hebrides, now known as Vanuatu
1981	Antigua and Barbuda; Belize
1983	St Kitts and Nevis
1984	Brunei

1949, the Dutch economy expanded remarkably, and it could be mooted that such expansion might not have been as significant had the country tried to hold on to a colony seventy times bigger than itself and seven times more populous.[179]

Between 1967 and 1984, Britain gave up, or was forced to give up, the remains of her empire. The list is a long one (see Table 15).

The list seems impressive, yet few in the United Kingdom took much notice of the end of British rule, or even knew where these places were. It was all done with little struggle – unlike in India, Kenya, Malaysia, and many other countries. For most British people the end of the empire had come about when India was 'lost' in 1947. Others could not ignore the price demanded by the end of British rule as easily as those at home. For instance, the Mau Mau rebellion (1952–60), which started as an uprising of the Kikuyu of Kenya (Mau Mau was the term used by the British), was violently and cruelly suppressed.[180] Thousands were imprisoned in harsh concentration camps, subject to torture and degrading conditions.[181] Eventually, in 1961, Kenya was 'granted' independence. No assessment was made to see whether they had been sufficiently 'civilized'; colonies were just costing too much. It was not until 2013 that the British (Conservative) government recognized that 'Kenyans were subjected to torture and other forms of ill-treatment at the hands of the colonial administration', and agreed to pay compensation.[182]

Colonies cannot all be lumped together. Some were certainly profitable: India for the British and the Maghreb (north Africa west of Egypt)

for the French. In 1914 the Maghreb took 61.7 per cent of French investment in their empire – Algeria on its own accounted for 41.5 per cent.[183] India, Algeria, and Indochina were colonies for which an economic case could be made – unlike, say, Madagascar or Uganda. Yet it is equally reasonable to suggest that empire-building had to be somewhat connected to the metropolitan economy.[184] Acquiring and developing a colony is, undoubtedly, a business; but who profits? Colonial development, like defence spending, often simply constitutes a transfer of resources from the public coffer to private purses.

It is sometimes argued that an empire cushioned countries from economic decline and delivered profits for investors, but the artificial survival of some economic sectors is not necessarily in the interest of the wider economy. The end of empire, when it happened, was not generally as economically catastrophic for the 'mother-country' as its proponents feared. Throughout the period of decolonization, that is, throughout the 1950s and 1960s, the main cost associated with colonies was that of defending them. The costs, military and financial, were always far greater if one had to face the problem of having one's settlers ensconced in the colonies and resisting decolonization: the French in Algeria, the British in Rhodesia and, to some extent, in Kenya. There were, of course, exceptions: the French had relatively few settlers in the whole of Indochina (23,700 in 1913 and 34,000 in 1940), and even fewer from metropolitan France, yet they fought to retain Vietnam from 1946 until their catastrophic defeat at Dien Bien Phu in 1954.[185]

The main practical argument for empires is that one could trade within them. This argument had some strength in countries such as Britain where dependency on imported food and raw materials was particularly pronounced.[186] Trading patterns, however, differed so much from country to country that it would be useless to generalize. The economic growth of much of western Europe did not rely on trade with the 'periphery' as the British did.[187] But that was because a significant part of British economic growth relied on manufacturing cotton cloth, which required importing raw cotton from India (a colony), Egypt (a semi-colony), and the United States (an ex-colony). Before the Second World War what we now call the 'Third World' was of limited importance to world trade (it absorbed only 17 per cent of total exports), but it mattered much more to the United Kingdom, whose exports to the periphery represented 40 per cent of its own trade, though only 4–6 per cent of total production (still much higher than other countries).[188] And, of course, it mattered more because if you have an empire, you are more likely to trade with it than if you have not got one. As in most things in life, empires benefited some, others thought they did benefit, still others remained indifferent, unable to calculate whether they had anything to gain. Yet empires did shape the fate of capitalism throughout the decades, the fate of countries that had empires, the fate of those that had no colonies and, of course, the fate of those who were colonized.

18
The Great Colonial Debate: The French and the British

Whether or not colonies were functional to capitalism has long been debated particularly in the two leading colonialist countries of the period: Great Britain and France. Were colonies useful for industry, commerce, and finance? Were they a useful outlet for functionaries and migrants from the mother country? Did colonies inspire pride and patriotism, thus contributing to the formation of a national community, and so toning down the anxieties caused by capitalism? Patriotic, racial, and humanitarian arguments, along with economic ones, were constantly deployed in the great colonial debates in Britain and France. It was not simple to balance the cost in human lives, in military spending, in subsidies, against the benefits – the acquisition of primary products, the protection of one's own markets, employment, and international prestige.[1] Colonies made some of the people who thought they were going to get rich poor – investing abroad was a risky business. Between 1900 and 1905 fourteen out of the fifteen companies that obtained mining concessions in Sudan failed.[2] Mining and prospecting attracted the ill-informed, the over-optimistic, and the unscrupulous.

One could always sell to the colonies, but the richest colonies were those settled by white colonists. It is a truism that one can make more money selling to the rich than to the poor since, as F. Scott Fitzgerald put it (*The Rich Boy*, 1926), the former have more money, though there is an ample market selling low quality to the lower income groups – but this was to be an achievement of the twentieth century. In the decades leading up to the First World War the prosperous were mainly in Europe and North America and so it is not surprising that, on the eve of the First World War, the industrial powers of the world were still one another's best customers.[3]

You could be an independent European state and still have a sizeable chunk of your economy controlled by foreigners: in Romania, at the close of the nineteenth century, foreign capital totally dominated gas and electricity production, metallurgy, chemicals, and forestry products. Anglo-Dutch and Franco-Belgian capital together held about 57 per cent of the capital invested in the country.[4] Still, by 1913, Romania ranked fourth in the world as a wheat exporter (after Russia, Canada, and the United States) and was the second largest oil producer in Europe.[5]

It is rare in history to have a situation where everyone gains or everyone loses. Colonialism was no different. The military expenditure involved in the defence of the colonies was a burden for all taxpayers, but the expenses were public, the profits substantially private. By the 1880s the rulers of Victorian Britain had devised a 'Treasury test' to decide whether a territory was worth taking over: the colony had to generate enough revenue to pay for its rule.[6] This was not always complied with, but one can see the logic: a little like asking the hanged man to pay for his rope. The Victorians wanted empire on the cheap.

Investing in the colonies might cost the taxpayer but it might benefit local enterprises, thus colonialism could also be seen as a major public subsidy to the private sector. During the Second Empire the French state launched a series of public-works programmes in conjunction with private capital to develop Algeria: lighthouses, roads, dams, and so on, thus contributing to private profits.[7] It may be possible to calculate who benefited, but exceedingly difficult to work out who lost since it would involve some rather tricky counter-factual calculations (e.g. the consequence of an alternative pattern of public spending).[8]

Throughout the expansion of the French Empire, Britain remained France's leading commercial partner. In 1906 the French Empire absorbed only 11 per cent of France's exports. Not enough to make it essential, but not so little to make it irrelevant. Of course, it depended who you were. If you produced beer, the empire was crucial since 75 per cent of French beer was exported to the colonies (for obvious reasons Britain, Belgium, and Germany were unlikely to import French beer).[9] But the French sub-Saharan colonies were never worth the effort and expense. Even in 1930 these colonies were unable to provide France with more than 5 per cent of the coffee it imported. The French blamed the innate laziness of the natives. In fact, many French colonies had been acquired for political reasons. Economic issues were an add-on.[10]

Nor should we forget that even at the height of empire-building there always was, even in Britain, some opposition to colonialism, particularly from those in favour of capitalism. Some of this opposition was inspired by older liberal ideas that originated in the eighteenth century from political thinkers such as David Hume (*Political Discourses*), Adam Smith (*The Wealth of Nations*, a third of which was about empires), and Adam Ferguson (*Essay on the History of Civil Society*).[11] Even a committed Tory such as Samuel Johnson praised, in 1744, the poet Richard Savage for censuring:

> those crimes which have been generally committed by the discoverers of new regions, and to expose the enormous wickedness of making war upon barbarous nations because they cannot resist and of invading countries because they are fruitful; of extending navigation only to propagate vice, and of visiting distant lands only to lay them waste. He has asserted the natural equality of mankind . . .[12]

Adam Smith, the first to refer to Britain as a 'nation of shopkeepers', wrote that:

> To found a great empire for the sole purpose of raising up a people of customers, may at first sight, appear a project fit only for a nation of shopkeepers. It is, however, a project altogether unfit for a nation of shopkeepers, but extremely fit for a nation whose government is influenced by shopkeepers.[13]

As the British Empire expanded, liberal opposition to it increased. Richard Cobden and John Bright, the champions of free trade, Gladstone, and J. A. Hobson (the liberal anti-imperialist economist author of *Imperialism: A Study*, 1902, a text that influenced Lenin) were among those who insisted that the possession of an empire brought no material rewards to the nation as a whole; indeed, it harmed its growth prospects. Hobson thought that the imperial acquisitions of the 1890s brought little or no increase in trade, that most trade was with European countries and with the United States, and that the dictum 'trade follows the flag' had no foundation at all.[14] He thought that free trade was under threat from both the advocates of protectionism and warmongering imperialists.[15] Hobson regarded Free Trade (his capital letters) as a stage of social evolution where 'militarism is displaced by industrialism' and where 'nationalism yields place to an effective internationalism based upon identity of commercial interests'.[16] There was a lofty purpose to Hobson's politics. Quoting approvingly Richard Cobden, Hobson explained that he advocated free trade not just because it would create prosperity but because it would 'unite mankind in the bonds of peace'.[17] Eventually, Hobson's opposition to imperialism mellowed, and, just before the First World War, he granted that the penetration of backward areas could be to the advantage of both the mother country and the colonies.[18]

Even liberals, however, had no doubts that colonized people were not ready for liberalism. John Stuart Mill, who, like Hobson, thought that Britain gained little from her colonies, wrote in *Considerations on Representative Government* (1861):

> less advanced populations . . . must be governed by the dominant country, or by persons delegated for that purpose by it . . . There are, as we have already seen, conditions of society in which a vigorous despotism is in itself the best mode of government for training the people in what is specifically wanting to render them capable of a higher civilization . . . Such is the ideal rule of a free people over a barbarous or semi-barbarous one.[19]

A little earlier, in December 1859, in *Fraser's Magazine*, he had written:

> To suppose that the same international customs, and the same rules of international morality, can obtain between one civilized nation and another, and between civilized nations and barbarians, is a grave error . . . To characterize any conduct whatever towards a barbarous people as a violation of the law of nations, only shows that he who so speaks has never considered the subject . . . barbarians have no rights as a *nation* . . .[20]

Years before he had explained that savages were savages, in spite of body strength and courage, and though 'often not without intelligence' they were unable to cooperate and were just too selfish.[21]

Such conviction of the superiority of one's nation or race was quite common at the time (and still persists), as was the idea that one can classify states in terms of how civilized they are, meaning how close they are to the Western notion of civilization (today we talk of Western values as espoused by 'the international community', i.e. the West). Thus James Lorimer, Regius Professor of Law at the University of Edinburgh, writing in the 1880s, divided humanity into three 'concentric zones': civilized, barbarous, savage.[22] The first, obviously, consisted of Europe and areas inhabited by people of 'European descent, such as North and South America'. These could enjoy 'plenary political recognition', in other words be fully fledged participants in international politics. The second tier (Japan, China, Persia, Turkey, etc.) could enjoy at best 'partial political recognition', while the unfortunate rest could only be granted 'natural or mere human recognition'. Lorimer admitted the possibility of upgrading (not a word he used): should the Japanese continue at their 'present rate of progress for another twenty years', he explained, then they could be granted plenary political recognition. The Turks, however, would probably be downgraded to the status of savages.

Such views were held even by distinguished poets. Here is Coleridge's complacent 'table talk': 'Colonisation is not only a manifest expedient, but an imperative duty for Great Britain – God seems to hold out his finger to us over the seas.'[23]

At the end of the nineteenth century the idea that natives were inferior was the consensus. The idea that Africa was just the 'Dark Continent' had barely changed since Hegel's bizarre assertion, in his *Philosophy of History* (1820s), that Africa:

> is no historical part of the World; it has no movement or development to exhibit . . . What we properly understand by Africa, is the Unhistorical, Undeveloped Spirit, still involved in the conditions of mere nature, and which had to be presented here only as on the threshold of the World's History.[24]

This dismal view of Africa was held also by Victor Hugo, who had been intransigent in his opposition to the despotism of Napoleon III. Back from his self-imposed exile of almost twenty years, Hugo welcomed the *mission civilisatrice* of the Third Republic. On 18 May 1879 during a speech at a banquet commemorating the abolition of slavery, he declared in tones that would have been unthinkable one hundred years later:

> There are only two faces to this wild Africa: barbarism when inhabited, savagery when deserted . . . Seize this land. Take it. From whom? No one. Take it from God . . . God offers Africa to Europe . . . Where kings brought war, bring harmony. Take it not for the gun but for the plough, not for the sword but for commerce, not for conquest but for fraternity. [*prolonged applause*] Send your excess labour to Africa and, at a stroke, you will resolve the social question, transform your proletarians into property-owners. Go and build! Build roads, cities, grow and multiply and on an earth with fewer priests and princes, the divine spirit will manifest itself through peace and the human spirit through freedom.[25]

Few would have objected to the view of Captaine Renard, Secretary-General of the *Union Congolaise* (the association of companies in French Congo), in his 1901 report *La colonisation au Congo Français*, that Africans were inferior, and that the Europeans were the 'elder brothers'.[26] He wrote what he thought was obvious: civilization would have to be imposed on the natives by force, '*le fusil en main*' (gun in hand), since the natives were of low intelligence and naturally lazy and should be forced to work and treated like slaves.

In French Congo the routine violence inflicted on the natives went largely overlooked (since it did not reach the horrific levels of the

Belgian Congo), until some sensational case would spark moral outrage in the mother country. The Toqué-Gaud affair was such a case and caused widespread scandal in Paris. It appeared that two colonial administrators, George Toqué and Fernand Gaud, decided to punish a recalcitrant native by exploding a dynamite stick tied around his neck on 14 July 1903 as a way of celebrating the French Revolution and the Universal Declaration of the Rights of Man. There was a trial and the two murderers were condemned to only five years' imprisonment. Regarded by local whites as martyrs, the men were released after a mere two years.[27] George Toqué was eventually executed in 1920 by a military squad at Vincennes for complicity with the Germans during the First World War.

In mainland France the light sentence was received with opprobrium. A committee of inquiry was set up under the explorer Pierre Savorgnan de Brazza, a fierce defender of the rights of natives. Brazza wrote his report but died on the way back from the Congo. In France he was given a state funeral, though there was also private relief. His report on the horrors of French colonialism was kept hidden from the public.[28]

Brazza was far from being an ordinary administrator. Born in Castel Gandolfo near Rome (as Pietro di Brazzà), he acquired French nationality and explored the Congo and Ogooué rivers on behalf of the French government, founding various settlements, one of which became Brazzaville. In November 1885 he was appointed *commissaire général* of French Congo. He protected the natives from excessive exploitation by private firms and offered decent working conditions to those who worked for the French state. He was a humanitarian colonialist whose rule was in sharp contrast to the horrific conditions on the other side of the river Congo (Belgian Congo).

Brazza had obviously gone 'native', to use an expression diffused in British colonial circles denoting colonial administrators who took the side of the locals instead of prioritizing the interests of the mother country. He was a gentle colonialist accused of practising 'philanthropy not colonization', in the words of one plantation owner. His downfall was inevitable: he was dismissed in 1897.[29] His successor, Émile Gentil, was not so philanthropic and allowed 'normal' colonial repression and exploitation until the Toqué-Gaud affair in 1903 led to Brazza's last mission of 1905.

Unsurprisingly, arch-imperialists such as Cecil Rhodes thought that, within the hierarchy of the 'civilized', the English had a special role. Well before he became fabulously rich thanks to the diamond trade and before becoming Prime Minister of the Cape Colony, in his *Confession of Faith* (1877), a kind of will, written at the age of twenty-five, Rhodes intoned:

> if we had retained America there would at this moment be millions more of English living. I contend that we are the finest race in the world and that the more of the world we inhabit the better it is for the human race. Just fancy those parts that are at present inhabited by the most despicable specimens of human beings what an alteration there would be if they were brought under Anglo-Saxon influence, look again at the extra employment a new country added to our dominions gives.[30]

Those who were clearly in the pro-colonial camp included conservatives, who had little faith in the free market since they regarded capitalism as an anarchic and unpredictable system: Disraeli, of course, but also liberals like Joseph Chamberlain and Sir Charles Dilke (once a republican, in favour of female suffrage and trade unions) who turned into Radical Imperialists.[31] They felt that an empire protected by the Royal Navy would be a positive factor in deterring others from acquiring their own colonies to the disadvantage of British trade.[32] In 1888, Joseph Chamberlain, who had broken with Gladstone over Irish Home Rule, declared:

> Is there any man in his senses who believes that the crowded population of these islands could exist for a single day if we were to cut adrift from us the great dependencies . . . the natural markets for our trade? . . . If tomorrow it were possible, as some people apparently desire, to reduce by a stroke of the pen the British Empire to the dimension of the United Kingdom, half at least of our population would be starved.[33]

The target of these 'new imperialists' were the ageing Gladstone and the shrinking band of free-trade Manchester liberals. Lord Rosebery had them in mind when, as a Liberal Prime Minister, in a speech in Sheffield (25 October 1894), he decried the party 'of small England, of a shrunk England, of a degraded England, of a neutral England, of a submissive England'.[34] His liberal imperialist followers would be in power in the years leading to the war: H. H. Asquith (Prime Minister 1908–16), Sir Edward Grey (Foreign Secretary 1905–16), and R. B. Haldane (Secretary of State for War 1905–12).

In Britain, and perhaps in Britain alone, colonialism and free trade went together. Britain consolidated its empire, acquired new colonies, *and* did not embrace the wave of protectionism sweeping the industrialized world. In Great Britain free trade was a genuinely popular movement, 'a national ideology' supported by industrialists and workers alike.[35] Free trade was seen by the trade unions as ensuring cheap food, and by the middle classes as the basis for low taxes and economic growth.[36] As Frank Trentmann has written, 'The pocket was never very far from the heart.'[37]

The new great British consensus around empire and free trade linked the aristocracy with finance (for some reason aristocrats thought that banking was nobler and more genteel than manufacturing, and the City a better place to be than Sheffield or Manchester – a traditional view going back to the late seventeenth century). This consensus made it possible for the Conservative Party to rule almost uninterruptedly between 1885 and 1905 and to hold at bay the rise of a working-class party until the First World War. Some complained that the government ignored domestic industry in favour of overseas enterprise, particularly as manufacturing began to falter in the 1880s, but no government would have ignored the immense flow of British investment abroad.[38] In the mid-1850s the stock of net assets overseas was 8 per cent of the total wealth owned by Britons, by 1870 it had reached 17 per cent, and by 1913 it was a staggering 33 per cent: 'Never before or since has one nation committed so much of its national income and savings to capital formation abroad.'[39]

One of the reasons the empire was attractive to British investors is that it was heavily subsidized by British taxpayers. This was particularly true of the cost of its defence.[40] The burden of paying for the Boer War, for example, fell entirely on the British taxpayer. This caused some perplexity. Thus Sir Garnett Wolseley (Governor of Natal in southern Africa), discussing in 1878 the impending assumption of British control over the whole of the Transvaal, warned that to rule such a large territory in the face of Boer opposition would require 'a large garrison of British troops here, the expense of which must be defrayed by the Imperial exchequer'.[41]

In September 1901 the Prime Minister, Lord Salisbury, in a letter to Lord Curzon, Viceroy of India, lamented that while once Britain could do what it liked, now managing the empire had become 'a question of money'. A few months earlier, in April 1901, Lord Hamilton, Secretary of State for India, also in a letter to Curzon, expressed his fear of what we would call now 'imperial overstretch':

> Our interests being so extended makes it almost impossible for us to concentrate sufficiently, in any one direction, the pressure and power of the Empire so as to deter foreign nations from trying to encroach upon our interests in that particular quarter.[42]

It is difficult to estimate the proportion of taxes that specifically went towards paying for the defence of the empire.[43] Britain spent more on defence than France and Germany, though India underwrote all of its own administrative costs as well as the costs of its 'defence'. But this was not so for the white dominions of Canada, Australia, and New Zealand.[44] Without the empire, the British taxpayer would almost certainly have had a smaller bill, even though India paid for itself.[45]

In 1914 the value of British investment abroad was still double that of the French and three times that of the German. Hardly any of it was in manufacturing (where it would have competed with domestic production). Only 12 per cent was in plantation and mining. The largest share went into infrastructures such as railways, docks, tramways, telegraphs and telephones, gas, and electricity.[46] Such projects were usually sponsored or guaranteed by governments.

That British investment abroad was excessive was an argument deployed by those who accused the City, as they still do, of disregarding the interests of the nation in favour of their own (a bizarre accusation which assumes, against centuries of evidence, that bankers should act like selfless patriots – tantamount to accusing bank robbers of being dishonest). Karl Marx, realist to the end, intoned in the third volume of *Capital*, 'If capital is sent abroad, this is . . . because it can be employed at a higher rate of profit in a foreign country.'[47] Yet it was not British investment in the British Empire that was disproportionate but rather, before the First World War, investment made in the United States – unsurprisingly since it was the fastest-growing economy in the world. Half of British overseas investment went to the western hemisphere, namely Canada, the USA, and Latin America. Only one-twelfth went to continental Europe. Australia and New Zealand, with barely 6 million people (fewer than London at the time), received 8 per cent, almost the same as the whole of Europe. Canada and Argentina were more valuable to Britain than the whole of Africa.[48] The majority of investment to Asia went to India. Africa got relatively little.[49] The so-called 'Dark Continent', from the British point of view, especially tropical Africa, was economically speaking of very little value. J. A. Hobson was right: trade did not follow the flag.

Niall Ferguson, a historian who has a positive view of empires, or at least of the British brand, thinks that before 1914 'the benefits of Empire had seemed to most people, on balance, to outweigh the costs'.[50] By 'most people' one assumes Ferguson means 'most British people'.

And the phrase 'had seemed' leaves open the question whether the benefits did outweigh the cost or whether this was just an impression, something almost impossible to measure. When it comes to the post-1914 era, Ferguson has fewer doubts: the costs *did* outweigh the benefits. Yet the empire went on for decades – in the Indian subcontinent until 1947, most of Africa until the 1960s – and was not vacated without some kind of struggle. It is therefore quite possible that popular support for imperialism grew simply because the empire, as it became established, could rely on a powerful propaganda machine, even though the gains from it (if any) were shrinking at a fast rate – further evidence that economics does not rule everything.

Opposition to empire declined in the years leading up to the First World War. The African continent was carved up in a relatively peaceful manner; it did not lead to war among European states (except for minor clashes); it did bring some discernible benefits and some unverifiable losses. Had colonial conquest entailed long and bitter wars there would have been a major shift in public opinion. Even the Italian defeat by Ethiopia at Adwa in 1896, though it had been a humiliation that rankled for a long time, involved only a few thousand troops. The only British colonial war serious enough to have an impact on public opinion was the Boer War, fought not to subjugate 'the natives' but against the Boers, the descendants of Dutch settlers. It took 300,000 men (20,000 of whom died) and a three-year campaign for the British to overwhelm the resistance of the Boers. It taught the British, in Rudyard Kipling's famous phrase, 'no end of a lesson':

> Let us admit it fairly, as a business people should,
> We have had no end of a lesson: it will do us no end of good.
> . . .
> It was our fault, and our very great fault – and now we must turn it to use.
> We have forty million reasons for failure, but not a single excuse.
> So the more we work and the less we talk the better results we shall get –
> We have had an Imperial lesson; it may make us an Empire yet![51]

There was considerable disquiet that the mightiest empire had taken so long and spent so much subduing a 'little' people of Dutch settlers. As Mr Brumley, a character in H. G. Wells's *The Wife of Sir Isaac Harmon* (1914), ruminates disconsolately, 'Our Empire was nearly beaten by a handful of farmers amidst the jeering contempt of the world . . .'[52] Sir Garnett (now Lord) Wolseley (see above) declared, 'if this war comes off it will be the most serious war England has ever had, when the size of our Army and the distance of the seat of war from England are taken into consideration'.[53]

But the Boer War and the Italian defeat in Ethiopia were exceptions. On the whole, imperial wars did not cost much, were usually won, and those who died were often professional soldiers or mercenaries or foreigners. It would have been unthinkable for a French general to address conscripted French troops and tell them what General Oscar de Négrier told the Foreign Legion (which recruited non-French soldiers) before going to Indochina in 1883 to finish off the conquest of the north of the country: *Vous, légionnaires, vous êtes soldats pour mourir, et je vous envoie où l'on meurt!* ('You, Legionnaires, are soldiers destined to die, and I send you where one dies!'). The historian John R. Seeley, in his 1883 Cambridge lectures, pointed out that 'It remains entirely incorrect to speak of the English nation as having conquered the nations of India. The nations of India have been conquered by an army of which on average about a fifth part was English.'[54]

Had colonial wars exacted a serious toll in casualties and money, support for colonization would have diminished. The empire was not as popular as it may appear from school textbooks, the parades, and the flag-waving. Many, not just in Britain but also in France, thought colonies too expensive.[55] Most just did not care. Harry Johnston, who became the first commissioner of Nyasaland (now Malawi) in 1891 (appointed by the arch-imperialist Cecil Rhodes), writing in the *Fortnightly Review* in 1890 at a time when Great Britain ruled the world, or most of it, lamented:

> A British Parliament which annually grumbles at voting a few thousand a year for British Bechuanaland . . . is hardly likely to find several hundred thousand pounds more for the administration of British East Africa, the Niger Protectorate, or Nyasaland. For this you, the stay-at-home British public, who give your votes at elections, are directly responsible . . . your representatives do and have done their utmost, with every government that has been in power for the last half-century, to hinder and hamper the extension and maintenance of the British Empire . . .[56]

Nor was the British Colonial Office particularly keen to spend money to protect investors overseas. As Sir Harry Ord, Governor of the Straits Settlement (Singapore and some coastal enclaves) explained to local businessmen: 'If persons, knowing the risks they run . . . choose to hazard their lives and properties for the sake of large profits . . . they must not expect the British Government to be answerable if their speculation proves unsuccessful.'[57]

There was never a British imperial project, that is, a decision to acquire an empire, and never an original starting point. As John Seeley famously mused:

> There is something very characteristic in the indifference which we show towards this mighty phenomenon of the diffusion of our race and the expansion of our state. We seem, as it were, to have conquered and peopled half the world in a fit of absence of mind.[58]

It took the Boer War to make a real impact.[59] Until the 1880s only the aristocracy and the desperate were seriously involved in empire-building; the majority of the middle classes did not care; the working classes were unenthusiastic; and the impact of the empire on British culture was slight.[60] Until the beginning of the twentieth century, and arguably even later, most people remained ignorant of the empire. Imperial history was not taught in universities.[61]

There had been imperial allusions in school magazines and there was a genre of popular 'colonial' literature where the hero was a Westerner, often helped by a 'noble savage', fighting against adversity and less noble savages. But such stuff was popular everywhere in the Western world, including in countries that had no real empire, such as Italy, where the adventure novels by Emilio Salgari sold very well at the turn of the century, when they were written, and well into the twentieth century. After 1880, and not before, British history and geography books became empire-friendly, but the empire was never central in such texts, unlike the Tudors or the Glorious Revolution of 1688. Only in 1911 did a real pro-empire textbook appear: C. R. L. Fletcher and Rudyard Kipling's *A History of England*, which mentioned the Industrial Revolution only twice, accusing it of having depopulated the English countryside.[62] Its smugness would make today's readers smile: 'other nations . . . have envied us' and are 'trying to copy us' in various fields, including on how 'to govern subject races well'.[63]

In France, history textbooks, such as the 'manuel Brossolette' (1907), dealt with the French conquest of Tunisia thus: 'In 1881 Jules Ferry decided to punish the Khoumirs [a Berber tribe], a turbulent people who constantly crossed into Algeria. In pursuit, it happened that our soldiers occupied Tunisia.'[64] The occupation of the Congo and Sudan, says another textbook, put an end to horrors such as the slave trade.[65]

A feeling of achievement was particularly felt by those members of the middle classes who went to the colonies. It gave them the possibility of enjoying an aristocratic lifestyle, taking pride in their 'origins', and 'doing good'; at home, of course, they had little to be proud of. They could do what they could never dream of doing in the 'mother country': have a large estate with ample provisions for hunting and shooting, indulge in conspicuous consumption, have servants, and adopt 'cultivated' modes of paternalistic behaviour.'[66] Why be against colonies when they provided jobs as administrators and officers for the middle classes and as soldiers for the unemployed; subsidies for colonially based enterprises and markets for exporters; as well as a pleasing feeling of superiority? The true imperialists, according to Bernard Porter, were a relatively small band of marginal misfits: Irish aristocrats, middle-class men with social pretensions, sexually frustrated men and women, rogues, ruffians, Scots, and so on.[67] There were a significant enough number of *déclassé* aristocrats to lead John Bright (the anti-imperialist Liberal MP) to regard the empire as 'a gigantic system of out-door relief for the aristocracy of Great Britain'.[68]

Hobson, writing in 1902, thundered against colonizers:

> As the despotic portion of our Empire has grown in area, a larger and larger number of men, trained in the temper and methods of autocracy . . . whose lives have been those of a superior caste living an artificial life removed from all the healthy restraints of ordinary European society . . . have returned to this country, bringing back the characters, sentiments, and ideas imposed by this foreign environment . . . everywhere they stand for coercion and for resistance to reform.[69]

In France it had been not much different. Hubert Jules Deschamps, a French colonial administrator in Madagascar, wrote in 1931, 'We leave [France] to become kings . . . And not do-nothing kings either, but artists at our job, enlightened despots organizing our kingdoms according to maturely reflected plans.'[70] Otherwise in France too there was much public indifference towards the empire, at least before 1914. Workers did not seem to connect their own interests to the acquisition of colonies. At the various trade union congresses in the two decades before the war the colonial issue was barely mentioned.[71] The pro-colonialist French geographer Maurice Zimmermann lamented that his countrymen seemed unwilling to settle in the colonies.[72]

Some of these mixed feelings (*mission civilisatrice* co-existing with indifference) appear to be the consequence of the lack of a 'colonial project' in both major imperial powers: there was no conscious, widely accepted establishment strategy to build an empire. John Seeley's famous 'absence of mind' remark could have been applied equally well to France.

However, once the empire had been built, it would take courage to call for its end. Colonies may not have been wildly popular, but they were not wildly unpopular either and so no campaign to relinquish even just some of them was ever mounted even by the staunchest anti-colonialists. Anti-colonialism was always a rearguard action, a demand not to extend the empire, never a demand to retrench it. Just as nationalism is constructed among the masses *after* the nation state comes into being, so imperialists are the consequences of empire-building, not the builders of empires.

An empire was the ultimate status symbol. It meant that one's country was one of the great powers. Status symbols have a long life that extends well past their sell-by-date. Take the present-day role of nuclear weapons: Great Britain, after the collapse of communism, had no conceivable nuclear foe. Yet, for years, no party in power, regardless of economic considerations, ever dared to suggest that it might be a good idea to stop wasting money on such weapons. The empire was certainly a far better investment than nuclear weapons for Britain, since, besides providing pride and prestige, it was, at the very least, 'an adjunct to British wealth'.[73]

The fruits of empire increasingly surrounded the average British household, especially in the twentieth century. The British might not have been very interested in the empire but they were 'comfortable with the idea of being imperial'.[74] By 1913, 45 per cent of their meat and dairy produce came from foreign, including colonial, sources. They drank Assam and Ceylon tea, Kenyan coffee – all sweetened with West Indian sugar – ate New Zealand butter, wrote on 'empire' typewriters, smoked Rhodesian tobacco, and wore clothes made of Australian wool or Egyptian cotton.[75] Of course, other Europeans did the same, but it was not 'their' tea, 'their' coffee, 'their' wool, 'their' tobacco. In practice it made little difference, except, perhaps, psychologically. The coffee could come from Brazil as well as Africa, the tobacco from Virginia or Kentucky, the chocolate from the Americas, the cotton from the United States, and the tea from China. The point was that all this had to cross the seas.[76] And Britain still 'ruled the waves'.

A popular imperial consciousness in France and Great Britain came into being only in the 1920s and 1930s, just as their empires began their gradual descent into extinction. Even then the central theme of patriotic history was freedom (Great Britain as the freest country in the world, etc.) rather than empire: 'Liberty not imperialism lay at the core of British history.'[77] The image foreigners often had of Great Britain was that of a powerful, arrogant imperial country (Perfidious Albion, etc.), but the British saw themselves as a 'free, moderate and peaceful nation'.[78] The idea was to lord it everywhere, but in a rather understated way. As Queen Victoria wrote, summarizing Lord Curzon's attitude to India (on his appointment as Viceroy of India), the Indians should be made to '*feel* that we are the masters, but it should be done kindly and not offensively, which alas! is so often not the case'.[79] This is not unlike the contrast between the image of the USA abroad in the late twentieth century (ruthless and ignorant imperialists) and that held by Americans of themselves (as well-meaning, honest, bent on saving the world from its follies).

Even Lord Salisbury, whose imperial credentials were unimpeachable (most of Britain's African empire had been acquired under his premiership), was far from being enamoured of the jingoistic aspects of imperialism. As early as 1859 he held onto an unemotional view of foreign policy, declaring that 'The only safe and dignified foreign policy for England, is to watch carefully over her own interests . . . to complain when they are wronged, to fight if that complaint is disregarded, and to concern herself with nothing else.'[80] Forty years later he still sounded more like a pragmatic shopkeeper than an imperialist – the empire was good for Britain, but one should not forget the profit and loss: 'The more our Empire extends the more our imperial spirit grows, the more we must urge on all who have to judge that those things are matters of business and must be considered upon business principles.'[81]

In defending an agreement with Germany in 1890, Salisbury thought it 'a very curious idea' that anyone would want to be able to control a territory 'extending all the way from Cape Town to the sources of the Nile', since 'this stretch of territory North of Lake Tanganyika could only have been a very narrow one', with no advantage to Britain and one that would have needlessly antagonized the Germans.[82] But this would have been seen by his detractors as a prestigious gain, shown on the map of Africa as an uninterrupted and pleasant stretch of pink from Alexandria to Cape Town – pink being the colour used by cartographers to represent British possessions. This is exactly what the map did look like after the First World War when the British acquired Tanganyika from Germany. Generations of schoolchildren were taught to look at the pink stretch with pride in their hearts.

Disraeli understood perfectly well the ideological value of empires and explained in his famous speech on 'Conservative and Liberal Principles' at Crystal Palace in London on 24 June 1872 that upholding 'the Empire of England' was one of the central purposes of the Conservatives because 'the people of England, and especially the working classes of England, are proud of belonging to a great country, and wish to maintain its greatness . . .', adding that though there may be a subversive element lurking among some British workers:

> the great body of the working class of England utterly repudiate such sentiments. They have no sympathy with them. They are English to the core. They repudiate cosmopolitan principles. They adhere to national principles. They are for maintaining the greatness of the kingdom and the empire, and they are proud of being subjects of our Sovereign and members of such an Empire.[83]

The question of costs Disraeli grandly tossed aside.[84] He knew that the recently acquired colonies in tropical Africa had limited economic significance.[85] The British explorer Daniel Rankin, for example, in his book on the Zambezi basin and Nyasaland, alternates between estimating 'the commercial and financial prospects of huge regions lately opened to the civilised world' and estimating 'to what a degree [our representatives] . . . have succeeded in carrying out the philanthropic and civilising policy they were deputed to represent'.[86]

Everyone flaunted their superiority: the liberal left, the conservative right, the holier-than-thou, and the cynics. Those who are convinced that they possess a superior culture have often been inclined to impose it on others (peacefully if possible, forcefully if necessary). Christians and Muslims in the Middle Ages (and now) were convinced of the nobility of their cause. In 1833, discussing the fate of India, the Whig historian Thomas Babington Macaulay, not yet famous but already an MP (he was only thirty-three at the time), intoned in the House of Commons:

> I see that we have established order where we found confusion . . . I see that the predatory tribes, which . . . passed annually over the harvests of India with the destructive rapidity of a hurricane, have quailed before the valour of a braver and sterner race, have been vanquished, scattered, hunted to their strongholds, and either extirpated by the English sword, or compelled to exchange the pursuits of rapine for those of industry.

And he then concluded with words that today sound unbearably smug (though the sentiment is not far off from that of contemporary liberal interventionists):

> What is power worth if it is founded on vice, on ignorance, and on misery; if we can hold it only by violating the most sacred duties which as governors we owe to the governed, and which . . . we owe to a race debased by three thousand years of despotism and priestcraft? We are free, we

> are civilised, to little purpose, if we grudge to any portion of the human race an equal measure of freedom and civilisation.[87]

A few decades later, in 1865, the notorious Eyre case further divided educated opinion about the proper relations between colonizers and colonized. Edward Eyre, the Governor of Jamaica, was accused of brutally killing 439 black people in the course of suppressing a riot, and subsequently flogging 600.[88]

A campaign under the name of the 'Jamaica Committee', led by John Stuart Mill and supported, among others, by John Bright, Charles Darwin, and Herbert Spencer, called for Eyre's prosecution. Charles Dickens, committed to the superiority of the white races (and supportive of the South in the American Civil War), denounced that platform of 'sympathy with the black – or the Native, or the Devil', holding that one should not deal with the 'Hottentots, as if they were identical with men in clean shirts at Camberwell'.[89] He joined the rival Eyre Defence and Aid Fund, led by Thomas Carlyle (author of *Occasional Discourse on the Negro Question*, 1849) and John Ruskin, and supported, among others, by the poet Alfred Tennyson and by the Anglican priest, academic, and author of *The Water Babies*, Charles Kingsley.

The 1880s and its accompanying 'colonial scramble' were the height of what came to be known as the 'new imperialism'. Joseph Chamberlain, formerly a progressive liberal Mayor of Birmingham, declared in the House of Commons, 'it is our duty to take our share in the work of civilisation in Africa'.[90] As Secretary of State for the Colonies in a Conservative-led coalition, Chamberlain, addressing the Imperial Institute on 11 November 1895, declared: 'I believe in the British Empire and, in the second place, I believe in the British race. I believe that the British race is the greatest of the governing races that the world has ever seen.'[91] Two years later, speaking at the Birmingham Chamber of Commerce, he added: 'In carrying out this work of civilization we are fulfilling what I believe to be our national mission', concluding, 'Great is the task, great is the responsibility, but great is the honour.'[92]

Lord Cromer, the all-powerful representative of the British Crown in Egypt for nearly thirty years (during which time he succeeded in *not* learning any Arabic), wrote in 1908 that 'I have lived too long in the East not to be aware that it is difficult for any European to arrive at a true estimate of Oriental wishes, aspirations and opinions.'[93] Yet he had no doubt that the English had been welcomed in Egypt not only 'by the lawful rulers' but also by the Egyptian people. After all, the English had come as 'the saviour of society'.[94] The Egyptians could not 'save' themselves on their own; the Englishman had to do it.[95] An entire chapter of his *Modern Egypt* is replete with disparaging comments of the 'typical' Egyptian, almost always compared unfavourably with the 'typical' Englishman. Egyptians lack logical thought and easily become the dupes of astrologers and magicians. They will accept as true the most absurd rumours. However, once the Egyptian is told what to do he will assimilate it rapidly, for he is a 'good imitator' in spite of his 'lethargic' mind.[96] These views were by no means unusual at the time, though that they should have been maintained after thirty years living in the country is astonishing.

Paternalistic European condescension was even embraced by women who were themselves fighting against dominant forms of patriarchy. Thus Millicent Fawcett, a leading Victorian feminist, defending herself from accusations that enfranchised women would set India 'on fire', wrote in *The Times* (4 January 1889) of the sterling work done by British women in India, which elicited 'the touching affection and reverence' of 'native women of India to the English women', and how valuable the work of these women would be 'if periods of storm and stress should arise for our Indian Empire'.[97] The Victoria League, a women's imperial propaganda society founded in 1901, organized war charities, provided 'imperial education' for the working classes, and aimed to strengthen the bond with the white dominions (i.e. Canada, Australia, and New Zealand) to ensure the preservation of the 'imperial race'.[98]

By not resisting, the natives confirmed their desire to submit to a greater and more civilized power. By resisting, they simply showed how barbaric they were. Thus, as the Indian 'Mutiny' gathered steam, *The Times* thundered (31 August 1857):

> The barbarities of the mutineers in India are so shocking, so atrocious . . . we are taken aback, as human nature must always be when it is outraged, when it meets with what is insufferable and inexpressible, and religion, we may say, may have something to do with this treatment. We are heretics in India, and therefore out of the pale of humanity. Religion is the pride of the Brahmin, and enters into his blood; the Mahomedan is a ferocious animal, and made so by his creed . . . These soldiers know that they have crossed the Rubicon, that they can never be friends with us . . . that it is a death struggle between us and them.

While *The Times*' correspondent in India, the famed Irish journalist William Howard Russell, denounced bravely the use of torture, summary punishment, and indiscriminate executions by the British, a cartoon in *Punch* (22 August 1857) depicted the 'Bengali tiger' (i.e. the mutineers) ravaging the body of a white woman saved by the intervention of the British lion. Another, also in *Punch* (12 September 1857) represented a vengeful Britannia engaged in violent but 'just' retribution against rebellious sepoys, protecting not just British women but also Indian women and children, thus justifying Britain's 'civilizing mission'.[99] It was the Indian 'Mutiny' of 1857 that led to the transformation of India into a colony and, in 1876, the crowning of Queen Victoria as 'Empress of India'. But the imperial mentality had existed well before.

Here too Charles Dickens, often regarded as a progressive writer (and so he was, but at home not overseas), was, once again, on the wrong side of history. In a letter to Angela Burdett-Coutts, a philanthropic baroness and one of the wealthiest women in England, he declared that if he were 'Commander in Chief of India', he would do his 'utmost' to exterminate the Indian race, 'to blot it out of mankind and raze it off the face of the earth'.[100]

*

By 1885, as colonial expansion was in full swing, France was still deeply divided ideologically, not just between left and right or liberals and conservatives but over the kind of constitutional regime it should have: a liberal republic or a conservative monarchy. This is why the French debate on colonization in the decades following the establishment of the Third Republic in 1870 is particularly interesting.

Born out of the defeat of Napoleon III by Prussia, the Third Republic had limited support. Catholic, monarchist, and rural France remained hostile to it. The expansion of the French colonial empire could provide a rallying point for most republicans and (some) monarchists. At first the pro-colonialists seemed to be winning the debate, but in February 1885 the French were defeated at the Battle of Lang Son in North Vietnam. It proved to be only a temporary embarrassment, but there is nothing like military humiliation to dampen interventionist ardours. Parliament refused to grant the Prime Minister, Jules Ferry, further funds for the Indochina campaign. Ferry had to resign. Ranged against him was a coalition of anti-colonialist republicans, led by Georges Clemenceau, and a Catholic-monarchist bloc of deputies reluctant to offer succour to the Third Republic that they despised so heartily. Business too was split. Bankers such as Henri Germain, founder of Crédit Lyonnais (1863), were strongly opposed to colonies.[101] Colonies, however, were not central to French politics and colonial politics was never consistent or coherent.[102] During the Second Empire virtually all republicans had been against Napoleon III's colonial policies. But when the Third Republic was established and they found themselves in power, many changed their mind. Jules Ferry (Prime Minister 1880–81 and 1883–5), the once-radical Léon Gambetta (Prime Minister 1881–2), and his follower Charles de Freycinet (four times Prime Minister) became born-again colonialists. Colonial policy seemed to provide an excellent platform for strengthening and uniting the young republic whose fate was still so uncertain. The Catholics too were on the move. The more intelligent among them, prompted by Pope Leo XIII, realized that an intransigent opposition to the republic was leading nowhere and it was in their interest to find some common ground with moderate republicans, who also wanted to make new friends to counterbalance the rising power of the socialists. The Abbé Pierre de Raboisson, virtually the spokesman for the Catholic Church in France, decreed that it was necessary to assure '*la grandeur de la France par la grandeur de ses colonies*'.[103]

Even among liberal economists there was some movement. Clément Juglar (one of the first theorists of the business cycle) and Joseph Garnier, editor of the liberal *Journal des économistes*, toned down their initial opposition. Paul Leroy-Beaulieu, author of *De la colonisation chez les peuples modernes* (1874), which inspired Jules Ferry, was far more outspoken.[104] A liberal admirer of British colonialism (he called the British '*le peuple colonisateur par excellence*'), he maintained that the French had failed to maintain their old possessions in the Americas because too few of them became settlers.[105] Settlers would maintain the customs and culture of the mother country, and hence a trading relationship, for a long time, even when the link with the old country was broken.[106]

There were actually few French settlers in the colonies. An exception was Algeria, which was regarded as an integral part of French territory in the Constitution of 1848. But even in Algeria there were few 'true' French settlers. In 1866, out of almost 218,000 settlers in Algeria only half had been previously resident in France, the others were non-Muslims who had settled in Algeria.[107] By 1870, thanks to the initiative of Adolphe Crémieux, a leader of the Jewish community in France, the Jews of Algeria were granted French nationality (the so-called Crémieux Decree), much to the alarm of the Muslim population. The majority of the Algerian population did not have the rights of French citizens. A proposed law in 1846 even declared that it was impossible to turn Muslims into French citizens, for cultural reasons.[108] In 1889 the right to French citizenship was conferred on all those born in Algeria, including foreign settlers, such as the Italians, Spaniards, and Maltese, but Muslims remained relegated to the status of *indigène* and hence excluded.[109] By the 1920s there were 850,000 'Europeans' in Algeria, 14 per cent of the total population.[110]

During the parliamentary debates of 1885 on colonialism, Jules Ferry on 28 July explained that colonization was important because France needed, more than ever, an outlet for her exports, now that Germany had embraced protectionism.[111] And of all the markets the most appetizing was that of China, opened thanks to the Opium Wars. Ferry rejoiced to have entered this market, a market of 400 million consumers who are not 'poor blacks' leading rudimentary lives but made up of 'one of the richest and more advanced peoples in the world'.[112] This was challenged by Jules Delafosse, an anti-colonialist conservative, who wondered why, if commercial outlets were so important, the French were trailing so far behind the British, the Germans, and the Americans in China – a market open to all.[113] Charles Freycinet, the pro-colonial Foreign Minister, declared that when it came to the conquest of Madagascar the 'real issue' was not the cost but the defence of 'our citizens in danger' (i.e. the French settlers) threatened by a government *à moitié barbare* (semi-barbaric). Since this was a matter of honour and national pride, it would be unbecoming to haggle about the cost.[114] He was obviously aware that the costs were in fact very high, the gains almost nil, and in any case very few French had settled in Madagascar.

Anti-colonialists argued that empires were too expensive. Georges Clemenceau, who was then against colonies in principle (he changed his mind as he progressed up the political ladder towards becoming Prime Minister), in his parliamentary intervention of 30 July 1885 questioned the lack of coherence in French colonial policies: why were some territories taken over and others not? Why did France spend as much on colonial policy as Britain, whose empire was much larger?[115]

René Lavollée, in an article in March 1877 in the liberal *Journal des économistes*, warned: 'Never in France has a regime spent so much for colonies and for so little profit . . . The time has come to react against such follies.'[116] Frédéric Passy, a liberal reformer, and eventually the first Nobel Peace Prize winner in 1901 (with Henri Dunant, a founder of the Red Cross), knowing full well that the ethical arguments would not convert the unconverted, declared in the parliamentary debate that 200 million francs was far too much to spend on expeditions in faraway countries.[117] Charles Gide, in 'À quoi servent les colonies' in *Revue de géographie* (15 October 1885), thought colonies were useless and emigration was not a valid reason since France needed to import labour, and its products, which tended to be high-quality luxury goods, would find no market in the colonies; besides, he added, French capitalists were risk averse, not audacious like the British.[118]

Some on the right were just as scornful of colonial aspiration, including right-wing supporters of Général Boulanger (a possible dictator until the decline of his popularity in January 1889); monarchists and anti-Semites, such as the Duc Albert de Broglie and Édouard Drumont, author of the best-selling and ferociously anti-Semitic *La France juive*; and revanchists such as Paul Déroulède, who lambasted Ferry's colonial policy, aimed at compensating for the defeat by Prussia in 1870 and the loss of Alsace and Lorraine with the sarcastic remark: '*J'ai perdu deux soeurs et vous m'offrez vingt domestiques*' ('I have lost two sisters and you offer me twenty servants').[119]

Socialists often opposed the unpalatable consequences of colonialism (such as its cost) rather than colonization per se. In the *Revue socialiste* (1897) Paul Louis, a socialist and later a communist, declared that colonialism was a waste of money, helped big capital, and was unjust towards black people.[120] Paul Henri d'Estournelles, another winner of the Nobel Peace Prize (1909), noted that French public opinion was increasingly demanding hard-headed business reasons to acquire colonies. 'France seems to be tired of being generous without any gain; our young writers no longer worry about the negroes of San Domingo or about the fate of Chinese children,' he wrote, 'they are no longer content with colonies that bring honour but demand that they should make us rich.'[121]

Jean Jaurès, future leader of the Socialist Party, was a 'humanitarian' colonialist. In the columns of the pro-colonialist *La Petite République* (17 May 1896), he denounced colonialism as a waste of resources while accepting its inevitability.[122] He thought it was necessary to 'reconstruct' (*refaire*) the Arab race, under France's 'noble tutelage'.[123] And, anyway, if Algeria had problems, he continued, it was the fault of the local Jews who monopolized the best jobs. In France, he went on, Jewish power was based on money and on their influence in the press and in finance, but in Algeria they also had strength in numbers.[124] (Yet when, a few years later, the Dreyfus Affair exploded, Jaurès, along with the novelist Émile Zola, took a clear stand against the detractors of the unjustly accused captain.)

In a speech in Parliament (1903), Jaurès explained that France had every right to remain in Morocco since the 'civilization she represents is certainly superior to that of the present regime in Morocco'.[125] The expansion of French markets, he claimed, would enable the French proletariat to obtain higher wages. The task of socialists was not to oppose colonialism per se but to ensure that indigenous people were treated humanely and that colonialism did not lead to war among colonial powers. Jaurès favoured international (i.e. Western) agreements to resolve extra-European 'problems'. He did not think the colonized should have a voice in this. So it is not surprising that, at the Seventh Congress of the Second International held in Stuttgart in August 1907, he voted against the anti-colonialist motion.[126] He was not the only one. Socialist delegates from colonialist countries, an outraged Lenin reported, voted in favour of 'civilized colonialism' or, rather, of a colonial policy 'which, under a socialist regime, may have a civilizing effect'. The anti-colonialist motion narrowly won (127 votes to 108).[127]

Few on the left argued against colonialism on the basis of human rights. The most favoured argument was that it was a waste of money, or that it enhanced the unhealthy relationship between government and particular business circles, or that the supporters of colonial policy had forgotten that the sacred duty of France was to recover the lost provinces of Alsace and Lorraine from Germany.[128] Thus the poet Charles Péguy, now well into his conservative phase, wrote, in 1913, that though he did not regret the support given to various oppressed people throughout the world: 'Why are we urged to be moved by the plight of oppressed people everywhere except for one, which happens to be the French people?'[129] Of course, for many, this is precisely what colonies were for: a compensation for the defeat in the Franco-Prussian War.[130]

Yet the *parti colonial* continued to grow in strength. In 1892 in the Chamber of Deputies there were ninety-one members of the vociferously pro-colonial *Groupe Colonial*. Ten years later there were almost 200 members. Thus, when, in 1912, France established a protectorate over Morocco, one of the last independent countries in Africa, there was virtually no opposition. The same noble motivations were trotted out: philanthropic humanitarianism, the sense of mission and destiny, the need to prevent Germany from taking over Morocco (thus threatening Algeria and Tunisia). French trade with Morocco was insignificant but the investments required to build up the country required loans from eager banks. The principal beneficiary was the Banque de Paris et des Pays-Bas (Paribas), a bank that grew mainly through government loan issues connected to colonialism.[131]

Whether indeed colonies profited France as a whole was doubtful. Between 1873 and 1913 well over half of French trade came from and or went to Great Britain, Germany, Belgium, Switzerland, Italy, and

Spain, Russia, the Balkans, and Latin America.[132] French trade with its colonies was small: between 12 and 14 per cent. Much French investment abroad went to central and eastern Europe and the Middle East, especially to Russia, where, by 1914, 25 per cent of total French investment was directed, against only 9 per cent to the empire.[133] Capital exports to the colonies did increase, but they increased far more to the Americas: 5 per cent in 1882, 26.3 per cent in 1913.[134] In other words the formal French colonial empire played a small part in France's foreign trade and foreign investment.[135]

In the 1880s it was still not quite taken for granted that France should become a fully fledged colonial power. The French parliamentary debates of 1885 centred on the acquisition of Madagascar and Tonkin (North Vietnam) but were really about whether France should follow the British. Economic lobbies such as the *Comité de l'Afrique Française*, supported by powerful economic interests (opium traders, the Banque d'Indochine, the *Société des mines du Tonkin*), wanted colonies. It is doubtful, however, that the initial impetus for the acquisition of Indochina in the 1880s was the pressure of economic interests.[136] The will to acquire the colonies existed among politicians, who then used economics as one of their many arguments. In 1885, however, it had become awkward to use naked economic interest, let alone the opium trade, as a good reason for acquiring Indochina.[137] It was felt preferable to invoke France's *mission civilisatrice* dressed up with the required humanitarian rhetoric. The opposition leader Albert de Mun, a monarchist and staunch Catholic who had originally voted against the war in Indochina, thus siding with the anti-colonialists, suggested in March 1884, during a debate on Madagascar, that colonialism might be desirable if the objectives were not lucrative, but civilizing: 'this would be the most noble and best justification for one's conquest'.[138] He detailed all the possible reasons for French intervention in the island.[139] In the first place, the *mission civilisatrice* was a French responsibility, since there are no duties and rights without responsibilities. It was not just a matter of money, it was a question of conscience. We have the duty to civilize these barbarians, we cannot treat them as equals because we are a superior race. Then there was the humanitarian angle: the inhabitants of Madagascar needed to be rescued from their perfidious local oppressors, who continued the work of the terrible Queen Ranavalona, responsible, according to de Mun, for the torture and death of some 200,000 of her own people thirty years previously. In fact, Queen Ranavalona (1788–1861) had been a remarkably modernizing sovereign who had the fault or merit of opposing the imposition of Christianity.[140] A clinching argument, for a good Catholic like Albert de Mun, was that colonization, be it in Madagascar or Indochina, provided great opportunities for the further expansion of Catholic missions.

Then a strategic factor was invoked: it was imperative to stop England from occupying Madagascar. England, warned de Mun, was already mistress of Gibraltar, Malta, and Cyprus, and was now ensconced on the banks of the Nile. France was a maritime nation but one could not be a maritime nation without being also a colonial power. Very similar arguments were produced by republicans opposing de Mun. François de Maby (future Minister of Colonies in 1887–8) supported the occupation of Madagascar on the grounds that it was an island easy to defend, very large, with good harbours, good fisheries, and plenty of coal, iron, and wood. Its 'few inhabitants' (there were actually 3 million of them), deeply divided by tribal rivalries, need not be exterminated, he magnanimously reassured his audience, only forced to join 'the ranks of civilization' by their deliverance from tyranny and superstition. Besides, and this was, as always, the clinching argument, if France did not take over Madagascar, 'others' would. From all sides they nodded; the 'others' were the British.[141] This was not an argument that required complex strategic calculation. The acquisition of colonies *might* not be necessary but they *might* become important because someone else *might* take them over.

A year later (28 July 1885) Jules Ferry, no longer Prime Minister but still powerful, took up the pseudo-humanitarian theme in a more robust language: 'Gentlemen . . . We must openly say that the superior races have a right with respect to the inferior races . . . because they have a duty, the duty to civilize the inferior races.'[142] Almost identical words were used by the socialist leader Léon Blum forty years later, in 1925, including the reference to the duty of 'superior races' towards those races still behind in culture and civilization – just like the monarchist de Mun.[143] One can, of course, list all the 'benefits' that colonization brought about: better transport, better roads, better infrastructures, public health. When Paul Doumer became Governor-General of French Vietnam between 1897 and 1902 (he eventually became President of the Republic in 1931 and was killed by a Russian émigré in 1932), he proceeded to restore Hanoi, the old imperial capital, to its 'ancient glory', turning it into the capital of French Vietnam (the capital had been moved to the more central city of Huế by the Nguyễn Emperor, Gia Long, in 1802). In reality, Doumer rebuilt Hanoi according to the prevailing ideology of the colonizers. It became 'French' in the sense that the natives were systematically regarded as inferior beings fit only to be servants and excluded from the beneficial aspects of colonial urban development. Being 'white' and a 'Westerner' was more central than being French since Russians, Italians, Germans, and the English enjoyed the same privileges as the French. In the words of a historian of Hanoi, 'imperial France created a white city of the Red River'.[144]

By 1906 the civilizing mission had become the most common defence of colonialism. Arthur Girault's *Principes de colonisation et de législation coloniale*, published in 1895, inspired by Herbert Spencer's 'pop' evolutionism, helped to train a generation of public functionaries.[145] The overwhelming assumption was similar to that expressed previously by Engels and de Tocqueville: colonization might hurt the indigenous people, but it is temporary and in the long run they will be better off. The white races were like severe yet kindly parents. Georges Leygues, Minister for Colonies, declared at the Colonial Congress (1906) that a colonization which did not intend to elevate the dignity, the morality, and the welfare of the colonized would be '*une oeuvre grossière et brutale, indigne d'une grande nation*' ('a vulgar and brutal endeavour, which did not become a great nation').[146]

One could have a racist view of history and still be against colonialism. Gustave Le Bon, the theorist of the psychology of the crowd (who also believed that the larger the skull the greater the intelligence), thought it was absurd to try to impose Western customs and ideas such as human rights on others. The French, he wrote in the 1880s in an overt attack on the liberal colonialist Paul Leroy-Beaulieu, have to use an army of 60,000 to control 6 million Muslims in Algeria, the same number required by the British to rule the whole of India. This is costly, childish, and useless, he exclaimed, urging the French to respect Islam and strengthen the authority of the mullahs without trying to transform Muslims into Frenchmen.[147] In other words the French should do as the British and eschew what today would be called cultural imperialism.

In elite circles this was not the dominant view. Albert Sarraut, Radical party politician, Governor-General of Indochina (1912–14 and 1917–19), Minister for Colonies in the early 1920s, briefly Prime Minister in the 1930s, and later, during the German occupation (1940–44), a supporter of Marshal Pétain, reflecting on French colonialism, basked in the idea that the French attitude towards the *indigènes* was far more egalitarian than that of the 'Anglo-Saxon'.[148] Such myth-making, common at the time, did not prevent him from describing the native as 'lazy, indolent, improvident. He likes to chat under the banyan tree or the baobab, singing, dancing, smoking, sleeping mostly.'[149] Inferior races were not going to be inferior for ever, he added, magnanimously, if appropriately cherished and nurtured.[150]

In France there was a popular belief that 'their' colonialism was humanitarian, whereas that of the British was mainly about plundering resources.[151] The British held a parallel view: their colonialism was better than that of anyone else. The British journalist and traveller Herbert Vivian writing in 1898 was shocked by the behaviour of the French in Tunisia:

> The more I have travelled about Tunisia the more impatient I have felt at the presence of the French. It is not mere patriotism which makes me say that an English occupation would have been a very different matter . . . we should, at least, have set up the full polish of civilization in its place.[152]

A British explorer claiming six years' experience in east Africa was equally shocked by the Portuguese:

> The Portuguese on this coast line have reached a depth of sexual immorality – indeed of sexual criminality – below which it is impossible for humanity to fall . . . The Portuguese morality in these dark regions is appreciably lower than that of the brute beasts.[153]

The imperialists, whether French or British, were not at all a force for modernization. Most of the time they allied themselves with local chieftains, princes, and potentates whose traditional powers they sought to preserve all the better to rule without too many problems. In Algeria the French used local sharia courts to maintain order. In Indonesia the Dutch authorities used Islamic courts and schools to administer the colony.[154] In Nigeria the Governor, Frederick Lugard, developed the concept of 'indirect rule', which involved coming to terms with local Muslim emirs, avoiding drastic reforms that would dislocate traditional rule. It was better, he explained, to rule the natives 'through their own chiefs and customs' rather than despotically and directly.[155]

The arguments, both 'humanitarian' and economic, raged backwards and forwards. Just as in England, in France too business interests were not too overt, as though greed and gain were unworthy motives in politics. The leader of the *Groupe Colonial* in the Chamber, Eugène Étienne, had no doubts that the empire was good for business but he did not feel it necessary or expedient to stress the matter. A far more formidable argument was the need to keep up with the other great powers. In a text published in 1897 he warned that 'our English, German and Italian competitors' were going after all the remaining 'virgin lands of the globe' (as lands inhabited by non-whites were called) and that, consequently, France must avoid imposing any restraints on her colonial ambitions.[156]

The pro-colonial discourse constantly used patriotic, humanitarian, and economic considerations. It is quite normal in politics to marshal all possible arguments to justify a policy around which the nation might rally. One pushes all the buttons available, hoping to get some right, in the knowledge that what might not convince some will convince others. The arguments may not be very good, or may be contradictory, but in the end, what matters in politics, particularly parliamentary politics, is winning today's battle. The arguments used to justify intervention in distant lands are familiar: Western politicians rehash them every few years, confident in the short-term memory of their citizens, thus keeping everyone apathetic and obedient: it's good for business, it's what great powers do; it's a moral duty; it's good for us; it's good for them.

19
The First Global Crisis

The scramble for colonies that started in the 1880s coincided with what might be called the first international crisis of capitalism, the so-called Long (or Great) Depression of 1873 to 1896; 'so-called' because there is considerable debate over whether it was a depression (it wasn't since growth continued), whether it was great, or long, or even a crisis. S. B. Saul in his aptly named book *The Myth of the Great Depression, 1873–1896* (1969) pointed out that there was no single pattern in that period and concluded by declaring that 'the sooner the "Great Depression" is banished from the literature, the better.'[1]

The Long Depression presents inconsistencies. Despite increases in production, contemporaries thought they were in the middle of a very serious crisis that would last a long time. It did: the economic turmoil actually lasted for over twenty years; the drop in prices threatened investments; interest rates fell; profits shrank.[2]

The significant decrease in prices was due to excess production: too many goods chasing too few buyers. It was, wrote David Landes, 'the most drastic deflation in the memory of man',[3] though he adds that deflation (falling prices) had started not in 1873 but after the Napoleonic Wars, briefly interrupted by the credit boom of the 1850s. In other words, deflation was normal throughout the nineteenth century.[4]

Deflation affected everybody differently. Wage earners benefited because they gained twice: first because prices went down, then because their wages went up (lower unemployment and stronger trade unions played a part). In Britain, in particular, average earnings increased by just over 40 per cent in the years 1880–1911, a remarkable improvement in living standards, higher than the continental average, though less than in the United States or Australia.[5]

The Long Depression was not a 'depression', i.e. a downturn in production: every country in Europe saw an increase in production (see Table 16).

Table 16 Per Capita Gross National Product in Europe, 1870–1910 (in 1970 US dollars)

	1870	1910
UK	904	1302
Belgium	738	1110
Denmark	563	1050
Germany	579	958
France	567	883
Sweden	351	763
Norway	441	706
Italy	467	548

Source: N. F. R. Crafts, 'Gross National Product in Europe 1870–1910: Some New Estimates', *Explorations in Economic History*, vol. 20, no. 4, October 1983, p. 389.

However, many entrepreneurs keenly felt the pessimism of those years. This is not surprising because increasing wages and falling prices resulted in lower *average* profits. But it did not happen uniformly. Clever or lucky industrialists, who took advantage of new technologies to reduce their costs, increased their profits. So unlike the more famous Great Crash of 1929, and the subsequent Great Depression of the 1930s, during the years of the 'Long Depression' there was economic growth and increased consumption. Between 1860 and 1913 manufacturing output constantly increased, as did globalization, as did capitalism. The pessimism of 1873–96 was followed, though only in some quarters, by the joyous optimism of the *Belle Époque*, which preceded the less joyous years of the Great War.

What changed was the league table of industrialized countries. Products that Great Britain could sell to others (rails, trains, steel, looms, cotton and silk products, etc.) were now made also in Germany, the United States, Italy, Austria, Russia, Australia, Japan, and India. Since technological improvements were global, the gap between the lead country (Great Britain) and the best of the rest narrowed and eventually vanished.[6] In 1860 the United Kingdom was well ahead of everyone, by 1913 it was trailing behind the USA, and, on a per capita basis, the gap with Belgium, Switzerland, and, more importantly, Germany was narrowing (see Table 17). The wages gap between British workers and those in other countries narrowed too (see Table 18).

Table 17 Industrialization Levels Per Capita, 1860–1913 (per capita volume of industrial production) (UK = 100 in 1900)

	1860	1913
Austria-Hungary	11	32
Belgium	28	88
France	20	59
Germany	15	85
Italy	10	26
Russia	8	20
Sweden	15	67
Switzerland	26	87
UK	64	115
USA	21	126
Japan	7	20

Source: Paul Bairoch, 'International Industrialization Levels from 1750 to 1980', *Journal of European Economic History*, vol. 11, no. 2, Fall 1982, p. 281.

Table 18 Relative Wages in Engineering, 1850–1905

	1850	1896	1905
Great Britain	100	100	100
France	42	61	78
Belgium	36	52	64
Germany	28	59	89

Source: Vera Zamagni, 'An International Comparison of Real Industrial Wages, 1890–1913: Methodological Issues and Results', in Peter Scholliers (eds), *Real Wages in 19th and 20th Century Europe: Historical and Comparative Perspectives*, Berg, Oxford 1989, p. 117.

In per capita terms Belgium had become, by 1913, the top exporting country in the world, followed by Switzerland, with the United Kingdom lagging in third place (see Table 19).

The British themselves had long tried to come to terms with the 'puzzling signs' that their own economic fate was without historical precedent and possibly fraught with danger.[7] The country had industrialized while sacrificing its agriculture. As a consequence, it needed to import cheap food, maintain a navy, and pursue international trade. The Royal Navy had been an essential part in the construction of the empire. It had seen

Table 19 Exports per Inhabitant, 1840–1910 (in dollars adjusted for 1990)

	1840	1880	1910
Belgium	7	43	85
Switzerland	18	50	60
UK	10	30	48
Denmark	6	20	45
Canada	10	16	34
France	4	15	29
Sweden	4	13	28
Germany	4	16	27
USA	7	16	19
Russia	1	3	7
Portugal	4	5	6
Japan	n/a	1	6

Source: Paul Bairoch, 'La Suisse dans le contexte international aux XIXe et XXe siècles', in Paul Bairoch and Martin Körner (eds), *La Suisse dans l'économie mondiale*, Droz, Geneva 1990, pp. 103–6.

off the Dutch and the Spaniards in the seventeenth and eighteenth centuries, and had emerged successfully from the Napoleonic Wars. This ensured for British business a disproportionate share of world trade, shipping, and commercial services.[8] Hence the popularity of the Royal Navy and the continuing popularity of the Scottish poet James Thomson's famous lines, 'Rule, Britannia! rule the waves', written in 1740 (see Chapter 7).

For Britain the expansion of world trade was a necessity. Its modern empire was connected to the internationalization of capitalism.[9] But trade was a necessity also for other industrializing states since Great Britain was a competitor for markets, raw materials, and agricultural products – all problems exacerbated by the 'Long Depression' of 1873–96.[10] This was one of the many paradoxes of the period: Britain needed a globalized world since it was a massive exporter, yet the globalization of the world meant an increase in competition and, with it, British decline.

This was the period of the great American industrial advance. By 1914 the United States was producing one-third of the world's industrial output.[11] But it was also then, as it is now, the greatest debtor country, with a $7.1 billion debt in 1914. The other countries trailed behind in indebtedness: Russia ($3.8 billion), Canada ($3.7 billion), and Argentina ($3 billion). Even in 2014 the USA was a major debtor country on a per capita basis (third after Japan and Ireland).[12] In 1912 an investment banker declared at the first Annual General Meeting of the Investment Banker's Association of America: 'We might as well face the situation. We cannot supply all the required capital in the United States. We must look to European countries for assistance, and while this demand for capital continues, we should be most careful not to frighten that capital from our shores.'[13] In 1913 the main lenders were the United Kingdom ($18 billion), followed by France with half that amount.[14] Much from these loans went to fund the American railways. In 1907 the financial editor of the *New York Evening Mail* declared:

> Without the accumulated and unemployed pound sterling of the Englishman, the francs of the Frenchmen, the Belgians and the Swiss, the guilder of the Dutchman and the marks of the German, the material progress that has been the lot of these United States ever since the close of the Civil War could not continue.[15]

There were some populist reactions at the prospect of foreigners owning American property, particularly land. On 24 January 1885, *The New York Times* spoke out against 'an evil of considerable magnitude – the acquisition of vast tracts of lands in the Territories by English noblemen'. But little was done. State legislatures enacted measures to prohibit alien ownership of land, but one could easily get round them. And, anyway, the populists were quite wrong: the American economy derived considerable benefits from such inward investments. The part played by foreign money and foreign business (and, of course, foreign labour) in making the United States the greatest industrial nation in the world at the end of the nineteenth century was considerable.

In Europe the 'left' condemned capital outflow. In Germany socialists denounced it because it brought oppression, in other words imperialism and colonialism, to weaker races.[16] According to Rudolf Hilferding, the leading social-democratic theorist and author of the classic *Finance Capital* (*Das Finanzkapital*, 1910), capital outflow encouraged an imperialist policy since all capitalists with interest overseas would want a strong state to protect their investments even in the most far-flung parts of the globe.[17] In France, various socialists deplored that French bankers sent money to the rest of the world, creating future competitors, instead of investing it at home.[18]

Borrowing from abroad was not always necessary for industrialization: Japan generated almost all its own capital in the nineteenth century – 'almost' because it used a British loan to build the first 18 miles of railway line between Tokyo and Yokohama. But then it used the indemnities extracted from China following the Japanese victory of 1895, a kind of war booty.[19] Only later did Western capital begin to pour into Japan.

There were numerous banking failures caused by the Long Depression: Jay Cooke and Company in the United States (1873), the Union Générale de France in 1882, and Baring Brothers in 1890 (due to the wheat failure in Argentina, the country's subsequent default and consequent 'Panic of 1893' in the USA). On 9 May 1873 the Vienna Stock Exchange crashed. In the 1880s the word 'depression' was used regularly in many French, British, and American official publications.[20] In 1880, *The Economist* wrote that 'It is very probable that the six years of depression will, in future, be reckoned from September 1873 to September 1879' and that the year 1879 had been 'one of the most sunless and cheerless of the century'.[21]

Economists had begun to speak a language that would become familiar to us: the language of globalization (though the word was not yet used). Previous crises were not so 'global'. Charles Kindleberger lists various 'panics' (as short economic crashes were then called) before 1825: five in England, one in Germany, one in France, and one in the Netherlands.[22] The 'Panic of 1825' occurred in the United Kingdom when the stock market crashed because of speculative investments in Latin America gone wrong (the new Latin American states had borrowed heavily). The crisis, however, affected mainly the English banking system, causing many bankruptcies. Scottish and Irish banks were barely affected.[23] The panic hardly manifested itself abroad. In fact, it was an intervention of gold from the Banque de France that saved the Bank of England from collapsing. Another major crisis, the American 'Panic of 1837', had minor implications outside the United States, though British bond holders were upset when some states, such as Pennsylvania, defaulted.

By the 1870s matters had changed considerably: a major crisis was unlikely to be self-contained. The huge waves of emigration, the remarkable expansion of direct investments, and the massive increase in exports marked a new era in the development of global capitalism, even though, from a global perspective, a large part of production, saving, and consumption was still outside this global market in that the majority of the world's producers were still small farmers selling to a relatively local market.

Hector Denis, a Belgian economist, writing in 1895, as the economy was finally improving, noted that what had been remarkable about the crisis of the previous years was that it had been a world crisis, one which involved all the nations *civilisées*.[24] He rightly saw that this was due to the growth of interdependence, which he attributed largely to the *révolution dans les moyens de transport*: the railways, the navy, postal system, and telegraph. But he thought that trade should be increasingly liberalized and that attempts to impose protectionist measures were unlikely to last long. He was wrong about protectionism, as we shall see. One consequence of the depression was an increase in calls for tariffs to protect the home economy. But he was right about transport. One of the consequences of the revolution in transport was that it made products more competitive, particularly agricultural products. It was now easier to import corn and wheat, especially American wheat, which, thanks to the much higher productivity of agriculture in the United States (tractors, harvesters, fertilizers), became cheaper and cheaper. The consequent decrease in international wheat prices damaged European agriculture. It forced Sweden, which had free trade in the 1850s and 1860s, to introduce protection; accelerated the decline of British farming; gave impetus to emigration in Italy; transformed Denmark from a grain-exporting country into an exporter of dairy products, bacon, and eggs; ruined peasants in Romania unable to compete with American cheap grain; and damaged Portuguese growth, which was based on agricultural exports.[25] This meant that protectionism could not fade away. In an era of growing democracy in which governments were expected to respond to changes in the economy, it was unrealistic to expect politicians to let the international markets ride roughshod over local interests and people.

In 1881, *The Economist* had warned that American cheap wheat was not an isolated incident but a permanent factor in the international economic landscape, and that from now on wheat production in the United States would 'entirely change the general situation of the wheat trade and of land value in the United Kingdom and France'.[26] One of the main consequences was an equalization of prices: in 1870 wheat in Liverpool was 57.6 per cent more expensive than in Chicago, by 1895 the difference had dropped to 17.8 per cent.[27] Prices dropped because more could be produced by fewer people and could be transported in huge quantities almost anywhere in the world.

The revolution in transportation meant that ships went faster and could cross the oceans more frequently. There was an improved knowledge of sea currents, the telegraph provided information that enabled ship owners to have a better sense of the stock required and did not need to wait too long in harbours. In the mid-nineteenth century sailing packets made the trip to Europe in twenty-one days, the fastest clippers in fourteen, and steamships in ten days. By the 1880s the Atlantic could be crossed in less than a week.[28] Similarly, the railways contributed to the lowering of freight rates. The cost of sending wheat from Chicago to New York fell by 35 per cent between 1868 and 1880.[29] There were, everywhere, massive rail-building programmes, all the more necessary since, in 1846, the trip from Paris to Marseille took longer than crossing the Atlantic.[30]

It was widely understood that the first global crisis of capitalism signalled a great readjustment in the international economy and had trans-national characteristics particularly affecting the great trading nations involved in a 'universal market'. Karl Marx's prediction in the *Communist Manifesto* ('the need of a constantly expanding market for its products chases the bourgeoisie over the whole surface of the globe') had turned out to be true. This was to be capitalism's destiny: from growth to crisis, from crisis to growth, with 'capitalism' usually emerging stronger but leaving on the roadside some victims, the poor, yes, but also unlucky or incompetent capitalists. What no one knew was when the next crisis would come about. Would crises occur in a regular cycle, like the seasons, or would they be totally unpredictable? Post-Enlightenment optimism, one of the hallmarks of capitalism, required some attempts to predict the unpredictable – repeated failures simply accelerated the search for a better crystal ball.

Since random events, by definition, cannot be predicted, theorists assumed patterns. The idea of economic cycles is generally attributed to the Swiss economist Jean-Charles de Sismondi in his *Nouveaux principes d'économie politique* (1819). The French statistician Clément Juglar, one of the earliest cycle theorists, warned in 1862 that it would be difficult to analyse such cycles because 'whenever we try to isolate the determinant causes, a crowd of occasional causes besiege us, trouble our perception and lead us into the error of taking what is accidental for the very essence of the problem'.[31] In fact, in spite of the considerable efforts by talented economists, it proved difficult, almost impossible, to predict the next 'panic'. This is still the case.

Obviously, for a crisis to become deeper there needs to be interconnectedness among states. If all states were completely self-sufficient, completely isolated from each other – no exports, no imports, no migration – then crises would, of course, still occur, but they would be self-contained. It is the world market that makes global crises possible. And there would be crises even if there were in the world a single state with a single market, with totally free movement of people and capital, no tariffs, no differences in taxes, and with costs only reflecting non-political or customary factors such as distances, weather, local conditions, and so on. For, in this imaginary world state there would still be regional disparities and inequalities in wealth, health, and conditions of existence (after all such differences exist within modern states). And such disparities would lead to political instability unless an effective system of political rules could be enforced between the regions.

Of course, there are those who believe that capitalism can adjust itself with relatively little interference from the political level, that regional and class inequalities sort themselves out (low wages in one part of the state attract investment and/or cause migrants to move to high-wage regions). For those who believe in the smooth functioning of markets the Leibnizian mantra of Professor Pangloss, mocked in Voltaire's *Candide* ('all is for the best in the best of all possible worlds'), holds true.

But what if capitalism itself is unstable, permanently, chronically? What if it does not develop harmoniously? What if the losers do not become winners? What if it is largely a matter of luck? After all, for centuries this is exactly what farmers, totally dependent on the weather (a force over which they have no control), have had to endure. They prayed to the gods and hoped for the best. Sometimes they were lucky and prospered, at other times they were not so lucky and starved. Traders too had to be lucky as they sailed with their goods across the seas. If they arrived safely they could sell their stuff at a good price and become wealthy. If they encountered a serious storm they drowned. Bad luck. And the more social mobility was restricted, as in the past, the more luck comes into the equation: some are born rich aristocrats and can afford to be lazy and do little; others are just born poor and will remain poor regardless of how hard they work.

What happens in the real world is that each state tries to protect 'its' economy and some of its citizens, or, at least, the citizens who 'matter', namely those who are electorally or economically significant and powerful. And each state must also agree to international rules in order to enable 'its' firms to conduct international business. Today there are international and regional agreements which are, in principle, acceptable to all the members, all sovereign states of unequal power. So each must be convinced that the agreements are also to their individual advantage (or that lack of an agreement would be a greater disadvantage) or they must be bullied or cajoled or bribed into submission. Usually economic benefits are very difficult to calculate and are unlikely to be evenly distributed, so that internal discussions and conflicts are almost inevitable. Each state will seek to minimize the negative impact of externalities and maximize their own impact. Protective tariffs are one way of achieving this; another is control over one's currency, enabling a state artificially to modify its export/import prices. But there are obvious problems with such exercise in sovereign power: if you devalue, or impose protective tariffs, others might do so and everyone would be back at the starting point.

That the world was becoming increasingly interdependent and that sovereignty was a relative concept was obvious to intelligent politicians. Thus, in 1896, as Italy was emerging from its worst crisis since unification, Giovanni Giolitti, five times Prime Minister of Italy, lectured his constituents on the meaning of national sovereignty.[32] He explained that a country which has borrowed abroad by selling bonds (such as Italy) was subject to the financial influence of the countries where the bond-holders reside as well as to the bond-holders themselves; crises and political events in those countries will have repercussions even if the debtor country is not responsible. In other words, the debtor country 'lacks financial independence which is the necessary complement to political independence'.[33]

Did anti-capitalist forces and the labour movement benefit from the Long Depression? It is difficult to say, since so many factors were involved. In Europe and in the United States strikes were frequent (and often successful) from the end of the Long Depression to the First World War. Trade unions in Europe vastly increased their membership from over 2 million in 1890 to 15.3 million in 1913. By 1919 the numbers had trebled again. The pre-war growth of trade unions was, for obvious reasons, more pronounced in the leading industrial countries: in Germany from 269,000 members in 1890 to nearly 4 million in 1913, in the United Kingdom from 1.5 million in 1890 to 4.1 million in 1913, and in the USA from a mere 50,000 in 1890 to 9 million in 1913.[34]

Virtually all of the main European socialist parties were formed in the last quarter of the nineteenth century (the British Labour Party is a notable exception) and virtually all of them saw their vote increase in the years leading up to the First World War. But since this was also a period of constant growth in the workforce and in urbanization, it is difficult to know how much to attribute to the effect of the depression and how much to capitalist development. Besides, as we have seen, wages went up and prices went down to the advantage of many workers.

Subsequent crises, such as the Crash of '29 and the downturn of 2008, far from constituting an ideal scenario for anti-capitalism, were followed by periods of retrenchment of working-class militancy. This, however, was not true for the decades following the 1880s, when unions and socialist parties became ever stronger, though in Britain nothing like the great Chartist movement of the 1840s materialized. In fact Britain, in terms of socialist politics, remained fairly backward, probably because it was home to an 'enlightened' Liberal Party that delayed the formation of a Labour Party. Besides, Britain was a beneficiary of the post-1896 recovery: 'As its industrial supremacy waned, its finance triumphed', as well as its services as a shipper, trader, insurance broker – all increasingly central to the global economy.[35]

This led to serious political problems for the governing classes, particularly for the Liberal Party, whose aim was to try to keep together the urban classes (workers and capitalists), while preventing the workers from embracing some kind of socialism. As for the Conservatives, their main problem was to defend landed interests (not just the landlords but also farmers and crofters in Wales and Scotland), while getting closer to the growing urban classes. Protectionism, the Conservatives believed, could be a solution since it would appeal to landed interests as well as to many in industry.[36]

In France the 'Long Depression' did not manifest itself fully until 1882. When it did, all official reports underlined its gravity. There was the fear of a right-wing coup led by Général Boulanger (who was, however, soundly defeated in the elections of 1889). There was a revival of anarchism.[37] There was an agricultural crisis, made worse by the ongoing destruction of vineyards by phylloxera (which, having first struck in 1860, reached prosperous Burgundy in 1880). The total areas cultivated with vines shrank by one-third and many small vine growers disappeared. (The problem was eventually resolved by importing aphid-resistant American vines.)[38] Commerce was hit and workshops closed. There was social unrest and an increase in strikes, especially at the end of the Long Depression: 634 strikes in 1893 (mainly in textiles and construction) compared to an annual average of 157 in the previous two decades.[39] A further increase in strikes occurred in 1899, coinciding with a progressive government, that of Pierre Waldeck-Rousseau, not surprisingly, since 'friendly' governments embolden working-class activity.[40]

In this crisis there were winners and losers. Lower interest rates penalized savers, and Émile Cheysson, a social Christian writer, declared euphorically in 1897 that the era of rentier capitalism was over.[41] But this was a little premature: profits already generated by previous generations sustained the development of a rentier class, which lived off interest on capital investments, even in 'advanced' England.[42] And as Thomas

Piketty shows, though inherited income dipped in the period we are examining, it revived massively after 1945.[43] Besides, in England, there was another kind of rentier class, denounced by John A. Hobson, the liberal arch-critic of colonialism, mainly domiciled in the south, in the 'home' counties, and in seaside towns, who lived off their overseas investments.[44]

Generally, industrialists regarded themselves as among the losers of the Long Depression, particularly in Germany, where pessimism was rife. Yet the 1873 fall in prices, though significant, was short-lived. The economy picked up during the winter of 1879–80, propelled by the resumption of railway construction in the United States that was profitable for German exports of iron, steel, and coal. But this revival was also short-lived. German producers had to find new markets for their ever cheaper goods, thus lowering their profits. The Long Depression gave impetus to pro-colonial sentiments, to mergers and the formation of vertical cartels, to industrialist pressure for government to compensate for falling profits and, ultimately, to protectionism.[45] Landowners were even more alarmed than industrialists, because of the fall in international wheat prices. Germany imported cheaper wheat from Russia and from the United States. German landlords were weakened.[46] The crisis of capitalism was far more serious for the aristocracy than for the capitalists.

For countries with a relatively low level of integration in the world economy (such as Russia) the crisis mattered less since exports were not as crucial as elsewhere. Some small countries, though well integrated in the global economy, did very well, and did not need protectionism. Belgium, for instance, exported coal and manufactures and imported food. The government did not have to face powerful rural interests. Its bourgeoisie was in full control.[47] Its working class was relatively prosperous. Its insertion in the world market, like that of Britain, meant that it was at the mercy of foreign demand, but not as much as those countries that depended on the export of food and were unable to develop technologically – countries such as those of Latin America or, to take a quite different example, Romania. There the bourgeoisie imported luxury goods (silks, fine cloth, clothing, carriages, glassware), exported primary products, and had a tiny home market. These countries were at the mercy of world markets, had a narrow fiscal basis and, at all times, found it difficult to raise taxes and hence develop a domestic capitalism.

Everyone was faced with a new phenomenon: a world economy governed by world prices; a changing economic power balance where

Great Britain was no longer supreme, though its trade was still far larger than that of its main European competitors, Germany and France; an ever-increasing involvement of the state in the economy; and industrialists the world over turning to their governments, begging for help, requesting protection, demanding subsidies, and pointing to other states protecting their economies. They used patriotism, nationalism, the spectre of socialism, and every argument they could find to obtain more 'state'. A few liberal intellectuals still complained about the state's being overweening, but most capitalists wanted more of it.

20
Protecting the Economy

The Long Depression of 1873 to 1896 had considerable transnational consequences, unsurprisingly, since the world was increasingly globalized. The most important of these was a turn towards protectionism. Not that the nineteenth century had been entirely committed to free trade. In the early part of the century, trade policy could be described 'as an ocean of protectionism surrounding a few liberal islands'.[1] But the gradual movement towards lower trade barriers that had started in the 1860s went into reverse. A wave of tariffs swept across the developed world.

Protective tariffs were increased or established in Italy, Spain, Austria-Hungary, and Romania in 1878; then in Greece, Switzerland, and Germany in 1879 (and again in Germany in 1890 and 1902); then in France in 1881, 1892, and 1902; and in Russia in 1882 and 1891. In Japan protectionism took the form of large-scale military production for the state.[2] The arms race that preceded the First World War was a great opportunity for subsidizing domestic manufacturing enterprises by awarding them military contracts, particularly when it came to shipbuilding. While there was not yet a powerful military-industrial complex able to determine policy, armaments firms, while pursuing a wider global market, were backed by their respective governments.[3] In the United States, where the level of protectionism was already high, new tariffs were set in 1883, and again in 1890 with the McKinley Tariff Act. By 1897 the Dingley Tariffs had increased duties to the highest level in the history of the USA (52 per cent) before lowering them again in the years leading to the First World War, though they still remained the highest in the developed world. Protectionism was so entrenched in the USA that even free traders never really expected to remove all trade barriers.[4] Even when the 1890 and 1892 elections showed that protectionism was unpopular, Congress did not find the courage to go against vested business interests keen to preserve a high tariff wall.[5] One of the consequences was that Great Britain, which in 1850 sent 20 per cent of its exports to the USA, saw these reduced to 6 per cent in 1900.[6] Yet Great Britain continued, almost alone (almost, because the Netherlands too had very low tariffs), to resist the trend towards protectionism.

Table 20 compares protective tariffs in 1875, at the onset of the Long Depression, with those in 1913, on the eve of the First World War.

High-exporting countries such as Belgium and Switzerland were always less protectionist than Italy, Spain, and Russia. In Germany, Bismarck abandoned his liberals allies, made peace with the Catholics, which he had persecuted during the so-called *Kulturkampf* (see Chapter 16), and turned against the 'free market' of which he had never been a fervent supporter. Having previously abolished most tariffs, he reintroduced them in 1879 to protect a wide range of agricultural and industrial goods: what became known as the 'marriage of iron and rye', i.e. an informal coalition of large-scale industrialists and the landed aristocracy (Junker). This shift was largely determined by the collapse, in the elections of 1878, of the two main pro-free trade parties, the National Liberal Party and the German Progress Party, and by the triumph of protectionist parties.[7] Bismarck followed the trend by casting aside the

Table 20 Protective Tariffs, c. 1875–1913, in percentage (average)

	c. 1875	1913
Austria-Hungary	15–20	18
Belgium	9–10	9
Denmark	15–20	14
France	12–15	20
Germany	4–6	13
Italy	8–10	18
Japan	5	30
Netherlands	3–5	4
Russia	15–20	84
Spain	15–20	41
Sweden	3–5	20
Switzerland	4–6	9
United Kingdom	0	0
USA	40–50	44

Source: Paul Bairoch, *Victoires et déboires*, vol. II: *Histoire économique et sociale du monde du XVIe siècle à nos jours*, Folio Gallimard, Paris 1997, p. 294.

liberal commercial bourgeoisie in favour of an alliance with protectionist-minded heavy industry.[8]

When, in 1890, Leo von Caprivi succeeded Bismarck as Chancellor and continued the policy of favouring heavy industry, he went one step further by proposing to lower duties on agricultural goods, thus ditching 'rye'. If one could find cheaper food elsewhere, Caprivi explained in 1891, one should import it and not force German workers to acquire expensive local food just to keep German farmers happy. Germany, he added, needed to export industrial goods: 'either we export goods or we export people. With our increasing population, if we do not have a similar increase in industry at the same time, we will not be able to continue to exist.'[9] The government, he added, had to think of the majority of the population who, as they earned less than 900 marks a year, needed cheap food.[10] He could have added that the Socialists had become the largest party with nearly 20 per cent of the vote in the 1890 elections and that they, along with the trade unions, favoured such trade liberalization since it would lower food prices (bread was more expensive in Germany than in free-trading Britain).

Since domestic agriculture could not entirely meet the country's grain needs, Germany had to establish good relations with grain-exporting countries by lowering tariffs on rye and wheat; other countries (Austria-Hungary, Italy, Switzerland, Belgium, Serbia, Romania) would reciprocate by lowering their tariffs against German industrial goods, much to the joy of German industrialists and German workers, and to the dismay of landowners.

The landowners fought back. They created lobbies and pressure groups such as the Farmers' League (*Bund der Landwirte*), most of whose 200,000 members were small farmers rather than large landowners.[11] Caprivi also had to face constant attacks from the embittered Bismarck, from liberals who thought he was too conciliatory towards the Catholics, and from Catholics who thought he was not friendly enough. In 1894, Caprivi was forced to resign. His enlightened social policies on child employment and trade union rights, and his progressive tax policies, were not sufficient to save him. Even with Caprivi gone, farming interests were doomed anyway:[12] the economic power of the Junker declined along with agriculture's share of the German economy.[13]

In spite of the wave of protectionism elsewhere, Great Britain remained committed to free trade. Frank Trentmann has explained how, though the Long Depression encouraged demands for protectionist policies, free trade was still viewed by much of British public opinion as the keystone of democracy, peace, and prosperity and, perhaps above all, cheap food.[14] An electoral Liberal poster of 1905 (the Liberals swept back into power the following year) depicted an anxious woman in poverty, with caricatures of capitalists and aristocrats in the background, and the caption: *Will You Go Back? Remember!!! The 'Hungry Forties'. Tariff 'Reform' Means Trusts for the Rich, Crusts for the Poor.* A Liberal Party election card pointed out that the average wage of a skilled worker in Britain was almost twice that of a German, bread was cheaper, while the Germans worked longer hours.[15] But many Conservatives too tried to present their proposed protectionist measures as a move to help the poor. The social reformer Charles Booth, a Conservative sympathizer, wrote in an article in the *National Review* in January 1904 that free trade was based on cosmopolitan, laissez-faire individualist principles, and he advocated a tariff of 5 per cent, arguing that it did not really amount to a tax on food (British agriculture as a share of GNP had fallen from 20 per cent in 1860 to 7 per cent in 1914).[16] Joseph Chamberlain depicted the free-trading Liberals as anti-working class, declaring in October 1903: 'What is the good . . . of prohibiting [sweated labour] in this country, if you allow sweated goods to come in from foreign countries?'[17]

The controversy between free trade and protectionism, unlike present-day debates, was concentrated on food prices since there were relatively few consumer goods. A policy of cheap food united almost all classes, except the farmers, but by then there were not many of those left in England. Free trade, in Britain, and perhaps in Britain alone, was a national policy that did not involve great sacrifices. This was not the case in Russia, where Ivan Vyshnegradsky, the Finance Minister, introduced a strong protectionist system in 1891, unparalleled in Europe, famously saying, when warned of an impending famine while the country was massively exporting grain to pay for industrial goods: 'we may not eat enough, but we will export'.[18] It is safe to assume that Vyshnegradsky went on eating normally (he was one of the richest men in Russia, of the self-made variety).[19] Some 400,000 people died in the famine of 1891, mainly due to a catastrophic harvest and the lack of adequate government support.[20] It was the most disastrous event to befall Russia in the period between the Crimean War and the First World War. The authorities – Ivan Vyshnegradsky in particular – were blamed because they did not immediately ban the export of cereals. The acquisition of foreign currency, crucial for the country's industrial growth, was a priority and it seemed that Vyshnegradsky delayed the ban as much as possible, though some claim that he did all he could to remedy the situation.[21] Eventually, the government, already behaving as a modern state, felt responsible and carried out a massive relief programme to help some 13 million peasants (10 per cent of the total population).[22] The prioritizing of exports exacerbating the famine was similar to Stalin's reaction to the Russian-Ukrainian famine of 1932 to 1933.[23]

The weather and Vyshnegradsky were not the only culprits. Russian agriculture was backward, its productivity low, and the railway system (essential for food distribution) inadequate. The famine, tremendous as it was, had relatively little impact on export trade. The reason for this is that the Russian economy in the 1880s was largely outside market relations, in other words not capitalist enough.[24] It was thus often possible to have famine in one area and abundance in another, as Amartya Sen famously argued in his *Poverty and Famines* (1981).[25] What had happened in Russia was that, as the price of grain shot up, the poor could not buy grain, so they starved while farmers preferred to sell their grain to foreigners. However, as the liberal Paul Milyoukov explained in lectures given in 1903, Russia could not hope to grow through exports. She had to expand her home market.[26] To do this she had to borrow from abroad. The architect of this policy was Count Witte. For him protectionism was a temporary measure, to be abolished when a home industry was developed and when Russia had finally caught up with the West. Every nation, he explained, traverses successive stages of development, the highest of which is the commercial industrial phase, and a policy of protectionism was merely a means to achieve this (a view that had been propounded by Friedrich List in 1841 in *The National System of Political Economy*; see Chapter 5).[27]

'My most notable achievement', as Witte put it with characteristic modesty, 'was a commercial treaty with Germany' limiting the import of some German products (1894): 'Everybody in Europe was surprised at the performance.' Then, he went on, he proceeded to borrow vast sums from foreign banks (1899) to develop domestic industry, much to the chagrin of the Emperor Nicholas II, who, for nationalistic reasons, opposed importing foreign capital.[28] Borrowing from abroad had already begun, but the percentage of foreign capital in industry increased steadily from 16 per cent in 1881 to 42 per cent in 1900.[29] Witte, the servant of the autocracy, was in reality a protectionist liberal who profoundly disliked landowners, whom he regarded as useless. He wanted to develop Russian capitalism, and to do so he had to impose tariffs. If foreign capital could not be obtained by export, he argued, then one had to borrow it.

Protectionism, in Russia and elsewhere, was seldom an ideological hallmark of 'left' or 'right', 'progress' or 'reaction', or even a position that always divided industrialists from landlords (as had been the case in Britain). In Spain, for instance, industrialists and landlords joined forces to demand state protection against foreign competition.[30] And in Latin America and the United States, as in Romania, it was the liberals, not the conservatives, who were the protectionists.[31]

In Romania, in the parliamentary debates of 1866 and 1867, when the possible avenues for economic developments were discussed, Ion Brătianu, the Liberal opposition leader and later Prime Minister (1876–88), took a stand against lowering tariffs, whereas Nicolae Golescu, the Conservative Prime Minister, in a kind of role reversal from the British prototype, was in favour of free trade, just like a classic Manchester liberal.[32] Fuller tariffs were introduced in 1886, granting special advantages to Romanian entrepreneurs at the expense of foreigners (i.e. Greeks, Jews, and Armenians), since in the preceding twenty years there had been an inflow of foreign goods, at first mainly luxuries (silks, fine cloth, clothing, glassware), then cheap goods intended for mass consumption.[33] But there were too few Romanian entrepreneurs: the native middle class was overwhelmingly made up of civil servants, lawyers, teachers, and academics, and other rather unproductive groups.[34] The liberals even opposed the free flow of foreign capital into the country, which they regarded as a threat to national sovereignty, thus erecting another obstacle to industrial growth.

Among the champions of protectionism in Romania were intellectuals such as Dionisie Pop Marţian and Alexandru Xenopol. Xenopol, an influential nationalist liberal historian, doubted that private enterprise could muster enough resources to industrialize the country.[35] Far from being in favour of a smaller state, Xenopol, Marţian, and other nationalist liberals believed that, because the country was a 'laggard' state, there was no alternative to industrialization from above with the state protecting domestic industry.[36] Further protectionist measures were introduced in 1904 by the Liberals, much to the distress of the Conservatives, because they did not sufficiently protect farm-based industries.[37] On the eve of the First World War, Conservatives pointed out, with considerable evidence, that protectionism had failed to industrialize the country and that it had harmed consumers.[38] Agriculture still continued to dominate the Romanian economy.

In a sense Romanian Liberals were in a trap. They were nationalists whose proud slogan was *prin noi înşine* (by ourselves).[39] But the protectionist principle of 'sheltered industrialization' was part of a wider nationalist package: nation-building, xenophobia, patriotism, anti-cosmopolitanism and anti-Semitism. The 'liberal' nationalist Xenopol himself became, in the 1930s, a close ally of Alexandru Cuza, leader of the fascistic Iron Guards.[40] The Conservatives were not particularly anti-Semitic, not any more so than the Liberals. And all defended the Orthodox Church against the Catholic Church. So the Romanian Liberals, unlike their counterparts in the West, were not even very secular.

If one worked in an industry that suffered from foreign competition, then it was rational to be in favour of protectionism; if one consumed cheaper imported goods then free trade made sense. And when the terms of trade changed, one's views would change. 'When events change, I change my mind', Keynes is supposed to have said (there is no evidence he ever did). Take French wine-growers: until the 1870s they were free traders; then, in the 1880s, as competition grew, they became protectionists.[41] At first, the best-organized wine-growers, those of Burgundy, wanted the state off their backs; then, alarmed at the competition from cheaper Italian, Spanish, and Algerian wines (as well as those from the Languedoc-Roussillon), they asked the state to intervene to regulate the quality of wines. Consequently, the Loi Griffe (14 August 1889) forbade the sale of products called wine not made exclusively with fermented grapes.[42] This was part of a process of the 'nationalization' of capital whereby capitalists defined their interests as being one with the nation state within which they operated.

Politicians tagged along, knowing only too well that part of their business was to help business. This was particularly true in France, under the Third Republic, where the main party, the Radical Party, was unmistakably pro-business while their opponents on the monarchist right had no economic programme.[43] The republicans had been in a minority at the start of the Third Republic (the National Assembly had a monarchist majority). Thirty years later, by 1902, the outright monarchists had virtually disappeared. The majority was, by then, solidly in the hands of the republicans of the Radical Party, which was at the time an essentially inchoate, unstable, and deeply divided coalition of centrists of various hues. They were held together, however, by an abiding identification of the destiny of France with that of French business, large and small. This had been clear for a long time even to the most radical among them, politicians such as Léon Gambetta, who, even before the birth of the Third Republic, had invoked the 'solidarity which now holds together politics and business and which, from now on, must keep us close for our common salvation'.[44]

The symbiosis between business and politics was well established in France, where there was a powerful tradition of state interventionism (it is common to refer to Louis XIV and his great *dirigiste* Minister of Finance, Jean-Baptiste Colbert). This tradition enabled politicians to make an uninhibited appeal to business interests. The career of Jules Ferry, one of the leading Third Republic politicians (and Prime Minister in the 1880s), was emblematic of opportunistic realism (not for nothing was his faction inside the republican group known as *les opportunistes*). Under Napoleon III, Ferry, then a young opposition politician, was an admirer of English liberalism, believing that the 'industrial spirit' could not thrive under the shadow of the state (under the Second Empire the state and business had been very close).[45] Then Napoleon III fell (1871) and Ferry was elected to Parliament as a deputy from the Vosges. Once elected he was expected to defend local textile interests from foreign competition (after all, they had bankrolled his campaign). And he did, becoming an enthusiastic protectionist.[46]

In Victorian England, where politics liked to parade in the clothes of ethical rhetoric, protectionism was never politically fashionable, at least not from 1850 onwards. While free trade seemed the natural way, the right way, and the British would add, the *British* way, the country had been at least until the first half of the nineteenth century a mercantilist country, a state of affairs that the fathers of economic liberalism, Adam Smith and David Ricardo, had never ceased to deplore. The considerable regulation and protectionist measures established during the period of British industrialization were abolished but only once British supremacy had become entrenched. The most important of such measures were the Navigation Acts of the seventeenth and eighteenth centuries, which established that all trade between England (or Great Britain after 1707) and the colonies should be conducted in English/British ships, operated by English/British sailors sailing between English/British ports. In other words British shipping, backed by massive government funding, had a virtual monopoly of trade, seeing off its main rivals: first the Dutch and then the French. Shipping costs were further reduced by the successful British suppression of piracy in the eighteenth century, since this cut the insurance premium and rendered it unnecessary to operate heavily armed ships.[47] Total supremacy, including colonial dominance, was achieved at the end of the Napoleonic Wars when Britain had achieved control, in addition to India, of key colonies in the West Indies.[48] Then, when everything was settled, in 1849, the Navigation Acts were repealed, bringing to an end two centuries of legislative protection for British commercial shipping.[49] Britain, as the first industrial nation, no longer needed to protect its industries, but it needed others not to protect theirs. The others, to catch up with Britain, needed to follow their own path and develop their own rules. And they did, adopting protectionism when it suited them.

In France the protectionists dressed up their economic arguments in nationalist clothing: it was necessary, they claimed, to defend the Nation, a nation of small producers united against the invasion of foreign products. French protectionists, unlike their British counterparts, were liberals not conservatives.[50] Yet by comparing trade figures it emerges that France's trade was less protectionist than that of Britain (contrary to prevailing assumptions) even in the decades 1840 to 1860.[51] It was only as a consequence of the 'Long Depression' of 1873 to 1896 and of the rapid growth of imports of wheat and other agricultural produce from the United States that France followed the general European drift towards protectionism.

In 1892, under the influence of Jules Méline, Minister for Agriculture from 1883 to 1885 and Prime Minister from 1896 to 1898, the French government imposed duties on agricultural products (the so-called 'Méline tariffs') to protect local produce, thus ending the Franco-British Trade agreement of 1860 (the Cobden-Chevalier agreement). This was seen as 'serious' turn towards protectionism, even though there had been tariffs for much of the nineteenth century.[52] France did not return to the high tariffs of the pre-1860 period.[53] Méline's main preoccupation was to placate both industrialists and landed interests alarmed by the continuing depression, but what he really wanted was for France to remain a country of small farmers and artisans. In a book published in 1905 he went further, looking forward to a return to the land, once workers and capitalists had recognized how unhealthy life in cities was and what a historical mistake the enormous increase in industrial development had been.[54] His rather utopian views remained confined to agrarian circles. The vast majority of the French moderates espoused the *politique d'affaire* unquestioningly, which underscored the power of the political and economic elites, to the detriment of the working classes.[55]

The problem with France was that, while its powerful and successful banks invested heavily abroad, it did not export much. There were regular complaints from official sources lamenting that French entrepreneurs were too narrow-minded, provincial, and self-satisfied, seldom adapting to the taste of foreigners in the belief that foreigners would always recognize the superiority of French taste (champagne, cognac, perfumes, and jewellery). Yet a modern industrial country could not base its export drive on such specialized luxuries.[56] Between 1880 and 1914

French external investments increased fourfold. Those who defended this movement claimed that in France there were insufficient opportunities for investment, but critics said it was the export of capital that starved France of capital.[57] Yet an encomium of the ability of banks to enmesh the world into an interconnected whole came from an unexpected source: Jean Jaurès, leader of the Socialist Party. In a famous speech in the Chamber of Deputies (20 December 1911, see Chapter 7) he explained that capital, 'like great migrating birds', has the freedom to fly 'over the barriers of race and custom walls', thus creating a network of interests so enmeshed that a single link broken in Paris has effects in Hamburg and New York. This, he continued, among cries of approval from the left-wing benches, is the 'beginning of a capitalist solidarity' (*un commencement de solidarité capitaliste*), to be feared when in the hands of base interests, but which, if inspired by the popular will, could guarantee peace.[58]

Protectionism also dominated the growing capitalist economy of the United States, today widely perceived as the champion of free trade. Here the southern states, which traditionally favoured free trade, since they exported cotton picked by slave labour, had been defeated in the Civil War by the protectionist and industrializing northern states. The end of slavery 'removed the social foundation for sustained opposition to bourgeois hegemony', explained Eugene Genovese, somewhat regretfully.[59] The North's victory led to an exceptionally high wall of tariffs (far higher than in any European country except Russia) behind which American industry continued its long journey towards global triumph. The USA's commitment to economic protectionism clashes with the popular image of American capitalism as uninhibited, go-getting, raw, and naked. In reality such fearless jungle capitalism could roar at will only because it was cushioned and protected by a state that made sure it never had to face international competition unless it could beat it. When Friedrich List explained in *The National System of Political Economy* (1841) that the industrialization of the latecomers could only be assured by protective tariffs, he was speaking with the voice of German nationalism and also in union with the sentiments of Alexander Hamilton, one of the Founding Fathers of the United States and author of well over half of the *Federalist Papers* (the main source for the interpretation of the Constitution). It was not in Germany but in the USA (he lived there as an exile between 1825 and 1832) where List refined his protectionist views.[60] Hamilton, the first US Secretary of the Treasury, realized that Britain's economic policy would compel the USA to remain a mere exporter of primary products and importer of manufactured goods (as was Latin America). Convinced that only industrialization could bring about prosperity, Hamilton, in his *Report on Manufactures* (1791), written for Congress, advocated protectionism as the instrument that would make the USA a leading agricultural *and* industrial power.[61] As it turned out, he was right. An unprotected American cotton-manufacturing industry could not have successfully withstood British competition: 'Removal of the tariff would have placed almost all American cotton textile producers . . . under severe pressure. Few would have survived the introduction of free trade.'[62]

American tariffs were high throughout the nineteenth century and beyond. During the 1870s and 1880s industrialists became ever more enthusiastic about protectionism because it kept European competitors at bay. The high tariffs provided benefits not so much to small firms as to 'the giant American corporations that were integrating vertically and gaining a long-term advantage over their European competitors, who were restricted to smaller markets'.[63] Protective tariffs were an essential element in the economic programme of the then dominant Republican Party, which stood for an industrially independent and self-contained prosperous nation.[64] The extent to which protectionism actually promoted industrialization in the southern states of the USA is uncertain, but it certainly was of benefit to the North.[65]

In the United States tariffs had also been virtually the sole way of raising revenue for the Federal government before the Civil War. Afterwards they were seen as a means of supporting the pension system for Union veterans, thus further strengthening Republican dominance in the North.[66] The first peacetime federal income tax, introduced only in 1894 (the Revenue Act) precisely in order to compensate for an eventual lowering of tariffs, was very low (2 per cent). On 4 March 1897, in his inaugural address, President William McKinley explicitly declared that direct taxation should always be avoided, except in time of war. What he called 'tariff taxation' (i.e. tariff duties) was much to be preferred. For this would 'give ample protection and encouragement to the industries and the development of our country'.[67]

Throughout Europe, whether in France or Russia, Germany or Italy, governments, in the decades preceding the First World War, took measures to encourage their own industries (steel in particular) and gave priority to their own domestic entrepreneurs in public-works programmes. This was the era of 'protected markets', markets made safe from foreign competition by a tariff wall, or made difficult to access by a mixture of political and economic measures. Great Britain had few tariffs, but its empire, formal and informal, was, in practice, a protected market. Spain, on the other hand, suffered from sluggish growth because it had lost much of its Latin American markets to the British.[68]

In Britain conservatives embraced protectionism once more. It seemed to offer a way out of the difficulties facing the country after a long period of supremacy, above all the challenges it faced from Germany, the United States, and other powers. British agriculture as a share of GNP had been declining throughout the nineteenth century, dropping from 20 per cent in 1860 to 7 per cent in 1914.[69] This is when British consumers started to consume Danish bacon, Dutch eggs, and New Zealand butter instead of producing it themselves.[70] In 1870 the UK's share of world manufacturing production was 31.8 per cent, the USA was second with 23.3 per cent, and Germany, the third manufacturing power, was at some distance with 13.2 per cent. By 1881 the USA was first with 28.6 per cent while Germany was still well below the UK. On the eve of the First World War, however, the USA had 35.8 per cent of world manufacturing, a greater share than the UK had had in 1870. Germany had 15.7, and the UK was now third with 14 per cent.[71] No wonder the British were alarmed.

Laggard countries were worried too. Catching up had become ever more difficult for them. After Unification in 1861, Italy had relatively low tariff barriers, but in 1878 the Italian government led by Agostino Depretis slammed tariffs on wheat to keep American wheat at bay, then introduced steel subsidies while Italian suppliers were given priority in awarding public-works contracts.[72] Further tariffs were introduced in 1887 by Francesco Crispi, Prime Minister after Depretis's death in July of that year. As a consequence, relations with France, Italy's main economic partner (in 1886, 44 per cent of Italy's export, went to France), deteriorated, giving way to a period of acrimonious relations. In this trade war Italy emerged the net loser, since Italian exports, particularly agricultural products from the south (wine, olive oil, and citrus), to France fell by two-thirds in the years immediately after 1887.[73] Some Italian industrialists, however, seemed to do reasonably well. Once tariffs were imposed, the country experienced considerable growth, particularly in textiles, whose export increased, though it is not easy to work out how much this was due to tariffs and how much to lower Italian wages.[74]

Other laggards outside Europe improved their position. Mexico experienced rapid economic growth in the years 1884 to 1900 thanks to a flood of foreign investments, based on an increase in the export of mineral products (copper, zinc, lead, and silver). Exported manufacturing was mainly textiles. There was little protectionism, certainly less than in

Europe, and there were no subsidies to industry. Yet very few of the gains were spent on economic modernization. The main culprits, in this case, were not foreign imperialists but local elites, who, like many in Latin America, 'were too preoccupied with hobnobbing with the haute couture of Paris, visiting the spas of Gstaad . . . or gambling in Monte Carlo', rather than developing manufacture.[75] Besides, since Mexican labour was cheap, there was little incentive to innovate. The beneficiaries, apart from the local elites, were European and American investors.

Protectionism did not interrupt either the constant growth of the world economy. Exports, as a proportion of national production, reached unprecedented levels: 14 per cent in 1913.[76] In 1830, European exports had been only 2 per cent of total production, rising to 9 per cent in 1860. Trade was propelled by growth and not the other way round.[77]

Globalization also increased. Until the 1880s, some 80 per cent of the trade of industrialized countries had taken place among themselves. Between 1880 and 1913 exports to what we later came to call the 'Third World' increased but only modestly in proportion to the overall growth of trade.[78] The last remaining free-trading nation, Britain, however, became more global, and by 1913 two-thirds of British exports went outside Europe, 21 per cent to the Americas and 43 per cent to Asia, Africa, and Oceania.[79]

By the outbreak of the First World War protectionism had run its course, and the international trading system had become multi-polar and extremely competitive. Capitalism had become global. Britain was still rich and powerful. The Edwardian era that followed, and its continental counterpart the *Belle Époque*, was a period of unprecedented prosperity, at least for the industrial classes of the Western world. But this prosperity was marred by competitive nationalism. Laggards and not so laggards, old and new hegemons, all were haunted by anxiety that erupted into frequent quarrels. They quarrelled over useless colonies as well as useful ones; they quarrelled over armaments, over who was threatening whom; they quarrelled over tariffs; they entered into alliances against each other. The French and the Italians clashed over Tunisia (1881); the French, British, and Germans clashed over Morocco in 1905 and in 1911. Germany, Austria-Hungary, and Italy established the so-called Triple Alliance (1881); Russia, France, and Great Britain retorted with the so-called Triple Entente (1907). After all, as if to prove Palmerstone's famous 1848 dictum ('We have no eternal allies, and we have no perpetual enemies'), Russia, which had been, in 1873, an ally of Austria-Hungary and Germany (the so-called League of the Three Emperors), now switched its allegiance to France and Britain;

Italy, one of Austria's allies, detested Austria (it still claimed that 'its' Trentino was still occupied by the Austrians) and, in fact, when Italy entered the First World War in 1915, a year after it had started, it did so against Austria, a fellow member of the Triple Alliance; Germany feared France's revanchist ambitions; Britain was worried about German naval rearmament.

In October 1912 the First Balkan War broke out. It pitted four Balkan states (Bulgaria, Serbia, Greece, and Montenegro) against the Ottoman Empire, forcing it out of most of its European territories. The Second Balkan War (1913) was a conflict among the victors of the first. Bulgaria, dissatisfied with its shares of the spoils, attacked Serbia and Greece. Romania intervened, as did the Ottoman Empire, which regained some of its lost territories. Bulgaria lost out. The so-called Great Powers were in disarray, unable to decide what were their priorities were: did Britain really want to preserve the territorial integrity of the Ottoman Empire, as it claimed? Did Russia want to weaken Austria-Hungary? Was France not ready to take on Germany? To what extent did Austria-Hungary want to expand further into the Balkans? Would Slav nationalism threaten the stability of the multinational Austro-Hungarian Empire? To what extent was Serbia following Russian policies? Would Germany back Austria in case of war? No wonder the Balkan Wars were seen as a dress rehearsal for the First World War.

Eventually, a 'world' war did start and it started in the Balkans. The immediate cause was of striking modernity: the action of a group of suicide bombers 'with a cult of sacrifice, death and revenge'.[80] Its repercussions were global, though the fighting was not. Most of it took place in Europe, some in the Middle East. Towards the end Japan entered the war to grab some of Germany's colonies, as did Siam (Thailand) for internal nationalist reasons. In 1917 Russia exploded in revolution and soon dropped out of the war. The United States joined the war in 1917, even though Woodrow Wilson, who, until then, had shown little interest in foreign affairs, had declared in August 1914, probably worried that the war would divide Americans between ethnic groups of different European parentage, that 'The United States must be neutral in fact, as well as in name, during these days that are to try men's souls.'[81] This largely European war signalled the end of European supremacy; it signalled the rise of Soviet Communism, the sole significant challenge to capitalism for the following seventy years; it signalled the end of the first wave of globalization; and it confirmed the supremacy of America.

The issue of protectionism, its timing, its extent, had been endlessly debated. Arguments varied and were more or less plausible according to the size of the country, the structure of its industry, and the relative strength of the various elites, particularly the industrial and financial classes. Yet the political establishment, at least in Europe, was still dominated by landed and aristocratic interests, though by then they had come to accept the desirability of industrialization. Capitalism was winning not because the capitalists were powerful, or better lobbyists, or more articulate or backed by a majority of public opinion, but because industrial power had become the unavoidable backbone of state power. The triumph of capitalism, in the decades before the First World War, meant that no government, regardless of its inclination, could ignore industrialization.

Protectionism, a return to mercantilism that would have horrified Adam Smith, altered fundamentally the relation between the state and the economy and the relations between states. Under free trade, the state could pretend to be 'outside' the economic sphere. It could look on, benevolently, as industrialists competed the world over for a larger share of markets. Trade seemed to be a private matter. If 'their' own industrialists did well, politicians could glory in their successes, attributing them to some national or ethnic superiority as they would glory in the success of their writers or scientists. Protectionism was different. It was a national state policy aimed at changing the rules of the game in favour of 'their' industrialists. It was the unmistakable sign that the state saw it as its duty to protect 'its' industrialists against those of other countries. It transformed the competition between firms into a competition between nations. In the era of globalized capitalism, protectionism linked, indissolubly, the fate of a nation's capitalism to that of a nation's government. Yet, at the same time, many capitalists were also 'internationalists' in the sense that they chose a globalizing strategy. Capitalism has no unifying logic. The controversy over free trade and protectionism could never be resolved, because their economic realities are diverse and variable. What may be advantageous at one time may be disadvantageous at another. Trade could facilitate capitalist development in one country while making it more difficult in another. Politics may demand what economics warns against. Protecting inefficient sectors may be economically undesirable but politically desirable.

Conclusion: Still Triumphant? Still Anxious?

The decades preceding the First World War were, for the industrialized countries, a time of progress and optimism. Looking back to those years and aware of the incipient conflict, we might surmise that any optimism was mixed with anxiety, perhaps even foreboding. Yet neither the people of Europe nor their leaders were particularly conscious of being on the eve of a major catastrophe. There was anxiety, of course, but it was inbuilt in the capitalist system, its dynamism, the speed with which it proceeded, the novelties it produced, and the rapidity with which old habits were destroyed. Capitalism moved on without a goal or a project. Its nemesis, socialism/communism, is/was not a system like capitalism; it was a political project devised by conscious political actors aimed at establishing a communally owned economy or, in its milder social-democratic version, a socially concerned, ethical, compassionate, and heavily regulated capitalism. Capitalism's predecessor, feudalism, did not have change at its core (though it changed continuously). In a feudal system, things remained exactly as they were, with day following night, spring following winter, and serfs paying their dues to landlords while living in the fear of God.

Capitalism is different. Although it too has no mind, no politics, and no unity, change is part of its own dynamic, its own history. Change comes from within itself. Capitalism's only criterion of success is its own survival, which in turn depends on constant change. 'Modern capitalism,' wrote Joan Robinson, 'has no purpose . . . except to keep the show going.'[1] Robinson was on the Keynesian 'left'. But on the neo-liberal 'right' Friedrich Hayek also argued, in *The Fatal Conceit* (1988) – his final *envoi* against socialism – that 'the extended order of human cooperation, an order more commonly, if somewhat misleadingly known as capitalism . . . resulted not from human design or intention but spontaneously.'[2] Hayek, perhaps unwittingly, was echoing Marx, for whom the 'only purpose' of capital was 'self-expansion'.[3] 'Accumulate, accumulate! That is Moses and the prophets!' Marx wrote, adding:

> Accumulation for accumulation's sake, production for production's sake: by this formula classical economy expressed the historical mission of the bourgeoisie, and did not for a single instant deceive itself over the birth-throes of wealth.[4]

And, as Keynes wrote in 1933, 'the . . . individualistic capitalism' that had emerged after the Great War, '. . . is not a success. It is not intelligent, it is not beautiful, it is not just, it is not virtuous – and it doesn't deliver the goods . . .' And he added: 'But when we wonder what to put in its place, we are extremely perplexed.'[5] Capitalism itself does not 'understand' what is going on.

To be anxious is not new, since the future is mysterious. For centuries there was plenty to be anxious about: the weather, pestilence, natural catastrophes, wars: all like acts of God. We knew these were inevitable, we just hoped they would not strike us, or not now. We prayed, tried to prevent diseases, prepared for self-defence, and accumulated stocks against eventual crop failures. With capitalism and modernity this changes. Dangers do not come from the gods (or not only from the gods) – but from human interaction.

The Great War enhanced the sense of peril since there had not been a major war on Europe's soil in living memory (if we exclude the Franco-Prussian War of 1870–71). 'I think we are in rats' alley / Where the dead men lost their bones,' wrote T. S. Eliot in *The Waste Land*, while Giuseppe Ungaretti in a short poem ('Soldati', 1918) remembers how it felt to be a soldier in that war:

Si sta come	We were as
d'autunno	in autumn
sugli alberi	leaves
le foglie	on trees

A literature of alarm emerged: everything was doomed; the barbarians were at the gates. W. B. Yeats, in his great poem 'The Second Coming', composed in 1919, with the war, the Russian Revolution, and the failure of the Irish Easter Rising in mind, warned:

> Things fall apart; the centre cannot hold;
> Mere anarchy is loosed upon the world,
> The blood-dimmed tide is loosed, and everywhere
> The ceremony of innocence is drowned;
> The best lack all conviction, while the worst
> Are full of passionate intensity.
> . . .

The darkness drops again; but now I know
That twenty centuries of stony sleep
Were vexed to nightmare by a rocking cradle,
And what rough beast, its hour come round at last,
Slouches towards Bethlehem to be born?

This poem has continued to resonate in English-language culture. The theme of doom is exciting. Lines of this poem have been used for a novel describing the end or decline of traditional life (Chinua Achebe's *Things Fall Apart*, 1958) and an essay critical of modern counter-culture (Joan Didion's 'Slouching towards Bethlehem', 1967).[6] Didion's essay begins thus:

> The center was not holding. It was a country of bankruptcy notices . . . of casual killings and misplaced children and abandoned homes . . . It was a country in which families routinely disappeared, trailing bad checks and repossession papers . . . children who were never taught and would never now learn the games that had held the society together . . . It was not a country in open revolution. It was not a country under enemy siege. It was the United States of America in the cold late spring of 1967, and the market was steady and the GNP high . . .[7]

This was San Francisco in the 1960s, one of the richest cities in one of the richest nations in the world.

Of course, doom-mongering has always existed. It's just that, after the First World War, the trope of 'decline and fall' became a fashionable genre, further popularized by writers such as Arnold Toynbee in his multi-volume *A Study of History* (1934–61). The most famous example was Oswald Spengler's best-selling *Der Untergang des Abendlandes* (*The Decline of the West*), published in 1918 (though actually written before the war). But even before Spengler, in 1904, Constantine Cavafy had published his poem (composed a little earlier), 'Waiting for the Barbarians', in which he imagines a city in decline whose people and rulers await the arrival of the 'barbarians' not just with some trepidation and fear but almost with a sense of deliverance from a mindless and visionless existence. The barbarians do not come and the citizens ask: 'What is to become of us without barbarians? Those people were a solution of a sort.'

Earlier than Cavafy, in 1892–3, Max Nordau (born Simon Südfeld), a physician and an early Zionist, had published in Berlin his *Entartung* (*Degeneration*), soon translated into Italian (1893), French (1894), and English (1895). *Degeneration* was dedicated to the celebrated Italian criminologist Cesare Lombroso (who believed that criminal traits were inherited). *Degeneration* was, as one would expect, a dirge about the end of civilization. The first chapter, entitled 'The Dusk of the Nations', provides us with some fin-de-siècle anecdotes: an exiled king who, short of money, renounces any claim and titles in exchange for money; a bishop who, prosecuted for insulting a politician, sells the transcript of his defence, obtaining more than the fine he has to pay; the head of the secret police, who turns the skin of an executed criminal into cigar cases that he sells to his friends; and so on. Nordau then adds: 'All these fin-de-siècle cases have . . . a common feature, to wit, a contempt for traditional views of custom and morality.'[8] And they are all about the transformation of everything into marketable commodities.

The use of the word 'decadence' in essays and books increased very rapidly, peaking in the decade before the First World War. This offered some evidence of the fact that intellectuals were alarmed; although, in a way, alarm is their default position. That pessimism should increase after the First World War was understandable, but there was relatively little reason for so much despondency before it. Despite the Long Depression of 1873 to 1896, the industrial world continued to grow, subduing much of the rest of the world. In the period 1871 to 1914, in the West, there were no major wars, revolutions, or regime changes. (The only important European conflict, the Balkan Wars of 1912–13, left the rest of the continent unperturbed.) And an unprecedented international migration of people to the Americas did not cause major political changes either in Europe (whence most of the migrants originated) or in the Americas (where most of the migrants went). This is all the more impressive since the flow of immigrants into the United States in the 1880s was, in proportion, three times that of the 1990s.[9]

Elsewhere, in the first years of the twentieth century, there was significant political unrest, even revolutions (see Chapter 11): Persia (1906), Turkey (1908), Mexico (1910), Portugal (1910), China (1911), the failed revolutions in Russia (1905) and in Albania (1910, against Ottoman rule), and the 'liberal' revolution in Paraguay (1904). Such turmoil and the hopes it inspired were designed to bring about modernity, democracy, and constitutional rule, and move 'forward' to a capitalist stage – not to return to a previous state of affairs.

Those enslaved by colonialism suffered considerably, but they often had suffered previously. The local rulers and their clients, though humiliated by the arrogance of their white masters, remained powerful. There were rebellions against colonial rule – as we saw in Chapter 17 – but only the Ethiopian resistance against Italy's attempt to take over the country in 1896 was successful.

In spite of the widespread fears, the panics, and the anxieties that at times seemed to overwhelm easily frightened elites in the 'advanced' countries, dissident anti-capitalist forces did not present a real threat before 1914. Anarchists, nationalists, conspirators, and various deranged individuals killed, in the decades between 1880 and 1914, a Tsar (Alexander II in 1881), two American presidents (James Garfield in 1881 and William McKinley in 1901); Abraham Lincoln had been murdered in 1865 and the presidents of France, Mexico, and Ecuador; the Prime Ministers of Russia, Bulgaria, Japan, and Persia; an Austrian Empress (Sissi) and the kings of Greece, Italy, Serbia (and his wife), and Portugal; but little of significance was achieved except, in some cases, to justify the subsequent repression. Then, in Sarajevo, on 28 June 1914, an Austrian archduke and his wife were killed by a Bosnian Serb.

Anarchist movements brought about no advance towards their utopian aims and not even limited success. Engels understood this well in 1895 when, in his introduction to Marx's *The Class Struggles in France, 1848–1850* (1850), he wrote that 'The time of surprise attacks, of revolutions carried through by small conscious minorities at the head of unconscious masses, is past.' One of the main aspects of capitalism is that it cannot be overturned by destroying or capturing its centre since it has none. It would take more than a few half-deranged terrorists and naive rebels to dismantle such a power structure. Terrorists are never in control of the consequences of their action. They can throw the initial stone but are quite unable to predict what ripples will occur. Those already powerful and against whom the action of terrorists are directed are the ones who decide how and when to respond, thus making the impotence of terrorism all the more evident.

Other forms of resistance, such as strikes and riots, were of far greater importance than plots and insurrections, but they succeeded, at best, in obtaining reforms that the elites should have had the intelligence to enact earlier. Socialist parties, as we have seen, were strong between 1880 and 1914 in only a few countries (such as Germany and Austria) and, though unable to form governments, had some influence on the pace of reforms (as did the trade unions in Great Britain). Only in Australia was a socialist party able to form a majority government before the First World War. Between the two world wars socialist parties became more politically significant and were occasionally in power (usually in coalition, as in Sweden, Denmark, Great Britain, Germany, France, Spain, and New Zealand). Only after 1945 would they become leading contenders for government in almost all Western European countries.

The improvement in literacy and education expanded the cohort of those who could be classified as members of the intelligentsia, but these were no more rebellious, if at all, than their forefathers, often entertaining the bourgeoisie with their harmless anti-bourgeois postures. Those of an artistic disposition, painters and sculptors, simply sold their wares to the nouveau riche who could not afford Renaissance masters. Modernism, whether embodied in stream-of-consciousness novels (prefigured in Laurence Sterne's *Tristram Shandy*, 1757), twelve-tone music, or abstract art, was no threat to the bourgeoisie and seldom claimed to be, though some naively claimed it was, for instance, Daniel Bell, who regarded modernism 'as the agency for the dissolution of the bourgeois world view . . .'[10]

Before the First World War, capitalism, in spite of its undoubted success, remained unpopular in culture (elite and non-elite) – as it still is today. The sheer accumulation of wealth, though the avowed goal of so many, was seldom celebrated in novels and poetry. Many of the revered writers of the nineteenth and twentieth centuries who wrote about money (Honoré de Balzac, Charles Dickens, Giovanni Verga, Wilhelm Raabe, Henrik Ibsen, Anthony Trollope, Émile Zola, Upton Sinclair, Jack London, Henry James, F. Scott Fitzgerald, John Steinbeck, and many others) could barely disguise their contempt for capitalists and financiers (see Chapters 9 and 15). These writers, on the whole, were far from being socialists, but they regarded competitive capitalism as irrational or inhuman, or vulgar, or a waste of resources or backward and belonging to the past. At a time when socialists were not thinking of a planned economy (this would come later, after the Russian Revolution and the crisis of 1929), many writers and thinkers were developing schemes for a planned and rational society ruled by technocrats – an ancient dream whose origins lie in Plato's *Republic* (where the rulers should be philosophers) and whose nineteenth-century antecedents could be found in the writings of Henri de Saint Simon and others (who thought that bankers and businessmen should be in charge). Much of this 'technocratic' anti-capitalism was expressed in novels about the future such as Edward Bellamy's *Looking Backward* (1888, see Chapters 14 and 15) and H. G. Wells's *A Modern Utopia* (1905) along with his book *Anticipations of the Reaction of Mechanical and Scientific Progress upon Human Life and Thought* (1901), as well as Thorstein

Veblen's *The Engineers and the Price System* (a collection of essays originally published in the journal *The Dial* in 1919).[11]

In the Cold War period as well as in the post-communist era that followed, anti-capitalism was far more present in popular culture than pro-capitalism. As the self-styled anarcho-libertarian pro-capitalist economist Murray N. Rothbard wrote, somewhat regretfully: 'It's true: greed has had a very bad press', adding with obvious glee as if trying to shock right-thinking people: 'I frankly don't see anything wrong with greed'[12] – a bon mot somewhat resuscitated in 1998 by the British Labour Party's guru Peter Mandelson when he declared to California computer executives that he was 'intensely relaxed about people getting filthy rich as long as they pay their taxes'.

People are envious and resentful of those who make money. Meanwhile the rich can just shrug their shoulders and go on counting their cash, since on the whole being envied for being rich is better than being pitied for being poor. In the West, traders in the City of London and on Wall Street earning huge bonuses are despised by many, while in post-communist Russia, among ordinary working people or the old, one could hardly hear a good word said about the so-called 'New Russians'.[13] Some may attribute this to the lingering success of Soviet propaganda, or to the nostalgia for the austere Soviet style of the 1960s; but the simplest explanation is that the rich are intensely disliked even when admired, and that rich capitalists are more disliked than the aristocracy of old, since being born an aristocrat like being born rich is a matter of luck, like winning the lottery, while self-made capitalists suggest that those who did not make it were incompetent or lazy.

There are exceptions to popular anti-capitalism in fiction. One is Ayn Rand's *Atlas Shrugged* (1957), preceded by another best-selling novel in 1943, *The Fountainhead*, celebrating an individualistic architect. In *Atlas Shrugged* the 'good guys' are tycoons and captains of industry and the 'bad guys' are 'collectivists' of various hues and bureaucrats. Ayn Rand (born Alisa Rosenbaum in St Petersburg in 1905) had written the novel precisely because she was dismayed that so little fiction had a positive attitude towards industrialists. While most fiction celebrates altruism and self-sacrifice (on behalf of one's faith, country, friends, family, or one's beloved), Ayn Rand celebrated selfishness, not always successfully.

The anti-capitalist genre was particularly prominent in popular science fiction and spy films produced in the United States and Great Britain, heartlands of capitalism. The anti-capitalist theme recurs constantly in Bond films, usually regarded as Cold War movies. In the third

James Bond film, *Goldfinger* (1964), the eponymous villain is not the usual Soviet agent but a crooked bullion dealer who plans to contaminate the gold held in Fort Knox to force up the value of his own gold. In *Tomorrow Never Dies* (1997), Bond forms an unlikely alliance with a (beautiful) Chinese spy who works for the Communist Party of the People's Republic of China to thwart the monstrous plans of a press magnate (a kind of Rupert Murdoch), who wants to provoke a third world war because wars are good for newspaper sales. In the film *Superman* (1978) the arch-criminal Lex Luthor (Gene Hackman) wants to nuke the California coastline since he's bought the adjoining desert land that he wants to develop and so make a fortune. In *Superman III* (1983) the nasty capitalist Ross Webster, in order to monopolize the world's coffee crop, wants to destroy the totality of Colombian coffee. In *Total Recall* (1990, with Arnold Schwarzenegger), malevolent capitalists exploit the 'mutants' on Mars. In James Cameron's *Avatar* (2009) the earth's resources have been depleted and a capitalist company exploits those of another planet endangering the natives and their harmonious way of life. In *Alien III* (1992) the Weyland-Yutani, a soulless, profit-driven corporation with no ethical values, runs extra-solar human colonies.

There are many such examples. The accumulation of wealth for its own sake is decried. The 'social' point of capitalism is consumption. Marx was aware of that when, in the opening lines of *Das Kapital*, he declared that the wealth of capitalist societies presented itself as 'an immense accumulation of commodities'.[14] We usually enjoy the commodities far more than the process of accumulating wealth, unless the job is particularly pleasurable and interesting. And it is the demand for commodities that propels the process of accumulation. Whether this process requires a system of (largely) private ownership, as capitalist ideologues claim, or whether it can work equally well (or better) under some form of communal or state ownership, as socialists maintain, was one of the major controversies of the twentieth century.

Although few people today defend communism, not many actually like capitalism. A survey commissioned by the World Service of the BBC in 2009, twenty years after the fall of the Berlin Wall, found widespread dissatisfaction with free-market capitalism in the twenty-seven countries surveyed. Only 11 per cent of those interviewed thought that capitalism worked well and felt that greater regulation was not a good idea. In only two countries did more than one in five feel that capitalism worked: in the United States (25 per cent) and, less predictably, in Pakistan (21 per cent). Worldwide, 23 per cent of all those surveyed felt that capitalism was fatally flawed, and that a new economic system was needed. This was the *average*: in France the anti-capitalists accounted for a staggering 43 per cent, in Mexico 38 per cent, in Brazil 35 per cent, and in Ukraine 31 per cent. In fifteen of the twenty-seven countries a majority thought that the government should own or control their country's major industries – a view strongly held in countries of the former Soviet Union such as Russia (77 per cent) and Ukraine (75 per cent). Among former communist countries a majority of Russians (61 per cent) and Ukrainians (54 per cent) thought that the breakup of the Soviet Union was a 'bad thing', unlike 80 per cent of the Poles and nearly two-thirds of Czechs.[15]

Be that as it may, popular anti-capitalism has never seriously affected the workings of capitalism; there has never been an anti-capitalist armed revolution in an advanced capitalist country. Perhaps capitalism requires, ideologically speaking, some enmity towards those who become wealthy to reassure the majority who are not and who will never be wealthy, hence sayings such as 'money does not make you happy'; 'the love of money is the root of all evil' (a passage addressed specifically to 'servants' and 'slaves' in First Timothy 6:10); 'You cannot serve both God and money' (Luke 16:13); money 'is the Devil's dung!', as Pope Francis declared in 2015, quoting Basil of Caesarea, a Church Father of the fourth century.[16] Even Margaret Thatcher told the General Assembly of the Church of Scotland that 'It is not the creation of wealth that is wrong, but the love of money for its own sake.'[17]

Reluctance to embrace a pro-capitalist ideology grew during the Great War (when the economy was put on a war footing) and even more in the interwar period. The Russian Revolution of 1917, the runaway inflation of the early 1920s (in Germany, Austria, and Hungary), the Wall Street Crash of 1929 and the subsequent Depression of the 1930s made capitalism more unpopular than ever. In those years the globalized economy, as it had developed between 1860 to 1914, contracted, as most countries resorted to protectionism and state intervention in the economy: the New Deal in the United States, planning in the USSR, the takeover of the banking system by Italian Fascism, and the massive rearmament programme in Japan and Nazi Germany. After the Second World War, the capitalist economies, in direct competition with the newly emergent communist world, followed variants of what came to be known, in Western Europe, as the 'Keynesian' welfare state, while in the USA a high-wage economy provided capitalism with its most formidable base of consensus: mass consumption.

Very little of this could have been perceived in the years 1860 to 1914. Historians tend to see the germs of what will happen in what has already happened and write about the past in the light of the consequences. One must try to resist the temptation. In 1910 hardly anyone seriously foresaw (though a few guessed) the First World War and the Russian Revolution. In the aftermath of the war not many foresaw the rise of Fascism and Nazism, the crash of 1929, the Japanese invasion of China in 1931, and the Second World War. In 1940 only a few perceived how the Cold War would shape the world or the end of colonial empires. In the 1970s and 1980s few predicted the fall of communism, the rise of China as a major economic power, and the advent of Islamic fundamentalism after the Iranian Revolution of 1979. Perhaps one should bear in mind Tocqueville's warning that 'Nothing is more apt to remind philosophers and statesmen of the need for modesty than the history of the French Revolution, for no event was greater or longer in the making or more fully prepared yet so little anticipated.'[18]

What was perfectly predictable and indeed widely predicted in the decades preceding the Great War was the triumph of capitalism, since even (or especially) its main opponents, the socialists, assumed that capitalist development was a 'natural' and inevitable stage in world history. Yet outright pro-capitalism was never a vote winner. If we examine the ideological basis of mass parties in the hundred years between 1880 and 1980, it is rare to find considerable popular support for what we might call today neo-liberal positions. There were social-democratic, socialist, and communist parties in most of Europe, New Zealand, and Australia; there were various social Christian parties: in Italy the *Partito Popolare* and, in 1943, its successor, the *Democrazia Cristiana*; in Germany, the Zentrum and, after 1945, the *Christlich Demokratische Union* and its Bavarian sister party, the *Christlich-Soziale Union*; in Austria the *Christlichsoziale Partei* and its successor the Austrian People's Party (*Österreichische Volkspartei*). There were in the Scandinavian countries various agrarian parties; in Greece and in some Latin American countries personality-based parties; and in the United States, Argentina, and Peru populist parties. There were 'national' or 'one-nation' parties such as the Gaullists in France, the Republicans and the Democrats (divided by policies such as 'states rights' versus 'big government') in the USA, the Conservatives in Britain, and, elsewhere, fascist parties of various hues.

Although capitalism was the only game in town, the electorate would not countenance a clear and direct appeal to free markets, and free-market liberals were in a minority throughout democratic Europe. A more positive view of the market economy emerged in the decades after 1945 and far more markedly only after the 1980s, when the second great globalization was under way. By then politics had changed considerably. What we called the 'reactionaries' (see the Introduction) have virtually disappeared. Only a few lovable eccentrics and some well-off 'hippies', almost all in prosperous countries, really harbour the dream of returning to the simplicities of pre-capitalism (when life chances were a fraction of what they are today).

The social Christians have almost gone. Christian Democracy, which in its German, Italian, and Austrian variants had presented itself as a barrier against both untrammelled individualism and mindless collectivism, has ended up being no more than compassionate conservatism. Outside Europe the main stronghold of political Christianity lies in the growing power of the fundamentalist Churches in the United States, where Jesus is recast as an unlikely supporter of free-market forces. While nineteenth-century evangelicals were concerned with social ills, such as alcoholism, slavery, or poverty, their modern followers are in love with capitalism. The Jesus who drove out 'all those who bought and sold' (the merchants) from the Temple (an episode that occurs in all four Gospels), and who would today threaten to do the same to bankers, would be lynched as a communist by some of today's fundamentalists.

Social democrats have not disappeared, but they are a shadow of their former selves. They find themselves compelled to defend the gains of the past (such as the welfare state) with no vision for the future, apart from spreading the benefits of capitalism more widely and more equally. A cautious conservative outlook has become their most obvious trait.

The trade unions are weaker than ever. The usual measure of union strength is the percentage of union members in the workforce (trade union density), an indicator that must be treated with caution since some countries with comparatively low density, such as France (only 7.7 per cent in 2014), have strong collective bargaining, and some of the former communist countries, such as the Czech Republic, with high union membership (for historical reason), have weak unions.[19] With this caveat in mind, it is significant that union density has been steadily declining throughout the OECD countries: in 1999 the average was 21 per cent and by 2014 it was down to under 17 per cent. In 1980, as a wave of neo-liberalism was about to be unleashed, trade union density in Germany was 34.8 per cent, in 1999 it was down to 25.3 per cent, and 18.4 per cent in 2011. In Italy density decreased from 49.5 per cent in 1980 to 35 per cent in 2011. In Israel, where the trade union federation (the Histadrut) was particularly powerful, union density dropped by half between 1999 and 2011. In Sweden, home of what is still the strongest trade union movement in the world, union density steadily declined from its peak of 86 per cent in 1995 to 67.7 per cent in 2014 (OECD data; the figures, however, include retired union members).

In the United Kingdom the drop was from 49.7 per cent in 1980 to 25.8 per cent in 2011. Legislation promulgated by Margaret Thatcher and her successor John Major further weakened the trade unions and reduced employment protection.[20] Much of this anti-union legislation was not repealed by successive Labour governments, though it was somewhat tempered by EU directives unenthusiastically implemented by Labour.[21] In the industrial relations field, as Colin Crouch, writing in 2001, has 'tentatively' suggested, 'New Labour represents a continuation of the neo-liberalism of the Conservative government.'[22]

Nevertheless the idea of untrammelled capitalism has remained unpopular in the United Kingdom, so much so that its main upholder, the Conservative Party, is embarrassed by it and in its manifesto for the election of 2017 declared that:

> Conservatism is not and never has been the philosophy described by caricaturists. We do not believe in untrammelled free markets. We reject the cult of selfish individualism. We abhor social division, injustice, unfairness and inequality.[23]

Much of this general decline was due to the significant shift away from manufacturing in the traditional industrial countries of the West, the drop in public-sector employment, and the proliferation of part-time and casual work and self-employment. In general, union membership has been more solid in the state sector than in the private sector; for instance, in Sweden union density is 83 per cent in the state sector and 65 per cent in the private sector.[24]

Free-market ideology has made inroads in countries that had originally appeared inured to it. Israel has ditched the ethnic-based Zionist socialism of its founding fathers (though it was never much more than a useful myth) in favour of an equally ethnic-based unbridled capitalism tempered by massive subsidies to West Bank settlers and immigrants (as long as they are Jewish).[25] In India the original socialistic inspiration of the Nehru-Gandhi Congress Party has metamorphosed into a market-oriented India led by the Hindu nationalist Bharatiya Janata Party (BJP, the Indian People's Party). Gandhism achieved few of its desired aims such as truth (*satya*), progress for all (*sarvodaya*), simple living, and national economic self-reliance (*swadeshi*). India today is as corrupt and violent as many other societies that never benefited from Gandhi's teachings. The BJP, as of 2016 India's largest political party, has long abandoned its commitment to 'integral humanism', which rejected individualism, in favour of an unabashed neo-liberalism under the banner of 'resurgent India'. In Turkey the secular authoritarian model imported by Mustafa Kemal Atatürk from Europe has given way to a popular authoritarianism committed to Islamic principles developed by Recep Tayyip Erdoğan, who, like Indian's Narendra Modi, the BJP leader, links neo-liberalism with religious values.

In the United States, President Bill Clinton, in his 1996 State of the Union address, declared that 'The era of big Government is over' while conceding that 'we cannot go back to the time when our citizens were left to fend for themselves'.[26] And Gordon Brown, when Labour Chancellor of the Exchequer in the United Kingdom, in 2006, a year before the beginning of the global downturn, congratulated the City of London for its achievements and for showing 'that Britain can succeed in an open global economy, a progressive globalisation, a Britain that is made for globalisation and a globalisation that is made for Britain'.[27]

In Japan large companies run along paternalistic lines guaranteeing lifetime employment (*shūshin koyō*) to their grateful employees and a wage system that rewarded seniority and loyalty to the company (*nenkō joretsu*) are under constant attack by the companies themselves. The old system, extant in some form since 1910, was credited for Japan's 'economic miracle'. Now that the miracle is over and the Japanese economy is stagnant, a new paradigm, in tune with neo-liberal beliefs, is emerging. 'Lifetime employment', glorified as the secret of success some decades ago, has turned into the alleged cause of stagnation.

Various 'socialist' variants, popular in the years of decolonization ('African socialism', 'Arab socialism', etc.), disappeared long ago, degenerating into generically pro-market dictatorial kleptocracies (such as those of Syria, Tunisia, Egypt, Algeria, and Zimbabwe). The Arab Spring of 2011 has ended up, in most cases, in bloodbaths, and, in the case of Syria, far worse than its main historical antecedent, the *Printemps des Peuples* (the Revolutions of 1848). The liberation of South Africa from the clutches of the apartheid regime in the years 1991 to 1994, the enfranchisement of the black majority, and the electoral victories of the African National Congress (ANC) in alliance with the South African Communist Party, have produced decidedly pro-business governments. As a result, in 2013, the largest trade union, the National Union of Metalworkers of South Africa (NUMSA), with well over 320,000 members, withdrew its support from the ANC.

Leftist hopes in Latin America, after the disappointments of its Cuban (communist) and Chilean (social-democratic) variants, were revived with Hugo Chávez in Venezuela (1999–2013), Luiz Inácio Lula da Silva (Lula) in Brazil (2003–11), the second wave of Peronism with Néstor and Cristina Kirchner in Argentina (2003–15), Evo Morales in Bolivia (2006–), and Rafael Correa in Ecuador (2007–17). Their advance was, at least in part, due to the fact that the expansion of the neo-liberal free market in the years 1980 to 2000 had not produced economic growth comparable to that of the much-reviled era of 'import substitution' (1960–80), except in the case of Chile.[28]

However, gradually, and in different forms, the hopes of a new Latin American anti-capitalism have been dashed: Nicolás Maduro, Chávez's successor, is ruling a country whose economy is in ruins. In Nicaragua the highly repressive regime of Daniel Ortega, once the darling of the left for having led the so-called Sandinista Revolution (1979–90), has turned out to be responsible for a repression of major proportions.[29] In Brazil, Lula was involved in financial scandals and his successor, Dilma Rousseff, was impeached for breaking Brazil's budget laws and had to give way to Michel Temer, widely held to be corrupt. He was succeeded by Jair Bolsonaro, nostalgic for the good old days of the dictatorship, self-confessed homophobe, misogynist, defender of torture, and racist. In Argentina, Cristina Kirchner was succeeded by a conservative, Mauricio Macri. Matters went better for the left in Bolivia when Evo Morales was re-elected for the third time in 2014; but in Ecuador, Lenin Moreno, once a loyal follower of Rafael Correa, turned to the right after winning the 2017 presidential elections. In Mexico, after prolonged drug wars that have cost the lives of 230,000 people (13,000 in 2011 alone), the anti-corruption candidate Andrés Manuel López Obrador was elected president in 2018. He faces an uphill task.[30]

Of course, nothing, in life or politics, ever proceeds smoothly. There is resistance to neo-liberalism, particularly neo-liberalism in international trade. Since free trade is a complex issue embraced historically by an array of political forces from left to right, the kind of trade liberalization promulgated by the IMF and the World Trade Organization, and embodied in free-trade treaties such as the North American Free Trade Agreement, the Trans-Pacific Trade Agreement, and the proposed Transatlantic Trade and Investment Partnership, encounter the hostility of populist movements of both the right and the left. The hostility of the 'anti-global' activists (who are themselves globalized, since they try to act on a worldwide scale and communicate using all the facilities of the international communication system) is far from being unjustified: in the 1980s (when Thatcher and Reagan ruled) the IMF and the World Bank became, as Joseph Stiglitz explained, 'the new missionary institutions' of free-market ideology and pushed these ideas 'on the reluctant poor countries that often badly needed their loans and grants'.[31] Yet the issues are never straightforward: as Joseph Stiglitz himself points out: 'Opening up the Jamaican milk market to U.S. imports in 1992 may have hurt local dairy farmers but it also meant poor children could get milk more cheaply.'[32]

Capitalism has coexisted with a variety of regimes, from Victorian Britain to republican France and Switzerland, from Fascism and Nazism to post-war European democracies, from post-Meiji Japan to south-east Asian dictatorships and communist China. It is difficult to imagine that, in the future, it would not be able, at the global level, to absorb and/or co-opt xenophobes, leftists, populists, and assorted anti-globalizers. After all, in order to survive, all that is required is for stuff to be made and sold to someone, somewhere. The ease with which Syriza, the Greek Coalition of the Radical Left, elected to power in 2015 on an anti-austerity platform, was compelled to accept the conditions imposed by the European Union is evidence of the severe external constraints that all elected governments face. No one wants to be permanently in opposition, but it is often easier than governing.

Anti-austerity movements, such as the *Indignados* in Spain or the *Kínima Aganaktisménon-Politón* in Greece, which surfaced in the years after 2010, as well as the 'no-global' left do not really propose an alternative to capitalism; only a more just capitalism. Unlike past socialist movements, it has little connection to 'the working class'; it is the champion of the poor, the marginalized, the victims of global capitalism, though it claims to be on the side of the 99 per cent against the top one per cent. Yet it has failed to mobilize most of the 99 per cent. The poor in Third World countries want to work for Western enterprises, since the alternative is to be poorer. A modern defence of these enterprises, such as that offered by the Nobel Prize winner Paul Krugman, would point out that the children offered 'exploitation' wages in sweatshops in the Third World would earn even less and work harder in poorer conditions on a plot of land or scavenging on a garbage heap.[33]

The wave of austerity policies of the twenty-first century that has paralleled the growth in inequalities has given rise to a crisis of 'normal' politics, as one might call the alternation in power between centre-left and centre-right parties. Parties that seemed to be solidly implanted in the Western political systems have disappeared or changed radically. In Italy virtually all the parties that dominated the politics of the country until 1990 (Christian Democrats, Communist, Socialist, etc.) gave way to a party led by a television tycoon (Silvio Berlusconi's Forza Italia), a centre-left party made up of ex-communists and Catholics (Partito democratico), a xenophobic party (Lega Nord, now called simply Lega), and a party founded by a comedian (Beppe Grillo's Movimento Cinque Stelle). In Austria the two candidates in the run-off for the presidency in 2016 did not belong to either of the two parties (Socialist and Social Christians) that had dominated the country almost uninterruptedly since the war: one was a Green, the other a right-wing populist (the Green won, just). In France, Emmanuel Macron, never before having held elected office, became President in 2017 by defeating the far-right candidate Marine Le Pen, while the traditional parties of the Fifth Republic, Socialists and Gaullists, were virtually annihilated. In the United States, Donald Trump, the Republican candidate whose politics were deemed 'peculiar' by most of the elites, won against the establishment figure of Hillary Clinton (though with a fewer votes). In the United Kingdom the referendum on membership of the European Union was won by those who wanted to leave, even though the majority of all the main parties wanted to remain, as did the City of London, the trade unions, the industrialists, and the cultural and intellectual elites. The Labour Party elected (twice) a veteran leftist (Jeremy Corbyn), widely contested by the party establishment and yet able to benefit from remarkable electoral support in the elections of 2017. In Greece and Spain the traditional parties of the left (PASOK in Greece and the PSOE in Spain) have been humiliated in elections by parties to their left: in Greece by Syriza (Coalition of the Radical Left, which became the leading force in the elections of 2015), and in Spain by Podemos ('We Can', founded in 2014), which, in the election of 2015 disrupted the two-party system extant since the end of the dictatorship. One can go on, but it seems that the kind of political consensus that had prevailed in the West for decades is being seriously challenged.

Some have attributed these remarkable changes not just to unpopular austerity policies and substantial immigration but also to the stagnation in wages throughout the advanced capitalist world. Deprived of the prospect of a constant increase in consumption, it is not surprising if many voters are angry and blame not only politicians, immigrants, and the rich but also 'globalization', by now a generic name for the present phase of capitalism.

The ancient citadels of Western capitalism feel besieged by the rise of new contenders. The idea that the periphery of the world (or 'the Rest', as some have called it) will challenge 'the West' has some connection with an older brand of 'third-worldism' associated with the Maoism of the 1960s. Lin Biao (then Mao's number two), in a pamphlet written in 1965 called *Long Live the Victory of the People's War!* drew a parallel between the Chinese Revolution where revolutionary 'red bases' in the countryside surrounded and captured the cities, and a future world revolution where the countryside of the world ('the oppressed nations and peoples in Asia, Africa and Latin America') would defeat 'imperialism and its lackeys'. Lin Biao died in mysterious circumstances in 1971, when a plane carrying him crashed in Mongolia, after he had attempted a coup against Mao – or so it was alleged by the Chinese authorities. The oppressed peoples did not rise up and China is doing all it can to join and overtake the cities of the world, namely the West.

Nowadays capitalism moves from crisis to crisis, emerging from each somewhat changed. Crises are vital to its perpetual regeneration. The global downturn of 2007–8 is an indication of the strength of capitalism, since a social system can be said to have really triumphed not when it is working well but when it is malfunctioning and *everyone* rushes to save it. Those who today harbour anti-capitalist views, in the face of the success of capitalism, focus on its failures, but many such failures consist in not having extended its benefits to all. And there is no way of knowing whether, in the longer run, benefits will be better distributed. Eventually, say the optimists, things will work out. On the contrary, say the pessimists, capitalism causes more problems than it resolves. The trouble is that history is the history of unintended consequences. 'Bad' things may turn, if one can wait long enough, into positive things. There is little doubt, for instance, that the enclosure of the common land in Britain (one of the preconditions for British industrialization) caused a deterioration in the conditions of life of those expelled from the land. But it is also true that their descendants are much better off now than if there had been no industrialization. This, of course, does not justify anything: some of the descendants of the slaves forcibly transported to the Americas may now be better off than if their ancestors had remained in west Africa – hardly a credible defence of slavery.

Ideologies of various hues have all floundered before the seemingly inexorable march of consumer capitalism. As it spread beyond the United States, Western Europe, Australia, and New Zealand, then Japan and, eventually, parts of Asia and Latin America, the solidity of capitalism has acquired a considerable material basis. It seemed that, for the first time in the history of humanity, there was a social system able to provide a high level of consumption for the majority of those who lived and worked within it. Its only rival, communism, had failed miserably in the test that mattered above all else, even more than basic civil liberties: the democratization of consumption. Without this failure there could have been no victory for neo-liberalism, however challenged and however partial. People have been increasingly metamorphosed into consumers and, through their demand for commodities, are able to signal their desires and preferences. They vote in elections but, above all, they vote on a daily basis with their dollars, pounds, euros, 'electing' this or that product, thus making citizenship of the consumer society more valued than that of the polity.

In the late 1940s, as the Cold War was rapidly developing, the sociologist David Riesman wrote a satire (at times self-mocking) called 'The Nylon War'. He imagined the United States dropping on the Soviet Union not nuclear devices but consumer goods on the assumption that if the Russian people could only sample the wonders of American capitalism, they would no longer put up with being regaled with statistics on steel and iron production, much preferring beauty salons and vacuum cleaners:

> Over 600 C-54s streamed high over Rostov, and another 200 over Vladivostok, dropped their cargoes . . . By today's standard these initial forays were small-scale – 200,0000 pairs of nylon hose, 4,000,000 packs of cigarettes . . . 20,000 yo-yos, 10,000 wrist watches . . . Yet this was more than enough to provoke frenzied rioting as the inhabitants scrambled for a share.[34]

Consumption was a major element in the West's Cold War propaganda. At the American National Exhibition held in Moscow in the summer of 1959, while many were still impressed by the Soviet success in launching the world's first satellite in 1957, the American exhibition was 'a consumer spectacle which showcased cosmetics, clothing, televisions, kitchens, soft drinks, mail order catalogues, fibreglass canoes and sailing-boats, automobiles and a prefabricated suburban house'.[35] The 'American kitchen' exhibited was the centre of the famous 'Kitchen Debate' between Richard Nixon, then Vice-President of the United States, and the Soviet leader, Nikita Khrushchev, in which the two, somewhat childishly, argued about the benefits of communism and capitalism for the ordinary household, and in which Khrushchev announced that the next Soviet seven-year plan would match the United States in consumer goods. In so doing he explicitly acknowledged Soviet underdevelopment and the transformation of communism into a mere 'catch-up ideology', the sure sign that consumer capitalism had been recognized as the standard against which the progress of communism should be measured. The USSR had won the initial phase of the space race, but lost the far more crucial consumer race, a race won, unequivocally, by the USA.

Of course, popular consumption was not everything in the triumph of capitalism. In the Introduction we noted the various strategies deployed towards the end of the nineteenth century to contain anxieties about capitalism: democracy, welfare, nationalism, the consolations of religion, state intervention. These helped to stabilize the system. But there were costs: welfare expanded the non-private sector and demanded high taxes. The former is popular, the latter are not. Economic nationalism (protectionism) is good for those who are protected but not for those who want cheaper goods, and it interferes with capitalists' wish to trade with anyone anywhere. Democracy introduced elements of equality but in a widely unequal system. It gave rise to expectations and constrained politicians. One could not just rule to please the powerful – at least, not all the time – one also had to please the people.

Besides, the bedrock of international capitalism, the United States, may well see its power wane. A massive literature has been produced to suggest that American economic and financial power is declining.[36] US manufacturing has been in decline for years: the sharp drop in manufacturing employment after 2000 has been directly linked to competition from Chinese imports.[37] Where America has been unquestionably a true 'hegemon' is in its domination of the international economy. The dollar is still the main international currency with no rival in sight, allowing the United States to run the largest external debt in the world, almost twice the size of the second debtor country (the United Kingdom).[38] Today the USA also exercises considerable power in the main international economic institutions. Its voting power in the World Bank and in the International Monetary Fund is the same or greater than that of the next three countries (Japan, China, and Germany).

American innovations have led the dot.com revolution of the past forty years or at least the commercialization of such innovations. In the field of popular culture the United States is still ahead of other countries to an extent unparalleled in the nineteenth century. American universities are regarded as among the very best in the world, with eight places in the top ten according to the 2016 Shanghai Ranking System (the other two are British: Oxford and Cambridge) and half of the top one hundred.[39]

America is still, by a long shot, the world's supreme military power. Its might is unequalled and unprecedented: as of 2015 its navy was superior to the next *ten* navies put together and its military spending was greater than that of the next *ten* countries.[40] Such military superiority has seldom translated itself into military gain: the USA was powerless to alter the division of Korea between North and South, in spite of enduring 35,000 casualties; it was humiliated in Vietnam; it was unable to defeat the Taliban in Afghanistan; it was incapable of securing a peaceful and democratic Iraq (the aim of the so-called 'humanitarian' intervention of 2003); and it has been unable (or unwilling) to solve the Israel-Palestine dispute. Its successes in the Cold War (collapse of communism, transformation of Communist China into a market economy) owe very little to military might.

Whether and for how long the United States will be able to maintain its hegemonic position is an open question. No one can predict the repercussions, political and military, of a further shift to the advantage of the East and above all towards China, or even what this shift might look like. No one can predict whether or to what extent there will be serious rivalries between capitalist states, or even wars among them (if any, there has not been a war between two advanced capitalist states since 1945). Whatever happens, it is highly likely that global capitalism will be able to adjust to such shifts, and adapt itself to new geopolitical circumstances as it has done in the last one hundred years. Some will suffer and some will gain, as usual. The United States may be the foremost capitalist state and the self-appointed defender of world capitalism, yet there is little doubt that capitalism can survive without American hegemonic power, as it was doing a century ago.

Much has changed since the decades of the fin-de-siècle. Capitalism today is somewhat different from the triumphant 'Western' capitalism described in this book. The most startling changes are to do with the shift to the East of manufacturing, the tremendous expansion of financial services, the size and scope of trans-national enterprises, the growth in the economic role of the state, the centrality of the United States as the chief defender of international capitalism, the collapse of communism – historically the only real global challenge to capitalism – and the transformation of China into a major economic power.

Today China is the second industrial country in the world, and catching up with the United States. Its interventionist policies and the preponderant role played by state-owned enterprises have created a huge domestic market. Soon China will become not just the largest market in the world, unsurprisingly given the size of its population, but also the largest market for luxury goods, to the delight of European brands such as Giorgio Armani, Louis Vuitton, and Cartier.[41] The Chinese advance (or return) to a high level of economic performance had been preceded by other oriental exploits: first that of Japan, then that of the so-called Asian Tigers (South Korea, Taiwan, Singapore, and Hong Kong). Manufacturing output as a percentage of national output has markedly declined in what were once the most industrialized countries in the world.[42] De-industrialization, in the sense of the declining share of industrial workers in the workforce, often attributed to the deliberate policies of neo-liberals, in fact started in the West in the 1970s, before the advent of Margaret Thatcher and Ronald Reagan and before the rise of China as a powerful economy. In 1965 (under Lyndon B. Johnson) the share of manufacturing employment peaked in the USA at 28 per cent and has declined ever since.[43] Charles Feinstein even claims that de-industrialization began in the late 1950s in the United Kingdom and in Belgium, the two countries that had been in the lead of early industrialization.[44] This has resulted in higher unemployment in the post-1980 period than in the golden age of capitalism (1945–75), greater inequalities, and relatively stagnant wages.[45] The increase in inequalities goes against a previous trend of decreasing inequalities in OECD countries.[46]

Taking the twentieth century as a whole, however, the most significant change in terms of employment in the top capitalist countries has been the massive shift from agriculture to services.[47] The most obvious consequence of this is that while in 1900 the typical worker was an unskilled male employed either in agriculture or in industry, now the new industries and services required a higher proportion of skilled professional and clerical labour and an increasing proportion of women.[48]

The shift away from industrial production to services is exemplified by a startling statistic. Uber, an internet 'taxi' service, launched in 2009, was, by 2015, worth more than the Ford Motor Car Company.[49] In 2017, Facebook, Amazon, Netflix, and Google were valued on Wall Street at more than $1.5 trillion – about the same as the Russian economy.[50] And more people were employed in US nail salons (68,000) than in the US coal industry.[51] In 1896, when the Dow Jones started, it listed only twelve companies. Of these, none are listed today – another example of the constant 'creative destruction' of the capitalist market economy first envisaged by Werner Sombart and then by Joseph Schumpeter. General Electric, the last to survive since 1896, was booted out in June 2018. By then most of the now thirty listed stocks are in retail (Wal-Mart), software (Apple and Microsoft), or finance (Goldman Sachs and JP Morgan). Amazon and Google are not included in the Dow Jones, because they are so big that to include them would skew the index too far away from the twenty-eight other companies.[52]

Today's capitalism has less to do with manufacturing and more to do with finance, and this, for now, is still dominated by the West (though the largest banks are Chinese, the top one in the world being the state-owned Industrial and Commercial Bank of China). Established well before modern industrial capitalism, banks in the nineteenth century were still institutions that lent money to businessmen to enable them to do business. The great economists of the past (Adam Smith, David Ricardo, Karl Marx) did not analyse them in depth. Adam Smith's discussion of banking is limited to a few pages of Chapter 2 of Book 2 of *The Wealth of Nations.* David Ricardo devotes only one chapter (Chapter 27 in the 1821 edition) of *The Principles of Political Economy and Taxation* to banks – largely to examine the possibility of panics caused by depositors simultaneously withdrawing their money. Banks are barely mentioned in the first volume of *Capital* (the only one Marx completed), while in the third volume he wrote: 'An exhaustive analysis of the credit system . . . lies beyond our plan.'[53]

Banks, by creating money via mortgages and loans, enabled the constant increase in household debt and hence of consumption. By the 1990s this reached record levels, 'making possible', as Robert Brenner warned before the downturn of 2008, a historic and explosive growth in consumption.[54] In the United States the growth of debt-driven consumption turned out to be a compensation for lower incomes. If wages do not increase at the same rate as previously, it makes perfect sense to borrow in order to sustain consumption, particularly in the most important asset for households: the purchase of homes. Rising inequality in the West and particularly in the United States has contributed to rising debt for the bottom 95 per cent of the American population who preferred to owe money than to consume less.[55]

The Western financial system has developed over the last fifty years into something akin to a casino, as Susan Strange perceived a few decades ago: 'As in a casino, the world of high finance today offers the players a choice of games.' Instead of roulette or blackjack, one 'may place bets on the future by dealing forward and by buying or selling options and all sorts of other recondite financial inventions'.[56] An element of gambling has always been part of industrial capitalism. Will the internal combustion engine really take off? Yes. Will people really spend money to buy televisions? Yes. How long will the success of Polaroid photography last? Polaroid was introduced in 1948; by 1978 the company had 21,000 employees; by 2001 it had been bankrupted by digital cameras. Will anyone buy DeLorean cars? No: production started in 1981 and ceased in 1982.

Some decades before the downturn of 2007, Hyman Minsky, the eminent economist, compared financialization to a Ponzi scheme (from the Boston fraudster involved in pyramid selling) because it rolls over the debt, increasing its size, while the actual settlement of the debt is constantly deferred. As a result, what can trigger a financial crisis in an inherently unstable financial system is not some entirely exogenous factor but normal events. Crises are 'normal': 'as long as an economy is capitalist, it will be financially unstable', but, Minsky, added, 'all capitalisms are unstable, but some capitalisms are more unstable than others'.[57] What can make the difference is the intervention of the regulatory authorities. The increase in total debt might not have happened or would not have happened to the same extent had not the Glass-Steagall Act of 1933 been repealed under the Clinton administration and the financial system deregulated by assorted neo-liberals.

Minsky's financial-instability hypothesis suggests that the more the system appears to be stable the more it is unstable: when everything works well, operators are more likely to run risks since they assume that matters will go on working well (just as gamblers might be tempted to increase their bets if they continue to win).

Of course, financial gambling is not new: in the early seventeenth century in the Netherlands, a famous 'Tulip mania' drove the price of tulip bulbs to absurd heights before it collapsed; in the early eighteenth century, in England, the South Sea Company, a private company created with state support to reduce the cost of the national debt, saw its stock rising enormously in value before collapsing a few years later, ruining many. Such panics, bubbles, crashes, and so on were described as early as 1841 by the Scottish journalist Charles Mackay in *Extraordinary Popular Delusions and the Madness of Crowds*, where he discussed speculators alongside medieval crusaders, witch-hunters, and alchemists. But in those days and even later in the nineteenth century, the financial system was not as intrinsic to the international economy as it is now.

In the absence of internal enemies of substance and with the unlikelihood of a series of anti-capitalist revolutions emerging in a number of countries, the rule of capitalism seems impregnable. Yet there is, as always, room for anxiety. Today, the main obstacles to the continuing expansion of capitalism is not the class struggle, or the revolutionary aspirations of the wretched of the earth, or Islamic fundamentalists. The main obstacles are the ecological limits to the development of a Western-style consumer society at the global level.

The problem for the West is that the 'Rest' want to be like the West: driving cars, using energy, eating meat, having holidays abroad, enjoying an endless supply of cheap clothes, cheap music, cheap food, as well as gadgetries, computers, and so on, in other words all the joys and pleasure of limitless consumption. If technical ways could be found to resolve the ecological problem, the real obstacles to limitless growth, then capitalism, as we know it today, will have acquired another lease of life.

There may be political ways: various forms of despotism and authoritarianism may put the clock back to a time where the vast majority are deprived, once again, of the pleasures of consumption. But this too would give rise to major problems of legitimacy. One cannot rule by guns alone, by prisons, and by torture. One must give the people hope for a better future.

Under conditions of democracy, the solution to the ecological problems are even more formidable, for it is difficult to imagine a scenario in which politicians and world leaders explain to their electorate, expecting to win votes, that consumption for the many has to be severely restricted while allowing the few to thrive and enjoy. This would wipe away the much recently acquired legitimacy of the system itself. Nor would it be realistic to expect the 3 billion people in China and in the Indian subcontinent, who have within their sight the lifestyle of 'the West', to return demurely and peacefully to the spartan consumption of yesterday, while Westerners continued to bask in the pleasures of capitalist consumption. The signs are ominous: China is already the largest car market in the world, the largest market for the internet, the second largest consumer of oil, the largest energy consumer, and the world's biggest carbon emitter, overtaking the United States. China burns half of the world's coal consumption. Meat consumption is increasing. In 2015 some 120 million Chinese went abroad for leisure and business (the combined population of France and Great Britain). China's rapid industrialization and urbanization means that there is a considerable reduction in the size of agricultural land (as happened in the West). Consequently, China may not be able to produce enough food to feed its citizens and will be forced to buy on the world market, with obvious consequences for world food prices.[58]

None of this is surprising, since China's population is so large. Should India's advances match those of China, the ecological problems would multiply still further.

The irony is that it is the triumph of capitalism itself which now threatens its future, and gives rise to endless further anxieties: the originator of consumption destroyed by the triumph of consumption, 'consum'd' as Shakespeare put it (in a different context) 'with that which it was nourish'd by'.

Bibliography

Abu-'Uksa, Wael, *Freedom in the Arab World: Concepts and Ideologies in Arabic Thought in the Nineteenth Century*, Cambridge University Press 2016

Ackroyd, Peter, *Dickens*, Vintage, London 1999

Adanir, Fikret, 'Turkey's Entry into the Concert of Europe', *European Review*, vol. 13, no. 3, 2005

Adas, Michael, *Machines as Measures of Men: Science, Technology and Ideologies of Western Dominance*, Cornell University Press 1989

Aerts, Erik, Claude Beaud, and Jean Stengers (eds), *Liberalism and Paternalism in the 19th Century* (Tenth International Economic History Congress, Leuven, August 1990), Leuven University Press 1990

Ageron, Charles-Robert, *L'anticolonialisme en France de 1871 à 1914*, Presses Universitaires de France, Paris 1973

Aglietta, Michel and Yves Landry, *La Chine vers la superpuissance*, Economica, Paris 2007

Agnew, Hugh, *The Czechs and the Lands of the Bohemian Crown*, Hoover Press, Stanford, CA 2013

Agulhon, Maurice, *La République 1880–1932*, vol. I, Hachette, Paris 1990

Ahmad, Aijaz, *Lineages of the Present: Ideology and Politics in Contemporary South Asia*, Verso, London 2000

Akarlı, Engin Deniz, 'The Tangled Ends of an Empire: Ottoman Encounters with the West and Problems of Westernization – an Overview', *Comparative Studies of South Asia, Africa and the Middle East*, vol. 26, no. 3, 2006

Alberti, Manfredi, *Senza lavoro. La disoccupazione in Italia dall'Unità a oggi*, Laterza, Rome-Bari 2016

Albrecht, Catherine, 'Rural Banks and Czech Nationalism in Bohemia, 1848–1914', *Agricultural History*, vol. 78, no. 3, Summer 2004, pp. 317–45

Allain, J.-C., 'L'expansion française au Maroc de 1902 à 1912', in Jean Bouvier and René Girault (eds), *L'imperialisme français d'avant 1914*, Mouton, Paris 1976

Allais, Maurice, *La crise mondiale d'aujourd'hui*, Clément Juglar, Paris 1999

Allen, Charles, *Duel in the Snows: The True Story of the Younghusband Mission to Lhasa*, John Murray, London 2004

Allen, Robert C., *The British Industrial Revolution in Global Perspective*, Cambridge University Press 2009

Amsden, Alice H., 'The State and Taiwan's Economic Development', in Peter B. Evans, Dietrich Rueschemeyer, and Theda Skocpol (eds), *Bringing the State Back In*, Cambridge University Press 1985

Amsden, Alice H., *Escape from Empire: The Developing World's Journey through Heaven and Hell*, The MIT Press, Cambridge, MA 2007

Anderson, Charles, *Politics and Economic Change in Latin America*, D. Van Nostrand Co., Princeton, NJ 1967

Anderson, Margaret Lavinia, 'The Limits of Secularization: On the Problem of the Catholic Revival in Nineteenth-Century Germany', *Historical Journal*, vol. 38, no. 3, September 1995

Anderson, Margaret Lavinia, *Practicing Democracy: Elections and Political Culture in Imperial Germany*, Princeton University Press 2000

Andersson, Lars-Fredrik and Liselotte Eriksson, 'The Compulsory Public Pension and the Demand for Life Insurance: The Case of Sweden, 1884–1914', *Economic History Review*, vol. 68, no. 1, February 2015

Anon., 'England's Outlook in East Africa', *Fortnightly Review*, no. 281, May 1890

Antonmattei, Pierre, *Léon Gambetta, héraut de la République*, Éditions Michalon, Paris 1999

Appleby, Joyce, *The Relentless Revolution: A History of Capitalism*, W. W. Norton & Co., New York 2011

Archer, Robin, *Why Is There No Labor Party in the United States*, Princeton University Press 2007

Ardant, Gabriel, *Histoire de l'impôt*, vol. 2: *Du XVIIIe au XXIe siècle*, Fayard, Paris 1972

Ardant, Gabriel, *Histoire financière. De l'antiquité à nos jours*, Gallimard, Paris 1976

Arion, Charles C., *La situation économique et sociale du paysan en Roumanie*, V. Giard & E. Brière, Paris 1895: https://archive.org/stream/lasituationcono00ariogoog#page/n13/mode/2up

Arjomand, Said Amir, *The Turban for the Crown: The Islamic Revolution in Iran*, Oxford University Press 1988

Armengaud, André, 'Population in Europe, 1700–1914', in Carlo M. Cipolla (ed.), *The Fontana Economic History of Europe*, vol. 3: *The Industrial Revolution*, Collins, Glasgow 1980

Arnold, Matthew, *Culture and Anarchy and Other Writings*, ed. Stefan Collini, Cambridge University Press 1993

Aron, Jean-Paul, *Le mangeur du XIXe siècle*, Payort, Paris 1989

Aron, Raymond, *Dix-huit leçons sur la société industrielle*, Gallimard, Paris 1962

Aronson, I. Michael, 'The Anti-Jewish Pogroms in Russia in 1881', in Klier and Lambroza (eds), *Pogroms: Anti-Jewish Violence in Modern Russian History*

Arrighi, Giovanni, *Adam Smith in Beijing: Lineages of the Twenty-First Century*, Verso, London 2007

Ascher, Abraham, *The Revolution of 1905: Authority Restored*, Stanford University Press 1992

Ascher, Abraham, *The Revolution of 1905: Russia in Disarray*, Stanford University Press 1988

Ashley, Susan A., *Making Liberalism Work: The Italian Experience 1860–1914*, Praeger, Westport, CT 2003

Asiwaju, A. I., *Partitioned Africans: Ethnic Relations across Africa's International Boundaries, 1884–1984*, C. Hurst & Co., London 1985

Asselain, Jean-Charles, 'La stagnation économique', in Lévy-Leboyer and Casanova (eds), *Entre l'état et le marché*

Asselain, Jean-Charles, 'L'expérience chinoise en perspective historique. Un regard occidental', *Revue d'études comparatives Est-Ouest*, vol. 30, nos 2–3, 1999, pp. 325–72

Asselain, Jean-Charles, 'Les résurgences du protectionnisme français', *Le débat*, no. 76, September–October 1993, pp. 148–66

Aston, T. H. and C. H. E. Philpin (eds), *The Brenner Debate: Agrarian Class Structure and Economic Development in Pre-Industrial Europe*, Cambridge University Press 1985

Atkin, Nicholas, *Pétain*, Longman, London 1998

Atkinson, A. B., 'The Distribution of Income in the UK and OECD Countries in the Twentieth Century', *Oxford Review of Economic Policy*, vol. 15, no. 4, 1999

Atkinson, A. B., *Incomes and the Welfare State: Essays on Britain and Europe*, Cambridge University Press 1995

Auerbach, Sascha, *Race, Law and 'The Chinese Puzzle' in Imperial Britain*, Macmillan, London 2009

Badie, Bertrand, *L'état importé. Essai sur l'occidentalisation de l'ordre politique*, Fayard, Paris 1992

Baglioni, Guido, *L'ideologia della borghesia industriale nell'Italia liberale*, Einaudi, Turin 1974

Bairoch, Paul, 'Europe's Gross National Product: 1800–1975', *Journal of European Economic History*, vol. 5, no. 2, 1976, pp. 273–40

Bairoch, Paul, 'International Industrialization Levels from 1750 to 1980', *Journal of European Economic History*, vol. 11, no. 2, Fall 1982

Bairoch, Paul, 'La Suisse dans le contexte international aux XIXe et XXe siècles', in Paul Bairoch and Martin Körner (eds), *La Suisse dans l'économie mondiale*, Droz, Geneva 1990

Bairoch, Paul, 'Le mythe de la croissance économique rapide au XIXe siècle', *Revue de l'institut de sociologie*, no. 2, 1962, pp. 307–31

Bairoch, Paul, 'Niveaux de développement économique de 1810 à 1910', *Annales*, vol. 20, no. 6, November–December 1965, pp. 1,091–1,117

Bairoch, Paul, 'Une nouvelle distribution des populations: villes et campagne', in Bardet and Dupâquier (eds), *Histoire des populations de l'Europe,* vol. 2

Bairoch, Paul, 'Urbanization and the Economy in Preindustrial Societies: The Findings of Two Decades of Research', *Journal of European Economic History*, vol. 18, no. 2, Fall 1989

Bairoch, Paul, *Economics and World History: Myths and Paradoxes*, Harvester, New York and London 1993

Bairoch, Paul, *Victoires et déboires*, vol. II: *Histoire économique et sociale du monde du XVIe siècle à nos jours*, Folio Gallimard, Paris 1997

Bairoch, Paul and Gary Goertz, 'Factors of Urbanisation in the Nineteenth-Century Developed Countries: A Descriptive and Econometric Analysis', *Urban Studies*, vol. 23, 1986, pp. 285–305

Baitenmann, Helga, 'Popular Participation in State Formation: Land Reform in Revolutionary Mexico', *Journal of Latin American Studies*, vol. 43, no. 1, February 2011

Balabkins, Nicholas W., *Not by Theory Alone . . .: The Economics of Gustav von Schmoller and its Legacy to America*, Duncker & Humblot, Berlin 1988

Baldwin, Peter, *Contagion and the State in Europe, 1830–1930*, Cambridge University Press 2005

Baldwin, Peter, *The Politics of Social Solidarity: Class Bases of the European Welfare State 1875–1975*, Cambridge University Press 1990

Baquiast, Paul, *La troisième République 1870–1940*, L'Harmattan, Paris 2002

Barbagallo, Francesco, *Napoli, Belle Époque*, Laterza, Rome-Bari 2015

Bardet, Jean-Pierre, 'La France en déclin', in Bardet and Dupâquier (eds), *Histoire des populations de l'Europe*, vol. 2

Bardet, Jean-Pierre and Jacques Dupâquier (eds), *Histoire des populations de l'Europe*, vol. 2, Fayard, Paris 1998

Barghoorn, Frederick Charles, 'The Russian Radicals of the 1860s and the Problem of the Industrial Proletariat', *Slavonic and East European Review*, vol. 2, no. 1, March 1943

Baring, Evelyn (Lord Cromer), *Modern Egypt*, vols 1 and 2, Routledge, London and New York 2000

Barkin, Kenneth, 'Adolf Wagner and German Industrial Development', *Journal of Modern History*, vol. 41, no. 2, June 1969, pp. 144–59

Barkin, Kenneth, *The Controversy over German Industrialization, 1890–1902*, University of Chicago Press 1970

Barzaghi, Ilaria, *Milano 1881: tanto lusso e tanta folla*, Silvana, Milan 2009

Bass, Jack and Marilyn W. Thompson, *Strom: The Complicated Personal and Political Life of Strom Thurmond*, PublicAffairs, New York 2005

Bastiat, Frédéric, *Harmonies économiques*, in *Oeuvres Complètes*, vol. VI, Guillaumin, Paris 1870 (6th ed.)

Batou, Jean, 'L'Égypte de Muhammad-'Ali: pouvoir politique et développement économique', *Annales*, vol. 46, no. 2, 1991

Bauerlein, Mark, *Negrophobia: A Race Riot in Atlanta, 1906*, Encounter Books, San Francisco, CA 2001

Baumol, William J., Robert E. Litan, and Carl J. Schramm, *Good Capitalism, Bad Capitalism, and the Economics of Growth and Prosperity*, Yale University Press 2007

Bayly, C. A., *Indian Society and the Making of the British Empire*, Cambridge University Press 1988

Bayly, C. A., *The Birth of the Modern World, 1780–1914*, Blackwell, Oxford 2004

Beasley, W. G., *Japanese Imperialism, 1894–1945*, Clarendon Press, Oxford 1987

Beasley, W. G., *The Meiji Restoration*, Stanford University Press 1972

Beaucarnot, Jean-Louis, *Les Schneider. Une dynastie*, Hachette, Paris 1986

Beauclerk, William N., *Rural Italy: An Account of the Present Agricultural Conditions of the Kingdom*, Richard Bentley & Son, London 1888

Beauvois, Daniel, *The Noble, the Serf and the Revizor: The Polish Nobility between Tsarist Imperialism and the Ukrainian Masses (1831–1863)*, Harwood, London 1991

Beck, Naomi, 'The Diffusion of Spencerism and its Political Interpretations in France and Italy', in Jones and Peel (eds), *Herbert Spencer: The Intellectual Legacy*

Becker, Sascha O. and Ludger Woessmann, 'Was Weber Wrong? A Human Capital Theory of Protestant Economic History', *Quarterly Journal of Economics*, vol. 124, no. 2, May 2009, pp. 531–96

Beckert, Sven, 'Emancipation and Empire: Reconstructing the Worldwide Web of Cotton Production in the Age of the American Civil War', *American Historical Review*, vol. 109, no. 5, December 2004

Beckert, Sven, *Empire of Cotton: A Global History*, Knopf, New York 2014

Beckert, Sven, *The Monied Metropolis: New York City and the Consolidation of the American Bourgeoisie, 1850–1896*, Cambridge University Press 2001

Becqué, Émile, *L'internationalisation des capitaux. Étude économique, financière et politique*, Imprimerie générale du Midi, Montpellier 1912

Bédarida, François, 'Perspectives sur le mouvement ouvrier et l'impérialisme en France au temps de la conquête coloniale', *Le Mouvement Social*, no. 86, January–March 1974

Beetham, David, *Max Weber and the Theory of Modern Politics*, Polity Press, Cambridge 1995

Bell, Daniel, *The Cultural Contradictions of Capitalism*, Basic Books, New York 1976

Bell, Duncan, 'John Stuart Mill on Colonies', *Political Theory*, vol. 38, no. 1, 2010

Bell, John D., *Peasants in Power: Alexander Stamboliski and the Bulgarian Agrarian National Union, 1899–1923*, Princeton University Press 1977

Bellamy, Edward, *Looking Backward: From 2000 to 1887*: http://www.gutenberg.org/files/624/624-h/624-h.htm

Bender, Thomas, *A Nation among Nations*, Hill and Wang, New York 2006

Benjamin, Walter, *On the Concept of History*, Gesammelten Schriften I:2. Suhrkamp Verlag, Frankfurt am Main 1974, Thesis 9, 1940: http://members.efn.org/~dredmond/ThesesonHistory.html

Bensel, Richard F., *The Political Economy of American Industrialization, 1877–1900*, Cambridge University Press 2000

Bentham, Jeremy, *An Introduction to the Principles of Morals and Legislation*, vol. 2, Pickering, London 1823

Bentley, Michael, '"Boundaries" in Theoretical Language about the British State', in Simon J. D. Green and Richard C. Whiting (eds), *The Boundaries of the State in Modern Britain*, Cambridge University Press 1996

Bentley, Michael, *Lord Salisbury's World: Conservative Environments in Late-Victorian Britain*, Cambridge University Press 2001

Bercken, Wil van den, *Holy Russia and Christian Europe*, SCM Press, London 1999

Berdahl, Daphne, 'The Spirit of Capitalism and the Boundaries of Citizenship in Post-Wall Germany', *Comparative Studies in Society and History*, vol. 47, no. 2, April 2005, pp. 235–51

Berdahl, Robert M., 'Conservative Politics and Aristocratic Landholders in Bismarckian Germany', *Journal of Modern History*, vol. 44, no. 1, March 1972, pp. 1–20

Berdyaev, Nicolas, *The Origin of Russian Communism*, Geoffrey Bles, London 1955

Berdyaev, Nikolai, *The Russian Idea*, Macmillan, New York 1946

Berend, Ivan T., *An Economic History of Twentieth-Century Europe*, Cambridge University Press 2006

Berend, Iván T. and György Ránki, 'Underdevelopment in Europe in the Context of East-West Relations in the 19th Century', *Études historiques hongroises*, ed. Dezső Nemes, Akadémiai Kiadó, Budapest 1980

Berend, Iván T. and György Ránki, *The European Periphery and Industrialization, 1780–1914*, Cambridge University Press 1982

Berg, Gerald M., 'Writing Ideology: Ranavalona, the Ancestral Bureaucrat', *History in Africa*, vol. 22, 1995

Berg, Maxine, 'Britain's Asian Century: Porcelain and Global History in the Long Eighteenth Century', in *The Birth of Modern Europe: Culture and Economy, 1400–1800. Essays in Honor of Jan de Vries*, ed. Laura Cruz and Joel Mokyr, Brill, Leiden 2010

Bergère, Marie-Claire, *Sun Yat-sen*, Fayard, Paris 1994

Bergeron, Louis (ed.), *Les capitalistes en France (1780–1914)*, Gallimard, Paris 1978

Berindei, Dan, 'The Nineteenth Century', in Dinu C. Giurescu and Stephen Fischer-Galaţi (eds), *Romania: A Historic Perspective*, East European Monographs, Boulder, CO, distributed by Columbia University Press 1998

Berkowitz, Michael, *Zionist Culture and West European Jewry before the First World War*, Cambridge University Press 1993

Berlanstein, Lenard R., *The Working People of Paris, 1871–1914*, Johns Hopkins University Press 1984

Berman, Sheri E., 'Modernization in Historical Perspective: The Case of Imperial Germany', *World Politics*, vol. 53, no. 3, April 2001, pp. 431–62

Berthe, Augustin, *Garcia Moreno, président de l'Équateur, vengeur et martyr du droit Chrétien (1821–1875)*, Retaux-Bray, Paris 1887

Bertolissi, Sergio, *Un paese sull'orlo delle riforme. La Russia zarista dal 1861 al 1904*, Franco Angeli, Milan 1998

Bethell, Leslie, 'Politics in Brazil: From Elections without Democracy to Democracy without Citizenship', *Daedalus*, vol. 129, no. 2, Spring 2000

Bethell, Leslie (ed.), *The Cambridge History of Latin America*, vol. III: *From Independence to c. 1870*, Cambridge University Press 1985

Bethell, Leslie (ed.), *The Cambridge History of Latin America*, vols IV and V: *c. 1870 to 1930*, Cambridge University Press 1986

Bew, Paul, *Ireland: The Politics of Enmity, 1789–2006*, Oxford University Press 2007

Bew, Paul, *Land and the National Question in Ireland, 1858–82*, Gill and Macmillan, Dublin 1978

Biagini, Eugenio F., *Liberty, Retrenchment and Reform: Popular Liberalism in the Age of Gladstone, 1860–1880*, Cambridge University Press 1992

Bickers, Robert, *The Scramble for China: Foreign Devils in the Qing Empire 1832–1914*, Allen Lane, London 2011

Biraben, Jean-Noël, 'Essai sur l'évolution du nombre des hommes', *Population*, vol. 34, no. 1, January–February 1979

Birch, Alan, *The Economic History of the British Iron and Steel Industry, 1784–1879*, Routledge, London 2005 (first published in 1967)

Birnbaum, Pierre, 'Le rôle limité des Juifs dans l'industrialisation de la société française', in *Les Juifs et l'économique, miroirs et mirages*, ed. Chantal Benayoun, Alain Médam, and Pierre-Jacques Rojtman, PUM, Toulouse 1992

Biskupski, M. B. B., *Independence Day: Myth, Symbol, and the Creation of Modern Poland*, Oxford University Press 2012

Bittlingmayer, George, 'Did Antitrust Policy Cause the Great Merger Wave?', *Journal of Law and Economics*, vol. 28, no. 1, April 1985, pp. 77–118

Black, Cyril E. et al., *The Modernization of Japan and Russia: A Comparative Study*, Free Press, New York and London 1975

Blackbourn, David, 'The Discreet Charm of the Bourgeoisie: Reappraising German History in the Nineteenth Century', in David Blackbourn and Geoff Eley, *The Peculiarities of German History: Bourgeois Society and Politics in Nineteenth-Century Germany*, Oxford University Press 1984

Blackbourn, David, *The Fontana History of Germany, 1780–1918*, Fontana Press, London 1997

Blackburn, Robin, 'State of the Union: Marx and America's Unfinished Revolution', *New Left Review*, no. 61, January–February 2010

Blackburn, Robin, 'The Subprime Crisis', *New Left Review*, no. 50, March–April 2008

Blackstone, William, *Commentaries on the Laws of England*, vol. 1, New York 1827 (1st edition, 1765–9)

Blanqui, Jérôme-Adolphe, *Histoire de l'économie politique en Europe depuis les anciens jusqu'à nos jours*, vol. 2, Guillaumin et Cie, Paris 1860

Blewett, Neal, 'The Franchise in the United Kingdom 1885–1918', *Past & Present*, no. 32, December 1965

Blobaum, Robert, 'The Politics of Antisemitism in Fin-de-Siècle Warsaw', *Journal of Modern History*, vol. 73, no. 2, June 2001

Bloy, Marjie, 'Victorian Legislation: A Timeline': http://www.victorianweb.org/history/legistl.html

Blum, Jerome, 'The Condition of the European Peasantry on the Eve of Emancipation', *Journal of Modern History*, vol. 46, no. 3, September 1974

Blum, Jerome, *The End of the Old Order in Rural Europe*, Princeton University Press 1978

Blum, Léon, 'Débat sur le budget des Colonies à la Chambre des députés, 9 juillet 1925', *Débats parlementaires, Assemblée, Session Ordinaire (30 juin–12 juillet 1925)*

Bock, Gisela and Pat Thane (eds), *Maternity and Gender Policies: Women and the Rise of the European Welfare States, 1880s–1950s*, Routledge, London and New York 1991

Boldetti, Ambra, 'La repressione in Italia. Il caso del 1894', *Rivista di Storia Contemporanea*, vol. 6, no. 4, 1977

Bolivar, Simón, *El Libertador: Writings of Simón Bolívar*, Oxford University Press 2003

Boltanski, Luc and Ève Chiapello, *Le nouvel esprit du capitalisme*, Gallimard, Paris 1999

Bolton, J. L. and F. G. Bruscoli, 'When did Antwerp Replace Bruges as the Commercial and Financial Centre of North-Western Europe? The Evidence of the Borromei Ledger for 1438', *The Economic History Review*, vol. 61, 2008, pp. 360–79

Bonakdarian, Mansour, *Britain and the Iranian Constitutional Revolution of 1906–1911: Foreign Policy, Imperialism, and Dissent*, Syracuse University Press 2006

Bonghi, Ruggiero, 'Leone XIII e il socialismo', *Nuova Antologia*, 1 June 1891: http://www.sintesidialettica.it/leggi_articolo.php?AUTH=207&ID=427&STYLE1=1

Boniece, Sally A. 'The Spiridonova Case, 1906: Terror, Myth, and Martyrdom', in Anthony Anemone (ed.), *Just Assassins: The Culture of Terrorism in Russia*, Northwestern University Press 2010

Bonjour, E., H. S. Offler, and G. R. Potter, *A Short History of Switzerland*, Clarendon Press, Oxford 1952

Bonneff, Léon and Maurice, *La vie tragique des travailleurs*, EDI, Paris 1984, first published 1908

Bonney, Richard, 'France, 1494–1815', in Richard Bonney (ed.), *The Rise of the Fiscal State in Europe, c.1200–1815*, Oxford University Press 1999

Booth, Charles, 'Enumeration and Classification of Paupers, and State Pensions for the Aged', *Journal of the Royal Statistical Society*, vol. 54, no. 4, 1891, pp. 600–643

Booth, Charles, *Life and Labour of the People in London*, First Series: *Poverty*, vol. 1, Macmillan, London 1902–4

Booth, William, *In Darkest England and the Way Out*, Charles Knight & Co., London 1970, first published 1890

Borman, Tracy, *Thomas Cromwell: The Untold Story of Henry VIII's Most Faithful Servant*, Hodder & Stoughton, London 2014

Bortolotti, Bernardo and Valentina Milella, 'Privatization in Western Europe: Stylized Facts, Outcomes, and Open Issues', in Roland (ed.), *Privatization: Successes and Failures*

Bouillé, Michel, 'Les congrès d'hygiène des travailleurs au début du siècle 1904–1911, *Le Mouvement Social*, no. 161, October–December 1992, pp. 43–65

Bourdieu, Jérôme and Bénédicte Reynaud, 'Factory Discipline and Externalities in the Reduction of Working Time in the 19th Century in France', in CNRS-CEPREMAP, Working Paper no. 2002–08, June 2002: http://www.cepremap.cnrs.fr/couv_orange/co0208.pdf

Bourgeois, Léon, *Solidarité*, Armand Colin, Paris 1896

Bourguignon, François and Christian Morrisson, 'Inequality among World Citizens: 1820–1992', *American Economic Review*, vol. 92, no. 4, September 2002, pp. 727–44

Bourke, Richard, *Empire & Revolution: The Political Life of Edmund Burke*, Princeton University Press 2015

Boutmy, Émile, *Éléments d'une psychologie politique du peuple américain*, A. Colin, Paris 1902

Bouvier, Jean, 'Les traits majeurs de l'impérialisme français avant 1914', *Le Mouvement Social*, no. 86, January–March 1974

Bouvier, Jean, 'Libres propos autour d'une demarche révisionniste', in Patrick Fridenson and André Straus (eds), *Le capitalisme français 19e–20e siècle. Blocages et dynamismes d'une croissance*, Fayard, Paris 1987

Bouvier, Jean and René Girault (eds), *L'impérialisme français d'avant 1914*, Mouton, Paris 1976

Bowen, H. V. *The Business of Empire: The East India Company and Imperial Britain, 1756–1833*, Cambridge University Press 2006

Boyer, John W., 'The End of an Old Regime: Visions of Political Reform in Late Imperial Austria', *Journal of Modern History*, vol. 58, no. 1, March 1986, pp. 159–93

Boyer, John W., *Political Radicalism in Late Imperial Vienna: Origins of the Christian Social Movement, 1848–1897*, University of Chicago Press 1981

Bramall, Chris and Peter Nolan, 'Introduction', in Xu Dixin and Wu Chengming (eds), *Chinese Capitalism, 1522–1840*

Brandeis, Louis D., *Other People's Money and How the Bankers Use It*, Frederick A. Stokes Co., New York 1914: https://archive.org/stream/otherpeoplesmoneoobran/otherpeoplesmoneoobran_djvu.txt

Brandes, Stuart D., *American Welfare Capitalism, 1880–1940*, University of Chicago Press 1976

Braudel, Fernand, *Civilisation matérielle, économie et capitalisme, XVe–XVIIIe siècle*, vol. 1: *Les structures du quotidien*; vol. 2: *Les jeux de l'échange*, Armand Colin, Paris 1979

Bray, Francesca, *Technology and Gender: Fabrics of Power in Late Imperial China*, University of California Press 1997

Brenner, Robert, 'Agrarian Class Structure and Economic Development in Pre-Industrial Europe', *Past & Present*, no. 70, February 1976

Brenner, Robert, 'Economic Backwardness in Eastern Europe in Light of Developments in the West', in Chirot (ed.), *The Origins of Backwardness in Eastern Europe*

Brenner, Robert, 'The Boom and the Bubble', *New Left Review*, no. 6, November–December 2000

Brenner, Robert P., 'The Low Countries in the Transition to Capitalism', *Journal of Agrarian Change*, vol. 1, no. 2, April 2001, pp. 169–238

Breton, Yves, 'La perception de la "grande dépression" de la fin du XIXe siècle (1873–1896) par les économistes français. Analyses et perspectives', *Économies et sociétés*, no. 8, 1993

Brewer, John, *The Sinews of Power: War, Money and the English State, 1688–1783*, Routledge, London 1994

Bright, John, *Speeches on Parliamentary Reform, & c. (delivered during the autumn of 1866)*, John Heywood, Manchester 1866

Broadberry, Stephen and Alexander Klein, 'Aggregate and Per Capita GDP in Europe, 1870–2000: Continental, Regional and National Data with Changing Boundaries', *Scandinavian Economic History Review*, vol. 60, no. 1, 2012, pp. 79–107

Broadberry, Stephen and Bishnupriya Gupta, 'The Early Modern Great Divergence: Wages, Prices and Economic Development in Europe and Asia, 1500–1800', *Economic History Review*, vol. 59, no. 1, 2006, pp. 2–31

Brocheux, Pierre and Daniel Hémery, *Indochine: la colonisation ambiguë, 1858–1954*, La Découverte, Paris 1995

Broder, Albert, Gérard Chastagnaret, and Émile Temime, 'Capital et croissance dans l'Espagne du XIXème siècle', in Jean-Pierre Amalric et al., *Aux origines du retard économique de l'Espagne, XVIe–XIXe siècles*, CNRS, Paris 1983

Brook, Timothy, *The Confusions of Pleasure: Commerce and Culture in Ming China*, University of California Press 1999

Brown, Gordon, Mansion House Speech, 22 June 2006: https://www.theguardian.com/business/2006/jun/22/politics.economicpolicy

Browne, Edward G., *The Persian Revolution of 1905–1909*, Cambridge University Press 1910

Brownlee, W. Elliot, *Federal Taxation in America: A Short History*, Cambridge University Press 1996

Brunschwig, Henri, *Mythes et réalités de l'impérialisme colonial français, 1871–1914*, Colin, Paris 1960

Bryan, William Jennings, *Letters to a Chinese Official*, McClure, Phillips and Co., New York 1906

Bryan, William Jennings, *The First Battle: A Story of the Campaign of 1896*, 2 vols, Kennikat Press, New York 1971 (originally published 1896)

Bryant, Joseph M., 'The West and the Rest Revisited: Debating Capitalist Origins, European Colonialism, and the Advent of Modernity', *Canadian Journal of Sociology*, vol. 31, no. 4, Autumn 2006, pp. 403–44

Bull, Malcolm, 'The Decline of Decadence', *New Left Review*, no. 94, July–August 2015

Bulmer-Thomas, Victor, *The Economic History of Latin America since Independence*, Cambridge University Press 2003

Bunge, Nicholas Khristianovich, *The Years 1881–1894 in Russia: A Memorandum Found in the Papers of N. Kh. Bunge. A Translation and Commentary*, ed. George E. Snow, in *Transactions of the American Philosophical Society*, vol. 71, part 6, Philadelphia, PA 1981

Burawoy, Michael, 'Karl Marx and the Satanic Mills: Factory Politics under Early Capitalism in England, the United States, and Russia', *American Journal of Sociology*, vol. 90, no. 2, September 1984, pp. 247–82

Buret, Eugène, *De la misère des classes laborieuses en Angleterre et en France*, 2 vols, Paulin, Paris 1840

Burke, Edmund, *Reflections on the Revolution in France*, Apollo Press, London 1814: http://books.google.co.uk/books?id=Y1wIAAAAQAAJ&printsec=frontcover&dq=burke+reflections+on+the+revolution+in+france&hl=en&sa=X&ei=LB3nUPybAYa-0QXPwYGQAg&ved=0CDwQ6AEwAQ#v=onepage&q=improvement%20of%20nations%20&f=false

Burke, Edmund, *Thoughts and Details on Scarcity, originally presented to the Right Hon. William Pitt, in the month of November 1795*, F. and C. Rivington, London 1800: https://archive.org/stream/thoughtsanddeta00pittgoog#page/n5/mode/2up

Buruma, Ian and Avishai Margalit, *Occidentalism: A Short History of Anti-Westernism*, Atlantic Books, London 2004

Bury, J. P. T., *Gambetta's Final Years: 'The Era of Difficulties', 1877–1882*, Longman, London 1982

Busino, Giovanni, 'Vilfredo Pareto sociologo della borghesia e dello sviluppo capitalistico?', *Rivista Storica Italiana*, vol. 83, no. 2, June 1971

Cafagna, Luciano and Nicola Crepax (eds), *Atti di intelligenza e sviluppo economico. Saggi per il bicentenario della nascita di Carlo Cattaneo*, Il Mulino, Bologna 2001

Cain, Peter, 'J. A. Hobson, Financial Capitalism and Imperialism in Late Victorian and Edwardian England', *Journal of Imperial and Commonwealth History*, vol. 13, no. 3, May 1985

Cain, Peter, 'Political Economy in Edwardian England: The Tariff-Reform Controversy', in Alan O'Day (ed.), *The Edwardian Age: Conflict and Stability, 1900–1914*, Macmillan, London 1979

Cain, Peter J., 'Variations on a Famous Theme: Hobson, International Trade and Imperialism, 1902–1938', in Michael Freeden (ed.), *Reappraising J. A. Hobson*, Unwin Hyman, London 1990

Cain, Peter J., 'Was it Worth Having? The British Empire, 1850–1950', *Revista de Historia Económica*, vol. 16, no. 1, Winter 1998

Cain, Peter J. and A. G. Hopkins, *British Imperialism: Innovation and Expansion, 1688–1914*, Longman, London 1993

Calder, Loren David, *The Political Thought of Yu. F. Samarin, 1840–1864*, Garland, New York 1987

Calhoun, Charles W. (ed.), *The Gilded Age*, Rowman & Littlefield, Lanham, MD 2007

Cameron, Rondo, with Olga Crisp et al., *Banking in the Early Stages of Industrialization*, Oxford University Press 1967

Candeloro, Giorgio, *Il movimento cattolico in Italia*, Riuniti, Rome 1982

Candeloro, Giorgio, *Storia dell'Italia moderna*, vol. 6: *Lo sviluppo del capitalismo e del movimento operaio 1871–1896*, Feltrinelli, Milan 1978

Cannadine, David, *Ornamentalism: How the British Saw their Empire*, Penguin, London 2002

Cantoni, Davide, 'The Economic Effects of the Protestant Reformation: Testing the Weber Hypothesis in the German Lands', *Journal of the European Economic Association*, vol. 13, no. 4, August 2015

Carlson, W. Bernard, 'Technology and America as a Consumer Society, 1870–1900', in Calhoun (ed.), *The Gilded Age*

Carlton, David L., *Mill and Town in South Carolina 1880–1920*, Louisiana State University Press 1982

Carlyle, Thomas, 'Signs of the Times', in *The Collected Works*, vol. III, Chapman and Hall, London 1858

Carnegie, Andrew, 'Wealth', *North American Review*, no. 148, June 1889

Carney, Judith A., *Black Rice: The African Origins of Rice Cultivation in the Americas*, Harvard University Press 2001

Caron, François, 'Dynamismes et freinages de la croissance industrielle', in Fernand Braudel and Ernest Labrousse (eds), *Histoire économique et sociale de la France*, Tome IV: *L'ère industrielle et la société d'aujord'hui (siècle 1880–1980)*, vol. 1, Presses Universitaires de France, Paris 1979

Caron, François, 'Essai d'analyse historique d'une psychologie du travail. Les mécaniciens et chauffeurs de locomotives du réseau du Nord de 1850 à 1910', *Le Mouvement Social*, no. 50, January–March 1965

Carozzi, Carlo, 'Le abitazioni nei capoluoghi di provincia italiani intorno al 1880: alla ricerca di alcune differenze tra Nord e Sud', in Andreina De Clementi (ed.), *La società inafferrabile*, Edizioni Lavoro, Rome 1986

Carreras, Albert, 'What Can We Learn from Long-Term Spanish Economic Performance?', in Pablo Martín-Aceña and James Simpson (eds), *The Economic Development of Spain since 1870*, Elgar, Aldershot 1995

Carter, Jimmy, Inaugural Address, 20 January 1977: http://www.presidency.ucsb.edu/ws/?pid=6575

Castel, Robert, *Les métamorphoses de la question sociale. Une cronique du salariat*, Fayard, Paris 1995

Castells, Manuel, *The Rise of the Network Society*, vol. 1 of *The Information Age*, Blackwell, Oxford 1996

Castillo, Greg, 'Domesticating the Cold War: Household Consumption as Propaganda in Marshall Plan Germany', *Journal of Contemporary History*, vol. 40, no. 2, 2005, pp. 261–88

Castles, Stephen and Mark J. Miller, *The Age of Migration: International Population Movements in the Modern World*, Palgrave, Basingstoke 2003

Cattaneo, Carlo, *Scritti filosofici*, vol. 1, ed. Norberto Bobbio, Felice Le Monnier, Florence 1960

Cépède, Frédéric, 'Les socialistes français et l'encyclique *Rerum Novarum*', in *Rerum Novarum. Écriture, contenu et réception d'une encyclique*, École Française de Rome, 1997

Challemel-Lacour, Paul, 'Hommes d'état en Angleterre: William Ewart Gladstone', *Revue des deux mondes*, 1 July 1870

Chamberlain, Joseph, *Foreign and Colonial Speeches*, Routledge and Sons, Manchester and London 1897

Chamberlain, Joseph, *Mr. Chamberlain's Speeches*, vol. 1, ed. Charles W. Boyd, Constable, London 1914

Chan, Jenny, Ngai Pun, and Mark Selden, 'Labour Protests and Trade Union Reforms in China', in Jan Drahokoupil, Rutvica Andrijasevic, and Devi Sacchetto (eds), *Flexible Workforces and Low Profit Margins: Electronics Assembly between Europe and China*, ETUI (Europe Trade Union Institute), Brussels 2016

Chan, Kenneth S. and Jean-Pierre Laffargue, 'Foreign Threats, Technological Progress and the Rise and Decline of Imperial China', *Pacific Economic Review*, vol. 17, no. 2, 2012, pp. 280–303

Chan, Wellington K. K., 'Government, Merchants and Industry to 1911', in Fairbank and Liu (eds), *The Cambridge History of China*, vol. 11: *Late Ch'ing, 1800–1911*, part 2

Chandler, Alfred D., Jr., *The Visible Hand: The Managerial Revolution in American Business*, Harvard University Press 1977

Chandler, Tertius, *Four Thousand Years of Urban Growth*, St David's University Press 1987

Chang, Hao, 'Intellectual Change and the Reform Movement, 1890–8', in Fairbank and Liu (eds), *The Cambridge History of China*, vol. 11: *Late Ch'ing, 1800–1911*, part 2

Chary, Frederick B., 'Agrarians, Radicals, Socialists, and the Bulgarian Peasantry: 1899–1905', in Volgyes (ed.), *The Peasantry of Eastern Europe*, vol. 1

Chastenet, Jacques, *Histoire de la Troisième République. L'enfance de la troisième, 1870–1879*, Hachette, Paris 1952

Chaumel, Guy, *Histoire des cheminots et de leurs syndicats*, Rivière, Paris 1948

Chaunu, Pierre, *Histoire, science sociale. La durée, l'espace et l'homme à l'époque moderne*, SEDES, Paris 1974

Chen, Liyan, 'How Uber Surpasses Ford and GM in Valuation in 5 Years', *Forbes Magazine*, December 2015: http://www.forbes.com/sites/liyanchen/2015/12/04/at-68-billion-valuation-uber-will-be-bigger-than-gm-ford-and-honda/#3fff593c5858

Chernow, Ron, *Titan: The Life of John D. Rockefeller, Sr.*, Little, Brown and Co., New York 1998

Chernyshevski, Nikolai (Nikolaï G. Tchernuishevsky), *A Vital Question; or, What Is To Be Done?*, trans. N. Haskell Dole and S. S. Skidelsky, Crowell, New York 1886

Chernyshevski, Nikolai, *Critique of Philosophical Prejudices against Communal Ownership* (1859), in Teodor Shanin (ed.), *Late Marx and the Russian Road: Marx and 'the peripheries of capitalism'*, Monthly Review Press, New York 1983

Chesnais, Jean-Claude, *La transition démographique. Trente ans de bouleversements (1965–1995)*, Les dossiers du CEPED, no. 34, October 1995

Chevalier, Louis, *Classes laborieuses et classes dangereuses à Paris pendant la première moitié du XIXe siècle*, Perrin, Paris 2002, first published 1958

Cheysson, Émile, *La crise du revenue et la loi du travail*, Comité de défense et de progrès social, Paris 1898

Chiarini, Roberto, 'Ambizioni e difficoltà di un progetto riformatore', in Roberto Chiarini (ed.), *Alle origini dell'età giolittiana*, Marsilio, Venice 2003

Chicherin, Boris, *Liberty, Equality, and the Market: Essays by B. N. Chicherin*, ed. and trans. G. M. Hamburg, Yale University Press 1998

Chirac, Auguste, *Les rois de la république. Histoire de Juiveries*, Dentu, Paris 1888

Chirot, Daniel, *Social Change in a Peripheral Society: The Creation of a Balkan Colony*, Academic Press, New York 1976

Chirot, Daniel (ed.), *The Origins of Backwardness in Eastern Europe: Economics and Politics from the Middle Ages until the Early Twentieth Century*, University of California Press 1989

Chirot, Daniel and Charles Ragin, 'The Market, Tradition and Peasant Rebellion: The Case of Romania in 1907', *American Sociological Review*, vol. 40, no. 4, August 1975

Chiswick, Barry R. and Timothy J. Hatton, 'International Migration and the Integration of Labor Markets', in Michael D. Bordo, Alan M. Taylor, and Jeffrey G. Williamson (eds), *Globalization in Historical Perspective*, University of Chicago Press 2003

Chlepner, B. S., *Cent ans d'histoire sociale en Belgique*, ULB, Brussels 1958

Chombart de Lauwe, Paul-Henry, *La vie quotidienne des familles ouvrières*, CNRS, Paris 1977 (first published 1956)

Chun, Lin, *The Transformation of Chinese Socialism*, Duke University Press 2006

Chung, Sue Fawn, 'The Much Maligned Empress Dowager: A Revisionist Study of the Empress Dowager Tz'u-hsi (1835–1908)', *Modern Asian Studies*, vol. 13, no. 2, 1979

Churchill, Ward, *A Little Matter of Genocide: Holocaust and Denial in the Americas 1492 to the Present*, City Lights Books, San Francisco, CA 1997

Churchill, Winston, *Liberalism and the Social Problem*, Hodder and Stoughton, London 1909: http://www.gutenberg.org/files/18419/18419-h/18419-h.htm

CIA, *World Factbook*, https://www.cia.gov/library/publications/the-world-factbook

Citron, Suzanne, *Le mythe national: l'histoire de France revisitée*, Éditions de l'Atelier, Ivry-sur-Seine 2008

Clarence-Smith, Gervase, *The Third Portuguese Empire, 1825–1975: A Study in Economic Imperialism*, Manchester University Press 1985

Clark, Christopher, *The Sleepwalkers: How Europe Went to War in 1914*, Allen Lane, London 2012

Clark, Gregory and Robert C. Feenstra, 'Technology in the Great Divergence', in Michael D. Bordo, Alan M. Taylor, and Jeffrey G. Williamson (eds), *Globalization in Historical Perspective*, University of Chicago Press 2003

Clark, Samuel, 'Nobility, Bourgeoisie and the Industrial Revolution in Belgium', *Past and Present*, no. 105, November 1984, pp. 140–75

Clay, Karen and Werner Troesken, 'Did Frederick Brodie Discover the World's First Environmental Kuznets Curve? Coal Smoke and the Rise and Fall of the London Fog', in *The Economics of Climate Change: Adaptations Past and Present*, ed. Gary D. Libecap and Richard H. Steckel, University of Chicago Press 2011

Clayton, Paul and Judith Rowbotham, 'How the Mid-Victorians Worked, Ate and Died', *International Journal of Environmental Research and Public Health*, vol. 6, no. 3, 2009, pp. 1,235–53

Clegg, H. A., Alan Fox and A. F. Thompson, *A History of British Trade Unions since 1889*, vol. 1: *1889–1910*, Clarendon Press, Oxford 1964

Clendenning, P. H., 'The Economic Awakening of Russia in the Eighteenth Century', *Journal of European Economic History*, vol. 14, no. 3, Winter 1985

Clinton, William J., Address Before a Joint Session of the Congress on the State of the Union, 23 January 1996: http://www.presidency.ucsb.edu/ws/?pid=53091

Cobbett, William, *Manchester Lectures*, 1832: http://books.google.com/books?id=HLouAAAAMAAJ&pg=PR3&source=gbs_selected_pages&cad=3#v=onepage&q&f=false

Cobden, Richard, *Speeches on Questions of Public Policy*: http://www.econlib.org/library/YPDBooks/Cobden/cbdSPP.html

Cohen, Mark R., 'Medieval Jewry in the World of Islam', in *The Oxford Handbook of Jewish Studies*, ed. Martin Goodman, Jeremy Cohen, and David Jan Sorkin, Oxford University Press 2002

Cohen, Nancy, *The Reconstruction of American Liberalism, 1865–1914*, University of North Carolina Press 2002

Cohen, William B., 'The Lure of Empire: Why Frenchmen Entered the Colonial Service', *Journal of Contemporary History*, vol. 4, no. 1, 1969

Cohn, Samuel Kline, Jr., *The Laboring Classes in Renaissance Florence*, Academic Press, New York 1980

Cole, Juan R. I., *Colonialism and Revolution in the Middle East: Social and Cultural Origins of the 'Urabi Movement*, American University in Cairo Press, Cairo 1999

Coleridge, Samuel Taylor, *Specimens of the Table Talk of the Late Samuel Taylor Coleridge*, vol. 2, John Murray, London 1835: http://archive.org/stream/specimensoftable02cole#page/n5/mode/2up

Colgrove, James, 'The McKeown Thesis: A Historical Controversy and its Enduring Influence', *American Journal of Public Health*, vol. 92, no. 5, May 2002, pp. 725–9: http://www.ncbi.nlm.nih.gov/pmc/articles/PMC1447153/

Collier, Paul and Anke Hoeffler, 'Greed and Grievance in Civil War', *Oxford Economic Papers*, no. 56, 2004

Collini, Stefan, 'The Idea of "Character" in Victorian Political Thought', *Transactions of the Royal Historical Society*, vol. 35, 1985

Collini, Stefan, *Liberalism and Sociology: L. T. Hobhouse and Political Argument in England, 1880–1914*, Cambridge University Press 1979

Collins, E. J. T., 'Why Wheat? Choice of Food Grains in Europe in the Nineteenth and Twentieth Centuries', *Journal of European Economic History*, vol. 22, no. 1, 1993

Conde, Roberto Cortés, 'The Growth of the Argentine economy c. 1870–1914', in Bethell (ed.), *The Cambridge History of Latin America*, vol. V

Condorcet, Marquis de, *Esquisse d'un tableau historique des progrès de l'esprit humain*, ed. Oliver H. Prior, Vrin, Paris 1970

Connor, Tim and Kelly Dent, *Offside! Labour Rights and Sportswear Production in Asia*, Oxfam 2006

Conservative and Unionist Party, *Manifesto 2017, Forward Together: Our Plan for a Stronger Britain and a Prosperous Future*

Constant, Benjamin, 'Principes de politique', in *Écrits politiques*, Gallimard, Paris 1997

Conte, Giampaolo and Gaetano Sabatini, 'The Ottoman External Debt and its Features under European Financial Control (1881–1914)', *Journal of European Economic History*, vol. 43, no. 3, 2014

Cook, Chris, *The Routledge Companion to Britain in the Nineteenth Century*, Routledge, London 2005

Cookey, Sylvanus, *King Jaja of the Niger Delta: His Life and Times, 1821–1891*, NOK publishers, New York 1974

Coolidge, Archibald Cary, *The United States as a World Power*, Macmillan, New York 1908

Cooper, John Milton, Jr., *Pivotal Decades: The United States, 1900–1920*, Norton, New York 1990

Copeland, Dale C., *Economic Interdependence and War*, Princeton University Press 2015

Coppa, Frank J., 'Economic and Ethical Liberalism in Conflict: The Extraordinary Liberalism of Giovanni Giolitti', *Journal of Modern History*, vol. 42, no. 2, June 1970

Cornet, Christine, *État et entreprises en Chine XIXe–XXe siècles. Le chantier naval de Jiangnan, 1865–1937*, Éditions Arguments, Paris 1997

Cortés, Juan Donoso, *Essay on Catholicism, Liberalism, and Socialism Considered in their Fundamental Principles*, J. B. Lippincott & Co., Philadelphia, PA 1862

Costantini, Dino, *Una malattia europea. Il 'nuovo discorso coloniale' francese e i suoi critici*, Pisa University Press 2006

Costantini, Massimo, *L'albero della libertà economica. Il processo di scioglimento delle corporazioni veneziane*, Arsenale, Venice 1987

Coyle, Diane, *GDP: A Brief but Affectionate History*, Princeton University Press 2014

Crafts, N. F. R., 'Gross National Product in Europe 1870–1910: Some New Estimates', *Explorations in Economic History*, vol. 20, no. 4, October 1983

Craig, F. W. S., *British Electoral Facts: 1832–1987*, Parliamentary Research Services, Darmouth 1989

Craig, Gordon A., *Germany 1866–1945*, Oxford University Press 1981

Crainz, Guido, *Padania. Il mondo dei braccianti dall'Ottocento alla fuga dalle campagne*, Donzelli, Rome 1994

Crawcour, E. Sidney, 'The Tokugawa Heritage', in Lockwood (ed.), *The State and Economic Enterprise in Japan*

Creel, H. G., 'The Beginnings of Bureaucracy in China: The Origin of the *Hsien*', *Journal of Asian Studies*, vol. 23, no. 2, February 1964

Crepax, Nicola, 'Tradizione Lombarda, industria tessile e sviluppo economico', in Cafagna and Crepax (eds), *Atti di intelligenza e sviluppo economico*

Crisp, Olga, *Studies in the Russian Economy before 1914*, Macmillan, London 1976

Crispi, Francesco, *Carteggi politici inediti di Francesco Crispi (1860–1900)*, ed. Tommaso Palamenghi-Crispi, L'Universelle imprimerie polyglotte, Rome 1912: https://archive.org/stream/carteggipoliticioocris/carteggipoliticioocris_djvu.txt

Crook, J. Mordaunt, *The Rise of the Nouveaux Riches*, John Murray, London 1999

Crook, Malcolm and Tom Crook, 'L'isoloir universel? La globalisation du scrutin secret au XIXe siècle', *Revue d'histoire du XIXe siècle*, no. 43, 2011

Crosby, Alfred W., Jr., *The Columbian Exchange: Biological and Cultural Consequences of 1492*, Praeger, Westport, CT 2003 (first published 1972)

Cross, Gary, *A Quest for Time: The Reduction of Work in Britain and France, 1840–1940*, University of California Press 1989

Crossley, Pamela Kyle, *Orphan Warriors: Three Manchu Generations and the End of the Qing World*, Princeton University Press 1990

Crossley, Pamela Kyle, *The Wobbling Pivot: China since 1800*, Wiley-Blackwell, Oxford 2010

Crouch, Colin, 'A Third Way in Industrial Relations?', in Stuart White (ed.), *New Labour: The Progressive Future?* Palgrave Macmillan, London 2001

Crouch, Colin, *Industrial Relations and European State Traditions*, Clarendon Press, Oxford 1993

Crouch, Colin, *The Strange Non-Death of Neoliberalism*, Polity, Cambridge 2011

Cunningham, William, 'Nationalism and Cosmopolitanism in Economics', *Journal of the Royal Statistical Society*, vol. 54, no. 4, December 1891, pp. 644–62

Curti, Merle and Kendall Birr, 'The Immigrant and the American Image in Europe, 1860–1914', *Mississippi Valley Historical Review*, vol. 37, no. 2, September 1950, pp. 203–30

Cynamon, Barry Z. and Steven M. Fazzari, 'Inequality, the Great Recession and Slow Recovery', *Cambridge Journal of Economics*, vol. 40, no. 2, March 2016

D'Azeglio, Massimo, *I miei ricordi*, G. Barbèra, Florence 1891 (first published 1867)

d'Estournelles de Constant, Paul, *La conquête de la Tunisie*, Sfar, Paris 2002

D'Ideville, (Comte) Henri, *Le maréchal Bugeaud, d'après sa correspondance intime, et des documents inédits, 1784–1849*, vol. 2, Firmin-Didot, Paris 1881

Da Costa, Emília Viotti, 'Brazil: The Age of Reform, 1870–1889', in Bethell (ed.), *The Cambridge History of Latin America*, vol. V

Dahrendorf, Ralf, *Society and Democracy in Germany*, Weidenfeld and Nicolson, London 1967

Dalla Vecchia, Giovanni, 'The Revolt in Italy', *Contemporary Review*, vol. 74, July 1898

Dallenne, Pierre, Alain Nonjon, and Cédric Tellenne (eds), *De l'internationalisation à la globalisation*, Ellipses, Paris 2007

Daniel, Jean-Marc, *Histoire vivante de la pensée économique: Des crises et des hommes*, Pearson, Paris 2010

Danilevskij, Nikolaj, *La doctrine panslaviste d'après N. J. Danilewsky* (including *La Russie et l'Europe*, based on the 4th edition, St Petersburg, 1889), ed. J. J. Skupiewski, Bureaux de la Liberté Roumaine, Bucharest, 1890 (an abridged version of the original)

Dardot, Pierre and Christian Laval, *La nouvelle raison du monde. Essai sur la société néolibérale*, La Découverte, Paris 2009

Darwin, John, *The Empire Project: The Rise and Fall of the British World System, 1830–1970*, Cambridge University Press 2009

Daumard, Adeline, 'Puissance et inquiétudes de la société bourgeoise', in Fernand Braudel and Ernest Labrousse (eds), *Histoire économique et sociale de la France*, Tome IV: *L'ère industrielle et la société d'aujourd'hui (siècle 1880–1980)*, vol. 1, Presses Universitaire de France, Paris 1979

Daunton, Martin, 'Creating Consent: Taxation, War, and Good Government in Britain, 1688–1914', in Sven H. Steinmo (ed.), *The Leap of Faith: The Fiscal Foundations of Successful Government in Europe and America*, Oxford University Press 2018

Daunton, Martin J., '"Gentlemanly Capitalism" and British Industry 1820–1914', *Past & Present*, no. 122, February 1989

Daunton, Martin J., 'Trusting Leviathan: The Politics of Taxation, 1815–1914', in Winch and O'Brien (eds), *The Political Economy of British Historical Experience, 1688–1914*

Daunton, Martin J., *Royal Mail: The Post Office since 1840*, Bloomsbury, London 2015

Daunton, Martin J. (ed.), *Housing the Workers, 1850–1914: A Comparative Perspective*, Leicester University Press 1990

Davidoff, Leonore, 'Mastered for Life: Servant and Wife in Victorian and Edwardian England', *Journal of Social History*, vol. 7, no. 4, Summer 1974

Davies, Norman, *God's Playground: A History of Poland*, vol. 1: *The Origins to 1795*, and vol. 2: *1795 to the Present*, Clarendon Press, Oxford 1981

Davis, Jennifer, 'From "Rookeries" to "Communities": Race, Poverty and Policing in London, 1850–1985', *History Workshop Journal*, vol. 27, no. 1, 1989

Davis, Lance E. and Robert A. Huttenback, *Mammon and the Pursuit of Empire: The Economics of British Imperialism*, Cambridge University Press 1988

Davis, Mike, *Late Victorian Holocausts: El Niño Famines and the Making of the Third World*, Verso Books, London 2001

Dawson, William Harbutt, *Bismarck and State Socialism: An Exposition of the Social and Economic Legislation of Germany since 1870*, Swan Sonnenschein & Co., London 1890

de Groot, Joanna, 'Metropolitan Desires and Colonial Connections: Reflections on Consumption and Empire', in Hall and Rose (eds), *At Home with the Empire*

de Molinari, Gustave, 'De la production de la sécurité', *Journal des économistes*, 15 February 1849: http://www.panarchy.org/molinari/securite.html

de Mun, Albert, *Discours*, Tome 3, Poussielgue, Paris 1888–95

de Staël, Germaine, *Considérations sur les principaux événements de la Révolution française, depuis son origine jusques et compris le 8 juillet 1815*, vol. 3, J.-A. Latour, Liège 1818

de Vries, Jan and Ad van der Woude, *The First Modern Economy: Success, Failure, and Perseverance of the Dutch Economy, 1500–1815*, Cambridge University Press 1997

Deane, Phyllis and W. A. Cole, *British Economic Growth, 1688–1959: Trends and Structure*, Cambridge University Press 1967

Deaton, Angus, *The Great Escape: Health, Wealth, and the Origins of Inequality*, Princeton University Press 2013

Debaenst, Bruno, 'Belgian Social Law and its Journals: A Reflected History', in *C@hiers du CRHIDI*, vol. 37, 2015: http://popups.ulg.ac.be/1370-2262/index.php?id=183

Debs, Eugene V., Campaign Speech, Lyceum Theatre, Fergus Falls, Minnesota, 27 August 1912: https://www.marxists.org/archive/debs/works/1912/1912-capsoc.htm

Debuisson, Marc, 'The Decline of Infant Mortality in the Belgian Districts at the Turn of the 20th Century', *Journal of Belgian History*, vol. 31, nos 3–4, 2001

Defoe, Daniel, *A Tour Thro' the Whole Island of Great Britain: Divided into Circuits or Journeys*, S. Birt, T. Osborne et al., London 1748 (first published 1724)

Defuisseaux, Alfred, 'Le catéchisme du peuple', 1886: http://users.skynet.be/roger.romain/Defuisseaux.html

Del Bo, Dino (ed.), *I cattolici italiani di fronte al socialismo*, edizioni Cinque Lune, Rome 1956

Del Panta, Lorenzo, 'Mortalité infantile et post-infantile en Italie du XVIIIe au XXe siècle: tendances à long terme et différences régionales', *Annales de démographie historique*, 1994

Delaet, Jean-Louis, 'Les émeutes de mars 1886 au Pays de Charleroi', in *Fourmies et les premier mai*, ed. Madeleine Rebérioux, Éditions Ouvrières, Paris 1994

Delalande, Nicolas, 'Le consentement à l'impôt en France: les contribuables, l'administration et le problème de la confiance. Une étude de cas en Seine-et-Oise (années 1860–années 1930)', *Revue d'histoire moderne et contemporaine*, vol. 56, no. 2, April–June 2009, pp. 135–63

Delalande, Nicolas, *Les batailles de l'impôt: Consentement et résistance de 1789 à nos jours*, Seuil, Paris 2011

Dell, Fabien, 'Top Incomes in Germany Throughout the Twentieth Century: 1891–1998', in A. B. Atkinson and Thomas Piketty (eds), *Top Incomes over the Twentieth Century: A Contrast Between European and English-Speaking Countries*, Oxford University Press 2007

Demo, Edoardo, 'Le manifatture tra medioevo ed età moderna', in *L'industria vicentina dal medioevo a oggi*, ed. Giovanni Luigi Fontana, CLEUP, Padua 2004

Denis, Hector, *La dépression économique et sociale et l'histoire des prix*, Huysmans, Brussels 1895

Département des études, de la prospective et des statistiques (French Government), *Cultures croisées. Références interculturelles des Allemands, des Italiens et des Français*, November 2008: http://www.culture.gouv.fr/depsculteuturdees

Derfler, Leslie, *Alexandre Millerand: The Socialist Years*, Mouton, The Hague 1977

Deringil, Selim, *The Well-Protected Domains: Ideology and the Legitimation of Power in the Ottoman Empire, 1876–1909*, I. B. Tauris, London and New York 1998

Dertilis, Georges B., 'Réseaux de crédit et stratégies du capital', in Georges B. Dertilis (ed.), *Banquiers, usuriers et paysans. Réseaux de crédit et stratégies du capital en Grèce (1780–1930)*, La Découverte, Paris 1988

Descours-Gatin, Chantal, *Quand l'opium finançait la colonisation en Indochine*, L'Harmattan, Paris 1992

Desolre, Guy, 'Un siècle de premiers mai et de réduction du temps de travail', in Van der Vorst (ed.), *Cent ans de droit social belge*

Deutsch, Karl W., *Nationalism and Social Communication*, MIT and Wiley, New York 1953

Dewerpe, Alain, *Le monde du travail en France, 1800–1950*, Armand Colin, Paris 1998

Dicey, A. V., *Introduction to the Study of the Law of the Constitution*, Macmillan, London 1889

Dicey, A .V., *Lectures on the Relation between Law and Public Opinion in England during the Nineteenth Century*, Macmillan, London 1962 (based on his 1898 lectures at the Harvard Law School, elaborated and published in 1905)

Dickens, Charles, *The Letters of Charles Dickens*, vol. 8, Clarendon Press, Oxford 2006

Didion, Joan, *Slouching towards Bethlehem*, Burning Man Books, Seattle 2009

Digby, William, *'Prosperous' British India: A Revelation from Official Records*, T. Fisher Unwin, London 1901

Diner, Hasia R., *Hungering for America: Italian, Irish, and Jewish Foodways in the Age of Migration*, Harvard University Press 2002

Diner, Steven J., *A Very Different Age: Americans of the Progressive Era*, Hill and Wang, New York 1998

Ding, X. L., *The Decline of Communism in China: Legitimacy Crisis 1977–1989*, Cambridge University Press 1994

Diogenes Laertius, *Lives of Eminent Philosophers*, trans. R. D. Hicks, vol. 2, Heinemann, London and New York 1925

Disraeli, Benjamin (Lord Beaconsfield), *Selected Speeches*, ed. T. E. Kebbel, 2 vols, Longmans, Green and Co., London 1882

Disraeli, Benjamin, *Sybil, or The Two Nations*, Penguin, London 1980

Disraeli, Benjamin, *The Letters of Disraeli to Lady Chesterfield and Lady Bradford*, vol. 1, Appleton and Co., New York 1929: https://ia800302.us.archive.org/14/items/lettersofdisrael009336mbp/lettersofdisrael009336mbp.pdf

Dmowski, Roman, *La question polonaise*, Armand Colin, Paris 1909

Dore, R. P., 'Talent and the Social Order in Tokugawa Japan', *Past & Present*, no. 21, April 1962

Doriot, Jacques, *Les colonies et le communisme*, Éditions Montaigne, Paris 1929

Dostoyevsky, Fyodor, *The Devils*, trans. Michael R. Katz, Oxford University Press 2008

Dostoyevsky, Fyodor, *The Diary of a Writer*, Ianmead, Haslemere 1984

Dowler, Wayne, *Russia in 1913*, Northern Illinois University Press 2010

Doyle, Peter, '"Nothing New and Nothing True": Some Socialist Reactions to *Rerum Novarum*', in *Rerum Novarum. Écriture, contenu et réception d'une encyclique*, École Française de Rome, 1997

Drake, Paul W., *Between Tyranny and Anarchy: A History of Democracy in Latin America, 1800–2006*, Stanford University Press 2009

Drapac, Vesna, 'Christians and Conservatives in Twentieth-Century France', *Historical Journal*, vol. 39, no. 3, 1996

Drumont, Édouard, *La France juive*, vol. 1, Éditions du Trident, La Librairie Française, Paris 1986

Du Bois, W. E. B., *Black Reconstruction in America*, Albert Saifer, Philadelphia, PA 1935

Du Camp, Maxime, *Expédition des Deux-Siciles*, Calmann Lévy, Paris 1881 (first published 1861)

Duara, Prasenjit, *Culture, Power, and the State: Rural North China, 1900–1942*, Stanford University Press 1988

Duclert, Vincent, *Jaurès 1859–1914. La politique et la légende*, Éditions Autrement, Paris 2013

Dudden, Alexis, *Japan's Colonization of Korea: Discourse and Power*, University of Hawai'i Press 2005

Duggan, Christopher, *Francesco Crispi, 1818–1901: From Nation to Nationalism*, Oxford University Press 2002

Duménil, Gérard and Dominique Lévy, *La grande bifurcation. En finir avec le néolibéralisme*, La Découverte, Paris 2014

Durand, Jean-Dominique, 'La réception de *Rerum Novarum* par les évêques français', in *Rerum Novarum. Écriture, contenu et réception d'une encyclique*, École Française de Rome, 1997

Durandin, Catherine, *Histoire des Roumains*, Fayard, Paris 1995

Dustūr. Aperçu sur les constitutions des états arabes et islamiques, Brill, Leiden 1966 – reprint of the entry *Dustūr* (constitution) in the *Encyclopédie de l'Islam*

Dutton, David, *One of Us? A Century of Australian Citizenship*, University of New South Wales Press 2002

Duval, Romain, 'Le rôle de l'idéologie et des croyances dans l'économie politique', *Revue d'économie politique*, vol. 117, no. 4, July–August 2007

Dwyer-Lindgren L., A. Bertozzi-Villa, R. W. Stubbs, C. Morozoff, J. P. Mackenbach, F. J. van Lenthe, A. H. Mokdad, and C. J. L. Murray, 'Inequalities in Life Expectancy among US Counties, 1980 to 2014', *JAMA Internal Medicine*, 8 May 2017: http://jamanetwork.com/journals/jamainternalmedicine/fullarticle/2626194

Echenberg, Myron, *Africa in the Time of Cholera: A History of Pandemics from 1817 to the Present*, Cambridge University Press 2011

Echenberg, Myron, *Plague Ports: The Global Urban Impact of Bubonic Plague, 1894–1901*, New York University Press 2007

Economist Intelligence Unit, *Democracy Index 2012*: http://pages.eiu.com/rs/eiu2/images/Democracy-Index-2012.pdf, and Economist Intelligence Unit, *Democracy Index 2014*: http://www.eiu.com/Handlers/WhitepaperHandler.ashx?fi=Democracy-index-2014.pdf&mode=wp&campaignid=Democracy0115

Edelstein, Michael, 'Foreign Investment and Empire, 1860–1914', in Roderick Floud and Donald McCloskey (eds), *The Economic History of Britain since 1700*, vol. 2: *1860 to the 1970s*, Cambridge University Press 1981

Edelstein, Michael, *Overseas Investment in the Age of High Imperialism: The United Kingdom, 1850–1914*, Columbia University Press 1982

Edgerton, David, *The Rise and Fall of the British Nation*, Allen Lane, London 2018

Edvinsson, Sören and Hans Nilsson, 'Swedish Towns during Industrialization', *Annales de démographie historique*, 1999

Eichengreen, Barry, *The European Economy since 1945*, Princeton University Press 2007

Eidelberg, Philip Gabriel, *The Great Rumanian Peasant Revolt of 1907: Origins of a Modern Jacquerie*, E. J. Brill, Leiden 1974

Einaudi, Luigi, 'La politica economica delle classi operaie italiane nel momento presente', in Luigi Einaudi, *Cronache economiche e politiche di un trentennio*, vol. 1: *1893–1902*, Einaudi, Turin 1959, originally in *Critica sociale*, 1 July 1899

Eldridge, C. C. (ed.), *British Imperialism in the Nineteenth Century*, Macmillan, London 1984

Eley, Geoff, *Reshaping the German Right: Radical Nationalism and Political Change after Bismarck*, Yale University Press 1980

Eliot, George, *Impressions of Theophrastus Such*, William Blackwood and Sons, Edinburgh and London 1879

Elkins, Caroline, *Imperial Reckoning: The Untold Story of Britain's Gulag in Kenya*, Holt and Co., New York 2005

Elon, Amos, *Herzl*, Weidenfeld and Nicolson, London 1975

Elshakry, Marwa, *Reading Darwin in Arabic, 1860–1950*, University of Chicago Press 2014

Elwitt, Sanford, *The Third Republic Defended: Bourgeois Reform in France, 1880–1914*, Louisiana State University Press 1986

Eng, Robert Y., 'Luddism and Labor Protest among Silk Artisans and Workers in Jiangnan and Guangdong, 1860–1930', *Late Imperial China*, vol. 11, no. 2, December 1990

Engels, Friedrich, 'Extraordinary Revelations. – Abd-el-Kader. – Guizot's Foreign Policy', *The Northern Star*, 22 January 1848, in Marx and Engels, *Collected Works*, vol. 6

Engels, Friedrich, 'Letter to Friedrich Sorge', 29 April 1886: https://www.marxists.org/archive/marx/works/1886/letters/86_04_29.htm

Engels, Friedrich, *Anti-Dühring*, Progress Publishers, Moscow 1969

Engels, Friedrich, *The Condition of the Working Class in England*, Oxford University Press 1993

Engerman, Stanley L. and Kenneth L. Sokoloff, 'Technology and Industrialization, 1790–1914', in Engerman and Gallman (eds), *Cambridge Economic History of the United States*, vol. 2

Engerman, Stanley L. and Kenneth L. Sokoloff, 'The Evolution of Suffrage Institutions in the New World', *Journal of Economic History*, vol. 65, no. 4, December 2005

Engerman, Stanley L. and Robert E. Gallman (eds), *The Cambridge Economic History of the United States*, vol. 2: *The Long Nineteenth Century*, Cambridge University Press 2000

Englander, David, *Poverty and Poor Law Reform in Nineteenth-Century Britain, 1834–1914: From Chadwick to Booth*, Routledge, London 2013

Etemad, Bouda, 'Grandeur et vicissitudes du débat colonial. Tendances récentes de l'histoire de la colonisation', *Tiers-Monde*, vol. 28, no. 112, 1987

Etemad, Bouda, *De l'utilité des empires. Colonisation et prospérité de l'Europe*, Armand Colin, Paris 2005

Étienne, Eugène, *Les compagnies de colonisation*, Augustin Challamel, Paris 1897

Eurostat Statistics, https://ec.europa.eu/eurostat/data/database

Evans, Peter B., Dietrich Rueschemeyer, and Theda Skocpol (eds), *Bringing the State Back In*, Cambridge University Press 1985

Evans, Robert, Jr., 'Evolution of the Japanese System of Employer-Employee Relations, 1868–1945', *Business History Review*, vol. 44, no. 1, 1970

Ewen, Elizabeth, *Immigrant Women in the Land of Dollars: Life and Culture on the Lower East Side, 1890–1925*, Monthly Review Press, New York 1985

Fairbank, John K. and Kwang-Ching Liu (eds), *The Cambridge History of China*, vol. 11: *Late Ch'ing, 1800–1911*, part 2, Cambridge University Press 1980

Fang Xing, 'The Retarded Development of Capitalism', in Xu and Wu (eds), *Chinese Capitalism, 1522–1840*

Farmer, Paul, *Infections and Inequalities: The Modern Plagues*, University of California Press 1999

Farrar, Marjorie Milbank, *Principled Pragmatist: The Political Career of Alexandre Millerand*, Berg, New York and Oxford 1991

Faujas-Saint-Fond, Barthélemy, *Voyage en Angleterre, en Écosse et aux Îles Hébrides*, 2 vols, H. J. Jansen, Paris 1797

Fawn, Rick and Jiří Hochman, *Historical Dictionary of the Czech State*, Scarecrow Press, Lanham, MD 2010

Federico, Giovanni, 'Italy's Late and Unprofitable Forays into Empire', *Revista de Historia Económica*, vol. 16, no. 1, Winter 1998

Fedor, Thomas Stanley, *Patterns of Urban Growth in the Russian Empire during the Nineteenth Century*, University of Chicago, Department of Geography, Research Paper no. 163, 1975

Feinstein, Charles, 'New Estimates of Average Earnings in the United Kingdom, 1880–1913', *Economic History Review*, vol. 43, no. 4, November 1990

Feinstein, Charles, 'Structural Change in the Developed Countries during the Twentieth Century', *Oxford Review of Economic Policy*, vol. 15, no. 4, 1999

Feldman, David, 'Was the Nineteenth Century a Golden Age for Immigrants?', in Andreas Fahrmeir, Olivier Faron, and Patrick Weil (eds), *Migration Control in the North Atlantic World: The Evolution of State Practices in Europe and the United States from the French Revolution to the Inter-War Period*, Berghahn Books, Oxford and New York 2005

Felice, Costantino, *Il disagio di vivere. Il cibo, la casa, le malattie in Abruzzo e Molise dall'Unità al secondo dopoguerra*, Franco Angeli, Milan 1990

Fenin, Aleksandr I., *Coal and Politics in Late Imperial Russia: Memoirs of a Russian Mining Engineer*, ed. Susan McCaffray, Northern Illinois University Press 1990

Fenoaltea, Stefano, 'Manchester, Manchesteriano . . . *Dekwakoncoz*?', in Cafagna and Crepax (eds), *Atti di intelligenza e sviluppo economico*

Fenwick, Carolyn C. (ed.), *The Poll Taxes of 1377, 1379, and 1381, Part 1: Bedfordshire-Leicestershire*, Oxford University Press for the British Academy, London 1998

Ferguson, Niall, 'Political Risk and the International Bond Market between the 1848 Revolution and the Outbreak of the First World War', *Economic History Review*, vol. 59, no. 1, 2006

Ferguson, Niall, *Empire: How Britain Made the Modern World*, Penguin, London 2004

Ferreira Duarte, João, 'The Politics of Non-Translation: A Case Study in Anglo-Portuguese Relations', *TTR: traduction, terminologie, rédaction*, vol. 13, no. 1, 2000: http://www.erudit.org/revue/TTR/2000/v13/n1/037395ar.pdf

Ferrier, R. W., *The History of the British Petroleum Company*, vol. 1: *The Developing Years 1901–1932*, Cambridge University Press 1982

Ferro, Marc, 'Introduction', in *Le livre noir du colonialisme*, ed. Marc Ferro, Robert Laffont, Paris 2003

Ferro, Marc, *Pétain*, Fayard, Paris 1987

Ferry, Jules, speech of 28 July 1885, in *1885: le tournant colonial de la République. Jules Ferry contre Georges Clemenceau*, introduction by Gilles Manceron, La Découverte/Poche, Paris 2007

Ferry, Jules, *Discours et opinions*, vol. V, ed. Paul Robiquet, Armand Colin, Paris 1898

Feuerwerker, Albert, 'Economic Trends in the Late Ch'ing Empire, 1870–1911', in Fairbank and Liu (eds), *The Cambridge History of China*, vol. 11: *Late Ch'ing, 1800–1911*, part 2

Fieldhouse, D. K., *The Theory of Capitalist Imperialism*, Longmans, London 1967

Figes, Orlando, *A People's Tragedy: The Russian Revolution 1891–1924*, Pimlico, London 1997

Figes, Orlando, *Crimea: The Last Crusade*, Allen Lane, London 2010

Figes, Orlando, *The Whisperers: Private Life in Stalin's Russia*, Allen Lane, London 2007

Finkel, Caroline, *Osman's Dream: The Story of the Ottoman Empire 1300–1923*, John Murray, London 2005

Finlayson, Geoffrey, *Citizen, State and Social Welfare in Britain, 1830–1990*, Clarendon Press, Oxford 1994

Finzi, Roberto, *Anti-Semitism: From its European Roots to the Holocaust*, Interlink Books, Northampton, MA 1999

Fischer, Lars, *The Socialist Response to Anti-Semitism in Imperial Germany*, Cambridge University Press 2007

Fishman, William J., 'The Condition of East End Jewry in 1888', West Central Lecture 1986, delivered at University College London, 24 June 1986

Flaubert, Gustave, *Correspondance*, vol. IV, Gallimard, Paris 1998

Fletcher, C. R. L. and Rudyard Kipling, *A History of England*, Doubleday, Page and Co., New York 1911

Fligstein, Neil, *Markets, Politics, and Globalization,* Acta Universitatis Upsaliensis: Studia Oeconomiae Negotiorum 42, Uppsala University 1997

Flint, John, *Cecil Rhodes*, Hutchinson, London 1976

Flora, Peter and Arnold J. Heidenheimer (eds), *The Development of Welfare States in Europe and America*, Transaction Books, Piscataway, NJ 1981

Flornoy, Eugène, *La lutte par l'association. L'action libérale populaire*, J. Gabalda et Cie, Paris 1907

Floud, Roderick and Donald McCloskey (eds), *The Economic History of Britain since 1700*, vol. 2: *1860–1939*, 2nd ed., Cambridge University Press 1994

Fogel, Robert W., *The Escape from Hunger and Premature Death, 1700–2100: Europe, America, and the Third World*, Cambridge University Press 2004

Fohlin, Caroline, 'Universal Banking in Pre-World War I Germany: Model or Myth?', *Explorations in Economic History*, vol. 36, no.4, 1999

Foner, Eric, 'Why is there no Socialism in the United States?', *History Workshop Journal*, no. 17, 1984

Foner, Eric, *Nothing but Freedom: Emancipation and its Legacy*, Louisiana State University Press 1983

Foner, Eric, *Reconstruction: America's Unfinished Revolution, 1863–1877*, Harper and Row, New York 1988

Fontana, Biancamaria, *Germaine de Staël: A Political Portrait*, Princeton University Press 2016

Fontana, Giovanni Luigi, 'Imprenditori, imprese e territorio dalla prima alla seconda rivoluzione industriale', in *L'industria vicentina dal medioevo a oggi*, ed. Giovanni Luigi Fontana, Centro Studi sull'impresa, Vicenza 2004

Ford, Henry, *My Life and Work*, Heinemann, London 1922

Fouskas, Vassilis K. and Constantine Dimoulas, *Greece, Financialization and the European Union*, Palgrave Macmillan, London 2013

Fox, Daniel M., *The Discovery of Abundance: Simon N. Patten and the Transformation of Social Theory*, Cornell University Press 1967

Fraile, Pedro and Álvaro Escribano, 'The Spanish 1898 Disaster: The Drift towards National-Protectionism', *Revista de Historia Económica*, vol. 16, no. 1, Winter 1998

Franceschi, Franco and Ilaria Taddei, *Le città italiane nel Medioevo, XII–XIV secolo*, Il Mulino, Bologna 2012

Francis I, (Pope), 'Address of His Holiness Pope Francis to Representatives of the Confederation of Italian Cooperatives', 28 February 2015: https://w2.vatican.va/content/francesco/en/speeches/2015/february/documents/papa-francesco_20150228_confcooperative.html

Frankel, Jonathan, *Prophecy and Politics: Socialism, Nationalism, and the Russian Jews, 1862–1917*, Cambridge University Press 1981

Franklin, Benjamin, 'Advice to a Young Tradesman, Written by an Old One', 1748: http://franklinpapers.org/franklin//framedvolumes.jsp;jsessionid=608ADED3CD5C773C127B274349F89A31

Freeden, Michael, *The New Liberalism: An Ideology of Social Reform*, Clarendon Press, Oxford 1978

Freeze, Gregory L., 'Church and Politics in Late Imperial Russia: Crisis and Radicalization of the Clergy', in Anna Geifman (ed.), *Russia under the Last Tsar: Opposition and Subversion, 1894–1917*, Blackwell, Oxford 1999

Freeze, Gregory L., 'Reform and Counter Reform 1855–1890', in Gregory L. Freeze (ed.), *Russia: A History*, Oxford University Press 2009

Fremigacci, Jean, 'L'état colonial français, du discours mythique aux réalités (1880–1940)', *Matériaux pour l'histoire de notre temps*, nos 32–3, 1993

Fridlizius, Gunnar, 'Sweden's Exports, 1850–1960: A Study in Perspective', *Economy and History*, vol. 6, 1963

Friedman, Max Paul, 'Beyond "Voting with their Feet": Toward a Conceptual History of "America" in European Migrant Sending Communities, 1860s to 1914', *Journal of Social History*, vol. 40, no. 3, Spring 2007

Friedman, Milton, *Why Government Is the Problem*, Hoover Press, Stanford, CA 2013; originally the Wriston Lecture presented in New York City, 19 November 1991

Fuchs, Rachel G., 'Morality and Poverty: Public Welfare for Mothers in Paris, 1870–1900', *French History*, vol. 2, no. 3, 1988

Fukuzawa, Yukichi, *The Autobiography of Yukichi Fukuzawa*, trans. Eiichi Kiyooka, Columbia University Press 2007

Fumey, Gilles and Olivier Etcheverria, *Atlas mondial des cuisines et gastronomies*, Éditions Autrement, Paris 2004

Fumian, Carlo, 'Per una storia della tecnocrazia. Utopie meccaniche e ingegneria sociale tra Otto e Novecento', *Rivista storica italiana*, vol. 124, no. 3, December 2012, pp. 908–59

Fung, Edmund S. K., 'State Building, Capitalist Development, and Social Justice: Social Democracy in China's Modern Transformation, 1921–1949', *Modern China*, vol. 31, no. 3, July 2005

Furlani, Silvio, 'Le riforme elettorali del 1882', in *Il parlamento italiano 1861–1988*, vol. V: *1877–1887*, Nuova CEI, Milan 1989

Gaillard, Jean-Michel, *Jules Ferry*, Fayard, Paris 1989

Gaillard, Jean-Michel and André Lespagnol, *Les mutations économiques et sociales au XIXe siècle (1780–1880)*, Nathan, Paris 1984

Gaillard, Jeanne, 'Les associations de production et la pensée politique en France (1852–1870)', *Le Mouvement Social*, no. 52, July–September 1966

Galambos, Louis, 'State-Owned Enterprises in a Hostile Environment: The US Experience', in *The Rise and Fall of State-Owned Enterprises in the Western World*, ed. Pier Angelo Toninelli, Cambridge University Press 2000

Galambos, Louis, *The Public Image of Big Business in America, 1880–1940*, Johns Hopkins University Press 1975

Galbraith, John Kenneth, *The Affluent Society*, Houghton Mifflin Harcourt, Boston 1998

Gall, Lothar, *Bismarck: The White Revolutionary*, 2 vols: *1815–1871* and *1871–1898*, Unwin Hyman, London 1990

Gallagher, J. and R. Robinson, 'The Imperialism of Free Trade', *Economic History Review*, 1953

Gallo, Ezequiel, 'Argentina: Society and Politics, 1880–1916', in Bethell (ed.), *The Cambridge History of Latin America*, vol. V

Galton, Francis, Letters to *The Times*, 26 December 1857 and 5 June 1873: http://galton.org/letters/africa-for-chinese/AfricaForTheChinese.htm

Gambino, Richard, *Vendetta: The True Story of the Largest Lynching in U.S. History*, Guernica Editions, Toronto 1998

Gandhi, Mahatma, *The Collected Works of Mahatma Gandhi* (electronic book), vol. 1: *1884–30 November 1896*, Publications Division Government of India, New Delhi 1999, p. 410: https://www.gandhiashramsevagram.org/gandhi-literature/mahatma-gandhi-collected-works-volume-1.pdf

Ganiage, Jean, 'North Africa', in *The Cambridge History of Africa*, vol. 6, Cambridge University Press 1985

Garelli, Alessandro, *I Salarj e la classe operaja in Italia*, Libreria Angelo Penato, Turin 1874

Garrigues, Jean, 'Un autre modèle pour la République: l'influence des Britanniques sur les libéraux français (1870–1880)', in Sylvie Aprile and Fabrice Bensimon (eds), *La France et l'Angleterre au XIXe siècle: échanges, représentations, comparaisons*, Creaphis éditions, Paris 2006

Gash, Norman, *Pillars of Government and Other Essays on State and Society, c. 1770–1880*, Edward Arnold, London 1986

Gasparri, Stefano and Cristina La Rocca, *Tempi barbarici. L'Europa occidentale tra antichità e medioevo (300–900)*, Carocci, Rome 2013

Gatrell, Peter, 'Industrial Expansion in Tsarist Russia, 1908–14', *Economic History Review*, vol. 35, no. 1, February 1982, pp. 99–110

Gatrell, Peter, 'The Russian Fiscal State, 1600–1914', in Bartolomé Yun-Casalilla and Patrick K. O'Brien (eds), *The Rise of Fiscal States: A Global History 1500–1914*, Cambridge University Press 2012

Gautier, Théophile, 'Eugène Plon. Thorvaldsen, sa vie et son oeuvre', *Le Moniteur Universel*, 8 July 1867

Gazeley, Ian and Andrew Newell, 'Urban Working-Class Food Consumption and Nutrition in Britain in 1904', *Economic History Review*, vol. 68, no. 1, February 2015

GB Historical GIS/University of Portsmouth, Population Statistics Total Population, *A Vision of Britain through Time*: http://www.visionofbritain.org.uk/unit/10076924/cube/TOT_POP

Geehr, Richard, *Karl Lueger: Mayor of Fin de Siècle Vienna*, Wayne State University Press 1990

Geifman, Anna (ed.), *Russia under the Last Tsar: Opposition and Subversion, 1894–1917*, Blackwell, Oxford 1999

Gélinas, Jacques B., *Dictionaire critique de la globalization. Les mots du pouvoir, le pouvoir des mots*, Ecosociété, Montréal 2008

Genovese, Eugene D., *The Southern Front*, University of Missouri Press 1995

Genovese, Eugene D., *The Southern Tradition: The Achievement and Limitations of an American Conservatism*, Harvard University Press 1994

Genovese, Eugene D. and Elizabeth Fox Genovese, *Slavery in White and Black: Class and Race in the Southern Slaveholders' New World Order*, Cambridge University Press 2008

Gentile, Emilio, *L'Italia giolittiana*, Il Mulino, Bologna 1990

George, Henry, Speech of 1 April 1885: http://www.historyisaweapon.com/defcon1/georgecripov.html

George, Henry, 'The Chinese in California', *New York Daily Tribune*, 1 May 1869

George, Henry, *Progress and Poverty*, J. M. Dent and Sons, London n.d.

Germain, André, *La bourgeoisie qui brûle. Propos d'un témoin, 1890–1914*, Sun, Paris 1951

Gernet, Jacques, *Le monde chinois*, 2 vols, Armand Colin, Paris 1972 and 2006

Gerő, András, *Modern Hungarian Society in the Making: The Unfinished Experience*, Central European University Press 1995

Gerschenkron, Alexander, 'Russia: Agrarian Policies and Industrialization, 1861–1917', in Alexander Gerschenkron, *Continuity in History and Other Essays*, Belknap Press, Cambridge, MA 1968

Gerschenkron, Alexander, 'The Rate of Industrial Growth in Russia since 1885', *Journal of Economic History*, vol. 7, *Supplement: Economic Growth: A Symposium* (1947), pp. 144–74

Gerschenkron, Alexander, *Economic Backwardness in Historical Perspective*, Belknap Press, Cambridge, MA 1962

Gibbons, (Cardinal) James, *A Retrospect of Fifty Years*, 1916: http://www.forgottenbooks.com/readbook/A_Retrospect_of_Fifty_Years_v1_1000611995#229

Giffin, Frederick C., 'The "First Russian Labor Code": The Law of June 3, 1886', *Russian History/Histoire Russe*, vol. 2, no. 2, 1975

Giffin, Frederick C., 'The Formative Years of the Russian Factory Inspectorate, 1882–1885', *Slavic Review*, vol. 25, no. 4, December 1966

Gildea, Robert, *Children of the Revolution: The French, 1799–1914*, Allen Lane, London 2008

Gilman, Marie-Hélène, 'L'empire colonial et la longue stagnation', in Yves Breton, Albert Broder, and Michel Lutfalla (eds), *La longue stagnation en France. L'autre dépression, 1873–1907*, Economica, Paris 1997

Gilmour, David, *Curzon: Imperial Statesman, 1859–1925*, John Murray, London 2004

Ginio, Eyal, '*El dovér el mas sànto*: The Mobilization of the Ottoman Jewish Population during the Balkan Wars (1912–13)', in Hannes Grandits, Nathalie Clayer, and Robert Pichler (eds), *Conflicting Loyalties in the Balkans: The Great Powers, the Ottoman Empire and Nation-Building*, I. B. Tauris, London 2011

Giolitti, Giovanni, *Discorsi extraparlamentari*, Einaudi, Turin 1952

Giolitti, Giovanni, *Discorsi parlamentari*, vol. 2, Camera dei Deputati, Rome 1953

Girardet, Raoul, *L'idée coloniale en France de 1871 à 1962*, Pluriel, Paris 1972

Girault, René, 'Place et rôle des échanges extérieurs', in Fernand Braudel and Ernest Labrousse (eds), *Histoire économique et sociale de la France*, Tome IV: *L'ère industrielle et la société d'aujourd'hui (siècle 1880–1980)*, vol. 1, Presses Universitaires de France, Paris 1979

Glade, William, 'Latin America and the International Economy, 1870–1914', in Bethell (ed.), *The Cambridge History of Latin America*, vol. IV

Gladstone, William, Speech in the House of Commons, 27 April 1866: http://hansard.millbanksystems.com/commons/1866/apr/27/adjourned-debate-eighth-night

Gladstone, William, Speech in the House of Commons, 11 May 1864: http://hansard.millbanksystems.com/commons/1864/may/11/second-reading

Gladstone, William, 'The Budget – Financial Statement' *The Times*, report of 17 April 1863. Also in Hansard: The Budget – Financial Statement, Ways and Means, *HC Deb*, 16 April 1863, pp. 244–5: http://hansard.millbanksystems.com/commons/1863/apr/16/the-budget-financial-statement-ways-and#S3V0170P0_18630416_HOC_22

Gladstone, William, *Gladstone Diaries*, vol. X: *January 1881–June 1883*, ed. H. C. G. Matthew, Clarendon Press, Oxford 1990

Glickman, Lawrence B., *A Living Wage: American Workers and the Making of Consumer Society*, Cornell University Press 1997

Goethe, J. W. von, *Werke*, vol. 1, Christian Wegner Verlag, Hamburg 1952

Goldin, Claudia D. and Frank D. Lewis, 'The Economic Cost of the American Civil War: Estimates and Implications', *Journal of Economic History*, vol. 35, no. 2, June 1975

Goldsmith, Raymond W., 'The Economic Growth of Tsarist Russia 1860–1913', *Economic Development and Cultural Change*, vol. 9, no. 3, *Essays in the Quantitative Study of Economic Growth*, April 1961

Goldstein, Melvyn C., 'Serfdom and Mobility: An Examination of the Institution of "Human Lease" in Traditional Tibetan Society', *Journal of Asian Studies*, vol. 30, no. 3, May 1971

Goldthwaite, Richard A. 'The Economy of Renaissance Italy: The Preconditions for Luxury Consumption', in *I Tatti Studies: Essays in the Renaissance*, vol. 2, Villa I Tatti and Harvard University Center, Florence 1987

Gómez-Galvarriato, Aurora and Jeffrey G. Williamson, 'Was it Prices, Productivity or Policy? Latin American Industrialisation after 1870', *Journal of Latin American Studies*, vol. 41, no. 4, November 2009

Gompers, Samuel and Herman Gutstadt, *Meat vs. Rice: American Manhood Against Asiatic Coolieism: Which Shall Survive?* (reprinted in 1908 by the Asiatic Exclusion League)

Gonjo, Yasuo, 'Le "plan Freycinet", 1878–1882: un aspect de la "grande dépression" économique en France', *Revue historique*, no. 503, July–September 1972

Gordadzé, Thorniké, 'La réforme du passé: l'effort historiographique de construction de la nation géorgienne', *Revue d'études comparatives Est-Ouest*, vol. 30, no. 1, March 1999

Gordon, Robert J., 'Does the "New Economy" Measure up to the Great Inventions of the Past?', *Journal of Economic Perspectives*, vol. 14, no. 4, Autumn 2000

Gordon, Robert J., *The Rise and Fall of American Growth: The U.S. Standard of Living since the Civil War*, Princeton University Press 2016

Gorlin, Robert H., 'Problems of Tax Reform in Imperial Russia', *Journal of Modern History*, vol. 49, no. 2 (June 1977), pp. 246–65

Gorshkov, Boris B., *Russia's Factory Children: State, Society and the Law, 1800–1917*, University of Pittsburgh Press 2009

Gott, Richard, *Britain's Empire: Resistance, Repression and Revolt*, Verso, London 2012

Gougeon, Jacques-Pierre, 'Les élites dirigeantes dans l'Allemagne des années 1890', in *Les limites de siècles. Champs de forces conservatrices et régressives depuis les temps modernes*, ed. Marita Gilli, vol. 1, Presses Universitaires Franc-Comtoises 2001

Gould, Lewis L., *Reform and Regulation: American Politics, 1900–1916*, John Wiley and Sons, New York, NY 1978

Gourevitch, Peter, *Politics in Hard Times: Comparative Responses to International Economic Crises*, Cornell University Press 1986

Gourou, Pierre, *Les Paysans du delta tonkinois* (Thèse de doctorat), Les Éditions d'art et d'histoire, Paris 1936

Graham, David, 'Developing into a Thing of the Past', *Toronto Star*, 3 April 2008: https://www.thestar.com/life/2008/04/03/developing_into_a_thing_of_the_past.html

Gramsci, Antonio, *Il Risorgimento*, Editori Riuniti, Rome 1971

Gramsci, Antonio, *Selections from Prison Notebooks*, ed. and trans. Quintin Hoare and Geoffrey Nowell Smith, Lawrence and Wishart, London 1971

Granozzi, Luciano, *Alla ricerca dei 'veri' capitalisti*, CUECM, Catania 2002

Grataloup, Christian, *Géohistoire de la mondialisation*, Armand Colin, Paris 2007

Gray, Peter, 'The Peculiarities of Irish Land Tenure, 1800–1914: From Agent of Impoverishment to Agent of Pacification', in Winch and O'Brien (eds), *The Political Economy of British Historical Experience, 1688–1914*

Green, E. H. H., *The Crisis of Conservatism: The Politics, Economics and Ideology of the British Conservative Party, 1880–1914*, Routledge, London 1995

Green, Simon J. D. and Richard C. Whiting (eds), *The Boundaries of the State in Modern Britain*, Cambridge University Press 1996

Gregory, Paul, 'Economic Growth and Structural Change in Tsarist Russia: A Case of Modern Economic Growth?', *Soviet Studies*, vol. 23, no. 3, January 1972, pp. 418–34

Griffin, Emma, *Liberty's Dawn: A People's History of the Industrial Revolution*, Yale University Press 2013

Grigg, David, 'The Nutritional Transition in Western Europe', *Journal of Historical Geography*, vol. 21, no. 3, 1995

Gubin, Eliane, 'Libéralisme économique et paternalisme en Belgique au XIXe siècle', in Aerts, Beaud, and Stengers (eds), *Liberalism and Paternalism in the 19th Century*

Guerra, François-Xavier, *Le Mexique. De l'Ancien Régime à la Révolution*, vol. 2, L'Harmattan, Paris 1985

Guerrazzi, Amedeo Osti, *Grande industria e legislazione sociale in età giolittiana*, Paravia, Turin 2000

Guerrero, Andrés, 'Naissance des bourgeoisies latino-américaines au XXe siècle: le cas de l'Équateur', *Annales*, vol. 35, no. 6, November–December 1980, pp. 1,171–93

Gueslin, André, *Gens pauvres, pauvres gens dans la France du XIXe siècle*, Aubier, Paris 1998

Gunton, George, 'The Economic and Social Aspect of Trusts', *Political Science Quarterly*, vol. 3, no. 3, September 1888

Guthrie, Doug, *China and Globalization: The Social, Economic and Political Transformation of Chinese Society*, Routledge, London 2012

Gutman, Herbert G., *Slavery and the Numbers Game: A Critique of 'Time on the Cross'*, University of Illinois Press 1975

Gutman, Herbert G., *Work, Culture, and Society in Industrializing America: Essays in American Working-Class and Social History*, Knopf, New York 1976

Guyot, Yves, *La famille Pichot. Scènes de l'enfer social*, Jules Rouff, Paris 1882

Gyáni, Gábor, 'Budapest', in Daunton (ed.), *Housing the Workers*

Ha-Joon Chang, *Kicking Away the Ladder: Development Strategy in Historical Perspective*, Anthem Press, London 2003

Habakkuk, H. J., *American and British Technology in the Nineteenth Century: The Search for Labour-Saving Inventions*, Cambridge University Press 1962

Habibi, Mariam, *L'interface France-Iran 1907–1938. Une diplomatie voilée*, L'Harmattan, Paris 2004

Hague, William, Statement of the Secretary of State for Foreign and Commonwealth Affairs, House of Commons, 6 June 2013, Mau Mau Claims (Settlement): http://www.publications.parliament.uk/pa/cm201314/cmhansrd/cm130606/debtext/130606-0002.htm#1306064600005

Hahamovitch, Cindy, 'Creating Perfect Immigrants: Guestworkers of the World in Historical Perspective', *Labor History*, vol. 44, no. 1, February 2003, pp. 69–94

Hahn, Steven, 'Class and State in Postemancipation Societies: Southern Planters in Comparative Perspective', *American Historical Review*, vol. 95, no. 1, February 1990

Halbwachs, Maurice, *La classe ouvrière et les niveaux de vie*, Gordon and Breach, Paris, London, and New York 1970 (reprint of 1st edition, 1912, published by Félix Alcan)

Hale, Charles A., 'Political and Social Ideas in Latin America, 1870–1930', in Bethell (ed.), *The Cambridge History of Latin America*, vol. IV

Hale, Charles A., *The Transformation of Liberalism in Late Nineteenth-Century Mexico*, Princeton University Press 1989

Hall, Catherine and Sonya Rose (eds), *At Home with the Empire: Metropolitan Culture and the Imperial World*, Cambridge University Press 2006

Hall, Michael M. and Hobart A. Spalding Jr., 'The Urban Working Class and Early Latin American Labour Movements, 1880–1930', in Bethell (ed.), *The Cambridge History of Latin America*, vol. IV

Hamerow, Theodore S., *The Birth of a New Europe*, University of North Carolina Press 1983

Hammurabi, *The Code of Hammurabi*, trans. L. W. King, 1915: http://www.sacred-texts.com/ane/ham/index.htm

Handcock, W. D. (ed.), *English Historical Documents*, vol. 10: *1874–1914*, Routledge, London 1996

Handford, Peter, 'Edward John Eyre and the Conflict of Laws', *Melbourne Law Review*, vol. 32, no. 3, 2008: http://www.austlii.edu.au/au/journals/MelbULawRw/2008/26.html

Hanham, H. J., *Elections and Party Management: Politics in the Time of Disraeli and Gladstone*, Harvester Press, Hassocks, Sussex 1978

Hanioğlu, M. Şükrü, *Preparation for a Revolution: The Young Turks, 1902–1908*, Oxford University Press 2001

Hannah, Leslie, 'Logistics, Market Size, and Giant Plants in the Early Twentieth Century: A Global View', *Journal of Economic History*, vol. 68, no. 1, March 2008, pp. 46–79

Hanousek, Jan, Evžen Kočenda, and Jan Svejnar, 'Privatization in Central and Eastern Europe and the Commonwealth of Independent States', in Roland (ed.), *Privatization: Successes and Failures*

Hao, Yen-P'ing, 'Cheng Kuan-ying: The Comprador as Reformer', *Journal of Asian Studies*, vol. 29, no. 1, November 1969

Hao, Yen-P'ing and Erh-min Wang, 'Changing Chinese Views of Western Relations, 1840–95', in Fairbank and Liu (eds), *The Cambridge History of China*, vol. 11: *Late Ch'ing, 1800–1911*, part 2

Harcave, Sidney, *Count Sergei Witte and the Twilight of Imperial Russia*, M. E. Sharpe, New York, NY 2004

Hardy, Anne, *The Epidemic Streets: Infectious Disease and the Rise of Preventive Medicine, 1856–1900*, Clarendon Press, Oxford 1993

Harkness, Margaret (under the pseudonym of John Law), *Out of Work*, Swan Sonnenstein & Co., London 1888

Harley, C. Knick, 'International Competitiveness of the Antebellum American Cotton Textile Industry', *Journal of Economic History*, vol. 52, no. 3, September 1992

Harris, Jose, 'Political Thought and the Welfare State 1870–1940: An Intellectual Framework for British Social Policy', *Past & Present*, no. 135, May 1992

Harris, José, 'The Transition to High Politics in English Social Policy, 1880–1914', in Michael Bentley and John Stevenson (eds), *High and Low Politics in Modern Britain*, Clarendon Press, Oxford 1983

Harrison, Austin, *England & Germany: Republished from 'The Observer'*, Macmillan, London 1907: http://archive.org/stream/englandandgermanoohARRUoft#page/n5/mode/2up

Harrison, Henrietta, 'Chinese and British Gift Giving in the Macartney Embassy of 1793', lecture at the School of Advanced Study, University of London, 6 February 2014, available as a podcast: https://www.youtube.com/watch?v=PDzHrQi8oTQ

Harrison, Henrietta, *China: Inventing the Nation*, Bloomsbury, London 2001

Harrison, Mark, *Disease and the Modern World*, Polity, Cambridge 2004

Hart, Robert, *'These from the Land of Sinim': Essays on the Chinese Question*, Chapman & Hall, London 1901

Harvey, Charles and Peter Taylor, 'Mineral Wealth and Economic Development: Foreign Direct Investment in Spain, 1851–1913', *Economic History Review*, vol. 40, no. 2, 1987

Hatzfeld, Henri, *Du paupérisme à la sécurité sociale (1850–1940)*, Presses Universitaires de Nancy 2004 (first published 1971)

Hau, Michel, 'Industrialization and Culture: The Case of Alsace', *Journal of European Economic History*, vol. 29, nos 2–3, Autumn–Winter 2000

Haxthausen, August von, *The Russian Empire, its People, Institutions, and Resources*, Chapman and Hall, London 1856, vol. 2: http://books.google.co.uk/books?id=1fAuAAAAYAAJ&printsec=frontcover&source=gbs_ge_summary_r&cad=0#v=onepage&q&f=false

Hayek, Friedrich, *The Fatal Conceit: The Errors of Socialism*, University of Chicago Press 2011

Hays, Samuel P., *The Response to Industrialism, 1885–1914*, University of Chicago Press 1995 (first ed. 1957)

Hayter, Susan and Valentina Stoevska, 'Social Dialogue Indicators: International Statistical Inquiry 2008–09. Technical Brief', ILO November 2011: http://laborsta.ilo.org/applv8/data/TUM/TUD%20and%20CBC%20Technical%20Brief.pdf

Hayward, Jack, *Fragmented France: Two Centuries of Disputed Identity*, Oxford University Press 2007

Hegel, G. W. F., *The Philosophy of History*, trans. J. Sibree, P. F. Collier and Son, New York 1901: http://babel.hathitrust.org/cgi/pt?id=coo1.ark:/13960/t5j96qh5b;view=1up;seq=5

Hegel, G. W. F., *Lectures on the Philosophy of World History*, vol. 1: *Manuscripts of the Introduction and the Lectures of 1822–23*, ed. and trans. Robert F. Brown and Peter C. Hodgson, Clarendon Press, Oxford 2011

Heikkinen, Sakari and Riitta Hjerppe, 'The Growth of Finnish Industry in 1860–1913: Causes and Linkages', *Journal of European Economic History*, vol. 16, no. 2, 1987

Helvetius, Claude-Adrien, 'Memoir on the Present State of the Government of the United Provinces', in *The Low Countries in Early Modern Times: A Documentary History*, ed. Herbert T. Rowen, Macmillan, London 1972

Hennock, E. P., 'Social Policy in the Bismarck Era: A Progress Report', *German History*, vol. 21, no. 2, 2003

Hennock, E. P., *The Origin of the Welfare State in England and Germany, 1850–1914: Social Policies Compared*, Cambridge University Press 2007

Herman, Arthur, *Gandhi and Churchill*, Random House, London 2010

Hermet, Guy, *Les populismes dans le monde. Une histoire sociologique (XIXe–XXe siècle)*, Fayard, Paris 2001

Hern, Alex and Nick Fletcher, 'Fangs: The Lighting Rise of Facebook, Amazon, Netflix and Google', *The Guardian*, 29 April 2017

Hervé, Gustave, *L'internationalisme*, Giard & Brière, Paris 1910

Herzen, Alexander, *My Past and Thoughts: The Memoirs of Alexander Herzen*, Chatto and Windus, London 1974

Herzl, Theodor, *The Diaries of Theodor Herzl*, Gollancz, London 1958

Herzl, Theodor, *The Jewish State*, Penguin, London 2010

Hewitson, Mark, 'German Public Opinion and the Question of Industrial Modernity: Wilhelmine Depictions of the French Economy', *European Review of History*, vol. 7, no. 1, Spring 2000

Higgs, Edward, 'Domestic Servants and Households in Victorian England', *Social History*, vol. 8, no. 2, May 1983

Higgs, Edward, 'Women, Occupations and Work in the Nineteenth Century Censuses', *History Workshop Journal*, vol. 23, no. 1, 1987

Higham, John, *Strangers in the Land: Patterns of American Nativism, 1860–1925*, Atheneum, New York 1973, first published 1955

Hilferding, Rudolf, *Finance Capital: A Study of the Latest Phase of Capitalist Development*, Routledge and Kegan Paul, London 1910

Hill, Christopher, *Reformation to Industrial Revolution: The Making of Modern English Society, 1530–1780*, Penguin, London 1969

Hilton, Rodney H., 'Introduction', in T. H. Aston and C. H. E. Philpin (eds), *The Brenner Debate: Agrarian Class Structure and Economic Development in Pre-Industrial Europe*, Cambridge University Press 1985

Hilton, Tim, *John Ruskin*, vol. 2: *The Later Years*, Yale University Press 2000

Hinde, Wendy, *Richard Cobden: A Victorian Outsider*, Yale University Press 1987

Hirata, Helena and Kurumi Sugita, 'Politique paternaliste et division sexuelle du travail: le cas de l'industrie japonaise', *Le Mouvement Social*, no. 144, July–September 1988

Hirschman, Albert O., *The Passions and the Interests: Political Arguments for Capitalism before its Triumph*, Princeton University Press 1977

Hirschmeier, Johannes and Tsunehiko Yui, *The Development of Japanese Business, 1600–1973*, Harvard University Press 1975

Hirshman, Charles, Samuel Preston, and Vu Manh Loi, 'Vietnamese Casualties during the American War: A New Estimate', *Population and Development Review*, vol. 21, no. 4, December 1995

Hitchins, Keith, *Rumania, 1866–1947*, Oxford University Press 1994

Hitler, Adolf, *Mein Kampf*, Hutchinson, London 1969

Hjerppe, Riitta, *The Finnish Economy, 1860–1985: Growth and Structural Change*, Bank of Finland, Helsinki 1989

Hobsbawm, Eric, *Industry and Empire*, Penguin, London 1968

Hobsbawm, Eric, *Nations and Nationalism since 1780*, Cambridge University Press 1993

Hobsbawm, Eric, *Primitive Rebels: Studies in Archaic Forms of Social Movements in the 19th and 20th Centuries*, Norton, New York 1959

Hobsbawm, Eric, *The Age of Empire 1875–1914*, Weidenfeld and Nicolson, London 1987

Hobson, J. A., 'Free Trade and Foreign Policy', *Contemporary Review*, vol. 74, August 1898

Hobson, J. A., *Imperialism: A Study*, James Pott and Co., New York 1902

Hochschild, Adam, *King Leopold's Ghost: A Story of Greed, Terror, and Heroism in Colonial Africa*, Macmillan, London 2000

Hoffmann, Christhard, 'Political Culture and Violence against Minorities: The Antisemitic Riots in Pomerania and West Prussia', in Hoffmann, Bergmann, and Smith (eds), *Exclusionary Violence: Antisemitic Riots in Modern German History*

Hoffmann, Christhard, Werner Bergmann, and Helmut Walser Smith (eds), *Exclusionary Violence: Antisemitic Riots in Modern German History*, University of Michigan Press 2002

Hoffmann, Stanley, *Essais sur la France. Déclin ou renouveau?*, Seuil, Paris 1974

Hofstadter, Richard, 'The Folklore of Populism', in *Antisemitism in the United States*, ed. Leonard Dinnerstein, Holt, Rinehart, and Winston, New York 1971

Hofstadter, Richard, *Social Darwinism in American Thought*, Beacon Press, Boston, MA 1992 (first published in 1944)

Holmes, Colin, 'The Tredegar Riots of 1911: Anti-Jewish Disturbances in South Wales', *Welsh History Review*, vol. 11, no. 2, December 1982

Holmes, Colin, *Anti-Semitism in British Society, 1876–1939*, Edward Arnold, London 1979

Holmes, Colin J., 'Laissez-Faire in Theory and Practice: Britain 1800–1875', *Journal of European Economic History*, vol. 5, no. 3, Winter 1976, pp. 671–88

Hopkins, A. G., 'Informal Empire in Argentina: An Alternative View', *Journal of Latin American Studies*, vol. 26, no. 2, May 1994, pp. 469–84

Hopkins, A. G., 'The Victorians and Africa: A Reconsideration of the Occupation of Egypt, 1882', *Journal of African History*, vol. 27, no. 2, 1986

Hoppen, K. Theodore, *Elections, Politics and Society in Ireland, 1832–1885*, Oxford University Press 1984

Horie, Yasuzō, 'Modern Entrepreneurship in Meiji Japan', in Lockwood (ed.), *The State and Economic Enterprise in Japan*

Horowitz, Daniel, *The Morality of Spending: Attitudes toward the Consumer Society in America, 1875–1940*, Johns Hopkins University Press 1985

Horowitz, Richard S., 'Breaking the Bonds of Precedent: The 1905–6 Government Reform Commission and the Remaking of the Qing Central State', *Modern Asian Studies*, vol. 37, no. 4, 2003, pp. 775–97

Hosking, Geoffrey, *Russia and the Russians: A History*, Harvard University Press 2001

Houang, François, introduction to Yan Fu (Yen Fou), *Les manifestes de Yen Fou*, Fayard, Paris 1977

Howland, Douglas, 'Society Reified: Herbert Spencer and Political Theory in Early Meiji Japan', *Comparative Studies in Society and History*, vol. 42, no. 1, January 2000

Howland, Douglas, *Borders of Chinese Civilization: Geography and History at Empire's End*, Duke University Press 1996

Hroch, Miroslav, *Social Preconditions of National Revival in Europe: A Comparative Analysis of the Social Composition of Patriotic Groups among the Smaller European Nations*, Cambridge University Press 1985

Hsü, Immanuel C. Y., 'Late Ch'ing Foreign Relations, 1866–1905', in Fairbank and Kwang-Ching Liu (eds), *The Cambridge History of China*, vol. 11: *Late Ch'ing, 1800–1911*, part 2

Hsü, Immanuel C. Y., *The Rise of Modern China*, Oxford University Press 1990

Huang, Philip C. C., 'The Paradigmatic Crisis in Chinese Studies: Paradoxes in Social and Economic History', *Modern China*, vol. 17, no. 3, July 1991, pp. 299–341

Huberman, Michael, 'Working Hours of the World Unite? New International Evidence of Worktime, 1870–1913', *Journal of Economic History*, vol. 64, no. 4, December 2004, pp. 964–1,001

Hughes, Robert, *The Culture of Complaint: The Fraying of America*, Oxford University Press 1993

Hugo, Victor, 'Discours sur l'Afrique', 18 May 1879, in *Actes et Paroles IV*, in *Politique*, Robert Laffont, Paris 1985

Hull, Isabel V., *Absolute Destruction: Military Culture and the Practices of War in Imperial Germany*, Cornell University Press 2004

Hume, David, *Selected Essays*, Oxford University Press 2008

Humphrey, Caroline, 'Creating a Culture of Disillusionment: Consumption in Moscow, a Chronicle of Changing Times', in Daniel Miller (ed.), *Worlds Apart: Modernity through the Prism of the Local*, Routledge, New York and London 1995

Humphrey, Caroline, 'Odessa: Pogroms in a Cosmopolitan City', in Caroline Humphrey and Vera Skvirskaja (eds), *Post-Cosmopolitan Cities: Explorations of Urban Coexistence*, Berghahn Books, New York and Oxford 2012

Hung, Ho-fung, *Protest with Chinese Characteristics*, Columbia University Press 2011

Huret, Jules, *Enquête sur la question sociale en Europe*, Perrin, Paris 1897: ftp://ftp.bnf.fr/002/N0024317_PDF_1_-1DM.pdf

Hutton, Patrick H., 'Popular Boulangism and the Advent of Mass Politics in France, 1886–90', *Journal of Contemporary History*, vol. 11, no. 1, 1976, pp. 85–106

Hutton, Will, *The Writing on the Wall: China and the West in the 21st Century*, Little, Brown, London 2007

Hyden-Hanscho, Veronika, 'Invisible Globalization: French Hats in Habsburg Vienna, 1650–1750', *Journal of European Economic History*, vol. 45, no. 3, 2016, pp. 11–54

Ichiko, Chuzo, 'Political and Institutional Reform, 1901–11', in Fairbank and Liu (eds), *The Cambridge History of China*, vol. 11: *Late Ch'ing, 1800–1911*, part 2

Iliffe, John, 'The Organization of the Maji Maji Rebellion', *Journal of African History*, vol. 8, no. 3, November 1967, pp. 495–512

Iliffe, John, *The Emergence of African Capitalism*, Macmillan, London 1983

Imai, Yoshio, 'N. G. Chernyshevskii: Pioneer of the Russian Cooperative Movement', in Don Karl Rowney (ed.), *Imperial Power and Development: Papers on Pre-Revolutionary Russian History*, Slavica Publishers, Columbus, OH 1990

Inagaki, Manjirō, *Japan and the Pacific, and a Japanese View of the Eastern Question*, T. Fisher Unwin, London 1890

Inglis, K. S., 'English Nonconformity and Social Reform, 1880–1900', *Past & Present*, no. 13, April 1958

Ingraham, Christopher, '15 Baltimore Neighborhoods Have Lower Life Expectancies than North Korea', *Washington Post*, 30 April 2015: http://www.washingtonpost.com/blogs/wonkblog/wp/2015/04/30/baltimores-poorest-residents-die-20-years-earlier-than-its-richest

Ingraham, Christopher, 'The Entire Coal Industry Employs Fewer People than Arby's', *Washington Post*, 31 March 2017: https://www.washingtonpost.com/news/wonk/wp/2017/03/31/8-surprisingly-small-industries-that-employ-more-people-than-coal/?utm_term=.38c8e500b1f3

Inkster, Ian, 'Technological and Industrial Change: A Comparative Essay', in *The Cambridge History of Science*, vol. 4, ed. Roy Porter, Cambridge University Press 2003

International Institute of Strategic Studies, *The Military Balance 2015*: https://www.iiss.org//media//images/publications/the%20military%20balance/milbal2016/mb%202016%20top%2015%20defence%20budgets%202015.jpg?la=en

International Monetary Fund (IMF), *World Economic Outlook Database*, April 2014: http://www.imf.org/external/pubs/ft/weo/2014/01/weodata/index.aspx

Iordachi, Constantin, 'The Unyielding Boundaries of Citizenship: The Emancipation of "Non-Citizens" in Romania, 1866–1918', *European Review of History*, vol. 8, no. 2, 2001

Iriye, Akira, 'Japan's Drive to Great-Power Status', in *The Cambridge History of Japan*, vol. 5: *The Nineteenth Century*, ed. Marius B. Jansen, Cambridge University Press 1989

Iriye, Akira, 'The Internationalization of History', *American Historical Review*, vol. 94, no. 1, February 1989

Iriye, Akira, *Pacific Estrangement: Japanese and American Expansion, 1897–1911*, Harvard University Press 1972

Israel, Jonathan I., *Dutch Primacy in World Trade, 1585–1740*, Clarendon Press, Oxford 1989

Israel, Jonathan I., *Radical Enlightenment: Philosophy and the Making of Modernity 1650–1750*, Oxford University Press 2001

Israel Ministry of Immigrant Absorption, http://www.moia.gov.il/English/FeelingIsrael/AboutIsrael/Pages/aliya2.aspx

Jacini, Stefano, *Pensieri sulla politica italiana*, G. Civelli, Florence 1889

Jacini, Stefano (ed.), *Atti della Giunta per la inchiesta agraria e sulle condizioni della classe agricola*, vol. XI, Tomo 1, *Province di Roma e Grosseto*, Forzani, Rome 1884. The author of this section of the Jacini Report was Senator Francesco Nobili-Vitelleschi: https://play.google.com/books/reader?id=Oi0oAAAAYAAJ&printsec=frontcover&output=reader&authuser=0&hl=en&pg=GBS.PA793

Jackson, Ashley, *The British Empire: A Very Short Introduction*, Oxford University Press 2013

Jacobs, Meg, 'The Politics of Plenty in the Twentieth-Century United States', in Martin Daunton and Matthew Hilton (eds), *The Politics of Consumption: Material Culture and Citizenship in Europe and America*, Berg, Oxford 2001

Jacobson, Lisa, *Raising Consumers: Children and the American Mass Market in the Early Twentieth Century*, Columbia University Press 2004

Jacquet, Olivier and Gilles Laferté, 'Le contrôle républicain du marché. Vignerons et négociants sous la Troisième République', *Annales*, no. 5, September–October 2006, pp. 1,147–70

James, Lawrence, *Churchill and Empire*, Weidenfeld and Nicolson, London 2013

Janos, Andrew C., 'Modernization and Decay in Historical Perspective: The Case of Romania', in Kenneth Jowitt (ed.), *Social Change in Romania, 1860–1940: A Debate on Development in a European Nation*, University of California Press 1978, pp. 72–116

Janos, Andrew C., *East Central Europe in the Modern World: The Politics of the Borderlands from Pre- to Postcommunism*, Stanford University Press 2000

Janos, Andrew C., *The Politics of Backwardness in Hungary, 1825–1945*, Princeton University Press 1982

Jansen, Marius B., 'Japan and the Chinese Revolution of 1911', in Fairbank and Liu (eds), *The Cambridge History of China*, vol. 11: *Late Ch'ing, 1800–1911*, part 2

Jansen, Marius B., 'Japanese Imperialism: Late Meiji Perspectives', in *The Japanese Colonial Empire, 1895–1945*, ed. Ramon Hawley Myers and Mark R. Peattie, Princeton University Press 1984

Jansen, Marius B., *China in the Tokugawa World*, Harvard University Press 1992

Jansen, Marius B., *The Making of Modern Japan*, Belknap Press, Cambridge, MA 2000

Janzé, Charles-Alfred de, *Les serfs de la voie ferrée. La vérité et les compagnies*, Tolmer, Paris 1881

Jaurès, Jean, 'En Algérie', in *Oeuvres de Jean Jaurès*, vol. 6, Fayard, Paris 2001, originally in *La Petite République*, 29 January 1898

Jaurès, Jean, 'Les compétitions coloniales', *La Petite République*, 17 May 1896: http://www.histoire.presse.fr/actualite/infos/jean-jaures-competitions-coloniales-in-petite-republique-du-17-mai-1896–22–11–2010–16782

Jaurès, Jean, *Les plus beaux discours*, Librio, Paris 2014

Jedlicki, Jerzy, *A Suburb of Europe: Nineteenth-Century Polish Approaches to Western Civilization*, Central European University Press 1999

Jefferson, Thomas, *Writings*, Memorial Edition, vol. 15: http://etext.virginia.edu/jefferson/quotations/jeff1325.htm

Jelavich, Charles and Barbara, *The Establishment of the Balkan National States 1804–1920*, University of Washington Press 1977

Jenco, Leigh, *Changing Referents: Learning Across Space and Time in China and the West*, Oxford University Press 2015

Jevons, William Stanley, *The Coal Question: An Inquiry Concerning the Progress of the Nation, and the Probable Exhaustion of our Coal-Mines*, Macmillan, London 1866 (first ed. 1865)

Jevons, William Stanley, *The State in Relation to Labour*, Macmillan, London 1882

Jewish Encyclopedia 1906: http://www.jewishencyclopedia.com/articles/12909-rothschild#anchor9, entry 'Alphonse de Rothschild'

Johnson, Paul, *Making the Market: Victorian Origins of Corporate Capitalism*, Cambridge University Press 2010

Johnson, Samuel, *The Life of Savage*: http://andromeda.rutgers.edu/~jlynch/Texts/savage.html

Johnston, H. H. (Sir 'Harry'), 'The Development of Tropical Africa under British Auspices', *Fortnightly Review*, no. 86, October 1890

Joly, Bertrand, 'Le parti royaliste et l'affaire Dreyfus (1898–1900)', *Revue historique*, no. 546, April–June 1983, pp. 311–64

Joly, Laurent, 'Les débuts de l'action française (1899–1914) ou l'élaboration d'un nationalisme antisémite', *Revue historique*, no. 639, July 2006

Jonas, Raymond, *The Battle of Adwa: African Victory in the Age of Empire*, Harvard University Press 2011

Jones, Colin, 'Perspectives on Poor Relief, Health Care and the Counter-Reformation in France', in *Health Care and Poor Relief in Counter-Reformation Europe*, ed. Ole Peter Grell and Andrew Cunningham, with Jon Arrizabalaga, Routledge, London 1999

Jones, Greta, 'Spencer and his Circle', in Jones and Peel (eds), *Herbert Spencer: The Intellectual Legacy*

Jones, Greta and Robert A. Peel (eds), *Herbert Spencer: The Intellectual Legacy*, The Galton Institute, London 2004

Jones, Stephen F., 'Russian Imperial Administration and the Georgian Nobility: The Georgian Conspiracy of 1832', *The Slavonic and East European Review*, vol. 65, no. 1, January 1987

Jouanique, Pierre, 'Three Medieval Merchants: Francesco di Marco Datini, Jacques Coeur and Benedetto Cotrugli', *Accounting, Business & Financial History*, vol. 6, no. 3, 1996, pp. 261–75

Juglar, Clément, *Des crises commerciales et de leur retour périodique en France, en Angleterre et aux États-Unis*, Guillaumin et Cie, Paris 1862

Jussila, Osmo, Seppo Hentilä, and Jukka Nevakivi, *From Grand Duchy to a Modern State: A Political History of Finland since 1809*, Hurst and Co., London 1999

Kahan, Arcadius, 'Government Policies and the Industrialization of Russia', *Journal of Economic History*, vol. 27, no. 4, December 1967

Kahan, Arcadius, *Russian Economic History: The Nineteenth Century*, Chicago University Press 1989

Kandiyoti, Deniz, 'End of Empire: Islam, Nationalism and Women in Turkey', in Deniz Kandiyoti (ed.), *Women, Islam and the State*, Temple University Press 1991

Kann, Robert A., *A History of the Habsburg Empire 1526–1918*, University of California Press 1974

Kant, Immanuel, 'On the Common Saying: That may be correct in theory, but it is of no use in practice', in Immanuel Kant, *Practical Philosophy*, ed. Mary Gregor, Cambridge University Press 1996

Kant, Immanuel, 'On the Use of Teleological Principles in Philosophy', in *Anthropology, History, and Education*, ed. Günter Zöller and Robert B. Louden, Cambridge University Press 2007

Kant, Immanuel, 'Perpetual Peace: A Philosophical Sketch', in *Political Writings*, ed. Hans Reiss, Cambridge University Press 1991

Kappeler, Andreas, *The Russian Empire: A Multi-Ethnic History*, Longman, Harlow 2001

Karabel, Jerome, 'The Reasons Why', *The New York Times*, 8 February 1979

Karl, Rebecca E., 'Creating Asia: China in the World at the Beginning of the Twentieth Century', *American Historical Review*, vol. 103, no. 4, October 1998

Kassab, Ahmed, *Histoire de la Tunisie. L'époque contemporaine*, Société tunisienne de diffusion, Tunis 1976

Katus, László, 'Economic Growth in Hungary during the Age of Dualism', *Social Economic Researches on the History of East-Central Europe, Studia Historica* 62, Budapest 1970

Katz, Friedrich, 'Mexico: Restored Republic and Porfiriato, 1867–1910', in Bethell (ed.), *The Cambridge History of Latin America*, vol. V

Kaufman, Burton I., 'The Organizational Dimension of United States Economic Foreign Policy, 1900–1920', *Business History Review*, vol. 46, no. 1, Spring 1972

Kaul, Chandrika, '"You cannot govern by force alone": W. H. Russell, *The Times* and the Great Rebellion', in Marina Carter and Crispin Bates (eds), *Mutiny at the Margins*, vol. 3, Sage, London 2013

Kay, James Phillips, *The Moral and Physical Condition of the Working Classes Employed in the Cotton Manufacture in Manchester*, Ridgway, London 1832: https://archive.org/stream/moralphysicalconookaysuoft#page/n3/mode/2up

Keddie, Nikki R., *Roots of Revolution: An Interpretive History of Modern Iran*, Yale University Press 1981

Kelly, Marjorie, 'The Incredibly Unproductive Shareholder', *Harvard Business Review*, vol. 80, no. 1, January 2002, pp. 18–19

Kelly, Morgan and Cormac Ó Gráda, 'Living Standards and Mortality since the Middle Ages', *Economic History Review*, vol. 67, no. 2, 2014

Kennedy, John F., Inaugural Address, 20 January 1961: http://www.jfklibrary.org/Research/Research-Aids/Ready-Reference/JFK-Quotations/Inaugural-Address.aspx

Kennedy, Paul, 'Continuity and Discontinuity in British Imperialism, 1815–1914', in Eldridge (ed.), *British Imperialism in the Nineteenth Century*

Kertzer, David, *The Popes against the Jews: The Vatican's Role in the Rise of Modern Anti-Semitism*, Knopf, New York 2001

Kévorkian, Raymond, *The Armenian Genocide: A Complete History*, I. B. Tauris, London 2011

Keynes, John Maynard, 'National Self-Sufficiency', originally in the *New Statesman* (8 July 1933), now in *Activities 1931–1939*, vol. XXI of *The Collected Writings of John Maynard Keynes*, Macmillan, London, and Cambridge University Press 1982

Keynes, John Maynard, 'The End of Laissez-Faire', 'Economic Possibilities for Our Grandchildren', in *Essays in Persuasion* in *The Collected Writings of John Maynard Keynes*, vol. IX, Macmillan, London 1972

Keynes, John Maynard, *The Economic Consequences of the Peace*, Harcourt, Brace, and Howe, New York 1920

Keynes, John Maynard, *The General Theory of Employment, Interest, and Money*, Macmillan, London 1967

Khoudour-Castéras, David, 'Welfare State and Labor Mobility: The Impact of Bismarck's Social Legislation on German Emigration before World War I', *Journal of Economic History*, vol. 68, no. 1, March 2008, pp. 211–43

Kiesewetter, Hubert, 'Competition for Wealth and Power: The Growing Rivalry between Industrial Britain and Industrial Germany 1815–1914', *Journal of European Economic History*, vol. 20, no. 2, Fall 1991

Kindleberger, Charles P., 'Review of *The Economy of Turkey; The Economic Development of Guatemala; Report on Cuba*', *Review of Economics and Statistics*, vol. 34, no. 4, November 1952

Kindleberger, Charles P., *Manias, Panics and Crashes: A History of Financial Crises*, 4th edition, Palgrave, London 2000

Kindleberger, C. P., 'The Rise of Free Trade in Western Europe, 1820–1875', *Journal of Economic History*, vol. 35, no. 1, March 1975

King, Desmond, *The Liberty of Strangers: Making the American Nation*, Oxford University Press 2005

Kingsley, Charles, *His Letters and Memories of his Life*, ed. his wife, vol. 1, Henry S. King & Co., London 1877

Kipnis, Ira, *The American Socialist Movement, 1897–1912*, Haymarket Books, Chicago, IL 2005, first published 1952

Kirzner, Israel M., 'Menger, Classical Liberalism, and the Austrian School of Economics', in *Carl Menger and his Legacy in Economics*, ed. Bruce J. Caldwell, Duke University Press 1990

Klein, Herbert S., *A Population History of the United States*, Cambridge University Press 2004

Klein, Maury, *The Genesis of Industrial America, 1870–1920*, Cambridge University Press 2007

Klessmann, Christoph, 'Long-Distance Migration, Integration and Segregation of an Ethnic Minority in Industrial Germany: The Case of the "Ruhr Poles"', in Klaus Bade (ed.), *Population, Labour and Migration in 19th- and 20th-Century Germany*, Berg, Leamington Spa 1987

Klier, John Doyle, *Russians, Jews and the Pogroms of 1881–1882*, Cambridge University Press 2011

Klier, John D. and Shlomo Lambroza (eds), *Pogroms: Anti-Jewish Violence in Modern Russian History*, Cambridge University Press 1992

Knight, Alan, *The Mexican Revolution*, vol. 2: *Counter-Revolution and Reconstruction*, Cambridge University Press 1986

Knight, Nathaniel, 'Was the Intelligentsia Part of the Nation? Visions of Society in Post-Emancipation Russia', in *Kritika: Explorations in Russian and Eurasian History*, vol. 7, no. 4, Fall 2006, pp. 733–58

Kochanski, Halik, 'Wolseley and the South African War', in John Gooch (ed.), *The Boer War: Direction, Experience and Image*, Frank Cass, London 2000

Koenig, Louis W., *Bryan: A Political Biography of William Jennings Bryan*, Putnam's Sons, New York 1971

Koestler, Arthur, *Promise and Fulfilment: Palestine 1917–1949*, Macmillan, New York 1949

Kolko, Gabriel, *The Triumph of Conservatism: A Reinterpretation of American History, 1900–1916*, Free Press of Glencoe, New York 1963

Körner, Martin, 'Expenditure', in Richard Bonney (ed.), *Economic Systems and State Finance*, Clarendon Press, Oxford 1995

Kossert, Andreas, 'Founding Father of Modern Poland and Nationalist Anti-semite: Roman Dmowski', in Rebecca Haynes and Martyn Rady (eds), *In the Shadow of Hitler*, I. B. Tauris, London 2011

Kōtoku, Shūsui, *L'impérialisme, le spectre du XXe siècle*, translated into French by Christine Lévy, CNRS éditions, Paris 2008

Kousser, J. Morgan, *The Shaping of Southern Politics: Suffrage Restriction and the Establishment of the One-Party South, 1880–1910*, Yale University Press 1974

Kristol, Irving, 'Urban Civilization and its Discontents', *Commentary*, July 1970

Krugman, Paul, 'In Praise of Cheap Labor', *Slate Magazine*, 21 March 1997

Krugman, Paul, 'Safer Sweatshops', *The New York Times*, 8 July 2013

Kubricht, A. Paul, 'The National-Economic Implications of the Formation of the Czech Agrarian Party (1899)', in Volgyes (ed.), *The Peasantry of Eastern Europe*, vol. 1

Kume Kunitake, *Japan Rising: The Iwakura Embassy to the USA and Europe*, ed. Chushichi Tsuzuki and R. Jules Young, Cambridge University Press 2009

Kurlander, Eric, 'The Rise of Völkisch-Nationalism and the Decline of German Liberalism: A Comparison of Liberal Political Cultures in Schleswig-Holstein and Silesia 1912–1924', *European Review of History*, vol. 9, no. 1, 2002

Kusmer, Kenneth L., *Down and Out, on the Road: The Homeless in American History*, Oxford University Press 2003

Kuznets, Simon, *Six Lectures on Economic Growth*, Free Press of Glencoe, IL, 1959

Lai, Cheng-chung, 'Adam Smith and Yen Fu: Western Economics in Chinese Perspective', *Journal of European Economic History*, vol. 18, no. 2, Fall 1989

Lains, Pedro, *L'économie portugaise au XIXe siècle. Croissance économique et commerce extérieur, 1851–1913*, L'Harmattan, Paris 1999

Lambroza, Shlomo, 'The Pogroms of 1903–1906', in Klier and Lambroza (eds), *Pogroms: Anti-Jewish Violence in Modern Russian History*

Lampe, John R., 'Imperial Borderlands or Capitalist Periphery? Redefining Balkan Backwardness, 1520–1914', in Chirot (ed.), *The Origins of Backwardness in Eastern Europe*

Lampe, John R., 'Varieties of Unsuccessful Industrialization: The Balkan States before 1914', *Journal of Economic History*, vol. 35, no. 1, March 1975, pp. 56–85

Lampedusa, Giuseppe Tomasi di, *Il gattopardo*, Feltrinelli, Milan 2002

Landes, David S., 'Japan and Europe: Contrasts in Industrialization', in Lockwood (ed.), *The State and Economic Enterprise in Japan*

Landes, David S., 'The Fable of the Dead Horse; or, The Industrial Revolution Revisited', in Mokyr (ed.), *The British Industrial Revolution*

Landes, David S., *The Unbound Prometheus: Technological Change and Industrial Development in Western Europe from 1750 to the Present*, Cambridge University Press 2003

Landes, David S., *The Wealth and Poverty of Nations*, Little, Brown and Co., London 1998

Langer, William L., *The Diplomacy of Imperialism, 1890–1902*, vol. 1, Knopf, New York 1935

Lansang, Jose A., 'The Philippine-American Experiment: A Filipino View', *Pacific Affairs*, vol. 25, no. 3, September 1952

Lanzaro, Jorge, 'La gauche en Uruguay: Le chemin vers le gouvernement', *Problèmes d'Amérique latine*, no. 55, Winter 2004–5

Larson, John, 'The Market Revolution', in Lacy K. Ford, *A Companion to the Civil War and Reconstruction*, Blackwell, Oxford 2005

Lawson, Philip, *The East India Company: A History*, Longman, London 1993

Layard, George Somes, *Mrs. Lynn Linton: Her Life, Letters, and Opinions*, Methuen, London 1901

Le Bon, Gustave, *La psychologie politique et la défense sociale*, Flammarion, Paris 1910

Le Play, Frédéric, *La réforme sociale en France déduite de l'observation comparée des peuples européens*, Mame, Tours 1874 (5th ed., revised), vol. 2 (first published 1864)

Leach, William R., *Land of Desire: Merchants, Power, and the Rise of a New American Culture*, Knopf Doubleday, New York 2011

Lebovics, Herman, *The Alliance of Iron and Wheat in the Third French Republic 1860–1914: Origins of the New Conservatism*, Louisiana State University Press 1988

Leduc, Jean, *Histoire de la France: l'enracinement de la République, 1879–1918*, Hachette, Paris 1991

Lees, Andrew, 'Critics of Urban Society in Germany, 1854–1914', *Journal of the History of Ideas*, vol. 40, no. 1, January–March 1979

Lehmann, Jean-Pierre, *The Roots of Modern Japan*, Macmillan, London 1982

Lehmann, Sibylle H., 'The German Elections in the 1870s: Why Germany Turned from Liberalism to Protectionism', *Journal of Economic History*, vol. 70, no. 1, March 2010

Leibniz, Gottfried, Preface to *Novissima Sinica*: http://www.zftrans.com/bbs/read.php?tid=15696

Lenin, V. I., 'The Agrarian Programme of Social-Democracy in the First Russian Revolution, 1905–1907'; 'The International Socialist Congress in Stuttgart', in *Collected Works*, vol. 13, Progress Publishers, Moscow 1972

Leo XIII, *Libertas* (1888): http://w2.vatican.va/content/leo-xiii/en/encyclicals/documents/hf_l-xiii_enc_20061888_libertas.html

Leo XIII, *Quod apostolici muneris* (1878): http://www.vatican.va/holy_father/leo_xiii/encyclicals/documents/hf_l-xiii_enc_28121878_quod-apostolici-muneris_en.html

Leo XIII, *Rerum Novarum* (1891): http://www.vatican.va/holy_father/leo_xiii/encyclicals/documents/hf_l-xiii_enc_15051891_rerum-novarum_en.html

Leonard, Carol S., *Agrarian Reform in Russia: The Road from Serfdom*, Cambridge University Press 2011

Lermontov, Mikhail, *Major Poetical Works*, ed. and trans. Anatoly Liberman, Croom Helm, London 1983

Leroy-Beaulieu, Anatole, *L'empire des Tsars et les Russes*, Laffont, Paris 1990 (reprint of the 4th edition, 1897–8)

Leroy-Beaulieu, Paul, 'De la nécessité de préparer une fédération européenne', *L'Économiste français*, 3 September 1898

Leroy-Beaulieu, Paul, 'Le prochain gouffre: le projet de loi sur les retraites', *L'Économiste français*, 11 May 1901

Leroy-Beaulieu, Paul, *De la colonisation chez les peuples modernes*, Guillaumin, Paris 1882 (2nd edition)

Leroy-Beaulieu, Paul, *Essai sur la répartition des richesses et sur la tendance à une moindre inégalité des conditions*, Guillaumin, Paris 1897 (4th edition, first published 1880)

Leroy-Beaulieu, Paul, *L'administration locale en France et en Angleterre*, Guillaumin, Paris 1872

Leroy-Beaulieu, Paul, *Le développement du socialisme d'état et le rachat des chemins de fer*, Debons, Paris 1880

Leroy-Beaulieu, Pierre, 'La Chine et les puissances', *L'Économiste français*, 10 September 1898

Leroy-Beaulieu, Pierre, 'Les États-Unis, puissance coloniale', *Revue des deux mondes*, January 1902, pp. 77–102

Letourneau, Charles, *L'évolution du commerce dans les diverses races humaines*, Vigot Frères, Paris 1897

Leuchtenburg, William E., *The American President: From Teddy Roosevelt to Bill Clinton*, Oxford University Press 2015

Leupp, Gary P., *Servants, Shophands, and Laborers in the Cities of Tokugawa Japan*, Princeton University Press 1992

Lévêque, Pierre, *Histoire des forces politiques en France, 1880–1940*, vol. 2, Armand Colin, Paris 1994

Levi, Carlo, *Cristo si è fermato a Eboli*, Einaudi, Turin 1946

Levi, Margaret, *Of Rule and Revenue*, University of California Press 1988

Levitt, Theodore, 'The Globalization of Markets', *Harvard Business Review*, vol. 61, no. 3, May–June 1983, pp. 92–102

Lévy, Christine, 'La naissance du mouvement ouvrier moderne au Japon', in Claude Hamon (ed.), *Entreprise et société dans le Japon d'avant-guerre*, Philippe Piquier, Arles 2011

Lévy-Leboyer, Maurice, 'La croissance économique en France au XIXe siècle', *Annales*, vol. 23, no. 4, July–August 1968

Lévy-Leboyer, Maurice and François Bourguignon, *L'économie française au XIXe siècle*, Economica, Paris 1985

Lévy-Leboyer, Maurice and Jean-Claude Casanova (eds), *Entre l'état et le marché. L'économie française des années 1880 à nos jours*, Gallimard, Paris 1991

Lewis, Bernard, *The Jews of Islam*, Princeton University Press 2016

Lewis, Colin M., 'Industry in Latin America before 1930', in Bethell (ed.), *The Cambridge History of Latin America*, vol. IV

Lewis, Paul H., *Authoritarian Regimes in Latin America: Dictators, Despots, and Tyrants*, Rowman & Littlefield, Lanham, MD 2006

Lewycka, Marina, *Various Pets Alive and Dead*, Penguin/Fig Tree, London 2012

Leymonerie, Claire, 'Le Salon des arts ménagers dans les années 1950', *Vingtième siècle*, no. 91, July–September 2006, pp. 43–56

Leys, Colin, *The Rise and Fall of Development Theory*, James Currey, London 1996

Li, Bozhong, *Agricultural Development in Jiangnan, 1620–1850*, Macmillan, Basingstoke 1998

Li, Lillian M., *Fighting Famine in North China*, Stanford University Press 2007

Liebman, Marcel, *Les socialistes belges, 1885–1914. La révolte et l'organisation*, Vie Ouvrière, Brussels 1979

Light, Alison, *Mrs Woolf and the Servants*, Penguin/Fig Tree, London 2007

Lincoln, Abraham, 'Second Inaugural Address', 4 March 1865: http://avalon.law.yale.edu/19th_century/lincoln2.asp, other speeches: http://www.abrahamlincolnonline.org/lincoln/speeches/fair.htm

Lind, Michael, *The Next American Nation: The New Nationalism and the Fourth American Revolution*, The Free Press, London 1995

Lindert, Peter H., *Growing Public: Social Spending and Economic Growth since the Eighteenth Century*, 2 vols, Cambridge University Press 2004

Linton, Eliza Lynn (E.L.L.), 'On the Side of the Maids', *Cornhill Magazine*, vol. 29, 1874: http://www.victorianweb.org/history/work/maids1.html

Linton, Eliza Lynn (E.L.L.), 'The Wild Women. 1. As Politicians', *Nineteenth Century*, vol. 30, no. 173, July 1891

Lipset, Seymour Martin and Gary Marks, *It Didn't Happen Here: Why Socialism Failed in the United States*, Norton and Co., New York 2000

Lis, Catharina and Hugo Soly, *Poverty and Capitalism in Pre-Industrial Europe*, Harvester Press, Hassocks, Sussex 1979

Lis, Catharina and Hugo Soly, *Worthy Efforts: Attitudes to Work and Workers in Pre-Industrial Europe*, Brill, Leiden and Boston, MA 2012

List, Frederick (Friedrich), *National System of Political Economy*, trans. G. A. Matile, J. B. Lippincott & Co., Philadelphia, PA 1856

Liu, William Guanglin, 'The Making of a Fiscal State in Song China, 960–1279', *Economic History Review*, vol. 68, no. 1, 2015, pp. 48–78

Livezeanu, Irina, *Cultural Politics in Greater Romania*, Cornell University Press 1995

Livi-Bacci, Massimo, *A Concise History of World Population*, Blackwell, Oxford 1997

Livi-Bacci, Massimo, *L'immigrazione e l'assimilazione degli italiani negli Stati Uniti*, Giuffrè, Milan 1961

Livi-Bacci, Massimo, *The Population of Europe: A History*, Blackwell, Oxford 2000

Livingston, Alexander, *Damn Great Empires! William James and the Politics of Pragmatism*, Oxford University Press 2016

Livy (Titus Livius), *Ab urbe condita*

Locke, John, *Second Treatise on Government*: http://www.gutenberg.org/files/7370/7370-h/7370-h.htm

Lockwood, William W. (ed.), *The State and Economic Enterprise in Japan: Essays in the Political Economy of Growth*, Princeton University Press 1965

Loginov, V. T., 'Stolypin as Reformer', *Russian Studies in History*, vol. 42, no. 4, Spring 2004

London, Jack, *The People of the Abyss*, Grosset & Dunlap, New York 1903

López-Campillo, Evelyne, *La crise de 1898*, Éditions Messene, Paris 1999

Lorenzo, David J., *Conceptions of Chinese Democracy*, Johns Hopkins University Press 2013

Lorimer, James, *Constitutionalism of the Future: or, Parliament the Mirror of the Nation*, Adam and Charles Black, Edinburgh 1865

Lorimer, James, *The Institutes of the Law of Nations: A Treatise of the Jural Relations of Separate Political Communities*, vol. 1, Blackwood, Edinburgh, 1883

Luckin, W., 'The Final Catastrophe – Cholera in London, 1866', *Medical History*, vol. 21, no. 1, 1977, pp. 32–42

Luo Guanzhong, *Three Kingdoms: A Historical Novel*, trans. Moss Roberts, University of California Press 1991

Luther, Martin, 'Ninety-Five Theses': http://www.luther.de/en/95thesen.html

Lyashchenko, Peter I., *History of the National Economy of Russia to the 1917 Revolution*, Macmillan, New York, NY 1949

Lynch, John, 'The Origins of Spanish American Independence', in Bethell (ed.), *The Cambridge History of Latin America*, vol. III

Lynn, Martin, 'British Policy, Trade, and Informal Empire in the Mid-Nineteenth Century', in *The Oxford History of the British Empire*, vol. 3: *The Nineteenth Century*, ed. Andrew Porter, Oxford University Press 1999

Lyons, F. S. L., *Internationalism in Europe, 1815–1914*, A. W. Sythoff, Leiden 1963

Macaulay, Thomas Babington, Speeches (5 July 1831; 10 July 1833), in *Miscellaneous Writings and Speeches*, vol. 4: http://www.gutenberg.org/files/2170/2170-h/2170-h.htm

Macey, David A. J., *Government and Peasant in Russia, 1861–1906: The Prehistory of the Stolypin Reforms*, Northern Illinois University Press 1987

Macfarlane, Alan, *The Savage Wars of Peace: England, Japan and the Malthusian Trap*, Palgrave, Basingstoke 2003

Macintyre, Stuart, *The Oxford History of Australia*, vol. 4: *1901–1942: The Succeeding Age*, Oxford University Press 1986

Mackerras, Colin, *Western Images of China*, Oxford University Press 1989

Mackinnon, Mary, 'Living Standards, 1870–1914', in Floud and McCloskey (eds), *The Economic History of Britain since 1700*, vol. 2

Macpherson, W. J., *The Economic Development of Japan c. 1868–1941*, Macmillan, London 1987

Maddison, Angus, 'Statistics on World Population, GDP and Per Capita GDP, 1–2008 AD': http://www.ggdc.net/maddison/oriindex.htm

Maddison, Angus, *Contours of the World Economy, 1–2030 AD: Essays in Macro-Economic History*, Oxford University Press 2007

Maddison, Angus, *Dynamic Forces in Capitalist Development: A Long-Run Comparative View*, Oxford University Press 1991

Madley, Benjamin, 'Reexamining the American Genocide Debate: Meaning, Historiography, and New Methods', *American Historical Review*, vol. 120, no. 1, February 2015

Madrick, Jeff, *The Case for Big Government*, Princeton University Press 2009

Maggi, Ruben Schindler, 'Indigenous Health in Brazil', *Revista Brasileira de Saúde Materno Infantil*, vol. 14, no. 1, January/March 2014: http://www.scielo.br/pdf/rbsmi/v14n1/en_1519-3829-rbsmi-14-01-0013.pdf

Maiguashca, Juan, 'The Electoral Reforms of 1861 in Ecuador and the Rise of a New Political Order', in Eduardo Posada-Carbó (ed.), *Elections before Democracy: The History of Elections in Europe and Latin America*, Macmillan, London 1996

Maliks, Reidar, *Kant's Politics in Context*, Oxford University Press 2014

Malthus, Thomas, *An Essay on the Principle of Population* (1798): http://www.gutenberg.org/files/4239/4239-h/4239-h.htm

Manoukian, Agopik, 'La famiglia dei contadini', in Piero Melograni (ed.), *La famiglia italiana dall'ottocento a oggi*, Laterza, Rome-Bari 1988

Mao Zedong, 'On the People's Democratic Dictatorship: In Commemoration of the Twenty-Eighth Anniversary of the Communist Party of China, June 30, 1949': https://www.marxists.org/reference/archive/mao/selected-works/volume-4/mswv4_65.htm

Marat, Jean-Paul, article in *L'Ami du peuple*, Wednesday, 30 June 1790: http://gallica.bnf.fr/ark:/12148/bpt6k1046480j

Marin, Séverine Antigone, '"L'américanisation du monde"? Étude des peurs allemandes face au "danger américain" (1897–1907)', in Dominique Barjot, Isabelle Lescent-Giles, and Marc de Ferrière Le Vayer (eds), *L'américanisation en Europe au XXe siècle: économie, culture, politique*, vol. 1, Centre de Recherche sur l'Histoire de l'Europe du Nord-Ouest, Université Charles-de-Gaulle, Lille 3, 2002

Maris, Bernard, *Des économistes au-dessus de tout soupçon ou la grande mascarade des prédictions*, Albin Michel, Paris 1990

Markoff, John, 'Where and When Was Democracy Invented?', *Comparative Studies in Society and History*, vol. 41, no. 4, October 1999

Marks, Shula, *Reluctant Rebellion: The 1906–8 Disturbances in Natal*, Clarendon Press, Oxford 1970

Marques-Pereira, Bérengère, 'Le Chili: les femmes et la gauche. Une relation amicale?', *Revue internationale de politique comparée*, vol. 12, no. 3, 2005

Marseille, Jacques, *Empire colonial et capitalisme français. Histoire d'un divorce*, Albin Michel, Paris 1984

Martin, Jean-François, *Histoire de la Tunisie contemporaine. De Ferry à Bourguiba, 1881–1956*, L'Harmattan, Paris 2003

Martin, R. Montgomery, *Opium in China, extracted from China; Political, Commercial, and Social*, James Madden, London n.d. (1847)

Martines, Lauro, *Furies: War in Europe 1450–1700*, Bloomsbury, London 2013

Marton, Silvia, *La construction politique de la nation. La nation dans les débats du Parlement de la Roumanie (1866–1871)*, Institutul European, Bucharest 2009

Maruyama, Masao, *Studies in the Intellectual History of Tokugawa Japan*, Princeton University Press 1974

Maruyama, Masao, *Thought and Behaviour in Modern Japanese Politics*, Oxford University Press 1969

Marx, Karl, *A Contribution to the Critique of Political Economy*, Progress Publishers, Moscow 1970

Marx, Karl, *Capital*, vol. 1, Progress Publishers, Moscow 1965

Marx, Karl, *Capital*, vol. 3, Progress Publishers, Moscow 1971

Marx, Karl, *Class Struggles in France, 1848–1850*, International Publishers, New York 1964

Marx, Karl, *Grundrisse: Foundations of the Critique of Political Economy (Rough Draft)*, Penguin, London 1973

Marx, Karl and Frederick Engels, *Collected Works*, vols 43 and 47, Lawrence and Wishart, London 2010, electronic edition

Marx, Karl and Friedrich Engels, *Correspondence 1846–1895: A Selection with Commentary and Notes*, Martin Lawrence, London 1934

Marx, Karl and Friedrich Engels, *Marx and Engels Correspondence*: https://www.marxists.org/archive/marx/works/1891/letters/91_10_24a.htm

Marx, Karl and Friedrich Engels, *The Communist Manifesto*, Penguin, London 2002

Masterman, Charles, *The Condition of England*, Methuen, London 1912, first published 1909

Mather, William, 'Labour and the Hours of Labour', *Contemporary Review*, vol. 62, November 1892

Mathias, Peter, 'La révolution industrielle en Angleterre: un cas unique?', *Annales*, vol. 27, no. 1, January–February 1972, pp. 33–45

Matthew, H. C. G., 'Introduction', in *The Gladstone Diaries*, vol. X: *January 1881–June 1883*, ed. H. C. G. Matthew, Clarendon Press, Oxford 1990

Mayer, Arno, *The Persistence of the Old Regime*, Croom Helm, London 1981

Mayer, Arno J., 'The Lower Middle Class as Historical Problem', *Journal of Modern History*, vol. 47, no. 3, September 1975

Mayeur, Jean-Marie, 'Catholicisme intransigeant, catholicisme social, démocratie chrétienne', *Annales*, vol. 27, no. 2, March/April 1972

Maynes, Charles William, 'Squandering Triumph: The West Botched the Post-Cold War World', *Foreign Affairs*, vol. 78, no. 1, January–February 1999

Mayo, Louise A., *The Ambivalent Image: Nineteenth-Century America's Perception of the Jew*, Associated University Presses 1988

McCagg, William O., Jr., 'Hungary's "Feudalized" Bourgeoisie', *Journal of Modern History*, vol. 44, no. 1, March 1972

McClelland, Keith and Sonya Rose, 'Citizenship and Empire, 1867–1928', in Hall and Rose (eds), *At Home with the Empire*

McCloskey, Deirdre N., *The Bourgeois Virtues: Ethics for an Age of Commerce*, University of Chicago Press 2006

McCormack, Noah, 'Civilising the Urban Other: Poverty as a National Problem', *Ritsumeikan Annual Review of International Studies*, vol. 6, 2007, pp. 21–43: http://www.ritsumei.ac.jp/acd/cg/ir/college/bulletin/e-vol.6/02Noah%20McCormack.pdf

McCormick, Richard L., 'The Discovery that Business Corrupts Politics: A Reappraisal of the Origins of Progressivism', *American Historical Review*, vol. 86, no. 2, April 1981

McCraw, Thomas K., 'American Capitalism', in Thomas K. McCraw (ed.), *Creating Modern Capitalism: How Entrepreneurs, Companies, and Countries Triumphed in Three Industrial Revolutions*, Harvard University Press 1997

McDaniel, Robert A., *The Shuster Mission and the Persian Constitutional Revolution*, Bibliotheca Islamica, Minneapolis, MN 1974

McDaniel, Tim, *Autocracy, Capitalism, and Revolution in Russia*, University of California Press 1988

McGovern, Charles, 'Consumption and Citizenship in the United States, 1900–1940', in *Getting and Spending*, ed. Susan Strasser, Charles McGovern, and Matthias Judt, Cambridge University Press 1998

McIvor, A. J., 'Employers, the Government, and Industrial Fatigue in Britain, 1890–1918', *Journal of Industrial Medicine*, vol. 44, no. 11, November 1987

McKeown, Thomas, *The Modern Rise of Population*, Edward Arnold, London 1976

McKinley, William, First Inaugural Address, 4 March 1897: http://avalon.law.yale.edu/19th_century/mckin1.asp

McMath, Robert C., Jr., *American Populism: A Social History, 1877–1898*, Hill and Wang, New York 1993

McNeill, J. R. and William H. McNeill, *The Human Web*, W. W. Norton, London 2003

McReynolds, Louise, *The News under Russia's Old Regime*, Princeton University Press 1991

Mearns, Andrew, *The Bitter Cry of Outcast London: An Inquiry into the Condition of the Abject Poor*, James Clarke and Co., London 1883

Medeiros, Marcelo de A., 'La gouvernance de gauche face aux processus de mondialisation: le cas du Brésil', *Revue internationale de politique comparée*, vol. 12, no. 3, 2005

Meiksins Wood, Ellen, *Empire of Capital*, Verso, London 2003

Meldini, Piero, 'A tavola e in cucina', in Piero Melograni (ed.), *La famiglia italiana dall'ottocento a oggi*, Laterza, Rome-Bari 1988

Méline, Jules, *Le Retour à la terre et la surproduction industrielle*, Hachette, Paris 1905

Mension-Rigau, Eric, *Aristocrates et grands bourgeois*, Plon, Paris 1994

Merger, Michèle, *Un siècle d'histoire industrielle en Italie, 1880–1998*, SEDES, Paris 1998

Merrill, Michael, 'Putting "Capitalism" in its Place: A Review of Recent Literature', *The William and Mary Quarterly*, vol. 52, no. 2, April 1995

Meslé, France and Jacques Vallin, 'Reconstitution de tables annuelles de mortalité pour la France au XIXe siècle', *Population*, vol. 44, no. 6, November–December 1989

Meyer, Stephen, III, *The Five-Dollar Day: Labor Management and Social Control in the Ford Motor Company, 1908–1921*, State University of New York Press 1981

Michalet, Charles-Albert, *Mondialisation, la grande rupture*, La Découverte, Paris 2007

Middleton, Roger, *Government versus the Market*, Edward Elgar, Cheltenham 1996

Mill, John Stuart, 'Miss Martineau's Summary of Political Economy', *Monthly Repository*, vol. VIII, May 1834, pp. 318–22, now in *The Collected Works of John Stuart Mill*, vol. IV

Mill, John Stuart, *Considerations on Representative Government*, Parker, Son, and Bourn, London 1861

Mill, John Stuart, *Dissertations and Discussions: Political, Philosophical, and Historical*, vols 1–3, Longmans, Green, Reader, and Dyer, London 1867–75

Mill, John Stuart, *Principles of Political Economy*, Longmans, Green and Co., London 1904

Miller, Alexei, *The Romanov Empire and Nationalism: Essays in the Methodology of Historical Research*, Central European University Press 2008

Millerand, Alexandre, *Le socialisme réformiste français*, Société nouvelle de librairie et d'édition, Paris 1903: http://ia600304.us.archive.org/9/items/lesocialismerefoomillgoog/lesocialismerefoomillgoog.pdf

Milyukov, Pavel (Paul Milyoukov), *Russia and its Crisis*, University of Chicago Press 1905: http://archive.org/stream/russiaitscrisisoomiliuoft#page/n3/mode/2up

Minsky, Hyman, *Can 'It' Happen Again? Essays on Instability and Finance*, Routledge, London 2016

Minsky, Hyman P., 'The Financial-Instability Hypothesis: Capitalist Processes and the Behavior of the Economy', in *Financial Crises: Theory, History, and Policy*, ed. Charles P. Kindleberger and Jean-Pierre Laffargue, Cambridge University Press and Éditions de la Maison des Sciences de l'Homme, Cambridge and Paris 1982

Misra, Amalendu, *Afghanistan: The Labyrinth of Violence*, Polity, Cambridge 2004

Missaggia, Maria Giovanna, *Stefano Jacini e la classe politica liberale*, Leo S. Olschki, Florence 2003

Mitchell, Brian R., *International Historical Statistics: Europe 1750–2005*, Palgrave Macmillan, New York 2007

Mitchell, Brian R., *International Historical Statistics: The Americas 1750–2005*, Palgrave Macmillan, New York 2007

Moch, Leslie Page, *Moving Europeans: Migration in Western Europe since 1650*, Indiana University Press 2003

Mokyr, Joel, *The Enlightened Economy: An Economic History of Britain, 1700–1850*, Yale University Press 2009

Mokyr, Joel, *The Lever of Riches: Technological Creativity and Economic Progress*, Oxford University Press 1990

Mokyr, Joel (ed.), *The British Industrial Revolution: An Economic Perspective*, Westview Press, Boulder, CO 1993

Mollan, S. M., 'Business Failure, Capital Investment and Information: Mining Companies in the Anglo-Egyptian Sudan, 1900–1913', *Journal of Imperial and Commonwealth History*, vol. 37, no. 2, June 2009, pp. 229–48

Möller, Jens, 'Towards Agrarian Capitalism: The Case of Southern Sweden during the 19th Century', *Geografiska Annaler: Series B, Human Geography*, vol. 72, no. 2/3, 1990

Mollier, Jean-Yves and Jocelyne George, *La plus longue des républiques, 1870–1940*, Fayard, Paris 1994

Montesquieu, Charles de Secondat, *De l'esprit des lois*, Gallimard, Paris 1995

Montias, John Michael, 'Notes on the Romanian Debate on Sheltered Industrialization: 1860–1906', in Kenneth Jowitt (ed.), *Social Change in Romania, 1860–1940: A Debate on Development in a European Nation*, University of California Press 1978, pp. 53–71

Montroni, Giovanni, 'La famiglia borghese', in Piero Melograni (ed.), *La famiglia italiana dall'ottocento a oggi*, Laterza, Rome-Bari 1988

Montroni, Giovanni, *La società italiana dall'unificazione alla Grande Guerra*, Laterza, Rome-Bari 2002

Moon, David, 'Peasant Migration and the Settlement of Russia's Frontiers, 1550–1897', *Historical Journal*, vol. 40, no. 4, December 1997, pp. 859–93

Moore, Barrington, Jr., *Injustice: The Social Bases of Obedience and Revolt*, Macmillan, London and Basingstoke 1978

Moore, Barrington, Jr., *Social Origins of Dictatorship and Democracy: Lord and Peasant in the Making of the Modern World*, Beacon Press, Boston, MA 1966

Moore, R. J., 'India and the British Empire', in Eldridge (ed.), *British Imperialism in the Nineteenth Century*

Morel, Jean-Paul, 'L'artigiano', in *L'uomo romano*, ed. Andrea Giardina, Laterza, Rome-Bari 1989

Morgan, Kenneth, 'Mercantilism and the British Empire 1688–1815', in Winch and O'Brien (eds), *The Political Economy of British Historical Experience, 1688–1914*

Mori, Giorgio, 'Blocco di potere e lotta politica in Italia', in *Storia della società italiana,* vol. 14: *Il blocco di potere nell'Italia unita*, Teti editore, Milan 1980

Mori, Giorgio, 'The Genesis of Italian Industrialization', *Journal of European Economic History*, vol. 4, no. 1, Spring 1975, pp. 79–94

Morishima, Michio, *Why Has Japan 'Succeeded'? Western Technology and the Japanese Ethos*, Cambridge University Press 1982

Morris, Edmund, *Theodore Rex*, Random House, New York 2001

Morris, William, Preface to *Signs of Change*, in *The Collected Works of William Morris*, vol. 23, Cambridge University Press 2012

Morris-Suzuki, Tessa, *Re-Inventing Japan: Time Space Nation*, M. E. Sharpe, Armonk, NY 1998

Morris-Suzuki, Tessa, *The Technological Transformation of Japan: From the Seventeenth to the Twenty-First Century*, Cambridge University Press 1994

Motadel, David, 'Islam and the European Empires', *Historical Journal*, vol. 55, no. 3, September 2012

Mote, F. W., *Imperial China, 900–1800*, Harvard University Press 1999

Moulder, Frances V., *Japan, China, and the Modern World Economy: Toward a Reinterpretation of East Asian Development ca. 1600 to ca. 1918*, Cambridge University Press 1977

Mouret, Arlette, 'La légende des 150,000 décès tuberculeux par an', *Annales de démographie historique*, 1996

Mouzelis, Nicos P., *Modern Greece: Facets of Underdevelopment*, Macmillan, London 1978

Mukerjee, Madhusree, *Churchill's Secret War: The British Empire and the Ravaging of India during World War II*, Basic Books, New York 2010

Mukherjee, Janam, *Hungry Bengal: War, Famine and the End of Empire*, Hurst & Co., London 2015

Mulhall, Michael G., *The Progress of the World in Arts, Agriculture, Commerce, Manufactures, Instruction, Railways, and Public Wealth since the Beginning of the Nineteenth Century*, Edward Stanford, London 1880

Muller, Jerry Z., *The Mind and the Market: Capitalism in Modern European Thought*, Knopf, New York 2002

Müller, Wolfgang, 'Foxconn Economics: How Much Room for Better Pay and Working Conditions?', in Jan Drahokoupil, Rutvica Andrijasevic, and Devi Sacchetto (eds), *Flexible Workforces and Low Profit Margins: Electronics Assembly between Europe and China*, ETUI (Europe Trade Union Institute), Brussels 2016

Mungello, David E., *The Great Encounter of China and the West, 1500–1800*, Rowman & Littlefield, Lanham, MD 2009

Munthe, Axel, *Letters from a Mourning City*, John Murray, London 1899

Murri, Romolo, *Battaglie d'oggi*, vol. 4, Società I. C. di Cultura, Rome 1904

Musgrave, Richard A., 'Reconsidering the Fiscal Role of Government', *American Economic Review*, vol. 87, no. 2, May 1997

Musil, Robert, *The Man Without Qualities*, Vintage Books, New York 1996

Musso, Stefano, 'La famiglia operaia', in Piero Melograni (ed.), *La famiglia italiana dall'ottocento a oggi*, Laterza, Rome-Bari 1988

Mussorgsky, Modest, *Boris Godunov*, text in CD Sony Classical Berliner Philharmoniker directed by Claudio Abbado, trans. Pamela Davidson

Nadal, Jordi, 'Un siglo de industrialización en España, 1833–1930', in Nicolás Sánchez-Albornoz (ed.), *La modernización económica de España 1830–1930*, Alianza Editorial, Madrid 1985

Nahavandi, Firouzeh (ed.), *Globalisation et néolibéralisme dans le tiers-monde*, L'Harmattan, Paris 2000

Najemy, John M., *A History of Florence, 1200–1575*, Blackwell, Oxford 2006

Nathans, Benjamin, *Beyond the Pale: The Jewish Encounter with Late Imperial Russia*, University of California Press 2004

Neal, Larry, 'How It All Began: The Monetary and Financial Architecture of Europe during the First Global Capital Markets, 1648–1815', *Financial History Review*, vol. 7, no. 2, 2000, pp. 117–40

Neal, Larry, 'The Financial Crisis of 1825 and the Restructuring of the British Financial System', Prepared for the 22nd Annual Economic Policy Conference at the Federal Reserve Bank of St Louis, 16–17 October 1997: https://www.researchgate.net/profile/Larry_Neal/publication/5047144_The_financial_crisis_of_1825_and_the_restructuring_of_the_British_financial_system/links/5457bb330cf26d5090ab5057.pdf

Neary, Ian, *The State and Politics in Japan*, Polity, Cambridge 2002

Nekrasov, Nikolay A., *Who Can Be Happy and Free in Russia?*: http://www.gutenberg.org/cache/epub/9619/pg9619.html

Neukomm, Edmond, *Voyage au pays du déficit (la Nouvelle Italie)*, Ernest Kolb, Paris 1890

Nietzsche, Friedrich, *Thus Spoke Zarathustra*, trans. R. J. Hollingdale, Penguin, London 2003

Noiriel, Gérard, *Les ouvriers dans la société française, XIXe–XXe siècle*, Éditions du Seuil, Paris 1986

Nolan, Peter, *China and the Global Business Revolution*, Palgrave, Basingstoke 2001

Nolan, Peter, *China at the Crossroads*, John Wiley, London 2013

Nonnis, David, 'Le attività artigianali', in Arnaldo Marcone (ed.), *L'età romana. Liberi, semiliberi, e schiavi in una società premoderna*, Castelvecchi, Rome 2016

Nord, Philip, 'The Welfare State in France, 1870–1914', *French Historical Studies*, vol. 18, no. 3, Spring 1994

Nordau, Max, *Degeneration*, University of Nebraska Press 1968

Norman, E. Herbert, *Japan's Emergence as a Modern State: Political and Economic Problems of the Meiji Period*, UBC Press, Vancouver and Toronto 2000 (1st edition 1940)

Normand, Charles, *La bourgeoisie française au XVIIe siècle*, Alcan, Paris 1908: http://ia700306.us.archive.org/BookReader/BookReaderImages.php?zip=/29/items/labourgeoisiefraoonormuoft/labourgeoisiefraoonormuoft_jp2.zip&file=labourgeoisiefraoonormuoft_jp2/labourgeoisiefraoonormuoft_0023.jp2&scale=6&rotate=0

North, Douglass C., *Institutions, Institutional Change and Economic Performance*, Cambridge University Press 1990

Nunes, Ana Bela, Eugénia Mata, and Nuno Valério, 'Portuguese Economic Growth 1833–1985', *Journal of European Economic History*, vol. 18, no. 2, Fall 1989

Nurdin, Jean, *Le rêve européen des penseurs allemands, 1700–1950*, Presses Universitaires du Septentrion, Paris 2003

Nye, John V. C., *War, Wine, and Taxes: The Political Economy of Anglo-French Trade, 1689–1900*, Princeton University Press 2007

Ó Gráda, Cormac, 'British Agriculture, 1860–1914', in Floud and McCloskey (eds), *The Economic History of Britain since 1700*, vol. 2

Ó Gráda, Cormac, 'Great Leap into Famine: A Review Essay', *Population and Development Review*, vol. 37, no. 1, March 2011

Ó Gráda, Cormac, *Famine: A Short History*, Princeton University Press 2009

O'Brien, Patrick, 'Do We Have a Typology for the Study of European Industrialization in the XIXth Century?', *Journal of European Economic History*, vol. 15, no. 2, Fall 1986

O'Brien, Patrick, 'European Economic Development: The Contribution of the Periphery', *Economic History Review*, vol. 35, no. 1, February 1982, pp. 1–18

O'Brien, Patrick, 'Fiscal Exceptionalism: Great Britain and its European Rivals from Civil War to Triumph at Trafalgar and Waterloo', in Winch and O'Brien (eds), *The Political Economy of British Historical Experience, 1688–1914*

O'Brien, Patrick, 'The Costs and Benefits of British Imperialism, 1846–1914', *Past & Present*, no. 120, August 1988

O'Brien, Patrick and Caglar Keyder, 'Les voies de passage vers la société industrielle en Grande-Bretagne et en France (1780–1914)', *Annales*, vol. 34, no. 6, November–December 1979

O'Brien, Patrick and Leandro Prados de la Escosura, 'The Costs and Benefits for Europeans from their Empires Overseas', *Revista de Historia Económica*, vol. 16, no. 1, Winter 1998

O'Rourke, Kevin and Jeffrey G. Williamson, 'Late Nineteenth-Century Anglo-American Factor-Price Convergence: Were Heckscher and Ohlin Right?', *Journal of Economic History*, vol. 54, no. 4, December 1994

O'Rourke, Kevin and Jeffrey G. Williamson, *Globalisation and History: The Evolution of a Nineteenth-Century Atlantic Economy*, MIT Press, Cambridge, MA 1999

O'Sullivan, John, 'Annexation', *United States Magazine and Democratic Review*, vol. 17, no. 1, July–August 1845

Obama, Barack, Inaugural Address 2009: https://obamawhitehouse.archives.gov/blog/2009/01/21/president-barack-obamas-inaugural-address

Observatory of Economic Complexity: http://atlas.media.mit.edu/en/visualize/tree_map/hs92/export/show/all/8471/2012

Obstfeld, Maurice and Alan M. Taylor, 'Globalization and Capital Markets', in Michael D. Bordo, Alan M. Taylor, and Jeffrey G. Williamson (eds), *Globalization in Historical Perspective*, University of Chicago Press 2003

Ochs, Michael, 'Tsarist Officialdom and Anti-Jewish Pogroms in Poland', in Klier and Lambroza (eds), *Pogroms: Anti-Jewish Violence in Modern Russian History*

OECD, *Economic Outlook*, no. 97, June 2015

OECD report: http://www.keepeek.com/Digital-Asset-Management/oecd/governance/government-at-a-glance-2015/general-government-debt-per-capita-2009-2013-and-2014_gov_glance-2015-graph21-en#page1

Offer, Avner, 'The British Empire, 1870–1914: A Waste of Money?', *Economic History Review*, vol. 46, no. 2, 1993

Office of National Statistics, *200 years of the Census in . . . YORKSHIRE*: https://www.ons.gov.uk/census/2001censusandearlier

Office of National Statistics, *Population Estimates for UK, England and Wales, Scotland and Northern Ireland, Mid-2015*, 23 June 2016

Ōgai, Mori, 'Yellow Peril', in Richard John Bowring, *Mori Ōgai and the Modernization of Japanese Culture*, Cambridge University Press 1979

Ohmae, Kenichi, *Beyond National Borders: Reflections on Japan and the World*, Dow Jones-Irwin, Homewood, IL 1987

Ohmae, Kenichi, *The End of the Nation State: The Rise of Regional Economies*, The Free Press, New York 1995

Ojeda Mata, Maite, 'Assimilation et différence. Les Juifs et l'état-nation hongrois, 1895–1914', in *Les limites de siècles. Champs de forces conservatrices et régressives depuis les temps modernes*, ed. Marita Gilli, Presses Universitaires Franc-Comtoises 2001

Okyar, Osman, 'A New Look at the Problem of Economic Growth in the Ottoman Empire (1800–1914)', *Journal of European Economic History*, vol. 16, no. 1, Spring 1987

Oliveira Marques, A. H. de, *Histoire du Portugal et de son empire colonial*, Karthala, Paris 1998

Olusoga, David and Casper W. Erichsen, *The Kaiser's Holocaust: Germany's Forgotten Genocide and the Colonial Roots of Nazism*, Faber and Faber, London 2010

Osterhammel, Jürgen, *The Transformation of the World: A Global History of the Nineteenth Century*, Princeton University Press 2014

Ostiguy, Pierre, 'Gauches péroniste et non péroniste dans le système de partis argentin', *Revue internationale de politique comparée*, vol. 12, no. 3, 2005

Owen, Roger, *Lord Cromer: Victorian Imperialist, Edwardian Proconsul*, Oxford University Press 2004

Owen, Thomas C., *Dilemmas of Russian Capitalism: Fedor Chizhov and Corporate Enterprise in the Railroad Age*, Harvard University Press 2005

Oyangen, Knut, 'The Gastrodynamics of Displacement: Place-Making and Gustatory Identity in the Immigrants' Midwest', *Journal of Interdisciplinary History*, vol. 39, no. 3, Winter 2009, pp. 323–48

Ozouf, Jacques and Mona, 'Le thème du patriotisme dans les manuels primaires', *Le Mouvement Social*, no. 49, October–December 1964

Paine, S. C. M., *Imperial Rivals: China, Russia, and their Disputed Frontier*, M. E. Sharpe, Armonk, NY 1996

Paine, Thomas, *Common Sense*, 1776: http://www.gutenberg.org/files/147/147-h/147-h.htm

Palat, Madhavan K., 'Casting Workers as an Estate in Late Imperial Russia', *Kritika: Explorations in Russian and Eurasian History*, vol. 8, no. 2, Spring 2007

Palmer, Sarah, *Politics, Shipping and the Repeal of the Navigation Laws*, Manchester University Press 1990

Pamuk, Şevket, 'The Evolution of Fiscal Institutions in the Ottoman Empire, 1500–1914', in Bartolomé Yun-Casalilla and Patrick K. O'Brien (eds), *The Rise of Fiscal States: A Global History, 1500–1914*, Cambridge University Press 2012

Pamuk, Şevket, *The Ottoman Empire and European Capitalism, 1820–1913: Trade, Investment and Production*, Cambridge University Press 1987

Paparazzo, Amelia, *I subalterni calabresi tra rimpianto e trasgressione. La Calabria dal brigantaggio post-unitario all'età giolittiana*, Franco Angeli, Milan 1984

Parize, René, 'Les militants ouvriers au Creusot pendant les grèves de 1899–1900', *Le Mouvement Social*, no. 99, April–June 1977

Parthasarathi, Prasannan, Review article: 'The Great Divergence', *Past & Present*, no. 176, 2002, pp. 275–93

Patten, Simon N., *The New Basis of Civilization*, Macmillan, London 1907 (Kennedy Lectures 1905)

Payne, Stanley G., *A History of Spain and Portugal*, vol. 2: *Eighteenth Century to Franco*, University of Wisconsin Press 1973

Pecchio, Giuseppe, *Osservazioni semi-serie di un esule sull'Inghilterra*, G. Ruggia & Co., Lugano 1831

Péguy, Charles, *L'Argent (suite)*, in Charles Péguy, *Oeuvres en prose, 1909–1914*, Bibliothèque de la Pléiade Gallimard, Paris 1961

Pei, Minxin, *China's Trapped Transition: The Limits of Developmental Autocracy*, Harvard University Press 2006

Pennock, Caroline Dodds, 'Mass Murder or Religious Homicide? Rethinking Human Sacrifice and Interpersonal Violence in Aztec Society', *Historical Social Research / Historische Sozialforschung*, vol. 37, no. 3, 2012

Perdue, Peter C., *Exhausting the Earth: State and Peasant in Hunan, 1500–1850*, Harvard University Press 1987

Perham, Margery, *Lugard: The Years of Adventure, 1858–1898*, Collins, London 1956

Perkin, Harold, *The Rise of Professional Society: England since 1880*, Routledge, London 2002

Perkins, Franklin, 'The Theoretical Basis of Comparative Philosophy in Leibniz' Writings on China', in Wenchao Li and Hans Poser (eds), *Das neueste über China. G. W. Leibnizens Novissima Sinica von 1697*, Fran Steiner Verlag, Stuttgart 2000

Perras, Arne, *Carl Peters and German Imperialism, 1856–1918*, Oxford University Press 2004

Perrenoud, Alfred and Patrice Bourdelais, 'Le recul de la mortalité', in Bardet and Dupâquier (eds), *Histoire des populations de l'Europe*

Perrot, Michelle, *Les ouvriers en grève*, vol. 1, Mouton & Co., Paris 1974

Pezeu-Massabuau, Jacques, 'La notion d'emprise sur le milieu géographique: l'exemple japonais', *Annales*, vol. 27, no. 1, January–February 1972, pp. 97–121

Pezeu-Massabuau, Jacques, 'Le Japon à l'ère mégalopolitaine: éclatement de l'espace traditionnel et insularité culturelle', *Annales*, vol. 36, no. 5, September–October 1981, pp. 815–40

Pflanze, Otto, *Bismarck and the Development of Germany*, vol. III: *The Period of Fortification, 1880–1898*, Princeton University Press 1990

Phillips, William H., 'The Economic Performance of Late Victorian Britain: Traditional Historians and Growth', *Journal of European Economic History*, vol. 18, no. 2, Fall 1989

Photinos, Christine, 'The Tramp in American Literature, 1873–1939': http://ejournals.library.vanderbilt.edu/index.php/ameriquests/article/viewFile/62/60

Piel, Jean, 'The Place of the Peasantry in the National Life of Peru in the Nineteenth Century', *Past & Present*, no. 46, February 1970

Pierce, Justin R. and Peter K. Schott, 'The Surprisingly Swift Decline of US Manufacturing Employment', *American Economic Review*, vol. 106, no. 7, July 2016

Pierrard, André and Jean-Louis Chappat, *La fusillade de Fourmies*, Miroirs, Nord/Pas-de-Calais 1991

Piketty, Thomas, *Capital in the Twenty-First Century*, Belknap Press, Harvard University Press 2014

Piketty, Thomas, Gilles Postel-Vinay, and Jean-Laurent Rosenthal, 'Wealth Concentration in a Developing Economy: Paris and France, 1807–1994', *American Economic Review*, vol. 96, no. 1, March 2006

Pinchemel, Philippe, *Structures sociales et dépopulation rurale dans les campagnes picardes de 1836 à 1936*, Armand Colin, Paris 1957

Pinol, Jean-Luc, *Le monde des villes au XIXe siècle*, Hachette, Paris 1991

Pipes, Richard, '"Intelligentsia" from the German "Intelligenz"? A Note', *Slavic Review*, vol. 30, no. 3, September 1971

Pipes, Richard, *Russia under the Old Regime*, Penguin, London 1984

Pipes, Richard, *Russian Conservatism and its Critics: A Study in Political Culture*, Yale University Press 2005

Pirenne, Henri, *Histoire de Belgique. Des origines à nos jours*, vol. 5, La Renaissance du Livre, Brussels 1975, original edition in seven volumes, 1900–1932

Pius IX's *Quanta Cura* and *The Syllabus of Errors*: https://archive.org/stream/QuantaCuraTheSyllabusOfErrors_247/pius_ix_pope_quanta_cura_and_the_syllabus_of_errors_djvu.txt

Plaggenborg, Stefan, 'Tax Policy and the Question of Peasant Poverty in Tsarist Russia 1881–1905', *Cahiers du Monde russe*, vol. 36, nos 1–2, January–June 1995, pp. 53–69

Plaggenborg, Stefan, 'Who Paid for the Industrialisation of Tsarist Russia?', *Revolutionary Russia*, vol. 3, no. 2, December 1990

Platt, D. C. M., 'Canada and Argentina: The First Preference of the British Investor, 1904–14', *Journal of Imperial and Commonwealth History*, vol. 13, no. 3, May 1985

Platt, D. C. M., 'Economic Factors in British Policy during the "New Imperialism"', *Past and Present*, no. 39, April 1968

Platt, D. C. M., *Finance, Trade, and Politics in British Foreign Policy, 1815–1914*, Clarendon Press, Oxford 1968

Plessis, Alain, 'Le "retard français": la faute à la banque? Banques locales, succursales de la Banque de France et financement de l'économie sous le Second Empire', in Patrick Fridenson and André Straus (eds), *Le capitalisme français 19e–20e siècle. Blocages et dynamismes d'une croissance*, Fayard, Paris 1987, pp. 199–210

Pobedonostsev, Konstantin P., *Reflections of a Russian Statesman*, trans. Robert Crozier Long, Grant Richards, London 1898

Podestà, Gian Luca, 'L'émigration italienne en Afrique orientale', *Annales de démographie historique*, no. 113, 1, 2007

Polanyi, Karl, *The Great Transformation: The Political and Economic Origins of Our Time*, Beacon Press, Boston, MA 2002

Pollard, Sidney, 'Factory Discipline in the Industrial Revolution', *Economic History Review*, vol. 16, no. 2, 1963

Pomeranz, Kenneth, *The Great Divergence: China, Europe, and the Making of the Modern World Economy*, Princeton University Press 2000

Pomeranz, Kenneth and Steven Topik, *The World that Trade Created: Society, Culture, and the World Economy, 1400 to the Present*, M. E. Sharpe, Armonk, NY 2006

Porter, Bernard, *The Absent-Minded Imperialists: Empire, Society, and Culture in Britain*, Oxford University Press 2004

Porter, Bernard, *The Lion's Share: A Short History of British Imperialism, 1850–1970*, Longman, London and New York, 1975

Porter, Glenn, 'Industrialization and the Rise of Big Business', in Calhoun (ed.), *The Gilded Age*

Posada-Carbó, Eduardo, 'Electoral Juggling: A Comparative History of the Corruption of Suffrage in Latin America, 1830–1930', *Journal of Latin American Studies*, vol. 32, no. 3, October 2000

Postan, M. M., 'L'expérience de l'industrialisation européenne et les problèmes actuels des pays sous-développés', in *L'industrialisation en Europe eu XIXe siècle*, Colloque international du CNRS, Lyon 1970, Éditions du CNRS, Paris 1972

Postel-Vinay, Gilles, 'L'agriculture dans l'économie française. Crises et réinsertion', in Lévy-Leboyer and Casanova (eds), *Entre l'état et le marché*

Potter, David M., *People of Plenty: Economic Abundance and the American Character*, University of Chicago Press 1973, first published 1954

Poullet, Prosper, *Les institutions françaises de 1795 à 1814. Essai sur les origines des institutions belges contemporaines*, Plon, Paris 1907

Powers, John, *History as Propaganda: Tibetan Exiles versus the People's Republic of China*, Oxford University Press 2004

Prazmowska, Anita, *Ignacy Paderewski*, Haus Publishing, London 2009

Prevenier, Walter, 'Conscience et perception de la condition sociale chez les gens du commun dans les anciens Pays-Bas des XIIIe et XIVe siècles', in *Le petit peuple dans l'Occident médiéval: Terminologies, perceptions, réalités*, ed. Pierre Boglioni, Robert Delort, and Claude Gauvard, Publications de la Sorbonne, Paris 2002

Prewitt, Kenneth, *What Is Your Race?: The Census and Our Flawed Efforts to Classify Americans*, Princeton University Press 2013

Prior, Christopher, *Edwardian England and the Idea of Racial Decline: An Empire's Future*, Palgrave, Basingstoke 2013

Procacci, Giuliano, *La lotta di classe in Italia agli inizi del secolo XX*, Riuniti, Rome 1978

Provost, Claire, 'The Industry of Inequality: Why the World is Obsessed with Private Security', *The Guardian*, 12 May 2017

Przeworski, Adam, 'The Last Instance: Are Institutions the Primary Cause of Economic Development?', *Archives européennes de sociologie*, vol. xlv, no. 2, 2004

Puissant, Jean, '1886, la contre-réforme sociale?', in Van der Vorst (ed.), *Cent ans de droit social belge*

Purcell, Victor, *The Boxer Uprising: A Background Study*, Cambridge University Press 1963

Pushkin, Alexander, 'To Chaadaev', trans. A. N. Matyatina: http://zhurnal.lib.ru/m/matjatina_a_n/tochaadaevaspushkin.shtml

Pushkin, Alexander, *Yevgeny Onegin*, trans. Anthony Briggs, Pushkin Press, London 2016

Qi Lin, 'The Poisoned Palace – Mystery of Last Emperor's Death', *China Daily*, 21 November 2008: http://www.chinadaily.com.cn/china/2008-11/21/content_7226663.htm

Qian Long: Letter to George III, 1793, from the Qianlong Emperor: https://legacy.fordham.edu/halsall/mod/1793qianlong.asp

Qian, Wen-yuan, *The Great Inertia: Scientific Stagnation in Traditional China*, Croom Helm, London 1985

Quataert, Donald, 'The Economic Climate of the "Young Turk Revolution" in 1908', *Journal of Modern History*, vol. 51, no. 3, September 1979

Quataert, Donald, 'The Age of Reforms, 1812–1914', in Halil İnalcık (ed.), *An Economic and Social History of the Ottoman Empire, 1300–1914*, Cambridge University Press 1994

Quilici, Nello, *Origine, sviluppo e insufficienza della borghesia italiana*, ISPI, Milan 1942

Rachman, Gideon, *Easternisation: War and Peace in the Asian Century*, Bodley Head, London 2016

Radtke, Kurt W., 'Ishibashi Tanzan: A Liberal Nationalist', *Japan Forum*, vol. 1, no. 1, April 1989

Ragionieri, Ernesto, *Storia d'Italia*, vol. 4: *Dall'Unità a oggi*, Einaudi, Turin 1976

Ralle, Michel, 'L'état de la Restauration et l'anti-étatisme ouvrier', *Le Mouvement Social*, no. 128, July–September 1984

Rankin, Daniel J., 'The Portuguese in East Africa', *Fortnightly Review*, no. 278, February 1890

Rankin, Daniel J., *The Zambesi Basin and Nyassaland*, Blackwood, London 1893

Rawski, Evelyn Sakakida, *Education and Popular Literacy in Ch'ing China*, University of Michigan Press 1979

Reagan, Ronald, First Inaugural Address, 20 January 1981: http://www.presidency.ucsb.edu/ws/?pid=43130

Rebérioux, Madeleine, *La République radicale? 1898–1914*, Éditions du Seuil, Paris 1975

Reeves, Maud Pember, *Round About a Pound a Week*, G. Bell and Sons, London 1913

Reid, J. H. Stewart, *The Origins of the British Labour Party*, University of Minnesota Press 1955

Reinert, Hugo and Erik S. Reinert, 'Creative Destruction in Economics: Nietzsche, Sombart, Schumpeter', in *Friedrich Nietzsche (1844–1900): Economy and Society*, ed. Jürgen Georg Backhaus and Wolfgang Drechsler, Springer, New York 2006

Reis, Jaime, 'How Poor was the European Periphery before 1850? The Mediterranean vs Scandinavia', in Şevket Pamuk and Jeffrey G. Williamson (eds), *The Mediterranean Response to Globalization before 1950*, Routledge, London and New York 2000

Renan, Ernest, 'Qu'est-ce qu'une nation?', lecture held at the Sorbonne on 11 March 1882: http://www.rutebeuf.com/textes/renan01.html

Renan, Ernest, *Histoire générale et système comparé des langues sémitiques*, première partie, Imprimerie Impériale, Paris 1855: http://gallica.bnf.fr/ark:/12148/bpt6k648895ov

Renard, (Capitaine), *La colonisation au Congo français. Étude sur les concessions accordées au Congo en vertu du décret du 28 mars 1899*, Kugelmann, Paris 1901

Renard, Didier, 'Assistance publique et bienfaisance privée, 1885–1914', *Politiques et management public*, vol. 5, no. 2, 1987, pp. 107–28.

Répaci, Antonino, *La marcia su Roma*, Rizzoli, Milan 1972

Rey-Goldzeiguer, Annie, *Le royaume arabe. La politique algérienne de Napoléon III, 1861–1870*, SNED, Algiers 1977

Reynolds, Lloyd G., 'The Spread of Economic Growth to the Third World: 1850–1980', *Journal of Economic Literature*, vol. XXI, September 1983, pp. 941–80

Rhodes, Chris, 'Manufacturing: International Comparisons', House of Commons Briefing Paper no. 05809, 5 January 2018

Ricardo, David, *On the Principles of Political Economy and Taxation*, John Murray, London 1821

Richardson, Bonham C., *The Caribbean in the Wider World, 1492–1992: A Regional Geography*, Cambridge University Press 1992

Rieber, Alfred J., *Merchants and Entrepreneurs in Imperial Russia*, University of North Carolina Press 1982

Riedi, Eliza, 'Women, Gender, and the Promotion of Empire: The Victoria League, 1901–1914', *Historical Journal*, vol. 45, no. 3, September 2002, pp. 569–99

Riello, Giorgio, *Cotton: The Fabric that Made the Modern World*, Cambridge University Press 2013

Riesman, David, 'The Nylon War', in David Ricsman, *Abundance for What? And Other Essays*, Chatto and Windus, London 1964

Riesman, David, *Abundance for What? And Other Essays*, Chatto and Windus, London 1964

Riis, Jacob, *How the Other Half Lives*, W. W. Norton, New York 2010

Riley, James C., *Rising Life Expectancy: A Global History*, Cambridge University Press 2001

Rioux, Jean-Pierre, *La France coloniale sans fard ni déni*, André Versaille, Brussels 2011

Robbins, Keith, *John Bright*, Routledge and Kegan Paul, London 1979

Robbins, Richard G., *Famine in Russia 1891–1892*, Columbia University Press 1975

Roberts, Andrew, *Salisbury: Victorian Titan*, Weidenfeld and Nicolson, London 1999

Roberts, Spencer E., *Essays in Russian Literature: The Conservative View: Leontiev, Rozanov, Shestov*, Ohio University Press 1968

Robins, Nick, *The Corporation that Changed the World: How the East India Company Shaped the Modern Multinational*, Pluto Press, London 2012

Robinson, Joan, *Economic Heresies: Some Old-Fashioned Questions in Economic Theory*, Macmillan, London and Basingstoke 1972

Robinson, Ronald, 'European Imperialism and Indigenous Reactions in British West Africa, 1880–1914', in H. L. Wesseling (ed.), *Expansion and Reaction*, Leiden University Press 1978

Robinson, Ronald and John Gallagher, *Africa and the Victorians: The Official Mind of Imperialism*, Macmillan, London 1965

Robles-Ortiz, Claudio, 'Agrarian Capitalism and Rural Labour: The Hacienda System in Central Chile, 1870–1920', *Journal of Latin American Studies*, vol. 41, no. 3, August 2009

Robson, Martin, *A History of the Royal Navy: The Seven Years War*, I. B. Tauris, London 2015

Rockefeller, John D., *Random Reminiscences of Men and Events*, Doubleday, Page & Company, New York 1909

Rodó, José Enrique, *Ariel*, ed. Belén Castro, Cátedra, Madrid 2000

Roe, Mark J., *Strong Managers, Weak Owners: The Political Roots of American Corporate Finance*, Princeton University Press 1994

Rogers, Donald W., *Making Capitalism Safe: Work Safety and Health Regulation in America, 1880–1940*, University of Illinois Press 2009

Rogger, Hans, 'America in the Russian Mind – or Russian Discoveries of America', *Pacific Historical Review*, vol. 47, no. 1, February 1978, pp. 27–51

Rogger, Hans, '*Amerikanizm* and the Economic Development of Russia', *Comparative Studies in Society and History*, vol. 23, no. 3, July 1981

Rogger, Hans, 'Conclusion and Overview', in Klier and Lambroza (eds), *Pogroms: Anti-Jewish Violence in Modern Russian History*

Rogger, Hans, *Russia in the Age of Modernisation and Revolution, 1881–1917*, Longman, London and New York 1983

Rohrbacher, Stefan, 'The "Hep Hep" Riots of 1819: Anti-Jewish Ideology, Agitation, and Violence', in Hoffmann, Bergmann, and Smith (eds), *Exclusionary Violence*

Rojas, Eduardo, 'Le socialisme au pouvoir au Chili: de la révolution sociale à la gouvernabilité du système', *Problèmes d'Amérique latine*, no. 55, Winter 2004–5, pp. 115–39

Roland, Gérard (ed.), *Privatization: Successes and Failures*, Columbia University Press 2008

Romano, Salvatore Francesco, *Storia dei Fasci siciliani*, Laterza, Rome-Bari 1959

Roosa, Ruth A., *Russian Industrialists in an Era of Revolution*, M. E. Sharpe, Armonk, NY 1997

Roosevelt, Theodore, 'Address at the Coliseum', 14 September 1912, San Francisco, California, in David M. Kennedy and Thomas A. Bailey (eds), *The American Spirit: United States History as Seen by Contemporaries*, Cengage Learning, Boston, MA 2009, vol. 2

Roosevelt, Theodore, 'First Annual Message' to Congress, 3 December 1901: http://www.presidency.ucsb.edu/ws/?pid=29542

Roosevelt, Theodore, 'Fourth Annual Message' to Congress, 6 December 1904: http://www.presidency.ucsb.edu/ws/?pid=29545

Roosevelt, Theodore, 'State of the Union Address', 6 December 1904: http://www.infoplease.com/t/hist/state-of-the-union/116.html

Roosevelt, Theodore, 'The Monroe Doctrine', *The Bachelor of Arts*, March 1896, in *American Ideals and Other Essays, Social and Political*, Putnam, New York 1897

Roosevelt, Theodore, 'The Strenuous Life' speech, the Hamilton Club, Chicago, IL, 10 April 1899: https://en.wikisource.org/wiki/The_Strenuous_Life

Rosanvallon, Pierre, *Le sacre du citoyen. Histoire du suffrage universel en France*, Gallimard, Paris 1992

Rosdolsky, Roman, 'The Distribution of the Agrarian Product in Feudalism', *Journal of Economic History*, vol. 11, no. 3, Summer 1951, pp. 247–65

Rosebery (Lord), Leader's Speech at the National Liberal Federation conference held at Cardiff on 18 January 1895: http://www.britishpoliticalspeech.org/speech-archive.htm?speech=5

Rosenthal, Caitlin C., 'From Memory to Mastery: Accounting for Control in America, 1750–1880', *Enterprise & Society*, vol. 14, no. 4, December 2013

Ross, Christopher N. B., 'Lord Curzon and E. G. Browne Confront the "Persian Question"', *Historical Journal*, vol. 52, no. 2, 2009, pp. 385–411

Ross, Ronald J., 'Enforcing the Kulturkampf in the Bismarckian State and the Limits of Coercion in Imperial Germany', *Journal of Modern History*, vol. 56, no. 3, September 1984

Rothbard, Murray N., 'A Future of Peace and Capitalism', in James H. Weaver (ed.), *Modern Political Economy: Radical and Orthodox Views on Crucial Issues*, Allyn and Bacon, Boston, MA 1973

Rothschild, Emma, *Economic Sentiments: Adam Smith, Condorcet and the Enlightenment*, Harvard University Press 2001

Rothschild, Emma, *The Inner Life of Empires: An Eighteenth-Century History*, Princeton University Press 2011

Rousseau, Jean-Jacques, *Discours sur l'économie politique*: http://classiques.uqac.ca/classiques/Rousseau_jj/discours_economie_politique/discours_eco_pol.html

Rousseau, Jean-Jacques, *Du contrat social ou Principes du droit politique*, in *Oeuvres*, vol. 5, Werdet et Lequin fils, Paris 1826

Rowntree, B. Seebohm, *Poverty: A Study of Town Life*, Macmillan, London 1901

Rowthorn, Robert and Ramana Ramaswamy, 'Deindustrialization – Its Causes and Implications', Economic Issues no. 10, IMF, Washington, DC 1997

Rowthorn, Robert and Ramana Ramaswamy, 'Growth, Trade, and Deindustrialization', *IMF Staff Papers*, vol. 46, no. 1, March 1999

Roy, Tirthankar, *The East India Company: The World's Most Powerful Corporation*, Allen Lane, Penguin Books India, New Delhi 2012

Roy, William G., *Socializing Capital: The Rise of the Large Industrial Corporation in America*, Princeton University Press 1997

Rozman, Gilbert, 'Social Change', in Marius B. Jansen (ed.), *The Cambridge History of Japan*, vol. 5: *The Nineteenth Century*, Cambridge University Press 1989

Rubinstein, W. D., 'Education and the Social Origins of British Élites, 1880–1970', *Past & Present*, no. 112, August 1986

Rudé, George, 'English Rural and Urban Disturbances on the Eve of the First Reform Bill, 1830–1831', *Past & Present*, no. 37, 1967

Rudé, George, *The Crowd in the French Revolution*, Oxford University Press 1959

Ruskin, John, *The Crown of Wild Olive. Munera Pulveris. Pre-Raphaelitism. Aratra Pentelici, etc.*, Dana Estes & Co., Boston, MA 1900

Russell, William Howard, *My Diary in India, in the Year 1858–9*, Routledge, Warne, and Routledge, London 1860

Sabato, Hilda, 'Citizenship, Political Participation and the Formation of the Public Sphere in Buenos Aires 1850s–1880s', *Past & Present*, no. 136, August 1992

Sachs, Jeffrey D. and Andrew Warner, *Economic Reform and the Process of Global Integration*, Brookings Papers on Economic Activity 1995

Saint-Bonnet, Antoine Blanc de, *La Restauration française*, Casterman, Paris 1872 (first published 1851 by Hervé)

Sainte-Beuve, Charles-Augustin, 'De la littérature industrielle', *Revue des deux mondes*, September 1839: http://fr.wikisource.org/wiki/La_Litt%C3%A9rature_industrielle

Salia, Kalistrat, *Histoire de la nation géorgienne*, Nino Salia, Paris 1980

Salisbury, Robert Cecil (Lord Salisbury), 'English Politics and Parties', *Bentley's Quarterly Review*, vol. 1, March 1859

Salisbury, Robert Cecil (Lord Salisbury), 'Labourers' and Artisans' Dwellings', *National Review*, no. 9, November 1883

Salisbury, Robert Cecil (Lord Salisbury), Speech to the House of Lords on the Second Reading of the Anglo-German Agreement Bill on 10 July 1890: http://hansard.millbanksystems.com/lords/1890/jul/10/second-reading-2

Salisbury, Robert Cecil (Lord Salisbury), *Lord Salisbury on Politics: A Selection from his Articles in the Quarterly Review, 1860–83*, ed. Paul Smith, Cambridge University Press 1972

Salzmann, Ariel, 'Citizens in Search of a State: The Limits of Political Participation in the Late Ottoman Empire', in Michael Hanagan and Charles Tilly (eds), *Extending Citizenship, Reconfiguring States*, Rowman & Littlefield, Lanham, MD 1999

Sammons, Jeffrey L., *Wilhelm Raabe: The Fiction of the Alternative Community*, Princeton University Press 1987

Sánchez-Albornoz, Nicolás, 'The Population of Latin America, 1850–1930', in Bethell (ed.), *The Cambridge History of Latin America*, vol. IV

Sand, Jordan, 'Subaltern Imperialists: The New Historiography of the Japanese Empire', *Past & Present*, no. 225, November 2014

Sandberg, Lars G., 'The Case of the Impoverished Sophisticate: Human Capital and Swedish Economic Growth before World War I', *Journal of Economic History*, vol. 39, no. 1, March 1979

Sarraut, Albert, *Grandeur et servitude coloniales*, L'Harmattan, Paris 2012, introduction by Nicola Cooper, originally published 1931

Sassen, Saskia (ed.), *Deciphering the Global: Its Scales, Spaces and Subjects*, Routledge, London 2007

Satya, Laxman D., *Cotton and Famine in Berar, 1850–1900*, Manohar, New Delhi 1997

Saul, S. B., 'The Export Economy 1870–1914', *Bulletin of Economic Research*, vol. 17, no. 1, May 1965

Saul, S. B., *The Myth of the Great Depression, 1873–1896*, Macmillan, London 1969

Saxton, Alexander, *The Indispensable Enemy: Labor and the Anti-Chinese Movement in California*, University of California Press 1971

Say, Jean-Baptiste, *Cours complet d'économie politique pratique*, vol. 5, Rapilly, Paris 1829

Say, Jean-Baptiste, *Traité d'économie politique ou simple exposition de la manière dont se forment, se distribuent et se consomment les richesses*, O. Zeller, 1841 (6th edition): http://fr.wikisource.org/wiki/Trait%C3%A9_d%E2%80%99%C3%A9conomie_politique/1841

Sayre, Robert and Michael Löwy, 'Figures du romantisme anti-capitaliste: une tentative de typologie', *L'homme et la société*, nos 73–4, 1984: http://www.persee.fr/web/revues/home/prescript/article/homso_0018-4306_1984_num_73_1_2169

Schorske, Carl E., *Fin-de-Siècle Vienna: Politics and Culture*, Cambridge University Press 1981

Schulz, Günther, 'Industrial Patriarchalism in Germany', in Aerts, Beaud, and Stengers (eds), *Liberalism and Paternalism in the 19th Century*

Schumacher, Aloys, 'L'Allemagne à la fin du XIXe siècle, l'illusion de la "Weltpolitik" et l'interrogation sur les limites de siècles', in *Les limites de siècles. Lieux de ruptures novatrices depuis les temps modernes*, ed. Marita Gilli, Presses Universitaires Franc-Comtoises 1998

Schumpeter, Joseph A., 'The Crisis of the Tax State' (1918), in Joseph A. Schumpeter, *The Economics and Sociology of Capitalism*, ed. Richard Swedberg, Princeton University Press 1991

Schumpeter, Joseph A., *Capitalism, Socialism and Democracy*, Unwin, London 1965

Schumpeter, Joseph A., *The Theory of Economic Development*, Transaction Publishers, New Brunswick 2011

Schwartz, Benjamin I., *In Search of Wealth and Power: Yen Fu and the West*, Harper, New York 1964

Schwartz, Michael, *Radical Protest and Social Structure: The Southern Farmers' Alliance and Cotton Tenancy, 1880–1890*, University of Chicago Press 1976

Schwartz, Pedro, *The New Political Economy of J. S. Mill*, Weidenfeld and Nicolson, London 1972

Secor, Philip, *Presidential Profiles: From George Washington to G. W. Bush*, iUniverse, Bloomington, IN 2008

Seeley, John R., *The Expansion of England: Two Courses of Lectures*, Macmillan, London 1914

Selim, Monique, 'Notes from Tashkent', *New Left Review*, no. 55, January–February 2009

Sen, Amartya, *Poverty and Famines: An Essay on Entitlement and Deprivation*, Oxford University Press 1981

Senior, Nassau W., *Letters on the Factory Act*, B. Fellowes, London 1837

Sennett, Richard, *Families against the City: Middle-Class Homes of Industrial Chicago, 1872–1890*, Harvard University Press 1970

Serrano, Carlos, 'Patriotismes, questions coloniales et mouvements ouvriers en Espagne à la fin du XIXe siècle', *Le Mouvement Social*, no. 128, July–September 1984

Seton-Watson, Hugh, *The Russian Empire, 1801–1917*, Clarendon Press, Oxford 1967

Shadwell, Arthur, *Industrial Efficiency: A Comparative Study of Industrial Life in England, Germany and America*, vol. 2, Longmans, Green, and Co., London 1906

Shah, Nayan, *Contagious Divides: Epidemics and Race in San Francisco's Chinatown*, University of California Press 2001

Shanghai Ranking Consultancy: http://www.shanghairanking.com/ARWU2016.html

Shanin, Teodor (ed.), *Late Marx and the Russian Road: Marx and 'the peripheries of capitalism'*, Monthly Review Press, New York 1983

Shanley, Mary Lyndon, *Feminism, Marriage, and the Law in Victorian England, 1850–1895*, I. B. Tauris, London 1989

Shapiro, Ann-Louise, 'Paris', in Daunton (ed.), *Housing the Workers*

Shaw, Flora, 'Nigeria', *The Times*, 8 January 1897, p. 6 (unsigned)

Shelokhaev, V. V., 'The Liberal Reform Model in Early Twentieth-Century Russia', *Russian Studies in History*, vol. 42, no. 4, Spring 2004

Shevzov, Vera, *Russian Orthodoxy on the Eve of Revolution*, Oxford University Press 2004

Short, John Phillip, *Magic Lantern Empire: Colonialism and Society in Germany*, Cornell University Press 2012

Shorter, Edward and Charles Tilly, *Strikes in France, 1830–1968*, Cambridge University Press 1974

Shpotov, Boris M., 'Russia and the Americanization Process (1900–1930s)', in Dominique Barjot, Isabelle Lescent-Giles, and Marc de Ferrière Le Vayer (eds), *L'américanisation en Europe au XXe siècle: economie, culture, politique*, vol. 1, Centre de Recherche sur l'Histoire de l'Europe du Nord-Ouest, Université Charles-de-Gaulle, Lille 3, 2002

Shubert, Adrian, *A Social History of Modern Spain*, Unwin Hyman, London 1990

Shuster, W. Morgan, *The Strangling of Persia: A Record of European Diplomacy and Oriental Intrigue*, T. Fisher Unwin, London 1912

Sidgwick, Henry, *The Elements of Politics*, Macmillan, London 1897, first published 1891

Sieyès, Abbé (Emmanuel), *Préliminaire de la Constitution françoise. Reconnaissance et exposition raisonnée des droits de l'homme et du citoyen*, Baudouin, Paris 1789: http://gallica.bnf.fr/ark:/12148/bpt6k41690g

Simmel, Georg, 'The Metropolis and Mental Life' (1903), in *Simmel on Culture*, ed. David Frisby and Mike Featherstone, Sage, London 1997

Simms, J. Y., 'The Economic Impact of the Russian Famine of 1891–92', *Slavonic and East European Review*, vol. 60, no. 1, January 1982

Singer, Milton, 'Religion and Social Change in India: The Max Weber Thesis, Phase Three', *Economic Development and Cultural Change*, vol. 14, no. 4, July 1966

Sirinelli, Jean-François, 'Guerre d'Algérie, guerre des pétitions?', in Jean-Pierre Rioux and Jean-François Sirinelli (eds), *La guerre d'Algérie et les intellectuels français*, Éditions Complexe, Brussels 1991

Skidelsky, Robert, 'Thinking about the State and the Economy', in Simon J. D. Green and Richard C. Whiting (eds), *The Boundaries of the State in Modern Britain*, Cambridge University Press 1996

Sklar, Martin J., *The Corporate Reconstruction of American Capitalism, 1890–1916: The Market, the Law, and Politics*, Cambridge University Press 1988

Skocpol, Theda, *Boomerang: Clinton's Health Security Effort and the Turn against Government in US Politics*, Norton, New York 1996

Sluga, Glenda, 'Narrating Difference and Defining the Nation in Late Nineteenth and Early Twentieth Century "Western" Europe', *European Review of History*, vol. 9, no. 2, 2002

Smith, Adam, *An Inquiry into the Nature and Causes of the Wealth of Nations*, Penn State Electronic Classics 2005: http://www2.hn.psu.edu/faculty/jmanis/adam-smith/Wealth-Nations.pdf

Smith, Adam, *Lectures on Jurisprudence*, ed. R. L. Meek, D. D. Raphael, and P. G. Stein, Clarendon Press, Oxford 1978

Smith, Helmut Walser, *German Nationalism and Religious Conflict: Culture, Ideology, Politics, 1870–1914*, Princeton University Press 1995

Smith, Michael S., *Tariff Reform in France, 1860–1900*, Cornell University Press 1980

Smith, Paul, 'Labour under the Law', *Industrial Relations Journal*, vol. 46, nos 5–6, November 2015

Smith, Paul, 'New Labour and the Commonsense of Neoliberalism: Trade Unionism, Collective Bargaining, and Workers' Rights', *Industrial Relations Journal*, vol. 40, no. 4, 2009

Smith, Paul, *Disraelian Conservatism and Social Reform*, Routledge and Kegan Paul, London 1967

Smith, S. A., *Russia in Revolution: An Empire in Crisis, 1890 to 1928*, Oxford University Press 2017

Smith, Timothy B., 'The Ideology of Charity, the Image of the English Poor Law, and Debates over the Right to Assistance in France, 1830–1905', *Historical Journal*, vol. 40, no. 4, December 1997, pp. 997–1,032

Smith, Timothy B., *Creating the Welfare State in France, 1880–1940*, McGill-Queen's University Press 2003

Smith, Tony, *The Pattern of Imperialism: The United States, Great Britain, and the Late-Industrializing World since 1815*, Cambridge University Press 1981

Smith, Woodruff D., 'The Ideology of German Colonialism, 1840–1906', *Journal of Modern History*, vol. 46, no. 4, December 1974

Snow, George E., 'Introduction', in *The Years 1881–1894 in Russia: A Memorandum Found in the Papers of N. Kh. Bunge. A Translation and Commentary*, ed. George E. Snow, in *Transactions of the American Philosophical Society*, vol. 71, part 6, Philadelphia, PA 1981

Snyder, Timothy, *The Reconstruction of Nations: Poland, Ukraine, Lithuania, Belarus, 1569–1999*, Yale University Press 2003

So, Alvin Y. and Stephen W. K. Chiu, *East Asia and the World Economy*, Sage, London 1995

Sohrabi, Nader, *Revolution and Constitutionalism in the Ottoman Empire and Iran*, Cambridge University Press 2011

Sombart, Werner, *Krieg und Kapitalismus*, Duncker & Humblot, Munich and Leipzig 1913

Sombart, Werner, *The Quintessence of Capitalism: A Study of the History and Psychology of the Modern Business Man*, Fisher Unwin, London 1915. Translation of his 1913 *Der Bourgeois*.

Sombart, Werner, *Why is there no Socialism in the United States?* Macmillan, New York and London 1976

Sorlin, Pierre, *Waldeck-Rousseau*, Armand Colin, Paris 1966

Sowerwine, Charles, *France since 1870: Culture, Society and the Making of the Republic*, Palgrave, Basingstoke 2009

Spahr, Charles B., *An Essay on the Present Distribution of Wealth in the United States*, Thomas Y. Crowell and Co., 2nd ed., Boston, MA 1896: http://archive.org/details/anessayonpresen01spahgoog

Spence, Jonathan, 'Opium Smoking in Ch'ing China', in Frederic Wakeman, Jr. and Carolyn Grant (eds), *Conflict and Control in Late Imperial China*, University of California Press 1975

Spence, Jonathan, *The Chan's Great Continent: China in Western Minds*, Penguin, London 2000

Spence, Jonathan, *The China Helpers: Western Advisers in China, 1620–1960*, Bodley Head, London 1969

Spence, Jonathan, *The Gate of Heavenly Peace: The Chinese and their Revolution, 1895–1980*, Faber and Faber, London and Boston, MA 1982

Spence, Jonathan, *The Search for Modern China*, Norton, New York 2013

Sperber, Jonathan, *The Kaiser's Voters: Electors and Elections in Imperial Germany*, Cambridge University Press 1997

Spulber, Nicolas, *Russia's Economic Transitions: From Late Tsarism to the New Millennium*, Cambridge University Press 2003

Stanford, Leland, Inaugural Gubernatorial Address, 10 January 1862: http://governors.library.ca.gov/addresses/08-Stanford.html

Stannard, David E., *American Holocaust: Columbus and the Conquest of the New World*, Oxford University Press 1992

Starr, S. Frederick, 'August von Haxthausen and Russia', *Slavonic and East European Review*, vol. 46, no. 107, July 1968

Stead, W. T., *The Americanization of the World, or The Trend of the Twentieth Century*, Horace Markley, New York 1902

Stedman Jones, Gareth, 'Rethinking Chartism', in Gareth Stedman Jones, *Languages of Class: Studies in English Working Class History, 1832–1982*, Cambridge University Press 1983

Stedman Jones, Gareth, *Outcast London: A Study in the Relationship between Classes in Victorian Society*, Clarendon Press, Oxford 1971

Steele, E. David, *Lord Salisbury*, Routledge, London 2002

Stella, Alessandro, *La révolte des Ciompi. Les hommes, les lieux, le travail*, Éditions de l'École des Hautes Études en Sciences Sociales, Paris 1993

Stendhal, *La Chartreuse de Parme*, Nelson, Paris 1839

Stepanov, V. L., 'Finance Ministry Policy in the 1880s and the Unrealized Potential for Economic Modernization in Russia', *Russian Studies in History*, vol. 42, no. 4, Spring 2004, pp. 14–21

Stepanov, V. L., 'Ivan Alekseevich Vyshnegradskii', *Russian Studies in History*, vol. 35, no. 2, Fall 1996

Stepanov, V. L., 'Nikolai Khristianovich Bunge', *Russian Studies in History*, vol. 35, no. 2, Fall 1996

Stephanson, Anders, *Manifest Destiny: American Expansionism and the Empire of Right*, Hill and Wang, New York 1995

Stern, Fritz, *The Politics of Cultural Despair: A Study in the Rise of the Germanic Ideology*, University of California Press 1974

Sternhell, Zeev, *Aux origines d'Israël. Entre nationalisme et socialisme*, Gallimard, Paris 2004

Sternhell, Zeev, *Maurice Barrès et le nationalisme français*, Éditions Complexe, Brussels 1985 (first published 1972)

Sternhell, Zeev, *The Founding Myths of Israel: Nationalism, Socialism, and the Making of the Jewish State*, Princeton University Press 1997

Stevenson, David, *Armaments and the Coming of War: Europe, 1904–1914*, Clarendon Press, Oxford 1996

Stiglitz, Joseph E., 'Foreword', in Roland (ed.), *Privatization: Successes and Failures*

Stiglitz, Joseph E., 'Is there a Post-Washington Consensus Consensus?', in *The Washington Consensus Reconsidered: Towards a New Global Governance*, ed. Narcís Serra and Joseph E. Stiglitz, Oxford University Press 2008

Stiglitz, Joseph E., *Globalization and its Discontents*, Norton, New York 2002

Stora, Benjamin, *Les trois exils. Juifs d'Algérie*, Stock, Paris 2006

Storti, Craig, *Incident at Bitter Creek: The Story of the Rock Springs Chinese Massacre*, Iowa State University Press 1991

Strange, Susan, *Casino Capitalism*, Blackwell, Oxford 1986

Strange, Susan, *The Retreat of the State: The Diffusion of Power in the World Economy*, Cambridge University Press 1996

Strasser, Susan, *Never Done: A History of American Housework*, Pantheon Books, New York 1982

Strasser, Susan, *Satisfaction Guaranteed: The Making of the American Mass Market*, Pantheon Books, New York 1989

Strauss, Julia C., 'Creating "Virtuous and Talented" Officials for the Twentieth Century: Discourse and Practice in *Xinzheng* China', *Modern Asian Studies*, vol. 37, no. 4, October 2003, pp. 831–50

Strikwerda, Carl, *A House Divided: Catholics, Socialists, and Flemish Nationalists in Nineteenth-Century Belgium*, Rowman & Littlefield, Lanham, MD, and Oxford 1997

Strinati, Valerio, 'Origini e istituzione della cassa di maternità (1875–1910)', *Studi Storici*, vol. 45, no. 2, April–June 2004

Suetonius (Gaius Suetonius Tranquillus), *On Grammarians* (*De Illustribus grammaticis*): http://penelope.uchicago.edu/Thayer/E/Roman/Texts/Suetonius/de_Grammaticis*.html

Sumner, William Graham, *The Challenge of Facts and Other Essays*, Yale University Press 1914

Sumner, William Graham, *War and Other Essays*, Yale University Press 1911

Sun Yat-sen, *The Three Principles of the People*, China Cultural Service, Taiwan 1981

Supple, Barry, 'The State and the Industrial Revolution, 1700–1914', in *The Fontana Economic History of Europe*, ed. Carlo M. Cipolla, vol. 3: *The Industrial Revolution*, Collins, Glasgow 1980

Szreter, Simon, *Health and Wealth: Studies in History and Policy*, University of Rochester Press 2005

Tabor, Nick, 'No Slouch', *The Paris Review*, 7 April 2015

Taft, Philip and Philip Ross, 'American Labor Violence: Its Causes, Character, and Outcome', in Hugh Davis Graham and Ted Robert Gurr (eds), *The History of Violence in America*, Praeger, New York 1969

Taine, Hippolyte, *Notes sur l'Angleterre*, 11th ed., Hachette, Paris 1899

Taira, Koji, 'Factory Legislation and Management Modernization during Japan's Industrialization, 1886–1916', *Business History Review*, vol. 44, no. 1, 1970, pp. 84–109

Takaki, Ronald, *Strangers from a Different Shore: A History of Asian Americans*, Little, Brown and Co., Boston, MA 1989

Talleyrand, Charles-Maurice de, *Mémoires du prince de Talleyrand*, vol. 1, Calmann Lévy, Paris 1891

Tamaki, Norio, *Yukichi Fukuzawa, 1835–1901: The Spirit of Enterprise in Modern Japan*, Palgrave Macmillan, London 2001

Tames, Richard, *Economy and Society in Nineteenth Century Britain*, Routledge, London 2013

Tapinos, Georges, 'Une seconde transition démographique? La population et l'emploi', in Lévy-Leboyer and Casanova (eds), *Entre l'état et le marché*

Taussig, F. W., *The Tariff History of the United States: A Series of Essays*, Putnam and Sons, New York and London 1892

Tawney, R. H., *Religion and the Rise of Capitalism*, Transaction Publishers, London 1998

Tawney, R. H., *The Acquisitive Soviety*, 1920: http://www.gutenberg.org/files/33741/33741-h/33741-h.htm

Temin, Peter, 'Globalization', *Oxford Review of Economic Policy*, vol. 15, no. 4, 1999

Teng, Ssu-yü and John K. Fairbank (eds), *China's Response to the West: A Documentary Survey, 1839–1923*, Harvard University Press 1961

Teschke, Benno, *The Myth of 1648: Class, Geopolitics and the Making of Modern International Relations*, Verso, London 2003

Tesnière, Lucien, 'Statistique des langues de l'Europe', in Antoine Meillet, *Les langues dans l'Europe nouvelle*, Payot, Paris 1928

Thackeray, David, 'Rethinking the Edwardian Crisis of Conservatism', *Historical Journal*, vol. 54, no. 1, 2011, pp. 191–213

Thackeray, William Makepeace, *The Complete Poems of W. M. Thackeray*, White, Stokes, and Allen, New York 1883

Thatcher, Margaret, 'Speech to General Assembly of the Church of Scotland', 21 May 1988: http://www.margaretthatcher.org/document/107246

Theis, Laurent, *Guizot. La traversée d'un siècle*, CNRS Éditions, Paris 2014

Thibaudet, Albert, *Les idées politiques de la France*, Librairie Stock, Paris 1932

Thiesse, Anne-Marie, *La création des identités nationales. Europe XVIIIe–XXe siècle*, Seuil, Paris 1999

Thompson, Alastair, *Left Liberals, the State, and Popular Politics in Wilhelmine Germany*, Oxford University Press 2000

Thompson, Andrew, 'Informal Empire? An Exploration in the History of Anglo-Argentine Relations, 1810–1914', *Journal of Latin American Studies*, vol. 24, no. 2, 1992, pp. 419–36

Thompson, F. M. L., 'Changing Perceptions of Land Tenures in Britain, 1750–1914', in Winch and O'Brien (eds), *The Political Economy of British Historical Experience, 1688–1914*

Thompson, F. M. L., *The Rise of Respectable Society: A Social History of Victorian Britain, 1830–1900*, Harvard University Press 1988

Thompson, James, '"A Nearly Related People": German Views of the British Labour Market, 1870–1900', in Winch and O'Brien (eds), *The Political Economy of British Historical Experience, 1688–1914*

Thompson, Roger R., *China's Local Councils in the Age of Constitutional Reform, 1898–1911*, Harvard University Press 1995

Tierney, Robert Thomas, *Tropics of Savagery: The Culture of the Japanese Empire in Comparative Frame*, University of California Press 2010

Tilly, Charles, 'War Making and State Making as Organized Crime', in *Bringing the State Back In*, ed. Peter B. Evans, Dietrich Rueschemeyer, and Theda Skocpol, Cambridge University Press 1985

Tocqueville, Alexis de, *De la démocratie en Amérique*, Pagnerre, Paris 1848

Tocqueville, Alexis de, *Mémoire sur le paupérisme*, Ministère de l'instruction publique et des beaux-arts, Imprimerie nationale, Paris 1835

Tocqueville, Alexis de, *Souvenirs*, Calmann Lévy, Paris 1893

Tocqueville, Alexis de, *The Ancien Régime and the French Revolution*, trans. Arthur Goldhammer, Cambridge University Press 2011

Tocqueville, Alexis de, *Travail sur l'Algérie*, in *Oeuvres complètes*, Gallimard, Bibliothèque de la Pléiade, Paris, 1991

Todd, David, *L'identité économique de la France: Libre-échange et protectionnisme 1814–1851*, Grasset, Paris 2008

Todorova, Maria, *Imagining the Balkans*, Oxford University Press 1997

Togliatti, Palmiro, 'Discorso su Giolitti', in Palmiro Togliatti, *Momenti della storia d'Italia*, Riuniti, Rome 1974

Tombs, Robert, 'How Bloody was *La Semaine Sanglante* of 1871? A Revision', *Historical Journal*, vol. 55, no. 3, 2012

Toniolo, Gianni, *Storia economica dell'Italia liberale, 1850–1918*, Il Mullino, Bologna 1988

Tooze, Adam, *The Deluge: The Great War and the Remaking of the Global Order, 1916–1931*, Allen Lane, London 2014

Torp, Cornelius, 'The "Coalition of Rye and Iron" under the Pressure of Globalization: A Reinterpretation of Germany's Political Economy before 1914', *Central European History*, vol. 43, no. 3, 2010

Tortella, Gabriel, 'Patterns of Economic Retardation and Recovery in South-Western Europe in the Nineteenth and Twentieth Centuries', *Economic History Review*, vol. 47, no. 1, 1994

Tortella, Gabriel, *The Development of Modern Spain: An Economic History of the Nineteenth and Twentieth Centuries*, Harvard University Press 2000

Toutain, Jean-Claude, *La population de la France de 1700 à 1959*, in *Cahiers de L'Institut de Science Économique Appliquée*, supplementary no. 133, January 1963

Treitschke, Heinrich von and Adolf Hausrath, *Treitschke: His Life and Works*, Jarrold & Sons/Allen & Unwin, London 1914: https://archive.org/stream/treitschkehislifootreiuoft#page/n11/mode/2up

Trencsényi, Balázs, Maciej Janowski, Mónika Baár, Maria Falina, and Michal Kopeček, *A History of Modern Political Thought in East Central Europe*, vol. 1: *Negotiating Modernity in the 'Long Nineteenth Century'*, Oxford University Press 2016

Trentmann, Frank, 'National Identity and Consumer Politics: Free Trade and Tariff Reform', in Winch and O'Brien (eds), *The Political Economy of British Historical Experience, 1688–1914*

Trentmann, Frank, *Free Trade Nation*, Oxford University Press 2008

Tribe, Keith, *Strategies of Economic Order: German Economic Discourse, 1750–1950*, Cambridge University Press 1995

Tristan, Flora, *Le tour de France. État actuel de la classe ouvrière sous l'aspect moral – intellectuel – matériel. Journal inédit 1843–1844*, Éditions Tête de feuilles, Paris 1973: http://gallica.bnf.fr/ark:/12148/bpt6k82507w

Troesken, Werner, 'Typhoid Rates and the Public Acquisition of Private Waterworks, 1880–1920', *Journal of Economic History*, vol. 59, no. 4, December 1999

Trump, Donald, Inaugural Address 2017: https://www.whitehouse.gov/inaugural-address

Tsuzuki, Chushichi, *The Pursuit of Power in Modern Japan, 1825–1995*, Oxford University Press 2000

Turner, Frederick Jackson, *The Frontier in American History*, Henry Holt and Co., New York 1921

Turner, Nat, *The Confessions of Nat Turner . . . As fully and voluntarily made to Thomas R. Gray . . .* : http://docsouth.unc.edu/neh/turner/turner.html

Uchida, Jun, *Brokers of Empire: Japanese Settler Colonialism in Korea, 1876–1945*, Harvard University Press 2011

Umemori, Naoyuki, 'The Historical Contexts of the High Treason Incident', in Masako Gavin and Ben Middleton (eds), *Japan and the High Treason Incident*, Routledge, London and New York 2013

UNICEF: https://www.unicef.org/gambia/Progress_on_drinking_water_and_sanitation_2014_update.pdf

United Nations, Department of Economic and Social Affairs, Population Division, *World Population Prospects: The 2015 Revision*, POP/DB/WPP/Rev.2015/POP/F01-1

USA Bureau of Labor Statistics: https://www.bls.gov/oes/current/oes339032.htm; https://www.bls.gov/oes/current/oes333051.htm; http://data.bls.gov/cgi-bin/cpicalc.pl; http://www.bls.gov/iag/tgs/iagauto.htm#iag31cesnsahourlyearnings.f.P

US Census Bureau: https://www.census.gov/population/censusdata/table-16.pdf

US Census Bureau Population Clock: https://www.census.gov/popclock/?intcmp=home_pop

US Census Office. *Report on Transportation Business in the United States at the Eleventh Census: 1890*

Van De Mieroop, Marc, 'Production and Commerce in the Old Babylonian Period', *Rivista di storia economica*, vol. 31, no. 1, April 2015, pp. 79–96

Van den Eeckhout, Patricia, 'Brussels', in Daunton (ed.), *Housing the Workers*

van der Eng, Pierre, 'Exploring Exploitation: The Netherlands and Colonial Indonesia 1870–1940', *Revista de Historia Económica*, vol. 16, no. 1, Winter 1998

Van der Vorst, Pierre (ed.), *Cent ans de droit social belge*, Bruylant, Brussels 1988

Van Reybrouck, David, *Congo: The Epic History of a People*, Fourth Estate, London 2014

Vandervelde, Émile, *Les crimes de la colonisation capitaliste. Interpellation de Vandervelde au Gouvernement*, Volksdrukkerij, Gand 1906

Vandervelde, Émile, *Les derniers jours de l'État du Congo. Journal de voyage (juillet–octobre 1908)*, Édition de la Société Nouvelle, Mons 1909

Vann, Michael G., 'Building Colonial Whiteness on the Red River: Race, Power, and Urbanism in Paul Doumer's Hanoi, 1897–1902', *Historical Reflections/Réflexions historiques*, vol. 33, no. 2, Summer 2007

Varouxakis, Georgios, *Mill on Nationality*, Routledge, London 2013

Vatikiotis, P. J., *The Modern History of Egypt*, Weidenfeld and Nicolson, London 1969

Veblen, Thorstein, *The Theory of the Leisure Class*, Random House, New York 2001

Velychenko, Stephen, 'Empire Loyalism and Minority Nationalism in Great Britain and Imperial Russia, 1707 to 1914: Institutions, Law, and Nationality in Scotland and Ukraine', *Comparative Studies in Society and History*, vol. 39, no. 3, July 1997

Verdès-Leroux, Jeannine, *Scandale financier et antisémitisme catholique. Le krach de l'Union générale*, Le Centurion, Paris 1969

Verley, Patrick, *Nouvelle histoire économique de la France contemporaine*, vol. 2: *L'industrialisation 1830–1914*, La Découverte, Paris 2002

Vernon, James, *Hunger: A Modern History*, Belknap Press of Harvard University Press 2007

Veuillot, Eugène, *Çà et là*, vol. 2, Gaume frères et J. Duprey, Paris 1860

Vichnevski, Anatoli, *La faucille et le rouble. La modernisation conservatrice en URSS*, Gallimard, Paris 2000

Vickers, Adrian, *A History of Modern Indonesia*, Cambridge University Press 2005

Victoria (Queen), *The Letters of Queen Victoria*, vol. 4, ed. George E. Buckle, Cambridge University Press 2014

Vidal, Jean-François, *Dépression et retour à la prospérité. Les économies européennes à la fin du XIXe siècle*, L'Harmattan, Paris 2000

Villari, Pasquale, 'Di chi è la colpa? O sia la pace o la guerra', in *Saggi di storia, di critica e di politica*, Tipografia Cavour, Florence 1868

Villari, Pasquale, *Le lettere meridionali ed altri scritti sulla questione sociale in Italia*, Le Monnier, Florence 1878

Villermé, Louis René, *Tableau de l'état physique et moral des ouvriers employés dans les manufactures de coton, de laine et de soie*, ed. Yves Tyl, UGE, Collection 10/18, Paris 1971: http://classiques.uqac.ca/classiques/villerme_louis_rene/tableau_etat_physique_moral/villerme_tableau_ouvriers.pdf

Vivian, Herbert, 'The French in Tunisia', *Contemporary Review*, vol. 74, October 1898

Voas, David and Mark Chaves, 'Is the United States a Counterexample to the Secularization Thesis?', *American Journal of Sociology*, vol. 121, no. 5, March 2016

Vögele, Jörg P., 'Différences entre ville et campagne et évolution de la mortalité en Allemagne pendant l'industrialisation', *Annales de démographie historique*, 1996

Vögele, Jörg P., *Urban Mortality Change in England and Germany, 1870–1913*, Liverpool University Press 1998

Volgyes, Ivan (ed.), *The Peasantry of Eastern Europe*, vol. 1: *Roots of Rural Transformation*, Pergamon Press, New York 1979

Voltaire, *Essai sur les moeurs et l'esprit des nations*, Tome 1 in *Oeuvres complètes*, vol. 15, Dupont, Paris 1823–7

Voltaire, *Histoire de Charles XII*, in *Oeuvres complètes*, vol. 22, Dupont, Paris 1823–7

Voltaire, *Histoire de l'Empire de Russie sous Pierre le Grand*, in *Oeuvres complètes*, vol. 23, Dupont, Paris 1823–7

Von Laue, Theodore H., 'A Secret Memorandum of Sergei Witte on the Industrialization of Imperial Russia', *Journal of Modern History*, vol. 26, no. 1, March 1954, pp. 60–74

Von Laue, Theodore H., 'Legal Marxism and the "Fate of Capitalism in Russia"', *Review of Politics*, vol. 18, no. 1, January 1956

Vries, P. H. H., 'Are Coal and Colonies Really Crucial? Kenneth Pomeranz and the Great Divergence', *Journal of World History*, vol. 12, no. 2, Fall 2001

Waddell, D. A. G., 'International Politics and Latin American Independence', in Bethell (ed.), *The Cambridge History of Latin America*, vol. III

Wade, Robert, 'Financial Regime Change?', *New Left Review*, no. 53, September/October 2008

Waines, David, 'The Failure of the Nationalist Resistance', in *The Transformation of Palestine: Essays on the Origin and Development of the Arab-Israeli Conflict*, ed. Ibrahim Abu-Lughod, Northwestern University Press 1987

Wakeman, Frederic, Jr., *The Fall of Imperial China*, The Free Press, New York and London 1975

Walicki, Andrzej, 'The Troubling Legacy of Roman Dmowski', *East European Politics and Societies*, vol. 14, no. 1, Winter 2000

Walicki, Andrzej, *The Controversy over Capitalism: Studies in the Social Philosophy of the Russian Populists*, University of Notre Dame Press 1989

Walicki, Andrzej, *The Slavophile Controversy: History of a Conservative Utopia in Nineteenth-Century Russian Thought*, Clarendon Press, Oxford 1975

Walker, Richard and Daniel Buck, 'The Chinese Road: Cities in the Transition to Capitalism', *New Left Review*, no. 46, July–August 2007

Wang, Haidong et al., 'Age-Specific and Sex-Specific Mortality in 187 Countries, 1970–2010: A Systematic Analysis for the Global Burden of Disease Study 2010', *Lancet*, vol. 380, no. 9859, 15 December 2012

Ward, William George, 'The Encyclical and Syllabus', *Dublin Review*, vol. 56, January–April 1865

Washbrook, David, 'South Asia, the World System, and World Capitalism', *Journal of Asian Studies*, vol. 49, no. 3, August 1990

Water Aid: http://www.wateraid.org/where-we-work/page/india

Webb, Sidney, 'A Plea for an Eight Hours Bill', Fabian Tract no. 16, 1890

Webb, Sidney, 'The Moral of the Elections', *Contemporary Review*, vol. 62, August 1892

Webb, Sidney and Beatrice, *Industrial Democracy*, Longmans, Green & Co., London 1902 (first published 1897)

Weber, Max, 'Politics as a Vocation', in Max Weber, *The Vocation Lectures*, ed. David Owen and Tracy B. Strong, Hackett Publishing, Indianapolis, IN 2004

Weber, Max, 'The Nation State and Economic Policy', in Peter Lassman and Ronald Speirs (eds), *Weber: Political Writings*, Cambridge University Press 1994

Weber, Max, *General Economic History* (1927), The Free Press, Glencoe, IL, 1950

Weber, Max, *The Protestant Ethic and the Spirit of Capitalism*, ed. and trans. Stephen Kalberg, Blackwell, Oxford 2002

Weber, Max, *The Religion of China: Confucianism and Taoism*, Macmillan, New York 1951

Webster, Richard A., *Industrial Imperialism in Italy, 1908–1915*, University of California Press 1975

Weeks, Theodore R., 'National Minorities in the Russian Empire, 1897–1917', in Anna Geifman (ed.), *Russia under the Last Tsar: Opposition and Subversion, 1894–1917*, Blackwell, Oxford 1999

Wehler, Hans-Ulrich, *The German Empire, 1871–1918*, Berg, Leamington Spa 1985

Weil, François, 'Les paternalismes aux États-Unis (1800–1930)', in Aerts, Beaud, and Stengers (eds), *Liberalism and Paternalism in the 19th Century*

Weil, Patrick, *Qu'est-ce qu'un Français?*, Grasset, Paris 2002

Weinberg, Robert, 'The Pogrom of 1905 in Odessa: A Case Study', in Klier and Lambroza (eds), *Pogroms: Anti-Jewish Violence in Modern Russian History*

Weiss, John H., 'Origins of the French Welfare State: Poor Relief in the Third Republic, 1871–1914', *French Historical Studies*, vol. 13, no. 1, Spring 1983

Weissbach, Lee Shai, 'Child Labor Legislation in Nineteenth-Century France', *Journal of Economic History*, vol. 37, no. 1, March 1977

Weissbach, Lee Shai, *Child Labor Reform in Nineteenth-Century France: Assuring the Future Harvest*, Louisiana State University Press 1989

Welch, William M., Jr., *No Country for a Gentleman: British Rule in Egypt, 1883–1907*, Greenwood Press, Westport, CT 1988

Werner, Karl Ferdinand, *Histoire de la France*, vol. 1: *Les Origines*, Fayard, Paris 1984

Wesseling, H. L., *Imperialism and Colonialism: Essays on the History of European Expansion*, Greenwood Press, Westport, CT 1997

West, Richard, *Brazza of the Congo: European Exploration and Exploitation in French Equatorial Africa*, Jonathan Cape, London 1972

Westad, Odd Arne, *Restless Empire: China and the World since 1750*, Bodley Head, London 2012

Weston, Timothy B., 'The Founding of the Imperial University and the Emergence of Chinese Modernity', in Rebecca E. Karl and Peter Zarrow (eds), *Rethinking the 1898 Reform Period: Political and Cultural Change in Late Qing China*, Harvard University Asia Center 2002

Whisenhunt, Donald W. (ed.), *Reading the Twentieth Century: Documents in American History*, Rowman & Littlefield, Lanham, MD 2009

Whitman, Walt, 'As I Sat Alone by Blue Ontario's Shores' and 'A Passage to India' (1870) from *Leaves of Grass*

Whitman, Walt, *Democratic Vistas* (1871): http://xroads.virginia.edu/~hyper/whitman/vistas/vistas.html

Wiener, Jonathan M., 'Review of Reviews: *Social Origins of Dictatorship and Democracy*', *History and Theory*, vol. 15, no. 2, May 1976

Wiener, Martin J., *English Culture and the Decline of the Industrial Spirit, 1850–1980*, Cambridge University Press 1981

Wileman, Donald G., 'Not the Radical Republic: Liberal Ideology and Central Blandishment in France, 1901–1914', *Historical Journal*, vol. 37, no. 3, September 1994, pp. 593–614

Wilkins, Mira, *The Emergence of Multinational Enterprise: American Business Abroad from the Colonial Era to 1914*, Harvard University Press 1970

Wilkins, Mira, *The History of Foreign Investment in the United States to 1914*, Harvard University Press 1989

Wilkinson, Richard and Kate Pickett, *The Spirit Level: Why More Equal Societies Almost Always Do Better*, Allen Lane, London 2009

Willard, Claude, *Le mouvement socialiste en France (1893–1905)*, Les Guesdistes, Éditions sociales, Paris 1965

Williams, Ernest Edwin, '*Made in Germany*', Heinemann, London 1896

Williams, Rosalind H., *Dream Worlds: Mass Consumption in Late Nineteenth-Century France*, University of California Press 1982

Williamson, Jeffrey G., *Globalization and the Poor Periphery before 1950*, MIT Press, Cambridge, MA 2006

Williamson, John, 'What Washington Means by Policy Reform', in *Latin American Adjustment: How Much Has Happened?*, ed. John Williamson, Institute for International Economics, Washington, DC 1989

Wilson, Andrew, *The Ukrainians: Unexpected Nation*, Yale University Press 2015

Wilson, Henry Lane, 'Errors with Reference to Mexico and Events that have Occurred There', *Annals of the American Academy of Political and Social Science*, vol. 54, July 1914

Wilson, Keith M., *The International Impact of the Boer War*, Routledge, London 2014 (revised ed.)

Wilson, Terry P., *The Cart that Changed the World: The Career of Sylvan N. Goldman*, University of Oklahoma Press 1978

Wilson, Woodrow, 'Democracy and Efficiency', *Atlantic Monthly*, vol. 87, no. 521, March 1901

Winch, Donald, 'Adam Smith's "enduring particular result": A Political and Cosmopolitan Perspective', in Istvan Hont and Michael Ignatieff (eds), *Wealth and Virtue: The Shaping of Political Economy in the Scottish Enlightenment*, Cambridge University Press 1983

Winch, Donald, *Riches and Poverty: An Intellectual History of Political Economy in Britain, 1750–1834*, Cambridge University Press 1996

Winch, Donald and Patrick O'Brien (eds), *The Political Economy of British Historical Experience, 1688–1914*, Oxford University Press 2002

Winkler, Heinrich August, *Germany: The Long Road West, 1789–1933*, Oxford University Press 2006

Winock, Michel, *La France et les Juifs*, Seuil, Paris 2004

Winter, James, *London's Teeming Streets, 1830–1914*, Routledge, London 1993

Witte, Sergei, *The Memoirs of Count Witte*, Heinemann, London 1921

Wohl, Anthony S., *The Eternal Slum: Housing and Social Policy in Victorian London*, Edward Arnold, London 1977

Wolf, Martin, 'How the Beijing Elite Sees the World', *The Financial Times*, 2 May 2018

Wolfe, Patrick, *Traces of History: Elementary Structures of Race*, Verso, London 2016

Wolff, Larry, 'Voltaire's Public and the Idea of Eastern Europe', *Slavic Review*, vol. 54, no. 4, 1995

Womack, John, Jr., 'The Mexican Revolution, 1910–1920', in Bethell (ed.), *The Cambridge History of Latin America*, vol. V

Wong, J. Y., *Deadly Dreams: Opium, Imperialism, and the* Arrow *War (1856–60) in China*, Cambridge University Press 1998

Wong, Roy Bin, *China Transformed: Historical Change and the Limits of European Experience*, Cornell University Press 1997

Woods, R. I., P. A. Watterson, and J. H. Woodward, 'The Causes of Rapid Infant Mortality Decline in England and Wales, 1861–1921, Part I', *Population Studies*, vol. 42, no. 3, November 1988, pp. 343–66

Woods, Robert, 'The Effects of Population Redistribution on the Level of Mortality in Nineteenth-Century England and Wales', *Journal of Economic History*, vol. 45, no. 3, September 1985

Woolf, Stuart, *The Poor in Western Europe in the Eighteenth and Nineteenth Centuries*, Methuen, London 1986

World Bank: http://data.worldbank.org/indicator/SP.URB.TOTL.IN.ZS?page=3

Wright, Mary Clabaugh, *The Last Stand of Chinese Conservatism: The T'ung-Chih Restoration 1862–1874*, Stanford University Press 1957

Wrigley, Chris, 'May Days and After', *History Today*, vol. 40, no. 6, June 1990: http://www.historytoday.com/chris-wrigley/may-days-and-after#sthash.qwns4XkK.dpuf

Wrigley, Chris (ed.), *British Trade Unions, 1945–1995*, Manchester University Press 1997

Wrigley, E. A., 'Brake or Accelerator? Urban Growth and Population Growth before the Industrial Revolution', in *Urbanization in History: A Process of Dynamic Interactions*, ed. Ad van der Woude, Akira Hayami, and Jan De Vries, Clarendon Press, Oxford 1995

Wrigley, E. A. and R. S. Schofield, *The Population History of England, 1541–1871*, Cambridge University Press 1989

Wu Chengming, 'A Brief Account of the Development of Capitalism in China', in Tim Wright (ed.), *The Chinese Economy in the Early Twentieth Century: Recent Chinese Studies*, St Martin's Press, New York 1992

Wu Chengming, 'On Embryonic Capitalism in China', in Xu Dixin and Wu Chengming (eds), *Chinese Capitalism, 1522–1840*

Wynn, Charters, *Workers, Strikes, and Pogroms: The Donbass-Dnepr Bend in Late Imperial Russia, 1870–1905*, Princeton University Press 1992

Xu Dixin and Wu Chengming (eds), *Chinese Capitalism, 1522–1840*, Macmillan, Basingstoke 2000

Yan Fu (Yen Fou), *Les manifestes de Yen Fou*, ed. François Houang, Fayard, Paris 1977

Yapp, Malcolm, 'Europe in the Turkish Mirror', *Past & Present*, no. 137, 1992

Zamagni, Vera, 'An International Comparison of Real Industrial Wages, 1890–1913: Methodological Issues and Results', in Peter Scholliers (ed.), *Real Wages in 19th and 20th Century Europe: Historical and Comparative Perspectives*, Berg, Oxford 1989

Zamagni, Vera, *Dalla periferia al centro. La seconda rinascita economica dell'Italia 1861–1981*, Il Mulino, Bologna 1990

Zamagni, Vera, *The Economic History of Italy, 1860–1990*, Clarendon Press, Oxford 1993

Zanichelli, Domenico, *Studi politici e storici*, Zanichelli, Bologna 1893

Zaridze, David et al., 'Alcohol and Mortality in Russia: Prospective Observational Study of 151,000 adults', *Lancet*, vol. 383, no. 9927, pp. 1,465–73

Zelnik, Reginald E., *Labor and Society in Tsarist Russia: The Factory Workers of St. Petersburg, 1855–1870*, Stanford University Press 1971

Zhang Zhidong (Chang Chih-tung), *China's Only Hope: An Appeal*, trans. Samuel I. Woodbridge, Fleming H. Revell Co., New York 1900

Zimmerman, Joshua D., *Poles, Jews, and the Politics of Nationality*, University of Wisconsin Press 2004

Zimmermann, Maurice, 'La ruine de l'empire colonial espagnol. Ses conséquences', *Annales de Géographie*, vol. 8, no. 37, 1899

Zimmermann, Maurice, 'Leçon d'ouverture du cours d'histoire et de géographie coloniales', *Annales de Géographie*, vol. 9, no. 43, 1900

Zolberg, Aristide R., 'Global Movements, Global Walls: Responses to Migration, 1885–1925', in Wang Gungwu (ed.), *Global History and Migrations*, Westview Press, Boulder CO, 1997

Zoppi, Sergio, *Dalla Rerum Novarum alla democrazia cristiana di Murri*, Il Mulino, Bologna 1991

Zürcher, Erik-Jan, 'Ottoman Sources of Kemalist Thought', in Elisabeth Özdalga (ed.), *Late Ottoman Society: The Intellectual Legacy*, Routledge, New York 2005

Notes

INTRODUCTION

1. Marc Van De Mieroop, 'Production and Commerce in the Old Babylonian Period', in *Rivista di storia economica*, vol. 31, no. 1, April 2015, p. 86. 2. See paragraph 23 in Gaius Suetonius Tranquillus, *On Grammarians*: http://penelope.uchicago.edu/Thayer/E/Roman/Texts/Suetonius/de_Grammaticis*.html. 3. David Nonnis, 'Le attività artigianali', in Arnaldo Marcone (ed.), *L'età romana. Liberi, semiliberi, e schiavi in una società premoderna*, Castelvecchi, Rome 2016, p. 276. 4. Catharina Lis and Hugo Soly, *Worthy Efforts: Attitudes to Work and Workers in Pre-Industrial Europe*, Brill, Leiden and Boston, MA 2012, p. 59. 5. Jean-Paul Morel, 'L'artigiano', in *L'uomo romano*, ed. Andrea Giardina, Laterza, Rome-Bari 1989, pp. 235, 243, 252, 266. 6. Stefano Gasparri and Cristina La Rocca, *Tempi barbarici. L'Europa occidentale tra antichità e medioevo (300–900)*, Carocci, Rome 2013, pp. 294–6. 7. Franco Franceschi and Ilaria Taddei, *Le città italiane nel Medioevo, XII–XIV secolo*, Il Mulino, Bologna 2012, pp. 73–7. 8. Samuel Kline Cohn, Jr., *The Laboring Classes in Renaissance Florence*, Academic Press, New York 1980, pp. 9–11, 69. 9. A thorough analysis can be found in Alessandro Stella, *La révolte des ciompi. Les hommes, les lieux, le travail*, Éditions de l'École des Hautes Études en Sciences Sociales, Paris 1993. Stella also discusses the historiography on whether the revolt could be qualified as an instance of the class struggle between the proletariat and the bourgeoisie, pp. 21–9; see also Walter Prevenier, 'Conscience et perception de la condition sociale chez les gens du commun dans les anciens Pays-Bas des XIIIe et XIVe siècles', in *Le petit peuple dans l'Occident médiéval: Terminologies, perceptions, réalités*, ed. Pierre Boglioni, Robert Delort, and Claude Gauvard, Publications de la Sorbonne, Paris 2002, pp. 177–8. 10. Massimo Costantini, *L'albero della libertà economica. Il processo di scioglimento delle corporazioni veneziane*, Arsenale, Venice, 1987, pp. 22–3. 11. Ibid, pp. 34–8. 12. Catharina Lis and Hugo Soly, *Poverty and Capitalism in Pre-Industrial Europe*, Harvester Press, Hassocks, Sussex 1979, p. 64. 13. See Pierre Jouanique, 'Three Medieval Merchants: Francesco di Marco Datini, Jacques Coeur and Benedetto Cotrugli', *Accounting, Business & Financial History*, vol. 6, no. 3, 1996, pp. 261–75. 14. Hammurabi, *The Code of Hammurabi*, trans. L. W. King, 1915: http://www.sacred-texts.com/ane/

ham/index.htm, and see also Van De Mieroop, 'Production and Commerce in the Old Babylonian Period', p. 88. **15.** Lis and Soly, *Worthy Efforts*, pp. 442–4. **16.** On Bruges and Antwerp see J. L. Bolton and F. G. Bruscoli, 'When Did Antwerp Replace Bruges as the Commercial and Financial Centre of North-Western Europe? The Evidence of the Borromei Ledger for 1438', *The Economic History Review*, vol. 61, 2008, pp. 360–79. **17.** Richard A. Goldthwaite, 'The Economy of Renaissance Italy: The Preconditions for Luxury Consumption', in *I Tatti Studies: Essays in the Renaissance*, vol. 2, Villa I Tatti and Harvard University Center, Florence 1987, p. 19. **18.** Ibid, p. 31. **19.** Jan de Vries and Ad van der Woude, *The First Modern Economy: Success, Failure, and Perseverance of the Dutch Economy, 1500–1815*, Cambridge University Press 1997, pp. 334–6 and 129. **20.** Ibid, p. 270. **21.** Ibid, p. 174. **22.** Robert P. Brenner, 'The Low Countries in the Transition to Capitalism', *Journal of Agrarian Change*, vol. 1, no. 2, April 2001, pp. 215–18, 224. **23.** See the analysis in Jonathan I. Israel, *Dutch Primacy in World Trade, 1585–1740*, Clarendon Press, Oxford 1989, p. 361. **24.** Daniel Defoe, *A Tour Thro' the Whole Island of Great Britain: Divided into Circuits or Journeys*, S. Birt, T. Osborne, et al., London 1748, p. 101 (first published 1724). **25.** E. A. Wrigley, 'Brake or Accelerator? Urban Growth and Population Growth before the Industrial Revolution', in *Urbanization in History: A Process of Dynamic Interactions*, ed. Ad van der Woude, Akira Hayami, and Jan De Vries, Clarendon Press, Oxford, 1995, p. 107. **26.** Eric Hobsbawm, *The Age of Empire 1875–1914*, Weidenfeld and Nicolson, London 1987, p. 343. **27.** See Kenneth Pomeranz, *The Great Divergence: China, Europe, and the Making of the Modern World Economy*, Princeton University Press 2000, p. 206. This important book has sparked a major debate. Stephen Broadberry and Bishnupriya Gupta argue that the advanced parts of India and China were similar to the less advanced parts of Europe; see their 'The Early Modern Great Divergence: Wages, Prices and Economic Development in Europe and Asia, 1500–1800', *Economic History Review*, vol. 59, no. 1, 2006, pp. 2–31. See also Prasannan Parthasarathi, 'Review Article: The Great Divergence', *Past & Present*, no. 176, 2002, pp. 275–93. The wider controversy on the 'West and the Rest' or 'eurocentrics' versus 'orientalists' is ably explored (but with little impartiality) by Joseph M. Bryant, 'The West and the Rest Revisited: Debating Capitalist Origins, European Colonialism, and the Advent of Modernity', *Canadian Journal of Sociology*, vol. 31, no. 4, Autumn 2006, pp. 403–44. A more favourable review is P. H. H. Vries, 'Are Coal and Colonies Really Crucial? Kenneth Pomeranz and the Great Divergence', *Journal of World History*, vol. 12, no. 2, Fall 2001. See also Fernand Braudel, *Civilisation matérielle, économie et capitalisme, XVe–XVIIIe siècle*, vol. 2: *Les jeux de l'échange*, Armand Colin, Paris 1979, esp. pp. 495–534; Joel Mokyr, *The Enlightened Economy: An Economic History of Britain, 1700–1850*, Yale University Press 2009, p. 100. **28.** Robert C. Allen, *The British Industrial Revolution in Global Perspective*, Cambridge University Press 2009, p. 81. **29.** Ibid, p. 82. **30.** Ibid, esp. chapter 6; on the amateur nature of British inventors see Joel Mokyr, *The Lever of Riches:*

Technological Creativity and Economic Progress, Oxford University Press 1990, p. 244. 31. Allen, *The British Industrial Revolution in Global Perspective*, chapter 4, esp. pp. 25–28ff. 32. Karl Marx, *Capital*, vol. 1, Progress Publishers, Moscow 1965, p. 759. 33. See Sven Beckert, *Empire of Cotton: A Global History*, Knopf, New York 2014, p. 244. 34. This is the substance of Joel Mokyr's explanation in his *The Enlightened Economy*, see esp. pp. 95, 106–23ff. Robert Allen disputed with considerable evidence any close connection between inventors and the Enlightenment; see his *The British Industrial Revolution in Global Perspective*, chapter 10. 35. Paul Bairoch, 'Le mythe de la croissance économique rapide au XIXe siècle', *Revue de l'Institut de Sociologie*, no. 2, 1962, pp. 312–17. 36. H. J. Habakkuk, *American and British Technology in the 19th Century: The Search for Labour-Saving Inventions*, Cambridge University Press 1962, pp. 4–5. 37. Firouzeh Nahavandi, 'Développement et globalization', in Firouzeh Nahavandi (ed.), *Globalisation et néolibéralisme dans le tiers-monde*, L'Harmattan, Paris 2000, p. 20. 38. See Adam Przeworski, 'The Last Instance: Are Institutions the Primary Cause of Economic Development?', *Archives Européennes de sociologie*, vol. 45, no. 2, 2004, pp. 165–67, and Douglass C. North, *Institutions, Institutional Change and Economic Performance*, Cambridge University Press 1990, p. 110. 39. Barry Supple, 'The State and the Industrial Revolution 1700–1914', in *The Fontana Economic History of Europe*, ed. Carlo M. Cipolla, vol. 3: *The Industrial Revolution*, Collins, Glasgow 1980, pp. 326–30. 40. Paul Johnson, *Making the Market: Victorian Origins of Corporate Capitalism*, Cambridge University Press 2010, p. 11. 41. Martin J. Daunton, *Royal Mail: The Post Office since 1840*, Bloomsbury, London 2015, pp. 19, 36. 42. Colin J. Holmes, 'Laissez-Faire in Theory and Practice: Britain 1800–1875', *Journal of European Economic History*, vol. 5, no. 3, Winter 1976, pp. 684–5. 43. R. W. Ferrier, *The History of the British Petroleum Company*, vol. 1: *The Developing Years 1901–1932*, Cambridge University Press 1982, pp. 190–201. 44. See data in Brian R. Mitchell's *International Historical Statistics: Europe 1750–2005* and *International Historical Statistics: The Americas 1750–2005*, Palgrave Macmillan, New York 2007. 45. Lloyd G. Reynolds, 'The Spread of Economic Growth to the Third World: 1850–1980', *Journal of Economic Literature*, vol. XXI, September 1983, p. 959. 46. *Eurostat*: http://epp.eurostat.ec.europa.eu/statistics_explained/index.php?title=File:Shares_in_the_world_market_for_exports,_2010_%28%25_share_of_world_exports%29.png&filetimestamp=20121008124241, and: http://epp.eurostat.ec.europa.eu/statistics_explained/index.php?title=File:Shares_in_the_world_market_for_imports,_2010_%28%25_share_of_world_imports%29.png&filetimestamp=20121008124249 47. Leslie Hannah, 'Logistics, Market Size, and Giant Plants in the Early Twentieth Century: A Global View', *Journal of Economic History*, vol. 68, no. 1, March 2008, p. 61. 48. Bernard Michel, 'La révolution industrielle dans les pays tchèques au XIXe siècle', *Annales*, vol. 20, no. 5, September–October 1965, pp. 984–1,105. 49. Michel Hau, 'Industrialization and Culture: The Case of Alsace', *Journal of European Economic History*, vol. 29, nos 2–3, Autumn–Winter 2000, pp. 295–9. 50. All figures in Paul Bairoch, *Victoires et déboires*, vol. II: *Histoire économique et sociale du monde du XVIe siècle à nos jours*, Folio Gallimard, Paris 1997, p. 16. 51. See data in Mitchell's *European Historical Statistics 1750–2005* and *International Historical Statistics: The Americas 1750–2005*. 52. Sven Beckert, 'Emancipation and Empire: Reconstructing the Worldwide Web of Cotton Production in the Age of the American Civil War', *American Historical Review*, vol. 109, no. 5, December 2004, p. 1,437. 53. World Bank (on the basis of ILO figures): http://data.worldbank.org/indicator/SL.IND.EMPL.ZS?end=2010&start=2006&view=map 54. UN: https://unstats.un.org/unsd/cr/registry/regcs.asp?Cl=17&Lg=1&Co=D 55. Hannah, 'Logistics, Market Size, and Giant Plants in the Early Twentieth Century', p. 53. 56. Patrick Verley, *La première révolution industrielle*, Armand Colin, Paris 2006, pp. 79–80, 106–7. 57. Théophile Gautier, 'Eugène Plon. Thorvaldsen, sa vie et son oeuvre', *Le Moniteur Universel*, 8 July 1867. '*D'un côté, la modernité la plus extrême; de l'autre, l'amour austère de l'antique.*' 58. John Stuart Mill, *Principles of Political Economy*, Longmans, Green and Co., London 1904, p. 351. 59. Joyce Appleby, *The Relentless Revolution: A History of Capitalism*, W. W. Norton & Co., New York 2011, p. 12. 60. Adam Tooze, *The Deluge: The Great War and the Remaking of the Global Order, 1916–1931*, Allen Lane, London 2014, p. 463. 61. Jenny Chan, Ngai Pun, and Mark Selden, 'Labour Protests and Trade Union Reforms in China', in Jan Drahokoupil, Rutvica Andrijasevic, and Devi Sacchetto (eds), *Flexible Workforces and Low Profit Margins: Electronics Assembly between Europe and China*, ETUI (Europe Trade Union Institute), Brussels 2016, p. 207, and, in the same collection, Wolfgang Müller, 'Foxconn Economics: How Much Room for Better Pay and Conditions?', p. 166. 62. Marx, *Capital*, vol. 1, pp. 254–5. 63. Jean-Charles Asselain, 'L'expérience chinoise en perspective historique. Un regard occidental', *Revue d'études comparatives Est-Ouest*, vol. 30, nos 2–3, 1999, p. 348. 64. E. A. Wrigley and R. S. Schofield, *The Population History of England, 1541–1871*, Cambridge University Press 1989, p. 210. 65. Thomas Carlyle, 'Signs of the Times', *The Collected Works*, vol. III, Chapman and Hall, London 1858, p. 100 (published in the *Edinburgh Review*). 66. Ibid, vol. III, p. 111. 67. Juan Donoso Cortés, *Essay on Catholicism, Liberalism, and Socialism Considered in their Fundamental Principles*, J. B. Lippincott & Co., Philadelphia, PA 1862, pp. 257, 175–6. 68. Jack Hayward, *Fragmented France: Two Centuries of Disputed Identity*, Oxford University Press 2007, p. 192. 69. Gabriel Ardant, *Histoire financière. De l'antiquité à nos jours*, Gallimard, Paris 1976, p. 329. 70. Alexis de Tocqueville, *The Ancien Régime and the French Revolution*, trans. Arthur Goldhammer, Cambridge University Press 2011, p. 157. 71. Giuseppe Tomasi di Lampedusa, *Il gattopardo*, Feltrinelli, Milan 2002, p. 41. 72. Michael Bentley, *Lord Salisbury's World: Conservative Environments in Late-Victorian Britain*, Cambridge University Press 2001, pp. 252–3. 73. Lord Salisbury, *Quarterly Review*, vol. 117, no. 233, 1865, p. 550, cited in *Lord Salisbury on Politics: A Selection from his Articles in the*

Quarterly Review, 1860–83, ed. Paul Smith, Cambridge University Press 1972, p. 24. 74. Werner Sombart, *Krieg und Kapitalismus*, Duncker & Humblot, Munich and Leipzig 1913, p. 207; Joseph A. Schumpeter, *Capitalism, Socialism and Democracy*, Unwin, London 1965, p. 83. Hugo Reinert and Erik S. Reinert trace the idea back to Nietzsche and before him to Hinduism, which so inspired Nietzsche; see their 'Creative Destruction in Economics: Nietzsche, Sombart, Schumpeter', in *Friedrich Nietzsche (1844–1900): Economy and Society*, ed. Jürgen Georg Backhaus and Wolfgang Drechsler, Springer, New York 2006. 75. Jerry Z. Muller, *The Mind and the Market: Capitalism in Modern European Thought*, Knopf, New York 2002, p. 295. 76. Richard Hofstadter, *Social Darwinism in American Thought*, Beacon Press, Boston, MA 1992, p. 8. This is the classic text on the subject, first published in 1944. 77. Kevin H. O'Rourke and Jeffrey G. Williamson, *Globalisation and History: The Evolution of a Nineteenth-Century Atlantic Economy*, MIT Press, Cambridge, MA 1999, p. 14 and esp. chapter 2. 78. Eric J. Hobsbawm, *Nations and Nationalism since 1780*, Cambridge University Press 1993, p. 132. 79. Jeffrey D. Sachs and Andrew Warner, *Economic Reform and the Process of Global Integration*, Brookings Papers on Economic Activity, 1995, p. 5. 80. Maurice Obstfeld and Alan M. Taylor, 'Globalization and Capital Markets', in Michael D. Bordo, Alan M. Taylor, and Jeffrey G. Williamson (eds), *Globalization in Historical Perspective*, University of Chicago Press 2003, p. 127. 81. Joseph A. Schumpeter, *The Theory of Economic Development*, Transaction Publishers, New Brunswick 2011, p. 156.

1. NEW STATES, OLD STATES

1. J. R. McNeill and William H. McNeill, *The Human Web*, W. W. Norton, London 2003, pp. 11–13. 2. See Kenneth Pomeranz and Steven Topik, *The World That Trade Created: Society, Culture and the World Economy, 1400 to the Present*, M. E. Sharpe, Armonk, New York 2006, p. 47; see also Geoff Wade, 'The Zheng He Voyages: A Reassessment', Asia Research Institute, National University of Singapore: http://www.hsse.nie.edu.sg/hum2008/conference%20paper/pdf/Wade%20zhenghe%20humanitiesconf.pdf; see also Christian Grataloup, *Géohistoire de la mondialisation*, Armand Colin, Paris 2007, pp. 107–9. 3. Pomeranz and Topik, *The World That Trade Created*, p. 21. 4. Pierre Chaunu, *Histoire, science sociale. La durée, l'espace et l'homme à l'époque moderne*, SEDES, Paris 1974, pp. 188–91. 5. Saskia Sassen (ed.), *Deciphering the Global: Its Scales, Spaces and Subjects*, Routledge, London 2007, p. 5. 6. See Manuel Castells, *The Rise of the Network Society*, vol. 1 of *The Information Age*, Blackwell, Oxford 1996, pp. 32–4. 7. Theodore Levitt, 'The Globalization of Markets', *Harvard Business Review*, vol. 61, no. 3, May–June 1983, pp. 92–102. 8. See GEMDEV (Groupement Économie Mondiale, Tiers-Monde, Développement), *Mondialisation. Les mots et les choses*, Khartala, Paris 1999, p. 7. 9. Susan Strange, *The Retreat of the State:*

The Diffusion of Power in the World Economy, Cambridge University Press 1996, p. xiii. 10. Judith A. Carney, *Black Rice: The African Origins of Rice Cultivation in the Americas*, Harvard University Press 2001. 11. Pomeranz and Topik, *The World That Trade Created*, p. xi. 12. Tracy Borman, *Thomas Cromwell: The Untold Story of Henry VIII's Most Faithful Servant*, Hodder & Stoughton, London 2014, Chapter 9. 13. Christian Boudan, *Géopolitique du goût. La guerre culinaire*, Presses Universitaires de France, Paris 2004, pp. 287–8. 14. Jean-Paul Aron, *Le mangeur du XIXe siècle*, Payot, Paris 1989, p. 109. 15. Ardant, *Histoire financière*, p. 333. 16. Veronika Hyden-Hanscho, 'Invisible Globalization: French Hats in Habsburg Vienna, 1650–1750', *Journal of European Economic History*, vol. 45, no. 3, 2016, pp. 11–54. 17. Jeffrey G. Williamson, *Globalization and the Poor Periphery before 1950*, MIT Press, Cambridge, MA 2006, pp. 12–15, 28. 18. Gregory Clark and Robert C. Feenstra, 'Technology in the Great Divergence', in Bordo, Taylor, and Williamson (eds), *Globalization in Historical Perspective*, p. 295. 19. Jeremy Bentham, *An Introduction to the Principles of Morals and Legislation* (originally printed 1780, first published 1789), vol. 2, Pickering, London 1823, p. 261; the Marquis de Condorcet, *Esquisse d'un tableau historique des progrès de l'esprit humain*, ed. Oliver H. Prior, Vrin, Paris 1970, p. 211. 20. See CIA, *World Factbook*: https://www.cia.gov/library/publications/the-world-factbook/appendix/appendix-g.html 21. F. S. L. Lyons, *Internationalism in Europe, 1815–1914*, A. W. Sythoff, Leiden 1963, p. 14. 22. Observatory of Economic Complexity, 2012 figures: http://atlas.media.mit.edu/en/visualize/tree_map/hs92/export/show/all/8471/2012 23. Orlando Figes, *The Whisperers: Private Life in Stalin's Russia*, Allen Lane, London 2007, p. 494. 24. Diogenes Laertius, *Lives of Eminent Philosophers*, trans. R. D. Hicks, vol. 2, Heinemann, London and New York 1925, p. 65. 25. See the study promoted by the French government: Département des études, de la prospective et des statistiques, *Cultures croisées. Références interculturelles des Allemands, des Italiens et des Français*, November 2008: http://www.culture.gouv.fr/depscultéuturdees 26. Kenichi Ohmae, *The End of the Nation State: The Rise of Regional Economies*, The Free Press, New York 1995, pp. 5, 80. 27. Kenichi Ohmae, *Beyond National Borders: Reflections on Japan and the World*, Dow Jones-Irwin, Homewood, IL 1987, p. 3. 28. Gustave Hervé, *L'internationalisme*, Giard & Brière, Paris 1910, pp. 5, 172: '*Les grandes patries modernes sont à peine nées, et voici que déjà elles sont minées par l'internationalisme.*' 29. Fernand Braudel, *L'identité de la France. Espace et histoire*, Arthaud-Flammarion, Paris 1986, pp. 288–90. 30. Anne-Marie Thiesse, *La création des identités nationales. Europe XVIIIe–XXe siècle*, Seuil, Paris 1999, pp. 50–51. 31. Karl Ferdinand Werner, *Histoire de la France*, vol. 1: *Les Origines*, Fayard, Paris 1984, p. 20. 32. Norman Davies, *God's Playground: A History of Poland*, vol. 1: *The Origins to 1795*, Clarendon Press, Oxford 1981, pp. 21ff. 33. Ibid, p. 24. 34. Tessa Morris-Suzuki, *Re-Inventing Japan: Time, Space, Nation*, M. E. Sharpe, Armonk, NY 1998, pp. 5–9. 35. Kalistrat Salia, *Histoire de la nation géorgienne*, Nino Salia, Paris 1980, p. 11; see also Thorniké Gordadzé's scathing criticism of this book in 'La réforme du passé: l'effort historiographique de construction de la nation géorgienne', *Revue d'études comparatives Est-Ouest*, vol. 30, no. 1, March 1999, pp. 53–80, esp. pp. 58, 63. 36. Andrew Wilson, *The Ukrainians: Unexpected Nation*, Yale University Press 2015, pp. 21–2. 37. Livy, *Ab urbe condita*, Book I, chapter 2: *'sub eodem iure solum sed etiam nomine omnes essent'*. 38. S. C. M. Paine, *Imperial Rivals: China, Russia, and their Disputed Frontier*, M. E. Sharpe, Armonk, NY 1996, p. 90. 39. Amalendu Misra, *Afghanistan: The Labyrinth of Violence*, Polity, Cambridge 2004, pp. 5ff. 40. A. I. Asiwaju, *Partitioned Africans: Ethnic Relations across Africa's International Boundaries, 1884–1984*, C. Hurst & Co., London 1985, pp. 2ff. 41. Flora Shaw, 'Nigeria', *The Times*, 8 January 1897, p. 6 (unsigned). 42. Paul Collier and Anke Hoeffler, 'Greed and Grievance in Civil War', *Oxford Economic Papers*, no. 56, 2004, p. 563. 43. Charles and Barbara Jelavich, *The Establishment of the Balkan National States 1804–1920*, University of Washington Press 1977, p. 66. 44. Keith Hitchins, *Rumania, 1866–1947*, Oxford University Press 1994, pp. 12–14. 45. Georges B. Dertilis, 'Introduction', in Georges B. Dertilis (ed.), *Banquiers, usuriers et paysans. Réseaux de crédit et stratégies du capital en Grèce (1780–1930)*, La Découverte, Paris 1988, p. 25; Catherine Durandin, *Histoire des Roumains*, Fayard, Paris 1995, p. 149. 46. Durandin, *Histoire des Roumains*, p. 148. 47. Caroline Finkel, *Osman's Dream: The Story of the Ottoman Empire 1300–1923*, John Murray, London 2005, p. 471. 48. Ibid, p. 486. 49. Stephen F. Jones, 'Russian Imperial Administration and the Georgian Nobility: The Georgian Conspiracy of 1832', *The Slavonic and East European Review*, vol. 65, no. 1, January 1987, pp. 54–5. In the nationalist version of Kalistrat Salia the Russian annexation of Georgia is portrayed as a unilateral initiative by the Tsar; see Salia, *Histoire de la nation géorgienne*, pp. 380–81. 50. Glenda Sluga, 'Narrating Difference and Defining the Nation in Late Nineteenth- and Early Twentieth Century "Western" Europe', *European Review of History*, vol. 9, no. 2, 2002, pp. 188–9. 51. Source: US Census Bureau, Internet release date: 13 September 2002. 52. http://www.census.gov/population/www/documentation/twps0029/twps0029.html 53. Frederick Jackson Turner, 'The Significance of the Frontier in American History', in *The Frontier in American History*, Holt, Rinehart and Winston, New York 1962, p. 4. 54. John Lynch, 'The Origins of Spanish American Independence', in Bethell (ed.), *Cambridge History of Latin America*, vol. III, p. 11. 55. Paul H. Lewis, *Authoritarian Regimes in Latin America: Dictators, Despots, and Tyrants*, Rowman & Littlefield, Lanham, MD 2005, p. 17 and p. 30n. 56. Nicolás Sánchez-Albornoz, 'The Population of Latin America, 1850–1930', in Bethell (ed.), *The Cambridge History of Latin America*, vol. IV, p. 122; Massimo Livi Bacci, *The Population of Europe: A History*, Blackwell, Oxford 2000, p. 8. 57. Simón Bolívar, *El Libertador: Writings of Simón Bolívar*, Oxford University Press 2003, p. 101. 58. Lewis, *Authoritarian Regimes in Latin America*, p. 17. 59. Emília Viotti Da Costa, 'Brazil: The Age of Reform, 1870–1889', in Bethell (ed.), *The Cambridge History of Latin America*, vol. V, p. 777. 60. Jean Piel, 'The Place of the Peasantry in the National Life of Peru in the Nineteenth Century', *Past & Present*, no. 46, February 1970, p. 120. 61. Benedict Anderson, *Imagined Communities*, Verso, London 2006, 2nd ed., pp. 50, 53ff. 62. Henrietta Harrison, *China: Inventing the Nation*, Bloomsbury, London 2001. 63. Rana Mitter, *A Bitter Revolution: China's Struggle with the Modern World*, Oxford University Press 2005, p. 30. 64. Amos Elon, *Herzl*, Weidenfeld and Nicolson, London 1975, p. 23. 65. Theodor Herzl, *The Jewish State*, Penguin, London 2010, pp. 29–30. 66. Ibid, pp. 38, 57. 67. Ibid, p. 96. 68. Sven Rubenson, 'Ethiopia and the Horn', in *The Cambridge History of Africa*, vol. 5, *From c. 1790 to 1870*, ed. John E. Flint, Cambridge University Press 1976, pp. 57–8. 69. Christopher Fyfe, 'Freed Slave Colonies in West Africa', in ibid, p. 192.

2. THE LIVES OF THE PEOPLE

1. Paolo Sorcinelli, 'L'alimentation et la santé', in *Histoire de l'alimentation*, ed. Jean-Louis Flandrin and Massimo Montanari, Fayard, Paris 1996, pp. 810–11. 2. Jean Leduc, *Histoire de la France: l'enracinement de la République, 1879–1918*, Hachette, Paris 1991, pp. 6–8. 3. Pierre Gourou, *Les Paysans du delta tonkinois* (Thèse doctorat), Les Éditions d'Art et d'Histoire, Paris 1936, pp. 306–9 and 568–9. 4. Robert J. Gordon, 'Does the "New Economy" Measure up to the Great Inventions of the Past?', *Journal of Economic Perspectives*, vol. 14, no. 4, Autumn 2000, pp. 49–74, esp. pp. 59–60; see also idem, *The Rise and Fall of American Growth: The U.S. Standard of Living since the Civil War*, Princeton University Press 2016, pp. 3–7. 5. Jean-Noël Biraben, 'Essai sur l'évolution du nombre des hommes', *Population*, vol. 34, no. 1, January–February 1979, p. 15, for data before 1950. For 1950, 1987, and 2015, see United Nations, Department of Economic and Social Affairs, Population Division, *World Population Prospects: The 2015 Revision*, POP/DB/WPP/Rev.2015/POP/F01-1. For 2018 see UN: births and deaths can be seen, as they happen, on this website: http://www.worldometers.info/world-population 6. Jacques Chastenet, *Histoire de la Troisième République. L'enfance de la troisième, 1870–1879*, Hachette, Paris 1952, pp. 260–62. 7. World Bank Data reporting UN data: http://data.worldbank.org/indicator/SP.URB.TOTL.IN.ZS?page=3 8. Ian Gazeley and Sara Horrell, 'Nutrition in the English Agricultural Labourer's Household over the Course of the Long Nineteenth Century', *Economic History Review*, vol. 66, no. 3, August 2013, pp. 757–84. 9. Jerome Blum, 'The Condition of the European Peasantry on the Eve of Emancipation', *Journal of Modern History*, vol. 46, no. 3, September 1974, pp. 410–12. 10. Paul Bairoch, 'La Suisse dans le contexte international aux XIXe et XXe siècles', in Paul Bairoch and Martin Körner (eds), *La Suisse dans l'économie mondiale*, Droz, Geneva 1990, p. 104. 11. Piero Meldini, 'A tavola e in cucina', in Piero Melograni (ed.), *La famiglia italiana dall'ottocento a oggi*, Laterza, Rome-Bari 1988, p. 435. 12. William N. Beauclerk, *Rural Italy: An*

Account of the Present Agricultural Conditions of the Kingdom, Richard Bentley & Son, London 1888, pp. 175, 107. 13. Stefano Jacini (ed.), *Atti della Giunta per la inchiesta agraria e sulle condizioni della classe agricola*, vol. XI, Tomo 1, *Province di Roma e Grosseto*, Forzani, Rome 1884, pp. 787–8, p. 793: https://play.google.com/books/reader?id=OiooAAAAYAAJ&printsec=frontcover&output=reader&authuser=0&hl=en&pg=GBS.PA793 14. E. J. T. Collins, 'Why Wheat? Choice of Food Grains in Europe in the Nineteenth and Twentieth Centuries', *Journal of European Economic History*, vol. 22, no. 1, 1993, p. 9. 15. Giovanni Montroni, *La società italiana dall'unificazione alla Grande Guerra*, Laterza, Rome-Bari 2002, p. 167. 16. Costantino Felice, *Il disagio di vivere. Il cibo, la casa, le malattie in Abruzzo e Molise dall'Unità al secondo dopoguerra*, Franco Angeli, Milan 1990, p. 49. 17. Agopik Manoukian, 'La famiglia dei contadini', in Piero Melograni (ed.), *La famiglia italiana dall'ottocento a oggi*, Laterza, Rome-Bari, 1988, p. 17. 18. Carlo Levi, *Cristo si è fermato a Eboli*, Einaudi, Turin 1946, p. 129. 19. Vera Zamagni, *Dalla periferia al centro. La seconda rinascita economica dell'Italia 1861–1981*, Il Mulino, Bologna 1990, p. 249. 20. Amelia Paparazzo, *I subalterni calabresi tra rimpianto e trasgressione. La Calabria dal brigantaggio post-unitario all'età giolittiana*, Franco Angeli, Milan 1984, pp. 79ff. 21. Ibid, p. 80. 22. Martine Segalen, 'Material Conditions of Family Life', in David Kertzer and Marzio Barbagli (eds), *Family Life in the Long Nineteenth Century, 1789–1914*, Yale University Press 2002, pp. 20–22. 23. Collins, 'Why Wheat?', p. 14. 24. Roberto Finzi, *'Sazia assai ma dà poco fiato'. Il mais nell'economia e nella vita rurale italiane. Secoli XVI–XX*, CLUEB, Bologna 2009, pp. 62, 95. 25. Arlette Mouret, 'La légende des 150,000 décès tuberculeux par an', *Annales de démographie historique*, 1996, p. 63. 26. Patrice Bourdelais, 'Épidémies et population: bilan et perspectives de recherches', in ibid, 1997, p. 17. 27. Georg Simmel, 'The Metropolis and Mental Life' (originally 'Die Grossstädte und das Geistesleben', in *Jahrbuch der Gehestiftung*, IX, Dresden 1903), in *Simmel on Culture*, ed. David Frisby and Mike Featherstone, Sage, London 1997, pp. 184–5. 28. Jean-Jacques Rousseau, *Émile ou de l'éducation*, vol. 2, Werdet et Lequien fils, Paris 1826, p. 267. 29. Andrew Lees, 'Critics of Urban Society in Germany, 1854–1914', *Journal of the History of Ideas*, vol. 40, no. 1, January–March 1979, pp. 62–3. 30. Ibid, pp. 70, 73. 31. Eugene Weber, *Peasants into Frenchmen: The Modernization of Rural France, 1870–1914*, Stanford University Press 1976, p. 286. 32. Robert Musil, *The Man Without Qualities*, vol. 1 (Chapter 76), Vintage Books, New York 1996, p. 349. 33. Fernand Braudel, *Civilisation matérielle, économie et capitalisme, XVe–XVIIIe siècle*, vol. 1: *Les structures du quotidien*, p. 431. 34. Paul Bairoch, *Economics and World History: Myths and Paradoxes*, Harvester, New York and London 1993, pp. 102–8. 35. Thomas Stanley Fedor, *Patterns of Urban Growth in the Russian Empire during the Nineteenth Century*, University of Chicago, Department of Geography, Research Paper no. 163, 1975, p. 24. 36. Ibid, p. 29. 37. Stephen Velychenko, 'Empire Loyalism and Minority Nationalism in Great Britain and Imperial Russia, 1707 to 1914:

Institutions, Law, and Nationality in Scotland and Ukraine', *Comparative Studies in Society and History*, vol. 39, no. 3, July 1997, p. 415. 38. Hippolyte Desprez, 'La Moldo-Valachie et le mouvement roumain', *Revue des deux mondes*, vol. 21, 1848, pp. 109–10. 39. Andrew C. Janos, 'Modernization and Decay in Historical Perspective: The Case of Romania', in Kenneth Jowitt (ed.), *Social Change in Romania, 1860–1940: A Debate on Development in a European Nation*, University of California Press 1978, p. 76. 40. Charles C. Arion, *La situation économique et sociale du paysan en Roumanie*, V. Giard & E. Brière, Paris 1895, p. 36 (for medical data), pp. 84–5: https://archive.org/stream/lasituationconoooariogoog#page/n13/mode/2up 41. Tertius Chandler, *Four Thousand Years of Urban Growth*, St David's University Press 1987, pp. 460–63; Lis and Soly, *Worthy Efforts*, p. 56. 42. Paul Bairoch, 'Urbanization and the Economy in Preindustrial Societies: The Findings of Two Decades of Research', *Journal of European Economic History*, vol. 18, no. 2, Fall 1989, p. 260. 43. Caroline Dodds Pennock, 'Mass Murder or Religious Homicide? Rethinking Human Sacrifice and Interpersonal Violence in Aztec Society', *Historical Social Research / Historische Sozialforschung*, vol. 37, no. 3, 2012, p. 282. 44. Jürgen Osterhammel, *The Transformation of the World: A Global History of the Nineteenth Century*, Princeton University Press 2014, p. 251. All such statistics should be taken with caution; Pomeranz and Topik, in *The World that Trade Created*, p. 82, say that Edo (Tokyo) was 'probably' the largest city in the eighteenth century. 45. Bairoch, 'Urbanization and the Economy in Preindustrial Societies', p. 244. 46. Leslie Page Moch, *Moving Europeans: Migration in Western Europe since 1650*, Indiana University Press 2003, p. 115. 47. Philippe Pinchemel, *Structures sociales et dépopulation rurale dans les campagnes picardes de 1836 à 1936*, Armand Colin, Paris 1957, p. 208; see also Moch, *Moving Europeans*, p. 128. 48. Herbert S. Klein, *A Population History of the United States*, Cambridge University Press 2004, pp. 119, 127. 49. Paul Bairoch, 'Niveaux de développements économique de 1810 à 1910', *Annales*, vol. 20, no. 6, November–December 1965, p. 1,109. 50. Robert A. Margo, 'The Labor Force in Nineteenth Century', in Stanley L. Engerman and Robert E. Gallman (eds), *The Cambridge Economic History of the United States*, vol. 2: *The Long Nineteenth Century*, Cambridge University Press 2000, pp. 215–16, and Klein, *A Population History of the United States*, p. 123. 51. Klein, *A Population History of the United States*, p. 129, and Michael R. Haines, 'The Population of the United States, 1790–1920', in Engerman and Gallman (eds), *The Cambridge Economic History of the United* States, vol. 2, p. 199. 52. Massimo Livi-Bacci, *L'immigrazione e l'assimilazione degli italiani negli Stati Uniti*, Giuffrè, Milan 1961, pp. 34–5. 53. Merle Curti and Kendall Birr, 'The Immigrant and the American Image in Europe, 1860–1914', *Mississippi Valley Historical Review*, vol. 37, no. 2, September 1950, p. 214. 54. Max Paul Friedman, 'Beyond "Voting with their Feet": Toward a Conceptual History of "America" in European Migrant Sending Communities, 1860s to 1914', *Journal of Social History*, vol. 40, no. 3, Spring 2007, pp. 558–9. 55. Léon and Maurice Bonneff, *La vie tragique des travailleurs*,

EDI, Paris 1984, first published 1908, p. 16. 56. Ibid, p. 21. 57. Ibid, p. 31. 58. Jennifer Davis, 'From "Rookeries" to "Communities": Race, Poverty and Policing in London, 1850–1985', *History Workshop Journal*, vol. 27, no. 1, 1989, pp. 68–9. 59. Maud Pember Reeves, *Round About a Pound a Week*, G. Bell and Sons, London 1913, p. 145. 60. Ibid, pp. 113–31. 61. Maurice Lévy-Leboyer and François Bourguignon, *L'économie française au XIXe siècle*, Economica, Paris 1985, pp. 24–5. 62. Claire Leymonerie, 'Le Salon des arts ménagers dans les années 1950', *Vingtième siècle*, no. 91, July–September 2006, p. 45; Paul-Henry Chombart de Lauwe, *La vie quotidienne des familles ouvrières*, CNRS, Paris 1977 (first published 1956), p. 75. 63. Allen, *The British Industrial Revolution in Global Perspective*, p. 33. 64. Friedrich Engels, *The Condition of the Working Class in England*, Oxford University Press 1993, p. 84. 65. Louis René Villermé, *Tableau de l'état physique et moral des ouvriers employés dans les manufactures de coton, de laine et de soie*, ed. Yves Tyl, UGE, Collection 10/18, Paris 1971, p. 314: http://classiques.uqac.ca/classiques/villerme_louis_rene/tableau_etat_physique_moral/villerme_tableau_ouvriers.pdf 66. Engels, *The Condition of the Working Class*, pp. 107–8. 67. Eugène Buret, *De la misère des classes laborieuses en Angleterre et en France*, vol. 1, Paulin, Paris 1840, p. 135. 68. Ibid, pp. 317–18. 69. Ibid, pp. 326, 340. 70. Ibid, p. 82; see comments in Karl Marx, *Economic and Philosophic Manuscripts of 1844*, Progress Publishers, Moscow 1967, p. 48. 71. Buret, *De la misère des classes laborieuses*, vol. 2, p. 27. 72. J. Mordaunt Crook, *The Rise of the Nouveaux Riches*, John Murray, London 1999, p. 62. 73. William J. Fishman, 'The Condition of East End Jewry in 1888', West Central Lecture 1986, delivered at University College London, 24 June 1986, p. 6. 74. Hippolyte Taine, *Notes sur l'Angleterre*, 11th ed., Hachette, Paris 1899, p. 9. 75. Ibid, p. 39. 76. Édouard Ducpétiaux, *De la condition des ouvriers mineurs dans la Grande-Bretagne et en Belgique*, Vandooren frères, Brussels 1843, p. 54. 77. Villermé, *Tableau de l'état physique et moral des ouvriers*, p. 176. 78. Jérôme Bourdieu and Bénédicte Reynaud, 'Factory Discipline and Externalities in the Reduction of Working Time in the 19th Century in France', CNRS-CEPREMAP, Working Paper no. 2002–08, June 2002, p. 15: http://www.cepremap.cnrs.fr/couv_orange/co0208.pdf 79. James Phillips Kay, *The Moral and Physical Condition of the Working Classes Employed in the Cotton Manufacture in Manchester*, Ridgway, London 1832, p. 9: https://archive.org/stream/moralphysicalconookaysuoft#page/n3/mode/2up 80. Ibid, pp. 10, 49, 71, 47, 39, 6–7, 12. 81. Sidney Pollard, 'Factory Discipline in the Industrial Revolution', *The Economic History Review*, vol. 16, no. 2, 1963, p. 260. 82. Marx, *Capital*, vol. 1, p. 670; *The Times*, 5 April 1867, p. 10 ('The Distress in Poplar'), mentions only 4,000–5,000 demonstrators. 83. William Gladstone, Speech to the House of Commons, 13 February 1843: http://hansard.millbanksystems.com/commons/1843/feb/13/distress-of-the-country, p. 4,801. 84. Pasquale Villari, *Le lettere meridionali ed altri scritti sulla questione sociale in Italia*, Le Monnier, Florence 1878, p. 83. 85. William Booth, *In Darkest England and the Way Out* (1890),

Charles Knight & Co, London 1970, pp. 11–12. 86. Originally published as *Captain Lobe: A Story of the Salvation Army* under the pseudonym of John Law. 87. Charles Booth, *Life and Labour of the People in London*, First Series: *Poverty*, vol. 1, Macmillan, London 1902–4, p. 33. 88. Ibid, p. 38. 89. Ibid, p. 36. 90. Anthony S. Wohl, *The Eternal Slum: Housing and Social Policy in Victorian London*, Edward Arnold, London 1977, p. 312. 91. Mokyr, *The Enlightened Economy*, p. 482. 92. Jack London, *The People of the Abyss*, Grosset & Dunlap, New York 1903, p. 168. 93. Guido Crainz, *Padania. Il mondo dei braccianti dall'Ottocento alla fuga dalle campagne*, Donzelli, Rome 1994, pp. 4–5. 94. Cited in Christopher Prior, *Edwardian England and the Idea of Racial Decline: An Empire's Future*, Palgrave, Basingstoke 2013, p. 41. 95. Ian Gazeley and Andrew Newell, 'Urban Working-Class Food Consumption and Nutrition in Britain in 1904', *Economic History Review*, vol. 68, no. 1, February 2015, p. 121. 96. Reginald E. Zelnik, *Labor and Society in Tsarist Russia: The Factory Workers of St. Petersburg, 1855–1870*, Stanford University Press 1971, pp. 269–71. 97. Ibid, pp. 241–8. 98. Hasia R. Diner, *Hungering for America: Italian, Irish, and Jewish Foodways in the Age of Migration*, Harvard University Press 2002, p. 13. 99. Knut Oyangen, 'The Gastrodynamics of Displacement: Place-Making and Gustatory Identity in the Immigrants' Midwest', *Journal of Interdisciplinary History*, vol. 39, no.3, Winter 2009, pp. 332–3. 100. Daniel Horowitz, *The Morality of Spending: Attitudes toward the Consumer Society in America, 1875–1940*, Johns Hopkins University Press 1985, p. 15, using Massachusetts Bureau of Statistics of Labor. 101. Jacob A. Riis, *How the Other Half Lives*, W. W. Norton, New York 2010, p. 65. 102. Elizabeth Ewen, *Immigrant Women in the Land of Dollars: Life and Culture on the Lower East Side, 1890–1925*, Monthly Review Press, New York 1985, p. 167. 103. Lévy-Leboyer and Bourguignon, *L'économie française au XIXe siècle*, p. 25. 104. George Rudé, *The Crowd in the French Revolution*, Oxford University Press 1959, p. 21. 105. Maurice Halbwachs, *La classe ouvrière et les niveaux de vie*, Gordon and Breach, Paris, London, and New York 1970 (reprint of 1st edition, 1912, published by Félix Alcan), p. 147. 106. US Deptartment of Labor Statistics, Office of Publication and Special Studies: http://www.bls.gov/opub/uscs/1901.pdf and http://www.bls.gov/opub/uscs/2002-03.pdf 107. Simon N. Patten, *The New Basis of Civilization*, Macmillan, London 1907, p. 18. 108. Ibid, pp. 19–20. 109. Osterhammel, *The Transformation of the World*, p. 233. 110. Susan Strasser, *Satisfaction Guaranteed: The Making of the American Mass Market*, Pantheon Books, New York 1989, p. 3. 111. Segalen, 'Material Conditions of Family Life', p. 21. 112. Stuart Woolf, *The Poor in Western Europe in the Eighteenth and Nineteenth Centuries*, Methuen, London 1986, p. 69. 113. Segalen, 'Material Conditions of Family Life', p. 27. 114. Robert Castel, *Les métamorphoses de la question sociale. Une cronique du salariat*, Fayard, Paris 1995, p. 11. 115. Charters Wynn, *Workers, Strikes, and Pogroms: The Donbass-Dnepr Bend in Late Imperial Russia, 1870–1905*, Princeton University Press 1992, p. 69. 116. Paparazzo, *I subalterni calabresi tra rimpianto e trasgressione*, pp. 66–7. 117. Jules Huret, *Enquête sur la question sociale en Europe*, Perrin, Paris 1897, p. 39: ftp://ftp.bnf.fr/002/N0024317_PDF_1_-1DM.pdf 118. Lenard R. Berlanstein, *The Working People of Paris, 1871–1914*, Johns Hopkins University Press 1984, p. 125. 119. Matsubara Iwagoro, *In Darkest Tokyo: Sketches of Humble Life in the Capital of Japan*, 'Eastern World' Newspaper Publishing and Printing Office, Yokohama 1897, p. 21. 120. Ibid, p. 13. 121. Noah McCormack, 'Civilising the Urban Other: Poverty as a National Problem', *Ritsumeikan Annual Review of International Studies*, vol. 6, 2007, pp. 34, 39: http://www.ritsumei.ac.jp/acd/cg/ir/college/bulletin/e-vol.6/02Noah%20McCormack.pdf; see also Chushichi Tsuzuki, *The Pursuit of Power in Modern Japan, 1825–1995*, Oxford University Press 2000, p. 149. 122. Louis Chevalier, *Classes laborieuses et classes dangereuses à Paris pendant la première moitié du XIXe siècle*, Perrin, Paris 2002, first published 1958, pp. 180–81. 123. Flora Tristan, *Le tour de France. État actuel de la classe ouvrière sous l'aspect moral – intellectuel – matériel. Journal inédit 1843–1844*, Éditions Tête de feuilles, Paris 1973, entry for 15 March 1843, p. 17: http://gallica.bnf.fr/ark:/12148/bpt6k82507w 124. Ibid, 16 April 1843, p. 28. 125. Chevalier, *Classes laborieuses et classes dangereuses*, p. 318. 126. GB Historical GIS / University of Portsmouth, Population Statistics Total Population, *A Vision of Britain through Time*: http://www.visionofbritain.org.uk/unit/10076924/cube/TOT_POP, accessed 3 May 2017. 127. Office of National Statistics, *Population Estimates for UK, England and Wales, Scotland and Northern Ireland, Mid-2015*, 23 June 2016. Retrieved 9 February 2017. 128. GB Historical GIS: http://www.visionofbritain.org.uk/unit/10097836/cube/TOT_POP 129. Greater London Authority: https://www.london.gov.uk/media/mayor-press-releases/2015/02/london-population-confirmed-at-record-high 130. Emma Griffin, *Liberty's Dawn: A People's History of the Industrial Revolution*, Yale University Press 2013, p. 52. 131. William Cobbett, *Rural Rides*, T. Nelson and Sons, London 1830, pp. 496–7: http://www.gutenberg.org/files/34238/34238-h/34238-h.htm 132. A. J. McIvor, 'Employers, the Government, and Industrial Fatigue in Britain, 1890–1918', *Journal of Industrial Medicine*, vol. 44, no. 11, November 1987, p. 725. 133. Axel Munthe, *Letters from a Mourning City*, John Murray, London 1899, pp. 31, 142–4. 134. Carlo Carozzi, 'Le abitazioni nei capoluoghi di provincia italiani intorno al 1880: alla ricerca di alcune differenze tra Nord e Sud', in Andreina De Clementi (ed.), *La società inafferrabile*, Edizioni Lavoro, Rome 1986, p. 137; for Chicago and New York, see Gordon, *The Rise and Fall of American Growth*, p. 51. 135. Maxime Du Camp, *Expédition des Deux-Siciles*, Calmann Lévy, Paris 1881, pp. 126 and 163. 136. André Gueslin, *Gens pauvres, pauvres gens dans la France du XIXe siècle*, Aubier, Paris 1998, pp. 84–5. 137. Alexis de Tocqueville, *Mémoire sur le paupérisme*, Ministère de l'instruction publique et des beaux-arts, Imprimerie nationale, Paris 1835, pp. 3–4. 138. Kume Kunitake, *Japan Rising: The Iwakura Embassy to the USA and Europe*, ed. Chushichi Tsuzuki and R. Jules Young, Cambridge University Press 2009, pp. 110–11. 139. Ellen Meiksins Wood,

Empire of Capital, Verso, London 2003, pp. 16, 18–19. 140. Buret, *De la misère des classes laborieuses*, vol. 2, p. 295. 141. B. Seebohm Rowntree, *Poverty: A Study of Town Life*, Macmillan, London 1901, p. 112. 142. Ibid, p. 118. 143. Ibid, pp. 119–21, 142. 144. Charles Booth, 'Enumeration and Classification of Paupers, and State Pensions for the Aged', *Journal of the Royal Statistical Society*, vol. 54, no. 4, 1891, pp. 600–643, 618. 145. Booth, *Life and Labour of the People in London*, p. 33. 146. Barthélemy Faujas-Saint-Fond, *Voyage en Angleterre, en Écosse et aux Îles Hébrides*, vol. 2, H. J. Jansen, Paris 1797, pp. 80–87. 147. Ibid, pp. 88–9, references to Miss Mac-Liane on pp. 22, 76, and 430. 148. Cited in Crook, *The Rise of the Nouveaux Riches*, pp. 47–8. 149. Berlanstein, *The Working People of Paris, 1871–1914*, p. 46. 150. Ardant, *Histoire financière*, p. 340. 151. Harold Perkin, *The Rise of Professional Society: England since 1880*, Routledge, London 2002, p. 29. 152. W. D. Rubinstein, 'Education and the Social Origins of British Élites, 1880–1970', *Past & Present*, no. 112, August 1986, p. 170. 153. Richard Sennett, *Families against the City: Middle-Class Homes of Industrial Chicago, 1872–1890*, Harvard University Press 1970, p. 86. 154. Pomeranz, *The Great Divergence*, p. 117. 155. Ibid, p. 118. 156. Data from Euromonitor International reported in the *Washington Post*, by Roberto A. Ferdman, 5 February 2015: https://www.washingtonpost.com/news/wonk/wp/2015/02/05/where-people-around-the-world-eat-the-most-sugar-and-fat/?utm_term=.708179dadd94, accessed 3 May 2017. 157. Adeline Daumard, 'Puissance et inquiétudes de la société bourgeoise', in Fernand Braudel and Ernest Labrousse (eds), *Histoire économique et sociale de la France*, Tome IV: *L'ère industrielle et la société d'aujourd'hui (siècle 1880–1980)*, vol. 1, Presses Universitaires de France, Paris 1979, p. 441. 158. Eliza Lynn Linton (E.L.L.), 'The Wild Women. 1. As Politicians', *Nineteenth Century*, vol. 30, no. 173, July 1891, pp. 79–80. 159. George Somes Layard, *Mrs. Lynn Linton: Her Life, Letters, and Opinions*, Methuen, London 1901, p. 349. 160. Eliza Lynn Linton (E.L.L.), 'On the Side of the Maids', *Cornhill Magazine*, vol. 29, 1874, pp. 299–300, 301–2, 305–6: http://www.victorianweb.org/history/work/maids1.html 161. Eric Mension-Rigau, *Aristocrates et grands bourgeois*, Plon, Paris 1994, pp. 390–91. 162. Daumard, 'Puissance et inquiétudes de la société bourgeoise', pp. 442, 460. 163. Alison Light, *Mrs Woolf and the Servants*, Penguin / Fig Tree, London 2007, p. xv. 164. For 1891 see Leonore Davidoff, 'Mastered for Life: Servant and Wife in Victorian and Edwardian England', *Journal of Social History*, vol. 7, no. 4, Summer 1974, p. 410; for 1871 see Edward Higgs, 'Domestic Servants and Households in Victorian England', *Social History*, vol. 8, no. 2, May 1983, p. 202. 165. Giovanni Montroni, 'La famiglia borghese', in Piero Melograni (ed.), *La famiglia italiana dall'ottocento a oggi*, Laterza, Rome-Bari 1988, p. 127. 166. Edward Higgs, 'Women, Occupations and Work in the Nineteenth Century Censuses', *History Workshop Journal*, vol. 23, no. 1, 1987, pp. 68–9. 167. Higgs, 'Domestic Servants and Households in Victorian England', p. 202. 168. Davidoff, 'Mastered for Life', p. 412. 169. Daumard, 'Puissance et inquiétudes de la société bourgeoise', p. 448. 170. Susan Strasser,

Never Done: A History of American Housework, Pantheon Books, New York 1982, p. 105. 171. Ibid, p. 86. 172. Jean-Luc Pinol, *Le monde des villes au XIXe siècle*, Hachette, Paris 1991, pp. 147–8. 173. Bairoch, 'Urbanization and the Economy in Pre-Industrial Societies', p. 261. 174. Sören Edvinsson and Hans Nilsson, 'Swedish Towns during Industrialization', *Annales de démographie historique*, 1999, p. 63. 175. Stefano Musso, 'La famiglia operaia', in Melograni (ed.), *La famiglia italiana dall'ottocento a oggi*, p. 67; *Histoire de la population française*, vol. 3: *De 1789 à 1914*, ed. Jacques Dupâquier, Presses Universitaires de France, Paris 1988, p. 294. 176. Robert Woods, 'The Effects of Population Redistribution on the Level of Mortality in Nineteenth-Century England and Wales', *Journal of Economic History*, vol. 45, no. 3, September 1985, p. 650. 177. Theodore Roosevelt, 'State of the Union Address', 6 December 1904: http://www.infoplease.com/t/hist/state-of-the-union/116.html 178. Jörg Vögele, *Urban Mortality Change in England and Germany, 1870–1913*, Liverpool University Press 1998, p. 35. 179. Ibid, p. 147. 180. Ibid, p. 35. 181. Jörg P. Vögele, 'Différences entre ville et campagne et évolution de la mortalité en Allemagne pendant l'industrialisation', *Annales de démographie historique*, 1996, p. 256. 182. Vögele, 'Différences entre ville et champagne', p. 253. 183. Gordon, *The Rise and Fall of American Growth*, pp. 51–2. 184. Alan Macfarlane, *The Savage Wars of Peace: England, Japan and the Malthusian Trap*, Palgrave, Basingstoke 2003, p. 126. 185. Ibid, p. 139. 186. Gordon, 'Does the "New Economy" Measure up to the Great Inventions of the Past?', p. 58; for France see Leymonerie, 'Le Salon des arts ménagers dans les années 1950', p. 45. 187. John Burnett, *Plenty and Want: A Social History of Food in England from 1815 to the Present Day*, Routledge, London 2013, p. 100. 188. Werner Troesken, *Water, Race, and Disease*, MIT Press 2004, p. 23. 189. John Milton Cooper, Jr., *Pivotal Decades: The United States, 1900–1920*, Norton, New York 1990, p. 99. 190. Louis Galambos, 'State-Owned Enterprises in a Hostile Environment: The US Experience', in *The Rise and Fall of State-Owned Enterprises in the Western World*, ed. Pier Angelo Toninelli, Cambridge University Press 2000, p. 282. 191. Figures from Water Aid: http://www.wateraid.org/where-we-work/page/india, and UNICEF: https://www.unicef.org/gambia/Progress_on_drinking_water_and_sanitation_2014_update.pdf 192. Pinol, *Le monde des villes au XIXe siècle*, p. 147. 193. Thomas Bethan, Danny Dorling, and George Davey Smith, 'Inequalities in Premature Mortality in Britain: Observational Study from 1921 to 2007', *British Medical Journal*, 22 July 2010: http://dx.doi.org/10.1136/bmj.c3639; Richard Wilkinson and Kate Pickett, *The Spirit Level: Why More Equal Societies Almost Always Do Better*, Allen Lane, London 2009, esp. pp. 15–26. 194. Alain Faure, 'Paris, "gouffre de l'espèce humaine"?', *French Historical Studies*, vol. 27, no. 1, Winter 2004, pp. 49–86. 195. James C. Riley, *Rising Life Expectancy: A Global History*, Cambridge University Press 2001, p. 2. 196. Adolf Hausrath, 'The Life of Treitschke', in Heinrich von Treitschke and Adolf Hausrath, *Treitschke: His Life and Works*, Jarrold & Sons/Allen & Unwin, London 1914, p. 9: https://

archive.org/stream/treitschkehislifootreiuoft#page/n15/mode/2up/search/colonisation 197. Marc Debuisson, 'The Decline of Infant Mortality in the Belgian Districts at the Turn of the 20th Century', *Journal of Belgian History*, vol. 31, nos 3–4, 2001, pp. 497–527. 198. Paul Clayton and Judith Rowbotham, 'How the Mid-Victorians Worked, Ate and Died', *International Journal of Environmental Research and Public Health*, vol. 6, no. 3, 2009, pp. 1,238–9. 199. Lorenzo Del Panta, 'Mortalité infantile et post-infantile en Italie du XVIIIe au XXe siècle: tendances à long terme et differences régionales', *Annales de démographie historique*, 1994, p. 47. 200. Riley, *Rising Life Expectancy*, p. xi, whose list is longer, and pp. 1–31; see Thomas McKeown, *The Modern Rise of Population*, Edward Arnold, London 1976; see also Robert W. Fogel, *The Escape from Hunger and Premature Death, 1700–2100: Europe, America, and the Third World*, Cambridge University Press 2004, p. 5. 201. Simon Szreter, *Health and Wealth: Studies in History and Policy*, esp. 'The Importance of Social Intervention in Britain's Mortality Decline c.1850–1914: A Reinterpretation of the Role of Public Health', University of Rochester Press 2005, pp. 98–145. 202. Werner Troesken, 'Typhoid Rates and the Public Acquisition of Private Waterworks, 1880–1920', *Journal of Economic History*, vol. 59, no. 4, December 1999, pp. 927, 931. 203. Haines, 'The Population of the United States, 1790–1920', p. 176. 204. United Nations, *Human Development Report*, 2006: http://hdr.undp.org/en/reports/global/hdr2006, p. 299; Riley, *Rising Life Expectancy*, p. 135. 205. Haidong Wang et al., 'Age-Specific and Sex-Specific Mortality in 187 Countries, 1970–2010: A Systematic Analysis for the Global Burden of Disease Study 2010', *Lancet*, vol. 380, no. 9859, 15 December 2012, pp. 2,075–84. 206. Riley, *Rising Life Expectancy*, p. 35. On Japan and Egypt see Jean-Claude Chesnais, *La transition démographique. Trente ans de bouleversements (1965–1995)*, Les dossiers du CEPED, no. 34, October 1995, p. 13. 207. Christopher Ingraham, '15 Baltimore Neighborhoods Have Lower Life Expectancies than North Korea', *Washington Post*, 30 April 2015: http://www.washingtonpost.com/blogs/wonkblog/wp/2015/04/30/baltimores-poorest-residents-die-20-years-earlier-than-its-richest 208. See this study from the University of Washington: L. Dwyer-Lindgren, A. Bertozzi-Villa, R. W. Stubbs, C. Morozoff, J. P. Mackenbach, F. J. van Lenthe, A. H. Mokdad, and C. J. L. Murray, 'Inequalities in Life Expectancy among US Counties, 1980 to 2014', *JAMA Internal Medicine*, 8 May 2017: http://jamanetwork.com/journals/jamainternalmedicine/fullarticle/2626194, accessed 10 May 2017; see also Wilkinson and Pickett, *The Spirit Level*. 209. Peter Nolan and John Sender, 'Death Rates, Life Expectancy and Economic Reforms', in Peter Nolan and Qimiao Fan (eds), *China's Economic Reforms: The Costs and Benefits of Incrementalism*, St. Martin's Press, New York 1994, p. 335. 210. WHO data: http://www.who.int/gho/publications/world_health_statistics/2016/EN_WHS2016_AnnexB.pdf?ua=1, accessed 10 May 2017. 211. Anne Hardy, *The Epidemic Streets: Infectious Disease and the Rise of Preventive Medicine, 1856–1900*, Clarendon Press, Oxford 1993, pp. 3ff. 212. Edmund A. Parkes, *Public Health*, J. & A. Churchill, London 1876, p. 17, published in the year of his death. 213. Figure for Africa in United Nations, *Human Development Report*, 2006, for Japan and Europe in Massimo Livi-Bacci, *A Concise History of World Population*, Blackwell, Oxford 1997, p. 121. 214. Nicolás Sánchez-Albornoz, 'The Population of Latin America, 1850–1930', in Bethell (ed.), *The Cambridge History of Latin America*, vol. IV, pp. 141–2. 215. Fogel, *The Escape from Hunger and Premature Death, 1700–2100*, p. 8. 216. David Grigg, 'The Nutritional Transition in Western Europe', *Journal of Historical Geography*, vol. 21, no. 3, 1995, p. 248. 217. Peter Baldwin, *Contagion and the State in Europe, 1830–1930*, Cambridge University Press 2005, p. 37. 218. Myron Echenberg, *Africa in the Time of Cholera: A History of Pandemics from 1817 to the Present*, Cambridge University Press 2011, p. 21. 219. Ibid, p. 75. 220. Geoffrey Hosking, *Russia and the Russians: A History*, Harvard University Press 2001, p. 9. 221. Montroni, *La società italiana dall'unificazione alla Grande Guerra*, p. 163. 222. Frank Snowden, *Naples in the Time of Cholera, 1884–1911*, Cambridge University Press 1995, p. 16. 223. László Katus, 'Economic Growth in Hungary during the Age of Dualism', *Social Economic Researches on the History of East-Central Europe, Studia Historica 62*, Budapest 1970, p. 41. 224. W. Luckin, 'The Final Catastrophe – Cholera in London, 1866', *Medical History*, vol. 21, no. 1, 1977, p. 32. 225. Livi-Bacci, *The Population of Europe: A History*; Snowden, *Naples in the Time of Cholera*, pp. 144–5; and Richard Evans, *Death in Hamburg: Society and Politics in the Cholera Years, 1830–1910*, Penguin, London 1990. 226. Evans, *Death in Hamburg*, p. 313. 227. Dhiman Barua and William B. Greenough III (eds), *Cholera*, Plenum Medical Book Company, New York 1991, p. 20. 228. Myron Echenberg, *Plague Ports: The Global Urban Impact of Bubonic Plague, 1894–1901*, New York University Press 2007, pp. 16–17 and 304, mortality statistics on p. 314. 229. Nayan Shah, *Contagious Divides: Epidemics and Race in San Francisco's Chinatown*, California University Press 2001, p. 2. 230. Echenberg, *Plague Ports*, p. 262. 231. Mark Harrison, *Disease and the Modern World*, Polity, Cambridge 2004, pp. 120–23. 232. Alfred W. Crosby, *America's Forgotten Pandemic: The Influenza of 1918*, Cambridge University Press 1989, p. 319. 233. John Womack, Jr., 'The Mexican Revolution, 1910–1920', in Bethell (ed.), *The Cambridge History of Latin America*, vol. V, p. 138. 234. France Meslé and Jacques Vallin, 'Reconstitution de tables annuelles de mortalité pour la France au XIXe siècle', *Population*, vol. 44, no. 6, November–December 1989, p. 1,136. 235. Klein, *A Population History of the United States*, p. 107. 236. Ibid, p. 109. 237. Ibid, p. 110. 238. For population statistics for England see National Statistics, *Focus on People and Migration*, Palgrave Macmillan, London 2005, pp. 2–4: http://www.statistics.gov.uk/downloads/theme_compendia/fom2005/01_FOPM_Population.pdf 239. Alfred W. Crosby, Jr., *The Columbian Exchange: Biological and Cultural Consequences of 1492*, Praeger, Westport, CT 2003 (first published 1972), p. 37. 240. Ibid, p. 39. 241. David E. Stannard, *American Holocaust: Columbus and the Conquest of the New World*, Oxford University Press 1992, pp. 33 and 267; see also Ward Churchill, *A Little Matter of Genocide: Holocaust and Denial in the Americas 1492 to the Present*, City Lights Books, San Francisco, CA 1997, pp. 134–6. Estimates of pre-contact native Americans vary widely: see Benjamin Madley, 'Reexamining the American Genocide Debate: Meaning, Historiography, and New Methods', *American Historical Review*, vol. 120, no. 1, February 2015, esp. footnote 1, p. 98. **242.** Stannard, *American Holocaust*, p. 145. **243.** Data from the IBGE (Instituto Brasileiro de Geografia e Estatística), cited in Ruben Schindler Maggi, 'Indigenous Health in Brazil', *Revista Brasileira de Saúde Materno Infantil*, vol. 14, no. 1, January/March 2014: http://www.scielo.br/pdf/rbsmi/v14n1/en_1519-3829-rbsmi-14-01-0013.pdf **244.** Carlo Cipolla, *Before the Industrial Revolution*, Cambridge University Press 1976, p. 75. **245.** Alain Dewerpe, *Le monde du travail en France, 1800–1950*, Armand Colin, Paris 1989, p. 99. **246.** Jean-Pierre Bardet, 'La France en déclin', in Jean-Pierre Bardet and Jacques Dupâquier (eds), *Histoire des populations de l'Europe*, vol. 2, Fayard, Paris 1998, pp. 287–325. **247.** *Histoire de la population française*, vol. 3, ed. Dupâquier (eds), p. 354. **248.** John C. Hunter, 'The Problem of the French Birth Rate on the Eve of World War I', *French Historical Studies*, vol. 2, no. 4, Autumn 1962, p. 494. **249.** Leduc, *Histoire de la France*, p. 101. **250.** Dewerpe, *Le monde du travail en France*, p. 100. **251.** Daumard, 'Puissance et inquiétudes de la société bourgeoise', pp. 458–9. **252.** Ibid, pp. 446–7. **253.** Ibid, 1906 figures on p. 457. **254.** François Caron, 'Dynamismes et freinages de la croissance industrielle', in Braudel and Labrousse (eds), *Histoire économique et sociale de la France*, Tome IV, vol. 1, p. 263. **255.** Janos, 'Modernization and Decay in Historical Perspective', p. 75. **256.** Ibid. **257.** Stephen Broadberry and Alexander Klein, 'Aggregate and Per Capita GDP in Europe, 1870–2000: Continental, Regional and National Data with Changing Boundaries', University of Warwick, 8 February 2008: http://www.cepr.org/meets/wkcn/1/1699/papers/Broadberry_Klein.pdf, p. 20. **258.** Jaime Reis, 'How Poor was the European Periphery before 1850? The Mediterranean vs Scandinavia', in Sevket Pamuk and Jeffrey G. Williamson (eds), *The Mediterranean Response to Globalization before 1950*, Routledge, London and New York 2000, pp. 20–21. **259.** Angus Maddison, *Dynamic Forces in Capitalist Development: A Long-Run Comparative View*, Oxford University Press 1991, p. 50. **260.** Paul Bairoch, 'Europe's Gross National Product: 1800–1975', *Journal of European Economic History*, vol. 5, no. 2, 1976, pp. 276–7. **261.** Ibid, p. 278. **262.** Ibid, p. 282. **263.** Ibid, p. 286. **264.** Ritta Hjerppe, *The Finnish Economy, 1860–1985: Growth and Structural Change*, Bank of Finland, Helsinki 1989, p. 51. **265.** Bairoch, 'Europe's Gross National Product: 1800–1975', p. 281. **266.** Ibid, p. 287. **267.** John Maynard Keynes, *The General Theory of Employment, Interest, and Money*, Macmillan, London 1967, p. 96. **268.** All Gini data from CIA *World Factbook*: https://www.cia.gov/library/publications/the-world-factbook/fields/2172.html **269.** Angus Deaton, *The Great Escape: Health, Wealth, and the Origins of Inequality*, Princeton University Press 2013, p. 1. **270.** François Bourguignon and Christian Morrisson, 'Inequality among World Citizens 1820–1992', *American Economic Review*, vol. 92, no. 4, September 2002,

p. 731. 271. Thomas Piketty, *Capital in the Twenty-First Century*, Belknap Press, Harvard University Press 2014, esp. Chapter 9. 272. Bourguignon and Morrisson, 'Inequality among World Citizens 1820–1992', p. 728. 273. Ibid. 274. Ibid, p. 733. 275. Paul Leroy-Beaulieu, *Essai sur la répartition des richesses et sur la tendance à une moindre inégalité des conditions*, 4th ed., Guillaumin, Paris 1897, p. iii. 276. Bourguignon and Morrisson, 'Inequality among World Citizens 1820–1992', p. 733. 277. Ibid, p. 734; Macfarlane, *The Savage Wars of Peace*, p. xix; Jacques Gernet, *Le monde chinois*, vol. 2: *L'époque moderne*, Armand Colin, Paris 2006, p. 238; see the discussion of Kenneth Pomeranz's *The Great Divergence*, and the survey of the literature in P. H. H. Vries, 'Are Coal and Colonies Really Crucial? Kenneth Pomeranz and the Great Divergence', *Journal of World History*, vol. 12, no. 2, Fall 2001, p. 411. 278. Roy Bin Wong, *China Transformed: Historical Change and the Limits of European Experience*, Cornell University Press 1997, p. 29. 279. Cited in E. N. Anderson, *The Food of China*, Yale University Press 1988, p. 96. 280. Adam Smith, *An Inquiry into the Nature and Causes of the Wealth of Nations*, Penn State Electronic Classics 2005, pp. 64, 161, 202: http://www2.hn.psu.edu/faculty/jmanis/adam-smith/Wealth-Nations.pdf 281. Bourguignon and Morrisson, 'Inequality among World Citizens 1820–1992', p. 737. 282. See calculation based on purchasing power parity in Vera Zamagni, 'An International Comparison of Real Industrial Wages, 1890–1913: Methodological Issues and Results', in Peter Scholliers (ed.), *Real Wages in 19th and 20th Century Europe: Historical and Comparative Perspectives*, Berg, Oxford 1989, p. 119. 283. Bairoch, 'Wages as an Indicator of Gross National Product', p. 58.

3. WESTERNIZING THE EAST

1. Maria Todorova, *Imagining the Balkans*, Oxford University Press 1997, p. 11. 2. Larry Wolff, 'Voltaire's Public and the Idea of Eastern Europe', *Slavic Review*, vol. 54, no. 4, 1995, pp. 932–42; Jonathan I. Israel, *Radical Enlightenment: Philosophy and the Making of Modernity, 1650–1750*, Oxford University Press 2001, p. 702. 3. Wolff, 'Voltaire's Public and the Idea of Eastern Europe', p. 936. 4. Voltaire, *Histoire de Charles XII*, in *Oeuvres complètes*, vol. 22, Dupont, Paris 1823–7, pp. 43–5. 5. Voltaire, *Histoire de l'Empire de Russie sous Pierre le Grand*, in *Oeuvres complètes*, vol. 23, Dupont, Paris 1823–7, p. 122. 6. Charles de Secondat Montesquieu, *De l'esprit des lois*, vol. I, Gallimard, Paris 1995, p. 180. 7. Yan Fu (Yen Fou), *Les manifestes de Yen Fou*, ed. François Houang, Fayard, Paris 1977, pp. 86–8. 8. Karl Marx and Friedrich Engels, *Correspondence 1846–1895: A Selection with Commentary and Notes*, Martin Lawrence, London 1934, p. 255. 9. Evelyn Baring (Lord Cromer), *Modern Egypt*, vol. 2, Routledge, London and New York 2000, pp. 539, 134, first published 1908. 10. Mary Lyndon Shanley, *Feminism, Marriage, and the Law in Victorian England, 1850–1895*, I. B. Tauris, London 1989, pp. 103–30, 131–55. 11. Cited in Jonathan D. Spence, *The*

Gate of Heavenly Peace: The Chinese and their Revolution, 1895–1980, Faber and Faber, London and Boston, MA 1982, p. 52. 12. Peter Zarrow, 'He Zhen and Anarcho-Feminism in China', *Journal of Asian Studies*, vol. 47, no. 4, November 1988, p. 799; see also Catherine Gipoulon, 'L'"intellectuel" au féminin: féminisme et révolution en Chine au début du XXe siècle', *Extrême-Orient, Extrême-Occident*, no. 4, 1984, pp. 159–73. 13. W. Morgan Shuster, *The Strangling of Persia: A Record of European Diplomacy and Oriental Intrigue*, T. Fisher Unwin, London 1912, pp. 187–8. 14. Ibid, p. 184. 15. Pomeranz, *The Great Divergence*, p. 9. 16. Ibid, pp. 43–4. 17. Mokyr, *The Lever of Riches*, pp. 210, 217; Donald B. Wagner, *Iron and Steel in Ancient China*, Brill, Leiden, New York and Cologne 1993, pp. 335–6. 18. On this last point see William Guanglin Liu, 'The Making of a Fiscal State in Song China, 960–1279', *Economic History Review*, vol. 68, no. 1, 2015, pp. 48–78. 19. This is the central argument of Kenneth S. Chan and Jean-Pierre Laffargue, 'Foreign Threats, Technological Progress and the Rise and Decline of Imperial China', *Pacific Economic Review*, vol. 17, no. 2, 2012, pp. 280–303. 20. Timothy Brook, *The Confusions of Pleasure: Commerce and Culture in Ming China*, University of California Press 1999, p. 201; Francesca Bray, *Technology and Gender: Fabrics of Power in Late Imperial China*, University of California Press 1997, p. 225. 21. F. W. Mote, *Imperial China, 900–1800*, Harvard University Press 1999, p. 947. 22. Bozhong Li, *Agricultural Development in Jiangnan, 1620–1850*, Macmillan, Basingstoke 1998, pp. 115, 159; Chris Bramall and Peter Nolan, 'Introduction', in Xu Dixin and Wu Chengming (eds), *Chinese Capitalism, 1522–1840*, Macmillan, Basingstoke 2000, pp. xxvi–xxvii. 23. Li, *Agricultural Development in Jiangnan*, p. 21. 24. See European data in Paul Bairoch and Gary Goertz, 'Factors of Urbanisation in the Nineteenth-Century Developed Countries: A Descriptive and Econometric Analysis', *Urban Studies*, 1986, vol. 23, p. 288. Of course, much depends on the definition of what constitutes an urban area. 25. Robert Y. Eng, 'Luddism and Labor Protest among Silk Artisans and Workers in Jiangnan and Guangdong, 1860–1930', *Late Imperial China*, vol. 11, no. 2, December 1990, p. 65. 26. Christine Cornet, *État et entreprises en Chine XIXe–XXe siècles. Le chantier naval de Jiangnan, 1865–1937*, Éditions Arguments, Paris 1997. 27. Jacques Gernet, *Le monde chinois*, vol. 2: *L'époque moderne*, Armand Colin, Paris 2006, p. 238. 28. Evelyn Sakakida Rawski, *Education and Popular Literacy in Ch'ing China*, University of Michigan Press 1979, p. 140. 29. Ernest Renan, *Essais de morale et de critique*, Michel Lévy frères, Paris 1859, pp. 361–2. 30. G. W. F. Hegel, *The Philosophy of History*, trans. J. Sibree, P. F. Collier and Son, New York 1901, p. 163: http://babel.hathitrust.org/cgi/pt?id=coo1.ark:/13960/t5j96qh5b;view=1up;seq=5 31. Wen-yuan Qian, *The Great Inertia: Scientific Stagnation in Traditional China*, Croom Helm, London 1985, p. 103. 32. See, in particular, Pamela Kyle Crossley, *Orphan Warriors: Three Manchu Generations and the End of the Qing World*, Princeton University Press 1990, pp. 8–10ff. 33. Pomeranz and Topik, *The World that Trade Created*, p. 12. 34. Qian Long, Letter to George III, 1793, from the Qianlong Emperor: https://legacy.fordham.edu/halsall/mod/1793qianlong.asp 35. See Henrietta Harrison's lecture of 6 February 2014 at the School of Advanced Study, University of London, and available as a podcast: 'Chinese and British Gift Giving in the Macartney Embassy of 1793': https://www.youtube.com/watch?v=PDzHrQi8oTQ 36. Robert Bickers, *The Scramble for China: Foreign Devils in the Qing Empire, 1832–1914*, Allen Lane, London 2011, p. 82. 37. Robert Hart, *'These from the Land of Sinim': Essays on the Chinese Question*, Chapman & Hall, London 1901, p. 61. 38. Jonathan Spence, 'Opium Smoking in Ch'ing China', in Frederic Wakeman, Jr. and Carolyn Grant (eds), *Conflict and Control in Late Imperial China*, University of California Press 1975, pp. 150–53. 39. Chang Chih-tung (Zhang Zhidong), *China's Only Hope: An Appeal*, Fleming H. Revell Co., New York 1900, pp. 72–3 (Chang Chih-tung is the Wade-Giles romanization for Zhang Zhidong). 40. Ssu-yü Teng and John K. Fairbank (eds), *China's Response to the West: A Documentary Survey, 1839–1923*, Harvard University Press 1961, pp. 25–6. 41. William Gladstone, Speech to the House of Commons, 8 April 1840, Hansard vol. 53, cc 749–837: http://hansard.millbanksystems.com/commons/1840/apr/08/war-with-china-adjourned-debate#S3V0053P0_18400408_HOC_6; see also Julia Lovell, *The Opium Wars: Drugs, Dreams and the Making of China*, Picador, London 2011, p. 107. 42. R. Montgomery Martin, *Opium in China, extracted from China; Political, Commercial, and Social*, James Madden, London n.d. (1847), p. 89. 43. Karl Marx, 'Trade or Opium?', *New York Daily Tribune*, 20 September 1858: http://www.marxists.org/archive/marx/works/1858/09/20.htm 44. Frances V. Moulder, *Japan, China, and the Modern World Economy: Towards a Reinterpretation of East Asian Development ca. 1600 to ca. 1918*, Cambridge University Press 1977, p. 108. 45. Ibid, p. 115. 46. Odd Arne Westad, *Restless Empire: China and the World since 1750*, Bodley Head, London 2012, p. 60. 47. Crossley, *Orphan Warriors*, p. 125. 48. Gernet, *Le monde chinois*, p. 316. 49. Wong, *China Transformed*, pp. 155–6. 50. Pamela Kyle Crossley, *The Wobbling Pivot: China since 1800*, Wiley-Blackwell, Oxford 2010, p. 109. 51. Peter C. Perdue, *Exhausting the Earth: State and Peasant in Hunan, 1500–1850*, Harvard University Press 1987, pp. 237–9. 52. Lillian M. Lil, *Fighting Famine in North China*, Stanford University Press 2007, pp. 268–77. 53. Ibid, pp. 308–9 and 469n. 54. Mary Clabaugh Wright, *The Last Stand of Chinese Conservatism: The T'ung-Chih Restoration, 1862–1874*, Stanford University Press 1957, p. 7. 55. Ibid, pp. 196ff. This author believes in the substantial incompatibility of Confucianism with a modern state. 56. Ibid, pp. 148–9. 57. Cited in ibid, p. 154. 58. Yen-P'ing Hao and Erh-min Wang, 'Changing Chinese Views of Western Relations, 1840–95', in *The Cambridge History of China*, ed. John K. Fairbank and Kwang-ching Liu, vol. 11: *Late Ch'ing, 1800–1911*, part 2, Cambridge University Press 1980, pp. 169–71. 59. Kenneth Pomeranz, *The Making of a Hinterland.: State, Society, and Economy in Inland North China,*

1853–1937, University of California Press 1993, p. 274. 60. Wong, *China Transformed*, p. 155. 61. Jonathan Spence, *The China Helpers: Western Advisers in China, 1620–1960*, Bodley Head, London 1969, p. 93. 62. Immanuel C. Y. Hsü, 'Late Ch'ing Foreign Relations, 1866–1905', in *The Cambridge History of China*, ed. Fairbank and Liu, vol. 11, pp. 70–72. 63. Spence, *The China Helpers*, p. 113. 64. Wu Chengming, 'A Brief Account of the Development of Capitalism in China', in Tim Wright (ed.), *The Chinese Economy in the Early Twentieth Century: Recent Chinese Studies*, St Martin's Press, New York 1992, p. 32. 65. Wright, *The Last Stand of Chinese Conservatism*, p. 177. 66. Max Weber, *The Religion of China: Confucianism and Taoism*, Macmillan, New York 1951, pp. 248, 227. 67. Text in Teng and Fairbank, *China's Response to the West*, pp. 52–3. 68. Jonathan D. Spence, *The Search for Modern China*, Norton, New York 2013, p. 187. 69. Crossley, *The Wobbling Pivot*, p. 119. 70. Douglas Howland, *Borders of Chinese Civilization: Geography and History at Empire's End*, Duke University Press 1996, p. 2, see also pp. 198ff. 71. Marius B. Jansen, *The Making of Modern Japan*, Belknap Press, Cambridge 2000, p. 433. 72. Chang Chih-tung (Zhang Zhidong), *China's Only Hope*, pp. 84–5. 73. Marius Jansen, 'Japan and the Chinese Revolution of 1911', in Fairbank and Liu (eds), *The Cambridge History of China*, vol. 11, pp. 345–6. 74. Hao Chang, 'Intellectual Change and the Reform Movement, 1890–08', in Fairbank and Liu (eds), *The Cambridge History of China*, vol. 11, pp. 285–91. 75. Ibid, pp. 323–7. 76. Spence, *The Search for Modern China*, p. 221. 77. Immanuel C. Y. Hsü, *The Rise of Modern China*, Oxford University Press 1990, p. 377. 78. Victor Purcell, *The Boxer Uprising: A Background Study*, Cambridge University Press 1963, p. 224. 79. Colin Mackerras, *Western Images of China*, Oxford University Press 1989, p. 68. 80. Crossley, *The Wobbling Pivot*, p. 139. 81. Chuzo Ichiko, 'Political and Institutional Reform, 1901–11', in Fairbank and Liu (eds), *The Cambridge History of China*, vol. 11, p. 375. 82. Crossley, *The Wobbling Pivot*, p. 118. 83. Text in Teng and Fairbank (eds), *China's Response to the West*, p. 199. 84. Ichiko, 'Political and Institutional Reform, 1901–11', pp. 376, 283. 85. Ibid, pp. 388–9. 86. Hsü, *The Rise of Modern China*, pp. 412–13. 87. Timothy B. Weston, 'The Founding of the Imperial University and the Emergence of Chinese Modernity', in Rebecca E. Karl and Peter Zarrow (eds), *Rethinking the 1898 Reform Period: Political and Cultural Change in Late Qing China*, Harvard University Asia Center, 2002, pp. 102–3. 88. Crossley, *The Wobbling Pivot*, p. 140. 89. Text in Teng and Fairbank (eds), *China's Response to the West*, p. 167. 90. Wellington K. K. Chan, 'Government, Merchants and Industry to 1911', in Fairbank and Liu (eds), *The Cambridge History of China*, vol. 11, pp. 419–20, 91. Yen-P'ing Hao, 'Cheng Kuan-ying: The Comprador as Reformer', *Journal of Asian Studies*, vol. 29, no. 1, November 1969, pp. 15–22. 92. Ibid, p. 20. 93. Hao and Wang, 'Changing Chinese Views of Western Relations, 1840–95', pp. 191–3. 94. Cheng-chung Lai, 'Adam Smith and Yen Fu: Western Economics in Chinese Perspective', *Journal of European Economic History*, vol. 18, no. 2, Fall 1989, pp. 373–5. 95. Frederic

Wakeman, Jr., *The Fall of Imperial China*, The Free Press, New York and London 1975, p. 39. 96. Benjamin I. Schwartz, *In Search of Wealth and Power: Yen Fu and the West*, Harper, New York 1964, p. 114. 97. Yan Fu (Yen Fou), *Les manifestes de Yen Fou*, p. 126; see also Hsü, *The Rise of Modern China*, pp. 422–3. 98. Leigh Jenco, *Changing Referents: Learning across Space and Time in China and the West*, Oxford University Press 2015, p. 28. 99. Cited by François Houang in his introduction to Yan Fu (Yen Fou), *Les manifestes de Yen Fou*, p. 27. 100. Mao Zedong, 'On the People's Democratic Dictatorship: In Commemoration of the Twenty-Eighth Anniversary of the Communist Party of China', 30 June 1949: https://www.marxists.org/reference/archive/mao/selected-works/volume-4/mswv4_65.htm, accessed 6 May 2017. 101. Richard S. Horowitz, 'Breaking the Bonds of Precedent: The 1905–6 Government Reform Commission and the Remaking of the Qing Central State', *Modern Asian Studies*, vol. 37, no. 4, p. 775. On the uses of Japan as a model for China see Roger R. Thompson, *China's Local Councils in the Age of Constitutional Reform, 1898–1911*, Harvard University Press 1995, pp. 39–52. 102. Roger R. Thomson, 'The Lessons of Defeat: Transforming the Qing State after the Boxer War', *Modern Asian Studies*, vol. 37, no. 4, 2003, pp. 769–73, esp. p. 770, suggesting that the reforms failed to convert the Qing state into one fit for the twentieth century. 103. Wong, *China Transformed*, p. 133. 104. Albert Feuerwerker, 'Economic Trends in the Late Ch'ing Empire, 1870–1911', in Fairbank and Liu (eds), *The Cambridge History of China*, vol. 11, p. 68. 105. See esp. Thompson, *China's Local Councils*, pp. 7–20. 106. Spence, *The Search for Modern China*, p. 235. 107. This claim seems to have been substantiated by a relatively recent investigation: see Lin Qi, 'The Poisoned Palace – Mystery of Last Emperor's Death', *China Daily*, 21 November 2008: http://www.chinadaily.com.cn/china/2008-11/21/content_7226663.htm, accessed 6 May 2017. 108. Ichiko, 'Political and Institutional Reform, 1901–11', p. 397. 109. Julia C. Strauss, 'Creating "Virtuous and Talented" Officials for the Twentieth Century: Discourse and Practice in *Xinzheng* China', *Modern Asian Studies*, vol. 37, no. 4, October 2003, p. 833. 110. 'Resolution on Certain Questions in the History of Our Party Since the Founding of the People's Republic of China adopted by the Sixth Plenary Session of the Eleventh Central Committee of the Communist Party of China on June 27, 1981': http://english.cpc.people.com.cn/66095/4471924.html 111. See Castells, *The Rise of the Network Society*, vol. 1 of *The Information Age*, p. 9, on the basis of Mokyr, *The Lever of Riches*, pp. 209–38. 112. John S. Gregory, *The West and China since 1500*, Palgrave, Basingstoke 2003, p. 116; see also Mackerras, *Western Images of China*, p. 44. 113. Hsü, *The Rise of Modern China*, p. 449. 114. Martin Lynn, 'British Policy, Trade, and Informal Empire in the Mid-Nineteenth Century', in Andrew Porter (ed.), *The Oxford History of the British Empire*, vol. 3: *The Nineteenth Century*, Oxford University Press 1999, p. 108. 115. Michael Adas, *Machines as Measures of Men: Science, Technology and Ideologies of Western Dominance*, Cornell University Press 1989, pp. 79–81; see also Jonathan Spence, *The*

Chan's Great Continent: China in Western Minds, Penguin, London 2000, pp. 81–100. **116.** Voltaire, *Essai sur les moeurs et l'esprit des nations*, Tome 1 in *Oeuvres complètes*, vol. 15, Dupont, Paris 1823–7, pp. 269–86. **117.** G. W. F. Hegel, *Lectures on the Philosophy of World History*, vol. 1: *Manuscripts of the Introduction and the Lectures of 1822–23*, ed. and trans. Robert F. Brown and Peter C. Hodgson, Clarendon Press, Oxford 2011, p. 212. **118.** Gottfried Leibniz, Preface to *Novissima Sinica*: http://www.zftrans.com/bbs/read.php?tid=15696; see also Franklin Perkins, 'The Theoretical Basis of Comparative Philosophy in Leibniz' Writings on China', in Wenchao Li and Hans Poser (eds), *Das neueste über China. G. W. Leibnizens Novissima Sinica von 1697*, Fran Steiner Verlag, Stuttgart 2000, p. 275. **119.** David E. Mungello, *The Great Encounter of China and the West, 1500–1800*, Rowman & Littlefield, Lanham, MD 2009, pp. 19, 31, 100. **120.** David Hume, 'Of Commerce', in David Hume, *Selected Essays*, Oxford University Press 2008, p. 164. **121.** Pomeranz, *The Making of a Hinterland*, pp. 19–22. **122.** Wu Chengming, 'On Embryonic Capitalism in China', in Xu Dixin and Wu Chengming (eds), *Chinese Capitalism, 1522–1840*, Macmillan, Basingstoke 2000, p. 19. **123.** Fang Xing, 'The Retarded Development of Capitalism', in ibid, p. 395. **124.** Hao and Wang, 'Changing Chinese Views of Western Relations, 1840–95', p. 175. **125.** See Li, *Agricultural Development in Jiangnan*, 'Conclusion', and also Philip C. C. Huang, 'The Paradigmatic Crisis in Chinese Studies: Paradoxes in Social and Economic History', *Modern China*, vol. 17, no. 3, July 1991, pp. 299–341. **126.** Michel Aglietta and Yves Landry, *La Chine vers la superpuissance*, Economica, Paris 2007, p. 1; World Bank data, *World Development Indicators*, retrieved 1 July 2014. **127.** Moulder, *Japan, China, and the Modern World Economy*, p. 151. **128.** Masao Maruyama, *Studies in the Intellectual History of Tokugawa Japan*, Princeton University Press 1974, pp. 327–30. **129.** Ibid, p. 340. **130.** Michio Morishima, *Why Has Japan 'Succeeded'? Western Technology and the Japanese Ethos*, Cambridge University Press 1982, pp. 73, 75, 85. **131.** Cited in W. G. Beasley, *The Meiji Restoration*, Stanford University Press 1972, pp. 266–7. **132.** Cyril E. Black et al., *The Modernization of Japan and Russia: A Comparative Study*, Free Press, New York and London 1975, p. 42; Jean-Pierre Lehmann, *The Roots of Modern Japan*, Macmillan, London 1982, p. 142; E. Sidney Crawcour, 'The Tokugawa Heritage', in William W. Lockwood (ed.), *The State and Economic Enterprise in Japan: Essays in the Political Economy of Growth*, Princeton University Press 1965, p. 18. **133.** W. J. Macpherson, *The Economic Development of Japan c. 1868–1941*, Macmillan, London 1987 pp. 24–31. **134.** Tessa Morris-Suzuki, *The Technological Transformation of Japan: From the Seventeenth to the Twenty-First Century*, Cambridge University Press 1994, pp. 73–4. **135.** Beasley, *The Meiji Restoration*, p. 74. **136.** Lehmann, *The Roots of Modern Japan* c. 1868–1941, pp. 242–3. **137.** Masao Maruyama, *Thought and Behaviour in Modern Japanese Politics*, Oxford University Press 1969, pp. 4–5. **138.** Tsuzuki, *The Pursuit of Power in Modern Japan*, p. 151;

Osterhammel, *The Transformation of the World*, p. 237. 139. Ian Neary, *The State and Politics in Japan*, Polity, Cambridge 2002, pp. 13–14; see also Morishima, *Why Has Japan 'Succeeded'?*, p. 88; Lehmann, *The Roots of Modern Japan*, p. 186; Macpherson, *The Economic Development of Japan*, p. 36; on Boissonade see Alexis Dudden, *Japan's Colonization of Korea: Discourse and Power*, University of Hawai'i Press 2005, pp. 106–7. 140. Johannes Hirschmeier and Tsunehiko Yui, *The Development of Japanese Business 1600–1973*, Harvard University Press 1975, pp. 75–6. 141. Neary, *The State and Politics in Japan*, pp. 15–16. 142. There is widespread agreement on this; see, inter alia, Hirschmeier and Yui, *The Development of Japanese Business, 1600–1973*, p. 70. 143. E. Herbert Norman, *Japan's Emergence as a Modern State: Political and Economic Problems of the Meiji Period*, UBC Press, Vancouver and Toronto 2000 (1st edition 1940), p. 46. 144. Ibid, p. 32. 145. Lehmann, *The Roots of Modern Japan*, pp. 267–8. 146. Jacques Pezeu-Massabuau, 'Le Japon à l'ère mégalopolitaine: éclatement de l'espace traditionnel et insularité culturelle', *Annales*, vol. 36, no. 5, September–October 1981, p. 831; Morishima, *Why Has Japan 'Succeeded'?*, p. 20; Jacques Pezeu-Massabuau, 'La notion d'emprise sur le milieu géographique: l'exemple japonais', *Annales*, vol. 27, no. 1, January–February 1972; Morris-Suzuki, *The Technological Transformation of Japan*, p. 17. 147. Manjirō Inagaki, *Japan and the Pacific, and a Japanese View of the Eastern Question*, T. Fisher Unwin, London 1890, p. 43; he dedicated the book to John Robert Seeley. 148. Robert Thomas Tierney, *Tropics of Savagery: The Culture of the Japanese Empire in Comparative Frame*, University of California Press 2010, p. 16. 149. Morris-Suzuki, *Re-Inventing Japan*, p. 24. 150. Yukichi Fukuzawa, *The Autobiography of Yukichi Fukuzawa*, trans. Eiichi Kiyooka, Columbia University Press 2007, p. 135. 151. See Norio Tamaki, *Yukichi Fukuzawa, 1835–1901: The Spirit of Enterprise in Modern Japan*, Palgrave, Basingstoke 2001, pp. 90–91; see also Akira Iriye, 'The Internationalization of History', *American Historical Review*, vol. 94, no. 1, February 1989 p. 7; see also Fukuzawa, *The Autobiography of Yukichi Fukuzawa*, pp. 373–9. 152. Tierney, *Tropics of Savagery*, pp. 27–8. 153. Fukuzawa, *The Autobiography of Yukichi Fukuzawa*, pp. 104, 116–17. 154. Norman, *Japan's Emergence as a Modern State*, pp. 176–7n. 155. Marius B. Jansen, *China in the Tokugawa World*, Harvard University Press 1992, p. 101. 156. Jansen, 'Japan and the Chinese Revolution of 1911', p. 342. 157. David S. Landes, 'Japan and Europe: Contrasts in Industrialization', in Lockwood (ed.), *The State and Economic Enterprise in Japan*, pp. 93–7. 158. Jansen, *The Making of Modern Japan*, p. 373. 159. Alvin Y. So and Stephen W. K. Chiu, *East Asia and the World Economy*, Sage, London 1995, pp. 74–5. 160. Lehmann, *The Roots of Modern Japan*, pp. 173–7. 161. Landes, 'Japan and Europe: Contrasts in Industrialization', pp. 101, 106–7, 115. 162. Norman, *Japan's Emergence as a Modern State*, p. 111. 163. Moulder, *Japan, China, and the Modern World Economy*, p. 179. 164. Lehmann, *The Roots of Modern Japan*, p. 209. 165. Macpherson, *The*

Economic Development of Japan, p. 35. 166. Tsuzuki, *The Pursuit of Power in Modern Japan*, p. 141, and Macpherson, *The Economic Development of Japan*, p. 34. 167. Tsuzuki, *The Pursuit of Power in Modern Japan*, p. 143. 168. Fukuzawa, *The Autobiography of Yukichi Fukuzawa*, p. 190. 169. Lehmann, *The Roots of Modern Japan*, p. 180. 170. Tsuzuki, *The Pursuit of Power in Modern Japan*, p. 138. 171. Macpherson, *The Economic Development of Japan*, p. 24. 172. Moulder, *Japan, China, and the Modern World Economy*, p. 179. 173. Morishima, *Why Has Japan 'Succeeded'?*, p. 60. 174. E. Sidney Crawcour, 'The Tokugawa Heritage', in Lockwood (ed.), *The State and Economic Enterprise in Japan*, pp. 42–3. 175. Kenneth B. Pyle, 'The Future of Japanese Nationality: An Essay in Contemporary History', *Journal of Japanese Studies*, vol. 8, no. 2. Summer 1982, pp. 238–9. 176. Yasuzō Horie, 'Modern Entrepreneurship in Meiji Japan', in Lockwood (ed.), *The State and Economic Enterprise in Japan*, p. 198. 177. Norman, *Japan's Emergence as a Modern State*, p. 71. 178. Ibid, pp. 7–8, 30. See also Hirschmeier and Yui, *The Development of Japanese Business, 1600–1973*, p. 1. 179. Hirschmeier and Yui, *The Development of Japanese Business, 1600–1973*, pp. 82–6. 180. Ibid, pp. 95–6. 181. Ibid, pp. 88–91. 182. Gary P. Leupp, *Servants, Shophands, and Laborers in the Cities of Tokugawa Japan*, Princeton University Press 1992, p. 176. 183. R. P. Dore, 'Talent and the Social Order in Tokugawa Japan', *Past & Present*, no. 21, April 1962, pp. 60–68. 184. E. Sidney Crawcour, 'The Tokugawa Heritage', in Lockwood (ed.), *The State and Economic Enterprise in Japan*, p. 34; such arguments had been advanced by T. C. Smith, *Agrarian Origins of Modern Japan* (1959), esp. pp. 71–2, 123. But this has been contested: see Bramall and Nolan, 'Introduction' to *Chinese Capitalism, 1522–1840*, pp. xxxiv–xxxv. 185. Cited in Akira Iriye, *Pacific Estrangement: Japanese and American Expansion, 1897–1911*, Harvard University Press 1972, p. 9. 186. Helena Hirata and Kurumi Sugita, 'Politique paternaliste et division sexuelle du travail: le cas de l'industrie japonaise', *Le Mouvement Social*, no. 144, July–September 1988, p. 75. 187. Christine Lévy, 'La naissance du mouvement ouvrier moderne au Japon', in Claude Hamon (ed.), *Entreprise et société dans le Japon d'avant-guerre*, Philippe Piquier, Arles 2011, p. 104; Hirschmeier and Yui, *The Development of Japanese Business, 1600–1973*, p. 110; Lehmann, *The Roots of Modern Japan*, p. 206. 188. Lehmann, *The Roots of Modern Japan*, p. 206; Tsuzuki, *The Pursuit of Power in Modern Japan*, p. 142. 189. Macpherson, *The Economic Development of Japan*, p. 18; Lehmann, *The Roots of Modern Japan*, p. 192, has slightly different figures; Moulder, *Japan, China, and the Modern World Economy*, pp. 183–8. 190. So and Chiu, *East Asia and the World Economy*, p. 53; also cited in Giovanni Arrighi, *Adam Smith in Beijing: Lineages of the Twenty-First Century*, Verso, London 2007, p. 342. 191. Wu Chengming, 'A Brief Account of the Development of Capitalism in China', in Tim Wright (ed.), *The Chinese Economy in the Early Twentieth Century: Recent Chinese Studies*, St Martin's Press, New York, 1992, p. 30.

4. THE ALLURE OF INDUSTRY

1. Osman Okyar, 'A New Look at the Problem of Economic Growth in the Ottoman Empire (1800–1914)', *Journal of European Economic History*, vol. 16, no. 1, Spring 1987, pp. 13–14. 2. Finkel, *Osman's Dream*, pp. 442–3. 3. Catherine Durandin, *Histoire des Roumains*, Fayard, Paris 1995, p. 101. 4. Selim Deringil, *The Well-Protected Domains: Ideology and the Legitimation of Power in the Ottoman Empire, 1876–1909*, I. B. Tauris, London and New York 1998, p. 135. 5. Finkel, *Osman's Dream*, p. 499. 6. Ariel Salzmann, 'Citizens in Search of a State: The Limits of Political Participation in the Late Ottoman Empire', in Michael Hanagan and Charles Tilly (eds), *Extending Citizenship, Reconfiguring States*, Rowman & Littlefield, Lanham, MD 1999, pp. 45–6. 7. Engin Deniz Akarli, 'The Tangled Ends of an Empire: Ottoman Encounters with the West and Problems of Westernization – an Overview', *Comparative Studies of South Asia, Africa and the Middle East*, vol. 26, no. 3, 2006, p. 357. 8. Şevket Pamuk, *The Ottoman Empire and European Capitalism, 1820–1913: Trade, Investment and Production*, Cambridge University Press 1987, pp. 13–14, 82ff. 9. Giampaolo Conte and Gaetano Sabatini, 'The Ottoman External Debt and its Features Under European Financial Control (1881–1914)', *Journal of European Economic History*, vol. 43, no. 3, 2014, pp. 69–96. 10. Pamuk, *The Ottoman Empire and European Capitalism, 1820–1913*, p. 61. 11. M. Şükrü Hanioğlu, *Preparation for a Revolution: The Young Turks, 1902–1908*, Oxford University Press 2001, esp. pp. 302–6. 12. Pamuk, *The Ottoman Empire and European Capitalism 1820–1913*, p. 83. 13. Finkel, *Osman's Dream*, pp. 504–9. 14. bertrand Badie, *L'état importé. Essai sur l'occidentalisation de l'ordre politique*, Fayard, Paris 1992, pp. 128, 168, 178ff. 15. Pavel Milyukov (Paul Milyoukov), *Russia and its Crisis*, University of Chicago Press 1905, p. 51: http://archive.org/stream/russiaitscrisisoomiliuoft#page/n3/mode/2up 16. Hitchins, *Rumania*, pp. 292–4. 17. Durandin, *Histoire des Roumains*, p. 192. 18. John Michael Montias, 'Notes on the Romanian Debate on Sheltered Industrialization: 1860–1906', in Kenneth Jowitt (ed.), *Social Change in Romania, 1860–1940: A Debate on Development in a European Nation*, University of California Press 1978, p. 60. 19. Iván T. Berend and György Ránki, *The European Periphery and Industrialization, 1780–1914*, Cambridge University Press 1982, p. 42. 20. Andrew C. Janos, 'Modernization and Decay in Historical Perspective: The Case of Romania', in Kenneth Jowitt (ed.), *Social Change in Romania, 1860–1940*, p. 84. 21. Ibid, p. 89. 22. Daniel Chirot, *Social Change in a Peripheral Society: The Creation of a Balkan Colony*, Academic Press, New York 1976, p. 144. 23. Dan Berindei, 'The Nineteenth Century', in Dinu C. Giurescu and Stephen Fischer-Galaţi (eds), *Romania: A Historic Perspective*, East European Monographs, Boulder, CO, distributed by Columbia University Press 1998, p. 225. 24. Janos, 'Modernization and Decay in Historical Perspective', p. 98. 25. Iordachi, 'The Unyielding Boundaries of Citizenship', pp. 162–3. 26. Janos, 'Modernization and Decay in Historical Perspective',

p. 93. 27. Ibid, pp. 100, 85. 28. Hitchins, *Rumania*, pp. 23–7. 29. Hippolyte Desprez, 'La Moldo-Valachie et le mouvement roumain', *Revue des deux mondes*, vol. 21, 1848, p. 112. 30. Hitchins, *Rumania*, p. 138. 31. Chirot, *Social Change in a Peripheral Society*, pp. 123, 130, 133. On the agrarian reform of 1864, see Durandin, *Histoire des Roumains*, pp. 164–6. 32. Daniel Chirot and Charles Ragin, 'The Market, Tradition and Peasant Rebellion: The Case of Romania in 1907', *American Sociological Review*, vol. 40, no. 4, August 1975, pp. 430–31. 33. Jeremy Attack, Fred Bateman, and William N. Parker, 'The Farm, the Farmer, and the Market', in Stanley L. Engerman and Robert E. Gallman (eds), *The Cambridge Economic History of the United States*, vol. 2: *The Long Nineteenth Century*, Cambridge University Press 2000, p. 257. 34. Simmel, 'The Metropolis and Mental Life', in *Simmel on Culture*, ed. Frisby and Featherstone, p. 176. 35. Iván T. Berend and György Ránki, 'Underdevelopment in Europe in the Context of East-West Relations in the Nineteenth Century', in *Études historiques hongroises*, ed. Dezső Nemes, Akadémiai Kiadó, Budapest 1980, p. 703. 36. Hitchins, *Rumania*, pp. 112–13; Durandin, *Histoire des Roumains*, pp. 183–7. 37. Durandin, *Histoire des Roumains*, p. 188. 38. Hitchins, *Rumania*, pp. 155–7. 39. Chirot, *Social Change in a Peripheral Society*, pp. 145, 148. 40. Walter Benjamin, *On the Concept of History*, Gesammelten Schriften I:2. Suhrkamp Verlag, Frankfurt am Main 1974, Thesis 9, 1940: http://members.efn.org/~dredmond/ThesesonHistory.html 41. Durandin, *Histoire des Roumains*, pp. 205–6. 42. On Spiru Haret see Irina Livezeanu, *Cultural Politics in Greater Romania*, Cornell University Press 1995, pp. 31–3. 43. Andrew C. Janos, *East Central Europe in the Modern World: The Politics of the Borderlands from Pre- to Postcommunism*, Stanford University Press 2000, pp. 77–8, 83–5. 44. Ibid, p. 91. 45. Victor Bulmer-Thomas, *The Economic History of Latin America since Independence*, Cambridge University Press 2003, pp. 53, 58, 72, and 74. 46. Ibid, p. 142. 47. William Glade, 'Latin America and the International Economy, 1870–1914', in Bethell (ed.), *The Cambridge History of Latin America*, vol. IV, p. 12. 48. Angus Maddison, *Historical Statistics of the World Economy: 1–2008 AD. Essays in Macro-Economic History*, Oxford University Press 2007. 49. Lehmann, *The Roots of Modern Japan*, pp. 192–4. 50. Bulmer-Thomas, *The Economic History of Latin America since Independence*, p. 128. 51. See Colin M. Lewis, 'Industry in Latin America before 1930', in Bethell (ed.), *The Cambridge History of Latin America*, vol. IV, pp. 277–8. 52. Claudio Robles-Ortiz, 'Agrarian Capitalism and Rural Labour: The Hacienda System in Central Chile, 1870–1920', *Journal of Latin American Studies*, vol. 41, no. 3, August 2009, pp. 493–526. 53. Aurora Gómez-Galvarriato and Jeffrey G. Williamson, 'Was it Prices, Productivity or Policy? Latin American Industrialisation after 1870', *Journal of Latin American Studies*, vol. 41, no. 4, November 2009, pp. 668–9. 54. Bulmer-Thomas, *The Economic History of Latin America since Independence*, p. 59; Glade, 'Latin America and the International Economy', pp. 16–17. 55. Andrés Guerrero, 'Naissance des bourgeoisies latino-américaines au XXe siècle: le cas de l'Équateur',

Annales, vol. 35, no. 6, November–December 1980, p. 1,172. 56. José Luis González, *Nuestra crisis y el Fondo Monetario Internacional*, p. 122, cited in Charles Anderson, *Politics and Economic Change in Latin America*, D. Van Nostrand Co., Princeton, NJ 1967, p. 28. 57. Glade, 'Latin America and the International Economy', pp. 7, 19, 48; see also Lewis, 'Industry in Latin America before 1930', pp. 268–70. 58. Charles A. Hale, 'Political and Social Ideas in Latin America, 1870–1930', in Bethell (ed.), *The Cambridge History of Latin America*, vol. IV, p. 414. 59. José Enrique Rodó, *Ariel*, ed. Belén Castro, Cátedra, Madrid 2000, pp. 180, 207, 215. 60. Bulmer-Thomas, *The Economic History of Latin America since Independence*, pp. 14–17. After the 1980s there was a return to export-led growth. See also Duncan Green, *Silent Revolution: The Rise and Crisis of Market Economics in Latin America*, Monthly Review Press, New York 2003, p. 11. 61. Joel Stillerman and Peter Winn, 'Introduction: Globalization and the Latin American Workplace', *International Labor and Working-Class History*, vol. 70, Fall 2006, p. 1. 62. Bulmer-Thomas, *The Economic History of Latin America since Independence*, p. 49. 63. Glade, 'Latin America and the International Economy', pp. 2–3. 64. Nicola Crepax, 'Tradizione Lombarda, industria tessile e sviluppo economico', in Luciano Cafagna and Nicola Crepax (eds), *Atti di intelligenza e sviluppo economico. Saggi per il bicentenario della nascita di Carlo Cattaneo*, Il Mulino, Bologna 2001, p. 244. 65. Giuliano Procacci, *La lotta di classe in Italia agli inizi del secolo XX*, Riuniti, Rome 1978, p. 8. 66. Stefano Musso, 'La famiglia operaia', in Piero Melograni (ed.), *La famiglia italiana dall'ottocento a oggi*, Laterza, Rome-Bari 1988, pp. 61–3. 67. Vera Zamagni, *The Economic History of Italy, 1860–1990*, Clarendon Press, Oxford 1993, pp. 81–2. 68. Francesco Barbagallo, *Napoli, Belle Époque*, Laterza, Rome-Bari 2015, p. 41. 69. Whether a form of serfdom existed in Tibet is controversial: see Melvyn C. Goldstein, who uses the term 'pervasive serfdom' in 'Serfdom and Mobility: An Examination of the Institution of "Human Lease" in Traditional Tibetan Society', *Journal of Asian Studies*, vol. 30, no. 3, May 1971, p. 521. 70. Jerome Blum, *The End of the Old Order in Rural Europe*, Princeton University Press 1978, pp. 377–86; Nicolas Spulber, *Russia's Economic Transitions: From Late Tsarism to the New Millennium*, Cambridge University Press 2003, p. 53. 71. Nicos P. Mouzelis, *Modern Greece: Facets of Underdevelopment*, Macmillan, London 1978, p. 15. 72. Ibid, p. 21. 73. Vassilis K. Fouskas and Constantine Dimoulas, *Greece, Financialization and the European Union*, Palgrave Macmillan, London 2013, p. 65. 74. *The Economist*, 17 October 2015: http://www.economist.com/news/economic-and-financial-indicators/21674507-merchant-fleets 75. Dertilis, 'Introduction', in Dertilis (ed.), *Banquiers, usuriers et paysans*, pp. 18, 28. 76. Albert Broder, Gérard Chastagnaret, and Émile Temime, 'Capital et croissance dans l'Espagne du XIXème siècle', in Jean-Pierre Amalric et al., *Aux origines du retard économique de l'Espagne, XVIe–XIXe siècles*, CNRS, Paris 1983, p. 64. 77. Ibid, pp. 64–73. 78. Charles Harvey and Peter Taylor, 'Mineral Wealth and Economic Development: Foreign Direct Investment in Spain, 1851–1913', *Economic*

History Review, vol. 40, no. 2, 1987, pp. 186–7. 79. Gabriel Tortella, *The Development of Modern Spain: An Economic History of the Nineteenth and Twentieth Centuries*, Harvard University Press 2000, pp. 75ff. 80. Harvey and Taylor, 'Mineral Wealth and Economic Development', p. 187. 81. Tortella Casares, *The Development of Modern Spain*, pp. 74, 89, 114. 82. Gabriel Tortella, 'Patterns of Economic Retardation and Recovery in South-Western Europe in the Nineteenth and Twentieth Centuries', *Economic History Review*, vol. 47, 1994, p. 5. 83. Bairoch, 'Niveaux de développement économique de 1810 à 1910', *Annales*, pp. 1,110, 1,092. The data were only for these eleven countries, but it is very unlikely that any other country would have warranted placement in the top eleven. This author is also careful to question some of the statistics available, in particular the low placement of Japan. 84. Bairoch, 'La Suisse dans le contexte international aux XIXe et XXe siècles', in Bairoch and Körner (eds), *La Suisse dans l'économie mondiale*, p. 106. 85. Lars G. Sandberg, 'The Case of the Impoverished Sophisticate: Human Capital and Swedish Economic Growth before World War I', *Journal of Economic History*, vol. 39, no. 1, March 1979, p. 225. 86. Paul Bairoch, 'International Industrialization Levels from 1750 to 1980', *Journal of European Economic History*, vol. 11, no. 2, Fall 1982, p. 293.

5. THE STATE

1. Cited in P. H. Clendenning, 'The Economic Awakening of Russia in the 18th Century', *Journal of European Economic History*, vol. 14, no. 3, Winter 1985, p. 470. 2. Ian Inkster, 'Technological and Industrial Change: A Comparative Essay', in *The Cambridge History of Science*, vol. 4, ed. Roy Porter, Cambridge University Press 2003, p. 862. 3. Malcolm Yapp, 'Europe in the Turkish mirror', *Past & Present*, no. 137, 1992, p. 154. 4. Yen-P'ing Hao and Erh-min Wang, 'Changing Chinese Views of Western Relations, 1840–95', in Fairbank and Liu (eds), *The Cambridge History of China*, vol. 11, p. 193. 5. Moulder, *Japan, China, and the Modern World Economy*, pp. 189–90. 6. This is the line taken by Charles Tilly in his 'War Making and State Making as Organized Crime', in *Bringing the State Back In*, ed. Peter B. Evans, Dietrich Rueschemeyer, and Theda Skocpol, Cambridge University Press 1985. 7. John Williamson, 'What Washington Means by Policy Reform', in *Latin American Adjustment: How Much Has Happened?*, ed. John Williamson, Institute for International Economics, Washington, DC 1989. 8. Adam Przeworski, 'The Last Instance: Are Institutions the Primary Cause of Economic Development?', *Archives européennes de sociologie*, vol. xlv, no. 2, 2004, p. 166. 9. Robert Wade, 'Financial Regime Change?', *New Left Review*, no. 53, September/October 2008, p.19; Arrighi, *Adam Smith in Beijing*, pp. 354–5. 10. Martin Wolf, 'How the Beijing Elite Sees the World', *Financial Times*, 2 May 2018. 11. Jean-Charles Asselain, 'L'expérience chinoise en perspective historique. Un regard occidental', *Revue d'études comparative Est-Ouest*, vol. 30, nos 2–3, 1999,

pp. 328, 353–4. 12. Chenggang Xu and Juzhong Zhuang, 'Why China Grew: The Role of Decentralization', in Peter Boone, Stanislaw Gomulka, and Richard Layard (eds), *Emerging from Communism: Lessons from Russia, China and Eastern Europe*, MIT 1998, pp. 183–7. 13. Ha-Joon Chang, *Kicking Away the Ladder: Development Strategy in Historical Perspective*, Anthem Press, London 2003, pp. 120–21; Joseph E. Stiglitz, 'Is there a Post-Washington Consensus Consensus?', in *The Washington Consensus Reconsidered: Towards a New Global Governance*, ed. Narcís Serra and Joseph E. Stiglitz, Oxford University Press 2008, p. 43. 14. Stiglitz, 'Is there a Post-Washington Consensus Consensus?', p. 44. 15. William J. Baumol, Robert E. Litan, and Carl J. Schramm, *Good Capitalism, Bad Capitalism and the Economics of Growth and Prosperity*, Yale University Press 2007, pp. 7–8. 16. Romain Duval, 'Le rôle de l'idéologie et des croyances dans l'économie politique', *Revue d'économie politique*, vol. 117, no. 4, July–August 2007, p. 594. 17. Frederick (Friedrich) List, *National System of Political Economy* (1841), trans. G. A. Matile, J. B. Lippincott & Co., Philadelphia, PA 1856, p. 267. 18. Ibid, p. 109. 19. Ibid, p. 262. 20. Ibid, p. 200. 21. Emma Rothschild, *Economic Sentiments: Adam Smith, Condorcet and the Enlightenment*, Harvard University Press 2001, p. 116. 22. Adam Smith, *An Inquiry into the Nature and Causes of the Wealth of Nations*, Penn State Electronic Classics 2005, pp. 363–4: http://www2.hn.psu.edu/faculty/jmanis/adam-smith/Wealth-Nations.pdf 23. Donald Winch, 'Adam Smith's "enduring particular result": A Political and Cosmopolitan Perspective', in Istvan Hont and Michael Ignatieff (eds), *Wealth and Virtue: The Shaping of Political Economy in the Scottish Enlightenment*, Cambridge University Press 1983, pp. 264–5. 24. Smith, *An Inquiry into the Nature and Causes of the Wealth of Nations*, p. 111. 25. Ibid, p. 83. 26. Angus Maddison, *Contours of the World Economy, 1–2030 AD: Essays in Macro-Economic History*, Oxford University Press 2007, p. 381. 27. Smith, *An Inquiry into the Nature and Causes of the Wealth of Nations*, p. 697. 28. Marina Lewycka, *Various Pets Alive and Dead*, Penguin/Fig Tree, London 2012, p. 61. 29. The full subtitle of Jean-Baptiste Say's *Cours complet d'économie politique pratique* (1829) was *ouvrage destiné à mettre sous les yeux des hommes d'État, des propriétaires fonciers et des capitalistes, des savans, des agriculteurs, des manufacturiers, des négocians, et en général de tous les citoyens l'économie des sociétés*, vol. 5. 30. Cited in Rothschild, *Economic Sentiments*, pp. 127–8; for the fuller citation see Smith, *An Inquiry into the Nature and Causes of the Wealth of Nations*, p. 213. 31. Smith, *An Inquiry into the Nature and Causes of the Wealth of Nations*, p. 602. 32. Ibid, pp. 537–8. 33. Keynes, *The General Theory of Employment, Interest, and Money*, pp. 46, 104. 34. Alexander Pushkin, *Yevgeny Onegin*, trans. Anthony Briggs, Pushkin Press, London 2016, p. 56. 35. Rothschild, *Economic Sentiments*, p. 81. 36. Colin J. Holmes, 'Laissez-Faire in Theory and Practice: Britain 1800–1875', *Journal of European Economic History*, vol. 5, no. 3, Winter 1976, p. 674. 37. Smith, *An Inquiry into the Nature and Causes of the Wealth of Nations*, p. 337. 38. David Hume, 'Of the Balance of Trade', in David Hume, *Selected Essays*, Oxford University Press 2008, p. 201. 39. John Stuart Mill, *Principles of Political Economy* (1848), Longmans, Green and Co., London 1904, p. 480; see also Pedro Schwartz, *The New Political Economy of J. S. Mill*, Weidenfeld and Nicolson, London 1972, p. 116, and, more generally, the whole of Chapter 6. 40. Eugenio F. Biagini, *Liberty, Retrenchment and Reform: Popular Liberalism in the Age of Gladstone, 1860–1880*, Cambridge University Press 1992, pp. 166–7. 41. Edmund Burke, *Thoughts and Details on Scarcity, originally presented to the Right Hon. William Pitt, in the month of November 1795*, F. and C. Rivington, London 1800, pp. 45–6: https://archive.org/stream/thoughtsanddetaoopittgoog#page/n5/mode/2up 42. John Maynard Keynes, 'The End of Laissez-Faire' (1926), in *Essays in Persuasion*, Macmillan 1972, p. 288. Keynes quotes Burke from one of the later editions of McCulloch's *Principles of Political Economy*, repeating McCulloch's mistake of writing 'exertion' instead of 'discretion' as Burke had written. 43. Burke, *Thoughts and Details on Scarcity*, p. 46. 44. Thomas Paine, *Common Sense*, 1776: http://www.gutenberg.org/files/147/147-h/147-h.htm 45. Friedrich Engels, *Anti-Dühring*, Progress Publishers, Moscow 1969, p. 333 (Part 3, Chapter 2). 46. Keynes, 'The End of Laissez-Faire', p. 291. 47. Herbert Spencer, *The Principles of Biology*, vol. 1, Williams and Norgate, Edinburgh 1864, pp. 444–5. 48. Herbert Spencer, *Social Statics*, together with *The Man versus the State*, D. Appleton and Co., New York 1897, p. 314. 49. David G. Ritchie, *The Principles of State Interference: Four Essays on the Political Philosophy of Mr. Herbert Spencer, J. S. Mill, and T. H. Green*, Swan Sonnenschein, London 1902 (1891), p. 3. 50. Ibid, p. 4. 51. Hofstadter, *Social Darwinism in American Thought*, pp. 31, 33. 52. Naomi Beck, 'The Diffusion of Spencerism and its Political Interpretations in France and Italy', in Greta Jones and Robert A. Peel (eds), *Herbert Spencer: The Intellectual Legacy*, The Galton Institute, London 2004, p. 42. 53. Ibid, pp. 51–2. 54. Schwartz, *In Search of Wealth and Power*, pp. 47–77. 55. Jansen, *The Making of Modern Japan*, p. 388. 56. Douglas Howland, 'Society Reified: Herbert Spencer and Political Theory in Early Meiji Japan', *Comparative Studies in Society and History*, vol. 42, no. 1, January 2000, p. 70. 57. Marwa Elshakry, *Reading Darwin in Arabic, 1860–1950*, University of Chicago Press 2014, pp. 82–3. 58. Charles A. Hale, *The Transformation of Liberalism in Late Nineteenth-Century Mexico*, Princeton University Press 1989, pp. 237, 251. 59. Greta Jones, 'Spencer and his Circle', in Jones and Peel (eds), *Herbert Spencer: The Intellectual Legacy*, p. 10. 60. Stefan Collini, *Liberalism and Sociology: L. T. Hobhouse and Political Argument in England, 1880–1914*, Cambridge University Press 1979, pp. 17–20. 61. Michael Freeden, *The New Liberalism: An Ideology of Social Reform*, Clarendon Press, Oxford 1978, pp. 35–6. 62. Collini, *Liberalism and Sociology*, pp. 20–21. 63. 'A Word for Laissez-Faire', *Pall Mall Gazette*, 14 October 1883, cited in Wohl, *The Eternal Slum*, pp. 223–4. 64. Sidney Webb, 'The Moral of the Elections', *Contemporary Review*, vol. 62, August 1892, p. 273. 65. Ibid, p. 275. 66. Ibid, pp. 280–81. 67. Joseph Chamberlain, *Mr. Chamberlain's*

Speeches, vol. 1, ed. Charles W. Boyd, Constable, London 1914, pp. 163–4. 68. Nicholas W. Balabkins, *Not by Theory Alone . . . : The Economics of Gustav von Schmoller and its Legacy to America*, Duncker & Humblot, Berlin 1988, p. 47; see also Kenneth Barkin, 'Adolf Wagner and German Industrial Development', *Journal of Modern History*, vol. 41, no. 2, June 1969, pp. 144–59. 69. Gary Cross, *A Quest for Time: The Reduction of Work in Britain and France, 1840–1940*, University of California Press 1989, p. 126. 70. David Blackbourn, 'The Discreet Charm of the Bourgeoisie: Reappraising German History in the Nineteenth Century', in David Blackbourn and Geoff Eley, *The Peculiarities of German History: Bourgeois Society and Politics in Nineteenth-Century Germany*, Oxford University Press 1984, pp. 178–81. 71. On Masaryk, Dobrogeanu-Gherea, and *Huszadik Század*, see Balázs Trencsényi, Maciej Janowski, Mónika Baar, Maria Falina, and Michal Kopeček, *A History of Modern Political Thought in East Central Europe*, vol. 1: *Negotiating Modernity in the 'Long Nineteenth Century'*, Oxford University Press 2016, pp. 332, 432, 465, 437–8, 468–9. 72. Michèle Merger, *Un siècle d'histoire industrielle en Italie, 1880–1998*, SEDES, Paris 1998, p. 21. 73. Guido Baglioni, *L'ideologia della borghesia industriale nell'Italia liberale*, Einaudi, Turin 1974, p. 129. 74. Antonio Gramsci, *Il Risorgimento*, Editori Riuniti, Rome 1971, p. 102. 75. Baglioni, *L'ideologia della borghesia industriale*, pp. 150–52. 76. Edmond Neukomm, *Voyage au pays du déficit (la Nouvelle Italie)*, Ernest Kolb, Paris 1890, p. 145. 77. Giorgio Mori, 'Blocco di potere e lotta politica in Italia', in *Storia della società italiana, vol. 14: Il blocco di potere nell'Italia unita*, Teti editore, Milan 1980, pp. 251, 264. 78. Nello Quilici, *Origine sviluppo e insufficienza della borghesia italiana*, ISPI, Milan 1942, p. 359. 79. Richard A. Webster, *Industrial Imperialism in Italy, 1908–1915*, University of California Press 1975, pp. 6–8, 12–15, 24–5, 41, 53. 80. Harrison, *Disease and the Modern World*, p. 115. 81. Paul Leroy-Beaulieu, *La question de la population*, F. Alcan, Paris 1913, p. 470. 82. Marx, *Capital*, vol. 1, pp. 16, 61, 81. 83. Keynes, 'The End of Laissez-Faire', p. 281. 84. Frédéric Bastiat, *Harmonies économiques*, in *Oeuvres Complètes*, vol. VI, Guillaumin, Paris 1870 (6th ed.), p. 557. 85. Ibid, pp. 553–5. 86. Ibid, pp. 541, 543–5. 87. Ibid, p. 566. 88. Eliane Gubin, 'Liberalisme économique et paternalisme en Belgique au XIXe siècle', in Erik Aerts, Claude Beaud, and Jean Stengers (eds), *Liberalism and Paternalism in the 19th Century* (Tenth International Economic History Congress, Leuven, August 1990), Leuven University Press 1990, pp. 83–5. 89. Gustave de Molinari, 'De la production de la sécurité', *Journal des économistes*, 15 February 1849: http://www.panarchy.org/molinari/securite.html 90. Jean Puissant, '1886, la contre-réforme sociale?', in Pierre Van der Vorst (ed.), *Cent ans de droit social belge*, Bruylant, Brussels 1988, p. 70. 91. Henri Pirenne, *Histoire de Belgique. Des origines à nos jours*, vol. 5, La Renaissance du Livre, Brussels 1975, p. 155, original edition in seven

volumes, 1900–1932. 92. Holmes, 'Laissez-Faire in Theory and Practice', p. 681. 93. John Stuart Mill, 'Miss Martineau's Summary of Political Economy', *Monthly Repository*, vol. VIII, May 1834, pp. 318–22 (a review of

The Moral of Many Fables by Harriet Martineau). The text can be found in *The Collected Works of John Stuart Mill*, vol. IV. 94. Keynes, 'The End of Laissez-Faire', p. 282. 95. Daumard, 'Puissance et inquiétudes de la société bourgeoise', p. 402. 96. William G. Roy, *Socializing Capital: The Rise of the Large Industrial Corporation in America*, Princeton University Press 1997, p. 83. 97. Olga Crisp, *Studies in the Russian Economy before 1914*, Macmillan, London 1976, pp. 153–4. 98. V. L. Stepanov, 'Nikolai Khristianovich Bunge', *Russian Studies in History*, vol. 35, no. 2, Fall 1996, p. 53. 99. François Caron, 'Dynamismes et freinages de la croissance industrielle', in Fernand Braudel and Ernest Labrousse (eds), *Histoire économique et sociale de la France*, Tome IV: *L'ère industrielle et la société d'aujourd'hui (siècle 1880–1980)*, vol. 1, Presses Universitaires de France, Paris 1979, p. 244. 100. Ibid, p. 252. 101. H. G. Creel, 'The Beginnings of Bureaucracy in China: The Origin of the *Hsien*', *Journal of Asian Studies*, vol. 23, no. 2, February 1964, p. 156. 102. Andrew C. Janos, *The Politics of Backwardness in Hungary, 1825–1945*, Princeton University Press 1982, pp. 90, 93–4. 103. OECD figures on the basis of ILO figures: http://www.oecd-ilibrary.org/sites/gov_glance-2011-en/05/01/gv-21-01.html?itemId=/content/chapter/gov_glance-2011-27-en&_csp_=6514ff186e872f0ad7b772c5f31fbf2f 104. Muller, *The Mind and the Market*, p. 234. 105. Mark Hewitson, 'German Public Opinion and the Question of Industrial Modernity: Wilhelmine Depictions of the French Economy', *European Review of History*, vol. 7, no. 1, Spring 2000, p. 59. 106. Max Weber, 'The Nation State and Economic Policy', in Peter Lassman and Ronald Speirs (eds), *Weber: Political Writings*, Cambridge University Press 1994, pp. 13, 15. 107. See Wolfgang J. Mommsen, *Max Weber et la politique allemande, 1890–1920*, Presses Universitaires de France, Paris 1985, p. 63. 108. David Beetham, *Max Weber and the Theory of Modern Politics*, Polity Press, Cambridge 1995, p. 38. 109. Ibid, pp. 56, 222–3. 110. Eric Hobsbawm, *Industry and Empire*, Penguin, London 1968, p. 135. 111. Cited in Martin Robson, *A History of the Royal Navy: The Seven Years War*, I. B. Tauris, London 2015, p. 52. 112. D. C. M. Platt, *Finance, Trade, and Politics in British Foreign Policy, 1815–1914*, Clarendon Press, Oxford 1968, pp. xiii–xiv. 113. David Edgerton, *The Rise and Fall of the British Nation*, Allen Lane, London 2018, pp. 113–19. 114. Christopher Hill, *Reformation to Industrial Revolution: The Making of Modern English Society, 1530–1780*, Penguin, London 1969, p. 226.

6. TAXATION

1. Edmund Burke, *Reflections on the Revolution in France*, Apollo Press, London 1814, p. 226. 2. Robert Brenner, 'Economic Backwardness in Eastern Europe in Light of Developments in the West', in Chirot (ed.), *The Origins of Backwardness in Eastern Europe*, p. 23. 3. Blum, 'The Condition of the European Peasantry on the Eve of Emancipation', pp. 398, 402. 4. Roman

Rosdolsky, 'The Distribution of the Agrarian Product in Feudalism', *Journal of Economic History*, vol. 11, no. 3, Summer 1951, pp. 263. 5. Cited in ibid, p. 264. 6. Carolyn C. Fenwick, (ed.) *The Poll Taxes of 1377, 1379, and 1381, Part 1: Bedfordshire Leicestershire*, Oxford University Press for the British Academy, London 1998, pp. xxiii–xxvi. 7. Ardant, *Histoire financière*, p. 196. 8. John Locke, *Second Treatise on Government*, Chapter XI, para. 142: http://www.gutenberg.org/files/7370/7370-h/7370-h.htm 9. Jean-Jacques Rousseau, *Discours sur l'économie politique*: http://classiques.uqac.ca/classiques/Rousseau_jj/discours_economie_politique/discours_eco_pol.html p. 28 10. Richard Bonney, 'France, 1494–1815', in Richard Bonney (ed.), *The Rise of the Fiscal State in Europe, c.1200–1815*, Oxford University Press 1999, p. 164. 11. Max Weber, 'Politics as a Vocation', in Max Weber, *The Vocation Lectures*, ed. David Owen and Tracy B. Strong, Hackett Publishing, Indianapolis, IN 2004, p. 33. 12. Jean-Baptiste Say, *Traité d'économie politique ou simple exposition de la manière dont se forment, se distribuent et se consomment les richesses*, O. Zeller, 1841 (6th ed.), Book 3, Chapter 9, pp. 507–8: http://fr.wikisource.org/wiki/Trait%C3%A9_d%E2%80%99%C3%A9conomie_politique/Livre_3/Chapitre_9 13. See a long-term study, limited to the department of Seine-et-Oise: Nicolas Delalande, 'Le consentement à l'impôt en France: les contribuables, l'administration et le problème de la confiance. Une étude de cas en Seine-et-Oise (années 1860–années 1930)', *Revue d'histoire moderne et contemporaine*, vol. 56, no. 2, April–June 2009, pp. 135–63. 14. Present league tables of failed states do not even consider tax collection as a key variable. See the yearly reports of the US-based Fund for Peace: http://www.fundforpeace.org/web/index.php?option=com_content&task=view&id=452&Itemid=900. In 2010 the top ten failures were: Somalia, Chad, Sudan, Zimbabwe, Congo, Afghanistan, Iraq, Central African Republic, Guinea, and Pakistan. 15. Joseph A. Schumpeter, 'The Crisis of the Tax State' (1918), in Joseph A. Schumpeter, *The Economics and Sociology of Capitalism*, ed. Richard Swedberg, Princeton University Press 1991, p. 100. 16. Jean-Marc Daniel, *Histoire vivante de la pensée économique: Des crises et des hommes*, Pearson, Paris 2010, p. 35. 17. John Brewer, *The Sinews of Power: War, Money and the English State, 1688–1783*, Routledge, London 1994, p. 22. See also Martin Daunton, 'Trusting Leviathan: The Politics of Taxation, 1815–1914', in Donald Winch and Patrick O'Brien (eds), *The Political Economy of British Historical Experience, 1688–1914*, Oxford University Press 2002, pp. 319–20. 18. Brewer, *The Sinews of Power*, p. 91. 19. Patrick O'Brien, 'Fiscal Exceptionalism: Great Britain and its European Rivals from Civil War to Triumph at Trafalgar and Waterloo', in Winch and O'Brien (eds), *The Political Economy of British Historical Experience, 1688–1914*, p. 262, and Martin Daunton, 'Creating Consent: Taxation, War, and Good Government in Britain, 1688–1914', in Sven H. Steinmo (ed.), *The Leap of Faith: The Fiscal Foundations of Successful Government in Europe and America*, Oxford University Press 2018, p. 131. 20. Margaret Levi, *Of Rule and Revenue*, University of California Press 1988, p. 97. 21. Thomas Mortimer, *The Elements of Commerce, Politics and Finances*, London 1772, pp. 321, 440. 22. Immanuel Kant, 'Perpetual Peace: A Philosophical Sketch', in *Political Writings*, ed. Hans Reiss, Cambridge University Press 1991, p. 95, my emphasis. 23. Peter Nolan, *China at the Crossroads*, John Wiley, London 2013, p. 142. 24. Levi, *Of Rule and Revenue*, pp. 123–4. 25. Daunton, 'Trusting Leviathan', pp. 323, 334. 26. Harriet Martineau, *A History of England: The Thirty Years' Peace*, Charles Knight, London 1849–50, vol. 2, p. 538, cited in Wendy Hinde, *Richard Cobden: A Victorian Outsider*, Yale University Press 1987, p. 106. 27. Norman Gash, *Pillars of Government and Other Essays on State and Society, c. 1770–1880*, Edward Arnold, London 1986, p. 53. 28. Gabriel Ardant, *Histoire de l'impôt*, vol. 2: *Du XVIIIe au XXIe siècle*, Fayard, Paris 1972, p. 343. 29. Daunton, 'Trusting Leviathan', pp. 335–40. 30. Roger Middleton, *Government versus the Market*, Edward Elgar, Cheltenham 1996, p. 86. 31. Smith, *An Inquiry into the Nature and Causes of the Wealth of Nations*, p. 691, see also p. 676. 32. Mill, *Principles of Political Economy*, 1904, p. 486. 33. Cited in Rothschild, *Economic Sentiments*, p. 29. 34. Burke, *Reflections on the Revolution in France*, pp. 286–7. 35. Montesquieu, *De l'esprit des lois*, vol. I, p. 416 (Book XIII, Chapter 1). 36. David J. A. Macey, *Government and Peasant in Russia, 1861–1906: The Prehistory of the Stolypin Reforms*, Northern Illinois University Press 1987, p. 36. 37. Pierre Antonmattei, *Léon Gambetta, héraut de la République*, Éditions Michalon, Paris 1999, p. 164. 38. Hewitson, 'German Public Opinion and the Question of Industrial Modernity', p. 54. 39. Middleton, *Government versus the Market*, p. 94. 40. Nicolas Delalande, *Les batailles de l'impôt: Consentement et résistance de 1789 à nos jours*, Seuil, Paris 2011, p. 215. 41. Caron, 'Dynamismes et freinages de la croissance industrielle', in Braudel and Labrousse (eds), *Histoire économique et sociale de la France*, vol. 1, book IV, p. 256. 42. Jean-Denis Bredin, *Joseph Caillaux*, Hachette, Paris 1980, pp. 95–6. 43. Delalande, *Les batailles de l'impôt*, p. 7. 44. Statistics of taxation come from the OECD database: www.oecd.org/ctp/taxdatabase 45. Stephen Vlastos, 'Opposition Movements in Early Meiji, 1868–1885', in Marius B. Jansen (ed.), *Cambridge History of Japan*, vol. 5: *The Nineteenth Century*, Cambridge University Press 1989, pp. 368–9. 46. Hirschmeier and Yui, *The Development of Japanese Business 1600–1973*, pp. 83–4; figure for land tax revenue in 1885–9 in Norman, *Japan's Emergence as a Modern State*, p. 77. 47. Berend and Ránki, *The European Periphery and Industrialization, 1780–1914*, p. 71. 48. Janos, *East Central Europe in the Modern World*, p. 92. 49. Janos, 'Modernization and Decay in Historical Perspective', p. 96. 50. Zamagni, *Dalla periferia al centro*, p. 219. 51. Şevket Pamuk, 'The Evolution of Fiscal Institutions in the Ottoman Empire, 1500–1914', in Bartolomé Yun-Casalilla and Patrick O'Brien (eds), *The Rise of Fiscal States: A Global History, 1500–1914*, Cambridge University Press 2012, pp. 329–30. 52. Robert H. Gorlin, 'Problems of Tax Reform in Imperial Russia', *Journal of Modern History*, vol. 49, no. 2, June 1977, p. 249, and Peter Gatrell, 'The Russian Fiscal State, 1600–1914', in Yun-Casalilla and O'Brien (eds), *The Rise of Fiscal States*, p. 203. Both authors present quite different figures but agree on the substance. 53. Sergei Witte, *The Memoirs of Count Witte*, Heinemann, London 1921, p. 55; see also Peter I. Lyashchenko, *History of the National Economy of Russia to the 1917 Revolution*, Macmillan, New York, NY 1949, p. 556. 54. Witte, *Memoirs*, p. 55. 55. Paul Gregory, 'Economic Growth and Structural Change in Tsarist Russia: A Case of Modern Economic Growth?', *Soviet Studies*, vol. 23, no. 3, January 1972, p. 421. 56. In 2005, 37 per cent of Russian men would die before the age of fifty-five, the comparable figure for the UK being only 7 per cent; see David Zaridze et al., 'Alcohol and Mortality in Russia: Prospective Observational Study of 151,000 Adults', *Lancet*, vol. 383, no. 9927, 26 April 2014, pp. 1,465–73. 57. Gorlin, 'Problems of Tax Reform in Imperial Russia', pp. 251, 261. 58. Wong, *China Transformed*, pp. 238–44ff. 59. Albert Feuerwerker, 'Economic Trends in the Late Ch'ing Empire, 1870–1911', in Fairbank and Liu (eds), *The Cambridge History of China*, vol. 11, p. 63. 60. Pomeranz, *The Making of a Hinterland*, p. 271. 61. Crossley, *The Wobbling Pivot*, p. 117. 62. Spence, *The Search for Modern China*, p. 231. 63. Richard A. Musgrave, 'Reconsidering the Fiscal Role of Government', *American Economic Review*, vol. 87, no. 2, May 1997, p. 156. 64. See the OECD database: https://stats.oecd.org/Index.aspx?DataSetCode=REV

7. LAGGARDS AND PATHBREAKERS

1. Hobsbawm, *Industry and Empire*, p. 13. 2. Maddison, *Dynamic Forces in Capitalist Development*, pp. 30–40. 3. Peter Mathias, 'La révolution industrielle en Angleterre: un cas unique?', *Annales*, vol. 27, no. 1, January–February 1972, pp. 37–8. 4. David S. Landes, *The Unbound Prometheus: Technological Change and Industrial Development in Western Europe from 1750 to the Present*, Cambridge University Press 2003, p. 219. 5. Charles Masterman, *The Condition of England*, Methuen, London 1912 (1st ed. 1909), p. 56. 6. Osterhammel, *The Transformation of the World*, p. 212. 7. Mokyr, *The Enlightened Economy*, pp. 99, 106–7. 8. F. M. L. Thompson, *The Rise of Respectable Society: A Social History of Victorian Britain, 1830–1900*, Harvard University Press 1988, p. 29. 9. See figures in Phyllis Deane and W. A. Cole, *British Economic Growth, 1688–1959: Trends and Structure*, Cambridge University Press 1967, p. 143. 10. Thompson, *The Rise of Respectable Society*, p. 43. 11. Supple, 'The State and the Industrial Revolution, 1700–1914', p. 302. 12. Jean-Michel Gaillard and André Lespagnol, *Les mutations économiques et sociales au XIXe siècle (1780–1880)*, Nathan, Paris 1984, p. 77. 13. Alan Birch, *The Economic History of the British Iron and Steel Industry, 1784–1879*, Routledge, London 2005 (first published 1967), p. 313. 14. Richard Tames, *Economy and Society in Nineteenth Century Britain*, Routledge, London 2013, p. 53. For a list of present-day steel-producing countries see: http://www.worldsteel.org 15. William H. Phillips, 'The Economic Performance of Late Victorian Britain: Traditional Historians and

Growth', *Journal of European Economic History*, vol. 18, no. 2, Fall 1989, p. 393, quoting D. N. McCloskey, *Economic Maturity and Entrepreneurial Decline: British Iron and Steel, 1870–1913*, Harvard University Press 1973, Chapter 5. 16. Bairoch, 'International Industrialization Levels from 1750 to 1980', pp. 330–31. 17. Patrick O'Brien and Caglar Keyder, 'Les voies de passage vers la société industrielle en Grande-Bretagne et en France (1780–1914)', *Annales*, vol. 34, no. 6, November–December 1979, pp. 1,287–8. 18. Gilles Postel-Vinay, 'L'agriculture dans l'économie française. Crises et réinsertion', in Maurice Lévy-Leboyer and Jean-Claude Casanova (eds), *Entre l'état et le marché. L'économie française des années 1880 à nos jours*, Gallimard, Paris 1991, p. 73. 19. Lévy-Leboyer and Bourguignon, *L'économie française au XIXe siècle*, pp. 268–9. 20. Leduc, *Histoire de la France*, p. 15. 21. Jean-Charles Asselain, 'La stagnation économique', in Lévy-Leboyer and Casanova (eds), *Entre l'état et le marché*, p. 220. 22. World Bank International Comparison Programme: http://web.worldbank.org/external/default/main?pagePK=60002244&theSitePK=270065&contentMDK=23562337&noSURL=Y&piPK=62002388 23. World Bank International Comparison Programme: http://web.worldbank.org/external/default/main?pagePK=60002244&theSitePK=270065&contentMDK=23562337&noSURL=Y&piPK=62002388 24. International Monetary Fund, World Economic Outlook Database, April 2014: http://www.imf.org/external/pubs/ft/weo/2014/01/weodata/index.aspx; World Bank: 'GDP per capita, PPP (current international $)', World Development Indicators database, updated 1 July 2014. 25. Berend and Ránki, *The European Periphery and Industrialization, 1780–1914*, pp. 31–3. 26. Gunnar Fridlizius, 'Sweden's Exports, 1850–1960: A Study in Perspective', *Economy and History*, vol. 6, 1963, p. 3. 27. Ibid, pp. 12, 21. 28. Ivan T. Berend, *An Economic History of Twentieth-Century Europe*, Cambridge University Press 2006, pp. 28–30. 29. Berend and Ránki, *The European Periphery and Industrialization, 1780–1914*, p. 64. 30. Sandberg, 'The Case of the Impoverished Sophisticate: Human Capital and Swedish Economic Growth before World War I', pp. 227, 230, 232. 31. Jens Möller, 'Towards Agrarian Capitalism: The Case of Southern Sweden during the 19th Century', *Geografiska Annaler: Series B, Human Geography*, vol. 72, no. 2/3, 1990, pp. 60ff. 32. Werner Sombart, *The Quintessence of Capitalism: A Study of the History and Psychology of the Modern Business Man*, Fisher Unwin, London 1915, pp. 141, 143. This is the translation of his 1913 book *Der Bourgeois*. 33. Sombart, *The Quintessence of Capitalism*, pp. 150–51. 34. Donald Winch, *Riches and Poverty: An Intellectual History of Political Economy in Britain, 1750–1834*, Cambridge University Press 1996, p. 165. 35. Austin Harrison, *England & Germany: Republished from 'The Observer'*, Macmillan, London 1907, p. 91: http://archive.org/stream/englandandgerman00harruoft#page/n5/mode/2up 36. Ibid, pp. 80–81. 37. Ibid, p. 93. 38. Ernest Edwin Williams, '*Made in Germany*', Heinemann, London 1896, pp. 162–3. 39. Arthur Shadwell, *Industrial Efficiency: A Comparative Study of Industrial Life in England, Germany and America*, vol. 2, Longmans, Green, and Co., London 1906, pp. 453–4. 40. Ibid, pp. 45–56. 41. Ibid, p. 456. 42. Ibid, p. 457. 43. Hubert Kiesewetter, 'Competition for Wealth and Power: The Growing Rivalry between Industrial Britain and Industrial Germany 1815–1914', *Journal of European Economic History*, vol. 20, no. 2, Fall 1991, p. 292. 44. Data for decadence in Malcolm Bull, 'The Decline of Decadence', *New Left Review*, July–August 2015, no. 94, pp. 83–6; the data for 'decline' in Google Books Ngram Viewer. 45. Baglioni, *L'ideologia della borghesia industriale*, p. 135. 46. Giovanni Luigi Fontana, 'Imprenditori, imprese e territorio dalla prima alla seconda rivoluzione industriale' in *L'industria vicentina dal medioevo a oggi*, ed. Giovanni Luigi Fontana, Centro Studi sull'impresa, Vicenza 2004, pp. 365–7. 47. As he acknowledges himself, not realizing this invalidates his thesis. See Luigi Einaudi, 'La politica economica delle classi operaie italiane nel momento presente', in Luigi Einaudi, *Cronache economiche e politiche di un trentennio*, vol. 1: *1893–1902*, Einaudi, Turin 1959, p. 164, originally in *Critica sociale* of 1 July 1899. 48. Ibid, pp. 165–9. 49. Zamagni, *Dalla periferia al centro*, pp. 207–9, see table on p. 207. 50. Ibid, p. 216. 51. Ilaria Barzaghi, *Milano 1881: tanto lusso e tanta folla*, Silvana, Milan 2009, pp. 185–6. 52. Ana Bela Nunes, Eugénia Mata, and Nuno Valério, 'Portuguese Economic Growth, 1833–1985', *Journal of European Economic History*, vol. 18, no. 2, Fall 1989, p. 301. 53. Pedro Lains, *L'économie portugaise au XIXe siècle. Croissance économique et commerce extérieur, 1851–1913*, L'Harmattan, Paris 1999, p. 48. 54. Stanley G. Payne, *A History of Spain and Portugal*, vol. 2: *Eighteenth Century to Franco*, University of Wisconsin Press 1973, p. 557. 55. Sakari Heikkinen and Riitta Hjerppe, 'The Growth of Finnish Industry in 1860–1913: Causes and Linkages', *Journal of European Economic History*, vol. 16, no. 2, 1987, pp. 227–9. 56. Hjerppe, *The Finnish Economy, 1860–1985*, pp. 51, 62–3. 57. David Moon, 'Peasant Migration and the Settlement of Russia's Frontiers, 1550–1897', *Historical Journal*, vol. 40, no. 4, December 1997, p. 893. 58. Berend and Ránki, *The European Periphery and Industrialization, 1780–1914*, p. 29. 59. Karl Marx, Preface to the first German edition, *Capital*, vol. 1, Progress Publishers, Moscow 1965, p. 9. 60. Adam Smith, *Lectures on Jurisprudence*, ed. R. L. Meek, D. D. Raphael, and P. G. Stein, Clarendon Press, Oxford 1978, p. 14. 61. Smith, *An Inquiry into the Nature and Causes of the Wealth of Nations*, pp. 310–11. 62. See these classic twentieth-century works: Karl Polanyi, *The Great Transformation: The Political and Economic Origins of Our Time* (1944), Beacon Press, Boston, MA 2002; Alexander Gerschenkron, *Economic Backwardness in Historical Perspective*, Belknap Press, Cambridge, MA 1962; and Barrington Moore, Jr., *Social Origins of Dictatorship and Democracy: Lord and Peasant in the Making of the Modern World*, Beacon Press, Boston, MA 1966. 63. Lucidly summarized by Jonathan M. Wiener in his 'Review of Reviews: *Social Origins of Dictatorship and Democracy*', in *History and Theory*, vol. 15, no. 2, May 1976, pp. 146–75. 64. Patrick O'Brien, 'Do We Have a Typology for the Study of European Industrialization in the XIXth Century?', *Journal of European Economic History*, vol. 15, no. 2, Fall 1986, p. 323. 65. Colin Leys, *The Rise and Fall of Development Theory*,

James Currey, London 1996, p. 49. 66. Luo Guanzhong, *Three Kingdoms: A Historical Novel*, trans. Moss Roberts, University of California Press 1991, p. 5. 67. Charles Kindleberger, 'Review of *The Economy of Turkey*; *The Economic Development of Guatemala*; *Report on Cuba*', *Review of Economics and Statistics*, vol. 34, no. 4, November 1952, p. 391, cited in Arrighi, *Smith in Beijing*, pp. 42–3. 68. M. M. Postan, 'L'expérience de l'industrialisation européenne et les problèmes actuels des pays sous-développés', in *L'industrialisation en Europe au XIXe siècle*, Colloque international du CNRS, Lyon 1970, Éditions du CNRS, Paris 1972, p. 48. 69. O'Brien and Keyder, 'Les voies de passage vers la société industrielle en Grande-Bretagne et en France (1780–1914)', p. 1,285. 70. Louis Bergeron (ed.), *Les capitalistes en France (1780–1914)*, Gallimard, Paris 1978, p. 125. 71. Rondo Cameron, 'France, 1800–1870', in Rondo Cameron, with Olga Crisp et al., *Banking in the Early Stages of Industrialization*, Oxford University Press 1967, pp. 100–128. But this is hotly disputed by Alain Plessis in his 'Le "retard français": la faute à la banque? Banques locales, succursales de la Banque de France et financement de l'économie sous le Second Empire', in Patrick Fridenson and André Straus (eds), *Le capitalisme français 19e–20e siècle. Blocages et dynamismes d'une croissance*, Paris, Fayard 1987, pp. 199–210. 72. Lévy-Leboyer and Bourguignon, *L'économie française au XIXe siècle*, p. 8. 73. Jean Bouvier, 'Libres propos autour d'une démarche révisionniste', in Fridenson and Straus, *Le capitalisme français 19e–20e siècle*, pp. 13–15. 74. Maurice Lévy-Leboyer, 'La croissance économique en France au XIXe siècle', *Annales*, vol. 23, no. 4, July–August 1968, p. 801. 75. Maurice Lévy-Leboyer, 'La décélération de l'économie française dans la seconde moitié du XIXe siècle', *Revue d'histoire économique et sociale*, vol. 49, no. 4, 1971, p. 486. 76. Patrick Verley, *Nouvelle histoire économique de la France contemporaine*, vol. 2: *L'industrialisation 1830–1914*, La Découverte, Paris 2002, p. 7. 77. Hewitson, 'German Public Opinion and the Question of Industrial Modernity', p. 48. 78. Ibid, pp. 49–52. 79. Leslie Hannah, 'Logistics, Market Size, and Giant Plants in the Early Twentieth Century: A Global View', *Journal of Economic History*, vol. 68, no. 1, March 2008, pp. 60–62. 80. Jean Garrigues, 'Un autre modèle pour la République: l'influence des Britanniques sur les libéraux français (1870–1880)', in Sylvie Aprile and Fabrice Bensimon (eds), *La France et l'Angleterre au XIXe siècle: échanges, représentations, comparaisons*, Creaphis éditions, Paris 2006, p. 182; see also Paul Challemel-Lacour's article 'Hommes d'état en Angleterre: William Ewart Gladstone', *Revue des deux mondes*, 1 July 1870, pp. 44–92; the citation is on p. 50. 81. Garrigues, 'Un autre modèle pour la République', pp. 182–7. 82. Bertrand Joly, 'Le parti royaliste et l'affaire Dreyfus (1898–1900)', *Revue historique*, no. 546, April–June 1983, pp. 311–64. 83. Michael G. Mulhall, *The Progress of the World in Arts, Agriculture, Commerce, Manufactures, Instruction, Railways, and Public Wealth since the Beginning of the Nineteenth Century*, Edward Stanford, London 1880, pp. 140–42. 84. Michael G. Mulhall, *Industries and Wealth of Nations*, Longmans, Green, and Co., London 1896, Table XIX for figures on trade and p. 391 for figures on earnings.

85. Germaine de Staël, *Considérations sur les principaux événements de la Révolution française, depuis son origine jusques et compris le 8 juillet 1815*, vol. 3, J.-A. Latour, Liège 1818, pp. 185, 230–2; see also Biancamaria Fontana, *Germaine de Staël: A Political Portrait*, Princeton University Press 2016, p. 229. 86. Cited in Laurent Theis, *Guizot. La traversée d'un siècle*, CNRS Éditions, Paris 2014, p. 178. On Guizot's Anglophilia see the whole of Chapter IX: http://www.guizot.com/wp-content/uploads/Les-Guizot-et-l-Angleterre.pdf 87. James Thompson, '"A Nearly Related People": German Views of the British Labour Market, 1870–1900', in Winch and O'Brien (eds), *The Political Economy of British Historical Experience*, pp. 95–8. 88. List, *National System of Political Economy*, pp. 437–8. 89. Barthélemy Faujas-Saint-Fond, *Voyage en Angleterre, en Écosse et aux Îles Hébrides*, H. J. Jansen, Paris 1797, vol. 1, pp. 113–14. 90. Ibid., pp. 58, 67–8, 44, 56. 91. Giorgio Mori, 'The Genesis of Italian Industrialization', *Journal of European Economic History*, vol. 4, no. 1, Spring 1975, pp. 91–2. 92. Giuseppe Pecchio, *Osservazioni semi-serie di un esule sull'Inghilterra*, G. Ruggia & Co., Lugano 1831, pp. 103, 124, 223. 93. Domenico Zanichelli, *Studi politici e storici*, Zanichelli, Bologna 1893, p. 15. 94. Ibid, p. 121. 95. Berend and Ránki, *The European Periphery and Industrialization, 1780–1914*, p. 21. 96. Ibid, p. 25. 97. Janos, *East Central Europe in the Modern World*, pp. 346–8, 353. 98. Katus, 'Economic Growth in Hungary during the Age of Dualism', pp. 55–6. 99. Ibid, pp. 57–8. 100. William O. McCagg Jr., 'Hungary's "Feudalized" Bourgeoisie', *Journal of Modern History*, vol. 44, no. 1, March 1972, p. 71. 101. Janos, *The Politics of Backwardness in Hungary*, pp. 120–21. 102. Cited in ibid, pp. 128–9. 103. Katus, 'Economic Growth in Hungary during the Age of Dualism', pp. 69–72. 104. Ibid, pp. 78–80. 105. Marx, *Capital*, vol. 1, p. 760. 106. Anatole Leroy-Beaulieu, *L'empire des Tsars et les Russes*, Laffont, Paris 1990, p. 279 (1st ed. 1881; the edition I am using is a reprint of the 4th ed. of 1897–8). 107. Karl Marx and Friedrich Engels, *The Communist Manifesto*, Penguin, London 2002, pp. 223–4. 108. F. M. L. Thomson, 'Changing Perceptions of Land Tenures in Britain, 1750–1914', in Winch and O'Brien (eds), *The Political Economy of British Historical Experience, 1688–1914*, pp. 133–4. 109. Bairoch, 'Niveaux de développement économique de 1810 à 1910', p. 1,096. 110. Karl Marx and Frederick Engels, *The German Ideology*, International Publishers, New York 1968, p. 38. 111. Kant 'Perpetual Peace', pp. 106–7. 112. Theodore S. Hamerow, *The Birth of a New Europe*, University of North Carolina Press 1983, p. 19, citing Franz Xaver von Neumann-Spallart, *Uebersichten der Weltwirtschaft: Jahrgang 1883–84*, Stuttgart 1887, p. 83. 113. William Cunningham, 'Nationalism and Cosmopolitanism in Economics', *Journal of the Royal Statistical Society*, vol. 54, no. 4, December 1891, pp. 649–50; noted in Frank Trentmann, 'National Identity and Consumer Politics: Free Trade and Tariff Reform', in Donald Winch and Patrick O'Brien (eds), *The Political Economy of British Historical Experience, 1688–1914*, Oxford University Press 2002, p. 215. 114. Cunningham, 'Nationalism and Cosmopolitanism in Economics', p. 651. 115. Hervé,

L'internationalisme, pp. 63–4. 116. Cited in René Girault, 'Place et rôle des échanges extérieurs', in Braudel and Labrousse (eds), *Histoire économique et sociale de la France*, Tome IV, vol. 1, p. 223. 117. Giovanni Dalla Vecchia, 'The Revolt in Italy', *Contemporary Review*, vol. 74, July 1898, p. 113. 118. Booth, *Life and Labour of the People in London*, p. 191. 119. C. A. Bayly, *The Birth of the Modern World, 1780–1914*, Blackwell, Oxford 2004, p. 172. 120. Arno J. Mayer, 'The Lower Middle Class as Historical Problem', *Journal of Modern History*, vol. 47, no. 3. September 1975, p. 419. 121. François Crouzet, *L'économie de la Grande-Bretagne Victorienne*, Société d'édition d'enseignement supérieur, Paris 1978, pp. 332–5. 122. Angus Maddison figures adjusted in international Geary–Khamis dollars (purchasing power parity), see www.ggdc.net/maddison/Historical . . . /horizontal-file_02-2010.xls (The Groningen Growth and Development Centre). 123. See Robert Brenner, 'Agrarian Class Structure and Economic Development in Pre-Industrial Europe', *Past & Present*, no. 70, February 1976, pp. 30–75, along with contributions to the debate sparked by the original article in T. H. Aston and C. H. E. Philpin (eds), *The Brenner Debate: Agrarian Class Structure and Economic Development in Pre-Industrial Europe*, Cambridge University Press 1985. 124. William Stanley Jevons, *The Coal Question: An Inquiry Concerning the Progress of the Nation, and the Probable Exhaustion of our Coal-Mines*, Macmillan, London 1866 (1st ed. 1865), p. 371. 125. William Gladstone, 'Financial Statement', 3 May 1866, House of Commons: http://hansard.millbanksystems.com/commons/1866/may/03/the-financial-statement pp. 399–400. 126. Stefan Collini, 'The Idea of "Character" in Victorian Political Thought', *Transactions of the Royal Historical Society*, vol. 35, 1985, p. 46. 127. Brenner, 'Economic Backwardness in Eastern Europe in Light of Developments in the West', pp. 15–52; see also Robert Brenner, 'The Agrarian Roots of European Capitalism', in *The Brenner Debate*, ed. Aston and Philpin; and Robert Brenner, 'The Origins of Capitalism: A Critique of Neo-Smithian Marxism', *New Left Review*, no. 104, July–August 1977. 128. Rodney H. Hilton, 'Introduction', in Aston and Philpin (eds), *The Brenner Debate*, p. 5. 129. Samuel Clark, 'Nobility, Bourgeoisie and the Industrial Revolution in Belgium', *Past & Present*, no. 105, November 1984, p. 167.

8. RUSSIA: THE RELUCTANT LAGGARD

1. Alexander Pushkin, 'To Chaadaev', trans. A. N. Matyatina: http://zhurnal.lib.ru/m/matjatina_a_n/tochaadaevaspushkin.shtml 2. Mikhail Lermontov, *Major Poetical Works*, ed. and trans. Anatoly Liberman, Croom Helm, London 1983, p. 47. 3. Hans Rogger, *Russia in the Age of Modernisation and Revolution, 1881–1917*, Longman, London and New York 1983, p. 100. 4. Orlando Figes, *Crimea: The Last Crusade*, Allen Lane, London 2010, pp. 484–8. 5. Gerschenkron, *Economic Backwardness in Historical Perspective*, p. 17. 6. Boris Chicherin, *Liberty, Equality, and the Market: Essays by B. N. Chicherin*, ed.

and trans. G. M. Hamburg, Yale University Press 1998, p. 133. 7. Milyoukov, *Russia and its Crisis*, p. 225. 8. Ibid, p. 226. 9. Alexander Herzen, *Selected Philosophical Works*, Foreign Languages Publishing House, Moscow 1956, p. 35 ('Dilettantism in Science', 1843). 10. S. V. Tiutiukin, 'Where Were the Socialists Leading Russia in the Early Twentieth Century?', *Russian Studies in History*, vol. 42, no. 4, Spring 2004, pp. 38–45. 11. Andrzej Walicki, *The Slavophile Controversy: History of a Conservative Utopia in Nineteenth-Century Russian Thought*, Clarendon Press, Oxford 1975, pp. 588–90. 12. Alexander Herzen, *My Past and Thoughts: The Memoirs of Alexander Herzen*, Chatto and Windus, London 1974, pp. 302–3. 13. Andrzej Walicki, *A History of Russian Thought: From the Enlightenment to Marxism*, Stanford University Press 1979, pp. 95–8. 14. Nikolai Berdyaev, *The Russian Idea*, Macmillan, New York 1946, p. 101. 15. Walicki, *A History of Russian Thought*, p. 92. 16. S. Frederick Starr, 'August von Haxthausen and Russia', *Slavonic and East European Review*, vol. 46, no. 107, July 1968, p. 462. 17. August von Haxthausen, *The Russian Empire, its People, Institutions, and Resources*, Chapman and Hall, London 1856, vol. 2, pp. 229–31; this is a shortened translation of the original. 18. Karl Marx, *Grundrisse: Foundations of the Critique of Political Economy (Rough Draft)*, Penguin, London 1973, p. 750. 19. Berdyaev, *The Russian Idea*, p. 104. 20. Ivan Turgenev, *Smoke*: http://ebooks.adelaide.edu.au/t/turgenev/ivan/smoke/chapter05.html 21. Fyodor Dostoyevsky, *The Devils*, trans. Michael R. Katz, Oxford University Press 2008, p. 35. 22. Yoshio Imai, 'N. G. Chernyshevskii: Pioneer of the Russian Cooperative Movement', in Don Karl Rowney (ed.), *Imperial Power and Development: Papers on Pre-Revolutionary Russian History*, Slavica Publishers, Columbus, OH 1990, pp. 136, 144; Nikolai Chernyshevski, *Critique of Philosophical Prejudices against Communal Ownership* (1859), extract in Teodor Shanin (ed.), *Late Marx and the Russian Road: Marx and 'the peripheries of capitalism'*, Monthly Review Press, New York 1983, p. 182. 23. Shanin (ed.), *Late Marx and the Russian Road*, p. 187. 24. Nikolai Chernyshevski (Nikolaï G. Tchernuishevsky), *A Vital Question; or, What Is To Be Done?*, trans. N. Haskell Dole and S. S. Skidelsky, Crowell, New York 1886, p. 185. 25. Walicki, *The Slavophile Controversy*, p. 403. 26. See text of letter in Shanin (ed.), *Late Marx and the Russian Road*, p. 98; the entire Zasulich–Marx exchange is on pp. 97–126. 27. Marx and Engels, *Correspondence 1846–1895*, p. 354. 28. Shanin (ed.), *Late Marx and the Russian Road*, p. 124. 29. Ibid, p. 131. 30. Milyoukov, *Russia and its Crisis*, p. 343. 31. Walicki, *The Slavophile Controversy*, p. 460. 32. Anatoli Vichnevski, *La faucille et le rouble. La modernisation conservatrice en URSS*, Gallimard, Paris 2000, p. 153. 33. Gerschenkron, *Economic Backwardness in Historical Perspective*, p. 17. 34. Rogger, *Russia in the Age of Modernisation and Revolution*, p. 76. 35. Arcadius Kahan, *Russian Economic History: The Nineteenth Century*, Chicago University Press 1989, p. 13; Rogger, *Russia in the Age of Modernisation and Revolution*, p. 3. 36. Spencer E. Roberts, *Essays in Russian Literature: The Conservative View: Leontiev, Rozanov, Shestov*, Ohio

University Press 1968, p. vii. 37. V. L. Stepanov, 'Finance Ministry Policy in the 1880s and the Unrealized Potential for Economic Modernization in Russia', *Russian Studies in History*, vol. 42, no. 4, Spring 2004, p. 16. 38. Gorlin, 'Problems of Tax Reform in Imperial Russia', p. 246. 39. Alexander Gerschenkron, 'Russia: Agrarian Policies and Industrialization, 1861–1917', in Alexander Gerschenkron, *Continuity in History and Other Essays*, Belknap Press, Cambridge, MA 1968, p. 145. 40. Jacob W. Kipp successfully rescues Reutern from oblivion in 'M. Kh. Reutern on the Russian State and Economy: A Liberal Bureaucrat during the Crimean Era, 1854–60', *Journal of Modern History*, vol. 47, no. 3, September 1975, esp. pp. 438–9. 41. Alfred J. Rieber, *Merchants and Entrepreneurs in Imperial Russia*, University of North Carolina Press 1982, p. 73. 42. Ibid, pp. 52–73. 43. Wynn, *Workers, Strikes, and Pogroms*, p. 21. 44. Modest Mussorgsky, *Boris Godunov*, text in CD Sony Classical Berliner Philharmoniker directed by Claudio Abbado, p. 232, trans. Pamela Davidson. 45. Nicolas Berdyaev, *The Origin of Russian Communism*, Geoffrey Bles, London 1955, p. 7. 46. Gerschenkron, 'Russia: Agrarian Policies and Industrialization, 1861–1917', p. 189. 47. Orlando Figes, *A People's Tragedy: The Russian Revolution 1891–1924*, Pimlico, London 1996, p. 106. 48. Nikolay A. Nekrasov, *Who Can Be Free and Happy in Russia?*: http://www.gutenberg.org/cache/epub/9619/pg9619.html 49. Leroy-Beaulieu, *L'empire des Tsars et les Russes*, pp. 427–8. 50. Figes, *A People's Tragedy*, pp. 107–8. 51. Charles Normand, *La bourgeoisie française au XVIIe siècle*, Alcan, Paris 1908, p. 9: http://ia700306.us.archive.org/BookReader/BookReaderImages.php?zip=/29/items/labourgeoisiefra00normuoft/labourgeoisiefra00normuoft_jp2.zip&file=labourgeoisiefra00normuoft_jp2/labourgeoisiefra00normuoft_0023.jp2&scale=6&rotate=0 52. Rogger, *Russia in the Age of Modernisation and Revolution*, p. 93. 53. Aleksandr I. Fenin, *Coal and Politics in Late Imperial Russia: Memoirs of a Russian Mining Engineer*, ed. Susan McCaffray, Northern Illinois University Press 1990, p. 114. 54. Witte, *The Memoirs of Count Witte*, pp. 209–10; see also Sidney Harcave, *Count Sergei Witte and the Twilight of Imperial Russia*, M. E. Sharpe, New York, NY 2004, p. 89. 55. Witte, *The Memoirs of Count Witte*, p. 52. 56. Ibid, p. 76. 57. Theodore H. Von Laue, 'A Secret Memorandum of Sergei Witte on the Industrialization of Imperial Russia', *Journal of Modern History*, vol. 26, no. 1, March 1954, pp. 101, 116–17. 58. Fyodor Dostoyevsky, 'Geók Tepé: What is Asia to Us', Fyodor Dostoyevsky, in *The Diary of a Writer*, Ianmead, Haslemere 1984, p. 1,044. 59. Beckert, 'Emancipation and Empire', p. 1,430. 60. Nikolaj Danilevskij, *La doctrine Panslaviste d'après N. J. Danilewsky* (including *La Russie et l'Europe*, based on the 4th edition, St Petersburg, 1889), ed. J. J. Skupiewski, Bureaux de la Liberté Roumaine, Bucharest 1890, pp. 46–7, 63, 71–2 (an abridged version of the original). 61. Stefan Plaggenborg, 'Who Paid for the Industrialisation of Tsarist Russia?', *Revolutionary Russia*, vol. 3, no. 2, December 1990, p. 183; see also, by the same author, 'Tax Policy and the Question of Peasant Poverty in Tsarist Russia 1881–1905', *Cahiers du Monde russe*, vol. 36, nos 1–2, January–June 1995, pp. 53–69. 62. Macey, *Government and*

Peasant in Russia, 1861–1906, p. 43. 63. Gregory, 'Economic Growth and Structural Change in Tsarist Russia'; Alexander Gerschenkron, 'The Rate of Industrial Growth in Russia since 1885', *Journal of Economic History*, vol. 7, *Supplement: Economic Growth: A Symposium* (1947), p. 145. 64. S. A. Smith, *Russia in Revolution: An Empire in Crisis, 1890 to 1928*, Oxford University Press 2017, p. 35. 65. Lyashchenko, *History of the National Economy of Russia to the 1917 Revolution*, p. 564. This text was regarded as so significant that its translation into English was sponsored by the American Council of Learned Societies. 66. Nicholas Khristianovich Bunge, *The Years 1881–1894 in Russia: A Memorandum Found in the Papers of N. Kh. Bunge. A Translation and Commentary*, ed. George E. Snow, in *Transactions of the American Philosophical Society*, vol. 71, part 6, Philadelphia, PA 1981, pp. 21, 51ff, 61–2. 67. George E. Snow, 'Introduction', in ibid, pp. 8–9; Plaggenborg, 'Who Paid for the Industrialisation of Tsarist Russia?', pp. 187–90. 68. See data in Plaggenborg, 'Who Paid for the Industrialisation of Tsarist Russia?', p. 203. For Gerschenkron's position, see 'Russia: Agrarian Policies and Industrialization, 1861–1917', pp. 140–254. 69. Stepanov, 'Nikolai Khristianovich Bunge', p. 61. 70. Rogger, *Russia in the Age of Modernisation and Revolution*, p. 79. 71. Harcave, *Count Sergei Witte and the Twilight of Imperial Russia*, p. 49. 72. See Macey, *Government and Peasant in Russia, 1861–1906*, p. 63. For Lenin's abuse, see *Comrade Workers, Forward to the Last, Decisive Fight!* (1918) in his *Collected Works*, Progress Publishers, Moscow, vol. 28, 1965, pp. 53–7. 73. Witte, *The Memoirs of Count Witte*, pp. 386–7. 74. Ruth A. Roosa, *Russian Industrialists in an Era of Revolution*, M. E. Sharpe, Armonk, NY 1997, p. 90. 75. Crisp, *Studies in the Russian Economy before 1914*, p. 23. 76. Spulber, *Russia's Economic Transitions*, p. 57. 77. Raymond W. Goldsmith, 'The Economic Growth of Tsarist Russia 1860–1913', *Economic Development and Cultural Change*, vol. 9, no. 3, *Essays in the Quantitative Study of Economic Growth*, April 1961, p. 441. 78. Gerschenkron, 'The Rate of Industrial Growth in Russia since 1885', p. 152. 79. Macey, *Government and Peasant in Russia, 1861–1906*, pp. 238, 121 and 214. 80. Quoted in Lyashchenko, *History of the National Economy of Russia to the 1917 Revolution*, p. 431. 81. Crisp, *Studies in the Russian Economy before 1914*, p. 21. 82. V. T. Loginov, 'Stolypin as Reformer', *Russian Studies in History*, vol. 42, no. 4, Spring 2004, pp. 22–4. 83. Carol S. Leonard, *Agrarian Reform in Russia: The Road from Serfdom*, Cambridge University Press 2011, p. 56. 84. See Alexander Gerschenkron, 'The Rate of Industrial Growth in Russia since 1885'. 85. Peter Gatrell, 'Industrial Expansion in Tsarist Russia, 1908–14', *Economic History Review*, vol. 35, no. 1, February 1982, pp. 100, 104–5. 86. Goldsmith, 'The Economic Growth of Tsarist Russia, 1860–1913', pp. 442–3. 87. Rogger, *Russia in the Age of Modernisation and Revolution*, pp. 102–3, 106–7, 113. 88. Fedor, *Patterns of Urban Growth in the Russian Empire during the Nineteenth Century*, p. 95. 89. Ibid, p. 175. 90. Ibid, p. 152. 91. Arcadius Kahan, 'Government Policies and the Industrialization of Russia', *Journal of Economic History*, vol. 27, no. 4, December 1967, pp. 461, 477. 92. Gerschenkron, 'The Rate of Industrial Growth in Russia since 1885', p. 156. 93. Gregory, 'Economic Growth and Structural Change in Tsarist Russia', pp. 420, 424. 94. Paul Bew, *Land and the National Question in Ireland, 1858–82*, Gill and Macmillan, Dublin 1978, p. 5. 95. Witte, *The Memoirs of Count Witte*, p. 388. 96. Sergio Bertolissi, *Un paese sull'orlo delle riforme. La Russia zarista dal 1861 al 1904*, Franco Angeli, Milan 1998, p. 37. 97. Rogger, *Russia in the Age of Modernisation and Revolution*, p. 81. 98. Rieber, *Merchants and Entrepreneurs in Imperial Russia*, pp. 137, 417. 99. Berdyaev, *The Origin of Russian Communism*, p. 65. 100. Spulber, *Russia's Economic Transitions*, p. 42. 101. Theodore H. Von Laue, 'Legal Marxism and the "Fate of Capitalism in Russia"', *Review of Politics*, vol. 18, no. 1, January 1956, pp. 28–9. 102. V. I. Lenin, 'The Agrarian Programme of Social-Democracy in the First Russian Revolution, 1905–1907', in *Collected Works*, vol. 13, Progress Publishers, Moscow 1972, p. 239.

9. THE AMERICAN CHALLENGE AND THE LOVE OF CAPITAL

1. Charles W. Calhoun (ed.), *The Gilded Age*, Rowman & Littlefield, Lanham, MD 2007, pp. 2 and 12; railways statistics from US Census Office, *Report on Transportation Business in the United States at the Eleventh Census: 1890*, pp. 3–6: http://www2.census.gov/prod2/decennial/documents/1890a_v14p1-01.pdf 2. Michael Schwartz, *Radical Protest and Social Structure: The Southern Farmers' Alliance and Cotton Tenancy, 1880–1890*, University of Chicago Press 1976, p. 5. 3. Cited in Hans Rogger, '*Amerikanizm* and the Economic Development of Russia', *Comparative Studies in Society and History*, vol. 23, no. 3, July 1981, p. 410. 4. Aleksandr Blok, 'Novaia Amerika', in *Sochineniia v dvukh tomakh* (Moscow 1955), vol. 1, cited in Rogger, '*Amerikanizm* and the Economic Development of Russia', p. 411; the translation is by V. de S. Pinto and is taken from *A Second Book of Russian Verse*, ed. C. M. Bowra (Macmillan, London 1948). 5. John Donne, 'To His Mistress Going to Bed', Elegy XX. 6. John Locke, *Second Treatise of Government*, Chapter 5, Section 49: http://www.gutenberg.org/files/7370/7370-h/7370-h.htm 7. W. T. Stead, *The Americanization of the World, or The Trend of the Twentieth Century*, Horace Markley, New York 1902, pp. 4, 442. 8. Alexis de Tocqueville, *De la démocratie en Amérique*, vol. 3, Pagnerre, Paris 1848, p. 70. 9. Walt Whitman, 'As I Sat Alone by Blue Ontario's Shores' (1867), from *Leaves of Grass*. 10. US Census Bureau, https://www.census.gov/population/censusdata/table-16.pdf; Census Bureau Population Clock: https://www.census.gov/popclock/?intcmp=home_pop, accessed 10 May 2017. 11. Karl Marx, 7 November 1861, *New-York Daily Tribune*: https://www.marxists.org/archive/marx/works/1861/11/07a.htm 12. Beckert, 'Emancipation and Empire', p. 1,409. 13. Eugene Genovese, *The Southern Tradition: The Achievement and Limitations of an American Conservatism*, Harvard University Press 1994,

p. 31. 14. Moore, *Social Origins of Dictatorship and Democracy*, p. 114. 15. Caitlin C. Rosenthal, 'From Memory to Mastery: Accounting for Control in America, 1750–1880', *Enterprise & Society*, vol. 14, no. 4, December 2013, p. 735. 16. Herbert Gutman's critique of this book centres on the alleged beliefs and behaviour of the slaves, not on the claim by Fogel and Engerman that slave plantations were more efficient than northern farms. See Herbert G. Gutman, *Slavery and the Numbers Game: A Critique of 'Time on the Cross'*, University of Illinois Press 1975. 17. Moore, *Social Origins of Dictatorship and Democracy*, p. 116. 18. Ibid, p. 118. 19. Ibid, p. 121. 20. Elizabeth Fox-Genovese and Eugene D. Genovese, *Slavery in White and Black: Class and Race in the Southern Slaveholders' New World Order*, Cambridge University Press 2008, p. 31. 21. Ibid, p. 47. 22. Glenn Porter, 'Industrialization and the Rise of Big Business', in Calhoun (ed.), *The Gilded Age*, p. 13. 23. Gutman, *Work, Culture, and Society in Industrializing America*, p. 5. 24. Michael Lind, *The Next American Nation: The New Nationalism and the Fourth American Revolution*, The Free Press, London 1995, p. 41. 25. See Irving Kristol, 'Urban Civilization and its Discontents', *Commentary*, July 1970; the text was based on Kristol's inaugural lecture on assuming the Professorship of Urban Values at New York University in 1969. 26. Maury Klein, *The Genesis of Industrial America, 1870–1920*, Cambridge University Press 2007, p. 12. 27. Eric Foner, *Nothing but Freedom: Emancipation and its Legacy*, Louisiana State University Press 1983, p. 40. 28. Ibid, pp. 46, 72. 29. Eric Foner, *Reconstruction: America's Unfinished Revolution, 1863–1877*, Harper and Row, New York 1988, pp. 213–14. 30. Foner, 'Why is there no Socialism in the United States?', *History Workshop Journal*, no. 17, 1984, p. 62. 31. W. E. B. Du Bois, *Black Reconstruction in America*, Albert Saifer, Philadelphia, PA 1935, p. 30. 32. Beckert, 'Emancipation and Empire', p. 1,409; see also Beckert, *Empire of Cotton*. 33. Moore, *Social Origins of Dictatorship and Democracy*, see Chapter 3, pp. 111–55. 34. Roy, *Socializing Capital*, p. 129. Note that some argue that the Civil War did not alter radically the path of industrialization: Claudia D. Goldin and Frank D. Lewis, 'The Economic Cost of the American Civil War: Estimates and Implications', *Journal of Economic History*, vol. 35, no. 2, June 1975, p. 321. 35. Foner, *Reconstruction*, pp. 461–3. 36. Barry R. Chiswick and Timothy J. Hatton, 'International Migration and the Integration of Labor Markets', in Bordo, Taylor and Williamson (eds), *Globalization in Historical Perspective*, pp. 67–70. 37. Jeff Madrick, *The Case for Big Government*, Princeton University Press 2009, p. 43. 38. W. Elliot Brownlee, *Federal Taxation in America: A Short History*, Cambridge University Press 1996, p. 23; for 2015, OECD data. 39. Brownlee, *Federal Taxation in America*, pp. 26–7. 40. Richard F. Bensel, *The Political Economy of American Industrialization, 1877–1900*, Cambridge University Press 2000, p. 13. 41. Robin Blackburn, 'State of the Union: Marx and America's Unfinished Revolution', *New Left Review*, no. 61, January–February 2010, p. 166; Anders Stephanson, *Manifest Destiny: American Expansionism and the Empire of Right*, Hill and Wang, New York 1995, p. 69. 42. Bureau of Labour

Statistics: https://www.bls.gov/oes/current/oes339032.htm and https://www.bls.gov/oes/current/oes333051.htm. See also Claire Provost, 'The Industry of Inequality: Why the World is Obsessed with Private Security', *The Guardian*, 12 May 2017: https://www.theguardian.com/inequality/2017/may/12/industry-of-inequality-why-world-is-obsessed-with-private-security 43. Glenn Porter, 'Industrialization and the Rise of Big Business', p. 15. 44. J. W. von Goethe, *Werke*, vol. 1, Christian Wegner Verlag, Hamburg 1952, p. 333. 45. Hegel, *Lectures on the Philosophy of World History*, vol. 1, p. 193. 46. Stendhal, *La Chartreuse de Parme*, Nelson, Paris 1839, p. 141. 47. Alexis de Tocqueville, *De la démocratie en Amérique*, vol. 1, Pagnerre, Paris 1848, p. 80. 48. Benjamin Franklin, 'Advice to a Young Tradesman, Written by an Old One', 1748: http://franklinpapers.org/franklin//framedvolumes.jsp;jsessionid=608ADED3CD5C773C127B274349F89A31 49. Charles Péguy, *L'Argent (suite)*, in Charles Péguy, *Oeuvres en prose 1909–1914*, Bibliothèque de la Pléiade Gallimard, Paris 1961, p. 1,267. 50. Thomas Jefferson, *Writings*, Memorial Edition, vol. 15, p. 23: http://etext.virginia.edu/jefferson/quotations/jeff1325.htm 51. This is the orthodox position; for a dissenting view see Caroline Fohlin, 'Universal Banking in Pre-World War I Germany: Model or Myth?', *Explorations in Economic History*, vol. 36, no. 4, 1999, pp. 305–43. 52. Noel Annan, 'The Possessed', *New York Review of Books*, 5 February 1976, cited in Martin J. Wiener, *English Culture and the Decline of the Industrial Spirit, 1850–1980*, Cambridge University Press 1981, p. 131. 53. John Maynard Keynes, 'Economic Possibilities for Our Grandchildren', in *Essays in Persuasion* in *The Collected Writings of John Maynard Keynes*, vol. IX, Macmillan, London 1972, p. 329. 54. Albert O. Hirschman, *The Passions and the Interests: Political Arguments for Capitalism before its Triumph*, Princeton University Press 1977, p. 9. 55. Cited in Robert Sayre and Michael Löwy, 'Figures du romantisme anti-capitaliste: une tentative de typologie', *L'homme et la société*, nos 73–4, 1984, p. 165: http://www.persee.fr/web/revues/home/prescript/article/homso_0018-4306_1984_num_73_1_2169 56. Quoted in Turner, *The Frontier in American History*, p. 211. The sentiments expressed in the quote are certainly those of Émile Boutmy, but the quote itself cannot be traced in Boutmy's main work on the subject: *Éléments d'une psychologie politique du peuple américain*, A. Colin, Paris 1902, see esp. pp. 48, 100, and 137. 57. Alexis de Tocqueville, *De la démocratie en Amérique*, vol. 4, Pagnerre, Paris 1848, p. 313. 58. Ibid, vol. 3, pp. 318–19 (an error in this edition makes it p. 218 instead of 318). 59. Mayer, 'The Lower Middle Class as Historical Problem', p. 422. 60. Lawrence B. Glickman, *A Living Wage: American Workers and the Making of Consumer Society*, Cornell University Press 1997, p. 1. 61. Ibid, pp. 11, 18. 62. Henry George, public lecture, 1 April 1885: http://www.historyisaweapon.com/defcon1/georgecripov.html 63. Henry George, *Progress and Poverty*, J. M. Dent and Sons, London 1879, p. 251. 64. Foner, *Reconstruction*, pp. 18–19. 65. Beckert, 'Emancipation and Empire', p. 1,427. 66. Foner, *Reconstruction*, p. 235. 67. Steven Hahn, 'Class and State in Postemancipation Societies: Southern Planters in Comparative

Perspective', *American Historical Review*, vol. 95, no. 1, February 1990, pp. 82, 92. 68. Sven Beckert, *The Monied Metropolis: New York City and the Consolidation of the American Bourgeoisie , 1850–1896*, Cambridge University Press 2001, pp. 299–300. 69. Gutman, *Work, Culture, and Society in Industrializing America*, p. 13. 70. Ibid, p. 323. 71. Bensel, *The Political Economy of American Industrialization*, p. 19. 72. Walt Whitman, 'A Passage to India' (1870), from *Leaves of Grass*. 73. Walt Whitman, *Democratic Vistas* (1871): http://xroads.virginia.edu/~hyper/whitman/vistas/vistas.html 74. Charles-Augustin Sainte-Beuve, 'De la littérature industrielle', *Revue des deux mondes*, September 1839: http://fr.wikisource.org/wiki/La_ Litt%C3%A9rature_industrielle 75. Herzen, *My Past and Thoughts*, p. 661. 76. Charles Letourneau, *L'évolution du commerce dans les diverses races humaines*, Vigot Frères, Paris 1897, pp. 541, 547, 550. 77. Simmel, 'The Metropolis and Mental Life', p. 177. 78. Sombart, *The Quintessence of Capitalism*, pp. 167, 171, 173–4, 181. 79. Richard L. McCormick, 'The Discovery that Business Corrupts Politics: A Reappraisal of the Origins of Progressivism', *American Historical Review*, vol. 86, no. 2, April 1981, p. 256. 80. Foner, *Reconstruction*, pp. 385–7. 81. Cited in Beckert, *The Monied Metropolis*, p. 308. 82. Foner, *Reconstruction*, pp. 465–7. 83. Bensel, *The Political Economy of American Industrialization*, p. 295. 84. Sombart, *The Quintessence of Capitalism*, p. 152. 85. Louis Galambos, *The Public Image of Big Business in America, 1880–1940*, Johns Hopkins University Press 1975, p. 120. 86. Ibid, p. 126. 87. Hofstadter, *Social Darwinism in American Thought*, pp. 50, 60. 88. William Graham Sumner, *The Challenge of Facts and Other Essays*, ed. Albert Galloway Keller, Yale University Press 1914, p. 90. 89. Ibid, p. 89. 90. Nancy Cohen, *The Reconstruction of American Liberalism, 1865–1914*, University of North Carolina Press 2002, pp. 149–50. 91. Jean-Louis Beaucarnot, *Les Schneider. Une dynastie*, Hachette, Paris 1986, pp. 32–5. 92. Bergeron (ed.), *Les capitalistes en France*, pp. 9–11. 93. Porter, 'Industrialization and the Rise of Big Business', pp. 18–19. 94. Ibid, p. 25. 95. Samuel P. Hays, *The Response to Industrialism, 1885–1914*, University of Chicago Press 1995 (1st ed. 1957), p. 94. 96. Cited in Gutman, *Work, Culture, and Society in Industrializing America*, p. 52. 97. Hays, *The Response to Industrialism*, p. 102. 98. Ibid, p. 79. 99. Ibid, pp. 72–3. 100. Gabriel Kolko, *The Triumph of Conservatism: A Reinterpretation of American History, 1900–1916*, Free Press of Glenco, New York 1963, pp. 12–14. 101. Jean Strouse, *Morgan: American Financier*, Random House, New York 2000, pp. xiii, 409; Steven J. Diner, *A Very Different Age: Americans of the Progressive Era*, Hill and Wang, New York 1998, p. 30. 102. John D. Rockefeller, *Random Reminiscences of Men and Events*, Doubleday, Page & Company, New York 1909: http://www.gutenberg.org/files/17090/17090-h/17090-h.htm, p. 144. 103. Ibid, p. 64. 104. George Bittlingmayer, 'Did Antitrust Policy Cause the Great Merger Wave?', *Journal of Law and Economics*, vol. 28, no. 1, April 1985, pp. 77–118. 105. Alfred D. Chandler, Jr., *The Visible Hand: The Managerial Revolution in American Business*, Harvard University Press 1977, pp. 134–7.

106. Bensel, *The Political Economy of American Industrialization*, p. 312. 107. Martin J. Sklar, *The Corporate Reconstruction of American Capitalism, 1890–1916: The Market, the Law, and Politics*, Cambridge University Press 1988, pp. 109–10. 108. William E. Leuchtenburg, *The American President: From Teddy Roosevelt to Bill Clinton*, Oxford University Press 2015, p. 32. 109. Lewis L. Gould, *Reform and Regulation: American Politics, 1900–1916*, John Wiley and Sons, New York 1978, pp. 31–2, 65–9. 110. Ron Chernow, *Titan: The Life of John D. Rockefeller, Sr.*, Little, Brown and Co., New York 1998, pp. 553–7. 111. Philip Taft and Philip Ross, 'American Labor Violence: Its Causes, Character, and Outcome', in Hugh Davis Graham and Ted Roberts Gurr (eds), *The History of Violence in America*, Praeger, New York 1969, p. 299. 112. Cohen, *The Reconstruction of American Liberalism*, pp. 198–200. 113. Taft and Ross, 'American Labor Violence', p. 281. 114. Stuart Brandes, *American Welfare Capitalism, 1880–1940*, University of Chicago Press 1976, pp. 1–3. 115. Bensel, *The Political Economy of American Industrialization*, p. 143. 116. Gould, *Reform and Regulation*, pp. 20–21. 117. Louis W. Koenig, *Bryan: A Political Biography of William Jennings Bryan*, Putnam's Sons, New York 1971, p. 335. 118. William Jennings Bryan, *The First Battle: A Story of the Campaign of 1896*, Kennikat Press, New York 1971, vol. 1, p. 203, and ibid, vol. 2, p. 319. 119. Reported in *The Times*, 10 March 1914, and cited in Gould, *Reform and Regulation*, p. 10. 120. Donald W. Rogers, *Making Capitalism Safe: Work Safety and Health Regulation in America, 1880–1940*, University of Illinois Press 2009, p. 172. 121. Theodore Roosevelt, 'Fourth Annual Message' to Congress, 6 December 1904: http://www.presidency.ucsb.edu/ws/?pid=29545 122. George Gunton, 'The Economic and Social Aspect of Trusts', *Political Science Quarterly*, vol. 3, no. 3, September 1888, esp. pp. 392–6. 123. Roy, *Socializing Capital*, pp. 4–5. 124. See US Bureau of Labor Statistics; for inflation calculation: http://data.bls.gov/cgi-bin/cpicalc.pl; for average hourly earnings: http://www.bls.gov/iag/tgs/iagauto.htm#iag31cesnsahourlyearnings.f.P 125. Stephen Meyer III, *The Five Dollar Day: Labor Management and Social Control in the Ford Motor Company, 1908–1921*, State University of New York Press 1981, pp. 1, 6. 126. Ibid, pp. 149–52. 127. Ibid, p. 156. 128. Ibid, pp. 167–8. 129. Klein, *The Genesis of Industrial America*, pp. 105, 116–22. 130. W. Bernard Carlson, 'Technology and America as a Consumer Society, 1870–1900', in Charles W. Calhoun (ed.), *The Gilded Age: Perspectives on the Origins of Modern America*, Rowan & Littlefield, Lanham, MD 2007, p. 31. 131. Carlson, 'Technology and America as a Consumer Society, 1870–1900', pp.31–2. 132. Klein, *The Genesis of Industrial America*, p. 48. 133. Ibid, pp. 41, 53. 134. Foner, *Reconstruction*, p. 463. 135. Klein, *The Genesis of Industrial America*, p. 134. 136. Thomas K. McCraw, 'American Capitalism', in Thomas K. McCraw (ed.), *American Capitalism: How Entrepreneurs, Companies, and Countries Triumphed in Three Industrial Revolutions*, Harvard University Press 1997, pp. 320–21. 137. Mira Wilkins, *The Emergence of Multinational Enterprise: American Business Abroad from the Colonial Era to*

1914, Harvard University Press 1970, pp. 9, 29, 37–44. 138. Séverine Antigone Marin, '"L'américanisation du monde"? Étude des peurs allemandes face au "danger américain" (1897–1907)', in Dominique Barjot, Isabelle Lescent-Giles, and Marc de Ferrière Le Vayer (eds), *L'américanisation en Europe au XXe siècle*, pp. 71–2. 139. Paul Leroy-Beaulieu, 'De la nécessité de préparer une fédération Européenne', *L'Économiste français*, 3 September 1898. 140. Burton I. Kaufman, 'The Organizational Dimension of United States Economic Foreign Policy, 1900–1920', *Business History Review*, vol. 46, no. 1, Spring 1972, p. 19, quoting the report of the Industrial Commission appointed by Congress in 1902.

10. BUILDING THE NATION

1. My emphasis; see John Markoff, 'Where and When Was Democracy Invented?', *Comparative Studies in Society and History*, vol. 41, no 4, October 1999, p. 666. 2. Ernest Renan, 'Qu'est-ce qu'une nation?', available in French at: http://www.rutebeuf.com/textes/renan01.html and in English at: http://ig.cs.tu-berlin.de/oldstatic/w2001/eu1/dokumente/Basistexte/Renan1882EN-Nation.pdf 3. Thiesse, *La création des identités nationales*, p. 11. 4. Friedrich Nietzsche, *Thus Spoke Zarathustra*, trans. R. J. Hollingdale, Penguin, London 2003, p. 75. 5. Carlo Cattaneo, *Scritti filosofici*, ed. Norberto Bobbio, Felice Le Monnier, Florence 1960, vol. 1, pp. 233–4. 6. Massimo D'Azeglio, *I miei ricordi*, G. Barbèra, Florence 1891 (first published 1867), p. 4. 7. Ibid, pp. 4–5. 8. Pasquale Villari, 'Di chi è la colpa? O sia la pace o la guerra', *Il Politecnico*, September 1866, in *Saggi di storia, di critica e di politica*, Tipografia Cavour, Florence 1868, p. 421. 9. Villari, *Le Lettere meridionali ed altro scritti sulla questione sociale in Italia*, p. 73. 10. Giovanni Busino, 'Vilfredo Pareto sociologo della borghesia e dello sviluppo capitalistico?', *Rivista Storica Italiana*, vol. 83, no. 2, June 1971, pp. 398–400. 11. Marie-Claire Bergère, *Sun Yat-sen*, Fayard, Paris 1994, p. 408. 12. David J. Lorenzo, *Conceptions of Chinese Democracy*, Johns Hopkins University Press 2013, p. 45. 13. Sun Yat-sen, *The Three Principles of the People*, China Cultural Service, Taiwan 1981, p. 61. 14. Ibid, p. 76. 15. Bergère, *Sun Yat-sen*, pp. 409–10. 16. Cited in Michael Berkowitz, *Zionist Culture and West European Jewry before the First World War*, Cambridge University Press 1993, p. 6. 17. Theodor Herzl, *The Diaries of Theodor Herzl*, Gollancz, London 1958, p. 10. 18. Herzl, *The Jewish State*, p. 68. 19. Carl E. Schorske, *Fin-de-Siècle Vienna: Politics and Culture*, Cambridge University Press 1981, p. 160. 20. Cited in Elon, *Herzl*, p. 69. 21. See statistical appendix in Robert A. Kann, *A History of the Habsburg Empire 1526–1918*, University of California Press 1974, pp. 606–8. 22. Lucien Tesnière, 'Statistique des langues de l'Europe', in Antoine Meillet, *Les langues dans l'Europe nouvelle*, Payot, Paris 1928, p. 307. 23. Helmut Walser Smith, *German Nationalism and Religious Conflict: Culture, Ideology, Politics, 1870–1914*, Princeton University Press 1995, pp. 174–5,

169. **24.** Ibid, p. 169. **25.** Ibid, p. 239. **26.** Ibid, p. 235. **27.** Gallup Poll: Religion: http://www.gallup.com/poll/1690/religion.aspx. David Voas and Mark Chaves maintain that there is a trend towards secularization in their 'Is the United States a Counterexample to the Secularization Thesis?', *American Journal of Sociology*, vol. 121, no. 5, March 2016. **28.** Peter H. Lindert, *Growing Public: Social Spending and Economic Growth since the Eighteenth Century*, vol. 1, Cambridge University Press 2004, pp. 90–92, 95; this does not include those privately educated, hence the low figure for the UK. **29.** Jacques and Mona Ozouf, 'Le thème du patriotisme dans les manuels primaires', *Le Mouvement Social*, no. 49, October–December 1964, pp. 12–13. **30.** Suzanne Citron, *Le mythe national: l'histoire de France revisitée*, Éditions de l'Atelier, Ivry-sur-Seine 2008, p. 161. **31.** Anita Prazmowska, *Ignacy Paderewski*, Haus Publishing, London 2009, p. 25. **32.** On the non-Romantic views of Dmowski see Andrzej Walicki, 'The Troubling Legacy of Roman Dmowski', *East European Politics and Societies*, vol. 14, no. 1, Winter 2000, esp. pp. 14–21. **33.** Prazmowska, *Ignacy Paderewski*, p. 29. **34.** Zeev Sternhell, *Maurice Barrès et le nationalisme français*, Éditions Complexe, Brussels 1985 (first published 1972), pp. 154–5, 173. **35.** Laurent Joly, 'Les débuts de l'action française (1899–1914) ou l'élaboration d'un nationalisme antisémite', *Revue historique*, no. 639, July 2006, p. 697. **36.** Ibid, p. 714. **37.** Ibid, p. 698. **38.** Anatoli Vichnevski, *La faucille et le rouble. La modernisation conservatrice en URSS*, Gallimard, Paris 2000, p. 322; Theodore R. Weeks, 'National Minorities in the Russian Empire, 1897–1917', in Anna Geifman (ed.), *Russia under the Last Tsar: Opposition and Subversion, 1894–1917*, Blackwell, Oxford 1999, p. 118. **39.** Timothy Snyder, *The Reconstruction of Nations: Poland, Ukraine, Lithuania, Belarus, 1569–1999*, Yale University Press 2003, pp. 119–20; Daniel Beauvois, *The Noble, the Serf and the Revizor: The Polish Nobility between Tsarist Imperialism and the Ukrainian Masses (1831–1863)*, Harwood, London 1991, p. 87. **40.** Spulber, *Russia's Economic Transitions*, pp. 8–9. **41.** Arno Mayer, *The Persistence of the Old Regime*, Croom Helm, London 1981, pp. 79–80, 84. **42.** Ibid, esp. Chapter 2. **43.** Robert M. Berdahl, 'Conservative Politics and Aristocratic Landholders in Bismarckian Germany', *Journal of Modern History*, vol. 44, no. 1, March 1972, pp. 14–16. **44.** Crook, *The Rise of the Nouveaux Riches*, pp. 37ff. **45.** M. J. Daunton, '"Gentlemanly" Capitalism and British Industry 1820–1914', *Past & Present*, no. 122, February 1989, pp. 121–3. **46.** Ibid, pp. 122, 125. **47.** Samuel Clark, 'Nobility, Bourgeoisie and the Industrial Revolution in Belgium' in *Past & Present*, no. 105, November 1984, p. 105. **48.** Deirdre N. McCloskey, *The Bourgeois Virtues: Ethics for an Age of Commerce*, University of Chicago Press 2006, pp. 470–71. **49.** This is where I agree with McCloskey, ibid, see esp. Chapter 38. **50.** Piketty, *Capital in the Twenty-First Century*, p. 292. Piketty barely deals with the nineteenth century, partly because the data are so unreliable. **51.** David Hume, 'Of Commerce' (1752), in David Hume, *Selected Essays*, Oxford University Press 2008, p. 164. **52.** Benjamin Disraeli, *Sybil, or The Two Nations*, Penguin, London 1980, p. 96, capitals in the

original. 53. Masterman, *The Condition of England*, p. 85; public penury/private ostentation can be found on p. 30. Kenneth Galbraith's own characterization is in *The Affluent Society*, Houghton Mifflin Harcourt, Boston 1998, p. 191. 54. Benjamin Disraeli (Lord Beaconsfield), *Selected Speeches*, ed. T. E. Kebbel, Longmans, Green and Co., London 1882, vol. 2, pp. 524–5, 531–2. 55. Paul Smith, *Disraelian Conservatism and Social Reform*, Routledge and Kegan Paul, London 1967, p. 44. 56. Ibid, p. 7. 57. Ibid, pp. 33–4. 58. William Gladstone, 'The Budget – Financial Statement', *The Times*, report of 17 April 1863. Also, somewhat toned down in Hansard: The Budget – Financial Statement, Ways and Means, *HC Deb*, 16 April 1863, pp. 244–5: http://hansard.millbanksystems.com/commons/1863/apr/16/the-budget-financial-statement-ways-and#S3V0170P0_18630416_HOC_22. 59. Marx, *Capital*, vol. 1, p. 651. 60. Alessandro Garelli, *I Salarj e la classe operaja in Italia*, Libreria Angelo Penato, Turin 1874, pp. 178 and 1. 61. Ibid, p. 13. 62. J. A. Hobson, 'Free Trade and Foreign Policy', *Contemporary Review*, vol. 74, August 1898, pp. 177–8. 63. Speech reprinted in Winston Churchill, *Liberalism and the Social Problem*, Hodder and Stoughton, London 1909, pp. 363–4: http://www.gutenberg.org/files/18419/18419-h/18419-h.htm; also cited in Geoffrey Finlayson, *Citizen, State and Social Welfare in Britain, 1830–1990*, Clarendon Press, Oxford 1994. 64. Booth, *In Darkest England*: http://www.jesus.org.uk/vault/library/booth_darkest_england.pdf 65. Andrew Mearns, *The Bitter Cry of Outcast London: An Inquiry into the Condition of the Abject Poor*, James Clarke and Co., London 1883, pp. 18–19. 66. Hitchins, *Rumania*, p. 163. 67. McCormack, 'Civilising the Urban Other', p. 30; see also Tsuzuki, *The Pursuit of Power in Modern Japan, 1825–1995*, p. 149. 68. McCormack, 'Civilising the Urban Other', pp. 30–31. 69. Leroy-Beaulieu, *Essai sur la repartition des richesses et sur la tendance à une moindre inégalité des conditions*, p. iii. 70. See discussion in Delalande, *Les batailles de l'impôt*, pp. 229–30. 71. Thomas Piketty, Gilles Postel-Vinay, and Jean-Laurent Rosenthal, 'Wealth Concentration in a Developing Economy: Paris and France, 1807–1994', *American Economic Review*, vol. 96, no. 1, March 2006, p. 239. 72. Ibid, p. 243. 73. Lincoln's speech can be accessed at: http://www.abrahamlincolnonline.org/lincoln/speeches/fair.htm 74. Andrew Carnegie, 'Wealth', *North American Review*, no. 148, June 1889, p. 654. 75. Ibid, p. 660.

11. A YEARNING FOR DEMOCRACY SWEEPS THE WORLD

1. Donald Quataert, 'The Economic Climate of the "Young Turk Revolution" in 1908', *Journal of Modern History*, vol. 51, no. 3, p. 1,147. 2. Fikret Adanir, 'Turkey's Entry into the Concert of Europe', *European Review*, vol. 13, no. 3, 2005, p. 407. 3. *Dustūr. Aperçu sur les constitutions des états arabes et islamiques*, Brill, Leiden 1966, p. 12 – this is the reprint of the entry *Dustūr* in the *Encyclopédie de l'Islam*. 4. Nader Sohrabi, *Revolution and Constitutionalism*

in the Ottoman Empire and Iran, Cambridge University Press 2011, pp. 41–2. 5. Salzmann, 'Citizens in Search of a State', p. 51; Sohrabi, *Revolution and Constitutionalism in the Ottoman Empire and Iran*, pp. 49–50. 6. Quataert, 'The Economic Climate of the "Young Turk Revolution"', pp. 1,148–9. 7. Deniz Kandiyoti, 'End of Empire: Islam, Nationalism and Women in Turkey', in Deniz Kandiyoti (ed.), *Women, Islam and the State*, Temple University Press 1991, p. 29. 8. *Dustūr*, p. 15. 9. Erik-Jan Zürcher, 'Ottoman Sources of Kemalist Thought', in Elisabeth Özdalga (ed.), *Late Ottoman Society: The Intellectual Legacy*, Routledge, New York 2005, p. 18. 10. Andrew Roberts, *Salisbury: Victorian Titan*, Weidenfeld and Nicolson, London 1999, p. 691. 11. Salzmann, 'Citizens in Search of a State', p. 55. 12. Sohrabi, *Revolution and Constitutionalism in the Ottoman Empire and Iran*, p. 319. 13. Ibid, p. 334; see also Nikki R. Keddie, *Roots of Revolution: An Interpretive History of Modern Iran*, Yale University Press 1981, p. 72. 14. Said Amir Arjomand, *The Turban for the Crown: The Islamic Revolution in Iran*, Oxford University Press 1988, pp. 37–8. 15. Keddie, *Roots of Revolution*, p. 77. 16. Sohrabi, *Revolution and Constitutionalism in the Ottoman Empire and Iran*, p. 336. 17. Arjomand, *The Turban for the Crown*, pp. 34–6. 18. Keddie, *Roots of Revolution*, p. 73. 19. Ibid, p. 64. 20. Mansour Bonakdarian, *Britain and the Iranian Constitutional Revolution of 1906–1911: Foreign Policy, Imperialism, and Dissent*, Syracuse University Press 2006, p. 167. 21. This was W. Morgan Shuster's verdict; see *The Strangling of Persia*, p. 21. 22. Robert A. McDaniel, *The Shuster Mission and the Persian Constitutional Revolution*, Bibliotheca Islamica, Minneapolis 1974, pp. 75–88. 23. Platt, *Finance, Trade, and Politics in British Foreign Policy, 1815–1914*, pp. 234–5. 24. Christopher N. B. Ross, 'Lord Curzon and E. G. Browne Confront the "Persian Question"', *Historical Journal*, vol. 52, no. 2, 2009, p. 390. 25. Ibid, p. 399. 26. Edward G. Browne, *The Persian Revolution of 1905–1909*, Cambridge University Press 1910, p. xx. 27. McDaniel, *The Shuster Mission*, p. 114. 28. Ibid, p. 125; Mariam Habibi, *L'interface France-Iran 1907–1938. Une diplomatie voilée*, L'Harmattan, Paris 2004, p. 55. 29. Shuster, *The Strangling of Persia*, p. 166. 30. Ibid, pp. 175–6. 31. Ibid, p. 192. 32. This is the thesis developed by Jean Batou in 'L'Égypte de Muhammad-'Ali: pouvoir politique et développement économique', *Annales*, vol. 46, no. 2, 1991, pp. 401–28; but see also Beckert, *Empire of Cotton*, p. 166. 33. P. J. Vatikiotis, *The Modern History of Egypt*, Weidenfeld and Nicolson, London 1969, pp. 58–60. 34. Ibid, pp. 62–5. 35. Beckert, *Empire of Cotton*, p. 169. 36. Vatikiotis, *The Modern History of Egypt*, pp. 87, 75. 37. Wael Abu-'Uksa, *Freedom in the Arab World: Concepts and Ideologies in Arabic Thought in the Nineteenth Century*, Cambridge University Press 2016, pp. 50–54. 38. Roger Owen, *Lord Cromer: Victorian Imperialist, Edwardian Proconsul*, Oxford University Press 2004, p. 236. 39. Letter of 14 December 1887, cited in ibid, p. 246. 40. Ibid, pp. 265–7. 41. Ibid, p. 273. 42. Ibid, p. 311. 43. William M. Welch, Jr., *No Country for a Gentleman: British Rule in Egypt, 1883–1907*, Greenwood Press, Westport, CT

1988, p. 8. 44. Lewis, *Authoritarian Regimes in Latin America*, pp. 17–18. 45. Alan Knight, *The Mexican Revolution*, vol. 2: *Counter-Revolution and Reconstruction*, Cambridge University Press 1986, p. 494. 46. Hale, *The Transformation of Liberalism in Late Nineteenth-Century Mexico*, p. 4. 47. Henry Lane Wilson, 'Errors with Reference to Mexico and Events that have Occurred There', *Annals of the American Academy of Political and Social Science*, vol. 54, July 1914, p. 148. 48. François-Xavier Guerra, *Le Mexique. De l'Ancien Régime à la Révolution*, vol. 2, L'Harmattan, Paris 1985, p. 305. 49. Ibid, p. 310. 50. Helga Baitenmann, 'Popular Participation in State Formation: Land Reform in Revolutionary Mexico', *Journal of Latin American Studies*, vol. 43, no. 1, February 2011, pp. 4, 11. 51. Knight, *The Mexican Revolution*, p. 496. 52. Guy Hermet, *Les populismes dans le monde. Une histoire sociologique (XIXe–XXe siècle)*, Fayard, Paris 2001, pp. 209–10. 53. Michael M. Hall and Hobart A. Spalding, Jr., 'The Urban Working Class and Early Latin American Labour Movements, 1880–1930', in Bethell (ed.), *The Cambridge History of Latin America*, vol. IV, pp. 326–7. 54. Roberts, *Salisbury*, p. 692. 55. Evelyne López-Campillo, *La crise de 1898*, Éditions Messene, Paris 1999, p. 17. 56. Ibid, p. 50. 57. Maurice Zimmermann, 'La ruine de l'empire colonial espagnol. Ses conséquences', *Annales de Géographie*, vol. 8, no. 37, 1899, pp. 93–4. 58. See Pedro Fraile and Álvaro Escribano, 'The Spanish 1898 Disaster: The Drift towards National-Protectionism', October 1997: http://e-archivo.uc3m.es/bitstream/10016/4126/1/wh980301.pdf 59. López-Campillo, *La crise de 1898*, pp. 56, 60. 60. Ibid, p. 41. 61. Cited in Richard Pipes, *Russian Conservatism and its Critics: A Study in Political Culture*, Yale University Press 2005, p. 116. 62. Loren David Calder, *The Political Thought of Yu. F. Samarin, 1840–1864*, Garland, New York 1987, p. 242. 63. Nathaniel Knight, 'Was the Intelligentsia Part of the Nation? Visions of Society in Post-Emancipation Russia', *Kritika: Explorations in Russian and Eurasian History*, vol.7, no. 4, Fall 2006, p. 735. 64. Louise McReynolds, *The News under Russia's Old Regime*, Princeton University Press 1991, p. 5. 65. Ibid, p. 204. 66. For the German antecedent of the word see Richard Pipes, '"Intelligentsia" from the German "Intelligenz"? A Note', *Slavic Review*, vol. 30, no. 3, September 1971, pp. 615–18. 67. Cited in Pipes, *Russian Conservatism and its Critics*, p. 140. 68. Konstantin P. Pobedonostsev, *Reflections of a Russian Statesman*, trans. Robert Crozier Long, Grant Richards, London 1898, p. 27. 69. Berdyaev, *The Origin of Russian Communism*, p. 156. 70. Cited in Walicki, *A History of Russian Thought*, p. 297. 71. Lyashchenko, *History of the National Economy of Russia to the 1917 Revolution*, p. 548. 72. Ibid, p. 549. 73. Sally A. Boniece, 'The Spiridonova Case, 1906: Terror, Myth, and Martyrdom', in Anthony Anemone (ed.), *Just Assassins: The Culture of Terrorism in Russia*, Northwestern University Press 2010, p. 128. 74. Ibid, p. 151. 75. Witte, *Memoirs*, p. 190. 76. Fyodor Dostoyevsky, *The Diary of a Writer*, p. 960, emphasis in the text; see also Knight, 'Was the Intelligentsia Part of the Nation?', p. 734. 77. Abraham Ascher, *The Revolution of 1905: Russia in Disarray*, Stanford University Press 1988, p. 54.

78. Witte, *Memoirs*, p. 367. 79. Ibid, pp. 389–90. 80. Ascher, *The Revolution of 1905*, pp. 71–2. 81. Milyukov, *Russia and its Crisis*, p. 296. 82. Ibid, pp. 327–8. 83. Ascher, *The Revolution of 1905*, pp. 87–9. 84. Hugh Seton-Watson, *The Russian Empire, 1801–1917*, Clarendon Press, Oxford 1967, p. 608. 85. Tim McDaniel, *Autocracy, Capitalism, and Revolution in Russia*, University of California Press 1988, pp. 58–9. 86. Rieber, *Merchants and Entrepreneurs in Imperial Russia*, pp. 346–7. 87. Ibid, p. 278. 88. V. V. Shelokhaev, 'The Liberal Reform Model in Early Twentieth-Century Russia', *Russian Studies in History*, vol. 42, no. 4, Spring 2004, pp. 29–33. 89. See text in Ascher, *The Revolution of 1905*, p. 229. 90. Witte, *Memoirs*, p. 312. 91. Figes, *A People's Tragedy*, p. 201. 92. Witte, *Memoirs*, p. 181. 93. David J. A. Macey, *Government and Peasant in Russia, 1861–1906: The Prehistory of the Stolypin Reforms*, Northern Illinois University Press 1987, p. 37. 94. Ascher, *The Revolution of 1905*, p. 43. 95. Ibid, p. 93. 96. Figes, *A People's Tragedy*, p. 216. 97. Ascher, *The Revolution of 1905*, p. 301. 98. Ibid, p. 318. 99. Ibid, p. 366. 100. Wayne Dowler, *Russia in 1913*, Northern Illinois University Press 2010, pp. 140, 188, *passim*.

12. KEEPING THE 'OUTSIDERS' OUT

1. Milton Friedman, *Why Government Is the Problem*, Hoover Press, Stanford, CA 2013; originally the Wriston Lecture presented in New York City, 19 November 1991, under the auspices of the Manhattan Institute, p. 17. 2. Alexei Miller, *The Romanov Empire and Nationalism: Essays in the Methodology of Historical Research*, Central European University Press, Budapest and New York 2008, p. 115. 3. Nicholas Khristianovich Bunge, *The Years 1881–1894 in Russia: A Memorandum Found in the Papers of N. Kh. Bunge. A Translation and Commentary*, ed. George E. Snow, in *Transactions of the American Philosophical Society*, vol. 71, part 6, Philadelphia, PA 1981, pp. 26–33. 4. Joshua D. Zimmerman, *Poles, Jews, and the Politics of Nationality*, University of Wisconsin Press 2004, p. 16; the figures are based on the 1897 census, the only census in Tsarist Russia. 5. Gregory L. Freeze, 'Reform and Counter Reform 1855–1890', in Gregory L. Freeze (ed.), *Russia: A History*, Oxford University Press 2009, p. 223. 6. Ibid, p. 222; see also Miller, *The Romanov Empire and Nationalism*, p. 116. 7. Benjamin Nathans, *Beyond the Pale: The Jewish Encounter with Late Imperial Russia*, University of California Press 2004, p. 4. 8. Schorske, *Fin-de-Siècle Vienna*, p. 129. 9. Dostoyevsky, *The Diary of a Writer*, p. 651, his emphasis, see also his diatribe on the Jewish Question on pp. 637–59. 10. Cited in Nathans, *Beyond the Pale*, p. 129. 11. Miller, *The Romanov Empire and Nationalism*, p. 118. 12. Michael Aronson, 'The Anti-Jewish Pogroms in Russia in 1881', in John D. Klier and Shlomo Lambroza (eds), *Pogroms: Anti-Jewish Violence in Modern Russian History*, Cambridge University Press 1992, p. 51. 13. Aronson, 'The Anti-Jewish Pogroms in Russia in 1881', p. 55. 14. Wynn, *Workers, Strikes, and Pogroms*, pp. 218–19.

15. Caroline Humphrey, 'Odessa: Pogroms in a Cosmopolitan City', in Caroline Humphrey and Vera Skvirskaja (eds), *Post-Cosmopolitan Cities: Explorations of Urban Coexistence*, Berghahn Books, New York and Oxford 2012, pp. 36–41. 16. Aronson, 'The Anti-Jewish Pogroms in Russia in 1881', pp. 44–5. 17. Shlomo Lambroza, 'The Pogroms of 1903–1906', in Klier and Lambroza (eds), *Pogroms*, p. 200. 18. Wynn, *Workers, Strikes, and Pogroms*, p. 200. 19. Robert Weinberg, 'The Pogrom of 1905 in Odessa: A Case Study', in Klier and Lambroza (eds), *Pogroms*, p. 248. 20. Miller, *The Romanov Empire and Nationalism*, pp. 122–3. 21. See the website of the Israel Ministry of Immigrant Absorption: http://www.moia.gov.il/English/FeelingIsrael/AboutIsrael/Pages/aliya2.aspx 22. Zeev Sternhell, *The Founding Myths of Israel: Nationalism, Socialism, and the Making of the Jewish State*, Princeton University Press 1997, p. 79. 23. Arthur Koestler, *Promise and Fulfilment: Palestine 1917–1949*, Macmillan, New York 1949, p. 3. 24. Patrick Wolfe, *Traces of History: Elementary Structures of Race*, Verso, London 2016, p. 216; see also David Waines, 'The Failure of the Nationalist Resistance', in *The Transformation of Palestine: Essays on the Origin and Development of the Arab-Israeli Conflict*, ed. Ibrahim Abu-Lughod, Northwestern University Press 1987, pp. 216–17. 25. Andreas Kappeler, *The Russian Empire: A Multi-Ethnic History*, Longman, Harlow 2001, pp. 270–71, 307. 26. Witte, *Memoirs*, pp. 378–9. 27. Michael Ochs, 'Tsarist Officialdom and Anti-Jewish Pogroms in Poland', in Klier and Lambroza (eds), *Pogroms*, p. 170. 28. Wynn, *Workers, Strikes, and Pogroms*, p. 36. 29. Ibid, p. 44. 30. Ibid, p. 63. 31. Snyder, *The Reconstruction of Nations*, p. 57. 32. Cited in Jonathan Frankel, *Prophecy and Politics: Socialism, Nationalism, and the Russian Jews, 1862–1917*, Cambridge University Press 1981, pp. 98–9. 33. John Doyle Klier, *Russians, Jews and the Pogroms of 1881–1882*, Cambridge University Press 2011, pp. 166–9. 34. Lars Fischer, *The Socialist Response to Anti-Semitism in Imperial Germany*, Cambridge University Press 2007, esp. pp. 41ff. 35. Stefan Rohrbacher, 'The "Hep Hep" Riots of 1819: Anti-Jewish Ideology, Agitation, and Violence', in Christhard Hoffmann, Werner Bergmann, and Helmut Walser Smith (eds), *Exclusionary Violence: Antisemitic Riots in Modern German History*, University of Michigan Press 2002, pp. 23–4. 36. See George Eliot, *Impressions of Theophrastus Such*, William Blackwood and Sons, Edinburgh and London 1879; this is the last essay by her imaginary scholar Theophrastus. 37. Hans Rogger, 'Conclusion and Overview', in Klier and Lambroza (eds), *Pogroms*, p. 319. 38. Kenneth D. Barkin, *The Controversy over German Industrialization, 1890–1902*, University of Chicago Press 1970, p. 159. 39. Davies, *God's Playground: A History of Poland*, vol. 2: *1795 to the Present*, p. 52; see also Walicki, 'The Troubling Legacy of Roman Dmowski', pp. 14, 28. 40. Snyder, *The Reconstruction of Nations*, p. 59. 41. Davies, *God's Playground*, vol. 2, p. 75. 42. Roman Dmowski, *La question polonaise*, Armand Colin, Paris 1909, pp. 180–81. 43. Ibid, p. 291. 44. Andreas Kossert, 'Founding Father of Modern Poland and Nationalist Antisemite: Roman Dmowski', in Rebecca Haynes and Martyn Rady (eds), *In the Shadow*

of Hitler, I. B. Tauris, London 2011, p. 98. 45. M. B. B. Biskupski, *Independence Day: Myth, Symbol, and the Creation of Modern Poland*, Oxford University Press 2012, p. 174. 46. Robert Blobaum, 'The Politics of Antisemitism in Fin-de-Siècle Warsaw', *Journal of Modern History*, vol. 73, no. 2, June 2001, p. 275. 47. Ibid, p. 287. 48. Ibid, pp. 275–80. 49. Colin Holmes, *Anti-Semitism in British Society, 1876–1939*, Edward Arnold, London 1979, pp. 97–100. 50. Colin Holmes, 'The Tredegar Riots of 1911: Anti-Jewish Disturbances in South Wales', *Welsh History Review*, vol. 11, no. 2, December 1982, pp. 214–25. 51. Fishman, 'The Condition of East End Jewry in 1888', p. 16. 52. James Winter, *London's Teeming Streets, 1830–1914*, Routledge, London 1993, p. 107. 53. András Gerő, *Modern Hungarian Society in the Making: The Unfinished Experience*, Central European University Press, Budapest 1995, pp. 182–3. 54. Maite Ojeda Mata, 'Assimilation et différence. Les Juifs et l'état-nation hongrois, 1895–1914', in *Les limites de siècles. Champs de forces conservatrices et régressives depuis les temps modernes*, ed. Marita Gilli, Presses Universitaires Franc-Comtoises 2001, p. 341. 55. Janos, *The Politics of Backwardness in Hungary, 1825–1945*, p. 141. 56. McCagg, 'Hungary's "Feudalized" Bourgeoisie', pp. 67–9. 57. Janos, *The Politics of Backwardness in Hungary, 1825–1945*, p. 116. 58. Gerő, *Modern Hungarian Society in the Making*, p. 174. 59. Irina Livezeanu, *Cultural Politics in Greater Romania*, Cornell University Press 1995, p. 193. 60. Constantin Iordachi, 'The Unyielding Boundaries of Citizenship: The Emancipation of "Non-Citizens" in Romania, 1866–1918', *European Review of History*, vol. 8, no. 2, 2001, pp. 167–8. 61. Hitchins, *Rumania*, p. 164. 62. Ibid, pp. 16 and 165–6; see also Janos, 'Modernization and Decay in Historical Perspective', p. 91; on the Belgian constitution as a model see Berindei, 'The Nineteenth Century', p. 223; on the Jews see Durandin, *Histoire des Roumains*, pp. 176–82. 63. Durandin, *Histoire des Roumains*, pp. 180–81. 64. Cited in Philip Gabriel Eidelberg, *The Great Rumanian Peasant Revolt of 1907: Origins of a Modern Jacquerie*, E. J. Brill, Leiden 1974, p. 204. 65. Chirot, *Social Change in a Peripheral Society*, p. 150; Hitchins, *Rumania*, p. 178; Chirot and Ragin, 'The Market, Tradition and Peasant Rebellion', pp. 434–5; Durandin, *Histoire des Roumains*, p. 192. 66. Schorske, *Fin-de-Siècle Vienna*, p. 116 and the whole of Chapter 3. 67. David Kertzer, *The Popes against the Jews: The Vatican's Role in the Rise of Modern Anti-Semitism*, Knopf, New York 2001, pp. 136–7. 68. Antoine Blanc de Saint-Bonnet, *De la Restauration française. Mémoire présenté au clergé et à l'aristocratie*, Hervé, Paris 1851, pp. 45–7, 234. 69. Werner Sombart, *The Jews and Modern Capitalism*, Transaction Books, New Brunswick and London 1997, pp. 188 and 248. 70. Édouard Drumont, *La France juive*, vol. 1, Éditions du Trident, La Librairie Française, Paris 1986, pp. 19, 34. 71. Michel Winock, *La France et les Juifs*, Seuil, Paris 2004, p. 91. 72. David Blackbourn, *The Fontana History of Germany, 1780–1918*, Fontana Press, London 1997, p. 308. 73. Muller, *The Mind and the Market*, p. 255. 74. Fritz Stern, *The Politics of Cultural Despair: A Study in the Rise of the Germanic Ideology*, University of California Press 1974, p. 61. 75. Roberto Finzi,

Anti-Semitism: From its European Roots to the Holocaust, Interlink Books, Northampton, MA 1999, p. 20. **76.** Sidney and Beatrice Webb, *Industrial Democracy*, Longmans, Green & Co., London 1902 (first published 1897), pp. 697–8. **77.** Auguste Chirac, *Les rois de la république. Histoire de Juiveries*, Dentu, Paris 1888, p. 135 (new edition). **78.** J. A. Hobson, *Imperialism: A Study*, James Pott and Co., New York 1902, p. 64. **79.** Jean-Yves Mollier and Jocelyne George, *La plus longue des républiques, 1870–1940*, Fayard, Paris 1994, pp. 129–30, 154. **80.** Pierre Birnbaum, 'Le rôle limité des juifs dans l'industrialisation de la société française', in *Les Juifs et l'économique, miroirs et mirages*, ed. Chantal Benayoun, Alain Médam, and Pierre-Jacques Rojtman, PUM, Toulouse 1992, pp. 174–5. **81.** Mark R. Cohen, 'Medieval Jewry in the World of Islam', in *The Oxford Handbook of Jewish Studies*, ed. Martin Goodman, Jeremy Cohen and David Jan Sorkin, Oxford University Press 2002, pp. 198–200. **82.** Bernard Lewis, *The Jews of Islam*, Princeton University Press 2016, p. 158. **83.** Eyal Ginio, '*El dovér el mas sànto*: The Mobilization of the Ottoman Jewish Population during the Balkan Wars (1912–13)', in Hannes Grandits, Nathalie Clayer and Robert Pichler (eds), *Conflicting Loyalties in the Balkans: The Great Powers, the Ottoman Empire and Nation-Building*, I. B. Tauris, London 2011, pp. 169–71ff. **84.** Raymond Kévorkian, *The Armenian Genocide: A Complete History*, I. B. Tauris, London 2011, pp. 11, 14. **85.** Ibid, p. 808. **86.** Ibid, p. 810. **87.** Mark Bauerlein, *Negrophobia: A Race Riot in Atlanta, 1906*, Encounter Books, San Francisco, CA 2001, p. 225. **88.** Ibid, p. 230. **89.** See report in NPR – formerly National Public Radio: http://www.npr.org/templates/story/story.php?storyId=6106285 **90.** Cited in Jack Bass and Marilyn W. Thompson, *Strom: The Complicated Personal and Political Life of Strom Thurmond*, PublicAffairs, New York 2005, p. 117. **91.** Craig Storti, *Incident at Bitter Creek: The Story of the Rock Springs Chinese Massacre*, Iowa State University Press 1991, esp. pp. 99–121. **92.** Ibid, pp. 23–4. **93.** Leland Stanford, 8th Governor, California, Inaugural Address, 10 January 1862: http://governors.library.ca.gov/addresses/08-Stanford.html **94.** Alexander Saxton, *The Indispensable Enemy: Labor and the Anti-Chinese Movement in California*, University of California Press 1971, p. 271. **95.** Ibid, p. 273. **96.** Foner, 'Why is there no Socialism in the United States?', p. 66. **97.** Samuel Gompers and Herman Gutstadt, *Meat vs. Rice: American Manhood Against Asiatic Coolieism. Which Shall Survive?* (reprinted in 1908 by the Asiatic Exclusion League), p. 22. **98.** Henry George, 'The Chinese in California', *New York Daily Tribune*, 1 May 1869. **99.** Riis, *How the Other Half Lives*, pp. 62–3. **100.** Archibald Cary Coolidge, *The United States as a World Power*, Macmillan, New York 1908, p. 62. **101.** Ibid, p. 66. **102.** Ronald Takaki, *Strangers from a Different Shore: A History of Asian Americans*, Little, Brown and Co., Boston, MA 1989, p. 201. **103.** John Higham, *Strangers in the Land: Patterns of American Nativism, 1860–1925*, Atheneum, New York 1973, p. 41. **104.** Kenneth Prewitt, *What Is Your Race?: The Census and Our Flawed Efforts to Classify Americans*, Princeton University Press 2013, p. 67 **105.** Desmond King, *The Liberty of Strangers: Making* *the American Nation*, Oxford University Press 2005, pp. 26–7. 106. The story is well told in Richard Gambino, *Vendetta: The True Story of the Largest Lynching in U.S. History*, Guernica Editions, Toronto 1998, see esp. pp. 96, 107–8. 107. Higham, *Strangers in the Land*, pp. 66–7, 92. 108. Richard Hofstadter, 'The Folklore of Populism', in *Antisemitism in the United States*, ed. Leonard Dinnerstein, Holt, Rinehart and Winston, New York 1971. See also Louise A. Mayo, *The Ambivalent Image: Nineteenth-Century America's Perception of the Jew*, Associated University Presses, London 1988. 109. Higham, *Strangers in the Land*, p. 93. 110. Edmund Barton, Australia's first Prime Minister, to the House of Representatives, discussing the 'Immigration Restriction Bill', House of Representatives, Debates, 12 September 1901, p. 48, cited in David Dutton, *One of Us? A Century of Australian Citizenship*, University of New South Wales Press 2002, p. 28; on the Labour Party's more racist line see Stuart Macintyre, *The Oxford History of Australia*, vol. 4: *1901–1942: The Succeeding Age*, Oxford University Press 1986, p. 89. 111. François Bédarida, 'Perspectives sur le mouvement ouvrier et l'impérialisme en France au temps de la conquête coloniale', *Le Mouvement Social*, no. 86, January–March 1974, p. 38. 112. Dewerpe, *Le monde du travail en France, 1800–1950*, p. 100. 113. Michelle Perrot, *Les ouvriers en grève*, Mouton & Co, Paris 1974, vol. 1, pp. 171–5. 114. Leroy-Beaulieu, *Essai sur la repartition des richesses*, pp. 473–4. 115. Beckert, *Empire of Cotton*, p. 271. 116. Hegel, *Lectures on the Philosophy of World History*, vol. 1, pp. 196–7. 117. Hegel, *The Philosophy of History*, p. 150. 118. Immanuel Kant, 'On the Use of Teleological Principles in Philosophy', in *Anthropology, History, and Education*, ed. Günter Zöller and Robert B. Louden, Cambridge University Press 2007, p. 211. 119. Voltaire, *Essai sur les moeurs et l'esprit des nations*, p. 9. 120. Ernest Renan, *Histoire générale et système comparé des langue sémitiques*, première partie, Imprimerie Impériale, Paris 1855, p. 4. 121. John Stuart Mill, *Considerations on Representative Government*, Parker, Son, and Bourn, London 1861, pp. 61–2, 64. For a lucid attempt to historize Mill's views on this theme see Georgios Varouxakis, *Mill on Nationality*, Routledge, London 2013, pp. 38–52, esp. p. 50. 122. Mahatma Gandhi, *The Collected Works of Mahatma Gandhi* (electronic book), vol. 1: *1884–30 November 1896*, Publications Division Government of India, New Delhi 1999, p. 410: https://www.gandhiashramsevagram.org/gandhi-literature/mahatma-gandhi-collected-works-volume-1.pdf. 123. Lawrence James, *Churchill and Empire*, Weidenfeld and Nicolson, London 2013, p. 48. 124. John Law (Margaret Harkness), *Out of Work*, Swan Sonnenstein & Co., London 1888, pp. 63–4. 125. Sascha Auerbach, *Race, Law and 'The Chinese Puzzle' in Imperial Britain*, Macmillan, London 2009, p. 39. 126. Ibid, p. 52. 127. Ibid, p. 50. 128. Ibid, pp. 74–5. 129. Mill, *Principles of Political Economy*, pp. 351–2. 130. Barkin, *The Controversy over German Industrialization, 1890–1902*, pp. 28–9. 131. Cindy Hahamovitch, 'Creating Perfect Immigrants: Guestworkers of the World in Historical Perspective', *Labor History*, vol. 44, no. 1, February 2003, pp. 73–4. 132. A. V. Dicey, *Lectures on the Relation between Law and Public Opinion in England during the Nineteenth Century*, Macmillan, London 1962, originally based on his 1898 lectures at Harvard Law School, elaborated and published in 1905, p. 298. 133. David Feldman, 'Was the Nineteenth Century a Golden Age for Immigrants?', in Andreas Fahrmeir, Olivier Faron and Patrick Weil (eds), *Migration Control in the North Atlantic World: The Evolution of State Practices in Europe and the United States from the French Revolution to the Inter-War Period*, Berghahn Books, New York 2005, pp. 170, 175. 134. Hahamovitch, 'Creating Perfect Immigrants', pp. 74–5. 135. Weber, 'The Nation State and Economic Policy', p. 9. 136. Ibid, p. 12. 137. Christoph Klessmann, 'Long-Distance Migration, Integration and Segregation of an Ethnic Minority in Industrial Germany: The Case of the "Ruhr Poles"', in Klaus Bade (ed.), *Population, Labour and Migration in 19th- and 20th-Century Germany*, Berg, Leamington Spa 1987, p. 102. 138. André Armengaud, 'Population in Europe, 1700–1914', in Carlo M. Cipolla (ed.), *The Fontana Economic History of Europe*, vol. 3: *The Industrial Revolution*, Collins, London 1980, p. 63. 139. Davis, 'From "Rookeries" to "Communities"', p. 69. 140. Armengaud, 'Population in Europe, 1700–1914', p. 67. 141. Aristide R. Zolberg, 'Global Movements, Global Walls: Responses to Migration 1885–1925', in Wang Gungwu (ed.), *Global History and Migrations*, Westview Press, Boulder, CO 1997, p. 288. 142. See figures on: http://esa.un.org/unmigration/documents/The_number_of_international_migrants.pdf

13. SUFFRAGE

1. Marcel Liebman, *Les socialistes belges, 1885–1914. La révolte et l'organisation*, Vie Ouvrière, Brussels 1979, p. 58, where it is claimed that twenty-four were killed; Jean-Louis Delaet mentions fourteen dead (including those injured who died later), see his 'Les émeutes de mars 1886 au Pays de Charleroi', in *Fourmies et les premier mai*, ed. Madeleine Rebérioux, Éditions Ouvrières, Paris 1994, p. 225. 2. André Pierrard and Jean-Louis Chappat, *La fusillade de Fourmies*, Miroirs, Nord/ Pas-de-Calais 1991, pp. 127–8. 3. Manfredi Alberti, *Senza lavoro La disoccupazione in Italia dall'Unità a oggi*, Laterza, Rome-Bari 2016, pp. 3–4. 4. Salvatore Francesco Romano, *Storia dei Fasci siciliani*, Laterza, Rome-Bari 1959, p. 1. 5. Ibid, p. 106. 6. Ibid, pp. 384–95. 7. Ibid, pp. 428–9. 8. Ibid, p. 471. 9. Ambra Boldetti, 'La repressione in Italia. Il caso del 1894', *Rivista di Storia Contemporanea*, vol. 6, no. 4, 1977, p. 491. 10. Ibid, p. 499. 11. Ibid, p. 503. 12. Romano, *Storia dei Fasci siciliani*, pp. 461–3. 13. Susan A. Ashley, *Making Liberalism Work: The Italian Experience, 1860–1914*, Praeger, Westport, CT 2003, p. 152. 14. Officially there were eighty-three dead, including a soldier, see 'La cessazione dello stato d'assedio', *Corriere della Sera*, 6–7 September 1898, p. 3; the journalist Eugenio Torelli Viollier, an eyewitness, thinks there were many more, see Lucio Villari, 'I fatti di Milano del 1898. La testimonianza di Eugenio Torelli Viollier', *Studi Storici*, vol. 8, no. 3, July–September 1967, pp. 534–49.

15. César de Paepe, *Le suffrage universel et la capacité politique de la classe ouvrière*, Gand 1890, p. 10, quoted in Liebman, *Les socialistes belges (1885–1914)*, p. 84. 16. David Hume, 'Of Refinement in the Arts' (1752), David Hume, *Selected Essays*, Oxford University Press 2008, pp. 174–5. 17. Yan Fu (Yen Fou), *Les manifestes de Yen Fou*, ed. François Houang, Fayard, Paris 1977, p. 96. 18. Ibid, p. 151. 19. William Jennings Bryan, *Letters to a Chinese Official*, McClure, Phillips and Co, New York 1906, pp. 54–5. 20. Eduardo Posada-Carbó, 'Electoral Juggling: A Comparative History of the Corruption of Suffrage in Latin America, 1830–1930', *Journal of Latin American Studies*, vol. 32, no. 3, October 2000, p. 623. 21. Paul W. Drake, *Between Tyranny and Anarchy: A History of Democracy in Latin America, 1800–2006*, Stanford University Press 2009, p. 112. 22. Leslie Bethell, 'Politics in Brazil: From Elections without Democracy to Democracy without Citizenship', *Daedalus*, vol. 129, no. 2, Spring 2000, pp. 3–6. 23. Posada-Carbó, 'Electoral Juggling', p. 612. 24. Juan Maiguashca, 'The Electoral Reforms of 1861 in Ecuador and the Rise of a New Political Order', in Eduardo Posada-Carbó (ed.), *Elections before Democracy: The History of Elections in Europe and Latin America*, Macmillan, London 1996, pp. 87–9. 25. Hilda Sabato, 'Citizenship, Political Participation and the Formation of the Public Sphere in Buenos Aires, 1850s–1880s', *Past & Present*, no. 136, August 1992, pp. 141–3. 26. Karl Marx, *Class Struggles in France, 1848–1850*, International Publishers, New York 1964, p. 54. 27. Osmo Jussila, Seppo Hentilä, and Jukka Nevakivi, *From Grand Duchy to a Modern State: A Political History of Finland since 1809*, Hurst and Co., London 1999, pp. 88–9. 28. James Lorimer, *Constitutionalism of the Future: or, Parliament the Mirror of the Nation*, Adam and Charles Black, Edinburgh 1865. 29. Barkin, *The Controversy over German Industrialization, 1890–1902*, p. 20. 30. Montesquieu, *De l'esprit des lois*, vol. I, livre 2, chapitre 2, p. 103. 31. Malcolm Crook and Tom Crook, 'L'isoloir universel? La globalisation du scrutin secret au XIXe siècle', *Revue d'histoire du XIXe siècle*, no. 43, 2011, pp. 41–55. 32. Margaret Lavinia Anderson, *Practicing Democracy: Elections and Political Culture in Imperial Germany*, Princeton University Press 2000, pp. 213–16, 242, 273. 33. Sheri E. Berman, 'Modernization in Historical Perspective: The Case of Imperial Germany', *World Politics*, vol. 53, no. 3, April 2001, p. 449. 34. Gerő, *Modern Hungarian Society in the Making*, p. 145. 35. H. J. Hanham, *Elections and Party Management: Politics in the Time of Disraeli and Gladstone*, Harvester Press, Hassocks, Sussex 1978, p. 263. 36. Economist Intelligence Unit, *Democracy Index 2012*: http://pages.eiu.com/rs/eiu2/images/Democracy-Index-2012.pdf; and *Democracy Index 2014*: http://www.eiu.com/Handlers/WhitepaperHandler.ashx?fi=Democracy-index-2014.pdf&mode=wp&campaignid=Democracy0115; and http://www.economist.com/blogs/graphicdetail/2017/01/daily-chart-20 37. In the 2017 French parliamentary elections turnout collapsed to below 50 per cent. 38. William Blackstone, *Commentaries on the Laws of England*, vol. 1, New York 1827, p. 127 (1st ed., 1765–9). 39. Reidar Maliks, *Kant's Politics in Context*, Oxford University Press 2014, p. 95. 40. Immanuel

Kant, 'On the Common Saying: That may be correct in theory, but it is of no use in practice', in Immanuel Kant, *Practical Philosophy*, ed. Mary Gregor, Cambridge University Press 1996, p. 292. 41. Ibid, p. 295. 42. Pierre Rosanvallon, *Le sacre du citoyen. Histoire du suffrage universel en France*, Gallimard, Paris 2001, p. 277. 43. Benjamin Constant, 'Principes de politique', in *Écrits politiques*, Gallimard, Paris 1997, pp. 367–8. 44. Ibid, pp. 344–6. 45. Ibid, pp. 347, 351, and *passim*. 46. Speech to the Assemblé nationale, 27 August 1789, quoted in Maliks, *Kant's Politics in Context*, pp. 83–4. 47. Abbé (Emmanuel) Sieyès, *Préliminaire de la Constitution françoise. Reconnaissance et exposition raisonnée des droits de l'homme et du citoyen*, Baudouin, Paris 1789, p. 16: http://gallica.bnf.fr/ark:/12148/bpt6k41690g/f18.item 48. Jean-Paul Marat, *L'Ami du peuple*, Wednesday, 30 June 1790, p. 6: http://gallica.bnf.fr/ark:/12148/bpt6k1046480j/f6.item 49. Rosanvallon, *Le sacre du citoyen*, pp. 267–8. 50. Alexis de Tocqueville, *Souvenirs*, Calmann Lévy, Paris 1893, pp. 15–16. 51. Cited in Rosanvallon, *Le sacre du citoyen*, pp. 286–7. 52. Claude Willard, *Le mouvement socialiste en France (1893–1905)*, Les Guesdistes, Éditions sociales, Paris 1965, p. 71. 53. Cited in Ronsavallon, *Le sacre du citoyen*, p. 353. 54. Ibid. 55. Letters of 30 April 1871 and 6 September 1871 in Gustave Flaubert, *Correspondance*, vol. IV, Gallimard, Paris 1998, pp. 314, 372. 56. Ibid, 7 October 1871, p. 384. 57. His emphasis, letter of 7 October 1871, in Flaubert, *Correspondance*, vol. IV, p. 384. 58. Cited in Hausrath, 'The Life of Treitschke', pp. 308–9, 311. 59. Jacques-Pierre Gougeon, 'Les élites dirigeantes dans l'Allemagne des années 1890', in *Les limites de siècles. Champs de forces conservatrices et régressives depuis les temps modernes*, ed. Marita Gilli, vol. 1, Presses Universitaires Franc-Comtoises 2001, p. 235. 60. See *The Miscellaneous Writings and Speeches of Lord Macaulay*, vol. 4: http://www.gutenberg.org/files/2170/2170-h/2170-h.htm 61. George Rudé, 'English Rural and Urban Disturbances on the Eve of the First Reform Bill, 1830–1831', *Past & Present*, no. 37, 1967, pp. 87ff. 62. Ibid, p. 98. 63. Chris Cook, *The Routledge Companion to Britain in the Nineteenth Century*, Routledge, London 2005, p. 68; Neal Blewett, 'The Franchise in the United Kingdom, 1885–1918', *Past & Present*, no. 32, December 1965, p. 31. 64. Mill, *Principles of Political Economy*, p. 460. 65. John Ruskin, *The Crown of Wild Olive. Munera Pulveris. Pre-Raphaelitism. Aratra Pentelici, etc.*, Dana Estes & Co., Boston, MA 1900, p. 195, his italics. 66. John Ruskin, *Time and Tide by Weare and Tyne: Twenty-Five Letters to a Working Man of Sunderland on the Laws of Work*, letter III, p. 9: http://www.gutenberg.org/files/31196/31196-h/31196-h.htm 67. Matthew Arnold, *Culture and Anarchy and Other Writings*, ed. Stefan Collini, Cambridge University Press 1993, p. 107. 68. William George Ward, 'The Encyclical and Syllabus', *Dublin Review*, vol. 56, January–April 1865, p. 473. 69. Bentley, *Lord Salisbury's World*, p. 73. 70. Lord Salisbury (signed Lord Robert Cecil), 'English Politics and Parties', *Bentley's Quarterly Review*, vol. 1, March 1859, pp. 28–9. 71. Smith, *Disraelian Conservatism and Social Reform*, p. 39. 72. E. David Steele, *Lord Salisbury*, Routledge, London 2002, p. 121. 73. Bentley, *Lord*

Salisbury's World, pp. 150, 152. 74. Originally in *Quarterly Review*, vol. 116, 1864, p. 269, cited in Smith (ed.), *Lord Salisbury on Politics*, p. 45. 75. Cited in Gareth Stedman Jones, 'Rethinking Chartism', in Gareth Stedman Jones, *Languages of Class: Studies in English Working Class History, 1832–1982*, Cambridge University Press 1983, p. 109. 76. Dicey, *Lectures on the Relation between Law and Public Opinion in England*, pp. 211–12. 77. Robert G. Gammage, *History of the Chartist Movement, 1837–1854* (first published 1854), cited in Stedman Jones, 'Rethinking Chartism', p. 100. 78. William Gladstone, House of Commons, 11 May 1864: http://hansard.millbanksystems.com/commons/1864/may/11/second-reading, cols 313–27. 79. Letter to Palmerston, 15 May 1864, *The Letters of Queen Victoria*, vol. 4, ed. George E. Buckle, Cambridge University Press, 2014, pp. 189–90. 80. William Gladstone, Speech in the House of Commons, 27 April 1866: http://hansard.millbanksystems.com/commons/1866/apr/27/adjourned-debate-eighth-night, col. 121. 81. John Bright, *Speeches on Parliamentary Reform, &c. (delivered during the autumn of 1866)*, John Heywood, Manchester 1866, p. 35. 82. F. W. S. Craig, *British Electoral Facts: 1832–1987*, Parliamentary Research Services, Darmouth 1989, pp. 9–10. 83. Smith, *Disraelian Conservatism and Social Reform*, p. 90. 84. Ibid, p. 102. 85. Ibid, pp. 96–7. 86. Dicey, *Lectures on the Relation between Law and Public Opinion in England*, p. 252. 87. Smith, *Disraelian Conservatism and Social Reform*, pp. 22–5. 88. Niall Ferguson, 'Political Risk and the International Bond Market between the 1848 Revolution and the Outbreak of the First World War', *Economic History Review*, vol. 59, no. 1, 2006, p. 94n. 89. Letter of 18 November 1868, in Karl Marx and Friedrich Engels, *Correspondence 1846–1895: A Selection with Commentary and Notes*, Martin Lawrence, London 1934, pp. 253–4. 90. Cited in Smith, *Disraelian Conservatism and Social Reform*, p. 103. 91. Webb, 'The Moral of the Elections', p. 287. 92. Lord Rosebery, Leader's Speech at the National Liberal Federation conference held at Cardiff on 18 January 1895: http://www.britishpoliticalspeech.org/speech-archive.htm?speech=5 93. Carl Strikwerda, *A House Divided: Catholics, Socialists, and Flemish Nationalists in Nineteenth-Century Belgium*, Rowman & Littlefield, Lanham, MD, and Oxford 1997, pp. 95–6. 94. Alfred Defuisseaux, 'Le catéchisme du peuple', 1886: http://users.skynet.be/roger.romain/Defuisseaux.html. On the sales of the pamphlet see Liebman, *Les socialistes belges, 1885–1914*, p. 68. 95. Strikwerda, *A House Divided*, p. 109. 96. Liebman, *Les socialistes belges, 1885–1914*, pp. 100–108. 97. Giorgio Candeloro, *Storia dell'Italia moderna*, vol. 6: *Lo sviluppo del capitalismo e del movimento operaio 1871–1896*, Feltrinelli, Milan 1978, pp. 154–5. 98. Silvio Furlani, 'Le riforme elettorali del 1882', in *Il parlamento italiano 1861–1988*, vol. V: *1877–1887*, Nuova CEI, Milan 1989, pp. 85–6. 99. Anderson, *Practicing Democracy*, p. 8. 100. Berman, 'Modernization in Historical Perspective', pp. 437–40. 101. Ibid, pp. 443–5. 102. Gilbert Rozman, 'Social Change', in Marius B. Jansen (ed.), *The Cambridge History of Japan*, vol. 5: *The Nineteenth Century*, Cambridge University Press 1989, p. 525.

103. Johannes Hirschmeier and Tsunehiko Yui, *The Development of Japanese Business, 1600–1973*, Harvard University Press 1975, pp. 73–4. 104. Neary, *The State and Politics in Japan*, p. 17. 105. Jansen, *The Making of Modern Japan*, p. 394. 106. Ibid, p. 415. 107. Norman, *Japan's Emergence as a Modern State*, p. 189. 108. Lehmann, *The Roots of Modern Japan*, pp. 247, 249, 267. 109. Yukichi Fukuzawa, *The Autobiography of Yukichi Fukuzawa*, trans. Eiichi Kiyooka, Columbia University Press 2007, p. 449 (in appendix). 110. Stanley L. Engerman and Kenneth L. Sokoloff, 'The Evolution of Suffrage Institutions in the New World', *Journal of Economic History*, vol. 65, no. 4, December 2005, pp. 906–9. 111. J. Morgan Kousser, *The Shaping of Southern Politics: Suffrage Restriction and the Establishment of the One-Party South, 1880–1910*, Yale University Press 1974, p. 12. 112. Foner, *Reconstruction*, pp. 235, 191. 113. Gould, *Reform and Regulation*, p. 7. 114. Kousser, *The Shaping of Southern Politics*, p. 39. 115. Gould, *Reform and Regulation*, p. 4.

14. PRIVATE AFFLUENCE, PUBLIC WELFARE

1. R. H. Tawney, *The Acquisitive Society*, 1920: http://www.gutenberg.org/files/33741/33741-h/33741-h.htm, p. 38. 2. John Maynard Keynes, *The Economic Consequences of the Peace*, 1920: http://www.gutenberg.org/files/15776/15776-h/15776-h.htm, Chapter 2. 3. Patten, *The New Basis of Civilization*, pp. 19–20. 4. Ibid, p. 6; see also Daniel M. Fox, *The Discovery of Abundance: Simon N. Patten and the Transformation of Social Theory*, Cornell University Press 1967, p. 11. 5. US Dept. of Labor Statistics, Office of Publication and Special Studies: http://www.bls.gov/opub/uscs/1901.pdf 6. Horowitz, *The Morality of Spending*, p. 30. 7. Charles McGovern, 'Consumption and Citizenship in the United States, 1900–1940', in *Getting and Spending*, ed. Susan Strasser, Charles McGovern, and Matthias Judt, Cambridge University Press 1998, p. 47. 8. Rosalind H. Williams, *Dream Worlds: Mass Consumption in Late Nineteenth-Century France*, University of California Press 1982, esp. pp. 303–10. 9. Bonneff, *La vie tragique des travailleurs*, p. 233. 10. Glickman, *A Living Wage*, pp. 5, 26–7. 11. Thorstein Veblen, *The Theory of the Leisure Class*, Random House, New York 2001, p. 55. 12. Hume, 'Of Refinement in the Arts', p. 170. 13. Diner, *Hungering for America*, p. 45. 14. Henry Ford, *My Life and Work*, Heinemann, London 1922, p. 73. 15. McGovern, 'Consumption and Citizenship in the United States, 1900–1940', pp. 44–5. 16. Brian Greenberg and Linda S. Watts, *Social History of the United States*, ABC-CLIO, Santa Barbara, CA 2009, p. 30. 17. Terry P. Wilson, *The Cart that Changed the World: The Career of Sylvan N. Goldman*, University of Oklahoma Press 1978, p. 85. 18. Klein, *The Genesis of Industrial America, 1870–1920*, p. 30. 19. Lisa Jacobson, *Raising Consumers: Children and the American Mass Market in the Early Twentieth Century*, Columbia University Press 2004, pp. 23–6. 20. William R. Leach, *Land of Desire: Merchants, Power, and the Rise of a New American Culture*,

Knopf Doubleday, New York 2011, p. 4. 21. Carlson, 'Technology and America as a Consumer Society, 1870–1900', pp. 29–30. 22. Edward Bellamy, *Looking Backward: From 2000 to 1887*: http://www.gutenberg.org/files/624/624-h/624-h.htm. The term 'credit card' appears in Chapter 9. 23. David M. Potter, *People of Plenty: Economic Abundance and the American Character*, University of Chicago Press 1973, first published 1954, p. 83, citing UN statistics in Karl W. Deutsch, *Nationalism and Social Communication*, MIT and Wiley, New York 1953, p. 40. 24. Ibid, pp. 84, 90, 95, 101, 175, 177, 195ff. 25. John Larson, 'The Market Revolution', in Lacy K. Ford, *A Companion to the Civil War and Reconstruction*, Blackwell, Oxford 2005, p. 41. 26. Lévy-Leboyer and Bourguignon, *L'économie française au XIXe siècle*, p. 38. 27. Charles B. Spahr, *An Essay on the Present Distribution of Wealth in the United States*, Thomas Y. Crowell and Co., 2nd ed., Boston, MA 1896, pp. 128–9: http://archive.org/details/anessayonpresen01spahgoog 28. Piketty, *Capital in the Twenty-First Century*, pp. 22–4, figure I.1. 29. Werner Sombart, *Why is there no Socialism in the United States?* Macmillan, New York and London 1976, p. 106. 30. Friedrich Engels, 'Letter to Friedrich Sorge', 24 October 1891, in *Marx and Engels Correspondence*: https://www.marxists.org/archive/marx/works/1891/letters/91_10_24a.htm 31. Cited in Foner, 'Why is there no Socialism in the United States?', p. 58. 32. For an overall assessment of the strength of these arguments see Seymour Martin Lipset and Gary Marks, *It Didn't Happen Here: Why Socialism Failed in the United States*, Norton and Co., New York 2000. 33. Robin Archer, *Why Is There No Labor Party in the United States*, Princeton University Press 2007, pp. 234–6. 34. Jerome Karabel, 'The Reasons Why', *The New York Times*, 8 February 1979; see also Foner, 'Why is there no Socialism in the United States?' pp. 60, 71. 35. Ira Kipnis, *The American Socialist Movement, 1897–1912*, Haymarket Books, Chicago, IL 2005, pp. 247–8, first published 1952. 36. Eugene V. Debs, Campaign Speech, Lyceum Theatre, Fergus Falls, Minnesota, 27 August 1912: https://www.marxists.org/archive/debs/works/1912/1912-capsoc.htm 37. Robert C. McMath, Jr, *American Populism: A Social History, 1877–1898*, Hill and Wang, New York 1993, p. 83. 38. Cohen, *The Reconstruction of American Liberalism, 1865–1914*, p. 177. 39. Theodore Roosevelt, 'Address at the Coliseum', 14 September 1912, San Francisco, California, in David M. Kennedy and Thomas A. Bailey (eds), *The American Spirit: United States History as Seen by Contemporaries*, Cengage Learning, Boston, MA 2009, vol. 2, p. 225. 40. Leuchtenburg, *The American President*, p. 61. 41. Sklar, *The Corporate Reconstruction of American Capitalism, 1890–1916*, pp. 401–4. 42. Theodore Roosevelt, 'First Annual Message' to Congress, 3 December 1901: http://www.presidency.ucsb.edu/ws/?pid=29542; see also Kolko, *The Triumph of Conservatism*, p. 66; Leuchtenburg, *The American President*, p. 30. 43. Gould, *Reform and Regulation*, p. 20. 44. Colin Jones, 'Perspectives on Poor Relief, Health Care and the Counter-Reformation in France', in *Health Care and Poor Relief in Counter-Reformation Europe*, ed. Ole Peter Grell and Andrew Cunningham, with Jon Arrizabalaga, Routledge,

London 1999, p. 216. 45. Mokyr, *The Enlightened Economy*, p. 440. 46. Thomas Malthus, *An Essay on the Principle of Population* (1798), Chapter 5, paragraph 3: http://www.gutenberg.org/files/4239/4239-h/4239-h.htm 47. Henri Hatzfeld, *Du paupérisme à la sécurité sociale (1850–1940)*, Presses Universitaires de Nancy 2004, pp. 34, 67–9. 48. Thomas Malthus, 'An Investigation of the Cause of the Present High Price of Provisions' (1800), cited and discussed in Morgan Kelly and Cormac O'Gráda, 'Living Standards and Mortality since the Middle Ages', *Economic History Review*, vol. 67, no. 2, 2014, p. 361. 49. Ibid, pp. 358–81. 50. David Ricardo, *On the Principles of Political Economy and Taxation*, John Murray, London 1821, p. 102 (Chapter 5: 'On Wages'). 51. David Englander, *Poverty and Poor Law Reform in Nineteenth-Century Britain, 1834–1914: From Chadwick to Booth*, Routledge, London 2013, p. 1. 52. Mokyr, *The Enlightened Economy*, p. 441. 53. Lindert, *Growing Public*, p. 8. 54. Castel, *Les métamorphoses de la question sociale*, p. 232. 55. Prosper Poullet, *Les institutions françaises de 1795 à 1814. Essai sur les origines des institutions belges contemporaines*, Plon, Paris 1907, p. 446. 56. Gareth Stedman Jones, *An End to Poverty? A Historical Debate*, Profile Books, London 2004, pp. 24–5. 57. Ibid, p. 20. 58. Poullet, *Les institutions françaises de 1795 à 1814*, p. 447; see also Lis and Soly, *Poverty and Capitalism in Pre-Industrial Europe*, pp. 209–10. 59. Jean-Baptiste Say, *Cours complet d'économie politique pratique*, vol. 5, Rapilly, Paris 1829, p. 347 (XXXII, 'Des sécours publics'). 60. Alexis de Tocqueville, *Mémoire sur le paupérisme*, Ministère de l'instruction publique et des beaux-arts, Imprimerie nationale, Paris 1835, pp. 12, 16. 61. Paul Leroy-Beaulieu, *L'administration locale en France et en Angleterre*, Guillaumin, Paris 1872, p. 237. 62. Ibid, p. 234. 63. Ibid, p. 251. 64. Leroy-Beaulieu, *Essai sur la repartition des richesses*, p. 437. 65. Ibid, p. 409. 66. Hatzfeld, *Du paupérisme à la sécurité sociale*, p. 34. 67. John H. Weiss, 'Origins of the French Welfare State: Poor Relief in the Third Republic, 1871–1914', *French Historical Studies*, vol. 13, no. 1, Spring 1983, p. 55. 68. Madeleine Rebérioux, *La République radicale? 1898–1914*, Éditions du Seuil, Paris 1975. 69. Albert Thibaudet, *Les idées politiques de la France*, Librairie Stock, Paris 1932, p. 184. Thibaudet, a literary critic, attributed the bon mot to 'a socialist'. 70. Donald G. Wileman, 'Not the Radical Republic: Liberal Ideology and Central Blandishment in France, 1901–1914', *Historical Journal*, vol. 37, no. 3, September 1994, pp. 593–614. 71. J. P. T. Bury, *Gambetta's Final Years: 'The Era of Difficulties', 1877–1882*, Longman, London 1982, pp. 355–6; Pierre Sorlin, *Waldeck-Rousseau*, Armand Colin, Paris 1966, p. 243. 72. Léon Gambetta, 'La politique et les affaires', *Revue politique*, 6 June 1868, cited in Jeanne Gaillard, 'Les associations de production et la pensée politique en France (1852–1870)', *Le Mouvement Social*, no. 52, July–September 1966, p. 77. 73. Antonmattei, *Léon Gambetta*, p. 168. 74. Ibid, pp. 175–6. 75. Jean-Michel Gaillard, *Jules Ferry*, Fayard, Paris 1989, pp. 160, 407–9. 76. Peter Baldwin, *The Politics of Social Solidarity: Class Bases of the European Welfare State, 1875–1975*, Cambridge University Press 1990, p. 102. 77. Timothy B. Smith, 'The Ideology of Charity, the Image of the English Poor Law, and Debates over the Right to Assistance in France, 1830–1905', *Historical Journal*, vol. 40, no. 4, December 1997, p. 999. 78. Sorlin, *Waldeck-Rousseau*, p. 270. 79. Leduc, *Histoire de la France*, p. 59. 80. Hatzfeld, *Du paupérisme à la sécurité sociale*, p. 34. 81. Didier Renard, 'Assistance publique et bienfaisance privée, 1885–1914', *Politiques et management public*, vol. 5, no. 2, 1987, p. 113. 82. Hatzfeld, *Du paupérisme à la sécurité sociale*, p. 72. 83. Ibid, p. 75. 84. Ibid, p. 74. 85. Robert Gildea, *Children of the Revolution: The French, 1799–1914*, Allen Lane, London 2008, p. 270. 86. Léon Bourgeois, *Solidarité*, Armand Colin, Paris 1896, pp. 12, 22. 87. Timothy B. Smith, *Creating the Welfare State in France, 1880–1940*, McGill-Queen's University Press 2003, pp. 13–14. 88. Paul Leroy-Beaulieu, 'Le prochain gouffre: le projet de loi sur les retraites', *L'Économiste français*, 11 May 1901. 89. William Stanley Jevons, *The State in Relation to Labour*, Macmillan, London 1882, p. 66; J. H. Stewart Reid, *The Origins of the British Labour Party*, University of Minnesota Press 1955, p. 14. 90. Henry Sidgwick, *The Elements of Politics*, Macmillan, London 1897, first published 1891, p. 40. 91. Sanford Elwitt, *The Third Republic Defended: Bourgeois Reforms in France, 1880–1914*, Louisiana State University Press 1986, p. 145, and Michel Bouillé, 'Les congrès d'hygiène des travailleurs au début du siècle 1904–1911', *Le Mouvement Social*, no. 161, October–December 1992, pp. 43–65. 92. Georges Tapinos, 'Une seconde transition démographique? La population et l'emploi', in Maurice Lévy-Leboyer and Jean-Claude Casanova (eds), *Entre l'état et le marché. L'économie française des années 1880 à nos jours*, Gallimard, Paris 1991, p. 96. 93. Perrot, *Les ouvriers en grève*, p. 166. 94. Philip Nord, 'The Welfare State in France, 1870–1914', *French Historical Studies*, vol. 18, no. 3, Spring 1994, pp. 827–8. 95. Rachel G. Fuchs, 'Morality and Poverty: Public Welfare for Mothers in Paris, 1870–1900', *French History*, vol. 2, no. 3, 1988, p. 289. 96. See Ida Bloom, 'Voluntary Motherhood 1900–1930: Theories and Politics of a Norwegian Feminist in an International Perspective', and also Anne-Lise Seip and Hilde Ibsen, 'Family Welfare, which Policy? Norway's Road to Child Allowances', both in Gisela Bock and Pat Thane (eds), *Maternity and Gender Policies: Women and the Rise of the European Welfare States, 1880s–1950s*, Routledge, London and New York 1991, pp. 21–39, 40–59. 97. Ann-Sofie Ohlander, 'The Invisible Child? The Struggle for a Social Democratic Family Policy in Sweden, 1900–1960s', in Bock and Thane (eds), *Maternity and Gender Policies*, pp. 60–72. 98. Bock and Thane (eds), 'Introduction' to *Maternity and Gender Policies*, p. 16. 99. Adrian Shubert, *A Social History of Modern Spain*, Unwin Hyman, London 1990, p. 50. 100. Peter Flora and Arnold J. Heidenheimer (eds), *The Development of Welfare States in Europe and America*, Transaction Books, Piscataway, NJ 1981, pp. 48–50. 101. Trencsényi et al., *A History of Modern Political Thought in East Central Europe*, p. 401. 102. Ha-Joon Chang, *Kicking Away the Ladder*, p. 104. 103. Edmund Morris, *Theodore Rex*, Random House, New York 2001, p. 507. 104. Baldwin, *The Politics of Social Solidarity*, pp. 5–8. 105. Ibid, pp. 62–3. 106. Ibid,

p. 66. 107. Lars-Fredrik Andersson and Liselotte Eriksson, 'The Compulsory Public Pension and the Demand for Life Insurance: The Case of Sweden, 1884–1914', *Economic History Review*, vol. 68, no. 1, February 2015, pp. 245–8. 108. William Harbutt Dawson, *Bismarck and State Socialism: An Exposition of the Social and Economic Legislation of Germany since 1870*, Swan Sonnenschein & Co., London 1890, pp. ix, 3–5. 109. Ibid, p. 28. 110. E. P. Hennock, *The Origin of the Welfare State in England and Germany, 1850–1914: Social Policies Compared*, Cambridge University Press 2007, p. 90. 111. E. P. Hennock, 'Social Policy in the Bismarck Era: A Progress Report', *German History*, vol. 21, no. 2, 2003, p. 234. On firing workers before pension see Barrington Moore, Jr., *Injustice: The Social Bases of Obedience and Revolt*, Macmillan, London and Basingstoke 1978, p. 268. 112. Lothar Gall, *Bismarck: The White Revolutionary*, vol. 2: *1871–1898*, Unwin Hyman, London 1990, pp. 165–6. 113. Hennock, *The Origin of the Welfare State in England and Germany*, pp. 87, 99. 114. Ibid, p. 89. 115. Ibid, p. 93. 116. David Khoudour-Castéras, 'Welfare State and Labor Mobility: The Impact of Bismarck's Social Legislation on German Emigration before World War I', *Journal of Economic History*, vol. 68, no. 1, March 2008, pp. 211–43. 117. Gall, *Bismarck: The White Revolutionary*, vol. 1: *1815–1871*, p. 29. 118. Gordon A. Craig, *Germany 1866–1945*, Oxford University Press 1981, p. 253. 119. Shubert, *A Social History of Modern Spain*, p. 50. 120. Barkin, *The Controversy over German Industrialization, 1890–1902*, p. 190. 121. Daumard, 'Puissance et inquiétudes de la société bourgeoise', p. 500. 122. Collini, *Liberalism and Sociology*, p. 33. 123. Peter Gray, 'The Peculiarities of Irish Land Tenure, 1800–1914: From Agent of Impoverishment to Agent of Pacification', in Donald Winch and Patrick O'Brien (eds), *The Political Economy of British Historical Experience, 1688–1914*, Oxford University Press 2002, p. 159. 124. Wohl, *The Eternal Slum*, p. 237. 125. Lord Salisbury, 'Labourers' and Artisans' Dwellings', *National Review*, no. 9, November 1883, pp. 301, 304. 126. Ibid, p. 310. 127. Wohl, *The Eternal Slum*, p. 232. 128. Roberts, *Salisbury*, pp. 284–6. 129. Gareth Stedman Jones, *Outcast London: A Study in the Relationship between Classes in Victorian Society*, Clarendon Press, Oxford 1971, p. 224. 130. Michael Bentley, '"Boundaries" in Theoretical Language about the British State', in Simon J. D. Green and Richard C. Whiting (eds), *The Boundaries of the State in Modern Britain*, Cambridge University Press 1996, p. 46. 131. Stedman Jones, *Outcast London*, p. 287. 132. Ibid, p. 292. 133. Mouret, 'La légende des 150,000 décés tuberculeux par an', pp. 64–9. 134. Dicey, *Lectures on the Relation between Law and Public Opinion in England*, p. 277. 135. Stedman Jones, *Outcast London*, p. 307. 136. José Harris, 'The Transition to High Politics in English Social Policy, 1880–1914', in Michael Bentley and John Stevenson (eds), *High and Low Politics in Modern Britain*, Clarendon Press, Oxford 1983. 137. E. H. H. Green, *The Crisis of Conservatism: The Politics, Economics and Ideology of the British Conservative Party, 1880–1914*, Routledge, London 1995, p. 254. 138. Ibid, pp. 4–6, 11. 139. A. B. Atkinson, *Incomes and the Welfare State: Essays on*

Britain and Europe, Cambridge University Press 1995, p. 134. 140. Harris, 'Political Thought and the Welfare State 1870–1940', p. 116. 141. Gramsci, *Il Risorgimento*, p. 102. 142. Francesco Crispi, Letter no. 427, 1891, in *Carteggi politici inediti di Francesco Crispi (1860–1900)*, ed. Tommaso Palamenghi-Crispi, L'Universelle imprimerie polyglotte, Rome 1912: https://archive.org/stream/carteggipoliticioocris/carteggipoliticioocris_djvu.txt 143. Christopher Duggan, *Francesco Crispi, 1818–1901: From Nation to Nationalism*, Oxford University Press 2002, p. 345. 144. Ibid, p. 576. 145. Ibid, p. 585.

15. MANAGING CAPITAL AND LABOUR

1. Edmund S. K. Fung, 'State Building, Capitalist Development, and Social Justice: Social Democracy in China's Modern Transformation, 1921–1949', *Modern China*, vol. 31, no. 3, July 2005, p. 320. 2. Frederick Charles Barghoorn, 'The Russian Radicals of the 1860's and the Problem of the Industrial Proletariat', *Slavonic and East European Review*, vol. 2, no. 1, March 1943, pp. 57–60. 3. Smith, *An Inquiry into the Nature and Causes of the Wealth of Nations*, p. 60. 4. Dicey, *Lectures on the Relation between Law and Public Opinion in England*, p. 266. 5. E. Bonjour, H. S. Offler, and G. R. Potter, *A Short History of Switzerland*, Clarendon Press, Oxford 1952, p. 307. 6. Lee Shai Weissbach, 'Child Labor Legislation in Nineteenth-Century France', *Journal of Economic History*, vol. 37, no. 1, March 1977, p. 269. 7. Ibid, p. 270; see also for non-implementation, Lee Shai Weissbach, *Child Labor Reform in Nineteenth-Century France: Assuring the Future Harvest*, Louisiana State University Press, 1989, pp. 213ff. 8. Daumard, 'Puissance et inquiétudes de la société bourgeoise', p. 471. 9. The traditional estimate of between 20,000 and 30,000 deaths seems exaggerated. A more accurate estimate is likely to be between 5,700 and 7,400; see Robert Tombs, 'How Bloody was *La Semaine Sanglante* of 1871? A Revision', *Historical Journal*, vol. 55, no. 3, 2012, pp. 679–97, esp. figures on pp. 693–5. 10. B. S. Chlepner, *Cent ans d'histoire sociale en Belgique*, Université Libre de Bruxelles 1958, p. 212; see also Puissant, '1886, la contre-réforme sociale?', p. 69. 11. Guy Desolre, 'Un siècle de premiers mai et de réduction du temps de travail', in Van der Vorst (ed.), *Cent ans de droit social belge*, p. 109. 12. Ibid, p. 111. 13. Census figures in Chlepner, *Cent ans d'histoire sociale en Belgique*, p. 111. 14. Ibid, pp. 114, 119, 125, 154, 213. 15. Marx, *Capital*, vol. 1, pp. 203, 299n, and 460–62. 16. Cross, *A Quest for Time*, pp. 56, 25. 17. Madhavan K. Palat, 'Casting Workers as an Estate in Late Imperial Russia', *Kritika: Explorations in Russian and Eurasian History*, vol. 8, no. 2, Spring 2007, p. 317. 18. Boris B. Gorshkov, *Russia's Factory Children: State, Society and the Law, 1800–1917*, University of Pittsburgh Press 2009, pp. 128–9. 19. Bunge, 'The Years 1881–1894 in Russia', p. 61. 20. Ibid, pp. 61–71. 21. Frederick C. Giffin, 'The "First Russian Labor Code": The Law of June 3, 1886', *Russian History/Histoire Russe*, vol. 2, no. 2, 1975, pp. 97–8. 22. Witte, *Memoirs*,

pp. 57–8. 23. Nassau W. Senior, *Letters on the Factory Act*, B. Fellowes, London 1837, p. 5; see also A. J. McIvor, 'Employers, the Government, and Industrial Fatigue in Britain, 1890–1918', *Journal of Industrial Medicine*, vol. 44, no. 11, November 1987, p. 725. 24. William Mather, 'Labour and the Hours of Labour', *Contemporary Review*, vol. 62, November 1892, p. 609; for his positive views of trade unions see pp. 616, 619. 25. Marx, *Capital*, vol. 1, p. 303. 26. Quoted in Chris Wrigley, 'May Days and After', *History Today*, vol. 40, no. 6, June 1990: http://www.historytoday.com/chris-wrigley/may-days-and-after#sthash.qwns4XkK.dpuf 27. Cross, *A Quest for Time*, p. 52. 28. Sidney Webb, 'A Plea for an Eight Hours Bill', Fabian Tract no. 16, 1890, p. 1. 29. Green, *The Crisis of Conservatism*, p. 257. 30. Ibid, p. 260. 31. Ibid, p. 243. 32. Yves Guyot, *La famille Pichot. Scènes de l'enfer social*, Jules Rouff, Paris 1882; the description of the manager, M. de Torgnac, is on p. 16. 33. On novels about tramps see Christine Photinos, 'The Tramp in American Literature, 1873–1939': http://ejournals.library.vanderbilt.edu/index.php/ameriquests/article/viewFile/62/60 accessed 16 May 2017; see also Kenneth L. Kusmer, *Down and Out, on the Road: The Homeless in American History*, Oxford University Press 2003, p. 44. 34. Jeffrey L. Sammons, *Wilhelm Raabe: The Fiction of the Alternative Community*, Princeton University Press 1987, pp. 270–71. 35. Daumard, 'Puissance et inquiétudes de la société bourgeoise', p. 501. 36. Guy Chaumel, *Histoire des cheminots et de leurs syndicats*, Rivière, Paris 1948, pp. 20–21. 37. Ibid, pp. 38–9. 38. Marx, *Capital*, vol. 1, pp. 253–4n. 39. François Caron, 'Essai d'analyse historique d'une psychologie du travail. Les mécaniciens et chauffeurs de locomotives du réseau du Nord de 1850 à 1910', *Le Mouvement Social*, no. 50, January–March 1965, pp. 10–11. 40. Barkin, *The Controversy over German Industrialization, 1890–1902*, pp. 140–41. 41. Michael Huberman, 'Working Hours of the World Unite? New International Evidence of Worktime, 1870–1913', *Journal of Economic History*, vol. 64, no. 4, December 2004, see table p. 976. 42. Ibid, pp. 982, 977. 43. Ibid, p. 966. 44. Smith, *Disraelian Conservatism and Social Reform*, p. 202. 45. Ibid, p. 217; see *The Letters of Disraeli to Lady Chesterfield and Lady Bradford*, vol. 1, Appleton and Co., New York 1929, pp. 337–8: https://ia800302.us.archive.org/14/items/lettersofdisrael009336mbp/lettersofdisrael009336mbp.pdf 46. Dicey, *Lectures on the Relation between Law and Public Opinion in England*, p. 238; see also Hennock, *The Origin of the Welfare State in England and Germany*, pp. 70ff. 47. A much fuller list of Victorian legislation can be found at Marjie Bloy, 'Victorian Legislation: A Timeline': http://www.victorianweb.org/history/legistl.html 48. Quoted in Dicey, *Lectures on the Relation between Law and Public Opinion in England*, p. 290. 49. Ibid, pp. 242, 249. 50. Hirata and Sugita, 'Politique paternaliste et division sexuelle du travail', p. 76. 51. Robert Evans, Jr., 'Evolution of the Japanese System of Employer-Employee Relations, 1868–1945', *Business History Review*, vol. 44, no. 1, 1970, p. 119; Neary, *The State and Politics in Japan*, p. 22. 52. Colin Crouch, *Industrial Relations and European State Traditions*, Clarendon Press, Oxford 1993, pp. 68–9, 96–7. 53. Sorlin,

Waldeck-Rousseau, p. 236. 54. Ibid, pp. 275–7. 55. Ibid, pp. 241, 125. 56. Ibid, pp. 295–6. 57. Ibid, p. 357. 58. Pierre Lévêque, *Histoire des forces politiques en France, 1880–1940*, vol. 2, Armand Colin, Paris 1994, p. 24. 59. Dewerpe, *Le monde du travail en France 1800–1950*, pp. 123, 129; British figures in H. A. Clegg, Alan Fox, and A. F. Thompson, *A History of British Trade Unions since 1889*, vol. 1: *1889–1910*, Clarendon Press, Oxford 1964, p. 1; on the trebling of trade unionists see Sorlin, *Waldeck-Rousseau*, p. 356. 60. Edward Shorter and Charles Tilly, *Strikes in France, 1830–1968*, Cambridge University Press 1974, p. 112. 61. Perrot, *Les ouvriers en grève*, p. 51; Shorter and Tilly, *Strikes in France, 1830–1968*, p. 69. 62. Daumard, 'Puissance et inquiétudes de la société bourgeoise', p. 523. 63. Marjorie Milbank Farrar, *Principled Pragmatist: The Political Career of Alexandre Millerand*, Berg, New York and Oxford 1991, p. 45. 64. Ibid, pp. 61–73. 65. Émile Cheysson, *La crise du revenu et la loi du travail*, Comité de défense et de progrès social, Paris 1898, pp.17–18. 66. Huret, *Enquête sur la question sociale en Europe*, pp. 39ff. 67. Ibid, p. 54; on the number employed in the steelworks see René Parize, 'Les militants ouvriers au Creusot pendant les grèves de 1899–1900', *Le Mouvement Social*, no. 99, April–June 1977, p. 97. 68. Ibid, pp. 97–8; Claude Beaud, 'Les Schneider au Creusot: un modèle paternaliste en réponse aux impératifs du libéralisme et à la montée du mouvement socialiste', in Aerts, Beaud, and Stengers (eds), *Liberalism and Paternalism in the 19th Century*, p. 15. 69. Brandes, *American Welfare Capitalism, 1880–1940*, pp. 4–5. 70. Ibid, p. 4. 71. François Weil, 'Les paternalismes aux États-Unis (1800–1930)', in Aerts, Beaud, and Stengers (eds), *Liberalism and Paternalism in the 19th Century*, p. 131. 72. See the entry 'Alphonse de Rothschild' in the *Jewish Encyclopedia* of 1906: http://www.jewishencyclopedia.com/articles/12909-rothschild#anchor9 73. Huret, *Enquête sur la question sociale en Europe*, pp. 64–9. 74. Günther Schulz, 'Industrial Patriarchalism in Germany', in Aerts, Beaud, and Stengers (eds), *Liberalism and Paternalism in the 19th Century*, pp. 62–6. 75. Ralf Dahrendorf, *Society and Democracy in Germany*, Weidenfeld and Nicolson, London 1967, pp. 49–50. 76. Charles-Alfred de Janzé, *Les serfs de la voie ferrée. La vérité et les compagnies*, Tolmer, Paris 1881, p. 15. 77. Koji Taira, 'Factory Legislation and Management Modernization during Japan's Industrialization, 1886–1916', *Business History Review*, vol. 44, no. 1, 1970, p. 89. 78. Lévy, 'La naissance du movement ouvrier moderne au Japon', pp. 122–3; see also Tsuzuki, *The Pursuit of Power in Modern Japan, 1825–1995*, p. 153. 79. Lehmann, *The Roots of Modern Japan*, p. 212. 80. Taira, 'Factory Legislation and Management Modernization during Japan's Industrialization, 1886–1916', pp. 87, 95, 109. 81. Alberti, *Senza lavoro*, p. 45; on the *Cassa di maternità* see Valerio Strinati, 'Origini e istituzione della Cassa di maternità (1875–1910)', *Studi Storici*, vol. 45, no. 2, April–June 2004, pp. 509–53. 82. Giovanni Giolitti, *Discorsi extraparlamentari*, Einaudi, Turin 1952, p. 173. 83. Webster, *Industrial Imperialism in Italy 1908–1915*, p. 344n. 84. Giovanni Giolitti, Speech to the Chamber of Deputies, 4 February 1901, in Giovanni Giolitti, *Discorsi parlamentari*, vol. 2,

Camera dei Deputati, Rome 1953, pp. 626–9. 85. Ibid, pp. 626ff. 86. Cited in Antonino Répaci, *La marcia su Roma*, Rizzoli, Milan 1972, p. 104. 87. Procacci, *La lotta di classe in Italia agli inizi del secolo XX*, pp. 83–5. 88. Giolitti, *Discorsi extraparlamentari*, pp. 105–6. 89. Giovanni Giolitti, Speech to the Camera dei Deputati, 4 February 1901, in Giolitti, *Discorsi parlamentari*, pp. 630, 633; see also Giolitti's speech of 29 October 1899, p. 1,186. 90. Giovanni Giolitti, Speech to the Camera dei Deputati, 21 June 1901, in *Atti parlamentari*, XX legislatura, p. 5,504. 91. For an overview of Giolitti's achievements, see Frank J. Coppa, 'Economic and Ethical Liberalism in Conflict: The Extraordinary Liberalism of Giovanni Giolitti', *Journal of Modern History*, vol. 42, no. 2, June 1970, pp. 191–215. 92. Palmiro Togliatti, 'Discorso su Giolitti', in Palmiro Togliatti, *Momenti della storia d'Italia*, Riuniti, Rome 1974, p. 94. 93. Ernesto Ragionieri, *Storia d'Italia*, vol. 4: *Dall'Unità a oggi*, Einaudi, Turin 1976, p. 1,870. 94. Alberti, *Senza lavoro*, p. 33. 95. Baglioni, *L'ideologia della borghesia industriale*, p. 163. 96. Ibid, p. 168; Amedeo Osti Guerrazzi, *Grande industria e legislazione sociale in età giolittiana*, Paravia, Turin 2000, p. 10. 97. Ragionieri, *Storia d'Italia*, vol. 4: *Dall'Unità a oggi*, pp. 1,866–97; Emilio Gentile, *L'Italia giolittiana*, Il Mulino, Bologna 1990, pp. 229–36; Amedeo Osti Guerrazzi, *Grande industria e legislazione sociale in età giolittiana*, Paravia, Turin 2000, p. 9. 98. See Louis D. Brandeis, *Other People's Money and How the Bankers Use It*, Frederick A. Stokes Co., New York 1914: https://archive.org/stream/otherpeoplesmoneoobran/otherpeoplesmoneoobran_djvu.txt 99. Mark J. Roe, *Strong Managers, Weak Owners: The Political Roots of American Corporate Finance*, Princeton University Press, 1994, p. 3. The separation between owners and managers was famously identified by Adolf Berle and Gardiner Means in their celebrated *The Modern Corporation and Private Property* (1932). 100. Marjorie Kelly, 'The Incredibly Unproductive Shareholder', *Harvard Business Review*, vol. 80, no. 1, January 2002, pp. 18–19. 101. Gérard Duménil and Dominique Lévy, *La grande bifurcation. En finir avec le néolibéralisme*, La Découverte, Paris 2014, p. 29.

16. GOD AND CAPITALISM

1. Charles Dickens, *Bleak House*, Chapter 15. 2. Martin Luther, 'Ninety-Five Theses', thesis no. 27, see: http://www.luther.de/en/95thesen.html 3. Brook, *The Confusions of Pleasure*, pp. 72–3; Ho-fung Hung, *Protest with Chinese Characteristics*, Columbia University Press 2011, p. 24. 4. Figes, *A People's Tragedy*, p. 63. 5. Richard Pipes, *Russia under the Old Regime*, Penguin, London 1984, p. 243 and the whole of Chapter 9. 6. Figes, *A People's Tragedy*, pp. 67, 65. 7. Vera Shevzov, *Russian Orthodoxy on the Eve of Revolution*, Oxford University Press 2004, p. 12. 8. Figes, *A People's Tragedy*, p. 69. 9. Marx, *Capital*, vol. 1, fn 92, Chapter 10, 'The Working Day', p. 206. 10. Max Weber, *The Protestant Ethic and the Spirit of Capitalism*, ed.

and trans. Stephen Kalberg, Blackwell, Oxford 2002, p. 66. 11. R. H. Tawney, *Religion and the Rise of Capitalism*, Transaction Publishers, London 1998, pp. 231–2. 12. Milton Singer, 'Religion and Social Change in India: The Max Weber Thesis, Phase Three', *Economic Development and Cultural Change*, vol. 14, no. 4, July 1966, p. 499. 13. John M. Najemy, *A History of Florence, 1200–1575*, Blackwell, Oxford 2006, p. 100. 14. Davide Cantoni, 'The Economic Effects of the Protestant Reformation: Testing the Weber Hypothesis in the German Lands', *Journal of the European Economic Association*, vol. 13, no. 4, August 2015, pp. 561–98. 15. Sascha O. Becker and Ludger Woessmann, 'Was Weber Wrong? A Human Capital Theory of Protestant Economic History', *Quarterly Journal of Economics*, vol. 124, no. 2, May 2009, pp. 531–96. 16. Max Weber, 'Prefatory Remarks' to *Collected Essays in the Sociology of Religion* (1920), in Weber, *The Protestant Ethic and the Spirit of Capitalism*, p. 153. 17. Blackbourn, *The Fontana History of Germany, 1780–1918*, p. 294. 18. Margaret Lavinia Anderson, 'The Limits of Secularization: On the Problem of the Catholic Revival in Nineteenth-Century Germany', *Historical Journal*, vol. 38, no. 3, September 1995, pp. 648, 652, 653, citing Richard J. Jensen, *The Winning of the Midwest: Social and Political Conflict, 1888–96*, Theodore K. Hoppen, *Elections, Politics and Society in Ireland, 1832–1885*, Oxford University Press 1984, p. 171, and Smith, *German Nationalism and Religious Conflict*, p. 94. 19. Blackbourn, *The Fontana History of Germany, 1780–1918*, p. 285. 20. K. S. Inglis, 'English Nonconformity and Social Reform, 1880–1900', *Past & Present*, no. 13, April 1958, pp. 74, 79. 21. Ibid, p. 83. 22. Ibid, p. 78. 23. Maruyama, *Thought and Behaviour in Modern Japanese Politics*, p. 4. 24. Augustin Berthe, *Garcia Moreno, président de l'Équateur, vengeur et martyr du driot Chrétien (1821–1875)*, Retaux-Bray, Paris 1887, pp. 620–21; this is a deeply Catholic book celebrating Moreno's achievements. 25. Charles A. Hale, 'Political and Social Ideas in Latin America, 1870–1930', in Bethell (ed.), *The Cambridge History of Latin America*, vol. IV, pp. 369, 377. 26. Gaillard, *Jules Ferry*, p. 182. 27. Chastenet, *Histoire de la Troisième République*, p. 223. 28. *Le Républicain de la Loire et de la Haute Loire* of 24 July 1876: http://www.memoireetactualite.org/presse/42LEREPUBLIC/PDF/1876/42LEREPUBLIC-18760724-P-0001.pdf 29. Marc Ferro, *Pétain*, Fayard, Paris 1987, pp. 255–6. 30. Maurice Agulhon, *La République 1880–1932*, vol. I, Hachette, Paris 1990, p. 25. 31. See text of Pius IX's *Quanta Cura* and the *Syllabus of Errors* in: https://archive.org/stream/QuantaCuraTheSyllabusOfErrors_247/pius_ix_pope_quanta_cura_and_the_syllabus_of_errors_djvu.txt 32. Eugène Veuillot, *Çà et là*, vol. 2, Gaume frères et J. Duprey, Paris 1860, pp. 279, 296; see Jean-Marie Mayeur, 'Catholicisme intransigeant, catholicisme social, démocratie chrétienne', *Annales*, vol. 27, no. 2, March–April 1972, p. 486. 33. Saint-Bonnet, *La Restauration française*, pp. 6, 203, 265; pp. vi, 13, 15 (first published in 1851 by Hervé Éditeur). 34. Puissant, '1886, la contre-réforme sociale?', p. 93. 35. (Cardinal) James Gibbons, *A Retrospect of Fifty Years*, 1916: http://www.forgottenbooks.com/readbook/A_Retrospect_of_Fifty_Years_v1_1000611995#229, p. 195.

36. Mayeur, 'Catholicisme intransigeant, catholicisme social, démocratie chrétienne', pp. 490–92. 37. Leo XIII, *Libertas* (paragraphs 10 and 14) in: http://w2.vatican.va/content/leo-xiii/en/encyclicals/documents/hf_l-xiii_enc_20061888_libertas.html 38. Leo XIII, *Quod apostolici muneris* (1878): http://wwwvatican.va/holy_father/leo_xiii/encyclicals/documents/hf_l-xiii_enc_28121878_quod-apostolici-muneris_en.html 39. All quotes from the Vatican translation into English of the original Latin text: Leo XIII, *Rerum Novarum*, 15 May 1891: http://www.vatican.va/holy_father/leo_xiii/encyclicals/documents/hf_l-xiii_enc_15051891_rerum-novarum_en.html 40. Ruggiero Bonghi, 'Leone XIII e il socialismo', *Nuova Antologia*, 1 June 1891: http://www.sintesidialettica.it/leggi_articolo.php?AUTH=207&ID=427&STYLE1=1 41. Jean-Dominique Durand, 'La réception de *Rerum Novarum* par les évêques français', in *Rerum Novarum. Écriture, contenu et réception d'une encyclique*, École Française de Rome, 1997, p. 295. 42. Ibid, p. 296. 43. On the socialist reactions see Peter Doyle, '"Nothing New and Nothing True": Some Socialist Reactions to *Rerum Novarum*', and Frédéric Cépède, 'Les socialistes français et l'encyclique *Rerum Novarum*', in *Rerum Novarum. Écriture, contenu et réception d'une encyclique*, École Française de Rome, 1997. 44. Lévêque, *Histoire des forces politiques en France*, p. 20. 45. Ibid, pp. 31–3. 46. Eugène Flornoy, *La lutte par l'association. L'action libérale populaire*, J. Gabalda et Cie, Paris 1907, p. 8. 47. Frédéric Le Play, *La réforme sociale en France déduite de l'observation comparée des peuples européens*, Mame, Tours 1874 (5th edition, revised), vol. 2 (first published 1864), pp. 107–13, esp. p. 110. 48. Le Play, *La réforme sociale en France*, pp. 7, 12–13. 49. Ibid, p. 36. 50. Dino Del Bo (ed.), *I cattolici italiani di fronte al socialismo*, Edizioni Cinque Lune, Rome 1956, pp. 64–5. 51. Giorgio Candeloro, *Il movimento cattolico in Italia*, Riuniti, Rome 1982, pp. 169–72. 52. Romolo Murri, *Battaglie d'oggi*, vol. 4, Società I.C. di Cultura, Rome 1904, p. 99. 53. Trencsényi et al., *A History of Modern Political Thought in East Central Europe*, p. 415. 54. Charles Kingsley, *His Letters and Memories of his Life*, ed. his wife, vol. 1, Henry S. King & Co., London 1877, p. 313. 55. Ibid, p. 314. 56. For Engels's characterization of William Morris see Friedrich Engels, 'Letter to Friedrich Sorge', 29 April 1886: https://www.marxists.org/archive/marx/works/1886/letters/86_04_29.htm 57. William Morris, Preface to *Signs of Change* (written March 1888), in *The Collected Works of William Morris*, vol. 23, Cambridge University Press 2012, p. 1. 58. Frederick B. Chary, 'Agrarians, Radicals, Socialists, and the Bulgarian Peasantry: 1899–1905', in Ivan Volgyes (ed.), *The Peasantry of Eastern Europe*, vol. 1: *Roots of Rural Transformation*, Pergamon Press, New York 1979, pp. 37–8, 44. 59. John D. Bell, *Peasants in Power: Alexander Stamboliski and the Bulgarian Agrarian National Union, 1899–1923*, Princeton University Press 1977, pp. 81–2. 60. Ibid, pp. 64–6. 61. Hugh Agnew, *The Czechs and the Lands of the Bohemian Crown*, Hoover Press, Stanford, CA 2013, p. 151; A. Paul Kubricht, 'The National-Economic Implications of the Formation of the Czech Agrarian Party (1899)', in Volgyes (ed.), *The Peasantry of Eastern Europe*, vol. 1, pp. 19–25. 62. Catherine Albrecht, 'Rural Banks

and Czech Nationalism in Bohemia, 1848–1914', *Agricultural History*, vol. 78, no. 3, Summer, 2004, p. 319. 63. Agnew, *The Czechs and the Lands of the Bohemian Crown*, p. 151; Rick Fawn and Jiří Hochman, *Historical Dictionary of the Czech State*, Scarecrow Press, Lanham, MD 2010, p. 37. 64. Janos, *The Politics of Backwardness in Hungary*, pp. 146–7. 65. Craig, *Germany 1866–1945*, pp. 72–4. 66. Heinrich August Winkler, *Germany: The Long Road West, 1789–1933*, Oxford University Press 2006, p. 201. 67. Blackbourn, 'The Discreet Charm of the Bourgeoisie', p. 262. 68. Anderson, 'The Limits of Secularization', pp. 647, 667, 669. 69. Ronald J. Ross, 'Enforcing the Kulturkampf in the Bismarckian State and the Limits of Coercion in Imperial Germany', *Journal of Modern History*, vol. 56, no. 3, September 1984, pp. 437ff, 468, 472. 70. Ibid, p. 480. 71. Anderson, *Practicing Democracy*, p. 118. 72. Jonathan Sperber, *The Kaiser's Voters: Electors and Elections in Imperial Germany*, Cambridge University Press 1997, p. 208. 73. Gall, *Bismarck*, p. 207. 74. John W. Boyer, *Political Radicalism in Late Imperial Vienna: Origins of the Christian Social Movement, 1848–1897*, University of Chicago Press, p. 410. 75. Richard Geehr, *Karl Lueger: Mayor of Fin de Siècle Vienna*, Wayne State University Press 1990, pp. 91–9. 76. Boyer, *Political Radicalism in Late Imperial Vienna*, pp. 185, 212. 77. Ibid, pp. 216–19. 78. Ibid, p. 409. 79. Geehr, *Karl Lueger*, p. 152. 80. Boyer, *Political Radicalism in Late Imperial Vienna*, pp. 419–20. 81. Adolf Hitler, *Mein Kampf*, Hutchinson, London 1969, p. 51. 82. Geehr, *Karl Lueger*, p. 144. 83. John W. Boyer, 'The End of an Old Regime: Visions of Political Reform in Late Imperial Austria', *Journal of Modern History*, vol. 58, no. 1, March 1986, pp. 165–9. 84. Boyer, *Political Radicalism in Late Imperial Vienna*, pp. 216–19; Boyer, 'The End of an Old Regime', p. 165. 85. Puissant, '1886, la contre-réforme sociale?', p. 73. 86. Bruno Debaenst, 'Belgian Social Law and its Journals: A Reflected History', in *C@hiers du CRHIDI*, vol. 37, 2015: http://popups.ulg.ac.be/1370-2262/index.php?id=183 87. Strikwerda, *A House Divided*, p. 241. 88. The texts can be found on the following websites: John F. Kennedy, http://www.jfklibrary.org/Research/Research-Aids/Ready-Reference/JFK-Quotations/Inaugural-Address.aspx; Jimmy Carter, http://www.presidency.ucsb.edu/ws/?pid=6575; Ronald Reagan, http://www.presidency.ucsb.edu/ws/?pid=43130; Barack Obama, https://obamawhitehouse.archives.gov/blog/2009/01/21/president-barack-obamas-inaugural-address; Donald Trump, https://www.whitehouse.gov/inaugural-address 89. Nat Turner, *The Confessions of Nat Turner . . . As fully and voluntarily made to Thomas R. Gray*: http://docsouth.unc.edu/neh/turner/turner.html 90. Eugene D. Genovese, 'James Henley Thornwell', in Eugen D. Genovese, *The Southern Front*, University of Missouri Press 1995, pp. 38–9; this essay is a spirited defence of Thornwell. 91. Abraham Lincoln, 'Second Inaugural Address', 4 March 1865: http://avalon.law.yale.edu/19th_century/lincoln2.asp 92. Eric Hobsbawm, *Primitive Rebels: Studies in Archaic Forms of Social Movements in the 19th and 20th Centuries*, Norton, New York 1959, Chapter 4.

17. EUROPE CONQUERS ALL

1. Friedrich Engels, 'Extraordinary Revelations. – Abd-el-Kader. – Guizot's Foreign Policy', *The Northern Star*, 22 January 1848, in Marx and Engels, *Collected Works*, vol. 6, p. 469. 2. William Thackeray, 'Abd-el-Kader at Toulon or, the Caged Hawk', in *The Complete Poems of William Makepeace Thackeray*, White, Stokes, and Allen, New York 1883, p. 25. 3. 'Abd-El-Kader and the United States', *The New York Times*, 20 October 1860: http://www.nytimes.com/1860/10/20/news/abd-el-kader-and-the-united-states.html 4. Henry D'Ideville, *Le maréchal Bugeaud, d'après sa correspondance intime, et des documents inédits, 1784–1849*, vol. 2, Firmin-Didot, Paris 1881, p. 486. 5. Alexis de Tocqueville, *Travail sur l'Algérie*, in *Oeuvres complètes*, Gallimard, Bibliothèque de la Pléiade, Paris 1991, pp. 704–5. 6. For the term 'melancholic colonialism' see Duncan Bell, 'John Stuart Mill on Colonies', *Political Theory*, vol. 38, no. 1, 2010, p. 37. 7. Joseph Chamberlain, *Foreign and Colonial Speeches*, Routledge and Sons, Manchester and London 1897, pp. 245, 242. 8. John O'Sullivan, 'Annexation', *United States Magazine and Democratic Review*, vol. 17, no. 1, July–August 1845. 9. Notable dependency theorists include the Argentinian Raúl Prebisch, the founding secretary-general of the United Nations Conference on Trade and Development (UNCTAD), Samir Amin's *L'impérialisme et le développement inégal* (1976), A. G. Frank, *Capitalism and Underdevelopment in Latin America* (1967), and Immanuel Wallerstein's multi-volume *The Modern World-System*. 10. Leys, *The Rise and Fall of Development Theory*, p. 49. 11. Paul Bairoch, 'International Industrialization Levels from 1750 to 1980', *Journal of European Economic History*, vol. 11, no. 2, Fall 1982, p. 277. 12. Giorgio Riello, *Cotton: The Fabric that Made the Modern World*, Cambridge University Press 2013, pp. 214, 228. 13. Beckert, *Empire of Cotton*, p. 247. 14. Bairoch, *Economics and World History*, pp. 88–9. 15. Beckert, *Empire of Cotton*, pp. 324–5. 16. Ibid, pp. 329–30. 17. Stiglitz, 'Is there a Post-Washington Consensus Consensus?', p. 50. 18. Beckert, *Empire of Cotton*, p. 299. 19. Laxman D. Satya, *Cotton and Famine in Berar, 1850–1900*, Manohar, New Delhi 1997, p. 141. 20. Beckert, *Empire of Cotton*, p. 255. 21. Satya, *Cotton and Famine in Berar, 1850–1900*, pp. 279–81. 22. Mike Davis, *Late Victorian Holocausts: El Niño Famines and the Making of the Third World*, Verso Books, London 2001, pp. 26–7. 23. Ibid, p. 7; Beckert, *Empire of Cotton*, p. 337. 24. William Digby, *'Prosperous' British India: A Revelation from Official Records*, T. Fisher Unwin, London 1901, pp. 118, 126–7: https://archive.org/details/ProsperousBritishIndiaARevelationWilliamDigby 25. Ibid, p. 24. 26. James Vernon, *Hunger: A Modern History*, Belknap Press of Harvard University Press 2007, p. 51. 27. Ibid, pp. 52–3. 28. Janam Mukherjee, *Hungry Bengal: War, Famine and the End of Empire*, Hurst & Co, London 2015, pp. 83, 251; Amartya Sen, *Poverty and Famines: An Essay on Entitlement and Deprivation*, Oxford University Press 1981, p. 52. 29. Mukherjee, *Hungry Bengal*, pp. 185–6; Wavell cited in Sen, *Poverty and Famines*,

p. 79. 30. Churchill's responsibility during the Bengal famine is not mentioned in Martin Gilbert's multi-volume biography of Churchill. For a full account see Madhusree Mukerjee, *Churchill's Secret War: The British Empire and the Ravaging of India during World War II*, Basic Books, New York 2010; see also Arthur Herman, *Gandhi and Churchill*, Random House, London 2010, p. 513. 31. C. A. Bayly, *Indian Society and the Making of the British Empire*, Cambridge University Press 1988, p. 201. 32. Paul Kennedy, 'Continuity and Discontinuity in British Imperialism, 1815–1914', in C. C. Eldridge (ed.), *British Imperialism in the Nineteenth Century*, Macmillan, London 1984, p. 26. 33. Bairoch, 'International Industrialization Levels from 1750 to 1980', p. 279. 34. Sylvanus Cookey, *King Jaja of the Niger Delta: His Life and Times, 1821–1891*, NOK publishers, New York 1974, pp. 101–3. 35. Ibid, pp. 119, 127. 36. Ibid, p. 167. 37. Beckert, *Empire of Cotton*, p. 131. 38. P. J. Vatikiotis, *The Modern History of Egypt*, Weidenfeld and Nicolson, London 1969, pp. 131, 137. 39. Cited in ibid, p. 141. 40. Ibid, pp. 141–4. 41. William L. Langer, *The Diplomacy of Imperialism, 1890–1902*, vol. 1, Knopf, New York 1935, p. 103. 42. Juan R. I. Cole, *Colonialism and Revolution in the Middle East: Social and Cultural Origins of the 'Urabi Movement*, American University in Cairo Press 1999, pp. 235–7. 43. See Gladstone's cabinet note of 3 July 1882 in *Gladstone Diaries*, vol. X, p. 291, and his letter to Bright, p. 298; see the discussion in A. G. Hopkins, 'The Victorians and Africa: A Reconsideration of the Occupation of Egypt, 1882', *Journal of African History*, vol. 27, no. 2, 1986, esp. pp. 380–85. 44. Keith Robbins, *John Bright*, Routledge and Kegan Paul, London 1979, p. 246; for Gladstone's urging him to reflect see his note to John Bright, in *Gladstone Diaries*, vol. X, p. 295. 45. Ahmed Kassab, *Histoire de la Tunisie. L'époque contemporaine*, Société tunisienne de diffusion, Tunis 1976, p. 8; Jean Ganiage, 'North Africa', in *The Cambridge History of Africa*, vol. 6, Cambridge University Press 1985, p. 184. 46. Kassab, *Histoire de la Tunisie*, p. 13. 47. Jean-François Martin, *Histoire de la Tunisie contemporaine. De Ferry à Bourguiba, 1881–1956*, L'Harmattan, Paris 2003, p. 52. 48. Niall Ferguson, *Empire: How Britain Made the Modern World*, Penguin, London 2004, pp. 365–6. 49. http://www.unohrlls.org/UserFiles/File/UN_LDC_Factsheet_053112.pdf 50. Sabato, 'Citizenship, Political Participation and the Formation of the Public Sphere in Buenos Aires 1850s–1880s', pp. 140–41. 51. Bonham C. Richardson, *The Caribbean in the Wider World, 1492–1992: A Regional Geography*, Cambridge University Press 1992, pp. 60–62, 33. 52. Alice H. Amsden, *Escape from Empire: The Developing World's Journey through Heaven and Hell*, The MIT Press, Cambridge, MA 2007, p. 11. 53. Jun Uchida, *Brokers of Empire: Japanese Settler Colonialism in Korea, 1876–1945*, Harvard University Press 2011, pp. 10–11. 54. Jordan Sand, 'Subaltern Imperialists: The New Historiography of the Japanese Empire', *Past & Present*, no. 225, November 2014, pp. 277–8, 285. 55. Iriye, *Pacific Estrangement*, pp. 130–32. 56. Marx, *Capital*, vol. 1, p. 751. 57. Charles-Maurice de Talleyrand, *Mémoires du prince de Talleyrand*, vol. 1, Calmann Lévy, Paris 1891, p. 237. 58. Max Weber, *General Economic History* (1927),

The Free Press, Glencoe, IL 1927, 1950, p. 298. 59. Montesquieu, *De l'esprit des lois*, vol. 2, livre XX, Chapter 1, pp. 609–10. 60. J. Y. Wong, *Deadly Dreams: Opium, Imperialism, and the Arrow War (1856–60) in China*, Cambridge University Press 1998, pp. 339–43. 61. Ibid, p. 350. 62. Ibid, p. 378. 63. Ibid, pp. 390 and 429. 64. The text can be read on: http://web.jjay.cuny.edu/~jobrien/reference/ob24.html 65. Rebecca E. Karl, 'Creating Asia: China in the World at the Beginning of the Twentieth Century', *American Historical Review*, vol. 103, no. 4, October 1998, p. 1,103. 66. Hsü, *The Rise of Modern China*, pp. 432–6. 67. Hans-Ulrich Wehler, *The German Empire, 1871–1918*, Berg, Leamington Spa 1985, p. 174. 68. Woodruff D. Smith, 'The Ideology of German Colonialism, 1840–1906', *Journal of Modern History*, vol. 46, no. 4, December 1974, p. 648. 69. Osterhammel, *The Transformation of the World*, p. 419. 70. Anon., 'England's Outlook in East Africa', *Fortnightly Review*, no. 281, May 1890, p. 770. 71. Joseph Chamberlain, Speech to the House of Commons, 20 March 1893, in *Mr. Chamberlain's Speeches*, ed. Charles W. Boyd, vol. 1, Constable, London 1914. 72. There is a long and interesting debate on the concept of informal empire. See, among others, J. Gallagher and R. Robinson, 'The Imperialism of Free Trade', *Economic History Review*, 1953; Platt, *Finance, Trade, and Politics in British Foreign Policy, 1815–1914*; Andrew Thompson, 'Informal Empire? An Exploration in the History of Anglo-Argentine Relations, 1810–1914', *Journal of Latin American Studies*, vol. 24, no. 2, 1992, pp. 419–36, and A. G. Hopkins, 'Informal Empire in Argentina: An Alternative View', *Journal of Latin American Studies*, vol. 26, no. 2, May 1994, pp. 469–84. 73. See the account on the British invasion of Tibet in Charles Allen, *Duel in the Snows: The True Story of the Younghusband Mission to Lhasa*, John Murray, London 2004, esp. pp. 1–2, 29–31, 111–27; see also John Powers, *History as Propaganda: Tibetan Exiles versus the People's Republic of China*, Oxford University Press 2004, p. 80; and, for an account more generous towards Curzon, see David Gilmour, *Curzon: Imperial Statesman, 1859–1925*, John Murray, London 2004, pp. 275–7. 74. Marius B. Jansen, *The Making of Modern Japan*, Belknap Press, Cambridge, MA 2000, p. 432. 75. Yukichi Fukuzawa, *The Autobiography of Yukichi Fukuzawa*, p. 415. 76. Mori Ōgai, 'Yellow Peril', in Richard John Bowring, *Mori Ōgai and the Modernization of Japanese Culture*, Cambridge University Press 1979, p. 120. 77. Inagaki, *Japan and the Pacific*, p. 47. 78. Ibid, p. 54. 79. W. G. Beasley, *Japanese Imperialism, 1894–1945*, Clarendon Press, Oxford 1987, p. 9; see also Marius B. Jansen, 'Japanese Imperialism: Late Meiji Perspectives', in *The Japanese Colonial Empire, 1895–1945*, ed. Ramon Hawley Myers and Mark R. Peattie, Princeton University Press, 1984, pp. 61–79. 80. Uchida, *Brokers of Empire*, p. 394. 81. Quoted in Jansen, 'Japanese Imperialism', p. 64. 82. Akira Iriye, 'Japan's Drive to Great-Power Status', in *The Cambridge History of Japan*, vol. 5: *The Nineteenth Century*, ed. Marius B. Jansen, Cambridge University Press 1989, pp. 753–5. 83. Dudden, *Japan's Colonization of Korea: Discourse and Power*, pp. 47–8; see also Naoyuki Umemori, 'The Historical Contexts of the High Treason Incident', in Masako Gavin and Ben

Middleton (eds), *Japan and the High Treason Incident*, Routledge, London and New York 2013, pp. 56–7. 84. Dudden, *Japan's Colonization of Korea*, p. 101. 85. Tierney, *Tropics of Savagery*, p. 44. 86. Ibid, pp. 38–9. 87. Kōtoku Shūsui, *L'impérialisme, le spectre du XXe siècle*, translated into French by Christine Lévy, CNRS éditions, Paris 2008, p. 127. 88. Iriye, *Pacific Estrangement*, p. 76. 89. Naoyuki, 'The Historical Context of the High Treason Incident', p. 52. 90. See figures in Patrick O'Brien and Leandro Prados de la Escosura, 'The Costs and Benefits for Europeans from their Empires Overseas', *Revista de Historia Económica*, vol. 16, no. 1, Winter 1998, p. 61. 91. An excellent survey can be found in Richard Gott, *Britain's Empire: Resistance, Repression and Revolt*, Verso, London 2012; see, for instance, pp. 138ff, 242, 108. 92. Shula Marks, *Reluctant Rebellion: The 1906–8 Disturbances in Natal*, Clarendon Press, Oxford 1970, p. 237. 93. John Iliffe, 'The Organization of the Maji Maji Rebellion', *Journal of African History*, vol. 8, no. 3, November 1967, esp. pp. 497–500. 94. Thomas Bender, *A Nation among Nations*, Hill and Wang, New York 2006, p. 230. 95. Ibid, p. 231. 96. See Marc Ferro, 'Introduction' to *Le livre noir du colonialisme*, Robert Laffont, Paris 2003. 97. On the massacre of the Herero people, see David Olusoga and Casper W. Erichsen, *The Kaiser's Holocaust: Germany's Forgotten Genocide and the Colonial Roots of Nazism*, Faber and Faber, London 2010. 98. Isabel V. Hull, *Absolute Destruction: Military Culture and the Practices of War in Imperial Germany*, Cornell University Press 2004, pp. 8, 11. 99. Ibid, pp. 25, 29, 33. 100. Ibid, pp. 57–9, 88. 101. BBC, 'Germany Admits Namibia Genocide': http://news.bbc.co.uk/1/hi/world/africa/3565938.stm 102. David Van Reybrouck, *Congo: The Epic History of a People*, Fourth Estate, London 2014, pp. 90–94. 103. Ibid, pp. 94–5. 104. Adam Hochschild, *King Leopold's Ghost: A Story of Greed, Terror, and Heroism in Colonial Africa*, Macmillan, London 2000, p. 227. 105. Ibid, p. 229. 106. Ibid, pp. 231–3. 107. Émile Vandervelde, *Les crimes de la colonisation capitaliste. Interpellation de Vandervelde au Gouvernement*, Volksdrukkerij, Gand 1906, p. 10. 108. Émile Vandervelde, *Les derniers jours de l'État du Congo. Journal de voyage (juillet–octobre 1908)*, Édition de la Société Nouvelle, Mons 1909, pp. 189–96. 109. Liebman, *Les socialistes belges, 1885–1914*, p. 221. 110. Ronald Robinson and John Gallagher, *Africa and the Victorians: The Official Mind of Imperialism*, Macmillan, London 1965. 111. Ronald Robinson, 'European Imperialism and Indigenous Reactions in British West Africa, 1880–1914', in H. L. Wesseling (ed.), *Expansion and Reaction*, Leiden University Press 1978, p. 144. 112. Bayly, *Indian Society and the Making of the British Em*[illegible]–114. [illegible] 115. Ashley Jackson, *The British Empire: A Very Short Introduction*, Oxford University Press 2013, pp. 4–5. 116. Bernard Porter, *The Lion's Share: A Short History of British Imperialism, 1850–1970*, Longman, London and New York, 1975, p. 2. 117. Spulber, *Russia's Economic Transitions*, p. 7. 118. Porter, *The Lion's Share*, p. 76. 119. Jules Ferry, speech of 28 July 1885 in *1885: le tournant colonial de la République. Jules Ferry contre Georges Clemenceau*, introduction by Gilles Manceron, La Découverte/Poche, Paris 2007, pp. 60–62. 120. Gougeon, 'Les élites dirigeantes dans l'Allemagne des années 1890', p. 244. 121. Treitschke and Hausrath, *Treitschke*, pp. 200, 210. 122. Smith, 'The Ideology of German Colonialism, 1840–1906', pp. 643–4. 123. Treitschke and Hausrath, *Treitschke*, p. 203. 124. Arne Perras, *Carl Peters and German Imperialism, 1856–1918*, Oxford University Press 2004, pp. 197–9, 247–9. 125. On *Weltpolitik* see Aloys Schumacher, 'L'Allemagne à la fin du XIXe siècle, l'illusion de la "Weltpolitik" et l'interrogation sur les limites de siècles', in *Les limites de siècles. Lieux de ruptures novatrices depuis les temps modernes*, ed. Marita Gilli, Presses Universitaires Franc-Comtoises 1998, pp. 225–36. 126. Wehler, *The German Empire, 1871–1918*, p. 174. 127. Geoff Eley, *Reshaping the German Right: Radical Nationalism and Political Change after Bismarck*, Yale University Press 1980, pp. 173, 366. 128. Engels to Bebel, in Karl Marx and Friedrich Engels, *Collected Works*, vol. 47: *Letters 1883–1887*, Lawrence and Wishart, London 2010, electronic edition, p. 55. 129. Smith, 'The Ideology of German Colonialism, 1840–1906', p. 655. 130. John Phillip Short, *Magic Lantern Empire: Colonialism and Society in Germany*, Cornell University Press 2012, p. 25. 131. Adrian Vickers, *A History of Modern Indonesia*, Cambridge University Press 2005, p. 13. 132. H. L. Wesseling, *Imperialism and Colonialism: Essays on the History of European Expansion*, Greenwood Press, Westport, CT 1997, pp. 79, 82. 133. Pierre van der Eng, 'Exploring Exploitation: The Netherlands and Colonial Indonesia, 1870–1940', *Revista de Historia Económica*, vol. 16, no. 1, Winter 1998, pp. 293, 299. 134. Duggan, *Francesco Crispi*, p. 695. 135. Raymond Jonas, *The Battle of Adwa: African Victory in the Age of Empire*, Harvard University Press 2011, pp. 3–4. 136. Giolitti, *Discorsi extraparlamentari*, p. 105. 137. Stefano Jacini, *Pensieri sulla politica italiana*, G. Civelli, Florence 1889, pp. 58ff; see also Maria Giovanna Missaggia, *Stefano Jacini e la classe politica liberale*, Leo S. Olschki, Florence 2003, p. 376. The term came to be used in French, *mégalomanie*, and from then in English. 138. Giovanni Federico, 'Italy's Late and Unprofitable Forays into Empire', *Revista de Historia Económica*, vol. 16, no. 1, Winter 1998, p. 381. 139. Gramsci, *Il Risorgimento*, p. 102. 140. Gian Luca Podestà, 'L'émigration italienne en Afrique orientale', *Annales de démographie historique*, no. 113, 1, 2007, pp. 59–60. 141. Webster, *Industrial Imperialism in Italy, 1908–1915*, p. 51; on the large size of Italian emigration to Argentina see Friedman, 'Beyond "Voting with their Feet"', pp. 558–9. 142. Zamagni, *The Economic History of Italy, 1860–1990*, p. 123. 143. Alberti, *Senza lavoro*, p. 26. 144. Pedro Lains, 'An Account of the Portuguese African Empire, 1885–1975', *Revista de Historia Económica*, vol. 16, no. 1, Winter 1998, pp. 238–40. 145. Gervase Clarence-Smith, *The Third Portuguese Empire, 1825–1975: A Study in Economic Imperialism*, Manchester University Press 1983, p. 61. 146. Ibid, p. 83. 147. João Ferreira Duarte, 'The Politics of Non-Translation: A Case Study in Anglo-Portuguese Relations', *TTR:*

traduction, terminologie, redaction, vol. 13, no. 1, 2000, p. 104: http://www.erudit.org/revue/TTR/2000/v13/n1/037395ar.pdf 148. A. H. de Oliveira Marques, *Histoire du Portugal et de son empire colonial*, Karthala, Paris 1998, p. 422. 149. Payne, *A History of Spain and Portugal*, p. 525. 150. Oliveira Marques, *Histoire du Portugal et de son empire colonial*, pp. 413–15. 151. Clarence-Smith, *The Third Portuguese Empire, 1825–1975*, pp. 105–6. 152. Fraile and Escribano, 'The Spanish 1898 Disaster', p. 265. 153. Ibid, p. 281. 154. Pierre Paul Leroy-Beaulieu, 'Les États-Unis, puissance coloniale', *Revue des deux mondes*, January 1902, p. 85. 155. Jose A. Lansang, 'The Philippine-American Experiment: A Filipino View', *Pacific Affairs*, vol. 25, no. 3, September 1952, p. 226. 156. Woodrow Wilson, 'Democracy and Efficiency', *Atlantic Monthly*, vol. 87, no. 521, March 1901, pp. 292, 297–8. 157. Theodore Roosevelt, 'State of the Union Address', 6 December 1904: http://www.infoplease.com/t/hist/state-of-the-union/116.html 158. The characterization of Roosevelt cited is Philip Secor's; see his *Presidential Profiles: From George Washington to G. W. Bush*, iUniverse, Bloomington, IN 2008, p. 283. 159. Hofstadter, *Social Darwinism in American Thought*, p. 175. 160. Full text of Roosevelt's speech 'The Strenuous Life', the Hamilton Club, Chicago, 10 April 1899: https://en.wikisource.org/wiki/The_Strenuous_Life; see also Hofstadter, *Social Darwinism in American Thought*, p. 184. 161. William Graham Sumner, 'The Conquest of the United States by Spain', originally in *The International Monthly* then in *War and Other Essays*, Yale University Press 1911, pp. 303–5. 162. Alexander Livingston, *Damn Great Empires! William James and the Politics of Pragmatism*, Oxford University Press 2016, p. 59. 163. 'Death of Mr. Cecil Rhodes', *Manchester Guardian*, 27 March 1902: https://www.theguardian.com/century/1899-1909/Story/0,,126334,00.html?redirection=century 164. For a more generous view of the East India Company see a view from India: Tirthankar Roy, *The East India Company: The World's Most Powerful Corporation*, Allen Lane, Penguin Books India, New Delhi 2012, esp. pp. 174–86. 165. Jeremy Bentham, *An Introduction to the Principles of Morals and Legislation*, cited by Nick Robins in the epilogue of *The Corporation that Changed the World: How the East India Company Shaped the Modern Multinational*, Pluto Press, London 2012. 166. Richard Bourke, *Empire & Revolution: The Political Life of Edmund Burke*, Princeton University Press 2015, p. 563. 167. Smith, *An Inquiry into the Nature and Causes of the Wealth of Nations*, p. 616. 168. Philip Lawson, *The East India Company: A History*, Longman, London 1993, p. 137. 169. Ibid, pp. 156–9. 170. H. V. Bowen, *The Business of Empire: The East India Company and Imperial Britain, 1756–1833*, Cambridge University Press 2006, p. 297. 171. Lawson, *The East India Company*, p. 162. 172. Bouda Etemad, 'Grandeur et vicissitudes du débat colonial. Tendances récentes de l'histoire de la colonisation', *Tiers-Monde*, vol. 28, no. 112, 1987, p. 804. 173. Bairoch, *Economics and World History*, p. 27. 174. See S. B. Saul, 'The Export Economy 1870–1914', *Bulletin of Economic Research*, vol. 17, no. 1, May 1965, pp. 5–18. 175. Robert Hughes, *The Culture of Complaint: The Fraying of America*, Oxford University

Press 1993, p. 88. 176. Jacques Marseille, *Empire colonial et capitalisme français. Histoire d'un divorce*, Albin Michel, Paris 1984, p. 35. 177. Jean-François Sirinelli, 'Guerre d'Algérie, guerre des pétitions?', in Jean-Pierre Rioux and Jean-François Sirinelli (eds), *La Guerre d'Algérie et les intellectuels français*, Éditions Complexe, Brussels 1991, p. 290. 178. See video of press conference: http://www.ina.fr/fresques/de-gaulle/fiche-media/Gaulle00218/conference-de-presse-du-11-avril-1961. 179. Marseille, *Empire colonial et capitalisme français*, p. 359. 180. John Darwin, *The Empire Project: The Rise and Fall of the British World System, 1830–1970*, Cambridge University Press 2009, pp. 617–18. 181. Caroline Elkins, *Imperial Reckoning: The Untold Story of Britain's Gulag in Kenya*, Holt and Co., New York 2005, pp. 144–5, 156ff. 182. William Hague, Statement of the Secretary of State for Foreign and Commonwealth Affairs, House of Commons, 6 June 2013, Mau Mau Claims (Settlement): http://www.publications.parliament.uk/pa/cm201314/cmhansrd/cm130606/debtext/130606-0002.htm#13060646000005 183. Bouda Etemad, *De l'utilité des empires. Colonisation et prospérité de l'Europe*, Armand Colin, Paris 2005, pp. 211–13. 184. R. J. Moore, 'India and the British Empire', in C. C. Eldridge (ed.), *British Imperialism in the Nineteenth Century*, Macmillan, London 1984, p. 74. 185. On the number of settlers see Pierre Brocheux and Daniel Hémery, *Indochine: la colonisation ambiguë, 1858–1954*, La Découverte, Paris 1995, p. 175. 186. Patrick O'Brien, 'The Costs and Benefits of British Imperialism, 1846–1914', *Past & Present*, no. 120, August 1988, p. 166. 187. Patrick O'Brien, 'European Economic Development: The Contribution of the Periphery', *Economic History Review*, vol. 35, no. 1, February 1982, pp. 1–18. 188. Bairoch, *Economics and World History*, pp. 72–3.

18. THE GREAT COLONIAL DEBATE: THE FRENCH AND THE BRITISH

1. An excellent survey of the debate is Avner Offer, 'The British Empire, 1870–1914: A Waste of Money?', *Economic History Review*, vol. 46, no. 2, 1993, pp. 215–38. See also Michael Edelstein, *Overseas Investment in the Age of High Imperialism: The United Kingdom, 1850–1914*, Columbia University Press 1982; Lance E. Davis and Robert A. Huttenback, *Mammon and the Pursuit of Empire: The Economics of British Imperialism,* Cambridge University Press 1988; Etemad, 'Grandeur et vicissitudes du débat colonial', p. 799. 2. S. M. Mollan, 'Business Failure, Capital Investment and Information: Mining Companies in the Anglo-Egyptian Sudan, 1900–1913', *Journal of Imperial and Commonwealth History*, vol. 37, no. 2, June 2009, p. 230. 3. Landes, *Unbound Prometheus*, p. 241. 4. Hitchins, *Rumania*, pp. 188–9. 5. Berindei, 'The Nineteenth Century', p. 230. 6. Robinson, 'European Imperialism and Indigenous Reactions', p. 142. 7. Annie Rey-Goldzeiguer, *Le royaume arabe. La politique algérienne de Napoléon III, 1861–1870*, SNED, Algiers

1977, pp. 584–5. 8. D. C. M. Platt, 'Economic Factors in British Policy during the "New Imperialism"', *Past & Present*, no. 39, April 1968, p. 125. 9. Marseille, *Empire colonial et capitalisme français*, pp. 40–41, 50–51. 10. Jean Fremigacci, 'L'état colonial français, du discours mythique aux réalités (1880–1940)', *Matériaux pour l'histoire de notre temps*, nos 32–3, 1993, p. 33. 11. Emma Rothschild, *The Inner Life of Empires: An Eighteenth-Century History*, Princeton University Press 2011, pp. 211–12. 12. Samuel Johnson, *The Life of Savage*, para 210: http://andromeda.rutgers.edu/~jlynch/Texts/savage.html 13. Smith, *An Inquiry into the Nature and Causes of the Wealth of Nations*, p. 498. 14. Hobson, 'Free Trade and Foreign Policy', pp. 172–5. 15. Ibid, p. 167. 16. Ibid, p. 168. 17. Ibid; see Richard Cobden's speech made at Wrexham, in Wales, under the auspices of the Peace Society on 14 November 1850, and the speech he delivered before the Manchester Chamber of Commerce on 25 October 1862: http://www.econlib.org/library/YPDBooks/Cobden/cbdSPP.html 18. P. J. Cain, 'Variations on a Famous Theme: Hobson, International Trade and Imperialism, 1902–1938', in Michael Freeden (ed.), *Reappraising J. A. Hobson*, Unwin Hyman, London 1990, p. 33. 19. Mill, *Considerations on Representative Government*, p. 322 (Chapter 18). 20. John Stuart Mill, 'A Few Words on Non-Intervention', in John Stuart Mill, *Dissertations and Discussions: Political, Philosophical, and Historical*, Longmans, Green, Reader, and Dyer, London 1867–75, vol. 3, pp. 167–8. 21. John Stuart Mill, 'Civilization', originally in *London and Westminster Review*, April 1836, reprinted in Mill, *Dissertations and Discussions*, vol. 1, p. 165. 22. James Lorimer, *The Institutes of the Law of Nations: A Treatise of the Jural Relations of Separate Political Communities*, vol. 1, Blackwood, Edinburgh 1883, pp. 102–3. 23. Samuel Taylor Coleridge, *Specimens of the Table Talk of the Late Samuel Taylor Coleridge*, John Murray, London 1835, vol. 2, p. 166: http://archive.org/stream/specimensoftable02cole#page/n5/mode/2up 24. Hegel, *The Philosophy of History*, p. 157. 25. Victor Hugo, 'Discours sur l'Afrique', 18 May 1879, in *Actes et Paroles IV*, in *Politique*, Robert Laffont, Paris 1985, p. 1,012. 26. Capitaine Renard, *La colonisation au Congo Français. Étude sur les Concessions accordées au Congo en vertu du décret du 28 mars 1899*, Kugelmann, Paris 1901, pp. 56ff. 27. See the account in Richard West, *Brazza of the Congo: European Exploration and Exploitation in French Equatorial Africa*, Jonathan Cape, London 1972, pp. 183–6. 28. Ibid, p. 188. 29. Ibid, p. 163. 30. John Flint, *Cecil Rhodes*, Hutchinson, London, 1976, pp. 248–9. 31. H. C. G. Matthew, 'Introduction', in *The Gladstone Diaries*, vol. X: *January 1881–June 1883*, ed. H. C. G. Matthew, Clarendon Press, Oxford 1990, p. xc. 32. Peter Cain, 'Was it Worth Having? The British Empire, 1850–1950', *Revista de Historia Económica*, vol. 16, no. 1, Winter 1998, p. 351. 33. Langer, *The Diplomacy of Imperialism, 1890–1902*, p. 77. 34. Ibid, p. 78. 35. This is the main thesis of Frank Trentmann's *Free Trade Nation*, Oxford University Press 2008. 36. P. J. Cain and A. G. Hopkins, *British Imperialism: Innovation and Expansion, 1688–1914*, Longman, London 1993, pp. 141–3. 37. Trentmann, *Free Trade Nation*, pp. 178, 321–2. 38. The argument is developed by Cain and Hopkins, *British Imperialism*, esp. Chapters 3 and 7. 39. Michael Edelstein, 'Foreign Investment and Empire, 1860–1914', in Roderick Floud and Donald McCloskey (eds), *The Economic History of Britain since 1700*, vol. 2: *1860 to the 1970s*, Cambridge University Press 1981, p. 70. 40. Davis and Huttenback, *Mammon and the Pursuit of Empire*, pp. 112–21. 41. Cited in ibid, p. 121. 42. Keith M. Wilson (ed.), *The International Impact of the Boer War*, Routledge, London 2014 (revised ed.), pp. 160–61. 43. O'Brien, 'The Costs and Benefits of British Imperialism, 1846–1914', pp. 189, 192, 197. 44. Davis and Huttenback, *Mammon and the Pursuit of Empire*, pp. 14–15; O'Brien, 'The Costs and Benefits of British Imperialism, 1846–1914', pp. 187, 188; see also the ensuing debate: Paul Kennedy's response in *Past & Present*, no. 125, November 1989, pp. 186–192, and Patrick O'Brien's reply, pp. 192–9. 45. According to Avner Offer, Great Britain spent less than France except during the Boer War; see his 'The British Empire, 1870–1914', p. 225. 46. Edelstein, 'Foreign Investment and Empire, 1860–1914', p. 74. 47. Karl Marx, *Capital*, vol. 3, Progress Publishers, Moscow 1971, p. 249. 48. D. C. M. Platt, 'Canada and Argentina: The First Preference of the British Investor, 1904–14', *Journal of Imperial and Commonwealth History*, vol. 13, no. 3, May 1985, p. 80. 49. All figures in Davis and Huttenback, *Mammon and the Pursuit of Empire*, pp. 43–52. 50. Ferguson, *Empire*, p. 317. 51. Rudyard Kipling, 'The Lesson', first published in *The Times*, 29 July 1901. 52. Green, *The Crisis of Conservatism*, p. 17. 53. Halik Kochanski, 'Wolseley and the South African War', in John Gooch (ed.), *The Boer War: Direction, Experience, and Image*, Frank Cass, London 2000, p. 59. 54. John R. Seeley, *The Expansion of England: Two Courses of Lectures*, Macmillan, London 1914, p. 233. 55. Gaillard, *Jules Ferry*, p. 357. 56. H. H. (Sir 'Harry') Johnston, 'The Development of Tropical Africa under British Auspices', *Fortnightly Review*, no. 86, October 1890, p. 687. 57. N. J. Ryan, *The Making of Modern Malaysia*, Oxford University Press, Kuala Lumpur 1967, pp. 122–3, cited in Porter, *The Lion's Share*, p. 5. 58. Seeley, *The Expansion of England*, p. 10. 59. Bernard Porter, *The Absent-Minded Imperialists: Empire, Society, and Culture in Britain*, Oxford University Press 2004, p. 53, who takes his title from John Seeley's remark cited above. 60. Ibid, p. 161. 61. Ibid, p. 49. 62. Wiener, *English Culture and the Decline of the Industrial Spirit, 1850–1980*, p. 84; see C. R. L. Fletcher and Rudyard Kipling, *A History of England*, Doubleday, Page and Co., New York 1911, pp. 246–7. 63. Fletcher and Kipling, *A History of England*, p. 299. 64. Ozouf, 'Le thème du patriotisme dans les manuels primaires', p. 23. 65. Ibid, p. 24. 66. David Cannadine, *Ornamentalism: How the British Saw their Empire*, Penguin, London 2002, p. 29. 67. Porter, *The Absent-Minded Imperialists*, p. 254. 68. The British MP John Bright (1811–89) in a speech to his constituents, Birmingham Town Hall, 29 October 1858, cited in Herman, *Gandhi and Churchill*, p. 29. 69. Hobson, *Imperialism*, p. 158. 70. Hubert Deschamps, 'La vocation coloniale et métier d'administrateur', *Afrique française*, September 1931, p. 499, cited in William B. Cohen, 'The Lure of Empire:

Why Frenchmen Entered the Colonial Service', *Journal of Contemporary History*, vol. 4, no. 1, 1969, p. 111. By 1960, Deschamps had reached the summit of the French colonial service as Gouverneur-Général des Colonies. 71. Bédarida, 'Perspectives sur le mouvement ouvrier et l'impérialisme', pp. 34–5. 72. Maurice Zimmermann. 'Leçon d'ouverture du cours d'histoire et de géographie coloniales', *Annales de Géographie*, vol. 9, no. 43, 1900, pp. 76–80. 73. Offer, 'The British Empire, 1870–1914', p. 236. 74. Catherine Hall and Sonya Rose (eds), *At Home with the Empire: Metropolitan Culture and the Imperial World*, Cambridge University Press 2006, pp. 2, 25. 75. Joanna de Groot, 'Metropolitan Desires and Colonial Connections: Reflections on Consumption and Empire', in Hall and Rose (eds), *At Home with the Empire*, pp. 172, 176–7. 76. Ardant, *Histoire financière*, p. 333. 77. Porter, *The Absent-Minded Imperialists*, pp. 238–40. 78. Ibid, p. 306. 79. Roberts, *Salisbury*, p. 694. 80. Lord Robert Cecil (Lord Salisbury), 'English Politics and Parties', *Bentley's Quarterly Review*, vol. 1, March 1859, p. 25. 81. Speech to the Constitutional Club, December 1898, cited in Roberts, *Salisbury*, p. 667. 82. See Lord Salisbury's speech to the House of Lords on the Second Reading of the Anglo-German Agreement Bill, 10 July 1890: http://hansard.millbanksystems.com/lords/1890/jul/10/second-reading-2 83. Benjamin Disraeli (Lord Beaconsfield), *Selected Speeches*, vol. 2, edited by T. E. Kebbel, Longmans, Green and Co., London 1882, pp. 523–35, esp. pp. 527–8. 84. Ibid, pp. 530–31. 85. Cain and Hopkins, *British Imperialism*, pp. 381–2. 86. Daniel J. Rankin, *The Zambesi Basin and Nyassaland*, Blackwood, London 1893, pp. 204, 263. 87. Thomas Babington Macaulay, Speech of 10 July 1833, in *Miscellaneous Writings and Speeches*, vol. 4: http://www.gutenberg.org/etext/2170 88. Peter Handford, 'Edward John Eyre and the Conflict of Laws', *Melbourne Law Review*, vol. 32, no. 3, 2008: http://www.austlii.edu.au/au/journals/MelbULawRw/2008/26.html 89. Letter of 30 November 1865, cited in Peter Ackroyd, *Dickens*, Vintage, London 1999, p. 1,025. 90. Joseph Chamberlain, Speech to the House of Commons, 20 March 1893, in *Mr. Chamberlain's Speeches*, vol. 1, p. 345. 91. Ibid, p. 89. 92. Ibid, pp. 244, 246. 93. Baring (Lord Cromer), *Modern Egypt*, vol. 1, p. 7; see footnote 2, where he says 'I do not speak Arabic'. 94. Ibid, vol. 2, p. 123. 95. Ibid, p. 124. 96. Ibid, pp. 132, 147, 151–4, 161. 97. Keith McClelland and Sonya Rose, 'Citizenship and Empire, 1867–1928', in Hall and Rose (eds), *At Home with the Empire*, p. 283. 98. Eliza Riedi, 'Women, Gender, and the Promotion of Empire: The Victoria League, 1901–1914', *Historical Journal*, vol. 45, no. 3, September 2002, p. 578. 99. Chandrika Kaul, '"You cannot govern by force alone": W. H. Russell, *The Times* and the Great Rebellion', in Marina Carter and Crispin Bates (eds), *Mutiny at the Margins*, vol. 3, Sage, London 2013, pp. 28–32; see also William Howard Russell's diary, where he recounts some of the atrocities of the war in India: *My Diary in India, in the Year 1858–9*, Routledge, Warne, and Routledge, London 1860, esp. pp. 215ff. 100. Charles Dickens, letter to Baroness Burdett-Coutts, October 1857, in *The Letters of Charles Dickens*, vol. 8, Clarendon Press, Oxford 2006, p. 459. 101. At least according to the recollections of his son the writer André Germain: see his *La bourgeoisie qui brûle. Propos d'un témoin, 1890–1914*, Sun, Paris 1951, p. 28. 102. Jean-Pierre Rioux, *La France coloniale sans fard ni déni*, André Versaille, Brussels 2011, pp. 20–21. 103. Gilman, 'L'empire colonial et la longue stagnation', pp. 386–9. 104. Raoul Girardet, *L'idée coloniale en France de 1871 à 1962*, Pluriel, Paris 1972, pp. 53–7; Charles-Robert Ageron, *L'anticolonialisme en France de 1871 à 1914*, Presses Universitaires de France, Paris 1973, p. 8. 105. Paul Leroy-Beaulieu, *De la colonisation chez les peuples modernes*, Guillaumin, Paris 1882 (2nd edition), pp. 91, 145. 106. Ibid, p. 347. 107. Rey-Goldzeiguer, *Le royaume arabe*, p. 552, and Etemad, *De l'utilité des empires*, p. 183. 108. Cited in Patrick Weil, *Qu'est-ce qu'un Français?*, Grasset, Paris 2002, p. 226. 109. Ibid, pp. 228–32. 110. Etemad, *De l'utilité des empires*, p. 184; see also Benjamin Stora, *Les trois exils. Juifs d'Algérie*, Stock, Paris 2006, p. 52. 111. Jules Ferry, Speech of 28 July 1885, in *1885: le tournant colonial de la République. Jules Ferry contre Georges Clemenceau*, introduction by Gilles Manceron, La Découverte/Poche, Paris 2007, p. 56. 112. Jules Ferry, *Discours et opinions*, vol. V, ed. Paul Robiquet, Armand Colin, Paris 1898, p. 185. 113. *1885: le tournant colonial de la République*, pp. 104–6. 114. Ibid, pp. 41–2. 115. Ibid, p. 77. 116. Marie-Hélène Gilman, 'L'empire colonial et la longue stagnation', in Yves Breton, Albert Broder, and Michel Lutfalla (eds), *La longue stagnation en France. L'autre dépression, 1873–1907*, Economica, Paris 1997, p. 386. 117. *1885: le tournant colonial de la République*, p. 45. 118. Ageron, *L'anticolonialisme en France de 1871 à 1914*, pp. 45–7. 119. Girardet, *L'idée coloniale en France de 1871 à 1962*, pp. 63, 100. 120. Ageron, *L'anticolonialisme en France de 1871 à 1914*, pp. 75–6. 121. Paul d'Estournelles de Constant, *La conquête de la Tunisie*, Sfar, Paris 2002, p. 258 (first published 1891 as *La politique française en Tunisie: Le Protectorat et ses origines*). 122. Jean Jaurès, 'Les compétitions coloniales', *La Petite République*, 17 May 1896. 123. Jean Jaurès, 'En Algérie', in *Oeuvres de Jean Jaurès*, vol. 6, Fayard, Paris 2001, p. 180, originally in *La Petite République*, 29 January 1898. 124. Jean Jaurès, 'La question juive en Algérie', *La Dépêche*, 1 May 1895, cited in Winock, *La France et les Juifs*, p. 91. 125. Girardet, *L'idée coloniale en France de 1871 à 1962*, p. 163. 126. Vincent Duclert, *Jaurès 1859–1914. La politique et la légende*, Éditions Autrement, Paris 2013, p. 239. 127. Lenin, 'The International Socialist Congress in Stuttgart', in *Collected Works*, vol. 13, pp. 76, 86. 128. Girardet, *L'idée coloniale en France de 1871 à 1962*, pp. 92, 99, 104–5. 129. Charles Péguy, *L'Argent (suite)*, in Charles Péguy, *Oeuvres en prose, 1909–1914*, Bibliothèque de la Pléiade Gallimard, Paris 1961, p. 1,238. 130. Henri Brunschwig, *Mythes et réalités de l'impérialisme colonial français, 1871–1914*, Colin, Paris 1960, p. 185. 131. J.-C. Allain, 'L'expansion française au Maroc de 1902 à 1912', in Jean Bouvier and René Girault (eds), *L'imperialisme français d'avant 1914*, Mouton, Paris 1976, pp. 39, 44, 53. 132. Jean Bouvier, 'Les traits majeurs de l'impérialisme français avant 1914', *Le Mouvement Sociale*, no. 86, January–March 1974, p. 9. 133. Rioux, *La France coloniale sans fard ni déni*, p. 15. 134. Jean

Bouvier and René Girault (eds), *L'imperialisme français d'avant 1914*, Mouton, Paris 1976, p. 9. 135. Bouvier, 'Les traits majeurs de l'imperialisme français avant 1914', pp. 20–22. 136. Brocheux and Hémery, *Indochine: la colonisation ambiguë, 1858–1954*, p. 41. 137. In any case the opium trade was used to defray some of the costs of colonization; see Chantal Descours-Gatin, *Quand l'opium financait la colonisation en Indochine*, L'Harmattan, Paris 1992, p. 9. 138. Albert de Mun, Speech to the Chambre des Députés, 24 March 1884, in *Discours,* Tome 3, Poussielgue, Paris 1888–95, p. 194. 139. Albert de Mun, Speech of 24 March 1884, in ibid; see esp. pp. 195–6, 202–3. 140. See Gerald M. Berg, 'Writing Ideology: Ranavalona, the Ancestral Bureaucrat', *History in Africa*, vol. 22, 1995, pp. 73–92. 141. *1885: le tournant colonial de la République*, pp. 34–7. 142. *1885: le tournant colonial de la République*, pp. 60–62; see also Ferry, *Discours et opinions*, p. 189. 143. Léon Blum, 'Débat sur le budget des colonies à la Chambre des Députés, 9 juillet 1925', in *Débats parlementaires, Assemblée, Session Ordinaire (30 juin–12 juillet 1925)*, in *Journal Officiel*, p. 848. 144. Michael G. Vann, 'Building Colonial Whiteness on the Red River: Race, Power, and Urbanism in Paul Doumer's Hanoi, 1897–1902', *Historical Reflections/Réflexions historiques*, vol. 33, no. 2, Summer 2007, pp. 277–304, esp. pp. 280–81. 145. Dino Costantini, *Una malattia europea. Il 'nuovo discorso coloniale' francese e i suoi critici*, Pisa University Press 2006, pp. 70–71. 146. Girardet, *L'idée coloniale en France de 1871 à 1962*, pp. 135–6. 147. Gustave Le Bon, *La psychologie politique et la défense sociale*, Flammarion, Paris 1910, pp. 227–8, 232, 241. 148. Albert Sarraut, *Grandeur et servitude coloniales*, L'Harmattan, Paris 2012, p. 137; the book was originally published in 1931. 149. Ibid, p. 90; see also the introduction by Nicola Cooper, pp. xxxv–xxxvi. 150. Sarraut, *Grandeur et servitude coloniales*, p. 74. 151. Girardet, *L'idée coloniale en France de 1871 à 1962*, p. 134. 152. Herbert Vivian, 'The French in Tunisia', *Contemporary Review*, vol. 74, October 1898, p. 569. 153. Daniel J. Rankin, 'The Portuguese in East Africa', *Fortnightly Review*, February 1890, no. 278, p. 161. 154. David Motadel, 'Islam and the European Empires', *Historical Journal*, vol. 55, no. 3, September 2012, pp. 834, 836, 839. 155. Margery Perham, *Lugard: The Years of Adventure, 1858–1898*, Collins, London 1956, p. 311. 156. Eugène Étienne, *Les compagnies de colonisation*, Augustin Challamel, Paris 1897, p. 8.

19. THE FIRST GLOBAL CRISIS

1. S. B. Saul, *The Myth of the Great Depression, 1873–1896*, Macmillan, London 1969, p. 55. 2. Vidal, *Dépression et retour de la prospérité*, pp. 169ff. 3. Landes, *Unbound Prometheus*, p. 231. 4. Ibid, p. 233. 5. Charles Feinstein, 'New Estimates of Average Earnings in the United Kingdom, 1880–1913', *Economic History Review*, vol. 43, no. 4, November 1990, pp. 607, 612; Mary Mackinnon, 'Living Standards, 1870–1914', in Roderick Floud and Donald McCloskey (eds), *The Economic History of Britain since 1870*, vol. 2:

1860–1939, Cambridge University Press 1994, p. 290. 6. See Peter Gourevitch's useful summary in *Politics in Hard Times: Comparative Responses to International Economic Crises*, Cornell University Press 1986, pp. 70–77. 7. Winch, *Riches and Poverty*, p. 165. 8. O'Brien, 'Do We Have a Typology for the Study of European Industrialization in the XIXth Century?', p. 296. 9. Arrighi, *Adam Smith in Beijing*, p. 137; see also David Washbrook, 'South Asia, the World System, and World Capitalism', *Journal of Asian Studies*, vol. 49, no. 3, August 1990, p. 481. 10. Tony Smith, *The Pattern of Imperialism: The United States, Great Britain, and the Late-Industrializing World since 1815*, Cambridge University Press 1981, p. 37. 11. Mira Wilkins, *The History of Foreign Investment in the United States to 1914*, Harvard University Press 1989, p. 141. 12. See OECD report: http://www.keepeek.com/Digital-Asset-Management/oecd/governance/government-at-a-glance-2015/general-government-debt-per-capita-2009-2013-and-2014_gov_glance-2015-graph21-en#page1 13. Wilkins, *The History of Foreign Investment in the United States to 1914*, p. 557. 14. Ibid, p. 145. 15. Ibid, p. 557. 16. Ibid, pp. 625, 600. 17. Rudolf Hilferding, *Finance Capital: A Study of the Latest Phase of Capitalist Development*, Routledge and Kegan Paul, London 1981, p. 322. 18. Émile Becqué, *L'internationalisation des capitaux. Étude économique, financière et politique*, Imprimerie générale du Midi, Montpellier 1912, p. 173. 19. Lehmann, *The Roots of Modern Japan*, pp. 173–4. 20. Jean-François Vidal, *Dépression et retour à la prospérité. Les économies européennes à la fin du XIXe siècle*, L'Harmattan, Paris 2000, pp. 9–10. 21. 'Commercial History and Review of 1879', *The Economist*, 13 March 1880, in *English Historical Documents*, vol. 10: *1874–1914*, ed. W. D. Handcock, Routledge, London 1996, p. 198. 22. Charles P. Kindleberger, *Manias, Panics and Crashes: A History of Financial Crises*, 4th edition, Palgrave, London 2000, pp. 253–9. 23. Larry Neal, 'The Financial Crisis of 1825 and the Restructuring of the British Financial System', Prepared for the 22nd Annual Economic Policy Conference at the Federal Reserve Bank of St. Louis, 16–17 October 1997, p. 37: https://www.researchgate.net/profile/Larry_Neal/publication/5047144_The_financial_crisis_of_1825_and_the_restructuring_of_the_British_financial_system/links/5457bb330cf26d5090ab5057.pdf 24. Hector Denis, *La dépression économique et sociale et l'histoire des prix*, Huysmans, Brussels 1895, pp. 2–4. 25. C. P. Kindleberger, 'The Rise of Free Trade in Western Europe, 1820–1875', in *Journal of Economic History*, vol. 35, no. 1, March 1975, p. 49; on Romanian wheat see Hitchins, *Rumania*, p. 189; Chirot, *Social Change in a Peripheral Society*, p. 122; on Portugal see Clarence-Smith, *The Third Portuguese Empire, 1825–1975*, p. 81; on Sweden see Berend and Ránki, *The European Periphery and Industrialization, 1780–1914*, p. 31. 26. 'Commercial History and Review of 1880', *The Economist*, 12 March 1881, in Handcock (ed.), *English Historical Documents*, vol. 10, p. 200. 27. Kevin O'Rourke and Jeffrey G. Williamson, 'Late Nineteenth-Century Anglo-American Factor-Price Convergence: Were Heckscher and Ohlin Right?', *Journal of Economic History*, vol. 54, no. 4, December 1994, p. 900. 28. Wilkins, *The*

Emergence of Multinational Enterprise, p. 35. 29. Barkin, *The Controversy over German Industrialization, 1890–1902*, p. 28. 30. Yves Breton, 'La perception de la "grande dépression" de la fin du XIXe siècle (1873–1896) par les économistes français. Analyses et perspectives', *Économies et sociétés*, no. 8, 1993, pp. 210–11. 31. Clément Juglar, *Des crises commerciales et de leur retour périodique en France, en Angleterre et aux États-Unis*, Guillaumin et Cie, Paris 1862, p. 1. 32. On the severity of the crisis see Gianni Toniolo, *Storia economica dell'Italia liberale, 1850–1918*, Il Mullino, Bologna 1988, pp. 139ff. 33. Giovanni Giolitti, Speech in Dronero, 19 October 1896, *Discorsi extraparlamentari*, p. 149. 34. All union membership figure in Bairoch, *Victoires et déboires*, vol. II, p. 491. 35. Arrighi, *Adam Smith in Beijing*, p. 101. 36. Daunton, '"Gentlemanly Capitalism" and British Industry 1820–1914', p. 155. 37. Breton, 'La perception de la "grande dépression" de la fin du XIXe siècle (1873–1896)', p. 205. 38. Jean Leduc, *Histoire de la France: l'enracinement de la République, 1879–1918*, Hachette, Paris 1991, pp. 132–3. 39. Shorter and Tilly, *Strikes in France, 1830–1968*, p. 112. 40. Ibid, p. 114. 41. Émile Cheysson, *La crise du revenue et la loi du travail*, Comité de défense et de progrès social, Paris 1898, p. 45, text of lecture held in Amiens, 6 April 1897. 42. Hobsbawm, *Industry and Empire*, p. 119. 43. Piketty, *Capital in the Twenty-First Century*, p. 421. 44. J. A. Hobson, 'The General Election: A Sociological Interpretation', *Sociological Review*, vol. 3, 1910, pp. 112–13, cited in Peter Cain, 'J. A. Hobson, Financial Capitalism and Imperialism in Late Victorian and Edwardian England', *Journal of Imperial and Commonwealth History*, vol. 13, no. 3, May 1985, pp. 8–9. 45. Smith, 'The Ideology of German Colonialism, 1840–1906', pp. 646–7. 46. Otto Pflanze, *Bismarck and the Development of Germany*, vol. III: *The Period of Fortification, 1880–1898*, Princeton University Press 1990, pp. 3–4, 7, 9, 14. 47. Puissant, '1886, La contre-réforme sociale?', p. 70.

20. PROTECTING THE ECONOMY

1. Bairoch, *Economics and World History*, p. 18. 2. Dale C. Copeland, *Economic Interdependence and War*, Princeton University Press 2015, p. 99. 3. David Stevenson, *Armaments and the Coming of War: Europe, 1904–1914*, Clarendon Press, Oxford 1996, pp. 26–7, 331. 4. Becker, *The Monied Metropolis*, p. 306. 5. F. W. Taussig, *The Tariff History of the United States: A Series of Essays*, Putnam and Sons, New York and London 1892, pp. 172–3, 174 ff, 320. 6. Smith, *The Pattern of Imperialism*, pp. 37–8. 7. Sibylle H. Lehmann, 'The German Elections in the 1870s: Why Germany Turned from Liberalism to Protectionism', *Journal of Economic History*, vol. 70, no. 1, March 2010, p. 149. 8. Barkin, *The Controversy over German Industrialization, 1890–1902*, p. 35. 9. Cornelius Torp, 'The "Coalition of Rye and Iron" under the Pressure of Globalization: A Reinterpretation of Germany's Political Economy before 1914', *Central European History*, vol. 43, no. 3, 2010, p. 411.

10. Barkin, *The Controversy over German Industrialization, 1890–1902*, pp. 52–6. 11. Winkler, *Germany: The Long Road West, 1789–1933*, pp. 240–41. 12. Torp, 'The "Coalition of Rye and Iron" under the Pressure of Globalization', p. 412. 13. Berman, 'Modernization in Historical Perspective', pp. 441–2. 14. Trentmann, *Free Trade Nation*, pp. 3–6, 15ff. 15. Ibid, Plate IV, 'The Hungry Forties' by Robert Morley, and Plate VIII. 16. Green, *The Crisis of Conservatism*, p. 244. 17. Cited in ibid, p. 246, from *Mr. Chamberlain's Speeches*, vol. 2, p. 206: http://archive.org/stream/mrchamberlainsspo2chamuoft#page/206/mode/2up 18. Richard G. Robbins, *Famine in Russia, 1891–1892*, Columbia University Press 1975, p. 6; Anatoli Vichnevski, *La faucille et le rouble. La modernisation conservatrice en URSS*, Gallimard, Paris 2000, p. 53; Lyashchenko, *History of the National Economy of Russia*, p. 561. 19. V. L. Stepanov, 'Ivan Alekseevich Vyshnegradskii', *Russian Studies in History*, Fall 1996, no. 2, vol. 35, p. 81. 20. Robbins, *Famine in Russia, 1891–1892*, p. 189. 21. Ibid, pp. 58–60; Stepanov, 'Ivan Alekseevich Vyshnegradskii', p. 97. 22. J. Y. Simms, 'The Economic Impact of the Russian Famine of 1891–92', *Slavonic and East European Review*, vol. 60, no. 1, January 1982, p. 69. 23. Cormac Ó Gráda, *Famine: A Short History*, Princeton University Press 2009, p. 236. 24. Simms, 'The Economic Impact of the Russian Famine of 1891–92', pp. 70–73. 25. Sen, *Poverty and Famines*, see esp. Chapter 4. 26. Milyoukov, *Russia and its Crisis*, p. 465. 27. Vichnevski, *La faucille et le* rouble, pp. 67–8. 28. Witte, *The Memoirs of Count Witte*, pp. 62, 71, 74. 29. Von Laue, 'A Secret Memorandum of Sergei Witte', pp. 98–9. 30. Jordi Nadal, 'Un siglo de industrialización en España, 1833–1930', in Nicolás Sánchez-Albornoz (ed.), *La modernización económica de España, 1830–1930*, Alianza Editorial, Madrid 1985, p. 93. 31. John Michael Montias, 'Notes on the Romanian Debate on Sheltered Industrialization: 1860–1906', in Kenneth Jowitt (ed.), *Social Change in Romania, 1860–1940: A Debate on Development in a European Nation*, University of California Press 1978, p. 53. 32. The debate is ably summarized by Silvia Marton in *La construction politique de la nation. La nation dans les débats du Parlement de la Roumanie (1866–1871)*, Institute European, Bucharest 2009, pp. 181–4. 33. Hitchins, *Rumania*, pp. 188–7. 34. Ibid, pp. 160–61. 35. Ibid, pp. 83–5. 36. Montias, 'Notes on the Romanian Debate on Sheltered Industrialization: 1860–1906', pp. 60–61. 37. Ibid, p. 66. 38. Janos, *East Central Europe in the Modern World*, p. 128. 39. Durandin, *Histoire des roumains*, pp. 183–4. 40. Joseph L. Love. 'Resisting Liberalism: Theorizing Backwardness and Development in Rumania before 1914', in Michalēs Psalidopoulos and Maria Eugéna Mata (eds), *Economic Thought and Policy in Less Developed Europe: The Nineteenth Century*, Routledge, London 2002, pp. 108–9. 41. Herman Lebovics, *The Alliance of Iron and Wheat in the Third French Republic, 1860–1914: Origins of the New Conservatism*, Louisiana State University Press 1988, p. 55. 42. Olivier Jacquet and Gilles Laferté, 'Le contrôle républicain du marché. Vignerons et négociants sous la Troisième République', *Annales*, no. 5, September–October 2006, pp. 1,149–51.

43. Bertrand Joly, 'Le parti royaliste et l'affaire Dreyfus (1898–1900)', *Revue Historique*, no. 546, April–June 1983, pp. 311–64. 44. Léon Gambetta, 'La politique et les affaires', *Revue politique et littéraire*, 6 June 1868, in *Discours et plaidoyers politiques*, vol. 11, p. 136. 45. Gaillard, *Jules Ferry*, pp. 157–8, 162. 46. Ibid, p. 301. 47. Pomeranz and Topik, *The World that Trade Created*, p. 54. 48. Kenneth Morgan, 'Mercantilism and the British Empire, 1688–1815', in Winch and O'Brien (eds), *The Political Economy of British Historical Experience, 1688–1914*, p. 173. 49. Sarah Palmer, *Politics, Shipping and the Repeal of the Navigation Laws*, Manchester University Press 1990, p. 162. 50. David Todd, *L'identité économique de la France: Libre-échange et protectionnisme, 1814–1851*, Grasset, Paris 2008, p. 415. 51. John V. C. Nye, *War, Wine, and Taxes: The Political Economy of Anglo-French Trade, 1689–1900*, Princeton University Press 2007, p. 3; Lucette Le Van-Lemesle, *Le Juste ou le Riche. L'enseignement de l'économie politique, 1815–1950*, Comité pour l'histoire économique et financière de la France, Paris 2004, p. 237; see also Paul Bairoch, *Economics and World History*, Harvester, New York and London 1993, pp. 22–3. 52. Jean-Charles Asselain, 'Les résurgences du protectionnisme français', *Le débat*, no. 76, September–October 1993, pp. 148–66. 53. Michael S. Smith, *Tariff Reform in France, 1860–1900*, Cornell University Press 1980, p. 196. 54. Jules Méline, *Le Retour à la terre et la surproduction industrielle*, Hachette, Paris 1905, pp. 201, 206, 310. 55. Lévêque, *Histoire des forces politiques en France, 1880–1940*, p. 24. 56. Girault, 'Place et rôle des échanges extérieurs', pp. 209–10. 57. Ibid, pp. 223–4. 58. Jean Jaurès, *Les plus beaux discours*, Librio, Paris 2014, p. 116. 59. Eugene Genovese, *The Southern Tradition: The Achievement and Limitations of an American Conservatism*, Harvard University Press 1994, p. 8. 60. Keith Tribe, *Strategies of Economic Order: German Economic Discourse, 1750–1950*, Cambridge University Press 1995, Chapter 3 and esp. pp. 49–50. 61. Tribe, *Strategies of Economic Order*, pp. 49–51; see also Donald Winch, *Riches and Poverty: An Intellectual History of Political Economy in Britain, 1750–1834*, Cambridge University Press 1996, p. 162. 62. C. Knick Harley, 'International Competitiveness of the Antebellum American Cotton Textile Industry', *Journal of Economic History*, vol. 52, no. 3, September 1992, p. 560. 63. Brownlee, *Federal Taxation in America*, p. 33. 64. Gould, *Reform and Regulation*, p. 33. 65. Bensel, *The Political Economy of American Industrialization, 1877–1900*, pp. 463–5. 66. Ibid, p. 457. 67. William McKinley, First Inaugural Address, 4 March 1897: http://avalon.law.yale.edu/19th_century/mckin1.asp 68. Albert Carreras, 'What Can We Learn from Long-Term Spanish Economic Performance?', in Pablo Martín-Aceña and James Simpson (eds), *The Economic Development of Spain since 1870*, Elgar, Aldershot 1995, pp. 40–43. 69. Cormac Ó Gráda, 'British Agriculture, 1860–1914', in Roderick Floud and Donald McCloskey (eds), *The Economic History of Britain since 1700*, 2nd edition, vol. 2: *1860–1939*, Cambridge University Press 1994, p. 145; there is typo in this edition, '1816' where it should have been '1860'. 70. The point, made by C. P. Kindleberger, is cited in Ó Gráda, 'British Agriculture,

1860–1914', p. 146. 71. Peter Cain, 'Political Economy in Edwardian England: The Tariff-Reform Controversy', in Alan O'Day (ed.) *The Edwardian Age: Conflict and Stability, 1900–1914*, Macmillan, London 1979, p. 36. 72. Merger, *Un siècle d'histoire industrielle en Italie, 1880–1998*, pp. 22–4. 73. Duggan, *Francesco Crispi*, pp. 518–23; Merger, *Un siècle d'histoire industrielle en Italie, 1880–1998*, pp. 31–2. 74. Stefano Fenoaltea, 'Manchester, Manchesteriano . . . *Dekwakoncoz*?', in Cafagna and Crepax (eds), *Atti di intelligenza e sviluppo economico*, pp. 493–9. 75. Friedrich Katz, 'Mexico: Restored Republic and Porfiriato, 1867–1910', in Bethell (ed.), *The Cambridge History of Latin America*, vol. V, pp. 29–31. 76. Bairoch, *Victoires et déboires*, vol. II, pp. 308–9. 77. Ibid, p. 310. 78. Ibid, p. 311. 79. Darwin, *The Empire Project*, p. 277. 80. Christopher Clark, *The Sleepwalkers: How Europe Went to War in 1914*, Allen Lane, London 2012, p. xxv. 81. *Reading the Twentieth Century: Documents in American History*, ed. Donald W. Whisenhunt, Rowman & Littlefield, Lanham, MD 2009, p. 21.

CONCLUSION: STILL TRIUMPHANT? STILL ANXIOUS?

1. Joan Robinson, *Economic Heresies: Some Old-fashioned Questions in Economic Theory*, Macmillan, London and Basingstoke 1972, p. 143. 2. Friedrich Hayek, *The Fatal Conceit: The Errors of Socialism*, University of Chicago Press 2011, p. 6. 3. Marx, *Capital*, vol. 3, p. 241. 4. Ibid, vol. 1, p. 595. 5. John Maynard Keynes, 'National Self-Sufficiency', originally in the *New Statesman* (8 July 1933), now in *Activities 1931–1939*, vol. XXI of *The Collected Writings of John Maynard Keynes*, Macmillan and Cambridge University Press 1982, p. 239. 6. See Nick Tabor's clever essay on cribs from Yeats' poem, 'No Slouch', *The Paris Review*, 7 April 2015. 7. Joan Didion, *Slouching towards Bethlehem*, Burning Man Books, Seattle 2009, p. 5. 8. Max Nordau, *Degeneration*, University of Nebraska Press 1968, pp. 4–5. 9. Peter Temin, 'Globalization', *Oxford Review of Economic Policy*, vol. 15, no. 4, 1999, p. 85. 10. Daniel Bell, *The Cultural Contradictions of Capitalism*, Basic Books, London 1996, p. xxi (Foreword 1978, the book was originally published in 1976). 11. A thorough discussion of modern 'technocratic' thinkers can be found in Carlo Fumian, 'Per una storia della tecnocrazia. Utopie meccaniche e ingegneria sociale tra Otto e Novecento', *Rivista storica italiana*, vol. 124, no. 3, December 2012, pp. 908–59. 12. Murray N. Rothbard, 'A Future of Peace and Capitalism', in James H. Weaver (ed.), *Modern Political Economy: Radical and Orthodox Views on Crucial Issues*, Allyn and Bacon, Boston, MA 1973, p. 423. 13. Caroline Humphrey, 'Creating a Culture of Disillusionment: Consumption in Moscow, a Chronicle of Changing Times', in Daniel Miller (ed.), *Worlds Apart: Modernity through the Prism of the Local*, Routledge, New York and London 1995, pp. 61–2. 14. Marx, *Capital*, vol. 1, p. 35; Marx had used the expression in 1859; see *A Contribution to the Critique of Political*

Economy, Progress Publishers, Moscow 1970, p. 3. 15. http://www.worldpublicopinion.org/pipa/articles/btglobalizationtradera/644.php?nid=&id=&pnt=644 and http://www.worldpublicopinion.org/pipa/pdf/ 16. Pope Francis I, 'Address of His Holiness Pope Francis to Representatives of the Confederation of Italian Cooperatives', 28 February 2015: https://w2.vatican.va/content/francesco/en/speeches/2015/february/documents/papa-francesco_20150228_confcooperative.html 17. Margaret Thatcher, 'Speech to General Assembly of the Church of Scotland', 21 May 1988: http://www.margaretthatcher.org/document/107246 18. Tocqueville, *The Ancien Régime and the French Revolution*, p. 11. 19. Trade union data are from the OECD. For technical issues on trade union statistics see Susan Hayter and Valentina Stoevska, 'Social Dialogue Indicators: International Statistical Inquiry 2008–09. Technical Brief', ILO November 2011: http://laborsta.ilo.org/applv8/data/TUM/TUD%20and%20CBC%20Technical%20Brief.pdf 20. See Chris Wrigley (ed.), *British Trade Unions, 1945–1995*, Manchester University Press 1997, pp. 161–80, for details of the legislation. 21. Paul Smith, 'Labour under the Law', *Industrial Relations Journal*, vol. 46, nos 5–6, November 2015, p. 358; see also Paul Smith, 'New Labour and the Commonsense of Neoliberalism: Trade Unionism, Collective bargaining, and Workers' Rights', *Industrial Relations Journal*, vol. 40, no. 4. 22. Colin Crouch, 'A Third Way in Industrial Relations?', in Stuart White (ed.), *New Labour: The Progressive Future?* Palgrave, London 2001, p. 104. 23. The Conservative and Unionist Party Manifesto 2017, *Forward Together: Our Plan for a Stronger Britain and a Prosperous Future*, p. 9. 24. ETUI: http://www.worker-participation.eu/National-Industrial-Relations/Countries/Sweden/Trade-Unions 25. On how Labour Zionism made socialism subordinate to nationalism see Zeev Sternhell, *Aux origines d'Israël. Entre nationalisme et socialisme*, Gallimard, Paris 2004, esp. Chapter 3. 26. William J. Clinton, Address before a Joint Session of the Congress on the State of the Union, 23 January 1996: http://www.presidency.ucsb.edu/ws/?pid=53091 27. Gordon Brown, Mansion House Speech, 22 June 2006: https://www.theguardian.com/business/2006/jun/22/politics.economicpolicy 28. William J. Baumol, Robert E. Litan, and Carl J. Schramm, *Good Capitalism, Bad Capitalism, and the Economics of Growth and Prosperity*, Yale University Press 2007, pp. 74–5. 29. https://www.amnesty.org/en/latest/news/2018/07/nicaragua-represion-estatal-ha-llegado-a-niveles-deplorables/ 30. See CNN: http://edition.cnn.com/2013/09/02/world/americas/mexico-drug-war-fast-facts/index.html; https://www.theguardian.com/world/2018/feb/10/mexico-drug-cartels-soldiers-military, and BBC Report: https://www.bbc.co.uk/programmes/p06cc1mm, and CNN: https://edition.cnn.com/2018/06/27/americas/mexico-political-deaths-election-season-trnd/index.html 31. Joseph E. Stiglitz, *Globalization and its Discontents*, Norton, New York 2002, p. 13. 32. Ibid, p. 5. 33. Paul Krugman, 'In Praise of Cheap Labor', *Slate Magazine*, 21 March 1997, and 'Safer Sweatshops', *The New York Times*, 8 July 2013. 34. David Riesman, 'The Nylon War', in David Riesman, *Abundance for What? and Other Essays*, Chatto and Windus, New York 1964, p. 69;

the C-54 Skymaster was a transport aircraft used by the US military. 35. Greg Castillo, 'Domesticating the Cold War: Household Consumption as Propaganda in Marshall Plan Germany', *Journal of Contemporary History*, vol. 40, no. 2, 2005, pp. 261–2, 282. 36. Last but not least is Gideon Rachman's *Easternisation: War and Peace in the Asian Century*, Bodley Head, London 2016. 37. Justin R. Pierce and Peter K. Schott, 'The Surprisingly Swift Decline of US Manufacturing Employment', *American Economic Review*, vol. 106, no. 7, July 2016, p. 1,632. 38. CIA, *World Factbook*: https://www.cia.gov/library/publications/the-world-factbook/rankorder/2079rank.htmlUS 39. Shanghai Ranking Consultancy: http://www.shanghairanking.com/ARWU2016.html 40. See data for 2015 from the International Institute of Strategic Studies: The Military Balance: https://www.iiss.org//media//images/publications/the%20military%20balance/milbal2016/mb%202016%20top%2015%20defence%20budgets%202015.jpg?la=en 41. Richard Walker and Daniel Buck, 'The Chinese Road: Cities in the Transition to Capitalism', *New Left Review*, no. 46, July–August 2007, pp. 50–51; *Jing Daily*, 16 February 2016, quoting a report by the Shanghai-based luxury consultancy Fortune Character. 42. Source: UNCTAD, cited in Chris Rhodes, 'Manufacturing: International Comparisons', House of Commons Briefing Paper no. 05809, 5 January 2018, Table 5. 43. Robert Rowthorn and Ramana Ramaswamy, 'Deindustrialization – Its Causes and Implications', Economic Issues no. 10, IMF, Washington, DC 1997; see also their 'Growth, Trade, and Deindustrialization', *IMF Staff Papers*, vol. 46, no. 1, March 1999, pp. 18–41. OECD figures cited by Charles Feinstein are different: the American peak was in 1966 and not in 1965 with 36 per cent and not 28 per cent, see Charles Feinstein, 'Structural Change in the Developed Countries during the Twentieth Century', *Oxford Review of Economic Policy*, vol. 15, no. 4, 1999, p. 39. 44. Feinstein, 'Structural Change in the Developed Countries during the Twentieth Century', p. 38. 45. Rowthorn and Ramaswamy, 'Deindustrialization – Its Causes and Implications', p. 5. 46. A. B. Atkinson, 'The Distribution of Income in the UK and OECD Countries in the Twentieth Century', *Oxford Review of Economic Policy*, vol. 15, no. 4, 1999, pp. 59, 60, 65. 47. Feinstein, 'Structural Change in the Developed Countries during the Twentieth Century', pp. 35–7. 48. Ibid, pp. 47–8. 49. Liyan Chen, 'How Uber Surpasses Ford and GM in Valuation in 5 Years', *Forbes Magazine*, December 2015: http://www.forbes.com/sites/liyanchen/2015/12/04/at-68-billion-valuation-uber-will-be-bigger-than-gm-ford-and-honda/#3fff593c5858 50. Alex Hern and Nick Fletcher, 'Fangs: The Lighting Rise of Facebook, Amazon, Netflix and Google', *The Guardian*, 29 April 2017. 51. Christopher Ingraham, 'The Entire Coal Industry Employs Fewer People than Arby's', *Washington Post*, 31 March 2017: https://www.washingtonpost.com/news/wonk/wp/2017/03/31/8-surprisingly-small-industries-that-employ-more-people-than-coal/?utm_term=.38c8e500b1f3 52. https://www.cnbc.com/2018/06/20/heres-why-google-and-amazon-probably-will-never-be-included-in-the-dow.html 53. Marx, *Capital*, vol. 3, p. 401. 54. Robert Brenner, 'The Boom and the Bubble', *New Left Review*, no. 6, November–

December 2000, pp. 6, 27, 39–40. 55. The argument is explained in detail in Barry Z. Cynamon and Steven M. Fazzari, 'Inequality, the Great Recession and Slow Recovery', *Cambridge Journal of Economics*, vol. 40, no. 2, March 2016, pp. 373–99; see also Robin Blackburn, 'The Subprime Crisis', *New Left Review*, no. 50, March–April 2008, pp. 64–6. 56. Susan Strange, *Casino Capitalism*, Blackwell, Oxford 1986, p. 1. 57. Hyman P. Minsky, 'The Financial-Instability Hypothesis: Capitalist Processes and the Behavior of the Economy', in *Financial Crises: Theory, History, and Policy*, ed. Charles P. Kindleberger and Jean-Pierre Laffargue, Cambridge University Press and Éditions de la Maison des Sciences de l'Homme, Cambridge and Paris 1982, pp. 22, 36; see also Hyman Minsky, *Can 'It' Happen Again? Essays on Instability and Finance*, Routledge, London 2016 (first published 1982), pp. viiff. 58. Doug Guthrie, *China and Globalization: The Social, Economic and Political Transformation of Chinese Society*, Routledge, London 2012; on the size of the car market see http://www.statista.com/statistics/416036/largest-automobile-markets-worldwide-based-on-new-car-registrations/; for statistics on carbon emissions and coal production see *The Guardian*, 30 January 2013, using data from US Energy Information Administration.

Index

ALLEN LANE

an imprint of

PENGUIN BOOKS

Also Published

John Tierney and Roy F. Baumeister, *The Power of Bad: And How to Overcome It*

Greta Thunberg, *No One Is Too Small to Make a Difference: Illustrated Edition*

Glenn Simpson and Peter Fritsch, *Crime in Progress: The Secret History of the Trump-Russia Investigation*

Abhijit V. Banerjee and Esther Duflo, *Good Economics for Hard Times: Better Answers to Our Biggest Problems*

Gaia Vince, *Transcendence: How Humans Evolved through Fire, Language, Beauty and Time*

Roderick Floud, *An Economic History of the English Garden*

Rana Foroohar, *Don't Be Evil: The Case Against Big Tech*

Ivan Krastev and Stephen Holmes, *The Light that Failed: A Reckoning*

Andrew Roberts, *Leadership in War: Lessons from Those Who Made History*

Alexander Watson, *The Fortress: The Great Siege of Przemysl*

Stuart Russell, *Human Compatible: AI and the Problem of Control*

Serhii Plokhy, *Forgotten Bastards of the Eastern Front: An Untold Story of World War II*

Dominic Sandbrook, *Who Dares Wins: Britain, 1979-1982*

Charles Moore, *Margaret Thatcher: The Authorized Biography, Volume Three: Herself Alone*

Thomas Penn, *The Brothers York: An English Tragedy*

David Abulafia, *The Boundless Sea: A Human History of the Oceans*

Anthony Aguirre, *Cosmological Koans: A Journey to the Heart of Physics*

Orlando Figes, *The Europeans: Three Lives and the Making of a Cosmopolitan Culture*

Naomi Klein, *On Fire: The Burning Case for a Green New Deal*

Anne Boyer, *The Undying: A Meditation on Modern Illness*

Benjamin Moser, *Sontag: Her Life*

Daniel Markovits, *The Meritocracy Trap*

Malcolm Gladwell, *Talking to Strangers: What We Should Know about the People We Don't Know*

Peter Hennessy, *Winds of Change: Britain in the Early Sixties*

John Sellars, *Lessons in Stoicism: What Ancient Philosophers Teach Us about How to Live*

Brendan Simms, *Hitler: Only the World Was Enough*

Hassan Damluji, *The Responsible Globalist: What Citizens of the World Can Learn from Nationalism*

Peter Gatrell, *The Unsettling of Europe: The Great Migration, 1945 to the Present*

Justin Marozzi, *Islamic Empires: Fifteen Cities that Define a Civilization*

Bruce Hood, *Possessed: Why We Want More Than We Need*

Susan Neiman, *Learning from the Germans: Confronting Race and the Memory of Evil*

Donald D. Hoffman, *The Case Against Reality: How Evolution Hid the Truth from Our Eyes*

Frank Close, *Trinity: The Treachery and Pursuit of the Most Dangerous Spy in History*

Richard M. Eaton, *India in the Persianate Age: 1000-1765*

Janet L. Nelson, *King and Emperor: A New Life of Charlemagne*

Philip Mansel, *King of the World: The Life of Louis XIV*

Donald Sassoon, *The Anxious Triumph: A Global History of Capitalism, 1860-1914*

Elliot Ackerman, *Places and Names: On War, Revolution and Returning*

Jonathan Aldred, *Licence to be Bad: How Economics Corrupted Us*

Johny Pitts, *Afropean: Notes from Black Europe*

Walt Odets, *Out of the Shadows: Reimagining Gay Men's Lives*

James Lovelock, *Novacene: The Coming Age of Hyperintelligence*

Mark B. Smith, *The Russia Anxiety: And How History Can Resolve It*

Stella Tillyard, *George IV: King in Waiting*

Jonathan Rée, *Witcraft: The Invention of Philosophy in English*

Jared Diamond, *Upheaval: How Nations Cope with Crisis and Change*

Emma Dabiri, *Don't Touch My Hair*

Srecko Horvat, *Poetry from the Future: Why a Global Liberation Movement Is Our Civilisation's Last Chance*

Paul Mason, *Clear Bright Future: A Radical Defence of the Human Being*

Remo H. Largo, *The Right Life: Human Individuality and its role in our development, health and happiness*

Joseph Stiglitz, *People, Power and Profits: Progressive Capitalism for an Age of Discontent*

David Brooks, *The Second Mountain*

Roberto Calasso, *The Unnamable Present*

Lee Smolin, *Einstein's Unfinished Revolution: The Search for What Lies Beyond the Quantum*

Clare Carlisle, *Philosopher of the Heart: The Restless Life of Søren Kierkegaard*

Nicci Gerrard, *What Dementia Teaches Us About Love*

Edward O. Wilson, *Genesis: On the Deep Origin of Societies*

John Barton, *A History of the Bible: The Book and its Faiths*

Carolyn Forché, *What You Have Heard is True: A Memoir of Witness and Resistance*

Elizabeth-Jane Burnett, *The Grassling*

Kate Brown, *Manual for Survival: A Chernobyl Guide to the Future*

Roderick Beaton, *Greece: Biography of a Modern Nation*

Matt Parker, *Humble Pi: A Comedy of Maths Errors*

Ruchir Sharma, *Democracy on the Road*